# LIFE AND EDUCATION IN EARLY SOCIETIES

THE MACMILLAN COMPANY
NEW YORK · BOSTON · CHICAGO
DALLAS · ATLANTA · SAN FRANCISCO

MACMILLAN AND CO., LIMITED
LONDON · BOMBAY · CALCUTTA
MADRAS · MELBOURNE

THE MACMILLAN COMPANY
OF CANADA, LIMITED
TORONTO

INDIAN BOWMEN
(L. Choris, *Voyage Pittoresque autour du Monde*, Pl. XIII)

# Life and Education in Early Societies

THOMAS WOODY

UNIVERSITY OF PENNSYLVANIA

THE MACMILLAN COMPANY : NEW YORK 1949

Charles M. Bakewell, *Sourcebook in Ancient Philosophy*, copyright, 1907, by Charles Scribner's Sons; copyright, 1935, by Charles M. Bakewell.

George W. Botsford and Lillie S. Botsford, *The Story of Rome as Greeks and Romans Tell It*, copyright, 1903, 1931, by The Macmillan Company, New York.

James Henry Breasted, *Development of Religion and Thought in Ancient Egypt*, copyright, 1912, by Charles Scribner's Sons; copyright, 1940, by Charles Breasted.

James Henry Breasted, *A History of Egypt*, copyright, 1905, by Charles Scribner's Sons; copyright, 1933, by James Henry Breasted.

Rhys Carpenter, *The Humanistic Value of Archaeology*, Harvard University Press, Cambridge, Mass., copyright, 1933, by the Board of Trustees of Oberlin College.

M. Cary, *A History of Rome*, copyright, 1935, by Macmillan and Co., Limited, London.

Havelock Ellis, *The Dance of Life*, Houghton Mifflin Company, Boston, copyright, 1923, by Havelock Ellis.

Clarence A. Forbes, *Greek Physical Education*, copyright, 1929, by The Century Co., New York.

W. Warde Fowler, *Social Life at Rome in the Age of Cicero*, copyright, 1909, 1937, by The Macmillan Company, New York.

Tenney Frank, *Roman Imperialism*, copyright, 1914, 1942, by The Macmillan Company, New York.

Tenney Frank, *Rome and Italy of the Empire*, copyright, 1940, by The Johns Hopkins Press, Baltimore.

George S. Goodspeed, *A History of the Babylonians and Assyrians*, copyright, 1902, by Charles Scribner's Sons; copyright, 1930, by Florence M. Goodspeed.

R. S. Greenshields, *The Ball and the Polo Stick or Book of Ecstasy*, a translation of Gui u Chaugān or Hālnāma by Mahmud 'Ārifī, copyright, 1932, by Luzac & Company, London.

Charles Hose, *Natural Man A Record from Borneo*, copyright, 1926, by Macmillan and Co., Limited, London.

A. V. W. Jackson, *Persia Past and Present*, The Macmillan Company, New York, copyright, 1906, 1934, by A. V. W. Jackson.

Harold Whetstone Johnston, *The Private Life of the Romans*, revised by M. Johnston, copyright, 1903, 1932, by Scott, Foresman and Company, Chicago.

William Cranston Lawton, *The Soul of the Anthology*, copyright, 1923, by Yale University Press, New Haven.

Walton Brooks McDaniel, *Roman Private Life and Its Survivals*, copyright, 1924, by Longmans, Green & Co., New York.

Philip Ainsworth Means, *Ancient Civilizations of the Andes*, copyright, 1931, by Charles Scribner's Sons, New York.

David Riesman, *The Story of Medicine in the Middle Ages*, copyright, 1935, by Paul B. Hoeber, Inc., New York.

Curt Sachs, *World History of the Dance*, translated by B. Schönberg, copyright, 1937, by W. W. Norton & Company, Inc., New York.

Grant Showerman, *Rome and the Romans*, copyright, 1931, by The Macmillan Company, New York.

John K. Shryock, *The Origin and Development of the State Cult of Confucius*, The Century Co., New York, copyright, 1932, by the American Historical Association.

Baldwin Spencer and F. J. Gillen, *The Arunta A Study of a Stone Age People*, 2 vols., copyright, Macmillan and Co., Limited, London, 1927.

*The Aeneid of Virgil*, translated by Harlan Hoge Ballard, Charles Scribner's Sons, New York, copyright, 1908, 1911, 1930, by Harlan H. Ballard.

John B. Watson, *The Ways of Behaviorism*, copyright, 1928, by Harper & Brothers, New York.

Arthur S. Way, *The Odes of Bacchylides*, copyright, 1929, by Macmillan and Co., Limited, London.

Edward Thomas Williams, *China Yesterday and Today*, copyright, 1923, by Thomas Y. Crowell Company, New York.

Robert S. Woodworth, *Psychology*, copyright, 1921, 1929, by Henry Holt and Company, Inc., New York.

*To* THE WORLD-FRATERNITY

OF STUDENTS AND TEACHERS

# PREFACE

Despite the fact that lip-service has been paid increasingly to the dictum "a sound mind in a sound body," ever since western Europe began to revive the educational concepts of the Graeco-Roman world, there is still a lack of balance between physical and mental culture, both in school programs and among those who write of education. This is evident in many quarters, even where a certain universality of outlook ought to reign. Turn where one will, it is impossible to find physical culture adequately presented in books dealing with the general history of education. Written in keeping with a dominant rationalism, these books have been concerned chiefly with intellectual movements and institutions for mental improvement. This tendency has been strengthened to some extent by an asceticism, which, though it declined sharply after the Middle Ages and is generally obscured by rival biases of the modern world, still affects the outlook of many. In certain instances, it is true, physical culture played such a prominent rôle that it could not be wholly ignored. Thus, Spartan education, being chiefly physical, came off better than that of other societies whose intellectual achievements provided absorbing interest and left scant space for attention to the physical life of man.

There has been much talk of educating the whole man. A modern psychology has emphasized the indivisibility of mind and matter. If history of education were studied from this point of view, if attention were fixed on the whole of man's past experience, a more faithful portrait would emerge. Grasberger's three volumes on *Erziehung und Unterricht im Klassischen Altertum* (1864–1881) thus presented the education of Greece and Rome. Sometime an inclusive, balanced history of man's educational efforts from the origins to the present time may be possible. Such a universal view of the matter, faithful to life, would contribute more to sound judgment than can be reasonably expected from piecemeal efforts.

The present volume makes no presumptuous claim to being that ideal, inclusive treatment of physical and intellectual educational history; rather, giving considerable space to physical aspects of man's life and education in certain ancient societies and combining therewith a sketch of the culture of the mind, it aims modestly to supplement existing histories. Perhaps the time will come when physical and mental culture can be brought together properly in a single work, and adequate time will be vouchsafed to such a study, as a phase of man's civilization.

Failing to find an adequate balance of the history of physical and other phases of education, those interested in the former aspect of it have been compelled to glean from varied and scattered sources. Some periods and phases of physical education have been studied, and are readily accessible in well-known standard works. This is especially true of the Greeks, for the interest and labors of classicists have for centuries contributed to the unfolding of their history. Physical culture in other lands has fared less well. To draw a general portrait of its development in antiquity, one must therefore go far afield. The few general accounts of physical culture that have appeared in English discuss Greek and Roman societies very briefly; and the Orient in a few words, or not at all.

In the day of Goethe many Westerners doubtless thought that "Chinese, Indian, and Egyptian antiquities are never more than curiosities." While this curt dismissal of early Eastern culture may have seemed reasonable to Occidentals who saw the Orient still wrapped in sleep, it appears quite indefensible to-day to all those who see that it is awake. Indeed, it is difficult to understand how anyone can study the development of culture in the West without attempting to see it in relation to what had taken place long before Greece and Rome became important centers of civilization. We have come to see that Egyptian, Babylonian, and other Eastern cultures formed "the bed rock of European institutions." Aristotle observed truly that "he who considers things in their first growth and origin, whether a state or anything else, will obtain the clearest view of them." To what field other than education could this judgment more properly apply? A poetic dream, "East is East and West is West, and never the twain shall meet," has been rudely dispelled. To-morrow it will be recalled only by historians. The history of education, in both physical and mental aspects, will serve coming generations best if it embraces both East and West.

Environment teaches man before schools do; it continues to do so after formal processes of education have risen to great importance. Recognizing in this book the integral character of social life, and that formal education, mental and physical, is constantly conditioned by man's economy, religion, and political and social systems, a survey is made of those factors which constitute the framework of all formal educational operations. Notwithstanding the prominence given to practical phases of life as forms of education, political and pedagogical theory affecting physical and mental education has been given space, albeit less than could have been assigned to it if political and social institutions were taken for granted. The view of Professor Mahaffy anent educational theory—"it is idle to transfer to a practical book, or to an historical account, what has never been realized"—seems dubious doctrine. To exclude the thought of the Greeks about education, their efforts at intellectual reconstruction of it and society, is to suppress an important part of their history. To attempt all this—a review of life and education, physical and mental, theoretical and practical—seems sounder; but it adds bulk to the history of education, an area wherein traditional practice has generally favored compendious treatment. Brevity is the spice of wit, and poetry has been called the best history; but Clio, though one of the Muses, does not aspire to the rôle of comédienne. In defense of length one is tempted to quote Plato's remark, "There is no reason to prefer the shorter to the better."

A distinguished man of letters once remarked that he'd as soon swim the Charles every time he needed to go to Boston as read all his books in the original. One would infinitely prefer to read in the original the *Mahabharata*, *Manu*, *Li Ki*, *Nei Zeh*, *Gilgamesh*, tablets of Boghaz-Koi, *Kiddushin*, *Baba Metzia*, and all the authors of Greece and Rome. But these are too many rivers to cross. The author is profoundly indebted to the world of scholars who have built bridges by which he has passed to many lands. Such bridges, fortunately, are never worn out by use; instead, like much used roads, they are apt to be kept in good repair. Those he has taken are indicated in notes and a bibliography.

A special toll of acknowledgment is gladly paid to authors, translators, editors, and publishers of works from which more or less extensive quotations or illustrations have been taken: (1) Jonathan Cape, Ltd., London, *Greek Athletics*, by F. A. Wright; (2) The Clarendon Press, Oxford, *The Works of Aristotle*, edited by J. A. Smith and W. D. Ross, with translations by them and J. I. Beare, I. Bywater, J. F. Dobson, L. D. Dowdall, E. M. Edghill, A. S. L. Farquharson, E. S. Forster, R. K. Gaye, R. P. Hardie, A. J. Jenkinson, H. H. Joachim, B. Jowett, F. G. Kenyon, T. Loveday, G. R. G. Mure, W. Ogle, W. A. Pickard-Cambridge, A. Platt, W. R. Roberts, G. R. T. Ross, J. Solomon, St. G. Stock, J. L. Stocks, D. W. Thompson, and E. W. Webster; *The Public Orations of Demosthenes*, translated by A. W. Pickard-Cambridge; *Athletics of the Ancient World*, by E. W. Gardiner; *Gregory of Tours: The History of the Franks*, translated by O. M. Dalton; *Horace for English Readers*, translated by E. C. Wickham; *The Works of Lucian of Samosata*, translated by H. W. Fowler and F. G. Fowler; *The Sacred Books of the East*, edited by F. M.

Müller; *The Letters of Sidonius*, translated by O. M. Dalton; *Thucydides*, translated by B. Jowett; (3) E. P. Dutton and Company, New York, *Martial: The Twelve Books of Epigrams*, translated by J. A. Pott and F. A. Wright; (4) Harvard University Press, Cambridge, for various translations in The Loeb Classical Library: *The Speeches of Aeschines*, by C. D. Adams; *Ammianus Marcellinus*, by J. C. Rolfe; *Appian's Roman History*, by H. White; *Aristophanes*, by B. B. Rogers; *Athenaeus: The Deipnosophists*, by C. B. Gulick; *Saint Augustine's Confessions*, by W. Watts; *Ausonius*, by H. G. Evelyn-White, with *The Eucharisticus* of Paulinus Pellaeus; *Marcus Porcius Cato: On Agriculture and Marcus Terentius Varro: On Agriculture*, by W. D. Hooper, revised by H. B. Ash; *Cicero: Brutus*, by G. L. Hendrickson and *Orator*, by H. M. Hubbell; *Cicero: De Finibus Bonorum et Malorum*, by H. Rackham; *Cicero: De Re Publica and De Legibus*, by C. W. Keyes; *Cicero: Letters to Atticus*, by E. O. Winstedt; *Cicero: The Letters to His Friends* and *Letters to Quintus*, by W. G. Williams; *Cicero: Philippics*, by W. C. A. Ker; *Cicero: The Speeches, Pro Lege Manilia, Pro Caecina, Pro Cluentio, Pro Rabirio, Perduellionis*, by H. G. Hodge; *Cicero: Tusculan Disputations*, by J. E. King; *Claudian*, by M. Platnauer; *Demosthenes: Private Orations*, by A. T. Murray; *Dio Chrysostom*, by J. W. Cohoon and H. L. Crosby; *Diodorus of Sicily*, by C. H. Oldfather; *Dio's Roman History*, by E. Cary; *Euripides*, by A. S. Way; *Lucius Annaeus Florus: Epitome of Roman History*, by E. S. Forster, with *Cornelius Nepos*, by J. C. Rolfe; *The Correspondence of Marcus Cornelius Fronto*, by C. R. Haines; *The Attic Nights of Aulus Gellius*, by J. C. Rolfe; *Hesiod: The Homeric Hymns and Homerica*, by H. G. Evelyn-White; *Hippocrates*, by W. H. S. Jones and E. T. Withington; *Isocrates*, by G. Norlin; *Select Letters of St. Jerome*, by F. A. Wright; *Josephus*, by H. St. J. Thackeray and R. Marcus; *Juvenal and Persius*, by G. G. Ramsay; *Livy*, by B. O. Foster, F. G. Moore, E. T. Sage, and A. C. Schlesinger; *Lucan: The Civil War*, by J. D. Duff; *Lucretius: De Rerum Natura*, by W. H. D. Rouse; *Lyra Graeca*, by J. M. Edmonds; *Martial: Epigrams*, by W. C. A. Ker; *Menander*, by F. G. Allinson; *Ovid: The Art of Love, and Other Poems*, by J. H. Mozley; *Ovid: Tristia and Ex Ponto*, by A. L. Wheeler; *Ovid's Fasti*, by J. G. Frazer; *Philostratus: Imagines and Callistratus: Descriptions*, by A. Fairbanks; *Philostratus: The Life of Apollonius of Tyana*, by F. C. Conybeare; *Pliny: Letters*, by W. Melmoth, revised by W. M. L. Hutchinson; *Pliny: Natural History*, by H. Rackham; *Plutarch's Lives*, by B. Perrin; *Plutarch's Moralia*, by F. C. Babbitt, H. N. Fowler, and W. C. Helmbold; *Polybius: The Histories*, by W. R. Paton; *Procopius*, by H. B. Dewing; *The Institutio Oratoria of Quintilian*, by H. E. Butler; *Sallust*, by J. C. Rolfe; *The Scriptores Historiae Augustae*, by D. Magie; *Seneca: Apocolocyntosis*, by W. H. D. Rouse, with *Petronius*, by M. Heseltine; *Seneca: Moral Essays*, by J. W. Basore; *Seneca ad Lucilium Epistu-*

lae Morales, by R. M. Gummere; The Geography of Strabo, by H. L. Jones; Suetonius, by J. C. Rolfe; Tacitus: Dialogus, by W. Peterson; Terence, by J. Sargeaunt; Tertullian: Apology and De Spectaculis, by T. R. Glover, with Minucius Felix, by G. H. Rendall; Varro: On the Latin Language, by R. G. Kent; Vitruvius on Architecture, by F. Granger; Xenophon: Memorabilia and Oeconomicus, by E. C. Marchant; Xenophon: Symposium and Apology, by O. J. Todd, with the Anabasis, by C. L. Brownson; and Xenophon: Scripta Minora, by E. C. Marchant; (5) The Johns Hopkins Press, Baltimore, Rome and Italy of the Empire, by T. Frank; (6) George Routledge & Sons, Ltd., and Kegan Paul, Trench, Trübner and Company, Ltd., London, The Sháhnáma of Firdausí, translated by A. G. Warner and E. Warner; (7) Kegan Paul, Trench, Trübner & Co., Ltd., London, G. Glotz, The Aegean Civilization, translated by M. R. Dobie and E. M. Riley; L. Homo, Primitive Italy and the Beginnings of Roman Imperialism, translated by V. G. Childe; and R. Karsten, The Civilization of the South American Indians; (8) Little, Brown and Company, Boston, Plutarch's Lives and Writings, translated by A. H. Clough and W. W. Goodwin; (9) Longmans, Green and Company, Inc., New York, Horace, translated by A. F. Murison; (10) The Macmillan Company, New York, and Macmillan & Co., Ltd., London, The Odes of Bacchylides and The Odes of Pindar, translated by A. S. Way; Pausanias's Description of Greece, translated by J. G. Frazer; Annals of Tacitus, translated by A. J. Church and W. J. Brodribb; (11) Macmillan & Co., Ltd., London, A History of Rome, by M. Cary; (12) Oxford University Press, Oxford, The Works of Plato, translated and edited by B. Jowett; (13) Charles Scribner's Sons, New York, The Aeneid of Virgil, translated by H. H. Ballard; (14) Yale University Press, New Haven, The Soul of the Anthology, by W. C. Lawton.

For reproductions from their works grateful acknowledgment is made to the following publishers and authors: Cambridge University Press, London, The Care of Books, by J. W. Clark; Heimeran, Munich, Antike Schwimmkunst, by E. Mehl; Luzac & Company, London, The Ball and the Polo Stick, by R. S. Greenshields; Macmillan & Co., Ltd., London, Atlas of Classical Antiquities, by T. Schreiber; The Palace of Minos at Knossos, by Sir Arthur Evans; Arthur Probsthain, London, Mohenjo-Daro and the Indus Civilization, by J. Marshall. Thanks are also tendered to The American Museum of Natural History, New York, The Metropolitan Museum of Art, New York, The University Museum, University of Pennsylvania, The New York Public Library, and The Philadelphia Museum of Art for permission to reproduce items in their collections, and to members of their staffs for generous assistance.

Obligations for friendly counsel, and for the inspiration of genial interest in my work, are numerous. Risking invidious distinction I name a few: Ralph M. Chait, Edward P. Cheyney, H. Lamar Crosby, Tung Yuen Fong, George

D. Hadzsits, James House, Jr., Isaac L. Kandel, William C. Lawton, L. Legrain, Frederick Luehring, Emile Malakis, James C. Miller, Paul Monroe, James Mulhern, John A. Pope, Ralph Preston, Nathaniel Reich, Theodore L. Reller, Richard Shryock, Ephraim Speiser, Wei-ts Zen. Aid of The Faculty Research Committee, University of Pennsylvania, for grants in connection with initial study of physical phases of ancient education is gratefully acknowledged. Reuben Goldberg and Victor Junette have generously helped me with photographic work. To Wilhelmine L. Woody, Sadie Bell, Elizabeth H. McKee, and Jeannette C. Weiss, I am indebted for faithful work on the manuscript. Especially am I deeply grateful to members of The Macmillan Company for many courtesies and for generous assistance at all times.

Thomas Woody

*Philadelphia, Pa.*

# CONTENTS

# ILLUSTRATIONS

# 1

# ORIGINS

He who thus considers things in their first growth and origin, whether a state or anything else, will obtain the clearest view of them.    ARISTOTLE

# 1

# INTRODUCTION

A n examination of primitive social organization exposes the roots of many institutions which, in a modified form, become the distinguishing features of more advanced societies. Though education is frequently regarded as the distinguishing mark of civilized society, the view is evidently an error. The basic needs of man are the same, but the mode of their satisfaction varies with his habitat and culture. Training and education are universal; but the quality of the educational process changes. Education—physical, moral, and mental— is seen to have been one of the prominent features of primitive life; although an apparently unconscious process, its significance is not for that reason to be minimized. The history of education, ranging from the blindly groping to the most highly purposive process, is the record of man's reconstruction of his ideals and institutions, and his efforts to mold each generation to them with such skill and insight as he could command. To note the central features of primitive society and the relation of physical education to them; to set forth how certain social groups effected social and educational changes, in transition from primitive life to early civilization; and to portray the evolution of the most advanced societies of the Mediterranean world, and their theories and practices in respect to the well-being of man—these are the purposes of this book.

How many thousand years man lived in a primitive condition before the phenomena of settled civilizations began to appear, it is impossible to say precisely. The time required to pass through Paleolithic and Neolithic cultures varied in different parts of the world, and the exact duration of either of them is unknown. In general, however, Neolithic culture and primitive agriculture are believed to have originated some fifteen thousand to twenty thousand years or more before the Christian era, in the river valleys of Mesopotamia and Egypt, and somewhat more recently in Europe—perhaps twelve thousand years ago. This hazy date line marks roughly the beginning of the great civilizations of the East, whose dominion lasted until the fifth century B.C. The battle of

3

Platæa (479 B.C.), terminating in favor of the Greeks, made certain that Greek civilization was not to be crushed by the weight of Persian power. The succeeding thousand years witnessed the full flowering of Greek genius, the fusion of ·Hellenic and Roman cultures, and finally their disintegration, which marked the end of ancient civilization in the Mediterranean basin.

The last five or six thousand years of the dominant Eastern cultures concern us most, naturally; for of man's education we can infer relatively little from an examination of his weapons, tools, and trinkets; and of his thoughts about his education we can know still less. These millenniums bear testimony to man's increasing capacity for social organization on a grand scale. Vestigial traits of his primitive life remain, but they are so much modified and overlaid that he seems a new person: once dependent on stick and stone, he now makes use of bronze and iron; once a free hunter, he becomes farmer, laborer, merchant, slave; once naked, he now clothes himself richly (or at least some do); once a dweller in cave and tent, he builds palaces and temples (for those who rule); once a wanderer, he builds cities and grows sentimental about "native soil"; once too poor and weak to supply even the most urgent needs, he becomes rich and powerful, lives luxuriously, overpowers his weaker neighbors and creates a great dominion; and, though once an awed believer in a multitude of spirits inhabiting all things seen, he now becomes so bold, on occasion, as to call them one. It is this city-builder and destroyer, this one-god-seeker, who most forcefully strikes our attention in Sumer, Akkad, Babylonia, Assyria, Egypt, India, Persia, and elsewhere in the ancient world. By these and many other traits we know that man, imperfect though he is, has gone far beyond first childhood.

In the small primitive tribal community there was little specialization of function, the clearest division being along sex lines. But when hunting gave way to herding, hoeing, and plowing, life became more and more settled, the group increased in size, wealth, and power, and in place of the fugitive camp the more or less permanent citadel arose. The necessities and opportunities of this larger settled community, interacting upon the variable capacities of man, stimulated the growth of functional classes. It is noteworthy, however, that while certain societies were sufficiently fluid to permit classes to form and sustain themselves by new recruits in each generation, others were bound by strict caste lines, decreed by conquerors who sought to perpetuate their dominion by proclaiming that caste determined the functions which one might perform. Thus, early India knew no strict class organization, but the chains of caste were gradually forged and came to have a nearly universal validity.[1]

---

[1] Manu, 1, 87 ff., in Müller: *The Sacred Books of the East*, xxv, 24; Dutt: *Ancient India*, pp. 8, 67 ff.; Davids: *Buddhist India*, pp. 56 f., 118 f. Consult the bibliography at the end of this volume for additional information concerning works cited.

Among the classes, gradually differentiated, that of priests was important; at times it held undisputed first place. If not that, its rôle was significant by virtue of its influence over other classes through its real or supposed knowledge, its mastery of the people's traditions, its ability to read, to expound, and to increase the literary heritage—all of which seemed like magic to the uninitiated. Next to the wise men in importance were the strong men, the king (sometimes also priest) and his soldiers who trained themselves to do his bidding. Supporting the spiritual and physical rulers was a basic class of workers—agriculturalists, herdsmen, artisans—whose labor made the soil bring forth its fruits, fostered the increase of domestic animals, and produced implements and other goods necessary to the community or valuable for trade. As trade developed, a more or less special merchant class emerged. China designated merchants as a fourth class; in India, the Vaisyas were to "tend cattle," "trade," "lend money," and "cultivate land." [2]

This functional stratification of society was an important phase of growing civilization. With it came differentiation of education. Whereas in primitive life the work of camp and field had been done by women, it came to be performed by a particular class of men, assisted more or less by their women and children; for others it was considered too menial or taboo. These folk, toiling early and late, had slight opportunity for any other education than apprenticeship to their tasks; and little superfluous energy or time for physical exercise and diversion, or for illumination of their minds. The kingly, noble soldier-folk, strong of body and inclined to heroic action, had appropriate professional training in feats of physical skill. Possessed of more leisure, they indulged in physical sports and pastimes, many of which, derived from remote origins in their savage past, served admirably as pre-professional and professional training. The priestly class, busy with its literary invention, was intent upon reading the past and prophesying the future; supported by the labor of one class and protected by the arms of another, it had no obvious or immediate need for physical exertion and training, save as some dance or other exercise of past ages might continue to be credited with religious significance. Naturally, such an elite came to think of education as pre-eminently mental and moral, and frequently exhibited an ascetic unconcern for physical well-being and excellence.

Though early civilizations differed from primitive life in many ways, more importance attaches to certain lines of advancement than to others. It was significant when man substituted a bronze implement for one of stone. Improved tools increased mastery of physical environment and helped to advance those who perfected them to wealth and power. It was still more significant, however, when man discovered his ability to tell stories in pictures, and devised a flexible technique whereby he could leave a record on the rude boulder, on

[2] Manu, I, 90; Smith: *Chinese Characteristics*, p. 28.

papyrus, or on pressed clay. This magic (for it seemed, indeed, powerful magic to make chips, stones, and ordinary clay the messengers of one's thought) extended the realm of man's mind. No longer was he doomed to remain just as poor, mentally, as his own generation; no longer must he remember simply from day to day, from moon to moon, or from year to year. Memory, tradition, "truth," lengthened into generations, centuries, and epochs; the merest youth glibly repeated the hard-won wisdom (and errors) of his ancestral dust, and marveled at the record of heroic exploits which clustered round some age-old name. Not the Hebrew alone, but Hindu, Chinese, Egyptian, and Persian became, in varying degree, the peoples of books. The book is the key to their cultures. The book of law, religion, ritual, custom, philosophy, science, and art became the true sovereign. A priest or king ruled for a lifetime; but the book ruled their children's children. Just as the development of conceptual intelligence and language marked man's divergence from the animal kingdom, so the art of writing and literature became a primary factor in his civilization.

The utilization of letters extended the range of man's mental operations by adding a vast store of vicarious experience to that which, previously, he gained from life directly. Stimulated and fed by these rich streams from out of his own past and also, at times, by those of neighbors whose languages and literatures he learned, man had the prime conditions for critical comparative study. Here and there appear fumbling efforts at critical examination of ideas, a reconstruction of experience, a projection of thinking into the future. In Greece this rise of a conscious philosophy of education is marked by a significant effort to find a happy balance of the education of the mind and the body; to justify the claims of the individual and the collective; and to discover a rational basis for functional social stratification. What had been among primitive and Oriental peoples a slavish following of traditional thought and practice, was subjected to close scrutiny by philosophers who sought the optimum development of the free citizen. The agencies to be utilized were old; but the idea of conscious control of the character of the citizen and the future of society was novel and inspiring, and has had a marked influence on Western education, physical and mental and moral. The notion of planning a better world has had a varying fortune. Likewise, the ideal of harmony of mind and body has been admired and praised, held in contempt, disputed, and ignored. Rome scarcely accepted it; Christian ascetics denied its validity; other folk of the Middle Ages took little heed of it, were even ignorant of it. Since the Renaissance, however, that ideal has increasingly interested men and women of Western Europe. In the modern world, of course, there is a clash between the professional and liberal conceptions of education, physical and mental, as there was in the ancient. Professionally, man is trained physically to be a soldier, for sake of country or for sake of class, according as he is a citizen of bourgeois or proletarian society; again, he is disciplined to become a professional dancer, ballplayer, wrestler, boxer, or bowler, for the entertainment of onlookers, and for the sake of fame, and "the pot." In accord with the liberal conception, however, public playgrounds and clubs for recreation provide increasingly for the normal physical exercise of boys and girls; and schools and colleges have sought, with some success, to combine physical and intellectual education, despite many hindrances that stand in the way.

To this point the relation of education in general to social evolution has been considered. Of physical education, in particular, of its sources, forms, and adaptations amid the shifting scenes of social development, something remains to be said. Physical culture, interpreting it broadly, as one must for a proper understanding, is one of the most ancient phases of man's education. Before his mind struggled after the fruits of reason; before his heart essayed the flights of song; before imagination peopled the world around him with invisible beings, man had cause to be physically active, in work and in play. Through informal physical activities he gained most of that which physical education provides in more formal fashion to-day. Such simple, primitive, natural forms of activity ran back far beyond man's written history; indeed, they were a continuous part of his experience long epochs before the dawn of settled civilization. Education through physical work and play has been, and is, shared by man with other animals; education of the mind has distinguished his societies from theirs.

Anthropology, history, and sociology show conclusively the influence of environment on physical culture. Biologists and psychologists emphasize the view that the primary bases of play are found in man's own nature, which is predisposed to physical exercise and also to a restless mental curiosity. To give exercise to muscles and to provide explanations for what one finds around him, are both fundamentally satisfying. This natural theory of the origin of sports, comprising, as it does, the factors of native endowment interacting with environmental forces, was not unknown to the ancient world. In its present outlines, however, it is a modern formulation which has evolved since the rise of naturalism and represents a sharp reaction against the ascetic conceptions of medieval Europe. Groos' *The Play of Man* and *The Play of Animals* set forth the native basis of play, the impulse to bodily and mental activity, and its educational significance. Translated into English at the beginning of this century, his work gave a great stimulus to further study and the recognition of play as a significant form of education.[3] Reid's *Principles of Heredity* also developed at some length the theory that random, apparently useless play activities of

[3] *Play of Man*, pp. 74 ff.

animals and humans are important agencies of early growth and are a natural basis for education. Indeed, play itself is education.[4] This view became all but universal in the next generation.

The origins of physical culture are to be found in tendencies that are native in man. These drives are numerous and complex; it is not necessary to present a complete analysis of them here. Psychologists differ somewhat in their analyses of man's native equipment.[5] James lists many reflexes, for example, sneezing, coughing, gagging, hiccuping, snoring; and more complex tendencies, which he is content to call instincts, such as sucking, biting, clasping, carrying to the mouth, crying, turning the head, holding the head erect, sitting up, standing, locomotion, vocalization, imitation, emulation, pugnacity, sympathy, hunting, fear of many things and experiences, appropriation, construction, play, curiosity, sociability and shyness, secretiveness, cleanliness, modesty and shame, love, jealousy, and parental love. Watson explains, at some length, why the behaviorist finds "none of the instincts listed by James," and accounts for all the observed tendencies in man by the "conditioning" process which has been studied by Pavlov, Twitmyer, and others.[6] Woodworth, too, agrees to "give up the word *instinct*," as applied to many of the tendencies named above; nevertheless, he refuses to call them *habits*. Each tendency has, he says, ". . . a nucleus that is unlearned, but each develops in the individual by a process of learning, though perhaps by maturation as well." [7]

Students of the history of physical education need not go far into the verbal differences of the psychologists. It is clear that many observe the same phenomena, yet call them by different names. Let it suffice to say that certain fundamental general tendencies in man have constituted, and do constitute, the starting point of his physical culture, informal and formal. Central in importance are these: (1) tendencies to satisfy hunger; (2) those that minister, directly or indirectly, to the preservation of the individual when opposed or pursued by foes; (3) complex and varied drives operative in mating and propagation; (4) the bent toward a degree of random manipulation of brain and brawn, which in itself appears to be satisfying to man and animals when they are in a state of health and freshness; [8] (5) an inclination to fear the strange, the untried, the unknown; and (6) a preference for gregarious behavior. There are, of course, intricate interrelations. From the tendency to satisfy the first need, there developed elaborate exercises connected with hunting, fishing, agri-

4 Reid: *The Principles of Heredity*, pp. 241 ff.

5 Cf. James: *Principles of Psychology*, II, chap. 24; McDougall: *Outline of Psychology*, chaps. 3–5; Thorndike: *Educational Psychology*, Vol. I, *The Original Nature of Man*; Watson: *The Ways of Behaviorism*, chap. 2; Woodworth: *Psychology*, chap. 6.

6 Pavlov: *Conditioned Reflexes; Lectures on Conditioned Reflexes;* Twitmyer: *A Study of the Kneejerk;* Woodworth: *Experimental Psychology,* chap. 5.

7 Woodworth: *Psychology*, p. 246.

8 Thorndike: *op. cit.*, I, 137 f., 146 ff.

culture, and the camp; from the second, the manifold activities of man, individual and collective, connected with the industries of peace and war; from the third, many forms of dancing; from the fourth, spontaneous play, dancing, and many sedentary pastimes as well; and from man's fears of the unknown, instinctive or learned as they might be, plus his capacity for mental manipulation, there sprang explanations of invisible causes, or supposed causes and controls, of the phenomena of the visible world. This body of explanations of the causes and controls of man's life made up the content of primitive religious belief. The beliefs of man influenced his actions. The invisible moving force must be propitiated; therefore he danced for it or made obeisance to it by some other ceremonial.

¶ Physical exercise is necessary to the growth, the health, and the happiness of man, mental as well as physical. For man is a unity. His "mind" may be isolated for the purpose of study and discussion, but not in actual life. Some profess to see, as a result of the development and application of science to the labor of man, the possibility of a gradual disintegration of his physical nature. Such a view is obviously fantastic. When all labor is done by machines, as it may sometime be, man will still need healthy muscles and vital organs as a condition of healthy life. Such a sturdy system, if not developed by the normal labor of the day, must be gained through various substitute forms of exercise.

The history of physical education reveals that, at various stages of development, particular modes of physical activity have ministered to man's health and happiness. In primitive societies there were manifold labors, made necessary by the struggle to gain a livelihood; exercises of a warlike character, both defensive and aggressive; spontaneous play, imitative and inventive in character; and dancing, which was generally closely correlated with the quest for food, military affairs, mating, and religion. Besides these categories may be noted sportive contests, developed to a point of perfection by a few for the entertainment of others, people whose wealth and position made them chiefly vicarious consumers, passive observers, of that which once they had themselves performed. Ultimately appear remedial exercises, "health gymnastics," designed to reclaim for man that priceless boon of health, of which a complex civilization so often robbed him. These forms of physical exercise, never mutually exclusive, have been characteristic of primitive societies, and have developed in advanced cultures as well. They are found to-day among Papuans, Borneans, Indians, Eskimos, and other nature peoples; they existed in the great empires of the Orient, at the beginning of recorded history; modified in some respects, they are found in the most highly developed societies of to-day. What aspect of man's life, indeed, has not borne the imprint of his physical propensities and the institutions that have arisen from them?

# 2

# PRIMITIVE LIFE AND EDUCATION

The origins of man's culture, physical and mental, are found in his original nature and in the environment with which he has had to cope. These factors have been interactive. Environment has shaped man, and he has modified the world into which he was born. Of the two, environment and man, the former appears to have been the more variable, the latter more constant.

An indelible picture has been fixed in our minds: the portrait of an age, "When wild in wood the noble savage ran." This picture of freedom, called to mind by the poet, is neither entirely accurate nor complete. Primitive man loved freedom and was in some ways free; in other respects he was bound by a life of struggle and imprisoned in a vast unknown. The love of freedom is noted by many observers of primitive life. The Californian Indians, Choris informs us, would come in troops to the mission in the winter, "but in the spring most of them abandon it. This manner of living does not please them; they become bored with constant work and . . . abundance. In their mountains they lead a life, free and independent though miserable. . . . After a few months' stay . . . they generally begin to be fretful, grow thin, and continually cast mournful glances toward the mountains which they see in the distance." [1]

The freedom of primitive man's life in woodland, prairie, or mountains impresses us less, however, than the difficulties which challenged his existence. The first need was food; to satisfy it, man had to forsake freedom and idleness, in some degree, for industry. In the friendliest environments, the industry required was not great, apparently, for primitive tastes were as simple as the means for satisfying them. One took what nature offered and used it with as little preparation as possible. Choris tells us that rats, snakes, insects, and roots served the Californian Indians for nourishment. This menu is, doubtless, in-

[1] Choris: Voyage Pittoresque autour du Monde, pp. 2 f.

complete: fish, rabbit, bear, beaver, buffalo, and other animals at times rewarded the skill of Indian hunters with a comfortable feeling around the waist. Papuans ate fish, turtle, prawns, dugong, crabs, crayfish, carpet-snake, crocodile, dog, cat; while sago, yams, sweet potatoes, bananas, and cocoanuts were also prepared with considerable skill.[2] The Aruntas of Australia lived on lizards, marsupials, emus, kangaroos, opossum, echidna, euros, rock-wallabies, rock-pigeons, eagle-hawk, and such vegetables as the bulbous Irriakura, pods of the acacia, the seeds of a kind of Claytonia, and other natural products which the environment afforded. In fact, everything edible, "animal and plant alike," was taken for food.[3]

In more advanced early societies, agricultural labor supplemented the chase. But there, too, life was still simple. Means,[4] remarks that, in Peru, needs of the people were few, and the Incas sought to keep them so. The mass of the people lived on dried llama, roasted and boiled corn and potatoes, certain combinations of these seasoned with red pepper, soups from leaves and roots, bread of maize, and occasionally fresh llama, huanaco, and venison. As beverages the Incas used brews made from maize, maguey leaves, and *mulli* berries. Tobacco was used in a limited way for medical purposes; and *cuca* was even more narrowly restricted because of its evil effects.

Among certain aboriginal groups of North America, agriculture was considerably advanced. This was notably true of the Zuñi of New Mexico and Arizona. Many tribes, one authority says, were essentially agricultural and ". . . all subsisted in much larger degree than is commonly supposed on the produce of the soil." Such foods as succotash, hominy, pinole, tamale, pemmican, corn, potatoes, beans, and squashes were generally used. Even "the indigenous modes of preparing food" have been thought by some students worthy of special study, with a view to their preservation and continuance.[5]

Clothing of primitives is simple. In the friendliest climates little mental or physical effort is required to provide it. The Indians of California, Choris asserted, "go absolutely naked." The Arunta, also, are commonly unacquainted with clothing. Punans and Kayans of Borneo generally wear a sort of sash or girdle around the waist, bands around the legs below the knee and, quite commonly, also around the lower or upper arm. A cloth wound round the head completes their outfit. The women are a little more fully covered than the men.[6] The peoples of Melanesia and Polynesia frequently go quite uncovered. When clothing is worn, it is a rude girdle, breechcloth, or a short skirt of grass.

[2] Riley: *Among Papuan Head-Hunters*, pp. 54 ff.
[3] Spencer and Gillen: *The Arunta*, I, 15 ff.
[4] *Ancient Civilizations of the Andes*, pp. 308 ff.
[5] Stevenson: "The Zuñi Indians," 23d *Ann. Rep. Bur. Am. Ethnol.*, pp. xi–xii, xxviii.
[6] Choris: *op. cit.*, pp. 2 f.; Hose, *Natural Man*, and Spencer and Gillen, *op. cit.*, show many illustrations.

The skirt of grass, or leaves, seems indispensable for females. At childbirth a grass cloak or mat, covering the body from head to foot, is worn by the women of some tribes.[7]

If the production of clothing causes little exertion, save in cold climates, implements, even though few in number, often require great pains to manufacture. The bow and arrow, spear, boat, snowshoes, all of which serve the chase; the ball-club, snow snake, ring-and-pin, and other implements used in sports; the trinkets for adornment; the rude plows, hoes, harrows, wagons, flails, stoves, buckets, baskets, basins, and pots which marked emergence into agricultural life—all these reveal man, the lover of activity and creation, impelled by necessity, yet often inspired with an aesthetic sense which produced a beautiful industrial art.[8]

Rivers, lakes, and small boats to ride upon them, constituted the earliest means by which man traveled from his campfire to distant places. To make use of these natural highways, man was compelled to become a boatbuilder. The elaborate preparation, the ceremonies, the skill, required to make a canoe among Papuan head-hunters, are described by Riley.[9] To build the biggest and best, experts well trained by experience are required; and they are not lacking, for boys of twelve are already able to imitate the craft of their elders. A vast amount of myth often came to envelop and embroider man's notions concerning his acquisition of knowledge and skill in various crafts and in social undertakings. In the mythology of the Onondagas a divine patron and counselor, Ta-ren-ya-wa-go, came and dwelt among them for a time. Hi-a-wat-ha, as he was known on earth, was wise and clever in every way. Good government, control of hunting and fishing grounds, and the cultivation of corn and beans, he brought to them and made the Onondagas exalted among the neighboring nations. Most remarkable of all was his magic light canoe.[10] A poetic portrait of man, the skillful, aesthetic builder of boats, is drawn in the story of Hiawatha, who girdles the tree, removes the bark, hews boughs of cedar, and shapes the framework . . . that he may—

> Build a swift Cheemaun for sailing,
> That shall float upon the river. . . .

Following the natural highways, man often came upon strange men and mores. Amalgamation by peaceful or by warlike means sometimes followed. Larger and more numerous communities had need of better paths, roads, bridges, bigger and better boats. Such an extension of building activity is found among

---

[7] Brown: *Melanesians and Polynesians*, pp. 202, 310–5.
[8] Means: *op. cit.*, pp. 70 ff., and chap. 11; Hose: *op. cit.*, Pt. IV; Furness: *Home Life of Borneo Head-Hunters*, pp. 146 ff.; Stevenson: *op. cit.*, *loc. cit.*, pp. 349–83.
[9] *Op. cit.*, chap. 8.
[10] Schoolcraft: *Archives of Aboriginal Knowledge*, V, 157 ff.

the Incas, whose excellent roads and footways formed a strong bond, uniting a great number of societies. Two chief highways ran through Cuzco and bound the whole coast and the highlands to the capital. These were supplemented by numerous "secondary roads," and even "causeways and suspension bridges" were built across swampy ground and rivers.[11]

The need of food was constant and universal; that of clothing and shelter, variable. The habitations of primitive men varied with the locality and the ingenuity of the people; but the best of them were crude. Architecture is one of the finest arts of civilization. The Indians described by Choris "had no fixed dwellings"; a rock, a bush, protected them amid all the vicissitudes of life. Other red men had well-constructed tepees of boughs, skins, and bark. Those of the Southwest, more advanced, built strong pueblos, with their "houses built one upon another in a succession of terraces, the roof of one forming the floor or yard of the one next above, and so on until in some cases five tiers of dwellings are successively erected . . . ," though generally there were only two.[12] Though they had advanced to an agricultural economy, Inca peasants had only thatched roofs and earthen floors, and generally lacked windows and chimneys. Though certainly not comfortable, their houses were substantial, the best of them, on the coast, being constructed of adobe. Means believes that they were probably not less comfortable than those of peasants in southern Europe up to the present century, though they had neither "chairs, tables, dressers," nor iron, glass, brass, or pewter objects and "wheeled tools" such as European commoners had long considered indispensable. Houses of the nobility were constructed of masonry, and were well furnished.[13]

In primitive life there was a rough division of labor: that allotted to men and that belonging to women. This plan resulted, naturally, in differentiation of education for boys and girls. Drudgery usually fell to the females. Women in some cases, however, were skilled in medical ceremonies, but these were the exception.[14] Schoolcraft [15] notes that the wife of the hunter had "entire control of the wigwam," while a large part of the hunter's time was "spent in seeking game." Among Dakotahs the women were reported as more industrious than the men. "The women do the cooking" and "construct and remove the lodges," which are "from eight to fifteen feet in diameter, about ten to fifteen feet high, and [are] made of buffalo-skins tanned." [16] Among agricultural peoples, such as the Incas, the sphere of women was the home, where all

[11] Means: op. cit., pp. 329 ff.
[12] Stevenson: op. cit., loc. cit., pp. 349 f.; cf. Choris: op. cit., for illustrations from the life of many primitives; Schoolcraft: op. cit., ii, 58, 63, 66, 80.
[13] Means: op. cit., pp. 310 f., 322 f.
[14] Corlett: The Medicine-Man of the American Indian, pp. 108, 202, 237, 244.
[15] Op. cit., ii, 63.
[16] Ibid., iv, 67 f.

domestic work was performed, including making "all the clothing of the family." [17] Stevenson reports that Zuñi Indian women delighted ". . . in house building, especially in plastering the houses. They consider this their special prerogative and would feel that their rights were infringed upon were men to do it. . . . Little girls assist in bringing the water used in mixing the mortar, working industriously . . . trudging from the river with their diminutive water vases on their heads. . . ." Men do the heavier work, however, laying foundations, dressing the logs, and placing them in position.[18]

In the restless quest for food and shelter, man is kin to the rest of the animal world, but he differs in that he is more adaptable, less fixed and limited in his reactions to the world around him. The quest for satisfactory adaptation, a greater degree of certainty and happiness, first blindly groping and then conscious, has made his history far more intricate and variable than the life cycle of his lowlier comrades. This quest after certainty characterizes primitive as well as modern man.

Beyond the outward struggles for food, for clothing, and for shelter, man waged a fourth conquest: to secure himself against a world invisible, which his curious, fearful, restless mind fancied in every visible thing. This quest after the essence of things, the effort to ferret out, explain, and control the causes of phenomena, marked man as a radical investigator and experimenter, even though his explanations and guesses, when once established as traditions, served to bar him temporarily from further improvement. Herein was the beginning of religion, philosophy, and science.

Man's efforts to unravel the mystery of the invisible was rooted in the necessity of controlling and using the visible world for his own needs. How could he control and use the substance if he did not first gain mastery of, or perhaps effect a friendly relation with, its shadow, its essence, its moving force? That there was such a double, he was convinced.[19] If a rock rolled down a declivity, what moved it? If water swept away his camp, did not some spirit stir it? If lightning flashed, what caused it to appear and disappear, leaving destruction behind it? If rain came not and crops withered, did not a spirit withhold it because of some displeasure with man? Since rocks, water, winds, lightning, thunder, indeed all the elements of nature, seemed mightier than he, and since it was impossible to live without them, man sought either to ease these processes by propitiating the spirits which controlled them, or, if possible,

[17] Means: op. cit., p. 311.
[18] Stevenson: op. cit., lôc. cit., p. 349.
[19] Cf. Tylor: Primitive Culture, 1, chap. 11; Levy-Brühl: Das Denken der Naturvölker, pp. 61 ff.; Im Thurn: Among the Indians of Guiana, chap. 17; Raum: Chaga Childhood, pp. 237 ff.; Opler: An Apache Life-way, pp. 186–315; Barnes: The History of Western Civilization, 1, 56 ff.

actually to gain ascendancy over the spirits themselves by the employment of powerful magic.

Prayers, dances, and a host of other ceremonies, designed to propitiate nature spirits, have developed among primitive peoples throughout the world. Mandan hunters sang and danced in reverent yet determined mood to cause buffalo herds to wander toward their village.[20] Pueblo Indian agriculturists invoked the thunder, lightning, and rain that corn might be plentiful and good:

> I am praying to the lightning to ripen my corn,
> I am praying to the thunder which carries the lightning.
> Corn is sweet where lightning has fallen.[21]

The multitude of nature gods and the songs and prayers addressed to them are indeed bewildering. Millenniums passed, and still man trembled before the powerful world of spirits that his mind had fashioned. The earliest literatures of ancient civilizations bear testimony to his constant concern with their propitiation. Ultimately, however, the conquest of the unknown, invisible, and mysterious forces was simplified and reduced to a systematic method. Science found law and order in the world instead of capricious willful spirits and inspired in men a fair serenity, such as that which animated the scientist-philosopher-poet Goethe, as he sang:

> Thou gavest me lordly Nature for a kingdom,
> And power to feel and to enjoy it. . . .

### EDUCATION OF PRIMITIVE PEOPLES

Education may be thought of as formal and informal, theoretical and practical, mental and physical, whether modern life or that of primitives is under consideration. The relative importance of the formal and the informal is altered significantly, however, as one passes from primitive to highly developed civilizations. Among nature peoples the informal, physical, and practical activities of life occupy an extensive place; in advanced societies man's more thorough intellectual comprehension of his world leads to an expansion of formal institutions which cultivate his hard-won areas of knowledge and seek consciously to extend their boundaries. This social metamorphosis and the shift to an emphasis on formal, intellectual education have not uncommonly been carried to an extent injurious to the physical well-being of society—at least, those members of it upon whom the incidence of the new learning fell.

MENTAL EDUCATION  Though one speaks of mind and body, yet understands that they are unitary, so speaking of mental and physical education

[20] Catlin: *Letters and Notes on the North American Indians*, I, 127 f.
[21] Lowell: "Songs of the Pueblo Indians," *The Dial*, LXIX, 250.

by no means implies a lack of interaction and interdependence. The interrelationships are, indeed, so ubiquitous and intricate as to render it impossible to draw a line between them. But though so often closely intermingled, mental education sprang from man's effort to subjugate his world by explanation of its motive forces; physical activities have been conditioned both by these explanations and by the potentialities and limitations of the body's mechanism. Since all things physical and sensible were held to be controlled by invisible powers, primitive man sought some explanation of this extremely significant relationship. Such reasons, beliefs, suppositions—right, wrong, or mixed as they doubtless were—constituted his mental furniture. In sickness and in health, in life and in death, he sought to make his peace with the invisible world, in the somewhat uncertain light of these explanations. To indoctrinate the young with these notions was the purpose of formal primitive education; yet some inkling of them must have been informally apprehended.

That this phase of education was thought to be of great importance, seems clear in light of the practices of nature peoples. Since it dealt with the occult, the mysterious, the intricate, the invisible, it was but natural that only the old men, wizards, shamans, or others who had profited by long experience or by special study of such things, were competent to direct it. Ultimately a special class arose which gave attention to such matters. Such a class, a priesthood, passed judgment on what was proper for their people to know, and elaborated its own body of beliefs about the invisible and the methods of controlling it. This class possessed more leisure for reflection and probably greater powers of reflection and intuition. Systematic use of their leisure produced an accumulation of esoteric wisdom, first preserved by oral tradition, later in written form.

Just as the character of the knowledge determined that only the experienced and expert could possess and impart it, so also it was a factor in fixing the occasion when instruction should be given. Wise men could not be ever at hand to inform the uninitiated; neither were the uninitiated always ready to be instructed. Hence, presumably, arose the practice of having ceremonial occasions when youths of an impressionable age were brought together in small groups to be acquainted with tribal taboos, secrets—things so sacred often as not to bear repetition.

This formal education which sought to impress tribal notions upon each generation was imparted chiefly through totemistic and initiatory ceremonies. Rites pertaining to the tribal totem were important to primitive peoples, since they regarded all things, phenomena, plants, animals, and men as kin. Spencer says of the Pueblos that they saw all as parts of one "system of all-conscious and inter-related life, in which the degree of relationship seems to be determined largely, if not wholly, by the degrees of resemblance." "The belief in relationship based on real or fancied resemblance is shown clearly in their symbolism. Thus the forked line represents both lightning and the serpent with its forked tongue, because it is believed there is a close relationship between them. Again, the swift arrow is related to the lightning, and generally has the zig-zag line representing this phenomenon painted on the shaft. The snake dance . . . has for its basis the belief in the close relationship between the serpent, the lightning and storm. It is an intercession for rain, and the snakes, by their peculiar relationship, become mediators. The Pueblo goes even fur-ther. Through his inability to distinguish between subject and object, he car-ries this relationship existing between form and function in either animals or inanimate beings so far as to construct objects of stone or wood in imitation of certain powerful animals, in the belief that he can, through his created re-sembling forms, gain power over these animals. Thus he has developed his fetichistic system of mediation, which is a prominent feature of his worship." [22]

The primitive's belief that all the world is animated is commented on by almost all observers. "Every object for him possesses a spiritual life," says Stevenson, "so that celestial bodies, mountains, rocks, the flora of the earth, and the earth itself are to him quite different from what they are to civilized man. The sturdy pine, the delicate sapling, the fragrant blossom, the giant rock, and the tiny pebble play alike their part in the mystic world of the aborig-inal man." [23]

Brown noted in *Melanesians and Polynesians* a tendency to stress the idea of kinship between men and their totems, which they were in the habit of call-ing "our relatives." [24] The totem is to them a "shadow" of their god. Proof of conversion from heathenism was given by one family by eating their former totem—albeit with fear and trembling. This belief in kinship between man and his totem is frequently, though not always, traceable to the fact that primitive man, not understanding his origin, was wont to ascribe it to various elements of his nonhuman environment.[25]

An understanding of the importance of initiatory ceremonies may be gained by a brief review of the description of certain of them in Spencer and Gillen's study of *The Arunta*.[26] Every native must pass through elaborate ceremonies before becoming a full-fledged member of a tribe. Though they vary as to de-tails the rites have much in common and serve similar purposes. Among the Arunta there are four great ceremonials, beginning about ten or twelve and extending, in some cases, until the mature age of thirty years. The first is called *Alkira-kiwuma* or "throwing up to the sky"; the second, *Lartna* or circum-cision; the third, *Arilta* or subincision; and the fourth, *Engwura*, a ceremonial

22 Spencer: *Education of the Pueblo Child*, pp. 69 ff.
23 *Op. cit., loc. cit.*, p. 20.
24 *Op. cit.*, pp. 27 ff., 218, 248, 278 f.
25 Todd: *The Primitive Family as an Educational Agency*, pp. 64 ff.
26 *Op. cit.*, 1, 175–303. The Sacred Pole (*Kauwa-auwa*) plays a prominent part in these rites.

ARUNTA SACRED POLE CEREMONY
(Courtesy, Australian National Travel Association)

ordeal of fire. Before the first ceremony the boy is called *Ambaquerka;* after it he is named *Ulpmerka.* During *Lartna* the initiate is known as *Wurtja;* after it he is *Arakurta.* When the next ceremony, *Arilta,* has been performed he becomes *Atua-kurka;* this he remains till after the fourth, *Engwura,* when he is recognized as *Urliara.*

The *Engwura,* the last of the initiatory rites, is made up of "series of ceremonies concerned with the totems," involving "tests both moral and physical," intended to strengthen and give "courage, wisdom, endurance and self-restraint" to those who go through them and make them more kindly and "less apt to quarrel." Naturally the rites have the effect also of causing the youth to look with greater awe and reverence upon the old men who are able to tell them so much and whom they are compelled to obey. The *Engwura* rituals vary considerably in the different totem groups which practice them. Some require only a day or two; another, the *Achilpa,* or wild-cat totem, demands four months. Spencer and Gillen report that every day of the four months was given over to a new ceremony or several of them, but that it was possible to recognize five distinct stages in the entire *Engwura:* the first, the dispatch of messengers, assembling of the people, and "dancing corroborees" participated in by men and women; the second, marked by the separation of men and women, and a performance of sacred ceremonies by the men on the specially laid-out *Engwura* ground, after which the initiates were known as *Illpong-worra;* third, the continuance of religious rites, during which the young men were forbidden to speak to certain of the elders; the fourth phase, marked by the ordeal of fire, after which initiates were given the name *Urliara;* and the fifth, in which men and women joined, when the initiates made an offering of meat to those with whom they had previously been forbidden to speak, the ban of silence was removed in a special ceremony, and the young men were recognized as full-fledged members of the tribe.

Spencer and Gillen describe at length the rôle of totems in the life of Australian natives. Every person "is born into some totem," that is, "belongs to a group of persons," all of whom are named for and are "especially associated with, some natural object." [27] Though the totems are generally plants and animals, they may also be clouds, water, wind, sun, and other elements. It is customary, moreover, to associate various features of the environment, such as a tree, a water hole, a mountain, a lake, a stream, with a particular totem; these, because of their totemic association, have a sacred meaning for members of that totem. Those who belong to the same totem are, then, members of a great family, unified by a common bond of belief and customary ceremonials. In general, totemistic ceremonies have as their purpose the promotion of growth and multiplication of the plant or animal for which the totem group is named, and are generally performed at the time of year when the animals breed, or when the plants bloom. Ceremonies of the water totem are apt to be held when there has been insufficient rain. Clearly, the natives desire to protect themselves against economic want by propitiation of the spirit world with whose welfare their own is always associated.

### PHYSICAL ASPECTS OF PRIMITIVE CULTURE

Physical and mental education cannot be completely separated. Initiatory, totemistic, and medical ceremonies frequently include dancing and other physical exercises, and so contribute somewhat to the development and testing of physical endurance, courage, and skill, either incidentally or by design. Thus Means, in his *Ancient Civilizations of the Andes,*[28] tells of the youth of "the land of the Four Parts," who were always adept in the art of running, and were called upon to exhibit their skill in it at the initiation ceremonies which marked

[27] *Ibid.,* I, 67–124.
[28] *Op. cit.,* pp. 332 f.

the pubertal age. But though they are thus closely interrelated, it is possible to distinguish between that type of education which sprang from man's natural tendency to mental activity and the explanation of things and that which was an outgrowth of his restless bodily powers.

The physical activities of primitive man fall naturally into two chief categories: (1) an informal apprenticeship by which he prepared for the various physical occupations essential to life and (2) play activities which may have served a utilitarian end ultimately, but were recreational and were engaged in primarily because they were fundamentally satisfying.

The terms "work" and "play" are adult conceptions. The basic rhythms of both are the same. Those tendencies and abilities which enable man to play, enable him to work also. But the psychology of work and that of play are quite different: the adult performs an exercise because of necessity and calls it work; the child imitates the same performance and calls it play. The motive in work is external, serious, and often compulsory; in play, internal and spontaneous. It is clear that in so far as compulsion be reduced, work becomes play; and that in so far as compulsion be introduced into play activities, they become work.

Among primitives the care of health and physical development in infancy and early boyhood was often not as good as it was in later years when the child was free to run about and imitate the various activities of its elders. The Inca mother carried her baby on her back, and took no thought of that original nature which so early prompts man to more or less random manipulation of the body; nor was the situation much better when the child, a little older, was wrapped in a bit of cloth and stood up in a hole just deep enough to come up to his armpits.[29] The children of North American Indians were similarly restrained from activity in infancy. Penn wrote of the Delawares that they wrapped the newborn "in a clout," laid it on a thin board, and swaddled it "fast upon the board to make it straight."[30] Numerous devices of modern civilization appear to have been invented to save the mother rather than to allow the child to grow.

*Apprenticeship*  Physical development through practical apprenticeship to labor could be illustrated voluminously by references to the life of any primitive people. Only in the case of leisure classes (in more highly developed societies) "who toil not, and neither do they spin," does ordinary, everyday labor fail to demand physical exercise.

One of the earliest types of practical physical apprenticeship to be found among primitives is hunting, to which man turned because of necessity. There

[29] *Ibid.*, pp. 365 f.
[30] Myers: *William Penn*, p. 30.

is every reason to believe, as Charles Hose says,[31] that the paternal hunter was proud of introducing the young lad to the mysteries and difficulties of the chase, which demanded both mental and physical prowess, and that he exulted and applauded when youth gave evidence of having acquired some skill. Among the Dakotahs, boys were taught "when young" to use bow and arrow. "Little boys" practiced shooting at small sunfish, using a string attached both to bow and arrow to pull up the fish when it had been impaled. Hunting larger game was begun about twelve years of age.[32] Among the Delawares, Penn tells us, boys were "ripe for the woods" about fifteen years of age.[33] A remarkable degree of skill with bow and arrow came from such early and continuous practice. Tixier says of the Osage that they seldom needed a second arrow when shooting bison.[34] Among the Arunta of Australia, "from earliest childhood boys and girls alike are trained to take note of every track made by every living thing." [35] This skill, throwing the spear and boomerang, and running are quite indispensable to sustain life. Among Papuan head-hunters boys are accustomed to make little canoes, excellent in "design and craftsmanship," as early as the age of twelve.[36] Borneans want their sons to be brave and fearless, and they accustom them early to the realistic use of weapons and the spilling of human blood.[37] Play at war games has been a part of the education of all warlike peoples.

Among those groups that have entered upon an agricultural existence, the apprenticeship of the body to physical toil assumes new forms. Of the Pueblos Spencer concludes:

"The principal occupations . . . such as agriculture, hunting, pottery and implement making, weaving and building, are all imitated in the plays of the children; at first very rudely of course, but later with considerable fidelity, for imitation has become almost instinctive with the Pueblos. They are tacitly encouraged in these plays by their elders, who provide those things which the child nature calls for when beyond the stage in which the bent stick suffices for a bow and the twig for the arrow, and when his plays become less purely symbolical. Thus, the Indian boy is provided with a bow and arrows and becomes a hunter, a battle axe and becomes a warrior, or he is given a plat of ground where he constructs miniature acequias and tills the soil or herds his flocks. With a few stones and some adobe he constructs miniature imitations

31 Hambly and Hose: *Origins of Education among Primitive Peoples,* p. xi.
32 Schoolcraft: *op. cit.,* IV, 61.
33 Myers: *op. cit.,* p. 30.
34 *Tixier's Travels,* p. 192.
35 Spencer and Gillen: *op. cit.,* I, 20 ff.
36 Riley: *op. cit.,* p. 108.
37 Furness: *op. cit.,* pp. 54–66.

of those buildings which have been the wonder of the ethnologist, or he may become a weaver, an arrow-maker or a skin-dresser. Very early, indeed, he will be expected to take an active part in the simpler of these occupations, for the Pueblo children are taught to work as soon as they can be of the least assistance. Likewise, the little girl imitates in her plays those occupations which fall to the woman's lot among the Pueblos; maternal duties, household cares, bearing of burdens, as well as the more skillful occupation of pottery making, basket and cloth weaving, bead and shell work, all find a place in her spontaneous activities. Like her brother, also, she is very early required to begin her life work. Little girls of five and six assist in caring for the younger children, carry water and wood, and even help to prepare the clay for the pottery and the material for the basket weaving. As the children grow older they gradually take a larger share in all the occupations common to the Pueblos." [38]

Many former activities may still hold some place among agricultural or industrial peoples, however, either because they still have some use, or because they have simply become a game. Thus hunting, wrestling, boxing, running, and many other sports and pastimes survive among societies which do not depend on them to provide food or to prepare for defensive or aggressive action.

Sufficient evidence has been cited to show that, besides the usual hunting, fishing, and fighting which are generally thought to have occupied his time, primitive man was active in many other ways. The conclusion seems well-founded that one thus active, and living on a simple diet in the open air, had no need of systematic physical training to stimulate him or to satisfy his natural urge to physical exercise. Life was sufficiently rigorous and varied to supply that which in more complex societies, especially those highly industrialized, must be gained by systematic, purposeful effort.

*Dancing* Though primitive life demanded that man be active in a directly useful way that he might not die of hunger, or by the hand of enemies, or by exposure, there were other factors that caused him to be active both in a playful and in a reverent, serious way. In fact, apparently nonpurposive, playful activities occupied a large place in an existence quite innocent of all chronometers save the sun. Frequently pleasure was mingled with a serious intent. Many games which have survived among modern peoples and which now have little or no serious purpose were not devoid of it in earlier days.

There is probably no better example of the survival of primitive practices in modern life than dancing. What causes this survival, long after certain of the previously assigned reasons for it have ceased to exist? The answer lies in human nature. In so far as any activity satisfies some original or "instinctive"

[38] Spencer: *op. cit.*, pp. 76 ff.

demand of man it has, and will continue to have, adequate reason for existence, though some of its early ideological associations and justification may have faded from his mind completely. Such an original satisfier rhythm seems to be. Life is a rhythm; dancing is life itself, as Havelock Ellis maintains in *The Dance of Life*. Young and old dance to-day chiefly for pleasure; they have laid aside some of the remoter purposes which moved the primitive to rhythmic expression. Highly developed peoples cease to implore their deities with ritualistic dances. No advanced "cultured" peoples, intent on killing their enemies, prepare seriously for war by treading martial measures; nor does the white-haired sage, when seized with pain, challenge the power of disease-demons by a devil dance. Civilized man takes more and better medicine; he fights bigger, more destructive wars, and says longer, wordier prayers.

The serious purpose of primitive dancing has been noted by many scholars. Karsten, in his *Civilization of the South American Indians*, reports that dances ". . . are generally no amusement, but a serious ceremonial performance." [39] Even among those Indians who are supposed by some students to know only "profane dances," Karsten believes that the original, serious, magical, or religious purpose has simply been forgotten. Hambly [40] maintains that the oldest dances are probably those "mimetic" rhythmic ceremonials which man employed to promote faunal and floral fertility, and which go back to the earliest hunting and crude, agricultural periods of his existence. To these are linked also those dances connected with the "main aspects of human endeavour," such as hunting, sex-life, and all dealing with the spirit world. In primitive society, "every branch of musical expression is a communal concern," a necessary element in all training of the young, whereas among more advanced peoples dancing commonly becomes a professional art or is regarded as a means to pleasure on the part of the individual. Hambly's classification recognizes two chief types of dances among primitives: social, and magic or religious. It is noteworthy, however, that all are, broadly considered, both religious and social, and have to do with all the important affairs of man from the time he is born till he takes his departure. The most prominent of them are those that concern birth, initiation into the tribe, marriage, war, worship of totems, getting food, the propitiation of good spirits and the exorcism of evil, and finally the advent of death. Ellis declares that it is dancing that "has socialized man." [41] It must not be overlooked, however, that though physical development, recreation, and health do not seem to have been consciously sought through dancing, they were probably the chief benefits derived from it. The hygienic importance

[39] *Op. cit.*, pp. 17 f.
[40] *Tribal Dancing*, pp. 77 ff.
[41] Ellis: *The Dance of Life*, p. 64; Hambly: *op. cit.*, pp. 15 f.

of certain primitive dances, by aiding organs of "generation, parturition, and evacuation," has been recognized by some ethnologists.[42]

Though it is impossible to present a full story of dancing in this work,[43] a number of illustrative citations, drawn from the life of widely scattered primitive groups, will convey a fair understanding of this phenomenon of primitive life. As noted, all dances were in a large sense religious: just as one cannot separate the primitive from his animistic conceptions, so one cannot isolate his dances from those things which they were thought to influence or control.

Hunger comes quickly and calls imperatively for satisfaction, whether one be savage or civilized, and it is an eminently persuasive view that the earliest dances were connected with the control of the game and plants which formed the chief source of food supplies. A few examples of this method of control will suffice to illustrate a fairly universal practice. The Mayas feasted and danced in honor of the gods of hunting, holding a deer's skull in one hand and an arrow in the other, the purpose being to "ensure a successful hunting season." [44] Catlin, who visited many Indian tribes and described their habits carefully, gives an instructive account of the Mandan buffalo-dance, in which the economic purpose is evident. His interesting description, which follows, gives many details of the setting and conduct of the dance:

"Buffaloes, it is known, are a sort of roaming creatures, congregating occasionally in huge masses, and strolling away about the country from east to west, or from north to south, or just where their whims or strange fancies may lead them; and the Mandans are sometimes, by this means, most unceremoniously left without any thing to eat; and being a small tribe, and unwilling to risk their lives by going far from home in the face of their more powerful enemies, are oftentimes left almost in a state of starvation. In any emergency of this kind, every man musters and brings out of his lodge his mask (the skin of a buffalo's head with the horns on), which he is obliged to keep in readiness for this occasion; and then commences the buffalo dance . . . which is held for the purpose of making 'buffalo come' . . . [i.e. to cause them to] change the direction of their wanderings, and bend their course towards the Mandan village, and graze about on the beautiful hills and bluffs in its vicinity, where the Mandans can shoot them down and cook them as they want them for food.

"For the most part of the year, the young warriors and hunters, by riding out a mile or two from the village, can kill meat in abundance; and sometimes large herds of these animals may be seen grazing in full view of the village. There are other seasons also when the young men have ranged about the coun-

42 Hambly and Hose: op. cit., p. 335.
43 Cf. Hambly: op. cit.; Grove: Dancing; Buttree: The Rhythm of the Redman; and numerous descriptions to be found in books on primitive life at the end of this volume and in Hambly's bibliography.
44 Gann and Thompson: The History of the Maya, p. 148.

try as far as they are willing to risk their lives, on account of their enemies, without finding meat. This sad intelligence is brought back to the chiefs and doctors, who sit in solemn council, and consult on the most expedient measures to be taken, until they are sure to decide upon the old and only expedient which 'never has failed.'

"The chief issues his order to his runners or criers, who proclaim it through the village—and in a few minutes the dance begins. The place where this strange operation is carried on is in the public area in the centre of the village, and in front of the great medicine or mystery lodge. About ten or fifteen Mandans at a time join in the dance, each one with the skin of the buffalo's head (or mask) with the horns on, placed over his head, and in his hand his favourite bow or lance, with which he is used to slay the buffalo."

Catlin noted ". . . that this dance always had the desired effect, that it never fails, nor can it, for it cannot be stopped (but is going incessantly day and night) until 'buffalo come.' Drums are beaten and rattles are shaken, and songs and yells incessantly are shouted, and lookers-on stand ready with masks on their heads, and weapons in hand, to take the place of each one as he becomes fatigued, and jumps out of the ring.

"During this time of general excitement, spies or 'lookers' are kept on the hills in the neighbourhood of the village, who, when they discover buffaloes in sight, give the appropriate signal, by 'throwing their robes,' which is instantly seen in the village, and understood by the whole tribe. At this joyful intelligence there is a shout of thanks to the Great Spirit, and more especially to the mystery-man, and the dancers, who *have been the immediate cause of their success!* There is then a brisk preparation for the chase—a grand hunt takes place. The choicest pieces of the victims are sacrificed to the Great Spirit, and then a surfeit and a carouse.

"These dances have sometimes been continued in this village two and three weeks without stopping an instant, until the joyful moment when buffaloes made their appearance. So they *never fail;* and they think they have been the means of bringing them in.

"Every man in the Mandan village . . . is obliged by a village regulation, to keep the mask of the buffalo, hanging on a post at the head of his bed, which he can use on his head whenever he is called upon by the chiefs, to dance for the coming of buffaloes. The mask is put over the head, and generally has a strip of the skin hanging to it, of the whole length of the animal, with the tail attached to it, which, passing down over the back of the dancer, is dragging on the ground. . . . When one becomes fatigued of the exercise, he signifies it by bending quite forward, and sinking his body towards the ground; when another draws a bow upon him and hits him with a blunt arrow, and he falls like a buffalo—is seized by the bye-standers, who drag him out of the ring by the heels, brandishing their knives about him; and having gone through the motions of skinning and cutting him up, they let him off, and his place is at once supplied by another, who dances into the ring with his mask on; and by this taking of places, the scene is easily kept up night and day, until the desired effect has been produced, that of 'making buffalo come.' " [45]

Many primitive dances rest upon the belief that human life has sprung from animals, plants, and other features of man's environment; and they are designed in one way and another to propitiate the animal spirit with whose welfare that of men is so intimately joined. The philosophy of the Ute Bear Dance, is thus explained by Verner Z. Reed:

"The Utes believe that their primal ancestors were bears; after these came a race of Indians, who, on dying, were changed to bears, and as bears they roamed in the forests and mountains until they died, when they went to the future land and lived with the shades, preserving the forms of bears, but having human wisdom and participating with the Indians in the pleasures of immortality. It is believed that this transmigration ceased long ago, but the bears of the present are believed to be descendants of the Ute bears of old, and are therefore related to the Indians. Bear worship, in one form or another, tinges many of their ceremonies. They regard the bear as the wisest of animals and the bravest of all except the mountain lion. They believe that bears possess wonderful magic power; that they can convey intelligence over long distances by means of po-o-kan-te, or magic. They believe that the bears are fully cognizant of the relationship existing between themselves and the Utes, and their ceremony of the Bear dance, being a form of animal worship, assists in strengthening this friendship. As the Utes consider that they are a higher order of beings than the bears, one of the purposes of the dance is to assist the bears to recover from hibernation, to find food, to choose mates, and to cast the film of blindness from their eyes. Some of the other motives of the ceremonies are to charm the dancers from danger of death from bears, to enable the Indians to send messages to their dead friends who dwell in the land of immortality, and one or two minor ceremonies are performed usually for the purpose of healing certain forms of sickness.

"The Bear dance is always held in the month of March, that being the time when the bears recover from hibernation. In former times the dance was more exactingly observed than it now is, and a dance was often held annually by each one of the Ute tribes. Of late years, however, a dance given by any one of the main tribes is deemed sufficient.

"The dance is always given under the direction of some one person, usually a medicine man or chief, although he may have any number of semi-official assistants. Sometimes two or three months are consumed in making the neces-

[45] Catlin: op. cit., I, 127 f.

sary preparations. After the annual winter hunt is over, when the time grows dull and the people listless from inaction, a man goes to the proper functionary and asks him to appoint the time for a Bear dance." [46]

Agricultural peoples lived a more complex life than those who depended on the chase for a living. Their religious rites, accordingly, took on a character befitting the new processes in which members of the community were engaged. The dances of such peoples form an important part of numerous fertility cults. Having become agriculturalists, these early men sensed a new significance in the sun, the warm south wind, the rain, thunder and lightning, and the flooding of lakes and rivers. In New Guinea an agricultural dance was held at the beginning of the seeding season. The Incas prayed to Ataguju and made sacrifices to him, saying, "Let not hail fall upon the maize," and "Give us many sons, llamas and much corn." Dances were a prominent part of the religious fertility rites, and were performed in sheltered places set apart for them. Among the Zuñi Indians elaborate winter solstice ceremonies were held; these lasted eleven days, when they were observed in 1891. Beginning about December 21, there began a long series of ceremonies, established by tradition, in which the sun priest was the chief director. Prayers to the rising sun were made at a certain stump which the priest sprinkled with holy meal. With the prayers and planting of prayer plumes, sacred dances were interspersed. Stevenson thus describes the purpose and character of the performance:

"The dancing continues in all the kiwitsiwe until long after midnight. . . . The visits of the Sälimobiya, with the dances and distribution of seeds, are repeated . . . every fourth night until . . . four visits have been made. Each member of the Kotikili carries a bowl of food to the road . . . praying as he goes that the gods will bless the Ashiwi with rain to fructify the earth, that she may bear to them the fruits of her being. The food is emptied into the river as offerings to . . . [all the deities]." [47]

Similar ceremonies, prayers, and dances mark the summer solstice; and throughout the season, at appropriate times, rain ceremonies, led by the rain priesthood, and ceremonies of thanksgiving for crops are held. One of the most famous of these is the Dance of the Corn Maidens, by which rain is brought to water the earth, that the corn may be made beautiful to look upon and all may have food.[48] Among the Peruvians, Karsten observed the maize-dance (ayrihua), in which "particularly good specimens of the plant" were used. The spirits inhabiting these stalks having been propitiated, it was believed that the "whole maize-field" would be favorably influenced. The same investigator reported also a dance of the Mataco Indians, performed at sugar factories in the

[46] Reed: "The Ute Bear Dance," Am. Anthrop., O.S., ix, 237 ff.
[47] Stevenson: op. cit., loc. cit., pp. 140 f.
[48] Ibid., pp. 180 ff.

Argentine, for the purpose of aiding the growth of sugar cane. In this dance, a bunch of canes was held erect by two men, while "other Indians danced and chanted around it, as they declared, to 'hurry on the cane.' . . ."[49]

Similar to the dances used to influence the fertility of the soil, were those devised to promote fruitfulness of the human stock. Such, doubtless, is the significance of many dances which make up a prominent part of primitive initiatory ceremonies. Karsten reports on the phallic dances of Brazilian Indians, the significance of which is not open to question. The Chorotis and the Ashluslays, he says, hold a feast about ". . . the time when the *algaroba* and some other important fruits reach maturity. . . . This is also the time when courtship and marriages take place among these natives. The Chorotis and the Ashluslays believe that the fruits are animated by 'good' spirits, and the dances performed at this season are supposed favourably to influence these spirits and to make the fruits abound. Likewise, sexual intercourse is promiscuously indulged in by the young men and women taking part in the dances, and seems to be essential to the feast. . . ."[50] After a study of dancing among many primitive groups throughout the world, Hambly concluded that it is of the greatest significance among them, and promotes the selection of mates by giving an opportunity for the exhibition of physical "charm, grace and endurance."[51]

A sequel to the dances promoting the selection of mates is one, apparently much less common, the purpose of which is to aid delivery. Charles Hose, in his *Natural Man*, says that during confinement the Kayans, especially in the Upper Rejang, sometimes perform a dance intended to "facilitate delivery." Those who perform such dances are generally friends or relatives of the mother. The dancer ". . . takes in her arms a bundle of cloth, which she handles like a baby while she dances, afterwards putting it into the cradle, in which a child is carried on the back. . . ."[52]

A practically universal form of dancing among primitives is associated with war. Unlike the dance at birth, at initiation, or at death, the war dance may be called for more or less throughout life. It is found among present-day primitives and is depicted in the industrial art of such people as the Incas.[53] In some cases the war dance may have become an exhibition to display the skill and art of the performers. Young George ·Washington wrote a brief account of an Iroquois war dance, performed by members of a war party on their way from

[49] Karsten: *op. cit.*, pp. 320 f.
[50] Karsten: *The Civilization of the South American Indians*, pp. 427 ff. Courtesy of Kegan Paul, Trench, Trübner & Co., Ltd., London.
[51] *Op. cit.*, p. 141.
[52] Hose: *op. cit.*, p. 58.
[53] Means: *op. cit.*, pp. 78 ff.

battle.[54] This was simply an exhibition to please the whites who had encouraged them with liquor. In the majority of cases, doubtless, the purpose was serious and realistic: to stimulate warlike attitudes, to intimidate the enemy spirit or get control of it, and to insure the successful outcome of battle. In a sense, the war dance was shadow-boxing: one imitated all the actions that would be performed in actual conflict, and thus gained a certain preparation for the fray, both physical and psychological. Evans refers to a solo war dance of a Tuaran youth, in which he went through "all the actions of a native engaged in warfare . . . the spying of a foe from a distance, the stealthy creep through bushes or tall grass, the gliding behind tree-trunks, the sudden rush of a surprise attack, the rout of the enemy and the swaggering bravado of the victors." [55] Among the Kayans there is a "display of warlike feeling" in the war dance: "The boy, in full panoply of war, and brandishing a sword and shield, goes through the movements of a single combat. He crouches beneath his shield, and springs violently hither and thither, emitting piercing yells of defiance and rage, cutting and striking at his imaginary foe or his partner in the dance. . . ." [56]

The common participation of boys in make-believe battles and scalp dances was an early conditioning, a practical training, for those activities which tribal life demanded of them. It was the counterpart of military or premilitary training in our schools and colleges. The scalp taken was the record of achievement in battle, which the Indian must keep himself, whereas among people of greater literary attainments martial successes are chronicled and praised by official statisticians and historians; and the scalp dance was like a march through some triumphal arch. It has been observed that females are drawn to the soldier and the uniform. The war and scalp dances of the primitive seem also to have played a part in sexual selection.

The sham fight and scalp dance were part of the regular education of Mandan Indian boys. A firsthand account of this vigorous phase of their training has been left us by Catlin:

"During the pleasant mornings of the summer, the little boys between the age of seven and fifteen are called out, to the number of several hundred, and being divided into two companies, each of which is headed by some experienced warrior, who leads them on, in the character of a teacher, they are led out into the prairie at sunrise, where this curious discipline is regularly taught them. . . . Their bodies are naked, and each one has a little bow in his left hand and a number of arrows made of large spears of grass, which are harmless

[54] Myers: The Boy George Washington, pp. 62 f.
[55] Evans: Among Primitive Peoples in Borneo, pp. 134, 243 ff.
[56] Hose: op. cit., pp. 64 f.

MANDAN INDIAN SHAM BATTLE

(G. Catlin, *Letters and Notes on the North American Indians*, 1, Pl. 57)

in their effects. Each one has also a little belt or girdle around his waist, in which he carries a knife made of a piece of wood and equally harmless—on the tops of their heads are slightly attached small tufts of grass, which answer as scalps, and in this plight, they follow the dictates of their experienced leaders, who lead them through the judicious evolutions of Indian warfare—of feints— of retreats—of attacks—and at last to a general fight. Many manoeuvres are gone through, and eventually they are brought up face to face, within fifteen or twenty feet of each other, with their leaders at their head stimulating them on. Their bows are bent upon each other and their missiles flying, whilst they are dodging and fending them off.

"If any one is struck with an arrow on any vital part of his body, he is obliged to fall, and his adversary rushes up to him, places his foot upon him, and snatching from his belt his wooden knife, grasps hold of his victim's scalp-lock of grass, and making a feint at it with his wooden knife, twitches it off and puts it into his belt, and enters again into the ranks and front of battle.

"This mode of training generally lasts an hour or more in the morning, and is performed on an empty stomach, affording them a rigid and wholesome exercise, whilst they are instructed in the important science of war. Some five or six miles of ground are run over during these evolutions, giving suppleness to their limbs and strength to their muscles, which last and benefit them through life.

"After this exciting exhibition is ended, they all return to their village, where the chiefs and braves pay profound attention to their vaunting, and applaud them for their artifice and valour.

"Those who have taken scalps then step forward, brandishing them and making their boast as they enter into the *scalp-dance* (in which they are also instructed by their leaders or teachers), jumping and yelling—brandishing their scalps, and reciting their *sanguinary deeds*, to the great astonishment of their tender aged sweethearts, who are gazing with wonder upon them." [57]

The scalp dance, celebrating the victory of adult warriors among the Sioux, is described by Catlin thus:

"The *Scalp-dance* . . . is given in celebration of victory; and amongst this tribe, as I learned whilst residing with them, [is] danced in the night by the light of their torches, and just before retiring to bed. When a war party returns from a war excursion, bringing home with them the scalps of their enemies, they generally 'dance them' for fifteen nights in succession, vaunting forth the most extravagant boasts of their wonderful prowess in war, whilst they brandish their war weapons in their hands. A number of young women are selected to aid (though they do not actually join in the dance), by stepping into the centre of the ring, and holding up the scalps that have been recently taken, whilst the warriors dance (or rather *jump*), around in a circle, brandishing their weapons, and barking and yelping in the most frightful manner, all jumping on both feet at a time, with a simultaneous stamp, and blow, and thrust of their weapons; with which it would seem as if they were actually cutting and carving each other to pieces. During these frantic leaps, and yelps, and thrusts, every man distorts his face to the utmost of his muscles, darting about his glaring eye-balls and snapping his teeth, as if he were in the heat . . . of battle!" [58]

An observer of Indian life once remarked that the Indians had a dance for everything. The generalization would be applicable to most primitive groups. Many forms of dancing have been cited. Two others, closely related, one dealing with the exorcism of evil spirits and disease demons and another connected with the final rites for those who have succumbed, may be mentioned briefly. Cure by dancing had its *raison d'être* in the notion that illness resulted from some evil spell that was cast by an enemy spirit, rather than from natural causes.[59] Such dances, therefore, could be directed successfully only by those cunning medicine men who had special knowledge of the spirit world and who, possessing mastery of certain charms, incantations, ceremonial dances, and other rituals, were thought able to wheedle the evil spirit, or to compel it by some means to leave its victim. Hambly [60] tells of the people of Ba Thonga who, by flattering words, attempt first to get the demon to reveal his name, for knowing the name is the first step toward power over him. When cajolery fails, they resort to threats. In Bori Dancing, the "patient himself has to undergo a

[57] Catlin: *op. cit.*, I, 131 f.
[58] *Ibid.*, I, 245 f.
[59] Corlett: *op. cit.*, chap. 3; Levy-Brühl: *op. cit.*, chap. 7.
[60] *Op. cit.*, pp. 257 f.

long period of training and initiation," for which he pays a fee to the wise tutor, "before undertaking his own curative treatment by means of gymnastic dances." [61]

The intricate character of magic medicine is evident in Navaho ceremonies. Nine major healing rituals and numerous minor ones are known. Though curing ailments is the primary purpose, numerous prayers for more general benefits—plentiful rainfall, crops, and general welfare of the people—are intermingled in the performances. Navaho magic medicine is a great social affair; it is also expensive, for the patient must pay both the head medicine man and his assistants, and provide all the materials that have been fixed by long-established usage. The chief ceremonies last nine nights and days; lesser ones may be a matter of hours, or may continue a day or so. An omission or error on any point renders the ceremony void, and it must be begun de novo. Dry painting of intricate designs in favorite Navaho colors, singing, and dancing occupy a prominent place in this system of magic cures. Washington Matthews described the Night Chant and the Mountain Chant in great detail many years ago, and other anthropologists have made extended studies.[62] The last night of the Mountain Chant culminated in eleven dances. The last of them, the fire dance, a vigorous, remarkable, and spectacular performance, is thus described by Matthews:

"The Eleventh dance was the fire dance, or fire play, which was the most picturesque and startling of all. Some time before the actors entered, we heard, mingled with the blowing of the buffalo horn, strange sounds, much like the call of the sand-hill crane; they will, for convenience, be called trumpeting. These sounds continued to grow louder and come nearer until they were heard at the opening in the east, and in a second after, ten men, having no more clothing on than the performers in the first dance, entered. Every man except the leader bore a long thick bundle of shredded cedar bark in each hand and one had two extra bundles on his shoulders for the later use of the leader. The latter carried four small fagots of the same material in his hands. Four times they all danced around the fire, waving their bundles of bark towards it. They halted in the east; the leader advanced towards the central fire, lighted one of his fagots, and trumpeting loudly threw it to the east over the fence of the corral. He performed a similar act at the south, at the west, and at the north; but before the northern brand was thrown he lighted with it the bark bundles of his comrades. As each brand disappeared over the fence some of the spectators blew into their hands and made a motion as if tossing some substance after

[61] Ibid., pp. 254 ff.
[62] Matthews: "The Mountain Chant," 5th Ann. Rep. Bur. Am. Ethnol., pp. 379–467; "The Night Chant," Memoirs, Am. Mus. Nat. Hist., Vol. VI; Wyman and Kluckhohn: Navaho Classification of Their Song Ceremonials; and An Introduction to Navaho Chant Practice, Memoirs, Am. Anthrop. Assoc., No. 50, 1938, and No. 53, 1940, respectively.

the departing flame. When the fascicles were all lighted the whole band began a wild race around the fire. At first they kept close together and spat upon one another some substance of supposed medicinal virtue. Soon they scattered and ran apparently without concert, the rapid racing causing the brands to throw out long brilliant streamers of flame over the hands and arms of the dancers. Then they proceeded to apply the brands to their own nude bodies and to the bodies of their comrades in front of them, no man ever once turning round; at times the dancer struck his victim vigorous blows with his flaming wand; again he seized the flame as if it were a sponge and, keeping close to the one pursued, rubbed the back of the latter for several moments, as if he were bathing him. In the mean time the sufferer would perhaps catch up with some one in front of him and in turn bathe him in flame. At times when a dancer found no one in front of him he proceeded to sponge his own back, and might keep this up while making two or three circuits around the fire or until he caught up with some one else. At each application of the blaze the loud trumpeting was heard, and it often seemed as if a great flock of cranes was winging its way overhead southward through the darkness. If a brand became extinguished it was lighted again in the central fire; but when it was so far consumed as to be no longer held conveniently in the hand, the dancer dropped it and rushed, trumpeting, out of the corral. Thus, one by one, they all departed. When they were gone many of the spectators came forward, picked up some of the fallen fragments of cedar bark, lighted them, and bathed their hands in the flames as a charm against the evil effects of fire." [63]

When death comes, whether by disease, old age, or by the hand of the enemy, many primitives resort to ritualistic ceremonies. Dancing plays a part in these; but death dances are not universal. Hose [64] reports little or no evidence of dancing in his discussion of "death and the hereafter," although it is obvious that the Kayan natives have a great fear of the spirits of the dead, perform many ceremonies, and take intricate precautionary measures to prevent the spirits from returning to the dwelling of the deceased member. Riley, writing of death and burial among the Kiwais, makes no reference to death dances, except in the case of a very "distinguished person" or an "only child," when, after the skull had been cut from the body, cleansed, and decorated, preparations were made for feasting and dancing, which began "at sundown and finished at daylight next day." [65] Stevenson's extensive account of Zuñi customs, too, makes no mention of dancing at death. Hambly,[66] however, who is especially interested in dancing, points to the prevalent use of death dances among

[63] Matthews: "The Mountain Chant," loc. cit., pp. 441 f.
[64] Op. cit., pp. 206–19.
[65] Op. cit., pp. 169 ff.
[66] Op. cit., chap. 7.

34 [ORIGINS]

the Shokas of Tibet, the Shans of Upper Burma, the Todas, the Veddas of Ceylon, the Boloki of the Congo, and many others.

*Games as education* To-day men and women participate in games for a variety of reasons. One plays for recreation, for exercise, for health; another plays just "for the fun of it"; still others turn play into professional activity. Historically considered, it is evident that many games that play so important a rôle in physical education programs to-day, have sprung in part from sources which are seldom thought of by those who direct them or engage in them. On the other hand, some bases of sport among primitive societies were the same that are recognized to-day. Chief among the original sources of sportive activities were the natural drives of man, religious beliefs and practices, and various ultilitarian purposes.

Running through voluminous descriptions of primitive games is the general conclusion, reached by most students, that many sports, perhaps all, had at some remote time a religious or animistic significance, and were played in connection with divination, or for the propitiation of the spirit world.[67] Games of chance, Tylor believes, are so closely similar to the "arts of divination" that there is good reason to consider them as a "sportive survival" of what was once a "serious practice." [68] Instead of figuring on the law of probability, primitive minds were inclined to hold that some invisible power determined the lot chosen, the dice that would turn up; and there is still, even among those who live in a materialistic, scientific age, a suspicious awe with respect to numbers, lots, and the turn of fortune's wheel. Culin, in his monumental *Games of the North American Indians*, says of the "hoop and pole" play that it has a distinct religious character among the Apache Indians. It seems, however, that this significance may be but little understood by the commonalty, for "only those medicine men . . . deeply versed in their folklore and traditions can give a minute explanation of the original meaning and symbolism of this game. . . ." [69] Elsewhere he says that the Indian origin myths often contain reference to games. These represent "the demiurge, the first man, the culture hero [who] overcomes some opponent, a foe of the human race, by exercise of superior cunning, skill, or magic." "The primal gamblers" are thus revealed "as those curious children, the divine Twins, the miraculous offspring of the Sun. . . . Always contending, they are the original patrons of play, and their games are the games now played by men." [70] Spencer, too, in his *Education of the Pueblo Child*, says of the Pueblos that they have a considerable number of games, all

---

[67] Stevenson: "Zuñi Games," Am. Anthrop., N.S., v, 468.
[68] Op. cit., I, 78–83.
[69] Culin: Games of the North American Indians, 24th Ann. Rep. Bur. Am. Ethnol., p. 453.
[70] Ibid., pp. 32 ff. and xxxix–xl.

"characterized by conjurations, divinations, prayers and incantations" which are "the most important features of each." [71]

A vast number of primitive games have an obvious utility. The early desire to train youth in certain useful, habitual acts of their elders was unquestionably a prolific source of childhood's games. The war game of Indian youths has been mentioned. The utility of it is not open to question. Among the Veddas boys make bows and arrows and learn the arts of the hunter; and the girls play at using mock vessels and instruments employed by their mothers. The children of British North America follow in miniature the occupations of hunting, housekeeping, and fighting as practiced by adults. In Central Africa the construction of play houses, making arrows, clay-modeling, baking, fighting, hunting and killing small animals and birds are among the pastimes of girls and boys.[72] Among certain Indian tribes the throwing of the "snow snake," a well-polished club which was hurled with force and accuracy across the surface of the snow, had doubtless a practical use. It is sometimes called a "rabbit club." [73] The accurate hurling of club or spear and the shooting of arrows were indubitably valuable as vocational training, and at the same time gave a sense of pleasure.

Numerous sports are simply vestigial survivals of what once was useful. To-day they have become purely recreational, a means of entertainment, and the original, serious reason for being is forgotten. Such are the archery contests of the present day.[74] Culin states that Indian ball games with racquets may be a dramatization of war, pointing out Mooney's observation that the Cherokees applied the same name to both war and ball game. Rivers,[75] too, says that in Polynesia, with two or three exceptions, the bow and arrow are used "only in sport or as a means of shooting fish, birds or rats" and not as a weapon. The rise of games to a place of importance as a means of recreation and entertainment and entirely apart from more serious purposes that may once have brought them into being, is also suggested by the report of those who have studied Inca civilization. Means quotes Blas Valera to the effect that the Incas decreed "three holidays every month," during which they diverted themselves "with various games" so that labor might not "become oppressive." [76] Among the Maya a favorite thrilling spectacle was pok-ta-pok, a game of great antiquity, closely associated with war and religion, and originated by the gods, according to tradition. From the Maya it came to the Aztecs, who called it tlax-ti. The

[71] Op. cit., pp. 37 ff.
[72] Hambly and Hose: op. cit., pp. 76, 80, 86, 95, 107 ff., 161.
[73] Culin: op. cit., loc. cit., p. 402.
[74] Tylor: op. cit., 1, 72 f.
[75] The History of Melanesian Society, 11, 446 ff.
[76] Means: op. cit., p. 314.

game was played in a long court, and engaged two parties, small in number or running up into hundreds. On opposite walls were two rings, about one and one-half to two feet in diameter, set vertically to the floor and from fifteen to twenty or more feet above it. The object of the game was to drive a solid rubber ball, about one foot in diameter, through the rings, using the buttocks and legs to propel it, or in some cases the hands. Spectators watched the contest from the top of the walls.[77]

The games of North American Indians were divided by Culin into two classes: those of chance and those of dexterity. Such a classification would serve for other primitive groups as well. The types of dexterity cultivated differ, of course, among different peoples, but dexterity, in some form, is always an element in some of their games. Games of chance are subdivided into two groups: those in which dice or sticks are thrown to determine numbers; and those involving guessing the location of a certain specially marked lot or dice. Games of dexterity include archery, snow snake, hoop-and-pole, ring-and-pin, racquets, shinny, double-ball, ball-race, football, hand-and-football, tossed-ball, foot-cast ball, ball juggling and hot ball. To these Culin added many "minor amusements" such as shuttlecock, tipcat, quoits, stone-throwing, shuffleboard, jack-straws, swing, stilts, tops, bull-roarer, buzz, popgun, bean-shooter, cat's cradle, running races, "unclassified games," and some "derived from Europeans." He was convinced that none of the games described, except the last group, "were imported into America at any time either before or after the Conquest." Moreover "games of all the classes designated are found among all the Indian tribes of North America and constitute the games par excellence of the Indians." [78]

These games were played by men and women, youth and maidens, generally "at fixed seasons as the accompaniment of certain festivals or religious rites." But children practiced "similar imitative sports." Eastman reported the same view: "Our sports were molded by the life and customs of our people . . . we practiced only what we expected to do when grown." He mentioned "feats with the bow and arrow," foot- and pony-races, wrestling, swimming, fights with mudballs and willows, top-spinning, hunting buffalo, "white man," lacrosse, coasting in winter on ribs of animals, and "war upon bees," the latter being a war game in which they imagined they were making an attack on their enemies, the Ojibways. To this, he added, "Sometimes we played 'medicine dance,'" which was disapproved of by our elders as "an act of irreverence." [79]

George Catlin's detailed firsthand account of certain Indian games conveys a clear impression of the stamina, poise, and skill that they involved. His obser-

[77] Gann and Thompson: op. cit., pp. 177 f.; Morley: "Chichen Itzá," Nat. Geog. Mag., XLVII, 71 ff.
[78] Culin: op. cit., loc. cit., pp. 31 f., 36 ff.
[79] Eastman: Indian Boyhood, pp. 63–75.

MANDANS PLAYING TCHUNG-KEE
(G. Catlin, *Letters and Notes on the North American Indians*, 1, Pl. 59)

vations on a few of them may be noted. *Tchung-kee*, a favorite game of the
Mandan Indians, was played thus:

"The game of Tchung-kee [is] a beautiful athletic exercise, which they seem
to be almost unceasingly practicing whilst the weather is fair, and they have
nothing else of moment to demand their attention. This game is decidedly
their favourite amusement, and is played near to the village on a pavement of
clay, which has been used for that purpose until it has become as smooth and
hard as a floor. For this game, two champions form their respective parties,
by choosing alternately the most famous players, until their requisite numbers
are made up. Their bettings are then made, and their stakes are held by some
of the chiefs or others present. The play commences . . . with two (one from
each party), who start off upon a trot, abreast of each other, and one of them
rolls in advance of them, on the pavement, a little ring of two or three inches
in diameter, cut out of a stone; and each one follows it up with his 'tchung-
kee' (a stick of six feet in length, with little bits of leather projecting from its
sides of an inch or more in length), which he throws before him as he runs,
sliding it along upon the ground after the ring, endeavouring to place it in such
a position when it stops, that the ring may fall upon it, and receive one of the
little projections of leather through it, which counts for game, one, or two, or
four, according to the position of the leather on which the ring is lodged. The
last winner always has the rolling of the ring, and both start and throw the

tchung-kee together; if either fails to receive the ring or to lie in a certain position, it is a forfeiture of the amount of the number he was nearest to, and he loses his throw; when another steps into his place. This game is a very difficult one to describe, so as to give an exact idea of it, unless one can see it played— it is a game of great beauty and fine bodily exercise, and these people become excessively fascinated with it; often gambling away every thing they possess, and even sometimes, when everything else was gone, have been known to stake their liberty upon the issue of these games, offering themselves as slaves to their opponents in case they get beaten." [80]

The Choctaws, Catlin says, "even in their troubles" seem to be happy and have "preserved with great tenacity their different games," such as "horse-racing, dancing, wrestling, foot-racing, and ball-playing." The last named, "the most beautiful . . . wonderful game," and their favorite, he says, "can never be appreciated by those who are not happy enough to see it." Catlin's word-picture, supplemented by drawings, is one of the best accounts of Indian lacrosse that has been preserved. A vast panorama of pulsing life is unrolled before our eyes:

"It is no uncommon occurrence for six or eight hundred or a thousand of these young men, to engage in a game of ball, with five or six times that number of spectators, of men, women and children, surrounding the ground, and looking on. And I pronounce such a scene, with its hundreds of Nature's most beautiful models, denuded, and painted of various colours, running and leaping into the air, in all the most extravagant and varied forms, in the desperate struggles for the ball, a school for the painter or sculptor, equal to any of those which ever inspired the hand of the artist in the Olympian games or the Roman forum.

"I have made it an uniform rule, whilst in the Indian country, to attend every ball-play I could hear of, if I could do it by riding a distance of twenty or thirty miles; and my usual custom has been on such occasions, to straddle the back of my horse, and look on to the best advantage. In this way I have sat, and oftentimes reclined, and almost dropped from my horse's back, with irresistible laughter at the succession of droll tricks, and kicks and scuffles which ensue, in the almost superhuman struggles for the ball. These plays generally commence at nine o'clock, or near it, in the morning; and I have more than once balanced myself on my pony, from that time till near sundown, without more than one minute of intermission at a time, before the game has been decided.

"It is impossible for pen and ink alone, or brushes, or even with their combined efforts, to give more than a caricature of such a scene; but such as I have

[80] Catlin: op. cit. I, 132 f.

been able to do, I have put upon the canvass, and in the slight outlines which I have here attached . . . I will convey as correct an account as I can, and leave the reader to imagine the rest; or look to *other books* for what I may have omitted.

"While at the Choctaw agency it was announced, that there was to be a great play on a certain day, within a few miles, on which occasion I attended, and made the three sketches which are hereto annexed; and also the following entry in my note-book, which I literally copy out.

" 'Monday afternoon at three o'clock, I rode out with Lieutenants S. and M., to a very pretty prairie, about six miles distant, to the ball-play-ground of the Choctaws, where we found several thousand Indians encamped. There were two points of timber about half a mile apart, in which the two parties for the play, with their respective families and friends, were encamped; and lying between them, the prairie on which the game was to be played. My companions and myself, although we had been apprised, that to see the whole of a ball-play, we must remain on the ground all the night previous, had brought nothing to sleep upon, resolving to keep our eyes open, and see what transpired through the night. During the afternoon, we loitered about amongst the different tents and shantees of the two encampments, and afterwards, at sundown, witnessed the ceremony of measuring out the ground, and erecting the "byes" or goals which were to guide the play. Each party had their goal made with two upright posts, about 25 feet high and six feet apart, set firm in the ground, with a pole across at the top. These goals were about forty or fifty rods apart; and at a point just half way between, was another small stake, driven down, where the ball was to be thrown up at the firing of a gun, to be struggled for by the players. All this preparation was made by some old men, who were, it seems, selected to be the judges of the play, who drew a line from one bye to the other; to which directly came from the woods, on both sides, a great concourse of women and old men, boys and girls, and dogs and horses, where bets were to be made on the play. The betting was all done across this line, and seemed to be chiefly left to the women, who seemed to have martialled out a little of everything that their houses and their fields possessed. Goods and chattels— knives—dresses—blankets—pots and kettles—dogs and horses, and guns; and all were placed in the possession of *stake-holders*, who sat by them, and watched them on the ground all night, preparatory to the play.

" 'The sticks with which this tribe play, are bent into an oblong hoop at the end, with a sort of slight web of small thongs tied across, to prevent the ball from passing through. The players hold one of these in each hand, and by leaping into the air, they catch the ball between the two nettings and throw it, without being allowed to strike it, or catch it in their hands.

" 'The mode in which these sticks are constructed and used, will be seen in the portrait of *Tullock-chish-ko* (he who drinks the juice of the stone), the most distinguished ball-player of the Choctaw nation . . . represented in his ball-play dress, with his ball-sticks in his hands. In every ball-play of these people, it is a rule of the play, that no man shall wear moccasins on his feet, or any other dress than his breech-cloth around his waist, with a beautiful bead belt, and a "tail," made of white horsehair or quills, and a "*mane*" on the neck, of horsehair dyed of various colours.

" 'This game had been arranged and "made up," three or four months before the parties met to play it, and in the following manner:—The two champions who led the two parties, and had the alternate choosing of the players through the whole tribe, sent runners, with the ball-sticks most fantastically ornamented with ribbons and red paint, to be touched by each one of the chosen players; who thereby agreed to be on the spot at the appointed time and ready for the play. The ground having been all prepared and preliminaries of the game all settled, and the bettings all made, and goods all "staked," night came on without the appearance of any players on the ground. But soon after dark, a procession of lighted flambeaux was seen coming from each encampment, to the ground where the players assembled around their respective byes; and at the beat of the drums and chaunts of the women, each party of players commenced the "ball-play dance." . . . Each party danced for a quarter of an hour around their respective byes, in their ball-play dress; rattling their ball-sticks together in the most violent manner, and all singing as loud as they could raise their voices; whilst the women of each party, who had their goods at stake, formed into two rows on the line between the two parties of players, and danced also, in an uniform step, and all their voices joined in chaunts to the Great Spirit; in which they were soliciting his favour in deciding the game to their advantage; and also encouraging the players to exert every power they possessed, in the struggle that was to ensue. In the mean time, four old *medicine-men*, who were to have the starting of the ball, and who were to be judges of the play, were seated at the point where the ball was to be started; and busily smoking to the Great Spirit for their success in judging rightly, and impartially, between the parties in so important an affair.

" 'This dance was one of the most picturesque scenes imaginable, and was repeated at intervals of every half hour during the night, and exactly in the same manner; so that the players were certainly awake all the night, and arranged in their appropriate dress, prepared for the play which was to commence at nine o'clock the next morning. In the morning, at the hour, the two parties and all their friends, were drawn out and over the ground; when at length the game commenced, by the judges throwing up the ball at the firing of a gun; when an instant struggle ensued between the players, who were some six or seven hundred in numbers, and were mutually endeavouring to catch the ball in their sticks, and throw it home and between their respective stakes; which, whenever successfully done, counts one for game. In this game every player was dressed alike, that is, *divested* of all dress, except the girdle and the tail, which I have before described; and in these desperate struggles for the ball, when it is *up*, . . . where hundreds are running together and leaping, actually over each other's heads, and darting between their adversaries' legs, tripping and throwing, and foiling each other in every possible manner, and every voice raised to the highest key, in shrill yelps and barks! there are rapid successions of feats, and of incidents, that astonish and amuse far beyond the conception of any one who has not had the singular good luck to witness them. In these struggles, every mode is used that can be devised, to oppose the progress of the foremost, who is likely to get the ball; and these obstructions often meet desperate individual resistance, which terminates in a violent scuffle, and sometimes in fisticuffs; when their sticks are dropped, and the parties are unmolested, whilst they are settling it between themselves; unless it be by a general *stampedo*, to which they are subject who are down, if the ball happens to pass in their direction. Every weapon, by a rule of all ball-plays, is laid by in their respective encampments, and no man allowed to go for one; so that the sudden broils that take place on the ground, are presumed to be as suddenly settled without any probability of much personal injury; and no one is allowed to interfere in any way with the contentious individuals.

" 'There are times, when the ball gets to the ground, . . . and such a confused mass rushing together around it, and knocking their sticks together, without the possibility of any one getting or seeing it, for the dust that they raise, that the spectator loses his strength, and everything else but his senses; when the condensed mass of ball-sticks, and shins, and bloody noses, is carried around the different parts of the ground, for a quarter of an hour at a time, without any one of the mass being able to see the ball; and when they are often thus scuffling for, several minutes after it has been thrown off, and played over another part of the ground.

" 'For each time that the ball was passed between the stakes of either party, one was counted for their game, and a halt of about one minute; when it was again started by the judges of the play, and a similar struggle ensued; and so on until the successful party arrived to 100, which was the limit of the game, and accomplished at an hour's sun, when they took the stakes; and then, by a previous agreement, produced a number of jugs of whiskey, which gave all a wholesome drink, and sent them all off merry and in good humour, but not drunk.' " [81]

The Indian's repertoire of games of skill included many "parlor tricks," some

<hr />

[81] *Ibid.*, II, 123 ff.; see also Schoolcraft: *op. cit.*, II, 78 f. for a description of ball games.

of which are quite familiar to us. Haddon,[82] mentions a number of "string figures" and explains how they are made. All are efforts at representation of some
feature of Indian experience, such as "tuktudqdjung" or caribou, "dressing a
skin," "pitching a tent," "crow's feet," "threading a closed loop," "hogan,"
"two hogans," "carrying wood," "many stars," the "owl," and "lightning."
Numerous similar tricks and string-games have been observed among other
primitive peoples.[83]

Gambling, though scarcely a form of physical exercise, is a favorite sport
both in primitive and civilized societies, and has been intimately associated
with religious life and athletic contests.[84] Probably all lot-games were originally
associated with divination. Whatever its true origin may be, gambling appears
to have been a universal satisfier, commonly indulged in by those who sit on
the side lines while the gods, the fates, or the players on the field determine
the outcome; a sort of vicarious experience whereby one identifies himself with
the game and secures at least some of the thrill of participation. Means refers
to certain artifacts of the Inca civilization which he thinks were used in a game
of dice.[85] Evans says that gambling in Borneo takes precedence even over cockfighting.[86] Schoolcraft reports the love of Indians, men and women, for the
game of "plum-stones"; that of "moccasins" is played by the men.[87] Culin cites
numerous travelers who observed the Indian's love of games of dice and betting
on the outcome of physical contests. The similarity between *pachisi*, a lot-
game of Hindustan, and the game of *patolli*, which was played in Mexico at
the time of the Conquest, was noted by Tylor. Both games are akin in principle
to European games such as trictrac, tables, backgammon, *jeu de l'oie* and other
games involving a throwing of dice and moving of pieces on a board from some
starting point to a goal.[88] Loskiel, quoted by Culin, thus described Indian gambling in western Pennsylvania and New York:

"The Indians are naturally given to gambling, and frequently risk their arms,
furniture, clothes, and all they possess to gratify this passion. The chief game
of the Iroquois and Delaware is dice, which, indeed, originated with them. The
dice are made of oval and flattish plum stones, painted black on one and yellow
on the other side. Two persons only can play at one time. They put the dice
into a dish, which is raised alternately by each gambler and struck on the table
or floor with force enough to make the dice rise and change their position,

[82] "A Few American String Figures and Tricks," Am. Anthrop., N.S., v, 213–23.
[83] Hose: op. cit., pp. 62 f.; Hambly and Hose: op. cit., pp. 45, 95; Culin: op. cit., loc. cit.,
pp. 761–79; Holmes: In Primitive New Guinea, pp. 279 ff.; Kidd: Savage Childhood, pp.
4, 176 f.
[84] Culin: op. cit., loc. cit., pp. 47 f., 115 f., 512 f.
[85] Op. cit., pp. 328 f.
[86] Op. cit., p. 240.
[87] Op. cit., IV, 64 f.
[88] Tylor: On American Lot-Games, pp. 3 f.; Culin: op. cit., loc. cit., pp. 45 f., 227, 382.

when he who has the greater number of winning color counts 5, and the first who has the good fortune to do this eight times wins the game. The spectators seem in great agitation during the game, and at every chance that appears decisive cry out with great vehemence. The gamblers distort their features, and if unsuccessful mutter their displeasure at the dice and the evil spirits who prevent their good fortune. Sometimes whole townships, and even whole tribes, play against each other. One of the missionaries happened to be present when two Iroquois townships, having got together a number of goods, consisting of blankets, cloth, shirts, linen, etc., gambled for them. The game lasted eight days. They assembled every day, and every inhabitant of each township tossed the dice once. This being done and the chance of each person noted down, they parted for the day; but each township offered a sacrifice in the evening to insure success to their party. This was done by a man going several times around the fire, throwing tobacco into it, and singing a song. Afterward the whole company danced. When the appointed time for the game was at an end they compared notes, and the winner bore away the spoil in triumph." [89]

A study of primitive games and pastimes reveals, that in so far as sportive tendencies are concerned, early man was not far different from his modern descendants; that he played many of the same games and, in many cases, probably played them for the same or similar reasons. Kidd, in his excellent study of *Savage Childhood*, expressed the belief that, if a Kafir child were suddenly dropped down on the sand at Margate, he could enter at once "into most of the games played there." [90] Besides showing that a bit of play makes the whole world kin, a study of primitive physical culture reinforces the view that play is natural, universal, and traditional in human societies. Perceiving its natural basis, its contribution to the satisfaction of the laws of man's individual and social nature, one is led perforce to the conclusion that a proper, balanced system of education must at all times be so designed as to make adequate provision for the proper functioning of body as well as mind, that there may be an inner harmony in man.

[89] Culin: op. cit., loc. cit., p. 105.
[90] Op. cit., p. 161.

# 2

# IN THE GREAT RIVER VALLEYS

With a mirror of brass you can adjust your hat; but with antiquity for a mirror you can predict the rise and fall of empires.    CONFUCIUS

# 3

# THE VALLEY OF THE NILE

A rolling stone gathers no moss. While primitives wandered from place to place, tarrying but a short while in any, they gathered but little of that which later distinguished human civilization. Only when man could settle, with a fair degree of permanence and security, could he forget the mores of hunting and fishing days. For permanent settlement he needed a reliable food supply, molested as little as possible by the forces of nature and by man's notorious enemy, man. Such a favorable situation was found in the valley of the Nile and in Mesopotamia, the land between the rivers Tigris and Euphrates. The time of this transition in Egypt is not precisely dated; wide variations in chronology appear among the best Egyptian scholars. Maspero maintained, however, that the emergence of early Egyptian culture must be placed at 8,000 B.C. to 10,000 B.C. to allow for the attainment of such perfection in art, government, and religion as meets our view at the beginning of the historic period about 5000 B.C.[1] The Egyptian calendar is credited by some to 4241 B.C.; while "true alphabetic *letters*" are said to have been known to Egyptians twenty-five hundred years earlier than elsewhere.[2]

Of what race or races, and from what place or places, the Egyptians came, is a debated question. Whether they were Asiatic or African; whether they came into the valley through Suez or across the Straits of Bab el-Mandeb and the Abyssinian range; whether they were of the Mediterranean race who conquered and destroyed, or evicted, a black people dwelling on the Nile, and were later reinforced by Asiatic migrations; or whether they were always there, "ever since the human race began"—these are some of the questions regarding their

---

[1] Maspero: *Dawn of Civilization*, pp. 43 ff.; Petrie: *History of Egypt*, I, 1–15; Baikie: A *History of Egypt*, I, chap. 2; II, 381 ff.
[2] Breasted: *History of Egypt*, pp. 32 f., 45; Sloley: "Primitive Methods of Measuring Time," *Jour. Egy. Archaeol.*, XVII, 168.

origin.[3] But whencesoever they came, and of whatsoever races, the Nile wrought its influence upon them and promoted the development of a unified people, a common life, religion, language, and literature.[4]

Since ancient days it has been a commonplace that Egypt was "the gift of the river." [5] Loaded with silt from the highlands, its rising flood begins to be perceptible at the first cataract in early June and continues till November, leaving, as it recedes, a rich deposit upon what would otherwise be barren sands. Warmed by a generous sun, this constantly replenished soil, fringing the ribbon of the Nile from the Delta southward for more than seven hundred miles, produced crops abundantly, even with a minimum of labor, and furnished a powerful inducement to the settlement and maintenance of communities by peaceful rather than savage, warlike means. Three crops matured each year: grains, such as wheat and barley; and grasses and vegetables. Wheat is said to have increased a hundredfold; and all crops in abundance. Wheat, barley, doora, peas, beans, lentils, hommos, gilbán, carthamus, lupins, bámia, figl, simsim, indigo, mustard, origanum, succory, flax, cotton, cassia senna, colocynth, cummin, coriander, cucurbitae, cucumbers, melons, leeks, onions, garlic, lotus, nelumbium, cyperus esculentus, papyrus, and a number of other plants were known to the Egyptians. Trees, such as the date, dôm, sycamore, acacia, tamarisk, cedar, fir, ebony, and balanite, either furnished food or supplied material for houses, furniture, implements, and artistic uses. From numerous plants a great array of medicinal drugs were prepared. A varied fauna supplemented agricultural foods, but the population subsisted chiefly on produce of the soil.[6] Add to this picture of plenty the advantages of clay fit for brick, abundant stone for permanent buildings, and not inconsiderable resources of copper, gold, and other metals, and it is difficult to imagine a more propitious theater for the genius of man. Here were food, raiment, and shelter, for himself and for his gods. By applying themselves consistently to labor, the Egyptians produced supplies that sufficed for a population which reached seven million in Roman times.[7] For whatever surplus was produced, and for anything needed from abroad, there were ready roads of commerce—the River, the Mediterranean, the Indian Ocean, the Red Sea—over which goods could be transported at little expense.

The dictum that Egypt was the gift of the Nile was a truth of many meanings. It was the source of sustenance of physical life; being the center of attention and admiration, it became the inspiration of religion; it was a problem the solution of which led to practical engineering feats; and the necessity of con-

---

[3] The History of Herodotus, II, 15; Diodorus of Sicily, I, 10; Baikie: op. cit., I, 50 f.

[4] Maspero: op. cit., pp. 44 ff.; Rawlinson: The Story of Ancient Egypt, pp. 23 ff.; Wilkinson: The Manners and Customs of the Ancient Egyptians, I, 1 ff.

[5] Herodotus, II, 5.

[6] Maspero: op. cit., pp. 32 ff.; Diodorus, I, 34–6.

[7] Breasted: op. cit., pp. 8 f.

trolling it in the interest of man actually shaped the political development of Egypt.[8] Though legend attributed the system of irrigation, dikes, and canals to Osiris, it was the product of many hands. Developed at many places simultaneously, without concerted plan, it was certain that sooner or later some communities would be injured by the efforts of others. An integrated, central control was needed, so that all communities might be served. This central authority was of necessity at first local; a strong local authority consolidated its gains and gradually extended its sway over other localities. Heliopolis became such a center in Lower Egypt. Its powerful kings traced their origin to Râ himself; its zealous priests "collected, condensed, and arranged the principal myths of the local religions"; and its geographical character and situation, being a "compact and restricted area," also contributed to the foundation of the kingdom of Lower Egypt.[9]

Settled long in this storehouse of nature, the people of Egypt developed a variety of specialized occupations. No longer did the simple, primitive division of functions between men and women suffice. Herodotus [10] noted seven distinct groups: priests, warriors, cowherds, swineherds, tradesmen, interpreters, and boatmen. These were not fixed castes; though the divisions were rather sharp, it was possible, even if difficult, to pass from one to the other. Sons commonly followed the occupation of their fathers, but this they were not compelled to do.[11] Having been trained for a particular employment, it was not easy to change; but there are instances of men who rose to high position from low estate. One who later became a high priest of Amon tells us that, till sixteen, he was educated for a military life and then entered Amon's temple.

Though class lines were not impassable, social classes were not by any means unimportant; indeed, the priests, the warriors, and the king made up a privileged order which possessed the wealth of Egypt. The country was divided into three parts. The first was the domain of the priests, who were free from taxes and impositions, were highly reverenced, and had great authority because of their wisdom, learning, and relation to the gods, all which enabled them to assist and advise the king. The second portion belonged to the king, to support his court in dignity, to defray the costs of war, and to reward those who were noted for courage and public service. The third part was assigned to the soldiers, as Diodorus [12] says, so that they might readily and cheerfully risk the dangers of war and that they might marry and raise children, who would imitate their valor and be trained to arms from very childhood.

Though little is known of the origin of the soldier class, it was possibly con-

8 Maspero: *op. cit.*, pp. 69 f.; Breasted: *op. cit.*, pp. 7 f.
9 Maspero: *op. cit.*, pp. 229 f.
10 Bk. ii, 164.
11 *Diodorus*, i, 81; Rawlinson: *op. cit.*, pp. 43 f.
12 Bk. i, 73.

stituted, at first, of a conquering people and their children; but later its strength was augmented by Bedouins, Negroes, Nubians, and captives taken in war. The mercenary supporters of the king were kept loyal by assignments of land, were not taxed, and were exempt from forced labor when on active service. That the soldiery might not become a powerful, permanent, landed aristocracy, Herodotus says, a change of land assignments was provided for each year. This effort to restrict their power was perhaps not continuous; at any rate, it was not wholly successful, for their importance at times nearly equaled that of priests, and "even kings and barons of highest rank could not ignore" it.[13]

More important than the soldiers, as a rule, was the priestly class, which gained political influence as early as the beginning of the Fifth Dynasty and occasionally could make and unmake kings.[14] Its functions were sacerdotal and secular. Though subject to the king, the priesthood was in a sense his master: by intercession with the gods, by advice to kings, and by instruction of ordinary men, it influenced all affairs. Naturally, though priests and soldiers contended for supremacy at times, each class strengthened the other against the mass of laborers who sustained them both. Like the soldiery, the priests were not a hereditary caste. Recruits came to the temples from many sources: some important positions were filled by the Pharaoh himself; lesser ones, by feudal underlings. Living on income from temple properties and the offerings made to the gods, the priests occupied an enviable position. Incumbents who married, having found the service of the gods pleasant and profitable, were not only loath to leave it, but brought in other members of their families and bred up their children to it, so that after generations there came to be "a sort of sacerdotal nobility." [15]

Below the owning, ruling classes, there was a vast laboring population, divisible into husbandmen, shepherds, artificers, boatmen—indeed a multitude of special functional classifications. Of these toiling masses some were slaves, others free. The slaves, purchased abroad or taken captive in war, were mere property, were moved about at will by the owner, received no regular pay, and had no hope of freedom. Some became serfs and were passed from hand to hand when the land changed owners. Royal slaves, of course, might rise to great power.[16] Free laborers and artisans, though theoretically able to dispose of themselves as they wished, were actually less free than they appeared to be; for, as elsewhere in feudal societies, it was necessary to pay allegiance to someone more powerful than oneself. Escape from subjection to another meant for-

---

[13] Maspero: *op. cit.*, pp. 305 ff.
[14] Breasted: *Development of Religion and Thought in Ancient Egypt*, p. 363.
[15] Maspero: *op. cit.*, pp. 301 ff.; Herodotus, II, 35–7.
[16] Maspero: *op. cit.*, pp. 326 ff.; Rawlinson: *op. cit.*, pp. 43 f., 60, 219 f.; Erman: *Life in Ancient Egypt*, pp. 105 f.

feiting the protection of one's superior and made one an easy victim of wrong-doers, from whom, without someone influential to plead for him, it was hard to get redress. Diodorus [17] states that the farmers tilled land, which they had from the king, priests, and soldiers on easy rentals, devoting their entire time to such labor. His view of their situation is perhaps too "easy." A modern critical scholar pictures them as extremely laborious, rarely entering "their houses except to eat and sleep," since their employments kept them constantly outside. Some of the laboring class had mud cabins, big enough for man and wife, and hired themselves for a daily wage; others leased land; still others, more able and fortunate, actually gained control of a little property which they could bequeath or sell. Upon all, however, rested the burden of taxes, requisitions, and forced labor. Taxes appear to have been a tithe of the gross produce, varying according as the inundation had been generous or scanty, and were collected with the stick when they could not be gathered without it. Forced labor was common whenever crops were to be planted and harvested, canals cleaned and repaired, stone quarried, temples built, or new monuments erected.[18]

Egyptian toilers appear to have been made of resilient stuff: though they labored hard, they sang at their work and feasted and drank at payday. But though spirits were brave, bodies were calloused, broken, bent, and diseased by inhuman labor, from which there was seldom any relaxation. The dolorous lot of artisans is pictured darkly by an ancient scribe: the smith's hands, "rugged as the crocodile"; the weaver "squatting, his knees against his chest"; the mason, his arms "worn out with work," since "he has no other bread than his fingers"; the dyer, his fingers reeking, his eyes weary, his hand never at rest; the stonecutter who is worn out "when at last he has earned something." In the country it is no better. The peasant works hard for others first, and for himself when he can, but he has nothing when the tax collector appears: "Dost thou not recall the picture of the farmer, when the tenth of his grain is levied? Worms have destroyed half of the wheat, and the hippopotami have eaten the rest; there are swarms of rats in the fields, the grasshoppers alight there, the cattle devour, the little birds pilfer, and if the farmer lose sight for an instant of what remains upon the ground, it is carried off by robbers; the thongs, moreover, which bind the iron and the hoe are worn out, and the team has died at the plough. It is then that the scribe steps out of the boat at the landing-place to levy the tithe, and there come the keepers of the doors of the granary with cudgels and the negroes with ribs of palm-leaves, who come crying: 'Come now, corn!' There is none, and they throw the cultivator full length upon the ground; bound, dragged to the canal, they fling him in head first; his wife is

[17] Bk. I, 74.
[18] Maspero: *op. cit.*, pp. 308 f., 320, 327 ff.

bound with him, his children are put into chains; the neighbours, in the meantime, leave him and fly to save their grain." [19]

In some respects Egyptian women enjoyed a high place in society. The law recognized their right to property. Certain women, indeed, held royal power, but this was the exception, not the rule. Though Herodotus says that a woman could not "serve the priestly office," there were priestesses of Hathor and Neith who danced and made music before them; indeed, high priestesses were appointed by the king and might share equally the perquisites of the office with men. Girls of noble families served in the temples at Thebes in the days of the Caesars.[20] Temple service was not a bar to later marriage. The Egyptian professed a regard for the purity of wives, held its protection desirable, its breach a sin. The "Negative Confession" proclaims among other virtues: ". . . I have not defiled the wife of any man"; again, "I have not committed any sin against purity." [21] Though in early times polygamy was not practiced in Egypt, in later days kings and men of great wealth had several wives and concubines. In general, however, there was no seclusion of the female sex, such as was common in other Oriental countries. As companion and helpmate of her husband, the wife governed his household, brought up the children, and was neither a slave nor a toy.[22] An elevated conception of mother and the love due to her is suggested by Dauuf's advice: "Give thy heart to learning and love her like a mother." Learning had, of course, very practical advantages among Egyptians. A certain prudential wisdom motivated the instruction of Ptah-hotep also, who said that a man, if wise, should love his wife, feed her abundantly, and clothe her well, for "as long as thou lookest to this, she is as a profitable field to her master." [23] Naturally, the rôle of women changed somewhat with the maturing of Egyptian society. In the Old and Middle Kingdoms the wife was dependent, though not slavish; while the New Kingdom saw something of a feminist tendency. A woman's club, at the time of Augustus, has been reported.[24]

Vocational opportunities for women were narrow. Generally, their education was slight and was gained through apprenticeship to their work. In upper- and middle-class families the heaviest work was done by slaves; but in the poorer, all household drudgery—spinning, weaving, mending, carrying water, feeding the fire, cooking, baking, grinding of corn—fell to woman's lot. To grind corn,

[19] Ibid., pp. 310 ff., 330 ff., 338 ff.; Wilkinson: op. cit., II, 418.
[20] Herodotus, II, 35, 54, 56; Blackman: "On the Position of Women in the Ancient Egyptian Hierarchy," Jour. Egy. Archaeol., VII, 8, 24, 28, 29; Breasted: History of Egypt, p. 63; Maspero: op. cit., pp. 50 ff.
[21] Wilson, E.: Egyptian Literature, p. 105.
[22] Rawlinson: op. cit., pp. 62 ff.
[23] Maspero: op. cit., p. 401.
[24] Edgar: "A Women's Club in Ancient Alexandria," Jour. Egy. Archaeol., IV, 253 f.; Spiegelberg: "Note on the Feminine Character of the New Empire," Jour. Egy. Archaeol.. XV, 199.

handfuls of grain were placed on a stone, "slightly hollowed," and then crushed with a stone "like a painter's muller." After an hour or more of such labor, which engaged "arms, shoulders, loins," indeed all the body, only "an indifferent result followed from the great exertion." [25] When this and other tasks, equally laborious, had been performed, there would be neither leisure nor inclination for more physical exertion.

Herodotus observed that the Egyptians were "religious to excess"; [26] theirs was the land of a thousand gods. The celestial domain reflected the terrestrial: as men were brought to one's service by promises, rewards, payments, so the gods contracted with men to assist them, give them health, happiness, and fortune in battle, and to replenish the supply of vitalizing Sa, a magical fluid which the gods could draw from the lake of Sa somewhere in the northern sky. The multitude of gods, associated more or less closely with natural forces, celestial bodies, and animals, represented the many localities and cities of Egypt. Each place had its god; each god, a college of priests. As the members of a community increased, and their wealth proportionately, so also the wealth of the god was augmented by the number of worshipers whose devotion was attested by gifts and sacrifices. At all times, says Maspero, "the domain of the gods formed . . . about one-third of the whole country." [27]

The gods were like men in some respects, but differed from them in others. They might marry and have children. Ultimately, they would die and forsake their cities for their tombs; but death came to them slowly, if inevitably, their bones turning gradually to silver, their flesh to gold, their hair to lapis lazuli. The long life, the relative permanence of influence and power of a god, served as a cohesive force, tending to effect and maintain a unity in the city or nome, more lasting than that secured by temporal powers. If misfortune and disintegration came to city or nome, it was around the local temple and its worship that the scattered remnants might be reunited. When the god, his temple, and his worship decayed, the strength and integrity of the community were indeed gone.

To enumerate even the principal gods would be supererogatory. Of the Osirian legends and worship, however, brief notice may be taken. Osiris represented the Nile River, descended from Râ himself, and was, at first, a wild, uncontrolled force, destructive and awe-inspiring to man. Later, however, as the Nile was harnessed to man's will, Osiris was transformed also into a benefactor of man; as the Nile ruled Egypt and made it what it was, so Osiris was the originator of good and useful arts. His primitive neighbor and sister, Isis, personifying the black earth of the Delta, dwelled at Buto. According to

[25] Maspero: op. cit., p. 320.
[26] Bk. II, 37.
[27] Maspero: op. cit., pp. 108 ff., 301 ff.; Rawlinson: op. cit., pp. 30 ff.

legend, Osiris married Isis, their union symbolizing the marriage of the flooding Nile and the thirsty soil. Since the fruit of this union nourished all creatures and, through the gifts of men, supported all the gods as well, Osiris came to be regarded as a chief deity.[28] The supreme importance of the Nile is beautifully portrayed in the hymn of "Adoration":

> Hail to thee O Nile!
> Thou showest thyself in this land,
> Coming in peace, giving life to Egypt. . . .

"Giving life" means many things: watering the soil; making wheat and spelt grow; giving life to animals; nourishing every creature; and maintaining the temples. The latter is important:

> If the gods in heaven are grieved,
> Then sorrow cometh on men.[29]

It has been said that belief in immortality was universal among the Egyptians. Practical as they were in earthly affairs, they were not less so in celestial matters. Belief in a continued existence led to a strong emphasis on the beauty, strength, and durability of their sepulchers, which they called "everlasting habitations," in contrast to the caravanserai where earthly life was spent. After the ultimate death of Osiris, it had seemed good to him that those who served faithfully in life should follow him to the Islands of the Blest. Thither the dead could go, if provided with adequate instructions, prayers, and passwords. Some learned them in life, so as to be ready; others studied them after death, from papyri deposited with the mummy, or were instructed by priests or relatives who recited the necessary passages into their ears. By reciting the "Negative Confession" before Osiris and his court of forty-two judges, one made his case acceptable in their sight. From this series of denials some insight into ideal standards of conduct may be gained. The prospective voyager to the Blessed Isles disavows being guilty of any kind of iniquity; specifically, he clears himself with respect to robbery, murder, lying, stealing food, injuring plowed fields, stirring up strife, cheating the measure, purloining and destroying property of the gods, cursing the gods, cursing the king, scorning the god of his local city, acting insolently, talking too much, judging hastily, abusing others, and many other faults.[30]

[28] Maspero: op. cit., pp. 23 f., 130 ff., 151 f.
[29] Wilson: op. cit., pp. 336 ff.
[30] Breasted: Development of Religion and Thought, chap. 8; Wilson: op. cit., pp. 104 ff.

### EDUCATION IN EGYPT

MENTAL EDUCATION Egypt's passing from primitive life to settled civilization entailed a great expansion of formal, intellectual education. This was occasioned by the increased complexity of life, the growing necessity for keeping records, the development of specialized professions, and especially the invention of writing (credited to the great god, Thoth) which made possible the preservation of vast accretions of knowledge. Formal education became a bookish matter, whereas it had once been limited to oral instruction and verbal repetition. A knowledge of letters became the path to power.

Education, formal no less than informal, was of a practical character. "Knowledge is indispensable to getting on in the world; hence . . . [Ptah-hotep] recommends knowledge." [31] Always enmeshed in the ideal of practicality, ever intent on getting ahead in respect to wealth and power, the Egyptians seem never to have been concerned with the notion of a disinterested pursuit of knowledge. Learning was prized because it opened the way to a superior station in life. Those who had ability were encouraged to prepare for the life of a scribe: "Give thy heart to learning"; "set to work and become a scribe"; the "ignorant man" is "unknown"; "like a heavily laden donkey, he is driven by the scribe"—these sayings and bits of advice reflect the certainty felt by an Egyptian that education would be profitable to him. The lack of prohibition against learning on the part of lower-class folk, and these words of encouragement to youth, must not lead us to conclude, however, that education was universally distributed. The school for scribes, attached to the court in olden days, would at best receive only a small part of the population.[32] The impecunious condition of the lowest class must have kept the majority from learning. Diodorus supports this view. After speaking of the education of the priests, he says that most of the common people are trained from infancy in all kinds of arts and crafts so as to get their living. Some of them are taught reading and writing, though only superficially. Chiefly craftsmen are thus instructed. But if most people of humble origin did not lift themselves by the bootstraps of learning to positions of importance, there were doubtless some who did.[33]

The wealth of priests, their near monopoly of the domain of learning, and the tendency to promote the interests of their relatives and benefactors had an important bearing on the accessibility of learning in Egypt. Maspero says that, though offices held by priests "were not necessarily hereditary," their children,

---

[31] Maspero: *op. cit.*, p. 401.
[32] Erman: *op. cit.*, p. 329; Rawlinson: *op. cit.*, p. 45.
[33] Diodorus, I, 81; Maspero: *op. cit.*, pp. 283–98.

A SCRIBE READING  *Thebes, c. 1450 B.C.–1400 B.C.*
(Courtesy, The Metropolitan Museum of Art, New York)

"born and bred in the shelter of the sanctuary, almost always succeeded to the positions of their fathers. . . ." [34] The more elaborate education of these, and others from whatever origin, who desired to prepare for the higher positions in life, was of two kinds, sacred and ordinary. The ordinary learning of the simplest scribe was quite limited: "Every one was a scribe who knew how to read, write, and cipher, was fairly proficient in wording the administrative formulas, and could easily apply the elementary rules of book-keeping." [35] Sacred learning included ultimately whatever esoteric knowledge the priesthood possessed. Aristotle credited Egyptian priests with the pursuit of knowledge for its own sake, for example, in mathematics, for they were the first to have leisure for such study.[36] Higher secular professions required arithmetic and geometry because of their bearing on practical problems of land surveys and the calculations of astrology.[37] The higher education of others than priests was naturally differentiated according as they were to become artists, architects, physicians, or engineers. The literary sources of advanced learning were to be found in the temples. Great priestly colleges were located in Thebes, Memphis, and Heliopolis. Under the New Kingdom certain government departments had divisions for training those who aspired to a career in them.[38] Professional training was acquired through apprenticeship to master physicians, engineers, and architects, supplemented by an acquaintance with the literature on the field in question. Since medicine continued to be so largely a matter of magic, and mathematics was limited to the solving of practical problems,[39] the learning involved in these areas was less imposing than the names ordinarily suggest to modern minds.

Of the organization of schools and the method of instruction, little can be said. Schooling began early in youth, about five or six years of age, and might continue as long as could be afforded and while attainments seemed promising. In Roman Egypt, training to be a scribe, like learning a trade, was gained under apprenticeship, as is shown by several contracts that have been recovered.[40] Copying classic instructions, such as those given by Amenemhait to his son, was a common mode of perfecting the style of the youthful aspiring scribe.[41] At the same time the instructions provided a guide to conduct. Thus "The Teaching of Amenophis the Son of Kanakht" concludes:

[34] *Op. cit.*, pp. 301 ff.
[35] *Ibid.*, pp. 283 ff.
[36] *Metaphysica*, I, 1.
[37] *Diodorus*, I, 81.
[38] Erman: *op. cit.*, p. 329.
[39] *Ibid.*, pp. 352 ff., 364 ff.
[40] Westermann: "Apprentice Contracts and the Apprentice System in Roman Egypt," *Class. Philol.*, IX, 304.
[41] Maspero: *op. cit.*, pp. 466 f.

> See for thyself these thirty chapters,
> They please, they educate;
> They are the foremost of all books;
> They instruct the ignorant.[42]

These patterns of perfection and exercises in numbers, bills, invoices, and other necessary business forms, were written first with a stylus upon a tablet of wood, and later upon papyrus. Learning was chiefly a process of drilling and memorizing, unalleviated by appeals to judgment, independent thinking, or originality. Discipline of the school was apparently severe. As among the Hebrews, the child was not to be spoiled by sparing the rod: "A boy's ears are on his back, he hears when he is beaten," summed up the disciplinary argument of Egyptian pedagogues.

### TRAINING IN PHYSICAL SKILL

*Humble occupations* The cultivation of physical skills was provided for by a more or less formal apprenticeship under those who were already competent, in much the same fashion as other attainments were passed on from teacher to learner. The goals of such an apprenticeship were doubtless about as varied as life's activities. Formal contracts have come to light which cover several occupations—weaving, making nails, hairdressing, shorthand, and flute-playing. These are dated from 18 B.C. to the third century A.D. The time of service ranges from six months (for the flute-player) to five years (for one of the weavers). The chief difference between the teaching contract (shorthand and flute-playing) and the apprentice contract (for weaving, etc.) is that, in the first, the master received a fee, while in the second he did not, owing to the fact that the work done by an apprentice in weaving, smithing, and similar occupations would itself be of economic value to the master.[43]

For the very lowest class of workers on farms, waterways, and in industries, the skill required might be limited indeed and very readily acquired. In families, a natural, informal apprenticeship prepared the young to assume, in due course, the labors of those already made competent by years of experience. Diodorus explains that the shepherds had looked after the flocks from generation to generation, the young learning from the old and adding something, perhaps, from their own experience. Likewise the husbandmen were trained from infancy by actual apprenticeship to all the labors of the land. In respect to invention, he says, they have learned to hatch chicks by an artificial method just as effectually as nature herself. Shifting occupations was not easily accomplished,

---

[42] Griffith: *op. cit., Jour. Egy. Archaeol.,* XII, 224; Simpson: "The Hebrew Book of Proverbs and the Teaching of Amenophis," *Jour. Egy. Archaeol.,* XII, 232–9.
[43] Westermann: *op. cit., loc. cit.,* IX, 296 f.

apparently. Mechanics and artificers, Diodorus says,[44] must practice such trades as their parents teach them, and not dabble in other things which might interfere with the improvement of their own proper trade.

*Heroic business* Strabo observed that the self-sufficiency of Egypt and her relatively sheltered situation in respect to her neighbors made her generally peaceful rather than distinguished in military affairs.[45] Modern scholarship, in general, confirms the view. It is obvious, however, that the tendencies of societies change, and a peaceful people may become ambitious of empire. Thus, under the Old and Middle Kingdoms, Egypt had been generally peaceful, and at last she suffered invasion and the establishment of Hyksos rule on the Nile. The effort to drive out the Hyksos, however, entailed a marked development of military spirit and power. At length, when success crowned that effort in the sixteenth century, Egypt had gained consciousness of her warlike potentialities. She proceeded forthwith to make a strong bid for empire, backed by the force of her armies. For two centuries (1600–1400 B.C.) Egypt was "the great military power of the ancient world." [46] Thereafter the drive to empire suffered a relapse and never regained great potency. Nevertheless, though war on a grand national scale was of rather brief duration, it is clear that petty local wars went on in various nomes of Egypt. Many were the border forays against the "nine bows," peoples of the desert, who from time to time raided the settled, prosperous Egyptian communities. Each nome had its "battle-house"; its militia; its contingent from the temple lands; and others from the "treasury department" and from friendly border peoples—all under the leadership of the monarch. The army drawn from the various nomes had perhaps nearly a half-million men, in Egypt's "most populous" days.[47]

Making war was the business of relatively few people, a fairly well-defined class of society. The native soldiers were settled upon farms in certain nomes when not on active service, so that their bodies might be made healthy by being inured to "habits of industry." Besides native Egyptian soldiers, there were numerous mercenaries. Tens of thousands of *Nashi*, Negroes, were being drilled for the Egyptian army about 2000 B.C. Even during the period of extensive wars under the New Empire, mercenaries made up the greater part of the Egyptian army.[48]

The soldiery prepared for their vocation by actual military maneuvers and exercises and by practicing many games, recognized as useful in the development of warlike attitudes and physical skill. It is said that Sesostris' father had many youths of his generation educated together, causing them to exercise un-

[44] Bk. I, 74.
[45] *The Geography of Strabo*, XVII, 1, 53.
[46] Baikie: *The Amarna Age*, p. 19; Erman: *op. cit.*, p. 521.
[47] Wilkinson: *op. cit.*, I, 187 ff.
[48] Erman: *op. cit.*, pp. 542 ff.; Tylor: *Anthropology*, p. 3.

ceasingly in all sorts of hardships, and not permitting anyone to eat until he had run 180 furlongs. The military school is often referred to as the "*stable for education.*" [49] Though the military position was not a hereditary one, its advantages were recognized as so great and so desirable that most of those engaged in fighting had their sons enrolled for military training. Even while yet young, boys ". . . were taken to the barracks, where they were taught not only the use of the bow, the battle-axe, the mace, the lance, and the shield, but were all instructed in such exercises as rendered the body supple, and prepared them for manoeuvring, regimental marching, running, jumping, and wrestling either with closed or open hand. They prepared themselves for battle by a regular war-dance, pirouetting, leaping, and brandishing their bows and quivers in the air. . . ." [50] At Beni-Hasan, soldiers of the Middle Kingdom are represented, armed with bows, going through the evolutions of a war dance.

The soldierly ideal was the mighty man of valor. Doubtless the heroic virtues were most prized under the great leaders of the New Empire, but praise of them is a common enough feature of Egyptian history. The king is usually portrayed as a model to be imitated; naturally, the heroic portrayal is subject to discount. He proved by his mighty deeds his wisdom and his right to rule. Usirtasen "is a hero who wrought with the sword, a mighty man of valour without peer: he beholds the barbarians, he rushes forward and falls upon their predatory hordes. He is the hurler of javelins who makes feeble the hands of the foe; those whom he strikes never more lift the lance. Terrible is he, shattering skulls with the blows of his war-mace, and none resisted him in his time. . . . None may escape his arrow; before he bends his bow the barbarians flee from his arms like dogs, for the great goddess has charged him to fight against all who know not her name, and whom he strikes he spares not; he leaves nothing alive." [51] The king, and his soldiers too—who fight only less spectacularly and less effectively than he—are the agents of civilization; they drive out the barbarians by virtue of their greater physical skill, the superiority of their arms, and compel them to recognize the power and superiority of gods whom they never knew before.

The equipment of Egyptian soldiers enables one to know something of the particular skills they endeavored to perfect. The strength of the army lay in the archers, who fought either on foot or in chariots. The cavalry, the charioteers, were a foreign importation into Egypt and highly valued. The chariot fighter commonly used bows and darts, for which he was entirely freed by the services of his driver. Chariot forces were housed in the royal stables, which were really schools for that branch of the armed forces. The infantry was divided accord-

---

[49] *Diodorus, I, 53; Erman: op. cit., pp. 330, 548.
[50] Maspero: op. cit., pp. 305 ff.
[51] Ibid., pp. 466 f.

ing to the arms used in various branches: "bowmen, spearmen, swordsmen, clubmen, slingers. . . ." Besides these offensive weapons they used "two species of javelin," the sling, daggers, knives, falchions, hatchets, battle-axes, poleaxes, maces, and the *lissán*, "a curved stick similar to that still in use" among Ethiopians.[52] For defense their bodies were protected by helmets (usually quilted rather than of metal), coats of armor, and a shield—generally equal in length to half the man's height, but sometimes great enough to hide the person completely. With such weapons, it is clear that the exercise of arms chiefly demanded the same types of physical excellence that had served the warriors of far more primitive civilizations. The handling of horses and chariots in battle, however, demanded a new skill, for one must be able not only to drive skillfully, but he must also care for his horses and be able to take to pieces and adjust his chariot. Of the use of such engines of war as the swinging battering-ram the Egyptians appear to have known nothing.[53]

The education of the soldier, or rather that of superior military officers, was not all physical. In the army as elsewhere in life, the learned person held a place that was most highly valued. The "scribes of the army" were of many different ranks, some serving only a company, while others had duties concerned with the entire army and ranked even above the "charioteer of the court." As Erman says, "according to Egyptian ideas, even in the profession of arms, a good education was the only thing that could bring men happiness and success." [54]

*Sports and recreation* As a preliminary to military training and as a supplement to it, the Egyptians engaged in many sports of the field and in gymnastic exercises; they amused themselves with mimic battles, wrestling, jumping, fist-fights, single-sticks, and other exercises, to develop strength and bravery in hand-to-hand encounter. Hunting, a vestigial remnant of a life long past, was still an excellent training for war, and hence was not only a pleasant sport but an obligation as well. The kings regarded the destruction of wild beasts as a royal duty to their realm, for the most dangerous beasts were a menace to settled communities. According to Diodorus,[55] if the hippopotamus had brought forth young every year, it would have ruined the husbandmen of Egypt. For the masters of the hunt, pursuit of wild beasts was of course a profession; but some kings led personally in hunting expeditions as they led in battle; and their achievements in the former appear to have been rated important, by themselves at least, if not equally significant as their exploits in the

---

[52] Wilkinson: *op. cit.*, I, 191 ff.
[53] Maspero: *op. cit.*, pp. 58 f., 452; Wilkinson: *op. cit.*, I, 186–278; Erman: *Aegypten und Aegyptisches Leben im Altertum*, chap. 20; Breasted: *History of Egypt*, pp. 234 f.; Herodotus, VII, 63, 69.
[54] *Life in Ancient Egypt*, p. 550.
[55] Bk. I, 35.

latter. Amenhotep declares that in ten years he had slain by his own hand more than one hundred kings of the forest; and Thotmes III is said to have killed or taken one hundred and twenty elephants.[56]

But hunting was not for kings and nobility alone. They led in the hunt of kingly beasts, of course; but smaller game, fish, and birds abounded, and furnished sport at least for the lesser warriors and doubtless, too, for some common folk. Wilkinson's full account of hunting and fishing maintains that "all classes of the Egyptians delighted in the sports of the field . . ."; and though some have considered that huntsmen were a definite class in Egypt, as did Plato, it is incorrect to consider hunting as limited to them entirely.[57] Peasants shot with arrows and trapped the hyena, not for sport alone, but to protect their crops. The ibex, wild ox, panther, gazelle, porcupine, antelope, fox, jackal, wolf, leopard, ostrich, wild boar, oryx, stag, wild sheep, hare, wildcat, giraffe, and crocodile figured often as objects of the chase. Fishing and fowling, too, appear to have been rather universal sports. The Egyptians acquired a marked skill in training dogs, lions, and even great cats to assist them in pursuing, capturing, and retrieving game. They became skillful in the use of the "throw-stick" or boomerang, which they were fond of hurling at birds; while nets and traps in great variety, the bow, the spear, the club, the harpoon, the fishing pole and line, the lasso, and knives, constituted their most effective instruments of capture and destruction. Some of these they wielded on foot, and others in chariots on appropriate occasions. The bola was a strap approximately five yards long, having a small stone attached to it, which caused it, when properly thrown, to wrap itself around the legs, horns, or neck of an animal, so that the huntsman could pull his prey to the ground.

For some, it must be remembered, fishing, fowling, and hunting were serious businesses rather than sport. There were, at certain periods at least, official birdcatchers and hunters. In such cases, an apprenticeship to a particular skill was an indispensable part of education. The weapons used depended, to some extent, on whether the purpose was vocational or recreational. The throw-stick was doubtless commonly used for sport; but nets were employed to take birds for food supply.[58]

In such a favorable physical environment fishing was inevitably important, first as a source of food supply, and then as a sport. Kings and priests might avoid fish, but commoners could not pass by such a source of food.[59] The wealthy, too, who were not restrained by priestly taboo, appear to have used fish for food in many ways. Tackle, spear, harpoon, net, hook and line, rod—

[56] Rawlinson: op. cit., pp. 194 f., 220 f.
[57] Op. cit., II, chap. 8; Klebs: Die Reliefs und Malereien des Neuen Reiches. Abhandlungen der Heidelberger Akademie der Wissenschaften, Nr. IX, 75 ff.
[58] Erman: Life in Ancient Egypt, pp. 236 ff.
[59] Radcliffe: Fishing from the Earliest Times, pp. 319 ff.

all were known to Egyptians about 2000 B.C. When Egypt became populous and had an extensive division of labor, there was a special class of boatmen—listed by Herodotus as the seventh, or lowest, class of people—of which group fishermen probably formed a part. There is no occupation which is not better than that of fisherman—such, apparently, was the opinion of Egyptians. Whenever he casts his net, "his fate is in the hands of God." [60] The leisure class fished for sport, employing both the primitive spear and the line. Those who fished for a livelihood, however, used the more efficient nets.

Upon reading, in Lane's *Modern Egyptians*,[61] that "gymnastic games, or such diversions as require much bodily exertion, are very uncommon among . . . [them]," one might expect to find little evidence of attention to physical sports in their past history. Gardiner says, in fact, that ". . . it is clear that they [Egyptians] had no claim to be an athletic people . . ." and gives as the reason that "they were not a military people . . ." but depended on recruits to the army from the Sudan.[62] This observation is true within limits; but perhaps it has been stressed too heavily. Mercenaries were certainly employed in great numbers; yet, according to Wilkinson, when "Egypt was most populous," the native army, drawn from the nomes, was not far from half a million men.[63] Moreover, as has been noted, Egypt had, for a time, a marked military interest and renown, and even sought for empire. Such a development was, of course, brief. It may be that Egyptians had a somewhat greater interest in physical sports than we have commonly believed. There has been, perhaps, an undue tendency to minimize their love of physical contests, because it is easy to be influenced by the accounts given of Egyptians by their Greek neighbors. Vogt holds, and his view may be a sound one, that the failure of Greek travelers and writers to relate much about Egyptian athletics probably means nothing more than that Greeks, whose athletic interests were profound and whose physical attainments were remarkable, found nothing particularly noteworthy in the sports and exercises of their neighbors.[64] That physical contests did not play the same rôle among Egyptians as among the Greeks is obvious; but that a variety of sports and exercises furnished recreation and amusement for the many, and served a more limited class as a conditioner of the body for the more arduous training for the profession of arms, seems a reasonable conclusion from the evidence which modern studies of Egypt have discovered.

Certain of the early references made by foreigners to the subject of Egyptian sports and contests may be noted briefly. That Egyptians generally laid little stress on gymnastic games is suggested by Herodotus, who took special cogni-

60 *Ibid.*, p. 333; Klebs: *op. cit., loc. cit.*, pp. 23, 86 ff.
61 Vol. II, 54.
62 *Athletics of the Ancient World*, p. 8.
63 *Op. cit.*, I, 187 ff.
64 Bogeng: *Geschichte des Sports*, I, 121.

zance of the celebration of gymnastic contests by the people of Chemmis, which was so ". . . unlike the rest of the Egyptians." To his inquiry as to the reason for their different practice, he was told that they celebrated thus in honor of Perseus, whom they claimed as ancestor, and that he had charged them to "institute a gymnastic contest in his honour." [65] With regard to Herodotus' report of the matter, Wilkinson holds that "it is . . . probable that he [Perseus] was not the only god in whose honor gymnastic exercises were performed; and the fondness of the Egyptians for such amusements is fully proven by the monuments . . . on which wrestling and other games are portrayed with great minuteness. Wrestling, indeed, was a favorite amusement in Egypt . . . and it is highly probable that games similar to those mentioned by Herodotus were celebrated in the nome of Heracleopolis, as well as in honor of other Egyptian gods." [66] But even if we accept the view that formal athletic contests were the exception rather than the rule, and that the celebrations at Chemmis were the most remarkable of all, other ancient authorities bear witness that recreations of various sorts were generally indulged in by the common people, whenever they were freed from their labor. Diodorus,[67] for example, says that, during the inundation, the common people, now at ease from all employments of the field, indulge themselves in idleness, feasting, sports, and pleasures of all kinds.

If some difference of opinion exists as to the extent of formal, physical contests, such is not the case when it comes to informal participation in games. The playthings buried with children, such as dolls, pigs, crocodiles, ducks, pigeons, boats, balls, play furniture, marbles, tops, bowls, hoops, jumping-jacks, and the like, suggest that games, both active and sedentary, were an important element early in life.[68] As age increased, more active games occupied their attention. At Beni-Hasan two figures are shown at a game with hoops, in which each person has a hooked rod wherewith he seeks, apparently, to take the hoop from the other. Other pictorial remains depict somersaults, pole climbing, and contestants throwing knives or spikes, trying to make them stick into a block of wood. Two figures, seated back to back, with two arms linked at the elbow, are striving to rise without touching their free hands to the floor. In another scene, two persons stand side by side, and whirl around them two others who are in a semi-reclining position, with their feet placed together at the center, while their hands are held by those standing.[69] Lifting and swinging weights, clubs, or sacks of sand, and fighting with the short single-stick, or with the

[65] History, II, 91.
[66] Wilkinson: op. cit., III, 370.
[67] Bk. I, 36.
[68] Maspero: op. cit., pp. 318 f.; Breasted: History of Egypt, pp. 89 ff.
[69] Klebs: op. cit., loc. cit., pp. 223 ff.; Wilkinson: op. cit., II, 62, 68 f.

*nebboot*, a pole five or six feet long, were common means of testing strength, skill, courage, and the hardness of the contestants' skulls. Such contests are represented on the ground and in boats, individually and in companies. The game of *gereed*, described by Lane,[70] as played by the peasants of Upper Egypt to-day, seems to be an adaptation of the long pole fight of the ancients. Lane says, however, that it is played commonly only by those who have more recently settled on the Nile and is derived from the "early Bedawees." The object of the fight with the *nebboot* was to strike the opponent's head, the pole being swung with both hands. In single-stick contests the free forearm, with which one warded off the blows, was protected by a wooden guard which extended to his finger tips, while the stick hand was protected by a sort of shield. Mimic battles, in which they attacked improvised strongholds, were not only a source of entertainment but a means of training among the soldiers. The wealthy encouraged bull-fighting, for which animals were especially trained, as Strabo reported at Memphis.[71] Prizes were given the winner, or to his owner or trainer. That men also fought bulls is certain, but this practice does not seem to have been common; nor does it appear, says Wilkinson, that "culprits, or captives taken in war" were compelled "to combat with wild beasts. . . ."[72]

Ball was played by men, women, and children; but, though different modes of play are frequently shown, there do not seem to have been very elaborate or intricate games. Racquets and handball do not seem to have been played, judging by the pictorial records. The balls commonly used were about three inches in diameter, were made of leather or skins, and stuffed with reeds, hay, bran, or other soft materials. Ball-play, it seems, might be simply a tossing-catching game; and again, a test of skill in juggling several balls. The players are shown in various positions. Though ball-play has more commonly been a sport for boys, in Egyptian records women are often represented as participants. One attractive graphic portrayal shows women, probably professionals, in a favorite game in which two players are borne on the backs of two others; the one who fails to catch the ball, becomes in turn the ass.

Wrestling was evidently a favorite amusement, and was remarkably highly developed so far as techniques were concerned. For soldiers, wrestling was one of the exercises employed for general physical conditioning.[73] Professional wrestling for exhibition and the entertainment of others seems to have become common. In the age of greatest professionalism which swept the Greek world, the Ptolemies, like rulers in Rome later, rewarded athletes handsomely. The athletes' privileges were, apparently, a sort of compensation for the "glory re-

70 *Modern Egyptians*, II, 54 ff.
71 Bk. XVII, 1, 31.
72 *Op. cit.*, II, 77.
73 Maspero: *op. cit.*, pp. 305 f.

flected upon the rulers" by their athletic achievements.[74] Wrestling was in a highly perfected state many centuries before Sparta and Athens came to prominence in the life of the Mediterranean. Many methods of attack and defense, indeed nearly all the holds and throws now used, are exhibited in the tombs of Beni-Hasan, which date back to about 2000 B.C. The contestants are wrestling naked, except for a narrow girdle. It is thought that wrestlers oiled their bodies, as did their Greek neighbors, thus increasing the difficulty of their art. The two contestants approached each other with arms inclined before them, each seeking the most favorable grip upon his adversary. When brought to the floor it was necessary to continue, apparently, till the shoulders were down. This is not certain, however. Whether defeat was acknowledged by a sign or by a word, is not known. It is also not clear whether striking, as in boxing, was allowed. Gardiner says there is ". . . no indication of hitting as in the Greek pankration"; but Wilkinson is less positive, and suggests that in one group at Beni-Hasan, "the combatants appear to strike each other." [75] If practiced at all, it would seem to have been uncommon.

Wilson has described in considerable detail the wrestling bouts and other contests of the New Kingdom, dealing with evidence in "five scenes of games in celebration of the appearance of the king," which range over a period of two hundred years.[76] One scene alone, he thinks, may represent boxers, but this is uncertain. His paper supports the view that "a full series of developed and effective wrestling holds was known" and used by the Egyptians. Wrestling was "skilled and governed by a definite code." The contestants, in these instances, appear to have been trained, professional grapplers. Wilson quotes the opinion of Harper, a technically qualified judge of wrestling, who says: "Egyptian wrestling was amazingly like our own. Some of the holds are carried out just as we should wish to do them now." One chief difference, in these representations, however, is that only upright wrestling is shown, and there is ". . . no wrestling on the mat." [77]

The extent to which swimming was practiced by the ancient Egyptians is difficult to ascertain. Certainly, few artistic portrayals of it have come to light. Mehl, however, has recently reproduced two hieroglyphs, one credited to about 3000 B.C. and the other to 2500 B.C., representing swimming figures.[78] The more ancient one shows the body quite horizontal in the water; the legs make rather high alternating strokes, while the arms alternate in a sort of crawl. The other

[74] Westermann: "The Ptolemies and the Welfare of Their Subjects," Am. Hist. Rev., XLIII, 272.
[75] Op. cit., II, 72 f.; Gardiner: op. cit., p. 7; Hyde: Olympic Victor Monuments, p. 228.
[76] Wilson, J. A.: "Ceremonial Games of the New Kingdom," Jour. Egy. Archaeol., XVII, 211 f.
[77] Ibid., XVII, 218 f.
[78] Antike Schwimmkunst, p. 97; Thomas: Swimming, p. 87. See figure, p. 68.

WRESTLERS

(P. E. Newberry, *Beni-Hasan*, Pt. ii, Pl. v).

portrays only the upper half of the body, in a semihorizontal plane, the right arm reaching forward, the left being thrown back. Pools, often built in the form of a "T," had become a common feature of the gardens of the nobility by the Eighteenth Dynasty. Surrounded by trees and flowers, they were sometimes large and deep enough for pleasure boats, and provided facilities for fishing and bathing, yet were not deep enough to be dangerous "for the least skillful wet-bob" of the harem. Numerous wood carvings are thought to represent swimmers who, swimming under water, seize birds by the legs and drag them under.[79]

In one of the groups on the south wall at Beni-Hasan there is possibly represented a game like prisoners' base.[80] Use of the bow and arrow in hunting scenes, warfare, and target shooting, is found in numerous instances. Erman reproduces a scene showing the god Seth teaching bow-shooting. Girls are shown here and there at target practice, as at Thebes.[81]

To-day it is common to think of sports and the physical training program in connection with health, cleanliness, and preventive medicine. Medical practice was highly developed among the Egyptians, Herodotus [82] tells us, there being specialists to treat diseases of the eye, the head, the teeth, the intestines, and many other parts of the body. Nevertheless, Egyptian medicine was still en-

[79] Klebs: *op. cit., loc. cit.*, pp. 23 ff., 82; Peet and Woolley: *The City of Akhenaten*, pp. 114–22; Erman: *Life in Ancient Egypt*, pp. 195 ff.; Luehring: *Swimming Pool Standards*, pp. 14 f.
[80] Newberry: *Beni-Hasan*, Pt. ii, 49.
[81] Erman: *Aegypten und Aegyptisches Leben*, p. 325; Wilkinson: *op. cit.*, i, 27.
[82] Bk. ii, 84.

thralled, to a remarkable degree, by magic. Belief in magic causation and cures of disease is not conducive to an understanding of the relation between exercise and health, and it is to be doubted whether the Egyptians arrived at that de-

THE EGYPTIAN CRAWL
(E. Mehl, *Antike Schwimmkunst*, p. 97, Ernst Heimeran Verlag, Munich, 1927)

gree of understanding. It is evident, however, that cleanliness and bathing were objects of concern, save among the lowest elements of society; and the relation of cleanliness to health may have been understood in some degree. Warm and cold baths were used, Wilkinson says, and they "were probably recommended and taken medicinally when occasion required." The "always fresh washed" linen, mentioned by Herodotus, was doubtless truly characteristic of the better-to-do Egyptians, but not of all. Wilkinson points to an example of a bath at Thebes, in which a woman, attended by four servants, is being bathed. Since bathing was forbidden during mourning, he concludes that baths must have been looked upon "as a luxury, as well as a necessary comfort." [83] Just how extensive was bathing, either as a "luxury" or as "necessary comfort," it is impossible to say. The extreme regulations of the priests to insure cleanliness were commented on by Herodotus, who said that they "shave their whole body every other day, that no lice or other impure thing may adhere to them when they are engaged in the service of the gods. . . . They bathe twice every day in cold water, and twice every night. . . ." [84] Shaving was not solely a priestly habit; the heads even of young children were shaved, and even slaves, when they came to Egypt, had to "conform to the cleanly habits of their masters, their beards and heads were shaved, and they adopted a close cap." [85] There were certain classes, however—such as herdsmen, boatmen, fishermen, bird-catchers—whose life and labors in the marshy areas were scarcely compatible with cleanliness. These "marshmen," who wore crude clothing, never shaved their heads, and even wore beards and mustaches, were regarded as "pariahs" by those more favorably situated.[86]

The prevalence of games of chance, guessing, and divination among primi-

[83] *Op. cit.*, II, 352 ff.
[84] Bk. II, 37.
[85] Wilkinson: *op. cit.*, II, 331 f.
[86] Erman: *Life in Ancient Egypt*, p. 439.

tive peoples has been noted.[87] Among Egyptians, games similar in nature and purpose had great popularity, and their origin may be explained in the same way. Dice, mora, "odd and even," draughts, and the "game of the vase" were evidently popular enough to gain a place in the scenes depicted by artists on ancient monuments. A game something like the Greek kollabismos was also played. At Beni-Hasan two figures are shown seated, holding their closed hands over the back of a third, who kneels with his face near the ground, and is supposed to guess the combined number of dice, stones, or shells held in their hands.[88] Múngala, a game of modern Egyptians, is supposed to have been derived from their ancient ancestors.[89] Dice are believed to have been anciently in vogue, being resorted to, according to mythical lore, as a means of determining the outcome of uncertain events. In the game of mora, as in the Italian game, two players simultaneously thrust out a hand while one of them guesses the total number of fingers extended. The manner of playing the "game of the vase" is obscure, despite an excellent representation of it in the tomb of Raséps. A "snake-game" was played, in which little figures of lions and dogs, and also small varicolored balls, were moved, in some unknown manner, over a board or table marked with the coiled design of a snake. Four small balls and nine vase-shaped stones, found by Petrie, have been regarded as evidence of a game of skittles. Remnants of spinning tops have also been discovered.[90]

Dancing    Dancing played an important rôle in primitive societies. In early Egyptian civilization its place continued to be prominent and of great significance. Certain important changes appear to have come about, however, when society became settled and considerably stratified. Whereas primitive peoples all danced, in historic Egypt dancing seems to have been considered improper for the upper class, and was "not customary" among them "either in public or private assemblies"; on the other hand, indulgence in dancing was general, perhaps almost universal, among the common people.[91] Even in the nineteenth century, Lane noticed that "Egyptian ladies" were "very seldom instructed either in music or dancing . . ." but took great delight in the performance of professionals.[92] The reasons against participation in dancing by the upper class, it appears, were that it was incompatible with their proper dignity. Being elevated above the masses by their wealth and social station, they left the dance to the more primitive, rude, uncultured peasants and artisans. The fact that pictorial remains sometimes depict kings dancing, is not

[87] Supra, pp. 36, 42 f.
[88] Wilkinson: op. cit., ii, 59 ff.
[89] Lane: op. cit., ii, 46 ff.
[90] Petrie and Quibell: Naqada and Ballas, pp. 11, 14, 35; Klebs: op. cit., loc. cit., p. 229; Erman: Aegypten und Aegyptisches Leben, p. 292; Falkener: Games Ancient and Oriental, pp. 9–111.
[91] Wilkinson: op. cit., i, 500 ff.
[92] Op. cit., i, 239 f.

MUSIC AND DANCING IN EGYPT *Tomb of Djeser-ka-Re-sonbe, Thebes, c. 1415 B.C.*
(Courtesy, The Metropolitan Museum of Art, New York)

out of harmony with the view stated. To participate in ceremonial dancing of a religious character was not incompatible with royal dignity, especially since king and priest might be one and the same person. King Semti danced, but it was a devotional dance; similarly, King Pepi danced before a god for the purpose of giving comfort and strength to the deity.[93]

But if dancing ceased to be customary among the upper classes, some of the purposes of dancing could be served by having others dance for them. Functional specialization of classes in Egyptian society has been noted; and professionalization of dancing is a marked characteristic of that society. The rich, powerful, educated, dignified folk could afford the luxury of entertainers to amuse them. Provision of musicians and dancers at private houses was a favorite means of entertaining. Supplying such services became a great business. Under the patronage of the court and others who were well to do, dancing became a highly developed art. Indeed, Egypt has been called the mother "of all civilized dancing." Dancers came to ancient Rome from the cities of the Nile.[94] The gods, as well as men, could be pleased better, served better, by the perfect dance of professional servants. The rich paid for this service to the gods, much as men and women of wealth in other societies purchase the service of professional preachers and priests to worship the gods in their behalf.

Professionalized dancing is thus an outstanding feature of Egyptian civiliza-

[93] Hambly: *Tribal Dancing*, pp. 58 f.; Kees: *Der Opfertanz des Ägyptischen Königs.*
[94] Ellis: *The Dance of Life*, pp. 53 f.

tion. Both men and women entered the business. Professional service of dancers fell generally into two classes: (1) religious and sedate; (2) secular, riotous, and indecorous, according to the occasion and the appetite of those who paid for it. Religious dances emphasized slow posturing and studied, artistic movement, joined with an accompaniment of hand-clapping and vocal and instrumental music. Secular dancing made use of rapid, even violent, movements, embodying feats of acrobatic prowess, though apparently not attempting anything like tightwire dancing. Profane dances, depicted on ancient tombs, show that the Egyptians were highly skilled, developed the pirouette, and practiced the *grand battement* or high kick.[95] Secular dances were often accompanied by much ribaldry. Wilkinson thinks that the "excesses were confined to the inferior class of performers, at the houses of the lower orders"; but considering the tendency of wealthy people to develop a taste for the spicy, at the same time that their ability to provide the means for its gratification increases, the inference is open to some doubt. The character of contracts made between professional entertainers and their patrons is well known, at least for later Egyptian history. Artemisia, of Philadelphia, asks Isidora, a castanet dancer, to perform at a festival for six days, beginning on a specified date. The castanets are believed to represent infiltration of Greek influence in the Hellenistic age, though an Egyptian clapper had been in use even in the earliest times in connection with dances wholly Egyptian in character. Isidora is to provide one other dancer, and they are to receive thirty-six drachmas a day. Four *artabas* of barley and twenty-four loaves of bread will be supplied them; their jewels and equipment will be guarded carefully; and two donkeys will be provided for transportation to the festival and back again.[96]

Slaves were trained as dancers for service at the court and in families; but free Egyptians also often turned to dancing, hiring themselves for the entertainment of those who would employ them on various festal occasions. In the temples female singers and dancers served the gods for whose service they were trained and by which they lived. The propitiation of nature spirits, which primitives practiced in the forest, had fallen into specialized hands, and had been removed to the temples, where the gods and their servitors dwelled. Education of all kinds in Egypt was of a highly vocational or professional nature; and since dancing had become a profession, whose devotees competed for a livelihood, dispensed at the hands of the upper class, one would expect to find a systematic training, in schools or through apprenticeship to masters and mistresses of the art, by which the most capable could develop the highest skill possible and thus gain the greatest reward. Pictorial remains about the begin-

[95] *Jour. Egy. Archaeol.*, II, 250.
[96] Westermann: "The Castanet Dancers of Arsinoe," *Jour. Egy. Archaeol.*, x, 134–44; Kraemer: "A Greek Element in Egyptian Dancing," *Am. Jour. Archaeol.*, xxxv, 135.

ning of the New Empire appear to represent a sort of dancing school. Dancing and music are inevitably closely associated. Training for flute-playing by apprenticeship to a master is attested by a contract, dated 13 B.C.[97] Music is said to have been taught, at least to some, in the army; and a sort of war dance played some part in the life of military folk. Wilkinson found "no instance of the . . . dance of armed men," except, perhaps, some figures at Beni-Hasan, "jumping with arms in their hands," that may have been "intended as an allusion to this exercise of the soldier. . . ."[98] Lexová, however, speaks of Egyptian war dances with more assurance, and distinguishes between a dance by Negro troops and another by Lybian soldiers. The dance of the Negro soldiers is " a wild mixture of undisciplined movements"; but the Lybians keep time by beating curved pieces of wood together and are "performing a dance, which is probably a representation of a duel. . . ."[99]

Dances, religious and profane, were performed singly, by pairs, and in companies, and by both sexes; more particularly they have been classified as purely movemental, gymnastic, imitative, military, dramatic, lyrical, grotesque, funeral, religious, the pair dance, and the group dance.[100] Dancing was accompanied by such primitive music as clapping and by vocal and instrumental rhythms. Such instruments as the castanets, tambourine, drum, cymbals, cylindrical maces, harp, pipes, lyre, and the guitar, were employed. Among the finds at Abydos, in tombs of the Twelfth Dynasty (fourth millennium B.C., according to Petrie's chronology), is a limestone figure of a female acrobat performing a "funerary dance," the khetebt. "She bends her body backwards till it forms a bow, her hands rest on the ground behind her, and her head and long hair hang down till they touch the ground."[101] On the south wall of Beni-Hasan one sees four male dancers and four men keeping time, followed by six female dancers with four girls beating time.[102] Generally, it seems, women played a more important rôle in dancing than did men. At Memphis fourteen women are represented in the "song of the ladies of the harem"; in another scene there are fifteen female dancers. Women dancers are generally depicted in long transparent robes, revealing the entire figure, belted occasionally at the waist. Some performers appear to have danced naked, unless, perchance, the faint lines used to denote their draperies have been effaced by time. Wilkinson does not believe that the Egyptians were so depraved as to have had naked dancing-girls in the presence of men, or that their priests would have allowed

---

97 Westermann: "Apprentice Contracts and the Apprentice System in Roman Egypt," loc. cit., IX, 296; cf. Klebs: op. cit., loc. cit., pp. 218 ff.
98 Wilkinson: op. cit., I, 503 f., 508; Erman: Life in Ancient Egypt, p. 524.
99 Lexová: Ancient Egyptian Dances, p. 30.
100 Ibid., pp. 21–42.
101 Peet: "The Year's Work at Abydos," Jour. Egy. Archaeol., I, 39.
102 Newberry: op. cit., loc. cit., Pt. II, 49.

it; but Birch, who revised Wilkinson's excellent volumes, adds his own conclusion that "it is certain . . . they sometimes danced naked, as their successors, the Alméhs, do. . . ." [103] The dance was sometimes employed to tell a continuous story, but this was true of private performances rather than public. The ballet, Birch says, was not developed by the Egyptians, though their figures and postures suggest the recent ballet.

The earliest evidence, drawn from the Egyptians themselves and from the comments upon them by their visitors in ancient days, bears witness to the prevalence of dancing among the common folk of the Nile. It is quite evident that the reserve in respect to dancing among the upper classes was not operative among the commoners. Speaking of the multitude who came to Canobus for the public festivals, Strabo says that they indulged in "singing and dancing, without restraint"; and, indeed, "with the utmost licentiousness." [104] As to their "solemn assemblies," Herodotus says, the Egyptians did not limit themselves to one, but had several in the year. To them there came great crowds of men and women (sometimes as many as 700,000), "sailing all together, vast numbers in each boat, many of the women with castanets, which they strike, while some of the men pipe during the whole time of the voyage." [105] At various stopping places, some danced, while others sang and clapped their hands. It was at these festivals and upon other similar occasions, when the common folk came together, that the "extravagant buffoonery, dancing in a ludicrous manner, standing on their heads," and similar stunts, referred to by Wilkinson and others, generally took place.[106] The continuance of the ancient practices of dancing, the drunkenness, buffoonery, and immorality associated with it, is described by Lane, who believes it probable that "the modern Ghawázee are descended from the class of female dancers who amused the Egyptians in the times of the early Pharaohs." [107] Something of ancient funerary dancing may have survived also. The movements of people after a funeral at a modern cemetery, reported by Mace, may be carried over from the dances of the priestesses of Hathor.[108]

Notwithstanding an extraordinary extensiveness, thoroughness, and specialization, Egyptian education remained essentially centered in present practicality. Even mathematics and other branches of their higher learning, which Aristotle thought the priests pursued for the sake of truth itself, seems to us rather closely associated with practical concerns, from which escape is rare. On the physical side, too, practical, professional goals of the soldier, dancer,

103 Wilkinson: op. cit., I, 500, 504 f.
104 Bk. XVII, 1, 17.
105 Bk. II, 58–60.
106 Op. cit., I, 394.
107 Op. cit., II, 86–92, 149, 237–42.
108 "Hathor Dances," Jour. Egy. Archaeol., VI, 297.

wrestler, acrobat, and bullfighter are evidently of highest importance, though many people played in numerous ways for sheer enjoyment. Of the idea that physical and intellectual exercises should be harmoniously joined to produce a harmony of soul and body, the Egyptians do not seem to have taken cognizance. Diodorus,[109] contrasting Egyptian and Greek practice in respect to combining intellectual and physical education, says that as for "wrestling and music," Egyptians were not inclined to approve of them at all. Wrestling, they held, would give only a temporary vigor, not robust health; and music would be useless, even harmful, tending toward effeminacy.

[109] Bk. I, 81.

# 4

# THE LAND BETWEEN THE RIVERS

When Layard began his travels and researches in Mesopotamia (1839), its ancient people, their life, occupations, architecture, art, and education were so little known that he could scarcely imagine what might lie hidden by the "stern shapeless mound"—the sole visible monument to the restless striving of a civilization long since dead. "The more he conjectures," says Layard, "the more vague the results appear. The scene around is worthy of the ruin he is contemplating; desolation meets desolation: a feeling of awe succeeds to wonder; for there is nothing to relieve the mind, to lead to hope, or to tell of what has gone by. . . ." [1] Since then research has succeeded research; by thoughtful, courageous labor, Sumer, Akkad, Babylon, and Assyria have been made to pass like a pageant before our eyes.

Civilization between the Tigris and Euphrates paralleled that of Egypt, having developed agriculture and city life to a marked extent by 4000 to 3500 B.C. To some extent the two cultures were interdependent.[2] Barley and wheat, considered indigenous to Babylonia, found their way to Egypt in neolithic times. A marked development had taken place long before writing and the keeping of records began. The earliest inscriptions reveal an intricate social and political scene: agriculture is the main occupation; irrigation canals serve to distribute water; people are living in settled communities; there are cities and states, under the rule of gods and kings; arts are developed; the priests have temples, which are the permanent habitations of the gods.[3] What millennia passed between the emergence from savagery and the early Sumerian cities built on artificial mounds, no one can say. The Sumerians were once denied a real existence by some; and the Sumerian language was considered

---

[1] Nineveh and Its Remains, i, 6 f.
[2] Speiser: Mesopotamian Origins, p. 2.
[3] Sayce: Babylonians and Assyrians, p. 12; Goodspeed: Babylonians and Assyrians, pp. 49 ff.

merely a special tongue of the priesthood. To-day the Sumerians are commonly regarded as the forerunners of Babylonian civilization; but that there were others who occupied Lower Mesopotamia before them is held to be no longer open to "serious doubt." Similarities between Sumerian and Chinese characters suggest a common origin.[4] The art work from the tomb of Queen Shoubad (3200 or 3500 B.C.) comprising numerous symbolic representations of music and dancing, and elaborate game boards, pawns, and dice, wrought with shell, lapis lazuli, and silver, suggests a civilization already old.[5] To the Sumerian culture were added Semitic and Kassite elements; but the time of such fusion is somewhat uncertain.[6] The wars of Semite and Sumerian reached a turning point, however, when Sargon conquered the Sumerians (in 2848 B.C., according to Meissner's chronology), absorbed their superior culture, and extended his sway from the Persian Gulf to the Mediterranean. The next thousand years saw a remarkable development of civilization in the land between the rivers, which reached a high point in the days of Hammurabi. Long wars with the Kassites, however, were shortly to put an end to the supremacy of Babylon. About 1750 B.C. Kassite conquerors seized the throne of Babylon for a time. After 1100 B.C. the center of power shifted northward to Assur and Nineveh. In 539 B.C. Babylon and Nineveh both came under the yoke of Cyrus.

As to the origin of Babylonian culture, the ancients gave a ready answer. Ignorant of fact, they wove a tale of early Chaos; the origin of gods; the struggle of creation; the establishment of order; the first king of Babylon, Alôros; and so on down to their contemporary civilization. That their turning from hunting and herding to a settled life of agricultural and industrial employments was influenced profoundly by the environment in which they found themselves, seems certain. There, between the rivers, was plenty of water, plenty of pasture, and a rich, alluvial soil which would grow crops in great abundance. Herodotus observed the rich character of the soil and related fabulous stories about the size of barley and wheat, and the magnificent annual yield of grain.[7] What Herodotus recorded was the result of labor throughout long centuries, which rescued the soil from the flooding waters. The river was at once a source of wealth and a powerful enemy. To make it serviceable, one must become irrigator and engineer, and, at the same time, an expert agriculturalist; to make it carry merchandise, one must become adept in building boats and operating them. The circular boats, built of willows and covered with skins, which carried cargoes down to Babylon, and the donkey on board which brought the

[4] Speiser: op. cit., p. 46; Ball: Chinese and Sumerian, pp. 35 ff.
[5] Legrain: "L'Art Sumérien au Temps de la Reine Shoubad," Gazette des Beaux Arts, ser. 6, VI, 1–26.
[6] Jastrow: The Civilization of Babylonia and Assyria, pp. 120 ff.; King: Sumer and Akkad, pp. 3 ff.; Sayce: op. cit., pp. 4 ff.
[7] The History of Herodotus, I, 193.

skins back up the river when the cargo had been unloaded, strike modern folk as crude and inefficient. Nevertheless, they served their purpose: the trade of Babylon increased, not only within her borders but with distant parts.[8] Thus, if Egypt was the "gift of the Nile," Babylon was similarly the product of the Tigris and the Euphrates; and the inhabitants properly called one the "life of the land" and the other the "bestower of blessings."

Food products, indigenous and introduced from outside, flourished in great abundance. Besides those named there were chick-peas, lentils, cucumbers, eggplant, onions, beans, pumpkins, vetches, rice, melons, figs, dates, the vine, apples, almonds, walnuts, apricots, and pistachio. Fish, animals, and birds of many kinds were also used for the table. Wild life of the air included the pelican, heron, crane, stork, cormorant, sea gull, duck, swan, wild goose, ostrich, bustard, partridge, quail, thrush, blackbird, ortolan, pigeon, turtledove, eagle, and hawk. Reptiles—mostly not harmful—the lion, elephant, gazelle, urus, leopard, lynx, wildcat, hyena, porcupine, beaver, ibex, deer, panther, onager, and wild boar provided excitement in the chase and, in some instances, a supplement to the larder. The dog, ass, ox, goat, and sheep, and later the horse and camel, were domesticated.[9]

The Babylonians were not so richly endowed with building materials as the Assyrians and the Egyptians. Neither metal nor stone was to be had in their valley; and to get them from northern Mesopotamia, the neighboring mountains, or from Egypt, required great toil. Timber, too, was not plentiful, but there were cypress, plane tree, tamarisk, and acacia; and cedar was brought from Lebanon. Because of lack of stone, the Babylonians turned to the soil and became makers of brick, which they baked in the sun and burned in kilns. Almost inevitably massiveness was a common characteristic of their public buildings—a monotony relieved somewhat by coloring, panels, towers, and gateways. Providing foundations for such huge structures was not easy, but it was accomplished generally by erecting great mounds, which imparted an even more ponderous appearance to the palaces of kings and the temples of the gods.[10]

The governments of Babylonia and Assyria were monarchies. The kings—the adopted sons of Bel Merodach, the god of the city, according to priestly representation—were priests as well as kings. In Assyria, though government and religion were by no means separate, and Assur was the god-city, the king was head of a military bureaucracy rather than a priestly one. In Babylonia as in Egypt there were many cities, and each had its god and its king. "One city,

[8] Ibid., 1, 194; Rawlinson: Five Great Monarchies, III, 14 ff.; Sayce: op. cit., pp. 8 f.
[9] Rawlinson: op. cit., III, 16 ff.; Maspero: Dawn of Civilization, pp. 554 ff.; Goodspeed: op. cit., pp. 9 f.; Rogers: A History of Babylonia and Assyria, 1, 421 ff.
[10] Sayce: op. cit., pp. 10, 90 ff.; Jastrow: op. cit., pp. 367 ff.

one god, one lord" was the rule.[11] As a city grew in power and wealth, its sway was extended over the weaker. Thus Babylon became supreme among the cities around it, her god-king took captive the gods of the conquered, proving, as it were, the superiority of Bel Merodach. At length, however, the god-kings of Babylon were forced to bow to the kings of Assur and Nineveh, whose chief arts were of war, rather than agriculture, industry, and commerce; [12] and in the sixth century B.C. all were brought under the sway of Cyrus. In the doleful phrase of the prophet, ". . . Babylon is taken, Bel is put to shame, Merodach is dismayed . . . for out of the north there cometh up a nation against her, which shall make her land desolate, and none shall dwell therein." [13]

In Babylonia and Assyria there was a nobility, a feudal aristocracy. Theoretically the land was the gods'; actually there were the sovereign's domain, the source of his wealth, and another realm constituted of fiefs held by noble families who fought for and otherwise served the king. With the growth of commerce a merchant class arose at Babylon, which, with the priests, became more influential than the feudal nobility. In Assyria, a military and civil bureaucracy, whose officials were named by the king, ultimately superseded the decadent feudal order.[14] Besides priests, soldiers, merchants, and an increasing class of professional folk (such as scribes and artists), there were peasants, artisans, and slaves at the base of the social pyramid.

Slaves were numerous and of three classes: some were attached to the soil; others were held by private masters; and still others were temple slaves who tilled the lands for the priests. Labor being hard and the climate enervating, slaves wore out quickly, but were readily replaced, for the supply was fairly regular. Slaves were so much property, counted like cows, sold, and resold at the wish of the master, but they were generally allowed to marry and rear children. To make them more profitable, a master might have them taught a trade, a business, or even the profession of scribe. In some cases, slaves were apparently able to buy their freedom; again, they received it as a gift from kind masters who wished to reward faithful service. In Assyria slaves were more commonly captives of war, were treated more severely than in Babylon, Sayce believes, and generally brought better prices.[15]

In theory the soil belonged to the gods; but the hands of the gods were stiff and could not wield hoe and mattock or guide the plow. For this they relied on ordinary men. The difficulties of farming, in the vicinity of the capricious rivers, are not easily imagined by those who perform its toil under easier conditions. Strabo described the incessant labor of building dams, clean-

[11] Maspero: op. cit., p. 595.
[12] Rogers: op. cit., I, 439 ff.
[13] Jeremiah, L, 2-3.
[14] Sayce: op. cit., pp. 173 f.; Maspero: op. cit., pp. 722 f.
[15] Sayce: op. cit., pp. 67 ff., 78 f.; Maspero: op. cit., pp. 742 ff.

ing canals, and opening and closing them at proper seasons, so as to provide sufficiency and avoid deficiency of water at all times.[16] Then came seeding and harvest. Since winters were mild, the peasant cannot have been idle even then.

PLOWING IN ANCIENT BABYLON

(Courtesy, The University Museum, University of Pennsylvania, Philadelphia)

Tools for soil culture were crude, the Babylonians and Assyrians having devoted more thought to the perfection of the war lord's implements than to those of the farmer. The clumsy plow was only a larger hoe, to whose lengthened handle oxen were yoked. Despite poor tools, however, the knowledge of agriculture is said to have been excellent; [17] treatises on it have been discovered in temple libraries; and the methods of the Babylonians were in turn transmitted to Greece, Arabia, and Irak. Scenes that have come down to us portray the peasants' life as a mixture of labor and plaintive melancholy. Thus the plodding plowman of Babylon follows the oxen home:

[16] *The Geography of Strabo*, XVI, 7, 9–11.
[17] Maspero: *op. cit.*, pp. 770 f.

> My knees are marching,
> My feet are not resting;
> Taking no thought,
> Drive me home.[18]

The chief occupations of the Assyrians, judging from monumental inscriptions, were fighting, hunting, construction work, and boating. Babylon, on the other hand, though her civilization was originally chiefly agricultural, developed a diverse commercial and industrial life whose fame was carried to the civilized world. Among skilled craftsmen one finds the weaver, dyer, fuller, tanner, cobbler; smiths working gold, silver, copper, and iron; the cutler, carpenter, joiner, stonecutter; the porcelain-maker, potter, brickmaker, vintner; the carver of artistic gems; and the manufacturer of crude tools. In this domestic industry the master made and sold his goods, utilizing the service of slaves, apprentices, and his own children whom he trained.[19]

The life of the city workers was little easier than that of the countrymen. Maspero has depicted the "progressive impoverishment" of the "small tradesman" and "free workman" who became involved in debt from which they could escape only "by strenuous efforts and incessant labor." "Life," he says, "was not so pleasant in Chaldaea as in Egypt," for the records reveal "a people greedy of gain, exacting, litigious, and almost exclusively absorbed by material concerns." [20] Only on some festal occasion, such as the opening of a new temple or the return of a victorious king, were they allowed relaxation from arduous, monotonous toil.

The position of women changed considerably as Babylonian society matured; it varied also according to the socio-economic level of the family. Generalization is thus difficult, as may be seen from views expressed by various authorities.[21] The Code of Hammurabi defined the rights and obligations of women as well as others in society in a remarkably thorough fashion.[22] On the whole, their position was an elevated and pleasant one, but prostitution and concubinage were practiced, and intimate relations between masters and maidservants were common. The rites of Venus, which shocked Herodotus and which Sayce attributed to the "invention of the Greeks," are treated with fairer realism by Jastrow.[23]

The family was apparently headed in early times by the mother; later the

---

[18] Sayce: op. cit., p. 87.
[19] Meissner: Babylonien und Assyrien, I, 231 f.
[20] Maspero: op. cit., pp. 750–60.
[21] Meissner: op. cit., I, 401 ff.; Jastrow: op. cit., pp. 233 ff., 272 f., 285 ff., 302 ff.; Sayce: op. cit., pp. 14–20, 23 f., 29 ff., 41 ff., 128; Maspero: op. cit., pp. 707 f., 732–42, 746 ff.
[22] Harper: The Code of Hammurabi, art. 127–67, 170–84, et passim.
[23] Op. cit., pp. 233, 272, 307; Herodotus, I, 199; Sayce: op. cit., pp. 30 f.

husband gained patriarchal sway, but it was not absolute. He performed religious ceremonies for the family and directed most business matters, though women could form partnerships, buy and sell, lend and borrow. Marriage was impossible without the father's signature; he gave his daughter a dowry proportionate to her rank, and demanded a price from her husband. In a marriage of equals, the husband swore not to take a second wife while the first lived. If the oath were broken, the wife was released and received damages. Such property as a woman possessed at marriage, whether gained by gift or through business, was retained by her in case of separation. Women of the poorer sort were free from certain restrictions which hampered the wealthy and noble; they did not face the intrigues of the harem; and unions could be made and unmade more easily where wealth and position were not at stake. The lot of the lower class, however, was one of continuous labor, perhaps not unlike that of lower-class women of that land to-day.[24] Education, of course, apart from apprenticeship to toil, was not for the poor.

Religious developments in the Tigris-Euphrates valley were in some respects similar to those in Egypt. The gods were numerous, had various characters, performed a wide range of functions, and were at first of local origin and habitation. Ninib, patron god of Nippur, later overshadowed by Enlil, was a sun-god who watched over harvests; but he was also a warrior, a god of the chase, a just judge, and a healer of diseases. Enlil was chiefly a god of battle, who ruled the nether world and gave magic powers to men. Ea, god of Eridu, was a deity of light, goodness, and wisdom, who gave arts and science to men, led them into the industries of civilized life, healed the sick, and revived the dead. Ishtar was goddess of fertility, both in the vegetable and the animal kingdom.[25]

Gods were numerous; so were the priests. Even one god might have many servants. In early days the ruler and the priest were one; but, by 2450 B.C. a mediator-priest had come between the ruler and the god. The number of priests and their specialization increased apace with the wealth of the temples. Among the "thirty classes of priests" were the "exorciser," "diviner," "singer," "anointer," "musician," and "snake charmer." Though not strictly a caste, the priests were set apart by learning, which gave them great authority in the state.[26]

As striving cities grew, the weaker were consolidated under the stronger. In similar fashion the conflicts of contending deities were harmonized, and the heavenly domain took on a more orderly appearance. Ninib became son of Enlil; and Merodach, when Babylon had become the chief city, became god

[24] Layard: op. cit., I, 360 f.
[25] Sayce: op. cit., p. 3; Jastrow: op. cit., pp. 194–99, 453 ff.
[26] Diodorus of Sicily, II, 29; Rawlinson: op. cit., III, 12 ff.; Jastrow: op. cit., pp. 271 f.

of gods. The priests fashioned a story of creation and evolution from chaos; of the creative power of Merodach, son of Ea, and his gift of divine blood which, mixed with clay, enabled men and beasts to live; of the coming of Oannes, the first being possessed of reason, who gave men agriculture, letters, law, science, art, cities, and temples; and of punishment by a flood from which only one human pair escaped. The versions we have of these events, crystallized, perhaps, by the seventh century B.C., have been developing for many hundreds of years. The psalm of a poet-priest, attributed to the third millennium, is full of fervid faith in a supreme god:

> In heaven who is supreme? Thou alone, thou art supreme!
> On earth, who is supreme? Thou alone, thou art supreme!

Centuries later a prayer, attributed to Nebuchadnezzar, appeals to Him "that art from everlasting, lord of all that exists." [27] Presumably few were able, however, to substitute one for the many.

FORMAL EDUCATION    Formal education became rather widespread in the course of many centuries of development and ranged from elementary reading, writing, and religion to advanced studies in law, medicine, and astrology. In general, education was the prerogative of the upper classes—those who could pay for it; there is no evidence of free public schools. Contract tablets show, however, that slaves were sometimes taught to read and write, to enhance their value. Sayce cites also the case of a "son of an 'irrigator,' one of the poorest and lowest members of the community," who copied a part of the "Epic of the Creation." In Assyria, education was more strictly limited to the upper classes than in Babylonia. At best education could probably be obtained by those who had most need of it, and who were willing and able to sacrifice time and money for it. Those who carried on business either had some knowledge of reading, writing, and counting, or they employed a scribe to perform these services for them. "Girls also shared in the education given to their brothers." Near the Babylonian colony of Kanis "there was even a sort of ladies' college." [28]

Schools taught by priests and scribes were numerous but not large. They were probably commonly closely associated with libraries; in any case school tablets have been found there. Individual instruction, oral repetition, and copying of models were probably characteristic methods of teaching. Sayce thinks children were well taught, judging from the "remarkably good spelling" found in letters. Certainly, pupils were encouraged to be diligent: a copybook motto

[27] Maspero: op. cit., pp. 537–47, 566–72; Sayce: op. cit., p. 261.
[28] Sayce: "The Early Geography of South-Eastern Asia Minor," Jour. Hellenic Studies, XLIII, 44; Sayce: Babylonians and Assyrians, pp. 47, 55, 214 f.; Meissner: op. cit., I, 231, 400.

ACCOUNT OF THE CREATION AND THE DELUGE   *Nippur*, c. 2200 B.C.
(Courtesy, The University Museum, University of Pennsylvania, Philadelphia)

advised that "he who would excel in the school of the scribes must rise like the dawn." Close application to the clay tablets must have been a sore trial. Play may have relieved the strain to some extent, but youth were probably more often persuaded to apply themselves by other hoary, tested means.

Education prepared youth for the work of scribes, who might be copyists, authors, secretaries, lawyers, librarians, teachers, public clerks, officials, in fact, members of any profession which demanded skill in writing. The number and size of libraries show the prevalence of literary arts. A library of about 2700 B.C., discovered at Tello, contained 32,000 books; that of Nineveh contained many thousands. All large cities of Babylon had libraries; possibly many of the smaller ones as well. Law, public and private letters, public and private legal documents, history, chronology, medicine, astrology, geography, grammar, philology, mathematics, natural history, theology, "science" of signs and portents, and some lighter subjects found a place in them.[29]

The libraries were commonly housed in temples, and were under the care of the influential priests, who cultivated the higher branches of learning. Diodorus

[29] Meissner: *op. cit.*, II, 330–5; Goodspeed: *op. cit.*, pp. 34 ff.; Maspero: *op. cit.*, pp. 723 ff.

says that these ancient Chaldaeans held about the same place as priests in Egypt, filled all "divine offices," and spent their time in the study of philosophy, astrology, and divination. As for the education of their children, they passed on learning from father to son. Being thus brought up from very childhood, and taught everything freely by their parents, the Chaldaean priests became most famous for their learning.[30] Besides the children of the priestly families, other persons, foreign as well as native, seem to have studied under them. The schools of priests were perhaps as numerous as the temples themselves. Among the more significant were Erech and Borsippa, to which Strabo refers.[31]

Details of the process of higher education are little known, but the products of the labor of the priestly class illuminate an extensive scene of intellectual advancement. Treatises on diseases and their remedies existed in the third millennium B.C. The *Illumination of Bel*, a collection of seventy-two books, brought together a vast store of "scientific" lore. *Hammurabi's Code*, the *Babylonian Chronicle*, the *Gilgamesh Epic*, the *Creation Epic*, and various treatises on grammar, mathematics, philology, geography, engineering, and surveying are the most notable proofs of the variety, range, and depth of Babylonian learning.[32]

INFORMAL EDUCATION OF WORK AND PLAY    From the foregoing it is evident that life in Babylonia and Assyria was of an eminently practical nature. Even formal literary and scientific education was largely a preparation for one's vocation in life. Diodorus' description of education in the family of the priest suggests an apprenticeship. Apprenticeship applies, however, more precisely to the training for tasks of the lower order of workers and the informal discipline in arms and feats of physical prowess required of the army. Apprenticeship of artisans was regulated by the Code of Hammurabi, which provided that "if an artisan take a son for adoption and teach him his handicraft, one may not bring claim for him"; but "if he do not teach him his handicraft, that adopted son may return to his father's house." [33] Thus an adopted son must be trained to the craft and have an equal opportunity with natural sons. The importance of the provision is clear when one considers that the followers of each occupation made up a sort of guild or family and that the craft itself was looked upon as hereditary. "Every workman," says Maspero, "taught his own trade to his children, and these in their turn would instruct theirs; families

[30] Diodorus, II, 29.
[31] Bk. XVI, 1, 6; Jastrow: op. cit., pp. 275 f.; Rawlinson: op. cit., III, 12 ff.
[32] Cf. Harper: op. cit.; Johns: Babylonian and Assyrian Laws, Contracts and Letters; Meissner: op. cit., I, chap. 9; and II; Maspero: op. cit., pp. 773–84; Goodspeed: op. cit., pp. 34 ff., 86–106; Sayce: Babylonians and Assyrians, pp. 44–66, 161 f., 195–263; Jastrow: op. cit., chaps. 5–6, 8.
[33] Harper: op. cit., p. 71.

which had an hereditary profession, or from generation to generation had gathered bands of workmen about them, formed themselves into various guilds, or, to use the customary term, into tribes, governed by chiefs and following specified customs. A workman belonged to the tribe of the weavers, or of the blacksmiths, or of the corn-merchants, and the description of an individual would not have been considered as sufficiently exact, if the designation of his tribe were not inserted after his name in addition to his paternal affiliation." [34] The women of lower-class families who bore the burden of all household labor, must have trained their daughters by an informal apprenticeship to the physical tasks they were to perform, even as masters trained boys in their shops.

Slaves were also apprenticed to trades, perhaps to another slave who was skilled. Penalties were provided for failing to instruct the apprentice according to legal requirements. The teacher received no fee for his work, but had the benefit of the apprentice's labor. Contracts for apprentices, in later Babylonian history, have been recovered which deal with the training of bakers, fullers, stonecutters, and weavers. The time involved in such training varied in these instances from fifteen months for the baker to six years for the fuller, but these do not constitute general, fixed terms of service in such trades. [35]

War was the chief business of the Assyrians; it was prominent also in the earliest history of Sumer, Akkad, and Babylon. [36] In a sense all wars were religious, or so they were regarded by those who made them. Was it not by favor of the gods that victory was won? Did not a victory of the ruler extend the sway of the gods of his city? And should not the gods be repaid for their assistance by gifts of spoils to the temples? Whether wars were fought for the service of the god or of mammon, the fact remains that military conquests rather than intellectual contributions marked the rise of Assyrian power; and when her greatness, thus forcefully built up, was ultimately destroyed, little else remained. Such culture as Assyria had was largely borrowed. Pride of race kept her ruling class from uniting with those they conquered; the vanquished were held together by force rather than by cultivation of a common mind and culture. It is therefore not surprising that when Xenophon passed the site of mighty Nineveh, two hundred years after her fall, he found nothing to tell him of her former greatness. Goodspeed has well remarked that "wisely to govern a peaceful empire had not yet come to stand among the glories of monarchs." Instead, it was generally their purpose "to strike terror into the heart of the opposer and to warn the intending rebel of his fate." [37]

The sculptured remains of Assyria which have been recovered, and from

---

[34] Maspero: op. cit., pp. 751 ff.
[35] Johns: op. cit., pp. 181 f.; Westermann: "Apprentice Contracts and the Apprentice System in Roman Egypt," Class. Philol., IX, 304 f.
[36] Meissner: op. cit., I, 80, 89.
[37] Goodspeed: op. cit., pp. 201 f.; Meissner: op. cit., I, 113 f.; Maspero: op. cit., p. 706.

which most reliable evidence of the organization and equipment of the army is to be gained, bear witness to the supreme stress placed upon military skill; but their story of the peaceful arts is brief indeed. The army was originally made up of native peasants; but under the Second Empire there was a standing army, partly composed of mercenaries. The strength of this military force lay chiefly in horsemen and charioteers (the king and others of high rank being thus equipped), and the infantry, who were of the lower classes.[38] From a brief review of the equipment of these classes one may infer what physical skills were necessary for the profession of arms.

Foot soldiers used small straight swords, daggers, spears, "rounded bows about four feet in length," slings, axes, maces of bronze or iron, and shields and helmets, according as they were swordsmen, spearmen, archers, slingers, or pioneers. Archers seem to have been considered an exceedingly important part of the infantry at all times; but the types of archers and their equipment varied considerably from time to time. Strabo [39] speaks of the Cossaeans and Elymaeans, warlike mountaineers, who were "all fighters." Indeed, the mountainous areas were a "nursery of soldiers," and the greatest part of them were archers. Thus it would appear that the great Assyrian army simply perfected the use of one of the favorite weapons of primitive mountain folk and made it an effective agent of its conquests.

Assyrian archers were well equipped and highly trained. They are represented as fighting singly and in pairs, one holding a shield and sword, while the other, protected from the enemy, used his bow and arrows. Archers were divided into two main classes, light and heavy. The light archers had no helmet, were naked to the waist, and were shod lightly or not at all. They neither carried shields nor had attendants to carry them. That these men were speedy and highly skilled in the use of their weapons is the impression conveyed by numerous illustrations which show them shooting, kneeling and standing, and often holding two extra arrows in the right hand at the same time that the string is being drawn to send a third. Heavy archers, of whom there were two types, were generally well clothed and protected by coats of mail and helmets, and were assisted by one or two attendants with shields, spears, and swords. The more simply armed heavy archers generally knelt while shooting, but those more heavily armed always stood.

Spearmen varied in respect to their equipment from time to time, but they generally wore a tunic, helmet, low boots or sandals, and were armed with a spear—four to six feet long, and weighted occasionally at one end to perfect its balance—and a circular shield, made of wicker, which was strengthened in the center by a wooden or metal plaque.

[38] Sayce: *Babylonians and Assyrians*, p. 181; Rawlinson: *op. cit.*, I, 406.
[39] Bk. XVI, 1, 18.

In addition to these classes of fighters Sennacherib made use of slingers, armed with a primitive sling, made of a piece of leather, to which two strings were attached. Slingers may have been introduced in imitation of Egypt; but the Assyrian slingers were heavily clad and wore a coat of mail, whereas those of Egypt and elsewhere were lightly dressed and seem to have played only an unimportant rôle. From the time of Sargon there are references to baggage troops and engineers. The latter were equipped with axes and other construction tools with which to prepare roads for other units of the army. Artisans to make and repair weapons were likewise an important support of the army. Last, but not least significant, were the soothsayers who accompanied the troops to consult the omens and tell of the prospective outcome of any undertaking.[40]

The king and his highest ranking men fought in chariots, being assisted by the chariot driver who handled the reins and by an attendant who protected the fighter from the missiles of the enemy, while he launched arrows from his bow against them. People of less importance were often assisted only by a driver. As early as the third millennium B.C., kings went to war in chariots drawn by onagers, or perhaps by horses, says Maspero. Just when horses were first used in the Land between the Rivers is unknown. They are not mentioned in the Code of Hammurabi, though they were then known to some extent. In the centuries following, their use for military and other purposes of state became widespread, and documents show their importation for the royal stables.[41] Having arrived at a city's walls and begun the siege, the king and other charioteers might dismount and fire their arrows from the ground, still protected by shield-bearers. In such an attack the besieging forces made use also of fire, the battering-ram, blunt spears with which to undermine the ramparts, and scaling ladders. In siege warfare the later kings of Assyria were much superior to the Greeks to the time of Philip. Making use of rams, and towers which enabled the bowmen to reach the height of the battlements, Assyrian warriors were able to take walled cities.[42]

On open, level ground chariots were useful; in hilly, rough, and partly wooded country, however, they were an encumbrance and could not be relied on so much, though their use in such terrain is sometimes shown. This lesson was learned, doubtless, by hard experience in fighting their mountaineer neighbors, such as the Kurds and Armenians. Consequently, the cavalry came to be an important part of the Assyrian army, and was sometimes equal in number to one-tenth of the infantry. The size of the armed forces is not known with

40 Meissner: op. cit., I, 89 ff.; Rawlinson: op. cit., I, 428–40; Layard: op. cit., II, 341–7.
41 Maspero: op. çit., pp. 721 f.; Sayce: Babylonians and Assyrians, pp. 221 f.; Meissner: op. cit., I, 217 ff.
42 Tarn: Hellenistic Military and Naval Developments, pp. 101 f.

much exactness. Some figures are rather fantastic. Layard says that Holofernes had 12,000 archers mounted on horses; other leaders had an even larger proportion of cavalry. Ninus is said to have had 1,700,000 infantry, 210,000 cavalry, and 10,600 chariots. The vast number of prisoners reported taken by Tiglath-pileser IV (60,500) and Sargon (208,000) would, of course, have required enormous forces. The horsemen, at first, had but little special equipment, and used only bows and arrows; but when cavalry was fully developed, they were well equipped with saddles, swords, spears, shields, leathern breeches, long leather boots to protect the legs, and, at the time of Sennacherib, coats of mail. The king is never shown fighting on horseback, but a warrior is often seen leading an extra horse, probably for his majesty in case the latter's chariot should be damaged or his horses killed.[43]

Hunting was at once a means of replenishing the food supply, the sport of kings, and a phase of military training. Husbandmen must have hunted those wild animals which were a menace to them, and used some of them for food. Fishing was probably not a pastime among early Chaldaeans, but a means of getting a living. Fish was an important article of diet, and there was no priestly ban upon it as there was in Egypt. The existence of sacred fishponds, fishing inspectors, and the fact that efforts were made to protect fishing rights in ancient Sumer and Akkad, all point to the importance of fishing. In the days of Hammurabi, fishing was a carefully regulated and protected business. Contracts for fishing rights in the time of Darius II have been discovered.[44] How extensively Assyrians fished it is impossible to say, but some illustrations show them fishing from the bank, from a raft, and also while floating upon an inflated skin or mussuk. A rod was not used, apparently, but line, hook, and net were common. Fishermen are usually represented as poorly dressed, and we may infer that they were folk who were working to eke out a too meager food supply and were not fishing just for the fun of it.

As a sport and as heroic exercise to keep men fit in time of peace, hunting was the delight of kings, nobles, and wealthy men. Others probably hunted, but less than those of great estate. One of the scenes portrayed on the royal harp, found in the tomb of Queen Shoubad, seems to draw its inspiration from heroic tales of Gilgamesh, the mighty hunter.[45] In destroying ferocious and destructive beasts, the king was thought to serve his people and his god, much as he was said to serve them by slaying their enemies in battle. For this reason the spoils of the chase were dedicated to Ninib, and libations to him were poured out "over the dead bodies of lions and wild bulls." The greatest kings

---

[43] Meissner: op. cit., i, 102; Layard: op. cit., ii, 319–408; Rawlinson: op. cit., i, 423–8; Sayce: Babylonians and Assyrians, pp. 177 ff.

[44] Radcliffe: Fishing from the Earliest Times, pp. 360 ff., 379; King: op. cit., pp. 181 f., 268; History of Babylon, p. 171.

[45] Legrain: op. cit., loc. cit., ser. 6, vi, 14.

ASHURBANIPAL HUNTING LIONS
  (Courtesy, Bettmann Archive, New York)

were renowned for hunting, no less than for war: Nimrod was a "mighty hunter before the Lord"; Tiglathpileser hunted elephants on the *chabur* and proudly asserted he had killed nearly a thousand lions; Ninus of Nineveh was noted for his slaughter of lions and leopards; and Ashurnaçirpal "as a hunter and warrior . . . was untiring and resistless." The lion, tiger, antelope, boar, bear, stag, hare, wild goat, gazelle, and onager were among the favored objects of the chase. The ostrich and other birds were also taken. The animals were pursued not only in the open field but also in special hunting paradises provided for royal enjoyment. As among the Persians, the Assyrian youth were brought up to hunt at an early age. Skill in the use of the bow, the favorite weapon, must have approached perfection, for it is said that hares and partridges were brought down while on the run and in flight.[46]

Hunting the wild onager was one of the most difficult of sports, because of its speed, but it was brought down by arrows and also by a noosed rope or lasso, thrown so as to wrap around its neck or legs. When thus taken, it could be tamed and put to use; in early days it was harnessed to chariots and used in hunting and in war. Pursuing the lion, king of the animals, was naturally the most favored sport of royalty when peace hung heavy on their hands. Hunting gazelles, hares, and other small animals and birds was generally thought unworthy of the king, but he is often represented as present while others of high degree amused themselves at such sport. For lion and bull-hunting the king's

[46] Meissner: *op. cit.*, I, 224 ff., 421 f.; Layard: *op. cit.*, II, 431 f.; Goodspeed: *op. cit.*, p. 201; Jastrow: *op. cit.*, p. 199; Maspero: *op. cit.*, pp. 705 f.

chariot was prepared; the king himself was accoutered as for war, being assisted by a driver and grooms for his horses; he was supported also by swordsmen, shield-bearers, and other attendants who kept him supplied with arrows. First he attacked from the chariot with the bow, and varied this with spear and shield, sometimes from the ground, if perchance the beast was only wounded and turned to attack its pursuer. The number of animals slain in a royal hunt was often great, or at least the artists, sculptors, and other keepers of the record represented the take magnificently. One relief shows eighteen. When game was brought to the hunting park and turned loose for the sportsmen, the destruction was apt to be much greater, since armed soldiers were drawn up around the park so that none might escape.[47]

Apart from the physical exercise of labor and an early apprenticeship thereto, little can be said on the score of physical training and sports among the lowest elements of the population. Some of them doubtless turned to play when opportunity offered; but opportunities for recreation were relatively rare. Public and private celebrations, of course, provided more or less sporadic opportunities for music and dancing; catching birds, fishing, and even hunting of lions and other larger game as well as smaller animals, are said to have been "not only for princes" but "for everyone a source of the greatest pleasure." For those who fought in the armies there was a physical discipline appropriate to that branch of service which they filled. The chief supplement to such physical preparation for their vocation was the chase.

Physical and mental education for the upper class seems to have assumed a more systematic character. That horsemanship and the use of the bow formed a prominent part of training, there is no reason to doubt. Just what else was included is largely a matter of speculation. Training in physical exercises went hand in hand with some instruction of an intellectual character, at least in the case of those who were born to rule. Assurbanipal is said to have learned "to shoot with bow and to practise other bodily exercises" as a regular part of his education. Sayce believed it was "probable that similar exercises were also customary in Babylonia." Precisely what these "other bodily exercises" included is not known. A contest in wrestling or boxing, accompanied by musicians, is thought by some to be represented in an ancient relief—though it may be a game of mora rather than a physical contest. Other reliefs show youth practicing bow-shooting at a target.[48]

In a society which had learned the use of horses, their feeding, training, and management became a necessary part of education for those who would employ them in war and in hunting. The work and training of horsemen and

[47] Rawlinson: op. cit., I, 505–28; Jastrow: op. cit., pp. 16, 123, 168, 399 ff.
[48] Meissner: op. cit., I, 420 f., and Plates 217–8; Jüthner: Körperkultur im Altertum, p. 5; Sayce: Babylonians and Assyrians, pp. 48, 52.

charioteers is an obscure subject; till recently it was even more so. A fitful light is shed, however, by four of the ten thousand fragments of cuneiform tablets, pertaining to the Ḫatti Kingdom whence came the movement against Babylon which overthrew the First Dynasty (Samsuditana, 1956–1926 B.C.) and ultimately established Kassite power. Dating from about the fourteenth century B.C., these fragments were recovered (1905–1907) 145 kilometers east of Angora, at the village of Boghaz-Koi. Though no complete picture referring to charioteers can be gained from the tablets of Kikkuli from Mittanni, they appear to form parts of a pattern of daily routine, involving chiefly the harnessing of horses; driving them at a trot and at a gallop over certain specified distances; unharnessing, quieting, rubbing down, and stabling them; plaiting their tails and taking them into the river for a bath; and feeding them grain and hay or fodder. Directions relative to driving the horses at a trot for a certain distance and then at a gallop for a limited space, imply training rather than a contest. Though competitions are not mentioned, there are references to the *vasanna*, by which Forrer understands a simple stadium, oval in shape, 300 to 360 meters long, and surrounded by a barrier or fence of wooden pickets.[49]

To meet the difficulties presented by watercourses, warriors had to be trained to handle crude boats, in which chariots might be transported; they must also know how to swim. Swimming seems to have been a practical necessity for many. There may have been swimming for pleasure as well, though a modern scholar and traveler has said that in fifteen years he did not see any Assyrians swimming for pleasure, but always on business of some kind. Certain artistic remains show warriors swimming across streams. An inscription of the early ninth century B.C. speaks of soldiers fleeing—swimming like fish through the water to safety. The figures are fully clad, and are frequently shown with shields, spears, and other equipment. Warriors are most commonly represented as using inflated skins (*mussuks*) such as are still employed in Mesopotamia. This, it appears, was by no means easy, especially if the swimmer had to keep the skin inflated as he went, keeping the aperture in his mouth. Grave doubt is expressed by some as to whether a swimmer really did have to blow into the *mussuk* while in transit. Whether he did or not, a special student of the history of swimming has declared that swimming on a *mussuk* is a sign of skill, not of the lack of it. To use a *mussuk* "skillfully so as to fish or swim, it requires to be learnt when a child." The stroke was probably "hand-over-hand," alternating with the stroke of the legs.[50]

Apart from cleansing gained incidentally in swimming, Babylonians prac-

[49] Forrer: "Die Inschriften und Sprachen des Ḫatti-Reiches," *Zeitschrift der Deutschen Morgenländischen Gesellschaft*, LXXVI, 174–269.
[50] Radcliffe: op. cit., p. 356; Thomas: *Swimming*, pp. 78 f., 83; Layard: op. cit., I, 40 ff., 128 f., 333–40.

ticed ceremonial washing, as Herodotus reports. Ruins of baths in Assur (c. 1350 B.C.) and at Sendschirli in northern Syria in the palace of Asarhaddon (681–668 B.C.) have also been discovered.[51]

QUEEN SHOUBAD'S HARP
(Courtesy, The University Museum, University of Pennsylvania, Philadelphia)

It is commonly said that Babylonians and Assyrians were more fully engrossed in practical business, and that pleasures occupied less place among them than among Egyptians. Though there is doubtless some truth in this generalization, it is probably best not to emphasize the view too much. Recent sources reveal a fuller life to-day than could be seen a generation ago. The pic-

[51] *Herodotus*, I, 198; Schleyer: *Bäder und Badeanstalten*, pp. 5 f.

HERDSMAN PLAYING THE LUTE  *Nippur*
(Courtesy, The University Museum, University of Pennsylvania, Philadelphia)

ture may be more complete to-morrow. Even as information stands to-day, it is evident that the peoples between the rivers held in some measure to a philosophy of pleasure, which they commonly associated with music and dancing. To leap and sing is to express one's joy in life. "Dance and play, night and day" epitomizes a philosophy of pleasure. Hambly noted that exhibition dancing is generally indicative of the decay of the original communal significance of the dance. In Babylonia and Assyria dancing and music appear to have been commonly associated with religion and feasting; but it is also linked with commonplace activities. In very early times music and dancing were favorite themes of artists: on Queen Shoubad's harp, animal figures are used to symbolize them. The donkey sits at the harp; the bear dances, and the jackal plays the sistrum. Below them a wild goat with the sistrum and a man-scorpion "symbolize the spirit of the dance."[52] Music, vocal and instrumental, was a concomitant of almost every occupation of life: a relief shows a shepherd making music, while animals draw near around him; music lightens the labor of the reaper and the

[52] Legrain: *op. cit.*, *loc. cit.*, ser. 6, vi, 9, 18; Hambly: *Tribal Dancing*, pp. 133 ff.

brick molder; the rhythm of drums and cymbals accompanies the wrestling or boxing (or *mora?*) match; and the king's triumphal return and the weary march of prisoners are marked by appropriate music. The Hebrews complained because their captors required of them a song. Disease demons and death were thwarted by song. The gods were refreshed and cheered: "Morning and evening, the musicians delight the heart of the gods." "A time when the old sing and the young make music," says Meissner, was held to be "especially happy and blessed of the gods." "Babylonian hymns and prayers were designed chiefly for musical accompaniment and were classified according to the instrument with which they were accompanied." Of musical instruments there were many: tambourines, harps, cymbals, pipes, guitars, drums, lyres, zithers, dulcimers, and a variety of trumpets. Men and women became musicians and served in the temples and at court. Sayce believed they formed a special guild or class, but was in doubt whether they should be considered as a profession.[53] There seems to be little reason to doubt their professional status. Music is more often represented in the remains than is dancing, which is commonly associated with religious ceremonies. In a procession, noted by Rawlinson,[54] the leaders lift their feet as in a slow rhythmic dance while those following in the train clap their hands in time. To-day rude tribal folk, heirs of a once proud civilization, dance the Debkè and the sword dance over the mounds that cover it.

### FROM UR TO JERUSALEM

Beyond the Arabian desert stood the city of Ur, "a Semitic center" on the margin of the Babylonian plain. Some two hundred years before the time of Hammurabi, the family of Terah is believed to have gone up out of Ur northward to Haran, in one of those periodic migrations which are characteristic of nomadic, pastoral folk. In the course of time Abraham and his followers came to Shechem and Beer-lahai-roi, where they pastured their flocks, moving back and forth over the range of hills. This movement out of Ur of Chaldaea was part of a larger migration to the west, which ultimately brought some of the Semitic folk into Egypt, about 1650 B.C.[55] There, for a time, the Israelites pursued their pastoral callings, somewhat as they had done in Asia, but acquired some of the civilization of the Egyptians. The similarities between *Proverbs* and *The Teaching of Amenophis* suggest an indebtedness of one to the other, or that both drew from a common source.[56] Later they were put to

[53] Sayce: *Babylonians and Assyrians*, pp. 165 ff.; Meissner: *op. cit.*, I, 332 ff.
[54] *Op. cit.*, I, 543.
[55] Petrie: *Egypt and Israel*, p. 17; Barton: *Archaeology and the Bible*, chap. 9; Smith: *Old Testament History*, chap. 3.
[56] Simpson: "The Hebrew Book of Proverbs and the Teaching of Amenophis," *Jour. Egy. Archaeol.*, XII, 232-9.

forced labor [57] by Rameses II who "knew not Joseph." From this bondage they escaped, under the leadership of Moses, about 1220 B.C., into the land of Canaan. Here, after nearly a century under the Judges (1150–1030 B.C.), the people became discontented and demanded "a king to judge us like all the nations." [58] With varying fortunes the kingship continued to the beginning of the Babylonian captivity, 586 B.C. A major calamity was the division of the kingdom (933 B.C.) into Judah, whose seat was at Jerusalem, and Israel, whose chief city was Samaria. The latter, often referred to as the "lost ten tribes," were swept away by the Assyrians (721 B.C.) and carried into Media. Judah continued to be the center of Jewish culture, although beginning with the Babylonian captivity it, too, became for several hundred years a subject people: under Babylon, 586–538 B.C.; under Persia, 538–333 B.C.; and under Greece, Egypt, and Syria, 332–175 B.C. From 175 to 63 B.C., having revolted against Hellenization at the hands of Antiochus IV, King of Syria, home rule was enjoyed under the Maccabees. Finally, internal dissension afforded an opportunity for Roman intervention, which resulted in the loss of Jewish independence and a continued decline until 70 A.D., when Jerusalem was taken, the temple demolished, and the people scattered.

Economic life of the early Hebrews was exceedingly simple; being semi-nomadic, they were dependent on bountiful pasturage and supplies of drinking water. While they were at Shechem and elsewhere to the south, before they entered Egypt, they moved back and forth along the ridge of hills many times in the course of a few generations. There is no indication that they had fixed locations and permanent houses; presumably they lived in tents, perhaps similar to those occupied by Bedouins of the region to-day. There was, apparently, no personal ownership of land. Flocks of sheep and goats and herds of cattle constituted their chief wealth, but they were acquainted with gold and silver. Arrived in Egypt, there took place some mixture with Egyptian stock. Certain customs of the Egyptians were adopted also, which had an influence upon later culture, as is to be observed in the temple at Jerusalem and the robes of the high priest; despite new elements, however, the imprint of Babylonian culture on the Hebrew mind was not obliterated. At first their occupations were presumably the same or similar to those they had known earlier; at length, however, they were put to forced labor, making brick and constructing defenses for the Egyptians.[59] Once out of Egypt, their life was marked by a growing tendency toward habitation in walled cities and to agricultural pursuits, mixed, of course, with sporadic warfare. Peritz says

[57] Petrie: op. cit., pp. 21, 30 f., 38.
[58] I Samuel, VIII, 5.
[59] Petrie: op. cit., pp. 31 ff., 60 ff.

of this period that "while hitherto not ignorant of field labor, they became now agriculturists with settled abodes, houses, lands, vineyards, and olive yards." [60]

Women appear to have occupied an important place in early Hebrew society. Descent was traced to them, as is to be seen in the case of Sarah, Rebekah, Leah, and Dinah; and Deborah and Miriam ranked as prophetesses and judges, to whom the people of Israel came for judgment.[61] Later, the patriarchal system prevailed, and woman's position became one of dependency. Polygamy was recognized as legal,[62] but was practiced only by those who could afford it. Though plurality of wives was approved of, adultery was condemned by law. As among many other people, girls were less desired than boys. "Well to him whose children are boys; woe to him whose children are girls," says the Talmud.

Though women became less important in public affairs in later times, their place in the household was highly regarded. No Oriental folk gave more thought to rearing children in morality than did the Hebrews; and of moral training, for daughters especially, the mother was the primary agent. As domestic economist the wife was important also, for upon her wise management the welfare of the family depended. Such is the picture of the "worthy woman" in the Proverbs, who "seeketh wool and flax," "worketh willingly with her hands," "bringeth food from afar," "giveth food to her household," "considereth a field and buyeth it," and "planteth a vineyard." She is good-natured and full of wisdom, the ideal homemaker, "who looketh well to the ways of her household, and eateth not the bread of idleness." [63]

The religious thought of the Hebrews reflects an evolution similar to that of Babylonians, Hindus, and other Oriental peoples, though a monotheistic tendency appeared early in their history and was ultimately carried to a purer form.[64] In the beginning, however, when they wandered about seeking better pastures for their flocks, many religious conceptions of the Hebrews closely resembled those of other nature peoples, herdsmen and primitive agriculturists; even at the time of their escape from Egypt old habits of thinking continued, which conflicted with the conception of one supreme God. The nomadic Semites, like other early peoples, had a profound belief in spirits, good and evil, which could bring all things to pass, make man and beast fruitful, or destroy them utterly. Hence arose a vast array of magic practices, based on belief in the potency of certain numbers, objects, and names, which were destined to have a long life.[65] Man, being weak and inferior, sought to discover

[60] Peritz: Old Testament History, p. 114.
[61] Petrie: op. cit., pp. 21 ff.; Renan: History of the People of Israel, I, chap. 8.
[62] Peritz: op. cit., p. 116.
[63] Proverbs, xxxi.
[64] Renan: op. cit., I, chaps. 3–4.
[65] Trachtenberg: Jewish Magic and Superstition, pp. 29 ff., 69 ff., 108 ff.

the strong and superior that he might worship it and live. Religion was an eminently practical matter. Man negotiated with the invisible power for material goods, and promised payment if his request succeeded. Jacob vowed that "if God will be with me, and will keep me in this way that I go, and will give me bread to eat, and raiment to put on . . ." then shall Jehovah "be my God"; and "this stone, which I have set up for a pillar, shall be God's house: and of all that thou shalt give me I will surely give the tenth unto thee." [66] Totemic beliefs survived in Hebrew religious literature. Unclean animals hark back to the time when animals were closely associated with gods or were gods themselves.[67] Sayce says, apropos of totems, that David was of the serpent totem, and some scholars hold that the "brazen serpent found by Hezekiah in the Solomonic temple was the symbol of it." [68] The worship at stones, bethels, on which a libation of oil had been poured; the sacrificing in high places; the holiness of blood [69]—all point to a primitive age of man.

Opposed to these primitive ideas and practices, there is a strong note of monotheism and a sharp protest on the part of the prophets against a religion of blood and sacrifices. For them, at least, primitive powers were absorbed by Yahweh, a great god, besides whom there is no other. To him these Hebrew leaders vowed undivided allegiance. The prophet Micah declared eternal loyalty on behalf of the people: "For all people will walk every one in the name of his own God, and we will walk in the name of the Lord our God forever and ever." At times, the vision of the prophets became world-wide: not only Hebrews but other nations were to bow down to Yahweh. Cyrus is commissioned "to subdue nations before him"; Yahweh has sworn by himself "that unto me every knee shall bow, every tongue shall swear"; Babylon and Chaldaea with Bel and his idols, the oppressors of Judah, are to be bowed down; and the daughters of Babylon and Chaldaea are to "sit in the dust." [70]

THE EDUCATION OF LIFE  The informal education of life was all the Hebrews knew before the Babylonian captivity, save after the monarchy had been established, when some formal instruction by private teachers may have been given in the larger towns. This informal education at the hands of fathers and mothers was partly moral and religious, being based upon such customs, religious and secular, as time and tradition had approved, and upon the laws said to have been given to Moses.[71] Thus Jehovah had commanded: "Thou shalt love Jehovah thy God with all thy heart, and with all thy soul,

[66] Genesis, xxviii, 20–2.
[67] Smith: op. cit., pp. 333 ff.
[68] Sayce: Ancient Empires, pp. 200 f.
[69] Genesis, xxviii, 18–22; Renan: op. cit., I, 43 f.; Petrie: op. cit., pp. 47 ff.; Smith: op. cit., p. 335.
[70] Isaiah, xlv, 1, 23; xlvi, 1; xlvii, 1–11.
[71] Klostermann: Schulwesen im Alten Israel, pp. 4 ff.

and with all thy might. And these words, which I command thee this day, shall be upon thy heart; and thou shalt teach them diligently unto thy children, and shalt talk of them when thou sittest in thy house, and when thou walkest by the way, and when thou liest down, and when thou risest up. And thou shalt bind them for a sign upon thy hand, and they shall be for frontlets between thine eyes, and thou shalt write them upon the door-posts of thy house, and upon thy gates." [72]

Accompanying this informal moral and religious instruction there was physical training through the labors that life imposed—the work of hunters, fishers, warriors, herdsmen, and agriculturists. It has been said that the Jews did "very little" for "the culture of the physical man." [73] Of systematic physical training and organized athletic contests there was, of course, nothing in their early history. The "culture of the physical man," however, was not ignored; it came merely through an informal apprenticeship to life rather than through a formal process. Biblical literature tells of the supreme hunter who became "a mighty one in the earth," similar to the Babylonian Gilgamesh, if, indeed, they are not one and the same. Nimrod was a mighty hunter, and Esau a "skillful hunter" and "man of the field." The bow and spear were their weapons. Pits, traps, and nets were also employed, apparently, but dogs and horses, if used, are not named.[74] There is little evidence of the pursuit of hunting as a sport, though King Herod is given the reputation of a sportsman by Josephus, who speaks of his pursuit of wild beasts, his master of the chase, and the royal hunting spears.[75]

Fishing is often referred to in ancient Hebrew literature, but, as with hunting, the end served was probably an economic one. The Hebrews used fish for food—everything with scales and fins being permitted to them—and recalled with longing that they had eaten it for nothing in Egypt. Though some have thought that the use of the fishing rod was known to them, Radcliffe found no evidence to justify such an interpretation. Spears, bidents, harpoons, lines, nets, and hooks, however, seem to have been employed.[76]

"From twenty years old and upward, all that are able to go forth to war in Israel" were to be drafted by the command of Jehovah, though mercenaries were also employed at times.[77] The skill of the hunter and the fighter were closely allied in Israel, as among other early peoples; and since the Israelites

---

[72] Deuteronomy, VI, 5–9.

[73] Ballin: "Gymnastics in the Bible," *Mind and Body*, II, 129; Brink and Smith: *Athletes of the Bible*, passim.

[74] *Genesis*, x, 9; xxv, 27; Butler: *Sport in Classic Times*, p. 17; II Samuel, XXIII, 20; *Isaiah*, LI, 20; *Proverbs*, XXII, 5; *Job*, XVIII, 9–10.

[75] *Jewish Antiquities*, XV, 7, 7; XVI, 10, 3.

[76] Deuteronomy, XIV, 9–10; Numbers, XI, 5; *Job*, XLI, 1, 7; Amos, IV, 2; Habakkuk, I, 15–7; Radcliffe: *op. cit.*, pp. 397 ff.

[77] Numbers, I, 2–3; II Chronicles, XXV, 6.

throughout their history were in the midst of a hostile environment, it is natural that the mighty man of valor, physical greatness, and military sagacity was their ideal. Thus it was Saul—who "was higher than any of the people from his shoulders" upward, and who led them and "smote the Ammonites until the heat of the day," when "not two of them were left together" [78]—to whom they turned for a king to rule over them. His successor, David, was likewise credited with numerous heroic exploits against wild beasts and human enemies—feats which paved his way to power. The biblical story runs: "Thy servant was keeping his father's sheep; and when there came a lion, or a bear, and took a lamb out of the flock, I went out after him, and smote him, and delivered it out of his mouth; and when he arose against me, I caught him by his beard, and smote him, and slew him." [79]

In days of hand-to-hand fighting, one army frequently sent forth its champion to challenge a representative of the other. Thus David, having convinced Saul by the story of his prowess with bears and lions, was named to go out for the Israelites against the Philistines. Not being able to bear the armor given him to wear, for he was unused to it and a mere stripling, "he took his staff in his hand, and chose him five smooth stones out of the brook, and put them in the shepherd's bag which he had, even in his wallet; and his sling was in his hand: and he drew near to the Philistine. . . . And . . . when the Philistine arose, and came and drew nigh to meet David, . . . David hastened, and ran toward the army to meet the Philistine. And David put his hand in his bag, and took thence a stone, and slang it, and smote the Philistine . . . and the stone sank into his forehead, and he fell upon his face to the earth. So David prevailed over the Philistine with a sling and with a stone, and smote the Philistine, and slew him; but there was no sword in the hand of David." [80] Because of the king's jealousy at his popularity, David soon fled from the court and hid away in the cave of Adullam, where he became captain of a band of outlaws—kinsmen of those who were "in distress," "in debt," and "discontented." With them he carried on guerrilla warfare against his enemies, levying for supplies upon the herders and farmers of the neighboring communities for the "protection" he afforded them. When his small band of warriors had increased in numbers and his reputation for power and courage had become widely known, he was chosen king, at Hebron, by the heads of certain clans. Ultimately by military measures he consolidated the kingdom with Jerusalem as the capital.[81]

While it is certain that training for warfare must have been the most promi-

[78] I Samuel, x, 23; xi, 11.
[79] Ibid., xvii, 34–5.
[80] Ibid., xvii, 40–51.
[81] Ibid., xxii, 2; xxv; Smith: op. cit., pp. 133–43.

nent phase of physical training in the period following the flight from Egypt and during the gradual establishment of the monarchy, it is impossible to get a clear-cut and complete picture of the physical regimen of fighters in the Israelitish army. Certain skills, however, may be inferred from the kinds of implements employed. The spear, bow and arrow, sling, sword and shield— the weapons of seminomadic tribes of that day and region—were at first used almost exclusively. The spear was probably the oldest weapon, but swords were commonly used after the Hebrews came to Palestine. Both were of bronze. A gladiatorial combat between twelve men "for Benjamin" and "twelve of the servants of David"—something learned, perhaps, from contact with the Philistines—was staged before Joab and Abner.[82] Of great importance was the bow. Arrows were tipped with flint and bronze. Iron was also known. Chariots had been familiar to them since first contact with the Egyptians and Canaanites. Although David won them as booty from the Syrians, Solomon seems to have been the first to have cavalry and chariots in great numbers—12,000 horsemen and 1,400 chariots.[83] With fortification the Hebrews of early times appear to have been unacquainted, but in the monarchy their knowledge of military affairs increased, they took Canaanitish walled cities, and they walled in their own. King Rehoboam fortified fifteen cities; in later times the Maccabees built extensive fortifications.[84]

The sling was employed since early times, both in hunting and in war. David's exploit with it was apparently not uncommon; when the people of Benjamin arrayed themselves in battle against Israel, there were 700 chosen men who were left-handed and every one of them could "sling stones at a hair-breadth, and not miss." The majority of the army, however—26,000 men— were swordsmen.[85]

The bow must have been a popular weapon both for war and hunting, judging from the frequency of references to it: Hagar's son grew up and became an archer; Jacob sent Esau to the field with his bow to get venison; Israel gave Joseph a portion of land he had taken from the Amorite with bow and sword; Ulam's sons were archers, mighty and valorous; the men who surrounded David were able to use the bow, and the sling as well, with both the right hand and the left; and Jehu drew his bow and sent an arrow right through Joram's heart. David is said to have charged the people to teach the children of Judah "the song of the bow." [86] Petrie, speaking of the warfare of the Hyksos, the Israelites'

[82] II Samuel, II, 14–6; Barton: op. cit., Plates, 57–8; Nowack: Lehrbuch der Hebräischen Archäologie, I, 362 ff.

[83] I Kings, X, 26; II Chronicles, I, 14; IX, 25.

[84] II Chronicles, XI, 5–12; I Maccabees, IX, 50–2.

[85] Judges, XX, 14–6.

[86] Genesis, XXI, 20; XXVII, 3; XLVIII, 22; I Chronicles, VIII, 40; XII, 2; II Kings, IX, 24; II Samuel, I, 18 et seq., respectively; Isaiah, v, 28; Job, XXIX, 20; Jeremiah, LI, 11; Ezekiel, XXXIX, 3.

kinsmen who had wrought havoc among the Egyptian hosts in an earlier day, says that by their archery, which "entirely outranged the Egyptian means of attack and defence," they could render useless any opposition.[87] The continued use of the bow among the Israelites in Palestine is suggested by a line from the song of Deborah and Barak—"far from the noise of archers"—which they sang after the defeat of the Philistine, Sisera, who was equipped with "even nine hundred chariots of iron." Whether he was defeated by chariots, arrows, and other implements of war, or simply "by the edge of the sword" and the power of Jehovah's cunning, is not known, but we are informed that "all the host of Sisera fell" and "there was not a man left." [88]

Though in early times there were neither formal training nor athletic contests, numerous biblical passages refer to physical activities, generally in association with war and religion. In many figures of speech the activities of life were reflected. Archery was important in warfare; certain references to it suggest shooting at targets also. Jonathan says that he will shoot three arrows "as though I shot at a mark"; Jeremiah laments that he has been set "as a mark for the arrow"; and Job makes a like complaint.[89] Runners were employed to carry messages from the king "throughout all Israel and Judah"; at times this service was performed on horseback.[90] Among the swiftest runners there was Naphtali, who ran like a hind let loose; Elijah is said to have outraced the chariot of Ahab; and Asahel, whom Jerome called "a most swift runner," was as fleet of foot as the roe and was said to have been able to beat horses as well as men in running.[91] As for wrestling, Jacob is said to have wrestled with a man and sustained a strained thigh.[92] Bathing in streams is attested in the case of Pharaoh's daughter; and David was overcome by the beauty of Bath-sheba when he saw her bathing in the river.[93] Swimming was doubtless a necessity for soldiers. Isaiah speaks of one who "spreadeth forth his hands to swim"; and Jonathan, having been turned back by Bacchides, leaped with his men into the Jordan and swam to the farther side.[94] Little is said about balls, but the Israelites were certainly acquainted with them after their sojourn in Egypt. Isaiah says that Jehovah will toss Shebna "like a ball"; a verse in *Ecclesiastes* is interpreted by the *Midrash*, "The words of the wise are as the balls with which girls play," i.e., they pass from hand to hand without falling to the ground.[95]

[87] Petrie: *op. cit.*, pp. 18 ff.
[88] *Judges*, IV, 13–6.
[89] I *Samuel*, xx, 20; *Lamentations*, III, 12; *Job*, xVI, 12.
[90] II *Chronicles*, xxx, 6; *Esther*, III, 13; VIII, 10.
[91] *Genesis*, XLIX, 21; II *Samuel*, II, 18; I *Kings*, xVIII, 44–6; Josephus: *op. cit.*, VII, 1, 3; *Bible* (Vulgate), II *Kings*, II, 18.
[92] *Genesis*, xxxII, 24–5.
[93] *Exodus*, II, 5; II *Samuel*, xI, 2.
[94] *Isaiah*, xxv, 11; I *Maccabees*, IX, 48.
[95] *Ecclesiastes*, xII, 11; Feldman: *The Jewish Child*, p. 360.

Dancing, another form of physical exercise common throughout the early history of the Hebrews, must have been learned in an informal manner. As elsewhere among early peoples dancing was always associated with singing and instrumental music, and both played a prominent part on religious and other festal occasions. Singing and dancing were symbols of joy. When Job complains of the wicked who flourish, he declares that they—

> . . . send forth their little ones like a flock,
> And their children dance.
> They sing to the timbrel and harp,
> And rejoice at the sound of the pipe.[96]

It was doubtless with a great release of emotion, when the Egyptian hosts were said to have been swallowed up in the sea, that Miriam, the prophetess, took the timbrels in hand, and all the women danced and sang:

> I will sing unto Jehovah, for he hath triumphed gloriously:
> The horse and his rider hath he thrown into the sea.

> .  .  .

> Jehovah is a man of war:
> Jehovah is his name.
> Pharaoh's chariots and his host hath he cast into the sea;
> And his chosen captains are sunk in the Red Sea.[97]

In like manner, when David had slain the Philistine, "the women came out of all the cities of Israel, singing and dancing, to meet King Saul, with timbrels, with joy, and with instruments of music. And the women sang one to another as they played," saying:

> Saul hath slain his thousands,
> And David his ten thousands.[98]

But it was not only in the excitement and pleasure at overcoming their enemies and welcoming home the gory warrior that they danced; dancing was recognized as a suitable way of approaching the deity. With singing and dancing they worshiped the golden calf they had set up, which caused Moses' anger to "wax hot" and the tables of stone to be cast down and broken.[99] Religious, joyful, and warlike sentiments are joined in the following invocation to praise Jehovah with dancing and singing accompanied by harp and timbrel:

[96] *Job*, xxi, 11–2.
[97] *Exodus*, xv, 1, 3–4.
[98] i *Samuel*, xviii, 6–7.
[99] *Exodus*, xxxii, 18–9.

Let them praise his name in the dance:
Let them sing praises unto him with timbrel and harp.

. . .

Let the high praises of God be in their mouth,
And a two-edged sword in their hand;
To execute vengeance upon the nations,
And punishments upon the peoples;
To bind their kings with chains,
And their nobles with fetters of iron. . . .[100]

Again and again the religious rites are associated with dancing, the character of which presumably did not differ markedly from that performed on ordinary occasions. When the ark was to be removed to the city of the king, "David and all the house of Israel played before Jehovah with all manner of instruments made of fir-wood, and with harps, and with psalteries, and with timbrels, and with castanets, and with cymbals." And as they carried the ark from the house of Obed-edom into the city, "David danced before Jehovah with all his might. . . ." Only one person made a wry face at all this celebration. Saul's daughter, Michal, ridiculed the dance of David before the ark, and was disgusted at his "leaping and dancing" in such an abandoned fashion before the people.[101] The story of this affair, with the jealous criticisms voiced by Michal, is suggestive of a later period—perhaps that of Hezekiah, as Renan says—and reflects the attitude of high society at the court toward such primitive and outgrown forms of worship in honor of Yahweh.[102] Domenichino has sought to catch the spirit of this notable occasion in his engraving of David dancing before the ark;[103] but his hero is heavily robed, while Michal complained that David danced shamelessly uncovered. According to Renan, the rhythm of the religious dance is preserved for us, in a more or less modified form, in the Sixty-eighth Psalm:

Let God arise, let his enemies be scattered;
Let them also that hate him flee before him.

. . .

Sing unto God, sing praises to his name:
Cast up a highway for him that rideth through the deserts;
His name is Jehovah; and exult ye before him.

. . .

O God, when thou wentest forth before thy people,
When thou didst march through the wilderness;

[100] *Psalms*, CXLIX, 3, 6–8.
[101] II *Samuel*, VI, 5, 12–4, 16, 20.
[102] Renan: *op. cit.*, II, 41 f.
[103] Grove: *Dancing*, p. 27.

> A mountain of God is the mountain of Bashan;
> A high mountain is the mountain of Bashan.
> Why look ye askance, ye high mountains,
> At the mountain which God hath desired for his abode?
> Yea, Jehovah will dwell in it for ever.
> The chariots of God are twenty thousand, even thousands upon thou-
>     sands. . . .[104]

With the passing of primitive life, the rise of formal schools, and the devotion of much effort to mental culture, dancing is thought to have declined in favor as a part of worship, although it continued as a form of recreation and celebration on various secular occasions.[105] Others maintain, however, that "legislation of the priestly code" had little effect on "the taste of the people for dancing," which "grew rather than waned in the later period." [106] It seems certain that, in spite of the fact that dancing came into disfavor with the legalistically minded, it continued long to be associated in the minds of the people with religious worship. The learning of dancing, whether in favor or out of favor for religious purposes, must have been an informal process, engaged in chiefly at home or on occasions when youth came together.[107]

Another form of physical exercise of an informal sort must have been the lot of Jewish boys and girls in the days of wandering, under the monarchy, and after the Exile. Work in the camp, with the flocks, and in the fields occupied the earlier period. After the sojourn in Egypt and the conquest of Canaan, came more settled life; thenceforth agriculture, vine culture, raising cattle, fishing, mining, building, carpentry, metal industry, tanning, making tents, manufacturing pottery, and constructing a wide variety of tools must have constituted, along with warfare, the chief fields for apprenticeship of young men.[108] Even the most highly educated carried on some art or trade besides his work as scribe; and the *Talmud's* prescription that each father should cause his son to learn a trade,[109] may simply have incorporated into law what was already a general practice. All work was said to be "necessary to the world," but some occupations were preferred as more worthy. Thus the perfumer stood in higher estimation than the tanner.[110] Apropos of the method of training, Swift concludes: "It seems reasonable to assume that in most cases . . . [the son] followed his father's occupation and acquired his earliest training by assisting his father or

---

[104] *Psalms*, LXVIII, 1, 4, 7, 15–7.
[105] Swift: *Education in Ancient Israel*, pp. 61 f.
[106] Grove: *op. cit.*, pp. 31 f.
[107] Swift: *op. cit.*, p. 25.
[108] Delitzsch: *Jewish Artisan Life*, passim.
[109] *Kiddushin*, 29 a, 30 b.
[110] *Ibid.*, 82 a.

elder brothers in shop or market-place. As he grew older he would assist more and more until at length he would enter upon a regular apprenticeship. After elementary education had been made compulsory, the major part of this training would necessarily be postponed until the boy had finished his studies at the elementary school. Then, unless he continued his studies at some higher professional school for the sake of preparing to become a scribe or rabbi, he would take up serious preparation for some commercial or industrial occupation." [111]

With political and military weakness, which more and more characterized the Hebrews in the last few centuries of the pagan era, there came a narrowing of education. Less emphasis was placed upon physical and military training, while more attention was given to mental pursuits, particularly to the mastery of the law. The influence of Hellenism was spreading, however; and there was one group among the Hebrews which sought to modify the exclusive tendency toward legalistic mental training by introducing Hellenic ideals and practices which had been known to them in some degree since the fourth century. This liberal movement gave proof of its Hellenic leaning, when Jason gained a license from the king, caused a gymnasium to be erected "under the tower itself," and "forthwith brought his own nation to the Greekish fashion." Soon "the height of Greek fashions and increase of heathenish manners" was such "that the priests had no courage to serve any more at the altar, but despising the temple, and neglecting the sacrifices, hastened to be partakers of the unlawful allowance in the place of exercise, after the game of Discus called them forth . . . liking the glory of the Grecians best of all." Moreover, when the quadrennial games were being held at Tyrus, the king attended them and the Greekling, Jason, sent messengers with a gift of three hundred drachmas of silver for the sacrifice in honor of Hercules.[112] Gamaliel the Second, Resh Lakish, and others were decidedly favorably inclined toward the gymnastic movement. Simeon ben Gamaliel was apparently able to juggle burning torches, and some teachers urged fathers to teach their boys to swim.[113] Josephus' account of the six hundred men who had to swim all night when their ship foundered on a voyage to Rome, suggests remarkable attainments in swimming.[114] Swimming and bathing in the river seem to have continued, although swimming baths were also used.[115] Wrestling, leaping, boxing, throwing the discus and javelin, various kinds of acrobatics, lifting weights, and running were among the exercises introduced. But the "heathenish manners," the "profaneness of Jason," and particularly the nakedness of the gymnasts,

---

[111] Swift: op. cit., p. 61.
[112] I Maccabees, I, 14–5; II Maccabees, IV, 9, 13–5, 18–9.
[113] Kiddushin, 29 a; Spiers: The School System of the Talmud, p. 36.
[114] Life of Josephus, p. 3.
[115] Baba Metzia, 84 a.

offended the sense of propriety of many people, and it was soon evident that the attempt to bring the Hebrews to gymnastics was doomed to ultimate defeat. A century after the time of Antiochus Epiphanes, however, bullfights, the circus, and gladiatorial contests had been introduced, but these were vigorously condemned by the rabbis because of their immoral influence.[116] In a somewhat similar fashion early Christians turned against pagan physical culture and all sorts of exhibitions that increasingly marked decaying Roman society.

Among the Jews, recreation, cleanliness, and health were of no slight consequence; indeed they were regarded as religious obligations.[117] The Sabbath was a time for recreation of mind and body; but idleness was condemned. Bodily cleanliness was the beginning of spiritual purity or godliness. Going to the bath was like going to a religious ceremony. Said Hillel: "If those that look after the statues and monuments of kings that are placed in theatres and circuses are very careful to keep those images of earthly kings clean, how much more should I keep my body clean that has been made in the image of God." [118] "No learned man may live in a town in which, among other things, there are no public baths or public conveniences" was a law of the Sanhedrin.[119] In view of this lively concern for the body, it must be recognized therefore that, despite their antagonism to certain aspects of the gymnastic exercises of the Hellenizers, the Jews seem never to have accepted an asceticism which would destroy the body that the soul might live.

In early biblical times disease was regarded as a punishment from God. The Hebrews were assured by Moses that if they would obey the commandments of Jehovah, none of the diseases would be put upon them which had been put upon the Egyptians; [120] Job was afflicted by Satan with boils, with the consent of Jehovah; [121] and Asa died of an "exceeding great" disease in his feet, presumably because he went to physicians instead of seeking the intervention of Jehovah.[122] Physicians were condemned from time to time by the theologically minded; nevertheless, their importance increased and Jewish physicians became renowned for their wisdom in dealing with disease. The *Sanhedrin* declares that no learned man should live in a city which was without a physician.[123] Ultimately the functions of rabbi and physician were commonly combined in the same person.[124] Whether they relied on physicians or upon

[116] Aboda Zara, 18 b; Graetz: *History of the Jews*, I, 444 ff.; Smith: op. cit., pp. 443 ff.; Peritz: op. cit., pp. 293 ff.
[117] Joseph: *Judaism as Creed and Life*, pp. 274 ff.
[118] Feldman: op. cit., p. 253.
[119] Sanhedrin, 17 b.
[120] Exodus, xv, 26.
[121] Job, II, 3–7.
[122] II Chronicles, XVI, 12–3.
[123] Sanhedrin, 17 b.
[124] Friedenwald: "The Relation of the Jews and Judaism to the Medical Art," Am. Med., N.S., XII, 621.

Jehovah, the Hebrews moved steadily toward scientific measures, establishing dietary regulations and measures for curbing the spread of disease. Numerous animals, birds, and shellfish were declared unclean and forbidden as food, as also were the fats of certain beasts and all blood.[125]

Highly important were the agencies established for preventing the spread of contagious disease or uncleanness (*tomeh*) such as leprosy and gonorrhea. "Thus shall ye separate the children of Israel from their uncleanliness that they die not in their uncleanness." [126] Brav concludes that there was "a complete and efficient system of isolation which differs from our modern system only in the details of procedure and mode of expression." [127] Aaron and his sons were the health officers charged to enforce the law.[128] Important features of the system were: the reporting of cases to the sanitary officers; detention of suspicious cases for two weeks; and permanent isolation outside the city, under the care of guards. When cases were reported as cured, an additional seven days of isolation were required.[129]

While girls' occupations in the early period were often outside the home, it appears that, with the increasing settledness of social life, they were more and more restricted to the household, and its duties constituted the chief part of their training. The spinning rod is the "only accomplishment proper for a girl" says the *Talmud*.[130] In Talmudic times, it was said that "a woman should take an active interest in the management of her household, and devote herself to the moral and religious training of her children. . . ." Spiers infers that "much attention was paid to the private instruction of girls," but views varied widely as to whether girls should be taught the *Torah*: Ben Azai held that every father should teach it to his daughter; Eliezer, on the contrary, would rather see it burned than given to women.[131] That women were light-minded; that they would put learning to evil uses; that intellectual greatness was not their proper pursuit—these were seemingly common opinions.[132] Though apparently higher education in the law was generally not for women, there were exceptions to the rule. Religious education and domestic duties, such as spinning, weaving, dyeing, and baking, were of greatest importance for them. The Greek tongue became a polite accomplishment for girls, but this must have been true only on high social strata.[133] To these may safely be added music and dancing. Besides

---

125 Leviticus, XI; VII, 23–7.
126 *Ibid.*, XV, 31.
127 Brav: "The Biblical Sanitary Code to Prevent the Spread of Contagious Diseases," *Am. Med.*, N.S., XII, 639.
128 *Leviticus*, XIII, 2 *et seq.*
129 Brav: *op. cit., loc. cit.*, N.S., XII, 644.
130 Yoma, 66 b.
131 Sotah, 20 a.
132 *Ibid.*, 21 b; *Kiddushin*, 29 b, 80 b.
133 Spiers: *op. cit.*, pp. 8, 54 f.; Feldman: *op. cit.*, pp. 294 ff.

work inside the house, women on the land included in their labors the care of animals and vineyards, harvesting, managing slaves, and grinding corn. Reading, writing, and knowledge of weights, measures, and money were in "later times added in some cases at least." [134]

FORMAL SCHOOLING  Formal school education probably did not begin until after the Babylonian exile, though private tutorial instruction was provided earlier in some families. The art of writing may have been acquired by the Hebrews from the Canaanites among whom they had settled. The author of *Sefer Yetzirah* is said to have invented an alphabet and aimed to ". . . emphasize the superiority of alphabetic writing over the non-alphabetic. . . ." [135] Petrie maintains that, even when they were making brick in Egypt (1400 B.C.), the Hebrews must have been able to use "a native Semitic cursive writing" in keeping records as overseers.[136] Whatever the true source may have been, writing was known to them.[137] In the pre-exilic period, with the rise of the priesthood and prophets, there was undoubtedly some special provision for their members, and they presumably dealt with written materials to some extent, since the earliest documents of the *Pentateuch* are generally believed to have been written about 800 B.C. Opinions as to chronology differ, however, and some of the elements may have been written earlier. The "schools of the prophets"—though they devoted themselves to law, chronicles, sacred literature, music and, as some have it, to astronomy and mathematics—were scarcely schools in the usual sense of the term.

Upon returning from Babylon—where formal education was considerably advanced—the Hebrews institutionalized education and built synagogues, in which colleges of scribes, the *Beth ha-Midrash*, developed. These afforded an opportunity for those who had literary and scientific tastes to become thoroughly familiar with the law, Greek and other tongues, philosophy, and sciences such as mathematics, astronomy, geography, and botany, introduced chiefly by Greek influence. The scribes embodied the new educational ideal. Since they alone knew ancient Hebrew, and ordinary folk understood only Aramaic and Greek, the scribes became a recognized class of professional teachers.

The development of higher literary education naturally produced an intellectual class. Nevertheless, rich and poor were to be treated alike; indeed, the *Talmud* urged great concern for the poor, since they would devote themselves to learning with greater assiduity.[138] Throughout the postexilic period the inter-

---

[134] Swift: *op. cit.*, p. 116.
[135] Mordell: *The Origin of Letters*, pp. 11, 55–63; Nowack: *op. cit.*, I, 279 ff.; Peritz: *op. cit.*, p. 118; Graetz: *op. cit.*, I, 3; Margolis: *History of the Jewish People*, p. 10.
[136] Petrie: *op. cit.*, pp. 31 f.
[137] Deuteronomy, VI, 9; Joshua, XVIII, 9.
[138] Spiers: *op. cit.*, pp. 28 ff., 34 f., 54.

est in formal educational facilities increased, first through religious instruction in synagogues (which had been practiced in the days of Ezra) and then in public elementary schools. It was not till the second century B.C., however, that public elementary schools appeared. These were ultimately made compulsory. In 75 B.C., Simon ben Shetah ordered children sent to school, but this decree seems to have referred only to Jerusalem (or perhaps also to other large cities), and the schools were only for youth sixteen or seventeen years of age. About 64 A.D. elementary education was made general and compulsory throughout Palestine for boys six or seven years of age.[139]

The studies of the elementary schools probably included reading, writing, arithmetic, and religion, the latter being in fact extremely broad and covering history, law, morals, literature, and music of the Hebrews. The *Pentateuch*, *Psalms*, *Proverbs*, *Ecclesiasticus*, and the *Mishna* were the chief studies to the age of fifteen, for which preliminary preparation had been made by considerable memorization of the scriptures in the family. Beyond the elementary studies, religion and law (*Torah*, *Mishna*, and *Gemara*) constituted the central element, but a critical examination of these took the place of mere memorization; and to them was added commonly, if not universally, an opportunity to study languages and sciences.

Under the dominion of the law and the leadership of teachers whose devotion to it was unbounded, it is not strange that mental discipline became of paramount importance, professions were praised, and the work of the plowman, carpenter, herdsman, potter, and smith was spoken of with contempt by the learned class. "How can he get wisdom that holdeth the plough, and that glorieth in the goad, that driveth the oxen, and is occupied in their labours, and whose talk is of bullocks? He giveth his mind to make furrows; and is diligent to give the kine fodder." [140] The *Talmud* laid stress on training the memory. This was accomplished by much repetition, supplemented by writing, singing, reading, and the use of mnemonic devices. Insight into the variable abilities of pupils is evident in the Talmudic classification of individuals: the winnow, the best, which gets the grain of argument; the sieve, which catches only illustrations; the funnel, which holds nothing; and the sponge, which absorbs everything. A friendly attitude on the part of teachers was valued; it was a common saying that "one who is choleric cannot be a teacher." Anecdotes were employed by some to awaken interest; and Rabbi Akiba is said to have taught through reason "as well as by frequent repetitions." In general, however, the rule seems to have been, "learn first, and then understand." [141]

The ancient Hebrews believed in a close correlation between physical pun-

139 Güdemann: "Education," *Jewish Encyclopedia*, v, 43.
140 *Ecclesiasticus*, XXXVIII, 1–4, 25–30.
141 Spiers: *op. cit.*, pp. 24 f., 38 f.

ishment and an upright life: "He that spareth his rod hateth his son; but he that loveth him chasteneth him betimes"; "Chasten thy son, seeing there is hope; and set not thy heart on his destruction." [142] Though "spare the rod and spoil the child" was a remarkably persistent doctrine, it seems to have lost its hold upon learned Hebrews, to some extent at least, by Talmudic times. Corporal punishment was not as a rule to be employed, though punishment with a strap was approved of in case pupils were not amenable to appeals to honor and self-respect. Older pupils were not to be beaten. Bright students, who were inattentive, were to be punished and made to develop their talents; but the "dull" should not be punished. Rewards and presents were sometimes used to stimulate the younger pupils to greater effort.

At all times there appears to have been a concern for physical health. Children were not to be sent to school before six, since it might be detrimental to health. Schools were often held in the open air, though certain rabbis objected to teaching in public. Playgrounds were provided. The Talmud specified that not more than twenty-five were to be taught by one master, and that an assistant must be secured if as many as forty children attended.[143]

It is evident that, after the Exile, the Hebrews cultivated a profound devotion to formal education. "The world exists only by the breath of school children"; "the duty of taking the child to study is prior to everything"; and "our principal care of all is this, to educate our children well"—these and similar expressions scattered throughout the Talmud suggest that schoolmasters were a ruling force in Hebrew society. Though it is impossible to know precisely their extent, the prevalence of schools is suggested by the Talmud, which declares, "They searched from Dan to Beersheba, but found not an illiterate person." The prestige of scholars and teachers was superior to all others. He who taught the law was as worthy as though he himself had received it on Horeb. To him who had little business, but became wise, the greatest reward was held out: "He shall serve among great men, and appear before princes. . . ." [144]

---

[142] Proverbs, XIII, 24; XIX, 18; XXIII, 13.
[143] Sabbath, 127 a; Baba Bathra, 21 a; Moed Katan, ✳5 ab.
[144] Ecclesiasticus, XXXIX, 4.

# 5

# ON THE YELLOW RIVER

EARLY CHINESE CULTURE

The origin of Chinese civilization is a matter of some uncertainty. Whether it was indigenous, whether it originated in Central Asia, whether it came with the Sumerian from a common source, and similar questions, must be left for specialists to determine. Jastrow's conclusion that Sumerians were not Semites, and that their features "reveal a Turanian type," [1] suggests an origin to the northward, possibly in Central Asia. Ball's study, which gives a comparative lexicon of Chinese and Sumerian terms, and shows relationships between 108 Sumerian ideograms and ancient Chinese characters, tends to the view of a common origin from which Sumerian and Chinese developed.[2] The discovery of cultural relics, near Merv and Askabad, assigned to the ninth millennium B.C., points in the same direction. These were left by a people who already cultivated wheat and barley, lived in houses of sun-dried brick, and kept domestic animals—long-horn cattle, sheep, and pigs.[3]

Early in the third millennium (2704–2595 B.C.), Huang Ti and his followers are said to have migrated into China because of increasing drought in Central Asia. Slowly they penetrated the valley of the Yellow River, where, after some centuries, the traditional capital of Yao was established in Shansi province at Pingyang. There is, of course, no reliable account of these remote ages. Legendary lore covers many centuries, even thousands of years, and it is difficult to tell where legend breaks off and authentic history begins. Some Chinese authorities trace public schools back to Emperor Ti K'u (2432 B.C.); the Confucian legends credit the Chinese with organized government in 2357 B.C.; but modern scholars, both Chinese and Western, look with doubt upon such sources

---

[1] Jastrow: *The Civilization of Babylonia and Assyria*, p. 106; Williams: *China Yesterday and Today*, pp. 32 ff.; Hirth: *Ancient History of China*, pp. 14 ff.
[2] Ball: *Chinese and Sumerian*, pp. 35 ff.
[3] Pumpelly: *Explorations in Turkestan*, I, 57 ff.

as the *Book of History*, and question whether the *Regulations of Chou* may not be forgeries of the early Christian era.[4] The picture of an elaborate system of education, taken from the *History* and the *Regulations*, may be somewhat overdrawn.

Lacking precise, accurate history, early Chinese authors gave a generalized account of their origins. In "the time of the highest antiquity," according to *Li Ki*, men had no houses, but lived in nests in summer and caves in winter, and clothed themselves in skins and feathers. They knew nought of flax and oil and the "transforming power of fire," but ate the fruits of plants and trees and the flesh of birds and animals.[5] Then sages arose, and men learned the use of fire, molded metals, and fashioned clay. Hunting was succeeded by agriculture, and Shonnung invented instruments to till the fields. The Emperor's wife, "Lady of Si Ling," cultivated silk and used it in manufacturing clothing. Trees were hollowed to form canoes; oxen and horses were yoked to carts and chariots; means of defense were perfected; the bow and arrow and the pestle and mortar were invented; houses took the place of caves; and "knotted cords" for keeping records were replaced by written characters.[6] Ts'ang Kie, state historian under Huang Ti, was said to have invented over five hundred hieroglyphs. Besides these and many other arts of peace, Huang Ti built the first temple, formed settled villages, towns and provinces, and placed governors over them.

Heading early society was the "son of Heaven," to whom the arts of civilization were credited. Below him were feudal princes. According to *Li Ki* there were in ancient China nine provinces, each with 210 states. These city-states were held by feudal princes and varied in size and importance. Lands not assigned to them were "imperial, or public property." The "son of Heaven," a tiller of the soil, had "his field of a thousand acres, in which he himself held the plough"; and each prince had a "field of a hundred acres," in which he labored. All had mulberry trees and silkworms, and by their labors measured up to "the height of filial piety." [7]

The subjects of the "son of Heaven" were commonly classed as scholars, farmers, workmen, and merchants. Soldiers were at times considered a fifth class. Scholars constituted a powerful, favored group, and played a great rôle in the patriarchal, bureaucratic government. Other classes were subdivided into small landholders, gardeners, woodmen, stock raisers, artisans, merchants, wives who labored in silk and hemp industries, servants; and a "miscellaneous class" with "no fixed profession." The farmers, tenants of the feudal lords, cultivated crops under the direction of officials, appointed by the government, and paid taxes

[4] Shryock: *State Cult of Confucius*, p. 65.
[5] Müller: *The Sacred Books of the East*, xxvii, 369.
[6] *Ibid.*, xvi, 383 ff.; Hirth: *op. cit.*, pp. 10, 14, 22 f.
[7] Müller: *op. cit.*, xxviii, 222 f. From *The Sacred Books of the East*, edited by F. M. Müller (The Clarendon Press); Williams: *op. cit.*, p. 37.

in kind to their superiors. All other businesses were likewise under the direction of government inspectors. These ordinances of the Chou dynasty (1122–249 B.C.) may have influenced the development of guilds which, it is believed, helped to check "the tyranny of officialdom." [8] The guilds, in any case, were ancient, and developed their crafts to a remarkable degree, as may be judged from their work in porcelain, gold, silver, bronze, brass, lacquer, cloisonné, and lace. In the Middle Ages these were known in Europe for their excellence. Marco Polo noted the intensive work of the twelve guilds of Hangchow. Of the Chinese, whom he saw at the Mongol Court of the Great Khan (1245 A.D.), Carpini said: "Their betters as craftsmen in every art practised by man are not to be found in the whole world." [9] Something akin to the family-guild system existed. Such were the organizations that produced the famous Foochow lacquer, Canton bronze drums, and the silk brocade of the Han period.

The work of the lower classes was incessant. The pains they expended upon labor are almost incomprehensible to Westerners. Their laborious habits seem to have persisted to the present day. The day begins early and seemingly has no end. "The copper workers of Canton, the tinfoil workers of Foochow, the wood-carvers of Ningpo, the rice-mill workers of Shanghai, the cotton-cleaners and workers in the tread-mill for bolting flour in the northern provinces, may all be heard late at night, and at a preposterous hour in the morning. Long before daylight the traveller comes upon a countryman who has already reached a distance of many miles from his home, where he is posted in the darkness waiting for the coming of daylight, when he will begin the sale of his cabbages. . . ." [10] If there be exaggeration in this, it is slight. The trait of wakeful diligence may be observed to-day in Central Asia. Who has not risen at what he considers an early hour, only to find the Asiatic going about the streets as though he had been there all night!

Woman's work in China was no less exacting than that of men. Care of silkworms, preparation of cotton, sewing, and other household tasks combined to make life busy. Though in her own home she was often called "slave-girl," [11] and though "everything good and superior, according to Chinese ideas, is male," [12] woman's position was not inferior to that of her sisters in other Oriental countries. In some respects it was better. In earliest times she had an important place, lineage being traced through mothers rather than fathers. Even after descent was traced through the male line, and despite the fact that boys were desired rather than girls, woman's social inferiority has perhaps been exaggerated. Nevertheless, women were in bondage to men: in youth the girl

8 Williams: op. cit., p. 188; Hirth: op. cit., pp. 109 f.
9 Douglas: China, p. 27.
10 Smith: Chinese Characteristics, pp. 32 f.
11 Smith: Village Life in China, pp. 261 f.
12 Hirth: op. cit., pp. 59 f.

was subject to her father or elder brother; in marriage, to her husband; and in widowhood, to her son. Female infanticide, though practiced, was frowned upon.[13] Said Kwei Chunk Fu: "To destroy daughters is to make war on Heaven's harmony." Monogamy was the general rule. Polyandry existed, but was not widespread. Concubines were common in the upper classes. Divorce was uncommon, but could be obtained by the husband on seven grounds. Marriage took place about the age of twenty. Wives were to obey their husbands, being instructed as to their obligations before marriage. Their chief virtues were filial piety, flexibility, humility, piety, fidelity, obedience, chastity, reticence, and diligent performance of domestic duties. The spheres of men and of women were explained by *Li Ki:* "Men should not speak of what belongs to the inside of the house, nor the women of what belongs to the outside." [14] Lady Tsao's warning, in *Nu Chieh*, is explicit: "If the wife does not serve her husband, the rules of propriety will be destroyed." A voice from the *Book of History* speaks ominously: ". . . for the hen to do the crowing at dawn brings ruin upon the family."

Three religious systems, Confucian, Buddhist, and Taoist, developed side by side in China. The first was chiefly the cult of the official-scholar class, and so of the government; the last two, though they numbered adherents among the socially exalted, were pre-eminently religions of the masses. Buddhism was introduced into China near the beginning of the Christian era, and was more influential and significant than Taoism. By the middle of the second century it was patronized by the Emperor. Neither Taoism nor Buddhism appear to have crowded out primitive deities and cults which had existed from the most ancient times among the masses. Being in some respects alike, Buddhism and Taoism made peaceable bedfellows. Both developed monasticism, taught the uselessness of worldly striving, held out hope of personal salvation, and thus offered solace to the hard-working, the impoverished, and the hopeless. Confucianism, the opposite of these in many respects, was an aristocratic, conservative, intellectual, politico-moral, doctrinaire system. It knew no priest, save as the father served the family, and the Emperor the state. It is not strange, therefore, that attempts at syncretism with Taoism and Buddhism, in the fifth and sixth centuries, were opposed by Confucians generally and ultimately failed.[15]

Confucius was born of noble family about 550 B.C., but it was not until the reign of Wu Ti (141–87 B.C.) that Confucian principles gained official recognition. A "regular cult of Confucius" is first mentioned in 37 A.D. Han Ming Ti

---

[13] Giles, H. A.: *Adversaria Sinica*, pp. 352, 360, 366 ff.
[14] Müller: *op. cit.*, xxvii, 454. From *The Sacred Books of the East*, edited by F. M. Müller (The Clarendon Press).
[15] Shryock: *op. cit.*, pp. 117 ff.

in 59 A.D. commanded sacrifices to Confucius in the official schools.[16] Once established, the worship of Confucius was obligatory upon officials and scholars. As he had exalted scholars, he was in turn exalted by them and became the center of a cult which he himself would not have approved.

CONFUCIUS
(A. Williamson, *Journeys in North China*, 1, 232)

The strength of Confucius lay in the fact that he built upon a tradition long established, at least as old as the Chou dynasty. This tradition, represented in the *Odes*, *Book of Changes*, and the *Book of History*, he set forth as a model for society, and contributed to its extension by his own work, the *Spring and Autumn Annals*. Significant additions were made by his disciples, such as the *Analects*, *Book of Filial Piety*, *Great Learning*, and *Doctrine of the Mean*.

The heart of the Confucian system, which served the patriarchal state so well for more than two thousand years, is found in the doctrine of relationships and correlative duties: those pertaining to sovereign and subject, father and son,

[16] *Ibid.*, pp. 33 ff., 99, 229.

husband and wife, elder brother and younger brother, friend and friend. The necessity of each dutifully performing his obligations to others is stressed. Confucius prized propriety, morality, and social order—all of which come from obedience to Heaven, the Supreme Ruler, the ultimate principle. Obedience to kings, the sons of Heaven, is a necessary corollary of this celestial order.[17] "What Heaven has conferred is called Nature: an accordance with this nature is called the path of duty: the regulation of this path is called instruction." Herein, it seems, past tradition becomes a god, before whom all must bow. The potentialities of this system of thought in rendering society relatively unchanging is clear. But, if Confucianism was unprogressive, it offered a practical rule to go by. A certain reasonableness, certainly, is to be found in the instructions of *Li Ki*: "What a man dislikes in his superiors, let him not display in his treatment of his inferiors; and what he dislikes in his inferiors, let him not display in his service of his superiors. . . ."[18]

### INTELLECTUAL CULTURE

Though the statement that "public schools were established" in the reign of Ti K'u (2432–2363 B.C.) cannot be accepted uncritically,[19] some sort of formal instruction must have developed after the invention of writing, which archaeological discoveries show was in existence prior to the Chou dynasty (1122 B.C.). Such instruction was probably in private families rather than in schools. Private schools seem to have been the rule in the time of Confucius. From 221 to 618 A.D. education declined, but there was no cessation of educational activity.[20] From the beginning of the T'ang period (620 A.D.) formal education was zealously promoted; with minor exceptions it continued to conform to much the same pattern till the end of the imperial régime.

The purpose of formal education was to serve the social order. Governments could be overthrown and new ones established by force; but only by training efficient loyal administrators could any system be long maintained. The old maxim, "Employ the able and promote the worthy," expressed the ideal of a government whose greatest officials and statesmen were also literary and philosophical contributors to China's intellectual heritage. This philosophy of education, judging by the conversations of Wu Ti with Tung Chung Shu, at the time when Confucian principles were first coming into official grace, animated those who aspired to a place in governmental services. The philosopher

[17] Hirth: *op. cit.*, pp. 79 ff.
[18] Müller: *op. cit.*, XXVIII, 419. From *The Sacred Books of the East*, edited by F. M. Müller (The Clarendon Press).
[19] Biot: *Essai sur l'Histoire de l'Instruction Publique en Chine*, pp. 11 ff.; Hirth: *op. cit.*, p. 25; Shryock: *op. cit.*, pp. 65 ff.; Kuo: *Chinese System of Public Education*, pp. 7 ff.
[20] Biot: *op. cit.*, pp. 209 ff.

instructed Emperor Wu as to how he might rehabilitate the state; the way which he advised was the Confucian way, based on knowledge of the *Spring and Autumn Annals. Tao* is the way; by it men succeed; one must know *Tao. Tao* does not apply itself; good government exists in proportion as men come to know *Tao* and are able to apply it. "Education is needed," therefore, "for without education you cannot make the people upright. They are selfish and seek their own profit, as water seeks its level. You must educate them, even as you build a dam to stop the flow of water. If you establish education, evil will vanish; while if you abolish education, evil will grow, and even punishments will not prevent it; for the dam will be broken. . . ." [21] Good officials would promote education; and good education would make good officials. To reform government Wu must begin by creating schools and securing scholars. An imperial academy would attract scholars and provide means of their development. Examinations must be instituted "to select the best." Without "able officials," education will decline, and force will be the sole safeguard of order. Poverty, unemployment, weakness, and disturbances of all kinds will come—"even the *Yin* and *Yang* will be confused"—all because of a "lack of educated officials." [22]

Sound education and good social order are rooted in a knowledge of things, according to *The Great Learning:* "Things have their root and their branches; affairs have their end and their beginning. To know what is first and what is last will lead near to what is taught in the Great Learning. The ancients who wished to illustrate illustrious virtue throughout the kingdom, first ordered well their states. Wishing to order well their states, they first regulated their families. Wishing to regulate their families, they first cultivated their persons. Wishing to cultivate their persons, they first rectified their hearts. Wishing to rectify their hearts, they first sought to be sincere in their thoughts. Wishing to be sincere in their thoughts, they first extended to the utmost their knowledge. The extension of knowledge is by the investigation of things. Things being investigated, their knowledge became complete. Their knowledge being complete, their thoughts were sincere. Their thoughts being sincere, their hearts were then rectified. Their hearts being rectified, their persons were cultivated. Their persons being cultivated, their families were regulated. Their families being regulated, their states were rightly governed. Their states being rightly governed, the whole kingdom was made tranquil and happy." [23]

Education, then, was the getting of knowledge; and knowledge led to virtue, that is, propriety. *Li Ki* recommended the ant as a model of continual diligence. An ideal education in the Chou period, it is said, consisted of six virtues, six

[21] Shryock: *op. cit.,* p. 52.
[22] *Ibid.,* p. 55.
[23] Müller: *op. cit.,* xxviii, 411 f. From *The Sacred Books of the East,* edited by F. M. Müller (The Clarendon Press).

good actions, and six arts. The virtues were "wisdom, benevolence, goodness, righteousness, loyalty, and harmony"; the actions were honoring parents, being friendly to brothers, cordial to relatives by marriage, neighborly, trustful, and sympathetic; and the arts were "rituals, music, archery, charioteering, writing, and mathematics." A liberal education was supposed to include "five kinds of ritual, five kinds of music, five ways of archery, five ways of directing a chariot, six kinds of writings, and nine operations of mathematics." [24] This formula for a liberal education was an ideal, clearly attainable only by an elite. Though selective in intent, and leading to the formation of an aristocracy of scholarship, it is said that persons were admitted without respect to birth or wealth to the schools set up by Wu Wang (1122–1116 B.C.), and that this democratic principle has been "characteristic of the system of education and the subsequent promotion to high offices among the Chinese." [25] Since government schools were few, however, and much dependence was put on private institutions supported by parents, educational opportunity must have varied with the economic status of families. Democracy meant essentially that those who were able to prepare themselves, by whatever means, to take the public examinations, were permitted to do so; and, having passed them, they could expect preferment at the hands of government.

Nei Zeh, or The Pattern of the Family, describes the ideal training of "young gentlemen of good families." Education began early, as soon as the child could "take its own food." When able to speak, he was taught to speak "boldly and clearly." At six, he learned "numbers and the names of the cardinal points." At ten, the boy went to a master, learned the classes of characters, calculation, proper behavior of a youth, "polite" conversation, and reading the Tablets. At thirteen, he learned music, odes, and how to dance the ko. When full grown, he learned the hsiang, and was taught archery and chariot-driving. At twenty, he was "capped," learned various ceremonies, danced the ta hsia, and performed "filial and fraternal duties." At thirty, he married, continued his learning, and performed "the business proper to a man"; and at forty, he was "first appointed to office," promoted, if successful, at fifty, and retired at seventy.[26]

The content of formal education was drawn from classical books, to which Confucius had contributed. Beginning with the Trimetrical Classic, and passing to the Century of Surnames, the Millenary Classic, Odes for Children, Canons of Filial Duty, and The Juvenile Instructor, the youth memorized the literary treasures of the past. The second stage of learning was to master the Four Books (The Great Learning, Doctrine of the Mean, Confucian Analects,

[24] Biot: op. cit., p. 36; Kuo: op. cit., p. 18.
[25] Hirth: op. cit., p. 99.
[26] Müller: op. cit., xxvii, 476 ff.

and the works of Mencius) and the *Five Classics* (*Book of Changes, Book of History, Book of Odes, Book of Rites,* and the *Spring and Autumn Annals*). Having learned the forms and names of characters in these books, the student proceeded to translate or to read them with understanding. The final stage of education involved the writing of compositions on classical themes, such as would be set in the public examinations. The art of writing was an exacting part of his training, since passing an examination depended upon calligraphy as well as upon the excellence of the essay and fidelity to classical modes of thought and expression.

Many an ancient story inspired youth to study: Confucius had learned something from a mere child; one had tied his book to the horns of a cow; another had studied by the light of a glowworm; and two persons, though girls, had been "intelligent and well-informed." The bee and the silkworm offered excellent examples; "if men neglect to learn, they are inferior to insects." What could one do but study, when men of renown, and even the lowest forms of life, pointed the way?

Examinations, of several grades, conducted by the government in county and provincial seats and at the capital, opened the way to public office and prestige. They were long, physically and mentally exhausting, and were passed by relatively few; titles—"Flowering Talent," "Promoted Scholar," and "Fit for Office"—rewarded the successful. A fourth examination, which might be taken by those who succeeded in the third, gave admission to the *Han Lin Yuan,* the Imperial Academy.

Literary education, save in families that were well to do and liberal-minded, was not for girls; even those who studied literature did not enter the examinations. *The Pattern of the Family* states that, at ten, the girl should cease to leave the women's apartments; she should learn pleasing speech, be obedient, work with hemp and silk, make garments, and attend sacrifices. In short, she should "learn all woman's work." At fifteen she "assumed the hair-pin"; at twenty, if there was no occasion for delay, she married. For three months before marriage a young lady was taught "the virtue, the speech, the carriage, and the work of a wife." [27] Nothing is said of literary culture, yet this is the ideal education for better-class families. There were exceptions, however: Jen Hsiao "studied poetry and classical books"; Lady Tsao, though "ignorant and stupid," was instructed by the special favor of her father; and Wang Chieh Fu was "well versed in literature." Martin [28] calls attention to educated mothers, who educated their sons, but agrees that literary education of women was uncommon. Lower-class women (70 per cent or more of all) were not taught to read; but of the upper 30 per cent the most fortunate may have gone as far as

[27] Ibid., xxvii, 479; xxviii, 432.
[28] Lore of Cathay, pp. 284 ff.

the *Trimetrical Classic,* the *Century of Surnames,* and the *Four Classics for Girls.*[29] Among those who had a literary education, some eminent women appeared. But Giles analyzed over twenty-four thousand biographies and found that in most cases women were distinguished for piety, filial respect, self-sacrifice, heroic suffering, fidelity to husbands, wisdom and capability, beauty and religious character.[30] Only 26 were noted for music and painting; 250 were "remarkable" for some reason or other, one being "distinguished at football"; 7 were "witty and clever"; and 510 were eminent in literature. The percentage is not high, yet it would compare favorably with other countries of that age and later: for, if the phrase, "a woman without ability is normal," expressed the ancient Chinese view, it also characterized the outlook of most of mankind down to recent days.

### PHYSICAL CULTURE

Even a hasty glance at the pattern of Chinese education suffices to discover a dominant stress on intellectual excellence. To encourage application to bookish learning, Chinese masters (like others elsewhere) applied the rod, and held that "to teach without severity, shows a teacher's indolence." Failure to learn might be punished by "hundreds of blows"; and "bad scholars" were "not infrequently punished every day." [31] The bearing of physical play on school discipline was apparently unknown, or little appreciated.

Viewing this extremely bookish education which for centuries demanded every moment and all of a student's energy from early morning till dark, and left no time for any other exercise or employment, it is difficult to realize that in an earlier age physical sport constituted one part of a scholar's education. Chinese literati, in contrast to learned priesthoods of other Oriental societies, had formulated a philosophy, indeed, which recognized the union of physical, moral, aesthetic, and intellectual elements in an ideal liberal education. Hoh, relying on ancient sources, maintains that four or five thousand years ago physical education was not unknown; only in recent times it came to have slight importance. The disesteem of physical activities that developed in China is credited to the influence of religions, Taoism, Confucianism, and Buddhism, all of which stressed the quiet, studious, contemplative life. "Beware of strength," said Lao Tse in the *Tao Teh Ching,* for ". . . he who in arms is strong will not conquer. . . ." These views, of course, were not equally operative among all classes and at all times, but when they were reinforced by the influence of generations of scholars, brought up in the exclusively bookish tradition, fixed upon the schools in the Tang dynasty, and accentuated even

[29] Lewis: *Education of Girls in China,* p. 14.
[30] Giles: *op. cit.,* pp. 374 ff.
[31] Smith: *Village Life in China,* pp. 78 f.

more after the Ming, the effect was general and profound.[32] In the Confucian *Analects*, which declared that "the accomplished scholar is not a utensil," the bookish scholar might find some justification for his inability to do any kind of physical work; but the narrowness of his training and attainments is far removed from the liberal education of scholars of more ancient days. The present generation, of course, has witnessed the overthrow of the narrow, classical, literary pattern. In the new China there is a marked interest in physical culture, which can find justification in classical doctrines that had long been forgotten. A revolutionary placard in the city of Ch'ang Sha, in 1906, brought Confucian doctrine of physical and mental culture up to date: "The 'six arts' of which Confucius spoke are ceremonies, music, archery, charioteering, letters, and calculating. Archery and charioteering have reference to the art of war, and mean, in modern terms, that we must practise drilling and physical exercises." [33]

In the evolution of a people's life, physical culture of an informal sort is prior to formal intellectual training. In China, when writing had been introduced and formal education had become a necessity, certain physical skills were carried along with it. According to the account given by early Chinese writers, Kuo says that in the legendary age of Yao and Shun (2357–2206 B.C.) and under the dynasties of Hsia and Shang (*i.e.* to 1122 B.C.), education was chiefly moral and religious; that in the "institution known as Hsu," archery was taught; and that "literary education, as we understand it to-day, hardly existed at that early epoch. . . ." [34] Under the succeeding Chou dynasty (1122–249 B.C.) the curriculum, according to the *Book of Rites*, was fully developed and included the "six virtues," the "six praiseworthy actions," and the "six arts." Among the arts were "music, archery, [and] charioteering," all of which were closely associated. The practical significance of these for the feudal prince is obvious. The harmonious development of mind and body was to be accomplished by combining these with the other arts—"rites," writing, and mathematics [35]—all of which were covered by government examinations. Later, under the Han dynasty (206 B.C.–221 A.D.), the range of subjects required for civil service increased, but physical tests were still retained.

Under the T'ang, Sung, Mongol, and Ming dynasties (620–1644 A.D.), the "six arts" were still considered necessary to a complete education. The increments of literary learning became enormous, however, as succeeding generations of scholars added their commentaries; and with the increase of emphasis on mental attainments, physical culture receded into the background. Func-

[32] Hoh: *Physical Education in China*, pp. 33 ff., 228 f.
[33] Giles, L.: "The Awakening of China," *Nineteenth Century*, LX, 526.
[34] Kuo: *op. cit.*, pp. 10, 13.
[35] Biot: *op. cit.*, pp. 36 ff.; Kuo: *op. cit.*, p. 18.

tional specialization was growing. Special schools for military training were set up from time to time; and in literary institutions the tests in archery and horsemanship became nothing more than "essays on the archery and horsemanship of the ancients." [36] A persistent respect for the ancient liberal ideal is reflected in the efforts of certain rulers to maintain it, despite the difficulties and divergent tendencies of the new age. At the beginning of the Ming dynasty (1368 A.D.), when the old ideal had begun to be difficult of attainment, the founder of the dynasty, T'ai Tsu, "being a fond admirer of ancient usages," determined to add "military arts and mathematics" to the classical literary studies; but "this plan of combining military and literary studies . . . did not produce very good results, and in the course of a short time the college course as well as the tests of the examination system became once more purely literary in character. In 1392 he still wished to compel the students of the imperial college to practice archery, and refused to create colleges for the instruction of military men on the ground that he could conceive of only one system of education applicable to all men." [37]

The pattern of physical and general education, provided in ancient days for the sons of the best families, is portrayed in many Chinese classics. Music and dancing held a prominent place in the order of studies. *The Pattern of the Family* informs us that at thirteen the youth learned music and danced the *ko*; and when full-grown, he danced the *hsiang* and learned archery and charioteering.[38] At the time of King Wan (1258 B.C.), says the *Book of Rites*, in teaching the sons of the king and feudal princes and young men chosen for "aptitude for learning," the subjects of study varied with the seasons. "In spring and summer they were taught the use of the shield and spear; in autumn and winter that of the feather and flute. . . . The inferior directors of Music taught the use of the shield aided by the great assistants. The flute masters taught the use of the spear. . . .

"The Grand director of Music taught how to brandish the shield and axe. . . .

"At all examinations in the suburban schools, the rule was to select the best and mark out the most talented. . . . Those who had studied minor arts were encouraged and told to expect a second examination. . . .

"In the education of the crown princes adopted by the founders of the three dynasties the subjects were the rules of propriety and music. Music served to give the interior cultivation; the rules to give the external. The two, operating reciprocally within, had their outward manifestation, and the result was a

---

[36] Martin: *op. cit.*, pp. 313 f.
[37] Kuo: *op. cit.*, pp. 53 f.
[38] Müller: *op. cit.*, xxvii, 478.

peaceful serenity—reverence of inward feeling and mild elegance of manners." [39]

According to *The Royal Regulations*, compiled about 179–157 B.C., which describe the regulations relative to feudal nobles and officers at the time of Emperor Wan, great stress was laid on examinations. Students were classified, first, as "select scholars"; second, at the "great college," as "eminent scholars"; and third, as "complete scholars." Archery was stressed. In all the six districts of the royal domain, the aged men were all assembled at the school, and "on a good day archery was practised and places were given according to merit. . . . The Grand Minister of Instruction conducted thither the eminent scholars of the state and along with them superintended the business." [40]

Various references to the conduct of archery contests are found in the *I Li* and *She I*. Legge says of the latter that the author attempted "to show the attention paid to archery in ancient times," and how it was to serve moral and general educational purposes.[41] Neither extract nor epitome or paraphrase would convey the nicety of detail, the spirit, and philosophy of the archery contest, explained in the *She I*, or *The Meaning of the Ceremony of Archery*:

"Anciently it was the rule for the feudal lords, when they would practise archery, first to celebrate the ceremony of the Banquet, and for the Great officers and ordinary officers, when they would shoot, first to celebrate the ceremony of the Drinking in the country districts. . . .

"The archers, in advancing, retiring, and all their movements, were required to observe the rules. With minds correct, and straight carriage of the body, they were to hold their bows and arrows skilfully and firmly; and when they did so, they might be expected to hit the mark. In this way (from their archery) their characters could be seen.

"To regulate the discharging of the arrows, there was, in the case of the son of Heaven, the playing of the Zau-yu; in the case of the feudal lords, that of the Li-shau; in the case of the dignitaries, the Great officers, that of the Zhai-pin; and in the case of officers, that of the Zhai-fan.

"The Zau-yu is expressive of joy that every office is rightly filled; the Li-shau is expressive of the joy at audiences of the court; the Zhai-pin is expressive of the joy in observing the laws (which have been learned); and the Zhai-fan is expressive of the joy in being free from all failures in duty. Therefore the son of Heaven regulated his shooting by keeping in his mind the right feeling of all officers; a feudal prince, by keeping in his mind the times of his appearing

[39] *Ibid.*, xxvii, 345 ff. From *The Sacred Books of the East*, edited by F. M. Müller (The Clarendon Press).

[40] *Ibid.*, xxvii, 231. From *The Sacred Books of the East*, edited by F. M. Müller (The Clarendon Press).

[41] *Ibid.*, xxvii, 56 f.

before the son of Heaven; a dignitary, being a Great officer, by keeping in his mind the observing of the laws . . . ; and an officer, by keeping in his mind that he must not fail in the duties of his office.

"In this way, when they clearly understood the meaning of those regulating measures, and were thus able to avoid all failure in their services, they were successful in their undertakings, and their character and conduct were established. When their characters were established, no such evils as oppression and disorder occurred; and when their undertakings were successful, the states were tranquil and happy. Hence it is said that 'the archery served to show the completeness of the archer's virtue.'

"Therefore, anciently, the son of Heaven chose the feudal lords, the dignitaries who were Great officers, and the officers, from their skill in archery. Archery is specially the business of males, and there were added to it the embellishments of ceremonies and music. Hence among the things which may afford the most complete illustration of ceremonies and music, and the frequent performance of which may serve to establish virtue and good conduct, there is nothing equal to archery: and therefore the ancient kings paid much attention to it.

"Therefore, anciently, according to the royal institutes, the feudal princes annually presented the officers who had charge of their tribute to the son of Heaven, who made trial of them in the archery-hall. Those of them whose bodily carriage was in conformity with the rules, and whose shooting was in agreement with the music, and who hit the mark most frequently, were allowed to take part at the sacrifices. When his officers had frequently that privilege, their ruler was congratulated; if they frequently failed to obtain it, he was reprimanded. If a prince were frequently so congratulated, he received an increase to his territory; if he were frequently so reprimanded, part of his territory was taken from him. Hence came the saying, 'The archers shoot in the interest of their princes.' Thus, in the states, the rulers and their officers devoted themselves to archery, and the practice in connexion with it of the ceremonies and music. But when rulers and officers practise ceremonies and music, never has it been known that such practice led to their banishment or ruin.

"Hence it is said in the ode . . .

> 'Small officers and Great,
> Not one will keep away.
> See them before their prince,
> All in their full array.
> They feast, and then they shoot,
> Happy and praised to boot.'

The lines show how when rulers and their officers earnestly devoted themselves together to archery, and the practice in connexion with it of ceremonies and music, they were happy and got renown. It was on this account that the son of Heaven instituted the custom, and the feudal lords diligently attended to it. This was the way in which the son of Heaven cherished the princes, and had no need of weapons of war in dealing with them; it furnished also to the princes an instrument with which they trained themselves to rectitude.

"Once, when Confucius was conducting an archery meeting in a vegetable garden at Kio-hsiang, the lookers-on surrounded it like a wall. When the proceedings reached the point when a Master of the Horse should be appointed, he directed Zze Lu to take his bow and arrows, and go out to introduce those who wished to shoot, and to say, 'The general of a defeated army, the Great officer of a ruler-less state, and any one who has schemed to be the successor and heir of another, will not be allowed to enter, but the rest may all enter.' On this, one half went away, and the other half entered.

"After this . . . he further directed Kung Wang Khiu and Hsu Tien to raise the horns of liquor, and make proclamation. Then Kung Wang Khiu raised his horn, and said, 'Are the young and strong . . . observant of their filial and fraternal duties? Are the old and men of eighty . . . such as love propriety, not following licentious customs, and resolved to maintain their characters to death? If so, they may occupy the position of guests.' On this, one half of those who had entered went away, and the other half remained.

"Hsu Tien next raised his horn, and proclaimed, 'Are you fond of learning without being tired? Are you fond of the rules of propriety, and unswerving in your adherence to them? Do those of you who are eighty, ninety, or one hundred, expound the way of virtue without confusion or error? If so, you can occupy the position of visitors.' Thereupon hardly any remained.

"To shoot means to draw out to the end, and some say to lodge in the exact point. That drawing out to the end means every one unfolding his own idea; hence, with the mind even-balanced and the body correctly poised, the archer holds his bow and arrow skilfully and firmly. When he so holds them, he will hit the mark. Hence it is said, 'The father shoots at the father-mark; the son, at the son-mark; the ruler, at the ruler-mark; the subject, at the subject-mark.' Thus the archer shoots at the mark of his ideal self; and so the Great archery of the son of Heaven is called shooting at the mark of the feudal prince. 'Shooting at the mark of the feudal prince' was shooting to prove himself a prince. He who hit the mark was permitted to . . . retain his rank as a prince; he who did not hit the mark was not permitted to retain his rank as a prince.

"When the son of Heaven was about to sacrifice, the rule was that he should celebrate the archery at the pool, which name suggested the idea of selecting the officers by their shooting. After the archery at the pool came that in the archery hall. Those who hit the mark were permitted to take part in the sacrifice; and those who failed were not permitted to do so. The ruler of those who did not receive the permission was reprimanded, and had part of his territory taken from him. The ruler of those who were permitted was congratulated, and received an addition to his territory. The advancement appeared in the rank; the disapprobation, in the loss of territory.

"Hence, when a son is born, a bow of mulberry wood, and six arrows of the wild raspberry plant are placed on the left of the door, for the purpose of shooting at heaven, earth, and the four cardinal points. Heaven, earth, and the four points denote the spheres wherein the business of a man lies. The young man must first give his mind to what is to be his business, and then he may venture to receive emolument, that is, the provision for his food.

"Archery suggests to us the way of benevolence. The archer seeks to be correct in himself, and then discharges his arrow. If it miss the mark, he is not angry with the one who has surpassed himself, but turns round and seeks for the cause of failure in himself. . . .

"Confucius said, 'How difficult it is to shoot! How difficult it is to listen to the music! To shoot exactly in harmony with the note given by the music, and to shoot without missing the bull's-eye on the target:—it is only the archer of superior virtue who can do this! How shall a man of inferior character be able to hit the mark? It is said in the book of Poetry . . .

> ' "Now shoot," he says, "and show your skill."
> The other answers, "Shoot I will,
> And hit the mark;—and when you miss,
> Pray you the penal cup to kiss." ' " [42]

Dancing formed a regular part of the instruction of youth in families of the better class, the boy beginning to dance the ko at thirteen, the hsiang when full-grown, and the ta hsia when capped at twenty. An ancient bit of Chinese wisdom has it that "one may judge of a king by the state of dancing during his reign." [43] Dancing was of several kinds. Under the Chou dynasty six types were officially recognized: the "split-feather dance," for exorcism; the "whole-feather dance," for worship; the "regulating dance," to prevail against drought; the "tail dance," in which an oxtail was held by the dancers, symbolizing agriculture; the "shield dance," signifying defensive action; and the "battle-axe dance," symbolizing readiness for aggressive action. To these, a seventh was

[42] Ibid., xxviii, 446–53; cf. iii, 374 f., 399 ff. From The Sacred Books of the East, edited by F. M. Müller (The Clarendon Press).
[43] Ellis: The Dance of Life, p. 64.

added, the "humanity dance." [44] Under the Ming dynasty, the shield and the feather were three and a half feet long. Shields, feathers, and other accessories of the dances were not customary in the earliest times; instead, the performers danced bareheaded and with empty hands.

History runneth not back to the origin of these dances. In the early legendary period, however, it is said that they formed a part of religious ceremonies, the Emperor Yao having "ordained the Han Ch'ih dance, for the enjoyment of God." All six types of dances had religious aspects. Dancing involved steps, posturing, swaying and whirling the body, and movements of the arms. All movements were made in harmony with music and recitation. The following poem, as represented in the dance, involved one hundred and sixty movements:

> Thou didst establish the multitudes of our people,
> To go forth to work at sunrise,
> To go in to rest at sunset,
> To bore wells for drink,
> And to till fields for food.[45]

The religious, defensive, and aggressive motifs recall the character of dances in many primitive societies, and bear witness to the tenacity of human thought and feeling which causes customs to persist long after original incentives have disappeared. What was once thought to exert a controlling influence on man and his environment, or on the spirits which animated it, is afterwards perpetuated as pure symbolism. But though their ancient dances recall the primitive, it is clear that the Chinese had taken a step which distinguished their culture from that of primitive folk. They had created a philosophy of dancing, and given it written expression.

The philosophy of the dance is united with that of music. The rhythms and steps are for the benefit, enjoyment, and cultivation of the body; the tones of music, the modulations of voice and instruments, are for the harmony of soul. The significance of the one is outer; of the other, inner. Each influences the other. According to Yo Ki, "All modulations of the voice arise from the mind, and the various affections of the mind are produced by things external to it. The affections thus produced are manifested in the sounds that are uttered. . . . The combination of those modulated sounds, so as to give pleasure, and the direction in harmony with them of the shields and axes, and of the plumes and ox-tails, constitutes what we call music." [46]

[44] Giles, H. A.: op. cit., p. 121.
[45] Ibid., p. 123.
[46] Müller: op. cit., xxviii, 92. From The Sacred Books of the East, edited by F. M. Müller (The Clarendon Press).

The power of music and ceremonies was recognized by ancient kings, who therefore established them in order to perfect government. According to *Yo Ki,* ancient kings instituted ". . . ceremonies to direct men's aims aright; music to give harmony to their voices; laws to unify their conduct; and punishments to guard against their tendencies to evil. The end to which ceremonies, music, punishments, and laws conduct is one; they are the instruments by which the minds of the people are assimilated, and good order in government is made to appear." [47]

A pantomimic dance (wu) is thus explained by Confucius to Pin Mau Kia: "Music is a representation of accomplished facts. The pantomimes stand with their shields, each erect and firm as a hill, representing the attitude of king Wu. The violent movements of the arms and fierce stamping represent the enthusiasm of Thai Kung. The kneeling of all at the conclusion of the performance represents the government of peace, instituted by the dukes of Kau and Shao.

"Moreover, the pantomimes in the first movement proceed towards the north to imitate the marching of king Wu against Shang; in the second, they show the extinction of Shang; in the third, they show the return march to the south; in the fourth, they show the laying out of the Southern states; in the fifth, they show how . . . Kau and Shao were severally put in charge of the states on the left and right; in the sixth, they again unite at the point of starting to offer their homage to the son of Heaven. Two men, one on each side of the performers, excite them with bells, and four times they stop and strike and thrust, showing the great awe with which king Wu inspired the Middle states. Their advancing with these men on each side shows his eagerness to complete his helpful undertaking. The performers standing long together show how he waited for the arrival of the princes." [48]

An individualistic turn to the philosophy of music is given by the author of *Yo Ki. Yi,* a music master, being asked what kind of music was appropriate to a particular man, replied that he was "but a poor musician" and could not tell what was appropriate to particular individuals; but he was willing to say what types of music were appropriate to certain types of men, and would leave the questioner to select that type which was suitable to his character. "The generous and calm, the mild and correct, should sing the Sung; the magnanimous and calm, and those of wide penetration and sincere, the Ta Ya . . . ; the courteous and self-restraining, the lovers of the rules of propriety, the Hsiao Ya . . . ; the correct, upright, and calm, the discriminating and humble, the Fang . . . ; the determinedly upright, but yet gentle and loving, the Shang;

[47] *Ibid.,* xxviii, 93. From *The Sacred Books of the East,* edited by F. M. Müller (The Clarendon Press).

[48] *Ibid.,* xxviii, 122 f. From *The Sacred Books of the East,* edited by F. M. Müller (The Clarendon Press).

and the mild and honest, but yet capable of decision, the Khi. The object of this singing is for one to make himself right, and then to display his virtue. When he has thus put himself in a condition to act, Heaven and Earth respond to him, the four seasons revolve in harmony with him, the stars and constellations observe their proper laws, and all things are nourished and thrive." [49] Having recognized the significance of music, says the author of Yo Ki, the kings established music schools of different grades for the learners. The Yueh Ling—proceedings of the government for different months—specified a particular month when "orders are given to the chief director of Music to enter the college, and practise the dances with his pupils," there being dances of war and dances of peace.[50]

In the time of Yung Ming (485 A.D.) dancing was decreed in honor of Confucius; it may have existed earlier. In any case the Confucian cult had been recognized long before that; and according to tradition, dancing had been a part of ceremonials since 2255 B.C. Military dances were incorporated in the Confucian rites in 650 A.D. by Chen Kuan. Till relatively recent times ceremonial civil and military dances were still performed. In the civil dance, a long feather was carried in one hand and a stick in the other. In the military, the shield and axe were carried. The sacrificial Confucian hymn begins:

> Great is Confucius!
> He perceives things and knows them before the time;
> He is in the same order with Heaven and Earth;
> The teacher of ten thousand ages.
>
> .    .    .
>
> I think of thy bright virtue.
> The jade music ends.
> The music of metal is first heard;
> Of living men there was none like him;
> Truly his teaching is in all respects complete.

Thus ends the song of sacrifice:

> The Fu and Yi mountains are very high;
> The Chu and the Ssu spread their waters far;
> So thy beautiful acts extend their influence above and around,
> Causing benefits without end.
> Now has been seen the glory of the sacrifice;
> The sacrifice has been made to appear great and beautiful.
> He renovates the thousands of our people;
> He fosters our schools and halls for instruction.

[49] Ibid., XXVIII, 129 f. From The Sacred Books of the East, edited by F. M. Müller (The Clarendon Press).
[50] Ibid., XXVII, 249, 255 f.

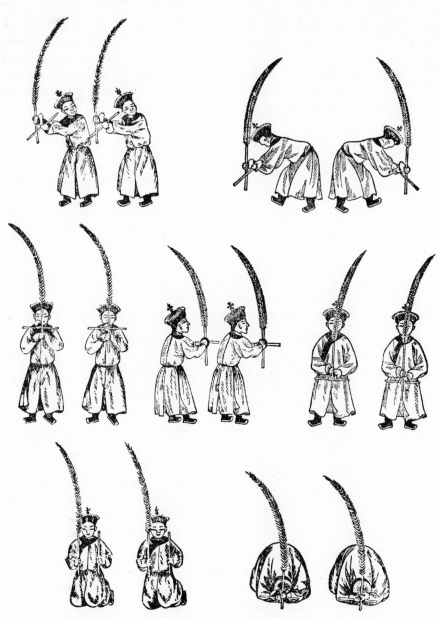

CHINESE RITUAL DANCE
(J. A. Van Aalst, *Chinese Music*, p. 32)

The hymn is composed of six strophes. The first marks the reception of the Spirit; the last, escorting the Spirit back. Intervening strophes mark the presentation of sacrificial viands and their removal. From the second to the fourth the dancers go through their movements. No movement marks the first and the last two strophes.[51]

Besides official ceremonial dances, cultivated for purposes of state, there were numerous kinds of rhythmic performances at private banquets and other special occasions. Men danced; women danced; at times, both danced together. There were paid·dancers and others who danced simply for pleasure. Some danced, apparently, just to astound the onlookers. It is said that a "high official" once danced before the emperor and finished by "standing on his hands and waggling his head about in a funny way." The emperor was amused, but a dignified statesman regretted such "sweeping the ground with the Five Classics." It is a far cry from the exalted philosophy of music and movement to these purely exhibitional dances, designed to astound and amuse the lordly master. There are always some discrepancies, naturally, between theory and practice. The philosophy was an expression of the noblest in dancing; but practice included the vulgar as well as the best. It was said that Madam Ta Ki, consort of Chou Sin (1154 B.C.), was lustful and cruel. The "most licentious songs were composed for her amusement, and the vilest dances exhibited." [52] Dancing and drunken carouse frequently went hand in hand at private banquets, where the dance was farthest removed from that high station which ritualists had sought to assign to it.[53]

So great was the prestige of dancing, so important was it as a criterion in judging of men, that in ancient feudal society it appears to have been thought strange, indeed a matter for complaint and suspicion, if a person of noble station refused to dance, or danced badly. The Prince of Chang Sha, for example, once danced before the Emperor at his birthday party. Being awkward and making an unsatisfactory, slight salutation to his superior, the prince was asked sternly what it meant. To this he gave answer in a witty excuse, "My fief is a very small one; [and] there is no room in it to turn round." This humorous explanation presumably let the prince out of the difficulty. For Akuteng, a Tartar prince, who refused to·dance before the last ruler of the Liao dynasty, it came near being more serious, for the Emperor said to his Privy Councillor: "At the banquet the other day, Akuteng was a little too haughty, and strange in his manner. Work up some complaint about frontier business, and take off his head; otherwise he will be giving trouble." [54]

51 Van Aalst: *Chinese Music*, pp. 31 ff.
52 Hirth: *op. cit.*, pp. 56 f.
53 Giles, H. A.: *op. cit.*, p. 127.
54 *Ibid.*, pp. 128 f.

The teaching of dancing continued long to be a part of the instruction of the scholar-official and of the nobility. Masters of dancing and music were held in high esteem. The decline, however, of the ideal of liberal education, which combined mental and physical excellence, meant inevitably that dancing would cease to be a part of the scholar's training. The heavy stress on extensive, formal, literary training, which was requisite for success in the public examinations, left no place for the balanced education of mind and body that ancient philosophy had extolled. The comments of observers at the beginning of the present century suggest that, though ancient dances were still performed occasionally, the youth who went through their evolutions showed a lack of training. Hoh observes that the "beautiful ideal of the dancing of ancient days has absolutely disappeared." Only at the birthday of Confucius can one "get a glimpse of the beautiful sentiment that belonged to ancient dancing." [55]

The literary works of the Chinese contain many references to the chase; they show that it was a means to secure food, a preparation for war, a pastime in intervals of leisure, a measure to safeguard crops, and was also regarded as an act of reverence. As in other matters of importance, the beginning of hunting was ascribed to great men. Fu Hi (2852 B.C.), said to have been the first emperor, was credited with teaching his people to hunt and fish. Hunting was a duty, but men of fifty, according to Li Ki, were not compelled to go on such expeditions.[56] A passage from Li Ki indicates the time, the purpose, and the observances of the chase, and also encourages a certain sympathetic concern for the order of nature:

"When the son of Heaven and the princes had no special business in hand, they had three huntings in the year. The first object in them was to supply the sacrificial dishes with dried flesh; the second, to provide for guests and visitors; and the third, to supply the ruler's kitchen.

"Not to hunt when there was no special business in the way was deemed an act of irreverence. To hunt without observing the rules . . . was deemed cruelty to the creatures of Heaven.

"The son of Heaven did not entirely surround the hunting ground; and a feudal prince did not take a . . . herd by surprise. When the son of Heaven had done killing, his large flag was lowered; and when the princes had done, their smaller flag. When the Great officers had done, the auxiliary carriages were stopped; and after this, the common people fell a hunting for themselves.

"When the otter sacrificed its fish, the foresters entered the meres and dams. When the wolf sacrificed its prey, the hunting commenced. When the dove

[55] Hoh: op. cit., pp. 32 f.
[56] Müller: op. cit., xxviii, 230; Hirth: op. cit., p. 9; cf. Lamb: Genghis Khan, chap. 17.

changed into a hawk, they set their nets, large and small. When the plants and trees began to drop their leaves, they entered the hills and forests with the axe. Until the insects had all withdrawn into their burrows, they did not fire the fields. They did not take fawns nor eggs. They did not kill pregnant animals, nor those which had not attained to their full growth. They did not throw down nests." [57]

The equipment of hunters, as well as a definite statement of purpose, makes clear the connection of hunting and war. The *Yueh Ling* designated a certain month as the time when "the son of Heaven, by means of hunting, . . ." taught "how to use the five weapons of war, and the rules for the management of horses." Subsequently "orders are given to the charioteers and the seven classes of grooms to see to the yoking of the several teams, to set up in the carriages the flags and various banners, to assign the carriages according to the rank of those who were to occupy them. . . . The Minister of Instruction, with his baton stuck in his girdle, addresses all before him with his face to the north. Then the son of Heaven, in his martial ornaments, with his bow in one hand, and the arrows under the armpit of the other, proceeds to hunt." As in Babylonia and Egypt, it was customary to perform some religious ceremony, "the superintendent of Sacrifices" being ordered "to offer some of the captured game to the spirits of the four quarters." [58]

The *Doctrine of the Mean* shows that Confucianism recognized the mean between two extremes as the way of virtue. The doctrine applied to hunting as well as other activities. Not to hunt was an evil; to lust after hunting, likewise. King Wan was noted for his avoidance of "excess in his excursions or his hunting." He enjoyed his throne for fifty years and his successors were advised to imitate his avoidance of excess.[59] Thai Khang, however, was noted for idleness, dissipation, and long hunting expeditions. "He went out to hunt beyond the Lo, and a hundred days elapsed without his returning." The people were discontented and, with the Prince of Khiung, resisted his return; and the mother of Thai Khang and his five brothers, hearing the discontent which arose against him, related the "Cautions" against excess:

> It was the lesson of our great ancestors:—
> The people should be cherished,
> And not looked down upon.

· · ·

[57] Müller: *op. cit.*, xxvii, 220 f.; cf. 106, 426. From *The Sacred Books of the East*, edited by F. M. Müller (The Clarendon Press).
[58] *Ibid.*, xxvii, 294 f. From *The Sacred Books of the East*, edited by F. M. Müller (The Clarendon Press).
[59] *Ibid.*, iii, 203.

It is in the Lessons:—
When the palace is a wild of lust,
And the country is a wild for hunting. . . .[60]

Elsewhere, a couplet from the *Li Ki* issues a warning:

He who loves hunting and women,
Brings his state to ruin.[61]

Numerous examples might be given of those who were virtuous in restraint; and of those, on the other hand, who erred by excess in hunting. T'ai K'ang (2188 B.C.) gave himself to the chase and other pleasures; and, had he not been the grandson of the great Yu, it is said, his subjects would have revolted against him. Like unto him was Hou I, who was murdered when he returned from a long hunt. Ch'ong T'ang (1766 B.C.), however, was noted for benevolence to men and animals, and was credited with the institution of good sportsmanship and proper regulations in hunting.[62] Confucius, it is said, would not shoot a sitting bird.

Among the objects of the chase were the wild goose or duck, boar, deer, wild ox, wolf, fox, and hare. Nets, dogs, and bows and arrows were used in hunting. On the "great hunts" of the chiefs, nets were fixed to the ground by stakes, and beaters drove the animals into them. Fires, too, were sometimes set, so as to drive animals to certain spots, that they might be shot easily.[63] One of the odes of Ch'ing depicts the daring of Shuh at the "grand chase," and also shows something of the accouterments employed by men of importance:

Shuh has gone hunting,
Mounted in his chariot and four.
The reins are in his grasp like ribbons,
While the two outside horses move [with regular steps] as dancers do.
Shuh is at the marshy ground;—
The fire flames out all at once,
And with bared arms he seizes a tiger,
And presents it before the duke.
O Shuh, try not [such sport] again;
Beware of getting hurt.[64]

---

[60] *Ibid.*, III, 78 f. From *The Sacred Books of the East*, edited by F. M. Müller (The Clarendon Press).
[61] *Ibid.*, XXVII, 433.
[62] Hirth: *op. cit.*, pp. 39, 42, 47.
[63] Legge: *Chinese Classics*, IV, Pt. I, Prolegomena, 148.
[64] *Ibid.*, IV, Pt. I, 129.

Hunting, in Biot's phrase, is the "image of war" and serves, in part, as a preparation for war. It is a common Western view that the Chinese were wholly pacific. The fact is, however, that their early history was marked by many clashes between feudal princes. Whether the Chinese have greater physical vitality, or less, than other peoples,[65] may be left to others to debate; but it is certain that they have survived many disasters, wars, pestilences, and barbarous slaughters. It would be possible to compile volumes of "heroic traditions" about "excellent archers" and the barbarities of war, in which strength, skill, and savage impulse triumphed over the higher, if less frequently extolled, faculties of man. In legendary days, before Yao and Shun, training for hunting and war, which alternately claimed their attention, began at an early age: "From early childhood they were taught to ride on sheep, to draw the bow and shoot birds and rats; when half grown they would shoot foxes and hares as game for food. Having grown to become soldiers, they would thus become excellent archers, when they were all supplied with armors on horseback. In easy times they would follow their cattle and live on the chase, but in times of trouble every man was trained to fight in battle and ready to make raids on other lands. This was their natural disposition. For distant fight their weapon was the bow and arrow; for close fight they used swords and small spears." [66] Ho, the father of Confucius, we are told, was "a soldier of great prowess and daring bravery," a veritable Samson, famed for having caught and held a falling portcullis while his companions were making their escape. More awe-inspiring to his enemies, perhaps, was Hsi Wang, credited at one time with the destruction of 30,000 literati and 600,000 other inhabitants of a city; and on another occasion, with the slaughter of 400,000 women who belonged to his army camp. Douglas reminds us that the Oriental delights in round numbers. It is a common human trait. Hence appropriate allowance may be made for exaggeration in respect to Hsi Wang's exploits.[67]

Passing from the days of primitive legends, when "every man was trained to fight" in the field, systematic preparation for war developed. The Pi Yung, an institution credited by some to the Chou dynasty, was, according to certain authorities, "merely a field of military exercise"—the Campus Martius of China.[68] Military examinations and degrees were established by decree in 702 A.D. Those who passed were classified as Ming Ching and Chin Shih. In the eleventh century, a military school was founded and staffed with instructors. Kao Tsung, in the next century, established competitive examinations in arch-

[65] Smith: *Chinese Characteristics*, pp. 144 ff.
[66] Hirth: *op. cit.*, p. 168.
[67] *Ibid.*, p. 229; Douglas: *op. cit.*, pp. 102 f.
[68] Biot: *op. cit.*, pp. 37 ff.; Shryock: *op. cit.*, p. 67; Kuo: *op. cit.*, p. 16.

ery, and "sanctioned" a military school in the capital. A little later military degrees were instituted in the army on the frontiers. Under the Ming dynasty, the military examinations, which had been "regarded as useless" by the Mongols, were re-established; they were conducted under "the high deputies of the ministry of war," but were not held "with much regularity" until 1506.[69]

So important in early feudal society was the business of war and ability to use its instruments, that the bow and arrow were regarded as symbols of power. A gift of these weapons to a prince by his sovereign "invested him with the power of punishing throughout the states within his jurisdiction all who were disobedient to the royal commands. . . ." Such a present was considered "a tribute to the merit of the receiver." [70] *Shu King*, one of the most ancient Chinese books, makes clear that military punishment of a feudal lord by the sovereign is simply the execution of "the punishment appointed by Heaven." The preparation for the battle, the advice, encouragement, and threats of the king to his followers, are described in a supposedly contemporary record. From it one may infer the types of training which were necessary for the army about the time of Khi, the son of Yu (2197–2189 B.C.): "If you, the archers on the left, do not do your work on the left, it will be a disregard of my orders. If you, the spearmen on the right, do not do your work on the right, it will be a disregard of my orders. If you, charioteers, do not observe the rules for the management of your horses, it will be a disregard of my orders. You who obey my orders, shall be rewarded before . . . my ancestors, and you who disobey my orders, shall be put to death before the altar of the spirits of the land, and I will also put to death your children." [71]

In *The Book of Poetry*, which contains contributions from 1766 B.C. to 586 B.C., one finds a laudatory description of the equipment of the prince of Lu, "unwaning, unfallen, unshaken, undisturbed," who will extend "the limits of the east, even the states along the sea." To him the tribes of Hwai will offer alliance, and all will offer allegiance: "Our prince's chariots are a thousand, and in each are the two spears with their vermilion tassels, and the two bows with their green bands. His footmen are thirty thousand, with shells on vermilion strings adorning their helmets. So numerous are his ardent followers, to deal with the tribes of the west and north, and to punish those of King and Shu . . . that none of them will dare to withstand us." [72]

*The Royal Regulations*, compiled about 179–157 B.C., give a glimpse of the

[69] Kuo: op. cit., pp. 44 f., 51, 56.
[70] Müller: op. cit., III, 267. From *The Sacred Books of the East*, edited by F. M. Müller (The Clarendon Press).
[71] Ibid., III, 76 f. From *The Sacred Books of the East*, edited by F. M. Müller (The Clarendon Press).
[72] Ibid., III, 344 f. From *The Sacred Books of the East*, edited by F. M. Müller (The Clarendon Press).

preparation of the scholar-soldier for service in war. "If any expedition of war were contemplated, orders were given to the Grand Minister of Instruction to teach the scholars the management of the chariot and the wearing of the coat of mail.

"In the case of all who professed any particular art, respect was had to their strength. If they were to go to a distant quarter, they had to display their arms and legs, and their skill in archery and charioteering was tested. All who professed particular arts for the service of their superiors, such as prayer-makers, writers, archers, carriage-drivers, doctors, diviners, and artisans . . . were not allowed to practise any other thing, or to change their offices. . . ." [73]

Biot's paper (1843) on the "Manners of the Ancient Chinese according to the She King," describes the make-up and conduct of a Chinese military force under the Chou dynasty:

"The principal element of a Chinese army was the chariot drawn by two or by four horses. It carried 3 mailed warriors, the officer to whom it belonged being in the middle. He had on his right his esquire, who passed to him his arms; and on his left the charioteer. A troop of soldiers followed the chariot to protect it. The term chariot was then a collective name like lance in our middle ages. The Li Ki reckons for every chariot 3 mailed warriors, 25 footmen in front and at the sides to guide the horses and the chariot, and 72 light-armed foot-soldiers following. . . . The number in the official list was never complete.

"The sovereign never marches without a guard of 2,500 men, called sze. Every dignitary or great officer had an escort of 500 men called leu. To employ our military terms, sze was a regiment and leu a battalion. Six sze, or 15,000 men, formed an ordinary army. They distinguished the soldiers on the left wing and the right, according to the division long used in the marching and encampments of the Tartar hordes. An army was divided into three troops. . . . The chief of each corps had his place in the middle of it.

"The chariot of the sovereign, or of the commander-in-chief, had four or six horses, yoked abreast. When there were four horses, which was the ordinary number, two of them were yoked to the pole, and two to the transverse bar of the chariot. The horses were covered with mail, or protected at the sides by bucklers. Those of the commanders had golden bits, with a small bell at each side of the bit. The reins were richly adorned and led through rings of leather on the backs of the horses. The sides of the chariots were covered with boards as a defense against the arrows of the enemy. They were adorned in the inside with mats of bamboo, or embroidered carpets. The axle-trees of the chariots of the chiefs were wrapped round with green silk, or with leather, probably to

[73] Ibid., xxvii, 18, 235. From The Sacred Books of the East, edited by F. M. Müller (The Clarendon Press).

strengthen them. The pole was also covered with leather, painted in 5 colors.

"The princes and regular warriors wore helmets. Those of the princes of the blood were adorned with a plume of red silk. The regular warriors had a sword, two lances (or spears) and two bows. The scabbards of the chiefs' swords were adorned with precious stones, or with other ornaments. The spears were of three kinds: maou, which was 4 meters long . . . and the kih, 16 cubits. These were set up in the war chariots. The javelin was 6 cubits 6 in. long, and was used by the foot-soldiers. All the lances had red pendants or streamers.

"Like the hunting bows, those used in war were of wood adorned with green silk. The bows of the chiefs had ornaments of ivory. There were also bows of horn, or strong as horn, which discharged several arrows at once. To preserve the bows, they were kept in cases of tiger skin, or of ordinary leather. Every case contained two bows, and they were closely fitted to bamboos, to hinder them from being warped by the damp. The bow-cases and the quivers were made of the skin of some marine animal called yu, which may have been a seal.

"The mailed warriors had bucklers, and battle-axes with handles of wood. The foot-soldiers were usually armed only with javelins and spears. . . . Besides the war-chariots, there followed the army carriages laden with sacks of baggage, and drawn by oxen. These sacks had one or two openings, and contained provisions. The chariots were unloaded, and arranged around the place of encampment. Then the feeble watched the baggage, while the strong advanced against the enemy.

"The expeditions against the indigenous tribes of the center, the west, and the north, were made in the 6th moon, the time of the year corresponding to the end of May and the beginning of June. They marched 30 le per day, about 11 kilometres, if we value the le at 1,800 cubits of 10 centimetres each. For a grand army of 300 chariots, 10 chariots formed the advanced guard.

"On the banners were figures of birds and of serpents. There were attached to them little bells and ribbons. On the royal standard there was the image of the sacred dragon. The princes of the blood, and secondary chiefs or viceroys had broad pennons or flags. One pennon, formed of an ox-tail upon a pole, was placed behind in the chariot of the chief of a squadron.

"The warriors wore colored cuisses, and buskins on their legs. . . . The commandant of a corps d'armée had the title K'ee Foo or of Shang Foo. Several odes designate the general by the name of 'the illustrious man'—meaning the Prince, the Dignitary.

"The drum gave the signal for departure, for attack, and for retreat. Large drums were covered with the skin of a fish called t'o. . . . Before the battle, the warriors excited one another by mock combats. They leaped, ran, and threatened one another with their weapons. . . ."

According to an ode, "King Wan causes the assault of a fortified city, and his soldiers ascend the wall by means of hooked ladders. He takes some prisoners and punishes them as rebels, proportioning their chastisement to the gravity of their offense. He causes one ear of his captives to be cut off, and in contenting himself with this punishment he passes for a just and humane man. In the State of Loo . . . the army, returned from an expedition, is assembled in the parade-ground. . . . They present to the prince the ears that have been cut off; they bring the captive chiefs in chains before the judge, by whom they are condemned by regular sentence. Like the tribes of America, the Chinese . . . made very few prisoners; they put the vanquished chiefs to death, and released the common soldiers after cutting off one of their ears, as a mark of dishonour, or that they might recognize them if they met with them again." [74]

It is a far cry from these harsh practices of warfare to the ideal principles of the *Doctrine of the Mean* and the pacifism of Taoism and Buddhism. "A state," says the *Tao Teh King*, "may be ruled by measures of correction; weapons of war may be used with crafty dexterity; but the kingdom is made one's own only by freedom from action and purpose. . . . I have three precious things which I prize and hold fast. The first is gentleness. . . . Gentleness is sure to be victorious even in battle, and firmly to maintain its ground. Heaven will save its possessor, by his very gentleness protecting him. . . . A master of the art of war has said, 'I do not dare to be the host to commence the war; I prefer to be the guest [i.e.] to act on the defensive. . . .' There is no calamity greater than lightly engaging in war. To do that is near losing the gentleness which is so precious. . . ."

> He who in Tao's wars has skill
> Assumes no martial port;
> He who fights with most good will
> To rage makes no resort.
> He who vanquishes yet still
> Keeps from his foes apart. . . .[75]

Some rulers professed Taoism, and most of them, after the Christian era, were followers of Confucius. It seems, however, in the light of history, that the doctrines did not go further in reducing war than did Christian doctrine in Christian states.

The feudal aristocracy of China patronized sports. As in ancient Rome and in western Europe during the Middle Ages, contests in swordsmanship were practiced. Even in the days of Huang Ti such combats are said to have been

---

[74] Legge: op. cit., IV, Pt. I, Prolegomena, 154 ff.
[75] Müller: op. cit., XXXIX, 100 f., 110 ff. From *The Sacred Books of the East*, edited by F. M. Müller (The Clarendon Press).

known, but authentic details are lacking. *Yueh Kien,* or "Delight in the Sword-Fight," tells us that King Wan of Kao delighted in a gladiatorial fight, staged for his benefit, in which "more than three thousand men, masters of the weapon, appeared as his guests . . . fighting together before him day and night." Of this he was never weary, and it continued for three years. His kingdom began to decay from neglect; other states had designs upon it; but still he did not improve his ways, until instructed by Kwang Zze that such behavior was unworthy of the son of Heaven.[76] Swordsmanship reached a high point between 618 and 1127 A.D., and many styles were developed. Thereafter it fell into gradual decay.

Wrestling is commonly ascribed by the Chinese to the earliest period of their athletic development—indeed to the days of Huang Ti. Under the Ch'in and the Han dynasties (255 B.C.–265 A.D.) wrestling was commonly employed in the army and became a popular exercise as well. This popularity increased from 265 to 618, and exhibition matches were arranged twice a year. As its rôle as entertainment grew, wrestling declined in importance, however, and became almost "unknown," till it was revived somewhat by Mongolian and Tibetan influence in North China.[77]

The gentle art of jiujitsu, made popular by the Japanese, seems to have had an earlier counterpart in China, from which the modern science may have developed.[78] Boxing, or "fisting and gripping," was practiced in China, and was "once a part of military training." Believed to have developed out of wrestling, the earliest "reliable" references to boxing run back to the seventh century B.C., when it was reputedly stressed by Kuan Chung, a minister of Duke Huan (685–645 B.C.). Only after 527 A.D., however, when Buddhidharma came to China, and used it as a daily exercise, was boxing extensively developed. In the tenth century, the manly art entered upon a golden age, and was made still more intricate by the expansion of Buddhidharma's "Eighteen Arahats" to 72, and then over 170, movements. Ten rules for training stressed systematic habits, self-discipline, vegetable diet, sexual restraint, and prohibition of stimulants. Under Mongol rule (1280–1368) boxing was extensively developed by monks rather than by townsmen. The Ming dynasty (1368–1644) saw the development of the "internal" system by Chang San Fung, which emphasized defensive and endurance tactics, in contrast to Buddhidharma's "external" system which had stressed the offensive. A noteworthy exception in the history of Chinese boxing is found in the fact that by the seventeenth century there were boxers even among the ablest literary scholars. Both internal and external

[76] *Ibid.,* XL, 186–91.
[77] Hoh: *op. cit.,* pp. 3, 12 f., 17, 30.
[78] Giles, H. A.: *op. cit.,* pp. 137 f.

systems are used to-day, and boxing is said to have been accepted as a good thing by all classes of people.[79]

The boxing of Buddhist monks of the Shao Lin monastery, developed, it is said, as a means of defense, seems to have had something in common with jiu-jitsu. Giles translates the term "boxing" "for convenience sake," but explains that it included "*la savate*, wrestling, quarterstaff, and even spear-play." As in boxing in Siam to-day, all strokes, grips, kicks, and punches were allowed! The *Topography* of Ningpo describes "the art of self-defence," which is twofold, as "exoteric and esoteric." "The exoteric style was that which was so greatly in vogue at Shao Lin, and consists chiefly in striking the adversary, and then by an acrobatic bound placing oneself out of reach. This style, however, often lays the striker open to serious risks. The esoteric style was that handed down by . . . Chang Sung Ch'i, and consists in opposing the adversary, but not letting fly unless actually compelled by stress of circumstances, and without giving any loophole of attack. This is the better style of the two." [80]

The skill of several "boxers" was widely heralded. Tales were told of the modest, unassuming Chang who, in the twelfth century, when the fame of monkish boxers had spread throughout the realm, was drawn into a bout with priests in a wine shop. Before agreeing to a contest, he made them certify that he would not be held responsible if any were killed. "This being settled, Chang folded his arms, and sat down on the ground. A priest then . . . came skipping around him, with a view to getting in a kick; Chang however slightly inclined his body and . . . let fly. The priest shot through the window like a ball, and fell so heavily outside that he was nearly killed." [81]

Similar to Chang, perhaps greater, was Pien Ch'eng, if the tale of his prowess may be trusted. That it was customary to embellish the feats of skill, as the chroniclers did those of kings and favorites, may be assumed. The following description conveys some idea of how "boxing" was regarded and how it was practiced in the sixteenth century. "Boxing seems to be an accomplishment of no real value in serious warfare. At the same time, inasmuch as a study of this art in its elementary stages involves flexibility of the arms and legs, together with activity of the body, I have included it for the sake of completeness. In boxing, the body must be quick to move, the hands quick to take advantage, and the legs lightly planted but firm, so as to advance or retire with effect. In the . . . flying leap of the leg lies the skill of the art; in turning the adversary upside down lies its ferocity; in planting a straight blow with the fist lies its

---

[79] Hoh: *op. cit.*, pp. 8, 13 f., 18 f., 30 f.; Liu: "Physical Education Movement in China," *Jour. Health and Phys. Educ.*, III, 62.
[80] Giles, H. A.: *op. cit.*, p. 135.
[81] *Ibid.*, p. 136.

rapidity; and in . . . deftly holding the adversary face upwards lies its gentle-ness." [82]

Giles refers to an early pastime known as "butting," said to have been prac-ticed two or three centuries before Christ. Some credit its introduction to 221 B.C. About 108 B.C., "a grand display of butting was organised under Imperial patronage." This sport, in which the participants covered their heads with ox heads and butted their antagonists like bulls, provided plenty of "smashed heads, broken arms" and "blood running in the palace yard." Nevertheless, em-perors themselves sometimes participated in it, as did Chuang Tsung.[83]

Football (ts'u chu), a kicking game played "with a round ball in a square field," was among the early sports of the Chinese, being attributed by some, like everything good, to the Yellow Emperor, Huang Ti, who used it to culti-vate alertness on the part of soldiers. Though such an early ascription may be open to doubt, football, it seems, had become a part of military preparation, or at any rate a sport of military men, in the third and fourth centuries B.C. A book on it is said to have existed at the time of the Han dynasty (206 B.C.–221 A.D.). An early historian declared that, in the third century B.C., Lin Tzu was a rich and powerful city, and that "there were none among its inhabitants who did not perform on the pipes, . . . fight cocks, race dogs, dice, or play foot-ball." Ts'u chu continued in popularity till the end of the Ming dynasty, but disappeared under the Manchus.

Numerous references to football are to be found. The ball was of leather and at first was stuffed, but later it was inflated so as to carry well when kicked. There were two or three types of play. In one game the ball was kicked over a net stretched between two poles, "several tens of feet in height"; in another, the object was to kick the ball through a hole, more than "a foot in diameter," in skins or cloth stretched between poles—something like football in Siam to-day, in which the ball is kicked through circular wreaths of flowers. A third game, which is somewhat obscure, seems more like the clever play of a juggler. In it the player performed remarkable feats with the ball, using "shoulders, back, breast, and belly, to take the place of his feet" and "making the ball run around his body without dropping." The score was counted by major and minor points, gained in various ways. An elaborate terminology, such as "ace," "deuce," and "tray," was used by the players. Seventy types of kicking were recognized; eleven conditions were indicated under which kicking was not per-mitted; and all play was forbidden in ten specified cases, for example, on windy days, after wine, and when the ground was wet.

Emperors and other famous personages played football. The sport seems to have been staged frequently for the amusement of monarchs, even when they

[82] Ibid., p. 137.
[83] Ibid., pp. 132 f.; Gardiner: Athletics of the Ancient World, p. 15.

FOOTBALL IN CHINA

(H. A. Giles, *Adversaria Sinica*, 1, 92)

did not participate. Near the end of the Eastern Han dynasty, the emperor gave himself up to archery, riding, and football to such an extent that literary studies were not attended to as before. Hsi Tsung, the *Mirror of History* says, was infamous for his constant devotion to football, cockfighting, and polo, and was not to be restrained. One of his ministers who reproved him for his pursuits, which savored so little of due propriety, was put to death. Wang Ch'i Sou, "a man of great talent," was skilled in the "nine branches of learning," and had a reputation in football that spread throughout the realm. "K'ung Kuei, a descendant of Confucius," is also credited with great skill in the game. Emperor Ch'eng Ti (32–6 B.C.) was fond of football and played it himself; when some of his officers suggested that it was "physically exhausting and also unsuitable to the Imperial dignity," he replied, "We like playing; and what one chooses to do is not exhausting." A philosophy of the value of football, and a parallel between playing the game and life, are found in the poetry of Li Yu, who lived about 50–130 A.D.:

> But there must be determination and coolness,
> Without the slightest irritation at failure . . .
> And if all this is necessary for football,
> How much more so for the business of life! [84]

Polo, a game developed, according to an eminent authority, "by Iranian tribes of Central Asia" near the beginning of the Christian era, is believed to have been introduced into China early in the seventh century. It is referred to definitely in 709 or 710 A.D., and was probably learned from the vanquished Tartars. Polo ponies were brought in from Khotan in 717.[85] The game was soon played by emperors, though the practice was disquieting to staid ministers. One of them gave his emperor three good reasons why he should not play, one being that it "is destructive of all ceremony between sovereign and subject." The emperor, it is said, sighed over the excellent memorial a long time. Again, a certain official was threatened with flogging if he did not cease teaching the emperor to play polo. Still they played. Everybody of importance, it is said, learned polo. In 1163, the emperor was so fond of the game that he ordered the grounds to be covered with "oiled cloth well sprinkled with sand" in case of rain. Under the T'ang dynasty, ladies learned to play polo on donkeys. A mortuary image of a mounted woman polo player, recovered from a Chinese grave, is in the Field Museum. In 881, the emperor compelled four candidates for official positions to play at polo, and gave the best post to the victor. The Kitan Tartars are said to have been the greatest polo players, but

---

[84] Giles, H. A.: *op. cit.*, pp. 93 f.; Hoh: *op. cit.*, pp. 4, 21, 30.
[85] Giles, H. A.: *op. cit.*, p. 94; Laufer: "The Early History of Polo," *Polo*, VII, 13 f.; Chait: "Relics of a Royal Sport in China," *Internat. Studio* (Nov., 1928), XCI, 33 ff.

POLO IN CHINA   *attributed to Ch'in Ying*
(Courtesy, *Asia*, June, 1923, XXIII, 431)

the Nu Chen Tartars upheld the custom that had been established. The following description gives some idea of the manner of play and the equipment:

"The players mounted . . . well-trained ponies, and each one was provided with a . . . club, of a good many feet in length, and shaped at one end like the crescent moon. They were then divided into two teams, the object of contention to both sides being a ball. Previously, at the south end of the ground, two poles had been set up, with boarding in between, in which a hole had been cut, having a net attached to it in the form of a bag. That side which could strike the ball into the bag, were the winners. Some say that the two teams were ranged on opposite sides of the ground, each with its own goal, and that victory was gained by driving the ball through the enemy's goal. The ball itself was as small as a man's fist, made of a light but hard wood, and painted red." [86]

Other active sports were popular in ancient China, at least at periods when military arts were of some importance. Tug-of-war exhibitions had considerable vogue under the Tang dynasty. Swinging was popular among ladies of the court. A variant form, "water swinging," in vogue in the Sung period, sometimes involved somersault dives from a boat. Other water sports are believed to be of early origin, because of necessity in naval warfare, but their early history is admittedly obscure. An author of the eleventh century says that boys

[86] Giles, H. A.: *op. cit.*, pp. 97 f.; Hoh: *op. cit.*, pp. 22 f.

of South China learned to tread water at seven, float at ten, and dive at fifteen years of age. Boating is traced back to the "Age of the Seven States," 481–221 B.C.[87]

A Chinese game, ch'ui wan, in some respects similar to golf, was played by soldiers under the Sung dynasty. Hui Tsung (1101–1126) is credited with being an enthusiast. Tees, holes marked by flags, balls of hardwood, and a club with bamboo shaft and a hardwood head, were necessary for playing. Any number might play. The rules covered such matters as choosing the order of hitting, positions and types of hitting, scoring, and the twenty-one penalties.[88]

The hilarious, manly sports of polo, football, and boxing, though indulged in by some emperors and others of the nobility in spite of official reproof and secret disapproval on the part of those who held to a staider tradition, are scarcely to be considered representative of Chinese physical culture. Nearer to its norm were the contests in archery, their best-loved achievement, in which shooting was joined with music, signifying the union of body and mind in perfect accomplishment. Archery, of course, was an approved part of military preparation. In the reign of T'ai Tsung (627–650) shooting from horseback was a regular part of a soldier's training, replacing the "archery ceremony" of the Chou period. Extraordinary skill was sought; shooting at a willow leaf became a popular test.[89]

For polite entertainment of one's guests the game of T'ou Hu, "pitch-pot," was highly esteemed. Rules of propriety were nicely prescribed for it, and the arrows were pitched while music played. From the description following, it is evident that behavior at the game was more important than winning:

"The host having bowed, and received the arrows for himself, advances to the space between the two pillars. He then retires, and returns to his station, motioning also to the guest to go to his mat for pitching. . . .

"The superintendent of the archery comes forward, and measures the distance of the pot from the mats, which should be a space of the length of two and a half arrows. He then returns to his station, sets forth the stand for the tallies, and with his face to the east, takes eight counters and stands up. He asks the guest to pitch, saying, 'When the arrow goes straight in, it is reckoned an entry. If you throw a second without waiting for your opponent to pitch, it is not reckoned.' The victor gives the vanquished a cup to drink; and when the cups of decision have been dispatched, the superintendent begs to set up what he calls 'a horse' for the victor. If he sets up one horse, then a second, and finally a third, he begs to congratulate the thrower on the number of his horses. He asks the host to pitch in the same way, and with the same words.

---

[87] Hoh: op. cit., pp. 24 ff.
[88] Ibid., pp. 27 f.
[89] Ibid., pp. 19 f.

PLAYING PITCH-POT   *a detail from* Ch'ing Ming, Spring Festival *on the* Yellow
River
(Courtesy, The Metropolitan Museum of Art, New York)

"He orders the cithern-players to strike up 'The Fox's Head,' with the same
interval between each repetition of the tune. . . .

"When the superintendent announces to them on the left and right that the
arrows are all used up, he requests them to pitch again. When an arrow enters,
he kneels, and puts down a counter. The partners of the guest are on the right,
and those of the host on the left.

"When they have done pitching, he takes up the counters, and says, 'They
have done pitching, both on the left and right; allow me to take the numbers.'
He then takes the numbers two by two, and leaves the single counters. After
this he takes the single counters, and gives the announcement, saying, 'Such
and such a side has the better by so many doubles, or naming the number of
the singles.' If they are equal, he says, 'Left and right are equal.'

"He then orders the cups to be filled, saying, 'Let the cup go round,' and
the cup-bearer of the successful side replies, 'Yes.' Those who have to drink all

kneel, and raising their cups with both hands, say, 'We receive what you give us to drink.' The victors also kneel and say, 'We beg respectfully to refresh you.'

"When this cup has gone round, according to rule, the superintendent asks leave to exhibit the 'horses' of the victorious side. Each 'horse' stands for so many counters. He who has only one 'horse' gives it to him who has two, to congratulate him on his superiority. . . .

"The number of the counters varies according to the place in which they kneel when playing the game. Each round is with 4 arrows. If the game be in the chamber, there are 5 sets of these; if in the hall, 7; if in the courtyard, 9. The counters are 1 cubit 2 inches long. The neck of the pot is 7 inches long; its belly, 5; and its mouth is 2½ inches in diameter. It contains a peck and 5 pints. It is filled with small beans, to prevent the arrows from leaping out. It is distant from the mats of the players, the length of 2½ arrows. The arrows are made of mulberry wood, or from the zizyphus, without the bark being removed.

"In Lu, the young people taking part in the game were admonished in these words, 'Do not be rude; do not be haughty; do not stand awry; do not talk about irrelevant matters; for those who stand awry, or speak about irrelevant matters, there is the regular penal cap.' " [90]

The ancient Chinese gave much attention to the subject of health, and the bearing of cleanliness and exercise upon it. To what extent this concern influenced practice is unknown; but among scholars and the devout, admonition to moderation in all things did not fall on deaf ears. In *Zu Hsing, The Conduct of the Scholar*, it is stated that the scholar "keeps his person free from stain, and continually bathes and refreshes his virtue." [91] An officer, serving the son of Heaven, "washed his hands five times a day" and combed his hair with a comb of wood or ivory; after bathing, he stepped from the tub onto a straw mat, washed his feet with hot water, and dried himself, using two towels.[92]

Health gymnastics were developed at an early date in China. The system of exercises termed *Kong Fu*, practiced about 500 A.D. by Buddhist monks and taught to others as a means to physical and spiritual health, was attributed by Tamo, its expositor, to the Yellow Emperor, Huang Ti, 2698 B.C. According to this doctrine, illnesses are due to internal stoppages and to the cessation of function of organs, which if taken in time, can be rectified by certain free exercises—sitting, kneeling, bending, lying, standing—all combined with proper prescribed respiratory training. Five types of breathing were associated with the

[90] Müller: *op. cit.*, xxviii, 397 ff. From *The Sacred Books of the East*, edited by F. M. Müller (The Clarendon Press). G. Montell gives many details in an article, "T'ou Hu—The Ancient Chinese Pitch-pot Game," *Ethnos* (1940), v, 70–83.
[91] Müller: *op. cit.*, xxviii, 407.
[92] *Ibid.*, xxviii, 5.

various forms of exercise in different positions. The similarity between Kong Fu, which is still followed by some in China, and the Swedish system is obvious. The assertion, however, that Ling borrowed his ideas from Kong Fu, through a French translation by Amiot, has been proved by Mehl-Wien to be unfounded.[93]

Since fish was an important article of food, fishing was a necessary form of labor. For many, it was also, doubtless, a source of recreation and enjoyment. Chinese literature abounds in references to fishing in many forms. Though fishing probably went back to earliest Chinese history, the first specific note of it is credited to 1122 B.C. The spear, hook, dredge, trap, line, rod, nets of many kinds, and boats were employed, and cormorants were trained to catch fish. Nets made of fine bamboo rods were seemingly in commonest use, but such wholesale methods were disapproved by some. Confucius is said to have fished with a line, but not with nets.[94] Chinese men of letters, at times, would stir the heart of Izaak Walton. One of the odes of Wei would lure him to the Ho:

> The waters of the Ho, wide and deep,
> Flow northwards in majestic course.
> The nets are dropt into them with a plashing sound,
> Among shoals of sturgeon, large and small. . . .[95]

As to hunting, it must be reckoned primarily a noble sport, though common folk must have hunted small birds and animals for food. A domestic ode portrays the wife seeking to rouse her drowsy husband to go afowling:

> Get up, husband, here's the day.
>
> .        .        .
>
> Shake off slumber, and prepare
> Ducks and geese to shoot and snare.
> All your darts and line may kill
> I will dress for you with skill.[96]

There appears to have been no systematic concern for the play and physical improvement of the masses of China. For them the exercise of labor left little leisure for recreation. Even in the late nineteenth century, it seemed to a Western observer that the children of the lower classes had relatively few games. The emphasis on propriety of behavior and a long-standing tradition of bookish education probably had much to do with restricting play activities.[97] Never-

---

[93] Bogeng: Geschichte des Sports, I, 119 ff.
[94] Legge: op. cit., IV, Pt. I, Prolegomena, 148 f.; Radcliffe: Fishing from the Earliest Times, pp. 449 ff.
[95] Legge: op. cit., IV, Pt. I, 96 f.
[96] Laurie: Historical Survey of Pre-Christian Education, p. 155.
[97] Smith: Village Life in China, pp. 243 ff.; Carus: Chinese Life and Customs, pp. 64 ff.

theless, in light of the recognized universal tendency to play, it is an error to generalize broadly on observations relative to the paucity of games in some localities. Hoh's listing shows that there were many common games.[98] Shuttle-cock, the national game, was of great antiquity. The bird was usually struck with the sole of the shoe, but might be played with the hand under certain circumstances. Flying kites, which were made to represent animals, birds, in-sects, men, serpents, ships, flower baskets, and the like, was a popular diver-sion, indulged in by young and old. Fighting kites (whose strings were sup-plied with bits of glass, so that one competitor might cut the string of another) and musical kites (equipped with metallic strings, so as to make music like an aeolian harp) were interesting variations, which show great ingenuity in de-velopment of the sport. A game of uncertain origin, similar to Western hand-ball, except that "dribbling" the ball any number of times was permitted be-fore striking it against the wall, was also played by Chinese children. The "eight graceful exercises," originated by Yo Fei (1102–1141) are also said to have been in use by many classes in China.[99]

A word may be added concerning the physical education of girls. In some families of the better sort girls were occasionally educated, but their training was pre-eminently that of propriety and literary and social graces rather than of the body. The slim, willow waist and the tiny foot, much admired, were scarcely compatible with vigorous physical life. Of all the manifold reasons that have been suggested for foot-binding, Giles held that the real one was sensual—to make the thighs large.[100] Whatever may have been the original source of a custom going back to the tenth century and probably long before that, it is evident that in certain respects women were weakened and made useless, except for ornamental and domestic purposes. So, at least, many Chi-nese came to think. A woman noted for ability in football; court ladies who played polo; and others who enjoyed the pleasures of swinging—these scarcely represent the general pattern of physical sports for women in old China. In-deed, it seems that apart from such exceptional cases, the physical exercise of girls came chiefly through dancing, which was, with music, a part of a polite education of accomplishments. Since the middle of the nineteenth century a new life of Chinese women has been coming into being; in the twentieth it has achieved a marked degree of maturity. In 1906, a revolutionary appeal in Hunan declared against the practice which compelled "200 million" women to be maimed, simply to be "nice" in appearance. The vigor of sentiment and the practical arguments of revolutionaries clash harshly, naturally, with the views of a feudal society in which women were highly regarded for decorative

[98] *Op. cit.*, chap. 3.
[99] Liu: *op. cit., loc. cit.*, III, 17 ff.
[100] Giles, H. A.: *op. cit.*, pp. 280 ff.

value. The "wasp-waisted," "pale-cheeked" woman is no longer admired. She has given way to the athletic type, better fitted to endure the storm and stress of China's new age.[101]

[101] Liu: *op. cit., loc. cit.*, III, 19 *ff.*

# 6

# IN THE INDUS VALLEY

Since 1922 a highly developed pre-Aryan civilization has been discovered, which compares favorably with that of the Nile and Mesopotamia. Mohenjo-Daro, on the Indus River, and Harappa, some four hundred miles distant, represent a culture, believed to have been general throughout the Sind and the Punjab; it may have extended into the valleys of the Jumna and the Ganges. These cities, which flourished five thousand years ago, appear to have had some intercourse with those in Mesopotamia.[1]

As in Egypt, Mesopotamia, and China, the ancient civilization of northern India was conditioned by the Indus River, which created a fertile valley conducive to the development of agriculture, and provided a ready means of transport. The river was at once a source of benefits and a menace to the city. Houses were built on firm foundations and terraces, which from time to time were raised to keep pace with the rising level of the plain, resulting from annual inundations. After an existence estimated at five hundred years, Mohenjo-Daro was abandoned, probably because of floods or the shifting of the river's bed—though other factors, pestilence and war, may have occasioned decline and removal.[2]

Whether the creators of Mohenjo-Daro were indigenous folk or came from elsewhere, is in doubt. That they were Vedic-Aryans has been suggested; that they may have derived from a common stock with Sumerians and proto-Elamites is another theory. Neither view is supported by anthropological or other evidence, says Marshall. Since few skeletal remains have been discovered, and these may have been slaves or prisoners, the answer to the question must wait upon further discoveries.[3]

[1] Marshall: *Mohenjo-Daro and the Indus Civilization*, I, 91 ff., 102 ff.

[2] *Ibid.*, I, 1, 6 f., 103; Mackay, E.: *The Indus Civilization*, pp. 15 f.; Mackay, D.: "Mohenjo-Daro and the Ancient Civilization of the Indus Valley," *Ann. Rep. Smithsonian Institution*, 1932, Pt. I, 434 f.

[3] Marshall: *op. cit.*, I, 42, 107; Mackay, E.: *op. cit.*, pp. 11 f.; Mackay, D.: *op. cit., loc. cit.*, pp. 436 f.

Though its authors are obscure, the culture of the Indus Valley proclaims its advancement in numerous ways. Mohenjo-Daro, which covered almost a square mile, implies a country able to produce food on a large scale, and also with adequately developed transport. Specimens of wheat and barley were found at Mohenjo-Daro. These, with melons, dates, pork, mutton, beef, poultry, turtles, tortoises, fresh and dried fish and shellfish, made up the diet, supplemented by milk—and perhaps also by many vegetables and fruits. Wild animals—such as the mongoose, shrew, black rat, several kinds of deer, Indian bison, rhinoceros, tiger, bear, monkey, and hare—were known, and some of them were used for food. Domesticated animals included the dog, sheep, zebu, buffalo, camel, and elephant—possibly also the pig and horse.[4]

The Indus civilization was marked by an extensive scene of industry. Cotton was used for clothing; spinning was practiced, apparently both in rich and poor families. As to the use of wool, there is some difference of opinion. Such metals as tin, lead, copper, bronze, silver, and gold were in use. Copper and bronze had largely superseded stone for various weapons, tools, and certain household utensils. Most household vessels, however, were of earthenware, made upon the wheel. Among the common domestic articles were spindle whorls, molds, dippers, ladles, flesh rubbers, needles, bodkins, leather-cutters, combs, razors, awls, knives, spoons, reamers, saws, adzes, axes, chisels, sickles, drinking cups, and dishes of many kinds. An object of chipped chert is believed to have served as a plowshare. The weapons of war and hunting included spears, daggers, axes, bows, arrows, maces, and slings; but there is no evidence of ·swords, shields, helmets, or greaves.[5]

Numerous bangles, earrings, bracelets, necklaces, anklets, girdles, and other articles testify to a love of personal adornment, and ingenuity in its manufacture. The art of the Indus is most characteristically represented by small square seal-amulets, evidently a common possession. Stone and terra cotta figurines of animals, chiefly children's playthings, are also plentiful; human representation is much less so. Most distinctive are a bronze dancing girl from Mohenjo-Daro and two statuettes found at Harappa. These last are excellent in design and execution. The bronze, though something like a caricature, is a spirited portrayal of a dancing nautch girl.[6]

Knowledge of the religion of the pre-Aryan folk is relatively limited, since no temple has been identified and no cemeteries unearthed. Other materials related to religion are not numerous. A number of figurines, however, are believed to be "effigies of the great Mother Goddess" or some local variant, whose worship is widespread and ancient in India. A male god, seated like a Yogi and

4 Marshall: op. cit., I, 27 ff.; Mackay, E.: op. cit., pp. 174, 188 f.
5 Marshall: op. cit., I, 29 ff., 35 ff.; II, chaps. 24–5; Mackay, E.: op. cit., pp. 121 ff., 173 f.
6 Marshall: op. cit., I, 43 ff.; III, Plate XCIV, 6–8; Mackay, E.: op. cit., pp. 106 ff., 161 ff.

surrounded by four beasts (rhinoceros, tiger, elephant, and buffalo) may represent a pre-Aryan prototype of the Siva of later date. The prominent featuring of animals, such as crocodiles, buffalos, tigers, and bulls on many small square seals, often associated with cult objects, prompts the thought that Indus gods were worshiped in animal forms. Marshall judges these elements of the pre-Aryan religion "so characteristically Indian as hardly to be distinguishable from still living Hinduism"—at least that part of it "which is bound up with animism and the cults of Siva and the Mother Goddess . . . still the two most potent forces in popular worship." [7]

Like the civilization itself, the language or languages must have been pre-Aryan. Since Dravidian culture was very widely spread over northern India, Dravidic was quite probably one of the tongues spoken. Nonalphabetic writing, similar to the pictographic scripts of Egypt, Mesopotamia, and China, was in use by the people of the Indus. This implies a significant step forward in education, the details of which can only be surmised. Though thus far undeciphered, 396 signs, chiefly seal inscriptions, have been distinguished. These are highly conventionalized and scarcely suggest the objects that may have been represented originally. Early *Brahmi* script is believed to have been derived from this pre-Aryan pictographic writing. No clay tablets have been found; presumably, writing was chiefly on leaves, bark, parchment, or other materials readily destroyed.[8]

The most remarkable features of this ancient Indus culture were its architecture, wells, baths, drainage systems, and public and private dust bins. There is evidence, too, that Mohenjo-Daro was built according to a plan.[9] Small houses (two rooms) as well as those of palatial size were built of burnt brick. Well-paved baths are found in private houses, both on ground and upper floors. The prevalence of well-constructed roomy houses, baths, wells, and excellent drainage systems suggests that "ordinary townspeople enjoyed . . . a degree of comfort and luxury unexampled in other parts of the then civilized world." Marshall believes that ". . . in no city of antiquity was so much attention paid to this matter of bathing as in Mohenjo-Daro." [10] The ubiquitous bathing facilities may point to a religious sanction supporting cleanliness. The Great Bath, most unique of all the structures unearthed, was 180 by 108 feet overall. Whether it was merely for pleasure or served a religious purpose is uncertain. While the latter is a probability, the Great Bath may have served the public much as did the bathing establishments of Rome. The tank itself, measuring approximately 39 by 23 feet, was excellently constructed. Its brick

[7] Marshall: *op. cit.*, I, vii, 49 ff., chap. 18, Plate XII, 17; Mackay, E.: *op. cit.*, chap. 3.
[8] Marshall: *op. cit.*, I, 39 ff.; II, chaps. 22–3.
[9] Mackay, E.: *op. cit.*, pp. 21 f.
[10] *Op. cit.*, I, vi, 75.

THE GREAT BATH, MOHENJO-DARO

(By permission of Arthur Probsthain, copyright, Government of India, from J. Marshall, Mohenjo-Daro, I, Pl. VIII)

walls, about 4½ feet thick, with waterproof backing, seem to have been sur-rounded with an ambulatory approximately 15 feet wide. The basin was sunk about 8 feet below the court level. At each end a flight of paved steps, covered with timbers, led down to the water. Just at the foot of the stairs a broad plat-form, 16 inches high and 39 inches broad, ran across the ends of the pool, pre-sumably to accommodate children or others for whom deep water was danger-ous. The pool may have been filled from a great well in a near-by room. A cov-ered drain provided easy removal of the water. Associated with the Great Bath, apparently, were a row of eight small bathrooms, each having a stairway leading to a room above. These, it is believed, may have served members of a priestly order. Another building is thought to have been a hot-air bath; vertical chases about 1¾ feet deep in its walls may have distributed hot air to the walls and floors of rooms above.[11]

Where wildlife was plentiful in field and stream, hunting and fishing might well be expected. Shooting antelope with arrows is depicted on amulets. Small balls have been found, proper for bow or sling, which may have been used in hunting birds. Dogs of several types are shown in models; some of them were apparently used for hunting. Game birds were probably used for fighting. That

[11] *Ibid.*, I, 24 ff., chap. 10; Mackay, E.: *op. cit.*, pp. 55 ff.

fishing was a common occupation is evident from numerous forms of fishhooks, the remnant of a fishing net, and net weights. What may have been a fishing boat is depicted on a seal.[12] In view of the many evidences of fishing in pre-Aryan India, it is interesting to note the scarcity of references thereto in the Rig-Veda, where fish is mentioned once.[13] In Sanskrit literature after 800 B.C., references to fish, fishermen, hooks, and nets are of more frequent occurrence.[14]

Games and toys of the Indus folk are known to us through a variety of objects, made of clay, stone, bone, shell, faience, bronze, and other material. Some were apparently made by children; others suggest the skill of toy specialists. Of children's toys there were rattles, whistles, marbles, chairs, bake pans, and various models of birds, animals, and male and female human figures. Toy animals were sometimes mounted on wheels or had stick legs; some were made with movable joints and heads. Balls of various sizes and ornamentation, made of clay, shell, and stone; and pieces of ivory or bone (varying in length from one and a fraction to more than three inches), which were probably used for throwing in games of chance, have been recovered. Cubical numbered dice, two game boards, and several pieces generally thought to be gamesmen, make it clear that in respect to amusements the people of the Indus civilization had much in common with those of other early lands.[15]

## ARYAN CULTURE IN INDIA

RISE OF ARYAN DOMINION  Views as to the relation between Aryan and pre-Aryan origins in India vary sharply. The Indus culture has been called Vedic-Aryan; others hold the Indus and the Vedic cultures "incontest-ably" related. Again, the common view has been that Aryan culture came from the outside; a rival theory holds that it was indigenous. The time of arrival of Aryans on the scene is naturally also disputed. Langdon believes Aryan origins in India are "far more ancient than history" admits, and that Indian Aryans may be "the oldest representatives of the Indo-Germanic race." A more common view is that Vedic culture appeared in India about the middle of the second millennium B.C.[16] as the result of a southward migration of Aryan peoples. In keeping with this theory the rich territory, whose fertility, crops, flora,

[12] Mackay, E.: op. cit., pp. 139, 186 ff.; Mackay, E. J. H.: Further Excavations at Mohenjo-Daro, I, 286, 290, 341, 356, 366, 435, 471 f., 641; II, Plates LXXXIX, A, XCI, 23-4, XCIII, 14.
[13] Grassmann: Rig-Veda, x, 68.
[14] Radcliffe: Fishing from the Earliest Times, pp. 48 f.; Macdonell: Sanskrit Literature, pp. 143, 217, 294.
[15] Marshall: op. cit., I, 39; Plate XIII, 3-6; II, 549-61; III, Plates CLIII-CLV; Mackay, E. J. H.: op. cit., I, 557-78; II, especially Plates LXXI, LXXVII-LXXXI, CV-CVI, CIX, CXL, CXLII.
[16] Marshall: op. cit., I, 110 ff.; II, 432; Venkateswara: Indian Culture through the Ages, pp. 9, 12 ff.

and fauna seemed so remarkable to Megasthenês,[17] was forcibly taken from the aboriginal dwellers, who for centuries offered stubborn resistance.

Political history, according to Hindu tradition, goes back to 3000 B.C., but the earliest reasonably certain date is the beginning of the Saisunaga dynasty about 600 B.C.[18] The preaching of Buddha (late sixth century B.C.); the invasion of India by Alexander (327 B.C.); Chandragupta (321–296 B.C.) and his grandson Asoka (c. 264–227 B.C.), who espoused Buddhism; the journeys of Fa Hien down the Ganges in the first decade of the fifth century A.D. and the travels of Hsuan Tsang in the second quarter of the seventh; the first Mohammedan invasion (664) and the establishment of Mohammedan sway in the thirteenth century—all these provide welcome definite anchorages in an otherwise highly uncertain chronology.

Much of the uncertainty of early Indian history is due to lack of written records. The earliest literature, the Rig-Veda, of great yet not definitely dated antiquity, seems to have been composed during the second millennium and was fairly crystallized by 1000 B.C. Writing, as noted, was known to the early Indus civilization. Brahmi script, fully developed apparently by 500 B.C., may have derived from the early Indus writing. At first used chiefly for business, writing is mentioned in a casual manner in Buddhist texts. Though Megasthenês (c. 300 B.C.) commented on the absence of writing among Hindus, Strabo says they wrote upon cloth but did not commit their laws to writing. Gautama encouraged his followers to learn his teachings in their vernacular and rebuked those who suggested that his works be put into Sanskrit. Buddhist texts were written down about the first century B.C. Brahmans were more reluctant than Buddhists to commit their intellectual treasures to writing, but by the seventh century A.D. learned works were commonly in written form.[19]

Whether Aryan civilization came from without or was indigenous, the Rig-Veda reflects the mingling of two peoples, a dark aboriginal folk and a fairer complexioned stock of tall, vigorous marauders who looked with contempt on the darker, against whom they were commonly arrayed in a struggle for dominion, though they also fought amongst themselves. The light-skinned conquerors were in a tribal stage of development. Caste was unknown. The father was warrior, priest, herder, and farmer.[20] Women enjoyed a position of

---

[17] McCrindle: Ancient India as Described by Megasthenês and Arrian, pp. 30 ff., 159 ff.
[18] Smith: Early History of India, pp. 9, 27.
[19] The Geography of Strabo, xv, 1, 66–7; Marshall: op. cit., I, 39 ff.; II, chaps. 22–3; Müller: The Sacred Books of the East, XIII, 201; xx, 150 f.; Venkateswara: op. cit., pp. 148 f., 213; Macdonell: op. cit., p. 17; Davids: Buddhist India, chap. 7; Keay: Ancient Indian Education, pp. 12, 37, 155.
[20] Dutt, R. C.: Ancient India, pp. 4 ff.

some freedom and dignity. Animistic in religion, the early conquerors worshiped nature forces, such as *Agni* (fire), *Indra* (thunder), *Rudra* (lightning), and the *Maruts* (storm gods).[21]

Though the new arrivals in the Indus Valley were vigorous and warlike, the hot climate, rainfall, and rich soil, conducive to agricultural life and an accumulation of wealth that made extended leisure possible, exerted a powerful influence upon them. Specialization of labor grew. Castes emerged and gradually exhibited a marked rigidity. The vigorous primitive religion, breathing a spirit fit to inspire the hearts of warriors, gave way to a contemplative, abstract religion, which undertook to expound the origin of all things, order the affairs of men, and show the relation of all to an ultimate goal. According to this architectonic scheme of things, Brahma, universal spirit, is the beginning and the end of all. The ultimate reunion of the soul with Brahma, after numerous reincarnations, is the distant goal of existence. Brahmanic theory recognized different levels of maturity in all things. Each individual has its beginning and its end. Being and nonbeing, integration and disintegration, birth and death, are the rhythmic pulsations of the cosmic order. Each thing occupies some point in the cycle of existence, higher or lower according to degree of maturity. Human life is only a higher point in that cycle. But individuals are not equally mature spiritually. According to their degrees of maturity, certain types are recognized: the masses, selfish, chiefly concerned with getting; a nobler few, less selfish, sensitive to duty, but keen for the rewards of fame and power; superior souls, numerically still more limited, whose spiritual capacity enables them to grasp the scheme of things entire, and whose passion is love and wisdom.[22]

Caste was not a ready-made system but the result of centuries of social evolution, involving a struggle of rival groups for dominion. Warriors were doubtless supreme in early days; but with more settled life, an intellectual caste claimed, and ultimately established, dominion, and assigned the stations of all below it. Brahmanic theory did not create divisions but rationalized, supported, and sought to render inviolate certain more or less natural cleavages. The source of *varna* (caste) and its meaning have been variously explained.[23] Originally it may only have differentiated Aryan conquerors and the conquered aboriginal population. *Brahmans* were poets and singers in early days, not members of a fixed priestly order. *Kshatriya*, designating the strong, was later applied to a soldier class. Eventually, however, *varna* indicated groups within the Aryan conquerors. The *Dharma Sastras* designate four castes: *Brahman*,

[21] Müller: *op. cit.*, XXXII, 14, 53, 81, 419, *passim*; XLVI, 1, 6, 8, *passim*; Griswold: *The Religion of the Rig Veda*, pp. 80–208.

[22] Coomaraswamy: *The Dance of Siva*, pp. 6 f., 10 f.; Pratt: *India and Its Faiths*, pp. 72–90.

[23] Dutt: *op. cit.*, pp. 68 f., 431 f., 673; cf. Senart: *Caste in India*, pp. 89–206; Davids: *op. cit.*, chap. 4; Griswold: *op. cit.*, pp. 45–52.

Kshatriya, Vaisya, and Sudra, the first three of which could perform religious ceremonies and study the Vedas. Buddhism was a significant protest on the part of the Gautama, born a Kshatriya, against the encroachments of caste regulations and ceremonialism of Brahmanism. Just as the four rivers that fell into the Ganges lost their names when they mingled with it, so those who accepted Buddha ceased to be Brahman, Kshatriya, Vaisya, or Sudra. With the rise of Buddhism even Sudras in some instances founded dynasties. Buddhist influence was great during the millennium, 250 B.C.–800 A.D., and left its impress on a modified Hinduism which superseded it.

Megasthenês, Strabo, Diodorus, and Arrian give various accounts of castes in India,[24] but the Laws of Manu, formulated about 200 A.D., though based on earlier works,[25] contain a more significant statement of the laws of caste. Duties are prescribed for all according to their origin from the mouth, the arms, the thighs, and from the feet of the "resplendent one."

"To Brahmanas he assigned teaching and studying the Veda, sacrificing for their own benefit and for others, giving and accepting of alms.

"The Kshatriya he commanded to protect the people, to bestow gifts, to offer sacrifices, to study the Veda, and to abstain from attaching himself to sensual pleasures;

"The Vaisya to tend cattle, to bestow gifts, to offer sacrifices, to study the Veda, to trade, to lend money, and to cultivate land.

"One occupation only the lord prescribed to the Sudra, to serve meekly even these other three castes." [26]

The superiority of the Brahman is everywhere stressed. His very birth "is an eternal incarnation of the sacred law," which he is to fulfill. Whatever exists belongs to the Brahman. Because of "the excellence of his origin" a Brahman is entitled to everything. The name of a Brahman must signify "auspicious"; of a Kshatriya, "protection"; of a Vaisya, "thriving"; and of a Sudra, "service." [27] Of value to the Brahman, doubtless, was the injunction that others should give to him. "Charity to Brahmans" was a constant theme of Hindu writings.[28]

Megasthenês and Arrian say the military caste was well paid and equipped. When "not in service," Strabo says, they spent their time in idleness and drinking, but were ever ready to march on an expedition.[29] Megasthenês was speaking of the court of Chandragupta, a prince famed for the splendor of his

24 Strabo, xv, 1, 39–41, 46–9; Diodorus of Sicily, ii, 40–1; Arrian: Indica, 11–2.
25 Macdonell: op. cit., pp. 260 f., 428.
26 Müller: op. cit., xxv, 24. From The Sacred Books of the East, edited by F. M. Müller (The Clarendon Press).
27 Ibid., xxv, 25 ff., 35, 55.
28 Dutt: op. cit., pp. 683 f.
29 McCrindle: op. cit., p. 43; Strabo (Jones), xv, 1, 47; Arrian, 12.

court and the excellent organization of his government. Soldiers were not every-where so liberally supported. Manu provided that Kshatriyas who had "fallen into distress" might subsist by certain lower occupations, but "must never arrogantly adopt the mode of life" of superiors.[30]

Vaisyas and Sudras, according to Manu, must perform the work prescribed for them, for to allow them to neglect their duties "would throw this whole world into confusion." The Vaisya must keep cattle, know the value of articles of trade, the soil, the sowing of seeds, weights and measures, the wages of servants, and the rules of business, so as to "increase his property in a righteous manner." The highest duty of a Sudra is to serve Brahmans; if he always does so, is gentle in speech, free from pride, and a good servant, he will attain a higher caste in the next life. Articles needed for sacrifices might be taken at pleasure by a Brahman or Kshatriya from a Vaisya or Sudra. For hope of a better fate in the next life, one must submit to the rules of caste in this: "It is better to discharge one's own appointed duty incompletely than to perform completely that of another; for he who lives according to the law of another caste is instantly excluded from his own." [31]

It is evident that the priestly legislators devised laws for the preservation of their privileges. A Brahman, though ignorant, was declared "a great divinity"; though he "committed all possible crimes," he was on no account to be pun-ished with death, but men of all other castes might "suffer capital punish-ment"; even though he engaged in mean occupations, yet he "must be hon-oured in every way." Let no one, not even a king, anger him for any reason, for the Brahman can "instantly destroy him together with his army and his vehicles." Kshatriyas and Brahmans must work together; neither prospers with-out the other; "being closely united, [they] prosper in this world and in the next." [32] Vaisyas were permitted religious knowledge and might perform sac-rifices. Sudras, however, except in rare instances, had no religious knowledge nor were admitted to sacrifices. A priestly rule declared that "the ears of a Sudra who listens, intentionally, when the Veda is being recited are to be filled with molten lead. His tongue is to be cut out if he recite it." [33] Pariahs (out-casts) had no rank in the social organization.

Agricultural labor was highly respected in the earliest days and was cele-brated in song and ceremonial. Merry, yet reverent, was the chant at the begin-ning of planting: "Fasten the ploughs, spread out the yokes, and sow the seed on this field which has been prepared. Let the corn grow with our hymns; let

[30] Müller: op. cit., xxv, 422 f.
[31] Ibid., xxv, 327, 400 f., 423, 432 f. From The Sacred Books of the East, edited by F. M. Müller (The Clarendon Press).
[32] Ibid., xxv, 320, 397 ff.
[33] Davids: op. cit., p. 118; Dutt: op. cit., p. 173.

the scythes fall on the neighbouring fields where the corn is ripe." [34] A stamp of degradation, however, was put by the priestly class upon many forms of labor, as may be seen in the *Dharma Sastras* and in *Manu*. Workers in leather, goldsmiths, sellers of arms, blacksmiths, weavers, dyers, washermen, and oil manufacturers were declared impure, along with prostitutes, drunkards, liars, liquor-vendors, eaters of dogs, and other evildoers. Under such discouragement it may seem remarkable that industry developed as it did. Weaving, spinning, dyeing, carpentry, preparing skins and fabrics for clothing, manufacturing plows, wagons, carts, and implements of war—the bow and arrow, swords, spears, and armor—were considerably advanced. There were at least eighteen guilds at the time of Buddha. Artisans of these groups belonged to the *Vaisyas*, as did the farmers; since the work of some of them was indispensable, they were well cared for by the state. Such was the case of armorers and shipwrights in the time of Chandragupta.[35]

The position of women changed from time to time. In days of primitive simplicity, they "joined in the worship, and helped in the performance of the ceremonies." The wife of Rama, often named as the ideal woman, and cer- tain poetesses and philosophers show that women of high social station might be distinguished for learning. Buddha wanted a maiden "accomplished in writing and in composing poetry . . . well versed in the rules of the *Sutras*." [36] His wife is said to have asked why a veil was necessary, if her character and behavior were correct. According to Megasthenês women still enjoyed much liberty in his day; and Strabo says that wives of *Brahmans* studied philosophy with their husbands.[37] The sphere and duties of women as wives and mothers were, however, held always in highest regard. The popular view that learned women would die widows or meet with some other calamity, was no encourage- ment to take risks, though exceptions appeared.[38] Priestly philosophers ex- pounded a philosophy of female subjection and inferiority. "Women, at all times," says *Manu*, "have been inconstant. . . . Infidelity, violence, deceit, envy, extreme avarice, a total want of good qualities, with impurity, are the innate faults of womankind." That such a creature should never be free, *Manu* provided: "In childhood a female must be subject to her father, in youth to her husband, when her lord is dead to her sons; a woman must never be inde- pendent." "Though destitute of virtue, or seeking pleasure elsewhere, or devoid of good qualities, yet a husband must be constantly worshipped as a god by a

[34] Dutt: op. cit., p. 40.
[35] Ibid., pp. 680 ff.; Rawlinson: *Intercourse between India and the Western World*, p. 53.
[36] Venkateswara: op. cit., pp. 110 ff.
[37] Strabo, xv, 1, 66.
[38] Ward: *Account of the Writings, Religion, and Manners, of the Hindoos*, 1, 194 ff.; Coomaraswamy: op. cit., pp. 82–102.

faithful wife . . . for that reason alone [she will] be exalted in heaven." [39]

EDUCATION

*Intellectual training* The home was the school, the mother the teacher, to about the age of five. Then, under a professional teacher, the elements of reading, writing, word study, grammar, arithmetic, and certain psalms and prayers were learned. According to the *Grhya Sutras*, a *Brahman* was initiated at the eighth year at the earliest, the sixteenth at the latest, into Vedic studies. The respective ages for *Kshatriyas* were the eleventh and the twenty-second years; and for *Vaisyas*, the twelfth and the twenty-fourth. Initiation was marked by a stricter regimen, a ceremonial feast, shaving, bathing, wearing a specially made garment, taking a staff, a new name, and binding with a sacred girdle. The *Brahman's* symbolic girdle was of sacred grass; the *Kshatriya's*, a bowstring; the *Vaisya's*, a thread of wool.[40]

Intellectual training centered in religious teaching; its purpose was to understand the *Vedas*, practice pious mortification, gain knowledge of law and philosophy, develop veneration for one's natural and one's spiritual father, and so attain harmony with *Brahma*.[41] Higher learning was chiefly a prerogative of *Brahmans*, though *Kshatriyas* and *Vaisyas* were entitled to study the *Vedas*, and *Manu* provided that "in times of distress" a student might learn the *Veda* from non-Brahmans. There were also several women of learning who became teachers in early Buddhist times.[42] Among Kurus and Panchalas, in early days, warriors learned the *Vedas*; [43] the Licchavis, too, though a military clan, were lovers of fine arts and the sons often went to distant countries for education. King Videha was instructed in law by four sages; and his son was educated at Taxila, a great seat of learning.[44]

When fully developed, higher education comprised linguistics, literature, theology, religion, philosophy, science, and law—drawn from the *Vedas* and commentaries thereon, the *Laws of Manu*, and the *Six Angas*. A *Brahman* family specialized, as a rule, in a particular *Veda*. The study of one *Veda* alone might occupy eight to twelve years; if the whole range of sacred literature and commentaries were attempted, it would require almost a lifetime.[45]

Educational organization was quite informal. Some teachers taught in their

---

[39] Müller: *op. cit.*, xxv, 195 f. From *The Sacred Books of the East*, edited by F. M. Müller (The Clarendon Press); Woody: *A History of Women's Education*, 1, 5 f.
[40] Venkateswara: *op. cit.*, pp. 69, 113–8.
[41] Müller: *op. cit.*, xxv, 24, 74; Venkateswara: *op. cit.*, pp. 70, 96 ff., 162 ff.
[42] Müller: *op. cit.*, xxv, 73; Venkateswara: *op. cit.*, pp. 111 ff., 220 f., 293 f.; Coomaraswamy: *op. cit.*, pp. 84 f.; Keay: *op. cit.*, pp. 80 ff.
[43] Dutt: *op. cit.*, pp. 128, 432 f.
[44] Law: *Ksatriya Clans in Buddhist India*, pp. 68 f., 148 f.; Venkateswara: *op. cit.*, pp. 166–71.
[45] Müller: *op. cit.*, xxv, 74 f.

own houses, or were followed by students to forest hermitages; others discoursed at court on learned matters, including winds, droughts, rains, and epidemics.[46] As higher education became more specialized, small groups of priests (three to twenty-one, it is said) gave instruction in colleges, *parishads*. Buddhist monasteries also became famed centers of learning. Nalanda, most renowned, drew thousands of students from India and from abroad. Certain centers became distinguished for specialization: Taxila, in medicine; Benares, in theology; and Ujjain, in astronomy.[47]

The study of literature was at first a process of committing to memory by oral repetition. When writing had come into use, it was usually taught by tracing characters in the sand, later upon leaves of palm and plane trees. Hindu psychology of learning in certain respects foreshadowed that of the present day: "Good instruction must be given without unpleasant sensations"; a teacher must "use sweet and gentle words." Discipline, accordingly, was customarily mild. Manu provided, however, that in case of necessity "a wife, a son, a slave, a pupil, . . . who have committed faults, may be beaten with a rope or a split bamboo, but on the back part of the body only, never on a noble part. . . ."[48]

*Physical culture*  Though a doctor felt two decades ago that he could "almost say positively . . . that we [Indians] are the sickest nation in the world to-day," and found the reasons therefor in climatic conditions, social and religious customs, and a certain reflective tendency, there was a marked concern for health in ancient India, and many sports and amusements were commonly enjoyed. After the tenth century A.D., however, a marked decline in physical education began, paralleling India's subjection to foreign rule. During the past hundred years, due chiefly to Western influences and the rise of Indian nationalism, physical education under both civil and military control has taken a new lease of life as a mass movement—especially since 1920.[49]

Health and physical culture were not sought through formal provisions among primitive Aryan conquerors. In Vedic hymns there were, however, constantly reiterated praise and supplication for food, strength, health, valiant heroes, and long life;[50] and the compulsions of life-activities provided sufficiently, doubtless, for physical exercise amongst the soldiers, farmers, and other lower industrial workers such as the *Sudras*, for whom nothing was provided

46 Strabo, xv, 1, 65–6; Diodorus, II, 40.
47 Venkateswara: op. cit., pp. 82 f., 159 ff., 227 ff.; Dutt: op. cit., pp. 175 ff.
48 Müller: op. cit., xxv, 306. From *The Sacred Books of the East*, edited by F. M. Müller (The Clarendon Press); Venkateswara: op. cit., pp. 37, 83, 100.
49 Gray: "Physical Education in India," *Am. Phys. Educ. Rev.*, xxiv, 376; Andrews: "Physical Education in India," *Jour. Health and Phys. Educ.*, iv, 10 ff.; Thomason: "Physical Education in India," *Mind and Body*, xxxv, 407 ff.
50 Müller: op. cit., xxxii, 108, 211, 347; xlvi, 277, 360, 376, 380, passim.

save training in the craft pursued by the father.[51] Megasthenês does mention a passive exercise, a massage: "Their favourite mode of exercising the body is by friction, applied in various ways, but especially by passing smooth ebony rollers over the skin." [52] Later literature placed great emphasis on diet and other physical care during the early years at the hands of the mother. A stricter regimen in respect to personal habits, washing, early retiring and rising, was prescribed for youth after initiation. Both Hindus and Buddhists imposed restrictions as to certain foods, partly for physical and mental effects, partly for ceremonial reasons. Fasting was stressed by Buddhists, especially, in order to restrain animal nature and to stimulate mental activity.[53]

Early rising, cleansing the teeth, rinsing the mouth, bathing in cold water once or even thrice daily were common features of Brahmanic and Buddhist systems of physical regimen. *Manu* prescribed bathing in the morning for *Brahmans*, and warned against bathing naked and taking baths immediately after meals and in pools which were not perfectly well known. Bathing, as a ritualistic cleansing, was prescribed for ascetics to atone for unintentional injuries to other living creatures.[54] Water and its cleansing and refreshing qualities occupied a place of importance in Indian life, owing largely doubtless to the hot climate and the accessibility of great rivers. When the summer has come, Aryuna says to Krishna, "Come, let us go" to the river Jumna and "sport there with our friends." [55] Provisions for oil baths are mentioned in the time of Chola I (c. 1023 A.D.). In Buddhist monasteries walking was a prescribed exercise; and pools were provided for bathing, to which the members were summoned each morning by a bell. Throwing water at, or chasing, each other in the water, or other sportive amusements, were not permitted. Special rules were promulgated for using and cleansing the hot bath. A steam bath was allowed to rheumatic sufferers. Separate bathing places were prescribed for men and women.[56]

The prohibitions laid by Buddha upon exercises, games, and amusements are an index to the pastimes common in India at that day: "games with eight pieces and ten pieces, and with tossing up, hopping over diagrams formed on the ground, and removing substances from a heap without shaking the remainder"; dice, trapball, drawing figures, throwing balls, blowing trumpets, plowing contests, tumbling, imitating windmills, guessing games, chariot races, shooting matches, marbles, mimicking others' actions, riding elephants and

---

[51] Keay: op. cit., pp. 57, 77 ff.; Venkateswara: op. cit., pp. 91, 155, 200 ff., 308 f.
[52] McCrindle: op. cit., p. 70.
[53] Venkateswara: op. cit., pp. 105 ff., 191 ff.
[54] Müller: op. cit., xxv, 136, 149, 152 f., 210; Schleyer: *Bäder und Badeanstalten*, pp. 3 ff.
[55] Dutt, M. N.: *Mahabharata*, Adi Parva, p. 300.
[56] Müller: op. cit., XIII, 44, 157 f.; XVII, 35, 56; XX, 102–10, 114 f., 296 ff., 367 ff.; Venkateswara: op. cit., pp. 232, 238, 278.

horses, swordsmanship, races with elephants, horses and carriages, running, wrestling, boxing, and enticing girls to dance.[57]

Yoga, unique Indian development, a systematic discipline of mind and body, involved numerous exercises in posture (asana) and regulated control and exercise of breathing, preferably performed in the open air at morning. To master with safety and benefit the intricacies and difficulties of Yoga required the instruction of experts. Breathing exercises were held especially valuable to those engaged in mental labor. When fully developed, Yoga included as many as eighty-four different postures, considered best. Thirty-two have been called useful for "this world." Fifteen are commonly recognized to-day. Though usually regarded merely as an extreme asceticism, Yoga was, at its best, a science of health, based on a philosophy of physical and mental control pointing toward the golden mean. According to Gautama, "There are two extremes which must be shunned. The one is a life of pleasure devoted to desire and enjoyment. That is base and ignoble, unworthy, unreal, and is the way of destruction. The other is a life of self-mortification, gloom, and torture. This is unworthy, unreal, and leads to nothing. The middle way of wise temperance and recollectedness is the way which ascends the mount of vision." [58]

Among the early warring Aryans in India the training for warfare was probably a rather informal but universal apprenticeship for all men. Non-Aryan girls, too, it is said, "joined the army in large numbers," but we know nothing of their training at that time or at later dates when certain women are reported to have "gloried in the military profession." [59] Megasthenês speaks of a host of women accompanying the army; and of the king's hunting, surrounded by women, armed as if for a campaign, some on horses, others on elephants and in chariots.[60]

That more or less formal contests at arms may have been held, even in the early days, is suggested by certain Vedic allusions.[61] In any case, as specialization of functional classes developed, the training of soldiers became more formal, extensive, and clearly defined. In the time of Gautama Buddha, who is said to have neglected "manly exercises" which sons of Kshatriyas commonly delighted in, military arts included fighting on horses and elephants and in chariots, archery, riding, walking, running, jumping, wrestling, swimming, and boxing. Dancing, also, was a part of early training. In the second century B.C.

[57] Müller: op cit., XVII, 348 f. From The Sacred Books of the East, edited by F. M. Müller (The Clarendon Press).
[58] Krishnayya: "The Yoga Asanas," Jour. Health and Phys. Educ., IV, 56; Bernard: Hatha Yoga, p. 6; Schmidt: Fakire und Fakirtum im Alten und Modernen Indien; Müller: op. cit., XIII, 94; Macdonell: op. cit., pp. 398 f.; Venkateswara: op. cit., pp. 141, 143.
[59] Venkateswara: op. cit., pp. 57, 66, 294.
[60] McCrindle: op. cit., pp. 38, 72 f.; Strabo, xv, 1, 55; Rawlinson: op. cit., p. 67.
[61] Rig-Veda, IV, 42, 5; Keay: op. cit., pp. 60 f.

military arts included forming various arrays, columns, and counter columns, heavy fighting, fist fighting, fighting with branches, the uses of the bow and the sword. According to one authority, a prince's training included such military arts as archery, elephant training, care and training of horses, battle formations, use of the lance, jumping, running, and crossing rivers.[62] Among the accomplishments recommended in the early Christian era as part of training for youth between five and sixteen years of age, were gymnastics, playing on musical glasses, dancing, swordstick combats, training cocks, quail, and rams for fighting, and teaching birds, such as parrots and starlings, to sing.[63] Polo was apparently introduced into India at the time of the Mohammedan conquest, and was extremely popular at the Mogul court in the sixteenth century. Since then it declined and all but disappeared, save on the borders near Burma and at a few places on the upper Indus, where it was played by commoners.[64]

It is not without interest that when functions had become specialized and castes clearly differentiated, literature reflected the fondly cherished view that all good gifts came from *Brahma* and his servants the priests. The *Mahabharata*, a great epic poem which grew by accretion through many centuries, had apparently achieved definite form by the fifth century B.C. According to this epic portrayal, the earth was once bereft of warriors, but *Kshatriya* women consorted with *Brahmans* and thus arose a race of *Kshatriyas* of greater power and ability. Drona, a *Brahman*, not a *Kshatriya*, is charged by Bhisma to teach princes the science of arms and meanwhile to enjoy the luxury of the Kuru household and receive the obedience of all Kurus. And Drona taught the sons of Pandu the use of all weapons, the bow, the club, the sword, the lance, the spear, the dart, and how to fight in chariots and on elephants and horseback. But of his pupils, Aryuna excelled them all; in bowmanship there was not his equal. To test their profit from his teaching, Drona held an examination in marksmanship, in which the object was to sever with an arrow the head of an artificial bird which he had placed as target in a tree top. All pupils but Aryuna see everything, the bird, the teacher, the tree. Aryuna, however, attention fixed only on the head he is to aim at, sees neither teacher, tree, nor even the body of the bird—and so he brings it down! Having completed the training of his pupils, Drona requests the king to hold a public competition to be viewed by all orders of society. Accordingly a great display of horsemen, charioteers, bowmen, fighters on elephants, swordsmen, was held in an arena, constructed by special order of the king. Thereafter, satisfied that all were now thoroughly accomplished in arms, Drona asks for his *dakshina*, payment for his services— nothing less than that his pupils seize Drupada, the king of Panchalas, and

[62] Venkateswara: *op. cit.*, pp. 170, 174 f., 199.
[63] Radcliffe: *op. cit.*, p. 49.
[64] Laufer: "The Early History of Polo," *Polo*, VII, 44.

bring him captive before him. This heroic labor, Aryuna dutifully fulfilled.[65]

The philosophy of power politics in the *Mahabharata* is Machiavellian and modern. A king should always extend his powers, avoiding his own faults, watching for faults of others. His own resources should be carefully concealed. The killing of an enemy, strong or weak, is always praiseworthy. If a king is weak, he should pretend to be blind and deaf, not noticing faults of others when he is not able to punish them. One must gain the confidence of one's enemies, then spring upon them like a wolf. Destroy enemies by every means: by arts of conciliation; by money; by fomenting disunion among them. By this jackal political science ". . . the timid, by exciting their fears, the courageous by the arts of conciliation, the covetous by gift of wealth, and the inferiors and the equals by the exhibition of prowess . . ." will be brought to subjection.[66]

The duties, virtues, and rewards of *Kshatriyas*, set apart by religion and custom as the protectors of society, were formulated more authoritatively in the *Laws of Manu*. A king, says *Manu*, though defeated by foes who are stronger than he, "must not shrink from battle, remembering the duty of *Kshatriyas*. Not to turn back in battle, to protect the people, . . ." is the greatest happiness. Those who "fight with the utmost exertion and do not turn back, go to heaven." Those who are "slain in battle," while turning back in fear, are condemned to bear the sins of their masters. Awards and booty come to the good *Kshatriyas*. Chariots, horses, elephants, parasols, money, grain, cattle, women, "all sorts of marketable goods and valueless metals belong to him who takes them . . ." singly; and what is taken jointly is to be divided among the soldiers. Always he must be prepared. "Let him be ever ready to strike, his prowess constantly displayed. . . . Of him who is always ready to strike, the whole world stands in awe; let him therefore make all creatures subject to himself even by the employment of force." [67]

The warlike spirit of the *Laws of Manu* harks back to the warrior's way of thinking and acting, portrayed in the earliest *Vedas*. *Indra* is the god of thunder, storm, and warlike fury. *Indra* protects his Aryan worshipers in war. "He subdues the people who do not perform sacrifices for the benefit of . . . Aryans. He flays the enemy of his black skin and kills him and reduces him to ashes." "O destroyer of foes! collect together the heads of these marauding troops, and crush them with thy wide foot!" [68] Another poem describes the preparation for war, the weapons and armor: chariots, horses, bows, quivers,

[65] Dutt, M. N.: op. cit., pp. 88, 190–203.
[66] Ibid., pp. 203 ff.
[67] Müller: op. cit., xxv, 230 ff., 238, 397 ff., 419. From *The Sacred Books of the East*, edited by F. M. Müller (The Clarendon Press).
[68] Dutt, R. C.: op. cit., p. 54.

and the poisoned arrows. "We will win cattle with the bow. . . . The string of the bow when pulled . . . whispers words of consolation to [the archer]. . . . The quiver is like the parent of many arrows. . . . The expert charioteer stands on his chariot and drives his horses wheresoever he will. . . . The horses raise the dust . . . and career over the field. . . . They do not retreat, but trample the marauding enemies under their feet. The arrow is feathered. . . . Well pulled and sent by the . . . string, it falls on the enemy. Wherever men stand together or are separate, there the shafts reap advantage. . . . We extol the arrow which is poisoned, whose face is of iron. . . ." [69]

The martial spirit that should pervade the breast of *Kshatriyas* is poetically portrayed by Bharavi, who points out that peace and submissiveness do not befit the warrior:

> Cast off thy sloth, assume thy native power,
> And, manlike, deal destruction to thy foe!
> Not kings, but hermits seek seclusion's bower,
> Forget their wrongs, and meekly bend in woe.
>
> If mighty men, whose treasure is their fame,
> Like thee consent their manhood to degrade,
> Then woe to warrior's pride and warrior's name,
> And honour, courage, chivalry be dead! [70]

The connection between religion and war is suggested by the following, in which the bow, "truly .. . . the nobleman's strength," is blessed at the royal inauguration: "Mitra's thou art—Varuna's thou art . . . may he slay Vritra by thee! . . . may he slay by thee his spiteful enemy!" [71]

The horse and war chariot, so indispensable to the conquering Aryans, both in war and in the chariot races of which the Indians were deeply enamored, occupy a large place in the earliest literature and in the later. Harnessing the two bays to the chariot that will carry the hero, prayers for strong fellies, chariots, horses, and reins, are recurrent themes of many Vedic hymns.[72] Religious sanctions appear in elaborate ceremonials held in connection with the war chariot and in sprinkling the horses with water: "Thou art Indra's thunderbolt; . . . the chariot is indeed a thunderbolt, and the sacrificer is Indra. . . . Thou art Indra's thunderbolt;—a winner of wealth, for the chariot is indeed a winner of wealth;—may this one win wealth by thee!—wealth means food: may this one gain food by thee. . . ." [73]

[69] *Ibid.*, pp. 60 f.
[70] *Ibid.*, p. 764.
[71] Müller: *op. cit.*, XLI, 88 f.
[72] *Ibid.*, XXXII, 14, 82, 337, *passim*.
[73] *Ibid.*, XLI, 18. From *The Sacred Books of the East*, edited by F. M. Müller (The Clarendon Press).

Lore dealing with the business of war grew with its growth and ultimately found expression in written form. *Dhanur-Veda,* meaning bow and science, gives numerous fanciful details of equipment and its uses. Brahma is said to have fashioned three bows from one bamboo. There were also bows of horn and ivory. They should be three and one-half or four cubits long. There were also bows for throwing pellets. Arrows about two cubits in length were tipped and feathered and were hung in a quiver on the back. The archer was to be equipped with protective thimbles of leather or other material to save his fingers and with a sleeve to protect the left arm. The novice must have a teacher, that he may learn to string and unstring the bow properly, draw the string, and take aim. He must practice throwing the bow in the air and catching it, and he must be able to draw with either hand. In addition to archery, such matters as wrestling, heavy staves (bludgeons equal to the length of both arms plus the body's width), shields, spears of several kinds, clubs, horses, elephants, camels, cows, and chariots are mentioned as agencies of war. Men engaged both in single combats and in massed assaults of infantry, horsemen, and charioteers, each group against a similarly organized opponent. The long heavy staff was used skillfully in warding off and in giving blows. Wrestling, primitive and brutal, with apparently no holds barred, emphasized skill in footwork, moving about the opponent, drawing in the neck if the antagonist tried to get a hold on it, avoiding being thrown on the back, and allowing the adversary to seize a foot. A wrestler should be able to walk on his hands and do somersaults. Kicking, hitting with closed or open hands, and butting with the head were allowed.[74]

It is said that a chivalrous code of fighting came ultimately to prevail amongst *Kshatriyas.* According to this standard, women, children, and the deranged were immune to attack. Likewise one should not attack an unarmed person, a lone charioteer who had lived through an encounter, one who declined fighting or gave himself up to the victors, those who were fearful, turned their backs and ran away, or who were already overcome by another fighter.[75]

Archery seems to have been the most loved implement of war and the chase. A hymn of the *Rig-Veda* pleads that the bow may bring spoils and oxen, success in battle, fear to the foe, and victory over the whole world.[76] Shooting seems at times to have been systematically taught. Of the Kurus and Panchalas it is said, "The relations and friends of the king and all the warriors of the nation learnt archery and riding and driving the war chariot from their early youth. . . ." [77] In the time of Buddha, the Licchavis, a *Kshatriya* clan, "were

[74] Ward: *op. cit.,* ii, 381 ff.
[75] *Ibid.,* ii, 390.
[76] Longman and Walrond: *Archery,* p. 1.
[77] Dutt, R. C.: *op. cit.,* p. 128.

hardy and active, ardent and strenuous in their military training, so that their enemies could have no chance of getting them at a disadvantage. They were fond of manly sport such as hunting . . . " but, on one occasion when they came upon the Buddha seated at the foot of a tree, they "threw away their bows and arrows. . . ." The Sakyas had "a school of archery at Kapilavastu where . . . [they] were trained." [78] Archery was expertly taught at Taxila.[79]

The Mallas clan was a martial race devoted to the "manly sport" of wrestling.[80] Strabo refers to some tribes who had the custom of giving virgins as prizes to the victors in boxing.[81] Arrian says that girls were exposed by their fathers in public, to be selected by the victor in wrestling, boxing, running, or any other manly exercise.[82]

Little of an exact character is to be learned from Megasthenês, Strabo, and other early writers regarding the training of Indian soldiers. The hints they offer, however, enable us to infer something of their exercise. At the time of Megasthenês, the soldiers of Chandragupta were maintained at the king's expense, just as were elephants, horses, chariots, and other equipment. All military affairs appear to have been under one governing body, of which there were six divisions, admiralty, transport, infantry, cavalry, war chariots, and elephants. All arms and animals were kept in armories and stables of the king. Chariots on the march were drawn by oxen; and the horses were led by halters, that they might be fresh when the battle began. Besides the charioteer, there were two fighting men to a chariot. The elephants carried four men, a driver and three archers.

Of the training of horses and the skill of charioteers, Megasthenês reported:

"When it is said that an Indian by springing forward in front of a horse can check his speed and hold him back, this is not true of all Indians, but only of such as have been trained from boyhood to manage horses; for it is a practice with them to control their horses with bit and bridle, and to make them move at a measured pace and in a straight course. They neither, however, gall their tongue by the use of spiked muzzles, nor torture the roof of their mouth. The professional trainers break them in by forcing them to gallop round and round in a ring, especially when they see them refractory. Such as undertake this work require to have a strong hand as well as a thorough knowledge of horses. The greatest proficients test their skill by driving a chariot round and round in a ring; and in truth it would be no trifling feat to control with ease a team of four high-mettled steeds when whirling round in a circle." [83]

[78] Law: op. cit., pp. 64 f., 185.
[79] Venkateswara: op. cit., p. 156.
[80] Law: op. cit., p. 171.
[81] Bk. xv, 1, 66.
[82] Indica, 17.
[83] McCrindle: op. cit., pp. 89 f.

From descriptions of equipment of the army, something may be inferred as to the training of soldiers of the several classes. Megasthenês says that Chandragupta's army numbered 400,000, which may have included, besides the regular fighting forces of infantry, cavalry, chariots, and elephants, the buglers, grooms, gong-ringers, drivers, mechanics, foragers, and sutlers who were all necessary for its comfort and conduct.

"The foot-soldiers carry a bow made of equal length with the man who bears it. This they rest upon the ground, and pressing against it with their left foot thus discharge the arrow, having drawn the string far backwards: for the shaft they use is little short of being three yards long, and there is nothing which can resist an Indian archer's shot—neither shield nor breastplate, nor any stronger defence if such there be. In their left hand they carry bucklers made of undressed ox-hide, which are not so broad as those who carry them, but are about as long. Some are equipped with javelins instead of bows, but all wear a sword, which is broad in the blade, but not longer than three cubits; and this, when they engage in close fight (which they do with reluctance), they wield with both hands, to fetch down a lustier blow. The horsemen are equipped with two lances like the lances called *saunia*, and with a shorter buckler than that carried by the foot-soldiers. But they do not put saddles on their horses, nor do they curb them with bits like the bits in use among the Greeks or the Kelts, but they fit on round the extremity of the horse's mouth a circular piece of stitched raw ox-hide studded with pricks of iron or brass pointing inwards, but not very sharp: if a man is rich he uses pricks made of ivory. Within the horse's mouth is put an iron prong like a skewer, to which the reins are attached. When the rider, then, pulls the reins, the prong controls the horse, and the pricks which are attached to this prong goad the mouth, so that it cannot but obey the reins." [84]

Houen Tsang described the armed forces of Silad-itya II, ruler of northern India. The military are selected from the bravest of the people, and, "as the sons follow the profession of their fathers, they soon acquire a knowledge of the art of war." Their business is to protect the frontiers and punish the rebellious. The tactics of the various branches of the army in battle are as follows:

"The elephants are covered with strong armour, and their tusks are provided with sharp spurs. A leader in a car gives the command, while two attendants on the right and left drive his chariot, which is drawn by four horses abreast. The general of soldiers remains in his chariot; he is surrounded by a file of guards, who keep close to his chariot wheels.

"The cavalry spread themselves in front to resist an attack, and in case of defeat they carry orders hither and thither. The infantry, by their quick move-

[84] *Ibid.*, pp. 220 f.

ments, contribute to the defence. These men are chosen for their courage and strength. They carry a long spear and a great shield; sometimes they hold a sword or sabre, and advance to the front with impetuosity. All their weapons of war are sharp and pointed. Some of them are these—spears, shields, bows, arrows, swords, sabres, battle-axes, lances, halberds, long javelins and various kinds of slings. All these they have used for ages." [85]

The hunters of whom early authorities speak, who cleared the fields of the tigers, boars, deer, birds, snakes, scorpions, and caught elephants and trained them for the army, undoubtedly had a physical apprenticeship to their task and learned to master the bow, the spear, and the club at an early age.[86] It is not to be assumed, however, that hunting was not followed by others besides those for whom it was an occupation. Even *Brahmans* at times engaged in the chase for profit; [87] and kings and nobles hunted for pleasure, if not for more utilitarian reasons. The Kuru princes, having the consent of their tutor, Drona, set out in their chariots on a hunting expedition. In the time of Chandragupta, says Megasthenês, the king left his palace to judge causes, to perform sacrifices, and to engage in the chase, being attended in hunting by armed women in chariots, on horses, and on elephants. He himself hunted from the back of an elephant, and sometimes shot animals with arrows from a platform.[88] King Asoka, who espoused Buddhism, published certain edicts which dealt disapprovingly with pastimes of kings, such as hunting. "Hundreds of thousands of living beings were killed every day," he records, for the table of the king; but he, after he had gained "true intelligence," found the proper pastime in philanthropy and religion.[89]

Hunting elephants was a difficult undertaking, "a task of immense labour," says Megasthenês,[90] requiring a vast amount of experience, bravery, and skill. Training them for riding, plowing, and military use also required patience, special knowledge, and skill, though the animals were reputedly docile. Strabo describes the Indian method of hunting and taming elephants:

"The chase of the elephant is conducted as follows: they dig a deep ditch round a treeless tract about four or five stadia in circuit and bridge the entrance with a very narrow bridge; and then, letting loose into the enclosure three or four of their tamest females, they themselves lie in wait under cover in hidden huts. Now the wild elephants do not approach by day, but they make the

[85] Dutt, R. C.: *op. cit.*, pp. 580 f.; Strabo, xv, 1, 66.
[86] Strabo, xv, 1, 41; Diodorus, ii, 39, 40; McCrindle: *op. cit.*, pp. 42, 84; Dutt, R. C.: *op. cit.*, pp. 272 f.; Rawlinson: *op. cit.*, pp. 52 f.
[87] Davids: *op. cit.*, p. 94.
[88] McCrindle: *op. cit.*, p. 72; Dutt, M. N.: *op. cit.*, p. 192.
[89] Dutt, R. C.: *op. cit.*, pp. 462, 465.
[90] McCrindle: *op. cit.*, pp. 136 f.

entrance one by one at night; and when they have entered, the men close the entrance secretly; and then, leading the most courageous of their tame combatants into the enclosure, they fight it out with the wild elephants, at the same time wearing them down also by starvation; and, once the animals are worn out, the boldest of the riders secretly dismount and each creeps under the belly of his own riding-elephant, and then, starting from here, creeps under the wild elephant and binds his feet together; and when this is done, they command the tamed elephant to beat those whose feet have been bound until they fall to the ground; and when they fall, the men fasten their necks to those of the tamed elephants with thongs of raw ox-hide; and in order that the wild elephants, when they shake those who are attempting to mount them, may not shake them off, the men make incisions round their necks and put the thongs round at these incisions, so that through pain they yield to their bonds and keep quiet. Of the elephants captured, they reject those that are too old or too young for service and lead away the rest to the stalls; and then, having tied their feet to one another and their necks to a firmly planted pillar, they subdue them by hunger; and then they restore them with green cane and grass. After this the elephants are taught to obey commands, some through words of command and others through being charmed by tunes and drum-beating. Those that are hard to tame are rare; for by nature the elephant is of a mild and gentle disposition, so that it is close to a rational animal; and some elephants have even taken up their riders who had fallen from loss of blood in the fight and carried them safely out of the battle, while others have fought for, and rescued, those who had crept between their fore-legs. And if in anger they have killed one of their feeders or masters, they yearn after him so strongly that through grief they abstain from food and sometimes even starve themselves to death.

". . . Nearchus says that in the hunt for them foot-traps also are put at places where tracks meet, and that the wild elephants are driven together into these by the tamed ones, which latter are stronger and guided by riders; and that they are so easy to tame that they learn to throw stones at a mark and to use weapons; and that they are excellent swimmers; and that a chariot drawn by elephants is considered a very great possession, and that they are driven under yoke like camels." [91]

Dancing in ancient India was intimately associated with religion, its music, and ceremonials. One of the earliest Vedic hymns addressed to Aurora likens her to a dancer, gay in a dress of many colors.[92] "Worship the Maruts with a

[91] *Strabo*, xv, 1, 42, 43. Trans. by H. L. Jones. The Loeb Classical Library. Quoted by permission of Harvard University Press, Cambridge, Mass.; *Arrian*, 13.
[92] Grassmann: *op. cit.*, II. 02.

SIVA
(Courtesy, Philadelphia Museum of Art)

174

song . . . O ye dancers, with golden ornaments, . . . take care of us, ye Maruts, for your friendship lasts for ever." [93] Numerous passages from their early literature show the Indian people's love of dancing and its integral rôle in religion. The figure of the dancer from Mohenjo-Daro and works of religious and other forms of art, show likewise the antiquity and the persistence of the love of rhythmic movement. The myriad forms of the dance of Siva celebrate with ecstasy "primal rhythmic energy," and become in time, however crude and unconscious its first manifestations may have been, the "image of the activity of God." [94] Siva, indeed, is Nataraja, the Lord of Dancers, one of whose dances represents his fivefold, godlike powers: creation, embodiment, preservation, destruction, and release.[95] The death dance itself, Venkateswara [96] says, is a symbol not of a final destruction, but of a transformation.

Dancing and music formed a part of youth's education in the time of Gautama and Goyame. Nevertheless, dancing was soon to fall into disfavor, perhaps because of growing stratification of society, professionalization of dancing, and its relegation to a low class of people who, because of excesses and irregularities said to have been common amongst them, were compelled in some places to dwell outside the city with other low elements of society.[97] Religious literature and law reflect this growing antagonism. Among the pastimes prohibited to Buddhist monks was entertainment by dancing girls.[98] The Laws of Manu put dancers, singers, liquor-dealers, cruel men, heretics, gamblers, and "those following forbidden occupations" all in one category, which the king should "instantly banish from his town." [99] Samvarta, a more recent work, listed dancers with leather-workers and washermen as impure.[100]

Despite the strictures of sacred books and legalistically religious minds, dancing continued to exert its popular appeal. Men danced and women danced; but dancing was by professional folk and lower social elements, not for respectable Hindu women or those of the Mohammedan faith.[101] Dances were of two classes, religious and profane. There were court dancers, temple dancers, and doubtless many who had no such favorable connections. Girls in the temple service were sometimes instructed in reading, writing, music, dancing, and singing. Under the Cholas of Tanjore, endowments made provision for four hundred temple dancers, whose duties also included music and

93 Müller: op. cit., xxxii, 402. From The Sacred Books of the East, edited by F. M. Müller (The Clarendon Press).
94 Coomaraswamy: op. cit., p. 56.
95 Ibid., p. 59.
96 Op. cit., pp. 28, 224, 271.
97 Ibid., pp. 170, 174, 200.
98 Müller: op. cit., xvii, 349.
99 Ibid., xxv, 381.
100 Dutt, R. C.: op. cit., pp. 659 f.
101 Hambly: Tribal Dancing, pp. 64 ff.

drama.[102] Temple women sometimes danced twice daily, once for their own sins, again for those of others.

Outside the court and temple circles, professional dancers and musicians served the fancy of men of wealth, by whom they were engaged to provide entertainment for guests. Grove describes such dancing, as observed in modern times: "In Bombay, the Asiatic Capua, the dancing-women, with their lithe figures and their languid eyes, remind us of the beautiful women of Greece. When a nautch takes place the young girls, at a signal given by the host, appear with bare feet. The music is generally monotonous, and the nautchees sing while they dance; in fact, the song is considered the chief part of the entertainment. They mostly express the passion of love with all the vicissitudes attendant on it—joy and fear, hope and jealousy, fury and delight; and every look, every attitude, every arm movement has been studied and exquisitely mimics the story. All dancing songs are not love songs, and occasionally some are introduced descriptive of incidents of Eastern life, such as war or the chase. The nautchees soon tire of their exertions, and generally several sets are hired for an entertainment ready to relieve one another. While they go through their gyrations the guests recline at their ease on couches, propped up with cushions, eating sweetmeats and fruit and drinking wines served by attendants." [103]

Besides such dances of an exhibitional character, numerous special dances may still be seen in parts of India, which are survivals of aboriginal customs. Such, for example, is the Khassia dance, described by Grove, in which the marriageable girls display themselves and choose, or are chosen by, "suitable" men: "A well-brought-up Khassia maiden of the superior class is taught that the perfection of dancing is to go round in a circle with the smallest possible amount of movement; not even an eyelid is to be lifted, her hands are to hang down by her side, and her feet are to be rigidly placed together, knees and ankle-bones touching each other. In this position she wriggles round the circle with a curious heel-and-toe motion—occasionally solemnly and slowly pirouetting round. The men amply compensate for the unexcited quietude of the girls; they jig, they leap, they hop, they wave arms, legs, umbrellas and knives about in the wildest confusion, accompanying their movements with the most savage war-whoops. . . ." [104]

[102] Venkateswara: op. cit., p. 295.
[103] Grove: Dancing, pp. 344 ff.; cf. Hambly: op. cit., pp. 21 f.
[104] Grove: op. cit., pp. 348 f.

# 7

# EMPIRE IN IRAN

The history of Medo-Persian greatness is brief. At the middle of the ninth century B.C. certain barbarous tribal folk, troublesome to their more civilized neighbor, Assyria, were brought under her subjection. Two centuries and a half later (606 B.C.), however, the tribes of the plateau having become united, Media and Babylonia became masters of the proud city of Nineveh. For half a century Media and Babylon lived peaceably with their two great neighbors, Lydia and Egypt. But peace, like calm preceding a storm, was not for long. On the southern marches of Media, a prince rose in revolt among the neighboring Persians, who till now had accepted the sway of Median kings.[1] Cyrus, characterized as "humane in disposition," "eager for knowledge," and "ambitious of honour," [2] was an intelligent, energetic, capable ruler. As head of the Persians he led them to victory over Media (550 B.C.), Lydia (546 B.C.), and Babylon (538 B.C.). Cyrus died (529 B.C.) but his successors brought Egypt, Armenia, Afghanistan, and the Indian Punjab under Persian sway. Darius and Xerxes made a protracted effort to force the Persian yoke on the reluctant Greeks, but were unsuccessful. Defeat at Plataea (479 B.C.) ended Persian hopes of conquering Hellas; they returned to Asia and, in 331 B.C., their Empire was destroyed by Alexander.

The organization and government of the Empire was probably the greatest achievement of Persian genius. Cyrus and some of his successors governed with a good deal of wisdom, albeit with severity. The kingship was hereditary; and the king's will was law. Disobedience, it is said, was punished by cutting off the head and arms.[3] Government was more centralized than it had been elsewhere.[4] Babylonia and Assyria had been rather loose organizations, mere aggre-

---

[1] The History of Herodotus, I, 123–30.
[2] Xenophon: Cyropaedia, I, 2, 1.
[3] The Geography of Strabo, xv, 3, 17.
[4] Sayce: Ancient Empires, pp. 247 ff.

gations of petty kingdoms which sometimes warred against each other without the approval of the "king of kings." Assyria had advanced, however, by dividing old kingdoms into satrapies under officers named by the king. The Persians extended and perfected this practice. Religion, customs, and laws of conquered peoples were left alone, but allegiance to the Great King was maintained through the payment of tribute, money, horses, and men. In each of the twenty provinces, a satrap governed, supported by a council and a general of the army. Check upon the satraps was constantly maintained through the "King's Ear," a royal secretary; the "King's Eye," a special agent of the king, investigated local governments from time to time, was armed with military authority, and could depose a satrap if necessary.[5]

Plato speaks highly of the degree of freedom which existed at certain times among the Persians, and says that the nation grew strong because of this "communion of soul." [6] Some degree of integration of mind may have resulted from a religion whose sacrificers were not permitted to pray for themselves alone, but "for the welfare of the king, and of the whole Persian people." [7] Too much stress should not be put upon this community of mind and of religion, however; for, though many accepted the religion of the Great King, the primary bond of union was one of steel; and when Persian rule was broken by Alexander, the union of peoples that had been effected by force, and held by force, readily disintegrated.

Linguistically, racially, religiously, the ruling class in India and the founders of the greatest empire before Alexander were related. Vedic literature and the sacred books of the Persians show that the ancestors of the creators of Brahmanism and Zoroastrianism once worshiped the same natural elements, wind and water, earth and sky, moon, sun, and fire.[8] "Unto Agni, son of the God Ormazd! Unto thee, O Agni, thou son of Ormazd, be grace, for thy worship, praise, propitiation, and glorification." As the ancient composers of the Vedas sang in praise of warrior, herdsman, and tiller of the soil, so, too, the poets of the Zend-Avesta celebrated the triumph of man over nature, of the good spirit over the bad, and of cultivation, which drives out the demon horde:

> When the corn grows, the demons hiss;
> When the shoots sprout, the demons cough . . .

From this common Indo-Iranian stock [9] those who dwelled in the high plateau of Iran developed, in the course of many centuries, a religion far different from Brahmanism. Zoroastrianism, so called from Zarathustra (dated

[5] Herodotus, III, 89–97.
[6] Laws, III, 694.
[7] Herodotus, I, 132.
[8] Ibid., I, 131–2; Strabo, XV, 3, 13–6.
[9] Müller: The Sacred Books of the East, IV, lvi–lxxxiii.

variously from the ninth to the seventh century), who is credited with formulating and crystallizing its teachings, was developed in Media by the Magi. After the conquest of Media by Cyrus, it became the official religion of the Persian rulers.

The central characteristic of Zoroastrianism or Mazdaism lies in the conception of a struggle between Ormazd—creator of all things, whose attributes are light, truth, goodness, life, wisdom, virtue, and purity—and Ahriman, the spirit of evil, sloth, death, decay, and darkness, who arose out of the conflict of forces when Ormazd created the world. All life is a struggle between the forces of good and those of evil. With one or the other men must ally themselves. Religion is, therefore, an individual matter. "Man, according to his deeds, belongs to Ormazd or to Ahriman." [10] This conception of choice between good and evil was the highest point to which the thought of the Medes and Persians rose. Mazdaism offered hope to the vigorous, struggling, striving individual—a blest eternity in the Abode of Song, where Ormazd dwelled with his angels; but the slothful and the evildoer would fall at death from a bridge into a nether world of torment. In its philosophical formulation Mazdaism must have been appreciated chiefly by its priestly creators, royalty, and nobility. The masses, who probably understood little of the conception of Mazda, must have continued to follow the primitive persuasions of their ancestors.

As a religion of activism, Mazdaism made a strong appeal to the soldierfolk whom Cyrus and Darius led to the founding of a mighty empire. By them its sway was extended, much as Christianity was extended by Constantine and Charlemagne, and as Mohammedanism was carried by the sword of Mohammed's followers. Certain texts of Mazdaism were like mottoes on their standards as they marched into battle: "Victory-making, army-governing, endowed with a thousand senses; power-wielding, power-possessing, and all-knowing; who sets the battle a going, who stands against armies in battles, who, standing against armies in battle, breaks asunder the lines arrayed. The wings of the columns gone to battle shake, and he throws terror upon the centre of the havocking host. He can bring and does bring down upon them distress and fear; he throws down the heads of those who lie unto Mithra, he takes off the heads of those who lie unto Mithra." [11]

The activism of Mazdaism was not limited to the field of battle. Instead of inviting men to idleness and reflection, it invited them to labor. Mazda is the god of "wide pastures" as well as of warfare. The irrigator, plowman, and harvester were all engaged in acts of righteousness; for he who labored "with his

---

[10] Ibid., IV, lxxiv. From The Sacred Books of the East, edited by F. M. Müller (The Clarendon Press).

[11] Ibid., XXIII, 128. From The Sacred Books of the East, edited by F. M. Müller (The Clarendon Press).

right arm and his left, with his left arm and his right" helped to subjugate the kingdom of darkness and death, and promoted the kingdom of life and light.[12]

Apart from religion, Persia contributed little to the culture of the world. Art and architecture were borrowed from her neighbors, Assyria and Babylon. Of her early literature, except the *Avesta*, we know little. In later centuries, of course, Firdausi, Sadi, Hafiz, Nizami lent luster to the Persian name. In commerce Persians were not distinguished; being busy fighting and ruling, they neither bought nor sold, as Strabo says, nor concerned themselves with markets.[13] From numerous early references to the gods' concern for agriculture, one might expect that it would have flourished; but such was not the case. The religion of the bow and spear transcended that of the plow and reaping hook, promising easier rewards. According to Herodotus, Cyrus promised his people that, if they would follow him, they would enjoy innumerable pleasures and "never condescend to any slavish toil." [14] A certain contempt for useful labor developed in privileged military circles, as pernicious in effect as that which marked the feudal aristocracy of western Europe at a later date. Moreover, in that high, arid plateau, where, in Strabo's fantastic phrase, lizards could not cross the streets of Susis fast enough at noonday to avoid being burned to death,[15] agriculture could not flourish generally (though in parts the temperature was mild and the valleys fertile) save by persistent, painstaking encouragement; and wealth, which might have been used for constructive development of the land, was squandered on the more heroic, exciting, dazzling project of conquering Europe as well as Asia. Persian military greatness was shortly blasted and eclipsed by the feats of another war lord. Probably no greater efforts have ever been expended for so little of lasting value.

Notwithstanding the futility of their ambitious empire-building, the Persians were an able, cheerful, rather carefree, pleasant, high-minded folk, whose private life reveals certain attractive features. Herodotus pictures them as ready to adopt foreign customs (even the "unnatural lust" of the Greeks), non-idolatrous in their worship, friendly and affectionate to those of their own rank, always ready to celebrate birthdays with a feast, and to make decisions in weighty matters only after double consideration—first when drunk, second when sober, or vice versa! To defile rivers,[16] tell lies, speak of anything that was unlawful to do, pray for one's self alone, and kill one's parents, were to them blameworthy. Less estimable, however, were their tendency to hold themselves "greatly superior in all respects to the rest of mankind," their religious persuasion that it was necessary to kill animals, and the subjection of women.

[12] Jackson: *Persia Past and Present*, pp. 25, 246.
[13] *Strabo*, xv, 3, 19.
[14] Bk. I, 126.
[15] Bk. xv, 3, 10.
[16] *Ibid.*, xv, 3, 16.

Polygamy and concubinage were quite common, says Herodotus.[17] The place of women was wholly domestic, the care of their children, to the age of five at least, their greatest concern. Sadi's estimate of women in the thirteenth century was still that of the ancient world: "Take your wife's opinion, and act in opposition to it"; "Choose a fresh wife every spring . . . for the Almanack of last year is good for nothing." [18]

## PERSIAN EDUCATION

MORAL AND INTELLECTUAL   Informal moral training, whether in the home or at a place of exercise, was emphasized in ancient Persia. Earliest influences were those of the mother, or her assistants in the case of the wealthy, for Persian boys were not seen by their fathers until they were five years of age. The purpose of this training, both in childhood and adolescence, was to inculcate certain habits and ideals, "piety in thought, word and action," that one might be a useful servant of the state.[19] The habit of obedience was fixed from the very outset; of equal importance was the habit of truthfulness, which impressed Herodotus as one of the three aspects of education between the ages of five and twenty years. Xenophon says that the Persians sought to insure by education that their citizens should not "be inclined to any action that is bad and mean." [20]

About the age of five, according to Herodotus and Strabo,[21] or at seven, as Plato says, speaking of the princes,[22] Persian boys began to receive a more systematic training, under teachers who were their "wisest men." There were no schools, however, in the usual sense, and little instruction of a literary character. For the lower class there was none, even of an elementary sort; and for wealthy and noble families, education seems to have been moral and physical rather than mental, being based upon direct teaching and examples of individuals rather than books. Strabo says that instruction at the age of five involved myths, the deeds of gods and the noblest men, rehearsed with and without singing. As for the Magi,[23] their wisdom was at first passed on by word of mouth. Ultimately, however, their knowledge of astrology, laws and customs, philosophy, medicine that was closely allied to primitive magic, and knowledge of the unseen world in general, was reduced to written form; thereafter, Magian education required the mastery of their sacred books, a part of which are known to us as the Zend-Avesta. The priests were the only formal teachers,

[17] Bk. I, 131–40.
[18] Costello: The Rose Garden of Persia, p. 94.
[19] Modi: Education among the Ancient Iranians, pp. 44 ff.
[20] Cyropaedia, I, 2, 3.
[21] Herodotus, I, 136; Strabo, xv, 3, 18.
[22] "First Alcibiades," Dialogues of Plato, IV, 541.
[23] Ragozin: The Story of Media, Babylon, and Persia, pp. 268 ff.

and since they were differentiated into several classes, education must have varied somewhat also. In the early medieval period, under the Sassanids, the nobles, too, learned at their hands, to "read, write, [and] reckon"; and the "wealthier townsmen," the merchants, were probably also taught.[24]

PHYSICAL CULTURE   Persian society was made up of three classes, priests, soldiers, and industrials (farmers, tradesmen, and mechanics)—though class lines were not rigidly fixed. For the latter, the poorer sort, knowledge and manual skills must have been acquired by a natural apprenticeship in the family, since children generally pursued the occupations of their fathers.[25] A plow with a share, a yoke, a whip for the oxen, a stone mortar, a mill for grinding corn by hand, and a spade for digging, are named as tools used by husbandmen.[26] Practice in their use probably constituted the chief part of training on the land. Physical culture of a more extensive and elaborate sort was primarily military in character, a phase of the apprenticeship to arms, designed to render the soldier class effective in the task of empire-building.

Our knowledge of Persian physical training is rather unsatisfactory, since there are but scattered references to it, and these are by foreign writers, Herodotus, Xenophon, Strabo, whose reporting often deviates from approved canons of historical writing, and must be constantly subject to discount. Xenophon's Cyropaedia, while it professes to describe the education of young Cyrus, and has been credited with varying degrees of significance as a portrait of Persian education,[27] is primarily an idealized portrait of Spartan education. Naturally, since Sparta and Persia both designed education for military ends, there was much in common between them, but Xenophon's portrayal was propaganda for a scheme of society and education which he admired; and while there is doubtless something of fact in the Cyropaedia, it is difficult to divine where fact leaves off and fancy begins. Fortunately, Persian religious books provide information on certain points and impart a degree of authenticity to the general portrait of ideals and practices in ancient Iran.

Somewhat akin to the Greek, the Persian ideal included the welfare of soul and body. Zoroaster prayed for victorious thinking, speaking, and acting, and Mazda gave him "fountains of manliness," strength of arms, keen sight, health, and sturdiness of the entire body. His pious followers likewise prayed first for heaven—the soul's welfare—and next for health and physical strength.[28] In harmony with this desire Persian leaders laid heavy stress on physical education. The three ends of training, says Herodotus, was "to ride, to draw the

---

[24] Huart: Ancient Persia, pp. 153 f.
[25] Modi: op. cit., pp. 52 f.
[26] Müller: op. cit., IV, 170.
[27] Letourneau: L'Évolution de l'Éducation, pp. 404 f.; Laurie: Historical Survey of Pre-Christian Education, p. 202; Forbes: Greek Physical Education, p. 94.
[28] Müller: op. cit., XXIII, 238 f.; XXXI, 236.

bow, and to speak the truth." Even being the father of many sons, which was encouraged by annual prizes, was put second "to prowess in arms." [29] Darius enumerated among his greatest achievements—things that future generations ought to know—that he excelled all others as horseman, archer, and hunter. In the next breath, however, he strains our credulity by adding, "I could do everything." [30] Though his boasting must be discounted, it reveals the pattern of physical skills most prized by a nation bent upon conquest—a pattern in which a king might be expected to excel.

The importance of the horse in Persian life could scarcely be exaggerated. In war, hunting, and polo its rôle was central. So much were Persians accustomed to move from place to place on horses that a common measure of distance was a day's journey on horseback. The devout prayed to Mithra for his own health, but at the same time begged strength and speed for his horses, that he might destroy his enemies completely.[31] He whose prayers to the goddess of Fortune were acceptable, was promised the reward of "horses swift and loud-neighing" and a swift, light chariot in battle.[32] Darius set up a monument to his horse, maintaining that he gained sway over Persia by virtue of his horse and groom.[33]

The soldiers' training was severe and long, though accounts vary somewhat as to its duration, and one must make allowance for the speculations of the Greeks. Herodotus says that from the fifth year to the twentieth they were taught to ride and use the bow; Strabo adds hurling the javelin to the list and spreads the period of training from five to twenty-four. Xenophon divides training into two periods: first, up to sixteen or seventeen; then an additional ten years of guard duty, hunting, and continued practice with bow and javelin which the men had learned as boys. According to Xenophon only those participated in this sort of training whose families were able to maintain them without putting them to labor. Strabo has the soldiers perform service in the army, both infantry and cavalry, between the ages of twenty and fifty. Xenophon makes the full-grown men spend twenty-five years after their second period of training subject to the orders of magistrates for military or other service in the interest of the state.[34]

The daily regimen, says Strabo, began with rising before dawn, and mustering in one place, as if to arm or to go hunting. Here they were divided into companies of fifty, each under a leader who put them through a race over a course thirty to forty stadia in length. Toughness was developed through watching herds, staying on guard all night, exposure to heat, cold, and rain, and

[29] Herodotus, I, 136; Strabo, xv, 3, 17.
[30] Strabo, xv, 3, 8.
[31] Müller: op. cit., xxiii, 122.
[32] Ibid., xxiii, 273.
[33] Herodotus, iii, 88.
[34] Ibid., i, 136; Strabo, xv, 3, 18–9; Cyropaedia, i, 2, 8–13, 15.

practice in crossing swift streams while keeping their clothes and weapons dry. According to Strabo's account the king gave prizes to encourage youth to excel in the exercises of the pentathlon. A certain amount of industrial labor and skill apparently was included in this early training of boys, for in the evening they are said to have worked at planting trees, cutting and collecting roots, and making armor, lines, and nets.[35]

Diet was simple and limited. Each day, when at home, their meals were of bread, cakes of barley, stewed or roasted meat, cardamom, salt, and water. Youth were expected to forage for wild fruits and nuts while on excursions away from home. Xenophon has it that the older youth, when hunting, might eat the flesh of wild animals they had killed; Strabo, however, who may be thinking of the younger boys, says they were not to eat the meat of wild animals taken in the chase, but were to bring their bag home.[36]

The education of young Cyrus, doubtless embellished considerably by his biographers, may be taken as an idealized pattern of a princely Persian's education. Herodotus says that when grown to manhood he was "the bravest and most popular of all his compeers." [37] Xenophon,[38] who refers to Cyrus as "most princely," modest, obedient, fond of horses and able to manage them, "assiduous in practising the warlike exercises of archery, and hurling the javelin," and fond of the chase, has described his education, showing the stress laid on skill in shooting, riding, and hunting:

"Thus he became more quiet, but was still in society extremely agreeable; for in whatever exercises he and his equals used to emulate each other, he did not challenge his companions to those in which he knew himself superior, but in those in which he felt himself inferior, he was the first to commence declaring that he would perform better than they. Accordingly, he would begin vaulting upon the horse, shooting with the bow, or hurling the javelin on horseback, while he was yet scarcely able to sit on a horse; and, when he was outdone, he was the first to laugh at himself; and as, on being unsuccessful, he did not shrink from attempting again the things in which he had failed, but assiduously employed himself in endeavouring to do them better, he soon attained an equality with his companions in horsemanship, and, by his love of the exercise, soon left them behind." [39]

A glance at the Persian army and its equipment tells us something of physical skills needed by those who filled its ranks. The *Vendidad* mentions the

[35] Strabo, xv, 3, 18.
[36] Ibid.; Cyropaedia, I, 2, 8, 11, 16.
[37] Bk. I, 123.
[38] Anabasis, I, 9.
[39] Cyropaedia, I, 4, 4–5. From Xenophon's Cyropaedia, or Institution of Cyrus, and The Hellenics. Trans. by J. S. Watson and H. Dale. George Bell & Sons, London, 1891.

javelin, knife, club, bow, quiver, shoulder belt and thirty brass-headed arrows, sling, thirty slingstones, cuirass, hauberk, tunic, helmet, girdle, and greaves as the implements of war.[40] These are mostly duplicated in the description of equipment by Herodotus, who says that Persian corselets were metal-plated like the Egyptian, and their tunics and trousers were leathern. Strabo mentions rhomboid-shaped wicker shields. Their deadliest weapon was the arrow, which they commonly discharged from a kneeling position with such effectiveness that the enemy was often beaten, or in any case thrown into confusion, before much hand-to-hand conflict could take place. Archers were assisted by swift-moving cavalry which outflanked and surrounded the enemy forces, or pursued them when they took to flight.[41] The army under the Sassanids had its chief strength in cavalry, both Persian and that of the tributary peoples. These knights commonly had for offensive equipment lances six feet long, bows and arrows, short straight swords, maces, axes, lassos, spears, and daggers. The chief strength of the Persian cavalry was always the bow, it is said; while that of their tributaries was in the spear, sword, and dagger. The infantry, at least at this time, was not very important; its members were but little trained in military skills and were armed only with wicker shields covered with skins. A reserve was provided of trained elephants, whose use had been learned from the Indians. They were also capable in siege-craft, which they are said to have learned from the Romans.[42]

In the Iranian mythology, hunting is traced back to Tahmurath, descendant of Hushang, first king of the oldest dynasty, who is credited with having taught his people to weave, keep domestic animals, and to train the snow leopard and falcon for use in hunting.[43] Whatever the merit of the myth, which is similar to that of many other peoples, hunting was as old as their earliest history and continued to be a favorite sport, of the privileged classes at least, when Persia rose to leadership of the empire. Probably because it was both useful as preparation for war and also destroyed many obnoxious animals, it constituted a part of the regular training of Persian youth.

Although Xenophon was a great enthusiast for hunting, the rôle which he credited to it as a schooling for war amongst the Persians can scarcely have exceeded the reality. "They attend to hunting," he says, "as a matter of public interest, and the king, as in war, is their leader, hunting himself, and seeing that others do so; because it seems to them to be the most efficient exercise for all such things as relate to war. It accustoms them to rise early in the morning,

---

[40] Müller: op. cit., IV, 169.
[41] Herodotus, I, 71, 135; VII, 61; Strabo, XV, 3, 18–9; Rawlinson: Five Great Monarchies, III, 238–43.
[42] Huart: op. cit., pp. 149 ff.
[43] Ibid., p. 206.

BAHRAM GUR HUNTING

(Courtesy, The Metropolitan Museum of Art, New York)

and to bear heat and cold; it exercises them in long marches, and in running; it necessitates them to use their bow against the beast that they hunt, and to throw their javelin, wherever he falls in their way; their courage must, of necessity, be often sharpened in the hunt, when any of the strong and vigorous beasts present themselves; for they must come to blows with the animal if he comes up to them, and must be upon their guard as he approaches; so that it is not easy to find what single thing, of all that is practised in war, is not to be found in hunting." [44]

Skill in hunting was a standard by which to measure kingly quality, whether in India, Egypt, Assyria, China, or Persia. It is not surprising, therefore, that Xenophon portrayed Cyrus as possessed of the greatest fearlessness and skill in hunting, so swiftly destroying all the wild animals in the paradise that the supply was not adequate to exercise his prowess. Seeing this, he besought his grandfather to allow him to hunt with others outside the park. Accordingly, Astyages, having learned of his desire to hunt abroad, "sent him out with his uncle, and sent some older persons on horseback with him, as guards upon him, to take care of him in the rugged parts of the country, and in case any beasts of the fiercer kind should show themselves. Cyrus, in consequence, was very earnest in inquiring of those that attended him, what beasts he was not to approach, and what sort of animals he might confidently pursue. They told him that bears had destroyed many that had ventured to approach them, as well as lions, wild boars, and leopards, but that stags, antelopes, wild sheep, and wild asses, were harmless creatures. They told him, likewise, that he must guard against rough places not less than the beasts; for that many men, with their horses, had been carried headlong over precipices. Cyrus attended to all these instructions very readily; but, as soon as he saw a stag leap forth, forgetting all that he had heard, he pursued, regarding nothing but which way the animal fled; and his horse, taking a leap with him, fell somehow upon his knees, and very nearly threw him over his neck. However Cyrus, though with difficulty, kept upon his back, and the horse got up again. When he reached the open ground he hurled his javelin, and struck the stag down, a fine large animal; and he was most highly delighted. But his guards, riding up to him, reproved him, told him into what danger he had run, and said that they must complain of him. Cyrus, having alighted from his horse, stood and listened to this with much uneasiness; but, hearing a shout, he sprang on his horse, as in a sort of enthusiasm, and seeing before him a boar advancing, he rode forward to meet it, and taking a good aim with his javelin, struck the boar in the forehead, and brought it down. But now his uncle, seeing his rashness, began to reprove him. Cyrus however, notwithstanding his uncle was finding fault with

<hr>

[44] Cyropaedia, I, 2, 10. From Xenophon's Cyropaedia, or Institution of Cyrus, and The Hellenics. Trans. by J. S. Watson and H. Dale. George Bell & Sons, London, 1891.

him, begged that he would allow him to carry off the beasts that he had taken, and to present them to his grandfather." [45]

Hunting was practiced both in open territory and in closed hunting parks or paradises, which were well stocked with lions, tigers, boars, stags, peacocks, pheasants, wild asses, gazelles, and ostriches. When hunting, the king was accompanied by a great retinue, frequently including even musicians. The bow and arrow were the favorite weapons for the chase, and fabulous stories are told of the accuracy with which they were used.[46] Nets, clubs, and spears were also used; and dogs for hunting were imported from India. The traditional sport had notable followers of royal blood as late as Chosroes II (590 A.D.) who is represented in contemporary sculptures as hunting the stag and the wild boar, assisted by beaters who drive the game toward him, while he is entertained by a company of harpists.[47]

In a nation dominated by warriors, approved sports were military or served some warlike end. Fishing, so commonly linked in modern times with hunting as a sport, had no place in Persia save as an occupation of commoners. "To fish" meant "to hunt fish"; and a fisherman was one who made his living by hunting and disposing of fish. For such a purpose the net was the only proper instrument. Herodotus [48] tells the fable, credited to Cyrus, of the piper who sought unsuccessfully to entice fish by his piping, but caught a great haul when he resorted to a net. Radcliffe says that native Persian has no word for "fish-hook," and there is no evidence of angling being practiced either in ancient or modern Persia.[49]

Competing with hunting in popularity among the warriors of ancient Persia was chugan or polo, from a Tibetan word pulu—a light ball of willow root. This ancient game, between which and golf, cricket, hurling, chicane of Languedoc, and calcio of Florence, a kinship has been claimed,[50] has been credited by certain historians to some time before the beginning of history, and by others more specifically to about 600 B.C., when heroic Siyawush and his Persian players astounded Afrasiab, king of Turania, with their remarkable equestrian skill and dexterity with gui (ball) and chugan (stick). Firdausi drew the picture:

> Now when the bright sun made the distance clear,
> And showed its face from heaven to all the land,

[45] Ibid., I, 4, 7–9. From Xenophon's Cyropaedia, or Institution of Cyrus, and The Hellenics. Trans. by J. S. Watson and H. Dale. George Bell & Sons, London, 1891.
[46] Nizami: The Haft Paikar, I, 48 ff.; Firdausi: Sháhnáma, VI, 382 ff.
[47] Julian the Emperor, p. 198; Huart: op. cit., pp. 33, 76 f., 145 f., 197; Jackson: op. cit., p. 222; Modi: op. cit., pp. 12 ff.
[48] Bk. I, 141.
[49] Fishing from the Earliest Times, pp. 50 f.
[50] Ouseley: Travels, I, 346.

> The prince went from his palace to the Ground
> To play at polo. Garsiwaz came up
> And drove the ball, which Siyawush pursued
> And caught it fairly with the polo-stick,
> While his opponent only found the dust.
> The ball struck by the prince was seen no more:
> Thou wouldst have said: "The sky hath drawn it up!" [51]

Discounting the early legends, Laufer credits polo's origin, about the beginning of the present era, to "Iranian tribes of Central Asia," whence it was carried into Persia and later into China.[52] Though certain of its derivative forms became the games of commoners, polo was originally a sport so hard and hazardous as to be thought worthy of kings and nobility. Naturally its expensive equipment made it the privilege of men of wealth. A host of traditions, apocryphal stories, and poetic utterances told of its royal associations. Hystaspes, half-legendary king of Persia, is represented by Firdausi as wielding his *chugan* so well that:

> The warriors paused, not one could see the ball,
> His stroke had made it vanish in mid air! [53]

Allegorical interpretation of the universe, creation, life, fate, destiny—in short, the whole of human *Tun und Streben*—runs through Persian literature on polo. As 'Ārifi says:

> Before I speak of the present state of things I
> must speak of the Glorious Creator . . .
> By Him the ball of the sphere is circling around
> the polo stick of the new moon . . .
> By His wisdom are set in action the polo stick
> of Fate and the ball of Destiny. . . .[54]

An oft-told story ran that, upon Alexander's succession to the throne, the Persian monarch (with no flattering intention) sent him a ball and polo stick with which to play. Alexander accepted, reading a fair meaning in the gift—that the ball was for him the earth and he, himself, the stick to drive it.

Under the Parthians, who came to power in Persia after Alexander, little is known of polo. Throughout the Sassanid dynasty, however, the game flour-

---

51 *Sháhnáma*, II, 292. Trans. by A. G. Warner and E. Warner. Courtesy of George Routledge & Sons, Ltd. and Kegan Paul, Trench, Trübner & Co., Ltd., London.
52 Laufer: "The Early History of Polo," *Polo*, VII, 13. For an excellent treatment of polo see Carl Diem, *Asiatische Reiterspiele*, Deutscher Archiv-Verlag, Berlin, 1942.
53 *Sháhnáma*, IV, 350.
54 Greenshields: *The Ball and the Polo Stick*, p. 5.

ished. Ardashir, its founder (226 A.D.), reputedly excelled in hunting and polo. Shapur, the son of Ardashir (241–272), is said to have revealed his kingly lineage by the unabashed recovery of a polo ball which fell right at the sovereign's feet. Bahram Gur, famed for his prowess in archery and hunting, is said to have been accomplished also in horsemanship and polo—everything, in fact, "useful or necessary for kings." At the end of the Sassanian period, perhaps earlier, ladies of the court are said to have played at polo with great skill. Under the Mohammedans, who for some time were too busy with warfare, polo apparently fell into disuse, but by the ninth century it had gained popularity among them as it had under the Sassanians. Harun-al-Rashid, still a mere boy, was described as unable to reach or hit the ball with a polo stick. In the twelfth century polo was popular at Constantinople, where Manuel Comnenus and his nobles were enthusiastic players. The conquering Tamerlane is credited with introducing a novel feature at Damascus, where his warriors used enemy heads for the game of *gui* and *chugan*.[55]

The ancient game, like the modern in all essential features, involved two opposing teams which, contending for the ball, sought to drive it through a goal (*mil*), using a long-handled mallet. The head of the stick varied: at times it was curved and spoonlike, so as to catch the ball; again there were crescent-shaped and straight transverse heads. Stone goal posts, nine feet high and twenty-four feet apart, still stand at Isfahan; the field (*maidan*) there measured 1,680 feet by 510 feet. The number of players was sometimes great, but four or six on a side probably constituted matches as a rule.

Persian traditions, recorded in their literature, are filled with heroic battles, feats of horsemanship, archery, and conquests of wild beasts in hunting. Of less warlike contests, little is said. Strabo [56] has it, however, that the king gave prizes to victors in running and the other contests of the pentathlon, but the nature and extent of such events is left obscure. Perhaps through contact with her neighbors wrestling gained ground in Persia. However that may be, as described by modern travelers it seems to have become a complex science. Ouseley shows two wrestlers being instructed by a master in some of the "tricks by which an antagonist may, without a blow, be extended backwards on the ground." [57] In the entire range of this Persian "jiujitsu" there were said to be 360 different ways by which to vanquish one's opponent. In this connection Ouseley relates the story of a master of wrestling who had taught his protégé every trick save one. The neophyte, becoming proud, insultingly challenged his teacher to a match before the governor. The contest was arranged; but,

---

[55] Ouseley: *op. cit.*, I, 345–55; Sykes: *Ten Thousand Miles in Persia*, chap. 29; Modi: *op. cit.*, pp. 20 ff.; Brown: *Polo*, chap. 1; Huart: *op. cit.*, pp. 143, 154; Jackson: *op. cit.*, p. 266.

[56] Bk. xv, 3, 18.

[57] *Op. cit.*, I, 234 ff.

A MASTER ABOUT TO THROW HIS PUPIL

(W. Ouseley, *Travels in Various Countries of the East*, I, Pl. XIII)

alas for the vain youth, all his skill and vigor could do nothing against the one trick which his master held in reserve. Completely undone, he was lifted bodily in the air above his master's head and hurled to the ground. The tale recalls the "house of strength" described by Buckingham in his *Travels in Assyria, Media, and Persia.* These gymnasia or athletic clubs, of which there were four or five at Shiraz and many others, he says, at Isfahan, Kermanshah, Teheran, and even Bokhara and Samarkand, were once subsidized by the government; but at the time of his visit, this was no longer true, and much of the support came from the public, which was attracted thither by the startling feats of skill that were performed. Champions went from place to place and challenged local talent. The skill and power of one of these, Melek Mohammed, who caught his opponent "by a single grasp, whirled him in the air, and threw him so violently on the ground that he expired on the spot," recall the scene of the professor of wrestling and his puffed-up pupil.[58]

Though dancing was characteristic of primitive Aryan life, and Xenophon says that Cyrus, though growing old, "made the usual sacrifices" and "led the dance among the Persians according to the practice of the country . . . as he had been accustomed," [59] there is no reference to dancing as a part of the education of Persian youth. In this, as in other matters, Xenophon may have had his eye on Sparta. However that may be, dancing had a strong hold in some circles. Certain Persian dance movements were introduced into Greece. A Persian dance, similar to one of the Cossacks, in which the dancer squats and alternately thrusts the legs forward horizontally, was known as *oklasma* to the Greeks, whose artists depicted it on certain vases about the fourth century B.C. Rumi, thirteenth century Persian poet, declared that he who knows "the power of the dance" knows God. The whirling dervish dances of his day, Sachs believes, must run back to primitive motifs thousands of years old in central Asia.[60]

With the development of Persian society, as in other Oriental civilizations, dancing appears to have become exhibitional in character and was associated with professional entertainers, generally of a low social status. Grove [61] asserts that "the religion of the country" sought to suppress dancing and even the records of it, but noted the continuance of professional dancing in great cities and also of certain dances of peasants in remote regions. Other modern observers of Persian life have commented on the prevalence of exhibition dancing, provided by professional entertainers. Some of the exhibitions at the

[58] Buckingham: *op. cit.*, II, 38–40.
[59] *Cyropaedia*, VIII, 7, 1.
[60] Sachs: *World History of the Dance*, pp. 4, 29 f., 42, 142; Keller: "An Oriental Dance on an Attic Vase," *Bul. Fogg Museum of Art*, IX, 56 ff.
[61] *Dancing*, p. 350.

"house of strength," described by Buckingham, were a mixture of wrestling, dancing, and acrobatics:

"At the sound of a drum and guitar, the men began to exercise themselves with large clubs held across their shoulders, moving in a measured dance: they next began to jump, and then stoop to the ground, as if about to sit, springing up again suddenly on their legs: they next swung one foot for a considerable length of time, and then the other; after which there was violent jumping and dancing, and afterwards a motion like swimming on the earth, by placing their breasts nearly to touch the soil, then drawing their bodies forward, and rising again, some even in this position bearing a man clinging fast to their loins. They next began to walk on their hands, with their feet in the air, falling from this position hard on the ground, turning head over heels in the air, and, last of all, wrestling with each other. All these feats were performed to measured tones of music; and each encounter of the last description was preceded by the recital of a poem, in order to encourage the combatants, which was done by the master of the place." [62]

Ouseley also reported dances, frequently acrobatic in nature, at the "houses of strength," in which boys, dressed in women's clothing, imitated dancing girls. Another "very extraordinary dance," which reminded him of the ancient Roman Salians, was performed by eighty or a hundred athletic men, accoutered with swords and knives and accompanied by music and a chant in praise of Mohammed.[63] Jackson reports dancing exhibitions somewhat like nautch dances of India, performed by handsome effeminate boys, and suggests that it may have been such as these whom Zoroaster's teaching condemned.[64]

Ceremonial cleansing and healing by incantation, with fees to the priests graduated according to the wealth and station of the person served, were provided in the sacred books of Persia. Numerous regulations concerning ablution of the face and hands, under various circumstances, appear in the Pahlavi texts. In certain cases propitiation required that the body and the clothes be thoroughly washed.[65] Apart from ritualistic cleansing, however, a superstitious regard for elements, such as fire, earth, and water, was prevalent in Persia and led to extraordinary efforts to keep them from pollution. Strabo says that the Persians neither bathed nor washed themselves in rivers, nor permitted pollution of them in any way. Elsewhere, however, Strabo casually drops a hint as to bathing: speaking of the intensity of the heat, he observes that cold water placed in the sun is quickly warmed for bathing. The taboo on bathing in

[62] Buckingham: op. cit., II, 36 f.
[63] Ouseley: op. cit., I, 190; III, 170 f., 402; Browne: A Year amongst the Persians, pp. 119 f., 320.
[64] Jackson: op. cit., pp. 52 f.; Müller: op. cit., IV, 100 ff.
[65] Müller: op. cit., IV, 84 f., 129 ff., 138 ff.; V, 259, 278, 293, 307, 333, 347.

rivers did not apparently interfere with the exigencies of war, since Strabo informs us that youth were trained "to cross torrential streams" in preparation for it, which implies learning how to swim. Herodotus says, however, that many of the barbarians lost their lives at Salamis because "they did not know how to swim." [66] Presumably the Magi were most meticulous about such taboos; a modern scholar asserts that the priests once overthrew a king because he built bathhouses, thus promoting the pollution of water.[67] The case, of course, does not establish a rule, but it shows the fanatical attitude of the priesthood and the extremes to which a principle might be carried before orthodoxy gave way to a more enlightened conception of sanitation. In modern Persia, Buckingham reported, the baths were "of a superior kind." [68]

[66] *Herodotus*, VIII, 89; *Strabo*, XV, 3, 10, 16, 18; Modi: *op. cit.*, p. 37.
[67] Müller: *op. cit.*, IV, xc.
[68] *Op. cit.*, I, 172, 185 ff., 349 f.; II, 65.

# 3

# EMPIRES OF THE SEA

Minos is the first to whom tradition ascribes the possession of a navy. He made himself master of a great part of what is now termed the Hellenic sea. . . . [later] the Hellenes likewise began to build navies and to make the sea their element.   THUCYDIDES

# 8

# ISLAND EMPIRE

THE PEOPLE AND THEIR CULTURE  A renowned traveler observed that the Greeks did not generally agree about their traditions.[1] Lacking exact history, they referred variously to the Pelasgians, "Peoples of the Sea," who by one account were a pre-Arcadian folk; by another, dwellers at the foot of Athens' Acropolis; and again, expellers of the Minyans from Lemnos.[2] Herodotus reported vestigial survivals of a "Pelasgic race" who still spoke a barbarous (i.e., non-Hellenic) tongue he could not understand.[3] Thucydides says that Pelasgians, the most widespread of pre-Hellenic tribes, gave their name to various districts.[4] Homer gives a place to the "stout Pelasgians" from Larissa, and elsewhere notes them among the many-tongued peoples of Crete.[5] Diodorus says that migrating Pelasgians found a haven in Crete, being the first outsiders to mix with indigenous Cretans.[6]

Certain modern scholars, partly in harmony with Hellenic tradition, find the perplexing Pelasgians a pre-Hellenic folk originally of northern Greece, some of whom were driven by invading Achaeans to the hills of Thessaly (perhaps about 2000 B.C.) and others to piracy on the sea. Some link them with Tyrrhenians, Lydians, Etruscans, and other peoples of the Mediterranean and its borders, as did the Greek historians.[7] As for the Eteo-Cretans, a non-Hellenic folk who, Diodorus and Strabo report, claimed to be the oldest population of

---

[1] Pausanias's Description of Greece, IX, 16, 7.
[2] Ibid., I, 28, 3; VII, 2, 2; VIII, 1, 4; 4, 1.
[3] The History of Herodotus, I, 57.
[4] Thucydides, I, 3.
[5] The Iliads of Homer, II, 747–9; The Odysseys of Homer, XIX, 244.
[6] Diodorus of Sicily, v, 80.
[7] The Cambridge Ancient History, II, 12, 476; Burn: Minoans, Philistines, and Greeks, pp. 58 ff., 132 f.; Glotz: The Aegean Civilization, p. 39; Herodotus, I, 57; Thucydides, IV, 109.

the Island sprung from the very soil, they are known to-day as members of the long-headed Mediterranean race which held sway before the advent of Indo-Europeans (the short-headed Achaeans and Dorians), who gradually mixed with them and rose to dominion. As for physical appearance the primitive Cretans were small, slender-waisted, athletic, and wiry. They are commonly represented with long hair, but with faces smooth-shaven.[8]

What the great river valleys were to the peoples of Egypt, Mesopotamia, India, and China, the sea was to the early Cretans—challenger and benefactor. Strabo [9] noted that the islanders were once rulers of the sea. Cretan Minos, Thucydides says,[10] was the first who created a navy, gained possession of most Hellenic waters, conquered the Cyclades and colonized them, and then sought to clear the sea of pirates. It seemed to Aristotle [11] that the Island, with one extremity near the Peloponnesus and the other reaching out to Rhodes and the Asian coast, was designed for dominion. Hence it was that Minos was able to create "the empire of the sea." Modern history and archaeology support the ancient authors' view that Cretan culture was made "possible only by the sea." With Crete as center, the eastern Mediterranean became the first great mixing bowl of early cultures of many lands.[12] Situated here, the neolithic Aegeans occupied a position of unsurpassed importance at the crossroads of the highways of the sea, reaching from the cities of the Nile to the mainland of Europe and to the little islands of the Aegean which lie like steppingstones to Asia Minor and the civilization of the fertile valleys beyond. In Crete, their island home, stone tools and weapons were soon laid aside, and a great bronze age culture arose, whose "ninety cities" were to "crown the famous shore." [13]

Though there are still many uncertainties, more is known to us to-day of that "Golden Age" which preceded historic Sparta and Athens than was known to the Greeks themselves. But until Schliemann dug up ancient Ilium, Tiryns, and Mycenae (1870–1884) [14] and Evans [15] bared the famous town of Knossos (1900–1905), little was known, save what Greek tradition vaguely told, of the great pre-Hellenic Aegean civilization centering on the Island of Crete and reaching out to numerous points of the Mediterranean basin. Thanks to them, their associates and successors, one may speak to-day with fair assurance of certain aspects of a bronze age civilization which arose on a base of neolithic cul-

---

[8] Diodorus, v, 64; The Geography of Strabo, x, 4, 6; Glotz: op. cit., pp. 57 ff.; Hall: Aegean Archaeology, pp. 34 f., 258; Mosso: The Dawn of Mediterranean Civilization, chap. 26.

[9] Bk. x, 4, 17.

[10] Bk. i, 4.

[11] Politica, ii, 10.

[12] Hall: op. cit., pp. 259 f.; Mosso: op. cit., p. 282; Glotz: op. cit., pp. 5, 44.

[13] Od., xix, 243–4.

[14] Schuchhardt: Schliemann's Excavations, pp. 6–15.

[15] The Palace of Minos at Knossos, i, v–vii.

ture, five or six millenniums before our era. In the development of this civilization four main periods are recognized: a neolithic age, 6000?–3000 B.C.; Early
Minoan, 3000–2100 B.C.; Middle Minoan, 2100–1500 B.C.; and Late Minoan,
1500–1200 B.C. In respect to metals, the Minoan civilization of Crete passed
through a transition Chalcolithic period, 3000–2400, and the bronze age,
about 2400–1200.[16]

Crete had developed extensive trade, built its first palaces, and reached an
advanced state of culture in many respects by 2000 B.C. After 1700 a vigorous
expansion took place, culminating in the "Golden Age" of Cretan culture,
about 1580–1400.[17] Thereafter, Crete lost her leadership following an apparently cataclysmic destruction of Knossos, when Minos, according to ancient
story, conducted a disastrous punitive expedition against Sicily.[18] If this was
the occasion of the collapse of Knossos, other forces may have been operative:
rapid expansion, with an attendant weakening of the native stock and spreading thin of policing power; growth of a population, whose food in some degree
depended on supplies from Egypt; rise of Mycenae, whose lords would naturally desire to eliminate the middlemen of Crete; development of a burdensome bureaucracy; excessive refinement, delicacy, and vice,[19] to which prosperous civilizations are commonly heir: decay of martial spirit and prowess, following centuries of internal harmony; and the introduction of mercenary service in place of that of native sons. Internal revolution, advanced by Evans as
the cause, is discounted by others. Invasion from the mainland seems a more
reasonable explanation.[20]

While Cretan society is known but imperfectly, certain tendencies in social
development are clear. From the large clan of the third millennium B.C. the
smaller family had developed at the height of Cretan power. Women occupied
a place of considerable importance and freedom. The pre-eminent cult of the
Mother Goddess, whose priestesses they were, suggests the central position of
women. There was no harem. Glotz infers a certain equality in marriage, which
must be within the clan. Kinship was determined by reference to the mother.
Spinning, weaving, and grinding corn were common occupations, and doubtless most employments were domestic, but women also made pottery, drove
chariots, engaged in the bull-grappler's art, went hunting, and attended exhibitions and festivals.[21]

Authority in early Cretan society was probably marked by an extreme local-

---

[16] *Ibid.*, I, 32 ff.; Glotz: *op. cit.*, pp. 20–8.
[17] Glotz: *op. cit.*, pp. 42 ff., 48 f.; Burn: *op. cit.*, pp. 48 f., 72, 83.
[18] Herodotus, VII, 170–1; Diodorus, IV, 79.
[19] Athenaeus, XIII, 602.
[20] Evans: *op. cit.*, II, Pt. II, 755 ff.; Burn: *op. cit.*, pp. 85, 96 ff.; C.A.H., II, 442 f.; Hall:
*op. cit.*, p. 260.
[21] Glotz: *op. cit.*, pp. 131 ff., 142 ff., 175.

ism, power being in the hands of tribal chiefs. Gradually, however, after centuries of growth, a degree of centralization emerged, cities being ranged against each other. Ultimately one of these, Knossos, gained supremacy. Her kings, whom tradition preserved in Minos, wielded an authority supported by a religious sanction, and each was at once ruler, priest, lawgiver, and judge.[22]

Archaeological investigations show that occupational activities reached a high state of development before the collapse of Cretan power, and later, for a time, at Mycenae and other centers of Aegean civilization. Though soil fit for cultivation was found only in small plots, and implements were rather crude, agriculturists grew barley and wheat and developed the olive, the vine, and many fruits. Bee culture and poultry-raising were also known. Of domesticated farm animals there were cattle, sheep, goats, and swine. Horses were in use in the late Minoan Age, about the same time they were brought into Egypt. Hunting and fishing supplemented the products of the soil. Certain natural resources were plentiful; those lacking, such as metal and stone of various kinds, were readily made good from near-by islands, Egypt, and more distant lands. Boat-building was indispensable to these island traders; native cypress was available for their craft, and cedar could be obtained from Lebanon. Copper came from Cyprus, and tin from distant Britain through Iberian ports. Iron was unknown till brought by the Dorians at the end of the Minoan Age. Manufactured goods reveal a thriving industrial scene of woodcutters, carpenters, founders, engravers, artists, sculptors, potters, armorers, builders, and masons, whose products were locally consumed or exchanged in trade. The Palace of Minos had its own extensive workshops.[23]

Out of primitive markets a large urban population gradually developed. Some communities were agricultural centers, while others developed industries and commerce. Homer speaks somewhere of ninety, elsewhere of a hundred, cities and a multitude of men. A host of communities have been excavated, the list of which already exceeds Homer's. Many of them had large populations. Evans thought Knossos might have had a population of 100,000. In such thriving cities, money, weights, measures, a numeral system, and writing were perfected as the needs of this world of traders expanded. By 2000, extensive trade had developed in the Aegean civilization; only at the decline of Cretan-Mycenaean power in the thirteenth century did trade with Egypt disappear. This commerce was carried by an extensive network of sea routes, connecting with well-developed roads on the Island of Crete. One of the most important, suited for wheeled traffic, ran north from Phaestos to the city of Knossos.[24]

22 Ibid., pp. 147 ff.
23 Mosso: op. cit., chap. 24; Glotz: op. cit., pp. 52, 154, 161 ff., 172 ff., 188, 191 ff., 224, 389, passim.
24 Evans: op. cit., II, Pt. II, 572–8; Burn: op. cit., pp. 72, 84 f., 146; Mosso: op. cit., p. 116; Hall: op. cit., pp. 211–32; Glotz: op. cit., pp. 138 f., 185.

INTELLECTUAL CULTURE   Diodorus [25] credited the origin of letters to the Muses, children of Zeus who had been nurtured by the priestly Cretan Curetes in a cave of Mt. Ida. The Phoenicians, he judged, borrowed and changed them, and received unearned credit for the invention of others. Though a half century ago Schliemann [26] found no evidence of writing at Mycenae, and the belief was expressed that there was no evidence of a written language in Cretan-Mycenaean culture, Evans' discoveries shortly showed that there had been an extensive use of writing which was "of indigenous and specifically Cretan origin"; and that not one but several scripts were distinguishable, one of which had been common to all Crete, the other a palace script of Knossos. Though Cretan is similar in some respects to Egyptian and other early pictographic scripts, experts differ as to their relationship and influence upon each other. Evans believes, however, that the Cretan was "essentially of home growth." [27] Knossos' burning had had the happy result of firing and thus preserving clay tablets that would otherwise have been destroyed. With their goods, Cretan traders carried their writing to distant places; Iberian script, Evans [28] believed, had been influenced by Cretan. Even after Knossos' loss of supremacy, the Island folk seem to have continued the use of writing, but its employment declined under the Achaeans, who appear to have had slight need of it.[29]

Though the stylus was commonly used, a few inscriptions in ink have been found. Hall supposes that pens and ink "must have been regularly used," and that papyrus was probably "imported from Egypt" and used for longer documents; but these have not survived. Clay tablets were presumably used chiefly for briefer matters, "accounts, bills, lists," and perhaps letters. The Cretan language, neither Semitic nor Indo-European, and the script still remain puzzles, though a few peculiarities of Cretan names and certain words are known through survivals in historic times.[30] The Cretan numerical system is understood; Hall remarks, "We can count in Minoan cyphers though we do not know how to pronounce their names." [31] The far-flung Cretan business world and the evident use of writing and a numerical system suggest the necessity of some sort of formal schooling. A room, thought to be a schoolroom, has

[25] Bk. v, 70, 74.
[26] Mycenae, p. 336.
[27] Evans: Scripta Minoa, I, 236–44; Hall: op. cit., pp. 211 f., 216 ff., 222. Dr. Bedrich Hrozny's claim to having deciphered the Cretan script and that of Mohenjo-Daro has aroused great interest, but doubt is entertained as to the soundness of his conclusions. See, for example, the review of his Die Älteste Geschichte Vorderasiens und Indiens (Prague, 1943) and Kretas und Vorgriechenlands Inschriften, Geschichte und Kultur (Stuttgart, Prague, 1943), by A. E. Kober, Am. Jour. of Archaeol. (Oct.–Dec., 1946), I, 493–5.
[28] Scripta Minoa, I, 99.
[29] Tsountas and Manatt: The Mycenaean Age, pp. 291 f.
[30] Glotz: op. cit., p. 387.
[31] Hall: op. cit., p. 217.

been unearthed, but it is open to question. Glotz thinks, however, that since writing was so very common, "schools and writing-masters must have existed all over Crete." [32]

PHYSICAL CULTURE AND AMUSEMENTS   The last palace at Knossos reveals in its art, vast stores of weapons, and tablets giving an account of the stock, a lively concern with the equipment of war. The panoramic Shield Fresco on the great stairway, depicting the military parade, was later imitated at the palace of Tiryns when power had shifted to the mainland. Armed forces on the Island were probably not large. While at first constituted of natives, contingents being supplied by local chiefs who recognized the sway of Knossos, mercenaries were later employed to some extent at least. Part of these were evidently Negroid, and may have served as a palace guard. War galleys were doubtless of great importance in an island empire. Clay models of boats appear in the early Minoan period. Many types are depicted throughout the centuries of Cretan power, but, being miniature, there are no full, detailed replicas. Some were equipped, however, with mast, sails, fixed rudders, and oars, even as many as twenty-eight pairs. Figures, interpreted as seated or squatting rowers, are found on seals as early as the third millennium.[33]

For defensive armor early Cretan soldiers had unwieldly, wide, towerlike shields, long enough to cover all but the head and feet. On the steatite chieftain goblet found at Hagia Triada only the heads are visible. These shields were a wooden framework, covered with skins. Later many variations occur: one, somewhat shorter, rounded at the ends, narrower in the middle, resembling in shape an "8" or an hourglass; another, narrow, semicylindrical; and a very small, circular, metal-covered shield, not native to Crete, but introduced from Asia and Cyprus. Cretan soldiers did not wear greaves, though these were a part of equipment in Mycenaean days. Helmets of leather or skin, sometimes covered with metal plates, and others wholly of metal were used, but were more common at Mycenae than on the Island. There the helmet was more often used by athletes, acrobats, and hunters than by soldiers. Corselets were used to some extent in Mycenaean days, but not commonly in Crete. Offensive equipment, more extensive and perfect, included the bow and arrow, spear, dart, dagger, and sword. The sling, commonly used by neighboring peoples, does not seem to have been employed by the Minoans.[34] Spears were made variously, both for close fighting and for throwing, the war spears or javelins being generally five to six feet long. Hunting spears were slightly longer. Bronze early supplanted flint for arrows and for spearheads. Cretan metal daggers were first of copper, then of bronze, but iron was unknown before the Dorian invasions. In

[32] Op. cit., pp. 378 f.
[33] Evans: Palace of Minos, II, Pt. I, 229–52; Pt. II, 755; IV, Pt. II, 520 f., 785 ff.
[34] Ibid., II, Pt. I, 344.

the manufacture of metal weapons Cretan armorers reached a high degree of perfection, joined with artistic embellishment. Mycenaean overlords seem to have depended on Cretan sources, for some time at least, for fine weapons, and other near-by and distant powers imported Cretan arms and then imitated them.

About the sixteenth century, when Crete was entering upon her "Golden Age," "thoroughbred horses" and chariots were introduced from Syria. From that time on they took a prominent place in war, and were also used in hunting, both on the Island and later in the Peloponnesus. The palace in Knossos was well supplied not only with entire chariots but also with an extensive array of parts, ready for assembling or for repairs.[35]

Judging from archaeology and from early literature, the bow seems to have been a most characteristic weapon. Mycenaeans and Cretans used it in war and in the chase. Tradition said that Apollo invented the bow and taught the Cretans its use; hence archery was "especially cultivated by the Cretans," and the bow itself was called Cretan.[36] Plato [37] credited archery with a prescribed place in Cretan education in his day. Pausanias thought the Cretans "the only Greek people" accustomed to use the bow, and spoke of a grave of Cretan bowmen at Athens. In historic times Lacedaemon had Cretan bowmen in her service, while Rome employed "a corps of Cretan archers" in the conquest of Greece.[38]

Of all sports, hunting was doubtless closest to the heart of Cretan and Mycenaean warriors, just as it was closely linked with the soldier class in other lands. A country abounding in wild life—deer, boars, lions, wolves, wild fowl—provided plentiful opportunities. Numerous artistic portrayals of hunting scenes have come to light. Most remarkable for their artistry are those on the bronze swords, inlaid with gold and silver, discovered by Schliemann at Mycenae. Hunters of the most dangerous animals, as commonly represented, are armed just like soldiers. The wild boar, lion, and deer were their choicest prey. Boar-hunting was practiced in early Cretan times, but at the close of the Minoan Age the sport was much more common on the mainland than on the Island. Boar-hunting scenes were a favorite theme of artists at Tiryns. A spirited scene from a Vaphio tomb represents a hunter spearing a long-tusked boar which is charging him in a headlong leap. The cups of Vaphio show that nets were also employed in hunting. Dogs, both male and female, which look like greyhounds, were used in hunting animals and birds. Large cats seem to have been trained for use in taking wild birds and smaller animals. Certain hunting

---

35 Ibid., I, 16; II, Pt. I, 155, 244; Pt. II, 576 f.; IV, Pt. I, 250 f.; Pt. II, 785–871; Tsountas and Manatt: op. cit., pp. 191–216; Glotz: op. cit., pp. 84–101.
36 Diodorus, v, 74.
37 Laws, I, 625.
38 Pausanias, I, 23, 4; 29, 6; IV, 8, 3; VII, 16, 1.

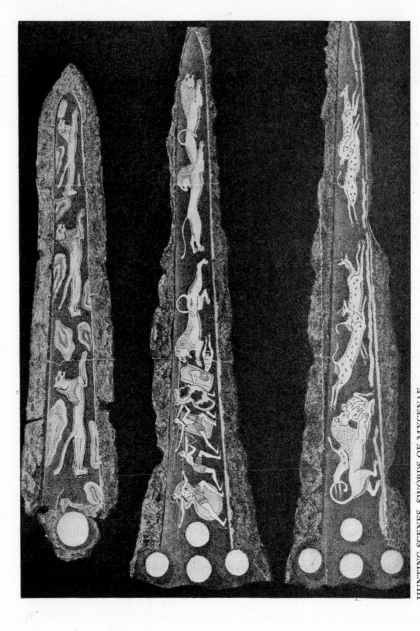

HUNTING SCENES, SWORDS OF MYCENAE
(Courtesy, Professor C. A. Robinson, from G. W. Botsford and C. A. Robinson, *Hellenic History*, Rev. Ed., Pl. 7, The Macmillan Company, New York, 1948)

scenes in which the cheetah is shown pursuing ducks in water filled with lotuses, parallel Egyptian scenes closely.[39]

Lion-hunting is commonly portrayed in late Minoan art, especially in remains found on the mainland. On a dagger blade from Mycenae four hunters, armed like soldiers with shields, bows, and spears, are engaging three lions, one of which turns on his pursuers. In many instances the beast himself is shown as hunter seizing his prey. In several lifelike scenes two lions are fighting for possession of a stag they have brought to ground.[40] Minoan hunters are also shown taking the semiwild great horned sheep by means of a lasso. A terrifying looking wild goat, the agrimi, was also an object of the chase.

Deer were common in Crete from early times, apparently, and furnished an entrancing subject for chase-inspired artists. Common red deer and the dappled deer are represented. Cretan artistic remains depict women engaging in hunting as did mythical Atalanta. Represented as Artemis or Dictynna, they are shown armed with bow and arrow, with quiver on the left shoulder, and dressed sometimes in hunting outfits such as were worn by men. A fresco from Tiryns represents women driving a chariot in a hunting scene. Deer-hunting in a chariot in full career is shown on a gold signet ring from a grave at Mycenae.[41] Though the use of the chariot in stag-hunting is commonly depicted, the nature of the terrain makes it reasonable to suppose that the artists were led into exaggeration by the attractiveness of the theme. Probably only the southern plain of Mesara on the Island, and the plain of Argos, were well adapted to the use of such a vehicle in hunting.[42]

Bull-grappling was highly developed in the Minoan Age. Believed by Evans [43] to have had its prototype in western Asia as early as 2400 B.C., evidences of it are found in Crete about 2100 B.C. or earlier. From the eighteenth century to the end of Cretan power, bull-grappling contests were a favorite theme of mural decorators and producers of a great variety of small art objects, jewelry, statuary, vases, cups, and seals, who reached their height of perfection in Crete's "Golden Age." When northern invaders first came to Knossos they must have looked in amazement at the marvelous frescoes on her palace walls. Under Mycenaean leaders these sports were carried to the mainland, or in any case were frequently represented at Mycenae, Vaphio, and Tiryns. The bull-baiting or hunting scenes depicted in Atreus' tomb at Mycenae are thought to be the work of Cretan artists using Cretan materials, though the work was probably done on the mainland. With the rest of Minoan culture, bull-grappling declined at the coming of the Dorians and all but disappeared. Its influ-

39 Gardner: New Chapters in Greek History, p. 66.
40 Perrot-Chipiez: Histoire de l'Art dans l'Antiquité, VI, 779 ff.
41 Schliemann: op. cit., p. 223; Evans: Palace of Minos, IV, Pt. II, 824.
42 Evans: Palace of Minos, I, 720; IV, Pt. II, 569–90.
43 Ibid., I, 15, 189 f.

ence may be reflected, however, in a modified form in Thessalian bull-fighting, involving horsemanship, which was so famous as to invite comment from Roman writers such as Pliny and Suetonius.[44] Memory of the Cretan sport was also kept alive in the traditions of Theseus' exploits with the Minotaur and the sacrifice of the bull of Marathon.[45]

Although the bull-grappling scenes have much in common, Evans convincingly distinguishes two varieties: one represents hunting wild, or semiwild creatures in more or less rugged, open terrain; another, a more formalized, perfected acrobatic performance which took place in an arena and had generally a religious ceremonial connotation. Such ceremonial grappling of sacred animals is depicted as early as the third millennium.[46] Early representations show the bull decorated with sacral coverings, blankets, or nets. In later times ceremonial exhibitions were viewed from grandstands in which the shrine of the Mother Goddess, "Our Lady of the Sports," had a central position. Performing acrobats, both male and female, may have been regarded as servants of the Goddess Mother who presided over them. The religious significance of the events is often indicated by certain conventional "Sacral Knots" and also, in some instances, by the presence of a deity, altar, and a long-robed sacrificing priest who plunges a dagger into the animal's neck. Save for these sacrificial scenes, where the priest, not the toreador, slew them, the animals were not slain—a feature which differentiates Minoan contests from Roman and Spanish beast fights of historic and present times.[47]

The famous Taureador Frescoes, which Evans placed not later than the sixteenth or fifteenth century, show the great perfection of Cretan mural decoration. An excellent restoration shows a gigantic, spotted, horned bull in full career, a male acrobat head over heels in a somersault over his back; and two female acrobats, one with her arms over the bull's horns, the other standing behind the animal holding outstretched arms to assist the vaulter as he comes to ground. The logical order of this "act" seems to be (1) seizure of the horns of the approaching bull, (2) a high swing in air as the animal tosses his head, (3) a backward somersault, landing on the bull's rump, and (4) a final leap to the arms of the assistant. This and similar stunts, Evans notes, have been called "impossible" by a modern expert "steer-wrestler." Many other artistic representations show athletes doing the "impossible": thus, certain gems from Mycenae show wrestlers apparently lifting bulls completely from the ground.[48]

These spectacular exhibitions were obviously most dangerous, and witnessing them evidently thrilled large audiences. They challenged the skill of many an

---

[44] Natural History (Rackham), VIII, 182; Claudius, 21.
[45] Pausanias, I, 24, 1; 27, 10; III, 18, 16.
[46] Evans: Palace of Minos, II, Pt. I, 260; III, 204, 223 f.
[47] Ibid., III, 207, 226 f.
[48] Ibid., III, 212 ff., 222, 231 f.

BULL-GRAPPLING ACROBAT

(A. Evans, *The Palace of Minos at Knossos*, III, Fig. 296, Macmillan & Co., Ltd., London, 1932)

artist who lavished his pains no less, perhaps even more, on representing the animals than the human performers. Yet the acrobats do not come off badly, whether in the frescoes or in statuettes. Of the latter, the most perfect specimen is found in a figurine of a youthful bull-leaper, executed in ivory pieces, ingeniously joined together. The excellence of this piece, in particular, led Evans to think that such "well-set arms and shoulders and strongly developed pectoral muscles" betoken a "careful physical training. . . ." [49]

As to who the performers were, no one knows. Some have thought them cap-

[49] *Ibid.*, III, 429.

tives, trained and forced to participate in dangerous exhibitions to please the caprice of their sovereign captors. The foremost authority admits that this may have been the case, but maintains that there is not the slightest evidence that they were captives. Perhaps there was a special class of bullfighters. The sport seems to have been in their blood. Evans believes the performers, both men and women, may have represented the best element of society, even as noble Spaniards and Roman emperors once entered the arena. Acting under a religious sanction and under the very eyes of the Mother Goddess, they represent a "glorification of athletic excellence," quite as Athenian artists delighted in showing Greek athletes as an embodiment of physical perfection. The rôle of women as performing acrobats, who are distinguishable from the boys chiefly by their striped sheath, their white color, curls, ribbons, and necklaces, harmonizes with their high social and religious station, which is reflected in the pre-eminence of the mother cult. Evans suggests that it may not be without significance that in historic Sparta, which was close to Minoan cultural influences, girls took a public part in athletics.[50]

Bull-grappling of a purely acrobatic type exhibited on festive occasions may have developed from ruder, utilitarian practice in throwing, roping, or otherwise catching wild animals; just as to-day one may see western cowhands rope animals on the range, or watch a like performance at professional rodeos. Scenes in which evidences of a "hunting" motif appear are found on cups from Vaphio, dating from the early fifteenth century or perhaps a little earlier. Credited to Cretan artists, these golden cups, which were found near Sparta in 1889, are among the finest specimens of the goldsmith's art, possessing a graceful naturalness and ease of line that shame the art of post-Mycenaean days. These scenes have been interpreted as episodes in "the capture of wild or half-wild bulls," [51] and also as "scenes of bull-grappling rather than of bull-hunting." [52] There may be something of both in them. Perhaps the artist seeks to represent the capture of wild creatures, to be trained for use in the arena. The same sort of expert grapplers are represented as in the ceremonial performances of the arena, but the terrain seems to be rocky, rugged, open country with some vegetation; and the taking of the beasts is marked by accidents. One scene seems to represent a "drive," bringing the animals into a heavy rope net stretched between two trees. Halted momentarily by the net, the grapplers try to take the bulls by the horns. One missed, apparently, and fell, or was tossed headlong, arms extended and feet in air, just escaping being trampled; another is being gored and tossed head over heels by the plunging beast, or perhaps he

---

[50] Ibid., I, 2; III, 231 f.
[51] Ibid., III, 177; Gardiner: Athletics of the Ancient World, p. 11; C.A.H., II, 455; Gardner: op. cit., p. 70.
[52] Hyde: Olympic Victor Monuments, p. 4.

has locked legs around the animal's horns, so as to prevent being gored to death. Behind these figures another bull is tangled in the net, while a third gallops off. The second cup exhibits a less exciting scene, which may be the taking of a wild bull by use of a decoy cow and a lasso. Likewise appearing to represent the taking of wild animals is an engraved onyx gem, on which a grappler leaps to seize a bull's horns while he is drinking.[53]

Though a generation ago it was confidently asserted that Mycenaeans were not fisheaters,[54] evidence shows that fish was an article of diet in the Minoan Age. Fish vertebrae have been found in a palace storeroom pot at Knossos. A fisherman with his catch, one of them a large fish like the Skaros, considered the finest of fish in the days of Pliny,[55] is represented on an engraved gem from Knossos. A Phylakopi vase shows four fishermen swinging along jauntily carrying their take in their hands. On fragments from Melos a well-dressed woman is represented sitting on a rock, pulling up a fishing net.[56]

Somewhat closer akin to later conceptions of athletics are various remains depicting boxers and wrestlers. Evans interprets certain fragments of athletic group reliefs from the palace at Knossos as remnants of "a group of two wrestlers," [57] though there can be no absolute certainty as to the type of sport represented. Boxing contests are more clearly depicted on a steatite rhyton, the so-called "Boxer Vase," dating from about 1600 B.C., found at Hagia Triada in 1901. Boxing is also shown on seals and on a fragment of steatite pyxis, found at Knossos and belonging to the same period. This sport, as well as bull-grappling, is represented in a theatral area, commonly associated in Cretan art with religious symbols. Evans regards the Minoan theater as definitely "a religious institution," and includes boxing and wrestling among the sacral sports. If held in the theatral areas excavated at Phaestos and Knossos, four to five hundred spectators could have witnessed such contests.[58]

The contestants are generally girdled by a tight belt around an abnormally small waist. Some wear helmets, others are without them. A cestus is indicated in some instances.[59] The helmeted boxers in the upper zone of the "Boxer Vase" appear to represent heavier, adult contestants, while those below, who are smaller and unhelmeted, may be boys or young men. Contestants are shown in conventional attitudes: the victor, aggressive, with left arm extended for defense, the right drawn back ready for a blow; the vanquished, either

[53] Evans: *Palace of Minos*, III, 177–232, 428 ff.; IV, Pt. I, 21 f., 39 ff.; Mosso: *The Palaces of Crete and Their Builders*, pp. 211–25; Tsountas and Manatt: *op. cit.*, pp. 51, 227 f., 352; Glotz: *op. cit.*, pp. 293 ff.
[54] Tsountas and Manatt: *op. cit.*, pp. 69, 334.
[55] *Natural History* (Rackham), IX, 29.
[56] Evans: *Palace of Minos*, I, 555 f., 677; III, 40, 43.
[57] *Ibid.*, III, 497 ff.
[58] *Ibid.*, I, 690; IV, 22; Glotz: *op. cit.*, p. 289.
[59] Evans: *Palace of Minos*, I, 688 ff.; Gardiner: *op. cit.*, pp. 12 f.

brought to his knees or to a sitting or prone position, with feet thrown high in the air. The well-developed muscles of the legs, arms, and shoulders of the competitors suggest a thorough athletic training.

Somewhat akin in spirit to the boxing scenes are certain representations of a more serious event, a combat of armed men. Of these the most realistic portrayal of a gladiatorial contest is found on a gold signet ring from Mycenae. Four men are engaged: one, already down, sits with dejected air, half supporting himself with left hand on the ground; another, wearing a plumed helmet or cap, is armed with a semicylindrical shield and spear; between them, engaged in a fight with heavy daggers, are two combatants, one of whom, just going down, is about to receive the fatal thrust.[60]

A Greek myth told that Idean Heracles, one of five brothers, set a race for the others and crowned the winner with wild olive.[61] Running contests may have been held, but evidence so far reported thereon is slight. Sealings found at Kato Zakro in eastern Crete show figures, apparently female, holding their arms as though running.[62]

Early Cretan religion was primitive and largely indigenous, though there was some borrowing, doubtless, from neighboring peoples. In any case, numerous similarities exist between Cretan, Egyptian, and Babylonian ideas, practices, and objects of worship. Among Cretans certain trees (olive, palm, pine), high places, pillars, caverns, rocks, heavenly bodies, the sea, sacred animals, and birds, were often held sacred. Kinship or identity of men and animals was acknowledged. A mural fragment found at Mycenae shows human figures masked in donkey heads, marching as though in a procession.[63] A host of cult objects—the double axe, cross, swastika, holy water, altar, dove, and bull—played an important rôle, indicating a highly developed symbolism which is understood but imperfectly to-day.

The most prominent feature of Cretan religion was the pre-eminent cult of the Great Mother, symbol of fruitfulness, patroness of war, hunting, fishing, navigation, games of chance, and contests of skill and daring, queen of earth and heaven, mistress of creation and dissolution. As chaste virgin she is Britomartis, as mother, Dictynna—so named because she is said to have invented nets (dictya) for hunting.[64] The male principle, though less prominent and apparently a later development, was commonly symbolized by the bull and humanly embodied in Minos. A great deal of space at the palace of Knossos was given over to his majesty's priestly functions. Libations, lustrations, private

[60] Schliemann: op. cit., p. 223; Evans: Palace of Minos, I, 691 ff.; III, 500, 502.
[61] Pausanias, v, 7, 7.
[62] Hogarth: "The Zakro Sealings," Jour. Hellenic Studies, xxii, 78, fig. 6; Glotz: op. cit., p. 293.
[63] Perrot-Chipiez: op. cit., vi, 886.
[64] Diodorus, v, 76.

and public sacrifices (some of blood, others bloodless), music, games, dancing, and processions were among the chief acts of worship, judging from artistic remains that have been preserved.

Music and the pipes to make it, according to Hellenic genealogy of the gods, were inventions of Athena, child of Zeus and Hera, whose marriage was celebrated in the Isle of Crete.[65] The genealogy may be worthless, but music and its kindred art, dancing, were of great antiquity in Crete, and were prominent in the worship of Dictynna, who had much in common with Athena. Homer placed Ariadne's dancing ground in "broad Knossos." It is amongst the Phaeacians that Demodocus' song and soulful lyre inspired the twinkling dance of youthful feet; there, too, the sprightly capering ball dance was staged to charm Ulysses.[66]

Music and dancing played a prominent rôle in Cretan life, and both, like sports, were intimately associated with religion. At times they appear as a simple, spontaneous expression of Cretan peasant life. A beautiful steatite vase from Hagia Triada is believed by Mosso [67] to represent harvesters singing and dancing as they return from the fields. The war dance, according to an ancient legend, had been instituted by the godlike Curetes, who also gave men knowledge of hunting, agriculture, law, and social concord.[68] Cretan dancing was lively, acrobatic feats being linked with it. Athenaeus says ". . . lively dances are called Cretan." [69] The theatral areas at Knossos and Phaestos were like a "religious institution," the pillar of the Great Goddess occupying a central position in the grandstands. There, amid a throng of worshipers, the goddess looked down on dancing, musical entertainments, and thrilling sporting festivals, filled with boxing and bull-grappling events. Music and dancing appear commonly in the festivals of the Great Mother. Women played a central rôle in Cretan religion and in its ritual dancing.[70] A fragment from Knossos shows beautifully dressed women apparently performing a processional dance in an enclosed grove of sacred olives. Their uplifted arms suggest adoration or entreaty. Looking on the scene is a remarkable host of upwards of five hundred figures, male and female.[71] On a gold signet ring from Isopata four women, in a setting of flowers, are performing a ceremonial dance, lifting their arms in adoration toward a small figure of the Great Goddess approaching from on high. The all-seeing eye of deity surveys all from the background.[72]

[65] Ibid., v, 72–3.
[66] Il., xviii, 536–49; Od., viii, 502–22.
[67] Palaces of Crete, pp. 166 ff.
[68] Diodorus, v, 65.
[69] Bk. v, 181.
[70] Mosso: Palaces of Crete, chap. 14.
[71] Evans: Palace of Minos, iii, 66 f.
[72] Ibid., iii, 68.

A gold ring from Mycenae represents devotees offering gifts to the goddess, seated under a sacred olive tree. A ceremonial picking of fruits, with attendant dancing, appears on rings from Vaphio and Mycenae.[73] An "arm-in-arm dance" is depicted in a terra cotta group from Palaikastro—three female dancers around a central figure playing the lyre. Before the musician is the sacred dove.[74] Group ritual dancing appears to be always represented by women only. In legends, as given by Greek writers, males and females united in the dance of Ariadne. The ritualistic, labyrinthine crane dance, which Theseus is said to have performed at Delos with youths and maids he had saved from the Cretan Minotaur and was bringing back to Athens, was held round an altar of horns,[75] such as Cretan remains show was in common use at sacrificial dances in prehistoric days. Solo dancers appear, however, in religious rôles: the ecstatic male dancer before the altar of the Goddess, shown on a steatite rhyton from Knossos; and a leaping, gesticulating, female dancer on a gem from Vaphio.[76]

In very early times Cretans had reed instruments, the syrinx, the salpinx, and the sistrum. The instruments most commonly represented in religious ceremonials are the flute and lyre. At the sacrifice of a bull, on a Hagia Triada sarcophagus, a youth is playing the double flute. A female dancer on a small gem from Vaphio holds a single flute in one hand.[77] The lyre, represented by an ancient legend as the invention of Cretan Apollo,[78] was known in several forms, with three, four, and even seven strings as later in classical times.[79]

Sanitary arrangements of Cretan palaces had been brought to a high state of perfection by experts in hydraulic engineering. Water was brought by conduits from near-by hills, and remarkable wells about thirty-three feet deep were also dug and walled up with terra cotta cylinders nearly two feet long, each constructed of three sections joined together. Water was also carried down stairways by runnels, built with easy parabolic curves to slow the current; and traps were placed at certain points to catch sediment, thus ensuring a good supply of clean rain water. Water pipes were constructed with tapering sections to guard against collection of sediment in them.[80]

Besides certain basins evidently designed for ceremonial lustrations, as in the Throne Room,[81] there were remarkably ingenious provisions for physical cleanliness. The Caravanserai, a sort of hostel where travelers may have put up

[73] Glotz: op. cit., pp. 236 ff.
[74] Mosso: Palaces of Crete, pp. 282 f.
[75] Plutarch: Theseus, 21; Pausanias, ix, 40, 3.
[76] Evans: Palace of Minos, ii, Pt. ii, 614; iii, 69.
[77] Ibid., iii, 39, 69.
[78] Diodorus, v, 74.
[79] Evans: Palace of Minos, iii, 66–80; Mosso: Palaces of Crete, pp. 309–23; Glotz: op. cit., p. 291.
[80] Evans: Palace of Minos, iii, 252 ff.
[81] Mosso: Palaces of Crete, pp. 64 ff.; Glotz: op. cit., pp. 117 f., 263 f.

as they arrived at Knossos by road from Phaestos, had provisions for foot baths and complete tubbings. Inside and outside entrances to the foot bath suggest its public character.[82] This foot basin was about six feet by four, and was deep enough to bring the water near the knees. Stone slabs around it and projecting somewhat over it, provided seats for bathers. Careful provisions were made for filling, emptying, and also for overflow.

Near to the foot bath was a room with tubs. Minoan bathtubs were of clay, beautifully decorated with painted designs. Considerably longer at the top than at the bottom, their length accommodated the ordinary Cretan man or woman comfortably; some tubs were apparently provided with crossbars to sit on. The rim of the tub was higher at the head than at the foot. The room just off the Queen's "Great Hall" at the Palace of Minos had a beautiful clay tub, whose upper rim sloped gently up from the foot to about twenty inches in height at the head. There is no evidence of a sink to carry off waste water from the bathroom, a negligence quite in contrast to the elaborate facilities for filling and emptying the foot basin. The toilet room, however, was equipped with a sink, and the latrine was flushed with water. At Tiryns the bath was wainscoted with wood and floored with a solid block of limestone, in which a gutter carried the water to stone piping running through the wall. At Mycenae, also, the bathroom had a sink.[83]

Swimming is represented on fragments of a tall silver rhyton, probably of Cretan workmanship, found in the Fourth Shaft Grave at Mycenae. It is part of a remarkable siege scene, certain features of which recall Hesiod's *Shield of Heracles*—"men fighting in warlike harness," and women on "well-built towers," weeping and tearing their cheeks.[84] Below the scene of fighting are naked swimmers, who are using a frog kick and breast stroke. Fragments of inlay work on a blade from a tomb at Vaphio also depict nude swimmers. While inferences regarding style of swimming must be somewhat uncertain, because of the nature of the evidence, the position of the legs and the upper part of the body suggest a flutter kick and a hand-over-hand side stroke, somewhat similar to that shown on the coin of Abydos.[85]

For quiet leisure hours Minoan folk had games of chance, some evidently played indoors, others outside. The first family of Knossos had a beautifully inlaid game board, about three feet long and more than half as wide, constructed of ivory, gold, silver, rock crystals, and imitation lapis lazuli. This board, which may have covered a box which held the men used in playing it, is assigned to the first half of the second millennium, but may have continued

[82] Evans: *Palace of Minos*, II, Pt. I, 116–23.
[83] Ibid., III, 385 f.; Tsountas and Manatt: *op. cit.*, pp. 48 f.; Glotz: *op. cit.*, pp. 116 ff.
[84] *Op. cit.*, 237.
[85] Evans: *Palace of Minos*, III, 89–98, 127; Tsountas and Manatt: *op. cit.*, pp. 212 ff.; cf. Mehl: *Antike Schwimmkunst*, Plates 4–6; Thomas: *Swimming*, p. 139.

in use in the late Minoan Age. The game almost certainly involved the throwing of dice or pebbles and the moving of pieces—similar, in some respects, to backgammon, Greek *polis*, Roman *latrunculi*, and Egyptian board games. Conically shaped ivory pieces were perhaps moved from one end of the board to the other, where there was a goal or "citadel," as Evans sought to interpret it. Sunray symbols on the base of these "men," similar to symbols used in Cretan script, suggest a religious association with the cult of the Minoan Mother Goddess, much as in other lands games of chance have been associated with religious ideas and practices.[86]

Likewise associated with religious antecedents, perhaps, and recalling the suitors' game on the oxhide at the palace gate [87] and the "pavement games" of Roman days [88] was a game, traces of which, more or less perfectly preserved, have been found in the Queen's "Great Hall" of Knossos, at the central palace at Mallia, the "Kavusi Table," and at the theatral areas in Knossos and Phaestos. A painted stucco fragment, in Evans' opinion, represents youths playing such a "pavement game." [89] The chief features of the game, as inferred from the several remains, were: a number of cups hollowed out in a stone slab or table, the number of which ranged from ten to thirty-nine. Generally they were arranged round a circle, but at the theatral areas they approximated a square. The best example, discovered at Mallia, was on a heavy slab about three feet in diameter, occupying a permanent position on a terrace. The cups, in this instance, were thirty-four in number, ranged around the entire circumference of the table. One of these, being somewhat larger, gave the circle a bulge at one point. The smaller cups were all of the same size, but in the center of the table was a larger cup, about six inches across and a little more than three deep. While the Mallia slab has been called a sacrificial table by some, who think the cups designed for offerings—libations, grain, cakes—Evans holds that it fits the pattern of the pavement games found elsewhere, though this does not preclude its having derived from some religious prototype.[90]

Widely divergent judgments have been expressed regarding the relationship between Cretan physical contests and the athletic festivals of Greece. A view, once widely held, denied Cretan influence. Gardiner thought there was "no evidence in Crete of anything from which Greek athletics could have developed." [91] In 1930 he expressed a like view: ". . . there is not a particle of evidence to connect with Crete the origin of the great athletic festivals of

[86] Evans: *Palace of Minos*, I, 471–85; *Scripta Minoa*, I, 221, no. 107 a; Falkener: *Games Ancient and Oriental*, pp. 9–111.
[87] *Od.*, I, 175–7.
[88] Falkener: *op. cit.*, pp. 364 ff.
[89] *Palace of Minos*, III, Plate xxv.
[90] *Ibid.*, III, 390–6.
[91] Gardiner: *Greek Athletic Sports and Festivals*, p. 11.

Greece." [92] Hyde recognized that "love of sport existed in Crete" as elsewhere, but contrasted it with the radically different world of Homer and the "atmosphere of true athletics." [93] At variance with these views, Glotz, reflecting a growing tendency to revise upwards the previous estimates of Minoan influence, contended that the feature of Cretan life which is most original—their love of "gymnastic and musical contests" accompanying their festivals—is precisely the one which distinguishes the Greeks also; that "there is as direct a connexion" between the boxing matches at Hagia Triada and the games given by Achilles and Alcinous as there is between the games described by Homer and the Olympic games. Minoan contests at religious festivals gave "birth to a national athletic tradition." "The theatre and *palaestra* of Hellas," Glotz concluded, "did no more than develop the legacy of the pre-Hellenes." [94] Ridington, who sought to test the validity of the thesis that Greek athletic festivals were a development from Cretan prototypes, came to agree substantially with Glotz, finding a "notable influence" exerted by Cretan culture. "Detail after detail" combine to build up a picture "till it seems that many of the basic elements of the Greek athletic festival were contributed to by the Minoan-Mycenaean culture." [95]

### THE MYCENAEAN AGE

FUSION OF MINOAN AND HELLENIC CULTURE   Opinions differ as to when Greeks first came to the Peloponnesus.[96] Unacquainted with exact history, they were apt to boast of an ancient tradition, saying that they had dwelled in their mountains before the moon was born. It is thought that Greeks may have entered the Peninsula to some extent about two thousand years before the Christian era; not till about 1500, however, or perhaps a little later, is there evidence of Achaeans moving into the lower Peloponnesus from northern regions above the Spercheus. These blond or brown-haired invaders gradually constituted themselves a ruling aristocracy. It may have been they who brought about the destruction of Knossos. In any case the Achaeans had gained mastery of certain centers of former Cretan power by the thirteenth century; in 1223 B.C., according to records of Merneptah, they reached out as far as the African coast, and assisted the Libyans in an attack on Egypt. Out of this mixture of Cretan and Achaean elements, the Mycenaean civilization evolved. Leadership passed from Knossos to Mycenae, in the plain of Argos; there ruled the Achaean hosts

---

[92] *Athletics of the Ancient World*, p. 14.
[93] Hyde: *op. cit.*, p. 7.
[94] Glotz: *op. cit.*, pp. 289, 392.
[95] Ridington: *The Minoan-Mycenaean Background of Greek Athletics*, pp. 86 f.
[96] Cf. *C.A.H.*, II, 473 ff.; Bury: *A History of Greece*, pp. 5 ff., 44 ff.; Jardé: *The Formation of the Greek People*, pp. 73 ff.

in that heroic "golden age," whose glories are thought by some to be reflected in part in Homeric verse. Wide differences of opinion exist, however, as to what is to be seen in the Homeric poems. Carpenter holds that Homer reflects "the only world which he knows," that is, "the late eighth and the seventh century," but recognizes that older elements may have entered into his work.[97] Bury, on the contrary, thinks Homer describes the life of the Mycenaean Age rather than that of his own day.[98]

After the fall of Knossos, Minoan culture approaches its eventide. Mycenae's Achaean lords, whose praises Homer sings, bask for a time in the sun of an older civilization. Theirs is a cruder, more lawless age, despite its reflected glory. War and piracy are their most engaging and profitable occupations. The last great act in their heroic drama, the expedition against Priam's rich city of Troy, appears to a recent historian as the final phase of an economic struggle. The grandiose accomplishment of Troy's destruction is the final heroic gesture of Achaean power.[99] The time of the Trojan war is uncertain. Greeks assigned it dates ranging from the early thirteenth to the early twelfth century. Burn thinks shortly before 1100 is a likelier date. Glotz prefers "about 1280," and maintains that the struggle may have spread over two centuries as well as one.[100] Though dates are problematic, more agreement is found as to the aftermath of the struggle. The Achaeans had extended themselves too far and spent themselves, as Knossos had done before. A protracted struggle must have weakened them. Petty quarrels were evident during the war, according to Homer's account; localism triumphed after it. Shortly after 1200 evidences of decline began to appear in Mycenaean culture. The Dorians, on the march southward, seem to have met only momentarily successful resistance. Powerful Mycenae, Tiryns, and other Achaean strongholds went down in flames. At the end of the eleventh century the darkness of the Greek Middle Ages was falling. Not for many centuries would another civilization of great brilliance arise, in Attica, and shed its light throughout the Mediterranean world.

CHARACTER OF SOCIETY REFLECTED IN HOMER This was preeminently an age of violence, despite some achievements in the arts of peaceful industry.[101] The lines of Hesiod fit them well:

> Their thoughts were bent on violence alone,
> The deeds of battle and the dying groan. . . .[102]

[97] The Humanistic Value of Archaeology, p. 72.
[98] C.A.H., II, 513 f.; cf. Glotz: op. cit., p. 393; Tsountas and Manatt: op. cit., p. 338; Gomperz: Greek Thinkers: A History of Ancient Philosophy, I, 28.
[99] Glotz: op. cit., pp. 219 f.; Keller: Homeric Society, pp. 308 f.
[100] Burn: op. cit., pp. 51 f.; Glotz: op. cit., pp. 53, 226, 405; cf. Carpenter: op. cit., p. 67.
[101] Keller: op. cit., p. 190.
[102] Davies: Hesiod and Theognis, p. 32.

The Achaeans had conquered the Cretans, partly at least because of superiority of their arms.[103] Piracy upon their neighbors of the sea continued to be one source of wealth. The strong triumphed over the weak. While Odysseus was away the suitors made themselves at home in his abode and consumed his wealth. Only at his return were matters righted, when the long-suffering master loosed his "bitter arrow"—

> Right at Antinous; and struck him just
> As he was lifting up the bowl, to show
> That 'twixt the cup and lip much ill may grow.[104]

At length, when the men were all "laid prostrate," the unfaithful women were strung up.[105] Thus order in the patriarchal domain was re-established.

The city was built upon conquest. Government sustained the power of victors over vanquished, and assured continuance of the fruits of victory. In the state, as in the household, government was by the strongest. The king, the strongest of all heads of houses, is recognized, even when among strangers, by his physical and mental alertness. Atrides assures his guests they wear "the portraiture of Jove-sustain'd and sceptre-bearing kings." [106] There may be bickering and criticism among those who wish to rule, but the principle is urged, and circumstances dictated its acceptance, that:

> We must not all be kings. The rule is most irregular,
> Where many rule. One lord, one king . . . and he,
> To whom wise Saturn's son hath giv'n both law and empery
> To rule the public, is that king.[107]

Though the ultimate appeal was to force, the unwritten law of *dike* and *themis* (what has been "pointed out" and "established") exercised restraint over action, and constituted a standard for judgment when wrongs were committed—a standard determined by, and in the interest of, the rich and powerful. Below the king ranged the nobles, *hetairoi*, commoners, and slaves. The nobles—simply lesser kings—were treated with consideration by their chief. In the assembly they constituted the *gerontes* or council. The *hetairoi*, closely associated with the nobility and serving them in a more or less professional capacity, might be noble foreigners, offspring of better families of the common

[103] Jardé: op. cit., p. 74.
[104] Od., xxII, 11–4. Though Chapman's version leaves something to be desired, Lawton's query, whether "prose is the proper form into which to translate a poem," is well-taken. See Lawton: "Womanhood in the Iliad," Atl. Mo., LXXI, 800. The passages quoted have been compared with generally approved prose versions, such as Butcher and Lang, The Odyssey of Homer; and Lang, Leaf, and Myers, The Iliad of Homer.
[105] Od., xxII, 588–602.
[106] Ibid., IV, 77–8.
[107] Il., II, 172–5.

people, or slaves who, for faithful service, had been raised to positions of trust. The commoners, though underprivileged, could attend the assembly (agora) and express their opinions—as Thersites did, though to no avail.[108] Slaves, commonly held by all who could afford them, were as a rule the women and children of foreigners, taken by force in war or bought like any other goods. Though without rights, except those granted by the caprice of masters, the treatment of slaves seems to have been mild. If the master willed it, a slave might marry, beget slave children, receive rewards for faithful service, and even buy a slave.[109]

Though nobility of character and loveliness are ascribed to certain women of Homer, their position was one of inferiority, as in other patriarchal and feudal societies. A woman was "not a person, but a thing . . . a perpetual minor." [110] A double standard required chastity of her before marriage, but not of the man. The wife had more rights than her husband's concubines, but she and they were both a sort of property: the wife was generally paid for and wed with ceremony; concubines, like slaves, were taken by force as prizes of war or as reward for skill. A woman's value was unblushingly computed as so many cattle; she was disposed of by her master like any other property. To appease sulking Achilles, sacred tripods, horses, gold, goodly caldrons are offered, and besides:

> Sev'n Lesbian ladies he shall have . . . the most select,
> And in their needles rarely skill'd, whom, when he took the town
> Of famous Lesbos, I did choose; who won the chief renown
> For beauty from their whole fair sex. . . .[111]

Moreover, if victory be theirs at Troy, Achilles with

> . . . that princely hand of his
> Shall choose him twenty Trojan dames. . . .[112]

Even if defeated they return from Troy, Achilles shall have his choice of three daughters, richly dowered with seven cities.

Homer's society knows of industry and commerce, but these are scarcely the business of heroes. Amid the waters

> . . . of the sable sea there lies
> An isle call'd Crete, a ravisher of eyes,

[108] Ibid., II, 194–210.
[109] Mahaffy: Social Life in Greece, pp. 44 ff., 57 ff.; Keller: op. cit., pp. 264 f., 273, 279.
[110] Keller: op. cit., p. 243; Lawton: op. cit., loc. cit., LXXI, 784–801; Seymour: Life in the Homeric Age, chap. 4; Mahaffy: op. cit., pp. 52 ff.; St. John: History of the Manners and Customs of Ancient Greece, I, 369–81.
[111] Il., IX, 132–5.
[112] Ibid., IX, 141–2.

> Fruitful, and mann'd with many an infinite store;
> Where ninety cities crown the famous shore,
> Mix'd with all-languag'd men.[113]

Homer's Greeks are given credit for agriculture and other attributes of settled life. The primitive Cyclops, however, have neither councils, councilors, nor laws; they are a race—

> Of proud-liv'd loiterers, that never sow,
> Nor put a plant in earth, nor use a plow,
> But trust in God for all things. . . .[114]

Neither is commerce pursued in the Cyclops' isle. They take no delight—

> In brave vermilion-prow-deck'd ships; nor wrights
> Useful, and skilful in such works as need
> Perfection to those traffics that exceed
> Their natural confines, to fly out and see
> Cities of men, and take in mutually
> The prease of others. . . .[115]

In contrast to the lawless Cyclops, Homer's Achaeans had beans, peas, lentils, wild asparagus, onions, wheat, and barley, which, with the flesh of sheep, cows, pigs, and goats, furnished the staples of diet. Grapes, olives, figs, apples, pears, plums, pomegranates, and such products as milk and honey were highly prized. Wine, generally diluted, was the common drink. To supplement the larder, recourse was had to the wild-life of land and sea. Boar, deer, and hare were plentiful, and hunting seems to have been common, for sport if not for necessity. Fishing was also a source of food, and a regular employment of commoners. Remains discovered by the archaeologists show that various kinds of sea food were eaten.[116]

Like other early peoples, the Greeks attributed many of their accomplishments to a legendary source. Aeschylus tells us that Prometheus first taught them to yoke animals for drawing and riding, harness horses to chariots and bring them to the rein, and to plow the "wine-dark" sea in "canvas-wingéd" ships. Whether taught by such a mythical pedagogue or no, Homer's Achaeans knew the use of horses, mules, and oxen. Horses were prized for riding, driving, and for drawing the war chariot, while mules were worked on farms. Oxen were the mainstay on the land, however, and so important an element of wealth

---

[113] Od., XIX, 240–4.
[114] Ibid., IX, 168–70.
[115] Ibid., IX, 194–9.
[116] C.A.H., II, 462; Seymour: op. cit., chap. 7; Keller: op. cit., p. 30; supra, p. 209.

that "ox" became a common unit of value. Plowing was done with a crude instrument, which appears to have been shod with iron, about the time of the Spartan invasion. Mention of the "thrice ploughed field" suggests that once over with such an imperfect tool was not enough to do a good job. Grain was cut with the sickle; it was threshed by driving oxen over it.

No degradation was associated with agriculture. On the contrary, plowing and harvesting were noble occupations, worthy even of men of great estate. Odysseus boasts to one of the suitors that he can best him, whether at plowing, mowing, or in the thick of battle. This, of course, is poetry. On the estates of great nobles, work was performed mostly by slaves, supplemented more or less by hired labor. The lot of hired workers was poor, doubtless, compared with other elements of society. Achilles would prefer it only to holding sway over all the dark, dank realms of death.[117]

The work of craftsmen was much sought after and well esteemed. Hephaestus, a god, is a cunning blacksmith. Fine workmanship was highly approved, and certain skillful-handed nobles are mentioned. Chief dependence, however, must have been put on the labor of others—skilled slaves, gained through war or purchase, and free artisans who worked for hire.[118]

Cosmological conceptions of Homer's Greeks were rather crude. To Zeus, son of Cronos and Rhea, belongs the broad heavens; to Demeter, the earth; to Poseidon, the sea; to Hades, the murky realm below. Earth, resting on water, is surrounded by the flowing stream of Oceanus; over all is the sky, upheld by the pillars of Atlas, across which is driven the chariot of the sun, which plunges at evening into ocean's stream. Beneath the earth lay the dim realms of Hades, the spirit afterworld; and below that, Tartarus.

Though marked by traces of primitive animism, the religion of the Achaeans transcends it. A product of long development, it embodies elements of Minoan civilization, primitive conceptions of the Hellenic conquerors, and influences from Egypt and the East. As in Babylonia, Egypt, and other lands, where certain local gods came gradually to enjoy a more general acceptance than others, so it was among the Greeks. The *Iliad,* the *Odyssey,* and the *Theogony* of Hesiod reveal that the company of the gods has been reduced to a sort of system—a rather loose one, indeed, which permits of variety, turmoil, and even a suggestion of revolt.[119]

Heavenly government reflects earthly rule: Zeus reigns as monarch, as Agamemnon holds sway among the lords of earth; like an earthly potentate he calls assemblies and presides. He has learned to divide and rule; his wife, Hera, and Athena, Apollo, Artemis, Poseidon, Ares, Aphrodite, Hermes, Demeter,

[117] *Od.,* XI, 641–6.
[118] Seymour: *op. cit.,* chaps. 9–10; Keller: *op. cit.,* pp. 84, 97 ff.
[119] Seymour: *op. cit.,* p. 413.

Hephaestus, and others have important spheres of influence. Reminders of animism and a certain localism, are the sacred hills, doves, trees—the "Oak of Zeus" at Dodona, the olive of Delos—and honors paid to the rivers, Cephisus, Scamander, and Spercheus.[120] But Zeus does not abide in the oak; and the river-gods and nymphs have relatively slight importance.

The gods are made in the likeness of men: they eat, drink, marry, and have issue; at times, they behave like brawling children; like feudal lords, they drive chariots and are wounded in battle. Though in most respects they are magnified men, there are other differences: the gods are immortal, live at ease, and feast on nectar and ambrosia; moreover, from their abode on high Olympus, they exert an influence against which mere humans strive in vain. Surrounded by such a company of supernatural agencies, the Greeks' fatalism, which they expressed in various ways, is not surprising. Says the ghost of Patroclos, "For me hath yawned that destiny grievous which at the very hour of my birth for me was appointed." "The Gods can raise, and throw men down, with ease"; [121] "He that fights with Heav'n hath never long to live." [122] It was often necessary, therefore, to learn the will of the gods by means of omens and the casting of lots.

Probably the most significant difference between the religion of the Greeks and that of early Oriental peoples lies in the fact that in Hellas is found neither authoritative sacred book, priestly caste, commandment, creed, nor dogma; neither revelation, inspired holy founder, nor religious reformer; neither reward in heaven nor punishment in hell. Homer's gods act disgracefully on many occasions; they think in a bemuddled fashion like men. Their common passions and vices led Gladstone to remark that not one in the whole lot could compare favorably with the herdsman Eumaeus. At a later period, doubt arose as to the propriety of permitting youth to learn about the scandalous lives of Homeric deities.[123]

The standard of the good life was determined not by appeals to holy books and priestly decrees, but by *dike* and *themis*—what has been "pointed out" and "established." These are enforced by men rather than by gods. Fear of the jealous anger of the gods at human fortune was real enough, but nemesis does not weigh very heavily with the fighting men of Homer.[124] Man's religious integrity, in a narrower sense, lay in the performance of ceremonies, not in the profession of belief. His duties to the gods were numerous, but the common man in his household, the king in the palace, and the soldier in the field might act as their own priests; for the gods were not far off, and neither occult wis-

---

120 Pausanias, I, 17, 5; 37, 3; VII, 21, 2; VIII, 23, 5.
121 *Od.*, XVI, 278.
122 *Il.*, V, 387.
123 Plato: *Republic*, II, 378.
124 Keller: *op. cit.*, pp. 115, 289 ff.

dom, acquaintance with unknown tongues, nor secret formulae such as develop in the hands of exclusive, hereditary, priestly organizations, were necessary to propitiate them. Priests there were, indeed, but they were secondary to civil authorities and were chosen by lot or by vote. Though certain reverence was due them, as the official representatives of the deities, they were servants of the state, not its masters.[125]

Greek graves bear evidence of a belief in an afterlife, and literature is full of allusions to it, but the conception of ascetic living as a preparation for it was to them foreign. Hades' realm was dark and gloomy, indeed, and Achilles preferred life as a mere hireling rather than "hold sway over all the dead," but Hades held no punishment for evildoers. It was the destiny of all.

EDUCATION, INTELLECTUAL AND PHYSICAL   Minoan civilization made extensive use of writing; it was known also for a time at Mycenae and other mainland centers. A marked decline occurred, however, as the unity of Minoan culture disintegrated under the sway of the northern conquerors.[126] Writing seems to have become nearly a "lost art" in Greek lands. Homer's heroes have been called "chivalrous" but "illiterate." [127] In casting lots each hero marked his own, but no one recognized the mark on the drawn lot save Ajax himself, whose mark it was.[128]

Under the circumstances formal education either was nonexistent or of very slight importance. Life and education were one. An apprenticeship to life's activities, which gave all needed knowledge and skill, might be gained at home or at a neighboring court. By fabled account, Asclepius and Achilles were sent to Chiron, the centaur, physician of the soul and body, who taught them and brought them ". . . to the highest degree of health, by exercising them in hunting, in journies on mountains, in the race, in sleeping on grassy beds, in eating rustic food, and in drinking river water." [129] Education at court befitted the social status of the recipient. The aged Phoenix, addressing Achilles, recalls his services as mentor, while employed by Peleus at the court of Atrides, to bring up the young prince to wisdom in speech and skill in action:

I, whom thy royal father sent as ord'rer of thy force,
When to Atrides from his court he left thee for this course,
Yet young, and when in skill of arms thou didst not so abound,
Nor hadst the habit of discourse, that makes men so renown'd.
In all which I was set by him, t'instruct thee as my son,

---

[125] Seymour: op. cit., chaps. 14–6; Keller: op. cit., chap. 3; Hyde: Greek Religion and Its Survivals, chap. 1.
[126] C.A.H., II, 437, 463, 508; Hall: The Oldest Civilization of Greece, pp. 138 ff.; Tsountas and Manatt: op. cit., pp. 291 f.; supra, p. 216.
[127] Burn: op. cit., pp. 129, 199.
[128] Il., VII, 153–68.
[129] Maximus Tyrius, diss. 18.

That thou might'st speak, when speech was fit, and do, when deeds
were done,
Not sit as dumb, for want of words, idle, for skill to move.[130]

Such training included all that befitted "manly youth" in a day when the
chief virtue was bravery and the noblest ambition was to attain renown in
war.[131] Homer's "verses are full of mighty shields, shining helmets, long spears,
and beautiful chariots, of brave men slaughtering, and of cowards that are
slain." [132] For the use of these one must be prepared:

> His sharpened spear let every warrior wield,
> And every warrior fix his brazen shield;
> Let all excite the fiery steeds of war,
> And all for combat fit the rattling car.[133]

Phoenix also looked after the food and drink of his charge, and was like a
father to him. Conversation, reciting favorite ballads of wandering rhapsodes,
and playing a simple instrument made a part of such a courtly education.
Achilles is represented as "singing the deeds of men." He was also taught the
uses of herbs by Chiron, which later he communicated to Patroclos. The flute,
shepherd's pipe, cithara, and other simple instruments were used. Paris played
the lyre. Wandering minstrels were specially skilled, and were looked to for
entertainment. Music and singing were constantly associated with dancing, and
both with religious ceremonies.

Children were the objects of marked affection; fathers wanted many, sons
especially. There appears to have been no exposure of children, as there was
later at Sparta and Athens. The boy attended feasts with his father, listened to
heroic recitals, and gradually absorbed an acquaintance with custom which had
the force of law. Girls, in a similar way, learned the duties of women. By such
association with elders youth seem to have acquired certain manual skills: a
prince is mentioned who built his chariot, Odysseus built his bed, and Paris
his palace. Nausicaa, though a princess, washed clothing; Helen and Penelope,
though queens, engaged in carding, spinning, weaving, and other domestic
pursuits.

Both boys and girls played many games. Nausicaa and her assistants played
at ball on the shore.[134] Girls and boys danced together.[135] Other games, such as
tops, draughts, knucklebones, were common for young children. When they
grew older, physical exercises and sports of great variety occupied an ever larger

[130] Il., IX, 417–23.
[131] Ibid., VI, 476–85; Burn: op. cit., p. 247.
[132] Maximus Tyrius, diss., 13.
[133] Ibid., quoting Il., II, 382.
[134] Od., VI, 139.
[135] Il., XVIII, 539.

place in the life of boys, but did not assume a systematic character. These sports were running, jumping, archery, horsemanship, hunting, hurling the spear and the discus, swimming, and driving the chariot—exercises which more or less directly gave a foretaste of military life. Pindar's portrayal of Achilles suggests that, in the case of precocious youth, at least, the transition from child-hood games to the sport of hunting came very early:

> In Phillyra's house a flaxen boy,
> Achilles oft in rapturous joy,
> His feats of strength essay'd.
> Aloof, like wind, his little javelin flew:
> The lion and the brinded boar he slew,
> Then homeward to old Chiron drew
> Their panting carcasses.
> This, when six years had fled.
> And all the after time
> Of his rejoicing prime,
> It was to Dian and the blue-eyed Maid
> A wonder, how he brought to ground
> The stag without or toils or hound:
> So fleet of foot was he.[136]

Hunting seems to have been both a necessity and a sport among Homer's Achaeans. It was necessary to kill certain wild beasts that were inimical to man; moreover, the spoils of the chase were a welcome supplement to the food supply. Certain legendary heroic names were associated with noted exploits in hunting with spear, bow, and club. Homer's heroes hunt in Hades, just as in life they had been famed for their destruction of wild beasts:

> Mighty Orion . . . was hunting there
> The herds of those beasts he had slaughter'd here
> In desert hills on earth. A club he bore,
> Entirely steel, whose virtues never wore.[137]

Dogs were specially bred to hunting, being particularly serviceable in taking the deer, lion, and wild boar. "Dog-leader" is sometimes used as a synonym for hunter.[138]

Fishing was common among folk of lower station, but was chiefly an occupation rather than a sport. The haul was used by them for food, but not generally

---

[136] Cary: *Pindar in English Verse*, pp. 139 f.
[137] *Od.*, XI, 775-8.
[138] Seymour: *op. cit.*, p. 358; Keller: *op. cit.*, pp. 29 f.

by those of higher position, unless necessity compelled it. Spears, lines, hooks, and nets were evidently commonly employed in fishing.[139]

The religion of Homer's Achaeans was intimately associated with everyday affairs. To them no high revelation was given. They were a vigorous, active people. When not engaged in conflict, they generally turned to games of rivalry for recreation. With these games religion was as closely joined as it was with the other activities of life. The gods themselves were the declared founders of gymnastic sports, the companions and competitors of mortal men. Their prowess, indeed, was greater than that of mortals, and therefore much honored of men. Odysseus admits that, though better than those around him, he could not have competed with Heracles or Eurytus, who dared contend with the immortal gods. The alleged divine authorship of their games suggests, if it does not prove, the great antiquity of Hellenic sports. Hermes, according to one tradition, was the originator of gymnastic training.[140] Heracles, Theseus,[141] and Apollo also were among the founding fathers. Apollo invented not only the lyre and the sort of music produced by it, says Diodorus,[142] but also the bow and how to use it. The "Hymn to Apollo" bears testimony to his reputation and the homage rendered to his name:

> I will remember and not be forgetful of archer Apollo,
> Who by the gods is dreaded within Zeus' halls as he enters.[143]

Apollo was also fond of the discus. Zeus challenged the other gods to a tug of war with a golden chain, to demonstrate his superiority against their united strength. Heracles was taught wrestling by Autolycos, son of Hermes. Thus in sport, as in other affairs, it is evident that the world of gods was not far from that of men.

Further evidence of the connection of Homeric sports with religion and life is found in the funeral games in honor of Patroclos. Such games, and also musical contests in honor of dead heroes, were common among the Greeks, and are generally accepted as the prototypes of later periodic festivals of sport, religious ceremony, dance and song. Thus the great athletic festivals originated in funeral games for particular heroes, but were subsequently celebrated in honor of deities.[144]

The Homeric poems portray the ideal of Achaean aristocracy, whose primary function is leadership in war. Sports practiced by this class reflect its interests

---

[139] Radcliffe: *Fishing from the Earliest Times*, pp. 63–85.
[140] Philostratos: *Concerning Gymnastics*, 16; Diodorus, v, 74.
[141] Pausanias, I, 39, 3.
[142] Bk. v, 74.
[143] Lawton: *Classical Greek Literature*, p. 53.
[144] Gardiner: *Greek Athletic Sports and Festivals*, pp. 27 ff.; Hyde: *Olympic Victor Monuments*, pp. 9 ff.; infra, pp. 365 f.

and physical skills, without which war could not be successfully conducted. Achaean sports, though spontaneous, serve an eminently practical end. In the games of the *Iliad*, warriors have a day off from bloody conflict with the enemy, and seek not only to honor the dead Patroclos but to cheer their mourning spirits with the gay rivalry of sport. In friendly yet energetic competition in "distressful," dangerous sports between comrades in arms, the edge is kept keen for genuine conflict in which there will be no quarter. This ideal of a life of conflict and conquest is ever close to the hearts of Greeks. Only by successful performance of strenuous, dangerous deeds, can men of this aristocratic, heroic world preserve their memory green. Pindar's beautiful metallic verse embodies this ideal:

> Deeds without danger wrought
> Neither in hollowed ships nor among men
> Are honored: but if aught
> Of glory be thro' peril sought
> Many remember then.[145]

The eulogies customarily bestowed upon things Greek should not obscure the fact that the beautiful may be linked with the ugly and savage in man's nature.[146] The funeral celebration arranged by Achilles reveals a noble, touching tenderness for his friend. For his opponent, however, whose corpse he madly tramps upon, there is only contempt and brutal treatment:

> Hector lies slaughter'd here
> Dragg'd at my chariot, and our dogs shall all in pieces tear
> His hated limbs. Twelve Trojan youths, born of their noblest strains,
> I took alive; and, yet enrag'd, will empty all their veins
> Of vital spirits, sacrific'd before thy heap of fire.[147]

The games following the cremation of Patroclos included the chariot race, boxing, wrestling, running, fighting with spears, discus-throwing, archery, and hurling the spear. Nestor, though too old to take part in games, boasts that, when young, not one could best him in boxing, wrestling, running, spear-throwing; and only Actor's sons outdid him in the chariot race.[148] Similar games followed the death of Achilles. Some have professed to see in the five sports named by Nestor a Homeric pentathlon, foreshadowing that of later times. This is clearly an exaggerated, erroneous interpretation. The exercises named are not the same as those later included in the pentathlon (wrestling, running,

---

[145] Lawton: *Greek Literature*, p. 147.
[146] *Ibid.*, pp. 9 f.
[147] *Il.*, XXIII, 17–21.
[148] *Ibid.*, XXIII, 551–9.

jumping, and throwing the discus and javelin). In the Homeric contests, more-over, there is an air of informality which ill comports with the fixed order of the Great Games of a later day.[149]

Of all Homeric sports chariot-racing is the most expensive and aristocratic; one must be rich enough to equip himself with horses and chariots. To com-petitors in this event the most attractive prizes are offered: the first, "a lady . . . gen'rally praiseful, fair and young, and skill'd in housewif'ries of all kinds fitting," and a large tripod; second, a young mare in foal; third, a caldron fair and bright; fourth, two talents of fine gold; and fifth, a great new urn. The contest is select; only five compete. Achilles himself will not make an entry: his horses are of a superior strain, and he doubts not that he would simply take back again the prizes offered. So to the others he proclaims:

> You then that trust in chariots, and hope with horse to crown
> Your conqu'ring temples, gird yourselves; now, fame and prize stretch for,
> All that have spirits.[150]

Old Phoenix, Achilles' tutor, is named to judge the race, the course of which is on the open plain—turning round an old stump and two white stones. Youth-ful Antilochos, who later disputes decisions and offers to fight if denied the second prize, is given a few hints by Nestor on how to drive. Thus runs his gar-rulous speech, as he tells how cleverness will outrun mere speed and power:

> But go on, show but thy art and heart
> At all points, and set them against their horses' heart and art;
> Good judges will not see thee lose. A carpenter's desert
> Stands more in cunning than in pow'r. A pilot doth avert
> His vessel from the rock, and wrack, tost with the churlish winds,
> By skill, not strength. . . .[151]

As to the stones which mark the course's turning—

> When near to these the race grows, then as right
> Drive on them as thy eye can judge; then lay thy bridle's weight
> Most of thy left side; thy right horse then switching, all thy throat,
> Spent in encouragements, give him, and all the rein let float
> About his shoulders; thy near horse will yet be he that gave
> Thy skill the prize, and him rein so his head may touch the nave
> Of thy left wheel; but then take care thou runn'st not on the stone
> (With wrack of horse and chariot) which so thou bear'st upon.[152]

[149] Gardiner: *Greek Athletic Sports and Festivals*, pp. 359 ff.; *infra*, Chap. XII.
[150] *Il.*, XXIII, 262–4.
[151] *Ibid.*, XXIII, 289–94.
[152] *Ibid.*, XXIII, 313–20.

Boxing, "that rough game," is the next attraction. For the victor, "a laborious mule" is offered; for the loser, "a round cup." Epëus, tall "man-mountain" and braggart that he is, lays hands on the mule, claiming him as his own before a blow is struck, and challenges all others:

> Now let some other stand
> Forth for the cup; this mule is mine, at cuffs I boast me best. . . .
> Who stands forth, I'll burst him, I will bray
> His bones as in a mortar. Fetch surgeons enow to take
> His corse from under me.[153]

Epëus knew whereof he boasted. So did his comrades in arms, apparently, for all were silent till, at last, Euryalus stood up, who once had bested all the Thebans at the funeral games of Oedipus. These, then, clad for the match with girdles and ox-hide thongs, fell to with might and main. Not all the encouragement and tricks taught Euryalus by Tydides could save him, when—

> . . . breast oppos'd to breast,
> Fists against fists rose, and they join'd, rattling of jaws was there,
> Gnashing of teeth, and heavy blows dash'd blood out ev'rywhere.
> At length Epëus spy'd clear way, rush'd in, and such a blow
> Drave underneath the other's ear, that his neat limbs did strow
> The knock'd earth, no more legs had he; . . .
> About whom rush'd a crowd of friends, that through the clusters bore
> His falt'ring knees, he spitting up thick clods of blood, his head
> Totter'd of one side, his sense gone; when, to a by-place led,
> Thither they brought him the round cup.[154]

So ended the "manly" sport. Hard upon it followed "painful" wrestling, no unimportant part of warlike training, in a day when man met man in hand-to-hand encounter. Two prizes, a tripod worth twelve oxen, and a woman worth only four, inspire the hearts of Ajax and Odysseus who measure power and cunning. They wrestle standing, not upon the ground:

> . . . forth they stepp'd, catch elbows with strong hands,
> And as the beams of some high house crack with a storm, yet stands
> The house, being built by well-skill'd men; so crack'd their backbones, wrinch'd
> With horrid twitches; in their sides, arms, shoulders, all bepinch'd,
> Ran thick the wales, red with the blood, ready to start out. Both
> Long'd for the conquest and the prize; yet show'd no play, being loth

[153] Ibid., xxiii, 582–8.
[154] Ibid., xxiii, 596–609.

To lose both. Nor could Ithacus stir Ajax; nor could he
Hale down Ulysses, being more strong than with mere strength to be
Hurl'd from all vantage of his sleight. Tir'd then with tugging play,
Great Ajax Telamonius said: "Thou wisest man, or lay
My face up, or let me lay thine; let Jove take care for these."
This said, he hois'd him up to air; when Laertiades
His wiles forgat not, Ajax' thigh he strook behind, and flat
He on his back fell; on his breast Ulysses. Wonder'd at
Was this of all; all stood amaz'd. Then the much suff'ring man,
Divine Ulysses, at next close the Telamonian
A little rais'd from earth, not quite, but with his knee implied
Lock'd legs; and down fell both on earth, close by each other's side,
Both fil'd with dust; but starting up, the third close they had made,
Had not Achilles' self stood up, restraining them, and bade:
"No more tug one another thus, nor moil yourselves. . . ." [155]

The contest is declared a draw; the prizes will be equal.

The poet does not spare his men! Odysseus proceeds at once to compete with Ajax and Antilochos in running. In this match the conception of sportsmanship, whether it be that of the gods, of men, or of the poet, seems a little below par. If Odysseus wins, it is because Minerva, divinely capricious, chooses to make "light his limbs"—an excellent description of the sensation, by the way—and makes his victory doubly probable, if not certain, by tripping Ajax, causing him to fall amid the filth of the funeral slaughter. Antilochos, moreover, makes us feel that it's not a genuine race at all: it was "fixed" in advance by the fact that the gods favor older men. All get prizes. Antilochos, who well employs his tongue, gets the third prize doubled by judicious praise of Achilles.

The combat of armed men, spear-throwing, hurling the *solus*, and the archery contest are said to be later additions to the *Iliad*. The armed combat, according to representations on the Clazomenae sarcophagus, the Amphiaraus Vase, and the Dipylon Vase, was a feature of the funeral games. In the games given by Achilles the combat in armor is entered only by Ajax and Diomed. Somewhat like the wrestling match, though both contestants "put looks on so austere, and join'd so roughly" that many feared the outcome, the event is terminated abruptly without a decision. Nevertheless, the sword from Thrace is bestowed on Diomed, and both dine generously at Achilles' tent.

Casting the weight, here simply a natural pig of stone and metal, is also a skill closely allied to primitive warfare, and clearly a popular sport. There are four contestants, but one prize, the weight itself, which Polypoetes flings so far beyond the rest that all around stand up and cheer.

[155] *Ibid.*, XXIII, 617-37.

Hurling the spear, which should have proved a beautiful event, turns out dull indeed, for Agamemnon and Meriones announce themselves as entrants, whereat Achilles, declaring none worthy to match the son of Atreus, awards him first prize, "a caldron new," and gives a lance to Meriones. The archery contest, whose object is to shoot a dove without touching the string which binds her to a pole, is won by Meriones, who succeeds in piercing the dove on wing amongst the clouds, after Teucer (who shot first, but, unlike Meriones, made no vow "to Him that rules the bow") had missed her, but cut the string.

Thus ended the games, whose rich prizes honored Achilles' generosity and the memory of his friend; and whose portrayals embellished the name of the poet or poets that gave them. What would Londos, Nurmi, Louis not do for such press agents—and for gods so attentive to mortals!

The care expended by Homer on the funeral games of Patroclos suggests both the importance of sports and the rôle of primitive rites among early Hellenes. References to such ceremonial games performed in the dim ages of mythology were common currency in later historic times. Plutarch [156] says that Minos instituted games in honor of Androgeos. Pausanias says funeral games were first celebrated for Azas, son of Arcas; Pelias was thus honored; and Mecisteus took part in those for Oedipus at Thebes.[157] The games in honor of Achilles by his mother, Thetis, were said to have excelled all others.[158]

Besides the sporting contests just described, numerous references in Homeric poetry and other literature deepen the conviction that the early Greeks were genuinely fond of physical competition. That they believed themselves superior to others, or that they were so depicted in their art, is not surprising. What people does not think itself more cultured, more skillful, than its neighbors? Almost any festal occasion that offered opportunity for recreation and entertainment was devoted to sport, music, and dancing. Individual prowess of many sorts, quite apart from formal contests, is often acclaimed. At the return of Odysseus, the boxing match with Irus and the contest with the bow are put on impromptu.[159] Trick horseback riding, leaping from back to back of four horses in full career, is mentioned in the *Iliad*.[160] Swimming and boating [161] though not mentioned as part of athletic competitions were doubtless common among people who had so many opportunities for them. Both warm and cold

---

[156] *Theseus*, 16.
[157] *Pausanias*, VIII, 4, 5; V, 17, 9; I, 28, 7.
[158] *Od*., XXIV, 122–8.
[159] *Ibid*., XVIII, 50–139; XXI. Whether Odysseus' feat was to shoot through twelve axheads, or through the holes in which the helves of the axes were inserted, has been debated.— Haynes: "Odysseus' Feat of Archery," *Am. Jour. Archaeol.*, VI, 487.
[160] Bk. XV, 625–30.
[161] *Od*., VIII, 46–7, 345; X, 100; Gardner: "Boat-races among the Greeks," *Jour. Hellenic Studies*, II, 90 f.

baths are familiar features of the domestic life of Homer's Greeks.[162] Rivers and the sea, however, provided the earliest facilities for bathing and swimming. Myth tells of Leander who swam the Hellespont nightly to his beloved Hero. Odysseus, when tempests destroyed his tipsy craft, swam wrestling with the sable seas to reach the Phaeacians' strand.[163]

The arrival of a stranger at the court of Alcinous, which some have thought to place in Crete, causes the Phaeacian king to order a feast with games and music.[164] The Phaeacians boast of their athletic prowess—until Odysseus has exhibited his—longing to give the visitor a show of their superiority in boxing, wrestling, leaping, running, and discus, that he may long remember it and carry their fame back home with him. Odysseus, too, is urged to show his skill; for, says Phaeacian Laodamas, none can prove his worth so well as by the strenuous arts of foot and hand. Odysseus at first modestly declines; then, stung by the taunt that he is only a seafaring merchant, unfit for noble, manly sports, he rebukes his accuser, seizes a stone, heavier than any yet thrown, and hurls it far beyond the best of them. Finally, his "spleen up," he challenges each and all, save Laodamas ("for he's mine host, and who will fight, or wrangle, with his friend?"), to compete with him in any sport "in use with men." The Phaeacian king thinks quickly and adroitly shifts the talk from manly sports to feasts, music, dancing, baths, and other features of luxurious life, in which the Phaeacians know no peer.

Dancing is a highly cultivated art amongst the Phaeacians, so spectacular in its evolutions, speed, and precision, that Odysseus is amazed at their twinkling feet, which moved so "swift, and fine, and beat the air so thin, they made it shine." [165] He is ready to grant them superiority in it at once, but is still to be entranced by a superb performance of an acrobatic ball dance by Halius and Laodamas:

> Then the rich-wrought ball,
> That Polybus had made, of purple all,
> They took to hand. One threw it to the sky,
> And then danc'd back; the other, capering high,
> Would surely catch it ere his foot touch'd ground,
> And up again advanc'd it, and so found
> The other cause of dance; and then did he
> Dance lofty tricks, till next it came to be
> His turn to catch, and serve the other still.

[162] Krause: *Die Gymnastik und Agonistik der Hellenen*, I, 624.
[163] *Od.*, v, 486, 504–5.
[164] *Ibid.*, viii, 48 *et seq.*
[165] *Ibid.*, viii, 372–3.

> When they had kept it up to either's will,
> They then danc'd ground tricks, oft mix'd hand in hand,
> And did so gracefully their change command,
> That all the other youth that stood at pause,
> With deaf'ning shouts gave them the great applause.[166]

These sports were practiced by folk of high degree. Commoners did not compete with their betters. Alcinous of the Phaeacian court sends fifty-two youth "chosen from the throng," the best at oars, to launch a ship, while others go to prepare a feast in honor of Odysseus. The "sceptre-bearing" kings are invited to feast and prove themselves in manly games.[167] Men who go avoyaging for cargoes and gain, and are concerned with favoring winds, are in a class apart from men "fit for contentions noble," says Euryalus.[168] That common folk had competitions among themselves, in imitation of their betters, there is no reason to doubt, though note is seldom taken of them. Homer sings of the great and for the great; reference to inferiors is often contemptuous, or they are ignored altogether. It may be that the boxing match between Irus and Odysseus justifies the conjecture that contests were arranged at times by nobles for their inferiors.[169] The evidence, however, is slight. The quarrel begun by Irus is really quite impromptu; the suitors, wishing to see some sport, egg on the opponents and promise favors to the winner.[170] The informal and spontaneous character of sports often appears, but there are distinctions; some are truly aristocratic, others of a humbler sort. While Achilles nurses his anger the leading men stalk about refusing to fight. Meanwhile, other folk—

> . . . yet pleas'd their hearts
> With throwing of the holéd stone, with hurling of their darts,
> And shooting fairly on the shore. . . .[171]

In such an aristocratic, regal sport as chariot-racing, commoners do not appear. Class distinctions are reflected in Homeric sport, as they are in other departments of life. Centuries later, when democracy had made some impress on the Hellenic world of sports, Alexander still thought it unworthy of royalty to compete with common men.

[166] Ibid., VIII, 509–22.
[167] Ibid., VIII, 44 et seq.
[168] Ibid., VIII, 210–23.
[169] Manning: "Professionalism in Greek Athletics," Class. Weekly, XI, 74.
[170] Od., XVIII, 51–68.
[171] Il., II, 685–7.

# 9

# DORIAN DOMINION

The bronze-age civilization which had centered at Knossos and Mycenae appears to have been profoundly disturbed about the twelfth century by migrations from the north. The Heraclids, as ancient legend put it, were returning to reclaim the heritage of Heracles. To this southward migration, which embraced Thessalians and Aetolians as well as Dorians, the name "Dorian" invasion is commonly given. Although, according to Greek accounts, the invasion occurred in 1104 B.C., the entire movement actually covered centuries. Evidence of infiltration is found as early as the fifteenth century in some localities, but the most destructive conquest seems to have occurred about the middle of the eleventh century.[1] Its effects are attested in many ways. The naturalness of Cretan-Mycenaean art gives way to crude "Geometric"; swords and other articles of iron become more common, bronze implements less so; new modes of clothing and adornments appear; communication is broken down; and the universal character which distinguished Cretan-Mycenaean civilization at its height is supplanted by a localism, evident in the varieties of Geometric art.[2] In short, Mycenaean culture declines, probably from internal decay as well as from external forces, and is followed by an age of darkness which continues until about the eighth century.

Prior to the seventh century lies the shadowland of many legends. The fascinating tale told by Pausanias about the Messenian wars,[3] built upon the accounts of Rhianus of Bene and Myron of Priene, is scarcely more satisfying than the mythical account of the Dorian invasion and the rise of Argolis, Sparta, and Messenia, according to which three great-grandsons of Hyllus

[1] Thucydides, I, 12; *The History of Herodotus*, I, 56; *The Cambridge Ancient History*, II, 519, 525.
[2] *C.A.H.*, II, 521; Jardé: *The Formation of the Greek People*, p. 75.
[3] *Pausanias's Description of Greece*, IV, 6–23.

(Temenus, Aristodemus, and Kresphontes) conquered the lower Peloponnesus and divided it by lot, Argolis falling to Temenus, Messenia to Kresphontes, and Sparta to the twin sons of Aristodemus who had just died. What is truth, what romance, in the tale of those laborious struggles whose heroes are let down safely by eagles' wings to the bottom of an abyss and escape from dark caverns by holding fast to foxes' tails?

Though one may distrust many details in the story of struggles that went on from the eleventh century to the seventh, and though the heroic embroidery and the doings of the gods may be discounted or entirely cast aside, the major consequences are sufficiently clear. What Knossos and Mycenae had been to the bronze-age civilization, Argos and Sparta became to the Dorian culture, which arose upon its ruins. But before Sparta established her iron sway over the Peloponnesus, the separatist tendencies, so ubiquitous at the end of the Mycenaean Age, produced scores of petty sovereign city-states. From the eleventh century to the eighth this divisive localism was at its height. Only gradually, by dint of great effort, Sparta rose to supremacy. The Achaeans first gave way before the Dorians or quasi-Dorians in the plain of Argos; to the south, on the River Eurotas, they established themselves at Sparta and ultimately conquered the Achaean stronghold of Amyclae, which "offered a long and not inglorious resistance"; and finally the town of "Helos by the sea." [4] By the middle of the eighth century, Sparta was mistress of Laconia. Westward, across the ridges of Tygaetus, lay fertile Messenia, whose subjection was brought about after two bitter, stubborn wars in the eighth and seventh centuries.[5] On this eminence of military power, extending throughout the lower Peloponnesus, Sparta stood till the fourth century, but not without the need of constant vigilance to put down revolts of the conquered populations. Then, after the battle of Leuctra (371 B.C.), as if to give the lie to the proud boast that Spartan women had never seen the smoke of enemy campfires, Theban Epaminondas ravaged their territory, even to the Eurotas and the environs of Sparta herself,[6] and refounded Messenia as a further means of weakening Spartan power.[7]

## SPARTAN SOCIAL INSTITUTIONS

When Polybius and Plutarch attributed the many centuries of Spartan law and order to Lycurgus, they honored a name traditionally revered ever since the Greeks began to write their history.[8] Whether Lycurgus ever existed, whether

[4] Ibid., III, 2, 6–7; Jardé: op. cit., pp. 122 f.
[5] Jardé: op. cit., pp. 117 f.; Bury: A History of Greece, pp. 127 f.
[6] Xenophon: Hellenics, VI, 5, 28; Plutarch: Agesilaus, 31.
[7] Pausanias, IV, 26.
[8] Polybius: The Histories, IV, 81; Plutarch: Lycurgus, 29; Agesilaus, 33.

his was a legendary name with which patriots associated certain aspects of their history, is open to question.[9] But though the reputed Lawgiver of Laconia be elusive, the character of Sparta's society and government during the centuries of her greatest power is fairly clear. Tradition said that Lycurgus lived about 855 B.C., and formed the nicely articulated system which came to be a symbol of oppression to enemies and a name to conjure with among later admirers and students of politics. It is evident, however, that Spartan society was a result of a long process of growth and not simply the embodiment of a design. A conspicuous feature of Laconian society, its stratification, was the result of conquest by the Dorian invaders. Because of the stubborn resistance of the inhabitants of Helos, they were reduced to serfdom. Hence, according to a common version, originated the designation "Helots," subsequently applied to other villages that fell subject to the conquerors' capricious will.[10] Their number, fluctuating from time to time, is not definitely known, but probably doubled as a result of the Messenian wars and exceeded the masters' ten to one.[11]

Hatred of the conquerors was intense and often flared into revolt. The Third Messenian War (464 B.C.), a revolt of Messenian Helots, lasted many years. Apropos of Cinadon's conspiracy against the Spartans, Xenophon says that Helots would willingly have eaten their Spartan lords alive.[12] Thucydides [13] declares that Spartan institutions were designed chiefly to keep the Helots down. By means of the Crypteia, Spartan youth spied upon Helots and did away with them; the ephors swore to make war upon them; and trickery was employed to betray their ablest members. Thus the Spartans announced on one occasion that those Helots who claimed they had rendered great service to the state would be freed. Thus chosen, about two thousand crowned themselves and went to the temples; soon after, however, these were done away with, and no one ever learned how they were destroyed.[14]

The Helots tilled the soil at the behest of their masters. By their labor Spartan citizen-soldiers were left free to devote themselves to public affairs. In war, Helots at times served their masters personally. Herodotus [15] says that, at the battle of Plataea, each Spartan was attended by seven Helots. Sometimes they were permitted to fight as light-armed, or even as heavy-armed, soldiers. For bravery they might be granted liberty; but if the story told by Thucydides be true, many must have feared "freedom" as a dubious gain. Manumission, executed by the state, was apt to be resorted to when soldiers were scarce. As time

[9] Bury: op. cit., p. 135.
[10] Pausanias, III, 20, 6.
[11] C.A.H., III, 538, 567; Müller: The History and Antiquities of the Doric Race, II, 44 f.; Wilkins: National Education in Greece, p. 12.
[12] Hellenics, III, 3, 6.
[13] Bk. IV, 80.
[14] Ibid.; Plutarch: Lycurgus, 28; Plato: Laws, I, 633.
[15] Bk. IX, 29.

went on and the aristocracy of free citizens dwindled, the Helots and the Perioeci were turned to more and more for warriors. Sending Helots to war was one way to get them away from Laconia! The army Brasidas led to Thrace included seven hundred heavy-armed Helots; and Agesilaus took two thousand newly enfranchised men on an expedition to Asia.[16] Cleomenes enfranchised the best Perioeci, organizing four thousand of them as heavy infantry; Helots, too, who could pay five Attic minas were freed, and two thousand of them were armed.[17]

Above the Helots were the Perioeci, distributed in many localities throughout Laconia, and derived probably from pre-Dorian groups which submitted more readily to the demands of their conquerors.[18] Perioeci were not serfs. They had certain privileges, served as heavy-armed troops under Spartan command, and exercised local control in their communities; but they had no voice in the determination of policy in Laconia. As a part of the subject population, they submitted to Spartan demands while Spartan strength compelled it, but were always ready to seize any favorable opportunity for revolt. A general uprising occurred among them when Epaminondas invaded Laconia after the battle of Leuctra.[19]

At the apex of the social pyramid were the Dorian conquerors, who had reduced pre-Dorians to the status of Helots and Perioeci. These Spartiates were citizens; they constituted the Spartan state. This relatively small group perfected and long maintained its hold upon the conquered by iron discipline of its members rather than by virtue of numbers. Plutarch says that nine thousand lots were assigned to genuine Spartan citizens by Lycurgus; Herodotus places the figure at eight thousand at the time of Thermopylae, while Aristotle says there were less than one thousand at the Theban invasion.[20] At the conspiracy of Cinadon, Xenophon says,[21] only forty Spartans were to be seen in the market place, compared with four thousand others.

Polybius [22] was of the opinion that Lycurgus, by judicious mixture of monarchy, aristocracy, and democracy, provided a constitution which safeguarded liberty longer at Sparta than had elsewhere been known. Aristotle,[23] however, found many flaws in the Spartan constitution. However one may judge it, good or bad, the system served the interest of a small class of conquerors, who sought

---

[16] Thucydides, IV, 80; Xenophon: *Hellenics*, III, 4, 2.

[17] Plutarch: *Cleomenes*, 11, 23.

[18] Herodotus, IX, 28; Isocrates: *Panathenaicus*, 177–81; C.A.H., V, 3 f.; Laistner: *A Survey of Ancient History*, pp. 129 f.

[19] Plutarch: *Cimon*, 16; *Agesilaus*, 32; Grote: *A History of Greece*, I, 478.

[20] Plutarch: *Lycurgus*, 8; Herodotus, VII, 234; Aristotle: *Politica*, II, 9; Laistner: *op. cit.*, p. 350.

[21] *Hellenics*, III, 3, 5.

[22] Bk. VI, 10.

[23] *Politica*, II, 9.

the preservation of their power and privileges amid a host of subjugated Helots and Perioeci.

The constitution of Sparta was democratic in a limited sense: at the age of thirty, every male Spartan became a member of the Apella, the assembly, which gave voice on war, peace, manumission of Helots, and other public matters. But the Apella enjoyed only a limited freedom: none could speak save the officials, those specially invited, and those approved by the magistrates. Moreover, though Lycurgus provided that the people should have the final decision,[24] this popular sovereignty was modified by Theopompus and Polydorus, so that, if the people voted "crookedly," their decision might be reversed by those above them. The Apella did not initiate policies, but approved or rejected them without modification, and was, as Grote says, "an inoperative formality." [25] But if the Apella's power was neutralized in this way, the common citizens gained real influence through the growth of the Ephorate—five men elected by the Apella, each for one year. The ephors had great power and often exercised it tyrannically.[26] They could convoke the Apella, pass upon complaints, control education, judge the conduct of men, levy and collect fines, perform judicial functions in many civil matters, and even cause the arrest of kings.

Aristocratic aspects of Spartan government were embodied in the Gerousia and the dual kingship. The Gerousia consisted of twenty-eight gerontes and the two hereditary kings, i.e., one member from each of thirty obes into which the three original tribes were divided. Its members, except the kings, were elected by acclamation in the Apella. Tenure was for life, but only old men of sixty were eligible for election. Life tenure in the Gerousia was recognized as a weakness by Aristotle, who pointed out that "the mind grows old as well as the body." [27]

The dual kingship was at once a source of dissension and a guarantee against successful despotism, the ambition of one being a check upon the other. Its origin is obscure, but probably may be traced to the two chief families, those of Eurysthenes and Procles, sons of Aristodemus. The kings were high priests of religion, dispensers of justice in important matters, and leaders of armies. In making war they were at first supreme, but it became customary, as their power diminished and that of the Ephorate was augmented, for them to gain the approval of the ephors for military undertakings. Ultimately their powers were so completely overshadowed by the Ephorate that, though they continued to enjoy honors, wealth and privileges, they were little better than hereditary generals who, even on campaigns, were accompanied by two of the ephors.[28]

24 Plutarch: *Lycurgus*, 6.
25 Grote: *op. cit.*, I, 473.
26 Aristotle: *Politica*, II, 9.
27 *Ibid.*
28 Herodotus, VI, 56–8; Xenophon: *Constitution of the Lacedaemonians*, 15; Aristotle: *Politica*, II, 9; Grote: *op. cit.*, I, 469 ff.; Abbott: *A History of Greece*, I, 203 ff.

The Spartan system at one time provided for a limited element of communism. Whether or not a Lycurgus or some other imposed these features, it is certain that they became real, and that they represented a drastic change in Spartan life. This change probably occurred, not in the ninth century, when Lycurgus was said to have lived, but shortly before the beginning of the sixth century.[29] It came when the Spartans by force of arms had extended their sway to Messenia and had thereby become great holders of land and masters of a vastly increased serf population. Wealth and established power are conducive to conservatism. This "lovely moment" of wealth and power the Spartan masters sought to seize and to hold fast. The *Eunomia*, the system of authoritative law which later opinion associated with Lycurgus, was the means by which dominion was to be preserved at the expense of strict self-discipline.

In the eighth and seventh centuries, Spartan society was brighter, more charming and hospitable, than it became in the sixth century and thereafter; the differences between Sparta and Athens, so much stressed by later writers, were a result of centuries of development.[30] Noted for hunting-dogs, horses, horsemanship—as well became a warlike, conquering people—and for its beautiful women (though one may distrust the voice of the oracle and the poet), this earlier age contrasted sharply with its successor, especially in respect to patronage of music and poetry. Thaletas of Crete, Alcman, Terpander of Lesbos, and Tyrtaeus, though not natives of Sparta, found her in the seventh century a patroness of their talents. Terpander, it is said, was invited to Sparta; there he taught music, and was oft a winner at the Pythian games. Alcman, from Sardis probably, was noted for his *partheneia*, choral songs for maidens. Tyrtaeus, reputedly a lame schoolmaster sent by Athenians upon request, became the inspirer of Spartan soldiers with his warlike songs, during the second Messenian War, and a guide to good citizenship through his stern, stately *Eunomia*. One of his marching songs appeals thus to the soldier:

> O youths of our populous Sparta,
> Ye children of citizen fathers,
> Thrust forward your shield in the left hand,
> Unterrified lift ye the lances,
> Nor be of your lives over-cautious,
> For 'tis not the tradition of Sparta! [31]

This age of culture passed away. Spartan soldiers continued to sing songs around the campfire, and 'tis said that those who sang them best were rewarded with a bit of meat, but Sparta ceased to be a patroness of arts. The cultural de-

[29] *C.A.H.*, III, 562; Laistner: *op. cit.*, pp. 131 f.

[30] Thucydides, I, 70; II, 35–46; *Lyra Graeca*, I, 27; Laistner: *op. cit.*, pp. 128 f., 153; Jardé: *op. cit.*, pp. 76 f.

[31] Lawton: *Classical Greek Literature*, pp. 88, 125 f.; Wright, W. C.: *A Short History of Greek Literature*, pp. 74, 93, 105 f.

cline of Sparta seems to harmonize with the reforms of Lycurgus, and it may be that its cause is to be found partly in them and the conditions that called them forth. Sparta became a great military barracks; her laws and her customs "were those of a garrison"; her sole virtue, that of courage in war.[32]

The Spartan system of discipline, attributed by Herodotus, Xenophon, Plutarch, and others to Lycurgus, was unique, differing even in certain respects from the Cretan, which it most resembled and from whence Lycurgus was said to have borrowed it.[33] The essential features of this social discipline were: an allotment of land to each citizen, sufficient to sustain him and enable him to contribute his share to the *syssitia* or public mess; prescription of a common diet (limited in quantity, so that one might feel hunger and have appetite for what otherwise would be unpalatable) and common, simple dress; restriction of active citizenship to those who observed the prescribed Spartan discipline and contributed their share to the mess; prohibition of the pursuit by citizens of any common or mechanical occupation, thus securing their devotion to public matters and weaning them from personal concern; withdrawal of gold and silver from circulation, and the substitution of iron money of great weight and of little value; prohibition of traveling and residing abroad, that none might contract a preference for foreign manners, views of government, or the "habits of ill-educated people"; provision that no strangers should be admitted to Sparta save for good reason, since with them would come strange words, feelings, ideas, and other novelties that might prove destructive to the harmony of the state; the institution of compulsory marriage, and the encouragement of such freedom that children might be produced by those who were thought fit to beget and to bear them; the public examination of the newborn and the rejection of those deemed unfit to become citizens; and finally, that all regulations might be faithfully observed by each new generation, the provision of a strict, common discipline—physical, mental, and moral—designed differentially so as to benefit both young men and maidens. Houses, moreover, were to be simple, that none might know luxury at home, or seek to show themselves better than others. Prohibitions were not for Spartans alone. Helots and Perioeci were enjoined to dance only vulgar dances and sing ridiculous songs, being warned against the use of songs and dances of freemen. Helots, when ordered by Theban invaders to sing the songs of Alcman and Terpander, are said to have refused because their masters had forbidden it.[34] The phrase "freemen's choirs and freemen's games" [35] reminds us that a line separated the slave from the freeman in other parts of Greece, though not so sharply as at Sparta.

[32] Wilkins: *op. cit.*, p. 9; Aristotle: *Politica*, II, 9.
[33] *Herodotus*, I, 65; Xenophon: *Lacedaemonians*, I, 2; Plutarch: *Lycurgus*, 4; *Pausanias*, III, 2, 4; Aristotle: *Politica*, II, 10.
[34] Plutarch: *Lycurgus*, 28.
[35] Aristophanes: *The Frogs*, 56.

## SPARTAN TRAINING

ITS CHARACTER AND PURPOSE  The *Eunomia* of Lycurgus gave meticulous attention to the training of youth. Aristotle, though critical of certain aspects of this regimen, approved of the Lacedaemonian solicitude for it—especially because it was considered a state function. In the public character of education may be seen a reflection and a symbol of Spartan life. Since everything was for the collective, rather than for the individual, education was public rather than private. Sparta trained youth to obedience to the laws, and made them submissive like colts that are broken. Thus she became famous as a "subduer of men." Lycurgus is said to have advised against building walls round the city, saying that a city is best fortified if it has a wall of men rather than of brick.[36] It is the strength of free men, trained in fidelity to law, of which Demaratus boasts to Xerxes: "For though they be free men, they are not in all respects free; Law is the master whom they own, and this master they fear more than thy subjects fear thee. Whatever he commands they do; and his commandment is always the same: it forbids them to flee in battle, whatever the number of their foes, and requires them to stand firm, and either to conquer or die." [37] Fidelity to law, as well as sadness, shines through the "teardrops of Simonides," who thus bears testimony to the effectiveness of Spartan training:

> Go, stranger, and to Lacedaemon tell
> That here, obeying her behests, we fell.[38]

All Spartan training was for a vocation—that of the soldier. To them the words of the poet might be applied:

> From their first youth unto their utmost age,
> Appointed the laborious wars to wage.

In time of peace, everything was sacrificed to prepare for war. Even the smallest matters were not neglected. After eating and drinking, says Plutarch, every man walked home "without a torch," so that he might habitually march boldly and fearlessly in the darkness.[39] They contrived ingeniously to make life in wartime more attractive than in peace. When engaged actively in war their exercises were easier, their diet less strict, and their officers more lenient; thus, it was said, they were the only people who found relaxation in war. Even in games, the Spartan aim was not recreation or personal enjoyment, but fitness

---

[36] Plutarch: *Lycurgus*, 19; *Agesilaus*, 1.
[37] *Herodotus*, VII, 104.
[38] *Ibid.*, VII, 228.
[39] *Lycurgus*, 12.

for war. Victory at Olympia was a high reward, indeed, but chiefly because it conferred the right to distinction in war. A Lacedaemonian, being asked what he had gained by his Olympic conquest, replied: "I shall stand in front of my King when I fight our enemies." [40] Success in war depended more upon individual skill and courage in hand-to-hand fighting than to-day. Physical strength and courage constituted, therefore, the primary ideals of Spartan training. To attain them they sacrificed certain other ends. Aristotle declared that Lacedaemonians brutalized their children by severe exercises which were calculated to heighten courage, but they failed to attain their goal.[41] Looking back to primitive practices of other lands, where physical prowess and courage were developed chiefly for war, one notes a close resemblance between them and those of Sparta. St. John observed that the spirit of Spartan training was "precisely the same" as that of certain warlike Indian tribes which produced numerous examples of "patience, fortitude, and magnanimity, together with . . . force, agility and suppleness of body. . . ." [42]

On the intellectual side, Spartan training seems to have been little beyond the primitive. The matter is rather obscure, however, and the evidence divergent. The judgments of those who were enemies of Sparta stress her brutal, unintellectual character; others, such as the "Laconizers," praise her uncritically and without stint. Plato's Hippias says that Spartans listened gladly to genealogies, tales of heroes, the settlement of tribes, and the founding of cities, but that "many of them know not, so to say, even how to reckon." [43] Isocrates [44] declares that the Spartans were so backward in education and general culture that they did not even learn letters, and that they would only be able to understand certain writings provided someone interpreted them. Plutarch says, however, that of "reading and writing" the Spartans had just "enough to serve their turn." He also informs us that Lycurgus introduced Homer into Sparta; and that "books and treatises," not deemed necessary to practical education, were "banned from the country." [45] Modern writers are scarcely more in agreement: one holds it "probable that most Spartans could read and write"; [46] another, that "writing . . . was never generally taught at Sparta"; [47] and still another, that "music, art, and literature counted for nothing . . ." unless in some way they served the practical ends of the state.[48] Wilkins, however, thinks that the "constant references in Herodotus, Thucy-

40 Ibid., 22.
41 Politica, VIII, 4.
42 St. John: History of the Manners and Customs of Ancient Greece, I, 270.
43 The Works of Plato (Cary, Davis, and Burges), IV, 219 f.
44 Panathenaicus, 209, 251.
45 Plutarch: Lycurgus, 4, 16; The Ancient Customs of the Spartans, 4.
46 Dobson: Ancient Education and Its Meaning to Us, p. 17.
47 Müller: op. cit., II, 322.
48 Forbes: Greek Physical Education, pp. 13 f.

dides, and Xenophon to written letters and treatises, without the slightest hint of any difficulty in reading them," and the practice of "communication between the Spartan authorities at home and their generals and ambassadors," must be interpreted to imply the possession of literary knowledge.[49] It seems probable that, though some literary training may have been gained, it was not provided for in an extensive or systematic manner, since time and effort devoted to physical training left slight opportunity for scholastic learning. At best, only a low level of intellectual culture prevailed, even if one interpret generously Plutarch's phrase, "enough to serve their turn."

Though letters apparently had little place in it, Spartan education was not entirely devoid of mental training. It is certain that, although Spartans knew little arithmetic, and though they may have been unable to read or appreciate the speeches of Isocrates, they prized and zealously cultivated an intellectual keenness, which, clothed in Laconic speech and scornful of sophistry, drove to the heart of a matter like a Spartan spear. The pithy speeches of Spartans led an admirer to say that one might regard intellectual exercise as even more characteristic of Spartans than physical.[50] Physical discipline was accompanied, moreover, by a marked stress on moral, religious, and aesthetic elements, which rendered Spartan training somewhat less narrow than might appear at first glance. Recital of passages from Homer, chanting the stirring poems of Tyrtaeus, performing the evolutions of religious and military dances, and repeating the well-conned phrases of the Lycurgan code (not to be reduced to writing),[51] constituted an important and potent education of heart and mind which was not less essential to the soldier than the discipline of physical powers. Plutarch believed that instruction in music and verse was not less careful than the cultivation of proper habits in speaking. Music and physical, military training were joined harmoniously. As Terpander said:

> There both the spear and music meet
> And justice walks along the street.[52]

Their songs stirred the spirit and inflamed men's minds with desire for action; the style was severe and restrained; and the thought, serious and elevating. There was praise in them for heroes who were happy; derision for cowards who were miserable; boasts as to what men would do and of what they had done. At a festival, three choirs, the old men, the youth, and the boys, intoned an ancient litany. The choir of old men solemnly proclaim:

> We once did deeds of prowess and were strong young men.

[49] Wilkins: op. cit., pp. 39 f.
[50] Plutarch: Lycurgus, 20.
[51] Ibid., 13.
[52] Cf. Lyra Graeca, I, 33.

The young men reply:

> We are so now . . . behold and see.

And the boys chime in:

> We shall be . . . mightier men by far. . . .

Pindar saw the union of wisdom in council, conquest in action, and joy in rhythmic expression, as the ideal of Spartan life and training:

> Councils of wise elders here,
> And the young men's conquering spear
> And dance, and song, and joy appear.[53]

Of the union of music, dancing, and physical training, which provided religious, ethical, and social education, Grote says:

"The training in which a Spartan passed his life consisted of exercises warlike, social, and religious, blended together. While the individual, strengthened by gymnastics, went through his painful lessons of fatigue, endurance, and aggression—the citizens collectively were kept in the constant habit of simultaneous and regulated movement in the warlike march, in the religious dance, and in the social procession. Music and song, being constantly employed to direct the measure and keep alive the spirit of these multitudinous movements, became associated with the most powerful feelings which the habitual self-suppression of a Spartan permitted to arise, and especially with those sympathies which are communicated at once to an assembled crowd. Indeed the musician and the minstrel were the only persons who ever addressed themselves to the feelings of a Lacedaemonian assembly. Moreover the simple music of that early day, though destitute of artistical merit and superseded afterwards by more complicated combinations, had nevertheless a pronounced ethical character." [54]

It is evident that Spartan education—physical, moral, and mental—looked toward a practical end: military dominion. From this vocational training, preparation for business was entirely excluded. Sparta was ruled by citizen-soldiers, not by businessmen or industrials. Lycurgus is said to have forbidden Spartans to engage in vulgar, mechanical trades. Helots did all necessary, laborious work; money-making was regarded as servile. Men under thirty "did not go into the market place at all," and it was thought improper for older men to loiter there, since they could be more fruitfully employed at the places of exercise and conversation, discussing matters of public import, instructing others, and being instructed themselves.[55]

[53] Clough: *Plutarch's Lives*, I, 113. Courtesy of Little, Brown & Company, Boston.
[54] Grote: *op. cit.*, I, 512.
[55] Plutarch: *Lycurgus*, 24–5.

PHYSICAL EDUCATION OF GIRLS  Spartan training of the citizen-
soldier was based, in the first place, upon a unique concern for the training of
girls, that they might become mothers of stalwart sons. Though details of this
training are not known, Plutarch describes the general provisions designed by
Lycurgus to achieve that perfection of women which would be most serviceable
to the military state:

"The truth is, he took in their case, also, all the care that was possible; he
ordered the maidens to exercise themselves with wrestling, running, throwing
the quoit, and casting the dart, to the end that the fruit they conceived might,
in strong and healthy bodies, take firmer root and find better growth, and withal
that they, with this greater vigor, might be the more able to undergo the pains
of childbearing. And to the end he might take away their over-great tenderness
and fear of exposure to the air, and all acquired womanishness, he ordered that
the young women should go naked in the processions, as well as the young
men, and dance, too, in that condition, at certain solemn feasts, singing certain songs, whilst the young men stood around, seeing and hearing them. On
these occasions, they now and then made, by jests, a befitting reflection upon
those who had misbehaved themselves in the war; and again sang encomiums
upon those who had done any gallant action, and by these means inspired the
younger sort with an emulation of their glory. . . . Nor was there anything
shameful in this nakedness of the young women; modesty attended them, and
all wantonness was excluded. It taught them simplicity and a care for good
health, and gave them some taste of higher feelings, admitted as they thus
were to the field of noble action and glory." [56]

Though the organization for girls' training was somewhat less exacting than
that for boys (they dwelled at home rather than in public barracks), they were
associated in herds (agelai) for the purpose of training, as were the boys, but
separate from them, and had their special gymnasia (dromoi) where they exercised in running, wrestling, jumping, dancing, hurling the javelin and discus,
and playing ball.[57] It was asserted, though on dubious authority, that they also
practiced the pancration.[58] Girls also learned to swim and ride horseback, and
at times entered horses in the races. At the festival of Hyacinthia girls took a
prominent part and participated in races on horseback.[59] Cynisca, daughter of
Archidamus, was "fond of the Olympic games, and was the first woman who
bred horses and won an Olympic victory." After her, "other women, chiefly
Lacedaemonian," won victories at Olympia, but none were more famous than

[56] Clough: Plutarch's Lives, I, 101 f. Courtesy of Little, Brown & Company, Boston.
[57] Grasberger: Erziehung und Unterricht im Klassischen Altertum, III, 503 ff.; Krause: Die
Gymnastik und Agonistik der Hellenen, I, 31 ff.; II, 688 f.
[58] Krause: op. cit., I, 55.
[59] Nilsson: Griechische Feste von Religiöser Bedeutung, p. 137; Freeman: Schools of Hellas,
p. 30; Forbes: op. cit., pp. 28 ff.

Cynisca.[60] One of these, Euryleonis, won a two-horse chariot race, and a statue was erected in her honor.[61]

Spartan Lampito boasts that she can jump and kick her buttocks,[62] an exercise known to other lands besides Sparta. According to Pollux [63] one Spartan girl could do the trick a thousand times, and it was recorded on her tomb. This exercise, which the Spartans called βίβασις, was regarded as belonging to dancing, both "boys and girls practising it diligently for strengthening the legs." [64]

Running was practiced by girls as well as by boys. Theocritus [65] pictures a band of 240 maidens, the flower of the land, who anoint themselves and run by the River Eurotas. In honor of Dionysus Colonatas a special race was run at Colona by eleven women, called Dionysiades.[66] At Olympia there was a special festival, the Heraea, for women, at which there were two choruses—the Hippodamia and the Physcoa—and races of girls of various ages. Pausanias describes them: "The virgins are not all of the same age; but the youngest run first, the next in age run next, and the eldest virgins run last of all . . . their hair hangs down, they wear a shirt that reaches to a little above the knee, the right shoulder is bare to the breast. The course assigned to them . . . is the Olympic stadium; but the course is shortened by about a sixth of the stadium. The winners receive crowns of olive and a share of the cow which is sacrificed to Hera; moreover, they are allowed to dedicate statues of themselves with their names engraved on them." [67] A unique, black-figured Attic vase, which shows three women in a running race, is believed to represent "the eldest of the three sets of maidens who raced in honor of Hera at Elis," as Pausanias described them, though certain details of dress do not agree with his account.[68]

Girls marched in religious processions, participated in choruses, and danced at certain festivals. At times young men and maidens danced together. Aristophanes portrays the dance. Thus runs the Laconian chorus:

> Leave Taygety, an' quickly
> Hither, Muse Laconian, come.
> Hymn the Gude o' braw Amyclae,
> Hymn Athana, Brassin-dome.
> Hymn the Tyndarids, for ever

[60] Pausanias, III, 8, 1.
[61] Ibid., III, 17, 6.
[62] Aristophanes: Lysistrata, 81–2.
[63] Onomasticon, IV, 14, 102.
[64] Grasberger: op. cit., I, 34; Krause: op. cit., I, 398.
[65] The Idylls, 18.
[66] Pausanias, III, 13, 7.
[67] Pausanias, v, 16, 2–3. Trans. by J. G. Frazer. Courtesy of Macmillan & Co., Ltd., London, and The Macmillan Company, New York.
[68] Kyle: "The Maidens' Race on Attic Vases," Am. Jour. Archaeol., VI, 53.

Sportin' by Eurotas river.
Noo then, noo the step begin,
Twirlin' licht the fleecy skin;
Sae we'se join our blithesome voices,
Praisin' Sparta, loud an' lang,
Sparta wha of auld rejoices
In the Choral dance an' sang.
O to watch her bonnie dochters
Sport alang Eurotas' waters!
Winsome feet for ever plyin',
Fleet as fillies, wild an' gay,
Winsome tresses tossin', flyin',
As o' Bacchanals at play.[69]

Lycurgus is said to have ordained that maidens should march in processions and dance at certain feasts while the young men looked on. Whether they danced naked, or only scantily dressed, has been disputed. It seems probable that they were not entirely unclad. Grasberger holds that the girls were attired in a *chiton*—somewhat longer than the boys' garment—which, slit at the side, permitted free exercise of the limbs and showed the thighs. Hence the reference to "thigh-showers." [70]

How long girls were given physical training is unknown, but Plato, who follows the Spartan system in certain respects, and may have done so in this, would continue physical training for women to the age of twenty, except those who married earlier.[71] Spartan girls may have begun exercises about seven, as did boys,[72] and one may infer that they continued gymnastics in public until marriage.

Spartan efforts in respect to the physical culture of women were a source of pride on their own part, and of ridicule, at times, at the hands of their neighbors. Spartan women are said to have been "the most beautiful in all Greece." [73] Gorgo, wife of Leonidas, is said to have boasted that only Spartan women brought forth men.[74] Athenian audiences would find the Spartan ideal of female physical perfection humorous. Aristophanes, doubtless, did not fail to raise a laugh at Spartan expense, when he made Lysistrata say of Lampito:

O the sweet girl! how hale and bright she looks!
Here's nerve! here's muscle! here's an arm could fairly throttle a bull!

[69] Aristophanes: *Lysistrata*, 1296–313. Trans. by B. B. Rogers. The Loeb Classical Library. Quoted by permission of Harvard University Press, Cambridge, Mass.
[70] Clough: op. cit., I, 101; Perrin: *Plutarch's Lives*, I, 246 ff.; Grasberger: op. cit., III, 504.
[71] *Laws*, VIII, 833.
[72] Forbes: op. cit., pp. 31 f.
[73] Müller: op. cit., II, 292.
[74] Plutarch: *Lycurgus*, 14.

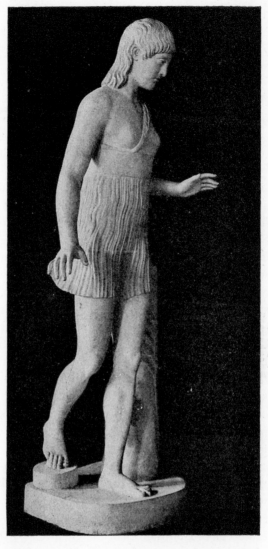

A GIRL RUNNER
Vatican, Rome (Courtesy, The Metropolitan Museum of Art, New York)

To which the buxom lass replies:

> Weel, by the Twa, I think sae.
> An' I can loup an' fling an' kick my hurdies.[75]

As to whether physical training of girls made them brave and serviceable to the state, there is a difference of opinion. Both favorable and unfavorable judgments may be partly true. Philostratos expressed a common opinion when he said that "Laconia became so great in war" because of her procedure in respect to the physical training of girls, who, united with men similarly trained, gave birth to sturdy children.[76] On occasion Spartan women showed initiative and courage. Cratesicleia and the wife of Panteus died bravely.[77] When Pyrrhus attacked Sparta, it is said that Archidamia went to the senate with a sword in hand, asked whether the men thought the women should survive the ruin of Sparta, and refused, on behalf of all the women, to be sent away to safety. Then the women and girls helped the older men dig a trench and sink the wagons, and sought to encourage the young men to fight bravely as befitted Spartans.[78] After the disastrous battle of Leuctra, it is said that Spartan women surpassed the men in puting on a brave front at the news of defeat and the death of their relatives. Soon there came a break, however. With the invasion of Laconia, which followed upon defeat at Leuctra, Plutarch reports that Agesilaus was profoundly distressed because of the chaos into which Sparta fell—the old men angry and critical of the state of affairs, and the women unable to keep still, being quite distracted at the noise of shouting and the sight of the enemies' fires.[79] Aristotle's judgment may be open to question, since he disapproved of the freedom which Laconian women enjoyed. Of the effect of Spartan discipline on the courage of women, and its serviceability when put to the extreme test of war, he says: "Even in regard to courage, which is of no use in daily life, and is needed only in war, the influence of the Lacedaemonian women has been most mischievous. The evil showed itself in the Theban invasion, when, unlike the women in other cities, they were utterly useless and caused more confusion than the enemy." [80] Plato, too, speaks disapprovingly of the lack of state regulation of the life of women at Sparta.[81]

PHYSICAL TRAINING OF BOYS    Although the public exercises of Spartan girls are said to have been promotive of marriages, and thus useful to

---

[75] Lysistrata, 78–82. Trans. by B. B. Rogers. The Loeb Classical Library. Quoted by permission of Harvard University Press, Cambridge, Mass.
[76] Philostratos: Concerning Gymnastics, 27.
[77] Plutarch: Cleomenes, 38–9.
[78] Plutarch: Pyrrhus, 27.
[79] Agesilaus, 29, 31.
[80] Politica, ii, 9. From The Works of Aristotle, translated by J. A. Smith and W. D. Ross (The Clarendon Press); cf. Müller: op. cit., ii, 298 f.
[81] Laws, vi, 781.

the state, it appears that this incentive was insufficient. Sparta had to resort to discrimination against those not married by the age of thirty, refusing them permission to witness public processions and the dances of young men and maidens, compelling them to march scantily clad around the market place in winter, and denying them such marks of respect as were commonly paid to married men.[82] But in spite of all efforts to encourage the breeding of citizen-soldiers, and the exemption from military service of fathers of three sons, the number of Spartan citizens declined, as may be judged from the testimony of Xenophon, Aristotle, and others. Perhaps the system of property distribution was at fault. Aristotle stated that, at the time of the Theban invasion, Spartan citizens numbered only one thousand; in his opinion "the want of men was their ruin." [83]

Children were looked upon as property—of the state, not of the parents—and the latter were to beget children for the state. Acrotatus, when he returned bloody and triumphant from battle, was urged by the old men to take to himself Chilonis and beget "brave sons for Sparta." [84] Women might be "lent" by old or childless husbands to other men to beget children; but it does not appear that the exchange could be initiated by women who desired excellent offspring. With this freedom in the marriage relation, it is said that amongst Spartans adultery was unknown.[85]

At the birth of the child, the state asserted its right of judgment. The infant was taken before certain "tryers"—elders of the tribe in which it was born—who ordered it to be brought up, if strong and well formed, and assigned it one of the shares of land; but, if puny and misshapen, they caused it to be exposed on Mount Taygetus, since it was deemed inconsistent with public welfare to preserve it. In case of exposure, or "putting away," the child might be taken and reared by Helots or Perioeci.[86] whose labor supported the Spartan military establishment.

Up to the age of seven the boy remained at home; even there, attention to physical strength and courageous temper was apparently uppermost. Mothers bathed the newborn child in wine, it is said, rather than water, to temper and test its body, and excluded swaddling bands, plentiful, dainty food, and all such care as would tend to develop weakness, fear, and peevishness. At this period, the boy might go to his father's mess, where, seated on a low stool, he received a "half share without any vegetables" and listened to the conversation. Though early training must have been chiefly in the mother's hands, since the father was compelled to spend much time in public pursuits, the instance of Agesi-

[82] Plutarch: Lycurgus, 15; Müller: op. cit., II, 294 ff.
[83] Politica, II, 9.
[84] Plutarch: Pyrrhus, 28.
[85] Plutarch: Lycurgus, 15; Xenophon: Lacedaemonians, I, 7–9.
[86] Plutarch: Lycurgus, 16.

laus, who is said to have ridden a stick-horse before his children, suggests that the father's influence in home-training was not lacking.[87]

At the age of seven the sons of Spartan citizens, rich and poor alike,[88] entered the *agoge*, a system of public, compulsory training, by virtue of which they were to become citizens. Failure to submit to this discipline resulted in loss of "all future honours." [89] Only the heirs apparent were exempt from the harsh rule of the *agoge*; they might submit to it, however, if they chose, as apparently Cleomenes, Leonidas, and Agesilaus did.[90] Besides sons of citizens, certain Helots (*Mothaces* as they were called) were admitted to the *agoge* at times as "foster-brothers" of young Spartans. Their number, however, was probably never large. If they finished the training, they were free, and might even attain full citizenship in some cases. Lysander, Callicratidas, and Gylippus are said to have arisen from this class.[91] Even foreigners might send their children for a Spartan education. Xenophon is said to have been persuaded by Agesilaus to bring his sons to Sparta that they might learn the best of all things, "how to obey, and how to command." [92]

Upon entering the *agoge* at seven, boys were enrolled in "herds" or *bouai*, each under a prefect or herd-leader, *bouagor*. These "herds" were grouped in larger troops or companies (*agelai*) for certain purposes, and each company was under one of the best of the prefects.[93] If each "herd" had 64 boys, as Freeman thinks, the number in a company would be 256, following Kahrstedt's opinion that there were four "herds" in each company.[94] Certain age groups were recognized in the agoge: "herd-children," the youngest, aged eight; "preparatory-youngsters," nine; "youngsters," ten; "preparatory boys," eleven; and "boys," twelve. From thirteen to fourteen, they were known as "preparatory-ephebi" (*melleirens*); and from fourteen to twenty, as "ephebi" (*eirens*).[95] The younger *eirens* were sometimes called *sideunai*; the older lads who were "just entering on manhood," [96] were called "ball-players" (σφαιρεῖς) perhaps because their chief sport was ball-play. This game, carried on with great enthusiasm, is said to have "resembled a battle rather than a diversion." [97]

---

[87] Müller: *op. cit.*, II, 288, 308.
[88] Plutarch: *Lycurgus*, 16; Aristotle: *Politica*, IV, 9.
[89] Xenophon: *Lacedaemonians*, III, 3.
[90] Plutarch: *Agesilaus*, 1–2; Müller: *op. cit.*, II, 308 f.
[91] Athenaeus, VI, 271; Clough: *op. cit.*, IV, 474; Xenophon: *Hellenics*, V, 3, 9; Freeman: *op. cit.*, pp. 15 ff.
[92] Plutarch: *Agesilaus*, 20.
[93] Xenophon: *Lacedaemonians*, II, 11.
[94] Müller: *op. cit.*, II, 310; Freeman: *op. cit.*, p. 18; Forbes: *op. cit.*, p. 22.
[95] Forbes, *op. cit.*, pp. 20 f., holds that the old notion that *melleiren* was applied from eighteen to twenty and *eiren* from twenty to thirty (cf. Abbott: *op. cit.*, I, 212; Grasberger: *op. cit.*, III, 58 ff.) is incorrect; Busolt-Swoboda: *Griechische Staatskunde*, II, 695 ff.
[96] Pausanias, III, 14, 6.
[97] Müller: *op. cit.*, II, 309 f.

The direction of the agoge was placed in the hands of a paidonomos, one of "the noblest and best men." This inspector of boys and their training was appointed by the ephors, and had authority to bring the boys together, take charge of them, and with the assistance of "whipbearers," to "punish them severely in case of misconduct." Xenophon comments soberly that "modesty and obedience" were "inseparable companions at Sparta." [98] The paidonomos continued to exercise some control, though less absolute, over the older youth, and under certain circumstances might turn them over to the ephors to be fined.[99] Immediate supervision of a company was placed in the hands of one of the ablest eirens, so that a leader was never lacking among the boys, even though no adult was present.[100]

Training the youth of Sparta was the duty of all citizens. If no particular work was appointed, the men went to watch the boys at their exercises, to teach them something, or to learn something themselves from those who were older and wiser.[101] While the ephors, the paidonomos, eirens, and "herd-leaders" had special functions of supervision and direction, in their absence any adult citizen might punish a youth for misconduct. Likewise the practice, common in Sparta as well as in Crete, of having adult citizens of good character act as "inspirers" of particular youths,[102] though liable to abuse, was promotive of social education, and gave to all citizens the work that is commonly done by paid teachers, or by fathers in societies where the family plays an important rôle. The relationship between "inspirer" and "hearer" was one of affection and mutual understanding, recognized by the state.[103] Kings had their "inspirers" and "hearers" as well as any of the "peers": Lysander was the "inspirer" or "lover" of Agesilaus; [104] Cleomenes III was the "hearer" of Xenares.[105] The responsibility of an "inspirer" was great; the social significance of the practice is suggested by the fact that, in case of faults, the "inspirer" might be punished [106] instead of the "hearer" who had committed them, on the assumption that the one most closely concerned with the boy's education was responsible for his failure in any aspect of manly behavior.

Clothing was extremely simple and limited, so that the body might be hardened. Dress and bedding were inspected frequently by the ephors.[107] It is said that boys were allowed one garment each year.[108] Sandals would soften the feet,

98 Plutarch: Lycurgus, 17; Xenophon: Lacedaemonians, II, 2.
99 Xenophon: Lacedaemonians, IV, 6.
100 Ibid., II, 10–1.
101 Plutarch: Lycurgus, 24.
102 Xenophon: Lacedaemonians, II, 10, 12–3; VI, 1–2.
103 Plutarch: Lycurgus, 17.
104 Plutarch: Agesilaus, 2.
105 Müller: op. cit., II, 301.
106 Plutarch: Lycurgus, 18.
107 Athenaeus, XII, 550.
108 Plutarch: Customs of the Spartans, 5.

hence they sought to harden them by going barefoot. Thus they would be able to climb hills and descend inclines more readily and with less danger; and boys who had learned to leap, jump, and run barefoot would be more nimble than those shod with sandals. Likewise, having just one garment a year, boys would grow up toughened to variations in temperature.[109]

The food at their public meals was so plain that "Spartan diet" became a byword. Barley meal, wine, cheese, figs or dates, meat (generally pork), and fish are mentioned as the compulsory contribution to the common meals. These, together with Spartan broth and special gifts at the time of religious sacrifices and after successful hunting trips, made up their diet. Cooks were hereditary in Sparta, which may account for the fact that cooking continued to be bad. Good cooks were not wanted. The famous Mythaecus, whose palatable concoctions were compared with the art of Phidias, was ordered to leave Sparta as soon as he came.[110] Spartan soup was so unappetizing, it was said, that only a plunge in the Eurotas could make it palatable.[111] A Sybarite who had been in Sparta and had eaten at the public mess, is said to have declared: "It is no wonder that Spartans are the bravest men in the world; for anyone in his right mind would prefer to die ten thousand times rather than share in such poor living." [112]

The diet of boys was in harmony with this same principle of simplicity; but they could supplement their spare rations by stealing, which was to make them more resourceful foragers and better fighters. Xenophon describes their practice thus: "As to the food, he required the prefect to bring with him such a moderate amount of it that the boys would never suffer from repletion, and would know what it was to go with their hunger unsatisfied; for he believed that those who underwent this training would be better able to continue working on an empty stomach, if necessary, and would be capable of carrying on longer without extra food, if the word of command were given to do so: they would want fewer delicacies and would accommodate themselves more readily to anything put before them, and at the same time would enjoy better health. He also thought that a diet which made their bodies slim would do more to increase their height than one that consisted of flesh-forming food." [113] At the time of Agis, in accord with this strictness of diet, young Spartan warriors were ordered to present themselves naked before the ephors every ten days, and

---

109 Xenophon: *Lacedaemonians*, ii, 3–4; Plutarch: *Lycurgus*, 16.
110 Maximus Tyrius, diss. 7.
111 Plutarch: *Lycurgus*, 12; Müller: *op. cit.*, ii, 285; Cicero: *Tusculan Disputations*, v, 34.
112 Athenaeus, iv, 138. Trans. by C. B. Gulick. The Loeb Classical Library. Quoted by permission of Harvard University Press, Cambridge, Mass.
113 Xenophon: *Lacedaemonians*, ii, 5–6. *Scripta Minora*, trans. by E. C. Marchant. The Loeb Classical Library. Quoted by permission of Harvard University Press, Cambridge, Mass.

those who were sturdy and strong, as a result of their gymnastics, were praised. If rolls of fat or any other sign of flabbiness betrayed indulgence and laziness on the part of any one, however, he was at once judged and beaten for his laxity.[114]

Life in the Spartan agoge was hard. The boys were all subjected to the same regimen and discipline, did their exercises, and played games together, their whole education being a continuous practice in prompt and perfect obedience, in harmony with the demands of the collective group. The members of a "herd" looked to their leader, obeyed his commands, and patiently submitted to whatever punishment he decreed. As they grew older, physical training became more strenuous. Their hair was cut short, they went unshod, and generally played naked. After twelve years of age they seldom had baths, wore no tunic, and slept on beds of reeds which they gathered along the Eurotas. These they broke off without the aid of knives. In winter, for greater warmth, they mixed thistledown with the rushes.[115]

Closely allied with the discipline of the agoge, as a means of developing unflinching courage and endurance, were the institutions of public flagellation and the Crypteia. The whip had a prominent place in Spartan training. Youths were beaten if they stole so awkwardly as to be detected.[116] Flagellation even to the point of death at the altar of Artemis Orthia was regularly and religiously performed; and youths vied with each other for the honor of proving themselves best in this test of hardness and endurance at the altar.[117] It was said that "Lacedaemonians were the most superstitious of all the Greeks." [118] However that may be, a religious superstition lay at the root of this practice which is said to have been established by Lycurgus as a substitute for human sacrifice, so that the altar might be wet with human blood as the oracle had bidden. Pausanias describes the ordeal thus: "The priestess stands by them holding the wooden image. It is small and light; but if the scourgers lay on lightly because a lad is handsome or noble, then the image grows so heavy in the woman's hands that she can hardly hold it, and she lays the blame on the scourgers, saying they are weighing her down. . . ." [119]

The Crypteia likewise served to harden Spartan youths by vigorous exercise under conditions of exposure and small supply of provisions; at the same time, it helped to keep the Helots in subjection. The vicious brutality of the system, as reported by the Lacedaemonian in Plato's Laws and as represented by

---

114 Athenaeus, XII, 550.
115 Plutarch: Lycurgus, 16.
116 Xenophon: Lacedaemonians, II, 8–9.
117 Plutarch: Lycurgus, 18.
118 Pausanias, III, 5, 8.
119 Pausanias, III, 16, 10. Trans. by J. G. Frazer. Courtesy of Macmillan & Co., Ltd., London, and The Macmillan Company, New York; Lucian: Anacharsis, 38; Cicero: Tusculan Disputations, II, 14.

Plutarch, though he is unwilling to ascribe it to Lycurgus, may be exaggerated.[120] It seems to harmonize, however, with the intention of the Spartan peers who would stop at nothing in their effort to harden future soldiers and hold in subjection a conquered population.[121] Plutarch gives this description of the Crypteia: "The magistrates from time to time sent out into the country at large the most discreet of the young warriors, equipped only with daggers and such supplies as were necessary. In the day time they scattered into obscure and out of the way places, where they hid themselves and lay quiet; but in the night they came down into the highways and killed every Helot whom they caught. Oftentimes, too, they actually traversed the fields where Helots were working and slew the sturdiest and best of them." [122]

Though Spartan training was chiefly physical and gave more attention to gymnastics than other Greek systems of education, there was less athletic specialization in it than might be expected. Such specialization was not allowed to compete with that purpose which mattered most—specialization for war. Aristotle, though critical of the brutality in Spartan training, reported that it did not fall into the error of making specialized athletes.[123] Xenophon thought that one could not easily find "healthier or handier" men than those of Sparta, since their exercises developed legs, arms, and neck equally well.[124] Plutarch relates that a Spartan, overcome by a wrestler from another country, remarked that his adversary was only a "cleverer wrestler," not a better man. A similar point of view is reflected in the attitude of Agesilaus toward a growing love of horse racing. This became a common sport after the Persian wars. At Sparta as at Athens it was indulged in by wealthy families rather than by all citizens. There were many Spartan winners at Olympia.[125] To show them that winning such a contest was no proof of manly virtue, but only of wealth and extravagant expense, Agesilaus had his sister enter a chariot at the Olympian Games.[126]

In the places of exercise, no one was permitted to be idle; and the oldest man present was charged to see that the tasks assigned should not be too easy, but hard enough for the food allotted, so that none might grow fat.[127] Professional teachers, *sophronistes*, *gymnastes*, and *paidotribes*, such as were employed at Athens, were unknown at Sparta; but the *Bideoi*, a board of five, had imme-

---

120 Müller, *op. cit.*, II, 40 ff., says that the Crypteia could not have amounted to legalized "assassination" of the Helots, otherwise Plato would not have given that name to his system of inspection by picked bodies of young men. Cf. Plato: *Laws*, I, 633; VI, 763; Plutarch: *Lycurgus*, 28; Krause: *op. cit.*, II, 674 f.
121 Thucydides, IV, 80.
122 *Lycurgus*, 28. Trans. by B. Perrin. The Loeb Classical Library. Quoted by permission of Harvard University Press, Cambridge, Mass.
123 *Politica*, VIII, 4.
124 *Lacedaemonians*, V, 9.
125 Krause: *op. cit.*, II, 670 ff.
126 Plutarch: *Agesilaus*, 20; *Pausanias*, III, 8, 1.
127 Xenophon: *Lacedaemonians*, V, 8.

diate oversight of gymnastic exercises, and arranged the ephebic contests. *Hoplomachoi*, gladiators who publicly exhibited and taught their skill at arms, were not at first permitted at Sparta, probably because their training was not thought useful in battle; but it seems that they were introduced in the late second or early third century of the Christian era.[128] Then, of course, professionalism engulfed Sparta as well as the rest of the Graeco-Roman world.[129] Not only at home, but on campaigns, the law required all Spartans to practice gymnastic regularly; consequently they took greater pride in themselves and had more dignity of bearing than other men. It was also provided that after the passage of youth, the men should wear their hair long so that they would look taller and be more impressive and terrifying to their enemies. It was the privilege of the warrior to comb his hair before going into battle. Herodotus describes the astonishment of the Persians at Thermopylae when they saw the Lacedaemonians grooming themselves and practicing gymnastics before beginning battle.[130]

Though the state system was hostile to athletic specialization, all kinds of physical contests seem to have appealed to the Spartans as to other Greek peoples. Zeus proposes a physical competition between himself and the rest of the gods—a tug of war with a golden chain.[131] Among the exercises and games of the Spartans were running, fighting, boxing, wrestling, pancration, hunting, riding, throwing the stone and javelin, dancing, archery,[132] and playing ball. Devotion to such sports and exercises was great, and the success of Spartans in them was remarkable. It has been said, indeed, that "Dorian Peloponnesus was the cradle" of festal athletic games; "the first victors at Olympian games, after these were recorded, were nearly all Dorians, or at least Peloponnesians," and "from the 15th to the 50th Olympiad most of them were Spartans." [133]

Walking, the most natural exercise of the lower extremities, was not regarded by the Greeks as a part of gymnastics, but it was a popular means of refreshment for the sick, weak, and old. Running, however, was among the earliest and most favored sports and assumed many forms—the stade-race, the *diaulos* (double race), the race in armor (important for military training), the torch-

---

128 Krause: *op. cit.*, II, 677; Plato: *Laches*, 183; Forbes: *op. cit.*, p. 26.

129 Forbes: *op. cit.*, pp. 40 f.

130 Xenophon: *Lacedaemonians*, XI, 3; XII, 5–6; Herodotus, VII, 208–9; Plutarch: *Lycurgus*, 22.

131 Seymour: *Life in the Homeric Age*, p. 400.

132 Although archery is included among the "regular exercises of the Spartans" (Forbes, *op. cit.*, p. 25), there is some difference of opinion as to the extent of its use. Homer's heroes were capable bowmen, and Apollo was said to have instructed Heracles in the use of the bow. In later times, however, shooting the bow is believed by some to have been "entirely excluded from the realm of gymnastic," save in Crete and certain other states. Against the Messenian light infantry, Sparta is said to have employed Cretan archers. Krause: *op. cit.*, I, 599 f.; Pausanias, I, 23, 4; 29, 6; IV, 8, 3; VII, 16, 1.

133 Krause: *op. cit.*, II, 660 f.

race, and the long race (δόλιχος). The simplest race, the *stadion* or *dromos*, had a prominent place as a separate contest at the great public festivals, where it was the most ancient event; [134] and it also formed a part of the pentathlon. The δόλιχος was seven, twelve, or even twenty-four stades long—a great test of speed and endurance. Pausanias says that Ladas, a Lacedaemonian, the swiftest runner of his time, won the Olympic crown in the long race, but died on the way home after the games.[135]

The prominent rôle of running at Sparta is suggested by the fact that gymnasia were at first nonexistent, but all exercises were performed in the open where the racecourse (δρόμος) was laid out. Pausanias says, "The Lacedaemonians give the name of the Course to the place where the youths are still in the habit of practising running." [136] In his day two gymnasia had been erected on the course. That running, wrestling, jumping, and throwing the discus and javelin constituted the chief elements of Spartan gymnastics is suggested by their numerous victories in the pentathlon and in separate contests at Olympia.[137] The victor in the men's pentathlon, at the Eighteenth Olympiad, was Lampis, a Spartan.[138] In the Thirty-eighth Olympiad, when the boys' pentathlon was instituted, Eutelidas, a Spartan, carried off the wild olive.[139] Pausanias refers to twenty-four stade-race victors at Olympia; seven winners of the double race; five victors in the long race; and twelve winners of the race in armor. Of these, it appears, a half were Laconians, among whom were such famous runners as Akanthos and Ladas, victors in the long race; and Chionis or Anchionis, who won the stade-race four times in succession and was thrice victor in the double race.[140]

Wrestling was one of the most popular contests. In the funeral games of Patroclos, it held an honored place. The origin of wrestling was pushed back to mythical times, and various accounts were given of it. Diodorus says that Hermes was the originator of wrestling schools; and Autolycos, son of Hermes, was said to have taught Heracles the art of wrestling.[141] Pausanias, however, says that Theseus invented the art of wrestling; before his time victory had depended more upon size and strength than upon science.[142] According to Philostratos [143] wrestling was developed for its utility in war. Spartans were renowned for wrestling, and had many victors at Olympia, among them

---

[134] Pausanias, v, 8, 6.
[135] Ibid., III, 21, 1.
[136] Ibid., III, 14, 6.
[137] Krause: op. cit., II, 662, 666 ff.
[138] Pausanias, v, 8, 7.
[139] Ibid., v, 9, 1.
[140] Hyde: Olympic Victor Monuments, pp. 191 ff.; Krause: op. cit., I, 339 ff.; II, 669.
[141] Diodorus of Sicily, v, 75; Apollodorus: The Library, II, 4, 9.
[142] Bk. I, 39, 3.
[143] Concerning Gymnastics, 11.

Heracles.[144] In the Eighteenth Olympiad, Eurybatos, a Lacedaemonian, was winner in wrestling; in the Thirty-seventh, prizes were offered for boys in wrestling, and Laconian Hipposthenes was the victor.[145] It was regarded as a special reproof to the coward that any Lacedaemonian would be ashamed "to be matched with him in a wrestling bout." [146] Though Xenophon says that Spartans were skilled in all kinds of wrestling, there seems to have been no highly specialized training, at least in early days. Plutarch [147] says that they did not have special masters to teach wrestling, because they wished Spartan boys to excel in courage rather than in clever tricks. Even in the days of Philopoemen, it is said that he did everything he could to discourage professional wrestling, and put aside all thought of engaging in it himself, because of its uselessness to prepare men for war.[148]

Boxing originated from the most natural form of hand-to-hand fighting with bare fists, and was one of the most ancient and favored of Greek sports. The contention that they invented it, however, is just another instance of the habit, which they shared with other peoples, of considering themselves the originators of all that seemed to them good. Early Cretan civilization, as we have seen, developed boxing [149] before the rise of the Greek states.

In the Homeric description of heroic days, boxing held an honored place. Mythology told of the gods who contended in the manly sport. Apollo had conquered Ares at Olympia; Tydeus was victor in boxing at the Nemean games; Heracles was instructed in the art of boxing by Harpalykos, son of Hermes.[150] Pollux, son of Spartan Tyndareus, was said to have won the boxing match at Olympia, in the days before "the unbroken tradition of the Olympiads" began.[151] Philostratos declared that boxing was encouraged for its value in war: "Boxing is an invention of the Lacedaemonians, and once found acceptance among the barbarian Bebryces. It was best practiced by Polydeuces, on which account the poets sang his praises. The ancient Lacedaemonians boxed, however, for the following reason: they had no helmets, and they considered that fighting with such was not according to the customs of the country; but the shield took the place of the helmet, if one understood how to carry it. In order, then, to parry blows directed at the face, and when they came to withstand them, they practiced boxing and sought, in this manner, to harden the face." [152]

144 Müller: op. cit., II, 315; Pausanias, v, 8, 4.
145 Pausanias, v, 8, 7 and 9.
146 Xenophon: Lacedaemonians, IX, 4.
147 Moralia, III, 403.
148 Plutarch: Philopoemen, 3.
149 Supra, pp. 209 f.
150 Krause: op. cit., I, 498.
151 Pausanias, v, 8, 4 and 6.
152 Philostratos: Concerning Gymnastics, 9.

Theocritus paints a vivid picture of the boxing match between Pollux and Amycus, a contest between scientific skill and brute strength: "Then Amycus came on furiously, making play with both hands; but Pollux smote him on the point of the chin as he charged, maddening him the more, and the giant confused the fighting, laying on with all his might, and going in with head down. . . . But the son of Zeus stepped now this side, now that, and hit him with both fists in turn, and checked his onslaught, for all his monstrous strength. Like a drunken man he reeled beneath the hero's blows, and spat out the red blood, while all the princes shouted together, as they marked the ugly bruises about his mouth and jaws, and saw his eyes half closed by puffy flesh. Next Pollux began to tease him, feinting on every side, and at last, seeing that he was now quite bewildered, he got in a smashing blow just above the middle of the nose beneath the eyebrows, and laid the bone of his forehead bare. Stretched on his back the giant fell amid the flowers; but he rose again, and the fighting went on fiercely. They mauled each other hard, laying on with the weighted thongs; but the giant was always busy with his fists on the other's chest and outside his neck, while Pollux, the invincible, kept on smashing his opponent's face with cruel blows." [153]

Notwithstanding the early prominence of boxing among Lacedaemonians, Freeman declares that it was "forbidden to the young Spartan"—and the pancration also—because it developed "a few particular muscles at the expense of the others." [154] Such an inference, based on statements of Plutarch and Aristotle,[155] may be open to doubt, though Philostratos also supports the view when he says that "in the course of time . . . [the Lacedaemonians] gave up boxing, and likewise the pancration. . . ." [156] Krause maintains that no Spartan was victor in boxing and pancration at the sacred games, and argues that if they had practiced these, they would certainly have produced winners.[157] Perhaps Spartans were only forbidden to engage in such competitions at the great games, where it would be unseemly for a Spartan to yield to an opponent. Philostratos must have had this in mind, for he states that they held it "disgraceful to participate in such contests, in which there was danger that, if a single one should yield, Sparta would be open to the reproach of cowardice." [158] This prohibition may have been responsible for a decrease in boxing at Sparta. Krause [159] says that "in later times" the Ionians, in contrast to the Dorians,

153 Theocritus: *Idylls*, XXII, 87–111, from F. A. Wright, *Greek Athletics*, p. 36, quoted by permission of the author; cf. Apollonius: *The Argonauts*, II, 30–97.
154 Freeman: *op. cit.*, p. 26.
155 *Politica*, VIII, 4; *Lycurgus*, 19.
156 Philostratos: *Concerning Gymnastics*, 9.
157 *Op. cit.*, I, 55; II, 666.
158 Philostratos: *Concerning Gymnastics*, 9.
159 *Op. cit.*, I, 499.

gave attention to boxing, and he wonders that the fame of Dorian ancestors in the art was not sufficient incentive to cause Spartans to devote themselves to it. Although the decline of boxing may have been real, popular opinion seems to have continued to associate the "painful" art with Spartan training. Plato says that the Laconizers of his day thought to imitate the Spartans by going about in short cloaks "with their ears bruised" and with the cestus bound on their arms, being "always in training." [160]

Though Lycurgus is said to have prohibited contests which involved the stretching forth of one's hand,[161] it does not appear that Müller, Freeman, Krause, and others are justified in their assertion that the pancration was not practiced at Sparta.[162] Spartan Heracles, according to tradition, was credited with victory in the pancration at Olympia in the days before the "unbroken tradition of the Olympiads" began.[163] Gardiner holds that the "primitive rough and tumble," the forerunner of the pancration, "unrestricted by law and un-refined by science, was allowed and encouraged as a test of endurance and a training for war," [164] but that Spartans were forbidden to enter such events with others at Olympia. Jüthner's view is to the same effect.[165] This contest, which was a combination of wrestling, boxing, kicking, gouging, and all natural efforts to overcome an opponent, is said to have been invented for its usefulness in war, and this was "demonstrated at Thermopylae when the Lacedaemonians, their lances and swords broken, fought with their naked hands." [166] Elsewhere Philostratos says, "The Lacedaemonians themselves explain that they do not practice these types of contest for the purpose of competition, but merely for the purpose of hardening, and this is entirely in harmony with their flagella-tion, for a law among them prescribes lashing at the altar." [167] The following description of the pancration has been preserved: "Those who engage in the pancratium . . . employ a wrestling that is hazardous; for they must needs meet blows on the face that are not safe for the wrestler, and must clinch in struggles that one can only win by pretending to fall, and they need skill that they may choke an adversary in different ways at different times, and the same contestants are both wrestling with the ankle and twisting the opponent's arm, to say nothing of dealing a blow and leaping upon the adversary; for these things are all permissible in the pancratium—anything except biting and goug-ing. The Lacedaemonians, indeed, allow even these, because, I suppose, they are

160 Plato: *Protagoras*, 342. The weighted cestus, known to later Roman times, was not worn in the early Greek games.—Hyde: *op. cit.*, p. 235.
161 Plutarch: *Lycurgus*, 19.
162 Müller: *op. cit.*, II, 315; Freeman: *op. cit.*, p. 26; Krause: *op. cit.*, II, 666.
163 Pausanias, v, 8, 4 and 6.
164 Gardiner: *Greek Athletic Sports and Festivals*, p. 435.
165 Jüthner: "Gymnastik," *Real-Encyclopädie*, VII, Pt. II, 2041.
166 Philostratos: *Concerning Gymnastics*, 11.
167 *Ibid.*, 58.

THE PANCRATION   C. 550–500 B.C.
(Courtesy, The Metropolitan Museum of Art, New York)

training themselves for battle, but the contests of Elis exclude them, though they do permit choking." [168]

For a nation whose education aimed primarily at preparation for war, throwing the discus furnished excellent training, since throwing stones or other missiles was common in warfare. Likewise hurling the javelin was of great importance to a people who still looked to the spear as their first weapon in war and in the chase.[169]

Spartan training is said to have more nearly approximated war itself than anything practiced elsewhere in Greece.[170] A common exercise of the Spartans, and one which provided the most direct preparation of the citizen-soldier, was organized fighting. To this they were early inured. Plutarch tells us that the old men, when inspecting the boys' performances, as they were charged to do, often encouraged them in quarrels and fights so as to have an opportunity to discover their various capacities in respect to bravery, boldness, and aggressiveness in the face of danger.[171] Organized fighting, in which the free range of the rough-and-tumble pancration apparently was permitted, was

[168] Philostratus: *Imagines*, II, 6. Trans. by A. Fairbanks. The Loeb Classical Library. Quoted by permission of Harvard University Press, Cambridge, Mass.
[169] Krause: *op. cit.*, I, 439 ff., 465 ff.; Grasberger: *op. cit.*, I, 327 ff.; II, 168 ff.
[170] Müller: *op. cit.*, II, 320.
[171] Lycurgus, 16.

arranged for, as well as individual contests. Certain officers, the *bidiaeans*, were charged with arranging athletic contests and "especially the games at the Plane-Tree Grove" or Platanistas. This spot, surrounded by water, was approached by two bridges. The fight is said to have followed rules laid down by Lycurgus; but apart from certain preliminary regulations, it seems to have been a rough-and-tumble, free-for-all fight. Before the contest the two competing groups of boys offered sacrifices to the war-god Enyalios, and staged a fight between two boars, the result of which was said to foretell the outcome of the coming battle. The next day they entered the grove by the bridges, the choice of which being determined by lot. Pausanias pithily summarized the method of fighting: "In fighting they strike, and kick, and bite, and gouge out each other's eyes. Thus they fight man against man. But they also charge in serried masses, and push each other into the water." [172]

The fight of the boys at the Plane-Tree Grove had a counterpart in contests for young men. Xenophon explains how these young men were divided into groups and were matched in valorous strife to attain a high degree of manly perfection: "The Ephors . . . pick out three of the very best among them," who are known as *hippagretai.* "Each of them enrolls a hundred others, stating his reasons for preferring one and rejecting another. The result is that those who fail to win the honour are at war both with those who sent them away and with their successful rivals; and they are on the watch for any lapse from the code of honour. . . . And they are bound, too, to keep themselves fit, for one effect of the strife is that they spar whenever they meet. . . ." [173]

Among the more or less undirected activities, hunting ranked high as a peacetime sport because of its value in keeping men fit for war. In the great kingdoms of the East, it has been noted, hunting was a royal sport for the same reason. By this standard every Spartan "peer" was a king in that he enjoyed the royal pastime. The labor of those held in subjection, and the prohibition against work on the part of Spartan citizens, left youths and adults free to enjoy the chase, though hunting was engaged in chiefly by those who had passed the age of twenty.[174] The rugged, wooded terrain of the Peloponnesus was an excellent hunting ground, where boars, deer, bears, wild goats, and other game were plentiful.[175] Laconian hunting dogs were famous throughout the Hellenic world. One is reminded of Argos, Odysseus' hunting hound, who

[172] Pausanias, III, 11, 2; 14, 8–10. Trans. by J. G. Frazer. Courtesy of Macmillan & Co., Ltd., London, and The Macmillan Company, New York; Lucian: *Anacharsis*, 38; Krause: op. cit., p. 676; Nilsson: op. cit., pp. 402 ff.
[173] Xenophon: *Lacedaemonians*, IV, 3–6. *Scripta Minora*, trans. by E. C. Marchant. The Loeb Classical Library. Quoted by permission of Harvard University Press, Cambridge, Mass.
[174] St. John: op. cit., I, 212; Bogeng: *Geschichte des Sports*, II, 592; Baumeister: *Denkmäler des Klassischen Altertums*, I, 709 ff.
[175] Pausanias, III, 20, 4.

ATTACKING A WILD BOAR    C. 460 B.C.
(Courtesy, The Metropolitan Museum of Art, New York)

> Never missed in deepest woods the swift game to pursue
> If once it glanced before his sight, for every track he knew.

Hunting dogs were shared to a certain extent in Lacedaemon. According to Xenophon, one invited the master to a hunt, who, if he were engaged, sent his dogs anyway.[176] Provision was also made for sharing food, in order that the needs might be met of those who were belated in the fields when hunting and when they had nothing at hand to eat.[177] The excellence of hunting must have been a great attraction to Xenophon who took up his residence in Lacedaemon. The *Cynegeticus*, a treatise on hunting commonly credited to Xenophon, though the authorship is disputed,[178] sets forth in enthusiastic fashion

[176] *Lacedaemonians*, VI, 3.
[177] *Ibid.*, VI, 4.
[178] Marchant: *Xenophon Scripta Minora*, xli–xliii.

the techniques of the chase and a philosophy of hunting as a phase of education as well. To Xenophon it seemed that game and hounds were a gift of the gods. These they bestowed upon men; and men, by giving heed to hounds and hunting, "excelled greatly and were admired for their virtue." [179] Youth are charged, therefore, "not to despise hunting or any other schooling. For these are the means by which men become good in war and in all things out of which must come excellence in thought and word and deed." The very first thing, "therefore, that a young man just out of his boyhood should take up is hunting, and afterwards he should go on to the other branches of education, provided he has means." [180]

"All men who have loved hunting have been good," thought Xenophon; so, too, have some women! [181] The Spartan lawgiver understood the value of hunting, as Xenophon says, and provided that those who had passed the time of youth and were ready to fill great public offices should continue their preparation by practicing hunting, "in order that they might be able to stand the fatigues of soldiering as well as the younger men." [182] It was in accord with ancient Spartan philosophy of practicality that Philopoemen, though physically able to excel in wrestling, shunned the expert training of the wrestling ground when told that the diet, sleep, exercises, and generally regular habits of professional athletes were out of keeping with the difficult and irregular demands made upon the soldier; and when he had nothing else to do, sought to develop strength and endurance by hunting and by work on his farm.[183] Xenophon recommends especially hunting on horseback, where the country is fit for it and big game is available, for in this way one becomes accustomed "to use his weapons properly on horseback" while "riding at top speed over all sorts of country." [184]

The value of hunting as military training is explained at some length: ". . . the advantages that those who have been attracted by this pursuit will gain are many. For it makes the body healthy, improves the sight and hearing, and keeps men from growing old; and it affords the best training for war. In the first place, when marching over rough roads under arms, they will not tire: accustomed to carry arms for capturing wild beasts, they will bear up under their tasks. Again, they will be capable of sleeping on a hard bed and of guarding well the place assigned to them. In an attack on the enemy they will be able to go for him and at the same time to carry out the orders that are passed along,

[179] Xenophon: On Hunting, I, 1–5.
[180] Ibid., I, 18; II, 1. Scripta Minora, trans. by E. C. Marchant. The Loeb Classical Library. Quoted by permission of Harvard University Press, Cambridge, Mass.
[181] Ibid., XIII, 18.
[182] Lacedaemonians, IV, 7.
[183] Plutarch: Philopoemen, 4.
[184] Xenophon: On the Art of Horsemanship, VIII, 10.

because they are used to do the same things on their own account when capturing the game. If their post is in the van they will not desert it, because they can endure. In the rout of the enemy they will make straight for the foe without a slip over any kind of ground, through habit. If part of their own army has met with disaster in ground rendered difficult by woods and defiles or what not, they will manage to save themselves without loss of honour and to save others. For their familiarity with the business will give them knowledge that others lack. Indeed, it has happened before now, when a great host of allies has been put to flight, that a little band of such men, through their fitness and confidence, has renewed the battle and routed the victorious enemy when he has blundered owing to difficulties in the ground. For men who are sound in body and mind may always stand on the threshold of success. It was because they knew that they owed their successes against the enemy to such qualities that our ancestors looked after the young men. For in spite of the scarcity of corn it was their custom from the earliest times not to prevent hunters from hunting over any growing crops; and, in addition, not to permit hunting at night within a radius of many furlongs from the city, so that the masters of that art might not rob the young men of their game. In fact they saw that this is the only one among the pleasures of the younger men that produces a rich crop of blessings. For it makes sober and upright men of them, because they are trained in the school of truth (and they perceived that to these men they owed their success in war, as in other matters); and it does not keep them from any other honourable occupation they wish to follow, like other and evil pleasures that they ought not to learn. Of such men, therefore, are good soldiers and good generals made. . . ." [185]

It has been said that, "in early times at least," "riding was one of the principal occupations of the youths of Sparta." [186] Though the evidence for this belief is held to be "slight" and "untrustworthy," [187] it is said that youth rode on gaily decked horses at the festival of Hyacinthia; [188] and the select band of three hundred youths were called *hippagretai*, "cavalry." [189] Strabo [190] noted, however, that these Spartan "knights" did not keep horses. These discordant views leave doubt as to the extent of the rôle riding may have played in Spartan training. Doubtless the importance of horsemanship varied from time to time. Krause states that "Sparta was not entirely without cavalry," and points out that Hipparchos was teacher of youth in the art of riding. [191] Plutarch cred-

[185] Xenophon: *On Hunting*, xii, 1–9. *Scripta Minora*, trans. by E. C. Marchant. The Loeb Classical Library. Quoted by permission of Harvard University Press, Cambridge, Mass.
[186] Müller: *op. cit.*, ii, 310.
[187] Wilkins: *op. cit.*, p. 23.
[188] Athenaeus, iv, 139.
[189] Xenophon: *Lacedaemonians*, iv, 3.
[190] *The Geography*, x, 4, 18.
[191] Krause: *op. cit.*, ii, 672.

ited Lycurgus with introducing a particular arrangement of the Spartan cavalry, the oulamos being a troop of fifty horsemen in quadrilateral formation. Xenophon says that the cavalry watched the enemy from positions commanding the widest view.[192] The pre-eminence of foot soldiers in Spartan military organization, however, must have caused riding to be less stressed than other exercises, for practicality was a first principle at Lacedaemon. The low estimation of cavalry in Spartan armies is recognized by Müller, though he credits riding with having been an important part in the training of youth.[193] Athens first formed a cavalry corps in the middle of the fifth century; and Sparta formed one in 424.[194] Sparta is said to have raised a force of four hundred horsemen and archers, "contrary to their usual custom"; later they had only six hundred cavalry as opposed to six thousand heavy-armed troops.[195] Xenophon expressed the view that such fame as the Lacedaemonian cavalry achieved dated "from the introduction of foreign cavalry"; and he therefore recommended a foreign contingent elsewhere as a means of economy and as a stimulus to rivalry in efficiency.[196] It seems, however, that the weight of Spartan horsemen did not bulk heavily. At the battle of Leuctra the Theban horse were in good trim, but Sparta's cavalry was in a "very inefficient condition," since the "richest," "weakest," and "least spirited" were on horseback and were "at once defeated." [197]

Probably no physical exercises assumed so many forms in Greece as did dancing. These may be classified as religious and profane, the latter including gymnastic, theatrical, and folk dances. There are also the dances of war and the dances of peace.[198] Theatrical dancing may be further classified as comic, tragic, and satiric. Though the numerous categories serve to call attention to the varied character of dancing and its significant rôle in Greek life, difficulties arise, since there is much overlapping of terms; what is called profane is not without its religious connection, and different names are often used by ancient authors for the same dances.[199] Certain dances which were intimately associated with significant aspects of Spartan life may be noted briefly. Like many other elements of Sparta's civilization, her dances bore a marked resemblance to the Cretan. Strabo [200] says, indeed, that the usual dance practiced in Lacedaemonia, the measures used, the songs sung, and many other customs, are commonly called Cretan, just as though they had come from Crete.

[192] Plutarch: Lycurgus, 23; Xenophon: Lacedaemonians, XII, 2.
[193] Müller: op. cit., II, 253.
[194] Busolt-Swoboda: op. cit., I, 344; Krause: op. cit., I, 589.
[195] Thucydides, IV, 55; Xenophon: Hellenics, IV, 2, 16.
[196] The Cavalry Commander, IX, 3–4.
[197] Xenophon: Hellenics, VI, 4, 10–3.
[198] Plato: Laws, VII, 815.
[199] Krause: op. cit., II, 822 ff.
[200] Bk. X, 4, 18.

Among the dances having a religious significance were the chorus at the Gymnopaedia; the chorus at the Caryae, in which Spartan maidens performed each year "their national dance" in honor of Artemis; [201] the *parthenia*, the chorus of maidens, said to have been "exceedingly grave and solemn"; [202] and the *hyporchema*, a lively dance accompanied by songs, which was performed by the Spartans around the flaming sacrifice in honor of Apollo.[203] Nowhere were music, dancing, and gymnastics more perfectly united than in the Gymnopaedia, a festival which was mainly athletic, and held in highest esteem by the Spartans.[204] Nothing was permitted to interfere with their performance; even when word of the calamitous defeat at Leuctra had been received, the ephors would not permit interruption of the chorus.[205] To participate in it was an honor; to be excluded from witnessing it was one means of disgracing the men who, though of marriageable age, were yet unwed.[206] At the beginning of the choral dance various exercises, especially those of wrestling and the pancration, were imitated; and these were followed by the Pyrrhic dance. Choruses of old men, youth, and boys participated in the Gymnopaedia, dancing naked, and singing the songs of Alcman, Thaletas, and other famous poets.[207]

Dancing was a prominent feature also in the three-day festival of Hyacinthia, religiously observed by Spartans in honor of Hyacinthos, whom Apollo was said to have killed accidentally by a throw of the discus.[208] Its beginning, marked by great restraint and solemnity, was followed at the middle of the second day by numerous events, music, dancing, and athletics, which were observed by many people. Athenaeus describes it: "Boys with tunics girded high play the lyre or sing to flute accompaniment while they run the entire gamut of the strings with the plectrum; they sing the praises of the god in anapaestic rhythm and in a high pitch. Others march through the theatre mounted on gaily adorned horses; full choirs of young men enter and sing some of their national songs, and dancers mingling among them go through the figures in the ancient style, accompanied by the flute and the voice of the singers. As for the girls, some are carried in wicker carts which are sumptuously ornamented, others parade in chariots yoked to two horses, which they race, and the entire city is given over to the bustle and joy of the festival. . . ." [209]

[201] Pausanias, III, 10, 7; Lucian: *Of Pantomime*, 10; Krause: op. cit., pp. 831 f.
[202] Müller: op. cit., II, 336.
[203] St. John: op. cit., I, 389; Müller: op. cit., I, 357 f.; Krause: op. cit., II, 825 f.; Athenaeus, XIV, 630.
[204] Pausanias, III, 11, 9; Lucian: *Of Pantomime*, 12; Nilsson: op. cit., pp. 140 ff.
[205] Xenophon: *Hellenics*, VI, 4, 16; Plutarch: *Agesilaus*, 29.
[206] Plutarch: *Lycurgus*, 15.
[207] *Ibid.*, 21; Krause: op. cit., II, 829 f.; Müller: op. cit., II, 334, 344; Athenaeus, XIV, 630–1.
[208] Pausanias, III, 10, 1; 19, 3–5; IV, 19, 4.
[209] Athenaeus, IV, 139. Trans. by C. B. Gulick. The Loeb Classical Library. Quoted by permission of Harvard University Press, Cambridge, Mass.

Dancing and music, closely associated at Sparta, constituted an important phase of moral and physical education, and were carefully regulated by the state. Music was chiefly choral, and thus contributed to the unity which Sparta so much desired. Probably few individuals studied music, or gained a scientific knowledge, but "without learning" it, Aristotle says, they were good judges of it.[210] Both music and dancing were intimately connected with war and religion. "Indeed," as one authority says, "the march of the Spartans and Cretans had, on account of its musical accompaniment, some resemblance to a dance." [211] Of all Spartan dances connected with war, the Pyrrhic dance in armor was pre-eminent. There was no agreement as to its origin, save that it was most ancient. Certain authorities traced it to Athena, some to Achilles, others to Castor, and still others to Pyrrhichos, a Cretan, or as others would have it, a Laconian. In fact, the mimic war dance was common to primitives, and some form of it was probably danced by the various Greek peoples.[212] The Pyrrhic dance had the same name as the expert armed combatant (πρύλις). It was quick and light in movement and was accompanied by the flute. Though not danced everywhere the same, the dancers generally imitated the action of defense (avoiding blows and missiles, giving way, leaping aside, rising up, falling down), and the mode of attack (hurling the javelin, giving blows, thrusting, shooting the bow).[213] Athenaeus says that at Sparta boys "from five years of age on" were thoroughly instructed in it.[214] It formed a part of the Gymnopaedia. Long after the Pyrrhic dance had ceased to have serious significance in other Greek states, the Spartans still danced it "as a warlike exercise."

The hormos is said to have been the most beautiful of all Spartan gymnastic dances. Young men and maidens participated in it, contrasting masculine courage and feminine grace. Though performed without weapons, the youths vied with each other in vigorous warlike movements, while the maidens followed with modest, graceful steps which were thought to befit them.[215]

The bibasis, a gymnastic exercise in favor at Sparta and practiced by boys, girls, and women, is generally considered a part of dancing.[216] In this, the dancer sprang into the air and sought to strike the buttocks with the heels as often as possible. Müller mentions the dipodia, deimalea, ithymbi, bryallicha, hypogypones, menes, tyrbasia, and the mimelic dance, all of which he regards as Laconian, but little is known of them save the name.[217] An acrobatic "ball

---

[210] Politica, VIII, 5.
[211] Müller: op. cit., II, 339.
[212] Lucian: Of Pantomime, 7–12, 18; Krause: op. cit., II, 836, 840 f.; supra, pp. 31, 211.
[213] Plato: Laws, VII, 815; Philostratos: Concerning Gymnastics, 19.
[214] Bk. XIV, 631; cf. Müller: op. cit., II, 343.
[215] Krause: op. cit., II, 842; Lucian: Of Pantomime, 12.
[216] Krause: op. cit., II, 842; supra, p. 245.
[217] Op. cit., II, 345 ff.

dance," such as was noted in Homer, was said by some ancient authorities to have been originated by Lacedaemonians.[218]

National songs and dances were the guarded heritage of Spartan citizens. The Helots, however, were forbidden to use such "noble" songs and dances; instead, they were often compelled to sing songs and dance dances of a vulgar and ludicrous character.[219] Though the national dances were generally marked by dignity and solemnity, even in the most solemn choruses of pagan Sparta there were elements which might be thought inimical to "female delicacy." [220]

The name "ballplayers" (σφαιρεῖς) was applied to Spartan youths who were "just entering on manhood," [221] presumably because ball-play was their chief exercise. Hippasus is said to have claimed that Lacedaemonians were "pioneers" in ball-playing "as in all gymnastic exercises." [222] Though Timocrates the Laconian was credited with a book on ball-play, only fragmentary references have been preserved, and neither the rules of the game nor the number of players are known to us. Nevertheless inscriptions show that there were yearly contests in the dromos, in which teams participated under the direction of the Bideoi, the same board that managed the contest in the Plane-Tree Grove. These matches seem to have taken place between teams composed of "about fifteen representatives of the obes." Victory was probably decided by matching the teams "in pairs in successive rounds until only one unbeaten team remained." [223]

Daily bathing seems to have been a part of Spartan physical regimen, but warm baths were in early times prohibited. Plutarch mentions bathing in the River Eurotas as an appetizer; his reference to the slight knowledge of "baths and unguents" doubtless refers to warm baths.[224] That river bathing was not merely an occasion for washing, but also for swimming, is a reasonable assumption. The Plane-Tree Grove contest was marked by an effort of each team to push its opponents into the water,[225] and suggests that the boys must have been able to take care of themselves. There is, however, no definite reference to instruction in swimming at Sparta, and some have doubted the prevalence of swimming there.[226] The lack of systematic instruction need not be so interpreted, however. Since Spartans did not favor professional gymnastic instruc-

[218] Athenaeus, I, 14.
[219] Plutarch: Lycurgus, 28; Müller: op. cit., II, 39, 349 ff.
[220] St. John: op. cit., I, 386 ff.
[221] Pausanias, III, 14, 6; Müller: op. cit., II, 309 f.
[222] Athenaeus, I, 14.
[223] Ibid., I, 15; Tod: "Teams of Ball-Players at Sparta," Ann. Brit. Sch. at Athens, x, 75; Lucian: Anacharsis, 38; Krause: op. cit., I, 301 f.; Grasberger: op. cit., I, 86.
[224] Lycurgus, 10, 12, 16; Customs of the Spartans, 2; Alcibiades, 23; Xenophon: Hellenics, v, 4, 28; Müller: op. cit., II, 283; Krause: op. cit., I, 625; Mehl: Antike Schwimmkunst, pp. 45 f.
[225] Pausanias, III, 14, 8.
[226] Cramer: Geschichte der Erziehung, I, 270.

tors, but relied on the older and more skilled boys to teach the younger, swimming may also have been learned in a similar informal fashion.[227] Krause holds that the Greeks were at all times ready swimmers; certainly those dwelling on the rivers and the coast were quite at home in the water which they were forced to encounter both in peace and war. That the Spartans "practiced themselves in swimming," Krause believes "certain." Freeman, too, maintains that the daily plunge in the Eurotas taught them swimming.[228] Numerous passages in ancient history show that swimming often stood the Greeks in good stead. Herodotus says that at Salamis only a few Greeks died, for "they were able to swim," and those not killed outright by the enemy escaped from the sinking vessels by swimming to Salamis.[229] Thucydides relates that a detachment of Spartans, blockaded on an island by the Athenians, offered a high price for corn, wine, and cheese that could be brought in, and promised freedom to any Helots who would bring in such food supplies. In connection with these efforts many swam in through the harbor, dragging by a cord skins filled with poppy-seed, linseed, and honey until they were observed, and precautions were taken against their daring exploits.[230]

FAILURE OF SPARTAN EDUCATION   Strict conformity with a fixed pattern of life was assiduously cultivated at Sparta by that class which had gained power and sought to preserve it. Having completed his reforms, Lycurgus is said to have forbidden any change in the constitution until he should return from Delphi.[231] No slight deviation was to be permitted lest such indulgence should lead to greater changes. Spartans are said to have opposed changing the number of strings on the lyre;[232] a cook who knew anything except approved Spartan cookery was not tolerated; even changing the rules of ball-play deserved punishment. Was it not from his admiration of Spartan fixity that Plato suggested that the people of his small state should always play the same games?[233]

That Spartan training was commonly regarded as the main source of power is suggested by the fact that Agis and Cleomenes, seeking to restore Sparta, endeavored to do so by re-establishing the ancient Lycurgan system of training;[234] and Philopoemen, when he wished to humble and destroy her, abolished the constitution of Lycurgus, and compelled the Spartans to bring up their children according to the Achaean fashion.[235] That the system of train-

227 Mehl: op. cit., p. 55.
228 Freeman: op. cit., p. 26; Krause: op. cit., I, 625, 630 f.
229 Bk. VIII, 89.
230 Thucydides, IV, 26.
231 Plutarch: Lycurgus, 29.
232 Plutarch: Customs of the Spartans, 17.
233 Laws, VII, 797.
234 Plutarch: Agis, 4–6; Cleomenes, 11.
235 Plutarch: Philopoemen, 16; Pausanias, VII, 8, 5.

ing was important and powerful is not to be denied; but systematic training is not the sole integrating force in any society. When other foundations had been destroyed, Spartan education, no matter how perfectly designed and faithfully carried out, could not really restore the city to its onetime power.

What results are creditable to the Spartan system? Modesty of demeanor appears to have been one result, if one may trust the assertions of admirers, ancient and modern.[236] Health, rugged beauty, agility, and physical endurance were certainly attained in generous measure. That Spartan training was brutalizing seems certain also, although Müller[237] holds to a contrary view. That a lack of independence of thought and action (save in a narrow range) and of intelligent imagination must have resulted from such a tight-laced system, seems inevitably true. The basic condition of freedom being denied, no critical philosophy of life or education arose. Spartans, however, gave a practical demonstration of a philosophy of both, which powerfully influenced the thinking of those Greeks who did seek to reconstruct human society nearer to the heart's desire.

Since loyalty to a system, and determination to preserve it unchanged, conditioned all their efforts, it was inevitable that Spartan success could only be temporary. All things change; nevertheless, for hundreds of years, Sparta was a marvel to all observers for her seemingly unchanging ways. After Plataea, she had not the adaptability nor the political intelligence to take advantage of the pre-eminence she had won by war.[238] She continued in splendid isolation, and impressed many observers by her firm control within her own borders. Polybius[239] thought she had the best government and the greatest power up to the time of Leuctra; but when change set in thereafter, she had more trouble and disorder than any other city knew. When circumstances changed around her, she was unable to meet them intelligently, yet could not escape their impact. Plutarch declared that, like a human body, she suffered from having "followed all the while too strict and severe a regimen; a single error turned the scale and brought down the entire prosperity of the city."[240]

Despite long, rigorous, ascetic training, Spartan citizens became weak and greedy. The prohibitions against changing the constitution, and other efforts to seize the present moment and hold it fast, were all in vain. Xenophon, Sparta's admirer, noted that, whereas once her citizens were compelled to live at home, in his day the best among them wished nothing more than to live abroad as governors of some foreign state. Yet no other Greek state wished to see Lacedaemon

---

[236] Xenophon: *Lacedaemonians*, III, 3; Freeman: *op. cit.*, p. 27.
[237] *Op. cit.*, II, 321.
[238] Bury: *op. cit.*, p. 323.
[239] Bk. IV, 81.
[240] Plutarch: *Agesilaus*, 33. Trans. by B. Perrin. The Loeb Classical Library. Quoted by permission of Harvard University Press, Cambridge, Mass.

regain supremacy, for whereas the Spartans once sought pre-eminently to be worthy rulers, they were now more anxious "to exercise rule than to be worthy of it." Such, Xenophon adds, is their fate, for "they obey neither their god nor the laws of Lycurgus." [241] The equality which Lycurgus had sought to impose in order that the state might be stable, gave way at length to inequality of wealth, by virtue of the purchase of land and the influx of wealth from the outside.[242] An old Laconic proverb ran: "Sparta will fall by love of wealth, naught else." Lycurgus had given the opinion that Lacedaemonians would prevail against their enemies "by continuing poor, and not coveting each man to be greater than his fellow." [243] In Xenophon's day, however, they boasted of their possessions, whereas formerly they had feared to possess gold. And with wealth, luxurious living became the fashion. The number of citizens declined to less than a thousand, says Aristotle, although large families were encouraged by military exemptions offered to fathers who had three sons. Even recruiting citizens from Perioeci and Helots was not sufficient to stay the process of disintegration.[244]

Courage of a kind the Lycurgan discipline did indeed develop. Herodotus attributes beautiful speeches to men of Lacedaemon on the subject of independence, liberty, and courage.[245] Plutarch says that Sparta's enemies for a time credited her with an "irresistible courage." [246] Spartans certainly were not cowards; most of them, doubtless, preferred to be "mourned at the mill" and "mourned at the mess," as Alcman says,[247] rather than be conquered. Archilochus, to be sure, is credited with the view that it were better to throw one's shield and run away than die upon the field; for—

> A better buckler one can soon regain,
> But who can get another life again?

But he was soon ordered from the city. Aristotle comments critically on the value of various kinds of courage, and concludes that the Spartans had only an inferior kind, the virtue of courage in war. As long as they were at war, they kept their power, but when they attained empire they fell, for they had learned nothing of the arts of peace.[248] Her soldiers and generals failed in the larger field of empire, though on the banks of the Eurotas they had done well. Polybius remarks that Lacedaemon, having long contended for the hegemony

[241] Xenophon: *Lacedaemonians*, xiv, 5, 7.
[242] Plutarch: *Lycurgus*, 30; *Agis*, 3. The communism, Bury thinks (*op. cit.*, pp. 134, 535), was "only superficial."
[243] Plutarch: *Lycurgus*, 19.
[244] Xenophon: *Lacedaemonians*, xiv, 3; Athenaeus, iv, 142; Aristotle: *Politica*, ii, 9.
[245] Bk. vii, 135–6.
[246] Plutarch: *Pelopidas*, 17.
[247] *Lyra Graeca*, i, 95.
[248] *Politica*, ii, 9.

of Greece, finally won it but was able to hold it uncontested scarcely twelve years.[249]

In war, which was the chief thing in which Spartans wished to excel, they were eminently successful for a time. Aristotle says, however: "It is notorious that the Lacedaemonians themselves, while they alone were assiduous in their laborious drill, were superior to others, but now they are beaten both in war and gymnastic exercises." For their superiority lay not just in the "mode of training" but in the fact that "they trained them when their only rivals did not." [250] War, the Spartans' vocation, was their own undoing. Agesilaus was reproached for having made the Thebans formidable foes by his constant excursions against them.[251] By constant warring with each other the Greeks weakened themselves. The words of Agesilaus are weighty: "O Greece, how many brave men hast thou destroyed; who if they had been preserved to so good a use, had sufficed to have conquered all Persia." To Sparta's sons, as to those of another "heroic age," the words of the poet aptly apply: "These dread battle hastened to their end." [252]

---

[249] Bk. I, 2.
[250] Politica, VIII, 4. From The Works of Aristotle, translated by J. A. Smith and W. D. Ross (The Clarendon Press).
[251] Plutarch: Lycurgus, 13.
[252] Davies: Hesiod and Theognis, p. 33.

# 10

# ATHENS

THE PEOPLE AND THEIR RESOURCES    By one of their popular traditions, related by Herodotus and fondly dwelt upon by great orators and others,
the Athenians credited themselves with being the "most ancient nation in
Greece," the only people who had "never changed their abode." [1] Attica had
always been inhabited by the same people; she alone, free from "savage monsters," had "brought forth man" who had "justice and religion," while other
lands had produced all kinds of animals, wild and tame.[2] There were, of course,
conflicting tales.

Modern archaeology and history show that neolithic man dwelt anciently at
Athens and elsewhere in Attica, as in other parts of Greece, and left his trace
in arrowheads, stone axes, and other implements. To the original inhabitants,
who spoke a barbarous (i.e., a non-Hellenic) tongue, the ancients gave the
name Pelasgians. Instead of remaining pure, however, as the story of autoch-
thony would have it, there was infiltration; and some of the great families later
traced their origin to Messenia and to Phoenicia. The tales of Egyptian
Cecrops, Cretan Minos, the legend of Ion, the evidence of language, Mycenaean remains in Attica,[3] the iron weapons, and the Dipylon pottery of the
period, all indicate the infiltration of influences from the outside—the touch
of Cretan and Mycenaean civilization and that of the conquering Dorians.
The last of these was potent enough to establish the Hellenic tongue among
the native population—a change which Herodotus infers must have taken
place.[4] A new art, the "Geometric," took the place of Mycenaean, as has been

---

[1] The History of Herodotus, VII, 161; Thucydides, I, 2; II, 36; Isocrates: Panegyricus, 23;
Panathenaicus, 124.
[2] Plato: Menexenus, 237.
[3] The Cambridge Ancient History, II, 459; III, 572 f., 596.
[4] Bk. I, 57–8; v, 76.

noted, and continued down to the sixth century. That the invading forces generally adjusted themselves gradually and rather peacefully among the native population seems probable: in any case, no such rift between conqueror and conquered is reflected in political institutions as in Laconia; nor is there evidence of a cataclysmic break between the old and the new cultures in Attica, as in the remains found in Argolis, Laconia, and Thessaly.[5]

Despite all evidence to the contrary, however, Athenians boasted of their autochthonous character, and claimed a certain cultural superiority—on which orators based persuasive propaganda during the Peloponnesian War. But if they were a pattern to others rather than imitators; if their government was liberal, and not for the few; if they enjoyed ease and recreation, while others devoted themselves to vigorous training; if they were open to foreign influences, whether of persons or of ideas; if they were a school for all Hellas; if they were quick to invent, plan, and execute, "bold even beyond their power," and ready to go abroad while the Spartans loved to stay at home [6]—if, indeed, they did possess these and other fair traits in a greater degree than the Lacedaemonians, they did so as a result of the interaction of many forces throughout several centuries. From the time of the Dorian invasion till the sixth century, it is generally believed, there was more similarity than difference between the cultures of Laconia and Attica.[7] Sparta had not then achieved that austere isolation which was to draw both derision and admiration from her neighbors; nor had Athens put on those refinements of art and letters which in the fifth and fourth centuries were to be her greatest distinction.

Geography and climate were important factors in preparing the later greatness of Athens. As Egypt was made by her river; as Crete, over the ever-ready Aegean and Mediterranean waters, was enabled to send her gifts of civilization far and wide; so Athens, because of her fortunate geography—a proportionately long seacoast, numerous inlets, and low-sloping beaches that were inviting to early navigators who pulled their boats ashore—seemed destined to be receptive to commercial and cultural advances from the south and east, to a degree not to be expected of less accessible parts of the Greek world. The most mountainous regions and those least accessible to the sea, in Hellas as well as in other countries, were culturally the most backward. At Athens the open invitation to adventure on the sea must have profoundly affected the temper and achievements of the peoples that shared it; this fact, taken in conjunction with the

---

[5] Burn: *Minoans, Philistines, and Greeks*, pp. 33 ff., 229 f.; Glotz: *The Aegean Civilization*, pp. 18, 47, 50, 53 ff., 201, 279, 292; Hall: *Aegean Archaeology*, pp. 17, 21; C.A.H., III, 571–7; Jardé: *The Formation of the Greek People*, pp. 151 ff.; Whibley: *Companion to Greek Studies*, pp. 228–34.

[6] Thucydides, I, 70; II, 37–41.

[7] Jardé: *op. cit.*, pp. 76, 166; Bury: *A History of Greece*, p. 342; Laistner: *A Survey of Ancient History*, pp. 128 f., 153.

relatively small amount of tillable land (though some areas were very fertile), the unnavigable rivers, and the mountains which made traffic by land with many cities either inconvenient or impossible at that immature industrial epoch, predisposed them in general to a career of colonization and foreign commerce. By the beginning of the sixth century Athens was already gaining superiority over her neighbors as a center of industry and commerce.[8]

Climatic influences were no less favorable than those of land and sea. Clear and stimulating, neither tropical nor extremely cold at any time, the climate of Attica enticed her people to a life of freedom out of doors, and made unnecessary heavy, unhygienic clothing. Small wonder that her poets sang her praises, and her soldiers and athletes won her fair renown. In that rare atmosphere Athenians stepped lightly, "as on wings uplifted." [9] Aristophanes is said to have credited his wit to the influence of Attic air!

Though chiefly a maritime city, Athens was also an outlet for an agricultural community. It is obvious, however, that while the fertile plains of Attica lay back of the city, most of her territory was scarcely capable of affording a living. Attica must have seemed poor in comparison with the fabulously fertile valleys of Mesopotamia.[10] The poverty of Attic soil impressed Thucydides; [11] Solon found the land scarcely rich enough to support those who worked upon it; [12] Plato,[13] however, thought it as fertile as any in the world, though it had once been better. Productivity differed, doubtless, with time and place. Farming with the primitive implements that were characteristic of Greek agriculture was laborious in any case; and hardships fell frequently upon husbandmen, owing to recurrent war.

The chief sources of Attica's agricultural wealth lay in olive groves and vineyards. Barley and wheat were grown; the former, the staple food of the peasants, capable of thriving even in very thin soil, led by a wide margin. In the fourth and fifth centuries grain was imported chiefly from the Euxine and other prime grain producing regions—a fact that affected profoundly the foreign policy of Athens.[14] In contrast with the meat-eating heroes of Homeric fame, Athenians depended chiefly on cereals and vegetables. Barley, wheat, oil, and wine were staples of diet. These were supplemented by millet, spelt, onions, garlic, beans, peas, leeks, mushrooms, lentils, lupines, spinach, lettuce, cabbage, radishes, asparagus, turnips, and many fruits and nuts. Cheese, various kinds of

---

8 Jardé: op. cit., pp. 149 f.; Lot: The End of the Ancient World, p. 61; Bury: op. cit., pp. 1 ff.
9 Euripides: Medea, 831.
10 Herodotus, 1, 193; Jardé: op. cit., p. 150; C.A.H., IV, 26.
11 Bk. 1, 2.
12 Plutarch: Solon, 22.
13 Critias, 111.
14 Laistner: op. cit., p. 288.

fish, oysters, snails, mussels, turtles, poultry, wild game and birds—such as hare, wild boar, deer, bear, ducks, geese, partridges, pigeons, quails, thrushes, black-birds—some beef, pork, goats' flesh, mutton, and honey gave further variety to Athenian fare.[15] Considering its importance in Athenian diet and in com-merce, it is not surprising that the olive was associated with religion—was re-garded, indeed, as a sacred gift of Athena herself. The vine was traced back to Dionysus. Moreover, great statesmen, such as Solon and Pisistratus, sought to encourage the cultivation of olives; and Athenian ephebi swore to protect vine-yards and olive groves, barley and wheat—the richest sources of agricultural wealth.[16]

Other natural resources Attica did not lack. Her mountainous regions (al-most half her territory), though unadapted to agriculture, provided timber for ships, houses, and fuel, as well as pasturage for goats and sheep, and harborage for birds and game. Quarries provided limestone, travertines, and Pentelic marble for public buildings and statuary; clay of the best quality for ceramics came from the base of Hymettos. The silver mines of Laureion, after the sixth century, were among the chief sources of Athenian economic pre-eminence.[17]

POLITICAL INTEGRATION AND DECLINE    Before the coming of Hellen, son of Deucalion, there was no unity, it was said, among the peoples of Greek lands. There were Danäans, Argives, Achaeans, but not Greeks; the very conception of Hellenes apart from barbarians had not arisen.[18] Particularism reigned within Attica herself in prehistoric times.[19] Unification, when it ulti-mately came about, was credited by Athenians to Theseus, much as Spartan hegemony was traced to Lycurgus. To us, however, the labors attributed to each of them seem to have been the work of many—the product of time, not the work of a moment.[20] The unification of rival communities of Attica under the leadership of Athens, though not definitely dated, was a gradual process, beginning as early as 1000, perhaps, and attaining its consummation near the beginning of the seventh century B.C. Prior to that time, localism was supreme; village warred against village till at length common interests brought them together, first in combinations of close-lying villages (as in the Tetrapolis of Marathon) and finally in a union with Athens. Politically considered, Athens and Attica became almost synonymous, though the memory of divisive local-ism was reflected in the fifth-century feast of Synoikia, unification. Attic unity

[15] Blümner: The Home Life of the Ancient Greeks, pp. 206 ff.; Gulick: Life of the Ancient Greeks, pp. 143 ff.; Davis: A Day in Old Athens, pp. 174–81.
[16] Plutarch: Solon, 23; Alcibiades, 15; Dio Chrysostom, xxv, 3.
[17] Glotz: Ancient Greece at Work, pp. 127 ff.; Jardé: op. cit., pp. 146 f.; Laistner: op. cit., p. 153.
[18] Thucydides, I, 3.
[19] C.A.H., III, 578.
[20] Ibid., III, 580; Bury: op. cit., p. 166.

was somewhat more perfect than that of any other Greek state. There were neither sharp stratification of the population, military overlords, nor subjugated peoples, as at Sparta. Of course, *synoikismos* did not equalize all citizens; in fact, it consolidated the power of the landed aristocracy, whose efforts had brought it about.[21] The political power of once powerful villages withered away, however, being merged in the sovereignty of Athens; and men of Thoricus, Icaria, Marathon, Cephisia—men of the hills, the coast, the plain—became Athenian citizens.

Government rang all the changes from monarchy to democracy. The earliest form was a primitive monarchy, whose kings had military, religious, and judicial functions. By the seventh century, monarchy was giving way before the wealthy landed Eupatrids who, jealous of the kingship, created an aristocratic republic. Kingship became elective for one year (683 B.C.); a *polemarch* was chosen to have charge of military affairs because some kings had proved weak in warfare; and an *archon eponymos* was named as chief magistrate. *Thesmothetae*—the six junior *archons*—named a little later, held office for one year. The Council of Areopagus, composed of those who had served as *archons*, was the aristocratic and autocratic guardian of law and order, its members serving for life.[22]

Private wealth at Athens was as significant as the common lot at Sparta. An *archon*, on taking office, proclaimed that no one should suffer diminution of possessions during his administration.[23] Euripides' *Medea* reminds us of the power of wealth:

> Gifts even win, 'tis said, the gods,
> Stronger than many words with men is gold.

Though blood and wealth first ruled the Attic land, their sway was disturbed at the outset by struggles among the wealthy themselves, and again, by the discontent of poor peasants and the rising power of the *thetes* (hired laborers), whose importance increased in proportion as Athens' sea power, industry, and commerce developed and coinage supplanted barter. Would-be tyrants showed their heads. Draco's code (621 B.C.), though it sought to diminish the uncertainty of life and property, and became a byword for severity, did not improve the situation fundamentally. An important legal distinction was made, indeed, between accidental and intentional killing. Far from easing the condition of the poor, however, Draco put into writing—what was doubtless practiced before—that the insolvent debtor's person should be at the disposal of his creditor.[24] The struggle between the landed aristocracy and those enslaved by debt

21 C.A.H., III, 586.
22 Aristotle: *Atheniensium Respublica*, 3; C.A.H., III, 590 ff.; Jardé: op. cit., p. 160.
23 Aristotle: *Ath. Resp.*, 56.
24 C.A.H., IV, 28 f., 33 ff.

increased in intensity. At length, in 594 B.C., with the consent of both parties, Solon was named *archon* and arbitrator-extraordinary between "the good and base." Wellborn, indeed, but not of the richest sort, his sympathy lay doubtless with the "good," who "in wealth were glorious and great." He scorned, however, the cruelty and greed of the wealthy who oppressed the poor, who had "no share in anything." For the poor extremists, likewise, whose "cravings knew no bound" and who wished a redistribution of land, he had contempt. Between these two extremes Solon saw himself,

> Turning at bay like wolf among the hounds.

According to certain fragments, Solon's reforms brought immediate relief by the cancellation of mortgages and the freeing of enslaved debtors:

> Dark Earth, thou best canst witness, from whose breast
> I swept the pillars broadcast planted there,
> And made thee free, who hadst been slave of yore.
> And many a man whom fraud or law had sold
> Far from his god-built land, an outcast slave,
> I brought again to Athens. . . .[25]

Remoter consequences flowed from the prohibition of loans secured by the debtor's person.[26] Numerous other reforms were credited to Solon: a new coinage, favorable to Athens' commercial advantage;[27] prohibition or restriction of certain exports and the encouragement of others; establishment of a system of weights and measures; limitation on the growth of large estates; provision that estates of Eupatrids were no longer indivisible; granting citizenship to alien craftsmen who settled permanently at Athens; levying a penalty on those who had no trade; and protection of slaves against reckless brutality of masters. Of far-reaching importance was the gift of political rights to *thetes*, permitting them a voice in the assembly and in choosing magistrates, though they were not eligible for office; and the establishment of courts of justice (*heliaea*) for all citizens, even *thetes*. To this, Aristotle believed, "the masses . . . owed their strength most of all, since, when the democracy is master of the voting-power, it is master of the constitution." [28]

Solon wrote his laws and departed. Tranquillity did not long prevail, however, for moderate measures could not restrain individual and class rivalries. Anarchy prevailed in 590 and 585 B.C. At length the struggle culminated in

[25] Aristotle: *Ath. Resp.*, 12. From *The Works of Aristotle*, translated by J. A. Smith and W. D. Ross (The Clarendon Press).
[26] *Ibid.*, 6.
[27] C.A.H., IV, 39 f.
[28] *Ath. Resp.*, 9. From *The Works of Aristotle*, translated by J. A. Smith and W. D. Ross (The Clarendon Press).

temporary peace under the tyrant Pisistratus who supported the landless hill men against those of the coast and the plain.[29] The constitution of Solon remained unchanged. Pisistratus rewarded his landless followers at the expense of the men of the plain, giving many a son of "aches and pains," who had tilled the stony upland soil, reason to be grateful to him. Under Pisistratus and his sons, peace and economic prosperity at home, and good relations with neighbors, were joined with literary and artistic advancement. Homer was edited and published "authoritatively"; competitions in epic recitals were incorporated in the Panathenian festival; Anacreon, Simonides, and other poets and artists made Athens famous as a patron of the arts.

The tyranny of Pisistratus and his sons formed a transition from the aristocratic government of Solon's day to the democracy of Cleisthenes, 510 B.C. Later generations credited numerous reforms to Cleisthenes. Those generally ascribed to him included a reform of the basis of citizenship by which the "maritime multitude"—commercial and industrial folk—could be taken into the political life of the city; the organization of a Council of Five Hundred in place of the Solonian Council of Four Hundred; the grant of the powerful weapon of ostracism to the mass of citizens; and extension of the right to hold offices, save the very highest, to those who had previously been excluded.[30] The first of these reforms was basic in importance. Citizenship no longer depended on membership in the *genos*. Clan and phratries henceforth had only social and religious rather than political significance. Attica was divided into administrative *demes*, registration in which constituted citizenship; and deme-membership was to be inherited. One *deme* or several made up a *trittyes*, of which there were thirty in all Attica. Each of the ten tribes were composed of three *trittyes*, one of which was urban, another coastal, while a third was from the inland.[31] Old loyalties and associations were thus disrupted; the noble and base in blood, the rich and poor, those from inland, from the coast, and Athens herself were mixed together, and the unification of Attica acquired a meaning it never had before.

Democracy, which Xenophon [32] so disdained, had not reached its zenith in the reforms of Cleisthenes; that would come with the years. The two lower classes of citizens were still excluded from the archonship, but in 487 B.C. sortition supplanted election, thus giving opportunity to the poor. Although changes in the army,[33] following naturally upon political reforms, were democratic in tendency, the growing importance of the ten generals (chosen by each

29 *Ibid.*, 14–6; *C.A.H.*, IV, 60–82.
30 Aristotle: *Ath. Resp.*, 21–2; Grote: A History of Greece, I, 563, 565; II, 386 f.; Bury: *op. cit.*, p. 214.
31 Aristotle: *Ath. Resp.*, 21; *C.A.H.*, IV, 141 ff.; V, 5 f., 102; Bury: *op. cit.*, pp. 211 ff.
32 *Polity of the Athenians*, I, III.
33 *C.A.H.*, IV, 154 f.; Aristotle: *Ath. Resp.*, 22.

of the ten tribes) shows the strength of the aristocratic element which persisted despite the rising tide of democracy to which events other than constitutional changes gave an impetus. Salamis (480) and Plataea (479) encouraged
democracy; the "maritime multitude," the "authors of the victory of Salamis,"
would scarcely permit privilege to be restored.[34]

Under the leadership of Themistocles, Athenians rebuilt their walls, and
proceeded rapidly to ascendancy in Hellenic affairs through leadership in the
Delian League—a naval confederacy founded to combat the Persian menace—
which was transformed gradually (478–454 B.C.) into an empire with over 260
tributary cities.[35] As commerce and naval power were conducive and necessary
to empire, and maritime folk were the reservoir of democratic tendencies,
growth of democracy and empire went hand in hand. Pericles offered Athenians empire on the seas, which neither "great king nor any nation" could
withstand;[36] at the same time, he encouraged the lower classes politically.
The aristocratic Areopagus was divested of political powers (enforcement of
laws, punishment, censorship), which were given to the people, represented
in the Council of Five Hundred, popular law courts, and the Assembly. Service
as *archon* was put on a paid basis, and, it appears, *zeugitae* (200-measure men)
and *thetes* (hired men) were soon admitted to membership. Payment for
judges in the people's courts was also introduced.[37]

The building of empire led inevitably to conflict with Sparta; scarcely had
it become a reality when its disintegration began, which ended in dissolution
at the close of the Peloponnesian War (404 B.C.). Athens destroyed her walls
and joined Sparta's League. Spartan rule proved worse than Athens' selfish sovereignty, however. After a brief trial of it, Thebes gained leadership (371 B.C.),
which lasted no longer than Epaminondas. When he fell (362 B.C.), sway
passed to Macedonian Philip, whom Epaminondas taught the latest arts of
war. At Chaeronea (338 B.C.) Philip triumphed, despite all that Demosthenes'
patriotic eloquence could stir against him. Under Alexander, Greek cities,
which had proved unable to rule themselves, were led on a heroic adventure
that was to make them rulers of the Nile and Mesopotamia. Alexander's hot
young dream vanished at his death; but it had paved the way for a far-flung
extension of Hellenic culture, if not of power. Macedonian, Seleucid, and
Ptolemy sought prestige through force and cunning; but all, at last, were drawn
under Roman sway.

Meantime, Athens, having left behind her dreams of empire, secured her
liberty as best she could from Egypt and from Rome. Within this "freedom"

---

34 Grote: *op. cit.*, II, 386.
35 Jardé: *op. cit.*, pp. 296 f.; Bury: *op. cit.*, pp. 331, 340.
36 Thucydides, II, 62.
37 Oman: *History of Greece*, pp. 269 f.; Bury: *op. cit.*, pp. 347 ff., 427.

she devoted herself to petty problems of local government and extending her empire of the mind. After the Peloponnesian War, Athens moved toward bankruptcy, contributed to by the ruinous expenses of war, numerous increasing internal drains on the treasury, and an injurious system of tax-farming. There were, however, certain periods of considerable prosperity.[38] Other momentous changes were taking place. Progressive bankruptcy of the state was paralleled by growth of personal fortunes. Agriculture never recovered from the destruction of the war. Countrymen poured into town and engaged in industry and commerce. Farm land fell into the hands of absentee owners. Citizen farmers decreased; slave labor, in some degree, took their place.[39] The gulf between rich and poor widened. Luxury supplanted simplicity in Athenian life. Population declined from the fourth century; in the second, according to Polybius, towns of Greece were desolate and the land barren. The lack of men was ascribed to a lack of children; folk wanted money and ease rather than work; wanting these, they avoided marriage; or if married, had few children.[40] Citizen-soldiers were replaced by professionals. Athletic training, once a part of the education of citizen-soldiers, became a profession, an end in itself.

POPULATION, CLASSES, AND LABOR  Though unification of Attica under Athenian leadership was accomplished by the beginning of the seventh century, economic class conflicts persisted and were a source of continual internal disorder. The constitution was "oligarchical"; the poor were "serfs of the rich" and had no "share in anything"; loans were secured by the debtor's person. Solon recognized four classes on the basis of wealth: *pentacosiomedimni* ( 500-measure men); *hippes* (knights, 300 measures); *zeugitae* (200 measures); and *thetes* (paid laborers). The political divisions at the time of Pisistratus—plainsmen, shoremen, and hillmen—were rooted in economic interests.[41] The lot of those sold into slavery for debt was improved by Solon's reforms, and the poorer citizens became more powerful as the fifth century wore on to its close. While this leveling of citizens was taking place, another cleavage in the population was developing. Attica was becoming half slave and half free.

Athens' citizen population at the time of Pericles has been estimated variously as 100,000, or even 170,000.[42] Perhaps a fifth succumbed during the Plague, whose agonies Thucydides portrayed.[43] Besides citizens there were

---

38 Aristotle: *Ath. Resp.*, 28; *Politica*, II, 7; Thucydides, VII, 28; Xenophon: *Memorabilia*, II, 7, 2; Rostovtzeff: *Social and Economic History of the Hellenistic World*, I, 95 f.; II, 628 ff., 1135 f.; III, 1329, 1354, 1604 f.; Busolt-Swoboda: *Griechische Staatskunde*, II, 1236 ff.; Glotz: *Ancient Greece at Work*, pp. 147 f.; Laistner: *op. cit.*, pp. 292 f.; Breasted: *Ancient Times*, pp. 396 f.
39 Glotz: *Ancient Greece at Work*, pp. 199, 202 f.
40 Lot: *op. cit.*, p. 67.
41 Aristotle: *Ath. Resp.*, 2, 7, 13.
42 Boeckh: *Public Economy of Athens*, pp. 36, 77; Bury: *op. cit.*, p. 408.
43 Bk. II, 47–54.

thirty or forty thousand metics (foreigners), a class that rose rapidly after the Persian War. Slavery, limited at first, increased rapidly during the fifth century. Trade and industry, requiring more laborers, purchased slaves and trained them for various specialized jobs.[44] Slaves were recruited from war captives, criminals, foundlings, and by slave raids. Athens became an important market, and her slave population may have numbered 80,000 or even 120,000.[45] Slaves were usually the property of individuals; but some were owned by the state. Their employments were mainly domestic and industrial, in mines and quarries; some were employed in agriculture.

The condition of those without citizenship (metics, freedmen, and slaves) was, in certain respects, favorable, compared with those in other Greek states. Metics were an important element at Athens. Though they seldom gained citizens' rights, were taxed heavily, could not hold real property, and were subject to war service and other burdens, they had considerable personal liberty and sometimes became prominent in Athenian affairs.[46] Slaves, too, enjoyed some consideration; in fact, they may have been better off than some "poor citizens of many an oligarchic State. . . ." [47] Xenophon [48] says they sometimes lived luxuriously, were excessively licentious, independent, and dressed just like free citizens. Aristophanes [49] refers to the shiftless servants whom the master fears to whip—at least in war. The slave could accumulate money and buy his freedom, or be freed for faithful service.

The cheapness of supplies, competition of numerous free laborers, metics, and slaves kept wages at a low level. Ordinary labor might earn six to ten cents a day; skilled artisans received as much as twenty cents.[50] Other employments were paid proportionately poorly; but musicians, actors, and hetairai were more richly rewarded.

Less is known of the condition of the poor than of the rich, whose exploits were gilded by the tongues of poets. Although in early times no citizen was so poor as to be without some trade or business, or be compelled to disgrace "the state by begging," later, particularly after the calamities of war, the poor increased in number, and a system of poor relief was instituted, with charitable institutions and free shelters supported at state expense. Public expenditures for building, in the Age of Pericles, may have been undertaken to alleviate un-

---

[44] Mahaffy: Social Life in Greece, pp. 57–62.
[45] C.A.H., v, 11; Glotz: Ancient Greece at Work, p. 198; Boeckh, op. cit., p. 77, estimated slaves in Attica at 365,000.
[46] Whibley: op. cit., pp. 435 f.; Laistner: op. cit., pp. 284 f.
[47] Glotz: Ancient Greece at Work, pp. 196 f.; St. John: History of the Manners and Customs of Ancient Greece, III, 18.
[48] Athenians, I, 10–1.
[49] Clouds, 4–6.
[50] Glotz: Ancient Greece at Work, pp. 166, 174; Boeckh: op. cit., pp. 116–23.

employment.[51] According to Aristotle, a law provided that persons having less than three *minas*, who were crippled and unable to work, were, upon public examination, to have "two obols a day from the State for their support." [52]

Conditions of labor were often bad, but self-interest of owners operated against brutal and complete neglect of workers. At the mines of Laureion, men worked in ten-hour shifts. In small shops conditions were better than in mines, but hours were longer, probably from morning light till sunset. Aristophanes pictures workers stirring at an early hour: "As soon as the cock sends forth his morning song, they all jump out of bed, blacksmiths, potters, leatherdressers, shoe-makers, bathmen, flour-dealers, lyre-turners, and shield-makers; they slip on their shoes and rush off to their work in the dark." [53] An anonymous bid for labor reform may be recognized in this plain-spoken couplet:

Six hours a day to tiresome tasks are quite enough to give.
The plain signs following after say distinctly *zethi*—live! [54]

Labor—certain types of it—was held worthy of free men. Socrates approves the smell of honest toil "which every free man loves." [55] In early times manual work was proper for a citizen. Solon sought to bring trades into good repute, and caused the Areopagus to scrutinize everyone's source of livelihood and whip the idle.[56] This view of labor and citizenship contrasted sharply with Sparta's conception. To Cleomenes, Hesiod was only the fit singer of Helots.[57] Ultimately, of course, increase of wealth and slavery encouraged idleness at Athens and undermined respect for labor. Free citizens had become only a minor element in the producing class in the fourth and fifth centuries.[58] Wealth became the measure of a man. Private gymnasia and baths,[59] as well as luxurious houses, were common appurtenances of men of fortune.[60] An Athenian audience could appreciate the speech of Jason:

For I knew
How every friend deserts the impoverished man.[61]

[51] Boeckh: op. cit., p. 486; St. John: op. cit., III, 69 f., 79, 89; Robinson: History of Greece, p. 152.
[52] Ath. Resp., 49.
[53] Glotz: Ancient Greece at Work, pp. 278 ff. Trans. by M. R. Dobie. Kegan Paul, Trench, Trübner, London, 1926.
[54] Lawton: The Soul of the Anthology, p. 128. Courtesy of Yale University Press, New Haven.
[55] Xenophon: Symposium, II, 4.
[56] Plutarch: Solon, 22.
[57] Symonds: Studies of the Greek Poets, I, 162.
[58] Laistner: op. cit., p. 285; Whibley: op. cit., p. 435.
[59] Xenophon: Athenians, II, 10.
[60] Mahaffy: op. cit., pp. 258 ff.; Breasted: op. cit., pp. 350 f.
[61] Lawton: Three Dramas of Euripides, p. 133.

Agricultural labor was in best repute, praised by poets and philosophers.[62] It escaped to some extent the debasement of slavery, which was not a very economical form of labor.[63] Hesiod, gifted singer who weaned the muse from heroes and taught her to speak of mundane matters, the struggle of the poor peasant against the crafty rich of the city, proclaimed: "Before excellence the immortal gods have placed toil and labor." [64] Idleness, not work, disgraces man. He who works is loved of gods and men. When to plow, prune, sharpen sickles, get fodder, winnow grain, cut grapes, build a house, geld boars and bulls, and other homely duties are set down. "Strip to sow and strip to plough and strip to reap" is the advice of Ascra's rustic poet; again,

> The work-deferrer never
> Sees full his barn, nor he that leaves work ever,
> And still is gadding out.[65]

All of which is good for his health and for his wealth. Centuries later, a lingering refrain of Hesiod's paean to rustic labor may be detected in old Archippos on his way to Hades:

> Sons, win your subsistence with the plough,
> And be ye faithful to the hoe, as now.[66]

Although poet and philosopher diligently extolled agricultural labor, it is evident that the rustic's lot was a hard one. Some lost their land and fell into slavery. Hesiod clearly advises that one should make the best of a hard life. His cruel Boreas, making "the old man round as a wheel," suggests a life under harsh conditions of nature; and the warning to "princes," that the deathless gods note "all those who oppress their fellows with crooked judgments," implies that tillers of the soil already felt the oppression of the landed nobles.[67]

### EDUCATION AT ATHENS

PHASES OF DEVELOPMENT   Education is the process and product of changes produced in man by the interaction of his original nature and all aspects of the environment in which he lives. The habitat of the Athenians, everyday activities, political development, relation with neighbors, class alignments and interests, traditions, and many other factors, operating informally, determined the character of Athenian society in broad outline, and constituted

[62] Aristotle: Oeconomica, I, 2; Xenophon: Oeconomicus, xv–xvi.
[63] Glotz: Ancient Greece at Work, pp. 199, 202 f., 211; St. John: op. cit., II, 273; III, 25 f.
[64] Symonds: op. cit., I, 181.
[65] Davies: Hesiod and Theognis, p. 41.
[66] Lawton: Anthology, p. 79.
[67] Jardé: op. cit., pp. 160 ff.; Bury: op. cit., p. 107.

a general frame of limitations within which education, in the more restricted scholastic sense, developed.

Athenian education, in this narrower sense, followed no single pattern. Changing conditions—social, political, economic—effected transformations in education which followed, more or less fitfully, in their wake. Broadly considered, three major periods are observable, which may be designated as Native Athenian, Transitional, and Cosmopolitan. These are not separated by cataclysmic changes; each, however, exhibits marked contrasts in respect to its central characteristics when fully matured. The Native Athenian, essentially provincial and self-sufficient, runs from earliest times (First Olympiad, 776 B.C.) to the emergence of Athens after the Persian War (479 B.C.) as empire-builder, center of wealth and commerce, rich in tributary cities, whirlpool of political changes, patron of arts, science, and philosophy. The Transition, a period of marked changes (notably, an increased stress on individual freedom, modification of institutions, decline of moral standards, and the emergence of critical educational philosophy), is clearly distinguishable by the middle of the fifth century, and continues till the end of Athenian national greatness and the success of Macedonia at Chaeronaea (338 B.C.). Tendencies of the Transition prepared the way for, and survived to some extent in, a Cosmopolitan epoch (338 B.C. to 529 A.D.) distinguished by the disappearance of state service as the *leitmotif* of education, and preoccupation with philosophical speculation and literary attainments. Athens became a cultural Mecca, looked to longingly by intellectuals, and visited by all who could afford the luxury of foreign study. Macedon and Rome made obeisance to her intellectual dominion, later shared with Alexandria. Christendom, too, despite fitful fluctuations in respect to views of pagan letters and philosophy, stood in her debt, and tolerated the existence of pagan institutions of learning till 529 A.D.

CHANGING VIEWS OF ATHENIAN CULTURE   Prior to 1870, it was customary to think of Greek civilization as a sudden development, a unique cataclysmic phenomenon of human history. Thanks to numerous discoveries since Schliemann and Evans began their work, this view has changed somewhat, and we see Athenian intellectual and aesthetic achievements, not as a meteor flashing through the sky, but as the maturing culture of a people that owed much to other climes and times.[68] With the gradual subsidence of this view, the "glory that was Greece," though glorious indeed, tends more and more to appear as a normal, accountable phase of social evolution.

The phenomenal interpretation, which offered startling contrasts between Greek society and others, was so universally and persuasively set forth as to gain general acceptance. Felton wrote: "The orient . . . required a thousand

68 Hyde: "The Religion of Greece," in Montgomery, *Religions of the Past and Present*, p. 257.

years for what Greece accomplished in a century." [69] It is true that Athens made rapid progress "in a century," but it is equally clear now that back of that development lay thousands of years of social evolution. To Hegel, Greece was "a point of light in history." If one look to a certain class at Athens, and to superior elements in that class at a certain period, the view is sustained; but other Greek states, and Athens, too, prior to the Enlightenment, scarcely shone with more brilliance than many other peoples at similar periods of development. Some observers found an "instinct" for knowledge, truth, and beauty in the "Greeks," and held that they were "first smitten with the passion for truth." [70] Aristotle, however, accorded priority in intellectual inquiry, mathematics, and science, to the priests of Egypt.[71] Most modern histories of education, written in accord with the cataclysmic interpretation of Greek history, took little or no notice of preceding developments as relatively unimportant. Drever thought the Greek, "as compared with other races, was imaginative, intensely intellectual, endowed with a fine sense of proportion, harmony, and restraint, and intensely 'human,' to use a term . . . to describe what was probably most characteristic of all. . . ." [72] What of Hindu, Chinese, Hebrew, Egyptian intellect, imagination, and "humanity"? William T. Harris declared: "In the beginning Greece is only aesthetic, worshipping beautiful individualities, the gods of Olympus. From the beginning it prizes its athletic games as a sort of worship of the beautiful by realizing gracefulness and physical freedom in the body." [73] Apart from the question whether the gods were always "beautiful individualities," this view of athletics stresses too exclusively aesthetic appreciation of the athlete, and appears to overlook the utilitarian military purpose which physical training served at Athens—not to mention the more strictly military ends of Sparta. War was a brutal, bloody business, "conducted without mercy" by Greek cities as well as by "barbarians," [74] and education was used to prepare mind as well as body for it. Isocrates maintained that even Homer had been given such a great place in education so that his constant praise of heroic fighters might stir up later generations to emulate them.[75]

Much stress has been laid on the view that Greek education was unaffected by caste, which so permeated Oriental society.[76] While no one would maintain that social cleavages in the Orient and in Greece meant precisely the same thing, the social stratification of freemen, noncitizens, and slaves should not

[69] Ancient and Modern Greece, I, 417.
[70] Butcher: Some Aspects of the Greek Genius, pp. 1 f.
[71] Metaphysica, I, 1.
[72] Drever: Greek Education, p. 9.
[73] Preface, Davidson's Education of the Greek People, p. viii.
[74] Jardé: op. cit., pp. 259 f.
[75] Panegyricus, 159.
[76] Felton: op. cit., I, 417.

be forgotten when speaking of Athenian education. As for Sparta, we have seen how meticulously the Spartiates trained themselves so as to maintain their power, and denied education to the conquered. Even the greatest of Athenian philosophers were unable to transcend, in theory, these class limitations of Greek experience and tradition. The Hellenic horizon was also restricted in regard to cultural potentialities of neighboring peoples and of women. Athenian education reveals an exalted self-esteem and contempt for neighbors, a "narrowness" and "exclusiveness," not only toward "barbarians," but often toward other Greek cities as well.[77] In regard to the intellect of women, Athens was normal rather than phenomenal; for, in practice (notwithstanding Plato's divergence), Athenian wives and daughters were about on a plane with those of many Oriental societies.

Far from underestimating the importance of Athenian education, the foregoing only serves to call attention to certain limitations of it; and emphasizes the fact that it was not inhumanly perfect, destitute of connection with ordinary social purposes, or completely out of harmony with educational development in the rest of the ancient world, as the phenomenal interpretation of Greek culture led many to believe.

CENTRAL TENDENCIES OF ATHENIAN EDUCATION    Certain central tendencies in Athenian education are observable in earliest practice and, though modified by social changes, color later theory: the ideal of state service; the harmony of mental, physical, aesthetic, and moral development; the cleavage between liberal education for those who could enjoy leisure and practical training for those compelled to do "ignoble" work.

Emphasis on service to the state permeated Athenian education as the norm of practice until the defeat of her political aspirations, and then was continued as an ideal. This was by no means narrow: it included the training of mind, body, moral integrity, and fidelity to the gods. Though one need not take Pericles at face value when he extols the virtues of Athenian life and contrasts them with the faults of others, there is persuasiveness in his assertion that the Athenian does not neglect public affairs because he takes care of private business; and that those so employed also have "a very fair idea of politics." The state they have created, he would have us believe, is proof of the excellence of the Athenian system, for it excels even the fairest reports of it when put to a severe test. For such a city men died; and all who live should be glad to labor in her service.[78] Individual life and happiness were as nothing compared with the supreme end, service to the state. Fidelity to the city, defense of temples and public property, obedience to laws and magistrates, and honor to the religion of their fathers were promised on oath by the ephebi. The ideal of indi-

[77] Mahaffy: op. cit., pp. 342 ff.
[78] Thucydides, II, 40–1.

vidual sacrifice, that the state might live, approximated the religious devotion and ascetic self-denial of a later age. Athenians served their city, as did the Spartans; the central difference lay in their conception of discipline that was to prepare them for such service.

Historian, philosopher, and statesman joined in praising early Athenian education for national ends. The comic poet, too, a critic of foibles of the Transition and joker at its expense, drew, in retrospect, a picture of sturdy excellence of body, moral integrity, and modesty that once prevailed. With an eye on his audience, Aristophanes tells again and again of the old fighting patriotism:

> Mine was then a life of glory,
> Never craven fear came o'er me
> Every foeman quailed before me
> As across the merry waters,
> Fast the eager galleys bore me.

What profit was there in such patriotic training? The answer is:

> Therefore we did batter down
> Many a hostile Median town.
> And 'twas we who for the nation
> Gathered in the tribute pay. . . .[79]

Aristophanes' weaklings were products of the watery, new education, whereas his stalwart heroes were—

Trained in music and palaestra, freemen's choirs and freemen's games.[80]

This "discipline rare," which once flourished at Athens, was always modest and decent, cultivated respectful concern for elders, stressed simple clothing and food, and employed the old music and manly exercises. This good old discipline, which taught "heroes of old to be hardy and bold," can even now be restored. If it is, the result will be as of yore:

> Your chest shall be white, your skin shall be bright,
> Your arms shall be tight, your tongue shall be slight,
> And everything else shall be proper and right.[81]

State-centered education was weakening at the Transition. All things were "just ready to burst with liberty," as Plato said; even horses and donkeys walked in the streets like freemen! It was hard for heirs to wealth and goodly names

[79] Aristophanes: Wasps, 1091–9. Trans. by B. B. Rogers. The Loeb Classical Library. Quoted by permission of Harvard University Press, Cambridge, Mass.
[80] Aristophanes: The Frogs (Murray), p. 56.
[81] Aristophanes: Clouds, 1009–14. Trans. by B. B. Rogers. The Loeb Classical Library. Quoted by permission of Harvard University Press, Cambridge, Mass.

to continue that self-denial and simplicity which had marked provincial Attic society. It was impossible, apparently, for the greatly increased body of citizens, the democracy of which Pericles boasts, to attain to the standards which an aristocracy had prized. After the Transition, social and economic changes combined with the waning of political power to weaken further and finally destroy the *raison d'être* of state education. Palaestra and gymnasium became centers of training for professional athletes instead of citizen-soldiers; and an intellectualism, individualistic rather than socially centered, ultimately supplanted the physical, moral, and aesthetic training of the earlier age.

A second ideal of Athenian education, a "balance of moral, mental, physical, and aesthetic development," gave a breadth to the state-centered training of citizens that differentiated it significantly from the citizen-training of Lacedaemon. The Athenian, like the Spartan, would be a soldier, but something more. Athenians owed much to the freer, more varied character of their institutions, which sought to liberate, rather than simply mold all in comformity with a rigid, narrow pattern. Plato portrayed this many-sided education: the discipline of the family; the music school for harmony and rhythm; gymnastic training, to make the body a fit servant of the mind, and to incline men to valor; and a study of the laws, to acquaint them with the requirements of social life.[82] Due allowance must be made, of course, for the fact that the authors of this ideal formulation and of others, were, by virtue of their own education, scarcely qualified as unbiased judges. The degree of success achieved in harmonizing aesthetic, intellectual, physical, and moral elements must be judged by the results. If, as Thucydides reported Pericles' view, Athenians did indeed enjoy what they themselves produced, and also what came from others; if they relished a degree of leisure unknown amid the laborious toil of Lacedaemon; if their devotion to public affairs did not preclude those of private life; if love of physical excellence was joined with an equal delight in the creations of the mind; and if many were, in fact, "qualified for the most varied kinds of action" —a "graceful versatility"—such an achievement deserves acclaim.[83] "Moderation in all things," "of nothing too much"—these philosophic formulae well express the ideal aimed at with some success, for a time, at Athens. "Man was a whole to the Hellenes," Freeman wrote, "and one part of him could not be sound if the other parts were not." [84] Though too inclusive as given, since not all Greeks understood or achieved it, the statement may properly be taken as an epitome of the cultural ideal of Athenian citizens at their best.

A third tendency of Athenian education, the cleavage between liberal education and utilitarian training, existed to some extent even in early days, and

[82] *Protagoras*, 325–6.
[83] *Thucydides*, II, 38–42.
[84] *Schools of Hellas*, pp. 279 f.

grew with the deepening differentiation of economic status. Solon's law, which required a father to teach his son a trade, was designed to keep an increasing population from idleness, stimulate trade, and supplement insufficient products of Attic agriculture.[85] As time went on, however, the widening gulf between rich and poor, absentee ownership, the prevalence of slave labor, and specialization in industry brought manual labor into disrepute. It became increasingly the lot of those outside the ranks of citizenship and of those citizens who were unable to escape from the laborious tasks which poverty imposed. The law of Solon became of no avail. Training for mechanical jobs came to be regarded as unworthy, servile, though philosophers continued to praise agriculture as worthy of free men. Liberal training itself, which theoretically, at least, was the lot of all freeborn youth—fitting them for the duties of their station—was in practice proportional to the economic status of the family. Plato says of it: "This is what is done by those who have the means, and those who have the means are the rich; their children begin to go to school soonest and leave off latest." [86] Demosthenes contrasts education of the rich and of the poor: "I then, Aeschines, had the advantage as a boy of attending the schools which became my position, and of possessing as much as one who is to do nothing ignoble owing to poverty must possess." But "you [Aeschines] . . . what has been your fortune when compared with this?—the fortune, thanks to which you were brought up as a boy in the depths of indigence, in close attendance upon the school along with your father, pounding up the ink, sponging down the forms, sweeping the attendants' room, occupying the position of a menial, not of a free-born boy! . . ." [87]

Philosophers stressed the principle of cleavage between liberal education and practical training which had been developing as a concomitant of the differentiation between upper and lower economic strata. "To be always seeking after the useful does not become free and exalted souls," says Aristotle.[88] Plato, too, praised arithmetic "if pursued in the spirit of a philosopher, not of a shopkeeper." [89] The theory of liberal studies was applicable to an economic class that could afford the leisure and employ the means; without them such culture could not be attained. Σχολή (leisure) came to mean school. Both implied wealth. The sausage-seller, lowly in origin, trained in the agora, knew nothing beyond his letters—and of them little "and that badly." [90] The rest of the

85 Plutarch: Solon, 22.
86 Protagoras, 326. From The Works of Plato, translated and edited by Benjamin Jowett (Oxford University Press).
87 On the Crown, 257–8. From The Public Orations of Demosthenes, translated by A. W. Pickard-Cambridge (The Clarendon Press); Bryant: "Boyhood and Youth in the Days of Aristophanes," Harvard Studies in Class. Philol., xviii, 108.
88 Politica, viii, 3.
89 Republic, vii, 525.
90 Aristophanes: The Knights, 188–9.

laborious crew that toiled long hours [91] probably fared no better in the culture of the mind.

INSTITUTIONS

Women and education of the home  The earliest education of children was conditioned by the status of women at Athens, which bordered upon Oriental seclusion. Women did not participate in the intellectual, social, or political life of men; they were completely lacking in independence—perpetual minors.[92] Though they took part in religious celebrations, attended tragic performances in the theater (but not comedies), went shopping occasionally, and, if unmarried, marched in the Panathenian Procession, they were neither permitted to attend the banquets of men nor to view the greatest athletic festival held at Olympia.[93] Widely divergent generalizations have been made, nevertheless, anent woman's sphere. Lawton concluded that "woman was to them an inferior, indispensable indeed, but only as the bearer of the man-child. The wife was not even a sharer in the lighter diversions of men. To the banquet came only the despised flute-players and dancing-girls, the playthings and the property of men. The true social club was the gymnasium or youths' palaestra: and here nothing feminine appeared at all." [94] Felton, recognizing that "purity of manners," "wise administration of the house," and "quiet and modest demeanor" were the chief female virtues at Athens, and that women were not as prominent as in Dorian communities, judged them "happy, respectable, and powerful in the sphere of domestic life"; their education, though not intellectual, imbued their minds "with the spirit of the national poetry, religion, and even the fine arts"; while "experience of life" prepared them to be the wise companions of men.[95]

Numerous poetic allusions reflect popular ideas concerning women, and harmonize with what is known of their actual social status. The Greek, like the Hebrew, traced man's infelicity and his inglorious fall to woman, Pandora. To this "beauteous evil" Zeus and his divine assistants gave wiles, beauty, desire, skill in domestic work, and a canine mind.[96] Yet Hesiod admits that there is "no nobler prize than a woman, if she be good . . ."; and, again, "nought else worse than a bad one." "Buy thou a woman, not wed her, that she may follow the oxen," [97] is his utilitarian advice; a house, an ox, and a woman appear to be

91 Glotz: Ancient Greece at Work, p. 278.
92 Becker: Charicles, p. 464; Woody: "The Fair Sex in Greek Society," Research Quarterly, x, 62–71.
93 Philostratos: Concerning Gymnastics, 17; Wright, F. A.: Greek Athletics, p. 25; Mahaffy: op. cit., p. 325.
94 Lawton: Classical Greek Literature, p. 148; Whibley: op. cit., p. 520.
95 Felton: op. cit., I, 432 f.
96 Hesiod: Works and Days, 60–105; Symonds: op. cit., I, 168 f.
97 Lawton: Greek Literature, p. 64; Successors of Homer, pp. 66 f.

on the same plane.[98] Simonides seems to have been faithful to the Hesiodic pattern in his cynical classification of female nature as like mud, salt water, swine, fox, dog, donkey, weasel, mare, and monkey; only a few are like bees, capable and industrious.[99] Woman's sphere was in the home. "I hate the gadding woman," says Theognis. With evident concern a visitor inquires of the husband whose wife has gone out of the house: "Great Zeus! What has she to do out?" In Syracuse, a law forbade a free matron to go abroad after sunset, lest she thereby confess herself an adulteress; in daytime, she must be accompanied by one maid, at least, and have permission of the Supervisor of Women.[100] Solon's law was to the same effect.[101] "Tis hard, you know, for women to get out," says Calonice, for one must mind a husband, another wake her servant. This one must put the child to sleep, that one wash him, and another "give him pap." [102]

Marriage was generally arranged by parents for reasons of convenience. The best marriageable age for girls was from sixteen to twenty, though marriage was often earlier. Divorce was easy for men and, under certain circumstances, compulsory. For women it was more difficult and less common, though for unfaithfulness and harsh treatment, they could leave their husbands and return with their property to the care of their fathers or nearest male relatives.[103]

The work of women varied with the times. In Homeric society women of noble birth served in many capacities. Washing, baking, grinding, weaving, and embroidery were among their employments. Penelope wove all day and unraveled her web at night. For the rustic family, Hesiod set a day for weaving:

> On this let careful woman's nimble hand
> Throw first the shuttle and the web expand.[104]

In later times, women of rich families depended on slaves or servants for most of the work of their sphere. In this domestic domain their power was rather complete, though Xenophon would have them instructed at marriage by their husbands.[105] In turn, they became the instructors of their children, the boys till ready for the palaestra, the girls until marriage. Training for any profession was rare, certainly, though Agnodice is said to have contrived by stealth

---

98 Works and Days, 405.
99 Symonds: op. cit., I, 281 ff.; Lawton: Greek Literature, pp. 101 f.; Wright, F. A.: Greek Social Life, pp. 19 ff.
100 Athenaeus, XII, 521.
101 Plutarch: Solon, 21.
102 Aristophanes: Lysistrata, 15–9.
103 Blümner: op. cit., pp. 134 ff.; Becker: op. cit., p. 473; St. John: op. cit., II, 4; Gulick: op. cit., chap. 9; Hesiod: Works and Days, 695–705; Whibley: op. cit., pp. 519 f.
104 Davies: Hesiod and Theognis, p. 53; Glotz: Ancient Greece at Work, pp. 15 f.
105 Oeconomicus, VII, 4–43; Woody: A History of Women's Education, I, 10 ff.; St. John: op. cit., II, 35.

to get a knowledge of medicine, built up a practice, and helped open the practice of midwifery to women at Athens.[106] The profession of skilled entertainers —musicians, jugglers, dancers, acrobats—seems alone to have been open to girls, but to those of a different social order.

How did women regard their lot? Most of them doubtless accepted it as a natural condition; but others, in the course of time, probably fretted at subjection. Economic changes that gave greater freedom to some women, the decay of patriarchal society, the views disseminated by certain philosophers, and the experience of intellectual opportunity on the part of a few women must have aroused serious concern as well as ridicule. There did indeed occur "a general stir about the position of women." [107] There is a conscious, pointed lament, if not a note of revolt, in *Tereus*: "We women are nothing—happy indeed is our • childhood, for *then* we are thoughtless; but when we attain maidenhood, lo! we are driven away from our homes, sold as merchandise, and compelled to marry and say 'All's well.' " [108] *Medea* echoes:

> Of all created things endowed with soul
> And sense, we women are the wretchedest.[109]

It seems certain that *Lysistrata* and the *Ecclesiazusae*, which ridicule the notion of woman's independence, must have owed their popularity to the existence of an audience well-acquainted with the disturbing question.

Though certain women at Athens became educated, few became famous. Lesbos produced a Sappho; Thebes, an Erinna and Corrinna; Diotima, Socrates says, taught him the "theory of love"; Aspasia of Miletus, concubine and wife of Pericles, drew a brilliant circle of men and women around her and is said to have taught Socrates rhetoric.[110] Pericles, however, although he delighted in her, seems to have held to the old Athenian ideal. In any case, Thucydides puts in his mouth praise of those women least spoken of, whether "for good or for evil among men." [111]

Education of an Athenian child to the end of the sixth year was in the home, in care of the mother, or of a nurse, usually a slave. The newborn was washed in tepid water and oil, and wrapped in swaddling clothes. On the fifth or the seventh day the Amphidromia was celebrated, the child was carried around the hearth, and the door was decorated with an olive wreath for a boy or a fillet of wool for a girl—provided the father, in whose hands lay the sole right of expo-

---

[106] St. John: *op. cit.*, i, 115; Abbott: *Society and Politics in Ancient Rome*, pp. 78 f.
[107] Mahaffy: *op. cit.*, pp. 274, 283.
[108] Davis: *op. cit.*, p. 36. From W. S. Davis, *A Day in Old Athens*, Allyn and Bacon, Boston, 1914.
[109] Lawton: *Three Dramas of Euripides*, p. 119.
[110] C.A.H., v, 389; St. John: *op. cit.*, ii, 43.
[111] Bk. ii, 45.

sure, authorized by law at Athens, had not decided, for one reason or another, to do away with the child.[112] On the tenth day family and friends joined in a happy festival, offered gifts to the child, and gave it a name. Exposure, when practiced, probably fell most heavily on females, the illegitimate, and the deformed. Economic factors were doubtless often decisive. Athenian families wanted children, but not too many. Numerous divisions of family wealth might be disastrous.

In poor or modestly situated families, mothers nursed their children, but wet nurses were commonly employed by the wealthy. Lacedaemonian women were in demand,[113] for they had a reputation for ability to manage children and form modest manners.[114] The day of aloofness to childish demands for attention had not yet come in Athens. Nurse or mother handled and dandled, sang, and told stories of "once upon a time" to engage the infant mind. Though philosophers disapproved of it,[115] stories of spirits, the "evil eye," the princess who ate children, and other bugaboos—as well as heroic legends of a past as old as the race itself—were related to wheedle or frighten infants into being "good." Proper behavior was secured by appeal to the slipper or more painful agencies, if necessary, for in the Athenian family it was axiomatic that manners make the man.

In spite of reliance on fright and corporal punishment, despite the cruelty of infanticide, there was a marked warmth of parental affection in the Athenian household, and parting brought deepest sorrow. Love and heartbreak at the death of a little son are poignantly set forth in Zonas' "Appeal to Charon":

> When the child of Kinyras stands
> At the ladder, extend thy hands,
> O Charon gloomy of face,
> And set him in his place.
> He slips in the sandal-bands:
> And across those pebbly sands,
> Barefoot, he fears to go.[116]

Besides physical care and moral, mental, and aesthetic influence of mothers and nurses, home education included numerous playthings and games which provided release of natural drives to activity. Most of them were similar to those of the present day. Pollux mentions a host of games, many of which were played by children, others engaged in by boys of school age. Grasberger has

---

[112] Becker: op. cit., pp. 217 ff.; Blümner: op. cit., pp. 78 ff.; St. John: op. cit., I, 118 ff.
[113] Plutarch: Alcibiades, 1.
[114] St. John: op. cit., I, 134 f.
[115] Plato: Laws, x, 887.
[116] Lawton: Anthology, p. 45.

A GIRL SWINGING
(Courtesy, The Metropolitan Museum of Art, New York)

classified the distinctly physical games (other than genuine gymnastics) according to their emphasis on hopping and jumping, running or catching, aiming and throwing.[117] The child's rattle (credited to Archytas), gocarts, whips, tops, hoops for rolling, whirligigs, kites, hobbyhorses, swings, seesaws, carved animals, swords, shields, bows and arrows, were all popular. Pets—dogs, goats, geese, ducks, monkeys, cocks—enlivened the scenes of play. Numerous games with balls, blindman's buff, hide-and-seek, knucklebones, *mora*, tug of war, duck and drake, tossing and spinning coins, running, jumping, skipping the rope, standing or hopping on a greased skin filled with liquid, shooting beans or pebbles, walking on stilts, tossing in a blanket, cockfighting, leapfrog, flying a beetle with a thread, guess-who-hit-you—all these appear to have been popular tests of fleetness, accuracy, poise, strength, and cunning. Of all games the many types of ball-playing were probably most favored.[118] Though little is known of the manner of play, the few hints given by ancient authors point to simplicity. There is much truth in the saying that "the Greeks danced everywhere and on any pretext." [119] Of the host of dances mentioned by Athenaeus [120] and others, some were perhaps learned informally by children at an early age, though special training would be given later to select groups.[121]

Among the clever feats, enjoyed by boys and girls and adults also, was a game played with five pebbles (πεντάλιθα), which were tossed from the palm of the hand and caught on the back of it.[122] Games of skill and calculation, such as *kottabos*, *khalkismos*, and *polis* or *petteia* (somewhat like checkers or chess), though commonly played by adults, doubtless found precocious imitators among children.[123]

The education of girls was carried on, as a rule, only in the household, and was limited to what mothers and nurses were able to convey, although Teos is named as an exception, where girls attended school with the boys.[124] Dancing and perhaps music were permitted for some girls in well-to-do families. A few seem to have known how to read and write; but modest behavior and some acquaintance with mythology and heroic tales, joined with practical knowledge

---

[117] *Erziehung und Unterricht im Klassischen Altertum*, I, 28–98; Pollux: *Onomasticon*, IX, 101 *et seq.; passim.*
[118] *Pollux*, IX, 103–7; Grasberger: *op. cit.*, I, 84–96.
[119] Vuillier: *History of Dancing*, p. 7.
[120] Bk. XIV, 628–31.
[121] Ussing: *Darstellung des Erziehungs-und Unterrichtswesens bei den Griechen und Römern*, pp. 58–64; Baumeister: *Denkmäler des Klassischen Altertums*, II, 778 ff.; Richter: *Spiele der Griechen und Römer*, chap. 1; Becker: *op. cit.*, pp. 222 ff.; Plummer: "Toys and Games for Children among the Ancient Hellenes," *Am. Phys. Educ. Rev.*, III, 157–69; Fuld: "Physical Education in Greece and Rome," *Am. Phys. Educ. Rev.*, XII, 2 ff.; Blümner: *op. cit.*, pp. 89–97.
[122] *Pollux*, IX, 126.
[123] Athenaeus, I, 16–7; XV, 666–7; Becker: *op. cit.*, pp. 349–55.
[124] Whibley: *op. cit.*, p. 505.

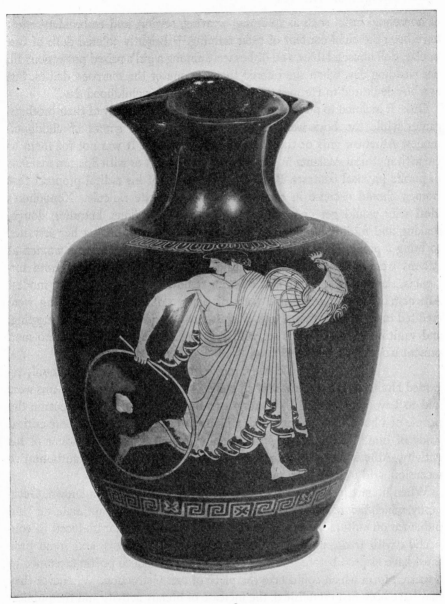

A YOUTH WITH HOOP AND COCK   C. 470–460 B.C.
(Courtesy, The Metropolitan Museum of Art, New York)

of household tasks, such as spinning, weaving, sewing, and embroidery, must have been the chief content of their training.[125] Brightly colored dolls of wax or clay, doll houses, tables, and dishes were among a girl's prized possessions till her wedding day, when she offered them to one of the marriage deities, just as a boy dedicated to Hermes the "companions of his childhood day."

Girls, if inclined to physical activity, no doubt shared many of their brothers' games while the boys were small. But beyond these games of childhood modest Athenian girls of the citizen-class did not go. It was not for them to vie with mythical Atalanta in hunting and running [126] or with Spartan maidens in public physical contests. Plato [127] recognized that his radical proposal that women should exercise in the palaestra would excite ridicule. Xenophon's ideal wife would get enough exercise from mixing flour, kneading dough, shaking and folding clothes, and walking about superintending her servants, to bring a proper glow to her cheeks and give her health.[128] Some women at Athens were expertly trained physically, but they were recruited from foreigners, slaves, and *hetairai*, and were far removed from the circle of modest Athenian women. Remarkable feats of poise, skill, grace, and daring were credited to these professional folk. Socrates marveled at their dancing, juggling, and vaulting through hoops set with bristling swords—a feat which no man present would have risked.[129]

*Exercise for the body; music for the soul* Greeks commonly regarded Homer as "the educator of all Hellas." In some dim past his poems were said to have been carried by Lycurgus to Sparta.[130] The Greeks became the people of a book, first, by committing Homer to memory, later by more critical study of him. Though seven cities, chiefly Ionian, dispute the honor of his nativity, Athens seems first to have subjected his poetry to an authoritative recension, said to have been made under Pisistratus.[131]

When literary institutions for youth first arose at Athens is unknown. Geography, which favored the development of her commerce, had ultimately a kind influence on cultural affairs as well. Letters, probably first introduced in connection with trade, must have preceded systematic schools; and some time must have elapsed before letters were employed to reduce poetic utterance to a written form which could take the place of oral instruction. Whenever they may have been first established, the increase of literary activity and the publica-

[125] Xenophon: Oeconomicus, VII, 4–43; Becker: op. cit., p. 465; Blümner: op. cit., p. 129.
[126] Ovid: Metamorphoses, VIII, 329 et seq.; x, 560 et seq.
[127] Republic, v, 457.
[128] Oeconomicus, x, 10–1.
[129] Xenophon: Symposium, II, 8–11; Becker: op. cit., pp. 101 ff.; Hermann: Lehrbuch der Griechischen Privatalterthümer, p. 503; Baumeister: Denkmäler, I, 249, 585.
[130] Plutarch: Lycurgus, 4.
[131] Wright, W. C.: A Short History of Greek Literature, pp. 22 f.

WOMEN LAYING AWAY CLOTHES   by *Douris*, c. 470 B.C.
(Courtesy, The Metropolitan Museum of Art, New York)

tion of laws in the seventh and sixth centuries imply the existence of some
sort of formal instruction. Schools may well have originated in the Ionian
islands where literary activity first became common. Herodotus [132] refers to a
school of 120 boys at Chios about 494 B.C. Pausanias [133] mentions one at
Astypalaea, a little earlier, with about sixty boys. Tyrtaeus (c. 640 B.C.), who
encouraged the Spartans with his heroic strains, was said, on dubious authority,
to have been a lame schoolmaster from Athens.[134] The laws attributed to
Solon, if the record be true, show the existence of schools, and imply a public

[132] Bk. VI, 27.
[133] *Description of Greece*, VI, 9, 6.
[134] Wright, W. C.: *op. cit.*, p. 74.

interest in them sufficient to demand some public regulation. Teachers of boys were required to open their schoolrooms not before sunrise and close them before sunset. No persons older than the boys were allowed to enter the school while pupils were present—except the teacher's son, brother, or daughter's husband—on pain of death. Places of exercise were also safeguarded. Superintendents of gymnasia were, under no condition, to allow persons who had reached the age of manhood to enter contests of Hermes along with boys. A gymnasiarch who failed in this respect was subject to the penalties fixed by law for seducing freeborn youth. Moreover, every choregus, appointed by the people, was to be over forty years of age.[135]

A balance of mental and physical education was sought at Athens. The palaestra (παλαίστρα, wrestling place) and the music school (διδασκαλειον, place of instruction) were to give that training in music and literature for the soul and exercise for the body which was thought essential for freeborn youth. At his seventh year a boy was permitted to enter school; he might continue there a long or a short period, depending on the wealth and wishes of his parents, up to the age of fifteen or sixteen.[136] Both palaestra and music school were private institutions, though Troezen is said to have provided Athenian refugees with free education.[137] They were not compulsory in the present sense of the term, though Plato [138] says that the laws required the father to have his sons taught music and gymnastic; and a law, credited to Solon, required all boys to learn to swim and to know their letters. Enforcement of the laws regarding safeguards of morals was under the jurisdiction of the Areopagus until its powers were curtailed, and the laws themselves fell into neglect.[139]

The laws did not create state schools, but they probably proved a stimulus to private masters. Many teachers, perhaps most of them, came from cities other than Athens. Schools differed in quality according to the character and attainments of their proprietor-masters. Fees varied likewise, but were low in all elementary schools; this, and the fact that foreigners and slaves were so commonly engaged in teaching, caused it to be regarded as a low, menial occupation. Demosthenes taunted Aeschines: your father was a slave in an elementary school and "wore shackles and a wooden halter"; "you taught letters; I attended school." [140] The poverty and servile status of schoolmasters were proverbial. Lucian portrayed the great folk of this world as so reduced in circumstances in

[135] Aeschines: Timarchus, 9–12.
[136] Becker: op. cit., p. 234; Whibley: op. cit., p. 510; Forbes: Greek Physical Education, p. 82.
[137] Plutarch: Themistocles, 10; Herodotus, VIII, 41; Boeckh: op. cit., p. 121.
[138] Crito, 50.
[139] Whibley: op. cit., p. 504; Becker: op. cit., pp. 228 f.
[140] On the Crown, 129, 265.

Hades that they must either sell fish or teach letters for a living, insulted by everyone like worthless slaves.[141]

When a son of good Athenian family went to school or to the gymnasium, he was in charge of a *paidagogos*, a slave who was perhaps worthless for other work, yet of as good character and manners as could be obtained by the parents. Solon thought the office of *paidagogos* important enough to receive attention in his laws.[142] His duties were to oversee the boy's behavior, habits of eating, dressing, walking, attitude toward elders, relation with lovers, and to punish him if necessary,[143] so as to further in every way that modest behavior which parents had sought to form in the household. The *paidagogos* carried his charge's books, musical instruments, and whatever was needful at the palaestra or the music school, and either remained there or returned thither to bring him home again.

The schoolmaster's domain was probably extremely simple, as a rule, though the room or portico of more "respectable" masters was well furnished. A high-backed chair for the teacher, low stools or benches for pupils, a reading stand, manuscripts, tablets, stylus, ferules, lyres, flutes, instrument cases, and the master's rod or strap are among the equipment generally mentioned or depicted in artistic remains. Decoration, simple in the extreme, was provided by representations of Apollo and the Muses; statues of Hermes adorned the places of physical exercise. A degree of informality was the rule: pets brought to school might be looked after by the *paidagogos*, while the boy had his turn with the master.[144]

School discipline was probably severe; some hold that it was "lax," however, since the social inferiority of the master would permit him to use little "real authority." Freeborn youth, with the prestige of breeding and perhaps of wealth behind them, would doubtless be contemptuous of the poor, ignoble, sometimes incompetent teacher, possibly incapacitated by age or other infirmity.[145] It seems fair to assume, however, that boys had respect for the rod and cat-o'-nine-tails in the hands of a competent person. Plato states that if a boy does not obey, "he is straightened by threats and blows, like a piece of warped wood." [146] The savagery of Lamprikos, who, at the mother's request, beats his pupil till "he's as mottled as a water snake" (while it may be some-

141 Menippus, 17.
142 Aeschines: *Timarchus*, 10.
143 Plato: *Protagoras*, 325–6; *Lysis*, 208; Xenophon: *Constitution of the Lacedaemonians*, II, 1.
144 Gerhard: *Auserlesene Griechische Vasenbilder*, Pt. IV, Plates CCLXXVI, CCLXXVIII–CCLXXIX.
145 Bryant: *op. cit.*, *loc. cit.*, XVIII, 109; Wright, F. A.: *Greek Athletics*, p. 71; Becker: *op. cit.*, p. 229.
146 *Protagoras*, 325. From *The Works of Plato*, translated and edited by Benjamin Jowett (Oxford University Press).

what discounted), is probably not sheer fantasy, but in keeping with measures sometimes used in Athenian schools. Freeman [147] holds, however, that the reference to "gags and fetters" could not hold true for Athenian schools. A "Schoolmaster's Valedictory" which makes reference to—

> The ferule that beside him lay
> Wherewith boys' silly heads to tap,
> His skull-cap, slippers, leathern strap . . .[148]

doubtless gives proper prominence to the "emblems of his trade," whether Callon taught at Athens or elsewhere in the Hellenic world where the cult of letters had made its way. Mahaffy [149] says there were "no eloquent protests against corporal punishment" among the Greeks. Plato, however, set forth the doctrine that one should ". . . not use compulsion, but let early education be a sort of amusement . . ."; and that ". . . knowledge which is acquired under compulsion obtains no hold on the mind." [150] Life changed, of course, and school discipline likewise. Those who tend to credit all changes in pedagogical mores to the influence of doctrines would, perhaps, trace the impudence of the schoolboy who will suffer no punishment but, himself, beats the tutor's head with a writing tablet [151] to the "soft" pedagogy of Plato's times.

Plato's Protagoras gives an account of what music school and palaestra sought to accomplish: "At a later stage they send him to teachers, and enjoin them to see to his manners even more than to his reading and music; and the teachers do as they are desired. And when the boy has learned his letters and is beginning to understand what is written, as before he understood only what was spoken, they put into his hands the works of great poets, which he reads at school; in these are contained many admonitions, and many tales, and praises, and encomia of ancient famous men, which he is required to learn by heart, in order that he may imitate or emulate them and desire to become like them. Then, again, the teachers of the lyre take similar care that their young disciple is temperate and gets into no mischief; and when they have taught him the use of the lyre, they introduce him to the poems of other excellent poets, who are the lyric poets; and these they set to music, and make their harmonies and rhythms quite familiar to the children, in order that they may learn to be more gentle, and harmonious, and rhythmical, and so more fitted for speech and action; for the life of man in every part has need of harmony and rhythm. Then they send them to the master of gymnastic, in order that their bodies may

---

[147] Op. cit., p. 98.
[148] Lawton: Anthology, p. 81. Courtesy of Yale University Press, New Haven.
[149] Old Greek Education, p. 39.
[150] Republic, VII, 536. From The Works of Plato, translated and edited by Benjamin Jowett (Oxford University Press).
[151] Plautus: The Two Bacchises, 438–49.

better minister to the virtuous mind, and that the weakness of their bodies may not force them to play the coward in war or on any other occasion. This is what is done by those who have the means, and those who have the means are the rich; their children begin education soonest and leave off latest. When they have done with masters, the state again compels them to learn the laws, and live after the pattern which they furnish, and not after their own fancies; and just as in learning to write, the writing-master first draws lines with a style for the use of the young beginner, and gives him the tablet and makes him follow the lines, so the city draws the laws, which were the invention of good law-givers who were of old time; these are given to the young man, in order to guide him in his conduct whether as ruler or ruled; and he who transgresses them is to be corrected, or, in other words, called to account, which is a term used not only in your country, but also in many others." [152]

Education stressed conduct, letters, literature and music, gymnastic exercises and games. The place of arithmetic in schools is open to doubt, and has been variously represented. The citharist, Davidson thought, "taught the elements of arithmetic," using "pebbles, a box of sand, or an abacus" to facilitate learn-ing.[153] Freeman's conclusion was that "simple arithmetic, with, probably, the weights and measures, and the outlines of the calendar, were taught by the letter-master. . . ." [154] The statement is open to doubt, however, as regards usual practice at the period when greatest stress was laid on character, and liberal, rather than practical, instruction was most favored.[155] Socrates recom-mended arithmetic, emphasizing "what was useful"; [156] Plato endorsed it, not for its practical value, though that is great, but as a preliminary to dialectic, and to quicken the mind.[157] With such high authority behind it, arithmetic, like certain other studies, may have claimed more of schooltime than in earlier days when character, letters, and music were supreme. Drawing and painting, too, had gained some place by the fourth century.[158]

Instruction in "music" included reading and writing; the poetry of Homer, Hesiod, Theognis, Solon, Alcman, Tyrtaeus, Pindar, Aeschylus, Euripides; pos-sibly, too, the fables of Aesop; singing, playing upon the seven-stringed lyre, and later, sometimes, the flute. The latter was open to objection, however, be-cause it excluded the voice, distorted the face, and stirred the emotions un-duly. Similarly, Phrygian and Lydian music, though they crept in, were thought

152 Protagoras, 325–6. From The Works of Plato, translated and edited by Benjamin Jowett (Oxford University Press).
153 Davidson: Aristotle and Ancient Educational Ideals, p. 77.
154 Op. cit., p. 103.
155 Whibley: op. cit., p. 508.
156 Xenophon: Memorabilia, IV, 7, 8.
157 Republic, VII, 536; Laws, V. 747.
158 Aristotle: Politica, VIII, 3.

THE MUSIC SCHOOL   *by Douris*
(G. Perrot and C. Chipiez, *Histoire de l'Art dans l'Antiquité*, IX, 551)

to be effeminate and of immoral influence, while the simple Dorian was favored for its supposed effect on manly, moral character. In the old music school, reading, writing, and music were sometimes taught by the lyre-master or citharist; but an elementary teacher of letters, reading, and writing, the *grammatistes*, was commonly employed.[159]

Instruction was given individually and also collectively. Reading, writing, and the lyre were probably taught individually, whereas singing might be imparted collectively. Instruction on the lyre was probably not begun till the age of about twelve or thirteen. In reading, the alphabetic-syllabic method seems to have been employed. An Attic terra cotta, probably indicative of school practice, contains the syllables of αρ, βαρ, γαρ, δαρ, etc. Rhythm came to be employed to facilitate learning, judging from the metrical alphabet of Callias of Athens.[160]

In teaching writing, copies were set, probably traced out faintly by the master in sand or on wax tablets, then followed and filled in by the pupil. Plato's statement that "the writing-master first draws lines" and makes the pupil follow them is somewhat obscure, and may be variously interpreted.[161] Writing was followed by dictation, first of simple words and phrases, then by extracts from approved authors. Memorization of long passages, even the whole of an author, was common practice. Homer was the indispensable first book,

[159] Whibley: *op. cit.*, pp. 507, 509; Freeman: *op. cit.*, p. 50.
[160] Athenaeus, X, 453; Freeman: *op. cit.*, pp. 88 ff.
[161] *Protagoras*, 326; Freeman: *op. cit.*, pp. 85 ff.

if one may trust the oft-told story that Alcibiades beat a schoolmaster for not having a copy of Homer in his school.[162] Xenophon makes Niceratus say that his father wanted to make him a good man, and so compelled him to learn the whole of Homer by heart—which, he assures us, he still can recite.[163] The fact that Athenian prisoners at Syracuse reputedly gained their liberty by reciting passages from Euripides suggests thorough memorizing in the days of their youth.[164]

Much that has been said of the music school is true of the palaestra, which was also a private institution, yet subject to public regulation.[165] The palaestras mentioned in *The Polity of the Athenians* were apparently private wrestling places or gymnasia, built by the rich for the sake of greater privacy, and not institutions for the physical education of boys.[166] Of fees, little is known, but Athenaeus [167] mentions a fee of one *mina*, about four pounds, which presumably covered the entire course of instruction.

While there is a difference of opinion about the matter, some holding that palaestra and music school were probably distinct, and that the training of the one preceded that of the other, the weight of evidence seems to favor the conclusion that both branches of education began at the same age, about the seventh year, and continued, at least for those who wished and could afford it, till about fifteen.[168] Just how the day was divided is uncertain. Activities of the music school may have occupied the morning hours and physical exercises the afternoon.[169] Perhaps there was no hard and fast rule; the order for some pupils may have been reversed. This would occasion no difficulty since there was much individual instruction in the music school, and few pupils appear to have been present at a time. Artistic remains show some coming from their physical exercises to the music master; others will go to the palaestra after they have had their turn with the citharist. In Lucian's portrayal of the school day's routine (of later date), early rising is followed by a visit to the music school, the palaestra, and then music school again after a bath and a light meal.[170]

Palaestra and music school may have been in the same place; if not, they were conveniently enough located so that both could be attended by the same pupils. In small villages and towns the palaestra was probably nothing more

162 Plutarch: *Alcibiades*, 7.
163 *Symposium*, III, 5.
164 Plutarch: *Nicias*, 29.
165 Aeschines: *Timarchus*, 9–11.
166 Xenophon: *Athenians*, II, 10; Forbes: *op. cit.*, pp. 80 f.
167 Bk. XIII, 584.
168 Cf. Grasberger: *op. cit.*, I, 239 ff.; Freeman: *op. cit.*, pp. 50 ff.; Forbes: *op. cit.*, pp. 60 f.; Mahaffy: *Old Greek Education*, p. 25; Wilkins: *National Education in Greece*, p. 65; Blümner: *op. cit.*, p. 115.
169 Richter: *op. cit.*, p. 29; Whibley: *op. cit.*, p. 506.
170 *Amores*, 44–5.

THE PALAESTRA

(F. W. E. Gerhard, *Auserlesene Vasenbilder*, IV, Pl. CCLXXI)

than a playground, where the boys turned naturally to some contest or other as a release from the restraints imposed by intellectual pursuits. Aelian pictures boys enjoying a tug of war on the playground after school. In larger centers, in later years at least, the palaestra became a more elaborate, systematic institution. It was generally an enclosed space,[171] having a sanded floor, open to air and sunlight, and located, as occasion permitted, near running water, which furnished natural bathing and swimming facilities. At Athens, where such nat-

[171] Girard: *L'Éducation Athénienne*, p. 186.

ural bathing facilities were not numerous, artificial facilities had to be provided.[172] When fully developed, the palaestra furnished privacy, protection against bad weather, a dressing room, storage space for oil, sand, specially constructed baths, perhaps also a place for dust with which to sprinkle and rub the body, and a *dromos* or racecourse, though some lacked this feature.[173] Equipment included pickaxes for loosening the ground for jumping, *halteres* to facilitate the jump and for use in connection with "gesticulation," discuses and javelins for boys of various ages, strigils for scraping the body, chains or tapes for measuring the jump, thongs for binding the hands in boxing, and caps to protect the head and ears.[174] Statues of Hermes and Heracles furnished decoration, betokening the constant association of religion and Greek games. Hermes, legendary founder of systematic gymnastic training and the palaestra itself—though another account credited Theseus with initiating scientific wrestling and systematic teaching of it—naturally occupied a central place.[175]

The paidotribe (*paidotribes*, boy rubber), the proprietor of the palaestra, directed the exercises and games of the boys. He was assisted by flute-players, since many exercises were conducted with music. Of his capacities little is known in the early period. Some were doubtless moderately or poorly qualified; others had a great reputation. The palaestras of Taureas, Timeas, and Siburtios were probably widely known. Some parents, it seems, thought more about the selection of a physical trainer than they did about a teacher for the mind.[176] According to Philostratos, the paidotribe's function was to "show all kinds of wrestling holds that exist, specifying the opportune moment, the degree of effort, and the extent of the movement; further, how one is to defend himself, or how one can overcome the defense of the other. . . ." But as for the purging of humors and other scientific matters, "The paidotribe will either not understand that at all, or, if he should have some knowledge, he will apply it improperly for boys. . . ." [177] He was then, according to Philostratos, much less informed and skilled than the gymnast; but we may think of him, at best, as one who was something of a specialist, understanding different physical constitutions and the exercises suited to them; how to develop beauty, strength, health, and the power of will; perhaps acquainted with dietary matters to some extent; and above all, a man to whom parents would entrust their boys for that training which was to make their bodies serve their minds, that they might not through physical weakness act like cowards in war or at any other time.[178]

172 Richter: op. cit., p. 28.
173 Philostratos: Concerning Gymnastics, 56; Grasberger: op. cit., 1, 245 f.
174 Freeman: op. cit., pp. 130 ff.
175 Pausanias, 1, 39, 3; Philostratos: Concerning Gymnastics, 16.
176 Plato: Protagoras, 313.
177 Philostratos: Concerning Gymnastics, 14; Grasberger: op. cit., 1, 263 f.
178 Plato: Protagoras, 326.

Since the paidotribe received boys who were quite young, and kept some at least till about fifteen, one infers that the exercises were graded somewhat to suit the development of the boys. Two general groups are distinguishable, "boys" seven to eleven, and "youths" eleven to fifteen years of age. On festival days, such as the Hermaea, however, the boys and youths were allowed to come together.[179] Aristotle says it is "an admitted principle, that gymnastic exercises should be employed in education, and that for children they should be of a lighter kind, avoiding severe diet or painful toil, lest the growth of the body be impaired." [180] He makes it clear, however, that the "admitted principle" was often infringed by the premature training of boys for the Olympian Games. Carriage and posture, with other matters pertaining to deportment becoming gentlemen's sons, were doubtless stressed in the palaestra. "Gesticulation," movements of the body, chiefly the upper extremities, designed as preliminary training for dancing and other gymnastic contests, particularly boxing, had a prominent place. Leapfrog, climbing a rope, tug of war, playing various games with balls, running, and jumping must also have belonged to the program for small boys. Even the javelin and discus, scaled down for youngsters, may have been used to some extent.[181] Running, jumping, wrestling, throwing the javelin and discus were the chief exercises of the palaestra.[182] The more strenuous exercises—wrestling, boxing, and pancration—made up the heavier parts of the program, at least for those who would enter public competitions. Boxing for boys was established at Olympia in 616 B.C.[183] While little can be said of swimming, it was commonly practiced, and may have been taught generally.[184] That it was regarded as necessary for general education, is suggested by the proverbial description of an uncultured person as one who knew neither swimming nor his letters. Though swimming may not have been as universal as the proverb suggests,[185] certain references [186] seem to indicate that its use was regarded as a commonplace. When artificial bathing facilities had become general, in private houses as well as in public institutions, swimming baths were commonly associated with them. Even women, who had no part in the life of the palaestra and gymnasium, are represented in swimming and shower baths on vase paintings of the late sixth century B.C. Bathing establishments naturally varied extensively in regard to facilities, depending on time and location, and whether

---

179 Grasberger: op. cit., I, 256; Plato: Lysis, 206; Charmides, 154.
180 Politica, VIII, 4. From The Works of Aristotle, translated by J. A. Smith and W. D. Ross (The Clarendon Press).
181 Freeman: op. cit., p. 130; Richter: op. cit., p. 29.
182 Grasberger: op. cit., I, 298–383; Becker: op. cit., pp. 85 f., 87 f.
183 Pausanias, v, 8, 9.
184 Grasberger: op. cit., I, 376 ff.
185 Thomas: Swimming, p. 88.
186 Herodotus, VII, 176; VIII, 89; Thucydides, IV, 25; VII, 25; Plato: Republic, v, 453; Pausanias, II, 35, 1; IV, 35, 9.

constructed prior to the advent of Roman influence. Polybius speaks of differentiation of facilities for the "more genteel people" so that they might bathe privately.[187]

Though dancing has been considered a part of elementary schoolwork by some, the opposite conclusion has been reached by many others. "In the regular system of education at Athens," says Freeman, "the boys learned only to sing and play, not to dance." [188] The fact that Socrates took instruction in dancing at an advanced age implies that it was not a part of general education in his youth. For a select group of boys, however, dancing would become an important part of education, if they were chosen by agents of the choregus of any of the ten tribes to be trained at his expense for the public festivals in which cyclic dancing had a prominent place. During the Transition and thereafter new dances came from abroad; likewise Greek dancing went abroad to influence others.[189]

At the regular school festivals, such as the Musea and Hermaea, pertaining to the music school and the palaestra respectively, there may have been some dancing, since festivals, religious celebrations, and dancing were generally closely associated by the Greeks. At the Hermaea, after religious rites, we may fancy the boys in festive dress, devoting themselves happily to the holiday, playing their favorite games. Thus we may leave them, just as Socrates is said to have found them as he entered a newly erected palaestra and engaged Lysis in conversation: "Upon entering we found that the boys had just been sacrificing; and this part of the festival was nearly at an end. They were all in their white array, and games at dice were going on among them. Most of them were in the outer court amusing themselves; but some were in a corner of the Apodyterium playing at odd and even with a number of dice, which they took out of little wicker baskets." [190]

*The gymnasium* From about fourteen or sixteen years of age, the training of music school and palaestra having come to an end, the sons of well-to-do Athenian families enjoyed a greater degree of liberty to the end of the eighteenth year. In any case this period had a definite termination, when systematic ephebic training had been established for the nineteenth and twentieth years.[191] During this interval almost exclusive attention was given to

---

[187] Schleyer: *Bäder und Badeanstalten*, pp. 26 f.; cf. infra, pp. 311, 314, 649–53; Sears: "A Greek Bath," *Am. Jour. Archaeol.*, viii, 216–26; Polybius: *The Histories*, xxx, 29.

[188] *Op. cit.*, p. 147; cf. Graves: *History of Education*, i, 163; Gulick: *op. cit.*, p. 84; Blümner: *op. cit.*, p. 320; Whibley: *op. cit.*, p. 510; Lucian: *Of Pantomime*; Scott: *Dancing in All Ages*, pp. 34–77; Vuillier: *op. cit.*, pp. 4–31.

[189] Keller: "An Oriental Dance on an Attic Vase," *Bul. Fogg Museum of Art*, ix, 56 ff.; Kraemer: "A Greek Element in Egyptian Dancing," *Am. Jour. Archaeol.*, xxxv, 125–38.

[190] Plato: *Lysis*, 206. From *The Works of Plato*, translated and edited by Benjamin Jowett (Oxford University Press); Grasberger: *op. cit.*, i, 256.

[191] Infra, pp. 317 f.

physical sports and exercises under special instructors at a public gymnasium. The poorer sort, though they may have managed to get some training at the palaestra and music school, were now compelled by economic circumstances to enter some remunerative occupation of the workaday world.[192] They were free, of course, to go to the public gymnasium and to exercise there, but fees would be charged for special instruction.[193] Of course, youths who were fortunate enough to be selected by the gymnasiarch for the *lampadedromia* (torch race) and those chosen by the *choregus* for the cyclic dances, would have a certain period of free training at the expense of the leaders of the respective liturgies.[194] Considering the fees for special "coaching" and the hours of labor, it seems doubtful whether youth of this age group, who were compelled to work, could participate to any great extent in the training of the gymnasium. Since public gymnasia were created by the city-state, were supervised by the gymnasiarch, and could be visited by all citizens, they must be regarded as evidence of recognition of public responsibility for physical education. There was, however, no compulsion save that which may have derived from social approval or disapproval and the imminence of war, in which, in the course of time, every male must be prepared to take part.

To the time of Pericles there were at least two public gymnasia, the Academy and the Kynosarges, both said to have been built in the time of Solon. A third, the Lyceum, though it is called the oldest and credited by some to Solon's time, is by others believed to be of later date, perhaps the Periclean age.[195] All were situated outside the city. The Academy, on the River Cephissus, under the patronage of Athena, was for freeborn Athenian boys, as was also the Lyceum, sacred to Apollo, located to the east of the city on the Ilissus. The Kynosarges, a shrine of Heracles, under the brow of Lycabettus, was for some time devoted to the sons of Athenian fathers by foreign mothers.[196] This distinction seems to have fallen into disuse by the fifth century, however. Themistocles, whose mother was a foreigner, is said to have helped undermine the old custom by getting a number of full-blooded youths to go with him to the Kynosarges for exercise.[197] Socrates seems to have visited it without attracting any special attention. Other public gymnasia were added in the course of time: the Ptolemeion, named for its founder and located near the *agora*; the gymnasium of

[192] Infra, p. 328.
[193] Freeman: op. cit., p. 142.
[194] Whibley: op. cit., p. 408.
[195] Krause: Theagenes oder Wissenschaftliche Darstellung der Gymnastik, Agonistik und Festspiele der Hellenen, p. 123; Die Gymnastik und Agonistik der Hellenen, 1, 90; Forbes: op. cit., p. 83.
[196] Pausanias, 1, 19, 3; Petersen: Das Gymnasium der Griechen nach Seiner Baulichen Einrichtung, p. 16.
[197] Plutarch: Themistocles, 1.

Hermes; the Diogeneion, in the center of the city; and another built by Hadrian. Of these, the Diogeneion and the Ptolemeion were reserved for the ephebi.[198] Besides the public gymnasia there were others, built privately. The author of *The Polity of the Athenians* (c. 425 B.C.), who had scant sympathy with the rising tide of democracy, noted that the rich, aristocratic citizens had suffered an eclipse by the "people," who built themselves "palaestras, dressing-rooms, and bathing establishments" at public expense, of which the "mob gets the benefit . . . rather than the select few or the well-to-do." But he added, "Rich men have in some cases private gymnasia and baths with dressing-rooms. . . ." [199]

The training of the gymnasium (for those fifteen to eighteen years of age) continued the exercises of the palaestra in a more strenuous fashion and perfected them. But in addition to these, youth now attended to riding, driving, the torch race, the race in armor, and hunting—though the latter was less encouraged in Athens than at Sparta, especially after wild game had become scarce. For riding there were special academies and, of course, special fees, which made it a sport for those who could afford to pay.[200] Rowing, swimming, and dancing in the public chorus were also a part of the education of many youths of this age. A knowledge of the laws was required, Plato [201] says, but we hear nothing of systematic instruction.

Instruction in the gymnasium was given by paidotribes and gymnasts and their assistants.[202] The distinction between paidotribe and gymnast was, doubtless, the result of many years' development and a tendency to refinement of specialization, which was inevitable when professionalism had become deeply rooted in the athletic world. Many athletes took up physical training of youth as a profession, after their own career as contenders for prizes had come to an end. To term one's self a "gymnast" may have become a fad, when the name had once been introduced "shortly before Plato's time." [203] Both terms seem at first to have been used rather loosely. In the course of time, however, certain distinctions between them were clearly recognized: the paidotribe had care of general physical training; the gymnast was an expert who trained youth for particular gymnastic contests. By the time of Galen and Philostratos, it would appear that the gymnast had come to be regarded as a scientific trainer, one who knew the "art of the paidotribe," something of medicine, and was also competent to deal with many questions pertaining to diet and health. Of

198 Pausanias, I, 2, 4; 17, 2; 18, 9; Dumont: *Essai sur l'Éphébie Attique*, I, 208.
199 *Athenians*, II, 9–10.
200 Petersen: *op. cit.*, pp. 4 f.
201 *Protagoras*, 326.
202 Krause: *Theagenes*, pp. 234 ff.
203 Forbes: *op. cit.*, pp. 90 f.

course, as Philostratos pointed out, many gymnasts did not truly know, or wisely practice, this complete science of gymnastic.[204]

The gymnasiarch, the chief official of the gymnasium, had general charge of its exercises and discipline, and directed the festivals.[205] He was one of those respected, wealthy citizens, appointed by each of the tribes to select and train runners to represent them in the torch races (hence also sometimes designated as lampadarch) and at such festivals as the Panathenaea and Hephaesteia. Since all this must be done at his personal expense, and the cost for such training might be as much as twelve hundred drachmas, the performance of such a public service was possible only for men of wealth. Xystarches, kosmetes, sophronistes, and many other functionaries assisted in the work of the gymnasium in connection with later ephebic training.[206] Epistatai, charged with supervision of the building and material equipment, had considerable responsibility, since a law prescribed that anyone who stole a cloak, oil cask, or any equipment worth more than ten drachmas from a gymnasium should be punished by death.[207]

Although there is no precise, contemporary description of a public gymnasium at Athens, fragmentary references in Greek authors and the detailed picture drawn by Vitruvius, at the time of Augustus, have been used to reconstruct a plan of this Greek institution.[208] Many points are doubtful, of course, and different interpretations are given of Vitruvius' text. Each gymnasium, moreover, must have had certain peculiarities, as did those of Pergamos and Ephesos. The gymnasium at Eretria, dating not earlier than the first century B.C., was "the simplest form" and had just the "bare essentials"—"an open space for exercising and porches or rooms about it for retiring." [209] Though many of the various facilities described by Vitruvius are known to have existed in Plato's day, the Roman's arrangement of them may follow some model (Naples, perhaps) that he had in mind. His picture, doubtless, is completer than the actual gymnasium of five hundred years before.[210] Following the reproduction,[211] certain features may be noted. The entire space, 360,000 square feet, is enclosed

204 Philostratos: Concerning Gymnastics, 14, 54; Grasberger: op. cit., I, 265.
205 Petersen: op. cit., p. 15.
206 Infra, pp. 321 ff.
207 Demosthenes: Timocrates, 736.
208 Petersen: op. cit., pp. 1–56; Krause: Gymnastik, I, 80–131; Baumeister: Denkmäler, I, 609–14; Becker: op. cit., pp. 293–309; Gardiner: Greek Athletic Sports and Festivals, pp. 467–500.
209 Richardson: "The Gymnasium at Eretria," Am. Jour. Archaeol. and Fine Arts, XI, 154 ff.
210 Krause: Gymnastik, I, 93 f., 98 f.; Gardiner, op. cit., p. 489, holds that the gymnasia daily frequented by Athenians probably "resembled the Vitruvian type more closely than did the gymnasia of Olympia and Delphi. . . ."
211 P. 313.

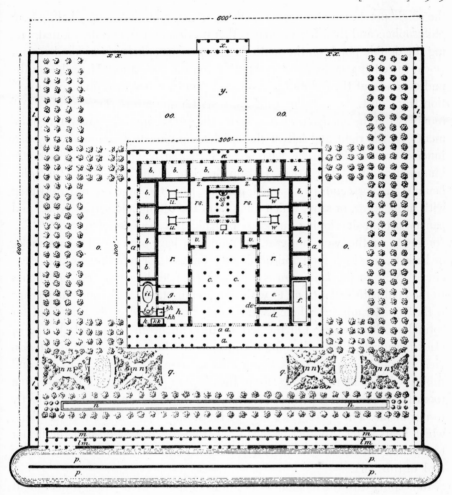

PLAN OF A GYMNASIUM
(C. Petersen, *Das Gymnasium der Griechen*, p. 57)

on three sides by walls 600 feet in length; on the fourth is a stadium (p) [212]
so arranged as to permit numerous spectators to witness athletic events. From
the entrance in the north wall (x x) a passageway (y) leads to the heart of the
gymnasium, the palaestra—a square structure, in this instance, the entire circumference of which is 1,200 feet. Three single porches are formed by the
peristyles on the north, east, and west sides (a); the fourth, a double porch
(aa), furnishing protection against stormy weather, is on the south. Within

[212] This deviates from the gymnasia at Athens which had no stadia attached to them.—
Petersen: *op. cit.*, p. 20.

the single porches are numerous *exedrae* (b), comfortable, roomy halls where philosophers and their hearers may gather for discourse. Centrally located, facing the double porch on the south, is the spacious *ephebeum* or *apodyterium* (c c), the chief exercise hall for wrestling and the pancration. Here the youths undress and put their clothing into bags or under coarse coverings for protection from dust. Around the walls are seats for spectators. Two small corner rooms (v) in the *apodyterium* may be for the safekeeping of gymnasium equipment. To the right and left of the *apodyterium* are two commodious, open inner courts (r) which may have served for ball-play, and as an aid to better illumination of interior spaces. Just on the right of the entrance to the *ephebeum* is the *koryceum* (d), named, perhaps, from the large bag or ball stuffed with meal, seeds, or sand, which hung from the ceiling and served boxers and pancratiasts in developing quickness of hand and firmness of footing.[213] According to another view, however, the room may have been used for bags, sacks, or baskets, in which food and drink were brought for refreshment after exercise.[214] Next to the *koryceum* is a passage (de) leading from the *ephebeum* to the cold bath or *loutron* (f) with a swimming tank.[215] Beyond the passage is the *konisterium* (e) where various kinds of fine sand or dust are kept for sprinkling the body.[216] On the left of the *ephebeum* is the oil storage or *elaeothesium* (g); and adjoining it conveniently the *tepidarium* or *aleipterion* (h), a heated room where, before or after exercise, one may be massaged and rubbed with oil by the *aleiptes*. From the *aleipterion* a passage (h h) leads to a room (k) where fuel is perhaps received, and which servants can enter directly from outside. The space (kk) may be for storing fuel for the furnace (kh), which heats water. Another passage leads from the *aleipterion* past the heater to a hot-air bath or *laconicum* (i k), the sweat bath (i), and warm swimming tank or tubs (ii).

In keeping with the religious associations of sports, each great gymnasium at Athens recognized a particular deity to whom it was sacred, and around whose shrine the gymnasium itself grew up. The innermost room, a sanctuary (s), has a statue of the deity (ss), and at the entrance an altar (t) for sacrifices. Around the temple are sacred precincts (rs) that separate it from other rooms (u) and (w)—living quarters for those employed in the baths, and for those who served in the temple, with the necessary kitchens, equipment, and storage space. From the sacred precincts one may pass (z) to the *exedrae* (b) and thence through the porch to large open spaces (oo), which were probably used for dangerous

---

[213] Cf. Krause: *Gymnastik*, I, 103; Philostratos: *Concerning Gymnastics*, 57; Gardiner: *op. cit.*, p. 492.
[214] Petersen: *op. cit.*, pp. 37 ff.
[215] Lucian: *Lexiphanes*, 4–5; cf. Stabian baths, Pompeii, *infra*, p. 653.
[216] Philostratos: *Concerning Gymnastics*, 56.

sports such as hurling the discus and javelin, shooting the bow, and also for military maneuvers on foot and horse. The smaller open spaces to right and left of the palaestra (o) were probably used for jumping, ball games (usually carried on out of doors by the Greeks), tug of war, and other favorite games. South of the palaestra is an open, sand-covered, rectangular space (q) probably devoted to wrestling, pancration, and possibly boxing. Flanking this on both sides are pleasant walks, hedged in by grassplots, plane trees, olives, and elms (n n). Near to these to the south is the open-air racecourse (n) surrounded by trees. Parallel to it, just inside the southern extremity of the gymnasium, is a double peristyle (lm) that connects the east and west colonnades and protects the twelve-foot wide xystos (m), depressed one and a half feet below the surrounding area, where athletes exercise under cover in inclement weather. Along the east and west walls, single peristyles (l) face pleasant gardens set with trees.[217]

*Ephebic training* A fourth phase of education for sons of Athenian parents began at the end of the eighteenth year and continued through the twentieth. The origin of this institution, the Ephebic College, has been a subject of dispute. Till recently it was credited with great antiquity. Girard [218] assigned it to the fifth century. Dumont [219] held that the ephebic institution lasted for eight hundred years, but recognized that no history existed of the early centuries. Mahaffy [220] had a fairly clear idea of the contrast between early informal practices and the later official system, though later researches have made the distinction much clearer.

The generally accepted view now is that the systematic institution of ephebic training arose in the late fourth century, though there were certain earlier practices similar to those of the later Ephebic College. These may have been the basis upon which more systematic training evolved. There is some ground for the evolutionary view. It was, indeed, an ancient custom for the state to educate the sons of those citizens who died in war, to present them publicly, and send "them to their several duties" in full armor clad.[221] If, however, systematic ephebic training, as later organized, had been in existence, special care for war orphans would have been superfluous. It is clear, moreover, that when definite provision had been made for general ephebic training, the old custom in respect to orphans appears to have fallen into disuse.[222] The very lack of recognition of the existence of such an institution as the Ephebic College on the part of Plato, Xenophon, Isocrates, and others suggests that it may not have

[217] Petersen: op. cit., pp. 54 ff.
[218] Op. cit., pp. 271–309; Freeman: op. cit., pp. 210–20.
[219] Op. cit., I, 33 f.
[220] Old Greek Education, pp. 73 ff.
[221] Thucydides, II, 46; Plato: Menexenus, 248–9.
[222] Bryant: op. cit., loc. cit., XVIII, 88.

316 [EMPIRES OF THE SEA]

existed in their day. The argument ex *silentio* has been carefully reviewed and sifted.[223] Silence is generally not very impressive evidence, but it may be significant under certain circumstances. In this case it is all but universal, and men who might be expected to praise such an institution, or recommend it as a model, or at least as a partial fulfillment of their ideal, do not in any way indicate knowledge of its existence. Xenophon, in fact, represents Socrates as saying that ". . . because military training is not publicly recognised by the state, you must not make that an excuse for being a whit less careful in attending to it yourself." [224] This implies that military training, to Socrates' day at least, was an individual responsibility, and harmonizes with the fact that orphans were made an exception by the state. Thucydides [225] represents Pericles as saying that the Athenians, in contrast to their enemies, prefer not to train themselves laboriously for war. Isocrates' remarks, too, imply the nonexistence of systematic training: ". . . although we seek to rule over all men, we are not willing to take the field ourselves, and although we undertake to wage war upon, one might almost say, the whole world, we do not train ourselves for war but employ instead vagabonds, deserters, and fugitives who have thronged together here in consequence of other misdemeanours, who, whenever others offer them higher pay, will follow their leadership against us." [226]

Besides the training of orphans, there are also early references to the service of young men as *peripoloi* (patrols), but the service is not known to have been definitely limited to a certain age group; there is no proof of its being systematic military and gymnastic training; it was not compulsory; and it may not have been viewed as a regular element of a citizen's education. Another practice, sometimes pointed to as evidence of the antiquity of ephebic training, is the soldier's oath of allegiance, referred to by Plutarch [227] in the time of Alcibiades. But the oath, even granting its great antiquity, would not prove the existence of systematic ephebic training. In fact, the treatment of orphans, the reference to *peripoloi* service, and the soldier's oath seem to conform with a pattern of individual initiative rather than a paternalistic state régime of compulsory, military training. These features were the forerunners of systematic training in the Ephebic College; they may, indeed, have suggested it when changes in the political and military life of Athens made a modification in education seem desirable to many.

[223] Wilamowitz-Moellendorff: *Aristoteles und Athen*, i, 191 ff.; Busolt-Swoboda: *op. cit.*, i, 577; Bryant: *op. cit., loc. cit.*, xviii, 84 f.; Forbes: *op. cit.*, pp. 113 ff.
[224] *Memorabilia*, iii, 12, 5.
[225] Bk. ii, 39.
[226] Isocrates: *On the Peace*, 44. Trans. by G. Norlin. The Loeb Classical Library. Quoted by permission of Harvard University Press, Cambridge, Mass.
[227] *Alcibiades*, 15.

Certain other facts, apart from these traditional usages, bear upon the origin of systematic military training. Athens, from a military standpoint, had declined markedly by the latter half of the fourth century. The "Social War" which ended in defeat (355 B.C.) proved she could not force her sway upon her confederates. Many became alarmed. Orators condemned her decadence. A movement for reform arose. Philosophers recommended ways and means whereby to strengthen the city by systematic training for defense. Particularly, after the battle of Chaeronaea (338 B.C.) and the death of Philip, Athens was moved to take practical steps, paternalistic in character, designed to rehabilitate her military power. It has been persuasively argued that Plato [228] fathered the Ephebic College. Xenophon's suggestions [229] may also have had some effect. Taking all evidence into consideration, Wilamowitz concluded that it was "the demands of the Socratics, which the demagogues now sought to carry out in their fashion." [230] Whether the propaganda for such an innovation was so influential or not, definite legalization of systematic training was attempted that was to prepare citizens for military service and rectify the situation which Isocrates [231] so scathingly criticized. The law establishing the ephebic system has been generally attributed to Epicrates, a wealthy citizen who may also have given something to support the institution. The earliest recovered inscription regarding the ephebi is from 334–333 B.C.[232] and concerns youths who were in their second year of training. Forbes believes the sum total of "evidence . . . is enough to convince even the most prejudiced person that there was no ephebia prior to 335." [233]

The establishment of systematic, compulsory ephebic training, provided by the state, marked the termination of reliance upon strength and loyalty developed through individual freedom, initiative, and choice. What life in a corrupt, selfish society no longer could confer, was now to be attempted by state officials. What Athenians had boasted did not exist among them; what, in better days, they had condemned in Lacedaemon [234]—they now imitated in some degree. The ephebic institution represents an effort to produce by a paternalistic system of education the strength and virtues of military efficiency. As an inscription stated, the people, being concerned for the training of the ephebi, ". . . enjoined by law that they should become acquainted with the

228 Laws, VI, 760.
229 The Cavalry Commander; On the Art of Horsemanship; Cyropaedia, I, 2, 4; Memorabilia, III, 5, 21–8.
230 Wilamowitz-Moellendorff: op. cit., I, 194.
231 On the Peace, 44.
232 Wilamowitz-Moellendorff: op. cit., I, 193 f.; Busolt-Swoboda: op. cit., II, 1189; Bryant: op. cit., loc. cit., XVIII, 86.
233 Op. cit., p. 119.
234 Freeman: op. cit., p. 220.

land, the fortresses, and the borders of Attica, and . . . perform in arms the exercises appertaining to war. . . ." [235]

Entrance to citizenship and ephebic training is described by Aristotle. The franchise, in his time, was open to all sons born of Athenian parents. At the age of eighteen they were enrolled among the demesmen, who voted on oath as to the candidates' age and parentage. If found younger than the law required, they were sent back to the boys; if parentage was not satisfactory, accusations were brought, the accused having the right to appeal to the court for a decision. If the court decided against a boy, he was sold as a slave; otherwise, he must be admitted to enrolment without further obstacle. When youths had passed these examinations, their fathers, assembled by tribes, nominated three men, over forty years old and most fit to have charge of the ephebi. From the nominees the Assembly chose one from each tribe to act as guardians to superintend everything, in conjunction with a director selected from the Athenian citizenry at large. In their charge the youths visited the temples, and then went to the Piraeus and garrisoned Munychia and Acte. Two trainers and assistants were named also by the Assembly to instruct them in fighting in heavy armor, the use of bow, javelin, and catapult. Guardians received a drachma, and the youths four obols each, their allowance being paid to the guardian, who purchased necessary provisions for the common mess. After thus training for a year, the ephebi had a military parade, and were armed by the city with shield and spear at a public ceremony in the theater. So equipped, the youth patroled the country and occupied certain fortresses, being for the time exempted, with a few exceptions, from taxes and court actions. After these two years of training the young men assumed their places in the ranks of citizens. [236]

A knowledge of Athenian law seems to have been required of those who were registered as citizens. When youth have done with schoolmasters, Plato says, "the state again compels them to learn the laws"; [237] and Aeschines says that "as soon as the young man has been registered in the list of citizens, and knows the laws of the state, . . ." [238] the lawgiver speaks to him directly rather than through another. Since we hear nothing of systematic instruction, acquaintance with laws may have been acquired informally, and by actual visitation of the courts.

The oath of allegiance, often credited to the time of Solon, which before the organization of ephebic training had been taken at the age of eighteen, was now administered at the beginning of the second year of training, at the time

[235] Forbes: *op. cit.,* p. 127.
[236] Aristotle: *Ath. Resp.,* 42.
[237] *Protagoras,* 326.
[238] *Timarchus,* 18. *The Speeches of Aeschines,* trans. by C. D. Adams. The Loeb Classical Library. Quoted by permission of Harvard University Press, Cambridge, Mass.

when the city gave arms to the cadet who was about to go out to patrol the country and occupy the fortresses. The pledges, taken on oath, make clear the association of piety, patriotism, and property: "I will never disgrace these sacred arms, nor desert my companion in the ranks, but will fight for the temples and public property, alone and with others. I will leave my fatherland, not less, but greater and better, than I received it. I will obey those who may at any time be in power, and both the existing laws and those which the people may unanimously make, and, if any one seeks to annul the laws or does not obey them, I will not allow him, but will defend them both alone and with others. I will honor the religion of my fatherland; let the gods, Agraulos, Enyalios, Ares, Zeus, Thallo, Auxo, and Hegemone bear witness." [239]

While too little is known of it to permit satisfactory generalization, the discipline of youth in the gymnasium and while on preliminary military service must have varied from time to time, depending upon the officers in charge of them. It was supposed to be strict; but while we hear of "slaves" and "a measureless amount of ills" at the hands of gymnasiarchs,[240] there is some indication of laxity or, at least, exceptions to the general rule. Demosthenes' account of an Athenian youth's experiences while on duty with the patrols (peripoloi) somewhat prior to the establishment of compulsory ephebic training, is illuminating. Abusive language, assaults, drunkenness, and other disorderly acts on the part of Conon's sons, when reported to the general, were only rebuked "with stern words"; which, far from being effective in restraining them, were followed that very night by a repetition of their outrageous conduct.[241]

That some degree of youth organization developed is suggested by the ephebic officers. In the time of Hadrian, when the ephebi were divided into groups, each division (systremma) had a leader from its own number, the systremmatarches. There were also from time to time, ephebic gymnasiarchs, chosen perhaps from the youths themselves, or from the teachers whose duty was to provide oil and other things necessary for the physical exercises of the ephebi. Other indications of youth organization are found under the Empire, when the college group was patterned upon the larger society outside—the student-citizens having their officials, such as archons, generals, astynomes, thesmothetae, heralds, chosen from the "best" families—the rich, the prominent.[242]

The exercises of the ephebic organization were physical, military, religious, and, in later times especially, intellectual. Mere mention of officials of the col-

[239] Pollux, VIII, 105; Grasberger: op. cit., III, 29 f.; Dumont: op. cit., I, 9 f.; Taylor: "The Athenian Ephebic Oath," Class. Jour., XIII, 499.
[240] Plato: Axiochus, 8.
[241] Demosthenes: Against Conon, 3–5.
[242] Dumont: op. cit., I, 220 ff., 231 ff., 306 ff.

lege reveals its devotion to physical culture and specifically military exercises. These included the maneuvers of fighting in armor, throwing the javelin, archery, the use of the sling, catapult, and *kestrosphendone*,[243] marches, running in various forms, wrestling, boxing, swimming, rowing, riding, driving the chariot, and the pancration.[244] The ephebi had contests of their own and received prizes; they competed also in the public games, although it is seldom possible to identify the winners from the College.[245] In the third century of the Christian era, gymnastic contests of the same sort were still carried on, but certain military exercises had disappeared.[246]

It is certain that the intellectual pursuits pertaining to a liberal education formed a part of the education of the ephebi; but it is impossible to distinguish their intellectual activities from the studies pursued by others who were not members of the Ephebic College.[247] Plutarch [248] names letters, geometry, rhetoric, and music as the studies of youth at Athens. "Letters," a broad term, included a wide range of studies: grammar, language, and philosophy. Youth attended lectures of the Academics, Stoics, Peripatetics, and other philosophers.

Considering the close association of patriotism, religion, and athletic festivals, it is not surprising that the members of the Ephebic College devoted considerable time to religious ceremonials. Religion, piety toward the gods, and defense of the temples were a part of civic duty. Throughout the year the life of the ephebi reflected this religious character as they participated in numerous celebrations. Even when the advancement of critical philosophy and other influences had combined to undermine ancient religious beliefs and practices, youths went through with ancient forms punctiliously, and even added new ones. Pre-eminent among these were the great public Eleusinian and Dionysian festivals; celebrations in honor of the great military achievements of their forefathers at Marathon, Munychia, Salamis, and Plataea; the Epitaphia, celebrated as a great Memorial Day in honor of all warrior dead; the Theseia, in honor of the Athenian hero. Other ceremonial occasions were peculiar to the college itself: exercises at entering and leaving; festivals in honor of Artemis Agrotere, Castor and Pollux, the Diogeneia, the Disoteria, and the Ptolemaia. These festivals continued to be honored under the Empire, but with diminished importance. In addition, Roman festivals, such as the Germania, Philadelphia, Adriania, the Antoniea, and several others were honored. Cyclic dances and athletic contests, such as the stade-race, double stade-

[243] *Polybius*, xxvii, 11; Livy, xlii, 65.
[244] Grasberger: *op. cit.*, iii, 92 ff.
[245] Dumont: *op. cit.*, i, 214 f.
[246] *Ibid.*, i, 236 f.
[247] *Ibid.*, i, 240–8; Grasberger: *op. cit.*, iii, 334–462.
[248] *Symposiacs*, ix, 1.

race, torch races, boat races, wrestling, pancration, and fighting in armor, in which the ephebi demonstrated the prowess gained by their training, played a prominent rôle in these religious celebrations.[249]

General relations of the ephebi to the state were in charge of the Senate, the Court of Areopagus, the Board of Generals (strategoi), and the gymnasiarchs. While military training was stressed, the relation of the generals to the work of the college was particularly close, certain activities of the ephebi being associated with the strategoi of special branches of the military service—the navy, the heavy-armed infantry, and the cavalry. More directly the administration of the college was in the hands of the kosmetes (director or president) and the sophronistai, one chosen from each tribe.[250] The latter, "moderators" or "discipline masters," appear to have had everything under their care, but were themselves subject to the authority of the Senate and kosmetes. Besides supervision of morals and instruction, each had to purchase supplies for the common mess.[251] Though the duty of looking after everything would seem to have been onerous, there were compensations, for the sophronistes was paid by the state and honored by the tribe if he performed his duties with faithfulness and energy. Not long after systematic ephebic training had been established, the number of ephebi became greatly reduced and the need for a sophronistes from each tribe disappeared. The office was discontinued, but was reintroduced in the reign of Hadrian, and continued to function till the college ceased to be.

The kosmetes, the head of the institution, was a magistrate elected from the "general body of Athenians," subject to a careful scrutiny to test his fitness for the office.[252] He held the position for one year and gave an account of his service on leaving office. Though no salary is mentioned, the kosmetes was commonly honored by the state and the ephebi themselves at the end of his service. Since he was of a prominent family,[253] salary would be of little moment compared with the honor. His duties were numerous; in fact not a single act was performed by the ephebi without his being associated with it. The kosmetes had general charge of their intellectual and physical exercise, preserved order, superintended health and morals, led public parades to the Piraeus and to other fortresses, and presided at religious festivals and at the presentation of the ephebi at the theater. At times he was particularly interested in furthering physical and military exercises. Shortly before the end of the second century B.C., the kosmetes was permitted to choose his staff. Unlike the sophronis-

---

[249] Dumont: op. cit., I, 260–305.
[250] Ibid., I, 165–206; Grasberger: op. cit., III, 462–85; Forbes: op. cit., pp. 141 ff.
[251] Aristotle: Ath. Resp., 42.
[252] Ibid.; Dumont: op. cit., I, 166.
[253] Dumont: op. cit., I, 170 f.

*tai*, who ceased to function when the college shrank to a mere shadow of its earlier self, the *kosmetes* continued throughout its entire existence.[254]

Eight additional functionaries of the college are named prior to the Empire: *paidotribes*, *hoplomachos*, *akontistes*, *toxotes*, *aphetes* and *catapaltaphetes*, *grammateus*, and *hyperetes*. Sixteen other new titles appear in the first century, a large number of them being assistants to the officials already named.[255] To the various masters, regardless of specialty, general terms were often applied, *didaskaloi* or *paideutai* (teachers, educators).[256]

While the *kosmetes* was concerned with the general direction of the college and with its relations to the state, the *paidotribes*, not to be confused with the trainer of a boys' palaestra, had specific charge of its internal affairs. His position was superior to theirs. Though in the day of Aristotle there were two paidotribes in the Ephebic College, the number decreased soon to one; assistants (*hypopaidotribai*) were appointed, however, in case of necessity, in the first century B.C.[257] While the list of known paidotribes is brief, it is certain that, unlike the *kosmetes*, they served for many years and were reappointed. Two of them together, Ariston and Abascantos, directed the college for nearly a century. At the beginning of the Empire, it became customary to appoint the paidotribe for life.[258]

The military character of the college at its beginning is reflected in the prominent position of the *hoplomachos*, teacher of heavy-armed fighting, who was next in rank to the paidotribe, and at times actually above him.[259] Under the Empire, however, when military instruction became perfunctory, the *grammateus* and the *hegemon* were occasionally listed above him, though he continued to have great importance. The *hoplomachos*, whose office appears in many other states besides Athens, but was disapproved of by the Spartans,[260] occupied his position for many years, was sometimes reappointed, and, at the time when Abascantos was paidotribe, was given the title for life.[261] His duties were to teach the whole art of fighting in armor, how to wear the helmet and the cuirass, and how to use shield, lance, and sword; how to fight in single combat and how to maneuver in mass; in short, everything except instruction in using the javelin, bow, and catapult, for which special instructors were provided. In fact, the *hoplomachos* caused youth to simulate "the various opera-

254 Forbes: *op. cit.*, p. 135.
255 Dumont: *op. cit.*, pp. 165 f.; Grasberger: *op. cit.*, III, 477 f.
256 Dumont: *op. cit.*, I, 175 ff.
257 Forbes: *op. cit.*, pp. 136, 138.
258 Dumont: *op. cit.*, I, 181 f.
259 *Ibid.*, I, 185 f.; Forbes: *op. cit.*, p. 139.
260 Dumont: *op. cit.*, I, 187 ff.
261 Grasberger: *op. cit.*, III, 143 f.

tions of war," and "claimed even to teach strategy and to discourse on military affairs," although this "was not his special function." [262]

The use of the javelin was taught by a special instructor, the *akontistes*.[263] Though Pausanias [264] asserts that the Cretans were the only Greeks accustomed to use the bow, it was given a place in the military instruction of ephebi. Plato [265] recommended it, with the javelin and sling, as part of the training for young people, boys and girls. The instructor in archery, the *toxotes*, is mentioned in ephebic inscriptions of the third century B.C., but, like the teacher of the javelin, he is not mentioned in inscriptions of 39 B.C. and thereafter.[266] The use of the catapult was taught by the *aphetes* or *catapaltaphetes*. Though important while military training was the dominant interest of the college, this position seems to have fallen vacant in the last century B.C.[267] When the positions of *akontistes*, *toxotes*, and *aphetes* disappear from the records, one need not infer that all exercises pertaining to them ceased altogether; but considering the perfunctory character of military training, its noncompulsory status, and the small number attending to it, these special exercises were left to the *hoplomachos*, the only military instructor remaining, if they were performed at all. The functions of the *grammateus* (secretary) and the *hyperetes* (servant) are suggested by their titles, but beyond that little is known.[268]

Many of the new officials of the college, under the Empire, were merely assistants to those previously named, such as the assistant paidotribe (*hypopaidotribes*); assistant *kosmetes* (*hypokosmetes* or *antikosmetes*); assistant secretary or recorder (*hypogrammateus* or *antigrammateus*). Promotion from an assistantship and from other lower positions to higher ones was practiced, save where hindered by too great a degree of specialization.[269]

Of other new functionaries little is known. The *hegemon* seems to have been one who marched at the head of the ephebic corps when they were on parade or attended some public ceremony; the *prostates*, too, found in later inscriptions, judging from his title and the prominence of his position on ephebic rolls, may have shared some duties previously performed by the *kosmetes*, and probably presided at certain ceremonies. The *hypozakoros* (chaplain), one of the latecomers, had charge of the elaborate, formal, religious observances,

262 Dumont: *op. cit.*, I, 186; Plato: *Laches*, 181–2; *Euthydemus*, 272–3.
263 Dumont: *op. cit.*, I, 190; Grasberger: *op. cit.*, III, 477.
264 Bk. I, 23, 4.
265 *Laws*, VII, 794.
266 Dumont: *op. cit.*, I, 192.
267 *Ibid.*, I, 191; Forbes: *op. cit.*, p. 141; on development of the catapult, Tarn, *Hellenistic Military and Naval Developments*, pp. 103 f.
268 Dumont: *op. cit.*, I, 165, 193; Grasberger: *op. cit.*, III, 477.
269 Dumont: *op. cit.*, I, 205 f.

which were given much attention in the last period of the college's existence. Like the *akontistes*, the *kestrophylax* was a specialist, his duty being to teach the art of throwing with a sling a short bolt or arrow tipped with metal. Though at first low in rank, his specialty was in high favor, apparently, at certain times.[270]

Plato and Galen stressed the importance of medical knowledge and the assistance of doctors for the paidotribe, if physical training was to be really beneficial to health. Philostratos,[271] too, laid emphasis on the relation of gymnastics to medical science, and the need for adjusting exercises to individual constitutions and states of health. The *iatros*, medical adviser of the college who appears near the end of the second century A.D., represents the accommodation of practice to theory, and suggests the great concern for health that had taken hold of those who could afford the luxury of worrying about it.

Among lesser newcomers were the *didaskalos* (music teacher)—not to be confused with *didaskaloi*, teachers in general, or with teachers of boys in the music school; the *lentiarios*, who had oversight of ephebic apparel; the *kapsarios*, bath attendant, who looked out for the bather's clothes; and the *thyroros*, janitor, i.e., doorman. The *xystarches*, although not a regular official of the college, was nevertheless associated with its work, since he had charge of the *xystos*, the covered place of exercise, where the ephebi performed in bad weather. He was generally a man of prominent family, but could be named from the ephebi themselves. Other titles, for example, the *epimeletes* and the *hypotaktes* [272] are obscure, though Dumont regards the latter as the head of a *taxis*, one of the classes into which the ephebi were divided.[273] The title *hieronikes* appears to have been applied to those ephebi who had conquered in the four great Greek athletic festivals.[274]

The gymnasia, the Ptolemeion in which the college library was located, and the Diogeneion, were reserved for ephebi; but prior to their erection, the older gymnasia, doubtless, were used by members of the college. Under the Empire the Ptolemeion ceased to be mentioned in the ephebic records;[275] while the Diogeneion was seemingly the center of military and physical exercises, and a general meeting point for the ephebi. The director of the Diogeneion and his staff—caretaker, assistant paidotribe, master of fighting in armor, secretary and his assistant, *kestrophylax*, music teacher, *hegemon*, and doorman—are mentioned in certain inscriptions of the second Christian century. This staff, dis-

[270] Polybius, xxvii, 11; Livy, xlii, 65, 9; Dumont: *op. cit.*, 1, 196 f., 199 f., 234.
[271] *Concerning Gymnastics*, 14–5, *et passim*.
[272] Dumont: *op. cit.*, 1, 203; Forbes: *op. cit.*, pp. 164, 168.
[273] *Op. cit.*, 1, 310.
[274] *Ibid.*, 1, 203; Suetonius: *Nero*, 25.
[275] Dumont: *op. cit.*, 1, 209.

tinct from that of the college itself, seems to have had charge of younger boys (*mellephebi*) about to enter the ranks of ephebi.[276]

With the decline of Athenian military power, under the dominion of Macedon and of Rome, there was little or no excuse for military training. Near the close of the fourth century, ephebic training was reduced to one year and ceased to be compulsory, partly because the financial plight of the state made it impossible to continue the provision wholly at public expense.[277] As a result, while once there had been upwards of a thousand cadets, the number declined to a mere twenty or thirty. Foreigners began to be admitted in the second century, and within less than a hundred years they were more numerous than native youth.[278] The number of native-born youth alone would scarcely have kept the institution alive.

These changes affected the program of exercises profoundly. When military efficiency on the part of Athenian youth had been the dominant *raison d'être* of the college, there had been little time for devotion to literary studies. At one time, before philosophy had been accepted as a proper study for youth, the Areopagus had summoned two Athenians for attending philosophical lectures and having no visible source of livelihood.[279] But with the passing of military power, physical training for military efficiency became more and more a perfunctory matter, often a mere entertainment or exhibition, and gave way to gymnastics and literary pursuits. Exercises and games did indeed continue; but the original spirit and purpose of athletics were dead.[280] In Cicero's time, even the military training of the ephebi seemed, to a Roman at least, "far from rigorous," and the "system of exercise for young men in gymnasiums," ridiculous.[281] A constantly increasing stress is noted on literary and philosophical studies. An inscription in the last quarter of the second century B.C. shows that throughout the year the ephebi were regularly attending philosophical lectures in the Ptolemeion, Lyceum, and Academy.[282] Finally, it became unnecessary to enroll among the cadets; one might attend the lectures of rhetoricians, philosophers, and grammarians without that formality. Moreover, on leaving college, it became customary for the ephebi to make a gift of a hundred books to the college library in the Ptolemeion.[283] With the development of intellectual facilities of various kinds, to which the name University of Athens has been

[276] Forbes: op. cit., pp. 168, 176 f.
[277] Busolt-Swoboda: op. cit., II, 1191; Dumont: op. cit., I, 66 f.
[278] Forbes: op. cit., pp. 154, 159 ff., 173; Freeman: op. cit., pp. 219 f.
[279] Athenaeus, IV, 168.
[280] Dumont: op. cit., I, 234 ff.; Philostratos: Concerning Gymnastics, 2, 44–5.
[281] Cicero: De Re Publica, IV, 4.
[282] Forbes: op. cit., p. 158.
[283] Freeman: op. cit., p. 219; Walden: The Universities of Ancient Greece, pp. 38 ff.

applied, we are not immediately concerned, beyond the fact that it was the outgrowth of the union of multifarious literary and philosophical studies that flowered in the age of Athenian enlightenment with the once exclusively physical and military system of training, established and prescribed for youth of the ephebic age. Ultimately, in the institution which had been pre-eminently a place for physical training, studies triumphed to such an extent that to turn from them to athletic contests was a matter of reproach—a deviation even punished by the masters. Libanius, in the fourth century, boasted that never while he was in Athens did he "engage in a game of ball." In a letter he tells a father that he punished his son because he forsook his books and "became a sprinter." Himerius, too, warned the boys against "playing ball" and "practising athletics" and other frivolities.[284]

It has been said that when two Greeks met they founded a gymnasium. While this may seem merely a fanciful exaggeration, there can be no doubt of Greek devotion to physical culture. Pausanias [285] mentions the gymnasium as one of the earmarks of a city. Excavations show that baths and gymnasia were central features of Hellenized Oriental cities. Even such an Egyptian city as Thebes had its Greek sports and gymnasium. Studies in schools and also the extensive development of clubs reveal the pervasive influence of Greek culture. The range of Greek authors read in Egyptian schools was wide, including "Homer, Demosthenes, Euripides, Menander, Plato, Thucydides, Aristophanes, Isocrates, Xenophon"; and to this fact is traceable the fortunate preservation of many works, especially Menander.[286] The spirit and purpose of gymnastic training was of course practical and professional, for professionalism overran all the Hellenistic world.[287]

The Ephebic College, when intellectual pursuits had balanced its original military exclusiveness, represented a union of mental and physical exercises which took place in or near the gymnasium. The ephebic organization at Athens is known from inscriptions to have been in existence until 262 or 266 A.D. Since it was then in a flourishing condition, and there is no reason to think it came to a cataclysmic end, it is probable that it may have continued to the end of the third century or even longer.[288] The vitality of the Greek influence and institutions, beyond Hellas, is well illustrated in the proliferation of the

[284] Walden: op. cit., pp. 319, 325.
[285] Bk. x, 4, 1.
[286] Oldfather: The Greek Literary Texts from Greco-Roman Egypt, p. 74; Milne: "Egyptian Nationalism under Greek and Roman Rule," Jour. Egy. Archaeol., xiv, 227; Bell: "Hellenic Culture in Egypt," ibid., viii, 142–50; "The Historical Value of Greek Papyri," ibid., vi, 234–46; Westermann: "Entertainment in the Villages of Graeco-Roman Egypt," ibid., xviii, 16–27.
[287] Gardiner: "A School in Ptolemaic Egypt," Class. Rev., xliv, 211 ff.
[288] Dumont: op. cit., i, 2 f.; Forbes: op. cit., p. 178.

Ephebic College in faraway lands, to which the armies of Alexander and other forces had carried Greek practices. Though there were numerous differences as to details—age of admission, length of course, the government of the institution—the college made a place for itself for a time at Alexandria, Massilia, Antioch, Jerusalem, and even by the distant rivers of Babylon. The latest specific reference to an ephebic institution comes from Alexandria (c. 323 A.D.), and urges the cadets "to put their best foot forward in their gymnastic exhibition." [289]

*The education of labor*  Solon's law, to the effect that "no son who had not been taught a trade should be compelled to support his father," and that the Areopagus should "examine into every man's means of livelihood and chastise those who had no occupation," [290] may have given a certain "dignity to all the trades" in his day. Ultimately, however, the divisive influence of a competitive system, combined with the growth of slavery and other factors, brought manual labor into discredit as something fit only for slaves or for citizens who were too poor to afford the luxury of idleness. While Pericles is credited with saying that those engaged in business have a fair notion of politics,[291] the low regard in which manual occupations came to be held generally by intellectuals and gentlemen is well known. Xenophon set forth the incompatibility of the life of the citizen with the "illiberal arts" of the worker: ". . . to be sure, the illiberal arts, as they are called, are spoken against, and are, naturally enough, held in utter disdain in our states. For they spoil the bodies of the workmen and the foremen, forcing them to sit still and live indoors, and in some cases to spend the day at the fire. The softening of the body involves a serious weakening of the mind. Moreover, these so-called illiberal arts leave no spare time for attention to one's friends and city, so that those who follow them are reputed bad at dealing with friends and bad defenders of their country. In fact, in some of the states, and especially in those reputed warlike, it is not even lawful for any of the citizens to work at illiberal arts." [292] Aristotle called "those arts vulgar which tend to deform the body, and likewise all paid employments, for they absorb and degrade the mind." Mechanics and tradesmen should not be citizens, since their life is "ignoble and inimical to virtue." [293] Plato, too, would permit no citizen to be an artisan. Neither should

---

[289] Forbes: *op. cit.*, p. 256; chap. 7 of Professor Forbes' work has given an excellent account of ephebic institutions in Greek cities and in others to which Greek influence spread.

[290] Plutarch: *Solon*, 22. Trans. by B. Perrin. The Loeb Classical Library. Quoted by permission of Harvard University Press, Cambridge, Mass.; Jardé: *op. cit.*, p. 166.

[291] Thucydides, II, 40.

[292] Xenophon: *Oeconomicus*, IV, 2–3. Trans. by E. C. Marchant. The Loeb Classical Library. Quoted by permission of Harvard University Press, Cambridge, Mass.

[293] *Politica*, VII, 9; VIII, 2. From *The Works of Aristotle*, translated by J. A. Smith and W. D. Ross (The Clarendon Press).

an artisan be permitted to be rich, though he should have enough to buy himself tools.[294]

The gulf between rich and poor, slave and free, had a major educational significance. "School" and leisure were interdependent; a Greek proverb ran, "There is no leisure for slaves." [295] The slave, of course, did not participate in the education of the citizen; but citizens, also, were clearly limited in respect to educational opportunities,[296] if poverty prohibited payment of fees for instruction in the palaestra, music school, and gymnasium. Even the Ephebic College became exclusive, aristocratic, and noncompulsory with the city's financial and political decline.

For those without leisure, whether slave or free, apprenticeship to life's labor stood in the place of a more extensive, generous education. Long hours and hard conditions of labor left little energy to be spent in liberal training of mind or body. In early days occupations were traditional or even hereditary, and sons learned by a natural apprenticeship the trade of the father.[297] The work of a statuary was thus learned by Socrates. A more formal apprenticeship developed, however, when technical specialization made it more and more necessary. Xenophon had observed the great degree of specialization in the industries of great cities, where a single, special task, e.g., in shoe manufacture, might suffice to occupy a person and give him maintenance.[298] Moreover, "If one wants to make a man a shoe-maker, a mason, . . . one sends him to a master who can teach him." Xenophon explains that a colt should be put out for breaking, and the terms of the agreement should be "put in writing," just as when one "apprentices his son to a profession." [299] Plato [300] mentions the craftsman who may be teaching his craft to others besides his own sons. Carpentry and medicine are noted as not only practiced but also taught.[301] The training of slaves for their duties in its service was undertaken by the state, and also by private persons for profit.[302] Apprenticeship to sculptors, painters, and other craftsmen is attested by artistic remains.[303]

The principle of learning to do by doing, an apprenticeship "in sport and in earnest" to what one would do when grown up, was recognized by Plato [304]

---

[294] Laws, VIII, 846; Republic, IV, 421.
[295] Aristotle: Politica, VII, 15.
[296] Plato: Protagoras, 326.
[297] Ibid., 328; Republic, V, 467.
[298] Cyropaedia, VIII, 2, 5.
[299] Art of Horsemanship, II, 2; cited incorrectly in Freeman, op. cit., p. 44, and Anderson, "Some Facts Regarding Vocational Training among the Ancient Greeks and Romans," Sch. Rev., XX, 194, as Revenues.
[300] Republic, IV, 421.
[301] The Works of Plato (Cary, Davis, and Burges), IV, 471.
[302] Aristotle: Politica, I, 7; Whibley: op. cit., p. 420; St. John: op. cit., III, 26.
[303] Glotz: Ancient Greece at Work, pp. 277 ff.
[304] Laws, I, 643.

as sound. Vocational training was not for everybody, however, for Plato was convinced that no artisan should be a citizen, and that vocational training was scarcely worthy of being called education.[305]

Though numerous allusions show that training was commonly gained through apprenticeship, there are few specific records of apprenticeship agreements. Those recovered pertain not to Athens but to Egypt, whither Greek culture spread. Westermann mentions "nine pure apprentice contracts," five for weaving and one each for "nail-making, flute-playing, short-hand writing, and hair-dressing." The master-workman is called *didaskalos* (teacher) and the apprentice *mathetes* (pupil). Neither the state nor guilds appear to have regulated the apprenticing of youth to masters, but the parties to a contract of apprenticeship were subject to a fine if the terms of agreement were not fulfilled. The length of apprenticeship varied, in the case of weaving, "from one to five" years. Holidays, the amount to be paid, the provision of food and clothes, fines for absence from work, and provision for making up time lost by absence, were generally specified in the contract. The exact age at which apprenticeship began probably varied, but in two contracts it seems to have been entered upon when the youth was about thirteen.[306]

For the laboring class one hears of no physical sports or exercises. Organized play is a compensation, developed for those who, one way or another, have escaped from the natural exercise of toil. Those who labored long in mine, quarry, or mill had little or no surplus energy to give to other physical exercises. For them labor was enough—indeed, too much—and they lightened it by chanteys of boatmen, songs of the vintners, flailmen, and grinders at the mill. Even beggars lightened their labor with the song of the crow:

> Or a well-kneaded loaf or an obolos give,
> Or what you will, for the crow must live.[307]

[305] *Ibid.*, I, 644; VIII, 846; Anderson: *op. cit., loc. cit.*, XX, 194.
[306] Westermann: "Vocational Training in Antiquity," *Sch. Rev.*, XXII, 601–10; "Apprentice Contracts and the Apprentice System in Roman Egypt," *Class. Philol.*, IX, 295–315.
[307] St. John: *op. cit.*, III, 92.

# 11

## FREEMEN'S GAMES

Physical exercises and contests were to the privileged class of citizens what "ignoble" labor was to the poor and the slave. Manly sports prepared the citizen for the exercise of his most important vocation, that of soldier. "The practical character of Greek sports indicates a nation of warriors," says Gardiner, who credits the rise of athletics to prominence to the influence of the northern invaders.[1] Taken altogether Greek athletic sports ". . . formed a complete and adequate training for what was to an ancient citizen the chief business of life—war." [2] Like other Greeks most Athenian citizens looked forward to the life of the soldier. At the middle of the fifth century, Athens had a standing army of about twenty-five hundred hoplites, one thousand cavalry [3] —aristocratic and exclusive—and a fleet of three to four hundred ships.[4] One hundred and eighty Athenian ships took part at Salamis, each with eighteen fighting men on deck.[5] The citizen might be called for active service between twenty and fifty years of age, and for garrison duty till sixty. The hoplite, heavily armed, must be strong, indeed, to carry all his equipment—helmet, cuirass, greaves, shield, spear, and sword.[6] Victory, then, depended much upon personal courage and prowess in hand-to-hand fighting,[7] for which physical training in

---

[1] Greek Athletic Sports and Festivals, pp. 8 f.; Freeman: Schools of Hellas, p. 57.
[2] Wright: Greek Athletics, p. 42.
[3] Tarn, Hellenistic Military and Naval Developments, pp. 55 f., discusses the relatively unimportant rôle of cavalry in Greek warfare, apart from Thessaly and Macedonia.
[4] Gulick: Life of the Ancient Greeks, pp. 190 ff.; Tucker: Life in Ancient Athens, pp. 193 ff.; Tarn, op. cit., p. 124, suggests that in dealing with Greek fighting ships we should think of "a glorified racing eight" rather than our usual conception of a war vessel. The comparison should not be stressed too much, however. A trireme might have a total personnel of about two hundred men, including oarsmen, navigators, and men under arms.— Tucker: op. cit., p. 198.
[5] Plutarch: Themistocles, 14.
[6] Wright: op. cit., pp. 42–55.
[7] Tarn: op. cit., p. 3.

330

contests afforded the best conditioning. Plutarch maintained that the Thebans beat the Spartans because they were better wrestlers. The names of famous early athletes were associated with military events. Milo of Croton, who won twelve prizes at Olympia and Delphi, fought against Sybaris in 511 B.C. Phaÿllus, likewise of Croton, thrice victor at the Pythian Games, fought against the Persians.[8] Philostratos held that ancient athletes who took part in eight or nine Olympiads were also "adapted to heavy military service and fought about the walls, by no means without success therein but rather distinguished by prizes and trophies, regarding war as preliminary practice for gymnastic, and gymnastic as preliminary training for war." [9]

Certainly nothing explains more directly their preoccupation with athletics than the fact that the Greek states were constantly engaged in war, a "seasonal occupation," as Tarn says,[10] ranging from petty struggles among themselves to major conflicts against outsiders. Undoubtedly the early prominence of Sparta, whose success in physical sports and prowess in war were commonly associated as cause and effect, had a stimulating influence on physical training at Athens. It is also worthy of notice that the conflict with Persia, the greatest threat to their freedom the Greeks had faced, produced a remarkable enthusiasm for athletics at Athens. The greatest vogue of physical culture is said to have been reached between the Persian and Peloponnesian wars.[11] When military strength waned, leaders urged systematic training of Athenian youth for war.

The influence of war is evident on every side. It is prominently reflected in Greek art, religion, poetry, history, athletics. Many Athenian men of letters, Aeschylus, Sophocles, Thucydides, Xenophon, and Socrates, played also the rôle of fighting men. Plutarch found no virtues more worthy of praise than those of the excellent soldier, the character he loved best to portray. Sport held the mirror up to this prominent aspect of Athenian life. The Greeks were not inoculated with the quiet, contemplative philosophy of the Hindu; the ascetic ideal of early Christianity was incomprehensible to them in the period of their greatness. It has been suggested that the infrequency of references to sheep in Greek literature may be due to the fact that the lamb, "dumb before her shearers," was not a Hellenic ideal.[12] Instead of flight from life, the Greek chose to live to fight and fight to live. Archilochus might leave his shield behind him and celebrate the fact poetically, but he died in battle, and his poetry generally breathes the warlike spirit of the Greeks:

[8] The History of Herodotus, VIII, 47; Pausanias's Description of Greece, X, 9, 1.
[9] Philostratos: Concerning Gymnastics, 43.
[10] Op. cit., pp. 2, 8.
[11] Gardiner: op. cit., pp. 4, 107 f.; Wright: op. cit., p. 27; Bondurant: Ancient Athletics, p. 7.
[12] Lawton: The Soul of the Anthology, p. 20.

> My spear is bread, white kneaded bread,
> My spear's Ismarian wine.
> My spear is food and drink and bed,
> With it the world is mine.[13]

Aeschylus celebrates the ubiquitous, heroic ideal of warlike activity, which runs continuously, with but few dissenting notes, from Homer till the voice of Greek spokesmen is mute:

> Their life was in shafts of ash and of elm, in bright plumes fluttering wide,
> In lance and greaves and corslet and helm and heart of seven bulls' hide.[14]

Specific and direct, as well as general and implied, recognition of sports as a training for war is not wanting. Tyrtaeus, reputed lame schoolmaster of Athens who stirred the Spartans with his warlike verses, extolled sport not for its own sake but for war. Speed in running, skill in wrestling, strength, beauty, kingly power, eloquence, fame—these are of no avail unless one is "a man of mettle in fight." [15] Ischomachos, though devoted to business and directing the work of his farm, says: "After this, I usually mount my horse and go through exercises, imitating as closely as I can the exercises needed in warfare." [16] Socrates is represented as recommending physical training pre-eminently for its value in war. To Epigenes he says there is no excuse for being in bad physical condition. He needs training just like any athlete training for Olympia. "Or do you count the life and death struggle with their enemies, upon which, it may be, the Athenians will enter, but a small thing? Why, many, thanks to their bad condition, lose their life in the perils of war or save it disgracefully: many, just for this same cause, are taken prisoners. . . . Many, again, by their bodily weakness earn infamy, being thought cowards." [17]

Solon, whom Lucian represents conversing with Anacharsis about the value of athletics, expresses the state's interest in physical culture as training for war: "Accordingly we devise elaborate gymnastic exercises, appoint instructors of each variety, and teach one boxing, another the pancratium. They are to be habituated to endurance, to meet blows half way, and never shrink from a wound. This method works two admirable effects in them: makes them spirited and heedless of bodily danger, and at the same time strong and enduring. Those whom you saw lowering their heads and wrestling learn to fall safely and pick themselves up lightly, to shove and grapple and twist, to endure

---

[13] Wright: op. cit., p. 45.
[14] Ibid., p. 47.
[15] Ibid., p. 46.
[16] Xenophon: Oeconomicus, XI, 17.
[17] Xenophon: Memorabilia, III, 12, 1–2. Trans. by E. C. Marchant. The Loeb Classical Library. Quoted by permission of Harvard University Press, Cambridge, Mass.

throttling, and to heave an adversary off his legs. *Their* acquirements are not unserviceable either; the one great thing they gain is beyond dispute; their bodies are hardened and strengthened by this rough treatment. Add another advantage of some importance: it is all so much practice against the day of battle. Obviously a man thus trained, when he meets a real enemy, will grapple and throw him the quicker, or if he falls will know better how to get up again. All through we are reckoning with that real test in arms; we expect much better results from our material if we supple and exercise their bodies before the armour goes on, so increasing their strength and efficiency, making them light and wiry in themselves (though the enemy will rather be impressed with their weight).

"You see how it will act. Something may surely be expected from those in arms who even without them would be considered awkward customers; they show no inert pasty masses of flesh, no cadaverous skinniness, they are not shade-blighted women; they do not quiver and run with sweat at the least exertion, and pant under their helmets as soon as a midday sun like this adds to the burden. What would be the use of creatures who should be overpowered by thirst and dust, unnerved at sight of blood, and as good as dead before they came within bow-shot or spear-thrust of the enemy?" [18]

With the rise of professional soldiers and the various improvements in warfare consolidated by the Macedonians—such as the increased use of cavalry, light-armed soldiers, and archers—the amateur citizen-soldier ceased to play an important rôle.[19] The two systems, the amateur and the professional, were put to the test, and the latter won at the battle of Chaeronaea. From that time onward physical education of the city-state lacked the most significant social purpose that had sustained it in preceding centuries.

Dangerous exploits are in themselves satisfying to primitive, natural instincts of those who perform them, and they are commonly approved and admired regardless of whether they serve a useful purpose. The Greeks idealized dangerous, "painful," manly exercises, apart from their utilitarian value as preparation for war. The terms "laborious," "painful," "contest," "struggle" are constantly associated with their sports. Much of their life was spent participating in, or observing, contests of physical strength and skill. The heroic exploits of Theseus and Heracles embodied this ideal. Courageous men court danger; they do not merely face it when it is inevitable. Theseus "refused to make his journey by sea," the easier way, and chose the dangerous way by land, no part of which was "clear nor yet without peril from robbers and miscreants." [20] He

---

[18] Lucian: *Anacharsis*, 24–5. From *The Works of Lucian of Samosata*, translated by H. W. Fowler and F. G. Fowler (The Clarendon Press).

[19] Tarn: *op. cit.*, pp. 8 ff., 21, 43 f., 50 ff.

[20] Plutarch: *Theseus*, 6.

went out of his way to meet Phaea, the Crommynion sow, so that it might not seem that he performed all his exploits because of sheer necessity. Alexander was admired for proving that he could ride the most unmanageable horse. His father wept for joy at his success, seeing in his courage, stubborn will, and skill, a proof that he must find a larger empire for his sway.[21] Success in sport was an earnest of success in life. Parallels between games and life are constantly drawn by the Greeks. "The world is all a stage, life is a sport: away with earnest and learn to play the game, or bear thy pains." [22] The uncertainties of the outcome of athletic contests are similar to the vicissitudes of life: ". . . to pronounce any one happy . . . while he is still living and running the risks of life," said Solon, "is like proclaiming an athlete victorious and crowning him while he is still contending for the prize." [23] Themistocles was told by faint-hearted, procrastinating Eurybiades, who thought to check his impatience, that "those who start too soon get a caning" at Olympia; to which Themistocles rejoined, "But those who lag behind get no crown." [24] To refuse to play the game, no matter how painful or laborious, was to rebel against life itself. Facing the element of danger enhanced the worth of every act. Pindar never wearies of singing of deeds of peril and "paths of dang'rous fame," where "trembling cowards never tread. . . ." [25]

In addition to idealization of the hazardous and "painful," the Greeks felt a deep appreciation of physical beauty, especially if joined with the glorious vigor of youth. Parmenides sings of—

Youth that art mated with charioteers and companions immortal,
Coming to us on the coursers that bear thee, to visit our mansion. . . .[26]

Tyrtaeus proclaims: "It is a shame for an old man to lie slain in the front of the battle, his body stripped and exposed. . . . But to the young all things are seemly. . . ." [27] "For beautiful boys there is no punishment when they do wrong" also expresses the idealization of physical beauty, so conspicuously associated with paedophilia.[28] Preference for the aesthetic is nowhere more evident than in matters pertaining to physical beauty. Wealth and power, however, are not excluded. They, too, are beautiful to the Athenian.[29] The Greek generally was no lover of the ascetic ideal of poverty. Love of beauty might find

---

[21] Plutarch: *Alexander*, 6.
[22] Butcher: *Some Aspects of the Greek Genius*, p. 172.
[23] Plutarch: *Solon*, 27. Trans. by B. Perrin. The Loeb Classical Library. Quoted by permission of Harvard University Press, Cambridge, Mass.
[24] Plutarch: *Themistocles*, 11.
[25] West: *Odes of Pindar*, "First Olympian," str. 6; Lawton: *Classical Greek Literature*, p. 147.
[26] Bakewell: *Source Book in Ancient Philosophy*, pp. 12 f.
[27] Gardiner: op. cit., p. 88.
[28] *The Cambridge Ancient History*, IV, 491; Gardiner: op. cit., p. 99.
[29] Mahaffy: *Social Life in Greece*, p. 327.

expression in the simplest concrete object and in the highest intellectuality, the love of the true and the good, according to Plato's views in the *Phaedrus* and the *Symposium*. The evidence of this appreciation of harmony comes, of course, primarily from artists, poets, and philosophers, whereas stress on military values as the goal of physical education is uppermost in the minds of statesmen.

Notwithstanding numerous references to the ideal of youthful strength and beauty, one need not hold that every Greek went into raptures over nude figures, nor "that ugliness was then an actual exception." [30] To do so would be to forget certain important limitations that have already been noted in Athenian life and education. Neither should we allow ourselves to translate effects into causes. Games and sports first gained their place on very realistic grounds, long before philosophers, poets, and sculptors voiced appreciation of the beauty which they did so much to foster. Moreover, in attempting to judge the results of physical education by the art of the Greeks, one must not forget that artists, as well as others, often tend to touch up their subjects.[31] Greek art imitated nature, but also idealized it. It was said that Zeuxis combined the best parts of several bodies because no single body could be perfect enough in every respect.[32] Artistic remains have often been less subjected to scientific doubt than other kinds of sources with which historians deal. Mahaffy wisely advised that one should "not exaggerate the matter" when trying to judge Greek physical beauty. "Very few boys really equalled the ideal types of the sculptor. . . ." [33]

Just as the Greeks extolled the virtues of youth, vigor, and beauty, and sought to hold them fast, so they shrank from old age and physical enfeeblement. Longing for death, so characteristic of early Christian ascetics and still found in Christian theory, was utterly foreign to them. Socrates' cheerful anticipation of death is an exception to the general rule; and he, of course, had already lived his life. The Greeks, generally, would not have sympathized with a modern poet's plea:

> Grow old along with me,
> The best is yet to be. . . .

At best they viewed death fatalistically and faced old age with as much stoical endurance or indifference as they could muster. The "grievous" destiny dawns, even as it has been appointed. The inevitability of one's end, however, instead of causing him to shrink from life, impels him, as Pindar says in the "First Olympian," to fill to the utmost its bright hour:

30 *Ibid.*, p. 326.
31 Wright: *op. cit.*, p. 106.
32 Venturi: *History of Art Criticism*, pp. 42, 44.
33 Mahaffy: *Old Greek Education*, p. 29.

> Yet since all of mortal Frame
> Must be number'd with the Dead,
> Who in dark inglorious Shade
> Wou'd his useless Life consume,
> And with deedless Years decay'd,
> Sink unhonour'd to the Tomb? [34]

A fatalistic view of death was not without some justification. A recent careful study shows that the average expectancy of life was only twenty-nine years, whereas to-day it is over fifty-seven for men and sixty-one for women.[35] Frequent wars, unsanitary conditions, the primitive character of medical knowledge, took a heavy toll of youth especially. A study of 2,022 inscriptions shows the age groups sixteen to twenty and twenty-one to twenty-five years to be hardest hit, while children, one to five, were in third place.[36]

It has been said that the Greeks were always young. Certainly they longed to be. Perhaps it was an earnest clinging to life that caused some of them to continue to "play the game" despite encroachments of the years. The ancient athletes, according to Philostratos, were apt to "grow old late" and took part in contests sometimes for eight or nine Olympiads;[37] in later days of decadence, however, contestants could not stand the strain.[38] Theophrastus would dissuade old men from dancing and the contests of the palaestra.[39] But obviously some seem to have persisted. Socrates took up dancing at an advanced age. Ephudion, "the game old man," fought the pancration with young Ascondas, says Aristophanes.[40] Plato mentions "the wrinkled old men who have anything but an agreeable appearance when they take to gymnastics." [41] Some corroboration of the participation in sports by old men is also found in artistic remains.[42]

It would be difficult to think of Greek art without nude Greek athletes. Football suits, tennis pants, and even bathing suits are scarcely conducive to artistic appreciation of the excellent physique developed by modern sports. Greek artists were more fortunate. Just when Greek athletes began to go nude is uncertain, but Thucydides says that Lacedaemonians "were the first who in their athletic exercises stripped naked and rubbed themselves over with oil. But this

---

[34] "First Olympian," str. 6.
[35] Richardson: Old Age among the Ancient Greeks, p. 234.
[36] Ibid., pp. 231 f.
[37] Concerning Gymnastics, 43.
[38] Ibid., 2.
[39] Richardson: op. cit., p. 41.
[40] Wasps, 1190–3.
[41] Republic, v, 452. From The Works of Plato, translated and edited by Benjamin Jowett (Oxford University Press).
[42] Richardson: op. cit., pp. 107 f.

was not the ancient custom; athletes formerly, even when they were contending at Olympia, wore girdles about their loins, a practice which lasted until quite lately." [43] Pausanias says that Orsippos was the first who won a race at Olympia, running without a girdle, either by accident or design.[44] The gymnasts at Olympia, according to Pausanias and Philostratos,[45] wore a cloak while performing their duties, until the discovery of Pherenike's deception caused the promulgation of a decree that they must appear unclad. The practice of competing nude doubtless grew gradually, and was not followed in all contests alike. Vase painters commonly depicted the girdle in the seventh century, and then gradually omitted it. Sculptors generally represented charioteers draped, but exceptions occur.[46] The barbarians of Asia, according to Thucydides, still continued to wear girdles when engaging in contests of boxing and wrestling. Herodotus observed that Lydians and barbarians generally held it a mark of disgrace "even to a man, to be seen naked." [47] Plato says that "not long ago" the Hellenes also believed that "a naked man was ridiculous and improper." Though he himself went so far as to propose physical training for men and women, he recognized that such an innovation would excite ridicule, just as nudity of men had once done.[48] Having become accustomed to nudity, the benefits of which were so obvious, the Greeks naturally prided themselves on sturdy, sun-tanned bodies—a distinction which set them off from their barbarian neighbors. Agesilaus sought to show his soldiers how inferior were the delicate, white, effeminate bodies of their adversaries.[49]

Emphasis on proportion and moderation is characteristic of the Athenian athletic ideal, in contrast with the one-sidedness of training in Lacedaemon.[50] That the mean is superior to either extreme became a common judgment. Theognis says: "Avoid excess; the mean is best." The theory of the mean, as applied to educational matters, is of course a product of the age of enlightenment. It appealed to the minds of philosophers, doubtless, as a prophylactic against the evils of professionalism that were beginning to appear. It must be understood, then, not as a description of what was, but as a guide to what ought to be. Socrates is said to have avoided excessive gymnastic exercises.[51] Though he recognized the practical utility of physical training for war, he had also a

[43] Thucydides, I, 6. From Thucydides, translated by B. Jowett (The Clarendon Press).
[44] Bk. I, 44, 1; Krause: Olympia oder Darstellung der Grossen Olympischen Spiele, pp. 339 ff.
[45] Concerning Gymnastics, 17; Pausanias, V, 6, 7–8; VI, 7, 2.
[46] Hyde: Olympic Victor Monuments, p. 48.
[47] Bk. I, 10.
[48] Republic, V, 452. From The Works of Plato, translated and edited by Benjamin Jowett (Oxford University Press).
[49] Plutarch: Agesilaus, 9.
[50] Forbes: Greek Physical Education, p. 10; Freeman: op. cit., pp. 279 f.; Davidson: Education of the Greek People, pp. 22 f.
[51] Grote: A History of Greece, III, 430.

profound appreciation of the beautiful for its own sake. "It is a disgrace," he said, "to grow old through sheer carelessness before seeing what manner of man you may become by developing your bodily strength and beauty to their highest limit." [52] This beauty lay essentially in proportion. Socrates noted that long-distance runners had thick legs and narrow shoulders, while gladiators and wrestlers had broad shoulders and small legs. He recommended dancing because no part of the ". . . body remained idle; neck and legs and hands together, one and all were exercised. That is how a man should dance, who wants to keep his body light and healthy." [53] Athletic exercises, moderately employed, are useful to men, but they are evil when carried to excess, said Aristotle; and he observed that Olympic victors, though they had gained prizes in youth, were rarely able to win them as men also, the early excessive training having "exhausted their constitutions." [54]

The highest general utility of physical culture, its function as governor that regulates the health of the body on which everything we do depends, was stressed by Socrates: ". . . in everything that men do the body is useful; . . . even in the process of thinking, in which the use of the body seems to be reduced to a minimum, it is matter of common knowledge that grave mistakes may often be traced to bad health. And because the body is in a bad condition, loss of memory, depression, discontent, insanity often assail the mind so violently as to drive whatever knowledge it contains clean out of it." [55]

While the state encouraged sport for the sake of military ends, and poets, artists, and philosophers extolled the dangerous, heroic, strong, and beautiful as attractive in themselves, the original and basic impetus to sports lay, as Philostratos said, within man's nature.[56] The conspicuous love of sports is preeminently an indication of the strength of the drive to activity, the will to life, to superiority, to victory, to power, that was characteristic of the Greeks. Similar primitive, natural tendencies, varying in intensity, existed in other ancient nations, as we have seen, but various factors—geographic, climatic, social, political [57]—led the Greeks to indulge in sportive, physical activity to a degree unknown to less accessible, less mobile, less democratic societies of the Orient.

This strong drive to activity, to life, linked men to the gods. The essence of the gods is power, superiority. The stronger, the more active, the more cunning are superior men. Religion reflects the life of a people; in it their aspira-

[52] Xenophon: Memorabilia, III, 12, 1–5, 8. Trans. by E. C. Marchant. The Loeb Classical Library. Quoted by permission of Harvard University Press, Cambridge, Mass.

[53] Xenophon: Symposium, II, 17. Trans. by O. J. Todd. The Loeb Classical Library. Quoted by permission of Harvard University Press, Cambridge, Mass.

[54] Politica, VIII, 4.

[55] Xenophon: Memorabilia, III, 12, 5–6. Trans. by E. C. Marchant. The Loeb Classical Library. Quoted by permission of Harvard University Press, Cambridge, Mass.

[56] Concerning Gymnastics, 16.

[57] Jüthner: "Gymnastik," Real-Encyclopädie, VII, Pt. II, 2035.

tions are revealed. An essentially religious nature is evident in Greek sports.[58] The origin of athletic contests, and even training for them, is credited to various gods and demigods—Prometheus, Hermes Enagios, the maid Palaistra, Theseus, Heracles—but, of course, the Greeks did not always agree about their own traditions.[59] Athletic festivals were first held in religious veneration of the dead. The Greeks fancied their gods playing, just as they themselves loved to do, except that they were more powerful, swifter, surer to win. Deities pursue such a royal sport as hunting, and also a democratic pastime like fishing.[60] "Painful" contests raised man's stock of heroic virtue to a higher level and brought him closer to the gods. To win victories in sport was godlike; on occasion it brought men honors commonly accorded to the gods. Herodotus tells of a certain Philip, "an Olympian victor," the "handsomest Greek of his day," for whom a temple was erected and divine honors appointed.[61] Generally, however, Greeks did not look favorably on such high fortune, since they remembered that the gods could both raise and throw men down with ease. Plutarch says that someone advised Diagoras, who had himself been crowned at Olympia, and had seen his sons and grandsons victors: "Die now, Diagoras; thou canst not ascend to Olympus." [62] Youth seems immortal, however; and play is the mirror of youth. Pindar, singer of victors, seems to see in men at play some kinship with the agelessness of the gods:

> So they take their delight, whenever the games are appointed.
> One would believe them to be immortal and ageless for ever. . . .[63]

### ATHENIANS AT PLAY BEFORE THEIR GODS

The union of sport and religion in festivals, wherein the Muses also had a part, had a definite bearing on the movement for unification within various Greek city-states and also throughout the nation. This relation is shown both in local and national athletic festivals. Though Athens was by no means most renowned for athletic prowess, her delight in festivals seems to have exceeded others, judging from the number of them and the amount of time devoted to them. Besides these there were many beyond her borders,[64] in which Athenians might participate as onlookers and as contestants, even as citizens from elsewhere came to share the sportive hospitality of Athens. Mommsen [65] has made

58 Lawton: Successors of Homer, pp. 133 ff.
59 Pausanias, I, 39, 3; Theocritus: The Idylls, 24; Philostratos: Concerning Gymnastics, 16; Forbes: op. cit., p. 7.
60 Butcher: op. cit., p. 263.
61 Bk. v, 47.
62 Pelopidas, 34.
63 Lawton: Successors of Homer, p. 134.
64 Nilsson: Griechische Feste von Religiöser Bedeutung, passim.
65 Feste der Stadt Athen im Altertum, passim.

up from a host of sources an extensive calendar of Athenian festivals that are known to us. Apart from various monthly sacrifices and ceremonies, he mentions forty festivals—some of them, the country Dionysia, for example, being observed independently in practically every village of Attica—ranging from the one-day Feast of Kronos, at the year's beginning, to the Diisoteria which came at its close. Of some of these little is known except the name; there may have been many others of which even that bare record has been lost. About seventy days of the year [66] are said to have been devoted to celebrations. These were to the Greeks days of rest, recreation, patriotism, and religious devotion, as Sundays and various national holidays are to peoples of the modern world. The "holy festivals," says Plato, were ordained of the gods, who pitied the laborious toils of men and sought thereby to "alternate rest with labour." [67]

To catalogue all the known festivals would be tedious and unprofitable, but a rough, twofold classification may be noted: first, festivals consisting of religious processions, sacrifices, feasting, drinking, and competitions in music, dancing, recitation, dramatic performances; and second, those whose religious and artistic features are known to have been combined with athletic contests. To the first category belong: the festival of Kronos, celebrated on July 12, marked by the feasting together of masters and servants in honor of the divinities of heaven and earth, Kronos and Rhea; [68] the Synoecia, in commemoration of the unification of Athens, attributed to Theseus, [69] and held in honor of him and Athena; the Thesmophoria, a joyous, five-day women's festival, held in October in honor of Demeter, for which a solemn nine-day preparation was required; the Lenaea, one of many lesser feasts in honor of the wine press, celebrated in January with drinking of new wine, a great banquet, and dramatic competitions; and the Great Dionysia, a March festival of five days or more, in which contests were held in boys' and men's choruses, tragedies, and comedies. [70] In the second category, in which athletic events had a place, were many of the most famous festivals and others less well known; the Panathenaea; the Heraclea at Marathon and in the Kynosarges at Athens; Eleusinia; Oschophoria; Thesea; Epitaphia; the Apaturia, with which were associated the Promethea and the Hephaestia; the country Dionysia; Munychia; Aiantea; the Athenian Olympia; Bendidea; and the Diisoteria.

The administration of public sacrifices and the taking of auspices were lodged, according to Aristotle, in the hands of Commissioners of Public Worship (hieropoei), elected by lot by the Assembly. Ten others, similarly chosen,

[66] Whibley: Companion to Greek Studies, p. 324.
[67] Laws, ii, 653. From The Works of Plato, translated and edited by Benjamin Jowett (Oxford University Press).
[68] Mommsen: op. cit., pp. 32 ff.
[69] Thucydides, ii, 15.
[70] Mommsen: op. cit., pp. 35 ff., 308 ff., 372 ff., 428 ff.

known as Annual Commissioners, had charge of certain sacrifices and administered all the quadrennial festivals, save the Panathenaea. These included the festival of Delos, which Athens had taken under her care, Brauronia, Heraclea, Eleusinia, and the Hephaestia.[71] Ten Commissioners of Games (*athlothĕtae*), also chosen by lot, after passing an examination, served four years. Their duties were to take charge of the Panathenian procession, the contests in music and gymnastics, and the horse races; and to provide the new *peplos* for Athena, as well as prize oil and vases for the victorious contestants.[72]

Little is known of the physical contests associated with these festivals, save the Panathenaea. The Heraclea at Marathon and in the Kynosarges at Athens were midsummer festivals. At the Marathonian, gymnastic contests were held and the victors well rewarded.[73] Whether athletic contests were conducted at the Kynosargean Heraclea, or Diomea,[74] is doubtful. The Eleusinian ceremonies were celebrated each year,[75] partly in Athens, partly in Eleusis. Though not a national festival, they drew such vast crowds from abroad as to give the appearance of a Hellenic festival.[76] Occupying altogether about two weeks' time, they were marked by an assemblage of the people in Athens, addresses, purifications, feasting, fasting, sacrifices, the procession of the holy child Iaachus to Eleusis—with dancing, games, and other aids to merriment. At Eleusis itself three to four days were devoted to celebrations, the most important feature being the dramatic unfolding of the Great Mysteries. The Eleusinian contests may have merited the claim to greater antiquity than those of Olympia itself. At any rate, an ancient *halteres*, belonging perhaps to the early sixth century, suggests a long tradition of competitive sports at Eleusis. The contests of the festival have been placed after the Mysteries by some; Mommsen, however, holds they must have preceded them.[77] The order may have varied at different periods. The program included gymnastic contests and horse races, the victors receiving as prizes certain measures of corn or barley at the hands of the Eleusinian priests.[78] Pindar names two who had conquered at Eleusis: Epharmostus in wrestling and Herodotus of Thebes, in the chariot race.[79]

The Oschophoria, Thesea, and the Epitaphia were closely associated, and all took place in October. At the Oschophoria two youths from each tribe, and from the better families, raced in pairs from the temple of Dionysius to Athena

[71] Aristotle: *Atheniensium Respublica*, 54; Mommsen: *op. cit.*, pp. 325 f., 340 f.
[72] *Ath. Resp.*, 60, 62.
[73] Mommsen: *op. cit.*, p. 167; Pindar: "Olympian" IX, str. 4; XIII, ep. 5.
[74] Aristophanes: *The Frogs*, 650–1.
[75] Mommsen: *op. cit.*, pp. 184, 244 f.
[76] Blümner: *The Home Life of the Ancient Greeks*, p. 378.
[77] *Op. cit.*, p. 184; Blümner: *op. cit.*, p. 382.
[78] Mommsen: *op. cit.*, pp. 190, 197.
[79] "Olympian" IX, str. 4; "Isthmian" I, ant. 4.

THE FOOT RACE

*Antikensammlungen*, Munich (Courtesy, Professor C. A. Robinson, from G. W. Botsford and C. A. Robinson, *Hellenic History*, Rev. Ed., Pl. 21, The Macmillan Company, New York, 1948)

Skiras, bearing vine branches laden with grapes. The ten winners were re-warded with a fivefold drink (*pentaploa*) of wine, honey, cheese, barley, and oil.[80] These races preceded the Thesea, a yearly festival primarily for Athenian youth, commemorating the home-coming of Theseus, first established about 475 B.C. when the bones of Theseus were brought from Skyros to Athens.[81] This festival was marked by a procession, sacrifices, a great, free feast for citizens, and many gymnastic contests—the long race, stade-race, double race, wrestling, boxing, pancration, race in heavy armor, hoplomachy, and throwing the javelin. The contests were arranged by groups according to age—a first, second, and third class for Attic boys, a fourth open to non-Attic youth as well, and a fifth class for men. The long race, race in heavy armor, javelin-throwing, and the contest in hoplomachy were entered apparently by older youth and the men. Only Attic victors are recorded for the first three classes; but in the fourth and fifth there were foreign victors, though few in number.[82] Besides these there were horse races and other cavalry competitions for several classes —in one record, a chariot race—and torch races for boys, youth, and men. The ceremonies of the Epitaphia, in honor of those fallen in battle, concluded the Thesea [83] and included similar exercises—foot races, a race in armor, torch races for youth and men, and military exhibitions—besides sacrificial and musical ceremonies.

The Apaturia was a three- or four-day festival about October 19 to October 21, celebrated generally in Attica as well as in Athens, at which was held a feast of the phratries where newborn children of citizens were presented before Zeus and Athena and legitimized. Closely associated with the Apaturia were the musical contests and torch races in honor of Hephaestus, in which the celebrants, dressed in their best, lighted torches at the hearth on which the sacred sacrifice was burning, and sang praises to the god of fire. Similar honors were paid to Prometheus.[84]

Throughout the winter, beginning with November, little attention was given to strictly athletic events; but festivals of a musical and dramatic character were numerous.[85] In December, and also later in some places, when country folk had little to do, the "lesser" or country Dionysia were celebrated by villages and individual families throughout Attica, as elsewhere in Hellas. At these village festivals there were choral and dramatic contests and such rural sports as ἀσκώλιασμός—trying to stand on one leg on an oiled wine sack.

April was a month of renewed activity, particularly on the sea. The Del-

80 *Athenaeus*, XI, 495–6; Mommsen: *op. cit.*, p. 283.
81 Mommsen: *op. cit.*, p. 289.
82 *Ibid.*, pp. 294 ff.
83 *Ibid.*, pp. 305 ff.
84 *Ibid.*, pp. 327 ff., 339 ff.
85 Gardner and Jevons: *A Manual of Greek Antiquities*, pp. 291 ff.

phinia, held on April 6, was sacred to Apollo and Artemis. At the Munychia, held on April 16 in honor of Artemis, and the Aiantea, named for Ajax and celebrating the victory at Salamis, there were boat races in the harbor and a procession; then a trip to Salamis, marked by a procession, sacrifices to Zeus, a boat race in honor of Ajax in specially constructed boats owned by the state,[86] a long race between youth of Salamis and youth of Athens, and torch races.[87] The Athenian Olympia, established by the Pisistratids, when the building of a temple to Olympian Zeus was begun, likewise fell in April. These games, equestrian and gymnastic in character, probably lapsed for a time, for Athens' resources declined and she was compelled to curtail festival as well as other expenses; but with the completion of the temple by Hadrian they were revived and extensively developed.[88] In May and June the sports calendar drew to a close with the Bendidea and the Diisoteria. The Bendidea, a festival in honor of the Thracian goddess Bendis, introduced in Athens about the time of Pericles, included processions by day, a novel, outlandish torch race on horseback in the evening, and revels at night.[89] The rites of Diisoteria, in honor of Zeus Soter, seem to have been celebrated partly at Athens but chiefly at the Piraeus, where a boat race by the ephebi was a prominent feature.[90]

Towering above all Athenian festivals in magnificence, variety of display, and cultural and political significance was the Great Panathenaea, symbolizing the unification of the Attic land and its inhabitants under the hegemony of Athens. The festival, held quadrennially in the third year of the Olympiad, lasted from July 21 to July 29. Though credited to Theseus, the Great Panathenaea was instituted or, in any case, greatly extended and perfected at the time of Solon and Pisistratus.[91] A less imposing festival of Athena, of earlier origin, the Little Panathenaea, continued to be held in the years between celebrations of the great festival. It is doubtless an outgrowth of these ancient "Athenian games" that we see in the Great Panathenaea, said to have been begun in 566 B.C. Solon, it is known, had encouraged athletics by establishing rules for gymnasia and by awarding prizes of five hundred drachmas to Olympian victors, and smaller ones to victors in less famous games.[92] Pisistratus, like many another tyrant, attached great importance to religious festivals. Ambitious for the commercial advancement, wealth, power, and leadership of Athens, he took under his care the old Delian festival, a religious event of great

[86] Gardner: "Boat-races at Athens," Jour. Hellenic Studies, II, 316; Dumont: Essai sur l'Éphébie Attique, I, 274 ff.
[87] Mommsen: op. cit., pp. 463 f.
[88] Ibid., pp. 465 ff.
[89] Ibid., pp. 488 ff.
[90] Ibid., pp. 524 ff.; Dumont: op. cit., I, 291.
[91] Pausanias, VIII, 2, 1; Plutarch: Theseus, 24; Mommsen: op. cit., pp. 41 ff., 153; Hyde: op. cit., pp. 17 f.
[92] Gardiner: op. cit., p 74.

moment to all Ionians since ancient days, purified the sanctuary, and established the quadrennial festival, introducing equestrian contests for the first
time. Language and literature kept pace with religion as unifying influences.
Understanding the significance of cultural matters, and hoping therein also to
make Athens the leader, Pisistratus is said to have provided for the first time
an authoritative edition of the Homeric poems and caused their recitation to
be made a regular part of the Great Panathenaea. In the Periclean age the
Odeon was erected, designed especially for the musical contests.

The program of the Great Panathenaea in the fourth century devoted three
days to musical contests, which Pericles is said to have instituted; [93] two, to
gymnastic contests; one, at least, to equestrian events; one, to Pyrrhic dances
and the manly beauty contest; one, to torch races, night revels, sacrifices, a great
feast, and the magnificent Panathenian procession in which a new peplos was
carried to the virgin goddess of the Acropolis; and another, the ninth day, to
a regatta.

Victors were rewarded with various gifts: oil from the sacred olives; vases,
often decorated with likenesses of Athena and a scene of the contest in which
victory was gained; silver and gold, in the case of musical contests; [94] and an
ox for victors in Pyrrhic dances.[95] The value of prizes varied naturally with the
contests, ranging from one amphora of oil (the second prize in the contest of
throwing the javelin on horseback) to 140 amphorae, which was first prize for
the chariot race with grown horses. First prizes were generally five times the
value of the second.[96] The oil was requisitioned by the archon from the groves
of sacred olives at the rate of three-fourths of a pint for each plant, and turned
over to the treasurers who gave it to the Commissioners of the Games, by
whom it was adjudged to the victors.[97]

That the athletic contests for boys and men existed in the sixth century and
included the usual contests of the Olympian festival is shown by early prize
vases. Later, by the fourth century, contests for boys, youths, and men were
distinguished. The contests for boys and youths and the oil prizes were as
shown in Table I in the early fourth century.

In the third century and the second, the events listed in Table II, open to

93 Mommsen: op. cit., p. 153; Plutarch: Pericles, 13.
94 Aristotle: Ath. Resp., 60.
95 Blümner: op. cit., p. 374.
96 Whibley: op. cit., p. 325; Mommsen: op. cit., pp. 70, 85.
97 Aristotle: Ath. Resp., 60.

BOYS WRESTLING

National Museum, Athens (Courtesy, The Metropolitan Museum of Art, New York)

TABLE I   EVENTS AND PRIZES FOR BOYS AND YOUTHS [98]

| Boys | | | Youths | | |
|---|---|---|---|---|---|
| Events | First Prize | Second Prize | Events | First Prize | Second Prize |
| Stade-race | [50] | 10 Amphorae | Stade-race | 60 | 12 Amphorae |
| Pentathlon | 30 | 6 " | Pentathlon | 40 | 8 " |
| Wrestling | 30 | 6 " | Wrestling | 40 | [ 8] " |
| Boxing | 30 | 6 " | Boxing | [40 | 8] " |
| Pancration | 40 | 8 " | [Pancration | 50 | 10] " |

TABLE II   CONTESTS FOR BOYS, YOUTHS, AND MEN [99]

| Boys | Youths | Men |
|---|---|---|
| Long race | Stade-race | Long race |
| Stade-race | Pentathlon | Stade-race |
| Double stade-race | Wrestling | Double stade-race |
| Wrestling | Boxing | Horse race |
| Boxing | Pancration | Pentathlon |
| Pancration | | Wrestling |
| | | Boxing |
| | | Pancration |
| | | Hoplite contest |

boys, youths and men, are believed to have occurred in the order indicated, beginning with the long race for boys and following through to the hoplite contest for men.

While the contests of the gymnasium were no respecters of wealth, the sports of the turf favored the long purse. In Homeric times equestrian events

---

[98] Mommsen: *op. cit.*, p. 70.
[99] *Ibid.*, pp. 70 f.

were associated with nobility and wealth. The four-horse and two-horse chariot races and the simple horse race were evidently a favorite pastime of the aristocratic element of Athenian society in the sixth century B.C., judging from the Panathenian amphorae; and though Solon may have sought to discourage such great devotion to it,[100] the love of the turf seems to have triumphed over gymnastics, as far as families of means were concerned. During the Transition period the popularity of the racecourse seems to have been extremely high. That this had something to do with depleting the palaestra and gymnasium seems quite probable; it may well be, too, that the morals of luxury-loving, spendthrift youth were undermined more effectively at the racecourse than in the circles of the new learning. That it contributed to the financial ruin of families, Aristophanes informs us in inimitable fashion. Old Strepsiades tells over the tale of indebtedness, incurred by his son for horses, chariots, and wagers, and solemnly concludes:

A galloping consumption caught my fortunes.[101]

At the Panathenian festival equestrian contests were evidently very popular, one day, or perhaps two, being given to them. That they increased in fame is attested by the number of wealthy and noble folk who came from abroad to participate in them. Even a few foreign women entered the races. In the second century B.C., when equestrian events sometimes numbered as many as twenty-four or more, the program for foreign visitors seems to have been more or less independent—a "contest within a contest." The number as well as the quality of folks from abroad seems to have varied from time to time; the splendor of races fluctuated sympathetically, a somewhat restricted program being offered when Athenians were more to themselves.[102]

Military displays and contests were prominent features of the local program. Though cavalry was not a strong branch of Athenian forces, at one time the well-to-do citizens furnished horses for the army, and the Council examined the condition of the cavalry.[103] These competitions must have had a serious significance in the fourth century, as a stimulus to interest in the cavalry forces of the city; but later, when Athenian military power was a thing of the past, they were nothing more than a show to delight the spectators. Indicative of the strength of the military tradition is the prominence of the apobates, a race which seems generally to have been first on the program,[104] though the order of the events varied. The apobates, associated with Attica and Boeotia, and tracing its origin back to Erechtheus, was a chariot race in which several teams participated, each consisting of a charioteer and a warrior. The latter, armed

[100] Gardiner: op. cit., p. 74.
[101] Clouds, 74.
[102] Mommsen: op. cit., pp. 86, 88 ff., 153.
[103] Aristotle: Ath. Resp., 49.
[104] Mommsen: op. cit., p. 95.

with triple-crested helmet and a small round shield, mounted and dismounted from the chariot at full speed. The finish of the race appears to have been unusual in that, having dismounted, the several warriors raced to the goal, while the charioteers themselves contended, there being thus two winners, a charioteer and an *apobates*.[105]

A splendid military display seems to have been provided by the *anthippasia*, a mass contest in which the cavalry of five tribes opposed that of the other five, the prize going to the best tribe or to its leader. Xenophon, zealous propagandist for improvement of cavalry, gives an account of the *anthippasia* as it ought to be conducted: "When the Hippodrome is the scene of the display, the right plan would be that the men should first be drawn up on a front broad enough to fill the Hippodrome with horses and drive out the people standing there. In the sham fight when the regiments pursue and fly from one another at the gallop in two squadrons of five regiments, each side led by its commander, the regiments should ride through one another. How formidable they will look when they charge front to front; how imposing when, after sweeping across the Hippodrome, they stand facing one another again; how splendid, when the trumpet sounds and they charge once more at a quicker pace! After the halt, the trumpet should sound once more, and they should charge yet a third time at top speed; and when they have crossed, they should all range themselves in battle line preparatory to being dismissed, and ride up to the Council, just as you are accustomed to do. I think that these manoeuvres would look more like war and would have the charm of novelty. It is unworthy of his high rank that a cavalry commander should gallop at a slower pace than the colonels, and ride in the same way as they do." [106]

From the sixth to the fourth century B.C. the Panathenian Games seem to have been held at Echelida, a deme near the Piraeus; but about 338 the gymnastic contests took place in the splendid Panathenian stadium built under Lycurgus. From Xenophon's account of the *anthippasia*, it appears that equestrian events were still held at times in the hippodrome at Echelida.[107]

Prizes for equestrian victors exceeded greatly those for gymnastic events, possibly because the maintenance of horses and chariots was expensive, and also because the prizes must be commensurate with the quality of noble, even royal, contestants. Even though liberal, the prizes certainly never covered expenses; for that reason, probably, the racecourse continued to be for those Athenians and foreigners who could afford to indulge luxurious tastes, and there was no host of professional equestrian contenders running from place to place to pick up prizes, a practice which grew more and more among pro-

[105] *Ibid.*, pp. 89 ff.; Hyde: *op. cit.*, pp. 272 ff.
[106] Xenophon: *The Cavalry Commander*, III, 10–3. *Scripta Minora*, trans. by E. C. Marchant. The Loeb Classical Library. Quoted by permission of Harvard University Press, Cambridge, Mass.
[107] *Ibid.*, III, 11; Mommsen: *op. cit.*, pp. 84, 97 f.

fessional boxers and wrestlers. A few figures, gleaned from the third and second centuries B.C., are significant of the intrusion of professional athleticism and the decline of general participation of Athenians in the gymnastic contests. Of "some sixty victors" whose native lands are recorded, only seven came from Athens, five of whom won the pancration.[108]

Though the equestrian events varied considerably from time to time, the following program, although clearly not complete, shows the order and the character of six of the contests and the prizes awarded in the early fourth century.

TABLE III   EQUESTRIAN EVENTS AND PRIZES [109]

| Events | First Prize | Second Prize |
|---|---|---|
| Colts: chariot race | 40 | 8 Amphorae |
| Horses: chariot race | 140 | 40 " |
| War horses: race | 16 | 4 " |
| War horses: chariot race | 30 | 6 " |
| Chariot procession | 4 | 1 " |
| Javelin contest on horseback | 5 | 1 " |

Next in the order of events, on the seventh day, came Pyrrhic dances, performed to the stirring notes of the flute, simulating the movements of warlike encounter and symbolizing the triumph of Athena and the Olympian gods over their enemies. These dances, which were perhaps instituted in the sixth century, following earlier Spartan usage, were given a place in both the "little" and the "great" Panathenaea. From about the time of Pisistratus, it seems, the Pyrrhic contests were engaged in by groups of eight against eight, at first in two, and later in three, age-classes—boys, youths, and men—each group of eight being selected, equipped, and led by a choregus, as was the cyclic chorus. The prize to the winners of each class was an ox worth one hundred drachmas, destined for sacrifice and perhaps led by the victors in the great procession on the following day. Whether each age-class contest took place separately or whether all three were performed simultaneously is uncertain, but the combined action would most vividly realize the purpose of the dance, i.e., portrayal of conflict on the field of battle.[110]

Contests in manly vigor and beauty (εὐανδρία) followed the Pyrrhic dances on the seventh day. There seems to have been different types of Euandria, peaceful and military, one for "old men" another for younger men.[111] The prizes, too, may have reference to two different contests, one prize being an ox worth a hundred drachmas, and another, a shield.[112] These contests in manly

---

108 Mommsen: op. cit., p. 83.
109 Ibid., p. 85.
110 Ibid., pp. 99 f.
111 Xenophon: Memorabilia, III, 3, 12; Symposium, IV, 17; Mommsen: op. cit., pp. 102 f. A beauty contest for women is revealed by inscriptional evidence, but in Arcadia, not Athens.—Ringwood: Agonistic Features of Local Greek Festivals, p. 7.
112 Aristotle: Ath. Resp., 60; Mommsen: op. cit., p. 101.

HORSEMEN, PANATHENIAN PROCESSION
(From a photograph in the author's collection)

beauty and vigor, like the Pyrrhic dances, were liturgies, performed under the direction of wealthy citizens and paid for by them.[113] The religious bearing of the contest is seen in the fact that the victors bore consecrated olive branches in honor of Athena.

Following the εὐανδρία there was another liturgical event, a torch race, under the direction of gymnasiarchs, the prize for the winner being a water jar worth thirty drachmas. The torch races began, apparently, in the evening and were followed by night revels, singing, and dancing.[114]

Probably the stateliest moment achieved by any Greek festival is the Panathenian Procession. In this, the crowning event of the nine-day festival, the whole of Athens and her realm seem to move forward—those who have competed, lost, and won: young men, old men, women, and girls; citizens and metics; armed men on foot, on horseback, and in chariots; musicians, choruses, archons, and other officials of the city. Under the amiable eyes of Zeus and the whole company of the gods, all move forward to make a great sacrifice, and to present the goddess with a new dress, woven by matrons and

[113] Blümner: op. cit., pp. 374 f.
[114] Euripides: Children of Hercules, 777–84; Mommsen: op. cit., pp. 101, 103 ff.; Blümner: op. cit., pp. 375 f.

daughters of her city, and borne in procession to Athena in her temple. There she stands, flanked by the priest and the Attic maidens with sacred vessels—a scene made vivid on the frieze of the Parthenon, and recalled by Ovid:

> 'Twas now the Feast when each Athenian maid
> Her Yearly homage to Minerva paid;
> In canisters, with garlands cover'd o'er,
> High on their head, their mystic gifts they bore. . . .[115]

Aristophanes tells us that the test of the old education, worthy of freemen, was not—

> Who can make a fine oration?

Instead—

> It was, who can row the best? [116]

Participation of the ephebi in boat races was a part of certain Athenian festivals.[117] On the final day of the Great Panathenaea, following the procession, feasting, and revelry, a regatta was held—an event added perhaps in the time of Themistocles and symbolic of Athenian ambitions on the sea. Little is known of the contest, but competition was by tribes, each presumably being represented by a ship. There were at least two prizes: the first, three hundred drachmas, or three oxen of that value, plus a sum of two hundred drachmas—the allowance for a feast; the second, two hundred drachmas. An ephebic relief of the Roman imperial period, dug up at Athens, depicting a boat race, torch race, and wrestling, may refer to the Panathenian contest; or it may be associated with the Munychia.[118] Pausanias mentions a ship near the Areopagus "made for the procession at the Panathenian festival." [119] If the mind's eye were to follow the comic poet Plato, in his allusion to the tomb of Themistocles on the promontory of the Piraeus, one might catch a glimpse of merchantmen—

> And watch the galleys as they race below.[120]

## PROFESSIONALISM AND THE DECLINE OF ATHLETICS

It has been noted that physical training was originally closely associated with service to the state. The flood tide of interest in it came with the rise of Athens

---

[115] Metamorphoses (Dryden), II, 711 et seq.
[116] Wasps, 1094–8. Trans. by B. B. Rogers. The Loeb Classical Library. Quoted by permission of Harvard University Press, Cambridge, Mass.
[117] Dumont: op. cit., I, 274 ff.; Gardner: "Boat-races among the Greeks," Jour. Hellenic Studies, II, 90–7; "Boat-races at Athens," ibid., II, 315 ff.
[118] Dumont: op. cit., I, 274; Mommsen: op. cit., pp. 145 f.
[119] Bk. I, 29. 1.
[120] Clough: Plutarch's Lives, I, 268.

to leadership in the world; the ebb began with her waning and decay. Just as success in the Persian wars and imperialistic expansionist ambitions had stimulated interest in physical training, so the Peloponnesian struggle, defeat, and subsequent contraction of Athens' sphere in the century following brought inattention to physical training and contempt for the soldierly ideal. For when the city had lost its independence, when it came at length to rely on the *Pax Romana*, what son of Athens could take seriously the ideal of military service on her behalf? The citizen-soldier had been replaced by the mercenary. The social purpose was lost; the individual became an end in himself. Amateur athletics went out; professional athletics came in. The decline of attention to physical fitness in the Transition was noted disapprovingly by Xenophon: Athenians "not only neglect to make themselves fit, but mock at those who take the trouble to do so." [121] Horses and chariots became more popular with the rich and aristocratic than the grueling exercises of the gymnasium. Isocrates declared that public festivals had become extravagant, ostentatious, empty shows in contrast to the "sane moderation" that previously characterized them.[122] The new intellectualism also offered serious competition. Aristophanes observed that the desire of all in the state was to "harangue" and "debate," and consequently the palaestras were "deserted and empty." [123] The disgruntled author of *The Polity of the Athenians* complained that "citizens devoting their time to gymnastics and to the cultivation of music are not to be found in Athens . . ." [124] as they were in the old days before the advent of democracy. Modern archaeologists corroborate these views, having found evidence of the decline in the fact that artistic remains of the latter part of the fifth century and the fourth show less and less attention to the exercises of the palaestra and more to "conversation scenes." [125]

Professionalism negated the ideals of early Athenian physical culture. Those ideals, doubtless, had never been fully realized. There was, from the very beginning, an element in athletics which, carried to excess, proved destructive. The hero-worship, accorded to the successful athlete of Pindar's day and earlier, led ultimately to the sacrifice of everything for the sake of success. Instead of harmony of development and general excellence in many sports, professionalism required specialization in particular sports for the sake of winning. This produced a one-sidedness previously unknown. Socrates noted the overdevelopment of the legs of runners and of the upper part of the bodies of boxers. Artis-

[121] *Memorabilia*, III, 5, 15.
[122] *Areopagiticus*, 53.
[123] *Frogs*, 1069–70.
[124] *Op. cit.*, I, 13.
[125] Manning: "Professionalism in Greek Athletics," *Class. Weekly*, XI, 76; Forbes: *op. cit.*, p. 89.

tic portrayals of athletes in the preprofessional period often do not in themselves indicate the sport in which the subject is engaging, unless symbolically by a thong for a boxer, discus and *halteres* for other sports; [126] but later statues show clearly the specialty of the athlete by his exaggerated characteristics. The seated bronze figure of a boxer by Apollonius, of the first century B.C.; the Farnese Heracles by Glycon, about 200 A.D.; and the mosaic figures of boxers in the baths of Caracalla—all show the effects of overspecialization. Galen's "Exhortation à l'Étude des Arts" calls attention to the brutalizing effect of the professional tendency. Of boxers and pancratiasts, he says, their "faces are disfigured and hideous to see . . . their limbs dislocated or broken," their eyes out of their sockets.[127] Pausanias cites the brutal practices of Sostratus, the pancratiast, and Leontiscus, a wrestler.[128]

Specialization changed also the habits of athletes. Philostratos says that the athletes of ancient days ate barley bread, unleavened wheaten bread, and other simple foods.[129] Vegetables, cheese, figs, and a limited amount of meat and wine seem to have been a part of their diet.[130] Dromeus of Stymphalus [131] and Pythagoras of Samos were credited, near the middle of the fifth century, with the discovery of the potency of a meat diet, and thenceforth the use of flesh in excessive quantities became common. Euripides declared the athlete a "slave to his jaw, and a victim of his belly." Athenaeus related fabulous tales concerning the capacity of famous athletes for food, and concluded: "In fact, it is no wonder that these men became gluttons; for all who go in for athletic contests are taught to eat heartily in connexion with their gymnastic exercises." [132] Philostratos looked with profound contempt upon the elaborate regulation of the diet of athletes, which made them fastidious yet voracious eaters, disinclined to activity, and utterly unfit for anything. Thus, for example, directions concerning the use of pork, prescribed "that pigs on the sea-coast are to be considered unusable, on account of the sea garlic of which the shores and the sand dunes are full; also to avoid those from near the rivers because they eat crayfish; and, for a strict diet, to use only those fattened on cornelian cherries and acorns." [133] Galen doubtless had the overstuffed professional boxers, wrestlers, and pancratiasts in mind when he said that most forms of exercise ". . . make men lazy, slow-witted, and fond of sleep." "Many wrestlers become so fat that

126 Pausanias, v, 26, 3; 27, 12.
127 Daremberg: Oeuvres de Galien, i, 40 f.
128 Bk. vi, 4, 1–3.
129 Concerning Gymnastics, 43.
130 Gardiner: Athletics of the Ancient World, p. 101; Blümner: op. cit., pp. 303 f.
131 Pausanias, vi, 7, 10.
132 Athenaeus, x, 413. Trans. by C. B. Gulick. The Loeb Classical Library. Quoted by permission of Harvard University Press, Cambridge, Mass.
133 Concerning Gymnastics, 44.

they have difficulty in breathing. . . ." They would not make good soldiers, or good servants of the state in any way. "You might sooner trust pigs than them." [134]

Professionalism involved, as a matter of necessity, a high development of the trainer's art. Many athletes doubtless employed their experience to good advantage and became trainers, as did Iccus, winner of the pentathlon at Olympia, who became "the best trainer of his day." [135] In early times the trainers had been nothing more than experienced, successful athletes. But with specialization and the development of medical and dietetic aspects of training, Philostratos says it became necessary, in order to improve athletics and safeguard the athletes, that trainers have a scientific preparation. These "scientific" experts became equal in importance to the athletes themselves, in fact, were often given credit for the victories of their protégés. [136] Trainers and those whom they trained eventually gained a monopoly in the world of competitive sports. Amateurs had little chance of success against them. [137] Athletics had become a career. Only at Olympia, where strict rules were enforced, did the repute of amateurism survive for long, despite the rising tide of professionalism and attendant pot-hunters. There "the contests remained under fairly honest management." [138]

In the course of time, as training became more and more complex, much was made of strict observation of set rules. To this highly developed system, combined with newfangled dietetic and medical notions, often little understood and irrationally followed, Philostratos traced the degeneration of athletics in his day. Boys were often excessively trained too early and thereafter were good for nothing—a practice which Aristotle condemned. [139] Most injurious, some thought, was a system of exercises which was developed and then followed slavishly, without due regard to individual requirements. Gerenos, from Naukratis, one of the best wrestlers of his day, Philostratos says, was killed by this stupid system, as applied by his trainer. [140] The fourfold series of exercises which have wrought such disaster, Philostratos describes as follows:

"By tetrads is to be understood a cycle of four days, on each of which something different takes place. On the first, the athlete is prepared; on the second, intensively engaged; on the third, given over to recreation; and, on the fourth, moderately exerted. The preparatory training is, however, an energetic, short and rapid movement, which arouses the athlete and prepares him for the com-

[134] Wright: op. cit., p. 117.
[135] Pausanias, VI, 10, 5.
[136] Concerning Gymnastics, 13–5, 20–3, 53–4.
[137] Real-Encyclopädie, II, Pt. II, 2050.
[138] Manning: op. cit., loc. cit., XI, 77.
[139] Politica, VIII, 4.
[140] Concerning Gymnastics, 54.

ing exertion; the intensive, an irrefutable test of the inner strength of constitution; the recreation, the period in which movement is again systematically
resumed; the day of moderate exertion teaches escape from the opponent, but
if he himself flees, not to relax. And since they plod through this entire method
of training systematically, and always repeat the tetrads, they deprive their
science of intelligent understanding in respect to the condition of the athlete
to be trained." [141]

How are these evils to be overcome? True science in place of pseudo science
is the only hope. Philostratos seems to think well enough of the profession of
gymnasts, but they who represent it must rise to superior heights. Training
must become more truly scientific if athletics are to be rid of the ruinous evils
and if stadia are to "flourish as a result of proper training." [142]

Hero-worship of successful athletes; the increase of athletic festivals that
engaged the attention of idle spectators; the augmented value of the purse
awarded; [143] the perfection of training (ten months' preparation—one month
in Olympia—was required); luxurious habits of an age of decadence; centering
the athlete's attention upon himself rather than on some useful, social end; and
the competition of cities for successful athletes [144]—all these combined to produce contempt for earlier standards of sportsmanship and morality. Sport must
have been a lucrative business to Theagenes of Thasos, who took fourteen hundred prizes.[145] Victories were bought and sold. Inscriptions reveal that there
was corruption in the lesser local festivals in the third century before Christ.[146]
Olympia itself was not untouched. Pausanias cited numerous cases of fines imposed on bartering athletes. The first instance, which occurred in the Ninety-
eighth Olympiad (388 B.C.), reflects the spread of professional venality. Strenuous efforts were made to discourage the evil. The Zanes, statues of Zeus set up
out of fines collected from offenders, were for the purpose of warning athletes
that "an Olympic victory is to be gained, not by money, but by fleetness of
foot and strength of body." [147] Aristophanes observed the growing weight of
gold in sports:

> Wealth can see, my boy!
> For Wealth is always highly sympathetic
> With literary games, and games athletic.[148]

---

[141] Ibid., 46–7.
[142] Ibid., 13, 53–4.
[143] Real-Encyclopädie, II, Pt. II, 2050; Gardiner: Athletics of the Ancient World, pp. 100, 111.
[144] Pausanias, VI, 13, 1; 18, 6.
[145] Ibid., VI, 11, 2–5.
[146] Ringwood: op. cit., pp. 8 f.
[147] Pausanias, V, 21.
[148] Plutus, 1159–63. Trans. by B. B. Rogers. The Loeb Classical Library. Quoted by permission of Harvard University Press, Cambridge, Mass.

Plato represented the soul of Atalanta choosing the body of an athlete for the next incarnation, because of the rewards that come to such a one.[149]

Writing many centuries later, when professionalism and venality had risen to proportions undreamed of by a more modest age, Philostratos (c. 170–245) gave vent to a bitter indictment of athletic practices: ". . . the wreath of Apollo or Poseidon, for which the gods themselves strove mightily, one can sell unpunished and purchase unpunished; . . . only among the Eleans is the olive-crown according to ancient belief still inviolable. As for the rest of the contests, however, I will mention among many examples the following one, which explains everything. A boy was victorious in wrestling at the Isthmian Games, after he had promised one of his opponents 3,000 drachmas for the victory. When they entered the gymnasium the next day, the one demanded his money; the other, however, declared that he owed him nothing, for he had conquered against his will. Since that settled nothing, they had recourse to an oath, and, arrived in the sanctuary of the Isthmian god, the one who had sold the victory swore he had sold the god's contest and that 3,000 had been promised him. And he made this confession with a loud voice, without the least hesitation. The truer the affair, even though witnesses were not lacking, the more ungodly and infamous it is. He swore to it, however, on the Isthmus, and in the face of Hellas. What then may not occur in Ionia, or in Asia, to the disgrace of the games. Of this corruption, I can not acquit even the trainers themselves. They come, of course, to training provided with money, make loans to athletes at a higher interest rate than is customary among merchants at sea, and take no concern for the honor of the athletes, but advise them to buy and sell and seek only their own advantage, whether it be in profitable loans to those who are inclined to buy, or in collecting after a successful deal. So much may be said concerning the haggling traders; for they hawk, as it were, the ability of the athletes, while they take good care of their own advantage." [150]

When athletics had become a lucrative career for which specialized training was required, the decision to be or not to be an athlete seems to have been weighed with care like any other momentous business choice. An expert trainer was supposed to know what sports a particular physique was good for, and could thus give valuable vocational guidance.[151] An interesting letter, dating from about 257 B.C., contains an inquiry about the probability of success on the part of a young athlete who is under training at a palaestra in Alexandria. The chief question is, Will he win? If the gymnast "is sure that the boy will win a victory, . . . [he is to] go on training him, otherwise not to incur useless ex-

149 *Republic*, x, 620.
150 *Concerning Gymnastics*, 45.
151 *Ibid.*, 25–6, 28.

pense or keep the boy from his letters. . . ." Hierocles answers, "Only the gods can be certain if the boy will win," but he is "promising" and "with the help of the gods" may turn out to be a winner.[152]

Extreme emphasis on training to win seems to have been fraught with inimical consequences to health. Even in the day of Hippocrates (460–377 B.C.) athleticism had been carried to such an extent that he called attention to the danger to health of "a perfect condition," that "highest pitch" of excellence sought by professional athletes. Since they cannot improve, and "cannot remain" at the same pitch of perfection, "the only possible change is for the worse." [153] The mind of athletes suffered as well as the body. Galen, once a surgeon for professional gladiators, advised definitely against entering athletics as a profession, for he held that the mind is superior to the body, and athletes of his day did not even enjoy the blessings of the body, having forgotten the ancient principle of moderation in all things. "Athletes have never enjoyed the goods of the soul . . . for, far from knowing whether their soul is rational they do not even know they have one." [154]

Given a certain degree of professional specialization, organization for the sake of professional benefits is apt to appear. Ultimately those who entered athletics as a career formed guilds, clubs, or associations, generally with Heracles as patron deity, and gained through them certain exemptions and privileges. The organization of athletes had gone far by the middle of the last pagan century. A document of 41 B.C. shows that Antony, on a visit at Ephesus, was requested by his gymnastic trainer and an official "of the corporation (σύνοδος) of the victors in the sacred games to confirm that body in the enjoyment of its traditional privileges, such as exemption from military service and civil burdens, together with the prerogatives attached to the festival of the games itself." The request was granted and authorized to be inscribed on a brazen tablet.[155] By the first century of the Christian era athletic guilds had become common. In the time of Hadrian, the Synod of Heracles, one of the most renowned organizations, originally established at Sardis, had its headquarters at Rome,[156] whence it appears to have directed athletic affairs throughout the Roman world, often sending its officials, who were the most famous athletes of the day, to officiate at various local athletic festivals. The relations of minor local associations to that at Rome are uncertain. The numerous, powerful unions were evidently effective in promoting the continuance and increase of privileges which had been begun in the pre-Christian era. Suetonius notes that

152 Gardiner: "A School in Ptolemaic Egypt," *Class. Rev.*, XLIV, 211 f.
153 Hippocrates: *Aphorisms*, I, 3.
154 Daremberg: *op. cit.*, I, 35.
155 Kenyon: "A Rescript of Marcus Antonius," *Class. Rev.*, VII, 477.
156 Real-Encyclopädie, II, Pt. II, 2057.

Augustus "maintained the privileges of the athletes and even increased them." [157] One of the most substantial encouragements to athletes was the right to pensions. By the middle of the third century, in the time of Gallienus, an allowance of 180 to 200 drachmas per month was due to any athlete who triumphed in the Sacred Games and made application for the benefit, this being secured by Roman law. Some athletes were so fortunate as to draw more than one pension.[158]

Though the poetry of Homer and of Pindar is full of encomia for winning athletes, the inscriptions concerning early winners are, nevertheless, exceedingly simple, with little or no boasting of record-breaking. According to Philostratos, however, many athletes of ancient days won contests in as many as eight or nine Olympiads.[159] Under the increased strains of professionalism, the athletes, beset by numerous ills, appeared not to last so long as a rule, though there were, naturally, individual exceptions. Galen says few reached old age.[160] But, if they did not last many years, the professionals often hung up notable series of victories in a short time. Their tendency to boastfulness, and the volubility of athletic associations, in sharp contrast to the modest demeanor of earlier days, enable us to know something of their spectacular achievements.[161] Demostratos, whose greatest athletic honors began in the days of Marcus Aurelius, enjoyed the citizenship of nine noble cities, including Alexandria, Athens, and Sparta. He was a marvelous athlete, having won crowns in Italy, Greece, Asia, and Africa. Twenty victories as a boy, and forty-eight when he had become a man, were credited to him in the Sacred Games. Numerous offices were showered on him; for some, it seems, he was not too abashed to ask. He was *xystarches* at the Capitolia and at certain provincial festivals; and the office of priest of the Synod of Rome was given him and his sons to enjoy. They, too, proved to be marvelous athletes and honored their father with a statue at Sardis. Similar to his was the career of Asclepiades of Alexandria. He was victor at Olympia; holder of the cherished title "Periodoneikes"; high priest of the Synod of Rome; chief guardian of the Great Serapis; citizen of Alexandria, Hermopolis, Puteoli; and councilor of Naples, Athens, Elis, and other cities. Asclepiades publicized himself as "pankratiast invincible, immovable, unrivalled," and took great pains to set his record straight. "I neither challenged any nor did any one in my time dare to challenge me, nor did I divide the crown with any nor did I decline a contest, or enter any protest, nor did I abandon any contest nor take part in any contest to please royalty, nor did

---

[157] *Augustus*, 45; infra, p. 751.
[158] Gardiner: *Athletics of the Ancient World*, p. 113.
[159] *Concerning Gymnastics*, 43.
[160] Daremberg: *op. cit.*, I, 38.
[161] Keil and Premerstein: *Bericht über eine Reise in Lydien*, pp. 19 ff.

I gain a victory in any new fangled games but in all the contests for which I ever entered my name I was crowned in the actual ring and was approved in all the preliminary trials." [162]

Just when the athletes were riding the crest of the wave of popularity, they and their organizations began to decline. They were naturally dependent upon the support of society and the favor of emperors. When Roman society began to give way before internal weakness and decay; when it faced in vain invasions from without; when Christianity, with its propaganda of ascetic disregard for the body and its furious attack upon the decadent morals of Rome, had gained the upper hand, and Roman government had become, at least nominally, Christian—then athletics were doomed to abolition. A decree of Diocletian and Maximian freed a victor (who won honestly) in three Sacred Games from all ordinary duties of citizenship. This seems to have been the last guarantee of privileges. Varazdates, an Armenian who won a boxing match in the 291st Olympiad, is the last known record of Olympia. Eight years later (393 A.D.) Theodosius the Great abolished the Olympian festival. With the discontinuance of the Great National Games, the basic support of professional athletics was removed.[163]

Occasional reference has been made to criticism of athletics.[164] Even at an early date, in the opinion of some at least, an exaggerated importance was attached by Greeks to physical prowess. On this favorable soil of preoccupation with games, professionalism gradually developed till it became clearly recognizable in the latter half of the fifth century. Ultimately it was powerful enough to drive out of the ring all amateur sport, finally invading even Sparta, "which resisted it longer than any other country." [165] A number of poets, essayists, philosophers, physicians, soldiers,[166] statesmen, from early times till the height of professionalism was reached under the Empire, gave expression to the low esteem in which they held mere physical excellence, although they regarded physical culture as an essential part of a free man's education. The similarity of criticism throughout the ages is striking, yet significant differences appear. Though seven hundred years separated them, the criticism of Xenophanes and Galen had much in common: both held the excellence of the athlete to be of an inferior sort, undeserving of the honors and rewards bestowed upon it. Xenophanes (c. 530 B.C.), however, criticized the "useless and unprofitable . . . idea of athleticism" from the standpoint of consequences to the city-state, whereas Galen deplored the evil effects of professional athletics

---

[162] Gardiner: *Athletics of the Ancient World*, p. 112. By permission of The Clarendon Press, Oxford.
[163] *Real-Encyclopädie*, II, Pt. II, 2053; *infra*, p. 399.
[164] *Supra*, pp. 288 f., 352.
[165] Forbes: *op. cit.*, pp. 40 f.
[166] *Infra*, pp. 431 f., 436 f., 442 ff., 453 f., 456 ff., 632 f.

on the mind and body of the individual. Xenophanes, who attacked many a received opinion and custom of the Hellenic world, thus put himself on record against even the favored heroes of Olympia:

"Nay, if a man should win victory by the swiftness of his feet, or in the pentathlum, where stands the precinct of Zeus by the streams of the Pisês at Olympia; or in wrestling, or because he hath skill in painful boxing, or in that dread contest which they call the pancratium, he would be more illustrious to look upon, in the eyes of his fellow-citizens, and he would win a conspicuous front seat at the contests, and would have bread from the public store, given by the city, and a present to be an heirloom for ever; yea, even if he won with horses, all these things would fall to his lot, though he be not so worthy as I. For my art is better than the strength of men and of horses. But there is no sense in all these opinions, and it is not right to prefer strength to good wisdom. Not though a man rise up among the people as a good boxer, or good at the pentathlum, or in wrestling, or even in swiftness of foot, which has preference among all men's deeds of strength in the contest—not for that reason can a city enjoy better laws. Small must be any joy that comes to a city for this, if a man wins in a contest beside the banks of the Pisês; for that cannot fatten the storehouses of a city." [167]

A century and a half later much the same criticism was expressed by Isocrates, who reflected in wonder and amazement that those who had established the great athletic festivals "should have thought the prowess of men's bodies to be deserving of so great bounties," [168] but had not provided any reward for those who had trained their minds for the service of their fellow men. If all the athletes were to become twice as strong as they are now, the world would not be a whit better; but if just one man should gain true enlightenment, all who chose to do so might profit by his wisdom. Euripides, too, product of the enlightenment that was sweeping over Athens, echoed in the Autolycus the views of Xenophanes. Though himself trained as an athlete, his attack is more vehement, due, perhaps, to the fact that he lived in an age of decline after the Peloponnesian War and was witness to a more advanced stage of athleticism:

> Of all the thousand ills that prey on Hellas
> Not one is greater than the tribe of athletes;
> For, first, they never learn how to live well,
> Nor, indeed, could they; seeing that a man,

[167] Athenaeus, x, 414. Trans. by C. B. Gulick. The Loeb Classical Library. Quoted by permission of Harvard University Press, Cambridge, Mass.; Bowra, "Xenophanes and the Olympic Games," Am. Jour. Philol., LIX, 257–79, examines various interpretations that have been given to these early criticisms.

[168] Panegyricus, 1.

Slave to his jaws and belly, cannot hope
To heap up wealth superior to his sire's.
How to be poor and row in fortune's boat
They know no better; for they have not learned
Manners that make men proof against ill luck.
Lustrous in youth, they lounge like living statues
Decking the streets; but when sad old age comes,
They fall and perish like a threadbare coat.
I've often blamed the customs of us Hellenes,
Who for the sake of such men meet together
To honor idle sport and feed our fill;
For who, I pray you, by his skill in wrestling,
Swiftness of foot, good boxing, strength at quoits,
Has served his city by the crown he gains?
Will they meet men in fight with quoits in hand,
Or in the press of shields drive forth the foeman
By force of fisticuffs from hearth and home?
Such follies are forgotten face to face
With steel. We therefore ought to crown with wreaths
Men wise and good, and him who guides the State,
A man well-tempered, just, and sound in counsel,
Or one who by his words averts ill deeds,
Warding off strife and warfare; for such things
Bring honor on the city and all Hellenes.[169]

Plato, too, in his ideal *Republic* would have none of the professional athletic training, for it makes men sleepy, dull, of poor health, slaves to a certain regimen, and quite incompetent to defend the state.[170] Similar criticism, mixed with biting sarcasm and an emphasis on a discipline of the spirit that will enable man to conquer in the greatest of all encounters, beside which the physical contests of athletes sink into pettiness, is attributed to Diogenes by Dio Chrysostom in the "Isthmian Discourse" and in "The Real Athlete." Being in Corinth, when the Isthmian Games were in progress, Diogenes roused the wrath of those around him by placing a crown of pine on his own head. To their protest against this impious act, and their assertion that he had won no crown, he replied:

"Many and mighty antagonists have I vanquished, not like these slaves who are now wrestling here, hurling the discus and running, but more difficult in every way—I mean poverty, exile, and disrepute; yes, and anger, pain, desire,

169 Symonds: *Studies of the Greek Poets*, II, 92 ff.; cf. Athenaeus, x, 413.
170 *Republic*, III, 404.

fear, and the most redoubtable beast of all, treacherous and cowardly, I mean pleasure, which no Greek or barbarian can claim he fights and conquers by the strength of his soul, but all alike have succumbed to her and have failed in this contest—Persians, Medes, Syrians, Macedonians, Athenians, Lacedaemonians —all, that is, save myself. Is it I, then, think you, that am worthy of the pine, or will you take and bestow it upon the one who is stuffed with the most meat? Take this answer, then, to those who sent you and say that it is they who break the law; for they go about wearing crowns and yet have won in no contest; and add that I have lent a greater lustre to the Isthmian games by having myself taken the crown, which ought to be a thing for goats, forsooth, to fight over, not for men." [171]

Diogenes lamented, moreover, "that men contended with one another in punching and kicking, but that no one showed any emulation in the pursuit of virtue." [172] To a crowned runner, being carried on the shoulders of enthusiastic fans, he declared that, though victorious, he was none the less inferior to the wild beasts, and that many of the swiftest were the most cowardly. As for winning the two-hundred-yard dash, he asked: ". . . What does that amount to? . . . For you certainly have not become one whit more intelligent for having outstripped your competitors, nor more temperate now than you were, nor less cowardly, nor are you less discontented, nor will your wants be less in the future or your life freer from grief and pain." And, though you are "fastest on foot of all the Greeks," you are "not faster than rabbits . . . nor deer. . . . I do not believe that you can outstrip even a fox." "As he spoke to the man in this vein," Chrysostom declares, "he made the business of foot-racing seem cheap in the eyes of many of the bystanders and caused the winner himself to go away sorrowing and much meeker." [173]

[171] Dio Chrysostom, ix, 11–3. Trans. by J. W. Cohoon and H. L. Crosby. The Loeb Classical Library. Quoted by permission of Harvard University Press, Cambridge, Mass.
[172] Diogenes Laërtius: "Life of Diogenes," 4.
[173] Dio Chrysostom, ix, 14–8, 20. Trans. by J. W. Cohoon and H. L. Crosby. The Loeb Classical Library. Quoted by permission of Harvard University Press, Cambridge, Mass.

# 12

# NATIONAL FESTIVALS

In the origin and development of the great national games of Greece three basic, formative factors are distinguishable, closely interwoven and functioning interdependently: a spontaneous delight in physical contests and an intense admiration of excellence therein; the ancient, traditional, religious practice of funeral games; and a sense of kinship and desire for unity that was never completely realized.

From the beginning to the end of their history, archaeological and literary remains show the Greeks preoccupied with sports—first spontaneously and without methodical arrangement, then according to orderly design. In their earliest history, when the use of letters was still limited or nonexistent, one sees their approval of excellence in physical contests in the graphic portrayal of such events. With the rise of literature, one hears the ecstatic acclaim of those who, at the funeral games of Patroclos, watch with bated breath the test of talents of swift runners, skilled wrestlers, cunning charioteers. When games have been organized and have become a fixed, recurrent business on the Greek calendar, the praise of physical prowess in stately moving rhythm becomes a business too, immortalizing at a stroke the sacred contest, noble dumb brutes, the manly victors, and the gifted pen as well. "Water of all elements is best; gold, of all metals; but of heroic, lordly contests, wherein the crown is won by manly merit, there is none greater than the Olympian Games." Such is the motif of Pindar's opening ode in praise of horseman Hiero, tyrant of Syracuse, victor at Olympia in 476 B.C. Eight years later, when to his already numerous conquests he added victory in the four-horse chariot race, we hear the paean of Bacchylides, "Cean nightingale":

> Glory went with them, and triumph victorious,
> As by wide-swirling Alpheus onward they sped,

363

FUNERAL SCENES   *Dipylon Vase, 8th century*
(Courtesy, The Metropolitan Museum of Art, New York)

364

And the name of Deinomenes' son they made glorious
With garlands of victory wreathing his head.[1]

Love of sports, acclaim of heroes living, and festive honors to them dead, are found in constant association in early Greek mythology. Whatever may have been the original factors in the development of funeral games, whether they were "a substitute for human sacrifice," or a memorial to a struggle for power, as has been suggested [2]—and both may have been true in one place and another—it is certain that they reflect an attitude thoroughly Greek. The doleful, Christian thought, "in the midst of life we are in death," was poles apart from the cheerful Greeks who, in the face of death, asserted the will to life and enjoyment. On this sturdy stock of natural impulse expressing itself in funeral games, there was ultimately engrafted a higher religious veneration and patriotic devotion. Strabo says that in Trojan times there were no games of the crown, or, if there were, they had no wide recognition: "Homer does not mention any of these, though he mentions another kind—funeral games." [3] Gardiner [4] holds that, despite the obscurity of their beginning, "there is no reason for discrediting the universal tradition" which traced the athletic festival to funeral games. Hyde says, "Even the athletic games were religious in origin and spirit, always associated with the worship of gods and heroes, and were among the strongest Pan-Hellenic influences, making not only for nationality, but also for a broader religion than that of tribe or city." [5]

The transition from early funeral practices to the great athletic festival was a gradual process, halting, hesitant, like the growth of social unity itself. Though the pattern is not the same in every case, the central tendency seems rather clear. The great man, successful as leader, renowned as fighter, a hero to those around him, is honored fittingly by games at his death; if great enough, the returning anniversary of his death becomes a fixed, memorial occasion; if his descendants are, like their ancestors, continuingly successful, contiguous peoples are brought under their sway, perhaps are amalgamated with them, accept their mores and think, in time, of a common (mythical) ancestor; the circle of festive celebrants at the recurrent rites is increased, and the tale of famous deeds as well. The process continues. A conventional myth, a convenient, serviceable story of the past grows up, crediting real fact to mythical causes: the ancestor is said to have had a certain number of sons from whom

1 Way: Odes of Bacchylides, III, ant. 1. Courtesy of Macmillan & Co., Ltd., London, and The Macmillan Company, New York.
2 Gardiner: Greek Athletic Sports and Festivals, pp. 31 f.; Hyde: Olympic Victor Monuments, p. 14.
3 The Geography of Strabo, VIII, 3, 30. Trans. by H. L. Jones.
4 Op. cit., p. 27.
5 Hyde: "The Religion of Greece," in Montgomery, Religions of the Past and Present, p. 253.

sprang the several branches of the present folk; the tribal hero has become the accepted progenitor of a whole people. At this point the hero is commonly credited with divinity, inherited or acquired. In such a case the celebration of his heroic, manly competence is at once a religious service to the gods.

Consider for a moment how legendary history accounted for the origin of the Greeks; and how a branch of that people associated honor to the gods, and the remembrance of their real or fancied ancestors, with a story of the conquest of power and the founding of the Olympic Games. The Greeks accepted a mythical Hellen from whose offspring came Ionians, Aeolians, Achaeans, Dorians.[6] The Dorians themselves traced their three tribes back to Dyman, Pamphylus, and Hyllus, who, by one story, were said to be the sons of Aegimius, Dorian king, in Thessaly. Great families often try to link themselves with great past events and personages, real or mythical, and so increase their fame. When the fame of Heracles, who was credited variously with Cretan, Hellenic, and Phoenician origins, had begun to be great in Greek cities,[7] the ruling family of Argos hitched their chariot to his rising star. By a modification of the story of Dorian ancestry, the tribe of Hyllus was traced back to Heracles, who was said to have fought for Aegimius against the Lapiths, for which he was rewarded with one-third of Aegimius' kingdom. When Heracles died, his son Hyllus was adopted by Aegimius; Heracles' grandchildren, sons of Hyllus, sought but failed to gain control of the domain that had been allotted Heracles; but his three great-grandchildren, of whom Temenus (head of the royal house in Argos) was one, resumed the effort and were successful, conquering all the Peloponnesus save Arcadia with the assistance of a one-eyed Aetolian, Oxylus, whom they set up as lord of Elis. Such was the fantastic reconstruction of history.

Now the Greeks often raised men to heroic stature, and their greatest heroes were commonly credited with godlike attributes. Heracles, at first a mighty man, the personification of unlimited strength and unfailing courage, gradually took on the character of a god and was honored as such, especially by athletes. A host of tales, often conflicting, were told of his exploits and the founding of the Olympian Games. Of the worship of Heracles among the Agyrineans, Diodorus says, "Every year with the utmost zeal they hold games which include gymnastic contests and horse-races," to which come bond and free, for they also teach their servants to worship him.[8] So great was his prowess that Zeus himself sought his aid against the giants. The two, Zeus and Heracles, were famed in legend as originators of the Olympian Games. Heracles, accord-

---

[6] Jardé: *The Formation of the Greek People*, p. 56; Bury: *A History of Greece*, pp. 79 f., 106.
[7] Gardner and Jevons: *A Manual of Greek Antiquities*, pp. 88, 157; supra, pp. 210, 233, 273.
[8] Diodorus of Sicily, IV, 24.

ing to one legend, set his brothers to run races, crowned the victor with wild olive, decreed the contests should be held quadrennially, and called them by the name Olympic. The descendants of Heracles set up an altar for him and

PELOPS AND HIPPODAMIA AS VICTORS

(From Furtwängler-Reichold, *Griechische Vasenmalerei*, ser. 2, Pl. 67, Verlag F. Bruckmann, Munich, 1904–1932)

held games at Olympia.[9] Pindar, in the "Tenth Olympian," [10] celebrates the story of Heracles' conquest of Pisa, the measuring of the ground with his foot, and the establishment of games in memory of the event. Diodorus says that after he had performed his various labors, Heracles established the Olympian Games in honor of Zeus, decreed the crown for a prize and won all the contests himself "without opposition," for "no one was bold enough to contend with him." [11] Zeus, likewise, was said to have wrestled there with Kronos for his kingdom, and celebrated his victory with games in which Apollo, Hermes, Ares, and others were contestants. Pelops, a Lydian, driven from Sipylus by Ilus, conquered Oenomaus in a chariot race by trickery and bribery, married Hippodamia, and acquired Pisa and Olympia. The previous unsuccessful suitors, who had lost their lives where he had been successful, he honored as heroes by a monument and sacrifices every year.[12] Pelops is said to have celebrated the Olympian Games more magnificently than any who had gone before him; and he, in turn, came to be honored by the Eleans more highly than any other heroes, just as they honored Zeus more than any other god.[13] Pindar, his mind on glorious past events at Olympia, says:

[9] *Pausanias's Description of Greece*, v, 7, 7–9; 8, 1.
[10] Str. 2 *et seq.*
[11] Bk. iv, 14.
[12] Pausanias, v, 1, 7; 7, 10; VI, 21, 9–11.
[13] *Ibid.*, v, 8, 2; 13, 1.

And his portion assured hath Pelops still
Where the priests the blood of the sacrifice spill;
And unto his tomb resorteth the throng
Of strangers from far who have heard his story.
From his grave-mound his spirit beholdeth the glory
Of the mighty Olympian strife of the strong
In the course that from Pelops its name hath ta'en,
Wherein be contending the swift to run
And the thews that be mighty in wrestling-strain.[14]

Strabo, who rejects the story of Heracles as founder, as "not much faith is to be put in" it, holds the games were founded by the Aetolians.[15] Oxylus, to whom it was said the Heraclids had given Elis as a reward for his aid in the conquest of the Peloponnesus, reputedly celebrated the Olympian Games; but after him they were discontinued, till revived, according to various accounts, by Iphitus of Elis, Cleosthenes of Pisa, and Lycurgus of Sparta. Pausanias says he saw a discus at the temple of Hera, on which was cut the decree of truce which the Eleans proclaimed at the Olympian festival.[16]

Thus run certain legends about Olympic beginnings prior to historic times. There were many and often conflicting stories; for, as Pausanias remarks, "not a few tales of wonder may be heard in Greece." [17] One and another, singly or collectively, they reflect the mixture of spontaneous love of physical contests, honor to dead heroes, a memory of territorial conquests, and the conquest of power by Zeus himself, in the Greeks' fanciful account of their greatest festival.

The destructive, divisive tendency among the Greek states is evident in the almost continuous warfare that marked their history. To their Persian enemies, it seemed extraordinary, as Mardonius said, that the Greeks "who spoke one language" almost invariably resorted to arms in settling their disputes. This divisive tendency, however, was not without a rival. Some sentiment favoring unity existed, and several factors were promotive of it, though they were never able to conquer the forces of a divisive character. Among the influences for unity were religion, common language and literature, similar social customs, and, not the least important, a devotion to sports that brought them together in frequent meetings, to compete in, and be spectators and admirers of, the same contests. One story of the founding of the Olympic contests reflects this view of the influence of the games on Greek unity: when the Argonauts were returning to their homes, Heracles is said to have proposed taking ". . . oaths

[14] Way: The Odes of Pindar, "Olympian" 1, str. 4. Courtesy of Macmillan & Co., Ltd., London, and The Macmillan Company, New York.
[15] Bk. VIII, 3, 30. Trans. by H. L. Jones.
[16] Bk. v, 4, 4; 20, 1; Plutarch: Lycurgus, 1.
[17] Bk. v, 10, 1.

among one another to fight at the side of anyone of their number who should call for aid; and that, furthermore, they should choose out the most excellent place in Greece, there to institute games and a festival for the whole race. . . ." [18] Isocrates says that the founders of the Great Games justly deserve high praise for their institution, for thereby peace and harmony were restored to a land harassed by struggles and disease.[19] Strabo says, owing to the games, the Eleans enjoyed profound peace and increased in numbers, while others were continually engaged in war.[20]

It would be difficult to name more powerful forces for unity than Homer and the Great Games. While frequent wars are a conspicuous feature of Greek history, it is even more remarkable to find the arbitrament of war set aside or postponed out of respect for the traditional festival of athletics and religion. While Leonidas was dying at Thermopylae, the Greeks without interruption went on with the usual ceremonies at Olympia. "Dorians, Ionians, folk of Athens, Sparta, and Thebes, despite their rivalries and hatreds, and in the midst of their most desperate wars, forgot for a moment, at the time of the festivals, their ancient quarrels, and at this pacific rendez-vous at which all gathered, spent a few days in happy harmony." [21] The "Truce of God" proclaimed at Olympia, the Isthmian truce, and similar periods of respite from war, enjoined in connection with the Pythian and Nemean festivals, were a gain, though of brief duration, to peoples so plagued with fratricidal struggles, even though the decreed cessation of hostilities might occasionally be of no avail, or be manipulated for political ends, and was sometimes infringed when it was inconvenient to observe it: as, for example, when Argive Pheidon seized control of Olympia by force; when Spartan Agesilaus invaded Corinth in the course of the Isthmian Games; and again, when Lacedaemonians attacked Lepreum during the Olympian truce.[22]

Quite apart from the periodic cessation of war, the Great Games furnished an excellent occasion for colonial Greeks to return to the homeland, and thus helped to keep alive a sense of common origin. The tie of common play among children and men, it is often observed, brings together even those who have little else to share. The influence of joint sportive festivals among the Greeks was great, partly in their own right, partly because they reinforced other cohesive tendencies: thus they provided the occasion, not for contests of athletes alone, but of artists, musicians, poets, orators, writers; and were the gathering place of people from all walks of life, royalty and common men, rich and

18 Diodorus, IV, 53. Trans. by C. H. Oldfather. The Loeb Classical Library. Quoted by permission of Harvard University Press, Cambridge, Mass.
19 Panegyricus, 43.
20 Bk. VIII, 3, 33.
21 Diehl: Excursions Archéologiques en Grèce, p. 206.
22 Strabo, VIII, 3, 33; Pausanias, III, 10, 1; Thucydides, V, 49.

poor, ignorant and learned. If the Olympian festival and others of national renown were not the most basic and powerful of unifying influences, and if, in the long run, they proved weaker than the forces operating against them, they constituted at least an unmistakable symbol of a unity temporarily achieved, and of an ideal whose permanent realization some Greeks were wise enough to see was the indispensable key to the continuance of Greek political integrity. They were to all Hellas a symbol of kinship and unification, as the Panathenian festival was to Athenians. The latter was realized; but the unity of Hellas fell short of fulfillment.

The importance attached to the national festivals, the political significance of the events, and faith in their potentialities may be read in the fact that Philip and Alexander both took advantage of the Olympian and Pythian festivals to consecrate their hold on Greece and unify it under their hands. Philip's horses and chariots won victories at Olympia as early as 356 B.C.; he caused the Philippeum to be built there after his victory at Chaeronaea.[23] Alexander, though no athlete in the Greek sense, and unwilling to enter contests with heterogeneous competitors,[24] recognized the importance of the festival, caused "Olympic games" to be celebrated at Dium, Agae, and elsewhere, and attached great significance to the victories of others. The Ptolemies, in their day, were ardent supporters of the Olympian Games; and Roman emperors, too, despite the low estimation of Romans for the Greek athletic ideal, regarded the great festivals as symbols of all Greece. At the Isthmian Games, in 196 B.C., Flamininus announced the freedom of Greece from Macedonia. Mummius, having destroyed the city of Corinth and subjugated Greece, dedicated at Olympia twenty-one gilded shields and a bronze statue of Zeus, from the spoils of the Achaean war, said to have been the first offering dedicated by a Roman in a Greek sanctuary.[25] The conquest of peace and unity, which Greece had been unable to achieve by rational, willing coöperation of her cities, had come in a superficial, equivocal sense by violence from without; Olympia, sacred shrine of free Greeks, and symbol of their common desire for peace and unity throughout centuries, was the scene where their weakness was memorialized in the solemn, bloodstained sacrifices of their conquerors.

The festivals were at once aristocratic and democratic. In origin aristocratic and exclusive, they became in the course of time more inclusive and democratic, reflecting the modification of Greek society by rising democratic tendencies which appeared in the midst of an aging aristocracy. The element of democracy is evident in the fact that all sorts of people came to Olympia, and all of proved Hellenic origin, rich or poor, of noble or common stock, were eli-

[23] Pausanias, v, 20, 10.
[24] Plutarch: Alexander, 4.
[25] Pausanias, v, 10, 5; 24, 4, 8.

gible to enter the contests. So great was the prestige of the games, particularly at Olympia, that the highest as well as the lowest might take pride in a victory crowned with the pale wild olive. Pindar held nothing among men more pleasant than the games, and victory in them the greatest any one could win. "For he that hath attained his heart's desire forgetteth death." [26] The praise of victory, ubiquitous in Homer, continued unabated in later centuries; most Greeks would have agreed with Homer's Phaeacian that—

> . . . whoever he be, for a hero no glory is greater
> Than whatever with hands, or again, with his feet he accomplish! [27]

There were, of course, a few dissenting voices among thinkers and men of action, who recognized that the growing tendency to athletic specialization was of no value to the state. Alexander, who declared he would be willing to compete in running at Olympia if he could run against kings, was certainly not in harmony with the old Greek tradition; he reflects, moreover, that aloofness toward athletic contests which was beginning to appear and continued to increase in proportion as the games became a field for professionals.[28] Philopoemen condemned and discouraged the pursuit of professional athletic training as useless.[29] Epaminondas held that soldiers ought not to be trained just like wrestlers, but by military exercises.[30]

Though one may speak of the democracy of the games, it was obviously limited. There was freedom, of course, for all Greeks to enter the contests; on the other hand, wealth and social position had an important bearing on success in the world of sports, and are constantly associated with the games in Greek literature. Menander reflects the common notion of relationship between high birth and manly sport:

> Maybe this boy here
> Was born above our station. Reared 'mongst working-folk
> He will despise our doings, his own level seek
> And venture on some action suiting noble birth:
> Will go a-lion-hunting; carry arms; or run
> A race at games.[31]

In so far as natural talent could emerge and prove its excellence without hindrance, the games were indeed democratic. Plato, however, makes it clear [32]

---

[26] Way: The Odes of Pindar, "Olympian" VIII, str. 4.
[27] Lawton: Classical Greek Literature, p. 146.
[28] Plutarch: Alexander, 4.
[29] Plutarch: Philopoemen, 3.
[30] Plutarch: Apophthegmata, "Epameinondas," 3; Nepos: Epaminondas, 2.
[31] The Arbitrants, 103–8. Trans. by F. G. Allinson. The Loeb Classical Library. Quoted by permission of Harvard University Press, Cambridge, Mass.
[32] Protagoras, 326.

that wealth and family affected adversely the equality of opportunity. The games were an exhibition and public test of that which education in home towns had produced,[33] plus intensive training at Olympia. Education in "music and palaestra" at Athens depended on the ability of the family to provide teachers and trainers. Certain public gymnasia were open to all citizens, and the Kynosarges to half-breeds; but money was needed to provide the service of special instructors. The most skillful teachers would offer the best instruction and receive the best pay. For a brief time the Ephebic College was free, but Athens sent few winners to the games at that period. At Sparta, under the laws of Lycurgus, the influence of wealth was apparently negated, at least for a time, but it appears that Spartan regimentation, with its emphasis on military arts, only gave a temporary advantage to Sparta and ultimately reduced her superiority in physical contests. From the early eighth century to 576 B.C. her victories topped all others to an extraordinary degree—if the records preserved are to be taken without too great discount. Then they came to an end. Prior to the reforms of Lycurgus, aristocracy and wealth must have had a decided influence in determining who would be best fitted for a contest, as in other states where aristocratic institutions prevailed. The arts and athletics of the more liberal type seem to have flourished together and declined together, attaining the highest level in the seventh and sinking to a low ebb in the fifth century.[34] This seems to harmonize with Aristotle's judgment of the benumbing, narrowing effect of the rigid, one-sided Spartan system.[35]

Thus it would appear that victories at Olympia were chiefly the triumphs of an aristocracy of wealth and family, which enjoyed sufficient freedom in which to grow. Both Spartan rigor and Athenian middle-class luxury and ease were in the long run detrimental. The Old Oligarch's complaint that the new democracy at Athens cares little for noble sports, and Aristophanes' thrusts at the flat-chested, glib-tongued products of the new education, both point to the influence of social change on the athletic tradition.[36]

The aristocracy of wealth and family that supported the old tradition was joined, of necessity, in the case of gymnastic events, with a genuine physical excellence decreed by nature. In horse racing and chariot contests, however, wealth sufficient to support a luxurious taste was the chief determiner. Agesilaus tried to demonstrate that winning chariot races at Olympia proved one's wealth only, not his excellence,[37] but equestrian sports continued to enjoy an aristocratic position, long after professionalism had invaded gymnastic contests and

[33] Gardner: New Chapters in Greek History, p. 268.
[34] Gardiner: op. cit., p. 57.
[35] Politica, VIII, 4.
[36] Supra, pp. 288, 352.
[37] Plutarch: Agesilaus, 20.

made them too ignoble for the participation of men of rank. It is significant that Philip of Macedon, kings of Egypt, and lesser royalty were pleased to have their entries of horses and chariots at Olympia. The wealth required to keep equipment and to train horses formed a barrier which separated effectively the nobler from the humbler sort, whose sports had become highly technical and professional. Cavalry events were not professionalized, for one reason, because even the good purses offered would not begin to support a stable. This must be kept in mind in reading Olympian history; for it, as well as other great festivals, reflects the gulf that existed in Greek society—a gulf that widened and deepened.

The two aristocratic elements—wealth and family, and superior natural physical endowment—are both celebrated in the matchless, immortal odes of Pindar and Bacchylides, whose rivalry for the honor of singing the victors' praises at the national festivals did not go unrewarded. Pindar was of aristocratic Theban family, and lived at the courts of Syracuse and Agrigentum. This "god-like bird of Zeus," who could ill endure the chatter of those he held less gifted, was well supplied from rich men's means. The singer of decaying aristocracy, Pindar had no sympathy for the rising tide of democracy that eddied round him,[38] though he once roused the anger of his Theban mother by singing the praises of "violet-crowned," glorious Athens, "bulwark of Hellas." Throughout the odes run constant encomia upon the noble, distinguished lineage, the heroic deeds or glorious victories achieved by the forbears of the victors whom he celebrates: they are hospitable to strangers, schooled in chivalry, occupied in noble pursuits, wiser than others, and ever warlike.[39] The sportsman's features and his deeds are not less worthy than his family's past. Pindar's athletic ideal is, of course, thoroughly in keeping with the old Greek tradition— more than that, it is almost universal in the world of sport wherever professionalism has not laid the hand of death. He does not tire of admiring the athlete, comely to look upon, whose looks are not belied by his performance, which causes the name of his fatherland to be proclaimed by the heralds. He was, after Homer, the most gifted singer of "a man fair-fighting," "ring-craft that shifteth its balance fast never falling," that the world has ever known. He saw every essential attribute of the great athlete, the aristocrat of nature, favored by Fate divine "with deftness of hand, with litheness of limb, with valour's light in his eyne. . . ." "The gifts that by Nature's self be given are ever the best. . . ." "Victory by aid of toil" is ever acclaimed; but mere training is decried, in athletes as well as in poets. Courage to face danger towers above all other

[38] Bury: op. cit., pp. 306 f.; The Cambridge Ancient History, IV, 512; Botsford and Sihler: Hellenic Civilization, p. 32.
[39] Way: The Odes of Pindar, "Olympian" XI, ep.; Butcher: Some Aspects of the Greek Genius, pp. 153 f.

excellence, and is celebrated in many passages: "Of man is the trial the one proof-test." [40] In praise of Arcesilas of Cyrene, winner in the chariot race, 462 B.C., he sings:

> . . . Mid those twoscore
> Drivers, who mid the throng
> Were hurled to earth, thou with a heart undaunted
> Didst drive unscathed thy chariot on. . . .[41]

Nowhere is the valorous aspect of the athletic ideal more fitly expressed than in the "Sixth Olympian": "if aught of glory be thro' peril sought many remember then." It leads, indeed, to that "honor," "sweet rest," and praise, "far beyond envy," that is "stored for victors at Olympia." [42]

It is evident that a practical purpose was served by the national games. They constituted the goal of, and gave significance to, one of the essential aspects of Greek education; indeed, from a realistic point of view, they were a part of that training.[43] The festivals differed from many modern sport gatherings,[44] having a serious origin and purpose rather than mere amusement as their end; but, though differing in details, they had much in common with the mass sport festivals that are zealously promoted in certain modern national states. They were to the Greeks, as they are to modern warlike peoples, "almost a duty towards the fatherland," as Diehl has said, "to which these exercises gave an élite of good soldiers and valorous citizens." [45] "With such men," it was said of Olympian victors, "there is no need of walls." The victorious athlete was indeed welcomed home from Olympia like a conquering general coming home from war.

### THE OLYMPIC GAMES

Various legends credited the establishment of the Olympian festival to Heracles, Zeus, and Pelops.[46] These fanciful reconstructions of history, though full of contradictions, take on a realistic color in the light of modern archaeological discoveries that point to Olympia as a site of festivals celebrated cen-

---

[40] Way: *The Odes of Pindar*, "Olympian" VIII, ep. 1; VII, ep. 1; IX, str. 4; ep. 4; ant. 4; II, str. 5; IV, ant. 1.

[41] Way: *The Odes of Pindar*, "Pythian" V, ant. 2. Courtesy of Macmillan & Co., Ltd., London, and The Macmillan Company, New York.

[42] Ibid., "Olympian" XI, ant.; Lawton: *op. cit.*, p. 147.

[43] Gardner: *op. cit.*, p. 268; Gardiner: *op. cit.*, pp. 1 f.

[44] C.A.H., IV, 509.

[45] *Op. cit.*, p. 207.

[46] *Supra*, pp. 366 f.; Diodorus, IV, 14, 53; Pausanias, V, 7, 6–10; VI, 21, 9–11.

turies before the accepted First Olympiad, 776 B.C. Olympia was a sacred place at least as early as the tenth or eleventh century, as many votive offerings testify.[47] "Olympia, . . . the port frequented by the Cretan sailors, worshipped the old deities of Mount Ida, Kronos, and Rhea, before it was consecrated to Zeus and Hera," and these pre-Hellenic Aegeao-Cretan people were noted for their love of gymnastic and musical festivals.[48] The palaestra of the Greeks, in Glotz's opinion, "did no more than develop the legacy of the pre-Hellenes." "In the religious festivals and funerary ceremonies there were contests which were to give birth to a national athletic tradition. . . ." [49] This view is plausible; though it does not help to fill the years prior to 776 with a chronicle of athletic development, it harmonizes with the legendary accounts that associated Olympia's gymnastic origins with Heracles from Ida in Crete, and it enables us to view differently the practices that once seemed to distinguish the Greeks so sharply from their neighbors of historic times.

Early in the eighth century, when islands of relative peace, quiet, and civilization were beginning to emerge from the sea of chaos that came with the Dorian invasion and swept Aegeao-Cretan and Mycenaean strongholds to destruction, Olympia was still nothing but a local festival, of less repute than the festival of Delos. But Olympia gained sway rapidly in the Peloponnesus, drew contestants from thence in the course of a dozen Olympiads, and by the end of a century, had gained recognition in the rest of Greece and the colonies.[50] Though her greatest prestige was not attained until the sixth century, it was then so great that other national festivals of the crown were officially recognized. Olympia remained the greatest national celebration in the Greek calendar, however, until the games were abolished by Theodosius I, in 394 A.D. In 426, the temple at Olympia was burned.[51]

According to Pausanias and Strabo the administrative control of the Olympian festival was from the beginning in the hands of the Eleans, though the Pisatans, aided by Argive Pheidon, seized control for a time.[52] This account, based on "the ancient writings of the Eleans," was doubtless a priestly chronicle, agreeable to the ears of the Eleans, since it credited them with original control. Xenophon, however, denied that original control was theirs,[53] and this view has been accepted by modern scholars who hold that original control

[47] Gardiner: *Athletics of the Ancient World*, p. 33; Hyde: *op. cit.*, pp. 14, 16.
[48] Glotz: *The Aegean Civilization*, pp. 296 f., 392. Trans. by M. R. Dobie and E. M. Riley. Courtesy of Kegan Paul, Trench, Trübner & Co., Ltd., London.
[49] *Ibid.*, p. 289. Courtesy of Kegan Paul, Trench, Trübner & Co., Ltd., London.
[50] *C.A.H.*, III, 547; Gardiner: *Athletics of the Ancient World*, p. 34.
[51] Baumeister: *Denkmäler des Klassischen Altertums*, II, 1061.
[52] Pausanias, V, 4, 5–6; 8, 5; 9, 4–6; Strabo, VIII, 3, 33.
[53] *Hellenics*, III, 2, 30; VII, 4, 28.

must have been exercised by the Pisatans and then by the invading Aetolians, the Eleans of later time. The transition of power involved a struggle, ended, it was said, on the advice of the Delphian Oracle [54] and by the joint efforts of Iphitus of Elis and Cleosthenes of Pisa, with whom Lycurgus was also later associated. From the dual administration of Iphitus and Cleosthenes came the two Hellanodicae, officials of the games, who wore purple robes signifying their royal origin. Dual administration, however, was beset with difficulties; in the fifth century the Eleans, aided by the Spartans, gained complete authority, which they maintained to the end.[55] At the time of Plataea the two officials were replaced by nine Hellanodicae, chosen by lot, each probably representing a tribe of Elis. The nine were divided into three groups: one had charge of the pentathlon; a second looked after the equestrian events; and the third directed other gymnastic contests. When the tribes of Elis increased to twelve, the Hellanodicae also numbered twelve; later, when the tribes were reduced to eight, and again increased to ten (108th Olympiad), the number of officials followed these fluctuations.[56]

The Hellanodicae were the executive officers of the Olympic Council, which originally probably represented local villages. Though the functions of the Council must have varied from time to time, it was the court of appeal, controlled the erection of new buildings, and approved the erection of victors' statues. The Hellanodicae were compelled to undergo a ten months' period of instruction by the Nomophylakes, after which they took an oath before the statue of Zeus in the Council House, being sworn to secrecy in matters pertaining to accepted and rejected candidates, and to upright judgments.[57] Delegates from Elis were said to have gone to Egypt to find out whether her wise men could suggest any improvement in administration of the games. They were advised that since Eleans were the judges, no Elean should be a competitor.[58] In the 102d Olympiad, one of the Hellanodicae won the chariot race; in consequence, the Eleans ruled that henceforth no horses of judges were to be entered.[59] Judges might be punished and fined, if an appeal against their judgments was successful.[60] Besides these chief authorities there were, of course, many lesser officials, trumpeters, heralds, and, in the Christian era, official guides (exegetae), who took care of the vast concourse of visitors.

The Olympian festival, held at the second or third full moon following the

---

[54] Pausanias, v, 4, 6; Krause: *Olympia oder Darstellung der Grossen Olympischen Spiele*, p. 37.
[55] Gardiner: *Greek Athletic Sports and Festivals*, pp. 46, 116.
[56] Pausanias, v, 9, 4–6; Krause: op. cit., pp. 126 ff.
[57] Pausanias, v, 24, 9–10; Krause: op. cit., pp. 130 f.
[58] *The History of Herodotus*, II, 160.
[59] Pausanias, VI, 1, 4–5.
[60] *Ibid.*, VI, 3, 7.

summer solstice, lasted five days at the time of Pindar,[61] the fourteenth or fifteenth of the month being the high point of the celebration.[62] Xenophanes, speaking of Olympic contests, mentions the foot race, pentathlon, wrestling, boxing, pancration, and horse racing.[63] Jumping, discus, and javelin would be included in the pentathlon. Foot races were of many kinds—stade-race, double race, long race, armed race, and torch race.[64] Views concerning the order of events in the pentathlon and the method of determining the victor vary considerably. The order may have been changed from time to time, though there is a strong probability of a fair degree of consistency. The best evidence seems to support the following order: running, jumping, discus, javelin, wrestling. But there is admittedly much uncertainty. Wrestling, in any case, seems certainly to have held the last place on the program of gymnastic contests.[65] Though the fantastic view was once held that to be crowned in the pentathlon one must win in all five of the contests, it has been more convincingly argued that victory in three out of five events determined the winner, and "in case of a tie account was taken of second and third places." [66] Probably no question has occasioned more controversy than the records made in the jump. Philostratos says that the *halteres* was invented by pentathletes for use in jumping, to give "wings" to the athlete and enable him to bring his feet "firmly and gracefully to the ground." [67] Despite their use, however, the records of Phaÿllus, who jumped fifty-five feet at Delphi, and of Chionis who leaped fifty-two (or fifty-four feet and eight inches by another calculation) at Olympia, have occasioned much speculation as to the reliability of the accounts and the method of jumping. Gardiner came to the conclusion that Phaÿllus' record jump was no more to be taken seriously than the feat of Milo who ate a whole four-year-old heifer.[68] Diels thought the record must be explained as "a three-fold jump." [69] Hyde, reviewing the evidence and the various theories that had been advanced, concluded that Gardiner's convictions regarding the falsity of the records were ill founded, and that the evidence "points conclusively to a multiple jump," probably a "hop, hop, jump." [70]

While wrestling and the pancration have been commonly contrasted, one being represented as a test of skill and science, the other as a trial of brute

[61] Way: The Odes of Pindar, "Olympian" v, ant. 1.
[62] Krause: op. cit., p. 69; Gardiner: Greek Athletic Sports and Festivals, pp. 194 f.
[63] Athenaeus, x, 414.
[64] Philostratos: Concerning Gymnastics, 3–8; Gardiner: "Notes on the Greek Foot-race," Jour. Hellenic Studies, xxiii, 261–91; Greek Athletic Sports and Festivals, pp. 270–94.
[65] Gardiner: Greek Athletic Sports and Festivals, pp. 363 f.
[66] Gardiner: "The Method of Deciding the Pentathlon," Jour. Hellenic Studies, xxiii, 69.
[67] Concerning Gymnastics, 55.
[68] "Phaÿllus and His Record Jump," Jour. Hellenic Studies, xxiv, 80.
[69] "Ancient Long Jump," Am. Jour. Archaeol., iv, 539.
[70] "The Pentathlum Jump," Am. Jour. Philol., lix, 406 f., 417.

JUMPING WITH HALTERES

Museum of Fine Arts, Boston (Courtesy, The Metropolitan Museum of Art, New York)

strength, Gardiner holds that the pancration was itself a "contest of skill," and "there is no ground" for so contrasting the two events.[71] Though Arrichion was killed in the pancration, certain ancient authors thought it even less dangerous than wrestling. Various other descriptions and the condemnation of it by Galen, however, have doubtless given rise to the general notion of its brutality. The fact that it included elements of boxing as well as wrestling, and that the struggle was carried on both standing and on the ground until one should acknowledge himself vanquished,[72] would also lend credence to the view that it was a more serious test. In wrestling, a "fair fall" was acknowledged if a contestant's "knee, hip, back, or shoulder" touched the ground. Three falls were necessary, i.e., the "best of five bouts," to win the crown. Tripping was permitted. Various hand and arm holds, neck holds, body holds, the arm lock, cross-buttock, and flying mare were evidently employed, but holds below the waist were not permitted.[73] The following description of the pancratic victory of Arrichion in the Fifty-fourth Olympiad [74] shows some of the features of the contest which set it off from wrestling and support its reputation for brutality.

"Accordingly the antagonist of Arrichion, having already clinched him around

[71] "The Pancration and Wrestling," Jour. Hellenic Studies, XXVI, 12.
[72] Philostratos: Concerning Gymnastics, 9, 21.
[73] Gardiner: "Wrestling," Jour. Hellenic Studies, XXV, 14–31, 263–93.
[74] Cf. Pausanias, VIII, 40, 2; Philostratos: Concerning Gymnastics, 21.

the middle, thought to kill him; already he had wound his forearm about the other's throat to shut off the breathing, while, pressing his legs on the groins and winding his feet one inside each knee of his adversary, he forestalled Arrichion's resistance by choking him till the sleep of death thus induced began to creep over his senses. But in relaxing the tension of his legs he failed to forestall the scheme of Arrichion; for the latter kicked back with the sole of his right foot (as the result of which his right side was imperilled since now his knee was hanging unsupported), then with his groin he holds his adversary tight till he can no longer resist, and, throwing his weight down toward the left while he locks the latter's foot tightly inside his own knee, by this violent outward thrust he wrenches the ankle from its socket." [75]

The beginning of the sacred truce, reputedly re-established by Iphitus,[76] which by the middle of the fifth century probably extended for three months rather than one, was announced by the Elean heralds, first in their own land and then in all Hellenic cities. As soon as the truce was proclaimed, contestants, official representatives, and visitors of all sorts traveling to Olympia were under the protection of the god, and no one was permitted to invade the sacred territory.[77] Those who transgressed the Olympian truce were subjected to judgments and penalties. Though sometimes honored in the breach rather than in observance, especially by Lacedaemon, its general effectiveness, particularly when Olympian prestige was at its height, was admittedly great. A fine of two *minas* for every hoplite was imposed on Sparta because of her invasion of the sacred territory and seizure of Lepreum during the Peloponnesian War. Upon her failure to pay, the Eleans refused her admission to the games and sacrifices.[78] An Athenian, Phrynon, who was robbed by Macedonian soldiers while on his way to the Olympic festival, received full restitution from the king and an apology, to the effect that the soldiers had not known of the beginning of the sacred truce.[79]

The regulations administered by the Hellanodicae at Olympia were numerous, precise, and generally strictly enforced. It was the business of these officials, who represented the chief judge of contests, Zeus himself, to ascertain the fitness of would-be contestants for the crown in respect to Hellenic parentage, age, physical condition, freedom from pollution by manslaughter, and from failure to perform any obligations owing to the Olympian god.[80] Evi-

[75] Philostratus: *Imagines*, II, 6. Trans. by A. Fairbanks. The Loeb Classical Library. Quoted by permission of Harvard University Press, Cambridge, Mass.
[76] Pausanias, v, 20, 1; 4, 5.
[77] Strabo, VIII, 3, 33; Krause: op. cit., pp. 35 ff.; Gardiner: *Greek Athletic Sports and Festivals*, pp. 43, 201 f.; Gardner: op. cit., p. 273.
[78] Thucydides, v, 49–50.
[79] Krause: op. cit., p. 41.
[80] Philostratos: *Concerning Gymnastics*, 25; Gardiner: *Greek Athletic Sports and Festivals*, p. 46.

dence of age and parentage must have been often unsatisfactory. Did Alexander, son of Amyntas, prove himself an Argive by such a genealogical account as Herodotus records? [81] Was it proof of his age, or the influence of a powerful friend, Agesilaus, that caused the Hellanodicae to admit an oversized Athenian to the boys' contests? [82] Giving false information, if discovered, was severely punished. Contestants must announce their intention to compete by a specified date, and a tardy appearance was punished by fine and exclusion from the games. Apollonius, surnamed Rhantes, was punished for late arrival, it being shown that he had taken time on the way to Olympia to make a little money at games held in Ionia.[83] Those who satisfied the officials as to these requirements must also make a sacrifice, and take an oath before Zeus Horkios that they would not use illegal tactics to win (to which fathers, brothers, and trainers must also swear), and that they had faithfully trained for the contests as prescribed. Olympic contestants were required to train for ten months,[84] one month's training being under the eyes of the Hellanodicae at Elis. Philostratos gives an idea of their strictness in the early third century A.D. They prescribed such training as seemed to them best, having themselves been trained for their service; and even the trainers were threatened with the lash if anything happened contrary to the rules. There was, indeed, no disputing their decrees, for to resist them meant disbarment from the games.[85] Training in wrestling at Elis was so severe a trial of ability that the rules expressly permitted a crown to be awarded without an "actual contest." [86] Having concluded training, when they were about to leave for the Olympic contests, the athletes were admonished by the Hellanodicae as follows: "If ye have laboured so hard as to be entitled to go to Olympia and have banished all sloth and cowardice from your lives, then march boldly on; but as for those who have not so trained themselves, let them depart whithersoever they like." [87]

Once enrolled for a contest, the athlete had no choice but to go through with it, or be shamed as a coward and punished, as was Sarapion, from Egypt, who became frightened the day before the pancration and ran away.[88] Physical unfitness, apparently, was not considered an adequate excuse. Thus, Theagenes, who entered his name in both boxing and the pancration in one Olympiad, but found himself so worn out after the first contest that he could not go on with

[81] Bk. v, 22; VIII, 136-7.
[82] Xenophon: Hellenics, IV, 1, 39-40; Plutarch: Agesilaus, 13.
[83] Pausanias, v, 21, 13-5.
[84] Ibid., v, 24, 9; Krause: op. cit., pp. 132 ff.
[85] Philostratos: Concerning Gymnastics, 54.
[86] Ibid., 11.
[87] Philostratus: The Life of Apollonius of Tyana, v, 43. Trans. by F. C. Conybeare. The Loeb Classical Library. Quoted by permission of Harvard University Press, Cambridge, Mass.
[88] Pausanias, v, 21, 18.

the second, was fined two talents, one for the god, and another to be paid to Euthymus whom, the judges held, he had wronged.[89]

Though the laws of Olympia punished venality severely, and officials were charged to be ever watchful, the evil crept in and increased. Philostratos traced its increase at the Great Games to the growth of professionalism, the habit of expensive, luxurious living, "Sicilian gluttony," and even to the trainers: "Some sell even their honor, as I believe, because they need much; others must buy themselves an easy victory, because they lead a luxurious life." Doubtless, too, excessive public adulation of victors caused many to desire a victory at any cost. Philostratos, however, regarded the games at Olympia as an exception to the rule: ". . . only among the Eleans is the olive-crown according to ancient belief still inviolable." [90] He goes on to cite what happened at the Isthmian Games. Considering the number of violations of Olympic rules, related by Pausanias and others, the statement of Philostratos means only that, relatively speaking, Olympia maintained the ancient ideal of sportsmanship with more success than others; indeed, the list of offenders does not seem large, considering the centuries of Olympian contests.

When venality was detected, the fact was published abroad; and a provision required the setting up of Zanes, bronze statues of Zeus, out of the fines imposed, so that contestants who came to Olympia could see them and be warned against like errors. Six were put up in the Ninety-eighth Olympiad, when Eupolus bribed his three opponents in boxing. These are said to have been the first fines imposed for such dishonesty. Verses were inscribed on one statue to the effect that an Olympic victory must be gained by fleetness and strength, not by money; another declared it was set up as "a terror to athletes who transgress"; a third praised the Eleans for their punishment of crooked athletes. Collecting the fines was sometimes difficult, as this instance shows: An Athenian pentathlete was fined for bribery in the 112th Olympiad; the Athenians asked for remission of the fine, which being refused, they neither paid nor attended the games, until compelled by an oracular voice from Delphi to do so. Six more Zanes were added—with verses, Pausanias says, no better than those on the punishment of Eupolus! Two others were erected in the 178th Olympiad for bribery in a wrestling match; again, in the 226th Olympiad, two boxers from Egypt increased the list of Zanes. The Eleans, Pausanias thought, should have been specially honorable in the games of Olympian Zeus, since they were under Elean jurisdiction; but an Elean father, wanting his son to win, bribed a father from Smyrna; this being known, both fathers were fined, rather than the sons.[91]

89 Ibid., vi, 6, 5–6.
90 Philostratos: Concerning Gymnastics, 45.
91 Pausanias, v, 21.

Sometimes athletes sold their abilities to cities which wished to increase their fame by having Olympic victors. Sotades, a Cretan, once victor in the long race, was bribed by Ephesus at the 100th Olympiad to proclaim himself an Ephesian, for which the Cretans banished him. Astylus, a Crotonian, victor at three Olympiads, allowed himself to be proclaimed a Syracusan to please Hiero, for which his townsmen made his house a gaol and took down his statue. Dicon, a Caulonian, many times a victor, sold himself to the Syracusans. Lichas, a Lacedaemonian, once entered his chariot under the name of Thebes, and for this he was whipped. Numerous other instances might be cited to show the spread of the golden blight at the Olympic and other great games. Virtue was not without her triumphs, however: Antipater of Miletus refused the bribe offered his father by the Syracusans to persuade him to proclaim himself from Syracuse, and set up a statue on which were inscribed his Milesian origin and the fact that he was the first Ionian to dedicate a statue at Olympia.[92]

A strict law imposed the penalty of death on married women who attempted to witness the Olympian Games, or even to cross the River Alpheus on forbidden days. Virgins were not hindered from observing the contests, however, according to Pausanias,[93] but this is thought at least open to question.[94] Two exceptions to the rule against women may be noted: the Priestess of Demeter Chamyne, a woman designated by the Eleans, who sat on a white altar opposite the Hellanodicae and witnessed the contests; and Pherenike of Rhodes, daughter of Diagoras, the boxer. Pherenike was the only woman who transgressed the law and yet escaped punishment. Her husband being dead, she disguised herself as a trainer and came with her son Pisirodus to the contests. When he was victorious, she became excited, leaped over the barrier which marked the space reserved for trainers, and in so doing exposed herself and betrayed her sex. Notwithstanding the seriousness of the offense, she was exempted from the punishment of being thrown from the Typaean rock because of the renown of her family, which had furnished many Olympic victors.[95]

The prohibition against women may be accounted for as a survival of an ancient religious taboo, antecedent to Dorian dominion. It was, in any case, out of keeping with Dorian practice in Lacedaemon and in other Dorian cities

[92] Ibid., VI, 2, 2, 6–7; 3, 11; 13, 1; 18, 6; Krause: op. cit., pp. 144 ff., 270, 285, 291; Hyde: Olympic Victor Monuments, pp. 33 f.; Gardiner: Greek Athletic Sports and Festivals, pp. 134 f., 174.

[93] Bk. VI, 20, 9.

[94] Krause: op. cit., pp. 54 ff.; Gardner: op. cit., p. 275; Gardiner: Greek Athletic Sports and Festivals, p. 47; Hyde: Olympic Victor Monuments, p. 49. Pausanias says, too, regarding the altar of Zeus, that maidens might ascend to a certain point; and women as well, "when they are not excluded from Olympia," i.e., when contests were not being held.—Bk. V, 13, 10.

[95] Pausanias, V, 6, 7–8; Philostratos: Concerning Gymnastics, 17.

such as Cyrene,[96] though it harmonized with Athenian discrimination against women.

A concession to women of wealth and rank was made in that they could enter horses and chariots at Olympia, though they could not themselves enter the contest. Those who took advantage of the opportunity were chiefly Lacedaemonians. Cynisca, daughter of Archidamus, was the first and the most famous woman, who won a victory in the four-horse chariot race at Olympia. A shrine was erected in her honor at the Plane-Tree Grove, and a memorial in stone of chariot, horses, charioteer, and a likeness of Cynisca herself was put up at Olympia.[97] Xenophon says that Agesilaus advised Cynisca to enter her horses at Olympia, so as to prove that victory in such matters depended on wealth and not necessarily on merit.[98] Euryleonis was also a winner with a two-horse chariot at Olympia. Macedonian women followed the Dorian fashion, and Belistiche was victor in the 129th Olympiad. Berenike Euergetis, wife of Ptolemy III, is also recorded as an Olympic winner.[99]

Though excluded from witnessing the contests in honor of Olympian Zeus, women had a festival of their own, athletic and religious in character, in honor of Hera. Her temple, of wood, stone, and sun-dried brick, more ancient than any other whose foundations remain at Olympia, is believed to date back at least to the tenth or eleventh century.[100] Like the men's contests, Hera's festival was traced back in legend to great antiquity, Hippodamia being credited with its institution in gratitude for her marriage with Pelops. Two choruses, the Physcoa and the Hippodamia, were under the direction of sixteen women, representing originally sixteen ancient cities of Elis. The matrons wove a robe for Hera every four years, and with their assistants conducted the Heraean Games, in which virgins of three age groups participated. These girls, with hair hanging down, dressed in a short shirt leaving the right shoulder bare to the breast and reaching a little above the knees, ran a course about one-sixth less than the length of the Olympic stadium. Victors were crowned with wild olive, received a share of a sacrificial cow, and were permitted to dedicate their statues in Hera's temple. Whether the marble statue of a girl runner, in the Vatican Museum, should be referred to the Heraean contests at Olympia, as many have thought, is open to question.[101]

In legendary lands and times the Greeks won prizes of more or less value in athletic contests. The prizes at the games in honor of Patroclos were commensurable in value with the merit of the dead and the generosity and dignity of

96 Krause: op. cit., p. 214; supra, pp. 244 ff.
97 Pausanias, III, 8, 1; 15, 1; VI, 1, 6; Krause: op. cit., p. 316.
98 Agesilaus, IX, 6; Plutarch: Agesilaus, 20.
99 Pausanias, III, 17, 6; V, 8, 11; Krause: op. cit., pp. 57 f., 258, 287.
100 Hyde: Olympic Victor Monuments, p. 16; Gardner: op. cit., p. 283.
101 Pausanias, V, 16; Hyde: Olympic Victor Monuments, pp. 49 f.; supra, p. 247.

the giver, and were offered to victors and to vanquished.[102] In early historic times, too, at festivals both of local and of wide renown, prizes of tangible value continued to be the rule. Only in the great national games of the crown did a slight, sacred symbol, a wreath of wild olive, laurel, parsley, or pine, become the sole, official reward for merit.[103] Dorian influence, which raised a local festival to national importance, also established the practice of giving a wreath as symbol of victory. In the earliest Olympiads prizes of real value must have been given as at other games. The substitution of the olive crown at Olympia may have been gradual; but, despite conflicting myths about its coming into use, it is generally held that it was given at the Seventh Olympiad, after the Pythian oracle had advised it, and was won in running by Daicles, a Dorian from Messenia.[104] Numerous other myths were associated with the wild olive. Heracles was said to have crowned his winning brother with it, and brought it first to Greece from the land of the Hyperboreans; it was said to have first sprouted on the banks of the Alpheus; Heracles, by another account, once leaned his club of wild olive against a statue of Hermes, and it struck root and flourished again.[105]

"Now on one, now on another, doth the grace that quickeneth look favourably," says Pindar.[106] On the head of the one thus favored, bound with a woolen fillet, was placed a wreath of wild olive, cut with a golden sickle by a boy whose parents were living, from the sacred "Olive of the Fair Crown," which stood within the Altis near the temple of Zeus. An imitation of the same crown adorned the head of the statue of Zeus, supreme judge of contests. In early times the seventeen crowns lay ready for the prospective winners on a tripod of bronze; later, on a magnificent table of ivory and gold. Whether the crown of victory was awarded immediately after each contest, or all of them together on the last day, the sixteenth of the festal month, has been disputed. Pausanias and others mention certain events which imply an immediate ceremony. Practice may have varied from time to time; but an immediate award seems most probable.[107]

Though a crown was the only award, various customary honors were the lot of the victor. In his right hand, he received a palm from the Hellanodik; [108] he heard his name, that of his father, and that of his country and city pro-

[102] Supra, pp. 226 ff.; Krause: op. cit., p. 169; Hyde: Olympic Victor Monuments, pp. 18 f.
[103] Pausanias, VIII, 48, 2.
[104] Müller: The History and Antiquities of the Doric Race, II, 314; Krause: op. cit., pp. 158, 262.
[105] Pausanias, II, 31, 10; V, 7, 7–8; 14, 3.
[106] Pater: Greek Studies, pp. 297 f.
[107] Pausanias, V, 11, 1; 12, 5; 15, 3; 20, 1–2; 21, 14; Krause: op. cit., pp. 162, 164 f.; Gardiner: Greek Athletic Sports and Festivals, pp. 200 f.
[108] Pausanias, VIII, 48, 2–3; Plutarch: Theseus, 21; Symposiacs, VIII, 4; Krause: op. cit., p. 168; cf. Tarbell: "The Palm of Victory," Class. Philol., III, 264–72.

claimed by the herald; above all arose the shouts of the multitude and the acclaim of his friends; and not less sweet was the song of a gifted singer, "sung in the victor's supper-room or at the door of his abode, or with the lyre and the pipe as they took him home in procession through the streets, . . . or in a temple where he laid up his crown. . . ." [109] Moreover, on the last day, he ate at the table of Zeus, as it were, when the Eleans feasted all victors at the Prytaneum; [110] if he liked, he might dedicate the sacred wreath, the instruments of his contest—discus, javelin, chariot, *halteres*—to the god of games; and he, his friends, relatives, or fellow citizens were free to put up at Olympia a personal statue, which would long remain as witness of his great day. To these monuments to personal triumph, Pausanias, in 173 A.D., and others in later years, returned to read the fascinating human story of Olympia.

For the vanquished, lucky perhaps to be alive, there was little or nothing to do but "slink homeward with scant sympathy, indeed thankful to be ignored," for Olympia honored the victor alone with a wreath.[111] Alcibiades boasts to the Athenians that in the chariot races he won first prize and also placed second and fourth, having entered seven chariots in one contest, more than any private individual theretofore; [112] Kallias, too, is said to have taken the prize in the horse race and also finished second in the four-horse chariot race; [113] but though second and fourth might be mentioned as an honor, no prize was connected with it.

Victories "without dust," *i.e.*, without an actual contest, were not unknown. A tardy arrival or failure to appear might give the crown to the opponent. Thus Heraclides was crowned in boxing because his opponent Apollonius of Rhantes came late.[114] Sometimes an entrant became frightened because of the reputation of his opponent and withdrew, thus acknowledging himself vanquished without a contest.[115] By a mythical account, Heracles was declared victor in "all the contests . . . without opposition." [116] A crown was occasionally won because an announced contestant, worn out with an earlier contest, was unable to meet his opponent. Thus Dromeus gained the crown for the first time in the pancration at the expense of Theagenes.[117] Excellence shown during the training period at Olympia could also win in certain cases. Though the award of a crown in the pancration without a contest was extraordinary, Philostratos says that training for wrestling at Olympia was so severe a trial that the rules

---

[109] Pater: *op. cit.*, p. 297.
[110] Pausanias, V, 15, 12.
[111] Krause: *op. cit.*, pp. 164, 169 ff.; Lawton: *op. cit.*, pp. 144 f.
[112] Thucydides, VI, 16.
[113] Herodotus, VI, 122.
[114] Pausanias, V, 21, 12–4.
[115] *Ibid.*, V, 21, 18.
[116] Diodorus, IV, 14.
[117] Pausanias, VI, 11, 4.

expressly permitted a victory therein without a contest, awarding the crown "to the best training—indeed, for training alone." [118]

Though Olympia safeguarded athletics against commercialism by awarding simply a symbolic wreath, Olympic heroes were not left long without other rewards. Solon encouraged Athenian athletes by a gift of five hundred drachmas to Olympian victors and fed them at public cost at the Prytaneum.[119] Crotonians reputedly offered lavish prizes to entice athletes to their city and thus "dim the glory" of the Olympic festival.[120] At Rome public maintenance was provided for Olympic victors and others.[121] Less tangible, though more spectacular, honors might come to an athlete if his city chose to erect a statue, greet him with a great procession, perhaps breach its walls for his triumphal entry, or even establish religious rites in his name.[122] Such gifts and extraordinary honors did much, doubtless, to encourage professionalism and a mercenary spirit. It is not strange that many came to want money above all else.[123] Though slight in the sixth century, compared with later times, these evils were sharply criticized by Xenophanes. Aristophanes wittily punctured the old belief that games were played for love of sport. His audiences well knew that "Wealth can see, my boy!" Euripides castigated the evil which had grown to formidable proportions in the fourth century. By the time of Galen and Philostratos professionalism and pot-hunting had brought ruin to athletics, though Olympia, despite numerous cases of venality, continued to award the crown until her honors to Olympian Zeus were cut off forever.[124]

### PYTHIAN, ISTHMIAN, AND NEMEAN GAMES

After a long history, when the concern over organized athletics had spread and a single great festival no longer sufficed, Olympia became the model for other festivals of national scope. By the early sixth century four national festivals had been recognized, the Pythian, Isthmian, and Nemean games having been instituted on a basis comparable to the Olympian.[125] None of these, however, achieved fame equal to Olympia.

From a religious and cultural standpoint the Pythia were second only to Olympia; in horse and chariot races they vied with Olympic events, but athletically they were probably inferior not only to Olympia but also to the

[118] Ibid.; Philostratos: Concerning Gymnastics, 11.
[119] Plutarch: Solon, 23; Aristides, 27.
[120] Athenaeus, XII, 522.
[121] Suetonius: Augustus, 45; infra, p. 751.
[122] Hyde: Olympic Victor Monuments, pp. 34 ff.
[123] Philostratos: Concerning Gymnastics, 45.
[124] Supra, pp. 354 f.
[125] Real-Encyclopädie, VII, Pt. II, 2042.

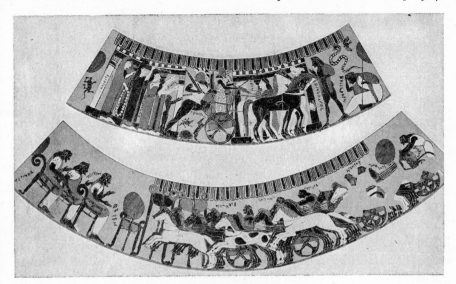

A FOUR HORSE CHARIOT RACE    6th century B.C.
Berlin Museum (Courtesy, The Metropolitan Museum of Art, New York)

Nemean and the Isthmian festivals.[126] Competitions in music gave the Pythia their greatest fame. There, since ancient times, the Hymn to Apollo was rendered in honor of the god's combat with the Python.[127] Ovid recalls the event, and the establishment of memorial games:

> Though every shaft took place, he spent the store
> Of his full quiver; and 'twas long before
> Th' expiring serpent wallow'd in his gore.
> Then, to preserve the fame of such a deed,
> For Python slain, he Pythian games decreed.[128]

Long celebrated as an octennial music festival,[129] the Pythia were reorganized in 582 B.C., after the ten-year Sacred War which arose out of the competing interests of Crissa, Cirrha, and Delphi.[130] Under the jurisdiction of the Amphictyonic league, they were administered by its council, the Hieromnemones, composed of two members from each of the twelve tribes, which had charge of all details pertaining to the holy place. The new festival, celebrated

126 Gardiner: *Greek Athletic Sports and Festivals*, p. 209; Hyde: *Olympic Victor Monuments*, pp. 24 f.
127 Strabo, IX, 3, 10.
128 *Metamorphoses* (Dryden), I, 21.
129 Krause: *Die Pythien Nemeen und Isthmien*, p. 29.
130 Grote: *A History of Greece*, I, 783.

quadrennially in the third year of each Olympiad, in the month of August, included gymnastic contests and chariot races on the Olympian pattern,[131] as well as musical events. Though little is known of the order of events, or the number of days devoted to the festival, the musical contests which were oldest and most important must have preceded gymnastic competitions, while equestrian contests followed them.[132] Just as prizes of value had been replaced by the olive wreath at Olympia, so at Delphi the reward of victory, after the festival's reorganization, was a crown of laurel and the symbolic palm.[133] The branches for the crown were to be cut from the Vale of Tempe by a boy whose mother and father were still living—again following Olympic precedent. The regulations governing the Pythian contests are little known, but it seems that, as at Olympia, failure in respect to promptness might exclude a contestant.[134] Dorieus, son of Diagoras, reputedly won a crown without a contest,[135] though Heliodorus [136] says that such an award was not permitted. Krause infers from these similarities to Olympian practice that other regulations introduced at Olympia were probably taken over by Delphi.[137] Just when the Pythian festival came to an end is unknown. In the 195th Pythiad the victor in tragedy was a Byzantine, Clemens; the Pythian Panegyric was mentioned at the time of the Emperor Julian; and it may well be that the festival continued till about 394 A.D., when the Olympic contests came to an end.[138]

The Isthmian Games, reputed by legend to have been founded by Theseus,[139] and reorganized about 582 B.C., were of less consequence as a religious festival than the Pythia, and of less importance athletically than the Olympic and Nemean festivals.[140] The earliest rites at the Isthmia were of a religious character, in honor of Melicertes. Their origin, like those at Olympia and Delphi, was shrouded in myths, the Isthmia being held by some to have antedated even Olympia, the Pythia, and the Nemea. According to one account the festival was first held by Poseidon and Helios; Castor had won the foot race; Calais the *diaulos*; Orpheus the contest with the cithara; Heracles the pancration; Polydeuces the boxing match; Peleus, wrestling; Telamon, throwing the discus; and Theseus the race in armor. The festival was also credited with equestrian contests in which Neleus and Phaeton were victors, and a boat race

---

[131] Krause: *Die Pythien*, p. 20.
[132] *Ibid.*, pp. 41 f.
[133] Pausanias, x, 7, 5; Krause: *Die Pythien*, pp. 49 f.
[134] Plutarch: *Symposiacs*, vii, 5, 1.
[135] Pausanias, vi, 7, 2.
[136] *Aethiopian History*, iv.
[137] *Die Pythien*, p. 47.
[138] *Ibid.*, pp. 53, 94 f.
[139] Plutarch: *Theseus*, 25.
[140] Krause: *Die Pythien*, pp. 182 f.; *Real-Encyclopädie*, vii, Pt. ii, 2042; *C.A.H.*, iii, 556.

wherein the Argo won the award.[141] Gardner says that of all the greater festivals ". . . the Isthmia alone probably included boat-racing." [142]

The frequency of the Isthmian festival, prior to its reorganization, is undetermined. The celebration may have been quite irregular; or it may have been an octennial event, as were other great festivals in early times. As reorganized, however, the Isthmia occurred every other year, in late April or early May, during the first and third years of each Olympiad.[143] The festival was celebrated in honor of Poseidon, whose temple on the Isthmus was surrounded by forests of pine.[144] Several days were probably occupied by the contests.[145] Gymnastic and equestrian events were included, and possibly boat races as well. Though musical events are not definitely known before the third century b.c., they probably existed from the very beginning. The order of events at the festival is unknown, but Livy tells us that the games were "regularly opened with a ritual chant. . . ." [146] Poetry, plays, and painting at one time or another were included among the events. Nero gained the crown as citharist and herald, though the manner of his winning was extraordinary.[147] Winners of the stade-race for men and boys are known; likewise, victors in the long race, wrestling, and boxing for men and boys, the pancration for men and youths, and the pentathlon. There were doubtless other gymnastic contests, but specific information is lacking in the scattered references that have been preserved. Equestrian events, similar to those at Olympia and Delphi, seem also to have had a place at the Isthmia, though only a few victors are known to us.

Though prior to the third century the Isthmian festival was little known, in later centuries its fame was noised abroad. The relative importance of Olympic and Isthmian games in Solon's time may be surmised from the fact that one hundred drachmas were decreed for Isthmian victors, and five hundred for those crowned at the Elean festival.[148] After the Persian War the Isthmia shared the heightened value that Greeks generally attached to Panhellenic festivals; nevertheless, Corinthians themselves appear to have had little athletic prestige, and their games did not draw as many great athletes from distant parts as did the Olympic and the Nemean. Isthmian popularity was greatest with Athenians, Aeginetans, Thebans, and other neighbors. Despite her inferior athletic stand-

[141] Krause: *Die Pythien*, pp. 170 ff.
[142] "Boat-races among the Greeks," *Jour. Hellenic Studies*, II, 92; *supra*, p. 351.
[143] Krause: *Die Pythien*, pp. 182, 184. The time has been disputed. Gardner, *Greek Athletic Sports and Festivals*, p. 214, holds with others that the Isthmia were held in the second and fourth years of the Olympiad.
[144] Strabo, VIII, 6, 22.
[145] Krause: *Die Pythien*, p. 192; Gardner: *Greek Athletic Sports and Festivals*, pp. 220 f.
[146] Livy, XXXIII, 32.
[147] Philostratus: *Apollonius of Tyana*, IV, 24; Krause: *Die Pythien*, pp. 189 ff.
[148] Plutarch: *Solon*, 23.

ing, however, the crowds that came to Corinth were so great as to excite comment by Strabo, Livy,[149] and others, and may have exceeded all festivals in size. This drawing capacity must be credited above all to the accessibility of the city of Corinth to merchants and to better accommodations for visitors. Dio Chrysostom says that ". . . when the time for the Isthmian games arrived," and everybody went to the Isthmus "to see the athletes and to gormandize," Diogenes went down also ". . . to make a study of the pursuits and ambitions of men. . . ." [150] Athenians especially had a high regard for the Isthmia—perhaps in connection with the legend that Theseus had made an agreement with the Corinthians by which a place of honor for Athenian representatives should be set aside as large as the fully stretched sail of the ship on which they came.[151] In light of this popularity of the Corinthian festival, it is interesting to recall that Socrates was said never to have left Athens save when he went on military service and again when he attended the Isthmian Games.[152] Aristophanes, in The Peace (421 B.C.), depicts the bubbling spirits of common folk at the prospect of a return to the ways of peace:

> What are you scribbling?
> Marking out a place
> To pitch my tent in, at the Isthmian games.[153]

Occasionally an ancient author conveys a vivid impression of popular reactions to the games and victorious athletes. Dio Chrysostom has described the enthusiasm with which a victor at Corinth was welcomed by the crowds. Diogenes, he says, ". . . saw a person leaving the race-track surrounded by a great mob and not even walking on the earth, but being carried shoulder high by the throng, with some following after and shouting, others leaping for joy and lifting their hands towards heaven, and still others throwing garlands and ribbons upon him. . . ." [154] Diogenes, not so much impressed by physical feats, is said to have put a crown on a horse's head because it had "won in kicking." [155] Though we are told that Diogenes thus caused many to ridicule the athletes, and that certain people actually went away without seeing the rest of the contests, his influence seems to have been of slight avail in breaking the

---

[149] Strabo, VIII, 6, 20; Livy, XXXIII, 32.
[150] Dio Chrysostom, VIII, 6–7; IX, 1. Trans. by J. W. Cohoon and H. L. Crosby. The Loeb Classical Library. Quoted by permission of Harvard University Press, Cambridge, Mass.
[151] Plutarch: Theseus, 25.
[152] Plato: Crito, 52.
[153] The Peace, 879 ff. Trans. by B. B. Rogers. The Loeb Classical Library. Quoted by permission of Harvard University Press, Cambridge, Mass.
[154] Dio Chrysostom, IX, 14. Trans. by J. W. Cohoon and H. L. Crosby. The Loeb Classical Library. Quoted by permission of Harvard University Press, Cambridge, Mass.
[155] Ibid., IX, 22.

Hellenic habit of excessive laudation of victorious athletes. Notwithstanding his views, Corinth would continue to welcome contestants and their supporters. It was both a pleasant and a profitable performance.

Due to the site of the Isthmian Games, commercialism seems to have been more pronounced than at any other national festival. It is probably not by chance that the worst instance of venality cited by Philostratos occurred at Corinth.[156] Perhaps, too, for this reason the Romans, famed for practicality and business, found a congenial atmosphere on the Isthmus. Under Roman rule the festival gained greater prominence. In 228 B.C. they were admitted to the Isthmian Games. Flamininus announced there, in 196 B.C., the freedom that Rome granted to Greek cities.[157] Even when the city was destroyed by Mummius, the Isthmian festival was not discontinued, though, for the time being, its direction was in the hands of the Sicyonians.[158] Caesar re-established the city, and the games were even more popular than before.[159] Nero competed at Corinth and boasted of his liberality to the Greeks. At the time of Julian, the Isthmia had taken on somewhat the character of Roman festivals, great sums being spent on animal combats. The festival may have continued to about the end of the fourth century, when the Olympian and Pythian contests also came to an end.[160]

Like other national festivals the celebration at Corinth, when it had been officially established, brought with it a moment of peace. Pausanias [161] cites the existence of a sacred truce at the Isthmia, even in legendary days. In historic times the truce was sometimes violated, as when Agesilaus invaded Corinth and took charge of the games then in progress.[162] Each Hellenic state was supposed to send a delegation (theoria) to the Isthmian as to other national festivals; but Elis neither sent representatives nor permitted Elean contestants to enter the lists at Corinth, a circumstance which still held true in the time of Pausanias, and for which various legendary reasons were assigned.[163]

Little is known of the Isthmian regulations, but they probably followed the Olympic pattern. Pausanias says that a person might compete as many as three times in one day; Cleitomachos, a Theban, won in wrestling, boxing, and the pancration.[164] Of the judges little is known, but they were Corinthians,[165] ex-

---

156 Philostratos: *Concerning Gymnastics*, 45.
157 Livy, XXXIII, 32.
158 Pausanias, II, 2, 2.
159 Krause: *Die Pythien*, pp. 180 f.
160 *Ibid.*, pp. 53, 181.
161 Bk. V, 2, 1.
162 Xenophon: *Hellenics*, IV, 5, 1–2.
163 Pausanias, V, 2, 2–5.
164 Bk. VI, 15, 3; Krause: *Die Pythien*, p. 194.
165 Way: *The Odes of Pindar*, "Nemean" II, str. 5.

cept for a few occasions when administration passed temporarily into other hands, as when the city of Corinth was destroyed. The judges themselves wore crowns while performing their functions,[166] and might serve more than once. The great liberality of entertainment of friends and of strangers, mentioned by Plutarch,[167] implies that the rôle of judge could only be played by wealthy men. Corinthian victors were crowned with parsley or pine, and like other winners at national games, received a palm branch from the judges. According to some of the ancients the crowns were first made of wild celery or parsley, and later of pine. It is most probable, however, that pine was first employed; later, parsley was used for a time; but afterwards, it was supplanted by the original pine.[168] Pindar refers to the victor crowned with wild celery.[169] It is said that Timoleon's soldiers, marching against the enemy, were met by mules laden with parsley. This they thought a bad omen, for the plant was commonly used to decorate graves of the dead. Timoleon reminded them, however, that the Isthmian crowns were made of the same thing, and commanded them to be of good courage and to twine wreaths for themselves, for the load of parsley was a clear augury of the victory that would be theirs.[170] In Roman times, certainly, pine came into its own again. Plutarch says it had recently come into use; but also that it had been the original reward of victory, and was only now restored to its ancient honor. A Corinthian coin from the time of Verus shows that pine was used. Writers of imperial times generally speak of it as the award for victory; Lucian speaks only of the crown of pine at the Isthmia, and it was used, presumably, till the festival was at an end.[171]

In many ways the development of the Nemean festival, though less well known, parallels the stories of Olympia, Delphi, and Corinth. Held in honor of Nemean Zeus, and associated mythologically with funeral rites and the slaying of the Nemean lion, the games were celebrated in the valley of Nemea, which lay between Cleonae and Phlius, about 120 stadia from Argos and 80 from Corinth.[172] There was the grave of the boy Opheltes, who, according to legend, was killed by a serpent while his nurse sought water to slake the thirst of Argive soldiers, whom Adrastus was leading against Thebes.[173] There, too, was the tomb of Lycurgus, father of Opheltes. The chief feature of the sacred place was the cypress-surrounded temple of Nemean Zeus—a sanctuary which,

---

[166] Dio Chrysostom, IX, 13.
[167] Symposiacs, VIII, 4, 1.
[168] Ibid., V, 3, 1–3; Krause: Die Pythien, pp. 197, 199 ff.
[169] Way: The Odes of Pindar, "Nemean" IV, str. 11; "Isthmian" II, ep. 1.
[170] Plutarch: Timoleon, 26.
[171] Anacharsis, 9; Krause: Die Pythien, p. 203.
[172] Strabo, VIII, 6, 19.
[173] Apollodorus: The Library, III, 6, 4.

though it had suffered the ravages of time and was bereft of its images, was still "worth seeing" in the time of Pausanias. Fifteen furlongs distant, in Mount Tretus, was the cave of the Nemean lion.[174]

Gymnastic contests, according to tradition, were instituted in honor of the dead boy. Legend had it that Adrastus, who first celebrated the games, won the horse race; Eteocles, the stade-race; Tydeus, the boxing match; Amphiaraos, throwing the discus and jumping (or the chariot race, ἅρματι, according to another reading); Laodokos, at throwing the spear; Polyneikes, in wrestling; and Parthenopaios in archery.[175]

When the Nemean Games were first celebrated is unknown, but Pausanias [176] speaks of victories at Nemea before the time when records were kept. Though certain Greek myths placed their origin before the First Olympiad, as early as the tenth century B.C. or even before,[177] there is nothing of authentic history. In the sixth century the enthusiasm for athletics, which stimulated the founding of national games elsewhere, may have caused the Nemean festival to be raised to Panhellenic rank. From the first Nemead, 573 B.C., after which records were kept, the games seem to have had an uncertain career, and less is known of them even in this historic period than of other national festivals. They continued under the Empire, however, and were celebrated at Argos.[178] Livy [179] called the Nemea "most popular" of all the games. In the reign of Hadrian they gained renewed renown, and may have continued, like other national games, till the time of Theodosius.[180]

By virtue of geographical location, the Nemean festival came naturally under the jurisdiction of Cleonae. Her management was often disputed by Argos, however, and about 460 B.C. control of the games passed to that city, whose tyrants gave them increased reputation, much as Pheidon of Argos brought renown to the Olympic Games, reorganized in the early sixth century. Though, save for brief intervals, the Nemean presidency was held by the Argives till the festival succumbed, there was a struggle over it, and the games were sometimes celebrated both by Argos and Cleonae.[181] Thus Aratus, leader of the Achaean League, drew Cleonae into it and re-established the games under its control, claiming the right from ancient custom. The Argives, against whom he was fighting, continued, however, to celebrate at Argos. Thus, in this instance, the

174 Pausanias, II, 15, 2–3.
175 Ibid., x, 25, 7; Apollodorus, III, 6, 4.
176 Bk. VI, 13, 8.
177 Krause: Die Pythien, p. 115.
178 Polybius: The Histories, v, 101; Real-Encyclopädie, VII, Pt. II, 2042.
179 Bk. XXXIV, 41.
180 Krause: Die Pythien, p. 119; Olympia, p. 50.
181 Krause: Die Pythien, pp. 108 ff.

games not only failed to promote peace and order, but were, in fact, a source
of conflict between cities. For the Achaeans, refusing to recognize the truce
proclaimed by the Argives for the safe passage of athletes to and from the festival, seized those who went through Achaean territory and sold them as captured enemies.[182] Notwithstanding the efforts of Aratus, however, the control
of the games passed finally from the hands of Cleonae.

Though the site of the Nemean Games has not been fully excavated, a stadium, gymnasium, and hippodrome may be assumed as indispensable for the
equestrian and gymnastic contests. A theater for musical contests is also indicated by Plutarch's casual reference to it, when Philopoemen attended the
competition of minstrels in 205 B.C.[183] The order of events is uncertain, but
probably followed the Olympic pattern. As elsewhere, musical contests may
have preceded gymnastic and equestrian events. The variety of Nemean contests outdid Olympia itself, since musical, gymnastic, and equestrian competitions were included. In athletic events Nemea was second only to Olympia,
and it is probable that most, if not all, Olympic contests were represented.[184]
The stade-race, wrestling, pentathlon, and pancration for youths and men; and
boxing, two-stade-race, the long race, and the race in armor are known events.
The race in armor at Nemea was reputed to be especially old. Pausanias mentions an armed race for men at the winter celebration.[185] Competitions for
younger persons were differentiated for youth (ἀγένειοι) and boys (παῖδες).
There was also a four-stade-race (δρόμος ἵππιος), variously interpreted as a race
for boys and as a boys' horse race. This race for boys is said to have been re-intro-
duced by Hadrian at the winter Nemean Games.[186] Equestrian contests are
mentioned at the founding of the games. Though there are few records of such
events, Alcibiades, Chromios, and Xenarches are known victors.[187]

After their establishment as a national festival, the Nemean Games were held
in the second and the fourth year of each Olympiad.[188] At its height the festival
must have occupied more than one day, and may have lasted for several.[189]
Livy mentions one day of the festival only, at the time when the victorious
Roman, Quinctius, presided over them; but by this he may have meant the
chief day of the festival. One day would scarcely have sufficed for the entire
celebration, which included musical, gymnastic, and equestrian contests, and
was, according to Livy, "the most popular" festival. Moreover, Livy speaks

[182] Plutarch: Aratus, 28.
[183] Plutarch: Philopoemen, 11; Pausanias, VIII, 50, 3.
[184] Krause: Die Pythien, pp. 133 f., 138.
[185] Bk. II, 15, 3; Philostratos: Concerning Gymnastics, 7.
[186] Pausanias, VI, 16, 4; Krause: Die Pythien, pp. 136 ff.
[187] Krause: Die Pythien, pp. 148, 150, 163.
[188] Ibid., p. 127.
[189] Gardiner: Greek Athletic Sports and Festivals, p. 225.

specifically elsewhere of a Nemean festival which was interrupted by a sudden foray of the Romans. Philip, he says, left the festival long enough to punish the invaders, and then returned to celebrate the remainder of the games.[190]

Little is known of the rules governing Nemean contests. Pausanias tells of Creugas, a boxer from Epidamnus, who was given a crown, though dead, while his antagonist, who had intentionally killed him, was expelled from the games as punishment. This parallels the decision of the Hellanodicae at Olympia, who crowned Arrichion in death.[191] It may be that, in other respects, Nemean rules were similar to those of Olympia. Victors were crowned with wreaths of wild celery or parsley, and received a branch of palm. The judges of the contests, perhaps twelve in number, were first of all from Cleonae, then from Argos, after the Argives had gained control. They wore somber mourning, befitting a celebration in honor of the dead.[192]

As a political purpose lay back of the national festival, and the Argives who controlled the games played a prominent rôle in Greek affairs, it was customary for the more important states to send impressive embassies to Argos. A Truce of God was proclaimed, as at other national festivals, permitting athletes, embassies, and other visitors to pass unmolested to and from the games during the sacred month. As has been noted, however, the truces were sometimes ignored, if it suited the purpose of some Greek city to do so. The Nemean truce was not exceptional in this respect. Xenophon says that on certain occasions a truce seems to have been "unjustly" proclaimed by the Argives as a means of protection against enemies; but, he says, the oracles approved of its being ignored by invaders when invoked for such a purpose.[193]

### INFLUENCE, FAILURE, AND DECLINE OF NATIONAL GAMES

The athletic habit grew; like begot like; the Olympian, Pythian, Nemean, and Isthmian festivals were a common heritage of all the Greeks, and where Greek culture went, its religious cults and festivals went also. Krause [194] thought the great number of Olympian and Pythian festivals a reliable proof of the respect which the Asiatic-Hellenic world continued to feel for the institutions of old Hellas. They were at least a symbol of kinship with a great past, which even the influence and power of Rome's empire could not quite obliterate.

The great national games had many imitators. Though most of these lesser festivals are but little known, save through an inscription, a coin, or a brief

190 Livy, XXVII, 31; XXXIV, 41.
191 Pausanias, VIII, 40, 2–5.
192 Krause: Die Pythien, p. 141.
193 Hellenics, IV, 7, 2; V, 1, 29.
194 Die Pythien, p. 84.

literary reference, others left records enough to show the renown which once was theirs. Their origin, as in the case of the great national festivals, was commonly associated with the worship of gods, sometimes with honors to great heroes who had acquired godlike status. Though usually celebrated annually, some of the local festivals were quadrennial; a number of them vied with the national games in solemnity. The management of local festivals was similar to that of the Panhellenic Games, at least for the last three centuries of the Pagan era and a like period of the Christian.[195] Many of the lesser festivals known to us were called Olympian or Pythian. Krause found evidence of only three lesser Nemea and the same number of Isthmia. Of local Olympian festivals, however, at least twenty-six are known;[196] and of local Pythian games, twenty-eight.[197] The wide dispersion of the Pythia is probably due chiefly to the general acceptance of the cult of Apollo and the renown of the Delphian Oracle. The prestige of the Olympian cult, the antiquity of its festival, and the reputation of the games held at Elis doubtless encouraged Olympic imitators. The fact, too, that Hadrian took to himself the name Olympian, may have affected the choice of designation, since cities might wish to honor the imperial person. Though little is known of the origin of these lesser festivals, some were designated as Sacred Games, the title being conferred by the Emperor in imperial times. The Olympic Games at Antioch, whose renown attracted considerable attention on the part of contemporary writers, were established about 45 A.D. by permission of the Eleans themselves, and continued till 521.[198]

Though some of the lesser Olympia may have been a sincere tribute to a great Greek tradition, the festivals were often a testimony to the desire of Roman and provincial rulers to capitalize a revered institution and attract favorable attention to themselves. The spirit, certainly, was no longer Greek but Roman. Leaders in the provinces vied with one another in the magnificence of their shows. Aemilius Paulus celebrated games in Macedonia; Antiochus sought to surpass him and proclaimed widely the games to be held at Daphne. Polybius thus describes the imposing procession which opened the festival:

"It was headed by five thousand men in the prime of life armed after the Roman fashion and wearing breastplates of chain-armour. Next came five thousand Mysians, and immediately behind them three thousand Cilicians armed in the manner of light infantry, wearing gold crowns. Next came three thousand Thracians and five thousand Gauls. They were followed by twenty

[195] Ringwood: *Agonistic Features of Local Greek Festivals*, pp. 3 ff., 9, 11.
[196] Krause: *Olympia*, pp. 202–35.
[197] Krause: *Die Pythien*, pp. 53–85, 146 f., 207 ff.
[198] Krause: *Olympia*, pp. 207 ff.

thousand Macedonians of whom ten thousand bore golden shields, five thousand brazen shields and the rest silver shields. Next marched two hundred and fifty pairs of gladiators, and behind them a thousand horsemen from Nisa and three thousand from Antioch itself, most of whom had crowns and trappings of gold and the rest trappings of silver. Next to these came the so-called 'companion cavalry,' numbering about a thousand, all with gold trappings, and next the regiment of 'royal friends' of equal number and similarly accoutred; next a thousand picked horse followed by the so-called 'agema,' supposed to be the crack cavalry corps, numbering about a thousand. Last of all marched the 'cataphract' or mailed horse, the horses and men being . . . in complete mail," and numbering about fifteen hundred. All these wore purple surcoats, embroidered "with gold and heraldic designs. Next came a hundred chariots drawn by six horses and forty drawn by four horses, and then a chariot drawn by four elephants and another drawn by a pair, and finally thirty-six elephants in single file with their housings."

Polybius felt the difficulty of giving an adequate description of the other parts of the procession, but gave the "main features":

"About eight hundred young men wearing gold crowns made part of it as well as about a thousand fat cattle and nearly three hundred cows presented by the various sacred missions and eight hundred ivory tusks. The vast quantity of images it is impossible to enumerate. For representations of all the gods and spirits mentioned or worshipped by men and of all the heroes were carried along, some gilded and others draped in garments embroidered with gold, and they were all accompanied by representations executed in precious materials of the myths relating to them as traditionally narrated. Behind them came images of Night and Day, of Earth and Heaven, and of Dawn and Midday. The quantity of gold and silver plate may be estimated from what follows. The slaves of one of the royal 'friends,' Dionysius, the private secretary, marched along carrying articles of silver plate none of them weighing less than a thousand drachmae, and six hundred of the king's own slaves went by bearing articles of gold plate. Next there were about two hundred women sprinkling the crowd with perfumes from golden urns, and these were followed by eighty women seated in litters with golden feet and five hundred in litters with silver feet, all richly dressed. Such were the more remarkable features of the procession.

"When the games, gladiatorial shows, and beast-fights, which lasted for the thirty days devoted to spectacles, were over, for the first five succeeding days every one who chose anointed himself in the gymnasium with saffron ointment out of gold jars: of those there were fifteen, and there were the same number of jars with ointment of cinnamon and spikenard. On the succeeding days ointments of fenugreek, marjoram, and orris were brought in, all of exquisite perfume. For banqueting there were sometimes a thousand tables laid and sometimes fifteen hundred, all furnished with the most costly viands." [199]

The athletic festivals, which grew out of ancient funeral customs and were associated with great events and personages of Greek history, are among the most significant indications of an aspiration for a larger unity than that of the city-state. That aspiration was never fully realized. Just as there was no salvation for the city-state itself in the cult of physical excellence, as we have seen in the case of Sparta and Athens, so, too, national athletic festivals, though they brought Greeks from all parts together, did not provide that which was necessary to Panhellenic solidarity and continued growth. Instead of focusing attention on matters essential to the welfare of the state, the athletic festival encouraged the cult of physical excellence to the point of professionalism, made successful competition an end in itself, and provided a magnificent entertainment for an increasing idle, luxury-loving class of society. Where political intelligence and capacity for social coöperation were unequal to the feat of rising from the level of city-state interests to that of Panhellenic requirements, one must have faith in magic to expect that larger unity to be gained by the pleasant means of athletic congresses. Panhellenic festivals, at best, provided a useful emotional basis for a larger unity—by no means unimportant; but beyond that they could not go. It is significant that the political thought of Plato and Aristotle did not rise above the ideal of the small city-state.[200]

The decline and ultimate decay of the Greek festivals were conditioned chiefly by (1) the loss of Greek freedom, (2) the growth of Roman power, (3) professionalism and commercialism, and (4) by the gradual rise of Christian will to the point of supremacy. The real significance of the athletic festival disappeared when Greek states lost their independence, even though they might continue to enjoy liberty in local affairs, and the emperors encouraged the festivals for one reason or another. Flamininus might use the occasion of the Isthmia to decree the Greeks' freedom from Macedonian rule, as he did in 196 B.C.; Mummius might honor Zeus and, at the Isthmia in 146 B.C., celebrate the "unity of Greece" after Corinth had fallen; but these were empty phrases, a mockery of liberty. The trend toward greater consolidation and unification continued to grow; under Constantine, it strangled what remained of city-state freedom. Even so, the athletic festivals might have continued under the patronage of Roman emperors had there not been another factor. Hadrian persecuted Christians and praised and promoted the pagan festivals. But Christianity grew in power and prestige throughout three centuries, despite all persecution

---

[199] Polybius, xxx, 25–6. Trans. by W. R. Paton. The Loeb Classical Library. Quoted by permission of Harvard University Press, Cambridge, Mass.
[200] Infra, pp. 432–58, 470.

and contempt. Under Constantine it became the official religion. A faith that had suffered persecution now appealed, through church leaders, to its imperial exponents for fanatical action against paganism. The ascetic disregard for the body which had characterized the Christian cult, and its natural opposition to pagan shrines and ceremonials, were now translated into effective instruments against those chief symbols of pagan culture—the shrines of the gods and their accompanying festivals. The sacred temple at Delphi was despoiled by Constantine, and its ornaments were removed to Constantinople.[201] The policy of Constantine was mild, however, compared with that of later emperors. Theodosius I moved energetically against heresy within the church, and laid about him lustily against opponents without. Pagan sacrifices were forbidden, temples closed, and sacred properties were confiscated.[202] The Olympic festival, greatest remaining symbol of pagan religion and culture, was abolished in 393. The temple of Olympia was destroyed later, whether by order of Theodosius II or by the Goths is uncertain.[203] The end of Olympia symbolizes the eclipse of paganism by the rising Christian star rather than the demise of Greek culture. What was vital in that culture found other tenements. The spirit of the festivals had long been anything but Greek; commercialism, professionalism, and Roman exhibitionism had made them a mockery of the Greek ideal. Outlanders rather than Greeks had long been most numerous amongst contenders and victors. The last known victor was Armenian instead of Greek—Varazdates, who took the prize in boxing at the 291st Olympiad, 385 A.D.

[201] Gibbon: The Decline and Fall of the Roman Empire, II, 23 f.
[202] Ibid., II, 599 f.
[203] The Cambridge Medieval History, I, 113.

# 13

# HEALTH GYMNASTICS

While physical training was being turned aside from its original social purpose to serve increasingly the ends of professionalism and entertainment,[1] a deviation in another direction was also taking place. From being the pastime of youth and a symbol and proof of manly vigor, physical sports were to become the crutch of old age, a physician to the injured and the diseased.

Essentially the growth of health gymnastics was stimulated by two sets of factors, scientific and social in character: the increase of scientific medical knowledge; and socio-economic changes which gave rise, as has been noted,[2] to a class of wealthy, idle folk who were deprived of the normal exercise that labor had once afforded in a more primitive, natural state of society.[3] For this class inadequate exercise and increased luxuries of the table meant ill health. Physical exercises, designed to suit the individual's state of health, were to become a substitute for the normal, vitalizing exercises of an earlier time. Plato's clear insight and forthright statement enable us to see the evil consequence of idle, luxurious living. When "intemperance and diseases" increase in a state, doctors and lawyers begin to see their own importance and put on "airs." Sharply disapproving of "Syracusan dinners, and the refinements of Sicilian cookery," he declared it is a proof of "a bad and disgraceful state of education" that even those who profess to "have had a liberal education" ". . . require the help of medicine, not when a wound has to be cured, or on occasion of an epidemic, but just because, by their lives of indolence and luxury, men fill themselves like pools with waters and winds, compelling the ingenious sons of Asclepius to give diseases the names of flatulence and catarrh. . . ." [4]

[1] *Supra*, pp. 351–62.
[2] *Supra*, pp. 281, 283.
[3] Crosby: "The Quest of Health in Ancient Greece," *Univ. of Pa. Lectures*, IV, 309.
[4] *Republic*, III, 404–5. From *The Works of Plato*, translated and edited by Benjamin Jowett (Oxford University Press).

The use of gymnastics as an auxiliary of medicine, diet, and hygiene may be distinguished as early as Herodikos (somewhat after the first half of the fifth century) and Euryphon, leader of the Cnidian school of physicians, who expounded and applied it. Its rise to a position of prominence kept pace with the decline of society. Its progress is best known to us through the work of physicians, philosophers, and literary folk, such as Hippocrates (460 B.C.), Erasistratos (c. 300 B.C.), Plato (427 B.C.), Aristotle (384 B.C.), Plutarch (c. 46 A.D.), Galen (131 A.D.), Philostratos (c. 170), Aretaeus (latter half of the second century A.D.), and others. Herodikos himself was a paidotribe from Selymbria, "of a sickly constitution," as Plato says, who, "by a happy combination of training and doctoring," [5] prolonged his own life, as he believed. Health gymnastics arose from the union of the science of the paidotribe and gymnast with that of the physician, and subsequently attained a position of importance as a phase of medical practice. This was the beginning of a long dispute on the part of physicians and gymnasts as to the relation of the several sciences, medicine, gymnastics, hygiene, and dietetics to each other and the proper scope of each. Into the various meanings assigned to these terms during the interval between Hippocrates and Galen it is not necessary to enter, but it may be noted that Galen maintained that gymnastics (whose scientific character he stressed more than his forerunners, and which he sharply distinguished from the professional training of athletes) is a part of hygiene, and hygiene in turn is subordinate to medicine. In so doing he accepted essentially the meaning and relationships recognized by Hippocrates, but employed the term hygiene in place of dietetics.[6]

The basic principle of health gymnastics was necessity of balance between nourishment and energy expended. Energy spent must be restored by appropriate food; superabundant nourishment must be expended by physical exertion, if one would avoid evil consequences to health.[7] Health gymnastics implied, therefore, attention to the regulation of diet and of exercise and the adaptation of both to the constitution and circumstances of the individual person. The principle of functional necessity was also recognized and seems to have formed the basis of many recommendations by experts on health exercises. Its formulation is one of the significant proofs of the advancement of medical thinking and observation among the Greeks. Hippocrates stated the principle thus: "All parts of the body which are designed for a definite use are kept in health, and in the enjoyment of fair growth and of long youth, by the fulfil-

---

[5] Ibid., III, 406. From The Works of Plato, translated and edited by Benjamin Jowett (Oxford University Press).
[6] Egger: Begriff der Gymnastik bei den Alten Philosophen und Medizinern, pp. 99 ff.
[7] Real-Encyclopädie, VII, Pt. II, 2054; Gomperz: Greek Thinkers: A History of Ancient Philosophy, I, 288.

ment of that use, and by their appropriate exercise in the employment to which they are accustomed." [8] Disuse leads to ill health, imperfect development, and premature aging.

Bathing, which in a simple fashion had been constantly associated with the exercises of the palaestra and the gymnasium, was included along with games in the array of the physician's remedies. But instead of mere washing at a fountain or basin, as youth are shown doing in various early artistic remains, bathing became a matter of great concern, requiring elaborate provision for hot and cold water, vapor baths, swimming baths, equal or superior in importance to the provisions for exercise. Bathing establishments began to play an important rôle in the life of all Athenians. Aristophanes notes the tendencies of the new day which lead youth to ". . . haunt the baths, and shun the manlier Games!" [9] The author of the *Polity of the Athenians* says that baths, gymnasia, and dressing rooms had been built at public expense for the populace, whereas the rich had exclusive private establishments.[10]

Like other peoples, the Greeks were naturally concerned with their health. Ailments afflict man both under natural, primitive conditions and in more highly developed, artificial society. Though Hellas occupied a favorable position climatically, it is obvious that, even in early times, there were numerous ills, and people resorted to primitive doctors for the performance of miraculous cures. Gardner cites marvelous "cures by Apollo and Asclepius": a certain man had but one good eye; the other was but an empty socket. While he slept, he dreamed that the god mixed a salve and poured it in. When day came, he saw with both eyes! Hermodicus of Lampsacus was paralyzed. While he slept, the god told him to carry the biggest stone he could get into the hall. He went out and "brought in the stone which still lies before the hall." The early miraculous cures of the Asclepiads, which both modern and the later Greek physicians would call charlatanry, were gradually supplanted to some extent by remedies more in harmony with the age of enlightenment. Asclepius, as founder of medicine, continued to be ranked as the very head of the Pantheon; he was described by such terms as μέγας (great), σωτήρ (savior), κύριος (master), and even Zeus, but he now recommended physical exercise, cold baths, bare feet.[11] Hippocrates, a member of the Asclepiads at Cos, became the great authoritative founder of the tendency, and laid the basis of scientific medicine, of which health gymnastics was a branch.

Galen, who had a knowledge of the various Greek philosophical systems before he took up the study of medicine, declared that "the good physician is a

---

[8] Gomperz: *op. cit.*, I, 315.
[9] *Clouds*, 1054.
[10] Bk. II, 10.
[11] Gardner: *New Chapters in Greek History*, pp. 358, 370 ff., 378.

philosopher." [12] It need not follow that good philosophers are also good physicians, but many philosophers gave advice regarding health. Socrates, Plato, Aristotle, Plutarch, and many others exhibit great concern for, and keen insight in respect to, problems of health, diet, and exercise. Socrates, Xenophon says, advised his friends to learn everything possible "from those who know"; however, "everyone should watch himself throughout his life, and notice what sort of meat and drink and what form of exercise suit his constitution, and how he should regulate them in order to enjoy good health. For by such attention to yourselves you can discover better than any doctor what suits your constitution." [13] With regard to the best health of the master, Aristotle advised that he ought sometimes to "rise while it is still night; for this helps to make a man healthy and wealthy and wise. . . ." [14] Early rising was the general custom at Athens. The Assembly, the jury courts, and the Council of Five Hundred, as well as the festival plays at the theater, began with the dawn.[15] The tendency of the new age to pay attention to the factors of basic importance for health is reflected not only in the study of bodily conditions, quantity and kind of food, appropriate exercises, and the like, on the part of doctors, paidotribes, and gymnasts, but also in advice concerning the construction of houses. Thus Aristotle says: "With a view to well-being and health, the house ought to be airy in summer and sunny in winter. This would be best secured if it faces north and is not as wide as it is long." [16] The city of his day had ten commissioners who regulated the disposal of sewage, fixed building restrictions, and looked after removal of bodies "of those who die in the streets." [17]

Hippocrates' concern with exercise and diet in relation to health, and their adaptation to types of individuals and their various states, is evident in many passages of his treatises. A few direct quotations will best exhibit the quality of medical insight in his day, which was to constitute a pattern of thinking for centuries to come. "Some exercises," he says, "are natural and some violent." Even "sight, hearing, voice and thought" are discussed among the "natural exercises." "The nature of sight is as follows. The soul, applying itself to what it can see, is moved and warmed. As it warms it dries, the moisture having been emptied out. Through hearing, when noise strikes the soul, the latter is shaken and exercised, and as it is exercised it is warmed and dried. By all the thoughts that come to a man the soul is warmed and dried; consuming the moisture it

[12] Daremberg: Oeuvres de Galien, I, 1 ff.
[13] Xenophon: Memorabilia, IV, 7, 9. Trans. by E. C. Marchant. The Loeb Classical Library. Quoted by permission of Harvard University Press, Cambridge, Mass.
[14] Oeconomica, I, 6.
[15] Davis: A Day in Old Athens, p. 11.
[16] Oeconomica, I, 6. From The Works of Aristotle, translated by J. A. Smith and W. D. Ross (The Clarendon Press).
[17] Atheniensium Respublica, 50.

is exercised, it empties the flesh and it makes a man thin. Exercises of the voice, whether speech, reading or singing, all these move the soul. And as it moves it grows warm and dry, and consumes the moisture.

"Walking is a natural exercise, much more so than the other exercises, but there is something violent about it. The properties of the several kinds of walking are as follows. A walk after dinner dries the belly and body; it prevents the stomach becoming fat for the following reasons. As the man moves, the food and his body grow warm. So the flesh draws the moisture, and prevents it accumulating about the belly. So the body is filled while the belly grows thin. The drying is caused thus. As the body moves and grows warm, the finest part of the nourishment is either consumed by the innate heat, or secreted out with the breath or by the urine. What is left behind in the body is the driest part from the food, so that the belly and the flesh dry up. Early-morning walks too reduce [the body], and render the parts about the head light, bright and of good hearing, while they relax the bowels. They reduce because the body as it moves grows hot, and the moisture is thinned and purged, partly by the breath, partly when the nose is blown and the throat cleared, partly being consumed by the heat of the soul for the nourishment thereof. They relax the bowels because, cold breath rushing into them from above while they are hot, the heat gives way before the cold. It makes light the parts about the head for the following reasons. When the bowels have been emptied, being hot they draw to themselves the moisture from the body generally, and especially from the head; when the head is emptied sight and hearing are purged, and the man becomes bright. Walks after gymnastics render the body pure and thin, prevent the flesh melted by exercise from collecting together, and purge it away.

"Of running exercises, such as are not double and long, if increased gradually, have the power to heat, concoct and dissolve the flesh; they digest the power of the foods that is in the flesh, making the body slower and more gross than do circular runnings, but they are more beneficial to big eaters, and in winter rather than in summer. Running in a cloak has the same power, but heating more rapidly it makes the body more moist but less tanned, because this is not cleansed by meeting the rush of pure air, but remains in the same air while it is exercised. So this kind of running is beneficial to those who have a dry body, to those who have excess of flesh which they wish to reduce, and, because of the coldness of their bodies, to those who are getting on in years. The double course, with the body exposed to the air, dissolves the flesh less, but reduces the body more, because the exercises, being concerned with the inner parts of the soul, draw by revulsion the moisture out of the flesh, and render the body thin and dry. Running in a circle dissolves the flesh least, but reduces and contracts the flesh and the belly most, because, as it causes the most rapid respiration, it is the quickest to draw the moisture to itself.

"Swinging the arms, for persons of dry flesh, and when jerky, is inexpedient, as it causes sprains, in the following way. The body having been warmed, this swinging makes the skin considerably thinner, but contracts the flesh less than running in a circle, and empties the flesh of its moisture. Sparring and raising the body heat the flesh least, but they stimulate both body and soul, while they empty the body of breath. Wrestling and rubbing give exercise more to the exterior parts of the body, but they warm the flesh, harden it and make it grow, for the following reason. Parts that are naturally hard are compressed by rubbing, while hollow parts grow, such as are veins. For the flesh, growing warm and dry, draws to itself the nourishment through the passages, and then it grows. Wrestling in the dust has effects like to those of ordinary wrestling, but it dries more because of the dust, and it increases flesh less. Wrestling with the fingers reduces and draws the flesh upwards; the punch-ball and arm exercises have like effects. Holding the breath has the property of forcing open the passages, of thinning the skin, and of expelling therefrom the moisture.

"Exercises in dust differ from those in oil thus. Dust is cold, oil is warm. In winter oil promotes growth more, because it prevents the cold from being carried from the body. In summer, oil, producing excess of heat, melts the flesh, when the latter is heated by the season, by the oil and by the exercise. In summer it is exercise in dust that promotes growth more, for by cooling the body it prevents its being heated to excess. But in winter dust is chilling, or even freezing. To remain in the dust after exercise in summer benefits by its cooling property, if it be for a short time; if it be for long, it dries the body to excess and renders it hard as wood. Rubbing with oil and water softens the body, and prevents its becoming over-heated." [18]

Hippocrates divided the year into the usual four seasons, specified the time of the beginning of each, and recommended suitable diet and exercise. In winter, which may be taken here as an example, there should be one meal a day, unless one has "a very dry belly," in which case there should be a light luncheon also. Food should be "warming" and "drying" in character; wheat bread, rather than barley, and roasted instead of boiled meats are recommended. Drink should be slightly diluted dark wine, limited in amount. Vegetables should be limited in amount, and be warming and drying in effect. The same is true of barley water and barley gruel. As for physical habits they ought to be as follows: "Exercises should be many and of all kinds; running on the double track increased gradually; wrestling after being oiled, begun with light exercises and gradually made long; sharp walks after exercises, short walks in the sun after dinner; many walks in the early morning, quiet to begin with, increasing until they are violent, and then gently finishing. It is beneficial to sleep on a

---

[18] Hippocrates: *Regimen*, ii, 61–5. Trans. by W. H. S. Jones. The Loeb Classical Library. Quoted by permission of Harvard University Press, Cambridge, Mass.

hard bed and to take night walks and night runs, for all these things reduce and warm; unctions should be copious. When a bath is desired, let it be cold after exercise in the palaestra; after any other exercise, a hot bath is more beneficial. Sexual intercourse should be more frequent at this season, and for older men more than for the younger. Emetics are to be used three times a month by moist constitutions, twice a month by dry constitutions, after a meal of all sorts of food; after the emetic three days should pass in slowly increasing the food to the usual amount, and exercises should be lighter and fewer during this time. Emetics are beneficial after beef, pork, or any food causing excessive surfeit; also after excess of unaccustomed foods, cheesy, sweet or fat. Further, it is better to take an emetic after drunkenness, change of food or change of residence. One may expose oneself confidently to cold, except after food and exercise, but exposure is wise in early-morning walks, when the body has begun to warm up, in running, and during the other times, though excess should be avoided. For it is not good for the body not to be exposed to the cold of winter, just as trees that have not felt winter's cold can neither bear fruit nor themselves be vigorous. During this season, take also plenty of all sorts of exercise. For there is no risk of excess, unless fatigue-pains follow; this is the sign that I teach laymen, and the reason I will now proceed to explain. As the season is cold and congealed, animals too have the qualities of the season. So the body perforce warms up slowly under exercise, and only a small part of the available moisture is excreted. Then the time devoted to exercise is little, and that devoted to rest is much, as in winter days are short and nights are long. For these reasons neither the length nor the character of the exercise can be excessive. So in this way should this season be passed, for forty-four days, from the setting of the Pleiads to the solstice." [19]

To athletes Hippocrates offered a special word of advice, warning them against overtraining, for the peak of training cannot be prolonged. Since the athlete cannot improve further and cannot stand still, he must perforce change for the worse. "For this reason it is an advantage to reduce the fine condition quickly, in order that the body may make a fresh beginning of growth," but reduction must not be carried too far.[20] Of athletes' training in winter, he says they should "both run and wrestle." In summer they ought to "wrestle but little and not run at all" but should walk "a good deal in the cool." "Such as are fatigued after their running ought to wrestle; such as are fatigued by wrestling ought to run. For by taking exercise in this way they will warm, brace and refresh best the part of the body suffering from fatigue. Such as are attacked by

[19] Ibid., III, 68. Trans. by W. H. S. Jones. The Loeb Classical Library. Quoted by permission of Harvard University Press, Cambridge, Mass.
[20] Hippocrates: Aphorisms, I, 3. Trans. by W. H. S. Jones. The Loeb Classical Library. Quoted by permission of Harvard University Press, Cambridge, Mass.

diarrhœa when training, whose stools consist of undigested food, should reduce their training by at least one-third and their food by one-half. For it is plain that their bowels cannot generate the heat necessary to digest the quantity of their food. The food of such should be well-baked bread crumbled into wine, and their drink should be as undiluted and as little as possible, and they ought not to walk after food. At this time they should take only one meal each day, a practice which will give the bowels the greatest heat, and enable them to deal with whatever enters them. This kind of diarrhœa attacks mostly persons of close flesh, when a man of such a constitution is compelled to eat meat, for the veins when closely contracted cannot take in the food that enters. This kind of constitution is apt sharply to turn in either direction, to the good or to the bad, and in bodies of such a sort a good condition is at its best only for a while. Physiques of a less firm flesh and inclined to be hairy are more capable of forcible feeding and of fatigue, and their good condition is of longer duration. Such as throw up their food the day after, whose hypochondria are swollen because of the undigested food, are benefited by prolonging their sleep, but apart from this their bodies should be subjected to fatigue, and they should drink more wine and less diluted, and at such times partake of less food. For it is plain that their bellies are too weak and cold to digest the quantity of food. When people are attacked by thirst, diminish food and fatigue, and let them drink their wine well diluted and as cold as possible. Those who feel pains in the abdomen after exercise or after other fatigue are benefited by resting without food; they ought also to drink that of which the smallest quantity will cause the maximum of urine to be passed, in order that the veins across the abdomen may not be strained by repletion. For it is this way that tumours and fevers arise." [21]

Plutarch, famed as philosopher and moralist, reflects the great concern of his day for personal happiness and health. Health of body, however, is not his sole concern; for glory is unstable, beauty fades, health is easily impaired, strength wanes under the assaults of old age and disease, and, in any case, is inferior to that of many lower animals. For these reasons men should prize philosophy above all things, for it is to the mind what medicine is to the body. But, though learning is "immortal and divine," "it is not proper, either, to overlook the exercise of the body. . . ." Children must be sent to the paidotribes for the cultivation of good, graceful carriage and for the improvement of their strength, "for sturdiness of body in childhood is the foundation of a hale old age." [22] Just

21 Hippocrates: Regimen in Health, 7. Trans. by W. H. S. Jones. The Loeb Classical Library. Quoted by permission of Harvard University Press, Cambridge, Mass.
22 Plutarch: The Education of Children, 8, 10. Moralia, trans. by F. C. Babbitt et al. The Loeb Classical Library. Quoted by permission of Harvard University Press, Cambridge, Mass.

as one should learn in fair weather that which will be useful in stormy, so habits of good order and temperance should be formed in youth, for they will be the best security in old age. Following Plato, however, Plutarch warns against too much physical exercise, since, if carried to the point of weariness and drowsiness, it will be inimical to study. It is most important that boys be exercised in throwing the javelin, archery, and hunting, which are valuable for warfare, since the wealth of the vanquished becomes the spoil of the victors. War offers too severe a test for those who have grown up indoors; one trained in military exercises is superior to those who have been given highly specialized training in wrestling, but are left ignorant of war. If someone objects that this advice is all very well for freeborn children of the rich only, Plutarch says he would wish education to be for all alike. He knows, of course, that the poor may be unable to avail themselves of that which he has set forth as desirable. They must, however, blame their misfortune, not him who gave good advice; they must provide the best education they can, within the limit of their means.[23]

Elsewhere Plutarch recommends attention to the study of medicine as a liberal art, "inferior to none in elegance, distinction, and the satisfaction which it yields . . . ," and able to repay all efforts by giving her devotees health.[24] Of diet, Plutarch has read that a thin one is best for the body; yet he advises a less rigorous course, saying simply that one ought to avoid excess in meat and drink. At a feast one should remember Philip's advice to leave a 'corner for cake'; one should not act like the stingy and greedy, who keep themselves under when at home, but enjoy the costly fare of another man's table "as though they were engaged in ruthless foraging in an enemy's country," and are next day rewarded for their immoderation with indigestion.[25] Solid food, such as meat, cheese, dried figs, boiled eggs, should be eaten sparingly, for they clog the digestive system. It were better to eat no meat at all, but since custom is almost second nature, and it is hard to deny one's self these, they should be only a foundation for other things that are "thin" and "light"—herbs, fowl, fish—and more conducive to health.[26] Particularly to be avoided are those foods and drinks that persuade to more eating and drinking when one is neither hungry nor thirsty.[27] Milk should be used as a food, not as a drink. Wine, the most beneficial of drinks, should be taken in moderation, diluted with water. In addition, water should be drunk, at least two or three glasses a day, to weaken the wine. When fatigued after work, physical or mental, water is better than wine.[28] Discourse

---

[23] Ibid., 11.
[24] Advice about Keeping Well, 1. Moralia, trans. by F. C. Babbitt et al. The Loeb Classical Library. Quoted by permission of Harvard University Press, Cambridge, Mass.
[25] Ibid., 7.
[26] Ibid., 18.
[27] Ibid., 6.
[28] Ibid., 19.

at meals and afterwards on light and merry subjects, history, poetry, natural philosophy, till digestion be well under way, is held to be beneficial, and may be used as restraint to brutish appetite by taking one's mind off eating. Though Plutarch does not share the views of professional trainers and gymnasts who would ban all books and intellectual things at meals, he recognizes that strenuous mental effort should be shunned. One should not try to "solve the Indian problem" at dinner; neither is logic a fit dessert; it may even give one a headache. To follow the gymnasts, however, and go to the extreme of avoiding all serious intellectual discussion, would render one, like the athletes, "as glossy and blockish as the pillars in a gymnasium." [29]

To those who pride themselves on taking a cold bath after exercise, Plutarch says it "is ostentatious and juvenile rather than healthful." A warm bath is more conducive to health and is an aid to digestion. However, ". . . when nature affords us a sense of a moderate and comfortable condition in our body, the bath had better be left alone." A gentle anointing by the fire is a preferable way to secure warmth of body. Sunshine is good, if the temperature of the air permits.[30]

Physical exertions for a man of learning should be light. For the scholar's exercise Plutarch recommends reading aloud and speaking. For the exercise of the voice "increases the warmth, tones down the blood, clears out every vein, opens every artery, and does not permit of any concretion or solidifying of superfluous fluid like a sediment to take place in the containing organs which take over and digest the food." Even when the scholar goes traveling or stops at an inn, he should not be silent, though those around him laugh at his performance; "for where it is not disgraceful to eat it is certainly not disgraceful to take exercise. . . ." When one has finished reading or speaking, "before going to walk, one should make use of rubbing with oil in a warm room," which makes the "flesh supple" and in general properly disposes the spirits if it be not carried beyond "what is agreeable to the senses and not discomforting." [31]

Emetics and physic should not be regularly employed, though occasionally they may be necessary. Plato held the same view.[32] The best way, says Plutarch, is to avoid the occasion for them by light eating, occasional fasting, and drinking water for a few days. "Periods of fasting according to a fixed schedule," however, are to be avoided as contrary to nature.[33] Health of mind and body is not to be secured by sloth, idleness, or abstention, but by a balance between activity and repose and an alternation of physical and mental exertion. For, in

---

[29] Ibid., 16, 20.
[30] Ibid., 17.
[31] Ibid., 16. Moralia, trans. by F. C. Babbitt et al. The Loeb Classical Library. Quoted by permission of Harvard University Press, Cambridge, Mass.
[32] Timaeus, 89.
[33] Keeping Well, 22, 24.

Plutarch's opinion, Plato was right in saying "that there should be no move-ment of the body without the mind or of the mind without the body, but that we should preserve, as it were, the even balance of a well-matched team. . . ." [34] "Eating not unto satiety, labouring not unto weariness, and observance of chastity, are the most healthful things." [35] This nice adjustment the scholar and the man of public affairs can manage by reason, for they are not circum-scribed and hindered by those inconveniences which sordidness and poverty force upon those who are compelled to do bodily labor. For these sons of toil there is apparently no remedy in Plutarch's Advice about Keeping Well.

Philostratos' treatise Concerning Gymnastics is devoted to athletes and ath-letic training rather than to exercises for the aged, diseased, or ordinary persons. For this special class, while he treats most extensively the types of physical con-stitution that are fitted by nature to succeed in particular contests, and lays great stress on careful examinations by scientifically prepared trainers,[36] he makes certain observations that are closely akin to the recommendations of those who, like Plutarch and Galen, wrote for men of everyday affairs. Respect-ing the luxurious tendencies in eating he is no less caustic than Plutarch. There are evil moral consequences as well as physical. Fancy foods are harmful; wine is detrimental. "Over-feeding will be betrayed by the pendulous brow, panting breath" and fullness of cavities at the collar bones and in the groins. Wine drinkers have a "thick paunch." Those who are gluttons at the table, as well as those who are immoderate in the enjoyment of sexual pleasures, are worth-less for the athletic trainer, for they can never "carry off a wreath at a con-test." [37] Still, he gives recommendations as to how they are to be handled, as well as those who are of a nervous temperament.[38] Sun treatment is urged as valuable, but must be used according to the natural temperament of the ath-lete, whether phlegmatic or choleric.[39]

Galen of Pergamum, thoroughly educated by travel and study of the liberal arts as a preliminary to medicine, had a firsthand acquaintance with the train-ing of gladiators, but exhibits a marked contempt for athletes and professional fighters. This is but natural, for he saw that the extremes of their training, the unnaturalness of their life, were neither conducive to health of the mind nor of the body, despite the prodigious physical feats which they were able to per-form. The best physical exercises from the standpoint of health, he maintained, are those which delight the mind while they engage the body. Coursing and

[34] Ibid., 27.
[35] Ibid., 15. Moralia, trans. by F. C. Babbitt et al. The Loeb Classical Library. Quoted by permission of Harvard University Press, Cambridge, Mass.
[36] Op. cit., 26–42.
[37] Ibid., 47–8.
[38] Ibid., 53–4.
[39] Ibid., 58.

hunting are so excellent, from this point of view, that they must have been invented by good philosophers! But they offer insuperable difficulties for ordinary men in business or public affairs: much time and plenty of money.

Galen, who has a sympathetic eye for "even the poorest," selects ball-play as the best of sports because it is "so democratic," demands "no nets, nor weapons, nor horses, nor hounds: all it requires is one small ball." Naturally, as the instance of Dionysius of Syracuse shows, ball-play was also used by those who could afford the most expensive play.[40] Other exercises are too violent, or demand too much or too little of one or another part of the body; and no sport is healthful which exercises the physical parts unequally. The game with a small ball, contrary to most others, requires that one be something of a runner, something of a wrestler, leaper, dodger. Moreover, one must be quick of eye and quick of mind. "Thought by itself makes a man thin," but joined with the exercise and rivalry of this sport, "it is of the very greatest benefit." [41] Most exercises have an opposite result: "they make men lazy, slow-witted and fond of sleep. The competitions of the wrestling school tend to make people corpulent rather than to train them in virtue." [42] But a ball game so quickens mind and body, so trains one to attack and seize every opportunity, to take from the opponent and to keep what one has gained, that Galen thinks it the best training even for generals, the very essence of whose business is to be "an expert thief" and "an expert guardian." One of the chief virtues of the game with the small ball is that it can be played for violent exercise, and just as easily for light. The origin of ball-play was ascribed variously to Lydians, Corcyraeans, Sicyonians, and Lacedaemonians.[43] Three types of games, which made use of somewhat different balls, seem to have been common: one game was played with the harpastum, a small, hard, stuffed ball; another with the follis or sphaira, a lighter ball, stuffed with feathers, which was passed from player to player while they were running; and in the game of trigon, the players threw balls to each other.[44] Those too old or too young for other games, and also persons who are convalescing, can engage in ball-play to good advantage. One worn out in some part by labor can rest that part by attending to a particular phase of ball-play: those whose legs are wearied can let them rest, while they exercise the upper extremities by throwing and catching; but if the upper extremities are tired, there can be more emphasis on running and less on throwing.[45] Not the least advantage of ball-play is the fact that one engages in it with

40 Wright: Greek Athletics, p. 114; Cicero: Tusculan Disputations, v, 20.
41 Wright: op. cit., p. 116.
42 Ibid., p. 117. ·
43 The History of Herodotus, I, 94; Pliny: Natural History, vii, 205; Athenaeus, I, 14.
44 Baumeister: Denkmäler des Klassischen Altertums, I, 247 ff.; Real-Encyclopädie, ii, Pt. ii, 2832 et seq.; Athenaeus, I, 15; infra, pp. 666 ff.
45 Wright: op. cit., pp. 119 f.

YOUTHS PLAYING BALL

National Museum, Athens (Courtesy, The American School of Classical Studies, Athens)

no fear of those dire consequences—lameness, dislocations, broken blood vessels, ruptures, and even death itself—which so frequently occur in other sports.

Ball-play, of course, pertains chiefly to one aspect of the entire science of hygiene. Galen regards physical exercise as one branch of hygiene, and hygiene is a part of the whole science of medicine. A brief reference to his views on other aspects of hygiene are therefore in place. Chief among his works pertaining to feeding and care of the body are these: *On the Powers of Foods; The Good and Bad Juices of Foods; Of an Attenuated Diet; Of the Knowledge and Cure of Mental Affections; On the Preservation of Health;* and *Whether the Preservation of Health Depends on Medicine or Exercise.* There is also a commentary on Hippocrates' treatise on diet. In his treatise *On the Powers of Foods,* Galen indicated the need for a new work on the subject, based on reason and experience, which would set forth the values and effects of different foods on the various types of individuals and under certain circumstances. Wheat, barley, oats, millet, rice, beans, vetches, lupines, and the seeds of poppy, hemp, and flax are discussed, and the several kinds of food prepared from them. Similar treatment, on an extensive scale, is devoted to all sorts of fruits and vegetables and to foods derived from the animal kingdom. The effect of various articles of food and drink on the fluids of the body, their vitiation and restoration, is explained in the work on *The Good and Bad Juices of Foods.* In the treatise on *Attenuated Diet,* its utility is especially noted in certain diseases, such as gout, dyspnoea, and other chronic ailments, where it is sometimes valuable as a cure, again as an ameliorative.

In the work on *Mental Affections,* which concerns the relation of the mental and moral self to the physical, various emotional states and mental habits are discussed which bear on a happy, contented life. Anger, intemperance of various kinds, quarrelsomeness, jealousy, ambition, inordinate desire for wealth and power, extreme partisanship in scientific matters, hastiness in conclusions, all these and many of their like, are condemned, whether they arise from nature, as in the case of some individuals, or from faulty education, as in others. Here, in the moral and intellectual realm, as in the physical, moderation is the principle which must steadfastly be observed.

In the treatise on *Preservation of Health* and in the one dealing with the dependence of health on medicine and exercise, Galen gives his most systematic view of the interrelation of medicine, exercise, and diet. Health is due to all of them; one cannot stand without the others. All three constitute the whole science of medicine. Health arises from two sets of factors: those that promote it positively and those that assist it by negating the power of disease. The environment—air, water, foods, natural, appropriate exercise of mind and body, and the like—if favorable, provides the best basis for health, for such proper conditions facilitate the performance of natural functions, which is the *sine qua non* of health. Irregularities and inadequacies in the environment, which tend to frustrate or distort the natural performance of function, lead to ill health. These factors (diet and exercise) must vary according to age and constitution; and they must also be in harmony with one's social condition. Those who are bound to labor incessantly in a condition of servitude, without regularity of refreshment and recreation, are peculiarly disposed to disease. In childhood, nursing, education, diet, and the formation of proper health habits are important. Exercises occupy a more prominent place in the years of adolescence and up to maturity. Many types of friction, varying according to time of day, season, and locality, are recommended both as a remedy and as preparatory exercises for the more strenuous work of the gymnasium. The varieties of exercise in the gymnasium and their proper ends are explained; likewise the effect of different types of bathing, hot and cold. The phenomena of fatigue and weakness, arising from a variety of causes, are examined and the optimum treatment of each is recommended. The fifth book of Galen's treatise on *Preservation of Health* is devoted to the hygiene of those advanced in years, discusses the diseases most to be apprehended, the diet most advantageous in certain diseases and for certain temperaments, and the exercises appropriate to those of waning strength. Of all that he has to say of exercise, however, probably nothing is more truly representative of his views of its relation to health than the treatise on *Exercise with the Small Ball,* wherein he sets forth the universality of its usefulness.

A profound faith in the efficacy of physical exercise in treating certain diseases is found in the pages of Aretaeus, who lived in the latter half of the second century. In his treatise *On the Cure of Chronic Diseases*, the use of halteres and jumping is recommended when treating "cephalaea." [46] In cases of vertigo, exercises which cause distention of the neck and vigorous exercises with the hands are recommended, as well as "raising the head, to exercise the eyes at chironomy," χειρονομία, a measured swinging of the arms, throwing quoits, boxing, and running. But exercises with both large and small balls are bad; in fact, such exercises "occasion vertigo." [47] In cases of gonorrhoea "every attention is to be paid to diet"; gestation, walks, and gymnastic exercises are to be permitted and encouraged, since they are warming in effect.[48] In coeliacs the diet and habits of life should be kept moderate. Plenty of sleep at night, walking in daytime, vociferation, and "gestation among myrtles, bays, or thyme" for the beneficial effect it has on the digestion, are recommended, as well as gymnastic exercises, rubbing, chironomy, and use of the halteres in connection with exercises of the chest and abdomen.[49] Elephas (elephantiasis) is to be treated with a plain wholesome diet, easily digested. Care must be taken of hours of sleeping, walking, and place of habitation. Such exercises as running, tumbling, use of the leather bag, and vociferation are to be employed, but with due moderation. Clothing must be clean, both to please the eye and also because dirty clothing irritates the skin.[50] On the treatment of epilepsy, Aretaeus offers the following regimen:

"Promenades long, straight, without tortuosities, in a well ventilated place, under trees of myrtle and laurel, or among acrid and fragrant herbs, such as calamint, penny-royal, thyme, and mint; so much the better if wild and indigenous, but if not, among cultivated; in these places, prolonged gestation, which also should be straight. It is a good thing to take journeys, but not by a river side, so that he may not gaze upon the stream (for the current of a river occasions vertigo), nor where he may see anything turned round, such as a rolling-top, for he is too weak to preserve the animal spirits (pneuma) steady, which are, therefore, whirled about in a circle, and this circular motion is provocative of vertigo and of epilepsy. After the gestation, a gentle walk, then rest so as to induce tranquillity of the agitation created by the gestation. After these, the exercises of the arms, their extremities being rubbed with a towel made of raw flax. Not much oil [is] to be used in the inunction. The friction [is] to be protracted, and harder than usual for condensation, since most of them are bloated and fat: the head to be rubbed in the middle of the process, while the patient stands erect. The exercises of the neck and shoulders, chironomy, and the others mentioned by me under the treatment of Vertigo,

---

[46] Aretaeus, The Extant Works of, p. 461.
[47] Ibid., p. 467.
[48] Ibid., p. 489.
[49] Ibid., p. 492.
[50] Ibid., p. 497.

with sufficient fulness of detail; only the exercises should be sharper, so as to induce sweat and heat, for all these attenuate. During the whole of his life he should cultivate a keen temper without irascibility." [51]

To attempt to appraise precisely the success of Greek health gymnastics would be a fruitless if not an impossible task; its popularity is not to be disputed, however. Remarkable results were often claimed. Plato says that Herodikos "dying hard, by the help of science," "struggled on to old age" by virtue of his "invention of lingering death." [52] Plutarch tells of Laomedon, the Orchomenian, who, on the advice of his physician, formed the habit of running long distances to rid himself of a disease of the spleen, and so far regained health by virtue of this regimen of labor and exercise that he was able to enter the games and "became one of the best runners of the long course." [53] Hysmon is said to have made himself sound in health by practicing the pentathlon.[54] Numerous other instances might be cited; for it is common knowledge that careful attention to physical condition and adaptation of food and exercises to it produce remarkable changes in health. Galen says he restored countless persons to health simply by the use of gymnastic exercises.[55]

The rise of health gymnastic and the expansion of medical practice did not take place without arousing much distrust of doctors and contempt for their achievements. The philosophic mind, which looked to social values, could not fail to ask, Cui bono? Of what significance is it to preserve mere existence, if life itself is useless, has no end beyond itself? The popular mind, too, which could understand neither the old medicine nor the new, would take more delight in the marvelous miracles of priestly medicine men than in the prosaic, unspectacular science of Hippocrates. Crosby says that "of the many words in Greek associated with pharmaca, medicines, most are either uniformly or usually of bad significance"; and he believes that this indicates a mistrust of the practitioners of medicine.[56] It may well be true that the Greeks, who had been favored by a generous nature with conditions propitious to health, were skeptical about a science which sought to provide by rule that which had once been taken for granted. There was, at any rate, considerable spoofing at the learned, or not so learned, doctors' expense. Perhaps some had suffered from their ministrations, for even the most up-to-date medical men could not always be successful. Then, too, charlatans must have frequently claimed more than their "science" could be expected to perform. A profession whose members were re-

51 Ibid., pp. 471 f.
52 Republic, III, 406. From The Works of Plato, translated and edited by Benjamin Jowett (Oxford University Press).
53 Plutarch: Demosthenes, 6.
54 Pausanias's Description of Greece, VI, 3, 9–10.
55 Euler: Encyklopädisches Handbuch des Gesamten Turnwesens, I, 362.
56 Op. cit., loc. cit., IV, 315.

warded in princely fashion, in some instances at least, would scarcely fail to attract a certain proportion of "wind bags and street corner prophets" who sought to effect cures by "purifications" and "incantations." Such failures, whether for good and sufficient reason or not, or for lack of knowledge, provided excellent targets for witticisms, and the jokesmiths were not slow to recognize it. Thus Nicarchos jibes at the medic who even kills marble Zeus:

> Yesterday Marcos the doctor was called to Zeus, there, over the way.
> —Even tho' marble he be, and Zeus, his funeral is today.[57]

But against the jibes of literary dilettantes, we may properly note their praise as well. One need not go far to find high praise for the physician. The encomium is doubtless intended for those true sons of Asclepius, not for those who are doctors in name only: "One man practiced in medicine verily outweigheth many other men."

[57] Lawton: *The Soul of the Anthology*, p. 127.

# 14

# IN UTOPIA

The Homeric poems, Hesiod's *Theogony* and *Works and Days* constituted the Greeks' storehouse of intellectual, moral, and aesthetic values until fundamental social and educational changes undermined and transformed them. Indeed, it has been said, "Homer was, to his own and later times, history, geography, genealogy, religion, morals, politics. . . ." [1] While this is true, in general, modifications took place in Athenian conceptions as society changed and intellectual life was broadened and deepened. Amid these changes, of course, certain old elements persisted: freedom from religious authoritarianism and asceticism. Greek minds continued to parry the authoritarianism of a priestly order and inspired holy book, though Orphism threatened for a time to engulf the Greek mind and bring it under the sway of authoritarian, religious absolutism. [2] Against such a tendency the philosophic influence of Xenophanes, Heracleitus, Parmenides doubtless served as an antidote, though Pythagoreanism, tending to unite mysticism and science, was difficult to withstand. [3] Euripides, too, added his weight against belief in divine perfection, teaching instead that—

> If gods be strong and wicked, man, though weak,
> May prove their match by willing to be good. [4]

Religious asceticism, like authoritarianism, so common in the Orient, found no firm footing among the Greeks, though Orphism appealed strongly to many

---

[1] Keller: *Homeric Society*, pp. 183 f.
[2] Reinach: *Orpheus*, p. 88; Gomperz: *Greek Thinkers: A History of Ancient Philosophy*, 1, 80 ff.
[3] Gomperz: *op. cit.*, 1, 123 ff.; Reinach: *op. cit.*, p. 97; Bury: *A History of Greece*, pp. 319 ff.
[4] Lawton: *Classical Greek Literature*, p. 225.

in the sixth century, gained prestige when received by Onomacritus and Pythagoras, and was encouraged by Pisistratus and his sons. On the whole, however, the Greeks continued to think of gods as good and bad; [5] held that men might be even better than gods; clung to certain notions of beauty and joyousness in their religion, quite incompatible with asceticism; and took little stock in judgments, rewards, and punishments hereafter—though these concepts were fostered by Orphism. Hades, of course, was dreary enough, but only somewhat more dolorous than life. "Earth is full of evils and the sea is full," says Hesiod.[6] Though the meanest life is better than death, Hades is no punishment. Both good and bad, the greatest heroes and the meanest men, have to face this "destiny grievous." Close to the Greek mind and heart, no doubt, though it is a pleasanter picture than the earlier Greeks contrived, is Pindar's portrayal of the dead who amuse themselves with horse races, athletics, and the lyre.

Though the Greeks lacked a religious authoritarianism, which might have imposed order on the realm of the gods and orthodoxy on the minds of men; and though they avoided religious asceticism, and had no teaching priesthood, they were nonetheless religious. Even when philosophy had taken on some maturity, it was still unsalutary for one to publish his disbelief in the gods, to disparage public worship, or to desist from it. This religious attitude was most clearly manifested by faithful attention to conventional, public worship, conducted by priests designated by civil authority, and by the prominence of the religious motif in athletic festivals.

In time, of course, both religion and athletics came in for criticism. Though the change was a slow one, religion and morals of the early days ceased to have their wonted significance. The seventh and sixth centuries, and the later ones even more, witnessed many economic, political, and social changes, tending toward wider distribution of privilege and power that once had pertained only to men of wealth and station. These changes, broadly educative for an increasing class of people, were important, since increased economic well-being for more and more people brought greater opportunity for leisure and contemplation. The significance of leisure is obvious. Those who labor constantly with their hands have little time or energy to devote to affairs of the mind. Aristotle attributed the foundation of mathematical arts to the leisure of the Egyptian priesthood.[7] Numerous factors operating powerfully at Athens made her in reality the School of Hellas, and ultimately, in a sense, a University of Mankind. A critical philosophy emerged, differentiated from religion and theology, and critically disposed toward them. Xenophanes faced the fact

[5] Burns: *Greek Ideals*, pp. 90 ff.
[6] *Works and Days* (Evelyn-White), 101.
[7] *Metaphysica*, I, 1.

that men had created gods in their own image. Homer and Hesiod represented the gods at times as disgraceful, dishonest, adulterous, thieving. He, however, professed belief in "One god, supreme among gods and men; resembling mortals neither in form nor in mind." [8] The theater, by dramatizing the gods and bringing mythology before one's very eyes, tended to make serious belief in them more difficult. History undermined the authority of traditions. Euripides paraded the most inhuman aspects of the old gods, showed them irrational, petty, childish, futile—on the whole inferior to men and women—and voiced an aspiration for a higher conception:

> O Thou
> That bearest earth, Thyself by earth upborne,
> Whoe'er Thou art, hard for our powers to guess,
> Or Zeus, or Nature's law, or mind of man,
> To Thee I pray, for all the things of earth
> In right Thou guidest on Thy noiseless way.[9]

As the city-state became progressively the instrument of the good life for a greater number of men, it took on an ever larger significance, required more service, and a sort of loyalty hitherto unknown. Indeed, as the state became thoroughly a part of Hellenic consciousness, service to it became the most vital religion of the citizen. "Man versus the State" was a concept unknown to the Greek. In the state he was complete, was enabled to enjoy a rational existence.[10] Plato, logically enough to men of his generation, regarded "service of the laws" as "also the service of the Gods. . . ." [11] To defend the city and preserve the vineyards was synonymous with religion itself. Man losing his identity in the state was no more difficult for Greeks than losing one's self in God was to the early Christians. Aristotle declared: ". . . men should not think it slavery to live according to the rule of the constitution; for it is their salvation." [12] Devotion to the state seems to have reached a degree of self-denial, which might well compare with the ascetic self-negation of religious fanatics: "Their bodies they devote to their country as though they belonged to other men; [and] . . . their mind . . . is most truly their own when employed in her service." [13]

Ultimately, critical philosophy would reach far beyond mere criticism of

---

[8] Bakewell: *Source Book in Ancient Philosophy*, p. 8.
[9] Lawton: *op. cit.*, p. 225.
[10] Butcher: *Some Aspects of the Greek Genius*, p. 52.
[11] *Laws*, VI, 762. From *The Works of Plato*, translated and edited by Benjamin Jowett (Oxford University Press).
[12] *Politica*, v, 9. From *The Works of Aristotle*, translated by J. A. Smith and W. D. Ross (The Clarendon Press).
[13] Thucydides, I, 70. From *Thucydides*, translated by B. Jowett (The Clarendon Press).

concepts of the old religion. It would deny, too, the legitimacy of man's worship of the state and his identification of himself with it. Man would become an end in himself, or seek some otherworldly goal, when the pomp and power of the city waned and withered away. Its vulnerability and destruction would prove its imperfection, its unworthiness as arbiter of life and death. Then men would find their answer to the age-old question, "What is the end of man?" in complete absorption in personal desires; or, perchance, not wholly satisfied with that, would dream of a City of God.

In the decline of pagan gods who delighted in feats of athletic prowess, and the contemporary emergence of the notion of the superiority of mind; in the decay of the powerful, political state and the rise of an otherworldly Utopia, offering escape from the toils, hardships, and miseries of earth, are to be found the central reasons for the decline of the athletic spirit, the cult of body worship, and the parallel rise to prominence of ascetic disregard for the beauty and strength of the physical self and disparagement of the worth of athletic attainments. In other countries religion and warfare had been basic conditioners of physical sports. Greece was no exception to the rule. Critical philosophy, which undermined the old religion, sounded the knell of the old athleticism as well. Between the spirit of the author of the hymn to Apollo, who sings—

There they do honor to thee with boxing, dancing and singing—

and that of Xenophanes and Euripides there is a world of difference.

## EDUCATIONAL RECONSTRUCTION

Education at any moment is limited fundamentally by the economic, social, political institutions which man has set up. All may be modified from time to time both by blind forces and by intelligent insight. Fundamental changes in the social framework render the old educational pattern outmoded, undermine it, make it appear incongruous and unserviceable, and condition the formation of a new pattern in harmony with the new age. The "new education" may offer to solve the problems of the new order. It may do so in some measure; it may fail to do so; it may facilitate changes already in process. Much depends on the degree of conscious application of attention to the problems that matter most.

The "new education" at Athens was many-sided. Like "new education" everywhere, it was in many ways harmonious with dominant tendencies in the changing social scene which gave it birth. At its worst and for most people it was but a concession to the demands of new generations that sought happiness, fame, wealth, luxury, power, and sank social duty in individual desire. At its best, in the hands of a few, the new education gave impetus to a critical examination and rational reconstruction of society, which was to save it from disintegration by correcting basic errors which had been incorporated in it in the long, blind processes of its evolution.

Viewing education as a means of adjusting an individual more or less comfortably to the life of his day, the new education, at its worst, was more or less successful, and Athenians jogged on their way more or less gaily to the banks of Lethe. Viewed as a means to social stability, the new education, even at its best, was ineffective. Conservative hands were not able to turn the clock back, despite their pleasing pictures of a happy, golden yesterday when everything was decent and in good order. Radical reformers, on the other hand, with eyes fixed on the future, were not able, for all their wit, to lead selfish, ignorant, practical politicians to adopt radical remedies for radical social ills, but had to content themselves with drawing the mental blueprints of Utopia. The work of these builders of more stately social mansions, though of little practical importance in their day, has had uncommon significance for all who have thought subsequently on politics and education.

The roots of the new education, so far as its serious efforts at reconstructing the life of man are concerned, run back to the dawn of Greek enlightenment, the rise of critical questioning which, in the course of time, was to invade the material and the immaterial world, bringing great consequent shock to men and necessitating revision of their notions of all things. Of first-rate importance was the acid of doubt thrown on traditional ideas and mores by Xenophanes' critical attack on the folly of excessive adoration of victorious athletes. No less harsh was his condemnation of religious views. A comparative method enabled him to see that gods had been constituted by men in their own likeness. Such a view of deity was unduly limited, distorted, and would not suffice. In place of anthropomorphic polytheism he set the view that God is One, unlike men in mind and body. The disintegrative effect of this critical spirit on religion was obviously inescapable. Aeschylus might strive to give old religious ideas a modern dress and make them palatable to a changing world, but Euripides, distinctly modern, knew that a reconciliation of the old and new was impossible, and declared roundly: "If gods do evil, then they are not gods." Inevitably the gods melt into unity, their human features vanish, they make way for the Vortex of Leucippus, the Nous of Anaxagoras, the air of Anaximenes. "There is no Zeus. Young Vortex reigns, and he has turned out Zeus"—so say the philosophers and emancipated youth.[14] In the earth itself Xenophanes sees a process of change going on rather than unchanging fixity. Fossils on mountain

14 Aristophanes: Clouds, 1470.

tops reveal marine life that once was in the sea. The mountains will sink into the sea again, and men will disappear. "And this change happens to all worlds." [15]

The bright gleam of reason's aurora also shines through Hecataeus of Miletus who had seen the ridiculousness of many conflicting traditions: "I have written everything down as it appeared to me to be true; for manifold and laughable are the sayings of the Hellenes, as they seem to me." [16] So far had the tendency to doubt old explanations gone by the time of Herodotus, that it had even claimed a part of the mind of the Father of History. For though, in general, he was inclined to accept the tall story and let it go at that, he appears occasionally as a positivist of the new age, requiring that a story told by the poet or some other authority be reasonable or capable of verification. He knows no river called Ocean, hence supposes that some poet must have invented it; he balks at the story of the Arimaspi, who were said to be born with but one eye; he doubts whether the Magi actually caused a storm to abate— it may have done so of its own accord. These and similar doubts arise occasionally in a mind that is on the whole piously humble toward ancient truth and finds no difficulty in the tale of giant ants of India, larger than foxes but smaller than dogs.[17]

One may recognize in this critical movement an effort to reduce the chaotic world of primitive myth to order, giving a more exact account of cause and consequence. The vast inclusive realm of mythical explanation is constantly diminished as enlightenment advances and the realm of scientific fact proportionately increases. Leucippus, in his work On the Order of the Universe, had already broken with the primitive world of caprice when he announced: "Nothing happens without a cause, but everything with a cause and by necessity." [18] From this it is not a long step to the idea of control. Luck or caprice, said Democritus, "seldom measures swords with wisdom. Most things in life quick wit and sharp vision can set right." The greatest Greek philosophers would one day make an effort, by "quick wit and sharp vision," to set things right in politics and education. The new intellectualism, though it undermined faith in old traditions, inspired faith in human reason and made men see the Golden Age in the future rather than in the past.

The new movement, which tended to reduce the capricious world of the gods and material things to order on the basis of common principles, also lent encouragement to a unifying, inclusive view of life which brought man into harmony with, and made him a part of, nature. This philosophic naturalism was

[15] Bakewell: op. cit., p. 11.
[16] Gomperz: op. cit., I, 255 f.
[17] The History of Herodotus, III, 102, 116; Gomperz: op. cit., I, 271.
[18] Gomperz: op. cit., I, 317.

formulated by the Stoic school. Zeno (c. 300 B.C.) held that "the chief good was confessedly to live according to nature; which is to live according to virtue, for nature leads us to this point." "For our individual natures are all parts of universal nature. . . ." Plants and animals live according to nature, pursuing what is appropriate to them. Man, too, must live according to nature's direction. "And as reason is given to rational animals, . . ." living according to reason is necessary for men.[19]

Of this philosophic naturalism there were two widely different interpretations: one, agreeable to aristocratic sensibilities and prejudices and serviceable to men of might who make cities, states, and empires, and label their laws "right"; another, acceptable to the temper of rising democracy and serviceable to its devotees. According to the first view, nature made some slaves and others free.[20] Plato, too, having no love for the democratic tendencies of his day, would make an intellectual elite the rulers of his ideal state, while others, less endowed by nature, would be warriors and artisans. Other writers, more in harmony with social and political tendencies of the new day, saw in the law of a common nature a sure indication of equality, at once a vindication of the claims of common men to a place of importance in the world as masters of their destiny and a key by which their chains might be unlocked. The rhetorician, the poet, the romanticist, and the religionist were most inclinable to this view. "Nature has enslaved no man," says Alcidamas. Laws and conventions are the tyrants of mankind, and compel men to do what is against nature, against reason. Slavery gives the lie to nature. Euripides declares:

> The name alone is shameful to the slave;
> In all things else an honest man enslaved
> Falls not below the nature of the free.

In nature all are kin. Barriers of race, of bond and free, and of nationality were all to sink into Lethe; men were to prepare the way for a common humanity, a universal culture.

A new age implies new, or re-educated teachers. What the greatest minds brought forth and gave to a few, ultimately reached the ears of many through popular teachers, whose lectures and conversations were attended by youth who could pay for the luxury of learning, or thinking they learned something.[21] To these popular teachers the term sophist (wise man) was applied. In general the sophists have been assigned a questionable character and mercenary habits. The demoralization of Athenian society has indeed been credited by some to their subversive teaching. Thus Davidson says, ". . . it may be fairly enough

19 Diogenes Laërtius: The Lives and Opinions of Eminent Philosophers, VII, 52–3.
20 Aristotle: Politica, I, 5.
21 Plato: Sophist, 233; Grote: A History of Greece, III, 427.

said that they largely contributed to demoralize Athens. . . ." [22] Such, too, was the general picture drawn by Aristophanes who contrasted—

. . . the Discipline rare which flourished in Athens of yore . . .[23]

with that offered by the "red-haired things of unknown breed"—the wandering sophists who came from many lands. This new teacher empties the gymnasium and palaestra, crowds the baths and lecture rooms, and produces dire results—

. . . to begin, a cold pallid skin,
Arms small and chest weak, tongue practised to speak . . .
And your mind he'll prepare so that foul to be fair
And fair to be foul you shall always declare. . . .[24]

Plato's view is not fairer. The sophist hunts young men, professes to teach virtue, gets "a round sum," is pre-eminently a disputer and teacher of disputation about things seen and unseen, and seems to have a knowledge of all things, but is in reality only an imitator.[25]

To accept such views of the sophists and their influence would place too much weight on the laughing contempt of the skillful, witty Aristophanes, whose own tongue and pen were not incapable of sophistical deception. Though serious, aristocratic Plato criticized sophists for taking fees, his own school, the Academy, was reputedly founded on land purchased with money given by rich friends for his ransom, was aided financially by wealthy patrons (Dion, for example), and may have been further supported by fees, either fixed or left to the choice of students.[26] Plato's complaints against the sophists because they received fees scarcely seem to merit the importance sometimes granted them. In fact, paying fees to teachers was not itself novel to Athenians. The old Athenian music school and the palaestra had been conducted by privately paid teachers. If there was any novelty in the practice of the sophists, it lay in the higher cost of their "higher" learning.

The notion of the sophists' destructive capacity seems to rest on an exaggerated view of the power of words to change the character of men and their society; it overlooks the deep-rooted tendencies in society itself, and vastly oversimplifies and glosses over the processes of social change.[27] It credits with an extraordinary power the teaching of a disorganized group of teachers, who

[22] Aristotle and Ancient Educational Ideals, p. 101; cf. Grote's summary of complaints against them, op. cit., III, 404.
[23] Clouds, 960 et seq.
[24] Ibid., 1017–21. Trans. by B. B. Rogers. The Loeb Classical Library. Quoted by permission of Harvard University Press, Cambridge, Mass.
[25] Sophist, 222–3, 225–6, 233–4; Laches, 186; Protagoras, 328.
[26] Laërtius: Plato, 14; Gomperz: op. cit., II, 269 ff.
[27] Grote: op. cit., III, 427; cf. Jaeger: Paideia: The Ideals of Greek Culture, I, 286–331; Windelband: History of Philosophy, pp. 87–94.

taught no common body of knowledge or opinion, and who, since their livelihood depended on their students, must have taught views more or less acceptable to the day rather than highly subversive doctrines. It seems more realistic
to think that the sophists were more or less keen observers of the changing
world around them; that they were both good and bad, shallow and profound;
that they brought certain insights into this world of change to their students;
that they were willing to sell their educational wares to those who wanted to
attain success; that they went along with the tendencies of the new day, and
were ready to ride the rising tide; and that they sometimes had an exaggerated
opinion of their own importance—an overestimate too readily accepted by
others.

Essentially the new learning represented an extension of education on a
higher and broader plane than had been known by the old order. It was in-
formative, critical, destructive, and constructive. The sanctions of the old
mores that comfortably fitted the old city were giving way. Athens was coming
of age intellectually. Age, with its decrease of physical power, sobers the joyous
enthusiasms and checks the reckless energies of youth. Thought of the future
and dreaming of the past become more characteristic; and vigorous action less
so. Athens was soon to be a nonentity in military and political affairs; intellectually, she was on the threshold of a school of higher learning, whose influence would penetrate to all corners of the world.

The new learning at its best, notwithstanding novelties, reflected a characteristic of education in old Athens: a concern with secular affairs. That which
had once motivated action was now the central motif of Greek thought. As
life had centered in the city (*polis*), the science of government (politics) and
the relation of the individual to the social collective were to be the central problems of philosophy. Protagoras, reputedly the most individualistic of the
sophists, was concerned with preparation for practical affairs, public and private, that one might "learn to order his own house in the best manner," and
"be best able to speak and act in affairs of the state." [28]

In a world of change, while some men are satisfied with specifics for the moment, others seek general principles, valid for all time. The best minds that
were devoted to education sought soberly a firm basis, some fixed principles, by
which to test all things, and thus make possible the attainment of the good
life by man and by society. Some turned to science, religious mysticism, and
ascetic discipline; others thought that true knowledge and individual integrity,
arrived at under the conditions of the greatest intellectual freedom, provided
that basis. To know one's self, to govern one's desire, to distinguish between
knowledge and opinion, constituted the best that men could hope for. Many

[28] Gomperz: *op. cit.*, I, 413.

found the basis for a settled social order in a return to some tested pattern of the past, or in an idealized pattern of contemporary neighboring states. Others, a few, sought a radically reconstructed social order, utilizing certain elements of past experience joined with innovations that were designed to correct essential errors of the past. While all the intellectual builders had more or less in common, they were often poles apart. Pythagoras represented the tendency to combine mysticism, asceticism, and science. Socrates explored the individualistic approach to the problem. Xenophon preferred the conservative patterns of the past. Plato and Aristotle, indebted directly and indirectly, like Xenophon, to Socratic teaching, examined more critically and comprehensively past and present experience, and set forth widely varying views of the ideal state.

Men looking for Utopia gaze both backward and forward. Radical reforms often embody tested, conservative features. Great importance has been credited to one who, influenced by the pervasive Orphism of his day, combined religious mysticism and asceticism with the most notable contributions to science. While Pythagoras, who was born in Samos and flourished in the sixth century B.C., was renowned for his investigations in mathematics, astronomy, music, and medicine,[29] his insight into political and other affairs seems to have been also significant. Accounts of his life are frequently contradictory, uncritical, and doubtless warped by the biases of later centuries. He is said to have visited Egypt, Crete, Chaldaea, and Syria, imbibing the wisdom of their learned men and being initiated into religious mysteries. After returning to Samos and finding affairs there incompatible with philosophic pursuits, he removed to Crotona. There he established a brotherhood, credited variously with three hundred to six hundred members, and exerted a great influence in the world of learning and in political life as well.[30]

Considerable importance attaches to Pythagoras as the early formulator and disseminator of certain doctrines more fully developed by later philosophers. Music, he held, purges the passions; and he is said to have demonstrated the soundness of the theory.[31] In this and the doctrine of moderation one recognizes the theories of the mean and of *katharsis*, later developed by Plato and Aristotle.[32] Pythagoras also recognized the value of eugenic mating, the necessity of restraint of sexual appetite, and the doctrine of transmigration of souls.[33] In everything the unifying principle is number,[34] which has a mystical significance; hence the all-embracing character of mathematical study. Since order, harmony, number, and proportion pervade the universe, they should also ob-

---

[29] Laërtius: Pythagoras, 11.
[30] Ibid., 3, 15; Iamblichus' Life of Pythagoras, 6–7; Gomperz: op. cit., I, 101.
[31] Iamblichus, 25.
[32] Protagoras, 326; Politica, VIII, 6–7.
[33] Iamblichus, 31; Laërtius: Pythagoras, 4, 12.
[34] Gomperz: op. cit., I, 103 ff.

tain in human society; each individual should find his place in a harmonious relationship as unchanging as the celestial realms. While the Pythagorean table of opposites—Limited, Unlimited; Unity, Plurality; Rest, Motion; Light, Darkness—and many other central ideas were sharply combated by scientists of the Heracleitian stamp, idealists of the Socratic-Platonic school, and later the Neo-Platonists, found great satisfaction in them. Plato's doctrines of metempsychosis, rule by a philosophic class, communism of property, importance assigned to mathematics and music, the equality of women and men in the circle of philosophers,[35] and mystical elements in much of his thinking closely parallel Pythagorean thought and practice, and suggest a definite indebtedness or that both drew from the same source. On the religious side, certainly, both were influenced by Orphism.[36]

Physical exercise was given a prominent place in the Pythagorean discipline.[37] Exercise, food, and repose ought to be in proper proportion to each other; on this the health of the body depends. The Pythagoreans were credited by the ancients as the first who devoted themselves to a careful study of diet in relation to medicine; thus they attended to the body that it might, through proper food and exercise and avoidance of superfluous desires and manifold varieties of food, always be in the same condition, never too lean, never too fat.[38] It is said that they disapproved of hunting, but devoted themselves to running, wrestling, pantomimic gesticulation, and jumping with the *halteres*.[39] To what extent the conspicuous success of athletes from Crotona at Olympia should be credited to Pythagorean influence is open to question. Crotona was renowned for its salubrious climate and the health of its people; Milo, a Pythagorean, undoubtedly attracted the attention of the athletic world to his city by his athletic fame.[40] Pythagoras himself was even credited with being the first to train athletes on a meat diet; others say, however, that this was another man. It was likewise said by Eratosthenes that Pythagoras was the first who practiced scientific boxing; and that he once sought to enter the boys' boxing contest at Olympia, but, being reiected, entered that of the men and won the crown.[41]

Besides his influence on later intellectual affairs, a marked importance attaches to the religious and moral teachings of Pythagoras. To read his *Life* by Iamblichus is to be impressed with the view that ethical teaching and religious asceticism bulked more heavily than his scientific work. Of course, one must

35 Seventeen women belonged to the circle of Pythagoras.—Iamblichus, 36.
36 Reinach: op. cit., p. 88; Gomperz: op. cit., I, 123–52; II, 369 f.
37 Iamblichus, 21.
38 Ibid., 31, 34.
39 Ibid., 21.
40 The Geography of Strabo, VI, 1, 12.
41 Laërtius: Pythagoras, 12, 25; Gardiner: Greek Athletic Sports and Festivals, pp. 58, 126.

not forget the bias of the Christian era. The religious bent, however, was in harmony with the Orphic tendencies that swept Greece in the sixth century and caused men more and more to give attention to personal happiness and salvation rather than to social welfare, whether by means of religion or an individualistic, self-centered philosophy which aimed at personal perfection. Though Pythagoras and his followers were concerned with political affairs from time to time, his teaching and manner of life both emphasize the importance of a life of self-denial, apart from the rest of the world. Pythagoras seems, even in the sixth century, to have sensed the futility of the struggle for wealth and power, the ends for which the state expends itself. The state cannot attain his ends; he aims at the harmony, integrity, and perfection of man, which can only be accomplished by creating within the great society a smaller, more perfect one, wherein everything is made subservient to the soul's welfare. This perfection can be attained only by the most rigorous discipline. Pythagoras is the first great ascetic leader of the West who imposed a severe discipline on himself and a band of followers, anticipating the thought and practice of Christian ascetic societies centuries later.

Pythagorean asceticism appears in the rule of silence imposed on neophytes for five years, the provision for common property, and the injunctions against meat, certain fish, beans, and all aspects of luxurious life.[42] Luxury, he held, is the first evil that comes into homes and into the city; insolence and destruction follow.[43] Every effort must be made to thwart its hold on men. Nothing should be done whose end is pleasure—for nothing leads into error so surely. No one should be permitted to do just what he pleases; hence the necessity of rigorous government and a strict education. The punishment of desire is a necessary means to perfection. Sumptuous food, he held, ought to be introduced at dinners and then hastily removed to punish the appetite. Indeed, a distinctly Orphic doctrine appears in the dogma that since "we came into the present life for the purpose of punishment, it is necessary that we should be punished." [44]

Despite numerous ways in which the Pythagorean community anticipated Christian asceticism, there were certain important differences. It has been compared with medieval orders of chivalry.[45] Pythagorean asceticism was markedly active; that of the early Christians chiefly passive. Probably the most conspicuous difference lay in the Pythagoreans' devotion to cleanliness, recognition of physical culture as a means to excellence, and their faith in the virtue of the mean—excellent prophylactics against the extremes that Christian asceticism

[42] Laërtius: Pythagoras, 8, 18–9; Iamblichus, 24.
[43] Iamblichus, 30.
[44] Ibid., 18, 31.
[45] Gomperz: op. cit., 1, 99.

was to reach. In the golden words of the philosopher an old Greek ideal survives:

> Follow a cleanly, simple mode of life, . . .
> Be not neglectful of thy body's health;
> But measure use in drink, food, exercise—
> I mean by "measure" what brings no distress.[46]

Socrates, born of humble parentage, seems to have been democratic in his dealing with all men. Though favorably inclined neither to the democracy of Athens nor to her oligarchs,[47] he was a loyal citizen and participated in certain military expeditions. Giving up his work as statuary, he assumed the rôle of teacher. He demanded no fees from his pupils, lived extremely simply, and held all wealth and nobility of birth in low esteem.

There is one good, knowledge, which Socrates claimed he sought constantly; and there is one evil, ignorance. There is one chief virtue, namely, avoidance of excess. An essential to this end is self-knowledge. "Self-control," he said, "is an exact science, and when discovered the whole world may become virtuous." Socrates' only wisdom, he said, lay in knowing that he did not know. This, if true, would be refreshing in the Athenian hothouse of opinion. Though he exhibits a tenacity of mind and leads others to accept his views, there is no appeal to any court save that of reason. While our knowledge of the method and content of Socrates' teaching rests on something less than satisfactory grounds, he is represented by Plato, Xenophon, Aristophanes, and other contemporaries as interested in all problems of human life, which he investigated by engaging men in conversation, drawing out their opinions, leading them to examine, compare, and to discriminate between the sound and unsound—between appearance and valid conception. In the use of this conversational dialectic, he is represented as diabolically clever in deception, a "shrewd Attic quibbler," one who can make the "worse appear the better reason," as Aristophanes declared.

Though Socrates was tried and put to death on the complaint of Melitus that he was disloyal to the gods and corrupted the youth of Athens, posterity has consistently held a highly favorable view of him, taken largely, of course, from the testimony of his pupils. Indeed, the Athenians themselves are said to have repented of their action against him, condemned his enemies, and erected a statue in his honor.[48] Whether this be true or not, if one-tenth of the

---

[46] Davidson: op. cit., p. 58.
[47] Grote: op. cit., III, 462.
[48] Laërtius: Socrates, 23; Windelband: op. cit., pp. 94 ff.; Jaeger: op. cit., II, 13–76; Ueberweg: History of Philosophy, I, 80–8; Gomperz: op. cit., II, 117 f.; Grote: op. cit., III, 481 ff.

SOCRATES

(Courtesy, Professor C. A. Robinson, from G. W. Botsford and C. A. Robinson, *Hellenic History*, Rev. Ed., Pl. 72B, The Macmillan Company, New York, 1948)

430

keenness, skill in questioning, and wise judgments given were really his, one must see that he was truly a gadfly that stung men's minds to activity. His contribution to the "new education" lay in this stimulus to a critical treatment of human problems, a lead which Plato and Aristotle followed up and in many ways carried to a greater degree of perfection.

Socrates was not solely concerned with intellectual culture. It is said that he gave close "attention also to the training of the body, and was always in excellent condition himself." [49] In this, as in other matters, the rule was "nothing to excess." He is said to have had great physical endurance, but he shunned excessive gymnastic training, because such training required that men eat heavily. Beauty, harmony, and proportion, both of mind and of body, should be striven for. Indeed, he said, ". . . it is a disgrace to grow old through sheer carelessness before seeing what manner of man you may become by developing your bodily strength and beauty to their highest limit. But you cannot see that, if you are careless; for it will not come of its own accord." [50] This beauty lay essentially in proportion. Socrates pointed out that, in his day, runners of the long-distance race had muscular legs and narrow shoulders, while boxers and wrestlers had broad shoulders and small legs. Dancing he recommended, because "by distribution of the toil throughout my limbs I seek to give an even balance to my body." [51] Physical culture improved women as well as men. Socrates was profoundly impressed by the physical skill developed by girls in dancing, acrobatics, and juggling, as well as by the fact that they exhibited courage in performing dangerous feats which no man could match. By their exhibition he was moved to suggest that "woman's nature" was "nowise inferior to man's." [52]

The general utility of physical culture and its highest purpose, as the governor which regulates the health of the body on which everything one does depends, were stressed by Socrates: "For in everything that men do the body is useful; and in all uses of the body it is of great importance to be in as high a state of physical efficiency as possible. Why, even in the process of thinking, in which the use of the body seems to be reduced to a minimum, it is matter of common knowledge that grave mistakes may often be traced to bad health. And because the body is in a bad condition, loss of memory, depression, discontent, insanity often assail the mind so violently as to drive whatever knowledge it contains clean out of it. But a sound and healthy body is a strong protection

[49] Laërtius: Socrates, 7.
[50] Xenophon: Memorabilia, iii, 12, 8. Trans. by E. C. Marchant. The Loeb Classical Library. Quoted by permission of Harvard University Press, Cambridge, Mass.
[51] Xenophon: Symposium, ii, 17–8.
[52] Ibid., ii, 8–13.

to a man, and at least there is no danger then of such a calamity happening to him through physical weakness. . . ." [53] The interrelations of diet, exercise, medicinal aid, and health seem to have been clear to Socrates; one must learn everything possible from others who have knowledge, but everyone can be a better judge of his requirements than any physician.

For a soldier and an Athenian citizen, physical training for war was accepted as axiomatic. Socrates' views on this matter were not exceptional, judging by Xenophon's account. He explained to Epigenes that there was no justification for his bad physical condition. He needed training just like any athlete training for Olympia. The life-and-death struggle with Athens' enemies must be prepared for; one must be able to defend her, and also able to save his own life and not play the part of a coward.[54]

Certain principles credited to Socrates, but which may or may not have been his, were accepted also by his pupil, Plato, who undertook to blueprint Utopia —something that Socrates never attempted, perhaps because he placed little faith in schemes of government, external regulations, but fixed his trust in self-knowledge and self-control. Plato, unlike his master, was an aristocrat. He is said to have traveled widely and was educated in Megara, Egypt, Cyrene, Sicily, and in Italy, where he made contact with Pythagoreans whose doctrines may have influenced his views on the importance of number, re-embodiment of the soul, rule by philosophers, relation of music and astronomy, and various other matters.[55] Plato is said to have been trained in gymnastics by Ariston of Argos, and to have wrestled at the Isthmian Games; he was of robust physique, fought in three campaigns, and at Delium showed conspicuous valor.[56]

The facts concerning Plato's aristocratic background may well be remembered in the light of his preference for government by an aristocratic, intellectual elite, his high regard for the soldier class, his contempt for the "men of business, stooping as they walk," and the low station of artisans in his ideal society. He had no faith in the capacity of the masses to attain to such high virtue as Socrates had in mind, was contemptuous of Athenian democracy,[57] and believed in a rigid system of governmental control. Plato was, of course, a many-sided genius. In educational theory alone he presented widely divergent views, notably in the Republic, product of his early years, and in the Laws, composed at the close of his career. In both of these works it is necessary to examine certain central features of the society he envisaged in order to understand the rôle which he assigned to education.

---

[53] Xenophon: Memorabilia, III, 12, 5–7; IV, 7, 9. Trans. by E. C. Marchant. The Loeb Classical Library. Quoted by permission of Harvard University Press, Cambridge, Mass.
[54] Ibid., III, 12, 1–2.
[55] Laërtius: Plato, 8; Plato: Republic, VII, 530; Gomperz: op. cit., II, 250 ff.
[56] Laërtius: Plato, 5, 10.
[57] Ibid., 17; Plato: Republic, VIII, 558.

PLATO

(H. Brunn and P. J. Arndt, *Denkmäler Griechischer und Römischer Skulptur*, Pl. 5)

While Socrates stressed the attainment of true knowledge and virtue as the chief end, Plato emphasized the establishment of justice as the supreme goal. To establish justice is to avoid injustice; to avoid injustice, one must know whence it arises. In a simple, primitive, healthy society, in which men were concerned with the satisfaction of primal needs—food, shelter, clothing—injustice did not exist. As society grew, however, in complexity, wealth, and luxury, division of labor was necessary and new occupations appeared—tradesmen, entertainers, doctors, lawyers, warriors, and the like—with injustice as a concomitant of the "relations of these citizens with one another." [58] The increase of lawyers and doctors in a state is an evil symptom: one points to lack of a sense of justice on the part of citizens; the other to luxury, intemperance, and resultant increase of disease. War is found "to be derived from causes which are also the causes of almost all the evils in States . . ." [59] i.e., it is occasioned by the struggle for territory and commerce which the demand for luxurious living entails.

The worst government is that which offers the greatest liberty to be a dicast, a soldier, something or nothing, just as one fancies, regardless of capacity, and which dispenses "a sort of equality to equals and unequals alike." [60] It arises from immoderate pursuit of wealth on the part of the oligarchic rulers of the state, for "the love of wealth and the spirit of moderation" cannot exist together in citizens of the same state.[61] That is to say, the rulers sell out the interests of the commonwealth for the sake of private gain, thus proving their unfitness to rule. The city falls into decay or faces revolution because of the struggle for gain on the part of citizens from the lowest to the highest and the weakening that ensues. It is, of course, necessary to recognize human nature for what it is, and there are many who "will not be satisfied with the simpler way of life. . . ." [62] But since those who are not satisfied with the simpler life have proved themselves incompetent and dangerous rulers, it is desirable to set up certain restraints and controls in a reconstituted society, so that each and every sort of work will be done by those who are best fitted by nature and perfected by training; and in particular it is necessary to place the guidance and the protection of the state in the hands of those who are pre-eminently qualified to serve its ends, and are by nature and training least inclined to use it for their personal gain.

There are essentially three great classes of employment in society, the work

---

[58] Republic, II, 372.

[59] Ibid., II, 373; III, 404–6. From The Works of Plato, translated and edited by Benjamin Jowett (Oxford University Press).

[60] Ibid., VIII, 558.

[61] Ibid., VIII, 555.

[62] Ibid., II, 372. From The Works of Plato, translated and edited by Benjamin Jowett (Oxford University Press).

of artisans and husbandmen, that of soldiers, that of rulers. Corresponding to these are certain types of human capacity, best suited to them, and three classes in society, for society is the individual writ large: the first, chiefly physical, ruled by appetite, whose virtue is strength; the second, great of heart, ruled by passion, whose virtue is courage; the third, intellectual, the virtue of which is wisdom. Men and women, regardless of sex, should be assigned to the rôle of producer, soldier, and ruler, according as they possess one capacity or another. When each person is in his right occupation, and each class does its work—the intellectual ruling, the courageous protecting, and the strong producing and getting wealth to support themselves and the others—then justice will prevail in the state.[63]

Of the selection and training of artisans and husbandmen Plato has little to say, though he alludes to the meanness of the "useful arts"; [64] for sake of efficiency and order, however, each must have an occupation and be trained for that alone,[65] presumably by apprenticeship to the task. The members of this lowest order of society can apparently be readily selected, for they have iron in their system, are without spirit, and have no mark of intellectual capacity.[66] The differentiation of the two higher classes, soldiers (auxiliary guardians) and rulers (chief guardians), is a more painstaking process, not completed till the age of twenty, when some (potential philosophers) are selected for advanced education. All above the husbandmen and artisans will be reared simply, live like soldiers, have no property of their own, eat at a common mess, and receive only enough pay to cover fundamental needs; they will be educated from seven to eighteen in music and gymnastic, and from eighteen to twenty in military gymnastics, to make them serviceable to society rather than to themselves.[67]

While there is a marked adherence to old Athenian education from seven to eighteen, consisting as it did of music and gymnastics, Plato introduces a number of important strictures. The poets must be purged of evil stories that depict the gods as immoral and thus promote immorality in the young. Poetry, however, which instills a martial spirit, such as certain passages in Homer, is approved pabulum for future guardians.[68] Music also comes under censorship because "any musical innovation is full of danger to the State, and ought to be prevented"; for "when modes of music change," the state changes with them.[69] Ionian and Lydian harmonies are banned, but Dorian and Phrygian are re-

[63] Ibid., IV, 434.
[64] Ibid., VIII, 522.
[65] Ibid., II, 370.
[66] Ibid., III, 415.
[67] Ibid., III, 416-7.
[68] Ibid., II, 376-83; III, 386-7; 389-90.
[69] Ibid., IV, 424. From The Works of Plato, translated and edited by Benjamin Jowett (Oxford University Press).

tained, since they are conducive to temperance and courage; likewise, the flute and other "curiously-harmonized instruments" are excluded, while the lyre, harp, and shepherd's pipe are approved.[70]

Music and gymnastic are approved, not as ends in themselves nor because one trains the soul and the other the body, but because "both have in view chiefly the improvement of the soul." [71] Either one by itself produces distortion. Music, pursued alone, produces effeminacy, "a feeble warrior." Gymnastic, if carried on exclusively, produces hardness and ferocity; Plato is convinced that the "mere athlete becomes too much of a savage. . . ." [72] The defense of the ideal state cannot be entrusted to athletes, for their exercise "is but a sleepy sort of thing, and rather perilous to health. Do you not observe that athletes sleep away their lives, and are liable to most dangerous illnesses if they depart, in ever so slight a degree, from their customary regimen?" Therefore, "a finer sort of training will be required for our warrior athletes, who are to be like wakeful dogs, and to see and hear with the utmost keenness; they will have to endure many changes of water and also of food, of summer heat and winter cold, and yet they must not be liable to break down in health." [73] Neither professional athletic training nor health gymnastics [74] would be of service to the state. For, ". . . in gymnastics . . . if a man works hard and is a great feeder, and the reverse of a great student of music and philosophy, at first the high condition of his body fills him with pride and spirit, until he is twice the man that he was." Then, after a while, if he never pursues the Muses, even the intelligence which was in him grows feeble, dull, blind, and he becomes "like a wild beast, all violence and fierceness, and knows no other way of dealing. . . ." [75]

Plato contents himself in the *Republic* with establishing guiding principles in respect to music and gymnastic. There is no need for going into details about dances, hunting, gymnastic, and horse racing, he says, "for these all follow the general principle, and there will be no longer any difficulty in discovering them." [76] A more definite indication of what his preferred gymnastic would be is found in Plato's leaning toward the Spartan system of military discipline, though he would avoid some of its excesses, and in his assertion that "the really

---

[70] *Ibid.*, III, 399.
[71] Plato: *Timaeus*, 88.
[72] *Republic*, III, 410–1. From *The Works of Plato*, translated and edited by Benjamin Jowett (Oxford University Press).
[73] *Ibid.*, III, 404. From *The Works of Plato*, translated and edited by Benjamin Jowett (Oxford University Press).
[74] *Ibid.*, III, 406.
[75] *Ibid.*, III, 411. From *The Works of Plato*, translated and edited by Benjamin Jowett (Oxford University Press).
[76] *Ibid.*, III, 412. From *The Works of Plato*, translated and edited by Benjamin Jowett (Oxford University Press).

excellent gymnastic," which "is twin sister" to the simple musical education he has described, is "military gymnastic." [77] This is always associated with the strictest simplicity and leanness of diet; for, just as simplicity in music produces "temperance in the soul," so simplicity of gymnastic is the source of "health in the body." Even the children are to be taken on expeditions, that they may see all of war and be of assistance to their elders. They must not become soft; for they are to be members of a military class, and they must learn to do by observing and doing.[78]

Plato has profound doubts about human goodness; he sees how little reason and justice is ordinarily exhibited by men. If they had the powers of a Gygian ring, they would do injustice for their own gain, for all believe in their hearts "that injustice is far more profitable . . . than justice. . . ." [79] In the myth of Er, the first one to choose, who had a choice of the entire range of lots in a new life, selected immediately the greatest tyranny; for his virtue was only habitual, and "he had no philosophy" to guide him.[80] The implication is clear; only philosophy can be a guide to wise choice. The ideal state cannot be established, justice cannot be made sure, until philosophers are kings, or kings philosophers. Hence, philosophers are to rule the Republic. Such is Plato's conclusion. The true students of philosophy should have a vocation.[81] Admiration is expressed for the Lacedaemonians, the truly best philosophers; theirs was the type of "primitive philosophy." [82] In Plato's ideal state the primitive philosopher in man must be discovered and prepared by education for his true vocation.

The philosophers will be but "a very small remnant," [83] akin by nature to that best element which avoids the dishonest, everyday political world, being unable successfully to oppose "the madness of the multitude." They are lovers of all knowledge, curious to learn, quick and capable in apprehending truth. Though not anxious to rule (which is a good sign), they will be persuaded to do so, recognizing their obligation to society.[84] Selected for their love of, and quickness in the apprehension of, knowledge, which can be best observed and judged, not by forcing them to study, but by letting them engage in it as "a sort of amusement," thus revealing their true bent, they must be trained from twenty to thirty in arithmetic (which he asserts makes the quick quicker and improves the dull), geometry (for all who have studied it are quicker than

[77] Ibid., III, 404.
[78] Ibid., V, 467.
[79] Ibid., II, 360.
[80] Ibid., X, 619. From The Works of Plato, translated and edited by Benjamin Jowett (Oxford University Press).
[81] Ibid., V, 473; VII, 535.
[82] Protagoras, 342–3.
[83] Republic, VI, 496.
[84] Ibid., V, 475–6; VII, 520.

those who have not), and astronomy and music, not in their practical but in their theoretical aspects. To these, dialectic is to be added, by whose aid alone one can learn absolute truth.[85] This thorough study of the quadrivium, it is explained, will correlate what has been studied earlier in a sporadic fashion. It is not to begin till after the intensive gymnastic training (about eighteen to twenty), for the two or three years passed in that "training is useless for any other purpose; for sleep and exercise are unpropitious to learning; and the trial of who is first in gymnastic exercises is one of the most important tests to which they are subjected." [86] From thirty to thirty-five, philosophy will be studied.[87] Then, for fifteen years, they may be put into any office, tested and tempted in the world of experience. After fifty, the select few, who have passed all tests with distinction, will devote the rest of their lives to government and philosophical studies.

Among Plato's significant innovations was the idea of essential equality of talents in men and women. Women might be weaker, but some of them possessed talents appropriate to philosophers, others the courage of the soldier,[88] still others, just like most men, were only fit to be artisans and husbandmen. All women worthy of the education of guardians should study "music and gymnastic and also the art of war, which they must practise like the men." [89] Though many will think it ridiculous to see "women naked in the palaestra, exercising with the men, especially when they get old . . . wearing armour and riding upon horseback," Plato would have women strip and exercise, and share the toils of war and the defense of the country.[90] That innovations respecting women's education were not entirely theoretical, is suggested by the report that a number of distinguished women were in the Pythagorean community, and two women attended Plato's school.[91]

Plato's theory of universal truth must be stated briefly. It is his answer to the individualistic opinionativeness of the day. Protagoras' doctrine, "Man is the measure of all things," was taken by some to mean, "What appears to each man to be true, is true for each man." Such a doctrine would doubtless be flattering and agreeable to most men in an age of extreme democracy which sought to equate equals and unequals. Obviously, the thesis might as well be interpreted

85 *Ibid.*, VII, 526–7, 532.
86 *Ibid.*, VII, 537. From *The Works of Plato*, translated and edited by Benjamin Jowett (Oxford University Press).
87 *Ibid.*, VII, 539.
88 *Ibid.*, V, 456.
89 *Ibid.*, V, 452. From *The Works of Plato*, translated and edited by Benjamin Jowett (Oxford University Press).
90 *Ibid.*, V, 457. From *The Works of Plato*, translated and edited by Benjamin Jowett (Oxford University Press).
91 *Iamblichus*, 36; Laërtius: *Plato*, 31.

to mean man collectively.[92] Socrates seems to have given it the broader meaning. The "knowledge" of an individual may be shown to be really only opinion. Truth must be sought through a critical, dialectical process whereby false, unsound, superficial opinions can be detected and discarded, leaving the heart of sound knowledge. Plato's truth transcends the relativism of the sophists. It is unique, fixed, eternal. True reality is defined as perfect ideas, abstractions, universals, "patterns fixed in nature" that have always existed and always will continue.[93] Truth does not lie in our sensations, for all senses are inaccurate and deceive us. Truth dwells in a world all her own,[94] transcends the world of obscurity, sense perception, and opinion, and is scarcely apprehensible by men, but may be partially grasped through examples and pursued through the use of dialectic. Education is the process whereby opinions, perceptions, unrealities (the things men have been in the habit of calling real), which Plato compares to shadows cast on the back wall of a cave in which men are held prisoner, may be seen to be unreal and be supplanted by knowledge of reality, i.e., by knowledge of the original, perfect, universal forms by which the shadows were cast.[95] This genuine, perfect knowledge, this sole reality, the philosopher-rulers of the state must strive for. Obviously the dull, dim-eyed, slow-witted among the inhabitants of the Republic must take an easier road.

Plato's Laws, written at the very close of his life, depicts a society in some respects milder and mellower than the Republic, though in others as harsh and rigid as its forerunner. This social order is a "second best," a rather conservative scheme, which the philosopher thought attainable, while not denying the radical innovations of the ideal Republic.[96] The setting is in Crete; the characters are a Cretan, a Spartan, and an old Athenian—through whom Plato speaks. The Laws shows the unmistakable influence of Cretan and Spartan institutions. There is a notable strictness of government and rigidity of education. Certain contrasts with the Republic give an idea of the social, economic, and political framework in which education operates. The idea of rule by philosophers is set aside in favor of a government, something between a monarchy and a democracy, in which all citizens participate to some extent, but not equally—a government constituted of monarchical, aristocratic, democratic, and even tyrannical elements. A college of twelve censors (having impeachment powers over lesser officials), elected guardians of the law, hereditary and elected priests, a council of 360, a minister of education, paid teachers, and a

---

92 Cf. Gomperz: op. cit., I, 455 ff.; Windelband: op. cit., pp. 94 ff.
93 Plato: Cratylus, 389; Parmenides, 132; Meno, 72, 81–6; cf. Windelband: op. cit., pp. 116–31; Jaeger: op. cit., II, 160–73; Ueberweg: op. cit., I, 115–28.
94 Republic, x, 596 et seq.
95 Ibid., VII, 515 et seq.
96 Laws, V, 739.

multitude of lesser officials are assigned a place. The theory of absolute ideas, so prominent in earlier dialogues, seems to have lost its hold on Plato. Dialectic through which philosophers of the Republic had been trained is in disrepute.[97] The religious note is strong; orthodoxy is safeguarded by rigidly controlled education and by numerous laws against heresy. The freethinker and the political innovator are taboo. There is to be no communism. Riches and poverty are to be avoided by numerous restrictions. The territory is to be divided into 5,040 lots, one for each citizen, and these are to be grouped in twelve regions. The same discrimination respecting mean occupations and commerce is still maintained. No citizen may be an artisan, but some form of toil, other than that of artisans, is approved of as conducive to health and restraint of passion.[98] Some attention is given to the principles governing the training of artisans. Slavery is a "necessary" institution. It will work best if the slaves are of different stock; they should be treated well, not just for their own sake, but more because of the master's self-interest, for "man is a troublesome animal." [99]

Education is to be compulsory for all citizens, male and female, the children being "regarded as belonging to the state rather than to their parents." [100] Schools for music and gymnastic are to be set up in town and in the country, taught by foreigners who are to be paid for the service. A minister of education, at least fifty years old and the father of children, is to be elected by the magistrates to serve five years. For this post, "the greatest" of "all the great offices of state," that citizen will be chosen from the body of guardians of the laws who is "in every respect the best." [101]

Education, though the "fairest thing" men have, may take a wrong course, but it can be reformed. What is the purpose of this all-important process? Just as there are several orders of interests, those of the soul, those of the body, and those pertaining to money-making,[102] one must discriminate between two types of education. That which really deserves the name is "education in virtue from youth upwards, which makes a man eagerly pursue the ideal perfection of citizenship, and teaches him how rightly to rule and how to obey." Training which "aims at the acquisition of wealth or bodily strength, or mere cleverness apart from intelligence and justice, is mean and illiberal, and is not worthy to be called education at all." [103] Good education "makes good men,"

---

[97] Ibid., VII, 820; X, 891; XII, 965; Gomperz: op. cit., III, 246 ff.
[98] Plato: Laws, VIII, 841, 846.
[99] Ibid., VI, 777. From The Works of Plato, translated and edited by Benjamin Jowett (Oxford University Press).
[100] Ibid., VII, 804.
[101] Ibid., VI, 765–6.
[102] Ibid., V, 743.
[103] Ibid., I, 644.

and "good men act nobly, and conquer their enemies in battle. . . ." [104]

Education should be carried on in an active way, should be an apprenticeship through play to what one will do in later life: ". . . he who would be good at anything must practise that thing from his youth upwards, both in sport and earnest, in the particular way which the work requires; for example, he who is to be a good builder, should play at building children's houses; and he who is to be a good husbandman, at tilling the ground; those who have the care of their education should provide them when young with mimic tools. And they should learn beforehand the knowledge which they will afterwards require for their art. For example, the future carpenter should learn to measure or apply the line in play; and the future warrior should learn riding, or some other exercise for amusement, and the teacher should endeavour to direct, the children's inclinations and pleasures by the help of amusements, to their final aim in life. The sum of education is right training in the nursery. The soul of the child in his play should be trained to that sort of excellence in which when he grows up to manhood he will have to be perfected. . . ." [105]

Prenatal care is recognized as highly important. Rapid growth without exercise is the source of much evil to the body. Expectant mothers should be vigorously active, and children, though too young to walk, should have the exercise of motion, being carried about till the end of the third year. From then till six, children "will require sports, . . ." such "natural modes of amusement which they find out for themselves when they meet." At six boys and girls should be separated, the boys living together and the girls together. The boys will now go to teachers to learn horsemanship, the bow, the javelin, the sling, and the use of heavy arms. Stress is laid on the cultivation of ambidexterity. Girls are to learn the use of weapons too—"if they do not object." Thus will all, "boys and girls alike," be sound of hand and foot and "not spoil the gifts of nature by bad habits." [106]

Education is of two kinds, music and gymnastic. The superintendent of education must observe the established laws; citizens are charged to look after youth and punish them if they do wrong, or else "incur the greatest disgrace." [107] At ten the study of letters, including reading, writing, poetry, and the law, begins and continues for three years. [108] The lyre is taken up at thirteen

[104] Ibid., I, 641. From The Works of Plato, translated and edited by Benjamin Jowett (Oxford University Press).
[105] Ibid., I, 643. From The Works of Plato, translated and edited by Benjamin Jowett (Oxford University Press).
[106] Ibid., VII, 793–5. From The Works of Plato, translated and edited by Benjamin Jowett (Oxford University Press).
[107] Ibid., VII, 809.
[108] Cf. Protagoras, 325–6.

and continued for three years, avoiding a great complexity and variety of rhythms.[109] Arithmetic, mensuration, and astronomy complete intellectual education, being taught to "the many" in a general way, utilizing games as in Egypt to make learning "a pleasure and amusement." Mental learning, Plato says elsewhere, cannot be successfully forced, whereas compulsory physical exercise does no harm.[110] Only "a few" are to pursue these studies "in a strictly scientific manner. . . ."[111]

Gymnastic has its *raison d'être* in the nature of man, which delights in motion and rhythm. This branch of education consists of two main elements: gymnastic exercises and dancing. Man, having a sense of rhythm, invented dancing which, with melody, constitutes the whole choral art. One who is properly educated will sing and dance well. Dancing is of two kinds, noble and ignoble. The latter (Bacchic dances and the like) are not suitable for citizens at all. Of the noble, there are two types: for war, the Pyrrhic, which imitates giving and avoiding blows, leaping up and falling down, using the bow and the javelin; for peace, the Emmeleiai, which are natural, graceful, and symbolic of prosperity and order.[112]

Gymnastic training is chiefly military drill, archery, hurling weapons, using the light shield and heavy arms, military evolutions, logistics, encampments, and everything belonging to horsemanship.[113] Wrestling, which is closest to the military art, is to be practiced for this reason, and not for its own sake.[114] Hunting is praised and recommended because it simulates war. But there are several kinds of hunting; that of animals, birds, and fish; that of men; that of armies; and that of robbers. Youth are warned against being ensnared by a love of fishing or fowling and against robbing, for these are unworthy of freeborn youth. Only the chase of land animals, "which is carried on with horses and dogs and men's own persons," is recommended for the future citizens, because this involves running down, throwing, striking, and seizing with one's hands.[115]

Training of a military or semimilitary sort is supplemented by recreations that serve the same end. "Every city which has any sense, should go out to war at least for one day in every month," more, if thought fit, without regard to heat or cold, summer or winter. Everyone—men, women, and children—should go out in mass, having games and tournaments, "imitating in as lively a manner

[109] *Laws*, VII, 810.
[110] *Republic*, VII, 536.
[111] *Laws*, VII, 817–9.
[112] *Ibid.*, VII, 814–6.
[113] *Ibid.*, VII, 813.
[114] *Ibid.*, VII, 814.
[115] *Ibid.*, VII, 823. From *The Works of Plato*, translated and edited by Benjamin Jowett (Oxford University Press).

as they can real battles." For wrestlers, boxers, and pancratiasts train for their matches, and should not citizens do the same? "Will the legislator not . . . ordain that every day the soldiers shall perform lesser exercises without arms, making dancing and all gymnastic tend to this end; will he not require that they shall practise some gymnastic exercises, great or small, as often as every month; and that they shall have contests one with another in every part of the country, seizing upon posts and lying in ambush, and imitating in every respect the reality of war; fighting with boxing-gloves and hurling javelins, and using weapons somewhat dangerous, and as nearly as possible like the true ones, in order that the sport may not be altogether without fear, but may have terrors and to a certain degree show the man who has courage and the man who has not; and that the honour and dishonour which are assigned to them respectively, may prepare the whole city for the true conflict of life? If any one dies in these mimic contests, the homicide is involuntary, and we will make the slayer, when he has been purified according to law, to be pure of blood, considering that if a few men should die, others as good as they will be born; but that if fear is dead, then the citizens will never find a test of superior and inferior natures, which is a far greater evil to the state than the loss of a few." [116]

Only warlike contests are to be practiced and rewarded with prizes; all others are to be given up. Military exercises are selected on the principle that "the most military of all qualities is general activity of body, whether of foot or hand." For escape from and capturing enemies, "quickness of foot is required; but hand-to-hand conflict and combat need vigour and strength." [117] Hence there must be races in armor (graded for boys, youth, and men), single and double races, the horse course, distance race, race in heavy armor, another in still heavier armor, and a race for the archers. Other contests include, "instead of wrestling," "conflicts in armour of one against one, and two against two, and so on up to ten against ten," and skilled persons are to determine the winners in these matches.[118] A military pancration is to be established in which bows, shields, javelins, and stones, thrown by hand and with slings, are the weapons.[119] Since the chariot is of but little use in war, such races are not approved; but prizes for colts and horses, as well as contests between archers and javelin-men in armor on horseback, are to be established.

The laws pertaining to physical education apply to women as to men: "Both

[116] *Ibid.*, VIII, 829–31. From *The Works of Plato*, translated and edited by Benjamin Jowett (Oxford University Press).

[117] *Ibid.*, VIII, 832. From *The Works of Plato*, translated and edited by Benjamin Jowett (Oxford University Press).

[118] Cf. *Laches*, 178–80. From *The Works of Plato*, translated and edited by Benjamin Jowett (Oxford University Press).

[119] *Laws*, VIII, 834.

THE RACE IN ARMOR   *vase painting, 5th century*
Berlin Museum (Courtesy, The Metropolitan Museum of Art, New York)

go through the same exercises. I have no sort of fear of saying that gymnastic and horsemanship are as suitable to women as to men. . . . And . . . nothing can be more absurd than . . . men and women not following the same pursuits . . . for thus the state, instead of being a whole . . . is reduced to a half. . . ." [120] Elsewhere Plato says: "While they are yet girls they should have practised dancing in arms and the art of fighting—when they are grown-up women, applying themselves to evolutions and tactics, and the mode of grounding and taking up arms; if for no other reason, yet in case the whole people should have to leave the city and carry on operations of war outside, that the young who are left to guard and the rest of the city may be equal to the task; and, on the other hand (what is far from being an impossibility), when enemies, whether barbarian or Hellenic, come from without with mighty force and make a violent assault upon them, and thus compel them to fight for the possession of the city, great would be the disgrace to the state, if the women had been so miserably trained that they could not like birds fight for their young. . . ." [121]

Women's physical recreation, like the men's, is in military sports. Girls must compete naked in the stade, double stade, horse course, and long race from thirteen to eighteen, and may do so when older. Till married, women are also to take part in the armed combat, one against one, two against two, and so on, as do the men; women are not compelled to participate in the contests on

[120] *Ibid.*, vii, 804–5. From *The Works of Plato*, translated and edited by Benjamin Jowett (Oxford University Press).
[121] *Ibid.*, vii, 813–4. From *The Works of Plato*, translated and edited by Benjamin Jowett (Oxford University Press).

horseback, but may do so if they like and their early training has become a habit with them.[122]

Plato, the innovator, expresses fear of innovations, in the Laws as he did in the Republic. Once laws are fixed, they must remain. Even changes in gymnastic, music, and dancing would inevitably undermine the laws: therefore, music and gymnastic shall be kept in "their original form"; [123] and "no one in singing or dancing shall offend against public and consecrated models, and the general fashion among the youth, any more than he would offend against any other law," under pain of punishment "by the guardians of the laws, and by priests and priestesses." [124] Games, too, have an effect on the permanence and stability of the state. Children who are permitted to make innovations in their games will want to make changes in laws and institutions when they grow up. Therefore, plays and games must remain the same, since "he who changes the sports is secretly changing the manners of the young, and making the old to be dishonoured among them and the new to be honoured. And I affirm that there is nothing which is a greater injury to all states than saying or thinking thus." [125]

Plato has depicted a thorough, military education. Yet it arises from necessity, he says, and is aimed at peace, not conquest. Neither an individual nor a state should wrong another, and they should not be wronged by others. Our state can attain the first, he says, but it cannot be guaranteed freedom from wrong by others. Therefore, the state must prepare for war while it is at peace. Nevertheless, Plato emphasizes the evils of war, even the evils of victory for the victors, and argues that ". . . every man of us should live the life of peace as long and as well as he can." [126] Though war is the "aim and object" of Cretan and Spartan institutions, Plato holds that lawgivers should aim to reconcile classes and individuals within the state rather than promote the destruction of one by the other. Civil war is, of course, more to be feared than external, but "war, whether external or civil, is not the best, and the need of either is to be deprecated; but peace with one another, and good will, are best . . . [and] no one can be a true statesman . . . who looks only, or first of all, to external warfare; nor will he ever be a sound legislator who orders peace for the sake of war, and not war for the sake of peace." [127]

122 Ibid., VIII, 834.
123 Republic, IV, 424.
124 Laws, VII, 800. From The Works of Plato, translated and edited by Benjamin Jowett (Oxford University Press).
125 Ibid., VII, 797. From The Works of Plato, translated and edited by Benjamin Jowett (Oxford University Press).
126 Ibid., VII, 803. From The Works of Plato, translated and edited by Benjamin Jowett (Oxford University Press).
127 Ibid., I, 628. From The Works of Plato, translated and edited by Benjamin Jowett (Oxford University Press).

ARISTOTLE
(H. Brunn and P. J. Arndt, Denkmäler, Pl. 378)

It was Plato's good fortune to have as pupil the greatest mind in antiquity. Aristotle's biographer says that he had thin legs, small eyes, a lisping tongue, and was inclined to foppish dress.[128] It seems to have been unimportant; more significant was his ingenuity and industry in seeking the relation of effects and causes, organizing and assaying the knowledge of his day, formulating the laws of thought and canons of poetry and eloquence, investigating the ways of animals, explaining the mysteries of the soul, and detailing the proper ordering of a household. Indeed, as a literary wit of later days declared, Aristotle knew even the nature of an oyster's soul.[129]

Aristotle was born at Stagira, studied under Plato, tutored Alexander, and established a famous school of philosophy at the Lyceum in Athens, where he taught for many years. Shortly before his death he fled from the city under a charge of impiety, saying that Athens must not be permitted to sin twice against philosophy.[130] Deeply concerned with the problems of everyday life, Aristotle turned his critical eye upon the past and the social, political turmoil around him, and examined them in the light of philosophic schemes for improvement. From the crucible of his thought there came forth thoughtfully formulated principles of the good life for man and for the state, which, though obviously marred by many prejudices and the inadequacies of his science, have been highly significant in political and educational thinking to the present day.

There are certain similarities between Aristotle's views and those of Xenophon and Plato; thus he recognizes certain strong points in Spartan and Cretan institutions, though he censures other aspects of these commonwealths. Unlike them he puts greater trust in democratic government, and has less faith than they in rigid forms and unalterable prescriptions. Plato's doctrine of universal ideas is rejected. Both democracy and oligarchy (as they exist) are criticized: for the sons of an oligarchic class live in luxury and become the worst enemies of the state; and the adherents of democracy think of nothing but freedom to do as they like and let the majority rule.[131] Aristotle regards tyranny, oligarchy, and pure democracy as perversions of the three true forms of government, the monarchical, aristocratic, and constitutional, respectively.[132] The best government would be a wise, benevolent monarchy, ruled by one so much better than any other as to be unique, "a god among men";[133] under circumstances as they are, however, a constitutional government, in which all citizens (but not all persons) share, is, for practical purposes, the best

128 Laërtius: Aristotle, 1–2.
129 Lucian: Sale of Creeds, 26.
130 Laërtius: Aristotle, 7; Gomperz: op. cit., IV, 24.
131 Aristotle: Politica, IV, 13; V, 9; VI, 7; Windelband: op. cit., pp. 132 f.; Ueberweg: op. cit., I, 157 f.
132 Politica, III, 7; IV, 2.
133 Ibid., III, 13, 17.

attainable, for thus may be combined some advantageous features of oligarchic and democratic rule.[134] Here, as elsewhere, Aristotle applies the doctrine of the mean. Too much diversity is an evil, a cause of disintegration; but there may also be too much unity in the state. Both extremes are to be avoided. The mean is best. Spartan government was excellent in that it combined elements of monarchy, aristocracy, and democracy.[135]

Aristotle would locate his commonwealth in a healthful, temperate climate, for climate influences the nature of men. A cold, inhospitable one makes men spirited, but unintelligent, unskilled, and incapable of rule; a hot climate is conducive to intelligence and inventiveness but occasions a lack of spirit, and makes men liable to subjection; while a temperate clime, combining both spiritedness and intelligence, makes men fit to rule. The land must be well watered, adequate to support life, and accessible by land and sea, yet easily defended. All land is to be the property of the state, but half of it will be assigned to citizens for private use, each citizen having one share in the city itself and another share on the frontier, thus securing his interest in defense against enemies. The population must be large enough to perform all work necessary for the welfare of the state, yet not so large but that it "can be taken in at a single view." [136]

Artisans are not to be citizens in the "best form of state." Citizens must not do "illiberal" work.[137] Their shares of land and certain freely provided services make it possible for them to live a life of leisure, which is necessary for those who devote themselves to the good life of the state. Priests, magistrates, soldiers, and other citizens have their meals in common.[138]

The labors of society are productive, protective, deliberative, and directive. Slaves, public and private, are to cultivate all lands held by the state or by individuals, and do all other productive work of an "illiberal" sort. They ought to be unspirited folk, preferably of a foreign race—naturally inferior to their masters. Protective, directive, and deliberative functions belong to the master-class, the citizens—"those who carry arms"—with a certain exception.[139] Naval force was associated, in Greek experience, with the rise of lower orders to prominence; excepting marines, Aristotle would have it drawn from the non-citizen Perioeci and husbandmen.[140] The younger men begin at twenty-one years to perform active military and civil duties; while older ones act as legisla-

---

[134] Ibid., IV, 8–9, 11.
[135] Ibid., II, 1–6.
[136] Ibid., VII, 4–5, 7, 10–1. Compare Plato's view of the effect of habitat, winds, heats, waters, foods, on the nature of man—Laws, V, 747—and that of Hippocrates—"Airs, Waters, Places," Hippocrates, I, 137.
[137] Politica, III, 5; VII, 9.
[138] Ibid., VII, 10, 12.
[139] Ibid., IV, 13.
[140] Ibid., VI, 7; VII, 6.

tors, judges, and priests, and progressively enjoy contemplative leisure, as befits those who are capable of the highest happiness.[141]

Aristotle turns often to the "experience of ages" past, "for almost everything has been found out, although sometimes . . . not put together. . . ." [142] The *Politica* is a well-informed book, a more conservative treatise on the state than Plato's *Republic*, perhaps because Aristotle approached the political life of man through a study of the constitutions of 158 cities. He does more, however, than collect and set forth old facts and institutions. Those features of the past that are given place in his best attainable state are utilized because they are in harmony with certain principles of man's nature. Sound or unsound, these were inevitably colored by experience and observation that had sharp limitations. Nevertheless, the method speaks eloquently of the scientific outlook of the philosopher, even when his hypotheses seem most at variance with recognized facts of to-day.

Aristotle, like others before him, attempted to fix upon some valid, ultimate good.[143] But whereas Socrates held knowledge, and Plato, justice, to be the end, the highest good, Aristotle says that happiness is the chief and final end, encompassing all immediate and lesser ones. This, of course, does not deny the importance of the others. Indeed, "no government can stand which is not founded on justice." [144] Happiness is an end, good in itself for all men, never a means, hence more final than those immediate ends that are also means. Knowledge, justice, and music and arithmetic are useful to man, for they and many other things are means to the chief end, happiness—which is the valid final end both for man and for the state. Politics, the science of government, is the master science, for it includes and directs all others, that they may be serviceable to the attainment of the chief end, individually and collectively.[145]

Happiness, of course, is a broad term, is variously interpreted, and may be misunderstood. Its many meanings and implications—prosperity, independence, security, good birth, plenty of friends, plenty of children, happy old age, health, beauty, good stature, athletic ability, fame, honor, luck, and virtue— are all recognized.[146] But to be serviceable as a formula of the greatest good, the true end of man and society, a more scientific conception of happiness must be formulated. Aristotle finds the key to happiness is the performance of function, the activity that properly (naturally) belongs to anything. Observing

[141] *Ibid.*, VII, 9.
[142] *Ibid.*, II, 5. From *The Works of Aristotle*, translated by J. A. Smith and W. D. Ross (The Clarendon Press).
[143] *Ethica Nichomachea*, I, 1.
[144] *Politica*, VII, 14.
[145] *Ethica*, I, 2, 7.
[146] Aristotle: *Rhetorica*, I, 5.

that the goods of a flute-player and a carpenter are playing the flute and building houses, Aristotle raises the question: What is the function of man, as a
man? "Is he born without a function?" [147] Do feet and hands have functions,
while man as a whole is without them? If man has many functions, which one
distinguishes him from the vegetable kingdom and from the animal, and makes
him man?

Nutrition and growth are functions common to the whole animate world.[148]
Sensation, too, is common to lower animals and man. The rational function,
however, is that which distinguishes man from other living things. It is the activity of soul, of the rational element of the soul, one should say, for the soul
is both irrational (impulsive) and rational (capable of reason and self-direc-
tion). To act in accord with reason, then, is man's particular function, his highest good. The good life is a life of activity in accord with reason. Neither knowledge nor a state of mind are synonymous with the good life. It is not "the most
beautiful" or "the strongest" who are crowned at Olympia, but those who
enter the lists.[149]

Man cannot live alone, save for a brief time and in an incomplete sense. He
"is by nature a political animal"; [150] and the state is the creation, the result of
this nature. Its function is to promote and direct well the several activities
proper to man: those of nutrition and growth, of sensation, and of reason.
In this way the state makes possible the good life, the highest happiness of
which man is capable. When it so functions, the state may be said to be happy,
for it fulfills its end. Nonfunctioning is failure to live according to the principles of man's nature, is a denial of nature; it signifies unhappiness for man,
individually and collectively.

In individual man, where nature is not perverted, the rational soul rules the
irrational soul and the body, making the virtuous life possible; so, in the state,
there is good order and happiness when those in whom the rational element
exists direct, and are masters of, those in whom it does not exist at all (slaves),
or is incomplete or undeveloped, as in women and children. Some men are
slaves by nature. They are destined to be and "deserve to be slaves." [151] Others
"are by nature free," marked to rule, by virtue of the kind of soul implanted
in them. It is right and just for them to rule over beasts and inferior men.
"Man" is the "most essential" of all possessions. Hunting and war are both
natural acts of acquisition, establishing dominion of the superior over the inferior, and hence "naturally just." [152] The relation of the master to the slave is

[147] Ethica, I, 7; Magna Moralia, I, 3–5.
[148] Ethica, I, 7; Galen: On the Natural Faculties, I, 7.
[149] Aristotle: Ethica, I, 8.
[150] Politica, I, 2.
[151] Ibid., VII, 14.
[152] Ibid., I, 8.

not only good and proper for the master; it is also best for the slave, since it promotes the only activity of which he is capable. In the interest of economy and for the sake of character, the master should rise earlier and retire later than the slave. Anything that would diminish or destroy the slave's efficiency must be avoided. "Work, punishment, and food" are the necessary elements for the life of the slave, but good usage will always serve the master's self-interest.[153]

In the household, women and children are fitted by nature for subjection to the male, somewhat as slaves are to their masters, since they have no faculty for self-rule or direction. For the virtue of a woman, Aristotle holds, contrary to Plato, is not the same as that of a man; hers lies "in obeying," and that of a man "in commanding." [154] Aristotle thinks that throughout the animal kingdom, though the female has some qualities more strongly developed than the male, she is less complete, less courageous, weaker, more impulsive, and the "differentiation is the most obvious in the case of human kind. . . ." [155] From the differences in capacities implanted in slaves and artisans of all kinds (who were once all slaves, and in many states still are), Aristotle concludes that a state composed of such would be impossible, for a state exists for the good life, not for mere life.[156]

Though from "one point of view," war is natural and just, establishing the dominion of the superior over the inferior, Aristotle does not believe that men should pursue war for the purpose of enslaving those who do not deserve (by nature) to be slaves.[157] Rather than striving for dominion over its neighbors by war, the state should provide against its own enslavement and maintain its sway only for the good of the governed. To establish tyranny, to rule unjustly is unlawful, for there may be might without right. Those who praise the Spartan legislator who made "conquest and war his sole aim," do so unwisely; for, though the Lacedaemonians were "trained to meet dangers" and "gained great power," "they are not a happy people" now that their empire is broken up. Such military states are safe only when at war; they fall when they gain empire, losing their temper like unused iron, for the chief virtue of war is unserviceable in times of peace. "Facts, as well as arguments, prove that the legislator should direct all his military and other measures to the provision of leisure and the establishment of peace." The inferior in art and in nature exists for the service of the superior. "Men must be able to engage in business and go to war," but

[153] Aristotle: Oeconomica, I, 5–6; Glotz: Ancient Greece at Work, p. 200; Butcher: op. cit., pp. 73 ff.; St. John: History of the Manners and Customs of Ancient Greece, III, 1 ff.
[154] Politica, I, 5, 13.
[155] Historia Animalium, IX, 1. From The Works of Aristotle, translated by J. A. Smith and W. D. Ross (The Clarendon Press).
[156] Politica, III, 5, 9.
[157] Ibid., I, 8; VII, 14.

the one is for the sake of leisure and the other for the sake of peace. The legislator must so educate that citizens will have the virtues requisite to the good life in leisure and in peace, for it is a disgrace for men to show excellent qualities in action and in war, and "when they have peace and leisure to be no better than slaves." [158]

Observation of nature and reflection upon the past have led Aristotle to recognize another principle, that of change. Hippodamus introduced the idea of planning cities, and proposed to honor those who discovered anything new that would be useful to the state. Planning implies change. "Great caution" is necessary, however, for laws command obedience only through habit, and too great readiness to make changes "enfeebles the power of law." Still, politics is an art, and change is as necessary in this as in any other; only thus has improvement come about. Moreover, considering the rational principle toward which men strive, it is natural for man to "desire the good . . . not merely what their fathers had. . . ." [159] The chief questions are, therefore, who should make changes, all or only a few; and how extensive should changes be.

The study of politics, planning a more perfect state, inevitably embraces education. Education is a branch of politics. Nothing provides more surely for the permanence of governments than education, if rightly instituted, since the best laws can accomplish little unless youth are trained and educated "in the spirit of the constitution." To this end, the principles of education and of politics must be in harmony. Moreover, since the state has one purpose, the attainment of the good life for its citizens, education to that end must be the same for all. Since an individual belongs not to himself but to the state, the state alone may direct and determine what education is to be. Athens has done badly in respect to this, permitting families to decide for themselves; Lacedaemon has done well, making education a function of the government. All educational matters—the stories children are to hear, the pictures and statues they may see, their plays, what they may witness at the theater, what they may do and say, with whom they may associate—are placed under the directors of public education. [160] For what is experienced first is apt to remain with us; the things that give us pain or pleasure, the things we love and those we hate—all these are rudders by which youths are steered to a virtuous, happy life. [161]

The periods of education, and the elements appropriate to each, are determined by nature herself. The physical body, the irrational soul, and the rational soul develop in due order; hence concern for the body must come first, training of the irrational self next, and the education of reason last, though that of

[158] Ibid., II, 9; VII, 15. From The Works of Aristotle, translated by J. A. Smith and W. D. Ross (The Clarendon Press).
[159] Ibid., II, 8.
[160] Ibid., V, 9; VII, 17; VIII, 1.
[161] Ethica, X, 1.

the body and the appetites is ultimately "for the sake of the reason." [162]

Since it is futile to speak of ultimate ends without considering means thereto, education of the rational soul must wait upon that of the body. Education can accomplish nothing without a good physical stock on which it may be engrafted; hence the legislator is concerned with the physical qualities of the children of citizens. This goes back to eugenic mating, the time when mating should occur, and other related matters. Women ought to marry at eighteen, men at thirty-seven. Athletes and others too, who engage in physical labor that is excessive and of only one kind, are not suited to be citizens or the fathers of citizens, "any more than the valetudinarian or exhausted constitution." The mean between the two is preferred. Neither the very young nor the old are fit to produce children, healthy in mind and body. Women, while bearing children, should exercise their bodies daily (walking to the temples is recommended), but their minds should be at rest. Diet should be nourishing.

No child that is deformed shall live. When there is an excess of children, abortion is to be practiced.[163] In the first years of life nature decrees that physical growth is of paramount importance; hence chief attention must be to nutrition, exercise, and inuring the body to cold by a gradual process. Milk is the best food, as the habit of animals and warlike peoples show. To five years of age, the child will have no studies, no tasks, for these might hinder normal growth. Crying and screaming are good physical exercise; childish amusements, too, are good, if not overdone, vulgar, or effeminate. Children should not be left with slaves. On the moral side, all care should be taken to prohibit any speech or action in their presence that has a taint of meanness.

From five until seven, while they are still at home, children are to "look on at the pursuits which they are hereafter to learn." [164] Since woman's rôle is sedentary and in the household; since she is not a citizen, although a free person; and since she is subject to her husband, and is "the proper possession of all freemen," [165] the education of girls will be only in the family, and for its duties, in accord with the political principles laid down for the state, which exclude women from any directive function therein.[166]

Formal education after seven falls into two periods: the first, to the age of puberty; the second, from puberty to twenty-one.[167] Here again, the training of the body takes precedence over that of the soul, for Aristotle holds that body and soul are closely interlinked, and mental faculties are affected by movements

[162] Politica, VII, 15.
[163] Ibid., VII, 16.
[164] Ibid., VII, 17. From The Works of Aristotle, translated by J. A. Smith and W. D. Ross (The Clarendon Press).
[165] Oeconomica, I, 2, 3.
[166] Politica, I, 13; II, 5.
[167] Ibid., VII, 17.

and states of the body. Indeed, he agrees with physiognomists that movements, form, and proportion of the body reveal the character of the soul.[168] Since practice should precede theory, youth are to be turned over "to the trainer, who creates in them the proper habit of body, and to the wrestling-master, who teaches them their exercises." [169] Till fourteen or fifteen they should engage in lighter exercises, "avoiding severe diet or painful toil," the heavier being postponed till nearer manhood, "lest the growth of the body be impaired." Dancing, running, jumping, throwing the javelin and discus would be included among these lighter exercises, but Aristotle is content to state principles and omit details. The principle of the mean must be adhered to, for, as he says,[170] excessive or deficient exercise injures strength, just as too little or too much food and drink is inimical to health. The evil of excessive, severe, early training, Aristotle believed, had been proved by the fact that of Olympic victors not more than two or three ever won prizes both as boys and men. Hence the "athletic habit" is not to be encouraged. Even the Lacedaemonians, wise in some respects, erred in giving too much attention to "laborious exercises," thinking thereby to make their citizens courageous. In reality, however, they only brutalized them; besides, Lacedaemon was not successful in war because of her severe training, but because her rivals gave slight attention to such training. That which "is noble, not what is brutal, should have the first place; no wolf or other wild animal will face a really noble danger; such dangers are for the brave man." [171]

The period of light physical training is to be followed by three years devoted to study, during which little attention will be given to gymnastics. Respecting the education that is appropriate, Aristotle says there is much doubt and dispute. Men disagree as to the relative stress on moral and intellectual education; they also differ "about the things to be taught." [172] To decide the question, one must keep in mind the goal of the citizen's life, and determine upon educational principles that are in harmony therewith. A key is found in an earlier distinction between occupations that are liberal and those that are illiberal. "Any occupation, art, or science, which makes the body or soul or mind of the freeman less fit for the practice or exercise of virtue, is vulgar; wherefore we call those arts vulgar which tend to deform the body, and likewise all paid employments, for they absorb and degrade the mind." Even some liberal arts are proper for a free man only to a certain degree, for if one is too devoted to them, or aims at "perfection in them," they become illiberal. Children ought, therefore, to "be taught those useful things which are really neces-

[168] Physiognomonica, 2, 4; Philostratos: Concerning Gymnastics, 25 et seq.
[169] Aristotle: Politica, VIII, 3.
[170] Ethica, II, 2.
[171] Politica, VIII, 4; Ethica, III, 6, 7. From The Works of Aristotle, translated by J. A. Smith and W. D. Ross (The Clarendon Press).
[172] Politica, VIII, 2.

sary, but not all useful things. . . ." "To be always seeking after the useful does not become free and exalted souls." [173]

Agriculture, which is highly praised by Aristotle in the *Oeconomica*, and is recommended because "it does not make men's bodies unserviceable, as do the illiberal arts," but, on the contrary, "conduces greatly to bravery," rendering men "adventurous against the foe," [174] does not appear in the *Politica* as a field for training or education—presumably because even such dignified and beneficial labor is to be performed in the ideal state by public and private slaves. It is admitted, of course, that the "good man" may learn the craft of an inferior, but only for his "own occasional use"; if it goes beyond that, there will cease to be any distinction between masters and slaves.[175] In addition to gymnastics, reading, and writing, music and drawing are recommended. Reading and writing are necessary in many ways. Drawing, too, while it may be useful in making purchases, is to be taught "because it makes them judges of the beauty of the human form." [176] Music is approved as a means to "intellectual enjoyment in leisure," which is liberal and noble. Aristotle is often at pains to controvert the idea that education is play: the beginning of education is bitter, the end sweet; "learning is no amusement, but is accompanied with pain." But music is a serviceable amusement, a sweetener of toil—not an amusement for its own sake, but a means to an end—which is to youth what the rattle is to the baby; it ought to be employed, therefore, for Aristotle thinks that youth "will not, if they can help, endure anything which is not sweetened by pleasure. . . ." [177]

Music, moreover, serves a greater, a remoter end; it is conducive to virtuous character of the soul, just as gymnastic gives a certain character to the body. This alone would be sufficient justification for the use of music in the education of the young. There is an affinity in our souls for various rhythms. By choosing the right music we can set the best chords of the soul vibrating. Only those melodies should be employed that produce an ennobling, harmonious effect. Remarkable perfection of execution, such as is acquired for professional purposes, is to be shunned, of course, for this makes music an end in itself, not a means of improvement. In explaining this use of music, Aristotle has recourse again to the theory of the mean.[178] The virtuous life is a mean between extremes. As music exerts an involuntary influence over the soul by virtue of the

173 *Ibid.*, VIII, 2–3. From *The Works of Aristotle*, translated by J. A. Smith and W. D. Ross (The Clarendon Press).
174 *Op. cit.*, I, 2. From *The Works of Aristotle*, translated by J. A. Smith and W. D. Ross (The Clarendon Press); in contrast with this view of the warlike qualities of countrymen and commoners, cf. Aristophanes: *The Peace*, 441 *et seq.*; *Acharnians*, 509 *et seq.*
175 *Politica*, III, 4; VII, 9.
176 *Ibid.*, VIII, 3.
177 *Ibid.*, VIII, 5. From *The Works of Aristotle*, translated by J. A. Smith and W. D. Ross (The Clarendon Press); Laërtius: *Aristotle*, 11.
178 *Ethica*, II, 2, 6.

affinity spoken of, those modes of music must be avoided that have extreme effects, such as the Phrygian, which is too exciting, and the "so-called Mixolydian," which is conducive to sadness. Dorian, the mean between these extremes, is recognized as "manliest" and best, and should therefore be taught to youth, though for very young children and men of advanced age, the Lydian is held to be appropriate and useful.[179]

Instruments must be chosen on the same principle: the flute and the harp are rejected, the latter partly for its difficulty, the former because it distorts the face, hinders the use of the voice, "is too exciting," and is not "expressive of moral character." Those instruments alone may be used which "will make intelligent students of music. . . ."[180]

The rôle of music is also important in connection with purgation—catharsis —of the irrational soul. Just as physical play and exercise in the palaestra furnish an outlet for animal spirits and are conducive to dignified, manly bearing, so the purgation of the irrational soul by music is conducive to the virtuous life, providing an agreeable, harmless outlet for the passions. When purgation rather than instruction is the purpose, other modes and instruments may be employed; thus the flute, though condemned for instruction, is permitted when the purpose is "relief of the passions."[181] Purgation may also be effected by means of tragedy which, through imitation of life, arousing fear and pity, provides by vicarious experience a "catharsis of such emotions."[182] Through these and music the emotions are cultivated and brought under subjection to the rational soul.

What would provide the education of the rational soul is largely a matter of speculation, for the treatise on politics is incomplete. Mind and ability to think were little known in his day, but Aristotle calls "mind" that by means of which the soul judges and thinks. Until soul thinks, mind is not anything real. Thinking, which is both judgment and imagination, is viewed as of many types: art, science, practical reason, intuitive reason, and philosophic, contemplative wisdom, the key to "perfect happiness." Development of mind, in light of Aristotle's functional conception of it, would logically be expected to be exercise of the rational soul in thinking and judging.[183]

When boyhood with its lighter gymnastic exercises is past, and when three years have been devoted to study of an intellectual and moral nature, youth on

[179] Politica, VIII, 7.
[180] Ibid., VIII, 6. From The Works of Aristotle, translated by J. A. Smith and W. D. Ross (The Clarendon Press).
[181] Ibid.
[182] Aristotle: De Poetica, 6.
[183] De Anima, I, 3; II, 2; III, 3–4; Ethica, VI, 3–7, 11; X, 7; Davidson: op. cit., pp. 198 f; Wilkins: National Education in Greece, pp. 160 ff.; Wright: A Short History of Greek Literature, p. 402.

the threshold of manhood should have three years of continuous physical train-ing—hard exercises and strict diet. From this period (eighteen to twenty-one) study is specifically excluded on the ground that "men ought not to labour at the same time with their minds and with their bodies; for the two kinds of labour are opposed to one another. . . ." [184] The harder exercises of this period would presumably include wrestling, riding, shooting, marching, and other military exercises, though details are not given in the Politica. Elsewhere, how-ever, Aristotle recognizes the all-round athlete as most beautiful, both swift and strong—one who is good at running, able at wrestling, clever at boxing, and able to combine the two last as a good pancratiast.[185] One would expect these to be part of the citizen's training; but keeping in mind Aristotle's criticism of the excesses, brutality, and ultimate ineffectiveness of Lacedaemonian prac-tice, none of them would be overdone, or become an end in themselves in his ideal state. It seems certain that this training would be under the care of com-petent gymnasts and sufficiently realistic to enable men to take up active mili-tary duties at twenty-one. That gymnastic exercises should be continued by the older men is clear from the reference to a freeman's agora, whence all trade, mechanics, and husbandmen are excluded—a place where the magistrates will congregate to witness the performances of young and old.[186]

Physical training, as Aristotle would have it, should serve the education of a citizen whose end is not conquest but the virtuous life. Too great stress on mili-tary life, as in Lacedaemon, or on physical prowess, as in the case of profes-sional athletes, is repeatedly condemned as incompatible with the ultimate goal. In connection with aesthetic and moral training, and in order that the highest happiness might be attained, Aristotle saw the need of a science of gymnastics. Great improvements had been made in this art, setting aside ancient traditional usage.[187] He distinguishes between the paidotribe and the gymnast. The one is a trainer, the other a scientist who understands the whole range of the art of gymnastic from its lowest elements to the highest—one who "considers not only the suitableness of different modes of training to different bodies, but what sort is absolutely the best . . . and also what common form of training is adapted to the great majority of men." [188] This science aims at health, or harmony of body,[189] and calls to its assistance, at times, the science

184 Aristotle: Politica, VIII, 4. From The Works of Aristotle, translated by J. A. Smith and W. D. Ross (The Clarendon Press).
185 Rhetorica, I, 5.
186 Politica, VII, 12.
187 Ibid., II, 8.
188 Ibid., IV, 1. From The Works of Aristotle, translated by J. A. Smith and W. D. Ross (The Clarendon Press); Philostratos: Concerning Gymnastics, 14; Chryssafis: "Aristotle on Kinesiology," Jour. Health and Phys. Educ., I, 14 ff.; "Aristotle on Physical Educa-tion," ibid., I, 3 ff.
189 Aristotle: De Anima, I, 4.

of medicine, as has been noted in the discussion of health gymnastics. Yet health is more than freedom from disease; for it is that harmonious physical state which includes size, proportion, beauty, and strength, and makes it possible to use the body generously, without having "to abstain from everything or nearly everything that men do." [190] For this harmony of health, beauty, and strength, the training of the all-round athlete is best, making him swift, strong, and fit "for the exertion of warfare" in his prime.

Xenophon, a contemporary of Plato and a member of the Socratic group, gave some attention to a portrayal of his ideal education. Though his talents as soldier, horseman, huntsman, and writer of descriptive prose seem to have outweighed his critical, philosophical capacity, his work merits attention as an example of another pattern of Athenian reaction at a time when changes were making rapid headway in social and educational affairs. Like Plato, Xenophon exhibits no sympathy with the current tendencies of Athenian democracy. His thought is of a conservative, rather uncritical pattern; he has scarcely been touched, save superficially, by the enlightenment of science and philosophy that shines so often through the pages of Plato and Aristotle. His mind is that of a self-sufficient, religious country squire, ambitious adventurer, boastful soldier, who, in retirement on his estate, devoted himself to writing prolifically and often skillfully, particularly when dealing with subjects of which he was a master. It has been well said that Xenophon is most the philosopher when "he least affects the title." [191] What he offers on education is neither original, scientific, nor constructive; nor is it faithful, critical, historical reporting. Xenophon sees that Athenian society is adrift from its ancient moorings. He has not the wit of Aristophanes to hold it up to ridicule; nevertheless, the only way to right it and stabilize it is to revert to thoroughly tested patterns.

Notwithstanding a host of differences, Xenophon is at times in agreement with Plato and Aristotle. He believes, for example, that much evil has arisen from too free an economy at Athens, and he follows a popular intellectual tendency of the day in seeking the remedy—security and stability—in stricter control of many aspects of life. Not only education, but the merchant marine, mines, and other economic agencies ought to be nationalized and strictly controlled, to the end "that every Athenian may receive sufficient maintenance at the public expense." [192] Like the Greeks generally, Xenophon thought constantly in terms of war; hence physical education should be above all concerned with preparation of the soldier.[193] The Laconizing tendency of the day, from

[190] Rhetorica, I, 5. From The Works of Aristotle, translated by J. A. Smith and W. D. Ross (The Clarendon Press).
[191] Gomperz: op. cit., II, 119; Laërtius: Xenophon, 11–3.
[192] Xenophon: Ways and Means, III, 14; IV, 33.
[193] Memorabilia, III, 12.

which Plato and Aristotle were not free, though they examined Spartan institutions in a more critical spirit and often rejected them, found in Xenophon a hearty friend. His ideal education is really the ancient Laconian system, credited to Lycurgus. He had seen it; he had lived at the Court of Agesilaus, had served with his forces against Athens and Thebes at Coronea (394 B.C.), and had been given an estate at Scillus by the Spartan leader; and he had sent his sons to be educated under the Spartan system. Xenophon's praise of Spartan discipline appears in the guise of a historical novel, the *Cyropaedia* or the education of Cyrus the Persian Prince, in the *Constitution of the Lacedaemonians*, and in many other minor essays. While the *Cyropaedia* is sometimes drawn upon for glimpses of Persian education and doubtless incorporates some features of Persian training with which he had had an opportunity to become familiar, it is of uncertain value in that connection. Neither is it a faithful portrayal of Spartan education, for Xenophon has taken liberties with fact, excising what does not please him, mixing Spartan and Persian, and utilizing the Persian setting for the portrayal of his ideal.[194] The *Constitution of the Lacedaemonians*, likewise, is not a straightforward account of Spartan institutions, but a panegyric devoted chiefly to those aspects of Lacedaemon which seemed to Xenophon most worthy of admiration, embodying, as he thought, the "utmost limit of wisdom."  [195]

Xenophon's keenest observations are drawn from horsemanship, country life, warfare and the chase. Impressed by the fact that cattle obey herdsmen, and horses their grooms, while men conspire against those who attempt to govern them, he points to monarchy as the best agency by which men may be brought to obedience and orderly action. Using Cyrus as the model, Xenophon seeks to demonstrate that rule over men is by no means impossible of attainment, provided one goes about it in the right way. The key to Cyrus' success lies in his natural endowments (handsome person, generous nature, ambition, courage, devotion to learning) and in his training "in conformity with the laws of the Persians."  [196] This education differs from that of other states. While elsewhere families are allowed to train their own children as they please (Athenian practice is his target) and the states make laws to punish those who commit crimes, the Persians "provide from the beginning, that their citizens shall not be such as to be inclined to any action that is bad and mean."  [197] This is the way they do it: They have a "Freeman's Square"  [198] near the government buildings, whence all trade is banned so as not to disturb the life of those who

---

194 Gomperz: *op. cit.*, II, 130 ff.; Wright: *op. cit.*, p. 322.
195 *Op. cit.*, I, 2.
196 Xenophon: *Cyropaedia*, I, 1, 6; 2, 1–2.
197 *Ibid.*, I, 2, 3.
198 Cf. Spartan system, *supra*, p. 243, and Aristotle's freeman's agora.—*Politica*, VII, 12.

are being instructed. In it there are four divisions, one for boys, one for youths, another for those of maturity, and a fourth for men beyond military service. Here the youths, save those who are married, spend the night in light armor. All, youth and men, must be there every day. Each division has twelve officers, corresponding to the number of tribes, the men selected being those who are thought best capable of cultivating the highest virtues in the several age groups.

Under such schoolmasters, "the boys attending the public schools, pass their time in learning justice. . . ." [199] Letters and music, in which Xenophon had himself been trained, seem to be of no moment in his ideal education. The day is spent chiefly in deciding cases, disputes, and accusations among the youth, and fixing punishments, so that they may know what is right and what wrong. The boys learn self-control by seeing their elders practice it; obedience by observing that of their own officers to those who are superior to them; temperate living by not eating with mothers, but with teachers, and having little to eat—bread, cress, and river water forming their diet. With this training in temperance, obedience, and justice is combined shooting and hurling the spear, until they are sixteen or seventeen, at which time they are enrolled among the young men.

After being promoted, these youths spend the nights doing guard duty for ten years; during the day they are at the command of the authorities for any service to the state. Several times a month half of this youthful garrison, armed with bows, arrows, sabre, light shield, and two spears, is taken hunting by the king. The expense of these expeditions is borne by the government, since hunting is the best training for war, accustoming the men to early rising, fatiguing journeys, endurance of hunger, cold, and heat, courageous facing of hazards, and the use of weapons. Those left at home, for the time being, perform service for the government, and devote themselves to practicing those exercises they have begun as boys and engaging in competitive contests. Prizes are given to the victors; but honors are bestowed also on the officers in charge of them and on those who previously taught them as boys.[200]

When ten years have thus passed, youths are promoted to the ranks of mature men, where they serve for twenty-five years. These perform services for the government, some acting as magistrates at home; and when necessary, they take the field, armed with corselet, a round shield, and sabre. At the end of this service, being a little over fifty years of age, they become "elders," elect all officers, and administer justice.[201]

Such is the "Persian" system, described by Xenophon. Into it may enter the sons of all the Persians who can afford to have them educated. Hence it is

[199] Xenophon: Cyropaedia, I, 2, 6.
[200] Ibid., I, 2, 10–2.
[201] Ibid., I, 2, 13–4.

a system for those who have wealth, presumably only for the nobility; it is the only path by which one may rise to positions of trust and distinction. Commoners, it seems, are trained as common soldiers, targeteers, bowmen, slingers.[202] Pheraulas speaks of the training of commoners "to walk and run under heavy burdens"—a training of endurance, hunger, and thirst so severe that the weight of arms borne later is like the "lightness of wings. . . ."[203]

Xenophon's ideal prince, of course, had a broader experience than that provided by these schools of justice, for he went to visit the court of his grandfather, Astyages, ruler of the Medes. There he saw manners and morals less primitive, less severe and exemplary, he thought, than those he had known at home. After a few years, during which he learned to ride and helped his grandfather win a battle with the Assyrians, he was recalled to Persia by his father to complete the regular curriculum of Persian boys. In this course he excelled all others; when he had completed a year with the boys and ten more with the young men, he was chosen to lead an army of forty thousand into Media to assist his uncle, Cyaxares. Having addressed his chosen men on the excellence of their military training and charged them to employ it now for the end for which it was designed,[204] he personally consulted the gods and omens; for, it seems, his father had also trained him in soothsaying, so that he could not be imposed on by those professing the art.

The rest of Cyrus' education is that of life itself, the life of a leader of soldiers who practices on the field the skills and virtues acquired in training. In lulls before and after battle, he prepares his men and keeps them fit in mind and body by drill, competitive sports, hunting expeditions, and sham battles.[205] The rôle of physical exercise for the soldier is thus described: "Cyrus also took care that they should never go in to their dinner or supper without previous exercise; for he either led them out to hunt, and gave them exercise in that way, or contrived such sports for them as would make them exert themselves; or, if he happened to want anything done, he so managed it, that they should not return without hard exercise; for this he judged to be of service, in order to make them eat with pleasure, and to render them healthy and able to undergo labour; and labour he judged to be of use in making them more gentle one towards another, because even horses, that labour jointly together, stand likewise more contentedly together. And certainly with regard to facing the enemy, those who are conscious of having duly exercised themselves, are inspired with more boldness."[206]

202 Ibid., I, 5, 5; II, 1, 16.
203 Ibid., II, 3, 14.
204 Ibid., I, 5, 7–14.
205 Ibid., II, 1, 20–2, 29; 3, 17–21.
206 Ibid., II, 1, 29. From Xenophon's Cyropaedia, or Institution of Cyrus, and The Hellenics. Trans. by J. S. Watson and H. Dale. George Bell & Sons, London, 1891.

Xenophon's references to hunting are numerous. He contrasts the good it produces in men with the evil that comes from the sophists—an inferior sort of huntsmen who hunt money and young men and make them worthless.[207] The

RABBIT HUNTERS
(From Paul Monroe's slide collection)

*Cynegeticus*, a treatise on hunting, whose authorship has been disputed, but was credited by Plutarch, Arrian, and other ancients to Xenophon,[208] ascribes the origin of the sport to the gods who gave it to men; and all men, from mythical followers of the chase to Xenophon's day, who received this good gift and made use of it, turned out to be the best men, most useful to their country.[209] The gift of prowess in hunting seems to be the chief determiner of excellence. Even a few women in mythical times, such as Atalanta and Procris, were good, for they derived this excellent boon from Artemis.[210] Therefore Xenophon charges the young not to despise hunting. It is "the first pursuit" a young man just out of boyhood should take up.[211] Ten books of this treatise are given over to a practical, masterly, detailed description of the nets, weapons, and dogs that are necessary and best for hunting hare, deer, fawn, and wild boar.

Xenophon's philosophy of hunting is expounded at some length. Its chief advantages are that it gives health to the body, sharpens vision and hearing, keeps men young, and is the best military training. Hunters will not be wearied

---

[207] *Ibid.*, II, 4, 19–21; VIII, 1, 34; Xenophon: *On Hunting*, XIII, 1–2, 9.
[208] Marchant: *Xenophon Scripta Minora*, p. xliii; Wright: *op. cit.*, p. 323.
[209] Xenophon: *On Hunting*, I, 1–5.
[210] *Ibid.*, XIII, 18.
[211] *Ibid.*, II, 1.

by marches over rough terrain, since they have been inured to the labor of carrying weapons on long tramps in the chase. They can sleep on hard beds, take orders and fulfill commands, and they will be forward in attacking enemies, for all these they have done in hunting. Endurance, sureness of foot, ingenuity in tight situations, and confidence will be theirs; a small band of huntsmen-fighters may even be able on occasion to save the day already lost by larger forces. For soundness of body and of mind are the first steps toward success. Because they knew what hunting would give to their young men, Xenophon says, the ancients would neither prohibit the chase even over fields of growing grain, nor allow night-hunting for some distance around the city which would seriously limit the amount of game. In short, they recognized that sobriety and uprightness were more to be derived from hunting than from any other pursuit to which youth are inclined. If the objection is raised that by giving themselves to hunting, men will be kept from other legitimate pursuits, Xenophon demurs: the best men in private, domestic affairs are those who first fit themselves for service to their city; and if hunting gives the best training for public service, providing good generals and good soldiers, it is also the best for private life.[212]

Xenophon's preference for the discipline of the past and the virtues of the gentleman farmer, huntsman, and horseman, which he sets over against the intellectual learning offered by teachers of the new day, is also given full rein in his treatises On the Art of Horsemanship, The Cavalry Commander, and the Oeconomicus. The Oeconomicus, treating of the management of an estate, portrays Xenophon's ideal home of the country squire, his virtues and those of his wife. Here again one meets the views found in Aristotle and elsewhere, derived from the ancient, aristocratic tradition of the Eupatrids of early Attica, that agriculture is the noblest occupation for freemen, fit even for a gentleman, while the crafts are not. It is pleasant and profitable for those who understand it; it teaches good nature and good manners. It makes men more valorous and produces the best citizens.[213] It is significant that the name Ischomachos, which Xenophon gives to his gentleman farmer, means "great fighter." Although praise is showered on the nobility of agriculture, Ischomachus seems to get his exercise from going to and from the town, overseeing and directing the work of the farm, making suggestions for improvement where he can, while the work is done by paid men or servants. For recreation, after this business, he mounts his horse and goes through exercises imitating as nearly as possible those "needed in warfare," avoiding "neither slope nor steep incline, ditch nor watercourse," but taking care not to lame the horse. And Xenophon adds, with

212 Ibid., XII, 1–19.
213 Xenophon: Oeconomicus, VI, 10; XV–XVI.

his usual emphasis on the virtue of meager fare, that luncheon is "just enough to get through the day neither empty-bellied nor too full." [214] For the wife of this pattern of agricultural, military, and gastronomic perfection, who is taught by her husband, there is nothing in life but the inside of a house with her man; she prays to the gods that she may learn from her teacher, make herself better than a slave, know what pertains to her proper sphere, be obedient and discreet,[215] teach and superintend the servants, and direct the making of clothes and the preparation of food. Xenophon reads sermons in pans; with truly religious devotion he bows before the troops of pots which, like choric dancers, take their proper place around the altar.[216] Small wonder that he thinks the little lady will have no time for trying to make herself taller or rosier, and will have no need for physical culture other than what she gets from making her rounds of inspection, mixing dough, and folding clothes.[217]

In the Art of Horsemanship, which, like some of his other works, may have been written as a guide for his sons,[218] Xenophon deals with the qualities to look for in a horse, when to put him out to be broken, how to feed, clean, saddle, bridle, and mount him, and the best kind of ground for the stable yard. Moreover, he discusses the best exercises to perform on horseback, and how the horseman is to be armed—for the treatise is based on the assumption that the horse is to be bought and trained for war.

The Cavalry Commander,[219] written when war was anticipated between Athens and Thebes (c. 365 B.C.), treats of the religious duties of the leader of cavalry, for none can succeed unless he "work with God." The qualities and training of the cavalry commander, how he should drill the young men under him,[220] the feeding and training of horses, the standards that ought to obtain in those approved for service by the Council, and the public exhibitions of the cavalry on festal occasions for the purpose of pleasing and impressing the spectators, are set forth in considerable detail. If any leader wonders how he may best secure the loyalty of his men, Xenophon gives good advice, saying that one must show "himself more capable than they of doing whatever he requires of them." [221] Those who may feel that this is a difficult and endless training are reminded that it is less severe than that undergone by those who wish victory in a gymnastic contest; and the victories to which it leads are eminently "more glorious" and profitable than victory in a boxing match, since the gods

---

[214] Ibid., XI, 17–8; Memorabilia, III, 14.
[215] Oeconomicus, VII, 22 et seq.; X, 1.
[216] Ibid., VIII, 20.
[217] Ibid., X, 2, 10–1.
[218] Marchant: op. cit., p. ix.
[219] Op. cit., IX, 8–9.
[220] Ibid., I, 17–20.
[221] Ibid., VI, 4–6.

crown such triumphs with the happiness of states. Hence Xenophon does not think that "any art should be more assiduously cultivated" than those pertaining to war. One must either work for a living or get it from those who do. Xenophon never hesitates to cast his vote for those who by "a long apprenticeship" enable themselves "to live at the expense of much stronger folk." [222]

Since the goal of so much educational thought from Socrates to Aristotle was fitness for war, the question naturally arises whether the views of the Socratic school had any effect on military training at Athens. As definite propaganda for a better cavalry, it has been suggested that Xenophon's treatise may have been influential; in any case, Athenian cavalry gave a better account of itself at Mantinea a few years later.[223] Moreover, since systematic military training of youth from eighteen to twenty had probably not yet been generally provided for by the government in Plato's day, but was being maintained at public cost by 334 B.C. (only shortly after his death), some powerful influences must have been at work in the meantime to effect the change. Among the intellectual forces that may have been effective, those of the Socratic group were conspicuous, and the present view of the most competent authorities is that the Ephebic College was the offspring of the Socratic school, particularly of Plato's Laws.[224]

---

222 *Ibid.*, VIII, 7–8. Xenophon: *Scripta Minora*, trans. by E. C. Marchant. The Loeb Classical Library. Quoted by permission of Harvard University Press, Cambridge, Mass.
223 Marchant: *op. cit.*, p. xxix.
224 *Supra*, p. 317; Wilamowitz-Moellendorff: *Aristoteles und Athen*, I, 194; Forbes: *Greek Physical Education*, pp. 104 f.

# 15

# RETROSPECT

Life and culture varied much in Greek states. On the northern frontier, Thessaly, a tightly landlocked state, was noted in peace for the produce of her fertile farms, in war for famous cavalry, rather than for mental and physical culture or for victories in the games. Thebes was renowned for wrestling, which was said to have brought her victory in battle, as she was for the odes of her poetic son, but the fame of Pindar is doubtless more permanent than that of the wrestler or even that of the warrior Epaminondas. Sparta, it has been observed, became a byword for military strength and unchanging institutions. Athens' greatest achievement lay in the many-sidedness, breadth, and depth of her culture, which, in many respects unmatched by that of predecessors and contemporaries, was to provide a powerful intellectual, aesthetic, and moral stimulus in centuries to come.

Educational development at Athens, considered socially and individually, mentally and physically, was a most important event in Greek history—indeed, in world history. Something like an Athenian type of education did, in fact, hold true in other Hellenic states, excepting notably Crete and Sparta,[1] there being generally some provision for music, letters, and gymnastic. But Athens alone, preserving a marked degree of balance between the intellectual and physical, was to become the School of Hellas, the School of Rome, and, in our own era, the University of Mankind. After the subsidence of the Athenian cult of physical and mental excellence, during a thousand years of ascetic, religious disapproval, it bloomed again like a hardy millennial in western Europe when humanists discovered that for which they were groping in Athenian thought and practice, laboriously drawn up out of a long-neglected past and exhibited by Erasmus, Ascham, Elyot, and a host of others. The conception of what properly belonged to the culture of mind and of body was, for centuries thereafter, little more than a variation upon the Athenian theme. And that ideal

[1] Freeman: *Schools of Hellas*, pp. 76 f.

466

lives to-day, though certain significant modifications have been made in its implications, owing to an extensive development of science and the advent of social and political conditions that the Greeks never knew or fancied.

Athenian ideals and attainments in physical culture form an impressive chapter of the past, a past which is, for all its antiquity, a living presence. These were significant not only in themselves, but for their bearing on the aesthetic achievements of Athens. The excellence of her art is said to be traceable to a long-continued, ubiquitous association with the living model. This, though important, was not the sole determiner. Though Spartans, according to tradition, first stripped the body for physical contests, the innovation wrought no aesthetic magic. Other factors at Athens—a difference in genius, in temper, a larger enjoyment of life, and a broader, more flexible ideal, flourishing under the greater freedom of cultural and political institutions—combined to school the masters and their men who were to give concrete embodiment to the Greek ideal of beauty. Some who have studied the art of the great temple in honor of Zeus at Olympia, where the greatest of all national festivals was held, have been at pains to explain why artistic execution at the most sacred shrine of the Greeks not only did not excel but did not equal that of the structures and adornments which commemorate in the Parthenon the greatest festival of Athens. Gardner says of the Olympian remains: "Indeed, an ordinary student of art will find, in an hour's study of these figures, faults which in our day an inferior sculptor would not commit. And, what is still worse to a modern eye, the figures are not only faulty, but often displeasing, and the heads have a heaviness which sometimes seems to amount to brutality, and are repellent, if not absolutely repulsive. . . . In fact, the composition as well as the execution is of provincial character. . . . The clearest result . . . is the perception how far Pheidias was in advance of his predecessors in the construction of groups and in all qualities of design, and how superior were the Athenian stonecutters in knowledge of their craft to those of other parts of Greece." [2]

But, though her intellectual and artistic attainments made all the world her debtor, Athens suffered a political fate which differed little in the last analysis from that of her sister states. Neither physical fitness nor intellectual, aesthetic, and political qualities, cultivated in palaestras, gymnasia, and in the school of life, which Pericles so much extolled, were competent to preserve her. If her appearance on the horizon of political greatness was meteoric, her decline was also swift. Unification within her borders was accomplished more successfully than in other states. Economic, social, and political readjustments during a century and a half increased her integrity and promised greater stability. After Plataea it seemed that she was destined to take the next step, bringing the

---

[2] Gardner: *New Chapters in Greek History*, pp. 280 f.

Greek states together in a national union. Her maritime position invited to empire; and her leadership in the war not only impressed others but gave Athens herself a conscious pride, confidence, and ambition for achievement transcending anything she had known before. Pindar, a Theban, might with justice sing the praises of a—

> Mighty city, her brow wreathed with violets, glorious Athens,
> rampart of Greece, city illustrious, truly divine.

But "great evils" were in store for Athens and the rest of Greece. For though she had unified her neighbors and had then turned the Confederacy of Delos into a limited Athenian Empire (but not without arousing enmity and suspicion),[3] she was not able to bring Sparta and Corinth and their adherents into unity with her, nor could she subject their interests to her own. From 460 to 404 B.C., save for an interval of thirteen years, Athens sought by force and by cunning to maintain her empire. Pericles attempted to bring about an association of the Greek states under Attic leadership about 448 B.C., which, had it succeeded, would have translated the temporary, fitful coöperation of the years of common danger in the Great War with Persia into a settled, permanent arrangement. The Congress of the Greeks was to decide about restoring the sacred precincts violated by the Persians, pay united homage to the gods, and fix upon ways and means for security on the sea.[4] All Greek cities, so the persuasive Delphic oracle ran, were to send their first fruits to Eleusis, and Athens was to make sacrifices to Demeter for all the Greeks. But Periclean magic did not work. The strength, pride, jealousy, and independence of Greek cities made national union impossible, as it had done before and would continue to do. It was in some respects, indeed, "a sublime project" and "truly liberal," but its sublimity was limited by a selfishness which other Greek cities well knew and feared.[5] Those who had seen how Athens used her headship of the Delian League would hesitate to join an imperial league which was to preserve the status quo. From this solemn failure Athens went on within a few years to wage a great and, it seems, unnecessary war—hoping to maintain her privileged, profitable position by force against the will of Corinth, Aegina, Sparta, and other cities—from which she would emerge in a state of ruin. Truly, as the departing Spartan ambassador said that day was ". . . to the Heilenes the beginning of great sorrows." [6]

Economic rivalry was fundamentally involved in this failure of integration,

---

[3] Plutarch: *Pericles*, 12.
[4] *Ibid.*, 17.
[5] Jardé: *The Formation of the Greek People*, pp. 283, 287 f.; Bury: *A History of Greece*, pp. 366 f.; Laistner: *A Survey of Ancient History*, pp. 250 f.
[6] Thucydides, II, 12.

though other sources supplied fuel to the conflagration that swept the Greek cities. For, as Athens gained supremacy after the Persian Wars, she pinched Aegina and Megara, and her lengthening shadow fell athwart the path of interest of neighboring Corinth, likewise favorably situated for commercial expansion overseas. At the beginning of the Peloponnesian War, Corinth was the leading spirit in uniting other malcontents—Aegina, Megara, Sparta—against her Athenian competitor. Jardé concludes, after a careful survey, that Athens could have avoided war "if she had not made Corinth uneasy by her policy of expansion." [7] The prophecy credited to Solon, "Never by doom of Zeus or will of the blessed gods shall our city be destroyed . . . but by the citizens themselves . . . devoting themselves to wealth, . . ." was to have a belated and perhaps unexpected manner of fulfillment. Intelligence had proved unequal to the task of discriminating between true and apparent interest, between greater interest and a lesser one. So passion reigned in place of reason and made its intoxicating appeal to the "law of nature." For nearly thirty years the pestles of war pulverized the cities of Greece. Aristophanes portrays the enthusiasm with which the commoners anticipate release from war's heavy burdens, planning a holiday with boxing, wrestling, pancration, races, tricks, and games of every kind.[8] But the Peace of Nicias (421 B.C.), which was to last for fifty years, lasted scarcely two.

When at length the Peloponnesian War ended, Athens and other cities knew impoverishment and destruction from which they never recovered. The population of Attica never regained the level (about 315,000) it is believed to have reached about 431 B.C. Depopulation became acute in the late third century and continued to the time of Augustus.[9] Polybius declared, in the second century, that towns were deserted, the country barren. Strabo said, a century later, that Thebes was scarcely a village even, and most cities of Boeotia were in a similar condition. Messenia was largely deserted; Laconia, too, had a small population and only about thirty towns, in sharp contrast with earlier centuries.[10] Wars and general uncertainty were neither conducive to population increase nor to prosperity. There were times of some prosperity, to be sure, and certain personal fortunes might flourish, but Athens, though she was the cultural center of the world, was sometimes said to be a " 'hungry' city, living on good air and hopes." [11]

Notwithstanding remarkable achievements, there were also notable failures on the part of the Greeks. They could, on occasion, put to death or drive out

[7] Op. cit., p. 311.
[8] The Peace, 894–904.
[9] Rostovtzeff: Social and Economic History of the Hellenistic World, I, 95 f.; II, 1135 f.; III, 1329, 1604 f.
[10] The Geography of Strabo, VIII, 4, 11; IX, 2, 5.
[11] Rostovtzeff: op. cit., II, 628 ff.; III, 1354.

their wisest and best, as the fate of Socrates and the banishment of Aristides show.[12] Too often the worse triumphed over the better. Deep-rooted, fatalistic distrust and fear of too great superiority or success are revealed in the old saying: "Let no man fly to Olympus, nor try to marry Aphrodite."

The greatest of all failures, shared by other Greek cities as well as Athens, was the inability to find the next step in political integration, which would have transcended the limits of the city-state. Unification of Attica under Athens was effected, and a world of commerce, colonies, and wealth of varied character lay at her feet. Attic Greek spread and replaced Ionic as a common language.[13] A marked degree of cultural unity began to appear in Greek cities. Isocrates declared that "Hellenes" meant "no longer a race but an intelligence," and indicated those possessed of a common culture rather than a "common blood." [14] In centuries to come, this Hellenic culture would leave its impress in distant countries on schools, gymnasia, clubs, and other aspects and agencies of social life.[15] But Athens never gained a clear vision of national unity, save on a selfish, imperialistic pattern. Nor was the intellectual groundwork laid for such a union. Plato and Aristotle sought indeed a more perfect integrity and stability, based on a rational plan; but they envisaged only a better small city, and even their ideal city-states were divided within themselves. The Greek world and subsequent ages as well suffered heavily for the failure of Athenian leadership to heed sufficiently the sinister warning:

Cruel are the wars of brethren.

Euripides might have faith in the power of words to—

. . . do what e'er is done by conquering swords,

but Athens, like other Greek cities, continued to put her trust in hoplites and horses. It has been remarked how much the world gained when the Athenians banished a general and made a historian. More such translations might have profited both Athens and the rest of the world. The stress on the military aspects of education, proposed in the ideal commonwealths of Plato and Aristotle, not to mention Xenophon, in whom one scarcely expects a vaulting intelligence, shows that the greatest minds had by no means escaped from the realm where reigns the "law of nature" and the strong triumph over the weak.

The cynic indeed dreamed of being a citizen of the world and living a life of reason, but return to nature, denial of one's own city, renunciation of pleas-

[12] Plutarch: Aristides, 7.
[13] Jardé: op. cit., pp. 233 f.; Laistner: op. cit., pp. 357 f.
[14] Panegyricus, 50.
[15] Supra, pp. 326 f., 329.

THE HORSE RACE  *vase painting, 5th century* B.C.
Museum of Ancient Minor Arts, Munich (Courtesy, The Metropolitan Museum of Art, New York)

ure, a beggar's wallet and a beggar's bed were, to say the least, hard conditions, save, perhaps, for the poor, the foreigner, the outcast, and the slave. Few would choose that road voluntarily. Zeno, founder of Stoicism, conceived of an integrated world community, having a common life and government.[16] But to most of the Hellenistic world some sort of speedy deliverance through faith would make a stronger appeal than self-denial or the long, hard path offered by systematic, rational reconstruction. Such a faith, assuaging the pains of reality, a religion was to offer, when Athens, Sparta, Macedon, and Rome had failed to provide peace, plenty, security and, in general, a normal functioning for the whole man.

Democritus is said to have been "concerned at heart," for, with the greatest pains, his fund of insight into nature's kingdom was still so small. If, in his realm of study, there were grounds for the dictum, "Truth dwelleth in the deep," and the observation that "reality is shut out from human ken," how much more might Athenian statesmen and educational leaders have recognized their inability to give adequate account of the vast area of individual and collective conduct? Some have held that progress of the critical philosophy went too far, and had much to do with, or was even chiefly responsible for, the disintegration of Athenian life. A clearer understanding of the nature of the social life cycle and a better knowledge of the rôle that intelligence, or lack of it, might play in social integration and disintegration would enable us to see that the critical spirit was neither too profoundly nor too generally encouraged and developed. The intellectual insights in the politico-educational domain, even had they been applied, were too meager, not too great; and even the greatest were not always wise enough, as were Democritus and Socrates, to know that they did not know. Falling short of reality, they dogmatized about the nature of man and his society, taking shapes and shadows for truth itself. The unfin-

---

[16] Plutarch: *On the Fortune of Alexander*, 6.

ished task of Athenian intellectuals is in no small degree still before us; for we have neither learned how to educate free men nor how to build them a city, a state, a world, in which their whole being may know the "good" life, and the fruits of mind and body be husbanded for themselves and for their posterity.

# 4

## EMPIRE OF THE EAST AND WEST

---

Some races wax, others wane; in brief space the tribes of men change, and, like relays of runners, pass from hand to hand the torch of life.     LUCRETIUS

# 16

# PRE-ROMAN FOUNDATIONS

O f the waxing and waning of Rome's culture there are many stories. Romans themselves saw various types of history come and go: the thin, dry chronicle of Quintus Fabius Pictor; the rhetorical, uncritical *Annales*, composed by Gnaeus Gellius; the critical history of Polybius, preoccupied with proportion, continuity, cause, and effect; the monument that Livy reared, to tell the grandeur of Rome's past; and the history of Orosius, written in the dolorous days of a dying Empire, to prove pagan errors and Christian rectitude.

Livy casts doubt upon Rome's early history: her founding is an obscure story because of "great antiquity," rarity of early writing, and the destruction of records. The early traditions, "suitable rather to the fictions of poetry than to the genuine records of history," he neither affirms nor denies. He does relate them, however; Romans, if any people, should be permitted to blend things human and divine; others may accept the tale of Rome's descent from Mars, just as they submit to her sovereignty. Of a later time (322 B.C.) Livy says frankly, as does Cicero, it is impossible to know the false from true, since families have corrupted records to make sure their fame.[1] Despite this uncertainty, traditional history, as received from Livy "who never lieth," Diodorus, Dio Cassius, and others, was seldom questioned before the seventeenth century. Since then, the tendency to doubt, encouraged by Beaufort, Niebuhr, Mommsen, and others, has reduced the old tradition to "ruins." [2] Under such a cloud of doubt, one would be inclined to follow Dante's injunction, "Abandon every hope, ye who enter," were it not that amid the "ruins" of an old tradition painstaking hands have reared a more substantial structure.

---

[1] Livy, I, preface; VI, 1; VIII, 40; Cicero: *Brutus*, 16.
[2] Homo: *Primitive Italy and the Beginnings of Roman Imperialism*, p. 2; Duff: *A Literary History of Rome*, p. 645.

That Italy became the seat of empire, and Rome first made East and West the limits of her sway [3] depended in no slight degree on geographical position. Strabo observed her "insular" location, "securely guarded" by the sea; her northern boundary, "fortified by almost impassable mountains"; her harbors "few," but "capacious and admirably situated," offering opportunity for operations, defensive and offensive, and the "reception of abundant merchandise." [4] Just as Italy occupied the strategic center of the Mediterranean, Rome, athwart the Tiber, a scant score of miles inland, had ready access to the best port, Ostia, and commanded the natural highway to the heart of Italy. Livy noted especially this central location, "singularly adapted by nature for the increase of a city"; and the "commodious river," bringing inland products to the sea and commerce from abroad, yet unpropitious to attack by foreign fleets.[5]

Stretching with Sicily across the center of the landlocked sea, Italy enjoyed a varied climate. The Apennines gave rise to numerous lakes and streams; foothills and plains invited tillage of the soil, promising food for man and beast. Melting Alpine snows fed steadier streams and made the Po valley the richest of all Italy. Italians seemed destined by geography and climate to be herdsmen and husbandmen, and such they were till lure of conquest beckoned beyond the sea. Cato, Varro, Columella, Strabo, and Pliny portray a many-sided culture of field and garden crops and the breeding of beasts and fowls. Wheat, grapes, olives—major sources of agricultural wealth—were supplemented by flax, hemp, alfalfa, vetch, farrago of barley, oats, fenugreek, bitter vetch, chickling vetch, clover, lupines, beans, lentils, chick-peas, cress, rue, asparagus, onions, scallions, turnips, garlic, leeks, allheal, elecampane, cucumbers, gourds, caper, beets, parsley, skirret, radish, lettuce, dill, mustard, cabbage, parsnips, artichokes, sorghum, figs, quinces, jujubes, apples, peaches, plums, pears, apricots, sorb apples, and cherries. Walnuts, chestnuts, almonds, and pine-cone seeds were also used for food. Cows, sheep, goats, and pigs provided food and clothing. Horses were bred for the army, the road, and the circus. Donkeys, mules, and oxen were the usual draft animals on the farm. The culture of bees and birds of many kinds was extensively developed to supply the table.[6] Fish of many kinds, salt, sponges, and shellfish—source of purple dyes—were taken from the encircling sea.

Many of Italy's products were introduced from abroad when Rome became mistress of the Mediterranean. Sorghum came from India; peaches from Persia; and cherries from Pontus. Olives were known to Columella in ten varieties. Pliny judged Italy first in olive culture, the Licinian being best. Though citrus

---

[3] Dionysius of Halicarnassus, The Roman Antiquities of, i, 3.
[4] The Geography of Strabo, vi, 4, 1.
[5] Bk. v, 54.
[6] Frank: An Economic Survey of Ancient Rome, v, 138–68.

fruit was yet unknown, Columella [7] says that Italy learned to raise the fruits of almost all the world.

In respect to subterranean wealth, Italy's advantages were less marked, but the island of Elba had iron ore which was turned into iron objects of all sorts. Strabo says that ore was brought to the mainland for processing. Copper came from Campania and elsewhere.[8] Extensive manufacture of bronze articles had developed by the last century of the pagan era.

### PRIMITIVE AND ETRUSCAN CULTURES

The people who mastered Italy were a mixture of diverse stocks; their culture, the result of a fusion which had been going on for several millennia. Paleolithic man, hunter and fisher, lived almost wholly in caves, perhaps about 10,000 B.C. He flaked stone for implements, and used horn, bone, and possibly wood and leather. His food, clothing, and ornaments came from wild animals; agriculture, domestic animals, and even crude pottery were to him unknown. Neolithic culture in Italy dawned slowly, bringing polished stone tools and weapons, a sewing needle, crude dark pottery, and a few domestic animals. Round or oval huts, with a central basin to catch rain, became common, though cave-dwelling continued.[9] The men who made this culture have been called "Ligurians," since they survived in that area to historic times. These "Mediterraneans," precursors of the Indo-Europeans, were dark and short of stature. They probably knew no social unit beyond the family. They inhumed their dead. At the end of the fourth millennium B.C., they were still hunters and herders, probably unacquainted with agriculture, without metal implements, ignorant of writing and the use of sailing ships for commerce.[10]

Copper gradually supplemented stone implements in the third millennium. Hard upon it came the age of bronze. Indo-European infiltrations, probably from the Danube area in the third and second millennia, built "pile-dwellings" on northern lake margins and the "Terremare" settlements in the Adige and Po valleys. By the end of the second millennium their culture was spread over most of Italy. These invaders practiced cremation, used bronze and the potter's wheel, tended crops, built compact villages, and apparently assimilated the conquered natives, judging from the mixture of Aryan and non-Aryan linguistic elements, diverse marriage rites, and mortuary customs.[11]

The Villanovan "iron-age" culture, result either of another infiltration or

---

[7] Of Husbandry, III, 8; v, 8; Pliny: Natural History, xv, 3; Gibbon: The Decline and Fall of the Roman Empire, I, 103.
[8] Strabo, v, 2, 6; Diodorus of Sicily, v, 13; Pliny: Natural History, xxxiv, 2.
[9] Peet: The Stone and Bronze Ages in Italy and Sicily, pp. 37 ff., 88 ff.
[10] Homo: op. cit., pp. 25 ff., 68; Peet: op. cit., p. 109; Frank: Roman Imperialism, p. 1; Sandys: Companion to Latin Studies, p. 27.
[11] Peet: op. cit., pp. 283, 320 f., 362, 510; Sandys: op. cit., p. 31.

fusion of "Terremare" and "Ligurian" peoples, arose probably about the eleventh or tenth century, and continued to the close of the sixth, giving way before the Etruscans in the late ninth. Differing little from their precursors, save in the extensive use of iron and a less concentrated village community, the Villanovans left their impress on the shores of lakes in Tuscany, in the Alban hills, and in "Rome itself." [12]

Etruscan origins were disputed in ancient times. Herodotus told of an exodus from Lydia, under Tyrrhenus, across the sea to the Umbrians. Dionysius discounted the Herodotean account, however, because of marked differences between Etruscan and Lydian tongues, customs, and institutions, and held to an Italic origin.[13] Neither the Asiatic nor the Italic theory has been proved. The dispute fluctuates between these poles to this day. Niebuhr opposed the Asiatic thesis and suggested a Danubian origin, to which Mommsen also subscribed.[14] This view, further developed by Helbig, regarded Etruscan as an outgrowth of the earlier Terremare and Villanovan cultures. Recently the Asiatic theory has swung into favor, partly on the ground that Etruscan luxury, architecture, tombs, metallurgic skill, use of matronymics, divination, physiognomy, dress, and other traits point to Eastern kinship rather than to a slow evolution from Italian and Danubian sources. While final solution must wait upon decipherment of Etruscan inscriptions or additional archeological evidence, it seems probable that Etruscan culture was a hybrid, produced by the mingling of Terremare and Villanovan elements with infiltrations from Asia Minor or other Eastern centers.[15]

The time of these Eastern infiltrations has been assigned variously from the eleventh century to the ninth. After some two centuries or more, the Etruscans invaded Latium in the seventh century; their kings—Tarquin the Elder, Servius Tullius, Tarquin the Proud—made Rome their seat of Empire. From Latium they pressed into Campania, founded Capua, Nola, and other smaller cities. In the late sixth century Etruscan power expanded northward into the Po valley and along the Adriatic coast, north and south of the Po delta.[16]

Dionysius says that Latins, Umbrians, and others in Italy were once all called Etruscans by the Greeks, and Rome an Etruscan city. Their power, famed from the Alps to the Sicilian straits, reached its height by the end of the sixth

[12] Randall-MacIver: Villanovans and Early Etruscans, pp. 3, 39, 91.

[13] Dionysius, I, 30; The History of Herodotus, I, 94.

[14] Niebuhr: Römische Geschichte, pp. 62 ff.; Weege: Etruskische Malerei, pp. 65 ff.; Mommsen: History of Rome, I, 150 ff.; The Cambridge Ancient History, IV, chap. 12; VII, chap. 12.

[15] Randall-MacIver: Etruscans, pp. 7 f., 105; cf. Cary: History of Rome, p. 22; Fell: Etruria and Rome, pp. 7 f., 18.

[16] Randall-MacIver: Villanovans and Early Etruscans, p. 3; Etruscans, pp. 13 f., 18 ff.; Homo: op. cit., pp. 101, 105 f., 111, 115; Fell: op. cit., p. 22.

century, and crumbled rapidly in the fifth.[17] Etruscan hegemony at Rome was the first step toward Italian unity. Based primarily on superior armed force and aggressive leadership, it was probably to some extent mixed with peaceful penetration. The conquerors established themselves a ruling class, and used the conquered to labor on the land, delve in mines, row galleys, build fortresses, and to serve in war. Failing to assimilate the vanquished, they prepared the way for revolt against their sway.[18]

Progressive weakening of Etruscan power—reflected in the revolt of Latium at the end of the sixth century, the loss of Campania, the Po region and, finally, Southern Etruria—was probably due to a decline of the military spirit that had inspired expansion, the increase of luxury and pleasure, and struggles between the ruling class and subjugated peoples. Of crucial importance was the failure to develop a larger political unity which might call individual cities to each other's defense. The federation of twelve cities had primarily a religious significance. United action, or even assistance by a powerful neighbor, Caere, might have saved Veii (396 B.C.). Failure to learn union was suicidal; politically incompetent to take the next step, Etruria bowed to Roman rule.[19]

### ETRUSCAN INFLUENCE ON ROMAN CULTURE

In many ways Etruria's culture influenced Roman development. The superior Etruscan military pattern seems to have served the Romans as a model.[20] City-building was given a powerful impetus. Latium, occupied by nomadic, pastoral folk, who knew nothing but tribal villages at the Etruscan invasion, had learned consolidation into cities by the end of Etruscan sway. Even the scattered settlements on the Seven Hills may have been first welded into a city by Etruscan leadership. In any case, Rome's hegemony had been established under Tarquin the Proud before he was driven out by the Latin revolt.[21] Inside the rising cities, a busy life went on. Rome became a walled city; the Cloaca Maxima was made the outlet for a system of drainage; the port at Ostia, Rome's exit to the sea, was improved. Stone replaced wood in building and fortification. Mines were exploited; metallurgy was highly developed. Etruscans wrought both bronze and iron more extensively and skillfully than had the

---

[17] Dionysius, I, 29; Livy, I, 2; Randall-MacIver: Etruscans, p. 5.
[18] Homo: op. cit., pp. 42 f., 61, 100, 115; Fell: op. cit., pp. 23, 25 f.
[19] Randall-MacIver: Etruscans, pp. 147 ff.; Fell: op. cit., pp. 131 f., 135 ff., 168 f., 172, 174; Homo: op. cit., pp. 153 f., 159 f.
[20] Randall-MacIver: Etruscans, p. 20; Homo: op. cit., p. 61; Fell: op. cit., pp. 23 ff.; infra, p. 493.
[21] Frank: History of Rome, pp. 14 ff., 26; Homo: op. cit., pp. 112 ff.; Cary: op. cit., pp. 23, 38 f.

Villanovans. Outside the cities, too, industrious effort drained the marshes and facilitated the transition from pastoral to agricultural pursuits.[22]

Wide differences of opinion exist as to the creative capacity of the Etruscans. One authority holds that, for all their "great ability," they were "fundamentally lacking in initiative." [23] Another calls Etruscan rock-tomb frescoes only "indifferent imitations of Greek painting"; in stone sculpture, too, he says, they had no hope of "attaining the proficiency of the Greeks." [24] Randall-MacIver considers it essential to recognize two phases of development: first, "a long and important" one, in which the outside influence exerted on the Etruscans was not Greek but "near-Asiatic"; and a second period, from the sixth century onward, when Hellenic influence was obviously of great moment, and Athenian pottery and probably also artisans came in extensively. Respecting Etruscan and Greek influence on Roman sculpture, he believes, far less was derived from the Greeks than from the Etruscans.[25]

Etruscan use of writing is assigned by some to the late eighth or early seventh century; but the origin of the alphabet and the relationship of the Etruscan tongue are still obscure. The alphabet, by one account, has been commonly traced to the Greek city, Cumae. This Chalcidian alphabet, modified by the Etruscans, left its influence in Latium and elsewhere in Italy and supplanted the parent Greek.[26] Another theory, discounting dependence on the Greeks, holds that the Etruscan alphabet was a "variant" of one "also used by the Greeks," but was brought by the Etruscan invaders "as an already completed and familiar instrument. . . ." [27] The relationship of the Etruscan tongue is more of a problem than the alphabet. Though theories vary, the tendency to-day is to assign its origin to some pre-Hellenic language or languages of Asia Minor, perhaps Lydian, Lycian, Phrygian, Mysian, or Hittite.[28] While it has been inferred that there was little Etruscan literature, the argument ex silentio is unsound. Certain Latin writers do mention Etruscan literature and education. Varro refers to an Etruscan author of tragedy; others speak of songs of wit, raillery, and buffoonery, traced back to Etruscan Fescennium; there is mention of histories and also of certain religious, ritualistic books, written presumably at a late date.[29]

22 Homo: op. cit., pp. 109 f., 113, 117; Fell: op. cit., p. 25.
23 Fell: op. cit., p. 137.
24 Cary: op. cit., p. 19.
25 Randall-MacIver: Etruscans, pp. 103 f., 106 f., 116.
26 Fell: op. cit., pp. 19 f.; Homo: op. cit., p. 37; Cary: op. cit., p. 23.
27 Randall-MacIver: Etruscans, pp. 81, 121 f.; Dennis: Cities and Cemeteries of Etruria, I, xlvi–li; Müller: Die Etrusker, I, Beilage II; II, Beilagen I and II.
28 Randall-MacIver: Etruscans, pp. 120 f.; Homo: op. cit., p. 59.
29 Varro: On the Latin Language, v, 9, 55; Livy, VII, 2; Dionysius, I, 21; Censorini De Die Natali Liber, XVII; Müller: op. cit., II, 293–9; Dennis: op. cit., I, lx–lxi; Randall-MacIver: Etruscans, p. 123; Johnstone: Etruria Past and Present, pp. 176 f.

There are certain fragmentary references to Etruscan education. Livy mentions Marcus Fabius, who had been schooled at Caere and was thoroughly acquainted with the Etruscan tongue; and he adds that, in early times, Roman youth were commonly instructed in the learning of Etruria, as they later were in Greek.[30] The Etruscans, by Livy's account, were greatly devoted to religious ceremonials and excelled in the conduct of them.[31] Etruscan occult wisdom was credited to a marvelous Tages, a child in appearance but an old man in prudence, who, being plowed up by a farmer in Tarquinium, imparted his learning to an assembled crowd, and then died. His teaching, treasured by soothsayers, formed the basis of their science of divination, which, in Cicero's day, existed in many books [32] known as Etrusca disciplina. Religious lore, ritual, and its administration lay in the hands of sacerdotal, patrician families, and was passed on from father to son.[33] Sometimes men of inferior station were instructed in priestly practices, as was Attius Nevius because he had shown unusual promise in divination.[34] Certain noble women also cultivated this mysterious lore, as Livy says of Tanaquil.[35] Under the sway of Rome, a decline occurred, apparently, in the cultivation of occult knowledge in Etruscan families. To prevent its loss, the Roman Senate is said to have decreed that six sons of selected families should be sent to study divination under Etruscan priests.[36] Cicero, recognizing their superiority in such matters, provided in his Laws that "prodigies and portents" should be passed upon by Etruscan diviners "if the Senate so decree," and that Etruria should "instruct her leading men in this art." [37]

The names and functions of many deities suggest Rome's debt to Etruria. From mighty Tinia (Jupiter), who heads the hierarchy, speaks in thunder, and has power to hurl three different bolts of lightning, down to the lowliest deities, a marked parallelism of functions and often of names appears: Uni (Juno), Menvra (Minerva), Nethuns (Neptune). Voltumna and Horta are associated with gardens. A number of kindly gods, the Penates, Fortuna, Ceres, Genius, Jovialis, and Pales rule the flocks and fields and man's own destiny.[38] Certain Roman practices, too, appear to have been derived from Etruscan rites. Mantus, horrible of face, winged, armed with a great hammer and, at times, a sword, carries off the dead to the lower world. Thus he long continued to be depicted, when in Rome slain gladiators were dragged from the arena. Human

[30] Bk. IX, 36.
[31] Ibid., V, 1.
[32] Cicero: On Divination, I, 33; II, 23; Müller: op. cit., II, 23 ff.
[33] Müller: op. cit., II, 3, 299.
[34] Dionysius, III, 70.
[35] Bk. I, 34; Dennis: op. cit., II, 179.
[36] Cicero: On Divination, I, 41.
[37] Op. cit., II, 9.
[38] Müller: op. cit., II, 1–195.

sacrifice seems to have been common in Etruria. To Mania, mother of the dead, boys were sacrificed. It was said that 307 Roman captives were once slaughtered as a sacrifice by the Etruscans. Human sacrifice at Rome is believed to be Etruscan in origin.[39]

The names and functions of many Etruscan and Roman gods suggest either a common origin, extensive borrowing, or both. The strictness of authoritarian, priestly control, the authority of occult books, reliance on divination, indulgence in human sacrifice, and a generally fearful, gloomy outlook suggest a closer relationship with Oriental religions than with Greek. The "practice of divining by the livers of sheep" points directly to Chaldæa. "Models of clay livers from Mesopotamia" correspond "exactly" to the "bronze model of a liver" found at Piacenza.[40] Certain sections of the organ were assigned to the various gods; a diseased part indicated a god's displeasure. Foretelling events by the flight of birds and reading the heavens also formed a part of the priestly craft of ancient Etruria, which was taken over by Roman haruspices.

### ETRUSCAN GAMES

Herodotus informs us that the Lydians claimed to be the inventors of all the games common to them and the Greeks excepting "tables." At the time of a great famine, so the tale ran, they resorted to games to help them endure its hardships, playing on one day continuously, so as not to feel hunger, and eating the next while abstaining from games. "In this way they passed eighteen years," but to no avail.[41] Were one to lend an ear to the story and its sequel—the exodus of Lydians to the Umbrians—the sports of Etruscans, which are so variously depicted in tombs and on ornamental goods, might be regarded simply as the continuation and development of those brought by the invaders from their homeland. But though it may be justifiable to trace many of them to such a source, it must be remembered that Attic influence was strong from the fifth century on, and the Etruscan and Attic elements constantly intermingled.[42]

Knowledge of Etruscan sports comes chiefly from remains found in tumuli, none of which, it is generally believed, antedate 700 B.C. Up to that time, Etruscans buried in trenches; and commoners continued to do so. In the same tumuli some tombs go back to this early date, while others are not older than the fourth century B.C.[43] That which is depicted in tomb paintings and elsewhere is, of course, neither all Etruscan nor does it represent all of Etruscan life. Art in a class society commonly depicts primarily the doings of the master

[39] Livy, VII, 15; Müller: op. cit., II, 20 ff.
[40] Randall-MacIver: Etruscans, p. 125.
[41] Herodotus, I, 94.
[42] Randall-MacIver: Etruscans, pp. 37 f.
[43] Ibid., p. 57.

class; in this case, the sports that amused the aristocratic ruling class while at leisure and those exercises associated with the religious practices of that class are extensively portrayed. Only occasionally are the commoners—the conquered natives—depicted, as in the decorations on a bronze vessel (c. 500 B.C.), which show the returning plowman, a worker dragging a pig, and boar and rabbit huntsmen.[44] The heavy-armed soldiers, too, are probably Italic peoples, who by this time had come to form a great part of Etruscan armies.

The Etruscan aristocracy associated sport with religious and funereal rites, as did the Greeks; Müller [45] is of the opinion, however, that the religious element was even more serious than among the Greeks. The people of Veii were offended at the impiety of a great noble who interrupted the annual games and made off with his slaves—the performers—because of his displeasure at not being chosen chief priest by the twelve states.[46] Games were entered upon with as much concern and precision as the taking of auspices and the making of sacrifices. An omission of games, commission of the slightest error, or a deviation from the traditional order of their performance were such serious matters that repetition from the very beginning was felt to be necessary to make amends.

Music is all but universally associated with religion. Music and musical instruments, which were credited by Herodotus to the Lydians, along with all sorts of games, are commonly featured in Etruscan tombs and mentioned by ancient authors. Artistic remains suggest that the flute, Phrygian double pipes, the syrinx with multiple pipes, and other wind instruments were commonly employed. The lyre is also represented. The Etruscan trumpet, used for war, in processions, and at sacrifices, funerals, and athletic contests, was perhaps even more celebrated, being commonly considered the Etruscans' own invention. Music of the flutes accompanied sacrifices, processions, the festal meal, dancing, and boxing; men beat slaves, bakers kneaded, and huntsmen went on the chase to their music.[47]

Music had a place also in scenic entertainments or plays, and these were joined with religion. Etruscans were famed, apparently, for their ludi scaenici, as they were for occult religious knowledge, both of which were drawn upon by their rude Roman neighbors. Livy asserts that Rome, having been visited by a terrible pestilence, sought to propitiate the gods and sent to Etruria for actors (364 B.C.), who danced to the music of flutes, exhibiting graceful movements in the Tuscan fashion.[48] Thus the histrionic art is said to have been inaugurated

[44] Ibid., p. 21.
[45] Op. cit., II, 197.
[46] Livy, V, 1.
[47] Randall-MacIver: Etruscans, pp. 23 f.; Müller: op. cit., II, 200 ff.
[48] Bk. VII, 2.

at Rome, the term *histriones* itself being derived from *hister* which in the Etruscan tongue corresponded to *ludio* in Latin.

Fighting between armed men was a custom of many early peoples. Athenaeus, for example, cites Poseidonius, who credited it to the Celts; Hermippus, who thought Mantineans invented it; and Ephorus, to the effect that Arcadians and Mantineans practiced it, the latter having instituted "regular courses of instruction in fighting under arms." Cassander is said to have honored royal dead by "a contest of single fighters which was entered by four of his soldiers." [49] Athenaeus thus describes the Celtic custom:

"The Celts sometimes have gladiatorial contests during dinner. Having assembled under arms, they indulge in sham fights and practise feints with one another; sometimes they proceed even to the point of wounding each other, and then, exasperated by this, if the company does not intervene, they go so far as to kill. In ancient times . . . when whole joints of meat were served the best man received the thigh. But if another claimed it, they stood up to fight it out in single combat to the death. Others, again, would collect silver or gold, or a number of jars of wine from the audience in the theatre, and having exacted a pledge that their award would be carried out, they would decree that the collection be distributed as presents to their dearest relatives; they then stretched themselves on their backs over their shields, and someone standing near would cut their throats with a sword." [50]

Such contests among peoples constantly engaged in war are readily understood. There were contests of *hoplomachy* among the Greeks. Contests to the death among medieval European knights had a similar *raison d'être*. War, religious worship, honor to the dead, and the desire to prove one's skill and courage are among the chief elements that provided their sanction. Nowhere in the ancient world, however, were gladiatorial combats so extensively known and so systematically prepared on a grand scale as in Italy.

Gladiatorial combats were commonly thought to be indigenous to Etruria, where they were long fostered by the master class and associated with funerals and other religious rites. Fully armed gladiators are frequently represented on the walls of tombs and on urns; and Müller holds that the use of gladiatorial combats at funerals goes back to Etruscans, or, in any case, such a bloody mode of appeasing the dead must, among a people so long devoted to human sacrifices, have seemed a proper oblation to the Manes.[51]

From Etruria gladiatorial contests spread wherever Tuscan arms prevailed and became common throughout Italy. Athenaeus,[52] following Nicolas of

---

[49] *Athenaeus*, IV, 155.
[50] *Ibid.*, IV, 154. Trans. by C. B. Gulick. The Loeb Classical Library. Quoted by permission of Harvard University Press, Cambridge, Mass.
[51] Müller: *op. cit.*, II, 224; Dennis: *op. cit.*, I, 71; II, 175.
[52] Bk. IV, 153.

Damascus, says that the Romans borrowed from Etruscans the habit of staging shows of fighting men, not only at festivals and theaters, but also at banquets. Moreover, a Tuscan term, *lanista*, continued to be used at Rome to designate the trainer or superintendent of gladiators. Such combats were said to have become even more common in Campania than in Etruria; and their employment for entertainment at feasts was improved upon. Strabo [53] says the luxury of the Campanians went so far that, when entertaining distinguished guests at supper, they arranged the number of pairs of gladiators to comport with their guests' distinction. Capua long continued to be a great training center for gladiators. Throughout Italy these contests became a common mode of entertainment. Vitruvius, telling how the forum should be constructed, says that, "because the custom of giving gladiatorial shows in the forum has been handed down from our ancestors," we must "in the cities of Italy" proceed on such a plan as will give a view of the spectacle, unhindered by columns so far as possible.[54] The oldest known kind of equipment for gladiators was the Samnian. The Campanians, according to Livy's account,[55] outfitted their gladiators in armor of the Samnites out of scorn for their enemies, and this practice was taken over by the Romans.[56]

That hunting is a sport suitable to warriors, and that killing dangerous beasts has commonly been considered particularly fitting for royalty is well known. Hunting was a popular sport in Etruria, if one may judge from artistic remains found in many tombs. Naturally, artistic representation may merely depict the setting of a mythical tale; again, it may portray a bit of life in other lands. It is obvious, however, that hunting themes must have been pleasing to the taste of Etruscan patrons.[57]

Boar-hunting, judging from its common representation, seems to have been a favorite sport of the Etruscans; it may, moreover, have had a religious significance. Macrobius, referring to boar hunts, says that the animal was a symbol of winter; hence boar-hunting may be shown on sepulchral walls to represent that season of the year when annual *parentalia* were held to honor the dead.[58]

Certain hunting scenes, like other features of Etruscan life and art, have a distinctly Oriental atmosphere, resembling particularly Egyptian and Assyrian art. The stag hunt, the archers on foot and horseback, the spearmen, the man-lion fight, the lion-bull fights—depicted on bowls at Caere and Praeneste, about 670 B.C.—are quite Asiatic in spirit and execution. Along with hunting and

---

[53] Bk. v, 4, 13; Müller: op. cit., II, 223.
[54] Vitruvius on Architecture, v, 1, 1–2.
[55] Bk. IX, 40.
[56] Baumeister: Denkmäler des Klassischen Altertums, III, 2096.
[57] Dennis: op. cit., II, 175.
[58] Ibid.; Macrobivs, I, 21.

fighting certain peaceful aspects of pastoral life are depicted—horses and cattle grazing in the fields, and a gardener pruning trees under his master's watchful eye.[59] A lively portrayal of life along the coast depicts boats, fowlers, fishermen, and divers.

Gymnastic exhibitions and the sports of the circus are commonly shown on Etruscan remains, and their employment at Rome is said to have come first from Etruria. In these exercises the Etruscans are obviously often imitators of the Greeks, or, at least, their art reflects a Greek connection. Boxers are depicted frequently. The contenders were probably of an inferior class, providing entertainment for the nobility. Unlike Greek contestants, Etruscan athletes are generally portrayed clad, as they were later in Rome.[60] But certain scenes, doubtless more Greek than Etruscan in spirit, depict nude boxers, wrestlers, and other contestants. Music probably accompanied many events, if not all. Athenaeus [61] says that the Etruscans conducted boxing matches to the music of the flute.

The spirit of sport scenes in the *Tomba del Colle Casuccini* at Chiusi is similar to that conveyed by events portrayed in Egyptian tombs; besides, there are certain Greek features. Here are boxers; a woman dancing and shaking castanets; a nude youth wearing a crested Greek helmet, executing the dance in armor; a grown man, likewise unclad, exercising with the *halteres*; wrestlers or tumblers, directed by a paidotribe with his wand. Excellent representations of wrestling are found in the *Tomba degli Auguri* [62] and in the *Tomba della Scimia* at Chiusi. In the first of these, naked, heavy-bodied, bearded figures, with widespread legs, seize each other by the hands; in the second, one contestant has the opponent over his shoulder and, holding the neck firmly with one hand and an arm with the other, is ready to toss him head over heels. The boxers, depicted in the Scimian tomb, have heavy, Asiatic features, are likewise bearded, and wear a narrow belt about their waists; with hands protected by laced thongs, they begin the fray with one hand open, the other clenched.[63] The decoration of the *Tomba delle Bighe* at Corneto, quite Greek in character, portrays circus events, boxing, wrestling, hurling the discus, Pyrrhic dancers, armed youths on horseback, and a young man who is preparing to jump with a pole, perhaps to mount a horse. The figures, excepting the equestrians, *paidotribes*, and *agonothetae*, are unclothed.[64]

Italy was suitable for horse-breeding; and horses were known there before the Etruscans appeared on the scene. The new, aristocratic master class, con-

[59] Randall-MacIver: *Etruscans*, pp. 29 ff.
[60] Müller: *op. cit.*, II, 220.
[61] Bk. IV, 154.
[62] Weege: *op. cit.*, Plates 91, 93 and 94.
[63] Dennis: *op. cit.*, II, 323 f., 332 f.
[64] Weege: *op. cit.*, Beilage II; Gardiner: *Athletics of the Ancient World*, pp. 119 ff.

stantly engaged in war, seems to have done much, however, to develop the stock and train horses for various purposes. That the sports of the circus flourished in ancient Etruria is shown by many sources. Extensive remains of chariots and bridle bits are found in the tombs; and chariot racing and other equestrian events are extensively portrayed on their walls. Circus scenes may represent the games held in honor of the dead; in one scene a man and a woman appear to be saying farewell at the *spina*, which may symbolize the soul's completion of its race. The *Tomba Golini* at Orvieto suggests that Etruscans went to the afterworld in a chariot, their speediest mode of transit on . earth.[65]

An eminent authority holds that the Tuscan horse races were quite Greek; [66] their artistic portrayal is evidently Greek in spirit, being done by Greeks or by natives trained on Greek models; but it is not necessary to infer Greek origin of the events themselves, which were natural enough in such a social setting. Whatever the facts may be regarding their origin and the amount of Greek influence, it is certain that Etruria became famous for equestrian entertainments. Fabulous tales were associated with them. According to an old Roman legend, a *quadriga* ran away with the driver from the games at Veii, and did not stop until they had reached the Capitol at Rome.[67] Horses and chariots (and also boxers) were sent for from Etruria at the time of Tarquin, according to Livy,[68] and the solemn Great Roman Games were thereafter celebrated annually. The participation of Etruscans at the Circus in Rome seems to have been common. Porsena, by one account, made a truce with the Romans on one occasion in order to take part in their circus games; moreover, he was given the victor's crown. Caecina, a friend of Augustus, is said to have sent a four-horse chariot from Volaterrae to Rome. Etruscan nobles outfitted their entries for the Roman races, but, unlike the Greeks, they did not themselves drive.[69]

Four-horse chariots were of course preferred, but two-horse teams and single horse races were also common. The *Tomba del Colle Casuccini* contains excellent portrayals of charioteers, there being, in one race, three *bigae* (two-horse chariots) with drivers in tunics, white skull caps, and reins around their bodies. One of the *bigae* is just finishing the race, a winner.[70] The *Tomba delle Bighe* shows many equestrian events, the harnessing of teams to chariots, the race itself, youths preparing to mount, armed boys on horseback, and the assembled company of spectators.[71] In the Scimian tombs, besides charioteers,

[65] Dennis: *op. cit.*, II, 54 ff., 176; Fell: *op. cit.*, p. 29.
[66] Müller: *op. cit.*, II, 221.
[67] Plutarch: *Publicola*, 13; Pliny: *Natural History,* VIII, 65.
[68] Bk. I, 35.
[69] Pliny: *Natural History*, X, 34; Müller: *op. cit.*, II, 222.
[70] Weege: *op. cit.*, Plate 97.
[71] *Ibid.*, *Beilage* II.

TWO-HORSE CHARIOT RACE

(F. Weege, *Etruskische Malerei*, Pl. 97, Max Niemeyer Verlag, Halle, 1921)

one sees races on horseback, the riders sitting "side saddle," one with a bow, the other holding a poised lance.

The Etruscan circus, as shown in numerous reliefs, had features similar to those later known at Rome, notably the *spina* with its row of obelisks or cone-shaped figures. Since the races themselves were taken thither from Etruria, it is probable that the Roman circus was patterned after the Etrurian.[72] Livy says that Tarquin first marked out the Circus, called Maximus, space being set aside for senators and knights, so that they might put up seats for their accommodation.[73] Tarquin, it is assumed, would probably have built at Rome something similar to what he knew in his Tuscan home. Since no remains, other than pictorial, have been found, the structures in Etruria were probably of wood, as was the first one at Rome, which had seats supported on a scaffolding twelve feet high. Moreover, the *Tomba delle Bighe* at Corneto shows patrons seated on rude platforms, apparently wooden, with a canopy over their heads.

Dancing and music had a prominent part in the *ludi scaenici*, and both were associated with religion. To judge from artistic representations, dancing was

[72] Dennis: *op. cit.*, II, 175.
[73] Bk. I, 35; Dionysius, III, 68.

also a favorite form of entertainment. When used for such a purpose, the per-formers were doubtless inferiors and slaves. Both male and female youth are shown dancing, with elaborate gesticulation, in the decorations of the *Tomba del Triclinio*.[74] Boys and men engaged in the dance in armor, bearing shields, swords, and lances, imitating the movements of war. The *Tomba della Scimia* at Chiusi gives some conception of accouterments of a Pyrrhic dancer, who, equipped with double-cockaded helmet, shield, cuirass, greaves, and a wavy wand, moves to the music of the double flutes. Though there is no agreement on the matter, the dance of the *salii*, which combined both singing and danc-ing and followed a certain rhythm set by a leader, as did the band of armed dancers in Etruria, is believed by some scholars to have been borrowed from the Etruscans, or to have been influenced by them in this respect at least.[75] Choral dances seem to have had no place among the Etruscans.

The remains of upper-class Etruscan culture show that the position of women was less secluded than at Athens; on the other hand, their place was by no means comparable with that of Spartan women. The wives and daugh-ters of a luxury-loving, ruling class probably enjoyed much leisure, depending on slaves or servants for work.[76] An urn on which a reclining girl is portrayed, surrounded by a number of figures with scrolls, is interpreted by Dennis to in-dicate that the girl died before finishing her education; [77] this interpretation, however, is open to doubt. The mother's genealogy seems to have been given careful attention, judging from records that have come down to us.[78] Dennis credits women of Etruria with great respect and honor, basing his judgment on certain well-known facts: children took the mother's name as well as the father's; her sepulchre was even more splendid than her husband's; in some instances, at least, she had expert knowledge of religious mysteries (Tanaquil, for example) and perhaps some knowledge of letters; and she is portrayed sit-ting with men at dinner. It may be true, as Dennis believes, that Etruscan society had a strong influence on Rome in respect to the position of women.[79] Banquets were ubiquitous, judging from the tomb records and the testimony of ancient authors. Athenaeus says that Etruscans prepared sumptuous tables twice a day, and nude slave girls served at them. Fell, however, thinks that this is not supported by evidence. Poulsen, too, avers that "not a single naked handmaid" is found in Etruscan paintings.[80] While much that is reported

---

[74] Weege: *op. cit.*, *Tafel* 31.
[75] Müller: *op. cit.*, II, 218; Baumeister: *op. cit.*, III, 1547; Fowler: *The Roman Festivals of the Period of the Republic*, pp. 36 ff.; Dennis: *op. cit.*, II, 332.
[76] Dennis: *op. cit.*, I, lii; II, 53, 58.
[77] *Ibid.*, II, 179.
[78] Randall-MacIver: *Etruscans*, pp. 34 f.
[79] Dennis: *op. cit.*, I, lxiv, 310; II, 162 f.
[80] *Athenaeus*, IV, 153; Fell: *op. cit.*, p. 140; Poulsen: *Etruscan Tomb Paintings*, p. 33.

about Etruscan debauchery by Athenaeus and others may be exaggerated, it is generally recognized that a great decline occurred in Etruscan life after Etruria had gained supremacy, and extravagant luxuries and loose morals of the fourth and third centuries overstepped the stricter bounds of propriety of the sixth and fifth.[81]

Women are shown in many banquet scenes, but the representations are sometimes open to widely different interpretations. Thus, at a dinner scene of the Grotta Querciola, the sole woman present is considered a hetaera by Dennis; the wife of the man, by Gerhard; and "afflicted mother" being comforted by her son, by Mrs. Gray.[82] Athenaeus cites Aristotle to the effect that the "Tyrrhenians dine in company with their women, lying back under the same robe." [83] Other scenes certainly represent women in less compromising society. Fell [84] refers to a scene in the Tomba dei Vasi Dipinti, which he interprets as "a family" dining in Elysium as in life. Women also attended public games, as may be seen from the paintings at Chiusi, Tarquinii, and Corneto. In the Tomba delle Bighe women are shown, seated with men on slightly elevated, backless benches; all exhibit an attentive interest in the sportive events before them.

The pattern of Etruscan origins and development, while significant in itself as the portrait of a people who strove for dominion and speedily decayed when it had been gained, takes on added importance from the fact that Etruscan influence on Roman culture was many-sided and far-reaching. In military organization, agricultural improvement, city-building, engineering and architectural construction; in religious practices, superstition, and divination; in music, the theater, luxurious banquets, and entertainments; in gladiatorial combats, circus performances, and athletic contests; in the formation of guilds, artistic creation, and education—in all of these, in varying measure, the Etruscans are acknowledged to have left their imprint on the life of those who, when the Tuscan tide receded, were to make a more successful effort at the unification of Italy, and were to extend their dominion even to those shores from whence the Etruscan builders are believed to have come.

81 Fell: op. cit., pp. 142 f.
82 Dennis: op. cit., I, 309.
83 Bk. I, 23.
84 Op. cit., p. 141; Weege: op. cit., Tafel 66.

# 17

# EARLY ROMAN CULTURE

The early folk of Latium had no accurate knowledge of their origin. Though traditions varied, Rome's founding was placed about the middle of the eighth century. The Trojan tale and those of Mars, Rhea Silvia, Romulus, Remus, and the Sabine women were told and retold in great detail.[1] Neither Livy nor Dionysius were very successful in separating fact from fancy. Archaeological research has discredited certain traditions, but confirms the ancient view that Rome was not a city of great antiquity. The first settlements in Latium were not much earlier than 1000 B.C. These pastoral folk of Latium dwelt in small villages. The Latin League probably depended originally on ties of blood and religion.[2] How these tribal communities (which, according to Pliny, numbered fifty-three) came to unite, the Latins did not know. Probably they coalesced in the seventh and sixth centuries under the pressure of expanding Etruscan power, forming ten or twelve cities on sites most capable of defense. Rome, most favorably situated, had become by the end of the sixth century, or early fifth, the chief city for almost a third of Latium. Etruscan rule at Rome, lasting perhaps two generations, came to an end with the expulsion of Tarquin the Proud, dated traditionally about 509 B.C.[3]

Florus compared Rome's political life to that of man: the kingship, "infancy"; to the consulship of Appius Claudius and Quintus Fulvius (212 B.C.), "youth"; to Augustus Caesar, "manhood"; and after Caesar, "old age."[4] Rome's nonhereditary monarchy was the instrument of a superior class, the

---

[1] Livy, I, 1 et seq.; Florus: *Epitome of Roman History*, I, 1; Sallust: *War with Catiline*, 6; Virgil: *Aeneid*, I; Ovid: *Fasti*, III, 59–86, 197–228.

[2] Pliny: *Natural History*, III, 9; Dionysius of Halicarnassus, *The Roman Antiquities of*, IV, 49; V, 61; Diodorus of Sicily, VIII, fr. 3; Homo: *Primitive Italy and the Beginnings of Roman Imperialism*, pp. 77 f.

[3] Livy, I, 60; Homo: *op. cit.*, p. 159; Frank: *Roman Imperialism*, pp. 3 f., 13 ff.; Cary: *History of Rome*, pp. 30 f., 39.

[4] Florus, introduction.

Patricians—older settlers, possessed of large estates and pride in family names. An inferior order, Plebeians, was made up of tradesmen, merchants, and poor peasants. Both Patricians and Plebeians were enrolled in three tribes, subdivided into thirty *curiae*, which may have represented diverse racial elements, or perhaps only geographical, administrative areas.[5] The Comitia Curiata, the curial assembly, approved a new king nominated by the Senate, pledged obedience to him, and convened at his call to vote on certain matters. The Senate, drawn from Patrician families, was the real source of authority; for though its functions were advisory during a king's reign, the new monarch was named by the Senate through its *interrex*. Royal power covered matters terrestrial and celestial. Men and money were at his command; war and peace hung on his decision; he promulgated laws and could take auspices, but many religious functions were assigned to others whom he chose from Patrician families.

After the kings were expelled, two consuls, chosen annually, functioned till the end of the Republic. Though their powers were "truly regal," Romans dated the origin of their liberty from this time.[6] In reality, of course, the revolt against kingship was by and for the nobility. Since only Patricians could be consuls, and Plebeians suffered numerous other disabilities, a conspicuous feature of the first two and a half centuries of the Republic was the class struggle. As early as 494 Plebeians demanded redress against unjust arrest, imprisonment, and other evils; when these were not met, they threatened "secession," refusing to enter the army unless promised by consular officers and Senate that they should have authority to name two Plebeian tribunes, annually, who should be spokesmen of the commoners. The number was gradually increased to ten, and their powers vastly extended. An important gain was made when the laws were codified and published (traditionally, in 451 B.C.), thus reducing the likelihood of arbitrary action.[7] Even more significant was the successful demand for the right of intermarriage, the restraint of which Canuleius condemned.[8] The financial officers (*quaestores*) were increased to four, the office was opened to Plebeians, and soon thereafter (409 B.C.) three were elected.[9] The consulship was closed to Plebeians, however, till 366 B.C. After 342 B.C. a Plebeian was chosen each year.[10] In 351 the censorship was opened to Plebeians;[11] since the censors had already taken over the making of Senate lists

5 Homo: *op. cit.*, pp. 117 f.; Cary: *op. cit.*, pp. 52, 55 f.
6 Livy, II, 1; Cicero: *The Republic*, II, 30–2.
7 Livy, III, 31–4.
8 *Ibid.*, IV, 1–6.
9 *Ibid.*, IV, 43, 54.
10 *Ibid.*, VI, 42; VII, 1, 32; *The Cambridge Ancient History*, VII, 529.
11 Livy, VII, 22.

(c. 366), the path to the Senate was clear, the Ovinian Law (c. 312 B.C.) having directed the censors to choose the best men from every rank.[12]

The struggle for improved political status was paralleled by efforts for economic relief. Laws were passed against usury, fixing maximum interest at 1 per cent (357 B.C.); ten years later it was reduced to 0.5 per cent; five years thereafter, proposals were made to abolish usury entirely.[13] In line with this was an act (about 321 or 326 B.C.) for the relief of the debtor's person from distraint.[14]

Changes in economic and political status were interrelated with others. Rome's wars of expansion had far-reaching consequences. Success in war required more soldiers; Plebeians were drawn upon; and with their service came demands. The Republic's army retained the Centuriate classification, established under Etruscan kings. This Centuriate army gradually became a political assembly, the Comitia Centuriata, which grew in power while the old Comitia Curiata, dominated by Patricians, declined. The influential Centuriata soon were able to name censors and even consuls. Moreover, since classification depended on having wealth enough to equip one's self for a particular service, an aggressive, better-to-do Plebeian could improve his status. Meantime, the Comitia Tributa, a tribal assembly presided over by the tribunes of the people, grew in importance in the fourth and third centuries and came to rank with the Comitia Centuriata as a legislative body by 287 B.C.[15] Another path to power opened: the dictatorship, which had been instituted at an uncertain date and was at first filled only by Patricians, was ultimately accessible to Plebeians, Gaius Marcius Rutulus being the first commoner to hold such power.[16]

While Plebeians were rising in importance, the Patricians were declining numerically, partly because wars had taken a heavy toll, perhaps, too, by reason of refusal to marry commoners. Of fifty-three Patrician families named in the fifth century, only twenty-nine appear in the fourth. By 300 B.C. the proportion of Patricians to Plebeians may have been "less than one in twenty." [17]

Almost two and a half centuries of warfare marked Rome's history between the expulsion of Etruscan kings and the unification of Italy. The cities of Latium, which had aided Rome's revolt, formed a Latin League and made a treaty with Rome about 493 B.C. In a century and a half of intermittent wars, however, the League was destroyed (338 B.C.), certain Latin cities were incor-

12 C.A.H., VII, 522 f.
13 Livy, VII, 16, 27, 42.
14 Ibid., VIII, 28; C.A.H., VII, 544 ff.
15 Frank: op. cit., p. 64.
16 Livy, II, 18; VII, 17.
17 Cary: op. cit., p. 107.

porated with Rome, and others were made dependent. While establishing supremacy in Latium, Rome also faced her onetime sovereigns, the Etruscans, and the common enemy of both Rome and Etruria—the Gauls. Near-by Veii, a city comparable to Rome, was conquered in 396 B.C.; further conquest of Etruscan territory was facilitated by Gallic inroads which pushed even into Rome (387 B.C.). In the middle of the fourth century, after Rome had defeated Tarquinii and Falerii and weaned away friendly Caere, a forty-year truce was imposed (351 B.C.) which left Rome relatively free to turn on sturdier opponents, the Samnites.

While she was engaged with Etruria, Rome had a treaty with the Samnites (354 B.C.); but when the Etruscans were weakened and a truce established, Rome scrapped the treaty (343 B.C.), and joining with Capua, began a series of wars against the Samnites. The first phase of the Samnian War (343–341 B.C.) was indeterminate; the second (325–304 B.C.) gave Rome access to the Adriatic, a firm hold on Apulia, and alliances with the cities of Umbria and Picenum; the third (298–290 B.C.) consolidated and extended the gains of the second, and made Rome mistress from the Arnus to the Greek areas of southern Italy. So destructive had been the struggle that Pyrrhus, crossing Samnium a little later, asked "whether the country had ever been inhabited." Two centuries later a Samnite referred to Rome as a den of wolves which "devour the peoples of Italy." Shortly after the Samnian struggle, by assisting the Greek city of Thurii (282 B.C.), the Romans drew on themselves retaliation by powerful Tarentum, thus beginning a conflict which soon brought the Greek cities under Roman sway (272 B.C.).[18]

Over a path cleared by iron and blood and strewn with broken pledges, Rome had moved steadily toward military and political hegemony. As mistress of all Italy, Rome gained recognition from distant Egypt in 273 B.C. With near-by Carthage, however, Rome was soon to enter a conflict which would end her provincial existence and decide the lordship of the western Mediterranean.

Was there a clear-cut plan and purpose in Rome's wars which unified Italy? Livy saw the Samnite War as a struggle to decide mastery of Italy; that was, indeed, its consequence. Later historians, too, credited Romans with such foresight; but that the ultimate outcome was foreseen is doubtful. The Samnian wars appear as struggles between powerful, growing peoples, striving for immediate ends; such, too, seem the others, rather than the elements of a grand design for sovereignty.[19] Instead of singleness of purpose, there was a conflict of rival forces in Rome: one class, already satisfied, wished to enjoy its privileges without further risk; another, underprivileged, hoped for gains from successful

18 Homo: *op. cit.*, pp. 189, 208 f.
19 Frank: *op. cit.*, p. 46.

war. The conservative Senate, thinking of "scores of treaties," "honorable traditions," "orderly conduct of state affairs," war levies, and the potential losses of
unsuccessful war, was disinclined toward expansionist adventures; the Plebeians, however, knowing little of past treaties, hoping for booty, land and
colonization, low-priced grain, home improvements, were "more eager for empire" and readier for the risks of war.[20] After the conquest of Veii, Etruscan
Juno was not the only thing removed; all wealth, even the gods and their offerings were taken to Rome. Soldiers were given land; increased wealth brought
influence, and Plebeians soon gained access to "the highest office of State." [21]
Fruits of successful conquest whetted the appetite. The alliance with Thurii,
leading to the Tarentine War, was opposed by the Senate; the Plebeian Assembly, however, which had gained legislative competence in 287 B.C., approved.
Later, when the Mamertines sought Rome's support, the granting of which
brought conflict with Carthage, the Senate, foreseeing danger, did not sanction
it; the commons approved it, however, because of the "plunder" which all
might gain.[22]

The conquered peoples lost their sovereignty, but Rome's sway freed Italy
from internal wars, and made all more secure against outside encroachments.
The conquered cities did not all enjoy equally dependent status. Rome divided
them, giving unequal privileges.[23] Some were annexed, receiving certain rights
of citizenship; others were associated with Rome, being bound by separate,
special agreements.[24] Rome also planted colonies, drawn from various cities.
These settlements provided trustworthy defenders of strategic points, gave land
to those sent out, and probably made for greater unity.[25]

Rome's expansion brought impressive gains in territory and population. Her
primitive villages, where men dwelt in caves and huts, each comprised but a
few square miles and a few thousand inhabitants.[26] Territory increased to
about 2,400 square miles at the middle of the fourth century; to 4,200 at the
destruction of the Latin League (338 B.C.); to 10,700 by the end of the century; and to 31,700 in 280 B.C. After the Tarentine War, territory amounted to
over 48,000 square miles. There were now probably about three-quarters of a
million men able to bear arms. Rome may have had 100,000 population, and
Tarentum and Capua, 60,000 to 70,000, respectively.[27] Slavery, which existed
to some extent in Etruscan days, had grown appreciably. A 5 per cent tax on

[20] Ibid., pp. 64 ff.
[21] Livy, v, 22; Frank: op. cit., p. 21.
[22] Polybius: The Histories, I, 10–1.
[23] Homo: op. cit., p. 241.
[24] Ibid., p. 223; C.A.H., VII, 658 ff.; Cary: op. cit., pp. 127 ff.
[25] Appian: Civil Wars, I, 23, 35; Frank: op. cit., pp. 18, 35 ff.
[26] Varro: On Agriculture, III, 1; Homo: op. cit., p. 84; Mommsen: History of Rome, I, 61.
[27] Homo: op. cit., pp. 186, 223, 243 f.; Mommsen: op. cit., I, 122 f.; Cary: op. cit., pp. 121,
    136.

manumissions was fixed in 357 B.C.[28] Slavery's rôle in Roman life, however, was relatively slight before the foreign wars.

### CHARACTER AND DESTINY OF THE PEOPLE

Latin literature and modern writers discover diverse desires on the part of the Roman people: they swing between the poles of rest and activity; extol pursuit of gain and the enjoyment of leisure; they praise war and the arts of peace. They distinguish themselves in war and build an empire; they attain distinction in agriculture, first among the peaceful pursuits of man. These diverse tendencies were doubtless present at the beginning of Roman life. The primitive peasant, busy amid flocks and fields, left his plow and seized his pike when it served his interest. If, having gained something by war, conquest became a habit, the Roman often turned back wistfully to contemplate the peaceful, rustic life—the happiness once possessed. Virgil, though called to praise warlike achievements, is a more persuasive exponent of tranquil, rustic joys:

> Happy are they, beyond man's lot, if aware of the blessing,
> Husbandmen, to whom, remote from clashing of armies,
> Earth, repaying her debts, accordeth an easy existence.[29]

Ovid recalls a time when Janus was guardian of peace and knew naught of war; when men had not put Justice to flight, when uncut forests and pasturing herds were known at Rome.[30] Horace asks,[31] Who knows a better place than the country—

> Where churlish Care breaks less the thread of sleep?

There he portrays—

> The sturdy farmers of the ancient days,
> Content with little, when their grain was stored,
> Relieving by a festal time their frames
> And hearts that toiled in hope of rest at last. . . .[32]

Martial acquires fame at Rome and even sits at Caesar's table, but he also sings of—

> A fertile farm, one hearth the whole year through,
> No strife, a tranquil spirit, coatless ease,

[28] Mommsen: op. cit., I, 389.
[29] Lawton: Classical Latin Literature, p. 160.
[30] Fasti, I, 243 et seq.
[31] Epistles, I, 10.
[32] Lawton: op. cit., p. 18.

> Vigorous muscles in a healthy frame,
> Informal social ties and simple fare. . . .[33]

Respecting Rome's martial character modern historians followed the ancients. Romans seemed, as Polybius [34] said of the Peloponnesians—

> Aye vexed with toil, their spears never at rest.

Their warring progress impelled apologists to read a warlike destiny in tales of a hazy past. Ovid makes Romulus address his father thus: "Umpire of war, . . . we name the beginning of the Roman year after thee. . . ." Mars was to be revered in Latium, for the sword gave "a fierce race empire and glory." [35] Livy tells of the hind fleeing to the Gauls, the "wolf of Mars" turning to the Romans—a portent of destiny. The gods had willed that Rome should rule the world: so let them cultivate war, and teach their sons that no human power can withstand Roman arms. Janus' temple, open in war, closed in peace, was shut but twice after Numa's day, says Livy, after the First Punic War and after the battle of Actium.[36] At the height of imperial power, Horace prays: "Be still in war supreme."

Romans portrayed their wars as a fight for liberty. In war one must be victor; to be vanquished is to be enslaved. Others can endure slavery; but the Roman people are assured liberty. The Romans, Florus says, took up arms first to secure liberty, then to increase their bounds, afterwards to defend their allies, and ultimately to gain "glory and empire." [37] That all peoples had an equal right to independence did not occur to the Romans. Their empire was founded on a belief in Latin race supremacy. The "immortal Gods" willed it.[38] Virgil promises endless sway:

> Neither a limit in time nor yet of power I assign them:
> Empire endless I grant.[39]

The superior race must establish its sway, "sparing those who submit, but crushing in battle the haughty." Florus recounted the exploits of those who, "after sanguinary encounters, taught submission to savage races who had hitherto been free and were, therefore, impatient of the yoke." Cato destroyed the "resistance of the Celtiberians, the flower of Spanish manhood. . . ." Gracchus punished the same people and destroyed "a hundred and fifty cities." [40]

---

33 *Ibid.*, p. 275.
34 Bk. v, 106.
35 Ovid: *Fasti*, iii, 59–86.
36 Bk. i, 16, 19; x, 27.
37 Bk. i, 3.
38 Cicero: *Philippic* vi, 7; Chapot: *Roman World*, p. 418.
39 Lawton: *op. cit.*, p. 168.
40 *Florus*, i, 33. Trans. by E. S. Forster. The Loeb Classical Library. Quoted by permission of Harvard University Press, Cambridge, Mass.

The prospect of plunder also motivated Rome's wars. "War and pillage" were common among the seminomadic dwellers of Latium. Quintus Fabius, preparing to lead forces into Etruria, wanted to enrich all his soldiers.[41] Promise of plunder, Polybius says,[42] led the Plebeians to favor aid to the Mamertines. Cicero traced provincial hatred of Roman officers to their "lust for plunder." [43] Mithridates credited the Romans with "one inveterate motive for making war upon all nations," a "deep-seated desire for dominion and for riches." [44] Rome's poet-philosopher declared that the quest for goods had stirred up from the depths mighty tides of war.[45]

Superior physical strength and bravery were commonly ascribed to the Italians. Polybius thought them naturally superior to Phoenicians and Africans; but if their courage and strength often gave them success, they relied too constantly "on force" in all undertakings, even making a fault of "daring and violence," which sometimes brought them "signal defeats." [46] Tales of heroic exploits, proving soldierly courage in this "civilizing" of others, fill many pages of Roman history. Florus relishes Marius' campaign against the Teutons: "What a defeat he inflicted upon them, ye heavenly powers. . . !" Even when faced by Pyrrhus' elephants, Roman soldiers died with wounds only on their chests and a "threatening mien" on their faces. "How easy were it for me to win the empire of the world if I had an army of Romans. . . !" Pyrrhus exclaimed. The eulogist portrayed the Romans as superior in honor as well as in bravery, for they "knew that the only true victory is that which is won with untainted honour and unimpaired dignity." Though "glorious," "honourable," "illustrious," "humane," "upright," and "high-minded" were fit terms to describe the wars against Africans, Macedonians, Sicilians, Spaniards, Gauls, Thracians, Armenians, because these were the proof of "imperial greatness," the historian found it "deplorable" and "disgraceful" when Roman warlike might and spirit were turned upon slaves and gladiators and even upon themselves.[47]

Though Roman readiness for war is a common theme, there are exceptions. Polybius says that Romans were slow to enlist for the war in Spain, because of reports of constant battles and great losses. This "fit of cowardice" was so extensive that there were neither enough officers nor men; when Scipio volunteered, however, others were ashamed and enrolled for the campaign.[48]

---

[41] Livy, x, 25; Homo: op. cit., p. 72.
[42] Bk. I, 11.
[43] Cicero: On the Manilian Law, 22.
[44] Sallust: Letter of Mithridates, 5.
[45] Lucretius: De Rerum Natura, v, 1435.
[46] Bk. I, 37; VI, 52.
[47] Florus, I, 6, 13, 34, 38, 47. Trans. by E. S. Forster. The Loeb Classical Library. Quoted by permission of Harvard University Press, Cambridge, Mass.
[48] Bk. xxxv, 4.

Cicero's philosophy of conflict expressed a general view of the Romans. Nature gives dominion to the best. Mind governs the lower, less worthy tendencies in man. Masters rule slaves. Men able to govern themselves cannot justly be enslaved; but peoples inferior by nature are properly brought under the dominion of the superior.[49] Cicero defends the "justice of war," when undertaken to "reclaim property" and if "proclaimed beforehand." [50] It must not be began without provocation, and reparations must first have been demanded.[51] Those who preside over affairs and determine upon action are as serviceable to the country as those who fight, for by their wisdom war may be avoided or ended. Wisdom in decision is better than courage in battle, but one must not avoid war because of an aversion to fighting; and when making war, it should appear that there is "no other view but peace." [52]

Nothing outranked duty to country, in Cicero's opinion. Who would not gladly die in her service? But the Roman code of fighting was strict; one should not fight unless he had taken the soldier's oath. Cato's son, who had been dismissed from service, stayed on in the army through love of military life. Cato protested that he must take a second oath, for the first one having been annulled, it was not lawful for him to engage the enemy.[53]

A conflict between those who favored war and those inclined toward peace is revealed in speeches during the Punic wars. The spokesmen for peace explain that peace creates and preserves wealth; war spends and destroys it. Those who direct affairs should not arouse the people to war, unless it can be proved really advantageous. Is it not absurd to seek success in a foreign war before we have first set our own city's affairs in order? It would be well, at least, to avoid all "appearance of beginning war" and to "seem forced rather to defend oneself against aggression." Lentulus argues, however, that war preserves our own possessions and wins others', but peace destroys even what previous wars had gained. We must treat our own people worthily; but the enemy must be humbled.[54] Reverberations of these arguments—the gains of war, the demoralizing effects of peace—continue long after Rome's conquests had ended. It seems to have become a theme of school essays. Valor in war had enabled Rome to grow, pull down Sicily and Carthage, and then seize "the whole world at once." Later she grew feeble and "gave loose rein to peace"; and "a long, heavy peace is the ruin of the sons of Romulus." [55]

[49] Republic, iii, 25; Philippic vi, 7.
[50] Offices, i, 11.
[51] Republic, iii, 23.
[52] Offices, i, 23.
[53] Ibid., i, 11, 17.
[54] Dio's Roman History, xiii.
[55] Sulpicia's "Complaint on the Condition of the State and the Times of Domitian," formerly credited to Ausonius.—Appendix to Ausonius, v.

War is ever more tempting to those who anticipate gains than to those who have already won them. That state which sees no more profitable fields to conquer is apt to view force merely as a means to restrain aggressors who would disturb the enjoyment of its gains. Praise of peace, on the basis of the *status quo*, arose in Rome. Ovid, amid the ease and plenty of post-Actian days, proclaimed: "Come, Peace, thy dainty tresses wreathed with Actian laurels . . . abide in the whole world . . . [and] thou shalt be unto our chiefs a glory greater than war. May the soldier bear arms only to check the armed aggressor. . . ." [56]

Certain Romans, though they praised Rome's "glorious" feats of arms, understood the aftermath of conquest. Would it not have been better to be satisfied with Sicily and Africa, or even with dominion of Italy, than to grow so great and be ruined by one's own power? What has caused "domestic strife but excessive prosperity"? It has debased "the morals of the age," and the state is "engulfed in its own vices as in a common sewer." [57] This is *post factum* wisdom; it is for the few, not the many. For most Romans, doubtless, the choicest epitaph would have been like that of Scipio Barbatus:

> . . . a man both wise and valiant, . . .
> Consul, censor and aedile he became among you,
> Taurasia, Cisauna, and Samnium he conquered,
> Reduced Lucania wholly, and hostages exacted.[58]

The Romans were an eminently practical, methodical, unimaginative people, excelling in deeds rather than in ideas. Thus they judged themselves. Sallust says that "the best citizen preferred action to words." [59] Virgil granted his city pre-eminence in affairs of empire, but conceded that others could "mould more deftly the breathing bronze" and excel in creative arts. Among the examples of Roman inferiority some would include part of Virgil's own poetry. Of course, opinions vary widely: Niebuhr judged the *Aeneid* a "misdirected thought" from beginning to end; Comparetti, on the other hand, viewed it as the greatest poem ever written. However one may rate a particular poem, many would agree that "conscious study of style, direct imitation of Hellenic models, even slavish translation, came first of all." [60] Indebtedness to Hellas is everywhere evident—Homer in Virgil, Menander in Terence, Plato in Cicero—yet, despite all this, there is a Roman stamp, a practical aspect in Cicero and Caesar, not

[56] *Fasti*, I, 709–24. Trans. by J. G. Frazer. The Loeb Classical Library. Quoted by permission of Harvard University Press, Cambridge, Mass.
[57] *Florus*, I, 47.
[58] Lawton: *op. cit.*, p. 17.
[59] *Catiline*, 8–9.
[60] Lawton: *op. cit.*, pp. 6, 155.

to be found in anything Greek; and who can match the great poem of Lucretius?

Even in empire-building, his greatest accomplishment, the Roman's "practical common-sense and lack of imagination" were outstanding traits. "The Roman had no subtle and far-reaching programme of foreign policy . . . did not look beyond the morrow." [61] In various other fields the Romans were borrowers rather than creators. Cato declared that, like sheep, they followed readily the lead of others.[62] Their early religion was a prosaic, primitive animism. Greek myths were borrowed and associated with Roman deities; certain Greek cults were taken over directly. Practical arts, too, in which they became most renowned, they first learned from others, inventing "little or nothing" on their own initiative.[63] The primitive peasants knew nothing of the sea and commerce, and, as some think, little of war. Army organization, fortifications, and improved methods of fighting were learned from Etruria and Hellas.[64] The Greeks brought to Italy, also, the cultivation of olives and vineyards and a modification of the Phoenician alphabet, and furnished models for sculpture, ceramics, and architecture. It is said that play is an index to the bent of a people. All peoples play, of course, but some more joyously and creatively. In this domain, too, Romans borrowed from Etruscans and Greeks, not only public amusements, but children's games as well.[65]

The relative lack of creative accomplishment may be due partly to the fact that man individually "counted for little in the Roman world." [66] Perhaps, too, the Romans were unfortunate in coming after the Greeks, with whom, to their disadvantage, they have been constantly compared. It was natural that they should turn to those who had gained predominance in creative arts. What might have happened had they developed more independently? [67] No one can say. There seems to have been a deep-rooted preference for active rather than contemplative life. Cicero, though he thought literary affairs suited his nature best, returned to them only because he saw no place in the Senate or forum for his former activities; because times were evil, and only study could ease his mind or bring surcease of sorrow.[68] Musonius is thoroughly Roman when he says that neither men nor women should devote themselves wholly to philosophy. Is it strange that such a people should have become more famous for

---

61 Homo: *Primitive Italy and the Beginnings of Roman Imperialism*, pp. 255 f. Trans. by V. G. Childe. Courtesy of Kegan Paul, Trench, Trübner & Co., Ltd., London.
62 Plutarch: *Cato*, 8.
63 Paul-Louis: *Ancient Rome at Work*, p. 5.
64 Frank: *op. cit.*, p. 3; Cary: *op. cit.*, p. 18.
65 McDaniel: *Roman Private Life*, p. 143.
66 Paul-Louis: *op. cit.*, pp. 20 f.
67 Abbott: *Society and Politics in Ancient Rome*, pp. 161 ff.
68 Cicero: *Letters to His Friends*, iv, 3–4; v, 15; *Letters to Atticus*, iv, 18.

baths, aqueducts, amphitheaters, gigantic shows, their empire, legal codes, and roads than for charting the highways of the mind?

Preoccupation with material possessions, a deep concern with business success, Horace thought, had been prejudicial to intellectual effort. Roman boys learned in school to divide an *as* into a hundred parts, and knew well what remained if one *uncia* were taken from five. With this love of gain dyed in the soul, as it were, who could hope for poems worthy of cedar oil and polished cypress? [69] Attitudes towards getting, having, and spending conformed to a certain pattern; not all wealth was highly regarded. There was contempt for one who squandered an inheritance and one who leaped from poverty to riches. Cato ridiculed a man who sold his seaside estate, for he had swallowed easily what the sea could not.[70] Scipio dealt generously with his family, but was regarded as exceptional; for Romans, being "excessively particular" about money, were not inclined to "pay a single talent before the appointed day." [71] Landed wealth was eminently respectable; petty business was decried. Commerce on a grand scale, however, was "not so despicable"; and a man who stepped from it into "an estate" justly deserved praise.[72]

Rome's wars were justified as a defense of property and as a means of getting the property of others. Though the aristocracy deprecated the vulgar pursuit of wealth, they went after it if ventures promised large returns. Excessive wealth produced a love of luxury that ultimately infected "most of the people"—a weakness which even Cato's measures could do little to rectify. It is hard, said he, to save a city where "a fish sells for more than an ox." [73] Lucilius (180–103 B.C.) depicts the vulgar spirit of contemporary Rome—the bustle from dawn till dark, competitiveness, craft, deception. His pattern of virtue is a fit summary of the early Roman ideal:

> Man's virtue is to know each thing's true worth,
> What's good or bad, useless, dishonest, base:
> To know the limits in our quest of gain,
> To pay the proper honor unto wealth,
> To grant to office that which is its due,
> To be the foe of evil men and deeds,
> To count one's country's welfare first of all,
> And next our parents'; after that our own.[74]

---

[69] Art of Poetry, Wickham's Horace, pp. 356 f.
[70] Plutarch: Cato, 8; Sulla, 1.
[71] Botsford, G. W., and Botsford, L. S.: The Story of Rome, p. 148.
[72] Cicero: Offices, 1, 42.
[73] Plutarch: Cato, 8, 18.
[74] Lawton: op. cit., p. 61.

### EARLY ROMAN EDUCATION

Educational development, broadly considered, falls into two main types.[75] The first, the old Roman education, continued relatively unchanged to about the middle of the third century B.C., when Rome's conquests spread beyond Italy. The second type, the "new" education, was a fusion of Roman and Hellenic elements gradually perfected after this time. In the process of mutation from the first type to the disintegration of the second, several more or less distinct stages appear: the purely Roman, to 240 B.C.; a transition from the old to the new, dating from about 240 B.C., when Andronicus translated the Odyssey, to 55 B.C., the date of Cicero's De Oratore; vigorous maturity of the perfected Hellenized Roman pattern, 55 B.C. to 95 A.D., when Quintilian's Institutio Oratoria appeared; and a decline, slight at first, then more and more pervasive, until Roman education was supplanted by a Christian pattern. Such a periodization, though useful, should not be overemphasized or interpreted so strictly as to obscure the fact that life moves in a continuous stream, and certain elements of old patterns survive amid the new. Some persist, indeed, long after the dissolution of Roman polity.

THE FAMILY AND EDUCATION Perhaps as early as 1000 B.C. the family had emerged from the gens.[76] Though the gens name still remained, the family became the most important educational agency. The family tie was strengthened by religious belief: souls of the dead lived on, haunting burial places and requiring sustenance. Children provided for the departed spirits, which, if cared for, guarded the living. To be without descendants was, under such circumstances, a curse.

Authority of the paterfamilias over his household was extensive. At birth the child was laid before him to be taken up and admitted to family membership or to be refused and exposed. The Twelve Tables gave the father power of life and death over his son; he might even sell him, but after the third sale the son was freed from paternal control. Neither age, rank, offices, nor honors released a son from filial bonds.[77]

Woman's sphere was one of subjection: in girlhood, to her father; in marriage, to her husband; if unmarried at her father's death, she was commonly under the guardianship of an older brother. About the age of twelve a girl might marry. Marriage was strictly guarded. Though the Canuleian Law (445 B.C.) legalized intermarriage, it scarcely succeeded in destroying Patrician exclusive-

---

[75] Marquardt: Das Privatleben der Römer, p. 81.
[76] Cary: op. cit., p. 14.
[77] Botsford: op. cit., p. 93; Cicero: Caecina, 34; Gibbon: The Decline and Fall of the Roman Empire, III, 682 f.; Johnston: The Private Life of the Romans, pp. 29 ff., 76 f.

ness.[78] Marriages were arranged by heads of families; a girl's consent was un-necessary. Though *confarreatio* symbolized union of body and soul, it was not a union of equals. The wife was legally under the hand of her husband, who could "with the approval of the family council" inflict physical punishment or even take her life.[79] Though her property and earnings became her hus-band's, the wife shared in his estate, her inheritance being controlled by a guardian, according to her husband's will.

Despite numerous restraints, Roman women enjoyed a more dignified status than did those of Greece. The mother cared for her children's education, lived with the rest of the family rather than in a separate apartment, ate with her husband and guests, shared in conversation (save for intellectual and political matters of which she was supposedly ignorant), and participated in certain religious affairs. Her behavior was marked by gravity and reticence; light ac-complishments were inconsistent with the age. The long-established custom of kissing her kinsfolk was conducive to sobriety. Drinking is said to have been punished no less severely than adultery.[80] Roman writers warm to the theme of wifely industry, rectitude, and courage. Lucretia is busy at her wool, late at night; with "manly courage" she chooses to die rather than live dishonored.[81] Horace portrays the labors of rural domestic life:

> . . . a modest wife that plays her part—
> That keeps her house, her children rears—
> Like Sabine wife, or like the sun-tanned wife
> Of some industrious Apulan,
> Piles up old faggots on the sacred hearth
> 'Gainst coming of her toil-worn man,
> And, shutting in the wattled pound the cattle,
> Milks their distended udders dry,
> And, drawing from the cask wine of the year,
> Prepares the meal she does not buy. . . .[82]

In contrast with this picture of domestic seclusion, certain women were credited with courageous action and an influence on public affairs. Hersilia per-suaded the Sabine king to pardon the Romans.[83] Veturia and Volumnia so

---

[78] Livy, IV, 3–4; Cary: op. cit., p. 118, n. 2.
[79] Aulus Gellius, The Attic Nights, x, 23; Abbott: op. cit., p. 52.
[80] Gellius, x, 23; Tertullian: Apology, VI, 3–6; Dill: Roman Society in the Last Century of the Western Empire, p. 163; Fowler: Social Life at Rome in the Age of Cicero, pp. 143 ff.
[81] Ovid: Fasti, II, 847; Livy, I, 57–9.
[82] Horace: Epode II. Trans. by A. F. Murison. Courtesy of Longmans, Green & Co., Inc., New York.
[83] Livy, I, 11; Ovid: Fasti, appendix, pp. 407 f.; Plutarch: Romulus, 19.

influenced Coriolanus' actions that the men of Rome praised them and erected a temple to "female Fortune" as a monument.[84] In the time of Camillus, women gained public esteem by voluntarily giving their ornaments to make up for a shortage of gold. As a reward the Senate set aside an old custom and provided that "thereafter, when women died, a suitable eulogy should be spoken over them, as over men." [85]

There were certain exceptions to the rule of feminine dignity and propriety. Even the solemn duties of Vesta's temple did not make all sober and severe. Postumia was suspected of unchastity because her dress was more gay, her manners less reserved, than befitted a virgin. Though acquitted, she was ordered to refrain in the future from indiscreet mirth and to dress with more regard for sanctity than for elegance.[86] During the First Punic War, the Plebeian aediles fined a woman of rank because of arrogant language inconsistent with the dignity of Roman conduct.[87]

The old Roman ideal survived (at least in letters) amid the social turmoil of the late Republic and the Empire, contrasting sharply with the degradations of the new age. Lucretius Vespillo portrays his wife as true, obedient, kind, gracious, sociable, friendly, industrious at spinning, faithful in religion, not given to magic, unostentatious, and caring for her husband's mother as for her own.[88] Claudia's epitaph reflects the old ideal:

> Her husband she did love with all her heart.
> Two sons she bore him. . . .
> Of gentle speech she was, and gracious mien.
> She kept her house, span wool. All's said. Farewell.[89]

Life in early Rome was marked by severe simplicity. Little clothing was needed because of mild climate and a life of vigorous exercise. The farmer in the field often wore nothing but a loincloth; for household wear a tunic, reaching to the calf, or shortened by the use of a belt, sufficed. A toga was necessary only for public affairs and formal occasions. Cato mentions a tunic three and one-half feet in length, stout wooden shoes, and a blanket, as the proper amount of clothing to be issued "every other year" to farm hands.[90] Clothing was made in the household from homespun wool, woven on crude looms by the women and girls or by slaves under their direction. Even under the Empire

---

84 Livy, II, 40; Plutarch: Coriolanus, 33, 37.
85 Plutarch: Camillus, 8.
86 Livy, IV, 44.
87 Gellius, x, 6.
88 Fowler: op. cit., pp. 160 ff.
89 Lawton: op. cit., p. 17.
90 Cato: On Agriculture, 59; Johnston: op. cit., pp. 176, 179.

domestic production, though no longer a necessity, was still practiced to some extent. Augustus, who sought to restore somewhat the integrity of a bygone age, had his daughter and granddaughters learn to spin and weave.[91]

Diet followed the rule of simplicity, vegetables and cereals being most common; food was often eaten cold. Water, the common drink, was mixed with wine if available. Wheat, bread, "after-wine," "wind-fall olives," "fish-pickle and vinegar," oil, and salt, Cato says, should be strictly meted out by the master to his field workers.[92] Service was provided by members of the family until household slaves became cheap and plentiful. Professional cooks were unknown in Rome before 174; bakeries did not appear till about 171 B.C.[93]

The primitive Roman house and its furnishings were crude. All domestic activities were carried on in a large room, the *atrium*. An opening in the center let the smoke out and light and rain in. Windows were at first unknown; there was only one door. A place for the fire, implements for spinning, weaving, and cooking, a strongbox for valuables, and pallets for sleeping were the chief furnishings.[94]

Glimpses of old Roman education, though somewhat meager and unsatisfactory, may be gained from later writers. Due allowance must be made, of course, for exaggeration and idealization, apt to be indulged in by those who look back at a receding age whose passing they deplore.

Early Roman education centered in the family. Life dictated the curriculum. Mothers and fathers were the teachers: the mother, in respect to the duties of little women; the father, in affairs pertaining to the farm, the army, the forum, and religion. Though education was by the family, it was for the state. Calvus, when offered the office of military tribune, urged the people to accept his son, brought up under his own discipline, whom he would dedicate to the commonwealth in his stead.[95] Cicero accepted the old purpose and recommended that knowledge which would make men "useful to the State." This is the noblest function of wisdom, for nothing is higher than one's duty to the state. Those who serve their country are assigned a place of rest in the Milky Way.[96] Plutarch cites, as proof of the nobility of Cato the Younger, that he "chose a public career" rather than the pursuit of riches.[97] Though for the state, education was not supported or controlled by it. The Romans, unlike the Greeks, never wanted a uniform "system of education," officially ordained and estab-

[91] Suetonius: Augustus, 64.
[92] On Agriculture, 56–8.
[93] Mommsen: op. cit., III, 123; Fowler: op. cit., pp. 32, 39.
[94] Sandys: Companion to Latin Studies, pp. 217 f.; Johnston: op. cit., pp. 133 ff.
[95] Livy, v, 18.
[96] Cicero: Republic, I, 20; VI, 16; Offices, I, 6, 17.
[97] Cato the Younger, 19.

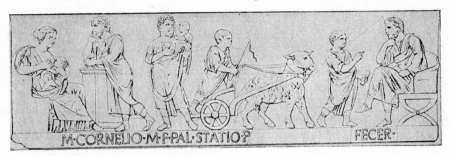

ROMAN FAMILY LIFE AND EDUCATION
(*Archäologische Zeitung*, XLIII, Pl. 148)

lished by law. This feature Cicero held to be best,[98] but Polybius criticized it as a weakness of Roman institutions.

What was the "old ancestral discipline" of the Roman Republic? We know it chiefly through sources from the late Republic and Empire. Pliny [99] informs us that "in the olden time" Roman youth learned by the precept and example of their elders how they should act and what they should in due time transmit to their own children. Cato (234–149 B.C.) was present while his wife washed and dressed their child, whom he taught himself rather than turn "such a priceless thing as education" over to a slave-schoolmaster. To this end he wrote out the history of Rome "in large characters," so that the boy might learn the ancient traditions of his country; and at a proper age he tutored him in Roman law.[100] Even when the "new education" had begun to flourish, the father still often assisted in his son's education. Aemilius Paulus trained his sons in the "ancestral discipline" to which he had been accustomed, adding Greek learning which had then become popular.[101] Cicero, having had an unsatisfactory master for his boys, gave them lessons himself.[102] Horace credited his good repute to his father who, though he had but a little farm, took his son to Rome for the best possible education, went with him daily to lectures, and was ever present to keep him safe from shameful deed or breath of scandal.[103] Suetonius says that even Augustus taught his grandsons "reading, swimming, and the other elements of education. . . ."[104]

In early times Roman mothers generally nursed their children, but wet nurses were sometimes employed. Though it was less common in her day, Cato's wife bathed, dressed, and nursed her own son, and even some of her

98 *Republic*, IV, 3.
99 *Letters*, VIII, 14.
100 Plutarch: *Cato*, 20.
101 Plutarch: *Aemilius Paulus*, 6.
102 *To Atticus*, VIII, 4.
103 Horace: *Satires*, I, 6.
104 *Augustus*, 64.

slaves' babies.[105] The diet of children was simple and spare in early days, as was that of the whole family. There was then no danger of "immature children" eating "a great deal" and sleeping "too much"—practices which Varro thought bad for their health.[106] The mother's concern went beyond physical care. As the first teacher and moral guide, her influence or that of some kinswoman was of paramount importance, according to Tacitus: "In the good old days, every man's son, born in wedlock, was brought up not in the chamber of some hireling nurse, but in his mother's lap, and at her knee. And that mother could have no higher praise than that she managed the house and gave herself to her children. Again, some elderly relative would be selected in order that to her, as a person who had been tried and never found wanting, might be entrusted the care of all the youthful scions of the same house; in the presence of such an one no base word could be uttered without grave offence, and no wrong deed done. Religiously and with the utmost delicacy she regulated not only the serious tasks of her youthful charges, but their recreations also and their games. . . . The object of this rigorous system was that the natural disposition of every child, while still sound at the core and untainted, not warped as yet by any vicious tendencies, might at once lay hold with heart and soul on virtuous accomplishments, and whether its bent was towards the army, or the law, or the pursuit of eloquence, might make that its sole aim and its all-absorbing interest." [107]

The moral influence of fathers and mothers became weaker, doubtless, under the pressure of great social changes, but Cornelia, Aurelia, and Atia are said to have educated their own children, the Gracchi, Caesar, and Augustus. In certain families this influence persisted under the Empire. Marcus Aurelius says that he owed to his mother "piety and beneficence," abstinence from evil deeds and thoughts, and simplicity of living.[108] Cato is said to have been as careful of speech in his son's presence as he would have been before the Vestal Virgins. In keeping with old Roman practice he never bathed with his son, being ashamed to appear naked.[109] Marcus Aurelius [110] credited to his father his modesty and manliness, and to his grandfather "good morals" and control of his temper.

The purpose of education in ancient Rome was thus to preserve the *mos maiorum*, to bring up youth according to an established pattern of life. As Ennius said:

[105] Plutarch: *Cato*, 20.
[106] *Gellius*, IV, 19.
[107] Tacitus: *A Dialogue on Oratory*, 28. Trans. by W. Peterson. The Loeb Classical Library. Quoted by permission of Harvard University Press, Cambridge, Mass.
[108] *The Meditations of the Emperor*, I, 3.
[109] Plutarch: *Cato*, 20.
[110] *Meditations*, I, 1–2.

The commonwealth of Rome is founded firm
On ancient customs and on men of might.[111]

In the formation of the future worthy father and citizen, obedience, piety to the gods, respect for law, physical health, strength, dexterity, good physical carriage, modesty in speech and behavior, practical ability, confidence in one's powers and the destiny of Rome, and native intelligence were all highly prized.[112]

The source of authority in all things pertaining to education lay in the powers of the father. If he accepted a child, it was given a name on the ninth day, if a boy; on the eighth, if a girl. The *dies lustricus*, significant of religious purification and dedication, was celebrated by an offering in the household or at a temple. To guard against enchantments a *bulla* was hung about the neck, to be worn by boys till manhood and on certain occasions afterwards; by girls, until marriage.[113] Not until manhood was the name officially registered.

To about seven years of age boys and girls were educated in the home, learning correct habits in manners and speech under the mother's care. Cicero thought that women, more than men, were apt to "preserve the ancient language unaltered"; and that rules for speaking Latin were unnecessary, since "the teaching given to children conveys" that in the home.[114] Reading, writing, and elementary arithmetic were also taught in the home.[115] The daughter's education usually came to an early end because of marriage. In spinning, weaving, and other housewifely arts she was duly instructed, "learning to do by doing." Horace portrays the countryman's wife, gracing his house with her children, piling the hearth with logs, drawing wine, and preparing the meal. Shutting the cows in the fold and milking them were also among her labors.[116] Cato's recipes for making cakes and preserving fruits suggest other phases of domestic economy [117] which girls must have learned betimes.

GAMES AND EXERCISES OF YOUTH    It has been said that the Greeks were always children, the Romans always men. At best it is only a half-truth. Though life in the Roman household, with its emphasis on duties, manners, correctness of speech, *pietas* and *gravitas*, may appear somber, subdued, and even severe, the cries of children at their play may be heard, if one but listen. When Quintilian expressed his approval of "play in the young" as "a sign of a

111 Cicero: *Republic*, v, 1. Trans. by C. W. Keyes. The Loeb Classical Library. Quoted by permission of Harvard University Press, Cambridge, Mass.
112 Marquardt: *op. cit.*, pp. 89 ff.
113 *Ibid.*, pp. 83 f.
114 *On Oratory*, III, 12–3; *Brutus*, 74.
115 Johnston: *op. cit.*, p. 84.
116 *Epode* II.
117 Plutarch: *Cato*, 25.

lively disposition," [118] he seems to be noting an observation made from life, not a bookish theory.

On the dies lustricus a ceremony of purification was performed, and friends, parents, and others of the household gave toys to the infant—miniature implements, axes, sickles, swords, half-moons, flowers—which were sometimes strung and hung about the neck. These toys, collectively called crepundia, were thought to have a magic charm against evil spirits—but children knew nothing of this till they grew older! Besides crepundia, dolls, wagons, carts, tops, balls, hoops, hobbyhorses, and stilts were common playthings of the young.[119] Pet animals and birds—dogs, cats, goats, geese, quails, doves, ducks, crows, pigeons, and even mice and monkeys, all helped to while away the long hours of childhood.

Roman children had a host of games, many of them common to other ancient lands and to primitive peoples the world over. Most of them, probably, were played by girls as well as boys, though not all. Among the physically less active were various games with dolls, nuts, knucklebones, "odd and even," "guess how many," tossing coins, dice, and many board games, the prototypes of checkers, chess, and backgammon. Cicero says that from antiquity the Romans had a proverb which they used to commend one's integrity: "He is one with whom you might play odd and even in the dark." [120] A favorite game with astragals, requiring much skill, was to toss up five and catch as many as possible on the back of one's hand. They were also thrown from the hand or a box, like dice, each of the various combinations having a special designation— the lowest, "Vulture," the highest, "Venus." So common were games with nuts that nuces relinquere (to take leave of nuts) was a common expression to denote the end of childhood.[121] Ovid mentions many games played by children with nuts. Six games are known to us. In one, several nuts were laid on the ground, and the player, trying to touch one or more of them, rolled another down an inclined board. Another game (ludus castellorum) consisted of laying three nuts together and throwing a fourth so as to lie upon them without moving them apart, the winner taking all. Again, a triangle, marked off with several parallel lines, was drawn upon the ground, and players threw or rolled nuts so as to cause them to touch as many lines as possible and yet remain within the delta. Another game was to toss nuts a certain distance into a dish or hollow cavity.

Children have played the "king game" in many lands. As Romans played it, a "king" was chosen by lot, who then commanded the others to do whatever

[118] The Institutio Oratoria, I, 3, 10.
[119] Sandys: op. cit., pp. 176, 227; Johnston: op. cit., pp. 78, 82 f.; McDaniel: op. cit., p. 67.
[120] Offices, III, 19; Ovid: The Walnut Tree, 73–86.
[121] Marquardt: op. cit., p. 839.

pleased him. Again, a winner in other group games seems to have been chosen king. Horace alludes to the custom when he speaks of schoolboys at their game, who say:

Do right the thing and you'll be king.[122]

Among the more active games were: seesaw; hide-and-seek; skipping stones; rolling hoops, with trinkets attached to warn the unwary; blindman's buff; whipping tops; riding stick-ponies; walking on stilts; building houses; driving goats or other pets, hitched to little carts; and various games with balls. Rolling the "Greek hoop" seems to have been considered a bit effeminate, unfit for older boys at any rate.[123] Virgil's pen picture of boys at their tops fits almost any age and any land:

> Just as at times a top, set a-twirl by the stroke of a whip-lash,
> Boys urge onward through vacant courts in widening circles,
> Deeply intent on the sport; impelled by the cord it is driven
> Round its bewildering track, while over it stand the untutored
> Throng of beardless boys admiring the musical box-wood,
> Giving their minds to the stroke. . . .[124]

Ball games, involving throwing up into the air, passing from one to another, striking with the hand against wall and ground, and bowling on the ground—a prototype of boccia of to-day[125]—became popular in Italy, but the time of origin of each and the rules for playing are for the most part obscure. The pila was a small ball; the pila paganica was larger and stuffed with feathers or similar material; the follis was still larger and inflated.[126] In early times, when exercise for military values was most stressed, ball-play must have been much less prominent than in the late Republic and under the Empire, when it became a common means of warming up for the bath,[127] and was a popular activity in every gymnasium.

As years advanced, more serious purposes were served by the games of youth: there was constantly a concern for mens sana in corpore sano, not for the sake of beauty, not for the satisfaction of the individual, but that the citizen might be serviceable in military affairs. To this end the most primitive and natural exercises known to man—hunting, running, jumping (height and distance), wrestling, boxing, throwing the stone, the ball and the pike, and riding horse-

---

122 Epistles, I, 1; Marquardt: op. cit., p. 838.
123 Horace: Odes, III, 24.
124 Aeneid, VII, 378–83. Trans. by H. H. Ballard. Courtesy of Charles Scribner's Sons, New York.
125 McDaniel: op. cit., p. 68.
126 Ramsay and Lanciani: A Manual of Roman Antiquities, pp. 486 f.
127 Martial: Epigrams, VII, 32.

back—were employed, constituting a premilitary training for older boys and young men. To these were added also exercising with sword, shield, and spear, on foot and on horseback. For this training the *Campus Martius* was set off along the Tiber, where youths and men might exercise every day. The early Romans knew no other places of exercise, whether of work or play, than the woods and farms and the Field of Mars.

Hunting and fishing were at first necessary to man's livelihood; he continued hunting when he became shepherd and farmer in order to save his flocks and crops and as a sport for leisure. Hunting is among the earliest named sports of Roman youth. The wild boar and smaller game were abundant. Romulus and Remus were said to have roamed the hills and dales for game, thus perfecting their strength and courage by encounters with wild beasts and by attacking robbers.[128] Tarquin, when seeking the crown, was said to have sent his predecessor's sons, who were almost grown up, away on a hunting trip.[129] Horace, looking back longingly to "early generations of mankind," portrayed convincingly the lure of hunting: "And then when the wintry months of Jove the Thunderer gather storms and snow, he either drives this way and that with his pack of dogs the wild boars into the toils set for them, or spreads on smooth pole the wide-meshed nets to catch the greedy fieldfares, or sets snares for the timid hare and the crane from over seas, sweet prizes." [130]

Swimming was a necessity for Roman soldiers and was presumably learned early by those who dwelled on Tiber's banks. Horatius, famed for prowess as fighter and swimmer, may well have been one of the heroes whose deeds were sung around the festive family board. Fathers taught their sons this pleasant, useful art. Cato, who sought to keep up old Roman practices, brought up his son to "swim lustily through the eddies and billows of the Tiber." [131] Augustus, likewise, is said to have taught his grandsons swimming.[132] In respect to bathing the Romans felt a modesty unknown to the Greeks. Cicero speaks of the well-established custom that ". . . sons grown up to manhood do not bathe along with their fathers, nor sons-in-law with their fathers-in-law." [133] Younger sons, one infers, did bath and swim with their fathers.

Though they had no sports or competitions peculiarly their own, girls evidently learned to swim, in some cases, at least, if credence be given to various references to Cloelia's swimming the Tiber with other girls. Accounts of her

---

[128] Livy, I, 4–5.
[129] Ibid., I, 35.
[130] Epode II. From *Horace for English Readers*, translated by E. C. Wickham (The Clarendon Press).
[131] Plutarch: *Cato*, 20.
[132] Suetonius: *Augustus*, 64.
[133] Offices, I, 35.

feat vary. Plutarch says that the girls "were seized with a desire to swim away" from their captors, despite "the depth and whirl of the strong current"; and he adds that "some say" Cloelia "crossed the stream on horseback, exhorting and encouraging the rest as they swam." [134]

Music and dancing ill comported with Roman *gravitas*. Though they played some part in Roman life, they had no such place in the education of early Roman youth as they occupied among the Greeks. It has been said that the Latins were "as nearly strangers to the Muses as any people well can be." [135] Some rudimentary songs, however, children may well have learned to repeat and imitate, since they were not excluded from the meals of their elders, and sons were even taken by their fathers when they dined out with friends. Cicero says of these old songs that it was a custom for "guests at table to sing one after the other to the accompaniment of the flute in praise of the merits of illustrious men." [136]

Both music and dancing were in early days chiefly associated with religious cults, funeral processions, triumphs, games, and other public affairs. The fact that these came to Rome from Etruria and later from Greece probably accounts, in no small degree, for Roman aloofness. Romans accepted dancing as a part of the *Ludi Magni*, the so-called Great Roman Games, and men, youth, and boys took part, armed with helmets, swords, and lances. These, however, were special occasions. They viewed with awe the religious processions and rites of the *Fratres Arvales*; and the sacred martial dances of the *Salii*, the Priests of Mars, who each year bore the sacred shields and chanted the *Saliaria Carmina* on the Kalends of March and following days.[137] But they did not join in these ritualistic movements and hymns. Dancing and music continued, even in later times, to be associated with a life unworthy of the good and noble. Sallust complains that Sempronia could "play the lyre and dance more skilfully than an honest woman need. . . ." [138] Dancers are reckoned by Cicero among others who follow mean professions.[139] Cicero thought highly of Socrates, but must have blushed to think of his learning to dance!

The gymnastic training of the Greeks seemed ridiculous to the Romans.

134 Plutarch: *Publicola*, 19. Trans. by B. Perrin. The Loeb Classical Library. Quoted by permission of Harvard University Press, Cambridge, Mass.; Livy, II, 13; Dio, XLV, 31; Florus, I, 4.
135 Lawton: *op. cit.*, p. 16.
136 *Tusculan Disputations*, IV, 2. Trans. by J. E. King. The Loeb Classical Library. Quoted by permission of Harvard University Press, Cambridge, Mass.; *Brutus*, 19; Plutarch: *Roman Questions*, 33.
137 Marquardt: *op. cit.*, p. 835; Fowler: *The Roman Festivals of the Period of the Republic*, pp. 35 ff.; Ramsay and Lanciani: *op. cit.*, pp. 381 f.
138 *Catiline*, 25.
139 *Offices*, I, 42.

Though they adopted the gymnasium when they grew older and turned to a more luxurious life, many of the most steadfast citizens could not contain their contempt. Tacitus vents disapproval of the shift from practice in "arms of legitimate warfare" to the exercises of the gymnasium.[140] Cicero, too, long before him, had expressed contempt for the absurd Greek system of training in gymnasia—such a ludicrous preparation for the burdens and dangers of war! The objection of Romans to gymnasia was doubtless due, in part, to their aversion to exposure of the body, for, as Ennius says: "Shame's beginning is the stripping of men's bodies openly." [141]

The young play games; the old mostly look on at them. If there be some truth in the saying, "Romans were always men," it seems to find partial support in the fact that they gave themselves so readily and consistently to watching the public games of the circus and amphitheater, and so little to participation in competitive sports, and then chiefly to those useful in war.

Public games of the circus are traced back, though somewhat vaguely, to the earliest days of Rome, but they continued in relatively moderate proportions during the early centuries of the Republic. At the end of the Republic, however, sixty-six days were given to games. Romulus is said to have arranged games in honor of Equestrian Neptune and called them *Consualia*, proclaiming them to neighboring towns, attracting among others the Sabines, whose women were then taken.[142] Etruscan Tarquin, having had a victory over the Latins at Apiolae and taken great booty, is said to have celebrated games with more splendor than the former kings, laid out the Circus Maximus, provided places where knights and senators could erect seats for themselves, and brought horses and boxers from Etruria. These games, *Ludi Magni* or *Ludi Romani*, were afterwards celebrated annually. Capitoline Games were ordered exhibited by Camillus (390 B.C.), and a special Collegium was created to care for their performance, in honor of Jupiter who had protected the citadel of the Romans against danger. The Plebeian Games were first celebrated in 220 B.C.[143] The Apollinarian Games, the first fixed, annual festival in honor of a Greek god, were instituted during the struggle with Hannibal (212 B.C.) in order to gain victory, the Romans being assured that, if the games were properly performed, Apollo would destroy the enemy. According to another account these games were set up to combat a pestilence. They were at all events made permanent, in 208 B.C., in an effort to counteract such an epidemic.[144]

---

[140] Tacitus: *Annals*, xiv, 20; Varro: *On Agriculture*, ii, introduction.
[141] Cicero: *Tusculan Disputations*, iv, 33; *Republic*, iv, 4.
[142] Livy, i, 9; Fowler: *Roman Festivals*, pp. 206 ff.; Johnston: *op. cit.*, p. 244.
[143] Livy, i, 35; v, 50; xxiii, 30; Wissowa: *Religion und Kultus der Römer*, pp. 111 f.; Fowler: *Roman Festivals*, pp. 215 ff.
[144] Livy, xxv, 12; xxvii, 23; Wissowa: *op. cit.*, pp. 239 ff.; Fowler: *Roman Festivals*, pp. 179 f.

THE SCHOOL OF LABOR ON THE LAND    The life of the shepherd "is the treble," and the farmer "plays the accompaniment," says Varro.[145] The Roman boy's education was attuned with these two occupations of the land as soon as he left his mother's care. While little is known of the life of herdsmen and farmers before the Punic War, a glimpse of it may be gained from later Roman writers. Tending the herds must have occupied many a youth's long days, for the terra Italia was filled with "a great abundance of cattle," and was said, by one account, to have derived its name from an old Greek word ἰταλοί, meaning oxen; by another, from vituli, meaning bullocks. So great was early Italy's concern with herds that wealth was judged in terms of cattle, and fines were fixed at so many oxen and sheep.[146]

Near the end of the Republic, Varro set forth certain requirements for herdsmen, young and old. The head herdsman must be literate, he says, "for one who does not know his letters is not fit for the place . . ." since he cannot keep correct account of his master's cattle.[147] Physical qualifications are stressed considerably, being differentiated for various types of work. "For herds of larger cattle older men; for the smaller even boys; but in both cases those who range the trails should be sturdier than those on the farm who go back to the steading every day. Thus on the range you may see young men, usually armed, while on the farm not only boys but even girls tend the flocks. The herdsmen should be required to stay on the range the entire day and have the herds feed together; but, on the other hand, to spend the night each with his own herd. They should all be under one herd-master; he should preferably be older than the rest and also more experienced, as the other herdsmen will be more disposed to take orders from one who surpasses them in both age and knowledge. Still, he should not be so much older that his age will prevent him from being as able to stand hard work; for neither old men nor boys can easily endure the hardships of the trail and the steepness and roughness of the mountains—all of which must be encountered by those who follow the herd, and especially herds of cattle and goats, which like cliffs and woods for pasturage. The men chosen for this work should be of a sturdy sort, swift, nimble, with supple limbs; men who can not only follow the herd but can also protect it from beasts and robbers, who can lift loads to the backs of pack animals, who can dash out, and who can hurl the javelin. . . ." [148]

Individual land ownership had been established at an early date. The beginning of agricultural pursuits, like many other useful arts of peace, was credited

145 On Agriculture, I, 2, 16.
146 Gellius, XI, 1; Varro: On Agriculture, II, 1, 9–10.
147 On Agriculture, II, 10, 10.
148 Varro: On Agriculture, II, 10, 1–3. Trans. by W. D. Hooper, rev. by H. B. Ash. The Loeb Classical Library. Quoted by permission of Harvard University Press, Cambridge, Mass.

to Numa, who sought to lead his people from warlike habits to the ways of peace, ". . . that they might be subdued and softened along with the soil they tilled." [149] To the time of the Punic wars, farming was still the all but universal peacetime occupation of Roman men, and senators drove their own oxen. Even in later days, when most labor had come to be looked upon with contempt, agriculture was praised as a worthy occupation for "a well-bred man." [150] Our ancestors put the countryman ahead of those who lived in cities, says Varro, and wisely so.[151] When Romans wanted to praise a man, Cato tells us, they called him a "good husbandman" or "a good farmer," and thought this the "greatest commendation." [152] For one's declining years rural labors were eminently fit, thought Cicero: "I come now to the pleasures of husbandmen, with which I am excessively delighted"; for these are not checked by "old age" and are best suited "to the life of a wise man," for they relate "to the earth, which never refuses command, and never returns without interest that which it hath received. . . ." [153]

The farm's hard labor was the school which strengthened body, limb, and hand.[154] The countryman worked for seven days and went to town on market days, nundinae, to sell his products, see friends, and learn of news. His farm was very small, perhaps as little as a half acre or as much as five; but with a primitive plow—"a tree trunk with a forked branch," in its earliest form— sickles, and axes, which were his chief implements, even so small a farm must have been enough to occupy the owner and perhaps an assistant or two.[155] Spelt, barley, and millet, the grains first cultivated, were supplemented by wheat about 450 B.C. The vine and the olive were so extensively grown in Varro's day that he asks: "Is not Italy so covered with trees that the whole land seems to be an orchard?" [156]

Horace, whose father's farm was a poor one, looked back with a wistful eye at the happy activities of the farmer, free from the "yoke of usury," far from "the insolent portals of the great"; plowing and replowing his ancestral acres; "wedding" the poplar and the vine; watching the lowing herds; pruning trees and grafting better stock; storing the freshly squeezed honey; clipping the passive sheep; and, in autumn, gathering the fruit of vine and tree.[157]

Cato followed farming "in earnest when he was young and poor," learning

149 Plutarch: Numa, 16–7; Livy, I, 19.
150 Cicero: Offices, I, 42; Varro: On Agriculture, III, 1, 4–5.
151 On Agriculture, II, introduction.
152 On Agriculture, introduction, p. 3.
153 Cicero: On Old Age, 15.
154 Lucretius, v, 1360.
155 Johnston: op. cit., pp. 355, 365; Paul-Louis: op. cit., pp. 51, 54.
156 Varro: On Agriculture, I, 2, 6–7.
157 Epode II.

to cultivate the stony soil of the Sabine country.[158] He is said to have regarded "farming and frugality" as the only paths to wealth—paths which he knew thoroughly and followed successfully. Farming, like other phases of life, had changed in some respects when he wrote his treatise on agriculture. Large farms had become common; slave labor was the rule, though some free labor was at times employed. Cato's directions as to kinds of work to be done, when and how, doubtless give an insight into farm activities with which he had been familiar in his youth.

Cato would choose a farm with "good, and naturally strong soil," well-watered; good, healthful climate, not beset by storms; and plenty of buildings. It should be at the foot of a mountain, facing southward, and preferably near a good town, on the sea or a navigable stream, or a good well-traveled road. There should be a plentiful supply of laborers. The farmer must have good neighbors and be able in certain seasons to secure voluntary assistance and hired labor.[159]

The owner is advised to look carefully into the condition of everything about the farm, and check upon the way in which all work has been performed: "When the master arrives at the farmstead, after paying his respects to the god of the household, let him go over the whole farm, if possible, on the same day; if not, at least on the next. When he has learned the condition of the farm, what work has been accomplished and what remains to be done, let him call in his overseer the next day and inquire of him what part of the work has been completed, what has been left undone; whether what has been finished was done betimes, and whether it is possible to complete the rest; and what was the yield of wine, grain, and all other products. Having gone into this, he should make a calculation of the labourers and the time consumed. If the amount of work does not seem satisfactory, the overseer claims that he has done his best, but that the slaves have not been well, the weather has been bad, slaves have run away, he has had public work to do; when he has given these and many other excuses, call the overseer back to your estimate of the work done and the hands employed. If it has been a rainy season, remind him of the work that could have been done on rainy days: scrubbing and pitching wine vats, cleaning the farmstead, shifting grain, hauling out manure, making a manure pit, cleaning seed, mending old harness and making new; and that the hands ought to have mended their smocks and hoods. Remind him, also, that on feast days old ditches might have been cleaned, road work done, brambles cut, the garden spaded, a meadow cleared, faggots bundled, thorns rooted out, spelt ground, and general cleaning done. When the slaves were

158 Plutarch: Cato, 25; Fowler: Social Life, p. 177.
159 Cato: On Agriculture, 1, 4.

sick, such large rations should not have been issued. After this has been gone into calmly, give orders for the completion of what work remains; run over the cash accounts, grain accounts, and purchases of fodder; run over the wine accounts, the oil accounts—what has been sold, what collected, balance due, and what is left that is saleable; where security for an account should be taken, let it be taken; and let the supplies on hand be checked over. Give orders that whatever may be lacking for the current year be supplied; that what is superfluous be sold; that whatever work should be let out be let. Give directions as to what work you want done on the place, and what you want let out, and leave the directions in writing. Look over the live stock and hold a sale. Sell your oil, if the price is satisfactory, and sell the surplus of your wine and grain. Sell worn-out oxen, blemished cattle, blemished sheep, wool, hides, an old wagon, old tools, an old slave, a sickly slave, and whatever else is superfluous. The master should have the selling habit, not the buying habit." [160]

A man with great estates did not do the work himself, but secured a trustworthy, capable slave to act as his overseer or *vilicus*. Such a steward must be a good manager, indeed, if he would measure up to Cato's requirements: "The feast days must be observed. He must withhold his hands from another's goods and diligently preserve his own. He must settle disputes among the slaves; and if anyone commits an offence he must punish him properly in proportion to the fault. He must see that the servants are well provided for, and that they do not suffer from cold or hunger. Let him keep them busy with their work—he will more easily keep them from wrongdoing and meddling. If the overseer sets his face against wrongdoing they will not do it; if he allows it, the master must not let him go unpunished. He must express his appreciation of good work, so that others may take pleasure in well-doing. The overseer must not be a gadabout, he must always be sober, and must not go out to dine. He must keep the servants busy, and see that the master's orders are carried out. He must not assume that he knows more than the master. He must consider the master's friends his own friends. He must pay heed to anyone to whom he has been bidden to listen. He must perform no religious rites, except on the occasion of the Compitalia at the cross-roads, or before the hearth. He must extend credit to no one without orders from the master, and must collect the loans made by the master. He must lend to no one seed-grain, fodder, spelt, wine, or oil. He must have two or three households, no more, from whom he borrows and to whom he lends. He must make up accounts with the master often. He must not hire the same day-labourer or servant or caretaker for longer than a day. He must not want to make any purchases without the knowledge of the master, nor want to keep anything hidden from the master. He must have no

---

[160] Cato: On Agriculture, 2. Trans. by W. D. Hooper, rev. by H. B. Ash. The Loeb Classical Library. Quoted by permission of Harvard University Press, Cambridge, Mass.

hanger-on. He must not consult a fortune teller, or prophet, or diviner, or astrologer. He must not stint the seed for sowing, for that brings bad fortune. He must see to it that he knows how to perform all the operations of the farm, and actually does perform them often, but not to the extent of becoming exhausted; by so doing he will learn what is in his servants' minds, and they will perform their work more contentedly. Also, he will be less disposed to gad about, will be in better health, and will enjoy his sleep more. He must be the first out of bed, the last to go to bed. Before then he must see that the farmstead is closed, that each one is asleep in his proper place, and that the stock have fodder.

"See that the draft oxen are looked after with the greatest care, and be somewhat indulgent to the teamsters to make them look after their stock with more pleasure. See that you keep your ploughs and ploughshares in good condition. Be careful not to plough land which is *cariosa* [wet on surface, dry below] or drive a cart over it, or turn cattle into it; if you are not careful about this, you will lose three years' crop of the land on which you have turned them. Litter the cattle and flocks carefully, and see that their hoofs are kept clean. Guard against the scab in flocks and herds; it is usually caused by underfeeding and exposure to wet weather. See that you carry out all farm operations betimes, for this is the way with farming: if you are late in doing one thing you will be late in doing everything. If bedding runs short, gather oak leaves and use them for bedding down sheep and cattle. See that you have a large dunghill; save the manure carefully, and when you carry it out, clean it of foreign matter and break it up. Autumn is the time to haul it out. During the autumn also dig trenches around the olive trees and manure them. Cut poplar, elm, and oak leaves betimes; store them before they are entirely dry, as fodder for sheep. Second-crop hay and aftermath should also be stored dry. Sow turnips, forage crops, and lupines after the autumn rains." [161]

The occupational groups, said to have been organized into guilds in the reign of Numa—"musicians, goldsmiths, carpenters, dyers, leather workers, curriers, braziers, and potters"—had probably been developing under the Etruscan kings. The scene of industrial activities, many of which had been learned from the Etruscans, probably changed slowly and not very extensively before the Carthaginian wars.[162] Romans continued to be almost wholly agricultural, and farmers were doubtless the artificers of their own crude implements in early days. Even in Cato's time and Varro's, though it was recognized that some manufactured goods, iron implements, pottery, and some textiles must be purchased, as much as possible was to be produced on the farm so that

161 Cato: *On Agriculture*, 5. Trans. by W. D. Hooper, rev. by H. B. Ash. The Loeb Classical Library. Quoted by permission of Harvard University Press, Cambridge, Mass.
162 Plutarch: *Numa*, 17; Fell: *Etruria and Rome*, pp. 70 f.; Paul-Louis: *op. cit.*, p. 67.

all workers would be kept busy.[163] Artisans, whether in towns or on the farms —when these became extensive and carried on industries themselves [164]—were mostly slaves or freedmen. Cato, who turned to all sorts of schemes to make money, is said to have bought "districts given over to fullers, pitch factories . . ." and purchased young slaves to be "trained like whelps or colts." Moreover, he lent money to some of his slaves that they might purchase boys to be trained and resold or kept for Cato's own service.[165] Little is known of the artisan's training in early days save that it was accomplished by active apprenticeship. At a later time, systematic instruction was employed "in at least some of the industrial arts." [166]

THE DISCIPLINE OF ARMS  Though Numa is said to have sought to divert his people from fighting to the ways of peace, the life of Romans continued to be divided between the fields of Ceres and those of Mars. Of them it might be said, in Homer's phrase, they were—

From youth to age, appointed the laborious wars to wage.[167]

Thus, the games of childhood were followed by the hardening exercise of rustic labor and the discipline of arms. Farming was consistently praised as the best nursery of "the bravest men and the sturdiest soldiers." [168]

Though Romans did not employ the modern, hard-worked term "propaganda," their ideals, institutions, deeds of heroes, and letters of great men acted as a powerful preparative of the Roman mind for war, its discipline, its glory, its inevitability. Later Christian writers might scoff and frown with contempt on Roman martial virtues and the warrior's love of public applause; they might urge, at their pleasure, that man's piety should not be seen of man, but the pagan Roman reveled in struggle and the subsequent triumph.

Warlike ability, physical sturdiness, readiness for discipline, and obedience to commands are among the most common traits singled out by biographers, historians, and tellers of tales to prove the greatness of Roman leaders. Like the work of a cartoonist, of course, their pictures may often bear slight resemblance to reality, but the effect on a people's mind was doubtless profound. Ovid draws the portrait of Romulus and Remus "exercising their naked bodies in the sunshine," trying their strength of arms with gloves and javelins and throwing heavy stones.[169] Corvus was on an easy footing with his soldiers, and in-

[163] Cato: On Agriculture, 135; Varro: On Agriculture, I, 22; Fowler: Social Life, pp. 217 ff.
[164] Varro: On Agriculture, I, 2, 21–3; Marquardt: op. cit., pp. 160 f.
[165] Plutarch: Cato, 21.
[166] Anderson: "Some Facts Regarding Vocational Training among the Ancient Greeks and Romans," Sch. Rev., xx, 197 f.
[167] Plutarch: Marcellus, 1; Numa, 16; Livy, I, 19.
[168] Cato: On Agriculture, introduction.
[169] Fasti, II, 365 et seq.

spired them by his example, because he performed all duties of the lowest; in military sports he met every competitor who offered, conquering and being conquered with equanimity.[170] Marcellus gained his name, 'tis said, because of his experience as a "man of war," his fondness of it, his "sturdy body" and "vigorous arm." [171] The physical strength and courage of Jugurtha, the Numidian outsider, which were developed by devotion to foot races, hurling the javelin, and hunting wild beasts, made him a great fighter and endeared him to Scipio and his men.[172]

Distinction in war was the path to greatness and service in the state. Fabius Maximus, understanding that "wars must be many," "trained his body for the wars" and his tongue "as an instrument of persuasion. . . ." [173] Cato wanted young men to get red, not pale; to use their feet on the march, their hands in conflict; to shout louder in battles than they snored in bed. Of a fat man, he said: "Where can such a body be of service to the state. . . ?" [174] Cicero declared, "It is glorious to fall when leading an army," and noted that "philosophers mostly die in their beds." [175] While he recognized that the ends sought through intelligence and reason were more important than those gained "by bodily strength," he maintained that a young man's chief title to fame came from military achievements, and pointed to the example of ancestors who "were almost always waging wars." [176]

To inspire them in their preparation for deeds of war, Roman youth heard told and retold the heroic exploits of days gone by. That of Horatius Cocles, who held back the foe while the bridge was cut behind him and then plunged in full armor into the Tiber, was an old, familiar favorite. Polybius, telling the tale once more, remarks: "Such, if I am not wrong, is the eager emulation of achieving noble deeds engendered in the Roman youth by their institutions." [177]

If Roman boys of later centuries had a more fastidious taste and required something other than the homespun sagas of earlier days, they did not need to go unsatisfied, for nothing in Roman literature could compare with Virgil's portrayal of war's feverish preparation:

Hitherto calm and unmoved, Ausonia blazed into fury.
Some set out for the plains on foot; high raised on their horses,

170 Livy, VII, 33.
171 Plutarch: Marcellus, 1.
172 Sallust: War with Jugurtha, 6.
173 Plutarch: Fabius Maximus, 1.
174 Plutarch: Cato, 9. Trans. by B. Perrin. The Loeb Classical Library. Quoted by permission of Harvard University Press, Cambridge, Mass.
175 De Finibus Bonorum et Malorum, II, 30.
176 Offices, II, 13.
177 Bk. VI, 55.

Others stormed on through clouds of dust; all calling for weapons;
Some with slippery lard fell to polishing buckler and javelin,
Rubbing them smooth and bright, or whetting the edge of their axes.
Gladly their standards they raised and heard the blare of the trumpet.
Five great cities were ringing aloud with the music of anvils
Forging new arms; Atina the strong and Tibur the haughty,
Ardea, old Crustumerium, too, and castled Antemnae.
Helmets they hollowed to cover their heads; into frames for their bucklers
Withes of willow they bent, and brazen breastplates they fashioned;
Others on burnished greaves laid plates of flexible silver:
All their devotion to sickle and share, all love for the furrow,
Yielded to this; their fires retempered the swords of their fathers;
Thundered the trumpets of war; sped swiftly the watchword of battle;
Nervously one from the wall was snatching a helmet; another
Yoked his whinnying steeds to the car, and in shield and in corselet
Triple with gold was clad, and girt with the sword he had proven.[178]

Even in later years of the Republic, when expensive domiciles and all their pertinent luxuries had become common among the rich, the old pattern of hard physical discipline of the army still found loyalty. Marius' early life was "temperate and in harmony with the rearing which the ancient Romans gave their children," and he "vied with the common soldiers in frugality and endurance. . . ."[179] He was conspicuous for diligence, honesty, military skill, courageous spirit in war, and ambition for glory. "Naturally virile and fond of war" and trained "in military rather than in civil life," he strove even against infirmities and a tendency to corpulence in old age and went daily to the *Campus Martius*. There he exercised "with the young men and showed that he was still agile in arms and capable of feats of horsemanship. . . ." He is said to have entered upon a campaign late in life, so that he might personally "give his son a military training."[180] Cato taught his son to throw the javelin, fight in armor, ride horseback, box, "swim lustily," and "to endure heat and cold." Aemilius Paulus also trained his sons in the "ancestral discipline," not willing to leave it to Greeks who were invading the precincts of hunting and horsemanship in his day.[181] Cato the Younger avoided the luxurious dress that had become fashionable in his day, and strengthened his body by strenuous exercises, habituating himself to withstand heat and cold with uncovered head,

---

[178] *Aeneid*, vii, 623–40. Trans. by H. H. Ballard. Courtesy of Charles Scribner's Sons, New York.
[179] Plutarch: *Caius Marius*, 3, 7. Trans. by B. Perrin. The Loeb Classical Library. Quoted by permission of Harvard University Press, Cambridge, Mass.
[180] *Ibid.*, 2–3, 7, 34; Sallust: *Jugurtha*, 63; Ihne: *History of Rome*, v, 61 f.
[181] Plutarch: *Cato*, 20; *Aemilius Paulus*, 6.

and to travel on foot in all seasons.[182] With the end of conquests, however, military exercises and strict discipline of youth appear to have declined. Pliny notes, in melancholy vein, that though in olden time youth "were inured from boyhood to service in the camp" and learned to command by being made to obey, there was in his own day "neither command nor obedience." [183]

The army in early times was small, having three regiments, each a thousand strong, supported by about three hundred cavalry. The whole of it was made up of Patrician landowners. Servius, however, increased the army, including all citizens who had property, and raised the cavalry to eighteen centuries, composed of the wealthiest men. Below these were five classes, determined on the basis of wealth, which ranged from one hundred thousand asses for those of the first class to eleven thousand for the fifth.[184] There were eighty centuries of the first class; twenty centuries each of the second, third, and fourth; and thirty centuries of the fifth class. All classes were divided into juniors—the abler-bodied, aged from seventeen to forty-six years—and seniors, ranging from forty-seven to sixty years of age. The junior soldiers went into the field; the seniors were to defend the city at home. Below these five classes were five centuries, two of which included artisans, smiths, and carpenters; two others, horn-blowers and trumpeters; and one, made up of unarmed men who served to fill up depleted ranks and function as scouts.[185]

The first-class centuries were armed with helmets, round shields, greaves, and corselets for defense; for offense they had swords and a long spear. The second class had a buckler in place of the shield and wore no corselet, but otherwise was the same as the first. The third class differed from the second in having no greaves; the fourth had only the long spear and a javelin; and the fifth was equipped with stones and slings. The two lowest classes had no armor for defense. Soldiers of these early days were property owners. Furnishing their own equipment and serving without pay, classification on the basis of wealth was of practical significance. Later, when small farmers declined and slaves were used on the land, Marius raised volunteers without respect to class, and assigned lands to his soldiers. Thus was forged a powerful, dangerous instrument for personal aggrandizement, since an army of men who had little or nothing were willing to fight for the best "paymaster," even though he might lead them against their own country.[186]

The earliest army probably engaged chiefly in hand-to-hand fighting. The Servian, however, fought in a mass formation, similar to the Macedonian phalanx. This being rather cumbersome and inflexible, the legion was later

---

[182] Plutarch: Cato the Younger, 5.
[183] Letters, VIII, 14.
[184] Livy, I, 43.
[185] Sandys: op. cit., pp. 458 f.
[186] Frank: op. cit., pp. 269 f.

divided into maniples, small units that could function more or less independently.[187] It was characteristic of the Romans that, in their effort to succeed in war, they were ever ready to learn from their enemies. With studied care, in the light of their own experience, they modified equipment and organization until they built up the most formidable infantry of the ancient world. Having built "a good military organization and a sound system of national tactics," says Oman, they had the "surest basis for a sustained career of conquest." [188]

Horsemanship was an important branch of military training for the aristocratic element of the army. Horses, selected for their natural fitness and spirit, were specially trained for army service in Varro's day.[189] Pliny says that his uncle, when he was commander of a troop of horse, published a treatise on the *Art of Using a Javelin on Horseback*.[190] Though at the time of the Carthaginian wars the cavalry had become well armed after the Greek fashion, Polybius says, in earlier times their equipment for defense and offense was poor. They had then "no cuirasses but fought in light undergarments," which made it easy to mount and dismount swiftly, but exposed them "to great danger in close combat, as they were nearly naked." [191] Their lances, too, were unserviceable, in his judgment, being too slender, pliant, and easily broken. Very imperfect, also, were their round bucklers of oxhide, too light for service in attack, and readily rotted by exposure to the rains.

Service in the Roman army was not a matter of choice but of compulsion. Servius completed his census, having expedited it by means of a law which threatened imprisonment and death to those not rated. To the third century B.C., only those citizens settled in the colonies were exempted from conscription, and they were already on perpetual duty.[192]

The discipline of the Roman army was severe. The sentry who nodded and failed to observe the approaching Gauls was thrown down from the citadel, with manifest approval on the part of all.[193] Sallust says that "in time of war punishment was more often inflicted for attacking the enemy contrary to orders, or for withdrawing too tardily when recalled from the field, than for venturing to abandon the standards or to give ground under stress. . . ." [194] Punishment of units which had been at fault might even be decimation. The severity of discipline, or rather the willingness to bear "galling discipline," com-

---

[187] Livy, VIII, 8; Chapot: op. cit., pp. 77 f.
[188] Oman: *The Art of War in the Middle Ages*, pp. 63 f.; Polybius, VI, 25; Cary: op. cit., pp. 124 f.
[189] Varro: *On Agriculture*, II, 7, 15-6.
[190] *Letters*, III, 5.
[191] Bk. VI, 25.
[192] Livy, I, 44; Homo: op. cit., p. 231.
[193] Livy, V, 47.
[194] *Catiline*, 9. *Sallust*, trans. by J. C. Rolfe. The Loeb Classical Library. Quoted by permission of Harvard University Press, Cambridge, Mass.

bined with persistence, rigorous training, and refusal to admit defeat, was doubtless a weighty factor in the conquest of imperial power.[195] Obviously, one must not credit too much to the effect of mere harsh discipline. Other peoples, also, had plenty of it. Hannibal is said to have beaten and crucified a guide in order to terrify all others, because he had mistaken Casinum for Casilinum and thus had misdirected the general.[196]

Fear of severe punishments is doubtless a great deterrent to undesired behavior. Roman military success, however, must, to a much greater degree, be traced to arduous training in certain games and exercises, selected for their military value. Romans of early centuries doubtless enjoyed their exercises, but there is no hint of recognition of personal enjoyment, or the cultivation of grace and beauty, as valid purposes.[197] The contests portrayed by Virgil are Greek rather than Roman in spirit.[198] To run, jump, ride, fence, swim, wrestle, throw the spear, hurl the stone or discus, box, hurl the spear on horseback, and hunt were useful in gaining health, strength, agility; and these, in turn, were necessary to the successful warrior. It was proper, therefore, that boys and young men should practice them. Tullus Hostilius, successor to Numa, was credited by historians with instituting "all military discipline" and the art of war, and "wondrously" training "the soldiers of Rome. . . ." [199] The *Campus Martius* was early set aside and dedicated to public use. Here the army, horse and foot, was assembled by Servius.[200] Throughout the coming centuries Roman youth and men would gather, practice themselves in warlike games, and cultivate skill in the use of weapons. The *Campus* was thus the Romans' first gymnasium; the fathers themselves, their sons' first gymnastic teachers. The father taught his son manly exercises and the use of arms, even as he inducted him by active apprenticeship into the labors of the farm and the duties of law and religion. Though Romans learned from the Greeks many things pertaining to war, they always were contemptuous toward Greek physical training. Caesar encouraged his troops, saying "the world you hope to win" will not cost much blood, for "you will meet an army enlisted from the training-schools of Greece, enfeebled by the practice of the wrestling-ground, and scarce able to carry the weight of their arms. . . ." [201]

So highly did the Romans prize training, they gave the same term to exercise and to army—*exercitus*. Polybius traced the strength of the Romans not only

195 Frank: *op. cit.*, p. 356.
196 Livy, XXII, 13.
197 Johnston: *op. cit.*, p. 238; Showerman: *Rome and the Romans*, p. 374.
198 *Aeneid*, V.
199 *Florus*, I, 1.
200 Livy, I, 44; II, 5.
201 Lucan: *The Civil War*, VII, 269 *et seq*. Trans. by J. D. Duff. The Loeb Classical Library. Quoted by permission of Harvard University Press, Cambridge, Mass.

to the fact that theirs was a citizens' army with natural physical superiority to begin with, but to their training which was carried to a higher degree of perfection than that of their enemies.[202] This training was acquired in ways already mentioned and also by early, active service in the field. Cicero, in praise of Pompey, says that he "left school and the studies of boyhood to join his father's army and study war in a serious campaign against formidable foes"; he had command of a large army even "in early manhood," learning warfare not from the instructions of others "but from the commands he held himself. . . ."[203] Early maturity in military affairs was a common phenomenon of Roman life, for it was gained from a training which was, in large part, life itself.

Not only at home, but in the field, intervals between actual movements and engagements were filled with strenuous training. Livy gives an account of Scipio's program for his soldiers and sailors during the stay at Carthage: "On the first day the legions under arms performed evolutions through a space of four miles; on the second day he ordered them to repair and clean their arms before their tents; on the third day they engaged in imitation of a regular battle with wooden swords, throwing javelins with the points covered with balls; on the fourth day they rested; on the fifth they again performed evolutions under arms. This succession of exercise and rest they kept up as long as they staid at Carthage. The rowers and mariners, pushing out to sea when the weather was calm, made trial of the manageableness of their ships by mock sea-fights. Such exercises, both by sea and land, without the city, prepared their minds and bodies for war."[204]

FORMAL SCHOOLING   Prior to 1000 B.C. the Italic peoples probably had no knowledge of letters, but about the eighth or early seventh century Greeks are believed to have introduced the alphabet at Cumae. In the sixth century writing was still rare, limited to political and religious documents of importance.[205] Cicero, Livy, and Dionysius thought they had seen "original texts" of fifth century treaties; and Polybius translated an old treaty with Carthage, credited to the first year of the Republic. Whether these texts were so old is doubtful. The publication of the Laws, commonly dated 451–450 B.C., is put as late as 300 or 200 B.C. by some scholars.[206] Certainly there was little writing prior to 290 B.C.—neither history, poetry, nor literary prose.[207] If schools existed before the Carthaginian wars, they had little material. Cicero's statement—"We learned the Law of the Twelve Tables in our boyhood as a

---

[202] Bk. VI, 52.
[203] Manilian Law, 10. Cicero: The Speeches, trans. by H. G. Hodge. The Loeb Classical Library. Quoted by permission of Harvard University Press, Cambridge, Mass.
[204] Livy (Spillan and Edmonds), xxvi, 51; Polybius, x, 20.
[205] Homo: op. cit., pp. 9, 66, 98; Lawton: op. cit., p. 13; Cary: op. cit., p. 14.
[206] Livy, III, 31–2, 34; Cicero: Republic, II, 36; Gellius, xx, 1; Cary: op. cit., p. 47.
[207] Frank: op. cit., pp. 59 f.

required formula"—suggests that the Law may have been a "first reader" in the early schools.[208]

References to schools, *ludi*, are few; they come from a much later date, and should be taken with caution. Plutarch's assertion that Romulus and Remus were taken to Gabii "to learn letters and the other branches of knowledge" [209] seems but a pleasing fiction. Tanaquil is said to have given Servius Tullius "a liberal education." [210] Virginia, the victim of Appius Claudius' plot, was taken as she was entering the forum, where there were schools of letters.[211] A teacher at Falerii (394 B.C.), who had the pleasant habit of taking his boys to walk beyond the town for the sake of play and exercise, on one occasion sought to deliver them to the Roman commander, and with them the entire city.[212] Camillus, pitching his camp before the city of the Tusculans (382 B.C.) noted, along with other signs of peaceful activity, the humming of pupils' voices at their lessons.[213] Marcus Fabius (310 B.C.) had been educated at Caere and was well acquainted with the Etruscan language and writing—according to Livy, a common accomplishment among Romans at that time.[214]

The fragmentary references to early elementary schools have been variously interpreted. Wilkins was uncertain about there being "any public schools at Rome" in the early Republic; Laurie, however, found no reason to doubt that many elementary schools existed.[215] After the Twelve Tables were published, there was, certainly, a real reason for acquiring an ability to read, and this was doubtless increasingly gained in schools. In better families, however, boys would continue to be taught the rudiments at home. Not till after Livius Andronicus had come to Rome and had Latinized the Odyssey,[216] was there enough literary matter to require extensive, specialized services of schoolmasters. The training of life, even in later times, often interfered with formal scholastic education, and apparently was held in higher regard, as Cicero's praise of Pompey, who left off the "studies of boyhood" to enter the school of military affairs, suggests.[217]

APPRENTICESHIP TO LAW    The family, farm, army, and the forum were at once phases of life and instruments of education. Romans held their constitution to be superior to those of other states, being the product of many

[208] Cicero: Laws, II, 23, 59; Lawton: op. cit., p. 14.
[209] Plutarch: Romulus, 6.
[210] Florus, I, 1.
[211] Livy, III, 44.
[212] Ibid., V, 27; Dio, VI, 24; Plutarch: Camillus, 10; Florus, I, 6.
[213] Livy, VI, 25; Plutarch: Camillus, 38.
[214] Bk. IX, 36.
[215] Wilkins: Roman Education, p. 8; Laurie: Historical Survey of Pre-Christian Education, p. 342.
[216] Infra, p. 572.
[217] Cicero: Manilian Law, 10.

rather than the work of one man.[218] Polybius praised it for its combination of despotic, aristocratic, and democratic features.[219] Cicero regarded Roman law as the foundation of intellectual training for men in all the affairs of public life; for in its Twelve Tables was comprised the whole "science of government," surpassing the learning of all philosophers, "both in weight of authority, and in plenitude of utility." Since Rome seemed to him pre-eminently "the seat of virtue, empire, and dignity," her "spirit, customs, and discipline" should be the "first objects of study," for "as much wisdom must be thought to have been employed in framing such laws, as in establishing so vast and powerful an empire." [220]

Training in knowledge of the law and the conduct of public and private affairs was gained by a direct apprenticeship under the father's hands, or, in his absence, under the care of "some person of years and dignity." The son of a senator attended with his father the sessions of the Senate. "Thus," says Pliny, "they were taught by that surest method of instruction, example, how far the right of proposing any law to the Senate extended; what privileges a senator had in delivering his opinion; the powers of senators who are magistrates, and the independence of the rest; where it is proper to yield, and where to stand firm; how long to speak, and when to be silent; how to distinguish conflicting motions, and how to discuss an amendment. In a word, they learnt by this means the whole conduct of a senator." [221]

With the growth of the state and numerous other changes in Roman life, training of youth for public life was more and more relegated to the schools. Cicero, Tacitus, Pliny, and others were in agreement that the old training was superior to the new. Cicero complained that "this generation of ours is ignorant of law." [222] The virtue of the old system, said Tacitus, lay in the fact that "they carried on their studies in the light of open day, and amid the very shock of battle, under conditions in which any stupid or ill-advised statement brings prompt retribution in the shape of the judge's disapproval, taunting criticism from your opponent—yes, and from your own supporters expressions of dissatisfaction." [223] Pliny declared that pleading before the centumviri gave him more "fatigue than pleasure"; the causes were "generally trivial and jejune"; those who pleaded were "impudent fellows, and the majority actually obscure young men," who had just migrated "from the schools, to practise declaiming.

[218] Cicero: Republic, II, 1.
[219] Bk. VI, 11–8; cf. Homo: Roman Political Institutions from City to State, pp. 123 f.
[220] On Oratory, I, 44.
[221] Pliny: Letters, VIII, 14. Trans. by W. Melmoth, rev. by W. M. L. Hutchinson. The Loeb Classical Library. Quoted by permission of Harvard University Press, Cambridge, Mass.; cf. Gellius, I, 23.
[222] On Oratory, I, 10.
[223] Tacitus: On Oratory, 34. Trans. by W. Peterson. The Loeb Classical Library. Quoted by permission of Harvard University Press, Cambridge, Mass.

. . ." [224] Even the time for pleading a case was measured out, an hour or two, or even a half of that, as though one could tell in advance how much time a cause required.[225]

RELIGION, A PHASE OF LIFE AND EDUCATION   Religion pervaded every aspect of early Roman life. Its hold upon youth was first fixed by the father, to whom obedience and honor were due. Youth learned to honor age; greater deference was shown to family men than to others. It was an old custom that young men should escort older men home.[226] Religion and morals were taught by example, by an apprenticeship in religious acts that were constantly performed in connection with all affairs, private and public. It had little to do with attendance at temples, for, though these later acquired importance, in early years there were none.[227]

The Romans were, in Sallust's phrase, *religiosissimi mortales*. Cicero thought them superior to all others in religious affairs; in this, Polybius concurred. It was their firm conviction that they were divinely destined to lead the world. Believing themselves the special beneficiaries of divine favor, it is not surprising that they were "lavish in their offerings to the gods. . . ." [228]

Rome's earliest religion was a primitive animism. A spirit, a moving force, *numina*, dwelled in everything. Its good will must be cultivated by appropriate, propitiatory rites to secure the safety, prosperity, and final happiness of man. To the indigenous animism were added, from time to time, various gods, religious practices, and beliefs from outside sources—particularly in time of pestilence or other disasters. Thus the *ludi scaenici* were brought from Etruria in 364 B.C.; and the cult of Apollo was established during the Punic War.[229]

Religious practices reflected Roman utilitarianism. Religion was essentially a practical business, a contractual relationship, established between men and spiritual powers.[230] The Roman asked not for spiritual improvement, but for prosperity in his undertakings and health to carry them through. To secure the approval of the gods, he was formal, scrupulous, businesslike, giving freely, even generously, what custom had decreed. "I give, and you give." Such was the spirit of his dealing with invisible powers. With the commercial outlook, however, there was mingled awe, fear, and reverence; these were indeed due to those greater than himself. The prescribed ceremonies, which were his obligation, were of long standing and were enjoined by pontifical authority. To make innovations would be dangerous, impious.

[224] *Letters*, II, 14.
[225] *Ibid.*, VI, 2.
[226] *Gellius*, II, 15.
[227] *Cf.* Plutarch: *Numa*, 8; Wilkins: *op. cit.*, p. 10.
[228] Sallust: *Catiline*, 9; Polybius, VI, 6; Livy, V, 54.
[229] Livy, VII, 2; XXV, 12; XXVII, 23.
[230] Showerman: *op. cit.*, pp. 288 f.

SUOVETAURILIA
(J. von Falke, *Greece and Rome*, p. 290)

In trivial affairs, as in the most important, man's dependence on other forces was recognized. Marriage was a solemn necessity. Childless men were considered accursed. By marriage one ensured successors, protection of one's burial place, and offerings to the hovering spirit. When taking such a momentous step the gods must be propitiated by proper ceremonies.[231]

To an agricultural and pastoral people the security of boundaries and the safety and fertility of plants and animals meant much. Boundaries were sacred. The "religion of Numa" condemned to the underworld one who molested boundary markers, *termini*; and a man forfeited his life for killing an ox. Every task of the herds and fields was entered on with due ceremony. After the "sacred feast" "begin the spring ploughing . . ." is Cato's instruction.[232] To purify the land, the *suovetaurilia* (sacrifice of pig, sheep, and bull) is prescribed, so that success may crown labor, while sickness, barrenness, and ruin may be averted, and the issue from flocks and fields may be plentiful. When thinning a grove, a certain formula must be repeated, and a pig sacrificed.[233] For the health of cattle, specified amounts of foods must be offered and eaten. Women may neither take part nor see the ceremony performed. Utmost nicety must be observed in all ceremonies. Certain trees must be grafted in the dark of the moon, in the afternoon, when there is no south wind. In doctoring an ox, both doctor and ox must fast, and both must stand.[234] Labor was forbidden

---

[231] Dill: *Roman Society from Nero to Marcus Aurelius*, pp. 256 f., 488; Johnston: *op. cit.*, p. 41.
[232] *On Agriculture*, 50; Paul-Louis: *op. cit.*, pp. 50 f.
[233] Cato: *On Agriculture*, 139, 141.
[234] *Ibid.*, 40, 71, 83.

on certain days; but some tasks—such as draining land, hedging grain fields, giving water, burning briars, dipping sheep, and setting snares for birds—were permitted even on holy days.[235]

War's uncertainties were too serious to face without the gods' approval. The making of war lay in the hands of the *Fetiales*, a priesthood of Numa, who called the gods to witness and invoked numerous evils on themselves and the country if they began war unjustly.[236] Military successes were credited to the gods and celebrated with appropriate ceremonies and games, sometimes promised in advance. Camillus solemnly vowed Great Games and the repair of Mother Matuta's temple upon the capture of Veii. After the Gauls' invasion, the temples were restored and purified, and Jupiter was honored by the Capitoline Games.[237]

An eminent scholar identifies Roman *religio* first of all with "awe, nervousness, scruple," meaning much the same as we do by superstition; and secondly, with the methods and rituals by which the spirits were appeased and fears were eased.[238] The service of superstition to the state was believed to have been great. Plutarch thought one should not be incredulous about fabulous tales of Rome, considering that the state would not have risen to such power "had it not been of a divine origin, and one which was attended by great marvels." [239] Numa had tamed the "fierce and warlike tempers" by "sacrifices, processions, and religious dances"; by "strange apparitions of divine beings and threatening voices," he had subdued and humbled their minds.[240] Polybius held that a scrupulous fear of the gods, "superstition," carried to such lengths that nothing could "exceed it," was the very thing which maintained "the cohesion of the Roman State." It was useful, he held, as a check on the fickle, lawless multitude which needs to be checked by invisible terrors and pageantry; the ancients were wise in introducing and cultivating such fears; moderns were "rash and foolish in banishing such beliefs." [241]

Whether or not superstitious beliefs and practices were thus consciously founded, fostered, and rendered effective, it is certain that they pervaded Roman society and motivated much of its activity. Later, of course, a Lucretius might find all superstitions odious; Plutarch might think it ridiculous that Romans should believe that a statue spoke; [242] but faith in capricious, super-

235 Columella: *Of Husbandry*, ii, 22; Virgil: *Georgics*, i, 268 *et seq.*
236 Plutarch: *Numa*, 12; Frank: *op. cit.*, pp. 8 f.
237 Livy, v, 19, 50; xxx, 27; Plutarch: *Camillus*, 5.
238 Fowler: *Social Life*, p. 319.
239 *Romulus*, 8.
240 Plutarch: *Numa*, 8. Trans. by B. Perrin. The Loeb Classical Library. Quoted by permission of Harvard University Press, Cambridge, Mass.
241 Bk. vi, 56.
242 *Coriolanus*, 37–8.

natural interference in all matters, great and small, was all but universal in early days and continued widespread even in the period of greatest enlighten-ment. A few examples give a hint of this aspect of the Roman mind. The cus-tom of driving a nail in the cella of Jupiter's temple was revived because of "great disasters." [243] When scenic plays, introduced from Etruria to combat a pestilence, were interrupted by a flood of the Tiber, the people were terrified, deeming it a sign of the gods' displeasure.[244] In the war with Veii, the Delphic oracle advised that the waters of the Alban lake must be prevented from join-ing the sea; otherwise Veii could not be taken. Priests directed ceremonies, accordingly, and sought to divert the waters.[245] Another tale of Veii forecast victory for the one who should cut up the entrails of a certain victim.[246] A man was warned by Jupiter that he must go to the magistrates, tell them that actions of a dancer in previous games had displeased the god, and cause the games to be repeated on a splendid scale; otherwise the city would be in danger. The man hesitated, and shortly lost a son; still delaying, he was stricken with paralysis; then, terrified, he was carried to the magistrates, to whom he told what Jupiter had commanded. Having discharged this duty, he was healed and walked away.[247] Appius Claudius lost his sight because he directed the Potitian family, which attended Heracles' altar, to teach the rites to outsiders. The whole Potitian family, thirty grownups and their offspring, died within a year. Such portentous events, Livy thought, ought to make people slow to change the established mode of religious rites.[248] A multitude of remarkable prodigies in Italy and at Rome during the Punic wars, Livy reports, were expiated with "full-grown victims," and supplications were ordered to those deities that had shrines in Rome.[249]

The encouragement of superstitions had its reward. Inured for centuries to belief in magic, the Roman populace was ready, when circumstances favored, to accept other magic than that which leaders held valid. As the Punic wars wore on, a veritable passion for superstitious rites, chiefly from abroad, took hold of Rome.[250] Roman rites fell into disuse; hosts of women sacrificed and offered prayers in public to strange gods in ways unusual. Finally, in order to get rid of these superstitions, the Senate ordered the surrender of all works on divination, prayers, and rituals, and forbade further public sacrifices accord-ing to novel, foreign rites.[251] The Senate itself was inconsistent, discouraging

---

[243] Dio, LV, 10, n. 2.
[244] Livy, VII, 2–3.
[245] Plutarch: Camillus, 4.
[246] Livy, V, 21.
[247] Ibid., II, 36–7.
[248] Ibid., IX, 29.
[249] Ibid., XXIV, 10.
[250] Ibid., XXV, 1.
[251] Ibid.

and again encouraging new worships, such as the Ludi Tarentini, approved in 249 and 207 B.C.[252]

Roman religion, originally a primitive animism, developed a more or less marked anthropomorphism. Jupiter ruled the heavens; Mars, war; Neptune, the sea; Mercury, commerce; Vulcan, the smithy; Ceres, grain; Janus, the changing year; Terminus, boundaries; Minerva, weaving, spinning, and arts of learning; Luna, the moon; Liber, fields; Flora, vegetables and flowers; Bona Dea, agriculture; Silvanus, woodlands; Pales, Lupercus, and Faunus, herds and herdsmen; Pomona, orchards; Saturn, the sown seed; Ops and Consus, the gathered crops. Robigus, a bad god, if not propitiated, would mildew crops. Vesta, special goddess of the hearth, and other spirits, lares and penates, constituted the focus of the domestic cult. The lares were guardians of roads, crossroads and common property boundaries, and were honored at festivals, Compitalia or Laralia, participated in by all of the district dwellers, free and unfree.[253] Travelers commended themselves to the protection of the lares viales. Public lares and penates were also worshiped.[254] Of the host of deities which ruled the much-partitioned Roman universe, many were native, others foreign, the latter element increasing as Rome became the center of the Mediterranean world.

Etruria, "mother of superstition," had a profound influence on Rome. Menvra, Losna, and Aplu are generally accepted as prototypes of Minerva, Luna, and Apollo. The Roman use of auspices has been called a "purely Etruscan element"; Romans appear to have trusted Etruscan ability to read signs and portents—a very serious, meticulous business—more than they did their own.[255]

The chief religious institutions were credited traditionally to Numa, who established the calendar of festivals, named the first flamines, and was himself first of the priests.[256] The machinery of the state cult was ruled by a supreme pontiff (Pontifex Maximus), subordinate pontifices, and flamines who presided over the cults of special deities. The chief flamines were those of Jupiter, Mars, and Quirinus. The Salii, dancing priests of Mars, had charge of twelve sacred shields, which they carried every March through the streets while they performed their dance; the Salii Collini directed the worship of Quirinus, the deified Romulus; the Fetiales were guardians of peace and war; the Augures explained the will of deities when auspices were taken; and the Quindecemviri had care of the Sibylline books. The Fratres Arvales, one of the oldest

252 Cary: op. cit., p. 273.
253 Cato: On Agriculture, 5.
254 Wissowa: op. cit., pp. 145–54; Fowler: Roman Festivals, pp. 136, 309, 335 ff.
255 Livy, XXVI, 23; Cicero: Laws, II, 9; On Divination, I, 41; Müller: Die Etrusker, II, 2 f.; Fell: op. cit., pp. 51 f.
256 Plutarch: Numa, 3, 9 et seq.

religious bodies, had as its first members the twelve sons of the foster mother of Romulus, Acca Larentia. All services of male gods were in the care of men. In the cults of Vesta, Juno, Ceres, and other goddesses, women took part. Six virgins, each serving Vesta for thirty years, lived in quarters by her temple and tended the holy fire. In later times numerous, new, foreign cults encouraged the service of women.[257] This state cult, though criticized as a "hard, narrow, unexpansive system of abstraction and personification," which aimed in legalis-. tic fashion to control all nature, man, and social relations, gained great hold upon the people, and, revived and perfected under Augustus, continued to the end of the Empire. Doubtless numerous festivals associated with Roman religion—the Ludi Romani in honor of Jupiter, the Saturnalia, the Cerealia and Lupercalia, designed to secure the safety and prosperity of herds and grain— were close to the hearts of the people, gave an opportunity for merrymaking, and contributed much to its hold upon them. The priestly colleges still met in the time of Theodosius; and certain of the oldest festivals, such as the Lupercalia, were still celebrated in the late fifth century.[258] Pagan cults and pagan games offered the most persistent resistance to Christian efforts to reform the ancient world.

[257] Abbott: op. cit., p. 78; Sandys: op. cit., pp. 152 f.; Johnston: op. cit., pp. 396 ff.
[258] Dill: Last Century, pp. 74 f.

# 18

# GROWTH AND DECAY OF EMPIRE

TRANSITION FROM REPUBLIC TO EMPIRE

Roman adventures beyond Italian shores (264 B.C.) inaugurated a period more reliably dealt with by early historians. Polybius, a Greek who was taken to Italy (167 B.C.), became intimately acquainted with Scipio Aemilianus, espoused Rome's cause, and spread on a broad canvas the story of her conquests. Livy also told the tale of those adventurous years more fully and reliably than that of the early Kingdom and Republic. Diodorus, Dionysius of Halicarnassus, Sallust, Lucan, Suetonius, Tacitus, Dio Cassius, Ammianus Marcellinus, Florus, Ausonius, Claudian, Spartianus, Capitolinus, Lampridius, Pollio, Tertullian, Jerome, and others embroidered the old story of Rome's beginning, the vicissitudes of the dying Republic and the early Empire, and depicted the lengthening shadows cast by Rome's setting sun. Theirs is a record of expansion by conquest and the subjection of other peoples, decay of self-government at Rome, and gradual social disintegration, from which, despite heroic efforts, no one was wise enough to save the Roman state. Besides this, it is a record of metamorphosis by which the crude culture of a primitive people, crossed with that of Hellenic cities, emerged as the crowning achievement of man in the Mediterranean world.

Having consolidated Rome's control over Italy, Romans developed aspirations for a wider domain, and popular leaders pointed out the advantages of empire to the Roman populace. This tendency, as it grew, eventually showed up the duplicity of the formulae of the priestly fetial board whose business had been to place Rome's cause in a favorable light, and that of her enemies in an unfavorable one.[1] Rome's imperialism and the Pax Romana were made possible by the destruction of other imperial forces, first of all Carthage and then other powers ringing the eastern Mediterranean. Her progress toward this

[1] Frank: *Roman Imperialism*, pp. 8 f.

end, described as "slow but implacable as a phenomenon of nature," [2] was frequently marked by ruthlessness toward others, as witness the destruction of Carthage (146 B.C.), the atrocities of Galba in Spain (151 B.C.), the plundering and enslavement of citizens of Epirus (167 B.C.). There were also cleverness, persistence, courage, heroism, and occasional examples of magnanimity, exemplified in the decree of freedom to the Greeks. Polybius, though friendly to the Romans, says that they had a way of extending their sway over others while "appearing to confer a benefit" on them. Of the Third Punic War, he says the Romans had long made up their minds to it, and were only watching for "a suitable opportunity and a pretext that would appeal to foreign nations." [3]

The unification of Italy, consummated in 272 B.C., was followed shortly by efforts to extend Rome's sway beyond the sea. The struggle for empire began with the first clash with Carthage (264–241 B.C.), which gave Rome Sicily, then Sardinia and Corsica. The destructive Hannibalic War (218–202 B.C.) ended in victory for Scipio Aemilianus, at Zama, with vassalage for Carthage, loss of her war fleet, and tribute to be paid to Rome. The Third Carthaginian War (149–146 B.C.) fulfilled Cato's fear-inspired injunction, "Carthage must be destroyed," and left Rome mistress of the western Mediterranean. During the last half century of the Carthaginian wars, Rome was engaged from time to time with Eastern powers as well. Macedonia, which had been in league with Hannibal in the Second Punic War, was turned upon at its close, defeated at Cynoscephalae, and made subject to Rome (197 B.C.). Philhellenism was strong in Rome at the time, and the Greeks, having favored Rome against Philip of Macedon, were given their freedom for the moment by a proclamation of the Senate, read at the Isthmian Games in 196 B.C.[4] Philip's ally, Antiochus the Great of Syria, next fell before the legions of the Scipios (190 B.C.), and gave Rome mastery to the River Halys. A third possible contender for sway, Egypt, long friendly toward Rome, came under Roman tutelage (168 B.C.) after the Senate intervened on her behalf against Antiochus IV. Two decades later (146 B.C.), the philhellenic bias of the Senate having subsided in favor of a return to the old Roman policy of ruling those they had conquered, the Greeks, who had been favored during the Roman-Macedonian conflict, were reduced to subjection. After the Achaean War, Corinth was destroyed.[5] In the brief space of 118 years Rome had added to her domain all the Mediterranean world—had become the crucible in which was to be mixed a cosmopolitan culture. Later conquests in Gaul, Britain, and elsewhere ex-

---

[2] Homo: *Primitive Italy and the Beginnings of Roman Imperialism*, p. x.
[3] *The Histories*, xxxvi, 2; xxxi, 10.
[4] *Ibid.*, xviii, 45–6; Frank: *op. cit.*, pp. 150 f.
[5] Frank: *op. cit*, pp. 190 ff.; Cary: *History of Rome*, pp. 210, 222 f., 252 f.

tended her territory, but brought nothing of moment to the culture of imperial Rome.

Having grasped potential wealth and power of empire the Roman future doubtless seemed bright to most observers. But to one of those who had helped bring these things to pass, the destruction of Carthage brought foreboding: Scipio is reported to have said to Polybius, ". . . some day the same doom will be pronounced upon my own country." [6]

Ancient authors viewed the growth of empire variously, but generally regarded it as a fulfillment of destiny. The gods willed that Rome should rule other nations; she was of "divine origin"; she must not forget her destiny. Florus, recounting the achievements of seven hundred years, declared that "Valour and Fortune" had "competed to establish the Roman empire." Tacitus and others seem to have accepted the Empire as a "desperate necessity." [7]

Livy [8] credits Hannibal with the wise observation that no great state is able to remain long at rest. Dionysius [9] understood the historic process by which the conquest of Italy emboldened Rome to go on to conquer Sicily, Sardinia, Corsica, Carthage, Macedon, Greece, and proceed even to universal dominion. Dio [10] believed that jealousy and fear, shared by both Rome and Carthage, led to war. Polybius noted the economic factors back of this restless striving, leading to new wars. Aid to the Mamertines, a forerunner of the Punic struggles, was urged by military leaders as a means of profit to the Roman people. Again, the financial interests of the *equites*, whose members enjoyed the income from contracts given out by the censors, were a powerful influence in foreign affairs; for everyone was interested in these contracts and the work they involved, and hence all elements tended to support each other wherever threatened by a common danger from abroad. [11] There is some truth in Polybius' interpretation, doubtless, but the unity of Roman decisions seems overdrawn. Certainly there were at times serious differences in respect to foreign policy; this is reflected in Cato's credo, "Carthage must be destroyed," and Nasica's dictum, "Carthage must be spared." [12]

Two widely divergent views are held respecting Roman imperial development: first, that it came about as a result of "the execution of grandiose 'plans' boldly conceived"; second, that empire resulted from steps, taken blunderingly,

---

[6] Polybius, xxxviii, 21–2; Appian: *Punic Wars*, 132.
[7] Lawton: *Classical Latin Literature*, p. 297; Florus: *Epitome of Roman History*, I, introduction; Cicero: *Philippic* vi, 7; Plutarch: *Romulus*, 8; Virgil: *Aeneid*, vi, 847 *et seq.*
[8] Bk. xxx, 44.
[9] *The Roman Antiquities*, I, 3.
[10] *Roman History*, xi, 1–3.
[11] Polybius, I, 11; vi, 17–8.
[12] Plutarch: *Cato*, 27.

which led to consequences unforeseen by the Roman Senate, which was slow, unimaginative, and fearful of adventures into unknown paths. Probably the Romans were neither as stupid as the second view suggests nor as superior as the first implies. But the view that Rome moved gradually and somewhat blindly into imperialism seems more reasonable than that there was an aggressive, consistent, planned program of foreign expansion. Romans probably regarded their wars as "preventive" and "defensive," as other imperial powers have done; that any Roman thought frankly of imperial power before the Punic wars seems improbable.[13] In the Second Punic War, Hannibal's determined pursuit of a war policy was indubitably a major obstacle to peaceful relations. The "democratic reformers" of the "Gracchan decade" were probably not aggressive imperialists, but they might have been forced into war, had they lasted longer, in order to secure improvements at home. In this "they differed but little from the senate." In the end, however, ". . . the free Roman people stumbled on falteringly and unwittingly into ever increasing dominion . . ." whose burden reduced them to servitude.[14] Rome's empire in the eastern Mediterranean may have been "even more the product of a chapter of accidents" than in the West. Had Greeks been united, the Romans would not have attempted their conquest, and could hardly have succeeded if they had.[15]

As to the influence of trade rivalries and financial interests on expansion in the second century B.C., there is wide difference of judgment. Mommsen, Mahaffy, and Wilamowitz hold that these factors played a leading rôle in determining foreign policy. Others maintain that Rome's treaty with Carthage (348 B.C.), lack of archaeological evidence of imports, Rome's inactivity against pirates prior to 67 B.C., and the belated improvement of the port of Ostia (42 A.D.), suggest that she was insignificant as a trader, and make it unreasonable to hold that commercial interests ". . . directed the foreign policies of the senate in the second century B.C., much less that it secured the destruction of Corinth and Carthage."[16] Frank estimates that foreign "collections and contracts" of the financial houses (publicani) in 150 B.C. amounted to only about 1 per cent of the wealth of the equites; that this was insignificant compared with investments in land at home; and that therefore the interest of the equites in foreign expansion in the second century was much less than is commonly believed. Their influence became a determining factor in the next cen-

---

[13] Homo: op. cit., pp. vii–viii, 259 f., 349; Frank: op. cit., p. 120.
[14] Frank: op. cit., pp. 257, 358.
[15] Cary: op. cit., p. 224.
[16] Frank: op. cit., pp. 277 f., 283 f., 286; Chapot: Roman World, p. 27; Mommsen: History of Rome, IV, 400 ff.

tury, however, largely because the Gracchan Law (123 B.C.) gave them improved status, and opened to them more extensive operations for the state.[17]

While Rome's dominion in Italy had generally gained approval, her management abroad fell short of it, for the fair dealing which she had exhibited toward conquered peoples at home was often lost sight of in the provinces. In Spain, for example, Roman generals frequently disavowed "treaty obligations," and the Senate was too apt to assent "to their double-dealing." [18] Moreover, whereas the Italian peoples gave military service, the provinces rendered tribute. The milch cow was far away, but Roman arms were long. Provincial governors and their aides recouped old losses and were ever alert for new gains. Besides collecting legal tribute, exemptions from supplying grain and quartering troops, the sale of "justice," and other devices were employed to enrich Romans who went to the provinces. Chief of the private profiteers were the tax gatherers, publicani, who collected as much beyond official allotments as they could, purchased grain at low cost and sold it at fabulous prices, and lent money at extortionate rates to oppressed provincials. Naturally, there were good as well as bad provincial agents. It was, of course, as far as many peoples were concerned, merely a substitution of one despotism for another, for Carthage was also a harsh master. Rome, however, was stronger than Carthage, and once her military machine had riveted the shackles, neither the periods of greatest disorder between rival domestic factions, which marked the demise of the Republic, nor even the faults and weaknesses of the worst emperors were the occasion of a single conquered people's regaining its liberty. The lot of the Greeks was somewhat happier than that of others, doubtless because of their cultural attraction for many Romans. Though they lost independence through Rome's conquest, they enjoyed a degree of peace unattainable while they fought amongst themselves. After the destruction of Corinth, Greek cities retained local government, trade between them was free, and Greek leagues were re-established for religious purposes.

The domestic effect of Rome's wars of conquest was felt in numerous ways. Economic consequences were inescapable, the damage done irreparable. A flood of grain, first from Sicily, later from the East, destroyed the well-being of Roman grain farmers, forced land out of the hands of small owners, and increased the holdings of large owners, who turned the land to grazing and vineyards. Etruria, though less injured than other farming regions in the Hannibalic War, first impressed Tiberius with the need for reforms. Marius raised six

[17] Frank: op. cit., pp. 292 f.
[18] Cary: op. cit., pp. 184, 186.

thousand men for his support in Etruria. The worst havoc struck southern Italy, where upwards of two million acres were laid waste and fell into the hands of the state. Land being a drug on the market, attempts were made to lease it for grazing, which required less manpower.[19]

There were other deficits; the cost of victories was great. The number of legions almost doubled after the battle at Cannae, money and slaves were contributed by the wealthier people, and coinage was depreciated. Spain, which had been conquered, had to be held; and holding it cost the state for two centuries more than it was able to take out. Though there were unprofitable ventures like Spain, victory in Africa and the East gave Rome an economic monopoly which she could exploit.[20] The chief problem became how best to divide the fruits of victory. Would the Romans be wise enough to devise a policy for the rational employment of their gains so as to strengthen the commonwealth?

Victories over Carthage and the Eastern powers gave great confidence to the Romans; internal tensions and violence, however, soon brought them to despair. The Senate's position was for a time greatly enhanced, and that of Plebeians, who had risen to political equality with Patricians (287 B.C.), was diminished.[21] According to Sallust, "Affairs at home and in the field were managed . . . [by] a few men" who had the "treasury, the provinces, public offices, glory and triumphs . . . [while] the people were burdened with military service and poverty." [22] But the prestige of the oligarchy of the Senate was short-lived; its rule was soon threatened by ominous forces, for foreign wars brought military leaders a prominence hitherto unknown. Varro received the thanks of the Senate for his services at Cannae, because he had not despaired of the Republic. Victorious generals brought money to their soldiers and new wealth to the treasury, and also enhanced private financial interests which, in turn, supported and sought to influence public affairs. Pompey's policy was in reality that of "Italian speculators" who gained influence in the government and swayed its destiny.[23] Looking back, it seemed to Florus that the age of conquests had been "golden, glorious," but that which followed was one of "iron and bloodshed," bringing the murder of the Gracchi and Drusus, wars against slaves and gladiators, and the struggles of Marius and Sulla, Pompey and Caesar. Extravagance and "profuse largesses," due to increased wealth, armed

[19] Fell: Etruria and Rome, pp. 161 ff.; Frank: op. cit., p. 130.
[20] Cary: op. cit., pp. 163, 178; Frank: op. cit., p. 129.
[21] Frank: op. cit., pp. 111, 132; Homo: Roman Political Institutions from City to State, p. 134.
[22] War with Jugurtha, 41. Sallust, trans. by J. C. Rolfe. The Loeb Classical Library. Quoted by permission of Harvard University Press, Cambridge, Mass.
[23] Chapot: op. cit., p. 31; Frank: op. cit., pp. 314 ff., 324 f.

Caesar and Pompey with "fatal torches" which lighted flames and destroyed the Republic.[24] War's successes brought military despotism. In the days of Marius, if not before, the real power of the state lay in the army; the civil wars were a struggle for its control, enjoyed for a day by a Sulla, a Pompey, a Caesar, who gained an empire but reduced the Roman people to servitude.

Certain developments leading to this loss of liberty require attention. Power lay theoretically in the people's hands, but in reality in the Senate, whose prestige had been enhanced by the wars. Most pressing of domestic concerns was the need for more free farmers, fewer slaves, distribution of land, and adjustment of Rome's relations with her Italian allies. The aristocratic, oligarchic Senate was satisfied with the *status quo*. The Licinian Law, which aimed to restrict the rich to five hundred acres of public land and a limited number of cattle and sheep to be pastured thereon, had been ineffective. Public lands, greatly increased by the wars, fell into the hands of a few nobles (hardly two thousand, by one account), unconcerned with anything but their own interests. Tiberius Gracchus, however, a noble who saw danger in such maldistribution of wealth, hoped to remedy the situation by rousing the dispossessed to a struggle on their own behalf. It was easy enough to find a following when he put the situation so boldly and bluntly: "The wild beasts that roam over Italy . . . have every one of them a cave or lair to lurk in; but the men who fight and die for Italy enjoy the common air and light, indeed, but nothing else; houseless and homeless they wander about with their wives and children. And it is with lying lips that their imperators exhort the soldiers in their battles to defend sepulchres and shrines from the enemy; for not a man of them has an hereditary altar, not one of all these many Romans an ancestral tomb, but they fight and die to support others in wealth and luxury, and though they are styled masters of the world, they have not a single clod of earth that is their own." [25]

Tiberius was elected tribune in 133 B.C. and secured an enactment similar to the Licinian Law, but was murdered by senators when he sought re-election. Gaius Gracchus, a brother, continued as tribune the same struggle ten years later. Recognizing that nothing could be done as long as the Senate's power remained supreme, Gaius sought to enhance the financial interests of the *equites* by securing them privileges as collectors of taxes in the provinces. The discontented allies, who had borne the burdens of war without having the rights of citizenship, were to be won over by that boon. Amid the disorders which followed, the reformer was slain in 121 B.C. The chief net results of reforms, therefore, were: an improved position of the *equites* at the expense of

---

[24] *Florus*, I, 34, 19; 47, 12.
[25] Plutarch: *Tiberius Gracchus*, 9–10. Trans. by B. Perrin. The Loeb Classical Library. Quoted by permission of Harvard University Press, Cambridge, Mass.; *Florus*, II, 1–3.

the senators; retention by the nobles of great estates, while the landless men were still landless; increase of the number of slaves on the land; and continued lack of citizenship of the allies.[26]

Of greatest moment for the future were the frustration of democratic procedure by the powerful nobility and the lesson in violence which the people were not slow in taking to heart. Increasingly they now turned to military men, rather than magistrates and laws for alleviation of injustices. Marius, a man of the people and a brilliant commander, was named by the assembly to replace Metellus, the Senate's general who had been fighting Numidian Jugurtha in north Africa. Having concluded the Jugurthine War, Marius became Consul again, and shortly after added to his renown by defeating the Germans and the Cimbrians (102 B.C.), who had long threatened northern Italy. Though successful in military affairs, Marius was less adept at politics; the Senate gained control once more, and reforms still waited. There were significant changes, however; for Marius put the pauperized people to work—in the army—breaking with the long-established property classifications, and establishing a professional, highly trained, military force, whose members had nothing to lose and were ready to follow the best paymaster. Pay for army service had been begun as early as the siege of Veii.[27]

The unrest of the Italian allies, the solution of whose problems had failed when Gaius Gracchus was slain, meanwhile increased. In 90 B.C., after the murder of Drusus who had become the champion of their cause, the Italians of the south and central regions formed a separate government. Civil war between Rome and Italica followed, resulting in a belated granting of citizenship by Rome (88 B.C.).

The remaining days of the Republic were marked by struggles between rival generals—conflicts which mocked the term "self-government." Sulla, who had just led Roman armies against the allies, was ordered by the Senate to take a command in Asia Minor; the people chose their favorite, Marius. Being without an army, Marius escaped to Africa, while Sulla gained passage of a law to the intent that the assembly must have the Senate's approval in the future, else it could not vote. On Sulla's departure for Asia Minor, Marius returned from Africa, placed himself at the head of a force, did execution on his opponents in the Senate, and was re-elected Consul in 86 B.C. At Sulla's return, the armies of the people at home were defeated one by one; Sulla became Dictator (82 B.C.), meted out "justice" to his enemies in the people's party, and stripped all power from the people's assembly and tribunes, transferring it to the Senate.

[26] Ihne: History of Rome, v, 10 f.; Cary: op. cit., pp. 293 f.; Frank: op. cit., pp. 251 f; Homo: Political Institutions, p. 153.
[27] Livy, IV, 59; Mommsen: op. cit., III, 413.

Uprisings of discontented slaves also plagued the Romans. Slave revolts, while not a novelty, took on a seriousness which they did not have in earlier days. In Sicily, some sixty thousand led by Eunus (135–132 B.C.) defied Roman arms successfully for a time. In 103 B.C. a second rising under Athenio had to be put down in Sicily.[28] Thirty years thereafter, Spartacus, a Thracian gladiator, escaped from the training school at Capua, raised and armed seventy thousand malcontents, and long resisted forces sent against him (73–71 B.C.).[29] These events had a profound effect: the Sicilian revolts were partially responsible for serious efforts at reform in the day of the Gracchi; that of Spartacus added fuel to fires already burning in Rome and helped to "precipitate a political crisis." [30]

The gains of the Senate, sealed only by Sulla's force, did not long stand. Pompey, victorious in Spain, was elected Consul (70 B.C.), having won popular support by promising repeal of Sulla's drastic legislation. Fulfilling his promise brought him greater power. In 67 B.C. he was given a large fleet to clear the pirates from the Mediterranean; speedily succeeding in this, he was given command of forces in Asia Minor, whence he returned in triumph, 61 B.C.[31] To secure land for his victorious soldiers and sanction for his acts in the East, he needed the Senate's stamp of approval. To this end, Pompey, the popular soldier; Crassus, a wealthy man, who knew that political ambition must be backed by a purse long enough to support an army; and Caesar, ambitious, friendly to the people, a good sport among inferiors, vigorous against opponents, quick to anticipate, judge, execute, and more aggressively expansionist than others Rome had known, formed a triumvirate which, though private, brought the government into their hands.[32] Caesar was elected Consul (59 B.C.), requited Pompey, secured certain land reforms, and was made provincial governor of Gaul and Illyricum.[33] In eight years the Gauls were conquered, and vast territories from the Rhine to beyond the Channel were made subject to Rome. Caesar, now ready to return, was a candidate for his second consulship; the Senate, fearful of returning victorious generals, opposed his re-election, gave Pompey command of home forces, and ordered Caesar to lay down the command of his Gallic army. Caesar refused and marched on Rome (49 B.C.). Pompey, knowing his forces unequal to Caesar's, fled from Italy to Greece; there he marshaled part of his men, while others still occupied Spain. Caesar, having been chosen Consul, turned first to Spain and defeated Pompey's followers; thence he crossed back to Greece, and overcame Pompey at Pharsalus

[28] Florus, II, 7.
[29] Appian: Civil Wars, I, 116; Plutarch: Pompey, 21; Crassus, 8–11; Florus, II, 7–8.
[30] Cary: op. cit., p. 365; Mommsen: op. cit., III, 102, 309 ff., 380 ff.; IV, 357–64.
[31] Mommsen: op. cit., IV, 400 ff.
[32] Plutarch: Caesar, 2; Suetonius: Julius, 19–20; Dio's Roman History, XLIV, 38; Frank: op. cit., pp. 329, 341, 344; Mommsen: op. cit., IV, 503 ff.
[33] Frank: op. cit., chap. 17; Mommsen: op. cit., V, 38–95.

(48 B.C.), thus ending a struggle which Lucan called "legality conferred on crime." [34] When Caesar returned to Rome three years later, after successes in Asia Minor and north Africa, he became permanent Dictator. Everything lay in Caesar's lap; honors were heaped upon him; but he was praised most roundly, it was said, when he refused a diadem at the Lupercalia. By mildness toward those who had opposed him, by quieting the fears of the Senate and the people, and by magnificent spectacles to divert them, Caesar sought to win the Romans.[35]

The Senate, whose incompetence and selfishness had been a major factor in bringing affairs of state to such a pass, was now more than ever a hollow mockery. Subservient to its masters, it had been enlarged at will by Sulla to six hundred and then by those whom Caesar honored. Caesar's murder (44 B.C.) introduced no new principle into Roman affairs; it continued faithfully the pattern of violence begun in the days of the Gracchi. The assassination of Cicero, bright symbol of an expiring age, followed the next year. In his death, though it has been called "a costly but necessary assurance of peace," the ablest voice of political reason was stilled.[36]

Unfortunately, peace did not come; the civil war for power went on. Octavian, Caesar's adopted son, joined Antony and Lepidus to form a new triumvirate; which, having increased its resources by confiscation of property and its security by murdering its opponents, continued the struggle against the last supporters of the Republic, Brutus and Cassius, and defeated them at Philippi, 42 B.C. The contest then narrowed to a struggle between Lepidus, Antony, and Octavian, the latter being finally victorious at Actium, 31 B.C.

The question was now whether the rule of one could cope with those problems which the leaders of the people and of the Senate had failed to solve. For the difficult task a new organization was about to be created. Octavian, adept at politics, conciliated the Senate and maintained many republican forms, being advised to let it appear that "full authority" lay in the Senate. Similarly, in the time of Julius, the Senate had solemnly granted him "permission to do whatever he wished . . . in order that he might seem to be acting with some show of legal authority." [37] Augustus, in fact, possessed power equal to Diocletian's, but for a time it seemed politic to preserve old forms.[38]

Certain restraints on freedom, however, were thought necessary: in some cities, the people were not to have "authority in any matter," nor "convene in

---

[34] The Civil War, I, 1 et seq.
[35] Plutarch: Caesar, 61; Dio, XLII, 30–3; XLIII, 14–8, 22–4, 45; XLIV, 6.
[36] Lawton: op. cit., p. 71; Chapot: op. cit., p. 34.
[37] Dio, XLII, 20; LII, 31. Trans. by E. Cary. The Loeb Classical Library. Quoted by permission of Harvard University Press, Cambridge, Mass.
[38] Homo: Political Institutions, pp. 218 f.; Frank: op. cit., pp. 348 f.

any assembly," for no good would come of it; in Rome, too, they were not to convene "in any meeting . . . to transact business." [39] The Senate might appear to be a power, but in reality it was not. Government resided in him who ruled the army, and continued so till the end, though in later centuries the army itself made and unmade emperors on numerous occasions.[40]

For an historic moment during the first two centuries of the Empire, the people of Rome experienced a degree of peace theretofore unknown. Many of the early imperial masters had "redeeming features." Even Domitian seemed praiseworthy compared with later emperors.[41] Government suffered, of course, from the incompetence and recklessness of Caligula (37–41 A.D.) and Nero (54–68 A.D.); the crimes of Domitian's "reign of terror" made happy the lot of one whose fate it was to die in his prime without witnessing them.[42] The Pax Romana was disturbed by occasional threats of civil war, as at the beginning of Vespasian's reign; by frontier wars; by Claudius' conquest of Britain; by the destruction of Jerusalem (70 A.D.); by war on the Dacians (101–106) and the Parthians (115–117); and by an effort to hold back the Germans in the reign of Marcus Aurelius. Still, in comparison with the bloody struggles from the days of the Gracchi to the time of Augustus, this was peace; [43] for the frontier wars were far from Rome, provincials chiefly made up the distant armies, and those at home felt no premonition of disasters that were to come.

A century of assassination, revolution, and civil war followed Marcus Aurelius. Internal decay and disorder invited intrusion of outside forces. Rome could not protect her conquered territories—Greece, Gaul, Spain, Africa, and even parts of Italy; soon she would be unable even to protect herself. After a century of portentous events, Diocletian (284–305) restored order by dint of heroic effort and despotic measures, and sought, though unsuccessfully, to provide for its continuance by creating two emperors (Augusti), to be supported by two Caesars who would come to power immediately at the termination of any reign. An army of governmental officials was created to administer the vast imperial machinery. To support such a bureaucracy and the army required vast increases in expenditure, heavier taxes, and more expert collection; and these, combined with fixed prices for commodities and labor, were ruinous to all kinds of business. Men sought freedom from such burdens, but were compelled by laws to follow their wonted occupations, having become in fact little better than slaves of the state. Rome's internal weaknesses were formidable in-

[39] Dio, LII, 30.
[40] Chapot: op. cit., pp. 66 f.; Lot: The End of the Ancient World, pp. 8 ff.
[41] Ammianus Marcellinus, XVIII, 4, 5.
[42] Tacitus: Agricola, 44–5.
[43] Dill: Roman Society from Nero to Marcus Aurelius, p. vi; Cary: op. cit., p. 663; Chapot: op. cit., pp. 51 f.

deed; yet, outwardly, her defenses were "never more complete than in A.D. 330. . . ." [44]

Constantine (324–337), victorious in the race to seize power after Diocletian's death, made Constantinople his capital. In the West the Empire struggled on uncertainly for two hundred years, witnessing increasing incursions of northern peoples, now generally superior to any force the Empire could muster. Many barbarians had long been settling on lands within imperial borders, and had been used to bolster up declining military forces, even to provide officers. Theodosius' success (379–395) in reuniting the Empire and restoring order was outwardly imposing, but by no means indicated new strength on the part of Rome; on the contrary, such power as it exhibited came largely from the vigorous barbarians whom Theodosius was able to employ in the Empire's services.[45] Claudian praises the Vandal, Stilicho, who has "dispersed the darkness that enshrouded our empire," "restored its glory," saved civilization, and enabled the poet to sing again of war and victory—"a Roman song to Roman ears." [46] Under Theodosius' two sons, Honorius and Arcadius, the Empire was again divided. Honorius, having destroyed his father's able friend, Stilicho, saw the victorious Goths sweep into Rome in 410. In rapid succession Gaul, Spain, Africa, and Britain were lost to the western Goths, Vandals, Burgundians, Angles, and Saxons; even Italy, tiny remnant of a powerful Empire, was faced by invasion of the Huns (450–453), and Rome was taken by a resurgent wave of Vandal forces from Africa in 455. Twenty years later (476) the Germans displaced the last Roman emperor, Romulus Augustulus, and gave power to their leader, Odoacer, who ruled with nominal approval from Constantinople. Barbarians themselves then struggled for the reins of government at Rome, simulating earlier factional wars of the Romans. Theodoric the Great dispossessed Odoacer of his seat (493); but the kingdom of the eastern Goths was in turn destroyed by the forces of Justinian in his efforts to reconstitute a united Empire.

Meanwhile, Rome, once the persecutor of Christians, emerged as a Christian tower of strength, to which men turned for refuge. The "City of God" was to be eternal, as pagan Rome had been alleged to be. Constantine turned to the fortress and found Christianity elastic enough to bless his arms and lead him, as he thought, to victory in 312; Christianity, in turn, won recognition. This gain in respectability made membership in the church attractive to many who had shunned it when it was a despised "subversive" movement. Men of ability, both Roman and "barbarian," were drawn increasingly to the work of organ-

---

[44] Cary: op. cit., pp. 735, 747; Lot: op. cit., pp. 20 ff.; Frank: An Economic Survey of Ancient Rome, v, 302 ff.; Thorndike: The History of Medieval Europe, pp. 70 ff.

[45] Lot: op. cit., p. 198.

[46] Claudian: The Gothic War, preface, 1–2; 36; On Stilicho's Consulship, II, 116–30.

ization and government in this ecclesiastical state which rose phoenix-like from
the ruins of the secular order.

### ATROPHY OF SELF-RULE

Polybius observed that all things are subject to mutation and decay, there being two sets of factors in the process, internal and external. Established supremacy, "uncontested sovereignty," and extended prosperity render life more
extravagant, increase rivalries, encourage "purse-proud display," [47] and condition the process of disintegration. Significant changes in the pattern of life began to appear when Rome turned to foreign conquests. The process of change
became rapid, moving like a flood in the last century of the Republic. Exter-
nally, Rome grew stronger, wealthier, more magnificent; internally, however,
decay made headway in political, economic, social, and religious life.

Mental anguish and despair were felt by many as the clash of warring factions foretold the Republic's end. Cicero gave the toga pura to his son at
Arpinum, his native town, for "Rome is no longer ours." In respect to the contest between Pompey and Caesar, he says, men everywhere are "gloomy and dejected." [48] Pompey, he confesses sadly, "has always won in a bad cause, but
fails in the best. . . . " "Absolute power is what he and Caesar have sought
. . . not . . . the happiness and honour of the community." "We are beaten,
ruined and utterly captive." [49] At the death of Cicero's daughter Tullia (45
B.C.), Sulpicius Rufus suggests a melancholy consolation: "She and the Republic passed away together." Many cities and states have crumbled, famous
men have perished, Rome's imperial sway has been "terribly impaired," and
the "provinces have been shaken to their foundations." [50] The note of sadness
and despair continues even amid the fanfare of empire. Livy [51] respects the
piety of Augustus, who restoreth the temples; but the times are bad, and
neither the evils nor the remedies are endurable; there is consolation, however,
in the reflection that in writing of Rome's great past one can withdraw from
the calamities which have long been witnessed.[52] Tacitus, bitter and contemptuous as he looked back to the breakup of free government, declared that at
Rome consuls, senators, and knights plunged into slavery—the greater the rank,
"the more eager" the hypocrisy.[53] Uneasiness, uncertainty, and distrust affected

[47] Bk. VI, 57.
[48] Showerman: Rome and the Romans, p. 104.
[49] Cicero: Letters to Atticus, VII, 23, 25; VIII, 11. Trans. by E. O. Winstedt. The Loeb
Classical Library. Quoted by permission of Harvard University Press, Cambridge, Mass.
[50] Cicero: Letters to His Friends, IV, 5. Trans. by W. G. Williams. The Loeb Classical
Library. Quoted by permission of Harvard University Press, Cambridge, Mass.
[51] Bk. IV, 20.
[52] Ibid., I, preface.
[53] Annals, I, 7.

CICERO  *Vatican, Rome*
(Courtesy, The Metropolitan Museum of Art, New York)

all; none could safely speak openly, honestly, their true opinions; even to do so privately was dangerous. Dio credited this solemn speech to Cato of Utica, when sending his son to Caesar: "I, who have been brought up in freedom, with the right of free speech, cannot in my old age change and learn slavery instead; but for you, who were both born and brought up amid such a condition, it is proper to serve the divinity that presides over your fortunes." [54]

The processes of democratic government, whose stabilization was accom-

_____

[54] Dio, XLIII, 10–1; XLII, 27–8. Trans. by E. Cary. The Loeb Classical Library. Quoted by permission of Harvard University Press, Cambridge, Mass.

plished by the law of 287 B.C. that equalized Patrician and Plebeian, had been slowly undermined during the foreign wars; the evidence of decline is writ large amid the violence which met the reformist efforts of the Gracchi and Drusus. Back of this political metamorphosis were deep-seated economic and social changes: decline of the once sturdy, free, agricultural class; growth of slavery; concentration of wealth, both of landed nobles and *equites*; the movement of rural folk into the city; and the increase of a city proletariat, dependent and undependable. This gulf between a small, independent, rich class and a large, dependent poor one would ultimately split the state and destroy it in civil war.

Numerous indications of danger appeared, apart from the increase of violence substituted for lawful action. Corruption grew; politics degenerated to a petty game.[55] Bribery and force reduced self-government to naught. Leaders organized those with votes to sell. Antibribery laws (67 B.C.) were of little avail; all consular candidates (54 B.C.) were indicted for bribery. Varro tells of the arrest of a man caught stuffing "the ballot-box." [56] The qualifications of a politician may be inferred from the fact that Cicero's son ran successfully for the aedileship at Arpinum, presumably because he was his father's son, hail fellow well met, had a reputation for athletic prowess, and was able to carry a load of liquor. Support of candidates was sought from ballplayers, who came to have great popularity with the amusement-loving populace, as inscriptions at Pompeii show. Places of amusement became the best barometers of public opinion; of three places where it could be gauged—public discussions, voting in assemblies, and at plays and games—playhouses and gladiatorial games were the best. Though Cicero "despised" the applause given to popularity-hunting citizens at the games, he regarded it not "as applause, but as a judgment," when it came from the highest, the middle, and the lowest.[57] Naturally, those who sought popular approval gained it more and more by lavish entertainment.[58]

Local government continued to some extent for a time under the Empire. Augustus preserved the "shadow of a free state" at Rome, allowing election of magistrates, but Tiberius (14–37) wiped out the semblance of government by the people.[59] Outside of Rome local government maintained a show of life longer than at the capital. A lively interest in politics persisted at Pompeii. Even women, though not voters, sometimes proposed candidates.[60] The second century, of course, saw a greater decline of self-government; the imperial régime absorbed local powers, and little dignity remained to make an office attractive. The chaos of municipal financial affairs in an age of luxury and reck-

---

55 Fowler: *Social Life at Rome in the Age of Cicero*, pp. 130 ff.
56 *On Agriculture*, III, 5, 18; Abbott: *Society and Politics in Ancient Rome*, pp. 104 f.
57 *Philippic* I, 15; Abbott: *op. cit.*, pp. 14 f., 100 f., 114, 201 f.
58 Rostovtzeff: *The Social and Economic History of the Roman Empire*, p. 33.
59 Tacitus: *Annals*, XIII, 28; Breasted: *Ancient Times*, p. 618.
60 Abbott: *op. cit.*, pp. 10, 19.

less spending deterred many who might have sought a public post; besides, one's private fortune was heavily taxed to provide lavish entertainments which the public had come to expect of officeholders. Since there was little to gain and much to lose, men increasingly avoided that for which they had once been ambitious. At Malaca, in the reign of Domitian (81–96), the magistrate in charge of elections was empowered to add names himself if candidates were not sufficient, and these candidates could then nominate others. As it had been earlier in Rome, so too in local towns it became impossible to preserve self-government. Men of ability and ambition went to Rome to win imperial favor and position. Even on petty, local matters the advice of the Emperor was sought.[61] Certain republican forms and practices were kept up in the second century, but local magistracies were nonexistent, or became mere titles at the end of the third. Even the fiction of senatorial approval, observed since Augustus, was ignored after 282; the faint afterglow of Roman freedom was completely obscured by the frank despotism of Diocletian.[62]

During the civil wars men had become distrustful of self-rule; the chaos of those days made them ready to submit to the authority of anyone who would relieve them of responsibility. Moreover, despite evil and brutality credited to Augustus, there were improvements in administration, which gave grounds for soaring popular confidence. Besides, Augustus was lavish with games.[63] Many were ready to forget.or forgive his deeds in the civil war for what he accomplished when he came to power. His long reign of forty-four years was an important factor. Many who had known the Republic died with it; the new generation knew it chiefly by tradition—a tradition of its most horrible days.[64] If there were those, then, who mourned the death of the Republic, there was no lack of others who sang the virtues of one-man rule. "Thine age, Caesar," says Horace, "has brought back plenteous crops . . . restored the standards . . . closed the gate of Ianus Quirinus . . . put a bridle in the mouth of license . . . banished vices and recalled the old ways of life. . . ."[65] In distant provinces men vowed to sacrifice all for the welfare of Augustus and his children.[66] His praises were engraved upon enduring stone: "Providence has marvellously enriched and adorned human life by giving us Augustus . . . our saviour, the benefactor of mankind . . . making wars to cease and order to reign everywhere."[67]

[61] Pliny: Letters, x, 17 A –24.
[62] Cary: op. cit., pp. 739 ff.; Dill: op. cit., pp. 246 ff.
[63] Suetonius: Augustus, 28–45, 62, 67–72; Chapot: op. cit., pp. 41 f.; Showerman: op. cit., pp. 416 f.
[64] Dio, LVI, 43–5.
[65] Odes, IV, 15. From Horace for English Readers, translated by E. C. Wickham (The Clarendon Press).
[66] Oath of Paphlagonians, 3 B.C., Botsford, Source-book of Ancient History, pp. 467 f.
[67] Chapot: op. cit., p. 41.

Senators vied with each other in proposing extraordinary honors at his death: consuls should celebrate his birth with Ludi Martiales; tribunes should care for the Augustalia; his cortège should pass through the triumphal gate, led by the Victory Statue; children of the best families were to sing dirges; iron rings, instead of gold, were to be worn the day of his funeral. The people, it was said, had done well to refuse to allow him to return to private life: "a democracy could never accommodate itself to interests so vast, but . . . leadership of one man would be most likely to conserve them. . . ." Besides, ". . . who would not choose to be safe without trouble, to be prosperous without danger. . . ?" [68]

Ecstasy over one-man rule was destined to be rudely disturbed. Peace, prosperity "without danger," and safety "without trouble" were precarious and fleeting. There were capable, sympathetic rulers from Augustus to Majorian, but government from first to last was more or less constantly disrupted by assassination: seven of the first twelve died by violence; and conspiracy dogged the heels of even the ablest in the first two centuries,[69] though these were the best years the Empire knew. The old mores could not be recalled; evils increased instead of declining. The private vices of Augustus were reputedly enormous, while publicly he sought to restore religion and restrict vice. Tiberius (14–37), though able, was suspicious, encouraged informers, prosecuted many for treason, and was credited with monstrous cruelties and immoralities.[70] Caligula (37–41) made the virtues of Augustus and Tiberius shine with renewed splendor, for he killed the wealthiest, confiscated their estates, and was himself assassinated. Romans had a foretaste of their disgrace and insecurity under capricious one-man rule, when Caligula made his horse a priest and consul, and wished the people had only one neck, that he might cut off all in one stroke! [71] Claudius (41–54), though considered little better than an imbecile, was generally kind, liberal-minded and well-intentioned toward his people; but he governed under the influence of his freedman, Pallas, had his wife, Messalina, killed, and was himself poisoned by Agrippina.[72] Nero (54–68), though well educated and restrained for a time by Seneca, left such a record of evil and so little of good that his name became synonymous with infamy.[73] Galba was assassinated; Otho took his own life; Vitellius (69) filled Rome with feasting, riot, and massacre during his scant year's rule, and was killed by Vespasian's troops.[74] Vespasian (70–79) restored somewhat the tar-

[68] Dio, LVI, 39–40, 46. Trans. by E. Cary. The Loeb Classical Library. Quoted by permission of Harvard University Press, Cambridge, Mass.; Suetonius: Augustus, 100.
[69] Dill: op. cit., p. 40.
[70] Suetonius: Tiberius, 41–5, 54–63.
[71] Dio, LIX, 5, 10, 13, 14; Suetonius: Caligula, 22–42.
[72] Suetonius: Claudius, 39, 44.
[73] Dio, LXI, 3–LXIII, 29; Suetonius: Nero, pass.
[74] Suetonius: Galba, 19–20; Otho, 11; Vitellius, 17.

nished imperial reputation, enjoyed a mild, constructive rule, and died a natural death, with a wisecrack on his tongue. Though credited with promoting learning, he revived the laws against philosophers when some of them sighed for the Republic, and caused Helvidius Priscus to be put to death.[75] Titus (79–81), though generally kindly, was also credited with cruelty and highhanded action.[76] Romans thought him fortunate in having a short reign. Domitian (81–96) sought to restrict licentiousness and even to enforce Augustus' laws on marriage. Suetonius thought his vices about equal at first to his virtues; later he turned all to vice, and was finally stabbed by one of his freedmen.[77] Nerva (96–98) compensated in some degree for the evils of Domitian; and the distinguished character and abilities of Trajan (98–117), Hadrian (117–138), Antoninus Pius (138–161), and Marcus Aurelius (161–180) gave the Empire more than four score years of orderly government. Commodus (180–192), however, vied with the worst emperors and emptied the treasury on beast fights and gladiatorial shows; Pertinax, in his brief reign (January to March, 193), was compelled to raise funds by selling at auction the possessions of his predecessor.[78]

### THE BURDENS OF EMPIRE

The evils of reckless private capitalism, at the end of the Republic, were conspicuous. One of the worst faults was corrected under Augustus by a census providing a more exact basis for provincial tax collection.[79] Tax-farming, though still employed to some extent, was carefully scrutinized and gradually came to an end; but government officials, too, proved harsh taskmasters. Increased regulation of life meant, of course, an increase of bureaucracy. Augustus created agencies for the care of buildings, roads, aqueducts, the Tiber, and grain distribution; for selecting senators, and to review the *equites*. The censorship was revived, the number of praetors increased.[80] Ultimately, this bureaucracy became a menace. The mechanism of government was so vast and intricate in the third and fourth centuries that it was a master rather than a servant, especially when emperors, raised up by the soldiers' choice, had little or no education or experience to prepare them for the onerous problems demanding solution.[81]

It is one of the most impressive facts of the imperial period that, notwithstanding the extent of power and the greatness of material resources, there was

---

[75] Suetonius: *Vespasian*, 15, 18, 23–4.
[76] Suetonius: *Titus*, 6–9.
[77] Suetonius: *Domitian*, 3, 10–2, 14–7; Ammianus, XVIII, 4, 5; Cary: *op. cit.*, p. 611.
[78] Dio, LXXIII, 9, 10, 14, 16–8; LXXIV, 5.
[79] Cary: *op. cit.*, p. 509; Fowler: *op. cit.*, pp. 95 f.
[80] Suetonius: *Augustus*, 37.
[81] Paul-Louis: *Ancient Rome at Work*, p. 230; Rostovtzeff: *op. cit.*, pp. 459 ff.; Cary: *op. cit.*, p. 743.

a conspicuous lack of continuity of policy, a failure to make government function so as to secure the well-being of the people. There were able, heroic men; there were individual and temporary successes; but, reviewing the period from Nerva (96–98) to Alexander Severus (222–235), Frank concludes that there were "very few intelligent plans though much honest endeavor. . . ." [82] One of the greatest evils lay in the tendency to get everything into imperial hands. Confiscation of property was pushed rapidly by Septimius Severus (193–211). Frank holds it probable that Septimius Severus "dealt the fatal blow to the Empire" by confiscating and centralizing the ownership of vast estates in the government. Imperial ownership injured agriculture, which was already badly off; increased wealth of the treasury made it even more attractive spoil to those of the army who might succeed to imperial sway, and thus encouraged the ". . . anarchy of the next fifty years." [83] From the middle of the third century there were continual disruptions and increasing awareness of insecurity. Business suffered, and many began to hoard money. Lot, speaking of the Council of State of Diocletian's day, pays tribute to the "praiseworthy" spirit of his twelve hundred edicts which aimed to end fraud and protect the workers, the weak, and the poor against the rich; but there was no originality, they merely repeated "old decisions." Aurelian, Diocletian, and Constantine, able as they were, recouped the losses of the third century and restored imperial finance and administration to a degree of order ". . . nearly as good as in the first century . . ."; but their heroic measures only delayed, and could not avert, the ultimate disaster of succeeding centuries.[84] Diocletian's plan to fix prices and wages (301) ended in failure, not necessarily because it was erroneous in principle, but because of errors in detail, rigidity, and oversimplification.[85]

By the middle of the third century various means were employed to meet the growing costs of government—depreciation of coinage, compulsory labor, levying of goods. Under Nero there was already some depreciation, the denarius being reduced from 3.90 to 3.41 grams; while the aureus weighed 7.40 or 7.60 grams, in contrast to 8.18 at the time of Caesar. Degeneration continued under the Antonines and reached lower levels in the time of Septimius Severus. Diocletian and Constantine restored coinage to a sound basis, but coin continued to be scarce, and soldiers were paid increasingly in kind. Lack of money to pay expenses led ultimately to greater dependence on barbarian soldiers.[86]

Taxation was an old problem; it grew with each increase of governmental functions. In the days of Camillus (446–365 B.C.) taxes had caused grumbling;

82 *Economic Survey*, v, 88.
83 *Ibid.*, v, 84 f.; Rostovtzeff: *op. cit.*, pp. 362 f.
84 Lot: *op. cit.*, pp. 20 ff., 59 f.
85 Frank: *Economic Survey*, v, 299 f.; Cary: *op. cit.*, p. 745.
86 Lot: *op. cit.*, pp. 55 f., 58 f.

even orphans were subjected to taxation to pay for military campaigns.[87] In the Republic and the early Empire, however, there was a degree of restraint. Tiberius sought to keep down governmental expenses, for he held that a shepherd ought only ". . . to shear his flock, not skin it." [88] As money became scarce and less stable in the third century, increasing dependence was put on taxes in kind, annona.[89] Growth of bureaucratic machinery, reaching unprecedented heights in Diocletian's time, meant inevitably still heavier taxation. Constantine's new Eastern court added to the burden. Getting money to support bureaucracy, army, shows, and public construction became the chief task of government, for those who lived on public money outnumbered those who provided it.[90]

Efficiency in gathering taxes was great. Had administrative ingenuity been directed equally energetically toward constructive ends and increasing the well-being and happiness of the people, the tale of Rome's grandeur might have been truly enhanced. Instead of the voice of contentment there was lamentation and despair. Lactantius (d. about 325 A.D.) drew a bleak picture: "Surveyors having been spread abroad, and occupied in a general and severe scrutiny, horrible scenes were exhibited, like the outrages of victorious enemies, and the wretched state of captives. Each spot of ground was measured, vines and fruit-trees numbered, lists taken of animals of every kind, and a capitation-roll made up. In cities, the common people, whether residing within or without the walls, were assembled, the market-places filled with crowds of families, all attended with their children and slaves, the noise of torture and scourges resounded, sons were hung on the rack to force discovery of the effects of their fathers, the most trusty slaves compelled by pain to bear witness against their masters, and wives to bear witness against their husbands. In default of all other evidence, men were tortured to speak against themselves; and no sooner did agony oblige them to acknowledge what they had not, but those imaginary effects were noted down in the lists. Neither youth, nor old age, nor sickness, afforded any exemption. The diseased and the infirm were carried in; the age of each was estimated; and, that the capitation-tax might be enlarged, years were added to the young and struck off from the old. General lamentation and sorrow prevailed." [91] Libanius (314–393) alludes to the "intolerable tax," the misery of people as the tax year approached. Laborers were ". . . crushed beneath the burden"; the poorest cobbler could not escape. Small tradesmen and even courtesans were taxed by Constantine. The people were "in tears and

[87] Plutarch: Camillus, 2; Livy, v, 10.
[88] Suetonius: Tiberius, 32; Frank: Economic Survey, v, 36.
[89] Rostovtzeff: op. cit., pp. 463 ff.
[90] Paul-Louis: op. cit., pp. 231 f.
[91] The Ante-Nicene Fathers, vii, 310.

grief"; the rack and whip extorted from the poor what they could not afford to pay. Children were sold, daughters made prostitutes, to secure money to pay taxes.[92]

Impoverishment has been justly called the "salient trait" of the declining Empire.[93] The *curiales* of the cities, compelled to bear most of the increasing weight of government, while senators were exempt from municipal taxes, ultimately found their position so odious that they fled from it by any path open to them. The richer at times gained admission to the senatorial order; the poorer sometimes found refuge among the artisans, a form of servitude itself, but less onerous than curial membership; others found respite in practical serfdom on great estates, or in the life of the religious recluse. Flight of the curial class was a grave danger to the state; this was enhanced by the fact that the landed aristocracy was clever in evading its obligations. In the early fifth century the Emperor warned the *curiales* against seeking senatorial rank, and their position became so hedged in by restrictions that it has been described as a form of "hereditary servitude," or even worse, an *ergastulum*.[94] Majorian (457–461), desirous of alleviating suffering of the poor, remitted back taxes and reinstituted the *defensores*, whose duty it was to inform the Emperor about abuses and to defend the poor; but he could really do little to improve their situation. The rich, however, were often able by various devious methods—bribes, delaying payments, and having their agents refuse information—to evade their taxes. As the government grew weaker, the landed aristocracy still pursued its own interests. Dill concludes that Majorian ". . . found his own nobles and civil servants as dangerous enemies of the state as the Vandals." [95]

### ECONOMIC, SOCIAL, AND RELIGIOUS CHANGES

POPULATION AND SOCIAL CLASSES  Rome's wars of expansion, though extensive, brought increased revenues up to a certain point; thereafter they became a losing game. Egypt was the last profitable accession. Augustus realized that Rome's expansion had reached its zenith.[96] The years of military expansion were also marked by increasing territory and population. The Empire's inhabitants have been estimated variously at 120,000,000 (Gibbon), 90,-000,000 (Von Wietersheim), 60,000,000 to 65,000,000 (Delbrück), and, by Beloch's painstaking calculation, at 54,000,000 in an area of 3,339,500 square kilometers. Gibbon's figure may have been too generous, Beloch's too small; the tendency to-day is to place the Empire at from 70,000,000 to 100,000,000

---

[92] Lot: *op. cit.*, pp. 174 f.
[93] Rostovtzeff: *op. cit.*, pp. 470 f.
[94] Dill: *Roman Society in the Last Century of the Western Empire*, pp. 249, 253 f., 259.
[95] *Ibid.*, pp. 231, 268, 276 ff.
[96] Frank: *Economic Survey*, v, 2; Paul-Louis: *op. cit.*, pp. 3 f.; Cary: *op. cit.*, pp. 247, 495.

in the time of Augustus. This population was widely dispersed: perhaps three-fourths of it was in the provinces; Italy may have had 15,000,000 or as little as 6,000,000; Rome herself, whose size was fantastically estimated by Vossius and Lipsius at 14,000,000 and 4,000,000, respectively, probably had approximately 1,000,000 inhabitants.[97] Despite her large numbers, heads of the state feared future depopulation, not without some reason: the wars had caused the loss of many men; and wealth, luxury, and a love of free, unburdened life were growing. Caesar "offered prizes for large families"; Augustus castigated the unmarried for rendering the state "barren and childless," increased penalties on them, and gave a cash bonus for each child.[98] Though these measures seem to have met with contempt, concentration of city populations increased at Rome and elsewhere until the third century; thereafter, cities declined, partly because of increasing celibacy, partly because of an exodus to the country, stimulated by growing burdens of taxation and various restraints which affected richer elements and artisans. Though statistics are not available from Constantine to Theodosius, it is believed that the population was less dense than at the beginning of the Empire and under the Antonines.[99]

Significant social mutations came inevitably as Rome expanded beyond her peninsular frontiers. The Punic wars brought many Plebeian families to prominence in military and political life. In 179 B.C. nearly three-fourths of the Senate were of Plebeian origin. Strangers flowed in from foreign shores; slaves increased rapidly, and many of them ultimately gained freedom, wealth, and influence; the old aristocracy declined relatively and was either submerged or united with new elements to form a new elite. Old names lost their meaning in a social revolution that made knights and senators of those who had been cobblers, barbers, slaves. Toward the "new men" there was, of course, contempt and anger.[100] Catiline derides Cicero, a "new man." Horace, himself the son of a freedman, berates the wealthy freedman who "now ploughs a thousand acres," drives his ponies, and sits in front at the theater. What can't money do? Pliny rails at the "impudent," "obscure young men" in the courts of law.[101] Rome never became a social democracy, however. Augustus established certain distinctions between free and freed: slaves were to have one name; slaves of the state, two; freedmen, three; while those born free "might have four names or more." Other restrictions made eligible for curule offices

---

[97] Beloch: *Die Bevölkerung der Griechisch-Römischen Welt*, pp. 38, 314, 507; Frank: *Economic Survey*, v, 218; Gibbon: *The Decline and Fall of the Roman Empire*, III, 34; Lot: op. cit., pp. 66 f., 69 f., 72; Cary: op. cit., pp. 486, 507.
[98] Dio, XLIII, 25; LVI, 1–2, 4–5; Suetonius: *Augustus*, 46.
[99] Paul-Louis: op. cit., p. 228; Dio, LVI, 6, 10.
[100] Homo: *Political Institutions*, p. xiii; Friedländer: *Roman Life and Manners under the Early Empire*, I, 108 f.; Dill: *Nero to Aurelius*, p. 61.
[101] *Letters*, II, 14; Appian: *Civil Wars*, II, 2; Horace: *Epode* IV.

only those whose forbears had held them, thus creating a hereditary nobility, to which, of course, names might be added by imperial favor.[102]

The free population was composed of three main divisions: senators, equites, and commoners. The senators, representing prestige of blood, wealth, and the distinction of long service, constituted a small, firmly intrenched aristocracy. In contrast to the Senate, made hereditary by Augustus, the equites rose and fell according to wealth. The order once comprised all those who could equip themselves for cavalry service; ultimately it included all outside the senatorial aristocracy whose wealth amounted to 400,000 sesterces (about 20,000 dollars). The wealth of this equestrian bourgeoisie, "born of war and founded on violence," was based on tribute from conquered peoples, the profits of wholesale trade, and numerous other large-scale undertakings, private and public. Big business gained the social approval of those who scorned the petty gain of little men. Huge fortunes made them powerful friends and dangerous enemies. One publican boasted "I have more gold than three kings." [103] Cicero advised Lentulus not to fall afoul of their interests, and reminded him of Scaevola who had gained their enmity.[104] By ability to finance needy, ambitious men, they shaped directly and indirectly the destiny of self-government. Caesar's debt of £280,000 was a modest one. As the Republic neared its end, the equites held "the balance of power." [105]

Senators and equites enjoyed wealth and social rank which set them off from the commoners, the bulk of the free population (comprising free workers, freedmen, idlers), soldiers who could not return to the simple, rural life, and petty farmers, forced from the land by the growth of great estates. Having citizens' rights, these were the object of solicitous vote-getters in the late Republic; since they constituted a potential danger to the privileged minority classes, they must be increasingly fed and occupied with circuses. Marius enrolled the proletariat extensively in his army, gaining support from those who had nothing to lose and much to gain.[106]

The ranks of citizens swelled rapidly. Under the Republic and during the first centuries of the Empire, citizenship was highly prized. Full citizenship gave two kinds of rights: jura publica and jura privata, rights pertaining to voting, holding office, marriage, and acquiring and holding property. An inferior order of citizenship conferred certain civil rights, but entailed no right of

---

102 Friedländer: op. cit., 1, 98 f.; Paul-Louis: op. cit., p. 229; Johnston: The Private Life of the Romans, p. 329.
103 Paul-Louis: op. cit., pp. 11, 122, 124; Cicero: Offices, 1, 42; Friedländer: op. cit., 1, 107, 134; Cary: op. cit., p. 263.
104 To His Friends, 1, 9.
105 Johnston: op. cit., p. 334; Paul-Louis: op. cit., p. 125.
106 Sallust: Jugurtha, 86; Fowler: op. cit., pp. 26 ff.; Abbott: op. cit., pp. 102 f., 132 f.; Johnston: op. cit., pp. 370 f.

suffrage. To gain these boons, persons of low estate sought the influence of powerful friends, or friends of friends. Pliny thanks Trajan for granting "complete privileges of a Roman to the freedwomen of a lady" and making Harpocras, his physician, a citizen.[107] The inclusiveness of citizenship finally became the butt of witticisms. Clotho suggests waiting an "hour or two" till Roman citizens can be made "of the half dozen" still outside.[108] In 212 A.D. all free men in the Empire were given citizenship. Ultimately citizenship and its duties and taxes became a burden from which men sought escape. To join the army, to be a rustic laborer, to become a monk, even to cross frontiers and dwell among barbarians, became more desirable than to suffer under the restraints and tax loads imposed by the emperors and the bureaucracy they had created.[109]

Slaves, though few in the early years of the Republic, increased as Rome extended her sway. A tax on manumissions (357 B.C.) suggests that they were already of some consequence; but not till after the wars of the third and second centuries did slavery become so general as to debase labor. While the number of slaves is unknown, there may have been 5,000,000 in Italy at the end of the Republic; 200,000 in Rome in Cicero's day, and 280,000 in the time of Augustus.[110] This would be about one slave to two freemen; other estimates make the proportion about one in four. Since the wars of expansion provided the bulk of the slave supply, the market dwindled when they came to an end, and prices soared to fantastic figures. If £100 became a not uncommon price, it is easy to understand why doubts arose as to the economic value of slave labor, and that it played a constantly declining rôle. Columella advised the use of free labor rather than slaves, wherever possible.[111]

In several ways slavery was injurious to the state. Inhuman treatment drove the ablest to revolt. Slave revolts commonly broke out where large, landed estates were most numerous, in Etruria, southern Italy, and in Sicily, and where the roughest, sturdiest types of men were employed. Though they were short-lived and failed to spread, the revolts in Etruria (196 B.C.), the Sicilian slave wars (140 B.C.), and the uprising under Spartacus (73 B.C.) were able for a time to defy Roman arms.[112] More important than armed revolts (for they could be

---

[107] *Letters*, x, 5–6.

[108] Seneca: *Apocolocyntosis*, 3.

[109] Chapot: *op. cit.*, p. 106; Paul-Louis: *op. cit.*, pp. 232 f.; Homo: *Primitive Italy*, pp. 223 f.

[110] Beloch: *op. cit.*, p. 404; Marquardt: *Römische Staatsverwaltung*, II, 123; Friedländer: *op. cit.*, IV, 19; Wallon: *Histoire de l'Esclavage dans l'Antiquité*, II, 72; Cary: *op. cit.*, p. 134; Barrow: *Slavery in the Roman Empire*, pp. 20 f.; Paul-Louis: *op. cit.*, pp. 9 f., 135; Fowler: *op. cit.*, pp. 215 f., 225.

[111] *Of Husbandry*, I, 7; Seneca: *Epistle* XXVII, 6; Marquardt: *Das Privatleben der Römer*, pp. 166 ff., 173 f.; Paul-Louis: *op. cit.*, pp. 39, 131 f., 241 f., 244.

[112] Appian: *Civil Wars*, I, 116; Ihne: *op. cit.*, IV, 424 ff.; V, 138 ff.; Chapot: *op. cit.*, pp. 132 ff.; Paul-Louis: *op. cit.*, pp. 144 ff.

put down) were the demoralizing influences of slavery, which prepared, in part, the ultimate decay of Roman society. The inimical effect of slavery was not erased by emancipation; those rendered vicious by a term of slavery could carry into Roman life nothing better than the habits and character already molded by their servitude. Moreover, since the state exercised no control, masters gave freedom to slaves as it pleased them, regardless of their qualifications for the station of free men. The unwisdom of pouring such a nondescript, unselected stream of slaves into the ranks of citizens seems self-evident.[113] In yet another way slavery was injurious: masters who knew no restraint save their own will in the punishment of slaves were themselves made vicious. Besides, being completely subject to the master's will, a large slave following might be used for political purposes, as was sometimes the case.[114]

By manumission and by purchase many slaves gained freedom; others won it by service in the army, as in Pompey's day. Manumissions may have reached three thousand a year in the third century. Despite taxes they became so extensive and indiscriminate that Augustus sought to stem the tide by new laws in 17 and 2 B.C.[115] Many freedmen gained wealth; some of them rose to positions of honor and trust. Augustus employed them in state service; and in the time of Caligula and Nero, freedmen, such as Callistus, Narcissus, and Pallas, played an even more important rôle. Claudius Etruscus served ten emperors before he died at the age of eighty.[116] But though freedmen rose rapidly in business and in state services, social ranks were closed against them. They might, as men of wealth, become members of the equites, but very seldom senators; and they could not legally marry into senatorial families. Their very success in business and other fields of endeavor doubtless inspired hatred and contempt toward them, such as Petronius, Martial, Juvenal, and others exhibited. "Freedman's wealth" became a byword, a term of reproach. Trimalchio boasts that he began with little, "left thirty millions," and "never listened to a philosopher." [117]

AGRICULTURE, INDUSTRY, AND BIG BUSINESS  The early Romans were simple farmers who performed all the various labors on the land. Great leaders came from the soil and returned to it again. Rome's wars changed all that, taking men from their homes and occupations. Atilius Regulus must have expressed the wish of many a Roman when he asked to return from Africa (c. 254 B.C.) because his little farm was going to ruin.[118] Conquest "enriched

---

113 Wallon: op. cit., ii, 435; Fowler: op. cit., pp. 228 ff.; Dill: Nero to Aurelius, pp. 101 f.; MacDaniel: Roman Private Life, p. 40.
114 Fowler: op. cit., pp. 223, 225, 227.
115 Appian: Civil Wars, v, 72; Wallon: op. cit., ii, 394 ff.; Marquardt: Privatleben, pp. 177 f.; Paul-Louis: op. cit., pp. 43, 140; Beloch: op. cit., pp. 403 f.; Cary: op. cit., pp. 260, 490; Frank: Roman Imperialism, pp. 7, 288.
116 Barrow: op. cit., pp. 202 ff.; Dill: Nero to Aurelius, pp. 103, 106 ff.
117 Petronius: Satyricon, 71.
118 Livy, summary xviii.

the wealthy and impoverished the poor," says Sallust. Fathers of families abandoned fields and plows, Varro says, found their way to Rome, and became more adept at clapping the circus than doing useful work. Tiberius Gracchus lamented those "masters of the universe" who own no soil and have nothing but daylight and the air they breathe. Virgil echoed the sadness of those forced from "pleasing fields and native home"; not all were as fortunate as he who had his "grounds . . . restored," their former flocks to feed.[119]

Romans left the soil, but they could not take leave of its problems. Repeated attempts were made to restore men to the land. Sulla, Caesar, and Augustus made some 370,000 assignments of land. Though designed to redistribute great estates, such efforts were less successful than desired, for many men, after long service in the army, preferred to sell their allotments or receive rents from others already occupying them. Buyers who had long purses were sufficiently numerous. Large-scale investors continued to prefer land investments for some time after the Punic War; owning an estate was thought to lend a distinction which other business could not confer.[120] Agriculture might be praised as suitable to free men, but they generally ceased to perform its toils. On great estates, because of the decline of free labor, slaves were indispensable and, in some respects, even preferable, since they were plentiful, cheap, easy to support, and would not be called for military service. Slave labor may have performed a valuable service to agriculture in the last pagan century, when free labor was not to be found; but Varro noted the inferiority of slaves and recommended "hired hands" where possible.[121] Columella thought it difficult to get profitable returns from slave labor on the land, though agriculture was more dependent on it than ever before. He defended the view that the soil does not fail man, but man fails the soil; and lamented that husbandry is in want of both teachers and students.[122] More scientific methods were gradually introduced, but it was hard to make grain crops profitable, since the chief market, Rome, was increasingly supplied from distant provinces.[123] Grain production declined, accordingly, being limited largely by local demands, and olive culture and vineyards became more important sources of income to farmers.

Pliny thought that large estates (latifundia) ruined Italy; others have shared his belief, but there is some difference of opinion. Frank, who discounts Pliny, thinks Italian agriculture was "still very prosperous in the seventies of the first century"; Paul-Louis, however, holds the words of Pliny and Sallust "pro-

119 Pastoral I; Paul-Louis: op. cit., pp. 171, 176 f.; Johnston: op. cit., pp. 340 f., 355 f.
120 Cicero: Offices, I, 42; Frank: Roman Imperialism, p. 287; Cary: op. cit., p. 450.
121 On Agriculture, I, 17, 1–5; Fowler: op. cit., pp. 220 ff.; Cary: op. cit., p. 259; Johnston: op. cit., pp. 329 f.
122 Bk. I, preface.
123 Frank: Economic Survey, v, 139 f., 218 f.; Cary: op. cit., p. 258.

foundly true." [124] Though the early effects of large estates on agriculture may be disputed, the ultimate consequences are clear: slave labor first replaced that of free men; when slaves became scarce, expensive, and unprofitable, Rome resorted to the colonate, a system of labor halfway between slavery and freedom. Initially the *coloni* were free tenants who paid a money rental for the land; after the third-century invasions, however, they became permanently fixed upon the land; if it was sold, the *coloni* went with it. The *latifundia* of the declining Empire, tilled by serfs, were the "forerunners of the medieval manor." [125]

Large private estates, tilled by serfs, were ultimately a failure. Laborers could not be drawn to the soil in sufficient numbers; many fled from it, for its burdens exceeded the rewards; efforts to stem the tide by reduction of taxes were unavailing. Extensive taxable acreage went out of cultivation in the fourth and fifth centuries. Symmachus (c. 345–410), a large owner, complained that agriculture had become a costly luxury.[126] Government estates, developed partly from lands confiscated during the early Empire and increased extensively under Septimius Severus, were no better than private ones; indeed, the imperial estates may have been a great menace, and Severus' land policy may have struck the Empire a "fatal blow." [127]

Though, according to tradition, eight guilds had been recognized in the days of Numa, they probably served religious, funerary, and social purposes primarily. As industrial life expanded, guilds increased but were not numerous until the second century B.C. Amid the social turmoil which marked the decline of the Republic, some guilds were involved in political movements and most of them were suppressed (64 B.C.); later, Caesar abolished all save those dating from the time of Numa.[128] The tendency to fear of organizations is reflected in Trajan's reply to Pliny anent a "guild of fire-men": other "means for extinguishing fires" should be found; for, no matter what the guild is called, men "banded together for a common end" will inevitably become a political organization.[129]

Associations increased nevertheless, and flourished under the Antonines. In the reign of Alexander Severus, there were thirty-two guilds at Rome; and emperors began to see them as potentially valuable assets. Severus sought to or-

[124] Pliny: *Natural History*, XVIII, 7; Paul-Louis: *op. cit.*, p. 171; Frank: *Economic Survey*, v, 171, 175.
[125] Cary: *op. cit.*, pp. 451, 744, 753; Paul-Louis: *op. cit.*, pp. 252, 256 f.; Lot: *op. cit.*, pp. 79 f., 108, 112 f.
[126] *Epistulae*, I, 5.
[127] Frank: *Economic Survey*, v, 84 f., 300; Paul-Louis: *op. cit.*, p. 272; Dill: *Last Century*, pp. 259 f.
[128] Plutarch: *Numa*, 17; Paul-Louis: *op. cit.*, pp. 49, 150 f.; Dill: *Nero to Aurelius*, pp. 253 ff.
[129] Pliny: *Letters*, X, 34.

ganize industrial associations and make them serviceable to the state.[130] From being merely tolerated in Gaul, the *collegia* became objects of approval in the third century, being useful in controlling the people and collecting taxes. This utilization of the guilds for support accompanied industrial collapse, which began in the third century. Ceramic production and glassware declined after 250 A.D., and Gaul and the Rhine region were bereft of most of their commerce and industry.[131]

As private industries declined, the state engaged more extensively in large-scale operations to equip its forces and supply its various needs, and resorted to more and more restrictions so that laborers might not escape from their occupations. Ultimately, the workaday world was completely enslaved by the government. Hundreds of thousands were reduced to compulsory labor; butchers, bakers, masons, boatmen, engravers, glass blowers, foundrymen, *coloni*, cobblers, and other artisans were knit into an intricate network of organizations, which became so burdensome that emperors on many occasions issued edicts (in 412, 450, and 455) requiring those who had fled from their guilds to return to them.[132]

Increased population, wealth, and power did not make Rome a great industrial center. The wealthy depended on their country estates for much produce, and gave little impetus to industry of the city; their luxuries came chiefly from abroad. Other factors operated against great industrial development at Rome. Metal and fuel were not at hand; transportation was slow and expensive. Since many of her conquered peoples were more highly developed industrially, more manufactured goods came to Rome than she sent out. The small domestic shop where articles were made and sold was a more common feature of industrial life at Pompeii and Rome than the factory. Spinning and weaving continued to be done by household slaves. Public bakeries at Rome and the state establishments for equipping the armies, maintained by "privileges, exemptions, and compulsion," should scarcely be regarded as large-scale industry. Lack of machinery may have held specialization in check. Some towns came to have a practical monopoly of certain manufactures, however; iron at Virunum and Puteoli, brick at Rome, and copper, bronze, and silver plate at Capua seem to have approached the factory system.[133]

Wages were doubtless low; but the matter is obscure. The penny a day (*denarius*, four sesterces), mentioned by Jesus, was probably considered a suffi-

[130] Rostovtzeff: *op. cit.*, p. 380; Paul-Louis: *op. cit.*, p. 264; Dill: *Nero to Aurelius*, pp. 256, 265.
[131] Cary: *op. cit.*, pp. 751 f.; Chapot: *op. cit.*, pp. 317 f.
[132] Paul-Louis: *op. cit.*, pp. 20 f., 232 f., 258 ff.; cf. Dill: *Last Century*, pp. 232 ff.; Cary: *op. cit.*, p. 753.
[133] Johnston: *op. cit.*, pp. 336 f.; Paul-Louis: *op. cit.*, pp. 184, 191; Lot: *op. cit.*, pp. 66 f., 74 f.; Frank: *Economic Survey*, v, 185, 187 f., 201, 216 ff., 222 f., 226, 229, 235.

cient wage. Owing to unemployment, even the small wage was an uncertain matter; without public largess laborers would have fared badly.[134] This aid fluctuated greatly from time to time. The difficulties of Rome's grain supply began early and increased with her expansion. The curule aediles distributed Spanish corn, so much to each street, about 202 B.C. In the time of Gracchus, relief was given by regulating prices and distributing free corn to citizens each month.[135] Though such regulation was criticized, and distributions were curtailed from time to time, even abolished in Sulla's day, controls and doles increased as the gulf widened between rich and poor. Three hundred and twenty thousand received free grain at the time of Caesar. Augustus distributed money at various times; grain was sometimes distributed free, and again at low cost.[136] Nerva created funds to provide maintenance for children of those in need. Such "alimentary institutions" were extended by Hadrian, Trajan, Antoninus Pius, and Marcus Aurelius. At the time of Septimius Severus about £480,000 were expended each year. From Caesar to Diocletian it is estimated that government had expended about £120,000,000 for doles of corn and bread alone.[137]

Under the emperors Rome put on a magnificent appearance. Augustus boasted that he found a city of brick and left one of marble. "Material splendour" was Rome's "greatest glory" in the age of the Antonines. Ammianus enumerated her beauteous marvels: the temple of Jove, baths, amphitheater, Pantheon, Temple of Venus and Roma, Forum of Peace, Pompey's Theater, Odeum, stadium, and, most magnificent, the Forum of Trajan.[138] In contrast with public magnificence and the luxurious houses and estates of the wealthy the quarters of the working population continued to be poor, being commonly in tenements (insulae), built as cheaply as possible and rented for as much as could be secured. Already numerous at the end of the Republic, such flats grew with impoverished masses. In the early fourth century there were over forty-four thousand tenements, but something less than eighteen hundred individual homes. These drafty cells were heated only by a brasero, if at all; furniture was limited and exceedingly primitive; water was carried from public fountains; light was furnished by a cheap lamp, a "wick floating in oil." [139] Small wonder that Juvenal advised the poor to live in the country, avoiding falling houses,

134 Frank: Economic Survey, v, 45; Davis: Influence of Wealth in Imperial Rome, p. 242; Rostovtzeff: op. cit., pp. 178, 419 f.; Johnston: op. cit., p. 345.
135 Livy, xxx, 26; Appian: Civil Wars, 1, 21; Rostovtzeff: "Frumentum," Real-Encyclopädie, VII, Pt. 1, 171 et seq.; Mommsen: op. cit., III, 76, 344.
136 Suetonius: Augustus, 41; Frank: Economic Survey, v, 8 f.; Mommsen: op. cit., IV, 110; Ihne: op. cit., v, 431 f.; Showerman: op. cit., p. 45.
137 Paul-Louis: op. cit., p. 239; Cary: op. cit., pp. 636 f.
138 Ammianus, XVI, 10, 13–5; Suetonius: Augustus, 28; Dio, LVI, 30; Dill: Nero to Aurelius, p. 4.
139 Friedländer: op. cit., 1, 144 f.; IV, 26 f.; Lot: op. cit., p. 73; Johnston: op. cit., pp. 172 f., 407.

fires, and nocturnal alarms. Men sicken and die for lack of sleep! Who but the rich can sleep in Rome? [140]

As a consequence of successful wars which gave her a "monopoly of power," wealth flowed to Rome. With the advent of financial imperialism the equestrian order acquired great weight in public affairs, its power being felt throughout the Empire. Two classes of capitalists may be distinguished: *negotiatores* and *publicani*. The first, private bankers and agents, provided exchange, gave letters of credit, and handled all sorts of business for their clients, particularly making loans. Everyone seems to have been borrowing, lending money, or perhaps doing both. Indebtedness was never greater. Cicero thought the amount of debts ought not to be so great as to injure the state, but fought efforts to liquidate the obligations of debtors. His censure of Caesar, who abolished one-fourth of all debts, was severe.[141] The *publicani* engaged in business for the state, making a profitable income out of collecting taxes in the provinces.[142] Newly acquired provinces offered quick wealth, especially to the nimble-witted and unscrupulous; consequently the *publicani* became ardent expansionists; so, too, did provincial governors who, despite restraints imposed by the Senate, lined their pockets by draining the provinces. *Publicani* also played a considerable rôle in other undertakings, such as building, road construction, and supplying the army. Sulpicius let contracts for horses, six thousand togas, and thirty thousand tunics. Polybius thought the profits of contracting were widely distributed: one could "almost say that everyone is interested in these contracts and the work they involved." [143]

The Senate had authority over the contracting companies, theoretically at least, and could grant them extensions of time or relieve them of obligations if necessary. That body's coöperation was therefore to be won. Cicero, though he well knew the hatred of provincials for Roman governors who bled them outrageously, defended the system and supported the Manilian Law, which was to give Pompey power. In his speech (66 B.C.) Cicero stressed the financial interests involved in the war against Mithridates. Surely the "interests and fortunes" of the "honourable and distinguished men who farm our revenues" ought "on personal grounds, to be your concern." For if our revenues are the sinews of the state, the ". . . class which farms those revenues is the mainstay of the other classes"; and if defeat and ruin be suffered in Asia, the result will be collapse and ruin in Rome.[144]

---

[140] *Satire* III, 232 *et seq.*
[141] *Offices*, II, 24; Rostovtzeff: *Social and Economic History*, p. 17; Homo: *Primitive Italy*, pp. 262 ff., 331 f., 341 ff.; Fowler: *op. cit.*, pp. 80 ff.; Lot: *op. cit.*, pp. 80 f.
[142] Fowler: *op. cit.*, pp. 69 f.
[143] Bk. VI, 17.
[144] *On the Manilian Law*, 7. Cicero: *The Speeches*, trans. by H. G. Hodge. The Loeb Classical Library. Quoted by permission of Harvard University Press, Cambridge, Mass.

Even if governors desired to deal justly with provincials, it was doubtless difficult to resist the appeal of interested *publicani* and their powerful friends. Cicero interceded because those whose interests were affected besought him to do so as a matter of "paramount importance to them." To his son-in-law he urged especial concern for the best interests of a Bithynian company, partly because of his personal relation to the head of it, and also because of the class of men in it; besides, owing to its relation to the *publicani* in general, he considered it "a most important factor in the State." Moreover, he felt sure that Crassipes, if compliant, would "find the Bithynian partners neither forgetful nor ungrateful." [145]

Though wealth flowed to Rome in consequence of successful wars, it brought no general well-being to the Roman people or to the state as a whole. Certain private individuals became extraordinarily wealthy, and passionately pursued greater wealth. Tax farmers and bankers did "incalculable harm" at home and abroad, for they put their great fortunes to little use, save for investments, chiefly abroad, and for ostentatious display. Provincial investments in land and mortgages determined the "chief economic drive during the Empire." [146] The "vast capital accumulated . . . was hardly ever used productively," either in the provinces or in Italy; "the new wealth" was chiefly held by a few "purse-proud parvenus"; "one of the most serious shortcomings of the Roman economic structure . . . was its failure to expand the basis of investment at home into manufacturing, trades, and production." [147] Rome became a great market, but only a one-sided one: her trade balance was unfavorable; everything came to her, but she produced little, "carried little and sold little." [148]

OLD FAITHS AND NEW   The transition from Republic to Empire was marked by disillusionment. Cato "wondered that when one soothsayer met another, he could help laughing." [149] Lucan's phrase, "dearer the victor's cause to the gods," suggests the distrust men felt toward the invisible powers. Cicero recognized that the "art and science of the augurs" had faded out, due to time's passage and human neglect.[150] Though he was a member of the Sacred College of Augurs, he ridiculed the notion of portents and superstitious fears; find out the true cause of anything, he believed, and there is no need to be terrified, no matter what comes to pass.[151] For two generations prior to 11 B.C. such a high

145 *To His Friends*, XIII, 9. Trans. by W. G. Williams. The Loeb Classical Library. Quoted by permission of Harvard University Press, Cambridge, Mass.
146 Frank: *Economic Survey*, v, 295 ff.
147 *Ibid.*, v, 29. Courtesy of The Johns Hopkins Press, Baltimore; Fowler: *op. cit.*, pp. 92 ff.
148 Lot: *op. cit.*, pp. 70, 76 ff.
149 Cicero: *On Divination*, II, 24.
150 *Laws*, II, 13; Augustine: *City of God*, VI, 2; Lawton: *op. cit.*, p. 262.
151 *On Divination*, II, 28; Lawton: *op. cit.*, p. 93.

office as the priesthood of Jupiter had not been filled; and many sacred edifices had fallen into ruin.[152] Despite official efforts to restore old faiths, Ganymede mourns the death of religion: "No one now believes that the gods are gods. There is no fasting . . . the gods are gouty . . . because we are sceptics." In the old days women prayed for rain, and it fell "by the bucket," and all were wet as "drowned rats." [153] Now the fields are baked dry.

The hold of the old religion on the common people was not universally dissolved, however. The religion of Numa, the sense of piety toward the gods, which had been inculcated throughout centuries, persisted long in rural regions where factors of decline were less potent. Pagan rites of the state cult lived to defy "the penal edicts of Theodosius and Honorius." Priestly colleges still convened at the time of Theodosius; Christian rulers, to the time of Gratian, bore the title "Pontifex Maximus"; and pagan festivals like the Lupercalia were still honored, despite Christian bishops, at the close of the fifth century. Pope Gelasius eradicated this "last stain of idolatry," but he is said to have appeased the Senate and people by a "formal apology." [154]

Numerous solvents promoted the decay of old beliefs. Increasing knowledge of Greek literature and philosophy, wherein doubts about the gods mingled with hostility and contempt, could not but undermine the old religion amongst the new intelligentsia.[155] The growing poverty of the thousands who crowded the city must also have been a stimulant to gnawing doubt. The old Roman had performed his part of a contract as a means to an end. If neither gods nor men show pity, wherefore should one have faith? For the proletarian in his cold, barren garret the rites of household gods became meaningless; the rites for the dead could have slight significance, for the poor "could no more afford a tomb . . . than a house." [156] On the other hand, great wealth and undisputed mastery over others may well have rendered men less attentive to gods on whom they once depended. A powerful disintegrating influence lay also in the prolific growth of foreign cults. Minds nurtured on superstition are a ready prey to new ones when the old are discredited. Intellectuals, schooled in reason, might throw all magic overboard; but ignorant, simple-minded folk were ready consumers of each strange novelty.

Certain new ceremonials were officially blessed: the *Ludi Tarentini* were approved (249 B.C.); games in honor of Apollo were introduced (212 B.C.) and became a fixed, annual festival in 208; Kybele, great mother of the gods, was introduced in 205 B.C., and the Megalesian Games in her honor grew

[152] Suetonius: *Augustus*, 30; *Dio*, LIV, 36.
[153] Petronius: *Satyricon*, 44. Trans. by M. Heseltine. The Loeb Classical Library. Quoted by permission of Harvard University Press, Cambridge, Mass.
[154] Gibbon: *op. cit.*, III, 240 f.; Dill: *Nero to Aurelius*, p. 529; *Last Century*, p. 74.
[155] Dill: *Nero to Aurelius*, p. 530; Abbott: *op. cit.*, pp. 184 f.
[156] Fowler: *op. cit.*, pp. 319 f.

rapidly in popularity.[157] The worship of Isis and Serapis developed in the first half of the last pagan century and gained such a popular hold that efforts were made to destroy it. In ten years (58 to 48 B.C.) four edicts were launched against it, and the temples were ordered razed.[158] Mithraism, though known after Pompey's destruction of the pirates' power in Cilicia,[159] had little influence in Rome before the end of the first century A.D.; in the next century, however, its vogue increased greatly. Commodus participated in its rites.[160] During this period the worship of Isis and Mithra quite obscured old Roman deities and Greek as well, and provided the most serious competition for the rising cult of the Christians.[161] Christianity, persecuted sporadically during its first three centuries, was officially recognized by Constantine and Licinius in 313.

Amid the decay of old gods and the kaleidoscopic scene of foreign infiltrations it is not remarkable to find the rise of man-worship, the identification of the great man and deity. It is an old popular notion that the great and powerful have traffic with the unseen, to other mortals denied. Even in life, Caesar accepted honors "too great" for mortals; at death, he was numbered among the gods, and it was alleged that a comet, seen for seven days running, was Caesar's soul in its celestial sphere. Two years later (42 B.C.) even greater honors were devised.[162]

The notion that a people must return to its forsaken faith, in order to rehabilitate itself, is ancient. The Romans owed their Empire to the gods, it was said; because they have forgotten old deities, Italy is afflicted by many woes. For this, says Horace, ". . . you must suffer, O Roman, till you have set up again the temples, the falling shrines of the gods and their images foul with sooty smoke." [163] Immediately after the battle of Actium, Augustus began the reorganization of the state religion. Priestly colleges, well-nigh forgotten, were revived and temples restored. Certain temples were rebuilt by private persons; Augustus is credited with rebuilding eighty-two. The restoration was evidently an insurance policy on Rome's established greatness.[164]

After the death of Lepidus, Augustus assumed the title of Pontifex Maximus, burned over two thousand religious books (by authors of little repute, it was said), preserving only a choice collection of Sibylline literature.[165] This

---

157 Livy, xxv, 12; xxvi, 23; xxix, 10; Wissowa: *Religion und Kultus der Römer*, pp. 239 ff., 255, 263 ff.; Ausonius, vii, 23; Ihne: *op. cit.*, v, 122 f.
158 Dio, xl, 47; xlii, 26; Wissowa: *op. cit.*, pp. 292 ff.
159 Plutarch: *Pompey*, 24.
160 Lampridius: *Commodus*, 9; Wissowa: *op. cit.*, pp. 307 ff.
161 Lawton: *op. cit.*, p. 235.
162 Suetonius: *Julius*, 76, 88; Plutarch: *Caesar*, 67; Dio, xliv, 6; xlvii, 19.
163 *Odes*, iii, 6. From *Horace for English Readers*, translated by E. C. Wickham (The Clarendon Press).
164 Suetonius: *Augustus*, 30; Dio, liii, 2; Wissowa: *op. cit.*, p. 67.
165 Suetonius: *Augustus*, 31.

effort to stamp out knowledge of foreign cults proved a failure, as did the re-habilitation of morality and religion of the early Romans.[166] The most com-pelling aspect of the new religious order lay in the state cult of emperor-worship, carried on by the seviri Augustales. Developing steadily after the deifi-cation of Julius, this cult was naturally reinforced by contact with Oriental countries, such as Egypt, where deity and temporal potentate had long been identified. Emperor-worship became a loyalty test; other cults were tolerated, provided loyalty to the state was demonstrated by performance of imperial re-ligious rites. As Pontifex Maximus the Emperor's authority was enhanced, for he controlled the filling of all priesthoods which previously had been chosen by the people, or in certain cases, coöpted. Into these reconstituted priesthoods, Augustus did not fail to put most of the chief men who supported his new régime.[167] The state cult continued and even waxed stronger when the official religion of the Empire became Christian, for the Emperor was worshiped, though no sacrifice was made to him. Through centralization of religion obedi-ence was due to the Emperor as to God himself.

That Romans were burdened with superstitious beliefs since earliest times is clearly written in their histories.[168] They were now living in a new world; but superstitions still lived. Men might find it difficult to believe in God, but it was easy to fear the devil and read assurance in the stars. Augustus, the creator of the new age, regarded certain omens as infallible. Putting his shoes on wrong in the morning was a bad sign; rain, at the beginning of a journey, was a good one; a palm tree growing in a pavement and an oak that suddenly began to grow impressed him mightily.[169] Centuries later Ammianus said: "Many . . . who deny that there are higher powers in heaven, neither appear in public nor eat a meal nor think they can with due caution take a bath, until they have criti-cally examined the calendar and learned where, for example, the planet Mer-cury is, or what degree of the constellation of the Crab the moon occupies in its course through the heavens." [170]

While there was much belief in magic, official and unofficial, some men flouted established practice by contemptuous unbelief. The impious Claudius Pulcher ignored an evil omen: when the sacred chickens wouldn't eat, he threw them into the sea, saying they might drink. He suffered defeat.[171] Caesar never

[166] Lawton: op. cit., p. 203.
[167] Wissowa: op. cit., p. 67; Homo: Political Institutions, pp. 227, 278 f.; Johnston: op. cit., p. 403; Thorndike: op. cit., pp. 29 f.
[168] Livy, xxv, 1, 12; xxvi, 23; xxxix, 8–19; Suetonius: Augustus, 94; Tacitus: Annals, I, 28, 76; II, 17; XII, 64; XIV, 12, 22; XV, 7, 44, 47; Dio, xxxvii, 9; xxxix, 20, 61; xlvii, 40; L, 10; LVI, 29; Plutarch: Sertorius, 11–2; Caius Marius, 17; Aemilius Paulus, 17.
[169] Suetonius: Augustus, 92.
[170] Ammianus Marcellinus, xxviii, 4, 24. Trans. by J. C. Rolfe. The Loeb Classical Library. Quoted by permission of Harvard University Press, Cambridge, Mass.
[171] Suetonius: Tiberius, 2.

allowed regard for religious scruples to deter him from any undertaking. To a soothsayer who reported bad omens, he said: "They will be more favourable when I wish it; it should not be regarded as a portent, if a beast has no heart." Laughing at Spurinna, and saying the Ides of March were come without harm, he was reminded that they had come but not gone.[172] Dio [173] noted that, despite many terrible omens in 31 B.C., the leaders disregarded them and continued preparations for war. Tacitus observed that, though there were many portents in the sky, which once would have broken up a public meeting, it did not deter Galba from going to his camp.[174] To a certain point Polybius held to a scientific principle: ". . . as for matters the efficient and final cause of which it is possible to discover we should not, I think, put them down to divine action." But beyond this, in respect to unusual events, ". . . impossible or difficult for a mere man to understand, . . ." we may ". . . naturally bow to popular opinion" in ascribing them to the gods or to chance.[175]

Among Roman intellectuals diverse tendencies developed as a consequence of their contact with a larger world, various religions, and philosophies. Some expound and appear to accept the theory of an afterlife, in which evil is punished and good rewarded; others doubt Providence, punishment, and reward; still others appear confused, uncertain as to what to think. With elements of Pythagoreanism and Platonism, Roman patriotism is mingled. Virgil [176] tells of those who, having freed themselves from the stains of a former existence by a thousand years of purgation, await a re-embodiment. Among these spirits are the heroes of Troy and the great names of Roman history. To what extent this mixture of Hellenic theory and Roman pride proved potable is a proper matter of speculation. Cicero and other intellectuals found the theory of immortality of the soul more or less inviting, as is suggested by Scipio's dream.[177] Presumably many held the view seriously. Lucretius would scarcely contend with imaginary foes. He earnestly entreats men to be rational: "Why doubt . . . that the soul when driven forth out of the body . . . not only cannot continue through eternity, but is unable to hold together the smallest fraction of time?" [178] Others, like Caesar and Pliny, took no stock in any existence but the present. To Caesar ". . . death is a relief from woes, not a punishment"; it leaves no room ". . . for sorrow or for joy." [179] Tacitus is somewhat

---

[172] Suetonius: *Julius*, 59, 77, 81. Trans. by J. C. Rolfe. The Loeb Classical Library. Quoted by permission of Harvard University Press, Cambridge, Mass.
[173] Bk. L, 11.
[174] *Histories*, I, 18.
[175] Polybius, XXXVI, 17. Trans. by W. R. Paton. The Loeb Classical Library. Quoted by permission of Harvard University Press, Cambridge, Mass.
[176] *Aeneid*, VI, 739–51.
[177] *The Republic*, VI, 9–26; cf. *On Old Age*, 23.
[178] *De Rerum Natura* (Munro), III, 592 *et seq.*
[179] Sallust: *War with Catiline*, 51, 20.

uncertain about Providence and design: most men, he thinks, continue to believe that a man's future is fixed from very birth; he, himself, must suspend judgment as to whether fate or mere chance governs human affairs.[180]

[180] Annals, III, 18; VI, 22; XIV, 12; cf. Cicero: De Natura Deorum, I, 1–2; II, 59.

# 19

## FROM PROVINCIAL
## TO COSMOPOLITAN CULTURE

The old order changeth, giving way to a new. A metamorphosis of education, informal and formal, mental and physical, paralleled Rome's political, economic, and social changes and interacted with them. The central feature of this transition was the Hellenization of education which took place
rapidly, despite opposition, as Rome moved from provincialism to cosmopoli-
tanism. Already distinguishable about the beginning of the Punic War, the
process was fairly complete by the middle of the first century b.c. The intervening period was marked by divergent stresses, antagonism to Hellenic culture
on the part of some, enthusiastic acceptance of it and energetic efforts to further it, on the part of others. One and the same person might exemplify in
himself the struggle between the old and new.

Cicero traced the mighty river of culture which flowed from Greece to Rome
to the days of Demaratus who fled from Corinth to Tarquinii, married a Tarquinian wife, and educated his sons in all the arts of the Greek system. Servius,
who later became king, was said to have been educated in the same way.[1] However that may be, through early contacts Romans gained some knowledge of
Greek. The alphabet had been known at Cumae since about the eighth or early
seventh century. For the learned, whose duty it was to consult Sibylline literature, Greek was indispensable. The rites of Ceres were taught the Romans by a
Greek priestess, on whom, Cicero says, the Senate conferred citizenship.[2]
Lucius Postumius, Roman envoy at Tarentum (282 b.c.), is said to have
spoken Greek; and the ambassador of Pyrrhus to Rome (281 b.c.) is believed

[1] Cicero: The Republic, ii, 19, 21.
[2] Cicero: Balbus, 24.

to have spoken to the Romans in Greek, perhaps without an interpreter.[3] The First Punic War (264–241 B.C.) went far to extend the acquaintance. Fabius Pictor (c. 254 B.C.) and his contemporary, Cincius Alimentus, the first Roman historians, wrote in Greek, which must have been understood by many. A Roman consul (131 B.C.) was considered unusually conversant with Greek, and even knew various dialects used in Asia Minor.[4]

Though Greek was known to some extent in early times, literary study at Rome, according to Suetonius, was not pursued, "still less held in any esteem," for the people were devoted chiefly to war and had little time for liberal employments. The earliest teachers of grammar were Italian Greek poets, Livius and Ennius, who gave instruction in both Greek and Latin "at home and abroad." [5] Andronicus, a Greek, taken as prisoner from Tarentum to Rome about 272 B.C., became the teacher of his master's sons and others, and continued active till about 207 B.C.[6] Since materials in Latin were scarce, the talented Greek translated the Odyssey into Latin (about 250 B.C.), thus introducing a textbook which supplemented and ultimately replaced the Twelve Tables of the Law.

Quintus Ennius, an Italian (b. 239 B.C.) who had imbibed Greek culture, was brought by Porcius Cato to Rome (204 B.C.), where he gave instruction in both Latin and Greek. Knowing Greek, Oscan, and Latin, Ennius boasted he had three hearts.[7] His talents as poet gained him the favor of the upper class, the friendship of the Scipios. Known as the father of Roman poetry, his importance for education is suggested by the fact that he is credited with bringing "to the Romans a full acceptance of Greek forms and taste." [8]

Suetonius regarded the beginnings of literary study under Andronicus and Ennius as quite "humble"; in his opinion the study of grammar was first introduced by Crates of Mallos, who came as ambassador to Rome in 169 B.C. or, as some think, about 159. During the performance of his duties and the delay occasioned by an accident, this learned Greek gave instruction in Greek literature, thus setting a pattern for Romans to follow.[9] Since Crates probably did not know Latin, the popularity of his lectures may indicate the extent to which Greek was already understood. The advent of Crates marked the beginning of philological study.[10] The foundations having been laid, grammatical studies "advanced in all directions." Suetonius names Lucius Aelius and Servius

---

[3] Plutarch: Pyrrhus, 14; Wilkins: Roman Education, p. 19.
[4] Duff: A Literary History of Rome, p. 114; Wilkins: op. cit., p. 25.
[5] Suetonius: Grammarians, 1.
[6] Mommsen: History of Rome, III, 136; Schanz-Hosius: Geschichte der Römischen Literatur, I, 45 f.
[7] Aulus Gellius, The Attic Nights of, XVII, 17; Schanz-Hosius: op. cit., I, 86 f.
[8] Lawton: Classical Latin Literature, p. 34.
[9] Suetonius: Grammarians, 1–2.
[10] Schanz-Hosius: op. cit., I, 231; Wilkins: op. cit., p. 22.

Clodius, statesmen and scholars, as leaders in the movement which became so popular that, at times, twenty schools were operating in Rome, and "grammar even made its way into the provinces." [11]

The introduction of Greek linguistic and literary studies stimulated interest in rhetoric and philosophy as well. Though these areas of learning became more or less clearly differentiated later, the lines were not at the outset strictly drawn. Suetonius says that, though rhetoric was introduced with greater difficulty, "grammarians of early days taught rhetoric as well," and many men wrote "on both subjects." [12] Opilius, a freedman, taught philosophy first, then rhetoric and grammar. Philologus, a freedman, was known as "a rhetorician among grammarians and a grammarian among rhetoricians." [13] In short, Greeks taught everything. In the time of Aemilius Paulus (c. 229–160 B.C.), grammarians, philosophers, rhetoricians, artists, and teachers of exercises and sports were Greeks.[14] At Cato's death (149 B.C.) Greek rhetoric was widely known. A keen interest in rhetoric and philosophy is reflected in Plutarch's account of the arrival of Carneades and Diogenes at Rome in 155 B.C. So great was the charm of Carneades in particular that ". . . the most studious of the city's youth hastened to wait upon them, and became their devoted and admiring listeners." All other pleasures were forgot; youth seemed as if "possessed" by philosophy.[15]

The growing influence of Greek culture on the Romans is shown in the lives of many individuals. Marcellus, who died in 208 B.C., was "a lover of Greek learning," though he was so occupied with war that he was unable to gain a proficiency in it commensurate with his desire. Aemilius Paulus trained his sons in the old Roman discipline, but more ardently in the Greek. Even Greeks were amazed at his concern for their pastimes, for he sacrificed to their gods, attended their feasts and contests, and made liberal financial allowances for them. Perhaps the greatest tribute to the power of Hellenic culture over the Romans is found in Cato who, even though he was a bitter critic, learned Greek late in life, devoted himself to Demosthenes and Thucydides, and frequently embellished his works with Greek thoughts and tales.[16]

Despite growing favor, evidences of distrust, antagonism, and contempt for things Hellenic were numerous and persistent. Cato brought Ennius to Rome and learned Greek, but he was sharply critical and contemptuous of Hellenic ways. He laughed at Albinus for writing his history in Greek and having to apologize for errors, since it was not his native tongue. The teaching of Socrates

11 Suetonius: *Grammarians*, 3.
12 *Ibid.*, 4; *Rhetoricians*, 1.
13 Suetonius: *Grammarians*, 6, 10.
14 Plutarch: *Aemilius Paulus*, 6.
15 Plutarch: *Cato*, 22.
16 Plutarch: *Marcellus*, 1; *Aemilius Paulus*, 6, 28; *Cato*, 2–3.

was not spared; likewise the school of Isocrates, whose students practiced their art till they were old men, as if they expected to plead their causes in Hades. Cato distrusted Greek physicians as well as philosophers, and warned his son against them, being convinced that "Rome would lose her empire when she had become infected with Greek letters." [17] When certain philosophers, Carneades and Diogenes, were pleading against a penalty imposed on the Athenian people, and had shown their great persuasive powers, Cato grew alarmed at their influence and declared, "We ought . . . to make up our minds one way or another, and vote on what the embassy proposes, in order that these men may return to their schools and lecture to the sons of Greece, while the youth of Rome give ear to their laws and magistrates, as heretofore." [18] Marius (155–86 B.C.) took a similar view of the Greeks, declaring it ridiculous to study the literature of a subject people. Though after his second triumph he gave the public Greek spectacles, he himself merely came, sat down a moment, and went away. Of his ignorance of Greek letters he said: "I did not greatly care to become acquainted with them, since they had not taught their teachers virtue." Instead, he boasted that he had learned the old Roman lesson "to strike down the foe. . . ." [19]

Disapproval of the Hellenizing tendency is shown in many ways. Calenus, ridiculing Cicero for his studiousness, calls him "Graeculus" and reproaches him for using "much more oil than wine. . . ." [20] Cicero, too, though a zealous promoter of Greek learning, had a low opinion of the people whom he credited with a ". . . natural aptitude for deceit." [21] Defending Flaccus, he praised their literary abilities, but decried their untrustworthiness as witnesses: ". . . a scrupulous regard to truth in giving their evidence is not a virtue that that nation has ever cultivated; they are utterly ignorant [as to] what is the meaning of that quality, they know nothing of its authority or of its weight. . . . They never reply precisely to a question. They always answer an accuser more than he asks them." [22] Elsewhere he refers to the "idle and talkative," though studious, learned Greeks—"that most learned nation" which abounds in impertinence.[23] "For more than 600 years," says Dill, "the Roman who had borrowed his best culture, his polish and ideas from the Greek, was ready to sneer at the 'Greekling.' " [24]

[17] Plutarch: Cato, 12, 23; Gellius, XI, 8.
[18] Plutarch: Cato, 22. Trans. by B. Perrin. The Loeb Classical Library. Quoted by permission of Harvard University Press, Cambridge, Mass.
[19] Sallust: War with Jugurtha, 85; Plutarch: Caius Marius, 2.
[20] Dio's Roman History, XLVI, 18.
[21] Letters to His Brother Quintus, I, 2.
[22] Cicero: Flaccus, 4.
[23] On Oratory, I, 22; II, 4.
[24] Roman Society from Nero to Marcus Aurelius, p. 90.

Probably no phase of the Hellenizing process came in for greater criticism than physical culture, as may be seen from Cicero, Cornelius Nepos, Horace, Seneca, and a host of other authors. Scipio was criticized by his enemies for dressing unlike a Roman, being unsoldier-like, walking around in the gymnasium in a robe and slippers, and giving time to light reading and the palaestra.[25]

Official efforts, put forth from time to time to stem the rising tide of Hellenism, testify both to its strength and the distrust felt by the Romans. In the consulship of Postumius (173 or perhaps 155 B.C.) the Epicurean philosophers, Alcaeus and Philiscus, were banished "because of the pleasures which they introduced." [26] In 161 B.C. the Senate passed a decree against "Latin speaking philosophers and rhetoricians." [27] Philosophy's servants continued to find rough sledding at Rome. Philosophers were apt to think independently and at times impudently; some of them were active politically. Helvidius, whom Vespasian banned and ordered put to death, denounced monarchy and praised democracy. Hostilianus and Demetrius were deported, in fact, "all the philosophers except Musonius," Dio says, because they took advantage of the name of philosophy to teach doctrines "inappropriate to the times." [28] Diogenes was flogged for denouncing Titus and Berenice, and Heras was beheaded for his "senseless yelpings." [29] Aulus Gellius says that philosophers were driven from Rome by a decree of the Senate (89) and were forbidden in all Italy; and that Epictetus left Rome for Nicopolis because of that decree.[30] Dio Chrysostom (c. 40–115), "golden mouthed" Greek rhetorician and philosopher, was also a victim of imperial displeasure. Antoninus (212) had a bitter hatred of the Aristotelians, burned their books, and abolished their common mess and other privileges at Alexandria.[31]

Criticism of the Greek influence continued long after Roman life had undergone a thorough transformation. The worst evils, regardless of their true source, were credited to the foreigner. Tacitus found the morality of the fathers forgotten, "utterly subverted by the introduction of a lax tone," "a degeneracy bred by foreign tastes." [32] Petronius portrayed the teachers of rhetoric, Encolpius and Agamemnon, in unattractive colors: their erudition, a mixture of robbery, murder—almost every roguery imaginable. The rhetoric schools are

[25] Livy, xxix, 19; Dio, xvii, 62; Cicero: Tusculan Disputations, iv, 23; Republic, iv, 4; Nepos: Epaminondas, 1; Horace: Odes, iii, 24; Seneca: Epistle lxxxviii; infra, pp. 646 ff.
[26] Athenaeus, xii, 547.
[27] Gellius, xv, 11; Suetonius: Rhetoricians, 1.
[28] Bk. lxv, 12–3; Suetonius: Vespasian, 15.
[29] Dio, lxv, 15.
[30] Gellius, xv, 11; Suetonius: Domitian, 10; Epictetus, The Discourses of, pp. 76 f.
[31] Dio, lxxviii, 7.
[32] Annals, xiv, 20.

the ruin of eloquence.[33] Juvenal, master of acid phrase, contemptuous of a Grecian Rome, pilloried the Greeks as a nation of actors, all ready to flatter by smiling, weeping, chilling, or sweating sympathetically with their patrons; all ready to ply any trade whether of grammarian, rhetorician, geometrician, artist, trainer, dancer, augur, physician, or magician.[34]

Long after the new education had gotten well under way, and even when it had triumphed, many Romans still clung to old educational practices and ideals. The persistence of the old is an index of the toughness of Roman character and the strength of their institutions; it is also a criticism of the new education, an expression of doubt, and again a definite conviction as to its inadequacy as a substitute for the old. Cato, typical of the best in old Rome, took personal charge of his son's education. The old, strenuous physical discipline of labor was prized both by Cato and Varro.[35] Aemilius Paulus trained his sons in the old discipline, though he valued and praised the new.[36] Augustus took care of his grandsons' education, physical and mental,[37] and in other ways prided himself on adherence to the old mores. Horace, though a product of the new learning, praised his father for attending him personally when he went to school.[38] Cicero, fine example of the effect of Hellenic learning on man's mental development, praised the old Roman training in law: Crassus was "proving himself in the law-courts" at an age when young men now are just winning applause as students of oratory.[39] Tacitus (c. 55-120 A.D.), discussing the question why there were many great orators in former ages, whereas in his own day there were only petty pleaders, declared that the excellence of the old was rooted in training at home and discipline in the realities of life, the boy being "taken by his father . . . and placed under the care of some orator who held a leading position at Rome." Nowadays, children are brought up at home by Greek servants; at school it is just as bad, ignorance meets ignorance, and the studies pursued defeat the object of genuine education.[40] Pliny, too, lauded the old training of the home, the camp, and the courts, and condemned the products of the rhetoric schools.[41] Martial disparaged the long-winded orator, and begged him to drink his "extra clock" and quench at once his thirst and eloquence.[42]

[33] Petronius: Satyricon, 1 et seq.
[34] Satire III, 58-125.
[35] Plutarch: Cato, 1-3, 20.
[36] Plutarch: Aemilius Paulus, 6.
[37] Suetonius: Augustus, 64.
[38] Satires, I, 6.
[39] Offices, II, 45, 47; On Oratory, I, 44.
[40] A Dialogue on Oratory, 1, 28-30, 34-5.
[41] Letters, II, 14; VIII, 14.
[42] Epigrams, VI, 35.

### INSTITUTIONS OF FORMAL EDUCATION

When Hellenic culture infiltrated Roman society, education, which previously had been chiefly an informal apprenticeship to life's duties, began to assume a formal, institutional aspect. The various types of institutions, largely borrowed from abroad, were fairly fixed by the last century B.C.; they continued on throughout the Empire, but suffered a marked deterioration in later centuries. From the lowest to the highest level, schooling proceeded from the *ludus* through Greek and Latin grammar schools, continued with the rhetoric school, and concluded with the university.[43]

Elementary education had been in the hands of parents in early Roman days. To some extent, as Cato, Augustus, Horace, and others suggest, the father's care for it continued despite the development of formal, educational institutions. Generally, however, a slave-tutor (*paedagogus*) was given charge of the Roman boy about the age of seven. The custom had become common in the days of Augustus, who assigned special seats for them at the theater, next to the section allotted to their charges.[44] Epictetus says: "When we are children our parents deliver us to a pedagogue to take care on all occasions that we suffer no harm." [45] While his duty was primarily supervision of manners and morals, the *paedagogus* (usually a Greek) might give instruction at times in Greek. Quintilian says that *paedagogi* "should have had a thorough education," or if not, they should know it; nothing is worse than thinking one has real knowledge when one knows only "the alphabet," for such a person disdains "the drudgery of teaching." [46]

Of the early elementary school (*ludus*) little is known. When, however, instruction in reading and writing had become a generally accepted necessity, such elementary institutions, taught by a *litterator* or *ludi magister*, became common.[47] *Litterator* meant a "dabbler in literature," one who had a "smattering of letters" in contrast to one thoroughly versed in letters. Though usage varied, Suetonius says that Romans commonly used *litteratus* and *litterator* as the Greeks did *grammaticus* and *grammatista*, the former of each pair of terms referring to a master, the latter to one moderately versed in literature. Augustine distinguishes carefully between elementary reading, writing, and ciphering, all which he detested, and those studies taught by the grammarians.[48]

[43] Becker: *Gallus or Roman Scenes of the Time of Augustus*, p. 9.
[44] Suetonius: *Augustus*, 44.
[45] Fr. 97.
[46] Quintilian: *The Institutio Oratoria*, I, 1, 8.
[47] Livy, III, 44; V, 27; VI, 25; Plutarch: *Camillus*, 38; *Real-Encyclopädie*, S.S., II, Pt. I, 763; Marquardt: *Das Privatleben der Römer*, pp. 92 ff.; *supra*, p. 527.
[48] Suetonius: *Grammarians*, 4; Gellius, XVI, 6; XVIII, 9; Augustine: *Confessions*, I, 13.

According to Plutarch,[49] Spurius Carvilius, a freedman, was the first "to open an elementary school" about 231 B.C. Considering earlier references to *ludi*, the character of this school and the precise meaning of Plutarch's words are somewhat uncertain. If this was, indeed, the first elementary school to charge fees, it may represent a certain expansion of elementary education in a public way. Earlier teachers may have taught only the children of certain households, receiving gifts instead of regular fees, whereas Carvilius admitted all who brought a fixed fee.[50]

Though *ludus* (sport, play, game) may have been employed, like the Greek σχολή, to attract rather than repel youth, the institution does not appear in attractive colors. Usually held in a *pergula*, an open porch or booth similar to that used for shops, it was exposed to the tumult of the street unless screened by a curtain. Juvenal calls school a "hole" that no blacksmith, no carder of wool, would use.[51] There was little equipment; though numerous materials—maps, historical handbooks, chronological tables—existed after the Republic, it is doubtful whether they were used in school.[52] Books became cheap, however, and pupils could have their own copies. The master occupied a small raised platform; the pupils sat upon the floor or on low wooden or stone seats, holding their writing tablets on their knees. One discounts satire; but, in general, the schools seem scarcely better than satirists painted them.

Elementary education became widespread under the Empire. Augustus made an exception of *praeceptores* and *medici*, allowing them to remain in Rome during a famine (10 A.D.) while other foreigners were expelled; he also educated many other children with his own.[53] When education was at its zenith in the third century, there were elementary schools in villages as well as cities, even in distant provinces.[54] Elementary teachers, however, did not share the privileges granted to certain learned classes after Nero.[55]

Elementary schooling usually began about seven and continued till about twelve. Boys and girls may have attended school together. A schoolmaster of Capua is shown with a girl and a boy on either side, but this proves nothing regarding coinstruction. School began before the cocks began to crow. Artificial light was used. Palaemon must have "snuffed up the odour of as many lamps"

[49] Roman Questions, 59.
[50] Grasberger, Erziehung und Unterricht im Klassischen Altertum, II, 211, thinks Carvilius' school represents a "higher stage of literary and rhetorical instruction"; cf. Jullien: Les Professeurs de Littérature dans l'Ancienne Rome, pp. 26 ff.; Wilkins: op. cit., p. 23.
[51] Juvenal, VII, 222 et seq.; Grasberger: op. cit., II, 208 ff.; Marquardt: op. cit., p. 93; Jullien: op. cit., pp. 114 ff.
[52] Marquardt: op. cit., pp. 109 f.; Sandys: Companion to Latin Studies, p. 230.
[53] Suetonius: Augustus, 42, 48.
[54] Rostovtzeff: The Social and Economic History of the Roman Empire, p. 375.
[55] Real-Encyclopädie, S.S., II, Pt. I, 764.

as he had scholars.[56] Discipline seems to have been harsh, but holidays were frequent. Regular festivals—Quinquatrus, Saturnalia, Floralia, Cerealia—market days (*nundinae*), and special triumphal days were probably free. A long vacation occurred in summer. The hot days of July having come, Martial bids the master let his "grim rod" keep holiday "till the Ides of October." Boys took the teacher their fees on the ides of eight months, the rest of the year supposedly being vacation time.[57]

In the early schools the Law of the Twelve Tables was at once the content of reading lessons and a political catechism. Later, attention was given to the Laws, the Latinized Odyssey, and other literary works as they increased and found favor with teachers. In Cicero's boyhood, however, the Laws were still learned as "a required formula." [58] The new materials seem to have quite displaced the Law at the middle of the first century B.C., for Cicero says "no one learns it nowadays."

Since education was private and was frequently begun at home, the time of learning to read must have varied with the family and the tutor. Some thought reading should not begin before seven, which was probably a common practice. Quintilian, however, would begin earlier. Children must be occupied in some way. Why neglect what can be gained before seven, since the young child's memory is most retentive? This early training ought not be too laborious, however; studies should be an amusement and involve some competition; praise and rewards should draw the pupils on to learning. Children should learn the forms of letters and their names at the same time, "just as they do with men." Have letters of ivory for them to play with; thus learning and pleasure may go hand in hand.[59] In learning reading and writing, model *sententiae* were used, hundreds of which have been preserved.[60]

In teaching writing, Seneca says, the "fingers are held and guided," following the outline of the letters; next, they "imitate a copy" and thus form a style.[61] Quintilian speaks of having children "trace" letters which others have made for them. As an improvement, when the child knows the shapes of letters, he recommends having them cut accurately upon a board, "so that the pen may be guided along the grooves" and not go astray.[62] St. Jerome recommended this old practice for Paula: "When she begins with uncertain hand to use the

[56] *Juvenal*, VII, 225 *et seq.*; *Martial*, IX, 68; XII, 57.
[57] Horace: *Satires*, I, 6; *Martial*, X, 62; Marquardt: *op. cit.*, pp. 113 f.; Sandys: *op. cit.*, p. 232.
[58] Cicero: *Laws*, II, 23; Grasberger: *op. cit.*, II, 297.
[59] *Quintilian*, I, 1, 18, 25–6.
[60] Fowler: *Social Life at Rome in the Age of Cicero*, pp. 184 f.
[61] *Epistle* XCIV, 51.
[62] *Quintilian*, I, 1, 27; V, 14, 31.

pen, either let another hand be put over hers to guide her baby fingers, or else have the letters marked on the tablet so that her writing may follow their outlines and keep to their limits without straying away." [63]

In keeping with the Romans' practical bent, reckoning had a prominent place in schools. Unlike the Greeks, Cicero says, the Romans limited mathematical study to its practical aspects, "measuring and reckoning." [64] A special teacher (*calculator*) was employed; his instruction, at least in later times, was rated higher and was better paid than that of the teacher of letters. In teaching numbers an intricate system of finger-reckoning and the abacus were used. One type of abacus had stone counters, *calculi;* another, movable buttons or knobs, set in grooves.[65] Knowledge of calculation was needed in court as well as in the counting house. An orator was thought "deficient in education" if he hesitated in making calculations, or if he contradicted his spoken calculations by "an uncertain or inappropriate gesture with his fingers." Knowledge of geometry was also necessary in cases involving "boundaries and measurements." [66]

Devotion to calculation was ridiculed by those who thought there was something better than knowing "how much." Places of business teach that "money is the first thing to seek," says Horace; the young and the old have this lesson on their lips. Romans learn in school "to divide the *as* by long sums into a hundred parts." [67] Mathematicians teach how to lay out estates, count, and adapt our fingers to avarice; it would be better, says Seneca, to learn that there is no value in such calculations, no use in wearing out bookkeepers keeping records of our wealth.[68] But learning that "one and one are two, two and two are four," was still part of Roman education in the youth of Augustine.[69]

Though the division between the elementary and the grammar school and between the grammar school and the rhetoric school was not definitely fixed, the generally approved time-allotment was from age seven to twelve for the *ludus;* twelve to the assumption of the *toga virilis,* for the school of the *grammaticus,* Greek and Latin; and the school of the *rhetor,* after donning the toga of manhood.[70]

Cato said that "the poetic art was not esteemed" in the old education, and anyone who turned to it was considered a "blockhead." [71] Now, however, all

---

[63] *Letter* cvii, 4. *Select Letters of St. Jerome,* trans. by F. A. Wright. The Loeb Classical Library. Quoted by permission of Harvard University Press, Cambridge, Mass.
[64] *Tusculan Disputations,* i, 2; Grasberger: *op. cit.,* ii, 325 ff.
[65] Marquardt: *op. cit.,* pp. 97 ff.
[66] *Quintilian,* i, 10, 35–6.
[67] *Art of Poetry,* Wickham's *Horace,* p. 356; *Epistles,* i, 1.
[68] *Epistle* lxxxviii, 10–1.
[69] *Confessions,* i, 13.
[70] Sandys: *op. cit.,* pp. 233 f. The age for putting on the dress of manhood varied widely from fourteen to seventeen.—Fowler: *op. cit.,* pp. 191 f.
[71] *Gellius,* xi, 2.

that changed. The early Greek grammar masters concentrated on reading and criticizing Homer. Gradually this was supplemented by other authors. The practical wisdom of the bard of Ascra made him acceptable in Roman schools. Paraphrasing Aesop's fables was recommended by Quintilian. Tragedy, lyric poetry, and comedy also had a place. Menander was especially favored. Erotic elegies and hendecasyllables (a meter commonly used in lampoons) were to be passed by entirely, or used only for older students.[72] Statius' father taught "the sons of Romulus" Homer, Hesiod, Pindar, Ibycus, Alcman, Stesichorus, Sappho, Battiades, Lycophron, Sophron, and Corinna.[73] A son's eulogy may have exaggerated; but Naples was strongly Greek.

For a time there was little at hand save Greek authors. The growth of Latin literature, however, soon made its study a matter of importance; consequently, grammar schools became more specialized in the early first century B.C., some being known as *grammatici Graeci*, others as *grammatici Latini*. Certain masters were able to teach both Greek and Latin literature. Gnipho (c. 116–66 B.C.) was well read in both tongues; Philologus, born at Athens, was famed as a "Latin grammarian." Stilo the Penman was reputedly the first Latin grammarian; after him, grammatical studies spread rapidly, many schools springing up at Rome and also in Roman provinces. Suetonius names many masters who gained prominence: in Gallia Togata, were Octavius Teucer, Pescennius Iaccus, and Oppius Chares; at Rome, Opilius, Gnipho, Marcus Andronicus, Orbilius, Philologus, Valerius Cato, Epicadus, Staberius Eros, Nicias, Lenaeus, Quintus Epirota, Verrius Flaccus, Crassicus, Aphrodisius, Hyginus, Melissus, Marcellus, Palaemon, and Probus.[74]

Certain grammar-school masters were also authors. Nicanor wrote commentaries and a satire; Opilius, a number of books on "learned topics"; Gnipho, *On the Latin Language*; Andronicus, *Criticisms of the Annals of Ennius*; Cato, grammatical works and poems; Aphrodisius, a criticism of Verrius' *Orthography*; Melissus, *Trifles* and *Fabulae Togatae*, scenes of Roman life; and Probus, *Observations on Our Early Language*. Palaemon was author of a grammar [75] and was a versatile versifier. Some grammarians gained immortality through the fame of their pupils and associates. Stilo taught Cicero; Gnipho was Caesar's tutor, and Cicero attended his instruction in rhetoric. Orbilius lives as Horace's "flogger." Philologus taught Sallust; Eros was the teacher of Brutus and Cassius; and Lenaeus was the freedman and companion of Pompey. Hyginus, an intimate friend of Ovid, was given charge of the Palatine Library by Augustus.[76]

[72] Quintilian, I, 8, 6–7; 9, 2; Jullien: *op. cit.*, pp. 205 ff.; Marquardt: *op. cit.*, p. 105.
[73] Statius: *Silvae*, v, 3.
[74] Suetonius: *Grammarians*, 4–24.
[75] *Ibid.*, 24; Juvenal, VI, 452.
[76] Suetonius: *Grammarians*, 7, 9–10, 13, 15, 20; Augustus, 29.

The question naturally arose as to whether Latin or Greek literature should come first. Several factors contributed to placing Greek first: the pre-eminence of Greek literature; the fact that it was the mother of Latin letters; and the priority of Greek teachers. Though Pliny [77] intimated that beginning with Homer was like beginning to climb at the top of a ladder, Quintilian, veteran schoolmaster and outstanding authority of the first century A.D., favored beginning with Homer and Virgil. One should begin with Greek; Latin, the everyday tongue, would be learned anyway; besides, Latin learning was derived from Greek. Latin instruction should follow shortly the beginning of Greek, both studies being then continued simultaneously. The common practice of studying only Greek, as "in the majority of cases," Quintilian considered bad, for it occasioned errors of accent and encouraged mixing foreign idioms with native speech.[78]

Latin masters used Andronicus' Odyssey. Horace did not regret learning it, but marveled that it should be praised as nearly perfect.[79] Virgil was linked with Homer by Quintilian. Some authors seem to have curried favor with the teachers; but Horace assures us that he would not "stoop" to canvassing schoolmasters; would not be so "senseless" as to want his works to be "lesson-books in cheap schools." [80] Virgil and other poets were reputedly introduced into schools by Epirota, "fond nurse of fledgling bards." [81] Horace came into the schools, too, presumably without currying favor. Though Quintilian would not like to explain certain passages, Juvenal mentions the "discoloured Horace" and "begrimed Virgil" of boys at school.[82] Quintilian considered Ennius, Accius, Pacuvius, Lucilius, Terence, and Caecilius valuable chiefly for "persons of riper years." Sallust's orations were read, but Quintilian warns against his style. Naevius, Afranius (known for his Fabulae Togatae), Lucan, Plautus, Statius, and others also gained a place. Quintilian thought one should not study poets alone; for vocabulary and subject matter all kinds of writers must be read.[83]

The method of teaching varied with the master. Verrius Flaccus gained renown for his use of rivalry, arraying those of equal advancement against each other, and giving prizes to the most successful.[84] Quintilian advised masters not to teach over the heads of pupils, for "vessels with narrow mouths" cannot

[77] Letters, II, 14.
[78] Bk. I, 1, 12–4; 8, 5.
[79] Epistles, II, 1.
[80] Ibid., I, 19; Satires, I, 10.
[81] Suetonius: Grammarians, 16.
[82] Satire VII, 226.
[83] Bk. I, 4, 4; 8, 6, 11 et seq.; IV, 2, 45.
[84] Suetonius: Grammarians, 17.

take liquids poured in too fast. Beginners should imitate their comrades rather than the master. His own teachers had had the boys compete for headship of the class, the leader being allowed to declaim first during the succeeding month, when another might be able to gain priority.[85] Repetition and expressing the same thought in various ways were common. Fronto advised Marcus Aurelius to follow his own tested practice: "You must turn the same maxim twice or thrice. . . . And so turn longer ones two or three times diligently, boldly. . . . This exercise will be the greatest help to you in speech making; undoubtedly, too, the excerpting of some sentences from the *Jugurtha* or the *Catiline*." [86] One must often use the blunt end of the stylus (*i.e.*, erase and rewrite), says Horace, to write anything worth a second reading.[87]

The teaching of literature, as Quintilian viewed it, involved practice in reading, attention to pronunciation, breathing, pauses, raising and lowering the voice, modulation, speed and vigor of speech. Orthography was not to be neglected. Proper attention must be given to the different qualities of poetry and prose. Poetry is song, but must not be read singsong. One must understand what he is trying to read. The teacher must be schooled in writing and speaking correctly and interpreting the poets; he must know music, astronomy, philosophy.[88] Given such a training, he can lead his pupils to understand grammatical and stylistic niceties, and any mythological, historical, musical, logical, ethical, geographical, and astronomical allusions and illustrations which a work may contain. Astronomy and other auxiliaries did not require thorough, detailed study. Quintilian did not recommend a complete, critical treatment of history, but only the "version which is generally received" or "rests upon good authority." [89] Tacitus thought that, in respect to knowledge of the past, there was "too little solid work." [90] Reading of authors was to be supplemented by oral and written paraphrases, more or less extensive, yet faithful to the author's meaning; and by writing aphorisms, moral essays, and delineation of character, based on subject matter already read.[91]

The place of prose in the grammar schools has been disputed, some writers holding that it was excluded, others that it was not. Becker [92] thinks prose writers were studied, and he names Cicero. Cicero, himself, referring to his

---

[85] Bk. I, 1, 23–4; 2, 26–8.
[86] Fronto, *The Correspondence of Marcus Cornelius*, I, 13 ff. Trans. by C. R. Haines. The Loeb Classical Library. Quoted by permission of Harvard University Press, Cambridge, Mass.
[87] *Satires*, I, 10.
[88] Quintilian, I, 4, 2–4; 7; 8, 1–3.
[89] *Ibid.*, I, 8, 18.
[90] *On Oratory*, 30.
[91] Quintilian, I, 9.
[92] *Op. cit.*, p. 192; Wilkins: *op. cit.*, pp. 56 f.; Jullien: *op. cit.*, pp. 211 f.

A ROMAN GRAMMAR SCHOOL
(From Paul Monroe's Slide Collection)

speech against Calventius Marius, wrote his brother that every schoolboy learns it "by rote as an exercise." [93] This might refer only to the rhetoric school, but such an interpretation is open to doubt. Cicero says that grammar includes study of poets and of history; and that the Romans, following Greek example, read and learned the poets by heart and regarded them as necessary for a free man's education. But Cicero adds that this pursuit of the poets is harmful, saps manliness, and that Plato was right in barring poets from his ideal state.[94]

Greek and Latin grammar schools provided general intellectual culture. The *rhetor* aimed at training public speakers. When fully developed, rhetoric-school training supplanted the earlier, practical apprenticeship of youth in the courts —a substitution which Cicero, Pliny, and Tacitus [95] criticized. Like the grammar school, training in rhetoric also came from Greek sources, but it was introduced with more difficulty. In 161 B.C. the Senate issued a decree against "Latin speaking philosophers and rhetoricians," authorizing Marcus Pomponius, the praetor, to proceed "in whatever way seemed to him in accord with the interests of the State and his oath of office," so "that they should not remain in Rome." [96] Seventy years later the subject still struck fire. In 92 B.C.

[93] To Quintus, III, 1, 4
[94] Tusculan Disputations, II, 11, 27; On Oratory, I, 42.
[95] On Oratory, I, 34–5; Cicero: On Oratory, I, 44; Offices, II, 45–7; Pliny: Letters, II, 14; VIII, 14.
[96] Gellius, XV, 11. Trans. by J. C. Rolfe. The Loeb Classical Library. Quoted by permission of Harvard University Press, Cambridge, Mass.; Suetonius: Rhetoricians, 1.

"Latin rhetoricians" were officially censured by the edict of Crassus and Aheno-barbus. Neither Senate nor Censors appear to have had much effect. Gradu-ally rhetoric came to be thought "useful and honourable," Suetonius says, many devoting themselves thereto for "defence and for glory." [97] Perhaps the decree of 92 B.C., ostensibly directed against Latin rhetoricians generally, was really aimed at Plotius Gallus, a teacher of Latin rhetoric who opposed Crassus and Ahenobarbus in politics.[98] Cicero, however, implies more than personal or political reasons for the decree; as a boy, he says, he desired to study Latin rhetoric under Plotius, the first Latin rhetorician, who was then famous, but was deterred by friends who thought training in Greek better.[99] According to the speech of Crassus, Latin rhetoricians were inferior; but he anticipated that the time would come when Latin eloquence might be preferable to the Greek.[100]

Some teachers taught both grammar and rhetoric; others became famed spe-cialists in oratory. Opilius taught philosophy, rhetoric, and then grammar. Gnipho taught grammar and also gave instruction in speaking and declaiming. Ateius, a grammarian, became a critic and taught declamation.[101] Plotius, once a slave, gained fame as Latin rhetorician and drew throngs to his school; Cicero says "the most diligent students of the subject were trained under him," though he himself did not have that privilege.[102] Marcus Antoninus (143–87 B.C.) was author of a work On Rhetoric.[103] Epidius taught Mark Antony and Augustus in his school of oratory. Clodius, a friend of Antony, was a teacher of Greek and Latin oratory. Silus won fame as a speaker, opened a lecture room, and gained notoriety as a pleader at court.[104]

The division between grammar school and rhetoric school was not adhered to strictly. Quintilian says that some rhetoricians—the Latin more than the Greek—abandoned certain of their proper functions and devoted themselves to declamation, while grammarians undertook much outside their province. The two schools should recognize their proper limits. To the chief elements—speaking correctly and interpreting authors—which are the proper business of the grammar master, Quintilian added "certain rudiments of oratory" for those not ready for the rhetoric school. When is one ready? Age does not de-termine; "when he is fit," says Quintilian, and only then, should the boy go to the rhetoric master.[105]

[97] Rhetoricians, 1.
[98] Gwynn: Roman Education from Cicero to Quintilian, p. 65.
[99] Suetonius: Rhetoricians, 2; Quintilian, II, 4, 42; III, 1, 19.
[100] Cicero: On Oratory, III, 24.
[101] Suetonius: Grammarians, 6, 7, 10.
[102] Suetonius: Rhetoricians, 2.
[103] Cicero: Brutus, 163; Orator, 18.
[104] Suetonius: Rhetoricians, 4–6.
[105] Bk. I, 9, 1 and 6; II, 1, 1–7.

Training in rhetoric, following Greek practice, fell into three divisions: *progymnasmata*, preliminary exercises; study of types of rhetoric; and declamation. *Progymnasmata* included narratives, fictitious, realistic, historical; critical treatment of the narrative, designed to confirm or refute it; praise of famous men and denunciation of evil.[106] Other exercises dealt with commonplaces, theses involving judgment and inventiveness of mind, and moral essays (*chriae*), in which pupils examined critically the sayings of the wise, or some notable action. Exercises in praise or denunciation of laws constituted one of the most important tasks of the rhetoric master.[107] The classifications of rhetoric, though disputed, were generally three in number: demonstrative, or laudatory; deliberative; and forensic, or judicial. All three types comprised five parts: invention (finding proper materials), arrangement, expression, memory, and delivery.[108]

Declamation, the culmination of the work of the *rhetor*, dealt with preparation of compositions on concrete cases (*causae*), and general, abstract propositions (*proposita*). Cicero thought this discrimination by the teachers a "capital error," for ". . . all controversies must have relation to the force and nature of the general position. . . ."[109] Later two classes of compositions were commonly designated: *suasoriae*, presenting a treatment of a certain course; and *controversiae*, defending or attacking a proposition. Jullien[110] calls *suasoriae* a training in deliberative eloquence; *controversiae*, a means of developing judicial oratory.

Seneca's *suasoriae* and *controversiae* furnish a fair idea of the questions treated by rhetoric schools.[111] It was, indeed, a test of inventiveness and language to reconstruct the situation of Agamemnon, deliberating whether to sacrifice Iphigenie; and of Hannibal, pondering whether to lead his army against Rome. Such puzzlers as these were also used: Young men, seeing fishermen drawing in nets, bargained with them and paid for the haul. The nets, being drawn up, contained not fish but gold. Both purchasers and fisherfolk claimed the haul. To whom did it belong? In another case, dealers in slaves, seeking to evade customs, dressed a slave in the *toga praetexta* with a *bulla* round his neck. Arrived at Rome, it was claimed that the slave was freed by the slave-dealers' action.[112] Was he free or not? Seneca observes, "We learn for school, not for life." Tacitus complains of the "subject-matter . . . so remote from real life," the "bombastic style" and "magniloquent phraseology" of the

---

[106] *Ibid.*, II, 4, 2, 18, 20.
[107] *Ibid.*, II, 4, 22–6, 33; Jullien: *op. cit.*, p. 317.
[108] Quintilian, III, 3, 1; 4, 12–5; Grasberger: *op. cit.*, III, 353 ff.
[109] On Oratory, II, 31.
[110] Op. cit., p. 318.
[111] Senecae Rhetoris Suasoriae, Controversiae, Declamationumque Excerpta.
[112] Suetonius: Rhetoricians, 1.

rhetoric schools.[113] Juvenal suggests the sad consequences of continually hearing pupils parade the same hackneyed themes: "Served up again and again, the cabbage is the death of the unhappy master!" [114]

The rhetoric school completed formal education for many Roman youths, but philosophical study grew in favor despite opposition. Wealthy families frequently maintained philosophers in their households, thus gaining informally an acquaintance with various aspects of Greek thought. The movement was stimulated by sporadic visits of Greek philosophers. Carneades won popularity at Rome in the middle of the second century B.C. Cicero, as a youth, listened to Epicurean Phaedrus at Rome; later he heard Philo the Academic. A taste for philosophy, thus acquired, was further satisfied by study at Athens, Rhodes, Alexandria, and elsewhere. Cicero spent two years on rhetoric and philosophy at Athens, and also studied in Asia Minor and at Rhodes. He sent his son to Athens at the age of twenty.[115] Caesar studied rhetoric at Rhodes; Horace and Ovid finished off their studies at Athens.

Western centers of oratory and philosophy also gained renown. In Strabo's day (c. 63 B.C.) elocution and philosophy flourished at Massilia, a veritable "school for the barbarians"; and some Romans preferred Massilia to Athens.[116] Cicero, though he liked Athens, thought her philosophy "topsy-turvy." [117] Rome, too, would one day have a university. Establishment of libraries, begun by Caesar, was extended under Augustus, Tiberius, and others. Vespasian founded a library in the Forum Vespasiani, probably in the Temple of Peace, erected 71–75 A.D.[118] This library furnished the basis of the Athenaeum, established under Hadrian, which became the "rallying-place" for Greek and Roman sophists and poets—the center of university life in Rome.[119] Literature, rhetoric, and law, together with mechanical, medical, and architectural science gained a place at the Athenaeum; but philosophy was somewhat neglected.

Cicero judged "all philosophy" "fruitful and profitable"; the part dealing with duties and living "consistently and virtuously" had no superior. To his son, whom he sent to Athens to garner philosophical treasures, he wrote: ". . . you have incurred a heavy responsibility both from Athens and Cratippus; and since you have gone to these as to a mart for good qualities, it would be most scandalous to return empty, disgracing the reputation both of the city and of the master." [120] Doubtless Marcus did not leave Athens quite "empty"; but

[113] On Oratory, 35.
[114] Juvenal, VII, 150 et seq.
[115] Plutarch: Cicero, 3–4; Grasberger: op. cit., III, 453.
[116] The Geography of Strabo, IV, 1, 5.
[117] Letters to Atticus, V, 10.
[118] Suetonius: Julius, 44; Vespasian, 9; Boyd: Public Libraries and Library Culture in Ancient Rome, p. 16.
[119] Walden: The Universities of Ancient Greece, pp. 85, 267; Grasberger: op. cit., III, 442.
[120] Cicero: Offices, III, 2.

neither did he profit so much, nor emulate the industry, honor, and fame of his father, as Cicero hoped he might. From his youth, Marcus needed the spur, not the curb.[121] When, at twenty, he went with an allowance of about £800 to Athens for philosophy, he acquired some fame for idleness and luxury. In a repentant mood, real or pretended, young Marcus wrote Tiro, his father's secretary, telling of the rectification of his ways, his serious devotion to study, and his need of a secretary—Greek preferred—to spare him the burden of writing his notes on lectures! [122]

Athens offered philosophy and frolic to well-to-do young Romans. The serious Horace, seeking truth in the groves of Academe, was poles apart from young Marcus. Many, however, combined study and pleasure. Gellius tells how young Romans spent the Saturnalia "very merrily yet temperately, not 'relaxing our minds' . . . for . . . to relax the mind is like losing it—but diverting our minds a little and relieving them by the delights of pleasant and improving conversation." Those who attended the same teachers dined together, each taking turn as host and providing prizes and laurel crowns for those who were able to answer the questions put to them. If one could not answer, the crown went to Saturn, god of the festival. Literary, historical, and sophistical questions mingled together, revealing the current devotion to erudition, clever phrase, and skillful argument: What early poet used the verb *verant*, signifying they speak the truth? "What you have not lost, that you have. You have not lost horns; therefore you have horns." "When I lie and admit that I lie, do I lie or speak the truth?" [123]

University life at Athens continued "merrily" but scarcely "temperately" in the fourth century. Lawlessness, increasing elsewhere, was reflected in student life. Students organized corps in support of rival sophists and sought by forceful methods to gain new members among those just arriving in the city. Gregory Nazianzus (329–389) described the seizure and initiation of new students. Libanius (314–393) was captured and confined in a "cell not much larger than a winejar," where he remained until he took an oath of allegiance to his captors. A spread, at the initiate's expense, commonly concluded initiation. Fighting, feasting, drinking, contracting debts greater than they could pay, playing ball, attending the theater and the racecourse, and raiding peoples' houses seem to have been common elements of gayety at the center of learning. Libanius regarded it as a distinguishing virtue that he himself never gave way to ball-playing, carousing, and raiding homes while he was a student at Athens.[124] As for intellectual fare at Athens, Libanius gave it a low rating.

[121] *To Atticus*, VI, 1.
[122] *Letters to His Friends*, XVI, 21.
[123] *Gellius*, XV, 2; XVIII, 2 and 13. Trans. by J. C. Rolfe. The Loeb Classical Library. Quoted by permission of Harvard University Press, Cambridge, Mass.
[124] Walden: *op. cit.*, p. 319.

The realization soon dawned that "it was nothing very wonderful that I had come to hear," for the teachers did not "differ much from boys." At Antioch, too, Libanius found students more interested in mimes, dancers, horses, drivers, fighting, and bathing than in his declamations. "On not a few occasions" he resorted to having the loafers seized by the necks and thrown out.[125]

### TEACHERS AND THEIR SELECTION

It is said, "One can always tell a teacher." Teachers of old Rome had some common traits; one of the commonest in early days was their slave origin. Suetonius [126] names a dozen or more grammarians who had been slaves. Palaemon was a "home-born slave" and learned weaving. Gnipho, though born free, was disowned. Melissus was born free, but was disowned and refused to return to freedom. Lucius Aelius and Servius Clodius, however, were knights. Lucius Plotus was freed because of his interest in letters, and became a rhetorician.[127]

Some masters had bad reputations, according to Suetonius.[128] Palaemon, one of the most famous, was given to luxurious living and "every kind of vice." Servius Clodius stole one of his father-in-law's books, was disowned, and left the city. Marcus Andronicus was indolent and not fit to have a school. Quintus Epirota was dismissed for improper conduct. Marcus Epidius, a rhetorician, was a blackmailer.[129] Quintilian warns against the influence of bad teachers and insists that the master should "be free from the grosser vices." [130] Other masters merely lacked decorum. Gellius found two grammarians of no small renown disputing violently in a park whether vir egregi or vir egregie were the proper vocative.[131] Cicero thought Dionysius (tutor for the boys) a "despicable cad," "an arch-chatter-box useless as a teacher," guilty of the highest ingratitude.[132]

With schoolmasters, as among other men, their evil doubtless "lives after them." There were those, however, whose goodness, heroism, uprightness, devotion, and esteem survived them. Numerianus, an elementary teacher, was rewarded for daring exploits in Severus' behalf.[133] Fronto seemed to Marcus Aurelius the "glory of Roman eloquence," "a man of mark," "most delightful," "master most sweet." [134] Persius paid tender tribute to Cornutus who, when

---

[125] Ibid., pp. 300 f., 304, 310, 319, 321 f.
[126] Grammarians, 6, 10–3, 15–20.
[127] Ibid., 3, 7, 21, 23; Rhetoricians, 3.
[128] Grammarians, 3, 8, 16, 23.
[129] Suetonius: Rhetoricians, 4.
[130] Bk. I, 2, 4; II, 2, 5 and 15.
[131] Bk. XIV, 5.
[132] To Atticus, VIII, 4.
[133] Dio, LXXVI, 5.
[134] Fronto, I, 129 ff.

life's path was doubtful, led him to virtue and reason.[135] Much seems to have
been expected of the teacher in the way of knowledge and molding of morals
and manners.[136] The most careful masters, it seems, looked after everything,
even their pupils' dress. Castricius, highly regarded by Hadrian for his character and knowledge was not unmindful of his pupils' attire: ". . . I should have
preferred to see you in your togas, or if that was too much trouble, at least with
girdles and mantles." [137]

Whether good or bad masters were in the majority, one cannot say; in any
case, it was necessary to select teachers with care. Pliny, seeking to establish a
school at Como, urged Tacitus to look out for teachers among men of letters
who might qualify and be willing to apply for the post.[138] Again, to find a tutor
for his nephews, he promised to visit "all the several professors" and give an
account of them, that a wise choice might be made.[139] When Corellia His-
pulla's son was ready for schooling outside the household, Pliny, though recognizing that eloquence, method, and discipline were not to be slighted, urged
first attention to the teacher's morals "at this dangerous period of life," and recommended Julius Genitor, especially for his grave behavior and irreproachable
morals—"too severe and rigid for the libertine manners of these times," perhaps.[140] Even though a good teacher were secured, one of the family might
have much to do with the teaching. Cicero urged his brother not to worry
about his son's education, for he himself would see to his application. The rhetoric master, Paeonius, is an "exceedingly well-trained and excellent fellow,"
but "my own system of instruction is somewhat more scholarly and argumenta-
tive." [141]

Boys differed then as now in respect to studiousness and conduct. Cicero's
son needed the spur; his nephew, the curb.[142] Boisterous, bellicose conduct was
not uncommon. Juvenal thought it a hard assignment to watch so many
charges: "Rufus and the rest are cudgelled each by his own pupils. . . ." [143]
Cassius beat Sulla's son, Faustus, because the boy had boasted of his father's
absolute power; when questioned, Cassius threatened to do so again.[144] Teachers commonly had recourse to the rod. Libanius sometimes ordered "the loafer"
thrown out; but, finding blows and stripes ineffective, he turned to "counsel

[135] Persius: Satire v, 30 et seq.
[136] Juvenal, VII, 197–243.
[137] Gellius, XIII, 22.
[138] Letters, IV, 13.
[139] Ibid., II, 18.
[140] Ibid., III, 3.
[141] To Quintus, III, 1, 4; 3.
[142] To Atticus, VI, 1.
[143] Satire VII, 213–5, 240–1.
[144] Plutarch: Brutus, 9.

and exhortation." [145] At Rome, too, some could rule by milder measures. Gnipho was known for kindliness and good nature. Verrius Flaccus used prizes as encouragement.[146] Quintilian disapproved of beating, as did Plutarch, con-

LΛBORΛ ΛSΕIIΕ QVOΜODOΕ(OLΛBORΛVi ΕΙΡRODΕRIITIꟼI

"GRIND ON, ASS, AS I HAVE DONE, AND MAY IT PROFIT YOU."

A BOY'S VIEW OF SCHOOL   *Palace of the Caesars*
(From Paul Monroe's Slide Collection)

sidering it a "disgraceful form of punishment," "fit only for slaves," and "an insult." He blushes at "the shameful abuse which scoundrels sometimes make of their right to administer corporal punishment." A good disciplinarian should not have to depend on such methods, he thought.[147] But most teachers depended on harsh discipline, perhaps all the more because the contempt of Romans for foreigners must have been acquired early by their sons. The classical portrait of the Roman schoolmaster is that of "the flogger." "He who is not flogged is not educated" summed up pedagogical practice. Horace's dour Orbilius thrashed with rod and whip of leather.[148] Martial pillories the bawling, howling schoolmaster, whose "savage howls and blows resound like thunder."[149] Martial would have the master rest his whip and rod until October.[150]

---

[145] Walden: *op. cit.*, pp. 321 f., 324.
[146] Suetonius: *Grammarians*, 7, 17.
[147] Quintilian, I, 3, 13–7; Plutarch: *The Education of Children*, 12.
[148] *Epistles*, II, 1; Suetonius: *Grammarians*, 9.
[149] Bk. IX, 68; cf. Plautus: *The Two Bacchises*, 430 *et seq.*
[150] Bk. X, 62.

## FROM PRIVATE TO IMPERIAL SUPPORT AND CONTROL

Carvilius is said to have been the first master to open an elementary school and teach for money.[151] The school from which hostages were taken and brought back in chains by Caligula was, perhaps, of this kind.[152] The pay of private teachers of letters, grammar, and rhetoric varied widely, but was commonly small and might be hard to collect.[153] Horace mentions centurions' sons, carrying "every Ides their fee of eight brass pieces [asses] each." [154] Every schoolboy worships Minerva "with a modest penny fee," says Juvenal.[155] Fees might be supplemented by gifts; some teachers taught for gifts alone. Gnipho received whatever his pupils offered. Some teachers died in misery. Pompilius Andronicus became poor and had to sell his book, *Criticisms of the Annals of Ennius*. Orbilius Pupillus had to live "under the tiles." Valerius Cato "could solve all questions," but "solvent could not be." [156] Juvenal bristles at the lot of teachers and literary folk. If one would earn a living by his tongue, he should go to Gaul or Africa. Juvenal remembers Quintilian, of course, but such a good fortune is "rarer than a white crow." [157] Even at Athens professors were "badly paid," though special privileges and allowances in kind improved their situation. Libanius, though he gave up charging fees for his own teaching, castigated both rich and poor students for failure to pay their teachers.[158]

Though some teachers were poverty-stricken, others were highly rewarded, especially when grammar became popular and the city had numerous well-attended schools. Lucius Appuleius, hired by a wealthy *equites* to teach a large school, received four hundred sesterces a year.[159] Much depended on the patron, but the master's talent and reputation were important factors. Verrius Flaccus, famed for his method of stimulating pupils to work, became tutor at the Court of Augustus and received 100,000 sesterces a year. Palaemon, widely known for his Latin Grammar, made 400,000 sesterces a year from his school.[160] Sosibius, teacher of Britannicus, received 1,000,000 sesterces from Vitellius,[161] but this tells nothing of regular fees.

Private venture schools were supplemented to some extent by others estab-

---

151 Plutarch: *Roman Questions*, 59.
152 Suetonius: *Caligula*, 45.
153 *Juvenal*, vii, 228 *et seq*.
154 *Satires*, i, 6; also read, "carrying their fee on the Ides of eight months."
155 *Juvenal*, x, 114 *et seq*.
156 Suetonius: *Grammarians*, 7–9, 11.
157 *Juvenal*, vii, 148 *et seq*., 202.
158 Walden: *op. cit.*, pp. 320 f.; Chapot: *Roman World*, p. 184.
159 Suetonius: *Grammarians*, 3; Jullien: *op. cit.*, pp. 172 ff.; sesterce = ¼ denarius or 2½ asses; the *as* weighed originally a pound (*libra*), later reduced to an ounce.
160 Suetonius: *Grammarians*, 17, 23.
161 Tacitus: *Annals*, xi, 4.

lished through the influence of persons who sought to encourage education as a public good. Pliny proposed to help establish a school at his native Como, so that sons might be educated near home, under parental control and oversight, and at less cost. Such an institution, he believed, might become famous enough to draw students from a distance, if sufficient care were given to its management and the choice of masters. He, himself, though still without children, would pay one-third of any sum the town might raise for the support of such a school; and the larger the sum demanded, the better pleased he would be.[162] Pliny's philanthropic proposal was probably not an isolated one.[163] Such schools, of course, did not make education public and free, in the commonly accepted meaning of to-day. There was neither compulsory education nor a system of schools supported by the state. Education had been and continued to be for the rich or well-to-do, not for the poor, though individual slaves and poor might in some cases be educated.[164]

When support of schoolmasters was provided by heads of state, education assumed more of a public aspect. Governmental encouragement of education began near the end of the Republic, when Caesar conferred citizenship "on all teachers of the liberal arts," so as to draw them to the city.[165] Augustus paid Verrius Flaccus 100,000 sesterces to bring his school to the palace; when he drove foreigners from Rome, an exception was made on behalf of teachers and doctors.[166] Under one-man rule, education, like other phases of life, became more and more dependent on imperial will and public purse—in fact, a public philanthropy. Vespasian, though no pretender to learning, and despite his banishment of all philosophers except Musonius, established a salary of 100,000 sesterces (about $5,000) for Greek and Latin rhetoricians, and relieved them and other learned folk of certain public duties. Quintilian was the first recipient; whether rhetoricians outside of Rome were thus paid is open to doubt.[167] Though these subsidies did not create a state "system" of education, they gave weighty support to a pattern of education which influenced Roman life throughout the Empire and, subsequently, western Europe.[168] Trajan built libraries, and was known as a "friend of learning in every department." [169] Hadrian developed the Athenaeum, subsidized teachers, endowed new chairs

---

162 Letters, IV, 13.
163 Dill: op. cit., p. 219.
164 Rostovtzeff: op. cit., p. 179; Wilkins: op. cit., pp. 37 f.; Abbott: Society and Politics in Ancient Rome, pp. 173 f.; Johnston: The Private Life of the Romans, p. 92.
165 Suetonius: Julius, 42; Mommsen: op. cit., v, 453.
166 Suetonius: Grammarians, 17; Augustus, 42.
167 Suetonius: Vespasian, 18; Dio, LXV, 12–3; Wilkins: op. cit., pp. 93 f.; Walden: op. cit., p. 81.
168 Dill: op. cit., p. 148.
169 Aurelius Victor: Roman Emperors, 13, in Botsford's The Story of Rome, pp. 288 f.; Dio, LXVIII, 16.

of learning in the provinces, and made grants to municipal schools. At the request of Plotina he removed the restrictions which required heads of philosophical schools at Athens to be Roman citizens. His fondness of learning, Greek as well at Latin, earned him the title "Greekling." [170]

Though imperial favor encouraged learning, it made the learned dependent on royal will. Teachers whom Hadrian thought "unfit for their profession" were given gifts and "then dismissed." [171] Antoninus Pius founded an institution for destitute girls, Faustinianae, similar to those for poor children begun by Nerva and Trajan. [172] "Rhetoricians and philosophers throughout all the provinces" were rewarded "with honours and money." [173] The number of sophists and grammarians was fixed according to the size of cities: in capital cities, five of each; in large cities, four of each; and in smaller cities, three. Under certain circumstances the number might be diminished, but not increased. Salaries were to be paid apparently by the municipalities, but if they were unable to do so, the imperial treasury was to supply the need. [174] Marcus Antoninus extended the work of Antoninus Pius, "established teachers at Athens in every branch of knowledge," and granted them annual salaries. [175] Several chairs were endowed, one or perhaps two, in each of the schools, Platonic, Peripatetic, Stoic, and Epicurean. [176] Theodotus, whom Marcus regarded as "a past master of political oratory and an ornament to rhetoric," was appointed to the chair of rhetoric at Athens at a salary of ten thousand drachmas.

Alexander Severus (222–235), broadening previous imperial policy somewhat, subsidized rhetoricians, grammarians, physicians, astrologers, engineers, and architects, "assigned lecture-rooms," and even "ordered rations" for freeborn pupils who were poor. [177] Royal munificence soon ran into difficulties, however; following Alexander Severus, the fortunes of teachers declined for a time, and state support appears to have been cut off. [178] Diocletian brought a degree of improvement, accompanied by stricter regimentation. Monthly fees for various classes of teachers were fixed by decree: 50 denarii for each pupil of the litterator; 200 per pupil of a grammaticus; and 250 for pupils of rhetoricians. [179] Constantine's edicts (321, 326, and 333) continued the policy of granting privileges and salaries to public teachers and physicians: the law of 333 included their wives and sons as well; salaries and fees were to be paid;

170 Spartianus: Hadrian, 1, 14; Dio, LXIX, 3; Walden: op. cit., pp. 84 f.
171 Spartianus: Hadrian, 16.
172 Capitolinus: Antoninus Pius, 8; Dio, LXVIII, 5.
173 Capitolinus: Antoninus Pius, 11.
174 Walden: op. cit., pp. 87 ff.
175 Dio, LXXII, 31.
176 Philostratus: Lives of the Sophists, II, 1; Walden: op. cit., p. 92.
177 Lampridius: Severus Alexander, 44.
178 Walden: op. cit., p. 105.
179 Sandys: op. cit., p. 231.

moreover, they were to be immune from all taxes, performance of civil duties, having strangers quartered upon them, legal processes, or any injustice. Anyone who molested them was to be punished by the judge.[180]

Julian (363) asserted the prerogative of supervising the naming of profes-sors [181]—a matter of importance to one seeking to restore paganism. His action, forbidding Christians to teach rhetoric and literature, was considered ob-noxious by some pagans as well as Christians. Ammianus thought it was "in-humane" and should be "buried in eternal silence." [182] Though ineffectual, the decree was in harmony with the growing tendency toward strict imperial control of teaching. In 376 Gratian decreed the salaries that were to be paid by towns, but left localities free to make their own appointments. Fifty years later (425), Theodosius and Valentinian forbade the opening of schools with-out governmental permission. In 529 Justinian issued an edict that no one should teach philosophy or law at Athens and specified that law should only be taught at Rome, New Rome, and Berytos.[183]

---

[180] Cubberley: Readings in the History of Education, p. 39.
[181] Dill: Roman Society in the Last Century of the Western Empire, p. 401.
[182] Ammianus Marcellinus, xxii, 10, 6.
[183] Procopius: The Anecdota or Secret History, xxvi, 1–7; Sandys: op. cit., p. 236; Gras-berger: op. cit., iii, 461.

# 20

# POLITICS, SCHOOLS, AND THE REPUBLIC OF LETTERS

## THE ORATOR AS IDEAL

The influx of Greek letters combined with the growth of Latin to effect a transformation in the Roman educational ideal. By 150 B.C. most Romans of the educated class were bilingual, and the earlier apprenticeship to farming, the army, and the court gave way to eloquence cultivated in schools. Cicero placed success won by intellect and "reasoning power" above that derived from physical excellence. Duty which is serviceable to society is preferred; and "well-directed action" always depends on "knowledge and prudence." Knowledge is "solitary and barren," if not joined with "service to mankind." [1] Thus, though letters were to occupy a central place in Roman education, the ideal of service to society was not to suffer. Plato convinced Cicero that those who rule should devote themselves to learning so that the state may be better governed; but studies should not encroach upon "public interest." Cicero knows that many hold literature in low esteem and think philosophical discussions unbecoming to statesmen, but he needs no further argument in favor of letters than that Cato studied Greek late in life and Publius Africanus took Panaetius the Stoic on his embassy to Egypt and Asia. Indeed, the Greeks by their learning "have rescued us from barbarism"; and we ought to be "willing exponents" of what we have gained from them. [2]

The combination of learning and statecraft became a phenomenon of marked importance, a phase of the individualism of the age. "When our empire over all nations was established," said Cicero, there was scarcely a youth, "ambitious of praise," who did not strive to learn the art of speaking. [3] Aemilius

---

[1] Cicero: Offices, I, 44–5.
[2] Cicero: Letters to His Brother Quintus, I, 1, 9–10; Academica, II, 2.
[3] On Oratory, I, 4, 8–10; Fowler: Social Life at Rome in the Age of Cicero, pp. 100 f.

Paulus, famed for military exploits, was a devotee of Greek learning; Sulla was well read in Greek and Latin; Brutus knew Greek philosophy well, and was particularly devoted to Plato.[4] Sallust, though of Plebeian origin, had a good education under Ateius Philologus, served as tribune, became quaestor, and entered the Senate.[5] Cicero and Caesar best exemplified the union of statecraft and attainments in the world of letters in the new age. Caesar studied under Apollonius at Rhodes, as did Cicero, and had the "greatest natural talent for political oratory," but he renounced first rank therein for sake of his career as commander and statesman. Cicero, though he early gave promise of being the best orator and felt that he could "with a certain degree of right" claim pre-eminence therein, asks: Whom, even of those who have given themselves wholly to oratory, can one rank above Caesar? [6]

Imperial heads of state, even bad ones, had excellent literary training, and some of them were distinguished for learning. Augustus devoted himself to oratory and liberal studies, gave personal attention to his grandsons' education, wrote many works in prose, attempted poetry and tragedy, and established libraries.[7] Tiberius was a constant visitor at the lecture halls of philosophers; Caligula gave attention to oratory; Nero's education was entrusted to Seneca about the age of eleven.[8] Vespasian, though of obscure birth, knew Homer, and initiated imperial subsidies to teachers; Hadrian was interested in Greek and Latin letters and also in modeling and painting.[9] Antoninus Pius was "a singularly gifted speaker and an elegant scholar." [10] Marcus Aurelius was in-structed in rhetoric by Fronto and Herodes, in philosophy by Rusticus and Apollonius. At the age of twelve he is said to have imitated the dress of philoso-phers and their ascetic mode of life.[11] Severus was schooled in Greek and Latin, studied at Athens when already in public life, and habitually engaged in dis-cussions in Greek and Latin.[12] Antoninus, his successor, was educated by him and studied philosophy after he became emperor, but later "forgot his intellec-tual training." [13] Severus Alexander was thoroughly trained in grammar, rhet-oric, and philosophy, but used Greek better than Latin in orations. He was also accomplished in painting and music. Plato's Republic, Cicero's Offices and political treatises, Virgil, and Horace were his favorites.[14]

[4] Plutarch: Aemilius Paulus, 6; Brutus, 2, 4; Sallust: War with Jugurtha, 95.
[5] Suetonius: Grammarians, 10; Rolfe: Sallust, pp. ix et seq.
[6] Suetonius: Julius, 55; Cicero: Brutus, 261; Offices, 1, 1; Plutarch: Cicero, 2; Caesar, 3.
[7] Suetonius: Augustus, 29, 64, 84–5.
[8] Suetonius: Tiberius, 11; Caligula, 53; Nero, 7; Dio's Roman History, LXI, 32.
[9] Suetonius: Vespasian, 2, 18, 23; Dio, LXIX, 3.
[10] Capitolinus: Antoninus Pius, 2, 11.
[11] Capitolinus: Marcus Antoninus, 1–3; Marcus Aurelius: The Meditations of the Emperor, I, 1–7; Dio, LXXII, 35–6.
[12] Spartianus: Severus, 1, 3; Dio, LXXVII, 17.
[13] Dio, LXXVIII, 11.
[14] Lampridius: Severus Alexander, 3, 27, 30–1.

At his best the orator was the fittest symbol of the new ideal. What was his natural character, what his learning? Dio thought Caesar embodied the ideal, for he combined "wonderful natural force" with "the most liberal education," which enabled him to understand readily, decide promptly, and arrange matters "most prudently." [15] Cicero's De Oratore (55 B.C.) expounded his conception of the ideal orator and education. This extensive treatise shows that Cato the Elder's definition of the orator—a "good man versed in speaking"—had been considerably expanded. It is significant of the change that was taking place that Cato regarded agriculture, war, oratory, law, and medicine as the proper fields of education, whereas Varro included grammar, rhetoric, dialectic, arithmetic, geometry, astronomy, music, architecture, and medicine.[16] The art of eloquence, Cicero says, is more vast and difficult and depends on more sciences than people imagine. There are many students and an abundance of masters, yet very few orators have been produced; the reason lies in the "incredible magnitude and difficulty" of oratory. In other arts less is required. The orator must have a logician's acuteness, a philosopher's wisdom, almost a poet's gift of language, an advocate's memory, a tragedian's voice, and the gestures of almost the best actor. They are good speakers who can express themselves accurately and perspicuously before a moderate audience; but he alone is eloquent who can admirably and nobly "amplify and adorn" any subject and know all the principles of oratory. Romans have been too busy in the forum and running for office to attain this high ideal; but Cicero judges the capacities of his countrymen such that the time may come when, with more leisure and devotion to study, a truly eloquent orator may appear.[17]

Cicero holds that "nature and genius" contribute most to speaking, for there must be natural acuteness in invention, retentive memory, ability to explain and adorn, good voice, strength of lungs, quickness of tongue, and a certain harmony of countenance and body. If one is not quick to learn, he can never thoroughly learn anything. One is improved by education, certainly, but those who are hesitant in speech, lack harmony of voice, and are awkward in bodily movements, can never rank amongst accomplished speakers. Those who lack certain natural endowments may achieve some honor and popularity; but the complete orator must be free from every fault, for he is to be the "high-priest" of the profession. Modesty and an inclination to embarrassment and timidity when beginning to speak are not improper or disadvantageous to the orator. Indeed, the better a man is qualified for speaking, the more he understands its difficulties and is likely to grow pale and tremble as he first begins to speak.[18]

[15] Bk. XLIV, 38.
[16] Sandys: Companion to Latin Studies, p. 229.
[17] On Oratory, I, 5, 21, 28.
[18] Ibid., I, 25–6, 46; III, 36.

The necessity for such a plentitude of natural gifts is obvious when one considers that the true orator's domain is vast, including everything relating to intercourse between citizens, the affairs of mankind in general, public administration, all civil matters, natural and moral laws, which he must be able to deal with judiciously in his pleading, though he may not know them as philosophers do.[19]

Oratory is divided into five parts: knowing what to say; arrangement of material; choice of language; fixing everything in the memory; and a dignified, graceful delivery. Before the main subject is touched upon, the audience should be prepared by an exordium; the case should then be stated clearly; the controverted point should be established; one's position should be proved, the adversary's refuted; and, in conclusion, everything favorable to one's cause should be amplified and reinforced, while all favorable to the opposition should be proved weak or invalid.[20] Successful speaking, according to Antonius, rests upon three things: proof of the facts stated; conciliation of one's hearers; and evocation in them of "whatever feeling our cause may require." The feelings on which the orator plays are love, hatred, anger, envy, pity, hope, joy, fear, and anxiety. Humor and jesting, important assets in speaking, "cannot be taught by any rules." [21] Since the orator weighs matters in the balance of "popular opinion," whereas philosophers require the goldsmith's scales, his highest attainment depends, in part, upon having a numerous audience.[22] His language should be pure, correct Latin, intelligible, perspicuous, graceful, and suited to the subject.[23]

Men do not become good speakers merely by speaking; indeed, "by speaking badly" they surely become bad speakers. To speak well it is necessary to write much. Writing is the best "teacher of oratory," for what is carefully considered, reduced to the best form and arrangement, and expressed in choicest language, will bring greatest applause when delivered. Even though one be compelled to speak at a moment's notice, what he says will retain something of the character of that which was previously written—will be better than if it had never been written. The imitation of excellent models is of first-rate importance.[24]

The true orator's preparation must be broad, for there is no "pursuit of greater difficulty" or one that requires more learning. He must study the use of voice, breath, tongue, and indeed the whole body. Actors as well as orators are to be studied, to put one on guard against awkward habits. The memory, if naturally strong, can be improved by exercise; and certain treatises thereon are

[19] Ibid., II, 16.
[20] Ibid., I, 31; II, 19.
[21] Ibid., II, 27, 51, 56, 60.
[22] Ibid., II, 38, 83.
[23] Ibid., I, 32; III, 12–4.
[24] Ibid., I, 33; II, 22.

recommended. If nature has given nothing, however, it cannot be called forth by practice.[25]

Studies are numerous, since "no man can be an orator possessed of every praiseworthy accomplishment" unless he knows everything important and "all liberal arts." [26] Poets, historians, writers, and teachers of all liberal arts and sciences must be read and used in all sorts of exercises, including praise, interpretation, correction, censure, and refutation. One must argue both sides of every question. Civil law, law in general, Senate usages, Roman government, rights of Roman allies, treaties, conventions—everything pertaining to the state and all antiquity must be known. Roman civil law "is indispensable to those who would become accomplished orators," for, in Cicero's judgment. "all civil law, except our own," is "undigested," "almost ridiculous." [27] An intellectual grace, distilled from all kinds of refinements, should season every oration. Though knowledge of the reason and nature of all things is necessary for the greatest eloquence, understanding is not all-sufficient. Issue is taken with Socrates' doctrine that "all men are sufficiently eloquent in that which they understand." Though plausible, it is not sound. No matter how perfectly a man understands a subject, if he does not know how to polish his expression, he cannot speak eloquently about it.[28]

The relation of learning to life is carefully considered. The attainment of great knowledge is difficult, and there is danger that extensive studies may draw one away from practice in speaking before the people and in the forum. Language and learning suited to the "tumults of the city and forum" are wanted, rather than that which is "florid" and "adapted for parade" in schools. The orator's "highest power" lies in stirring men's minds to anger, hatred, grief, or in leading them from these emotions to gentleness and pity; to do these things he needs a thorough knowledge of "the nature of mankind," "the passions of humanity," and those forces which impel or restrain men's minds. To investigate these arcana is the philosophers' province, but what they discover belongs to oratory, whose practical business is to sway the mind and feelings.[29] The distinction between him that uses knowledge and him that seeks to discover it is important: ". . . all arts are handled in one manner by those who apply them to practice; in another by those who, taking delight in treating of the arts themselves, never intend to do anything else during the whole course of their lives." [30]

[25] Ibid., I, 34; II, 87–8; III, 22.
[26] Ibid., I, 6.
[27] Ibid., I, 44.
[28] Ibid., I, 14, 18, 34.
[29] Ibid., I, 12–3, 18.
[30] Ibid., III, 23.

Cicero's ideal of liberal education is embodied in the complete orator—one well endowed by nature, enlarged by learning, and capable of using his natural talent and acquired learning effectively in public affairs. The true orator is more than a literary prodigy produced by grammarians; more than a glib speechmaker turned out by rhetoricians. Pericles was not taught "to bawl for hours by the water-clock." The "grandeur of the sciences" is diminished by "the distribution and separation of their parts," [31] i.e., by that specialization which knows nothing beyond its own borders. The complete orator is more than the philosopher. In a graceful figure Cicero suggests that learning flowed from a common eminence (Socrates) in two directions, like rivers from the Apennine divide; philosophers went, as it were, into the Ionian sea, and orators into barbarian, Tuscan waters, full of "rocks and dangers," wherein even Ulysses lost his way. The two must be united: if anyone would "call that philosopher, who instructs us fully in things and words, an *orator*," there is no objection; again, if anyone prefers to consider the orator, who has "wisdom united with eloquence, a *philosopher*," there is no reason to quarrel about the name.[32]

After examining several schools of philosophy Cicero comes to judgment. The Epicurean, though it appears true to some, is unsuitable to the orator,[33] who must be a leader in government. Since Epicureans deny the propriety of a wise man's devoting himself to public affairs, let them retire to the gardens for their own pleasure. The Stoics, too, are dismissed; for to speak after their manner and accept their notions of good, evil, honor, ignominy, rewards, and punishments would prevent the orator from carrying through any public business by speaking.[34] Though these offer no fit pattern, there is some truth in their systems, and the true orator cannot avoid philosophy. Should statesmen debate property rights in the child of a hired female slave and let questions pertaining to the whole conduct of man lie neglected? [35] If one be satisfied with modest eloquence, merely enough legal knowledge to see a case through the courts, and the ready rules of rhetoric masters, the would-be orator is reduced to a small domain indeed; but, if one would emulate Pericles or Demosthenes, he must have the powers of Carneades or of Aristotle.[36]

Quintilian (c. 35–95), educated under the grammarian Palaemon and the rhetorician Domitius Afer, viewed the ideal orator as the embodiment of a liberal education. Though he had served in the courts and gained consular rank, the erudite character of his treatise on oratory suggests the schoolroom

---

31 *Ibid.*, III, 33–4.
32 *Ibid.*, III, 19, 35.
33 Cicero: *De Finibus Bonorum et Malorum*, II, 22.
34 Cicero: *On Oratory*, III, 18.
35 Cicero: *De Finibus*, I, 4.
36 Cicero: *On Oratory*, III, 19, 21.

and the study more than the forum. Quintilian acknowledged [37] that he devoted a vast amount of research to a practically unlimited field.

Oratory is already in decay, as Quintilian's lost work, De Causis Corruptae Eloquentiae, suggests. The Institutio blames the grammarians and rhetoricians, who do not adhere to their proper spheres. Besides this trespass there are numerous other ills. The earliest stages of education are too commonly taken for granted. Flogging is general, but it is disgraceful, fit only for slaves. Immorality of masters must have been common, considering Quintilian's injunction to be on guard against it. Pupils applaud each other effusively and are spiteful toward teachers who fail to praise their efforts. There is too much bellowing "with uplifted hand," which appeals to the "dingier" part of an audience, but does not reflect a proper education of the speaker.[38] There is much pedantic insistence on minutiae, and too much attention to such matters makes "mincemeat of the mind." Such tiresome pedantry arouses Quintilian's ire; and he is depressed when the thought strikes him that his readers may find him pedantic too. His book is heavy, technical; he fears it will be a bitter dose for his readers! The task is laborious, even to himself; but he steers "straight on," inspired by his patron Prince and the importance of doing a piece of work more thorough than any yet attempted.[39]

Though oratory is more remote from the scene of struggle than it was in Cato's and Cicero's times, the ideal remains the same: the man of action. Oratory has revived courage and spurred on the soldier. The "art of rhetoric" "is realised in action." It aims to persuade to right action; if courts, senate, and assembly were filled with philosophers, there would be small need of eloquence.[40] "The man who can really play his part as a citizen and is capable of meeting the demands both of public and private business, the man who can guide a state by his counsels, give it a firm basis by his legislation and purge its vices by his decisions as a judge, is assuredly no other than the orator of our quest." [41]

The aim of education is to develop the perfect orator; nature and training must be joined, to that end.[42] The orator must first of all be a good man, endowed with unusual gifts for speaking. Individual capacities vary, and all men profit to some extent by education; but rules are futile unless there is natural talent. Good voice, power of lungs, health, endurance, and grace are neces-

[37] The Institutio Oratoria, II, 12, 12.
[38] Ibid., I, preface; 3, 13 et seq.; II, 1, 1–6; 2, 1–5, 9–13; 12, 9–10.
[39] Ibid., I, 5, 14; 7, 33; II, 17, 24; III, 1, 5; IV, preface; XII, preface.
[40] Ibid., II, 16, 7–8; 17, 25, and 28.
[41] Ibid., I, preface, 10. Quintilian's Institutio, trans. by H. E. Butler. The Loeb Classical Library. Quoted by permission of Harvard University Press, Cambridge, Mass.
[42] Ibid., II, 19, 1–3; XII, 1, 19.

sary and can be improved; if lacking, study cannot make up the deficit.[43] A good memory and powers of imitation are among the surest indications of educability. Play, too, is nature's index of a "lively disposition" and should be reasonably encouraged.[44] The good teacher will judge the natural bent of his pupils, even as a competent gymnast judges the types of contests for which a boy should be trained. Youth should exhibit a tendency to a profusion of capacities. It is easier to prune away excess than develop what is barren.[45]

The minutiae of oratory are multitudinous; though the origin of rhetoric lay in nature, experience and education have developed it to a high degree. The parents should both be educated as highly as possible; the nurse should be of good character, speak correctly and, ideally, should be a philosopher. The *paedagogus* ought also to be educated; if not, he should be cognizant of his lack. The child should begin to learn as soon as he begins to speak.[46] Public schooling is preferred to that of the household, for the disadvantages of a private tutor outweigh those of public tuition. Private learning is that of a hermit; in a larger circle youths learn from others and face conditions more nearly like those that will confront them in public life.[47]

After careful initiation in reading and writing, boys should go to grammar school, beginning with the Greek first.[48] This was a general practice. Echion's son makes "a hole in his Greek" and then begins to "relish Latin." [49] All kinds of writers are to be studied for a knowledge of words. One should read the best authors from the first, rather than select inferior ones because they are easier. From among the best, the simpler would come first; and passages should be memorized to improve style and vocabulary.[50] Music, astronomy, and philosophy must have a place, in so far as they are necessary to understand literary allusions.[51] Besides speaking and learning to interpret authors, youths should have some practice in writing paraphrases, moral essays, and character sketches on themes taken from their reading, before they go to the rhetoric master.[52] The Greek cycle of studies is approved; hence, geometry has a place. Quintilian uses the term in an inclusive sense, comprising arithmetic and astronomy. It has practical values, since the orator must speak on all subjects; as a discipline of the mind it sharpens the wits and cultivates the powers of percep-

43 Ibid., I, preface, 9, 26–7; I, 1, 1–3.
44 Ibid., I, 3, 1–3, 10–1.
45 Ibid., II, 4, 6–8; 8, 1–5.
46 Ibid., I, 1, 4–8, 15–9; 10, 4; III, 2, 1.
47 Ibid., I, 2.
48 Ibid., I, 4, 1.
49 Petronius: Satyricon, 46.
50 Quintilian, II, 5, 18–20; 7, 2–4.
51 Ibid., I, 4, 4.
52 Ibid., I, 9.

tion.[53] Music is to be included, but not "modern music," which is effeminate; the actor's art will also contribute to the future orator's delivery, but one must borrow with care.[54] Though Quintilian is disgusted by the mad devotion "to the cultivation of the body" that is so prevalent, he finds instruction in the gymnast's art and favors some use of physical training, since it can improve poise and develop ease of movement. Dancing should be employed (not too extensively), for it contributes to graceful bearing.[55]

After the solid, fundamental arts of the grammar school, the boy is ready for the rhetoric master. The five parts of oratory—"*invention, arrangement, expression, memory,* and *delivery* or *action*" [56]—receive extensive treatment. No slight detail is overlooked: even the orator's haircut and toga are touched upon; [57] all knowledge should be pursued, and there would be plenty of time, if so much were not wasted on ceremonial calls, idle talk, attending shows, running from place to place, drinking, feasting, and striving after physical cultivation. Besides literature and technical aspects of rhetoric, civil law, morals, religion,[58] acquaintance with the noblest deeds and sayings of the past, and philosophy are necessary. The ideal orator should be qualified to claim the "genuine title" of philosopher, for the principles of philosophy properly belong to oratory, though they come from philosophers. Philosophy and oratory are so united, in practice and theory, that Cicero thought they might be found in the same man. Though the orator is nourished upon philosophy, Quintilian holds it unnecessary that he should be bound to any one school.[59] Notwithstanding the extensiveness of the field, Quintilian hopes none will be appalled at the burden and abandon hope. One should remember that man's mind has astonishing power and capacity for the execution of our desires. If one but rises "to the height of this conception," the way will be found not "impassable or even hard." [60] Such a man in whom nature, study, and practice have been combined will have the greatest facility in speaking, and will be ever ready for action: "He stands armed for battle, ever ready for the fray, and his eloquence will no more fail him in the courts than speech will fail him in domestic affairs and the daily concerns of life: and he will never shirk his burden for fear of failing to find words, provided he has time to study his case: for all other knowledge will always be his at command." [61]

[53] *Ibid.,* I, 10, 34–49.
[54] *Ibid.,* I, 10, 31; 11, 1–14.
[55] *Ibid.,* I, 11, 15–9; II, 8, 7 and 15; XII, 11, 18.
[56] *Ibid.,* III, 3, 1; *supra,* p. 599.
[57] *Ibid.,* XII, 10, 47.
[58] *Ibid.,* XII, 3.
[59] *Ibid.,* I, preface, 11, 13, 18; XII, 2, 4–10, 26–7.
[60] *Ibid.,* XII, 11, 9–11.
[61] *Ibid.,* XII, 9, 21. Quintilian's *Institutio,* trans. by H. E. Butler. The Loeb Classical Library. Quoted by permission of Harvard University Press, Cambridge, Mass.

Tacitus' reference to the general, who was so surprised by an assault that he was unable to address his troops or marshal them into line,[62] suggests the old ideal of eloquence joined with action—an ideal that was honored more in word than in deed, however, after the first century B.C. The discrepancy between the eloquence of the forum and camp and that of the rhetoric school had been noted by Cicero.[63] As zeal for scholastic learning increased, the discrepancy grew greater, and the sturdier eloquence disappeared; literature, too, was deeply affected. The central theme of Tacitus' *Dialogue* is the decadence of oratory and the causes of this decay. The art of the rhetoric school came to be used "utterly without discretion" and was detrimental to state and individual.[64] Its chief use was to enable one to win fame as a lawyer in the criminal court. The "venal oratory" of the delator in the days of Nero brought men rich fees.[65] Cicero found Atticus' letters "sprinkled with the salt of refinement," in the phrase of the rhetoric school.[66] Ingenuity and refinement became the goal of the rhetoric master and public speaker. Romans were intoxicated by oratory; to be praised for eloquence was ardently desired. Pliny, writing to Arrianus about the trial of Marius Priscus which had called forth much good oratory, reported joyously that he had spoken nearly five hours, and the applause he received was equal to his fears experienced at the beginning of the speech.[67] Pleading had degenerated, however; youth rushed to the courts unintroduced or uninvited, and, to get applause, were ready to pay flattering clappers so much per head. Under such conditions, says Pliny, "he that has the loudest commendations is the worst orator." [68]

Divorced from life, speaking became an end in itself; the art of the orator became a popular form of entertainment. Merely to have heard a man speak became a matter of pride. Pliny had heard of Isaeus' coming to town, the advance accounts of his prowess, but reality outran report. Isaeus had the greatest "facility and copiousness," used "genuine Attic," let his audience select the subject, handled every point almost equally readily, and gave to his extemporaneous addresses the elegance of elaborate, finished compositions. Pliny regarded him as the "most eloquent" and "most happy" of mortals, and urged Nepos to come to Rome for the pleasure of hearing him and being able to say that he had heard him.[69]

62 *Histories*, IV, 33.
63 *On Oratory*, I, 18.
64 Fowler: op. cit., p. 196.
65 *Ibid.*, p. 173; Dill: *Roman Society from Nero to Marcus Aurelius*, pp. 35 f.
66 *Letters to Atticus*, I, 13.
67 *Letters*, II, 11.
68 *Ibid.*, II, 14.
69 *Ibid.*, II, 3.

### DIVORCE OF LIBERAL ARTS FROM LIFE

Economic and social divisions colored the conception of liberal education. Romans were conditioned by the existence of a slave class and a master class. Liberal studies were those worthy of a free man, which fitted him to perform the duties of his station. But wealth determined the extent of a free man's education; it supported leisure, without which extensive education was impossible. Without leisure one was not genuinely free. "He does not seem to me to be a free man," says Cicero, "who does not sometimes *do nothing*." [70] Men of wealth, such as Cicero, Quintilian, and others of their class, found it easy and natural to believe that liberal studies should not aim at money-making. They were economically secure; free to cultivate the arts of the mind in leisure. The taking of fees was a difficult question for Quintilian: the noblest thing for the orator would be to defend clients without regard to fees; but he may be rewarded, since one good turn deserves another. [71] For him whose economic status makes fees imperative, they are permissible; but they should be moderate —just enough to suffice for one's needs.

The conception of liberal education varied as Rome changed from a provincial to a cosmopolitan state; for when the Republic gave way to one-man rule, the political arena no longer offered a wide field to Roman citizens. Though in theory Cicero and Quintilian could combine the philosopher and orator in one man, Roman preference was for the man of action. Cicero was able to lose himself in study only after the arena of political action was closed to him, when there was "nothing else in which to find repose." [72] The divorce of liberal arts from life became more and more complete as public service through the agencies of self-government declined. Quintilian drew the orator as a fighting, public leader, yet his portrait was not of reality but an ideal, and he must constantly turn to Cicero's age to find anyone like the masterful figure he would conjure up. Under such conditions liberal studies became ends in themselves, a means to personal satisfaction; philosophy, a personal guide to virtue rather than a light to statecraft, as Plato and Aristotle had conceived it. Philosophers fixed their gaze on the distant goal of virtue; the outlines of the intermediate way-stations on the road grew dim and ultimately were obscured to view.

Asked to clarify his views on liberal studies, Seneca first defined them negatively: no study is to be included among the good which results in money-making. " 'Liberal studies' are so called . . . because they are studies worthy

[70] *On Oratory*, II, 6.
[71] Bk. XII, 7, 8–12.
[72] Cicero: *Letters to His Friends*, IV, 3 and 4; *To Atticus*, IV, 18; Plutarch: *Cicero*, 40.

of a free-born gentleman. But there is only one really liberal study,—that which gives a man his liberty. It is the study of wisdom, and that is lofty, brave, and great-souled. All other studies are puny and puerile." [73] The scholar, engrossed with details of language, poetry, history, falls short of liberal education: for what does "pronouncing syllables, investigating words, memorizing plays, or making rules for the scansion of poetry" have to do with eliminating fear, desire, or controlling passion? [74] Just as it is not the part of liberal education to discover whether Homer or Hesiod was the older poet, or to know whether Penelope was a "pattern of purity," so too a knowledge of treble and bass, the rules of arithmetic and geometry, the distances of the stars, a knowledge of painting, wrestling, and the like are not liberal. Seneca is surfeited with books; the reading of many leads to distraction, cloys the mind as numerous dishes do the appetite. One should read and reread "standard authors." [75] Without philosophy the body is sickly; even though it be strong, its strength is that of a madman.[76] It is possible to gain wisdom without so-called liberal studies— grammar, music, geometry, arithmetic, astronomy, rhetoric, logic—for though virtue must be learned, "it is not learned by means of these studies." [77] Such studies contribute much to our welfare in some respects, but "nothing at all as regards virtue." Seneca grants, however, that they "prepare the soul for the reception of virtue." [78] Those studies alone are really "liberal," or more truly called "free," whose "concern is virtue." [79] The studies of philosophers, who have descended to hair-splitting niceties and knowledge of "non-knowledge," fall short of being liberal. Zeno of Elea asserts that nothing exists, and so ends all difficulties! "You may sweep all these theories in with the superfluous troops of 'liberal' studies; the one class of men give me a knowledge that will be of no use to me, the other class do away with any hope of attaining knowledge." [80]

### GROWTH AND ATROPHY OF LETTERS

Greece made Rome a Republic of Letters. Nevertheless, in Horace's day, there still lingered "traces of the farmyard." [81] The transformation began significantly in the third century B.C., when classical meters gradually supplanted the rough Saturnian rhythm of native Latin. Thenceforward, for cen-

---

[73] Epistle LXXXVIII, 1–2. Seneca, Epistulae Morales, trans. by R. M. Gummere. The Loeb Classical Library. Quoted by permission of Harvard University Press, Cambridge, Mass.
[74] Ibid., 3–4.
[75] Epistle II.
[76] Epistle XV.
[77] Epistle LXXXVIII, 32.
[78] Ibid., 20.
[79] Ibid., 23.
[80] Ibid., 44–5. Seneca, Epistulae Morales, trans. by R. M. Gummere. The Loeb Classical Library. Quoted by permission of Harvard University Press, Cambridge, Mass.
[81] Epistles, II, 1.

turies, there was "little or no trace of truly native poetry." [82] Greece furnished textbooks and schoolmasters. From Andronicus' arrival at Rome (c. 272 B.C.) to the time of Augustus, Latin literature was like a child dependent on its mother. Translations and paraphrases from the Greek of Homer, Menander, and others formed the best part of the growing Latin book-shelf. Ennius drew from Homer; Afranius, from Menander. Terence (c. 185 B.C.) imitated Menander and Apollodorus. Criticized for having combined "Greek plays and written few Latin ones," he made no denial and was unrepentant.[83] Cicero found the themes for The Republic and The Laws in Plato; he, too, defended borrowing, holding it a "patriotic service" merely to translate Plato and Aristotle, and thus bring them to the knowledge of his countrymen, "as our poets have done with the plays." [84] Rome's borrowings were not in vain. If Virgil's indebtedness is truly "astonishing," he made the materials his own, by virtue of "graceful fitness in use," in an epic portrayal of a great nation's rise to power.[85] Perhaps in one field alone, as Quintilian implied, the Romans could properly claim originality. Horace, Juvenal, Persius, Seneca, and Petronius are sufficient warrant of their attainments in the realm of satire. Theirs was a natural talent for it, and times were propitious. Others might have said with Juvenal, "It is hard not to write satire."

In consequence of this cultural exchange, Latin developed and soon claimed equality with Greek as a world language.[86] Ovid recommended the two tongues, even for the art of love! [87] Varro (116–27 B.C.), like other literary folk, was much indebted to Greek authorities, but "preferred to derive Latin words from Latin sources, rather than to refer practically all to Greek origins." [88] The sense of nationality and independence toward foreign sources increased in Roman letters during the age of Augustus and was strong throughout the first century. Ultimately, however, the two cultures fused and the purely Roman element became less and less evident, till it was difficult to say whether a writer was more Greek or more Roman. Aulus Gellius (c. 130–180) represents "the all but complete fusion." [89] The union, of course, was never perfect. Rome became the center of a bilingual culture and swayed the nations by her power, but was herself enthralled. Marcus Aurelius ruled Rome: but his mind was ruled by Athens.

From Andronicus to Fronto, tutor of Aurelius, the rôle of teachers in de-

[82] Lawton: Classical Latin Literature, p. 19.
[83] Terence: The Self-Tormentor, prologue.
[84] Cicero: De Finibus, I, 2–3.
[85] Lawton: op. cit., p. 174.
[86] Cary: History of Rome, p. 587.
[87] Art of Love, II, 117 et seq.
[88] Kent: Varro On the Latin Language, I, xi.
[89] Lawton: op. cit., p. 311; Cary: op. cit., p. 580.

veloping Latin language and literature was of paramount importance—by reason of their influence on pupils who became eminent authors, and through their own contributions. The first teachers were also poets. Gnipho wrote *On the Latin Language* and was a teacher of Cicero. Praeconinus taught Varro, author of a treatise *On the Latin Language* and numerous other works on grammar. Palaemon, first among grammarians at Rome,[90] taught Quintilian, and he, in turn, had Pliny the Younger as a pupil. As author of the most complete treatise on oratory, Quintilian encouraged an "effort to revive a better rhetorical taste."[91]

Marcus Cornelius Fronto, who gained renown as an authority on linguistic questions, well illustrates the extreme trend of education toward minute scholarship. Gellius saw him as the center of a learned circle, possessed of marvelous erudition in the precise meaning of words.[92] A host of followers "imitated his methods in oratory and language";[93] his fame was still bright in the days of Jerome. Some three hundred years after his time, Sidonius[94] remembered the Frontonian school. Fronto's correspondence with Marcus Aurelius reveals a "scrupulous anxious care" in choosing words—especially the old, the unexpected word, one which requires searching and which, once found, admits of no substitute. Even the right syllable claims attention; and the order of words is a weighty matter. Bookishness and nicety of scholarship had become the hallmark of Roman education. The gulf between schools and swirling life had widened. It is significant that Fronto criticized even Cicero, the best pattern of eloquence in a man of action, because he was "far from disposed to search out words with especial care. . . ." Education of the Frontonian school was less for life than for letters; but if life suffered, the world of letters profited, for he left Latin "a freer and more plastic instrument" than it had been, and "by minute accuracy" in using words and "careful definition of their meaning," "gave precision and clarity" to it.[95]

Aemilius Paulus began the practice of transporting libraries to Rome, along with other booty of Eastern wars, in 167 B.C. Lucullus gathered many books together and made his house a place of welcome for Greeks at Rome. Sulla seized the treatises of Aristotle and Theophrastus in the library of Apellicon.[96] Caesar planned libraries of Greek and Latin works and set Varro to gathering and classifying them; two public libraries were established by Augustus.[97]

90 Suetonius: *Grammarians*, 1, 7, 23.
91 Lawton: *op. cit.*, p. 285.
92 *The Attic Nights*, II, 26.
93 Haines: *The Correspondence of Marcus Cornelius Fronto*, I, xxvi, xl.
94 *Letters*, I, 1.
95 *Fronto*, I, xli, 5. Trans. by C. R. Haines. The Loeb Classical Library. Quoted by permission of Harvard University Press, Cambridge, Mass.
96 Plutarch: *Aemilius Paulus*, 28; *Lucullus*, 42; *Sulla*, 26.
97 Suetonius: *Julius*, 44; *Augustus*, 29; *Dio*, XLIX, 43.

Domitian rehabilitated the libraries destroyed by fire, sought copies of lost works, and had scribes prepare new copies at Alexandria; Trajan also built libraries; in Hadrian's day there were twenty-nine public libraries in Rome,

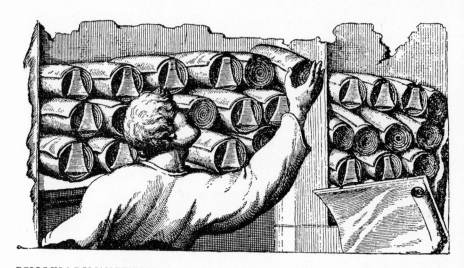

ROLLS IN A ROMAN LIBRARY

(From J. W. Clark, *The Care of Books*, p. 35, Cambridge University Press)

besides smaller collections at public baths.[98] Elsewhere libraries were established by private philanthropy or imperial aid. Pliny gave 100,000 sesterces for a library at Comum; others were founded at Volsinii and Suessa Aurunca; private philanthropy provided a library of 23,000 books at Timgad.[99] The numerous libraries imply "a very large reading public," since they "cannot have been intended" for "literary men" or "the well-to-do." Men of wealth had excellent private collections: Lucullus' library was like a "hostelry of the Muses"; Trimalchio boasted of two libraries, Greek and Latin.[100]

Education, though paid for privately, was generally inexpensive, since fees were low. The support of schools by the emperors was designed to aid the bourgeoisie, not the proletariat; children of the middle class were presumably able to get at least the rudiments of learning. "The average citizen," Abbott thinks, was probably literate; [101] in the second century, Cary says, the "ratio of illiterates in the population was never lower"; books became cheap, costing

[98] Suetonius: *Domitian*, 20; Dio, LXVIII, 16; Abbott: *Society and Politics in Ancient Rome*, pp. 175 f.
[99] Pliny: *Letters*, I, 8; Frank: *An Economic Survey of Ancient Rome*, v, 102; Cary: *op. cit.*, p. 691.
[100] Abbott: *op. cit.*, p. 176; Plutarch: *Lucullus*, 42; Petronius: *Satyricon*, 48.
[101] Abbott: *op. cit.*, p. 174.

probably not "more than twice what they do to-day." [102] Martial's first poems cost thirty or forty cents; the *Xenia* about twenty.

The aesthetic judgment of the Roman populace has been questioned. Commenting on Rome's crudities, Polybius cites Lucius Anicius who put on a performance by the most celebrated artists from Greece, placed all the flute players and the chorus on the stage and "ordered them to play all together." After a brief interval, the artists were told that they were not doing well; they should show more "competitive spirit." Not till they understood what was wanted, divided themselves into opposing parties and "engaged in a pitched battle" was there tremendous applause.[103] Terence's *Hecyra* was first interrupted by a stormy scene, the audience being diverted by a rope dancer; again, Ambivius says, "the vaunting of pugilists, the gatherings of their claque, the din, the clamour of the ladies" drove him "from the boards." A fresh attempt was made; but, it being reported that there was to be a gladiatorial show, the people rushed in with an "uproar and clamour and a struggle for seats" too great to withstand.[104]

The dramatists' art had difficulty in getting a hearing at Rome; its popularity was also to be brief. In Attius, whom Cicero knew as an old man, tragedy reached its zenith; with the demise of political freedom, it became "a mere literary exercise"; it might be written, but was seldom acted. The slave origin of actors and playwrights could only handicap a career, which, at best, seemed dubious in the eyes of Romans.[105] During the period of its greatest popularity the Roman government stood like adamant against the building of permanent theaters—too much like those of the Greeks whom they hated and distrusted. In 154 B.C. one of stone was begun, and then abandoned, because of anti-Hellenic sentiment. The first permanent theater was not erected until 55 B.C., when serious drama was in decline. Even then Pompey was censured for building it.[106] In a population of perhaps a million, at the time of Augustus, there were only three permanent theaters.[107]

The experiences of Ambivius and Rome's enduring love of the brutalities of the amphitheater have often been cited as proof of her aesthetic shortcomings. It has been said, in fact, that the rise of gladiatorial sports was partially responsible for the decline of Hellenistic tragedy at Rome. The games and the mimes, with their singing and dancing, offered increasingly keen and successful com-

[102] *Ibid.*, p. 175; Cary: *op. cit.*, p. 691; Rostovtzeff: *The Social and Economic History of the Roman Empire*, pp. 178 f.

[103] Polybius: *The Histories*, xxx, 22; Athenaeus, xiv, 615.

[104] Terence: *The Mother-in-Law*, prologues. Trans. by J. Sargeaunt. The Loeb Classical Library. Quoted by permission of Harvard University Press, Cambridge, Mass.

[105] Duff: *A Literary History of Rome*, pp. 231 f.; Lawton: *op. cit.*, pp. 38 f., 59.

[106] Tacitus: *Annals*, xiv, 20.

[107] Duff: *op. cit.*, pp. 157 f.; Fowler: *op. cit.*, pp. 309 f.

petition for the attention of the Roman populace.[108] Another critic, however, recalls the religious origin of gladiatorial games, observes that they were to the Roman what a bullfight is to the Spaniard, and questions their validity as a criterion for judging the aesthetic appreciation of the Romans. Moreover, he holds that the reaction of the Roman audience to the *Hecyra* showed good judgment rather than "an absence of literary taste." [109] There being no charge for admission, the success of plays really depended on their popularity, their appeal to all, rich and poor, and the quality of the actors. The triumph of the mime "over the tragic and comic actor" between the middle of the second and the middle of the first century B.C., Abbott believes, reflects the victory of realism over idealism and the transition from aristocracy to democracy.[110] Certainly as schooling and literacy increased, and ever wider intellectual horizons opened to men and women, it is only reasonable to expect that more and more weight attached to the voice of the growing audience, whether of hearers or readers. Cicero, Quintilian, Pliny, and others show that great weight was given to the opinion of the collective group on various matters. Cicero's comments on the judgment of the Roman populace are significant: when applause comes from the highest, the middle, and the lowest ranks, he says, it amounts to a "judgment" rather than mere "applause." [111] Pliny, too, credited the collective judgment of the crowd, even though individual opinion might be defective. He noted that Pomponius Secundus, the best tragic poet Quintilian had seen, always appealed "to the people" and followed their judgment, as expressed by "silence or applause in the theatre," if a question arose about including any particular passage in a play.[112] Pliny recognized, however, that the interest of audiences in his day was less than "in the time of our ancestors," there being "little disposition in the public to attend assemblies" for the recital of poetic products. Still, "men of genius" persevere. Despite the apathy toward poetry, he feels, nonetheless, that "if ever polite literature flourished at Rome, it certainly does now." [113] His was indeed an age of "polite" learning; but letters had lost the rugged qualities they once had known.

Back of the divorce of life from learning and the growing apathy in the Republic of Letters there were factors more potent than schools and schoolmasters. The arts of intellect flourish best under freedom. The teachers' position was always somewhat precarious; under the Republic it had been so, as rhetoricians and philosophers could witness; under one-man rule, the dependency of teachers grew apace. Even Quintilian bows before Domitian, "most righteous

[108] Lawton: *op. cit.*, pp. 23, 137.
[109] Abbott: *op. cit.*, pp. 165 ff., 176 f.
[110] *Ibid.*, p. 170.
[111] *Philippic* I, 15, 37.
[112] Pliny: *Letters*, VII, 17; Quintilian, X, 1, 98.
[113] *Letters*, I, 10, 13.

of censors," declaring "there is no deity that looks with such favour upon learning. . . ." [114] Dio received a "complimentary acknowledgment" of his little
book on the "dreams and portents" which gave Severus hope for supreme rule;
and under its spell he had a vision in which the "Divine Power commanded
. . . [him] to write history." [115]

The collapse of the Republic and the growth of despotism had a deleterious
effect on the minds of Romans and produced a progressive decay in education,
a "rapid decline" of literature. Men of learning became dependent on imperial
favor. "The patronage accorded by Augustus to men of letters," says Ramsay,
"may have done something to arrest the decay of literature; but with . . . the
accession of Tiberius the truth could no longer be concealed that the days of
liberty were over, and the natural results followed in every department of life
and thought. Deprived of the inspiration of reality, literature and oratory descended from the public to the private stage, and lost alike their meaning and
their manliness." [116] Just as schoolboys more and more debated threadbare
theses that had no contact with actual life, so literary folk applied themselves
with utmost nicety to remote arcana. If, in Domitian's reign, Statius preoccupied himself with extravagant phrases and phantoms, he finds forgiveness at
the hands of the modern critic who understands that "no one could fairly look
for any manifestation of daring originality at such a period. Freedom of speech
was stifled. Speech of any kind had to be prefaced with extravagant flattery to
the throne." [117] Of certain prose works by contemporaries of Seneca, Lawton
says, all reveal a "prudent effort to select subjects so remote, [and] colorless
. . ." as not to be "displeasing even to the most jealous imperial censorship."
The *gravitas* of Latin letters was ebbing away, "undermined by the loss of freedom and long capricious persecution"; "after Tacitus" no Latin author regained "the pedestal." [118] A revival of sorts did indeed take place in the second
century under good emperors whose reigns were marked by unwonted orderli-
ness; but after the middle of the third century the situation grew worse. "Books
in the libraries rotted," says a careful scholar, appraising the age of Diocletian;
though he created a degree of order, this "savior" denied "all the ideas that
had made Rome worthy of rule." [119]

There were voices of lament, bitterness, despair. One thinks of Lucan, Persius, Juvenal, Petronius, Tacitus, Seneca. Lucan, schooled with Persius under
the Stoic Cornutus, experienced both the encouragement of imperial favor and

[114] Bk. IV, preface, 3, 5.
[115] Bk. LXXIII, 23.
[116] Ramsay: *Juvenal and Persius*, p. xxvii. The Loeb Classical Library. Quoted by permission of Harvard University Press, Cambridge, Mass.
[117] Slater: *Silvae of Statius*, introduction, pp. 16 f.
[118] Lawton: *op. cit.*, pp. 253, 312.
[119] Frank: *op. cit.*, v, 303.

its malignant blight. Though his writing is "pervaded," or even "poisoned," with "the rhetoric of the schools," [120] he praised the Republic in the face of Nero, lamented the loss of liberty, and joined in a plot to slay the tyrant. His fate was doubtless a warning to others who might have been tempted to play his rôle. Persius flayed the decadence of Roman letters. Writers produce stuff that requires a lot of breath to recite, seek praise and enjoy it, regardless of its source or quality, and think it of importance if their utterances be pored over by a "hundred curly-headed urchins." [121] There is no honesty of criticism as there was in the day of Lucilius, father of Roman satire. Nobody wants it, but Persius, at least, will give it: everyone has the "ears of an ass." [122] The cause of decadence Persius finds in moral decay. All men are different, but all alike run after their own desires—games, love, dice, sleep, food—and "no two men offer the same prayers." [123] If Persius understands the relation of political to literary decadence, he does not speak out roundly about it. He does, of course, ridicule the Roman citizen who is made by "one twirl of the thumb," and thus is entitled to a measure of rotten corn.[124] The liberty he cries for is not political but moral in character—the freedom of the Stoic philosopher.

### PHILOSOPHY IN RETREAT

Though the Romans were not gifted with philosophic originality, they began, with the advent of extensive, literary education, to taste philosophies from abroad, and proved diligent, capable students. As long as the Republic lasted, however, and the great arena of public affairs was open to citizens, philosophy took no deep hold upon them. Lucullus [125] sought in philosophy leisure and repose. When Cicero found no longer "scope either in the senate-house or in the forum" for oratory, he turned his attention and energy to philosophy, for "the times are evil." [126] But, though he turned to study as to a "haven of refuge," and thought all philosophy profitable, Cicero preferred the practical aspects of it, namely that which treats of "duties" and teaches how to live consistently and virtuously.[127] Greek philosophical subtleties were generally given short shrift by the Romans.[128] Cicero thought philosophy had a genuine service to perform: to enable men to rule the state more wisely. He was profoundly influenced by Plato's *Republic* and *Laws*. Virtue was not simply a personal

---

[120] Duff: *Lucan*, p. viii; Schanz-Hosius: *Geschichte der Römischen Literatur*, ii, 492 ff.
[121] Persius: *Satire* i, 13 et seq.
[122] *Ibid.*, 114 et seq.
[123] *Satire* v, 52 et seq.
[124] *Ibid.*, 73 et seq.
[125] Plutarch: *Lucullus*, 1.
[126] *To His Friends*, iv, 3 and 4; Plutarch: *Cicero*, 40.
[127] *Offices*, iii, 2; *To His Friends*, v, 15.
[128] Seneca: *Epistle* cxi.

possession; its existence depended on its use; and its "noblest use" lay in "the government of the State." [129] Both Cicero and Quintilian considered philosophy necessary for the education of the ideal orator, the man of action.

Through the demise of the Republic, philosophy lost that sociopolitical *raison d'être* which Cicero thought so important; there was no free political life which it could serve. What paths could philosophers pursue? They might espouse a philosophy of revolt and seek to change the social order; they might lead men to goals other than political and social. It is commonly held that Tiberius Gracchus had been influenced to some degree by Blossius, his Stoic teacher, and Diophanes, a rhetorician, to take the reformer's path; but, in general, philosophy never stirred Romans profoundly toward any serious efforts to improve the condition of the lower classes. As individuals the slave and the impoverished might claim its healing: a slave's epitaph announced, "I have learned the doctrines of Pythagoras"; [130] and Epictetus,[131] a slave, taught a philosophy of freedom.

In general, even Stoics, whose philosophy embraced all men, led no movement for social reform or political revolution.[132] There was a moment, however, in the days of Nero and Domitian, when philosophy became something of a "revolutionary force," but it was aimed chiefly against "unworthy princes, rather than at the foundations of their power." [133] Helvidius Priscus, who with Flaccus and Lucan had been taught by Cornutus the Stoic, and was one of the Stoic circle of Thrasea,[134] cultivated the "favour of the rabble," denounced "royalty," praised "democracy," and banded "various men together, as if it were the function of philosophy to insult those in power, to stir up the multitudes, to overthrow the established order of things, and to bring about a revolution." [135]

Such a movement, if really as revolutionary as Dio believed, was a deviation from the rule. Persius' criticism of his times, his charge that every evil comes from moral decay, and his appeal for the inner freedom of the Stoic, were in harmony with the tendency of intellectuals to find solace in flight from reality. Philosophers took leave of social problems and devoted themselves to the quest of personal well-being, personal happiness.[136] Whether one turns to the Stoic, the Epicurean, or the Cynic, the result for social matters is substantially the same. The Cynic sets himself above the established laws of the state, and

129 *The Republic*, I, 2.
130 Abbott: *op. cit.*, p. 186.
131 *The Discourses*, IV, 1.
132 Fowler: *op. cit.*, pp. 26 ff.
133 Dill: *op. cit.*, p. 40.
134 Tacitus: *Annals*, XVI, 21–2, 28 *et seq.*
135 Dio, LXV, 12. Trans. by E. Cary. The Loeb Classical Library. Quoted by permission of Harvard University Press, Cambridge, Mass.
136 Seneca: *Epistle* XIV.

adheres to the "law of virtue"; denies all its duties, that he may be a citizen of the world. Pleasure as an end is evil; virtue is the only good; its essence is self-rule. Peregrinus plans his self-destruction, to prove his triumph over death. To Epicureans pleasure and pain are the measures of what is to be sought, what avoided. Happiness of the individual is the supreme good. Man finds how he should act by consulting his own advantage.[137] Such egocentrism afforded no succor to a sick society.

Personal virtue is the end toward which Seneca, Musonius, and Epictetus point. The old faith in the gods decayed; Augustus restored only its external forms. Philosophy serves the purpose of religion, is a means of the soul's salvation. Life is mean, contemptible; the philosopher becomes a personal guide to a "higher life," a "pedagogue of the human race," who leads man to "perfect beauty," "to the stars"; "the gods are not disdainful . . . they open the door . . . they lend a hand as you climb." [138] Musonius finds the essence of Stoic moral teaching in this: "If thou doest good painfully, thy pain is transient, but the good will endure; if thou doest evil with pleasure, thy pleasure will be transient, but the evil will endure." [139] Epictetus holds that "man is not the master of man; but death is, and life, and pleasure, and pain. . . ." [140]

Seneca, "millionaire philosopher," satiated with wealth and luxury, bids man give them up and lead a life of self-denial. Wealth is slavery; poverty is freedom from care.[141] Greed and luxury caused man's transition from happiness to misery. Man was happy in a state of nature.[142] His philosophy of moral discipline is for men of his own class; they are the ones enslaved by wealth and luxury; preachments of abstemiousness are meaningless, empty words to the underfed. Seneca's is a philosophy of disillusionment; his pessimism is unbounded. All men, high and low, are bad. There, in the populace, are as many vices as there are men. "Every place is full of crime and vice." [143] It must be so. Wicked we have been, are, and always will be.[144] There is lifelong conflict between spirit and matter; life is punishment; we die gradually every day; the greatest proof of the soul's exalted origin is that, if it judges its habitation strait and lowly, it fears not to take its departure. "He is truly great who not only has given himself the order to die, but has also found the means." Even gladiators, "abandoned and dangerous men"

137 Diogenes Laërtius: The Lives and Opinions of Eminent Philosophers, vi, 5; Ueberweg: History of Philosophy, i, 92 f., 211.
138 Seneca: Epistle LXXIII, 15–6; LXXXIX, 13.
139 Ueberweg: op. cit., i, 190.
140 Bk. i, 29.
141 Epistle XVII.
142 Epistle XC, 4 et seq.
143 Seneca: On Anger, ii, 8–9.
144 Seneca: On Benefits, i, 10.

as they are, can show others the way. "If you do not lack the courage, you will not lack the cleverness, to die." [145]

To Marcus Aurelius Stoicism is pre-eminently a personal philosophy, but it has social meaning as well. Philosophy alone is able to guide man, keeping the spirit "free from violence and unharmed, superior to pains and pleasures. . . ." [146] Aurelius settles the conflict between flesh and reason thus: let reason rule; "despise the flesh"; be not dissatisfied with the present nor fear the future.[147] Why should man fear change, dissolution? They are "according to nature, and nothing is evil which is according to nature"; considering changes that are implicit in the order of nature, one should despise all that is perishable, and not rate "life a thing of any value." [148] When all is done, be satisfied: "thou hast made thy voyage, thou hast come to the shore, quit the ship." Say not, "I have not finished the five acts, but only three . . . in life the three acts are the whole drama. . . ." [149]

Stoicism has certain social implications: Aurelius knows that his nature is social as well as rational; as a citizen he belongs to Rome; as a man, to the world.[150] From his first principle that one is "part of the whole which is governed by nature," it follows that he is "intimately related to the parts which are of the same kind . . ."; this being so, he will "do nothing unsocial," but rather turn all "efforts to the common interest, and divert them from the contrary." So motivated and directed, a citizen's life should be happy.[151] The concept of the relation of individual to social good is well put; but it does not lead Aurelius to expect social reform. Do not look for Plato's Republic, "for who can change men's opinions?" And without that power, what is to be expected in the way of improvement? Better be content if one small thing goes well. What hope was there for a Rome whose most enlightened prince, committed to a belief in indomitable will and the philosophy of labor,[152] with all the reins of power in his hands, could not see the way to translate his philosophy of social good will into action?

---

145 *Epistle* LXX, 22 *et seq.*; *Epistle* CXX, 15. Seneca, *Epistulae Morales*, trans. by R. M. Gummere. The Loeb Classical Library. Quoted by permission of Harvard University Press, Cambridge, Mass.
146 *Meditations*, II, 17; Windelband: *History of Philosophy*, p. 213.
147 *Meditations*, II, 2.
148 *Ibid.*, II, 17; IV, 50; IX, 28.
149 *Ibid.*, XII, 36.
150 *Ibid.*, VI, 44.
151 *Ibid.*, X, 6.
152 *Ibid.*, V, 1, 10; IX, 29.

# 21

# WOMAN'S SPHERE AND EDUCATION

Facing the fact of social decline, it is natural to ask whether it was caused by deterioration of human stock. Was Nature herself unkind to the Romans, robbing them of the enjoyment of that which they had been strong enough to win? Whatever may have happened ultimately to Roman stock, it seems probable that Nature was not at fault. Decadent tendencies were widespread in Roman society during the last two centuries B.C., but the human stock was evidently not "old or worn-out," judging from the strength of military force which continued victorious till the whole world within reach submitted to the Roman yoke. But if there is no sign of a natural weakening of physical stock, it is evident that great changes were in progress: Rome's wars were depleting man power; luxury was corroding and undermining the basic, social, educational institution, the family; marriage was declining, the birth rate falling.[1] Even in the days of Camillus, efforts were made to increase marriages by persuasion and by fines, for widows "were many because of the wars."[2] "Continuous military service" tended to weaken the marriage bond.[3] In Cato's day the notion that one should get wealth and keep it, and not have too many children, was gaining headway. Pursuit of a life of freedom, without the burdens of a family, seems to have been a significant factor in the decline. Marriage among the Romans had been a union de convenance rather than of love. When the old pattern of the family fell into decay, and the practical benefits of marriage declined with the increasing independence of women, cynicism increased among Roman men. It is reflected in the speech on marriage, liberorum creandorum

[1] Mommsen: History of Rome, v, 393; Fowler: Social Life at Rome in the Age of Cicero, p. 353.
[2] Plutarch: Camillus, 2.
[3] Cary: History of Rome, p. 264.

618

*causa*, credited to Metellus Numidicus, 102 B.C.: "If we could get on without a wife, Romans, we would all avoid that annoyance; but since nature has ordained that we can neither live very comfortably with them nor at all without them, we must take thought for our lasting well-being rather than for the pleasure of the moment." [4] Augustus strove (9 A.D.) to offset this celibate tendency by law. Declaring bachelors guilty of murder and sacrilege in not begetting children, and guilty of a crime against the state as well as themselves, he increased penalties against them and offered subsidies of 1,000 sesterces for each child.[5] Despite threats and indictments, however, the enactments fell short of their aim.[6]

Fundamental changes were taking place in the status of women and in the nature of the marriage relationship, the effects of which were to decrease the prestige and power of men and to emancipate women from many of the bonds which previously restricted their freedom. In early Rome the father's power had been supreme, and the notion of a husband's importance lingered: "In wedlock mischief often follows if too great is the wife's *dot*. Each sex has its powers, but in authority paramount is the *male*." [7] But Ausonius played on memories of a distant past. After the Punic wars woman had gained a certain moral and social equality, freedom from her husband, and possession of property, though political rights were still denied. Increased marital freedom for women is reflected in the growth of civil marriage (*matrimonium consensu*) which, though it existed even before the Twelve Tables, was not approved by Patrician families, among whom the religious marriage (*matrimonium confarreatione*) prevailed. After the Punic wars marriage "without *manus*" became the rule.[8]

Divorce had been difficult and exceedingly rare in the early Republic. The first reputedly occurred 519 years after the founding of the city, when Spurius Carvilius divorced his wife on the grounds of barrenness; [9] now it became "an everyday occurrence." [10] Matrimony was more and more exploited for ulterior ends. Antony married Fulvia, a woman who was not content with a man of private station, but wanted to "rule a ruler and command

---

[4] Aulus Gellius, *The Attic Nights*, I, 6. Trans. by J. C. Rolfe. The Loeb Classical Library. Quoted by permission of Harvard University Press, Cambridge, Mass.; a similar address was credited to Metellus Macedonicus, 131 B.C.—Suetonius: *Augustus*, 89.

[5] Suetonius: *Augustus*, 46; *Dio's Roman History*, LVI, 1–10.

[6] Tacitus: *Annals*, IV, 66; Dill: *Roman Society from Nero to Marcus Aurelius*, pp. 35 f.; Cary: *op. cit.*, p. 489.

[7] Ausonius, XII, 7. Trans. by H. G. Evelyn White. The Loeb Classical Library. Quoted by permission of Harvard University Press, Cambridge, Mass.

[8] Marquardt: *Das Privatleben der Römer*, pp. 63 f.; Mommsen: *op. cit.*, I, 112; Ihne: *History of Rome*, I, 565; Gibbon: *The Decline and Fall of the Roman Empire*, III, 686 f.; Dill: *op. cit.*, pp. 78–88; Abbott: *Society and Politics in Ancient Rome*, p. 41.

[9] Gellius, IV, 3; XVII, 21, 44; Tertullian says 600 years.—*Apology*, VI, 3–6.

[10] Mommsen: *op. cit.*, IV, 186.

a commander."[11] Greater freedom of marriage and divorce was conducive to the forming of alliances for wealth and power in the political world. The greatest men at the end of the Republic married like movie stars in our own day. Caesar had four wives; Pompey and Sulla, five each; Ovid, Octavian, and Pliny the Younger married three times.[12]

The wife had no property of her own under the old custom, nor had widows and fatherless maidens any control of property. Near the beginning of the second century B.C., however, by the use of "mock marriages," wives gained control of property and gradually escaped from the power of their husbands. Women got so much wealth in their hands, indeed, that it was declared a danger to the state, and the Voconian Law (169 B.C.) limited their inheritance to 100,000 sesterces. Doubtless women's wealth and growing influence lay back of Cato's caustic remark: ". . . we rule all other men, and our wives rule us."[13]

Certain Roman women of olden times had shown initiative and independence in a public way, as well as excellence in domestic virtues. With the relaxing of old customs their self-assertion increased. When the repeal of the Oppian Law against feminine luxuries was an issue (195 B.C.), women sought to influence the vote. Neither persuasion, modesty, nor the power of husbands, it was said, could keep them at home. The law was repealed; and they put on adornments then and there, and left the assembly dancing.[14] Again, during the Civil War, when an edict was published requiring fourteen hundred of the richest women to make a valuation of their property and to submit to an assessment to help pay for the war, they protested against sharing "the penalty" when they "did not share the guilt," and against paying taxes when they had "no part in the honours."[15] Notwithstanding the increase of their influence, women did not gain political status; had self-rule continued, they might possibly have done so. Under one-man rule all self-government atrophied. Women, to be sure, gained prominence occasionally by virtue of their connections with men of prominence. Agrippina, mother of Nero, was present when senators came to the palace, but was hidden by a screen; at one time, when she was about to mount the tribunal and preside with him, the scandal was forestalled.[16] Elagabalus in-

11 Plutarch: Antony, 10.
12 Abbott: op. cit., pp. 55 ff., 64; Friedländer: Roman Life and Manners under the Early Empire, I, 243; Cary: op. cit., pp. 456 f.
13 Plutarch: Cato, 8; Dio, LVI, 10; Marquardt: op. cit., p. 64; Mommsen: op. cit., III, 122; Gibbon: op. cit., III, 702; Fowler: op. cit., p. 147.
14 Dio, XVIII, 17; Livy, XXXIV, 1–8.
15 Appian: Civil Wars, IV, 32–4.
16 Tacitus: Annals, XIII, 5.

vited his mother to the Senate; and he formed a "women's senate," which laid down regulations on precedence, the clothes to wear in public, and who should use chariots, horses, carriages, litters, and other modes of conveyance.[17]

Wealth brought idleness to women as it did to men. Fulvia "took no thought for spinning or housekeeping." [18] If Augustus encouraged household industry by wearing clothing made by his sister, wife, or daughter,[19] it was so exceptional as to call for comment. A host of slaves degraded labor, and there was little to be done by free women of the household. Baking at home declined when public bakeshops began to flourish. Columella observed that wives generally gave way to luxury and idleness, avoided the labor of making wool, and disdained homemade clothing, preferring that which was very expensive. On farms it was necessary to have stewardesses who performed the duties of the wife.[20]

By expensive dress, gems, a grand equipage, and many slaves the "new woman" sought to impress and please. "Slimming," too, gained vogue. Mothers gave daughters "falling shoulders and straight bosoms to make 'em slim. If one of 'em is the least bit plump she's called a boxer and is docked of her rations. She's all right by nature but treatment makes her like a bulrush." [21] Many "unnatural women," Favorinus says, sought to preserve "their beauty" by abortion and refusal to nurse their babes.[22] That ground is made fruitful by cultivation and that the face may be improved by painting was not unknown to women of the new day. "Learn, O women," says Ovid, "what pains can enhance your looks, and how your beauty may be preserved." [23] Juvenal wonders whether to call it "a face or a sore" when all medicaments have been applied.[24]

The growing disinclination to marriage, increased opportunities for busy idleness in social life and at public entertainments, ready divorce, the desire of some like old Cato to get wealth and keep it, and many other factors bore unfavorably on the life of children. Exposure of babes was an ancient practice, but those accepted by the family had been most carefully nurtured. Mothers then nursed their own children; and this practice doubtless continued amongst the poor. In rich families, however, Tacitus says, children were turned over at birth to silly Greek serving-maids and male slave-attendants, apt to be the

[17] Lampridius: Elagabalus, 4.
[18] Plutarch: Antony, 10.
[19] Suetonius: Augustus, 73.
[20] Of Husbandry, XII, preface.
[21] Terence: The Eunuch, 312 et seq. Trans. by J. Sargeaunt. The Loeb Classical Library. Quoted by permission of Harvard University Press, Cambridge, Mass.
[22] Gellius, XII, 1.
[23] On Painting the Face, 1–2.
[24] Satire VI, 457–73.

"most worthless" members of the household. Though there were doubtless exceptions, the wet nurse took the place of the mother.[25] Favorinus' plea that mothers nurse their own children must have found scant approval on the part of upper-class women.

The growth of Rome was early marked by increasing lawlessness; and this affected women as it did men. A poison ring (c. 331 B.C.), involving 20 and then 170 women, caused the death of many; but so unusual was it at that date that people judged the whole thing a prodigy. A conspiracy was discovered (186 B.C.) which was associated with Bacchanalian rites, introduced from Etruria. Seven thousand men and women were allegedly drawn into this net of evil which spread through all Italy and aimed at controlling the state. The prominence credited to women in it—they were called "the source" of the "mischief"—reflects a growing restiveness and breaking with the old pattern of matronly sobriety. A few years later (180 B.C.) Hostilia was convicted of poisoning her husband, Piso.[26] In 154 B.C. two women were executed for poisoning their husbands.

Laxity of sex morals became noticeable. Polybius says that vicious tendencies, boy lovers, and courtesans were common, and Scipio was outstanding because of his "ambition to lead a virtuous life." [27] Men played the rôle of women; women sold their virtue. Dissoluteness in women doubtless evoked more comment, since moral standards had long been lower for men than for women. Sempronia, Sallust says, committed crimes of masculine daring, held nothing so cheap as her virtue and sought men even more than she was sought.[28] Princess Julia, said to have been "the most dissolute and shameless woman of her day," led Rome "into every form of brutalizing vice." [29] Though Augustus was "given to adultery," he made laws against it; but women avoided punishment under them by sacrificing the rank and privileges of matrons and registering as prostitutes.[30] In the time of Severus adultery became unusually common, further laws were enacted against it, and there were many indictments but few prosecutions. Dio says that three thousand cases were on the docket when he became consul.[31]

Though women were esteemed for domestic virtues, and were sometimes praised for courage, numerous casual remarks reveal a low estimate of their capacities. Lucretius considered "the male sex" in general "far superior in skill

---

[25] Tacitus: A Dialogue on Oratory, 29; Friedländer: op. cit., I, 229; Johnston: The Private Life of the Romans, pp. 80 f.; Gibbon: op. cit., III, 685.
[26] Livy, VIII, 18; XXXIX, 8–19; XL, 37.
[27] The Histories, XXXI, 25.
[28] Sallust: War with Catiline, 13, 25.
[29] Lawton: Classical Latin Literature, pp. 203 f.
[30] Suetonius: Augustus, 34, 69; Tiberius, 35.
[31] Dio, LXXVII, 16.

and more clever." [32] Livy expressed a common view in his reference to women, who he said were influenced by mere trifles. Elsewhere, describing the Romans' incompetence, delight in present ease, and failure to look to the future, he says that they sat idly quarreling just like women.[33] Polybius noted casually "a woman's natural shortness of view." [34] Dio recounted how one soon "demonstrated the weakness of the female sex, which quickly flies into a passion through lack of judgment, and quickly becomes terrified through cowardice." [35] Cato's declaration, "All other men rule their wives; we rule all other men, and our wives rule us"—a mocking recognition of their power—was not spoken in praise of women but in contempt for their growing wealth and independence. More sincere, probably, was his remark that he regretted only three things in his whole life, one being that he had trusted his wife with a secret.[36]

It is not surprising, considering the prevalent notions of female inferiority and the rapid spread of crime and vulgar practices among women, that many bitter attacks were made upon them. Petronius viewed "women one and all" as "a set of vultures." [37] Juvenal attributed almost every form of meanness and crime to them; "in the days of Saturn," humble fortunes, labor, chastity, and short slumbers preserved a general sobriety of conduct, but now no more. Wealth and luxury have made every crime familiar. Why be so mad as to take a wife, when ropes, windows, bridges, and other modes of exit are handy? Is there one woman in all the seats of all the theaters whose fidelity one can trust? The better the husband, the worse the wife. She will order everything, cause every quarrel, and have eight husbands in five autumns. To-day women are athletes and gladiators! What modesty can you expect from them? Mannish women at the baths; the woman musician; the female intellectual who disputes grammatical niceties and quotes philosophers and poets; she who beats her maids for a misplaced curl; women who know everything that's taking place, and all that is rumored; those skillful with poison, and many others—all fall under his withering satire. Juvenal looks through a dark glass, indeed, and lumps all "new women" together indiscriminately; the intellectual is no better, apparently, than the poisoner, the tyrant, the libertine.[38] Martial lacks the acidity of Juvenal, but his epigrams reveal the same evil tendencies of the day. Seneca, too, bares a scene of corruption, in which women are as guilty as men. The most famous founder of medicine had said that women never suffered baldness or gout, but now they are affected by both. Nature has not changed,

[32] Lucretius: De Rerum Natura, v, 1354 et seq.
[33] Livy, III, 68; VI, 34.
[34] Bk. II, 4.
[35] Bk. XII, 4.
[36] Plutarch: Cato, 8.
[37] Satyricon, 42.
[38] Satire VI.

624 [EMPIRE OF THE EAST AND WEST]

but she has been conquered. By matching men's indulgences, women reap the same harvests. They stay up as late, drink and vomit as much, vie with men in carousing and wrestling, and imitate them in their passions. Hence they are heirs to the ills of men.[39] Tertullian's attack on feminine weaknesses runs the gamut, but adds little; in fact, little could be added to the sweeping indictments of Juvenal and Seneca. Everything that "protected modesty or sobriety" has vanished. "Between matrons and harlots," he finds "not a vestige of distinction in dress left." [40]

Every shield has two sides. Even in the worst days of the Republic and Empire, some women were distinguished for fidelity, nobility, culture, and refinement, and men honored them for their high qualities. Caesar honored his wife by a funeral oration; nobility, strength of character, and fidelity were credited to Porcia.[41] Seneca thought the same standard of conduct should apply to husband and wife, and recorded the greatest fidelity and devotion on the part of Paulina.[42] Women, he believed, have as great a talent for goodness and education as men. Helvia and Marcia are both portrayed in the fairest colors.[43] Pliny [44] praised Calpurnia for discernment, thrift, purity, affection, and her devoted interest in his literary pursuits. Even though the state of society generally grew worse, and immorality was prevalent, the tale of excellence in women continued. Much depends on the writer and what he sees. Symmachus (345–410) extolled the ancient Roman ideal of women. Salvian reported gross laxity of morals in the fifth century. Sidonius (431–489) praised Filimatia for obedience, kindliness, and capability in her family. Religious works, he thought, were most suitable for ladies, but piety was found mingled with breadth of learning in some women of his acquaintance. To a friend about to marry he offered the reassurance that a wife would not necessarily hinder his studies, but assist them; and he cited Marcia and Hortensius, Terentia and Tullius, Calpurnia and Pliny, Rusticana and Symmachus, Corinna and Ovid, Argentaria and Lucan, Cynthia and Propertius, and other couples as proof.[45]

If the new day offered opportunity for license, it also gave many women a degree of enlightenment and a scope of useful activity in the world of affairs previously unknown.[46] A few women owned ships, perhaps by virtue of inheritance. Several women of the upper class were interested in the manufacture of brick; indeed, that business seems to have been dominated by women. Some women of lower classes and freedwomen assisted husbands in their shops;

[39] Seneca: *Epistle* xcv, 20–1.
[40] Tertullian: *Apology*, vi, 4–6.
[41] Plutarch: *Caesar*, 5; *Brutus*, 13, 15.
[42] *Epistle* xciv, 26; civ, 1–2; Tacitus: *Annals*, xv, 63.
[43] Seneca: *To Helvia*, xvi, 3–5; xix, 2, 6; *To Marcia*, xvi.
[44] *Letters*, iv, 19.
[45] Sidonius: *Letters*, ii, 8–10.
[46] Abbott: op. cit., pp. 95 ff.; Frank: *An Economic Survey of Ancient Rome*, v, 272.

others engaged in costuming, sewing, washing, weaving, selling fish, tending bar, managing estates. Cato devoted some attention to the duties and proper conduct of the wife of an overseer.[47] Many women, mostly Greek, were em-

A GIRL ACROBAT    *Naples Vase Painting*
(T. Schreiber, *Atlas of Classical Antiquities*, LXXVIII, 5, Macmillan & Co., Ltd., London, 1895)

ployed as mimes and musicians after the first century B.C.; Eucharis is said to have initiated the use of musical monologues. Some women took part in public gymnastic contests, though this apparently aroused opposition, and an edict was issued against it.[48] Medical practice, mostly in foreigners' hands, was entered by women, chiefly Greeks, who probably combined midwifery, magic, and beauty treatments. Scantia Redempta was described on her tomb as a "leader in the science of medicine." Magic and science were mingled rather indiscriminately. Though standards were low and quackery abounded, Soranus, writing in the second century A.D., said women wishing to enter medical practice should have ability to write, good memory, health, even temper, discretion, and knowledge of dietetics, of pharmacy, and (to some extent) of surgery. That women doctors were generally recognized is implied by the reference to "physicians of either sex" in Justinian's Code.[49] Women did not gain the right to practice law, which was the most fully developed profession,[50] but that there was a movement in that direction is to be inferred from Ulpian's edict which prohibited their service as pleaders in courts. Valerius Maximus mentions two

[47] Cato: *On Agriculture*, 142 et seq.
[48] Dio, LXXVI, 16.
[49] Abbott: *op. cit.*, pp. 80 ff.; Friedländer: *op. cit.*, I, 171, 175, 182 ff.; Dill: *op. cit.*, pp. 92 f., 457 f.; Mommsen: *op. cit.*, III, 193 f.; Marquardt: *op. cit.*, pp. 771 ff.
[50] Mommsen: *op. cit.*, IV, 254.

women, however, who used the privilege of arguing their own defense, much to his disapproval.[51] As for religious offices, some, such as the vestal service and the rites of Juno and other goddesses, had been open to women in early times. Women took part in the Bacchanalian conspiracy (186 B.C.), and the cult seems to have grown despite opposition. As new religions from the East overran Rome, women played an increasing rôle in their ceremonials.[52]

### WOMEN AND LETTERS

The education of women, which had been directed solely toward domestic employments, was gradually modified after the second century B.C. in conformity with the prevalent tendency toward literary and aesthetic culture.[53] This was true, of course, chiefly for girls in upper-class society. Some educated women became the center of intellectual circles and exerted great influence on public life. The power of Clodia over the coterie which she drew around her on the Palatine and at Baiae was enormous, and well merited the fear and hatred of those she opposed. Cornelia's influence on her sons' education and on public affairs made her one of Rome's most celebrated characters—credited with initiating the revolution at the end of the second century. Through her circle at Misenum she kept in touch with public affairs after her sons' death.[54] Livia, it was said, advised Augustus to pursue a policy of leniency and conciliation—a suggestion which he heeded.[55]

There is no ground for thinking that all women ceased to be concerned with their families. Some continued to be home-centered bodies; others combined public and private interests; while many, doubtless, were led by influences of the new age to avoid domestic duties. Horace refers to the years that crawl for "minors burdened by a mother's irksome tutelage." [56] Agricola imbibed his education from his mother, Julia Procilla.[57] Quintilian thought both parents should be thoroughly educated, and cited Cornelia, Laelia, and Hortensia as educated women, urging that those less educated than they should not, on that account, give less attention to their sons' education.[58]

The education of girls, like that of boys, began in the household. When families could afford it, a *paedagogus* had charge of each child; or an old slave woman might be assigned to the girl.[59] Since girls married early, usually be-

[51] Abbott: *op. cit.*, pp. 84 f.
[52] Livy, xxxix, 8–19; Friedländer: *op. cit.*, I, 255 ff.; Dill: *op. cit.*, p. 82.
[53] Dill: *op. cit.*, p. 79.
[54] Plutarch: *Tiberius Gracchus*, 1; *Caius Gracchus*, 19; Abbott: *op. cit.*, pp. 53 ff., 90 f.
[55] Dio, LV, 16–22.
[56] *Epistles*, I, 1.
[57] Tacitus: *Agricola*, 4.
[58] The *Institutio Oratoria*, I, 1, 6.
[59] Wilkins: *Roman Education*, p. 42.

tween thirteen and sixteen, their opportunity for schooling, whether inside or outside the family circle, was more limited than boys'. At twenty a woman was subject to Augustus' regulations directed against childlessness.[60] Due to the growing custom of having tutors and philosophers attached to the household, women could continue their education privately. Epirota taught his patron's married daughter.[61] Some husbands took the responsibility for educating their wives. Pliny encouraged his wife's learning. The wife of his friend Pompeius Saturninus, he says, wrote so well as to simulate Terence and Plautus—which Pliny thought highly creditable to Pompeius, who had "so highly improved and refined" her genius, for she had been only a girl at marriage.[62] Household education for girls seems to have continued to be the mode, at least for the best families. The *Faustinianae*, established by Antoninus Pius, and a similar institution, founded by Marcus Aurelius in honor of the younger Faustina, were for destitute girls.[63] In the early fifth century St. Jerome advised placing Paula's education in the hands of a "man of approved years, life and learning." [64]

Opinions vary as to whether girls were educated in schools with boys. Friedländer holds that they were taught together at schools, though perhaps only "to a certain age." Marquardt's view is similar. Paul of Aegina said that reading and writing should be taught to both sexes together at six or seven years of age. A schoolmaster's tomb at Capua, showing a girl at one side of the master and a boy on the other, suggests, but does not prove, coinstruction. Jullien and Wilkins hold that there is no clear evidence of coeducation.[65] Coeducation may have been the rule in country places, but only the exception at the capital. Certain scattered, fragmentary allusions to girls' and boys' education have thus been divergently interpreted. Martial refers to the "bawling pedant," whom "generous youth and ripening maiden hate"; the "schoolmaster," he says, "girls and boys abhor. . . ." [66] Ovid observes that even Menander is "wont to be read by boys and girls"; [67] his own book alone has brought punishment upon its author.

The extent of women's education varied greatly. Learning appeared among the best and the worst. Sophonisba, beloved by Masinissa and Syphax, was noted for literary and musical talents, as well as physical beauty.[68] Pompey's Cornelia was well versed in literature, played the lyre, knew geometry, and

---

[60] Friedländer: *op. cit.*, I, 232.
[61] Suetonius: *Grammarians*, 16.
[62] Pliny: *Letters*, I, 16; IV, 19.
[63] Capitolinus: *Antoninus Pius*, 8; *Marcus Antoninus*, 26.
[64] Letter CVII, 4.
[65] Jullien: *Les Professeurs de Littérature dans l'Ancienne Rome*, pp. 147 ff.; Wilkins: *op. cit.*, pp. 42 f.; Friedländer: *op. cit.*, I, 230; Marquardt: *op. cit.*, p. 110.
[66] *Epigrams*, VIII, 3; IX, 68.
[67] *Tristia*, II, 361-70.
[68] *Dio*, XVII, 50-1.

listened to "philosophical discourses with profit," yet was free from officious-ness which such attainments were "apt to impart to young women." [69] Hor-tensia's oration before the triumvirs was still read for its own merit in Quin-tilian's day, not simply out of honor to her sex.[70] Sempronia was possessed of "no mean endowments" and was "well read in the literature of Greece and Rome." [71] Ovid notes that ". . . there are learned women too, a scanty num-ber; and others are not learned, but wish to be so." [72] Fundania, though scarcely thirteen, according to Pliny,[73] had the wisdom of age and the sedateness of a matron. To her nurses, her paedagogus, and her teachers she was exemplary in behavior; at books she was intelligent and studious; in play she indulged sparingly and discreetly. Calpurnia was carefully educated, incomparably dis-cerning and thrifty, had a turn for books, read Pliny's compositions and even learned them by heart, listened to his speeches, sang his verses and set them to the lyre.[74] Pliny felt sure she would always be everything he could desire. Polla Argentaria, wife of Lucan, was credited with intellect and virtue as well as youth, beauty, and wealth.[75]

Dancing and music began to play some part in Roman education, along with letters. Disparaging remarks about them indicate something of their spread in Roman society. Music, "according to our ideas," says Nepos, is thought unfit for persons of importance, and dancing is even considered a vice; Cicero names dancers, butchers, cooks, and perfumers as examples of those who engage in "illiberal" occupations.[76] Scipio was distressed because free boys and girls were "going with lute and psaltery to the training schools of professional actors" and were learning songs and dances unfit for them. He himself has seen "more than fifty boys and girls" at "one of these dancing schools." [77] Sempronia could "play the lyre and dance more skilfully than an honest woman need. . . ." [78] Seneca speaks of "those whose daughters dance upon the stage and wed with a dowry of a million sesterces. . . ." [79]

Despite contempt and opposition, music and dancing gained great vogue. Approval of them grew with longer acquaintance. Demetrius and Tigellius, famous musicians, had many women followers; boys and girls of the best fam-

---

[69] Plutarch: Pompey, 55.
[70] Quintilian, I, 1, 6.
[71] Sallust: Catiline, 25.
[72] Art of Love, II, 279 et seq. Trans. by J. H. Mozley. The Loeb Classical Library. Quoted by permission of Harvard University Press, Cambridge, Mass.
[73] Letters, v, 16.
[74] Ibid., IV, 19.
[75] Statius: Silvae, II, 7; Duff: Lucan, p. viii.
[76] Nepos: Epaminondas, 1; Cicero: Offices, I, 42.
[77] Gwynn: Roman Education from Cicero to Quintilian, p. 55.
[78] Sallust: Catiline, 24–5.
[79] To Helvia, XII, 6.

ilies joined in singing a dirge in honor of Augustus.[80] Statius' stepdaughter was well educated and would soon marry, he thought, for with other excellencies she combined playing the lute, singing, and dancing. When Christian asceticism appeared in Roman society, dancing and music were among the arts prohibited. St. Jerome advised emphatically against "sporting in the dance." Paula must be deaf to musical instruments, such as the lyre, flute, and harp, and must not even know why they came into being.[81]

Though Romans were slow to take up philosophy, it gradually gained ground, and women turned to it; to have a philosopher in the household ultimately became the height of fashion. Cornelia, wife of Pompey, profited from philosophic study; and Caerellia, deeply interested in philosophy, copied the De Finibus. Julia Domna, wife of Septimius Severus, gathered a learned circle at court and devoted herself to science and philosophy; to her influence Philiscus reputedly owed his chair of rhetoric at Athens.[82] Theophila seems to have known both Stoic and Epicurean systems; Plotinus had many women disciples of Neo-Platonism in the third century.[83]

Certain writers praised the capacities of women and defended the view that they should be educated as were men; others were opposed. Quintilian wanted fathers and mothers both educated. Seneca's father opposed philosophic studies for his wife, because certain women did not "employ learning as a means to wisdom," but sought it for display. Nevertheless, owing to her turn of mind, she gained more than "might have been expected" and had "the foundations of all systematic knowledge." [84] Plutarch [85] praised women's bravery, thought the virtues of men and women were the same, and believed that women should be known not for their form but for their fame. In his Advice to Bride and Groom he recommended that they study philosophy, geometry, and astronomy together, which would be a safeguard against vanity, futility, and vulgarity in thought and conduct. Such studies would "divert women from all untoward conduct," and make them ashamed to be dancers, or to swallow beliefs in magic while under the charm of Plato or Xenophon.[86] Women have talent for education, according to Seneca; they have as much force, as much capacity for virtuous action as do men, he wrote to Marcia, while bidding her remember Cornelia, who lost twelve children. To Helvia he recommended philosophic studies as a refuge, despite the fact that his father had permitted

[80] Horace: Satires, I, 10; Suetonius: Augustus, 100.
[81] Jerome: Letter cvii, 6, 8; Friedländer: op. cit., I, 231.
[82] Plutarch: Pompey, 55; Cicero: Letters to Atticus, XIII, 21 a; Dio, LXXVI, 15; Philostratus: Lives of the Sophists, II, 30.
[83] Martial, VII, 69; Friedländer: op. cit., I, 254 f.
[84] Seneca: To Helvia, XVII, 4.
[85] Bravery of Women, introduction.
[86] Plutarch: Advice to Bride and Groom, 48.

her only "a mere smattering" of philosophy.[87] Musonius, too, defended philosophical study for women, as did Stoics generally, for virtues belong equally to men and women; and since "without philosophy no man can be rightly instructed, so neither can any woman." [88]

Since rhetoric schools aimed to develop orators and pleaders, and women never gained the right to practice law, it is readily understood that they had little reason to strive for such professional learning. Had this professional domain not remained closed to them, the customary limitation of their education to letters and philosophy would probably have been altered, and there might have been more than isolated examples of women distinguished for oratorical attainments.

What contribution did Roman women make to the world of letters? A number of interesting references testify to their attainments. Hortensia's oration was still read for its own merit.[89] Ovid's daughter, gifted with "native wit," learned to write poetry under his teaching and criticism, and would only be surpassed by Sappho if she kept alive the sacred flame.[90] The wife of Saturninus simulated Terence and Plautus.[91] Martial, though he wanted "a kind but simple wife," praised the poetry of Sulpicia, member of Messalla's coterie, who left a few elegies on her love of Cerinthus, which are judged "graceful in form and sincere in tone." [92] Theophila, steeped in Attic learning and far above most women, was skilled in poetry like Sappho, and would make, says Martial, an excellent critic.[93] Such compliments, though fairly common, should, presumably, not be taken too seriously. Tacitus mentions memoirs of Agrippina, mother of Nero, which he had used.[94] The most extensive literary effort known to us is an account of a fourth-century pilgrimage to Palestine, written by Silvia, sister of a Roman prefect, or by Aetheria, an abbess of Spain. Though valuable as a unique chronicle by a female zealot of early Christian days, her record is said to be "monotonous and repetitious," and lacks literary skill. Abbott concludes a survey of the slender remains of literary contributions from the pens of Roman women with the observation that it shows "pretty clearly that women made no important contributions to Latin literature." [95]

The effect of the "new learning" on women was viewed in various ways. In many instances learning in women deserved and called forth praise, even

[87] To Helvia, xvii, 3–5; To Marcia, xvi, 3.
[88] Laurie: Historical Survey of Pre-Christian Education, pp. 427 ff.
[89] Quintilian, i, 1, 6.
[90] Tristia, iii, 7.
[91] Pliny: Letters, i, 16.
[92] Abbott: op. cit., p. 91; Martial, ii, 90; x, 35.
[93] Bk. vii, 69.
[94] Annals, iv, 53.
[95] Abbott: op. cit., pp. 94 f.

though their contributions to Roman letters were slight, so far as can be judged to-day. Opposition to the new learning, keen even when men turned to it, was still greater when it was desired by women. The elder Seneca's objection to higher studies on the part of Helvia was by no means unique. The old, deep-set conviction of Romans that women's capacities were weak and inferior did not quickly or generally pass away. Theophila was "so little like the common female kind" in literary capacity that Martial praised her.[96] If we add to this notion of limited capacity the fact that a little learning would puff up many—women as well as men, and especially those who had had none before —and make them appear ridiculous, it is easy to understand that the result would be credited to the influence of education in general rather than to the character and extent of that which had been acquired; and to the nature of women in general rather than to the strength or weakness of particular persons. Juvenal's satire is at once a testimony to the increase of women's education and the contempt which many felt for those who paraded their accomplishments in an unpleasant manner. His temper, of course, is by no means judicial; he delights in the castigation of his day's ways; the intellectual woman as well as the vicious is condemned. He finds intolerable the woman who praises Virgil, forgives Dido, weighs the merits of Virgil and Homer; scatters the grammarians and rhetoricians, even the lawyers and auctioneers, or reduces them to speechlessness; defines propositions, lectures like a philosopher, hurls the crooked enthymeme, knows all history and even little-known poets; constantly delves into Palaemon, and will not even permit her women friends to make grammatical errors. She is a bore; a wife should have no special style; there should be something that she does not know; husbands should at least be allowed to make mistakes in grammar![97] But Juvenal was fighting a losing battle. In fact, as Dill says, the battle had been "lost long before he wrote."[98] The place of women in learning, as in Roman life, had been altered; to war against it was not unlike attempting to sweep back the tides of ocean with a broom.

96 Bk. vii, 69.
97 Juvenal, vi, 434–56
98 Op. cit., p. 81.

# 22

## GROWTH AND DECAY OF MILITARY DISCIPLINE

A s Rome became a great military force, her army and navy—the instruments of empire—became for many Romans an epitome of life and education. This was true for an increasing number until the peak of power was reached; thereafter, it declined in significance, quantitatively and qualitatively, till finally the very name "Roman legion" became obsolete; fifty years after Justinian, it had "completely vanished" as "a form of military efficiency." [1]

Notwithstanding ultimate decay, the military ideal and discipline were remarkably persistent; even after the cessation of conquests had removed their chief raison d'être, the broad expanse of the Campus Martius was a place of serious preparation for war's fatigues, and many shunned the easier regimen of the Greek gymnasium which was thought less valuable as training for war. Cato (234–149 B.C.) is sometimes called the last of the old Romans. Certainly, by his own discipline and that of his sons,[2] he proved himself worthy of that name. But those who, like Marius (155–86 B.C.), came up from the soil, kept the old discipline alive quite as well as Cato.[3] Varro's early regimen was simple and severe. Cicero, though less inclined to military life, trained for it, and served in one campaign.[4] Military distinction, he knew, was still the chief path to public recognition. His son, trained to arms, gained Pompey's praise by his skill in horsemanship and use of the javelin.[5] Caesar, educated both for the forum and the field, distinguished himself in sports and military exercises, such as swimming, horsemanship, use of arms, indifference to diet, and his powers of endurance.[6] Octavius, notwithstanding all the divine prodigies associated

[1] Oman: *The Art of War in the Middle Ages*, p. 3.
[2] Plutarch: *Cato*, 1, 3–4, 20.
[3] Plutarch: *Caius Marius*, 2, 34; Sallust: *War with Jugurtha*, 85.
[4] Fowler: *Social Life at Rome in the Age of Cicero*, pp. 177, 194.
[5] Cicero: *Offices*, II, 13.
[6] Plutarch: *Caesar*, 2, 17, 49; Suetonius: *Julius*, 57.

with his birth, exercised in the *Campus Martius* like other youths of his day, and "was thoroughly trained in military service" as well as in government and the new studies.[7] After he came to power, he held to the old ancestral discipline in his own household, and sought especially to prepare young men of senatorial families for war by giving them a tribunate and the command of a division and experience of camp life.[8] From time to time, even centuries after Augustus, certain emperors zealously maintained the old ideal of military exercise by personal example. Thus, Hadrian is said to have kept "in training," constantly exercising at arms and throwing the javelin.[9] In the middle of the fourth century, Constantius Augustus still kept up the old tradition, being skilled with the javelin, the bow, and in all exercises of the foot soldiers.[10]

The very fact that writers stressed so much the fidelity of certain leaders to the old discipline suggests the weakening of its hold upon others. Sallust's praise of the soldiers' rigorous discipline in duties of the camp and their "pleasure in handsome arms and war horses" is contrasted with the indulgence in "harlots and revelry." [11] Sybaris is weaned from "the sunny Campus," riding in "martial exercises," swimming in Tiber's stream, and using manly weapons.[12] As one turns the pages of imperial centuries, one becomes increasingly aware of the fact that, though there is elaborate praise of training citizens for war as a valuable asset for Rome,[13] there are fewer and fewer examples of it in practice. Certain of the emperors were, indeed, noted for their prowess in military training and in sports such as hunting, valued for military reasons; but lack of military merit and slight attention to vigorous, physical hardening for war's labors became common. Domitian, for example, was not interested in arms, but was excellent at archery, in which he engaged for sport.[14]

In the day of Polybius, the Roman army was made up of four legions of citizen-soldiers, drawn from propertied classes. Toughened by labor on the land in peacetime, these men made excellent soldiers. The infantryman served sixteen years before he became forty-six, or, in time of danger, twenty years; the cavalryman served ten. Military service preceded the holding of any political office. The legion was placed at 4,200, or at 5,000 in time of danger; to each legion were added 300 cavalry.[15] Foot soldiers were allowed two obols *per diem*; a centurion, four; and a cavalryman, one drachma. A foot soldier was entitled to two-thirds of an Attic *medimnus* of corn each month; a cavalryman had

---

[7] Dio's *Roman History*, XLV, 2; Suetonius: *Augustus*, 94; Plutarch: *Cicero*, 44.
[8] Suetonius: *Augustus*, 38, 64.
[9] Spartianus: *Hadrian*, 26.
[10] Ammianus Marcellinus, XXI, 16, 7.
[11] Sallust: *War with Catiline*, 7.
[12] Horace: *Odes*, I, 8.
[13] Juvenal: *Satire* XIV, 70–2.
[14] Suetonius: *Domitian*, 19.
[15] Polybius: *The Histories*, VI, 19–20.

seven *medimni* of barley and two of wheat. The cost of food and clothing was subtracted from their pay. Allies were allowed free rations.[16]

To the time of Marius, Roman soldiers were still drawn from the propertied class; but the decline of small farmers, growth of slave labor, and the increase of the proletariat compelled a change in the method of recruitment. Marius turned to volunteers from all classes, and assured them that he was unwilling to live in luxury while treating his troops stingily.[17] His immediate success insured the popularity of the new system, as long as sufficient rewards and satisfactory terms of service could be offered. In employment of the poor for pay lay the beginning of a standing army, for many of the proletariat who had nothing else to do were quite willing to remain in service. The way was also opened for political adventurers to gain power through the army, for poor men were ready to follow the most generous leader. In Caesar's time the soldiers' pay was perhaps equivalent to $40 or $50 *per annum*; even though small, it offered the soldier a more attractive life than that of laborers, whose status had been degraded by slavery.

At the time of Augustus an army of twenty legions, each consisting theoretically of 5,620 infantry, including 120 horse (save in time of great danger), was deemed sufficient to preserve the *Pax Romana*. Tiberius, according to Tacitus, had twenty-five legions; in the second century there were thirty. With the same number of auxiliaries, this would mean an army of 360,000 men.[18] Since the days of Marius it had grown to be a professionalized, regular army, and was made up of men who had volunteered, serving twenty years in the legion and twenty-five years in the auxiliary corps. Regular pay, permanence of service, a share in spoils, a bonus at retirement, allotment of land, and Roman citizenship (an attraction to foreigners who might enter the service) were among the chief rewards. The marriage of soldiers to women of the localities where they were stationed was first tolerated, and later legalized by Septimius Severus.[19]

Citizens whose census was under 400 drachmas went into naval service, according to Polybius.[20] In 256 B.C., at Ecnomus, the Romans' 330 ships were manned by approximately 150,000—fighters and crews together. A few years before the battle of Actium there were altogether about 1,000 vessels in the hands of the contenders for power; and in eighteen years prior to 31 B.C. almost 1,000 are said to have been destroyed. To maintain the *Pax Romana* and insure the flow of goods to Rome, ten standing fleets, two Italian and eight provincial, were maintained up to near the end of the second century. The total strength

---

[16] *Ibid.*, VI, 39; Attic *medimnus*, about 12 gallons.
[17] Sallust: *Jugurtha*, 85; Frank: *Roman Imperialism*, pp. 269 f.
[18] Showerman: *Rome and the Romans*, p. 457; for an account of auxiliaries, see Cheesman, *The Auxilia of the Roman Imperial Army*.
[19] Chapot: *Roman World*, pp. 79 ff.
[20] Bk. VI, 19.

of these fleets is unknown, but the Rhine fleet, operating on the river and the North Sea, where the heaviest demands were then being made upon sea power, is said to have had 1,000 ships in 16 A.D. Service in the fighting forces of the sea during the early Empire was for twenty-five or twenty-six years.[21] Human power propelled the Roman vessels, more or less aided by a sail or two. A trireme probably had about 170 at the oars, 20 sailors, and 10 men for combat; the quinquereme had about the same proportion, 310 oarsmen and 65 sailors and fighters. At the oars of their many-banked ships the Romans employed captured enemies, convicts, slaves, freedmen, some of their allies, and any others whom they could force into the laborious, killing toil.[22]

Pay, in the early Empire, was 225 *denarii* for ordinary soldiers; 375 for urban cohorts; and 750 for the Praetorian Guard. The pension, on leaving the army, was 12,000 sesterces for legionnaires, and 20,000 for Praetorians. Later emperors increased the pay of soldiers beyond what the treasury could bear. Caracalla's father paid legionnaires 500 *denarii*. Severus Alexander adopted a popular epitome of political wisdom—'The soldier must have a full purse.' Unfortunately, no policy of bribe or favor could save him when the soldiers decided to get rid of him. The army did in fact rule the Empire, when it could place the most liberal master on the throne. It forced Nerva to adopt Trajan, and placed Septimius Severus in the palace. One of Severus' gifts to the Praetorians was about £4,000,000. The game of "emperor-making" has been called "the chief proximate cause" of Rome's decline.[23] Ultimately money payments became impossible, and the government resorted to payment in kind.

A paid army, composed of the poorest and some of the worst elements and excluding the best—the senatorials—was doubtless a factor in destroying the military spirit that had marked the armies of the Republic. After the third century that spirit was little more than a memory. There being insufficient Roman volunteers in the late Empire, landed proprietors were compelled to furnish soldiers according to their holdings, just as they were levied upon for horses and pigs. These conscript soldiers came mostly from the *coloni*.[24] Opposition by landowners secured a degree of relief in that, in 397, they were authorized to pay 25 *solidi* in lieu of each man demanded by the army. Recruited by compulsion, branded like slaves upon their induction into the army, many sought to avoid service by self-mutilation and by desertion. Between 396 and 412 there were nine edicts regarding punishment of desertion and those who abetted the act. Such conscripts were allowed to marry; this circumstance was a source of

21 Sandys: *Companion to Latin Studies*, pp. 496 ff.
22 Showerman: *op. cit.*, pp. 481 ff.
23 Cary: *History of Rome*, p. 779; Paul-Louis: *Ancient Rome at Work*, p. 222; Lot: *The End of the Ancient World*, p. 58.
24 Dill: *Roman Society in the Last Century of the Western Empire*, pp. 235 f.

new soldier supply, since their children, born into the army, as it were, had no choice—at least after the time of Constantine—but to continue in the occupation of their fathers. The strength of the Roman legion, described by Vegetius as 6,000, fell in reality to about 1,500 men. His ideal and antiquarianism seem to have caused him to portray the army more in terms of the first than of the late fourth century.[25]

Considering such difficulties of recruitment, with military service a badge of servitude which Romans sought by all possible means to avoid, it is not strange that late barbarian enemies began to enter the Roman army for pay. After all, they had shown themselves the best fighters! Why not pay the best? Six years after Adrianople (378) there were 40,000 Goths in the Eastern army. After the middle of the fourth century, the quality of Roman armies appears to have depended on the number of barbarians in their ranks. "Julian's army was entirely German," says Lot; it entered the fray in the "boar's head" array of the barbarian and followed numerous German military customs. The best commands came to be held by Germans. Lot concludes that in the time of Syagrius, "King of the Romans" (464–486), it was necessary for a commander to "speak German in order to be understood by the best 'Roman' soldiers of Gaul!" Ever since Augustus, of course, Germans had been in the armed services to some extent; after Constantine, the "Roman army" became little more than a band of armed men, paid for their service in the Roman name.[26]

At the time of Polybius the youngest soldiers (velites) of the legion carried a sword, a javelin, and a small round shield (parma), and wore a plain helm. The hastati were equipped with a complete panoply, having a convex shield (scutum) four feet long and two and a half wide; a sword, suitable for thrusting; two heavy spears; a brass helm and greaves; and a breastplate of brass, or a coat of chain mail. The principes and triarii had the same armor, save that the latter carried long spears (hastae) instead of the pila. The cavalry was armed like that of Greece in Polybius' day.[27]

With relatively minor modifications, the Roman legions of the Empire used equipment similar to that at the close of the Republic.[28] Since the days of Archimedes at Syracuse (214 B.C.) the Romans had good reason to know something of the value of missile weapons.[29] Though in siege they used the ram, the ballista, the smaller onager, and the catapult, their employment of slings and bows was apparently chiefly in the hands of their auxiliaries, such as

[25] Oman: op. cit., pp. 8 f.; Lot: op. cit., p. 105; Cary: op. cit., p. 708.
[26] Lot: op cit., pp. 106, 231, 234 f.; Dill: op. cit., pp. 235 f.
[27] Bk. VI, 21–3, 25; Couissin: Les Armes Romaines, passim.
[28] Parker: The Roman Legions, pp. 250 ff.; Gibbon: The Decline and Fall of the Roman Empire, I, 55 ff.
[29] Livy, XXIV, 34; Plutarch: Marcellus, 14–7.

the Balearic slingers and Syrian bowmen.[30] Vegetius says that, in his day, the legionnaires had ceased wearing helm and cuirass because of their weight in reviews and sham battles. The real reason, probably, was that it had been found impossible to resist barbarian cavalry with the organization and weapons of earlier days; hence, more and more use was being made of missile weapons. In the fifth century the Roman army's equipment was much like that of their former enemies—soldiers on horseback, fighting with lance and bow. The forces of Ricimer and Aetius who met the Huns at Chalons were thus armed.[31]

The discipline and courage of the Roman army at its best evoked the praise of many competent judges. Polybius says that the Romans had an excellent way of teaching young recruits to face danger boldly, namely, by calling forward before the troops the most courageous, who had voluntarily and deliberately risked danger, and publicly praising their heroic acts and distributing appropriate prizes, a spear, a cup, horse trappings—even a "crown of gold" to him who first scaled the wall in storming a city.[32] The army's very name (exercitus), as Cicero says, suggests its discipline, its toil, the march, the bearing of heavy burdens—more than two weeks' provisions, stakes for entrenchment, shield, sword, and helm. "Look at the training of the legions, the double, the attack, the battle-cry, what an amount of toil it means! Hence comes the courage in battle that makes them ready to face wounds. Bring up a force of untrained soldiers of equal courage: they will seem like women. . . . Recruits have usually the advantage in age, but it is habit which teaches men to endure toil and despise wounds." [33]

Josephus, writing a history of the "Jewish War," expressed his admiration for Roman military training, and described it thus: ". . . Their nation does not wait for the outbreak of war to give men their first lesson in arms; they do not sit with folded hands in peace time only to put them in motion in the hour of need. On the contrary, as though they had been born with weapons in hand, they never have a truce from training, never wait for emergencies to arise. Moreover, their peace manoeuvres are no less strenuous than veritable warfare; each soldier daily throws all his energy into his drill, as though he were in action. Hence that perfect ease with which they sustain the shock of battle: no confusion breaks their customary formation, no panic paralyses, no fatigue exhausts them; and as their opponents cannot match these qualities, victory is the invariable and certain consequence. Indeed, it would not be wrong to describe their manoeuvres as bloodless combats and their combats as sanguinary

---

30 Showerman: *op. cit.*, pp. 458 f.
31 Oman: *op. cit.*, p. 11.
32 Bk. VI, 39.
33 *Tusculan Disputations*, II, 15–6. Trans. by J. E. King. The Loeb Classical Library. Quoted by permission of Harvard University Press, Cambridge, Mass.

manoeuvres." [34] The strenuous training prescribed by Scipio for naval and land forces during lulls between engagements at Carthage, as described by Polybius and Livy, supports Josephus' view that the Romans had "never a truce from training." [35]

Though Vegetius wrote ostensibly of his own times in his *Epitoma Rei Militaris*, the recruits' laborious training, which he depicted,[36] was probably more closely pertinent to the army of centuries past. Strenuous exercise of all kinds is urged as necessary to toughen men to pain and toil; they must be inured to heat and cold, that they may not become sick from being unprepared for the hard uncertainties of war. Caesar is said to have had poor health in certain respects, but found a remedy for it in marches, simple diet, and sleeping in the open air.[37] Soldiers should know a trade and be hardened by natural labor. They must be able to build fortifications, bridges, palisades, and dig ditches and tunnels. Dio says that Roman soldiers constantly practiced building pontoon bridges, just as they perfected themselves in all other military exercises.[38] Polybius [39] describes the Roman method of building palisades with stakes which the soldiers carried with them. In the school of arms described by Vegetius, the young Roman is made strong by wrestling, jumping ditches, throwing the spear, using shield, axe, sword, sling, and bow, and by bearing heavy burdens. The use of slings and bows was not extensive in Caesar's time, but became more important when Rome's armies learned that they must use missiles against their mounted foes.[40] The soldier must be able to swim across rivers and endure a long march under heavy burdens. Judson estimates the day's march as from fourteen to nineteen miles; the weight carried by the infantryman may have ranged from thirty to forty-five pounds, depending on the amount of rations, exclusive of armor.[41] Throwing the javelin on horseback required special training; according to Pliny, his uncle wrote a treatise on the subject.[42] The foot soldier must be able to throw the javelin even on the run, since the running attack gave an advantageous impetus to the onslaught.

When the power of Rome had brought a more or less submissive peace to her realm, the greatest test of the Roman army came: Could it long remain strong, without the exercise, the incentive of real warfare, the anticipation of

[34] *The Jewish War*, III, 5, 1. *Josephus*, trans. by H. St. J. Thackeray and R. Marcus. The Loeb Classical Library. Quoted by permission of Harvard University Press, Cambridge, Mass.

[35] *Polybius*, x, 20; Livy, xxvi, 51.

[36] Bk. I.

[37] Plutarch: *Caesar*, 17.

[38] Dio, LXXI, 3.

[39] Bk. xviii, 18.

[40] Judson: *Caesar's Army*, p. 58; Oman: *op. cit.*, pp. 9 f.

[41] Judson: *op. cit.*, pp. 36, 63; Vegetius, I, 9.

[42] *Letters*, III, 5.

ROMAN SOLDIERS FELLING TREES  *Trajan's Column, Alinari Photo*
(Courtesy, The Metropolitan Museum of Art, New York)

new conquests? Considered from a short-time view, yes; from a long-time view, no. Vegetius knew full well that Rome had brought all others to her sway by the force of her armies. He also knew that a long peace rendered men, trained to the rigors of war, careless and inattentive thereto. Hence he laid down a pattern of peacetime activities.[43] The best leaders, of course, turned to various kinds of labor, and kept up constant drilling to keep men busy who otherwise would have been idle. Roads were built, e.g. from Theveste to Carthage; troops put up their own buildings; and much more work of a constructive character was carried on in north Africa. Vetus (58 A.D.) dug a canal between the Moselle and Saône. Corbulo dug a canal twenty-three miles long between the Meuse and the Rhine, "to keep his soldiers free from sloth. . . ." Curtius Rufus worked the troops in mines, which did not sit well with the warriors.[44] Less wise and energetic leaders, however, allowed their commands to become easygoing, knowing nothing of work or discipline. Corbulo sought to restore strict discipline among troops in Germany "which had for-

[43] *Epitoma Rei Militaris*, I, 1, 26–8; II, 23.
[44] Tacitus: *Annals*, XI, 20; Parker: *op. cit.*, pp. 224 f.

gotten the labours and toils of the soldier and delighted only in plunder." [45]
The Eastern troops were probably always less well-disciplined than those of the
West. Of the Syrian legions, Tacitus wrote: "His [Corbulo's] legions indeed,
transferred as they had been from Syria and demoralised by a long peace, endured most impatiently the duties of a Roman camp. It was well known that
that army contained veterans who had never been on piquet duty or on night
guard, to whom the rampart and the fosse were new and strange sights, men
without helmets or breast-plates, sleek money-making traders, who had served
all their time in towns." [46]

While regimentation of the soldiers through constant drilling and practice
in all kinds of employments was a means to good behavior, the strictest discipline was also maintained by harsh punishment. Vegetius made clear that
punishment must be severe.[47] It was "an inflexible maxim of Roman discipline," says Gibbon, "that a good soldier should dread his officers far more
than the enemy." [48] Polybius was impressed with the strictness of discipline
and severity of punishments in his day. A general could punish with death insubordination, mutiny, and desertion on the battlefield. Decimation might
be resorted to in case of a legion or cohort which deserted. For insubordination,
troops might be compelled to camp outside the protected area, where they
would be first to meet the attack of enemies. Polybius describes the punishment
by *bastinado*, meted out to those found guilty of negligence in guard duty,
stealing anything from the camp, giving false testimony, self-abuse, or having
already been punished three times for the same offense: "The tribune takes a
cudgel and just touches the condemned man with it, after which all in the
camp beat or stone him, in most cases dispatching him in the camp itself. But
even those who manage to escape are not saved thereby: impossible! for they
are not allowed to return to their homes, and none of the family would dare
to receive such a man in his house. So that those who have once fallen into this
misfortune are utterly ruined. The same punishment is inflicted on the *optio*
and on the *praefect* of the squadron, if they do not give the proper orders at
the right time to the patrols and the praefect of the next squadron. Thus,
owing to the extreme severity and inevitableness of the penalty, the night
watches of the Roman army are most scrupulously kept." [49] Boasting of one's
valor to gain distinction, leaving a covering force because of fear, and throwing

---

[45] Tacitus: *Annals*, XI, 18.
[46] *Annals*, XIII, 35. Trans. by A. J. Church and W. J. Brodribb. Courtesy of Macmillan &
 Co., Ltd., London, and The Macmillan Company, New York.
[47] Bk. III, 10.
[48] *Op. cit.*, I, 53.
[49] *Polybius*, VI, 37. Trans. by W. R. Paton. The Loeb Classical Library. Quoted by permission of Harvard University Press, Cambridge, Mass.

away arms in battle, were regarded as disgraceful, and many would remain in a covering force and face certain death rather than risk punishment for leaving it. Others, having lost sword or shield in the fray, would risk life to recover the same rather than face the inevitable disgrace of returning without them.[50]

Numerous changes occurred near the end of the Republic, which tended to undermine discipline. Even in the days of Cato the complaint was made that Scipio's generosity undermined the soldiers' simplicity and encouraged them to engage in "wanton pleasures" with pay in excess of their actual need.[51] Leaders whose every expectation for future power depended on their personal hold upon their troops could scarcely enforce as harsh a discipline as those who had no ulterior ends. It is commonly accepted that discipline became laxer during the Civil War. Augustus sought to re-establish it.[52]

With the establishment of one-man rule and the substitution of mercenaries for the citizen army, however, strict discipline was restored at least for a time. Suetonius informs us that Augustus "exacted the strictest discipline" and gives as instances that he was reluctant to allow even generals to visit their wives; sold a knight who had cut off the thumbs of two sons to render them unfit for military service; dismissed the tenth legion in disgrace for insubordination; decimated cohorts that gave way in battle, and fed the rest barley instead of wheat; and punished centurions, just like ordinary soldiers, with death, if they left their post.[53] Tiberius, too, demanded the "strictest discipline" and revived punishments that had fallen into disuse.[54]

While, in general, discipline of the armed forces was doubtless better during the early Empire, it varied much from one régime to another. Pliny (c. 61–113) says that when he himself served in the army as a young man, "it was at a time when courage was suspected, and cowardice at a premium; when the generals were without authority, and the soldiers without awe; when there was neither command nor obedience; when our whole military system was relaxed, disordered, and actually turned upside down—in short, when it was better to forget than to remember its lessons." [55] Seneca, in sharp contrast, speaks of "those who are in the army" whose "camp discipline prohibits every luxury!" [56] Spartianus says, on the contrary, that discipline grew slack after Augustus, but a strong Emperor, Hadrian, "kept the soldiers in training just as if war were imminent," hardened them to fatigue, and gave them a personal example of mili-

---

[50] Ibid.
[51] Plutarch: Cato, 3.
[52] Judson: op. cit., p. 38; Parker: op. cit., p. 232.
[53] Suetonius: Augustus, 24.
[54] Suetonius: Tiberius, 19.
[55] Pliny: Letters, viii, 14. Trans. by W. Melmoth, rev. by W. M. L. Hutchinson. The Loeb Classical Library. Quoted by permission of Harvard University Press, Cambridge, Mass.
[56] To Helvia, xii, 2.

tary virtue and simplicity, even going to the extent of eating common soldiers' fare.[57]

Though Pliny and Spartianus are doubtless right in pointing to weakening of discipline after the time of Augustus, it was on the whole restored during the reign of the Antonines. Marcus' military discipline is said to have seemed harsh.[58] After them, it became weaker and more uncertain than ever before.[59] Dio Cassius declared that (about 227) the troops were so marked by wantonness, arrogance, and freedom from reproof that those in Mesopotamia killed their leader; and the Praetorians found fault with him because he ruled the Pannonian troops with a strong hand, for they feared that they might be compelled to submit to a like discipline. So serious was the discontent and want of order that Alexander allowed Dio to spend the period of his consulship "somewhere outside of Rome," lest he be killed.[60] Following Alexander Severus, the third century was marked by constant turmoil, due to an undisciplined army's making and unmaking emperors. The fourth century often witnessed even worse conditions. Ammianus [61] shows the abject fear felt by those leaders who had to pacify troops, angered because of the delay of provisions. To be chosen Emperor by such a lawless soldiery was indeed a "tragic fate" which men might accept as a "decree of death." [62]

Closely related to the problems of recruiting and disciplining young men to the ways of military life was the development of a number of associations, collegia, for young men. Under the Empire encouragement was given to a youth organization, Juventus. The desire of Augustus to restore discipline and order to the army doubtless made him friendly to such a movement. These municipal collegia iuvenum existed independently and were ultimately to be found in numerous cities of the realm. Their purpose was to train young men for physical and military fitness, and doubtless also to look to their loyalty and religious conformity.[63] They flourished best under the Julio-Claudian emperors; and under the Flavians they appeared in the western provinces. After the Flavians, the recruitment of armed forces depended much upon Romanized populations of former hostile provinces, and Rome's sovereigns sought to foster physical fitness, military capacity and loyalty among young men, whether in Gaul, Germany, Spain, or Africa.[64] Though their purpose is clear, details of physical activi-

---

[57] Hadrian, 10.
[58] Capitolinus: Marcus Antoninus, 22.
[59] Chapot: op. cit., p. 80.
[60] Dio, LXXX, 4–5.
[61] Bk. XIV, 10, 4.
[62] Lot: op. cit., p. 9.
[63] Rostovtzeff: The Social and Economic History of the Roman Empire, pp. 99, 500 f.; Della Corte: Ivventvs; Ziebarth: "Iuvenes," Real-Encyclopädie, x, Pt. II, 1357 et seq.
[64] Rostovtzeff: op. cit., pp. 103, 122, 287, 378 f., 551, 610; Ziebarth: op. cit., loc. cit.; Della Corte: op. cit.

ROMAN CAVALRY   *Trajan's Column, Alinari Photo*
(Courtesy, The Metropolitan Museum of Art, New York)

ties are but little known. Probably they were not much different from those of the Greek ephebi and the gymnasium, though their membership was not so democratic as that in the ephebi. Certainly the exercises of young men on the *Campus Martius* in an earlier day found in these institutions systematic encouragement.

Horsemanship was probably one of the most popular exercises, for the cavalry was an aristocratic branch of military service since the early days of Rome; and the *Juventus* was not only made up of freeborn youth of the best families, but depended also on the patronage of the men of wealth and position. The origin of the game of Troy,[65] often associated with this military organization of youth and one of the most popular equestrian displays at Rome

[65] Della Corte: *op. cit.*, pp. 29 ff.; Büdinger: "Die Römischen Spiele und der Patriciat," *Sitzungsberichte der Philosophisch-Historischen Classe der Kaiserlichen Akademie der Wissenschaften,* Vol. cxxiii, *Abhandlung,* iii, 28 ff.; Gardiner: *Athletics of the Ancient World,* pp. 126 f.

in the days of the Empire, is uncertain. It may, indeed, have been very old. Virgil, following the archaizing tendency of his age, portrayed the assembly of boys on horseback, under Ascanius' direction: the throng of spectators; clearing the course; the gleaming troops; the sharp crack of the whiplash; the interweaving lines of the riders, wheeling in intricate circles,

> Forming a picture of war, an image of actual battle.

Credited by Virgil to the time when the ramparts of Alba Longa were builded, the game was revived in the days of Rome's glory:

Still is the game called "Troy"; still "Trojan" the band of young troopers.[66]

Modern scholars have associated the game with the Etruscan *Truia*, preserved in an inscription on a sixth century Etruscan vase.[67] Little is known of it, although the parades are often mentioned in imperial times. The earliest historical reference to *Troia* is apparently that of Sulla's day. According to Plutarch, he exhibited the game of Troy and appointed two leaders, one of whom proved unacceptable to the boys, who refused to obey him and demanded Cato the Younger as their leader.[68] Agrippa performed "Troy" in 40 B.C.[69] in conjunction with a two-day celebration of Circensian Games. Along with a multitude of other entertainments, when he celebrated his five triumphs, Caesar had the game of Troy performed by two troops, a younger and an older.[70] Suetonius says that Augustus gave frequent performances of the game of Troy "by older and younger boys, thinking it a time-honoured and worthy custom for the flower of the nobility to become known in this way." [71] At the dedication of a temple to Mars (2 B.C.), the equestrian game of Troy was performed by sons of the best families.[72] Tiberius as a youth at the age of puberty (*pubescens*) took part in the Troy game, being leader of the older group of boys; [73] Caligula, eccentric in many ways, exhibited the game of Troy along with panther-baiting between races at the circus.[74] Claudius exhibited the *Troia* along with races and beast hunts.[75] Nero, when but a "young, half-grown boy," participated in it at a circus performance with marked success.[76]

That riding in the *Troia* involved some danger is evident from Suetonius'

---

[66] *Aeneid*, v, 548–603.
[67] Della Corte: *op. cit.*, p. 30.
[68] *Cato the Younger*, 3.
[69] *Dio*, XLVIII, 20.
[70] Suetonius: *Julius*, 39.
[71] *Augustus*, 43. Trans. by J. C. Rolfe. The Loeb Classical Library. Quoted by permission of Harvard University Press, Cambridge, Mass.
[72] *Dio*, LV, 10.
[73] Suetonius: *Tiberius*, 6.
[74] Suetonius: *Caligula*, 18.
[75] Suetonius: *Claudius*, 21.
[76] Suetonius: *Nero*, 7.

references to a protest made by Pollio to Augustus because his grandson had been injured, and also from the fact that Nonius Asprenas was lamed in the game. That it was not a serious part of training, but a public spectacle, is suggested by Suetonius, who says that Augustus gave up that sort of entertainment soon after because of the complaints.[77]

[77] Suetonius: *Augustus*, 43.

# 23

# ROMAN RECREATION

While the intellectual influence of Hellas was remaking the mind of the Romans, the cult of the body, which had made great progress in Hellenic cities, also began to penetrate Roman life. This infiltration of physical culture was slow, and the amalgamation of Greek and Roman elements was never fully consummated. Nevertheless, after Roman contact with the Greeks had once been established, it was inevitable that the old Roman physical education should undergo a marked change. The slow tempo and the imperfect character of such fusion as did take place were due in considerable degree to differences in the life of the two peoples. Chief of these were the eminently practical bent of the Romans, their continuous pursuit of war as an instrument of empire-building, and their lack of an ancient tradition of sports, such as the Greeks enshrined in the Homeric poems and in great athletic festivals. The contests which Virgil introduced into the *Aeneid* were more Greek than Roman. War at once destroyed the freedom of Italian cities, which might have developed competitive athletics, as had been done in Greece, and brutalized the Romans to such a degree that they preferred the bloody excitements of the arena to the milder entertainment of athletic competitions. Doubtless, too, the degenerate character of Greek athletic contests at the time of the Roman conquests and the evident military weakness of the Greeks inspired contempt among the conquerors for the practices of the conquered. Why should they hasten to approve that which seemed to have been of slight utility to its creators?

Physical culture in the early Republic served utilitarian ends almost entirely —was a discipline to labor on the land and service on the field of Mars. Such physical exercises and sports as formed a valuable, preliminary conditioner for these activities of adult life were approved and energetically practiced. Like Sparta, Rome subordinated natural play tendencies to military ends. To par-
646

ticipate in physical exercise beyond this aim, the practical-minded Romans had little inclination or leisure. Of themselves they instituted no competitive sports between cities, built no gymnasium or palaestra where men might train for such competitions. These came later, in some measure, with Greek influence; but competitions at Rome and in thoroughly Romanized cities were spectacles to be applauded, not contests for dignified Roman citizens to enter. It has been claimed that the difference between Greek and Roman views of sports is implied in the terms *ludi* and ἀγῶνες. Roman *ludi* were amusements, provided by "slaves or hirelings" for their betters; Greek ἀγῶνες were contests between free men.[1] Gibbon contrasted the Greek and Roman views thus: "The most eminent of the Greeks were actors, the Romans were merely spectators." [2] Butler held that ". . . in their love of sport, as in their love of art and of nature, the Romans followed but never rivalled the Greeks." [3] A Roman citizen, whether of high or low degree, would have been disgraced by a public appearance in the lists. The injunction, "Die, Diagoras, for you are not destined to ascend to heaven" (addressed to him when he had seen his two sons triumph in one day at Olympia) would have meant little or nothing to a Roman. Cicero regarded the Greek love of physical contests with disapproval: "Such achievements the Greeks think glorious—too much so perhaps. . . ." [4] Elsewhere he said: "At this very day, [when philosophers speak in all the gymnasia, the Greeks] would still rather hear the discus than a philosopher; and as soon as it begins to sound, they all desert the philosopher in the middle of his discourse . . . to anoint themselves for exerçise. . . ." [5]

The Romans had had some opportunity to become acquainted with Greek contests from early days. Greek influence upon the Etruscans has been noted; [6] likewise, in southern Italy, after the war with Pyrrhus, the Romans had ample opportunity to witness Greek contests in such cities as Tarentum and Paestum. Greek customs soon began to be accepted by prominent Romans. Scipio Africanus (c. 237–183 B.C) introduced the Greek habit of shaving and frequented the palaestra. Aemilius Paulus (c. 229–160 B.C.) trained his sons after the Greek pattern, though he did not neglect the old ancestral discipline. Moreover, he gained favor with the Greeks by giving games and sacrificing to the gods, and is said to have compared the capacity for arranging games well with ability to marshal troops in battle.[7] It was not until 186 B.C., however, according to

---

[1] Gardiner: *Athletics of the Ancient World*, p. 119.
[2] Gibbon: *The Decline and Fall of the Roman Empire*, III, 422.
[3] *Sport in Classic Times*, p. 207.
[4] *Tusculan Disputations*, I, 46. Trans. by J. E. King. The Loeb Classical Library. Quoted by permission of Harvard University Press, Cambridge, Mass.
[5] *On Oratory*, II, 5.
[6] *Supra*, p. 482; Cicero: *The Republic*, II, 34, 39.
[7] Plutarch: *Aemilius Paulus*, 6, 28; Polybius: *The Histories*, XXX, 14.

Livy, that "a contest of athletes," probably at wrestling or boxing, was first introduced in Rome.[8] Antony played the rôle of gymnasiarch for the Athenians.[9] Augustus exhibited contests of armed warriors in his sons' name at the Panathenian festival, was most attentive to the exercises of the ephebi at Capreae, and enjoined the Romans to use the Greek dress and language and the Greeks to use the Roman.[10] In Varro's day (116–27 B.C.) "the citified gymnasia of the Greeks" had taken hold in Rome; Romans had abandoned sickle and plow, and had gone to the city. Every villa must have its own gymnasium, palaestra, dressing rooms, and other apartments.[11] Cicero's delighted concern over the palaestra and gymnasium at his own place and at his brother's, tends to support Varro's views as to how Greek ways were getting on, notwithstanding frequent disparaging references to Greek athletics made by Cicero elsewhere. To Atticus he writes (68 B.C.): Pick up "any articles of vertu fit for my Gymnasium" that can be found. Early in 67 B.C. he is enthusiastic about certain "figures of Hermes in Pentelic marble with bronze heads," and has raised 20,400 sesterces for statues of Megaric marble. As to the things intended for the gymnasium he says: "The more the merrier, the sooner the better." Again he writes that he is impatiently waiting for the statues, his "purse is long enough," and he wants to indulge this "little weakness." The same year, writing as he sits in the palaestra, he again urges Atticus to speed statues for beautifying the palaestra and gymnasium. Years later he informed Atticus that "in these days, when every honest man's life hangs in the balance, I set high store by the enjoyment of my Palatine palaestra for a summer. . . ." [12] To his brother, Cicero writes with almost equal enthusiasm about the excellence of the statues, palaestra, pond, and other arrangements at Arcanum, one of Quintus' estates —it's all Caesar could wish, or even someone "more fastidious." [13]

Under the Empire many rulers exhibited a marked philhellenism, and this tendency, combined with open-handed generosity in expenditures, resulted in the building of numerous gymnasia, baths, and other aids to the enjoyment of new-found peace and leisure, not only at Rome but throughout the more populous parts of the realm. Agrippa built a sudatorium about 25 B.C., to which the name Laconian was given, because the Lacedaemonians "had a greater reputation at that time than anybody else for stripping and exercising after anointing themselves with oil." [14] Damascus was given a gymnasium by Herod.

---

[8] Bk. XXXIX, 22.
[9] Plutarch: Antony, 33.
[10] Suetonius: Augustus, 98; Dio's Roman History, LIV, 28.
[11] Varro: On Agriculture, II, introduction.
[12] Letters to Atticus, I, 6, 8–10; II, 4. Trans. by E. O. Winstedt. The Loeb Classical Library. Quoted by permission of Harvard University Press, Cambridge, Mass.
[13] Letters to His Brother Quintus, III, 1 and 9.
[14] Dio, LIII, 27.

Nero is said to have established the first permanent gymnasium at Rome (60 A.D.) and furnished oil to knights and senators "after the lax fashion of the Greeks." [15] In the second century the popularity of gymnasia became still greater, and every city wanted as much as possible to spend on such public institutions. Trajan tells Pliny that the Greeks "have a foible for Gymnasia; hence, perhaps, the citizens of Nicaea have been somewhat too ambitious in planning one; but they must be contented with such a one as will be sufficient to answer their occasions." [16] Every province, he goes on to say, has plenty of ingenious, skillful architects; and it is not necessary to send to Rome for them, for usually such specialists come from Greece to Rome.

The gymnasium and its activities came to occupy a most important place in the Hellenic-Roman world. It is said, indeed, that having a gymnasium distinguished the "metropolis" from other populous villages in Egypt. The most important city official was the gymnasiarch, who with numerous assistants supervised the games, provided oil, heated the baths, and attended to all matters pertaining thereto. Despite the fact that his office entailed heavy expenditures, the position was much sought after and was often "monopolized by certain families" which constituted "a sort of local nobility." In some cases endowments were provided, and donors may have become "permanent gymnasiarchs." [17] The dignity of the office is suggested by the fact that Antony, when celebrating a victory, served as gymnasiarch for the Athenians, wearing "a Greek robe and white shoes," and carrying the wand of office.[18]

Changes in habits of bathing kept pace with other innovations at Rome. In olden times, the sturdy Romans bathed only their arms and legs daily, and had a complete bath but once a week. In the last century of the Republic, the daily bath had become the rule. As a bathing place the Tiber alone sufficed at first; but when the growing city was supplied by aqueducts with more abundant water, cold swimming pools (piscinae) were built, the first in 312 B.C. All early bathing establishments were small and crude, compared with later standards. Scipio had at Liternum only a small bath, "buried in darkness according to the old style. . . ." [19] With the advent of great fortunes and the influx of Greek customs, however, the villas of the rich had spacious, luxurious baths with which palaestra and gymnasium were commonly associated. Cicero assures Atticus that he will have the bath heated in anticipation of his arrival.[20] Of this extravagance Seneca declared: "We think ourselves poor and mean if our

---

[15] Tacitus: Annals, XIV, 47; Suetonius: Nero, 12; Chapot: Roman World, p. 227.
[16] Pliny: Letters, X, 40. Trans. by W. Melmoth, rev. by W. M. L. Hutchinson. The Loeb Classical Library. Quoted by permission of Harvard University Press, Cambridge, Mass.
[17] Chapot: op. cit., p. 261.
[18] Plutarch: Antony, 33.
[19] Becker: Gallus or Roman Scenes of the Time of Augustus, p. 366.
[20] To Atticus, II, 3.

walls are not resplendent with large and costly mirrors; if our marbles from Alexandria are not set off by mosaics of Numidian stone, if their borders are not faced over on all sides with difficult patterns, arranged in many colours like paintings; if our vaulted ceilings are not buried in glass; if our swimming-pools are not lined with Thasian marble, once a rare and wonderful sight in any temple—pools into which we let down our bodies after they have been drained weak by abundant perspiration; and finally, if the water has not poured from silver spigots. I have so far been speaking of the ordinary bathing-establishments; what shall I say when I come to those of the freedmen? What a vast number of statues, of columns that support nothing, but are built for decoration, merely in order to spend money! And what masses of water that fall crashing from level to level! We have become so luxurious that we will have nothing but precious stones to walk upon." [21] Pliny describes the bath at his villa, Laurens, seventeen miles from Rome. From one apartment one enters ". . . the grand and spacious *cooling-room* belonging to the baths, from the opposite walls of which two basins curve outwards as though the wall were pressed into half-hoops; these are fully large enough, if you consider that the sea is close by. Contiguous to this is the anointing room, the furnace adjoining, and boiler-room; then come two other little bathing-rooms, which are fitted up in an elegant rather than costly manner: annexed to this, is a warm bath of extraordinary workmanship, wherein one may swim, and have a prospect at the same time of the sea. Not far from hence stands the tennis-court, which lies open to the warmth of the afternoon sun." [22]

Wealth, public and private, was turned to the erection of public bathing establishments, to some extent in the late Republic and in vast proportions under the Empire. Public baths (*balneum*, bathroom) began to appear after the Second Punic War; shortly before the close of the pagan era (33 B.C.) there were 170 of them in Rome.[23] Ultimately, it seems, every town of Italy had "at least one public bath." [24] At Pompeii there were three. Pliny says that a small village near his country villa had "no less than three public baths," which were very convenient if he had not time to prepare his own.[25]

The building of fine public baths early engaged the attention of Roman emperors. Under Augustus, Agrippa erected the first great *thermae* near the

---

[21] Epistle LXXXVI, 6–7. Seneca, *Epistulae Morales*, trans. by R. M. Gummere. The Loeb Classical Library. Quoted by permission of Harvard University Press, Cambridge, Mass.

[22] Pliny: *Letters*, II, 17. Trans. by W. Melmoth, rev. by W. M. L. Hutchinson. The Loeb Classical Library. Quoted by permission of Harvard University Press, Cambridge, Mass.; infra, p. 672.

[23] Mau: "Bäder," *Real-Encyclopädie*, II, Pt. II, 2747 et seq.; Marquardt: *Das Privatleben der Römer*, pp. 272, 274; Varro: *On the Latin Language*, IX, 68.

[24] Frank: *An Economic Survey of Ancient Rome*, V, 98.

[25] *Letters*, II, 17.

Pantheon, on the *Campus Martius*, which were dedicated in 25 B.C. but not actually used until 19 B.C., when the *Aqua Virgo* was ready to supply water.[26] These public *thermae* and their long line of successors—those built by Nero (64), Titus (81), Domitian (95), Caracalla (212–217), Alexander Severus, Diocletian (305–306), Constantine, and others—were after the Greek proto-type, but they were much more extensive and had elaborate arrangements and paraphernalia of the palaestra and gymnasium, as well as bathing and swimming facilities of every kind. In fact the bath of Agrippa was called the Laconian gym-nasium.[27] Building baths, like giving games and other entertainments, was a popular way to win public approval: the more grandiose the baths, the greater the acclaim. The baths of Titus were fit for an emperor, and he bathed in them with commoners sometimes. Severus is said to have built a bath in every part of the city which had none.[28] The elaborate baths of Caracalla measured nearly a quarter of a mile on each side. Diocletian outdid even the stupendous structures of Severus and Caracalla. Sixteen hundred marble seats had been provided for bathers in the baths of Caracalla; Diocletian's are said to have had twice that number, and the *natatorium* was two hundred feet long. At Bath, England, there was a quadrangular pool eighty-three feet long and forty in width.[29]

Public baths were built in far-flung areas of the Empire as well as in Italy and at Rome, as is evident from numerous classical references and from ruins which have been discovered in France, England, Germany, and elsewhere.[30] That the building and repair of baths in the provinces provided serious prob-lems for imperial heads to ponder, is evident from Pliny's correspondence with Trajan. He recommends that the Prusenses be permitted to repair their "an-cient and ruinous bath," which he has examined personally and thinks ought to be rebuilt. Trajan grants the request, provided, first, that it will not be too expensive for the people; and second, that no new taxes be levied and no tax money be diverted from other uses. Again Trajan writes to Pliny about the bath of the Claudiopolitani, which "they have placed, it seems, in a very im-proper situation. . . ." [31]

Public baths were first of all established for the profit of entrepreneurs. Later they were built by the government, by philanthropically minded citizens, and by combined public and private means. In the course of time, the building and support of public baths is said to have become one of the commonest objects of private philanthropy. The exact, proper construction of the bath seemed to

[26] Baumeister: *Denkmäler des Klassischen Altertums*, III, 1510.
[27] Dio, III, 27.
[28] Suetonius: *Titus*, 8; Lampridius: *Severus Alexander*, 39.
[29] Becker: *op. cit.*, p. 376; Breasted: *Ancient Times*, p. 645.
[30] Marquardt: *op. cit.*, pp. 276 f.
[31] Pliny: *Letters*, x, 23–4, 40.

Vitruvius important enough to justify devoting a special chapter to it.[32] Though baths were everywhere available, they were generally not free. The cost of admission was, however, extremely small—a quarter of an *as* at Rome, Seneca informs us.[33] Men at Vipasca, Spain, paid half an *as*, and women a double amount. Children were admitted free at Rome, but not everywhere. All persons were presumably free to use the public baths, if they could pay the stipulated fee. Fronto says that "gymnasia, and baths, if public ones, are thrown open free to all, but if private, are kept under strong lock and key with a door-keeper to boot, and a fee is exacted from the bathers." [34] In many instances endowment funds were provided, permitting the discontinuance of fees entirely. Such was the case at Bononia; and at Suessa Senonum, free baths were provided for everyone, even female slaves. Agrippa is said to have kept 170 baths open free to the public in 33 B.C.[35]

The Roman bath was commonly equipped with many rooms, each serving a special purpose: the *apodyterium*, for undressing; the *frigidarium*, a cold bath; the *tepidarium*, a warm room; the *caldarium*, a hot bath; the *laconicum*, a hot room for sweating; the *unctorium*, for anointing the body; the *destrictarium*, where oil and sweat might be removed with the strigil.[36] Besides the usual facilities for recreation in the palaestra and swimming pool, a bowling alley, on which stone balls were rolled, was provided in the Stabian baths of Pompeii. The great public baths provided facilities not only for bathing, swimming, and various physical exercises and sports, but also other means of enjoyment. Foods, eating places, and even libraries were provided in them from the time of Agrippa to Constantine. Suetonius says that Augustus composed most of his "Epigrams" at the bath.[37] Indeed, the bath became the athletic club of the Romans.

Considering the Roman people's preoccupation with baths and their refinements, it is small matter for wonder that poets devoted their talents to their praise. Statius [38] pours out a stream of eloquence over the beauties of the baths of Claudius Etruscus. Even though one came from Baiae, even if he had bathed in Nero's baths, he would not scorn their loveliness. "If you do not bathe in

---

[32] Vitruvius: On Architecture, v, 10.
[33] Epistle LXXXVI, 9; Becker: op. cit., pp. 370 f.
[34] Fronto, The Correspondence of Marcus Cornelius, I, 271. Trans. by C. R. Haines. The Loeb Classical Library. Quoted by permission of Harvard University Press, Cambridge, Mass.
[35] Rostovtzeff: The Social and Economic History of the Roman Empire, p. 178; Frank: op. cit., v, 104; Dill: Roman Society from Nero to Marcus Aurelius, p. 227; Johnston: The Private Life of the Romans, pp. 297 f.
[36] Mau: op. cit., loc. cit., II, Pt. II, 2750 et seq.
[37] Augustus, 85; Becker: op. cit., p. 390.
[38] Silvae, I, 5.

the warm baths of Etruscus," says Martial, "you will die unbathed, Op-pianus." [39] Claudian praises the bath of Quintius, set by the dusty road for the traveler's refreshment.[40]

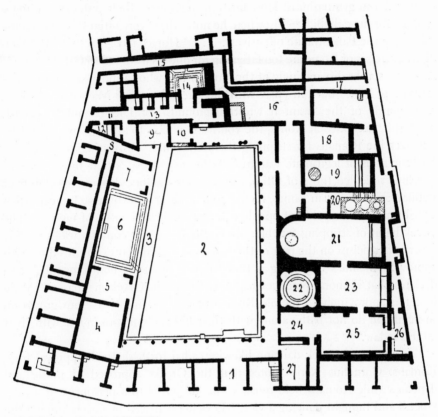

THE STABIAN BATHS, POMPEII

Pauly's *Real-Encyclopädie*, II, 2751–4, designates certain areas as follows: 1, main en-trance; 2, palaestra; 3, flag-paved alley; 9, room where stone balls were found, opening on the alley; 10, supervisor of the palaestra(?); 11, street entrance; 13, hall, off which is a lavatory, 14; 4, dressing-room; 5, 7, wash-rooms with shallow basins; 6, swimming pool; 8, side entrance; 15, 17, street entrances to women's bath; 16–19, bathing facilities for women —16, undressing-room, with a cold bath basin in corner; 18, tepidarium; 19, caldarium, with tub and wash basin; 21–25, men's baths—24, 25, undressing-rooms; 26, 27, anterooms, with benches for waiting servants; 20, heat plant; 21, caldarium with tub and wash basin; 22, frigidarium; 23, tepidarium.

The Roman's contempt for Greek gymnastics, dancing, and music is shown in many ways. Indications of disapproval appeared early and continued long; even when the old Roman system was quite devoid of vitality, criticism of the

39 *Epigrams*, VI, 42.
40 Claudian: *Shorter Poems*, 12.

new was vigorous though ineffective. Scipio aroused comment, because he gave time to the palaestra and walked about the gymnasium in a Greek robe and slippers.[41] Cicero exclaims at the absurdity of the Greek "system of exercise for young men in gymnasiums! How far from rigorous is their system of military training for the ephebi!" [42] Elsewhere he notes that "very often the movements learned in the Palaestra are offensive. . . ." [43] Horace recognizes that the "soldierly exercises of Rome are too fatiguing for one accustomed to Greek ways."[44] Again he speaks disparagingly of the Roman boy who cannot "sit a horse, and is afraid to hunt" but can "play with the Greek hoop." [45] Martial speaks contemptuously of the "wanton wrestling-grounds" of Lacedaemon.[46] Tacitus notes the "lax tone" at Rome, the youths' devotion to athletic sports; and he criticizes the Romans for stripping themselves and substituting boxing-gloves for "the arms of legitimate warfare." [47] Plutarch declares that the soldiers of Vitellius ridiculed those of Otho, calling them "actors, dancers, spectators at Pythian and Olympian games, men who had never known or seen a campaign or fighting" and "would not openly enter a conflict and battle of men." [48] The Greek habit of stripping for their athletic training and contests was a prolific source of criticism on the part of the Romans. Cicero quotes Ennius' line with approval, "Shame's beginning is the stripping of men's bodies openly," and declares that immoral practices had their origin in Greek gymnasia.[49] Again he refers approvingly to the old Roman practice, saying that "sons grown up to manhood do not bathe along with their fathers, nor sons-in-law with their fathers-in-law." [50]

The advent of Greek dancing likewise called forth sharp disapproval from Romans. Cornelius Nepos notes that the Greeks approved of music and dancing, while Romans held music to be "unsuited to a personage of importance," and thought dancing a vice.[51] Dancing is placed by Cicero among the illiberal occupations; one should not rashly "call a consul of the Roman people a dancer . . . for no man, one may almost say, ever dances when sober, unless perhaps he be a madman. . . ." [52] Even if one were offered a legacy, on the

[41] Livy, XXIX, 19.
[42] Republic, IV, 4. Trans. by C. W. Keyes. The Loeb Classical Library. Quoted by permission of Harvard University Press, Cambridge, Mass.
[43] Offices, I, 36.
[44] Satires, II, 2. From Horace for English Readers, translated by E. C. Wickham (The Clarendon Press).
[45] Odes, III, 24.
[46] Bk. IV, 55.
[47] Annals, XIV, 20.
[48] Plutarch: Otho, 6. Trans. by B. Perrin. The Loeb Classical Library. Quoted by permission of Harvard University Press, Cambridge, Mass.
[49] Tusculan Disputations, IV, 33.
[50] Offices, I, 35; Plutarch: Cato, 20.
[51] Epaminondas, 1.
[52] Cicero: Murena, 6; Offices, I, 42.

condition that "he should dance openly by daylight in the forum," he should refuse it; or, if he promised to do so, then he should break his word rather than dance, unless perchance by dancing he should be able to make some contribution "to some great occasion of the state"—in which case "it would not be disgraceful even to dance. . . ." [53]

Notwithstanding there was much criticism of it, dancing grew in popularity. Scipio, although himself criticized for frequenting the palaestra, expressed alarm that Roman boys and girls were learning dances unfit for freeborn youth. Sempronia, it was said, could dance better than "an honest woman need." Statius recognizes the advantages of dancing and music as accomplishments for the girl about to marry.[54] Quintilian finds a limited justification for dancing in the training of the orator, though he does not want gestures of the speaker to be patterned on movements of the dance.[55] Columella laments that the Romans study dancing and other polite accomplishments but have neither students nor teachers of the science of agriculture.[56] As for dancing in public, Cicero could not have imagined that within a century Caligula, a ruler of the Roman state, would stoop even to that; [57] and that, in Nero's reign, dancing would become so polite and common as to completely eclipse the once-famed *gravitas* of the old Romans.

## PHILOSOPHERS GLANCE AT PHYSICAL CULTURE

Roman philosophy was more marked by its borrowing from the Greeks than for its originality. In respect to philosophical views on physical culture the same was to some extent true; but, though their physical habits were greatly modified by the infiltration of Greek practices, Roman conceptions of physical education never came close to the Greek. It would scarcely be true to say that the Romans ever developed a philosophy of physical education, other than that which was implicit in their early vigorous life of the farm and the camp. The influence of this utilitarian outlook is constantly felt in their views of physical exercise.

Roman thought in respect to physical exercise is often marked by a negativism; the philosopher is busy decrying Greek principles, to which he traces many of the evils he finds at Rome. Cicero, as has been seen, has much of this negative criticism; but there are positive views, too, in his work that require notice.

[53] *Offices*, III, 24.
[54] Sallust: *War with Catiline*, 25; Friedländer: *Roman Life and Manners under the Early Empire*, I, 231; Gwynn: *Roman Education from Cicero to Quintilian*, p. 55.
[55] *The Institutio Oratoria*, I, 11, 15–9.
[56] *Of Husbandry*, I, preface.
[57] Suetonius: *Caligula*, 54.

Speaking of man's nature, Cicero lays hold of a fundamental principle of life, a principle which operates throughout the whole and in all the parts of his being. The whole figure of man and its several parts are adapted to man's nature, and it is necessary that the organs be healthy and vigorous. Basic in man's body is the principle of action, by which the parts and the whole function "in harmony with nature." There is in man, and also in every living creature, "a positive craving for constant activity. Perpetual repose is unendurable on any terms. This is a fact that may be readily detected in children of the tenderest age. . . . Nature reveals her plan . . . most clearly in childhood. Even infants, we notice, are incapable of keeping still. Children of a somewhat more advanced age delight in games involving considerable exertion, from which not even fear of punishment can restrain them. And this passion for activity grows as they grow older. The prospect of the most delightful dreams would not reconcile us to falling asleep for ever. . . ." [58] Even the least ambitious and vigorous, even the idlers, constantly seek something to do: a game board, a spectacle to watch, someone to chat with—these are needed to occupy their time. Private business, public, political, and military affairs, and devotion to learning are the chief avenues through which man finds the exercise of his various drives to activity.

Cicero holds that, as man's bodily structure surpasses that of other animals, so his mind is equipped both with senses and also the "predominant factor of intellect, which commands the obedience of the whole of man's nature . . ."; and the "attributes of the body are not comparable in importance with the parts of the mind. . . ." [59] This scale of values helps to explain Cicero's views of many matters. Successes won "by the use of our intellect and reasoning power are more gratifying than those which come from physical excellence." [60] Again, he says, "mere corporeal pleasure is unworthy the excellency of man's nature . . . [and one] ought to be extremely observant of limits in its indulgence." Satisfaction of physical desires should always be with respect to "our health and our strength"; everything should contribute to and conform to the "excellency and dignity of our nature," and what pertains to voluptuousness, effeminacy, and immodesty should be avoided. Our appetites need to be "contracted and mitigated." "Sport and merriment" are not man's true end, but they have a proper place; we ought, therefore, "to use them as we do sleep and other kinds of repose, when we have dispatched our weighty and important affairs." The sports of the *Campus Martius* and hunting are, to Cicero's way

[58] Cicero: *De Finibus Bonorum et Malorum*, v, 12, 20. Trans. by H. Rackham. The Loeb Classical Library. Quoted by permission of Harvard University Press, Cambridge, Mass.
[59] *Ibid.*, v, 11–3.
[60] Abbott: *Society and Politics in Ancient Rome*, pp. 199 f.

of thinking, "creditable examples" [61] of recreation and pleasure. Constantly the goal of utility is kept in mind: even the orator—his perfect man—will be able to play his part better if his gestures are strong and manly, not imitations of the theater and actors but rather of the camp and the palaestra.[62]

The disciplinary doctrines of Stoicism appealed strongly to the Roman, whose whole life, until near the end of the Republic, had been a discipline of toil. As his had not been a life of pleasure, but one of painful struggle, a philosophy of severe discipline seemed eminently sound and sensible. Spartan contempt of pain was a significant object lesson. Cicero says that "pain seems to be the most active antagonist of virtue. . . ." The way to gain virtue is to conquer pain. Will the "wise and steadfast man" give way before pain, when Spartan boys cry not, though they be "mangled with painful blows"? [63] Lycurgus' training of boys to hardship, by hunting, running, and exposure to heat, cold, hunger, and thirst, evidently met with Cicero's approval.[64] Marcus Aurelius says that he learned from Diognetus to desire a "plank bed and skin, and whatever else of the kind belongs to the Grecian discipline." [65]

Old Roman practice, as well as Greek precedent and the teachings of Plato, to whom Cicero was strongly drawn, would seem to compel him to devote some attention to physical exercise in his works on the state. It is significant that the references are relatively slight, and pertain largely to public exhibitions and their control. The *Republic* is almost wholly devoid of references to physical exercise, but in brief space the Greek system is condemned. Cicero notes, of course, that Numa Pompilius established games as a part of his effort to reform and regulate the life of the Romans.[66] In the *Laws*, Cicero also provides that the aediles shall, among other duties, have charge "of the customary games." At public games in the theater, held without chariot racing or athletic games, the pleasure of the public is to be provided for in moderation by "song to the music of harp and flute," "combined with honour to the gods." Moderation is insisted on, for music has the power to rouse the languid, calm the excited, restrain desires, or give them "free rein." The public games in the circus are to include "contests of body with body"—that is, such athletic events as boxing, wrestling, and running—and horse racing.[67]

Sallust's philosophy, not unlike that of Cicero, stresses the utility and propriety of physical exercise as a means to an end, not an end in itself: "I have

[61] *Offices*, I, 29–30.
[62] *On Oratory*, III, 59.
[63] *Tusculan Disputations*, V, 27.
[64] *Ibid.*, II, 14; V, 34.
[65] *The Meditations of the Emperor*, I, 6.
[66] *Republic*, II, 14; IV, 4.
[67] *Laws*, II, 9, 22; 15, 38; III, 3, 7.

no great admiration for mere athletic training or muscular prowess: but a man whose mind has sovereign control over a body neither weakened by self-indulgence nor debased by wealth to sloth and luxury may take his sport on the mountain or on the sea, and I will admire his body rejoicing in hard work and his limbs growing under his toil. . . ." [68]

Quintilian's view of physical activity differs little from that of Cicero, both in positive and negative aspects. He regards the tendency to "play in the young" as an index of vitality, likely to be associated with quickness of mind, whereas one who lacks "the impulse most natural to boys" is likely to be gloomy, depressed, and dull at study.[69] Gymnastics can be of value in the education of the complete man—the orator. Justification for some attention to gymnastics is found in Greek authors like Plato and Socrates, and also in the priestly dances approved by the early Romans. Quintilian does not want the gestures of oratory to be modeled on the dance: "Such training should not extend beyond the years of boyhood, and even boys should not devote too much time to it." But "such boyish exercises should continue to exert a certain influence, and . . . something of the grace which we acquired as learners should attend us in after life. . . ." Probably no Roman went so far as did Quintilian in admitting dancing as a proper part of education. As for physical development in general, one must avoid, certainly, the extremes of those who spend their life rubbing in oil and drinking in wine and killing the mind by too much concern for the body.[70] The elaborate attention that some in his day paid to the physical cult he regarded as nothing short of "insane." [71] Gymnastics have left, however, an excellent model of that which is proper—a pattern of all-round training, exemplified in Nicostratus who was trained so evenly and well in both boxing and wrestling that in the space of a few days he won the prize in both events—a model useful not only to the physical trainer, but worthy to be imitated by the teacher of oratory.[72]

The more completely that Greek practices swept the field, the more bitterly did some of the keenest Romans condemn them. Greek gymnastics, professional athleticism, and hot baths were all doubtless associated by many in a causal relationship with the moral degeneracy of Nero's day. Seneca wants to know "what 'liberal' element is there in these contemptible vomiters of our day, whose bodies are fed to fatness while their minds are thin and dull? Or do we really believe that the training which they give is 'liberal' for the young men of Rome, who used to be taught by our ancestors to stand straight and hurl a

[68] Butler: *op. cit.*, p. 201.
[69] *Quintilian*, I, 3, 10. Trans. by H. E. Butler. The Loeb Classical Library. Quoted by permission of Harvard University Press, Cambridge, Mass.
[70] *Ibid.*, I, 11, 15–9.
[71] *Ibid.*, XII, 11, 18.
[72] *Ibid.*, II, 8, 14.

spear, to wield a pike, to guide a horse, and to handle weapons? Our ancestors used to teach their children nothing that could be learned while lying down." [73] Seneca excludes from "liberal studies wrestling and all knowledge . . . compounded of oil and mud. . . ." [74] His professed concern is for moral rectitude. Even the old stress on strenuous physical exercises, though they were serviceable to the state, could not teach virtue. The new physical training, of course, frustrates the pursuit of virtue at every point. The hot baths which have replaced the cold plunge are enervating. If Hannibal's fiber was weakened by a brief relaxation, what can be said for the hot bath and the sweat room, "where they shut in the dry steam which is to draw your strength? Perspiration should flow only after toil." [75]

The mind's health should come first, that of the body second, says Seneca. Without the first, the strong man is only a madman. One should "limit the flesh as much as possible" and leave the spirit free. Much exercise wastes vital force, and much eating dulls the keen edge of the mind. To strive to develop big muscles, strong lungs, broad shoulders, is "foolish . . . and very unsuitable for a cultivated man." Even should one accept the goal of the athlete as worthy, one must recognize that, no matter how much he eats, how strong he becomes, he can never match a bull.[76] There are some exercises that Seneca approves and recommends to Lucilius, judging them by a proper Roman standard— their utility. These are the "short and simple exercises" that "tire the body rapidly, and so save our time" [77]—such as walking, running, jumping (high and broad jump, the leaping dance of the Salii, or what he calls the "clothes-cleaner's jump"), swinging weights, riding in a litter, and vociferation. Such exercises are desirable, for the "mind must have a change" which relaxes but does not unnerve. Any one of these exercises, Seneca says, will suffice, but whichever is chosen, one must "come back soon from body to mind." [78]

### ROMANS AT PLAY

LOVE OF PLAY SHOWN BY ROMANS  Roman inclination to play has been frequently contrasted with that of the Greeks. The Romans are said to have played chiefly for the sake of health rather than the joy of playing. Certainly health and strength through engaging in games and exercises were commonly accepted goals; but it must not be forgotten that Greek sports, too,

[73] Epistle LXXXVIII, 19. Seneca, Epistulae Morales, trans. by R. M. Gummere. The Loeb Classical Library. Quoted by permission of Harvard University Press, Cambridge, Mass.
[74] Ibid., 18.
[75] Epistle LI, 5–6.
[76] Epistle XV, 2–3.
[77] Romans frequently want to "save time"; thus Pliny goes on horseback, gets "as much exercise" as possible and loses "less time."—Letters, IX, 36.
[78] Epistle XV, 4–8.

served utilitarian ends. It was only natural that, both in Greece and in Rome, when there was no longer need of physical excellence for state service, play became more of an end in itself. Health gymnastics were encouraged both in Greece and in Rome when individual happiness and welfare began to transcend the importance of service to the commonweal. As for love of watching contests, that too became characteristic of Greece as well as of Rome in the days of decadence. Doubtless the Roman's love of public exhibitions and gladiatorial combats, of which an extensive and imposing record has been preserved, has tended to obscure the less conspicuous evidence of individual delight in play. This circumstance, combined with the fact that Rome did not develop such a love of organized public athletic contests (ἀγῶνες) as did the Greeks, has led to an undervaluation of their inclination to play.[79]

The Roman's love of play is variously displayed in hunting, running, ball games, swimming, wrestling, riding, and many other exercises. The exile's thoughts turn wistfully from Pontus to Italy in springtime, and he pictures the crowding festivals, horse races, play in light arms, play with ball and hoop, and well-oiled young men bathing in the waters of the Virgo. The time came, indeed, when, by Seneca's account, some Romans spent their whole life in play at chess, at ball-play, and baking themselves in the sun.[80] When not indulging in play of some kind himself, the wealthy Roman, who had put on the new life of luxury, loved to entertain his guests with acrobats, muscians, dancers, and other artists.[81]

Even the greatest and gravest Romans delighted in all manner of sports. Scaevola, Cato the Younger, and Maecenas indulged in ball-play.[82] Caesar, when made a captive, joined in the "sports and exercises" of his captors with perfect readiness.[83] Augustus is said to have given up military exercises in the Campus Martius after the civil wars, and turned to "pass-ball," "balloon-ball," and then to riding, walking, running and jumping, sometimes to fishing, and even to little games with children.[84] Antoninus Pius enjoyed walking, hunting, fishing; Marcus Aurelius loved boxing, wrestling, running, hunting, fowling, and is said to have been skillful at playing ball.[85] Commodus is said to have equalled his most skillful instructors in the use of bow and javelin, and was inordinately fond of hunting wild animals.

Even when the fortunes of state declined, the Romans' love of sports lin-

[79] Cf. Showerman: Rome and the Romans, p. 375; Gardiner: op. cit., p. 117.
[80] On the Shortness of Life, XIII, 1; Ovid: Tristia, III, 12, 19 et seq.
[81] Petronius: Satyricon, 53; Marquardt: op. cit., pp. 302, 337 f.
[82] Cicero: On Oratory, I, 36; Seneca: Epistle CIV, 33; Horace: Satires, I, 5.
[83] Plutarch: Caesar, 2; Suetonius: Julius, 4.
[84] Suetonius: Augustus, 83.
[85] Capitolinus: Antoninus Pius, 11; Marcus Antoninus, 4.

gered. Though Ausonius' praises of Gratian, who had raised him to consulship, are doubtless not to be trusted as to detail, it is not likely that he invented all the excellencies in physical sports—running, wrestling, jumping, throwing the javelin, riding—which he attributed to his patron.[86] Sidonius, Janus-like, looking back upon Rome's declining years and forward to the Middle Ages, presents entrancing glimpses of Roman Gaul at play in the fifth century. By no means ruled by asceticism, so widely heralded in Christian sermons, Sidonius enjoys a cheerful life, recalls the games of childhood—running, jumping, swimming, hunting with horse and bow, hawking, fishing, riding, boating, ball, dice, backgammon—and makes clear that he is no mere observer of the sports of others.

The Roman passion for order is exemplified by the daily routine, in which games played a prominent part: after the morning's affairs, a siesta (at least for the more fortunately situated), exercises (more or less severe), bathing, and then eating—such was the usual order. In the routine of Martial's day, the eighth hour is given to sports and the bath.[87] The public baths, though open earlier, "at the sixth hour," glow "with Nero's heat." [88] Horace mentions the Campus, the "game of three," the baths, and then the meal—all part of the day's routine, though he is content to take it less seriously than others do. Pliny considers Spurinna's daily round—walking, riding in a chariot, exposing himself to the sun, playing ball vigorously, and bathing—ideal, for it has kept him hale and hearty to old age.[89] Severus, in time of peace, after laboring till noon, would ride, take gymnastic exercise (playing ball, running, wrestling), bathe and swim, and then eat luncheon. Toward evening he bathed again and dined.[90] For the lower classes, doubtless, there was less time for such a leisurely routine, even though public baths became everywhere available. For many, labor probably left little desire for exercise. For them, says Showerman, work "did not cease with the seventh hour, but continued after the siesta until the setting of the sun." [91]

The vigorous preparation for the bath comes in for frequent verbal ridicule. Petronius' satirical portrait of the life of the vulgar rich depicts a bald old man playing at ball (with plenty of assistants), then sweating in the bath, and finally at dinner.[92] Martial declares that to "trifle with games in a square" is just idleness, and he commends Atticus, because,

[86] Ausonius: "Thanksgiving for His Consulship," 14.
[87] Bk. IV, 8; Becker: op. cit., pp. 65 f., 398.
[88] Martial, x, 48.
[89] Letters, III, 1; Horace: Satires, I, 6.
[90] Dio, LXXVII, 17; Lampridius: Severus Alexander, 30.
[91] Op. cit., pp. 139 f.
[92] Satyricon, 27–8.

> . . . you don't prepare for your bath with a ball—
> Whether bladder or feather or solid withal—
> Nor strike with blunt sword at some poor dummy image,
> Nor darting with speed snatch the ball from the scrimmage,
> Nor yet waste your time at the wrestler's toil
> With arms set akimbo all covered with oil.[93]

In early days the open *Campus Martius* and the near-by Tiber sufficed for physical sports; and there, in later times, public gymnasia and baths catered to the desires of those who had taken on the habits of a cosmopolitan existence.[94] For many of the rich the private palaestra and bath rivaled, or even excelled, the public establishments in the elegance of their appointments.

Increased crowding of the city population, combined with concentration of wealth and the availability of plenty of land for country estates, led many Romans to seek refuge in the country, where they found recreation and relaxation for more or less extensive intervals. Cato, who had been a farmer in earnest when young, became a "fancy farmer" for "recreation and amusement" in his old age.[95] Writers delight in extolling life in the country, even though they probably would not relish a return to the land in any truly realistic sense. Cicero praises cultivation of the land as an amusement fit for old age.[96] Martial sighs for "country pleasures" and declares he wants only "some acres few to till," where he can take the "country's spoils" with line and net—while slaves till the garden with right good will! [97] Juvenal declares that only the rich can sleep in town; for who can sleep in the wretched hired lodgings? The poor, especially, should long ago have migrated to the country, where one can get a house for what one pays for a dark hole in town. There on the land he can live with his hoe, irrigate his garden, and easily provide enough fare for "a hundred Pythagoreans." [98]

Some who fled to the country may have led a simple life; but many, perhaps most, could not easily lose their city habits. The routine of exercises, bath, and then dinner was followed there much the same as in town, though it could be varied by rambling, driving, or riding about the villa. The concern of Cicero and his brother for equipping the palaestras and gymnasia on their estates has been noted. Pliny's bath, ball-court (*sphaeristerium*), gymnasium, and other

[93] *Epigrams*, VII, 32. Trans. by J. A. Pott and F. A. Wright. Courtesy of E. P. Dutton & Co., Inc., New York.
[94] *The Geography of Strabo*, V, 3, 8.
[95] Plutarch: *Cato*, 24–5.
[96] *On Old Age*, 16.
[97] Bk. I, 55; III, 58.
[98] *Satire* III, 223 *et seq.*

recreational facilities at his estates left nothing to be desired.[99] His day's routine is: early rising, dictation, riding in his chariot, repose, walking, reading some Latin or Greek orations for the sake of digestion, walking again, then anointing, exercises, bath, and supper. Sometimes the order includes horseback riding in place of the chariot, and hunting—but he takes his tablets along when hunting, so that, though he catches nothing, he can at least bring something home![100]

### GAMES, MENTAL AND PHYSICAL

*Mental* The play tendency in man finds an outlet in games, mental as well as physical. The people of Italy were no exception to the rule. Of mental games, various forms of gambling were most preferred in early as well as in later times. The ancient Romans at once gave evidence of the widespread character of gambling and probably enhanced the sport's attractiveness by attempting to discourage it by legal prohibition, though restraint was relaxed at the Saturnalia. Domitian is said to have enforced the prohibition, but enforcement must have been rare. Many modern Italian homes, it is said by a careful observer, are more likely to shelter a book on the winning numbers than a Bible.[101] Young and old at Rome were inordinately fond of gambling. Gambling games are recommended to women by Ovid.[102] In the city, the public games, especially chariot races, provided an admirable stimulus; but even he who lived in the country and could wear a single suit for ten seasons, would "stake a nut or two" at knucklebones.[103] Huge sums were squandered in high society. The recklessness of Augustus at the game board is reported by Suetonius.[104] Juvenal declares that men go to the gaming table not with mere purses but with whole treasure chests at their side. One may lose 100,000 sesterces, and not have a shirt to give a "shivering slave." [105]

A favorite game, *micare digitis* (*mora*), in which two players sought to outsmart each other by guessing the number of fingers simultaneously extended, provided an ever-ready opportunity for wagers, and was also sometimes used to determine one's lot or future in the political or business world. Cicero suggests that two equally wise and valuable men, afloat on the sea with only one small plank between them, might decide who should get it by lot, or a game of odd

99 *Letters*, II, 17; V, 6.
100 *Ibid.*, IX, 36; cf. I, 6.
101 Johnston: *op. cit.*, p. 241; Becker: *op. cit.*, p. 501; McDaniel: *Roman Private Life*, p. 144.
102 *Art of Love*, III, 349 *et seq.*
103 *Martial*, IV, 66.
104 *Augustus*, 71.
105 *Satire* I, 88 *et seq.*

and even. Augustus is said to have bidden a father and son to cast lots, or play
mora, to determine which one should die. The popularity of the game gave
rise to a proverbial description of an honest man as one "with whom you can
safely play at odd and even in the dark." [106]

Of board games there were various forms, two of which, ludus latrunculorum
and the ludus duodecim scriptorum, are more or less clear to us. Both games
employed counters, calculi: the first, sometimes called "robbers," was somewhat similar to chess or draughts, being a contest between two parties of men,
each divided into different classes (pawns and officers). Duodecim scripta,
sometimes referred to as the game of tables (from tabula) was similar to backgammon, and was also played with counters upon a board divided into twenty-
four places. The moves were determined by throws of dice, by which one progressed from the first to the twenty-fourth place.[107] Some game boards were
made so that one side served for the ludus latrunculorum, the other for duodecim scripta.[108] Such games were extraordinarily popular amusements in the
houses of the wealthy. Trimalchio delays eating his dinner, but urges his guests
to begin, while he finishes his game on an unusually exquisite board, using gold
and silver coins for counters.[109] The Emperor Claudius was so fond of gaming
that he wrote a book on it and fitted up a board in his carriage so that he could
play while out driving.[110] Numerous references to board games show that they
were still popular in France in the fifth century. Sidonius has left an interesting
portrait of Theodoric, King of the Goths, playing at "tables." [111]

*Physical* Ball games enjoyed an undoubted popularity with the
Romans. Some type of ball-play was the most common means of warming up
before the bath. Martial [112] calls one an awkward rustic who is ignorant of how
to play the game of three. An illuminating insight into the importance of ball
in Roman life, and the influence which players might have, is gained from an
inscription which asks ballplayers to support a certain candidate, A. Vettius
Firmus, for the aedileship.[113] Cicero, knowing that such a figure will be perfectly comprehended, likens the power of the state to a ball that is snatched
from one by another.[114] Other allusions show that Romans commonly recognized a certain parallelism between ball games and politics. Cornelius Lentulus,
when an accounting for public money was demanded of him by Sulla in the

---

[106] Cicero: Offices, III, 19, 23; Suetonius: Augustus, 13.
[107] Marquardt: op. cit., pp. 855 ff.; Gregory of Tours: History of the Franks, II, 596.
[108] Martial, XIV, 17.
[109] Petronius: Satyricon, 33.
[110] Suetonius: Claudius, 33.
[111] Sidonius: Letters, I, 2, 7–8.
[112] Bk. XIV, 46.
[113] Abbott: op. cit., pp. 14 f.
[114] Cicero: Republic, I, 44.

Senate, declared he would not give it, "but would offer his leg, as boys were accustomed to do when they were playing ball and made a miss." [115] Seneca, though frequently contemptuous of ball-play and other forms of excessive devotion to physical exercise, makes a comparison between the giving of benefits and the throwing of a ball from one player to another.[116]

The greatest figures in Roman public life and in the world of letters were fond participants in ball games, which they carried on from their boyhood to man's estate. One player boasts on his epitaph that he had played ball with an emperor. Caesar, Augustus, Marcus Aurelius, and Alexander Severus played ball.[117] Cicero says that Publius Mucius was skilled in the game.[118] Stopping at Capua on the journey to Brundisium, Maecenas turns to a game of ball, but Virgil and Horace sleep, because ball-play is neither good for "sore eyes" nor for dyspepsia. Elsewhere, Horace notes the place of the "game of three" in the usual day's routine as a preparation for the bath; hunting hares and breaking horses are of course more soldierly and suited to the simple pattern of life, but for those who desire something less strenuous than the exercises of old Rome, he recommends "a game of ball," whose interest negatives the taste of toil.[119] Cato the Younger unconcernedly passes off a political defeat in an election and goes to the *Campus Martius* to practice ball.[120]

Even the old men indulged in ball-play for the sake of health. Galen's treatise on the "Small Ball" and his defense of ball-play for recreation and health testify to the extent and popularity of such exercises.[121] Spurinna combated the effects of old age by "prolonged and violent" playing at ball.[122] Cicero considers other amusements better for old age, however, than ball-play, swimming, and such sports—which are, in his opinion, more suited to the young.[123]

To this preference for ball-play, there were no doubt exceptions, which serve to throw the general practice into clearer relief. Such was Cicero, apparently, who says that he has devoted as much time to studies as others would to ballplay.[124] There is a note of contempt in Seneca, who declares that many men spent their whole life at chess, ball, or "baking their bodies in the sun." [125]

[115] Plutarch: *Cicero*, 17.
[116] *On Benefits*, II, 17, 3–5.
[117] Suetonius: *Augustus*, 83; Capitolinus: *Marcus Antoninus*, 4; Lampridius: *Severus Alexander*, 30.
[118] *On Oratory*, I, 50.
[119] *Satires*, I, 5–6; II, 2.
[120] Plutarch: *Cato the Younger*, 50.
[121] Galen: "De Parvae Pilae Exercitio," *Opera*, v, 899–910.
[122] Pliny: *Letters*, III, 1.
[123] *On Old Age*, 16.
[124] *Archias*, 6.
[125] *Shortness of Life*, XIII, 1.

In the "short and simple" exercises recommended by Seneca for saving time, ball-play is not included.[126]

Numerous literary allusions to ball-play attest the game's popularity. Fronto tells Appian that he who sends too great a gift offends as much as one who gives his partner in ball-play "too heavy a return." [127] Petronius [128] depicts the rich old man in red shirt and house shoes, playing busily with green balls, which are supplied to him and his companions by a slave, who stands with a bagful ready for replacement as soon as one is dropped to the ground. Martial's "Angler," seeking an invitation to dine, obsequiously chases through the dust after the balloon ball and politely hands it back, even though he has already bathed and dressed. In a hot game of *trigon* he catches everything, right and left, and scores his catches to the one he courts. The gift of a warm Spartan *endromis* is praised, for, even in December, it will defy rain and cold when one plays *trigon, harpastum,* or bats the *follis* to and fro.[129]

Games of ball were played in the open air in the *Campus Martius*,[130] and doubtless also by boys in the streets. When baths and gymnasia were established, a special court, *sphaeristerium*, was an important feature, but other exercises were practiced therein also. Pliny's *sphaeristerium* is open to the warm sun, and is large enough for several different games to be played at once, each with its own group of observers.[131]

Ball-play permits of many variations, and many were known to the Romans. One might simply throw up the ball and catch it, playing alone or with a companion. Games in which several balls were employed simultaneously suggest jugglery, something like that depicted in Egypt, rather than competitive ball games which were so common. The use of glass balls undoubtedly refers to the juggler's art.[132] Contests in which the ball was thrown or struck against the ground or against a wall—resembling modern handball—were known, but the exact manner of play is obscure. It appears that the old Romans "practised a bowling game that anticipated the play at *boccia*," commonly known to-day. Bats or racquets seem to have been practically unknown.[133] Though numerous passages in Latin works have been translated "tennis," it seems misleading, to say the least; some of the games, however, may be considered the forerunners of modern tennis.[134]

---

[126] *Epistle* xv, 4–8.
[127] *Fronto*, I, 277.
[128] *Satyricon*, 27.
[129] *Martial*, IV, 19; XII, 82.
[130] *Strabo*, V, 3, 8.
[131] *Letters*, II, 17; V, 6; Becker: *op. cit.*, pp. 93, 406 f.
[132] Marquardt: *op. cit.*, p. 844.
[133] McDaniel: *op. cit.*, p. 68; Johnston: *op. cit.*, p. 240.
[134] Dalton points out that the references in Sidonius' letters cannot properly relate to tennis as we know it, since no bat or racquet is mentioned.—*Letters of Sidonius*, I, cxii. Play

Literature abounds in references to ball-play, but the allusions are usually rather casual, and relatively little is known of the way games were played. Several different balls are distinguishable, however, and something of their use. Though several kinds of balls and ball games are mentioned, the distinction between the ball and the game is not always clear. Martial names four balls, *pila paganica* (stuffed with feathers, originally used in the country), *pila trigonalis* (used for the game of *trigon*), the *follis* (balloon, or bladder ball), fit for old men to play with, and *harpasta* (scrimmage balls).[135] Becker holds that there were really only three types of balls, the *pila*, the small ball, varying in hardness for different kinds of games; the *follis*, a large inflated balloon ball; and the *paganica*. Marquardt is of the opinion, however, that there were as many as five different balls, varying in size and contents.[136] The game of three, *trigon*, was very popular, if one may safely judge from literary allusions to it. Three players stood at the corners of an equilateral triangle and threw balls to each other at will, so that a player might have to handle two balls at once. Three, or even six, balls might be kept in play. It may be that the three players were assisted by three persons who picked up balls that dropped to the ground, and by three others who counted the balls dropped. In such a game nimble use of the left hand as well as the right would obviously be a great advantage. Martial's references to "nimble left-handers" indicate that left-handed plays were a proof of expertness.[137]

Marquardt distinguishes three different types of mass ball games, *sphaeromachiae*, but the differences in them are little known. In one play (ἐπίσκυρος) two equal sides oppose each other, separated by a line marked with stones, each having a barrier at its back, beyond which it cannot go. The ball, lying on the stone barrier, is thrown as far as possible by the side which first gets possession of it; the opponents catch it and throw it back again as far as they can. The ablest throwers thus press their opponents farther and farther back, until they reach the barrier in their rear and thus lose the game. In another game (φενίνδα) players are divided into two parties; one throws the ball, calling on a particular person of the opposing party to catch it, but throws in a different direction making it difficult to catch; failure to catch the ball loses the point.

with the *pila* has been translated as tennis and simply as ball-play. Pliny's *sphaeristerium*, open to the sun, is called a "tennis-court" (Hutchinson: *Pliny*, ii, 17) and "ball-court," Bk. v, 6. Watson makes Cicero—*On Oratory*, i, 16—speak of "those who play at tennis" (*qui pila ludunt*) and mentions Titius who was a "great tennis-player" (*qui, cum studiose pila luderet*).—*On Oratory*, ii, 62; iii, 23; cf. translation by E. W. Sutton and H. Rackham, Heinemann, London, 1942.

135 *Martial*, xiv, 45–8.

136 *Op. cit.*, p. 842; Becker: *op. cit.*, p. 399; cf. Mau: "Ballspiel," *Real-Encyclopädie*, ii, Pt. ii, 2832 *et seq.*; Ramsay and Lanciani: *A Manual of Roman Antiquities*, pp. 486 f.

137 Bk. xiv, 46; vii, 72; Marquardt: *op. cit.*, pp. 844 f.; Becker: *op. cit.*, pp. 402 f.; Johnston: *op. cit.*, p. 241.

This, some authorities believe, is the game referred to by Sidonius in his letter to Eriphius.[138]

The *harpastum* is but slightly known to us; various references give no clear impression of it, other than that it involved a vigorous, even violent scrimmage. Athenaeus explains that "great are the exertion and fatigue attendant upon contests of ball-playing, and violent twisting and turning of the neck." [139] Martial also refers to *harpasta*, used by him who "with empty labour makes big his neck . . ." and those who snatch the "scrimmage-ball" in the dust.[140] It may be that the game was simply to throw one ball, or perhaps more, up into the air and then scrimmage for the chance to catch it. Galen [141] speaks of the vigorous exertion required in certain ball games, especially one in which players form sides, oppose each other and scrimmage for the ball. In this violent form of small ball-play there is plenty of all-sided exercise for head, neck, ribs, chest, abdomen, loins, and legs. One must be a good runner, dodger, and jumper; indeed the small ball game is the best exercise for the legs, Galen holds, as it is for all parts of the body.

Though it would appear that no sport equaled ball-play in popularity, exercises with the *halteres* and the fencing post (*palus*), running, jumping, wrestling, and boxing provided variety in the physical recreation of Romans. Horace mentions flinging the quoit through "the yielding air." [142] Quintilian refers to throwing the spear and archery as exercises with which his readers were perfectly familiar.[143] Bathing, swimming, boating, hunting, and fishing provided exercise in less formal fashion.

Running and jumping were commonly practiced, both for utility and for recreation. Running "where the clear Virgo flows" is preferred by Martial to the various games played in every open square; and he also refers to one who hopes to conquer swift Athas in the foot race.[144] There were competitions in running, but such mild entertainment was no great attraction at Rome. Petrified remains of bodies of athletes, recently discovered under the ruins of Pompeii, are believed to have been runners who were exercising when the city was destroyed by the eruption of Mt. Vesuvius. Marcus Aurelius is said to have been fond of running.[145] Seneca recommended running as a good exercise for the studious. He also favored three types of jumping—the high, the broad

---

[138] Bk. v, 17; Marquardt: op. cit., pp. 845 f.
[139] Bk. I, 15.
[140] Bk. IV, 19; XIV, 48.
[141] De Parvae Pilae Exercitio, 2.
[142] Satires, II, 2.
[143] Bk. IX, 4, 8–9.
[144] Bk. IV, 19; VII, 32.
[145] Capitolinus: Marcus Antoninus, 4.

jump, and leaping like the Salii, the priests of Mars—as good exercises for the scholar.[146]

Walking, and riding on horseback, in carriages, and in litters, gave easy exercise to the old and infirm. Sometimes, however, even old men continued to exercise at games of ball, as did Spurinna. Augustus left off other exercises and turned to riding, walking, running, and leaping.[147] Riding in a litter is especially recommended by Seneca, because it shakes the body and does not interrupt study. Walking is also good.

Swinging the weights is recommended by Seneca to the studious, but he hates the fellow who swings them at Baiae and disturbs him with his puffing and grunting. Juvenal berates the woman who frequents the gymnasium and whose arms hang exhausted by swinging the heavy weights.[148]

Thrusting at a post (palus) with a wooden sword was apparently a common exercise. Vegetius refers to its use by young recruits (tirones); and Martial refers to those who strike at a "poor dummy image" with a blunt sword.[149] Juvenal refers to women who smite ". . . a stump, piercing it through and through with a foil, lunging at it with a shield, and going through all the proper motions. . . ."[150] Quintilian[151] also refers to training in fencing, which he associates with other contests of the wrestling school.

References to boxing abound in Latin literature. They shed little light on the science, indeed, but do reflect general interest in it and suggest that boxing was a common matter, understood and appreciated by the general public. Cicero's clever reference to Bestia, whom he had six times defended, as "that boxer's dummy on which I tried my lungs and voice,"[152] would, he knew, be thoroughly appreciated by a Roman audience. Suetonius[153] says that Marcus Pomponius Marcellus, a grammarian, had once been a boxer, and understood "head to the left," having a fighter's skill but no real talent. Quintilian says that the gymnast will turn his pupils into runners, boxers, or wrestlers, according to their different abilities, and will teach a pancratiast all the tricks of every branch of the science, and not merely how to use his fists and his heels.[154] Boxing was both a private exercise of the gymnasium and also a public spectacle. Martial praises Domitian for the revival of pugilism; Marcus Aurelius was fond of box-

[146] Epistle xv, 4.
[147] Suetonius: Augustus, 83; Pliny: Letters, iii, 1.
[148] Satire vi, 419 et seq.; Seneca: Epistle xv, 4; lvi, 1.
[149] Bk. vii, 32; Vegetius: Epitoma Rei Militaris, i, 11.
[150] Satire vi, 246 et seq. Trans. by G. G. Ramsay. The Loeb Classical Library. Quoted by permission of Harvard University Press, Cambridge, Mass.
[151] Bk. ix, 4, 8.
[152] Philippic xiii, 12.
[153] Grammarians, 22.
[154] Bk. ii, 8, 7, 13.

ing and wrestling, even though his interest in philosophy is said to have turned his attention from them.[155]

Virgil gives great space to the boxing match between Dares and Entellus,[156] whose powerful blow fells the bull awarded him as the prize of victory. He portrays his boxing competitors wearing heavy gauntlets, which really belong to his own era rather than to the primitive age of which he was professedly writing. Those of Entellus were of sevenfold seasoned bull's hide, "stiffened in rigid coils, insewn with lead and with iron," so terrifying in appearance that Dares, his competitor, drew back in consternation, whereat Aeneas considerately provided gauntlets of similar character for both boxers. The cauliflower ear became a common sight to the Romans. Martial contrasts Atticus with other youths who attend the instructions of a battered-eared boxer.[157] The destructiveness of the formidable cestus is suggested by the lines of Lucillius:

> This Victor, glorious in his Olive Wreath,
> Had once Eyes, Eye-brows, Nose, and Ears, and Teeth:
> But turning Caestus Champion, to his Cost,
> These, and, still worse! his Heritage he lost.[158]

Numerous literary references to wrestling testify to its common practice. Martial speaks of the "well-oiled" who "wrestle in the lists," and complains of wrestling masters who "waste the precious oil." [159] Suetonius tells us that there was bitter feeling toward Nero because, while people were suffering hunger at Rome, a ship came from Alexandria with a cargo of sand for the use of wrestlers at the court.[160] Quintilian's references [161] to the contests of the wrestling school and the tricks of attack and defense were doubtless made to an audience which he knew would understand them perfectly. Men of high station continued to wrestle. Severus Alexander engaged in a mild form of wrestling for recreation, and was a "wrestler of the first rank," according to his biographer.[162]

Swimming was common among the Romans from the earliest days, and numerous sources indicate its continued popularity. Cato taught his son to swim, and Augustus is said to have instructed his grandsons. Antoninus practiced swimming "even in rough water." [163] Cicero refers to his friend Trebatius as an enthusiastic swimmer; and Horace puts in Trebatius' mouth the advice

---

[155] Capitolinus: *Marcus Antoninus*, 4; Martial, VIII, 80.
[156] *Aeneid*, V, 362–484.
[157] Bk. VII, 32.
[158] West: *Odes of Pindar*, p. lxix.
[159] Bk. III, 58; IV, 19 (Pott and Wright).
[160] Suetonius: *Nero*, 45.
[161] Bk. IX, 4, 8.
[162] Lampridius: *Severus Alexander*, 27, 30.
[163] Plutarch: *Cato*, 20; Suetonius: *Augustus*, 64; Dio, LXVIII, 11.

that one must rub in oil and swim three times across the Tiber, if he would sleep well.[164] Literary allusions to swimming are numerous. Ovid's *Art of Love* [165] offers the advice that it is hard to swim against the current. Pliny [166] relates to Caninius a marvelous story about Hippo, in Africa, where people constantly diverted themselves with contests to see who could swim farthest into the sea. Martial, Statius, and others allude to the attractions of swimming at Baiae.[167]

Roman history abounds with references to swimming, there being many instances of its utility in time of war. Vegetius speaks of its value to all soldiers.[168] One of the oldest tales was that of Horatius Cocles, who fought the Etruscans at the Tiber bridge and then swam to safety. When the Cimbri and Teutons invaded Gaul and defeated the Romans (105 B.C.), Sertorius, although wounded, swam with shield and breastplate across the Rhone against an adverse current, and escaped. Publius Scaevius, one of Caesar's forces, though severely wounded and having lost his shield, leaped into the water and escaped by swimming.[169] In the Civil War, Lucan [170] says, Caesar bade his men arm and cross the river by "hard swimming," without waiting to look for bridge or ford. Dio tells us that in a sea fight (36 B.C.) the excellent swimming and light equipment of Sextus' men enabled them to escape from damaged ships to others, and thus helped to counterbalance certain of Caesar's advantages. At the signing of a pact by Sextus, Caesar, and Antony (39 B.C.), it is said that joy so affected their men that many who were in small boats jumped into the sea, and others on land rushed into the water to meet them, and they embraced each other while swimming and diving.[171] Caesar, driven from the Peninsula of Pharos into the sea, is said to have succeeded in swimming to one of his vessels, leaving his cloak in the water as a target for his assailants.[172] Suetonius declares that he swam two hundred paces, "holding up his left hand all the way, so as not to wet some papers," and dragged his cloak in his teeth so that the enemy could not get it for a trophy.[173] Dio says that Roman soldiers in Hadrian's day "swam the Ister with their arms." [174] Ammianus tells of Roman soldiers fleeing from their enemies across the Tigris, lying on their broad, curved shields and steering them as best they could; elsewhere he mentions

---

[164] Cicero: *Letters to His Friends*, VII, 10; Horace: *Satires*, II, 1.
[165] Bk. II, 181–2.
[166] *Letters*, IX, 33.
[167] *Epigrams*, VI, 43; *Silvae*, III, 5.
[168] Bk. I, 10.
[169] Livy, II, 10; Plutarch: *Sertorius*, 3; Dio, XXXVII, 53.
[170] *The Civil War*, IV, 148 *et seq.*
[171] Dio, XLVIII, 37; XLIX, 3.
[172] Florus: *Epitome of Roman History*, II, 13.
[173] Suetonius: *Julius*, 64; Dio, XLII, 40; Plutarch: *Caesar*, 49.
[174] Bk. LXIX, 9.

some who were either lost in the river, "being unskilled in swimming," or were seized by Saracens or Persians if they succeeded in crossing the water. Julian's soldiers, fighting against the Germans on the Rhine (357 A.D.), swam on their shields, using them like canoes, and surprised and butchered the enemy on one of the islands.[175] According to Libanius "the Rhine" was "hidden by the bodies of those [enemies] drowned through their want of knowing how to swim. . . ."[176]

When public and private baths were built, they were commonly provided with pools, large enough for swimming, and with both cold and warm water. The first warm pool in Rome was said to have been built by Maecenas. In the great public baths, the pools were magnificent; in Diocletian's, the *natatorium* was two hundred feet long and one hundred wide. The use of baths and swimming pools was very extensive. Augustus' body is said to have been calloused from much use of the strigil. Some who had plenty of leisure resorted to the baths two or three times a day. Even greater extremes are reported: Commodus bathed seven times a day; on one occasion he shoved his praetorian prefect into a swimming pool, toga and all. Severus Alexander was in the habit of bathing in a swimming pool for about an hour after his exercise.[177] Public pools at resorts were noisy places, according to Seneca's bitter testimony, who found the splash of those plunging into the swimming tank at Baiae very annoying.[178]

The luxuriousness of swimming pools built by men of wealth on their private estates was truly remarkable. Pliny's villa at Laurens had a "warm bath of extraordinary workmanship," wherein one might swim, having a view "at the same time of the sea." His Tuscan villa, at the foot of the Apennines, had a similar warm swimming pool in the court.[179] Elagabalus, his biographer says, would not swim in a pool unless it was perfumed with saffron or some other essence.[180]

The handling of boats was a matter of practical importance for the Romans, and became also a means of recreation and amusement. Literary references are numerous. The boat race is one of the most exciting contests portrayed by Virgil.[181] Cicero [182] turns to rowing to find a fitting illustration of the correct meaning of *inhibitio*. It is, he says, an "exclusively nautical word," and means

[175] *Ammianus Marcellinus*, XVI, 11, 9; XXIV, 6, 7; XXV, 8, 1–3.
[176] *Julian the Emperor*, pp. 141, 192.
[177] Dio, LV, 7; Suetonius: *Augustus*, 80; Lampridius: *Commodus*, 11; *Severus Alexander*, 30; Becker: op. cit., pp. 93, 376; further information on baths, supra, pp. 649–53.
[178] *Epistle* LVI, 2.
[179] *Letters*, II, 17; V, 6.
[180] Lampridius: *Elagabalus*, 19.
[181] *Aeneid*, V, 114 et seq.
[182] *To Atticus*, XIII, 21.

a vigorous motion to "back water," not simply resting on the oars, as he once thought. Seneca [183] remarks on the boatswain marking time in high-pitched tones to his crew; it's unpleasant, but he has steeled his nerves to bear it; in any case, it's not so bad as intermittent noises. Pliny [184] refers to sailing as one of the constant diversions of the people at Hippo. In the fourth and fifth centuries Ausonius and Sidonius refer to boating in Gaul, on the Moselle, and at Avitacum, near Clermont.[185]

It has been said that Romans were "never keen sportsmen," but they caught some of the love of sport from the Greeks. Some believe that it was "probably a proof of Greek tastes," even in Sulla's time, if a man was given to laborious hunting.[186] The Romans were "not greatly addicted" to hunting, says Fowler.[187] There is some truth in this, doubtless; but another fact is not to be forgotten. Hunting is often both work and play to primitive people; Romans in their primitive simplicity were no exception. While actively at work upon their farms, or busily pushing forward the bounds of empire, there was no occasion for extensive and elaborate recreation. But when the Empire was consummated; when wealth flowed in, enabling men to purchase ease; when popular political activity atrophied, or was delegated to one man and his agents—then hunting, along with many other activities, seems to have become a popular way of employing superabundant leisure.

Hunting, traditional sport of fighting men and of kings, might well grow in popularity among the Romans when they rested from war's labors. The traditional Roman emphasis upon the serious, practical business of life, however, kept them from going to extremes in devoting time to sports, even though congenial. Sallust declares that a man who spends his whole life hunting is performing a "menial service" rather than taking "lawful exercise." [188] Three hundred years later an entirely different point of view was to find expression, for, as Rome declined and public life made fewer demands upon them, recreation might consume most of a man's time. Ausonius (c. 310–393) takes pride in the fact that his father-in-law spent his whole life "in hunting, and husbandry, and all the pleasures of a refined life, despising public affairs." [189] Such is the contrast in attitudes at the end of the Republic and in the age of imperial decline. To this extreme devotion to the chase and other pleasures, Christian asceticism brought some check, at least in principle. Paulinus Pellaeus regrets his youthful

[183] Epistle LVI.
[184] Letters, IX, 33.
[185] Ausonius, X, 200 et seq.; Sidonius, II, 2, 19.
[186] Ihne: History of Rome, V, 445.
[187] Social Life at Rome in the Age of Cicero, p. 104.
[188] Butler: op. cit., p. 201.
[189] Ausonius, IV, 8.

desire to have a fine horse, a speedy hound, and a goodly hawk; only Christ's mercy, he says, saved him from breaking his neck when riding.[190]

The growth of a love of hunting and the stimulus given to it by Greek influence may be seen in several historical characters. Aemilius Paulus had his son, Scipio Aemilianus, taught all the elements of Greek education, including hunting; in this, as in other branches, it appears the teachers were Greek.[191] After the battle of Pydna, while the army remained in Macedonia, Scipio was put in complete charge of all matters pertaining to hunting, for Lucius Aemilius believed "hunting was the best training" for the bodies and courage of his soldiers. It is said that Scipio developed a love for the chase that lasted all his life, and he gave the time to it that other men gave to politics.[192]

Great concentration of wealth at Rome made large estates possible. These came to be supplied frequently with lakes for fishing, and hunting parks, not unlike those of Macedonian and Persian princes. Hortensius had a park on his estate near Laurentum, containing about fifty *jugera*, well stocked with all kinds of wild animals. Sulla is said to have devoted himself to hunting and fishing when he retired to his estate at Cumae.[193]

Cicero [194] mentions hunting, along with the exercises of the *Campus Martius*, as a creditable form of amusement. As the Empire became established and leisure reigned, more and more evidence of love of hunting is found in persons of prominence and in literary allusions. Hadrian was an enthusiastic huntsman, killed lions "with his own hand," and is said to have been injured physically at the sport. When his favorite hunting horse died, he built him a tomb with an inscription on it.[195] Antoninus Pius delighted in hunting and fishing.[196] Marcus Aurelius compared to robbers the spider with its prey, the armed leader with his Sarmatian prisoners, the hunter with his captive bear and boar and hare, and the fisherman with his catch; yet he himself seems to have loved these sports. Capitolinus says that Marcus engaged in fowling and "hunted well"; Dio says that he "would strike down wild boars while on horseback. . . ." [197] Perhaps his teacher had something to do with it. Fronto reminded him, in any case, that his ancestors for three generations back had mingled serious business with love of sport and other pleasures. When inaugurating his game preserve, Fronto advised him that he must be careful, if he struck a beast, to set the "horse at full gallop." Again he tells him of a hunting expedition and "doughty

---

[190] *The Eucharisticus*, 141 *et seq.*
[191] Plutarch: *Aemilius Paulus*, 6.
[192] Polybius, XXXI, 29.
[193] Appian: *Civil Wars*, I, 104; Fowler: *op. cit.*, p. 250.
[194] *Offices*, I, 29.
[195] Spartianus: *Hadrian*, 26; Dio, LXIX, 10.
[196] Capitolinus: *Antoninus Pius*, 11.
[197] *Meditations*, x, 10; Capitolinus: *Marcus Antoninus*, 4; Dio, LXXII, 36.

deeds," but admits that though they heard of boars being bagged, they themselves did not see any.[198] To praise emperors for their great prowess in the royal sport was, naturally, the height of propriety. Domitian is said to have been so skilled in archery that he was wont to shoot animals in such a way as to give them the appearance of having horns.[199] Ausonius quotes lines inscribed under a picture showing a lion, slain by Gratian with a single arrow: "The death which the lion suffers through so frail a reed is due, not to the weapon's power, but to the wielder's." [200]

Numerous literary allusions refer to the sports of field and stream. Horace portrays the thrill of hunting the boar with nets and hounds,[201] and his convincing portrait of country life and the joys of the sturdy chase testifies to the hold that hunting had on the hearts of Romans.[202] Unfortunately, he fears, some of the younger generation are "afraid to hunt." [203] Virgil [204] advises to feed the swift Spartan hounds and those of Molossis, that they may protect the flocks, hunt hare, wild boars, hinds, and wild asses, and drive great stags into the nets. Martial [205] sings of country pleasures—the spoils of the hunter's net and snaring the leaping trout. To him who lives in the country, the field and woods offer boar, hares, and other field fare, and the streams supply fish.

Even bookish Pliny tells us that he has turned sportsman and has bagged three boars—but, while he watched the nets, he had tablets at hand and wrote, so that, if he caught nothing, he could at least take something home. He advises Tacitus to do the same thing next time he goes hunting. Minerva is in the hills, as well as Diana! His Tuscan villa is preferred to several others, because there his mind is exercised by study, and his body is kept in health by hunting. To Caninius he writes asking whether he is engaged in study, fishing, or hunting, and adds that he, too, longs for such amusements as the sick do for wine, baths, and springs.[206]

Fishing, like hunting, would be work rather than sport, if done for making a living. It was doubtless both to two different classes of people in old Roman days, as now. Though often considered a plebeian sport, it sometimes occupied members of the imperial household. Augustus sometimes fished. Rufrius Crispinus, stepson to Nero, was ordered drowned by his slaves while he was en-

---

[198] *Fronto*, I, 173, 179; II, 9.
[199] Suetonius: *Domitian*, 19.
[200] *Ausonius*, XIX, 30. Trans. by H. G. Evelyn White. The Loeb Classical Library. Quoted by permission of Harvard University Press, Cambridge, Mass.
[201] *Odes*, I, 1.
[202] *Epode* II.
[203] Horace: *Odes*, III, 24.
[204] *Georgics*, III, 404 *et seq.*
[205] Bk. I, 55; IV, 66.
[206] Pliny: *Letters*, I, 6; II, 8; V, 6.

FISHING   *Leptis Magna Mosaic*
(Courtesy, Bettmann Archive, New York)

gaged in fishing. Antoninus Pius delighted in fishing and hunting.[207] Fishhooks were found by archaeologists at Pompeii.[208] Fishing is spoken of by Pliny [209] as one of the constant diversions of the people at Hippo. Some people, probably the poorest, got their living by fishing. To them it was not sport, but it occupied the hours devoted by others to such recreation. Plautus portrays the poverty-stricken fisherfolk:

These hooks that you see, and bamboo poles, are our means for attaining a living;
And every day from the city we come, to secure a subsistence, hither.
Instead of gymnastics and boyish games, this toil is our exercise only.[210]

Riding horseback and in chariots was naturally an important accomplishment for those who were wealthy enough to equip themselves with horses for army service; and horsemanship was a means of recreation for those who could afford the expense when the business of war declined. Horace expresses a regret that some of the younger generation have not been taught "how to sit a horse"; [211] this, while doubtless true of those who preferred a sedentary exist-

[207] Suetonius: *Augustus*, 83; *Nero*, 35; Capitolinus: *Antoninus Pius*, 11.
[208] Showerman: *op. cit.*, p. 375.
[209] *Letters*, IX, 33.
[210] Lawton: *Classical Latin Literature*, p. 45.
[211] *Odes*, III, 24.

ence, probably does not describe a tendency. Pliny's Tuscan villa had a spacious hippodrome, lined with bay, box, cypress, and plane trees. Sometimes he rides his horse about the farm, instead of taking exercise in the allée. Again, he rides in a chariot, or varies the day's program and rides horseback, getting as much exercise with less loss of time.[212] Certain early leaders and later emperors are credited with extraordinary feats in riding. Caesar was especially skilled at horsemanship, even from boyhood, and would ride his horse at a full gallop while holding his hands behind his back. Antoninus, it is said, "would ride on horseback as much as a hundred miles." [213] Ausonius, with fulsome praise for him who made him Consul, says that Gratian would drop his reins, draw his bow, urge his horse on with the whip, and could likewise check him with it. Paulinus Pellaeus, grandson of Ausonius, regretfully remembered how, in his careless pagan youth, he loved to ride his racing horse at a gallop.[214]

Certain instances of women, such as Cloelia and others, who performed feats of physical prowess in early Roman days were preserved in old traditions. In somewhat later times, women appeared more in public, but generally in an inactive rôle. With the coming of an increased degree of freedom for women, though they took advantage of the opportunity to witness public spectacles, there was generally little attention apparently to their physical recreation. Ball-play, however—at least the less violent forms, involving throwing up and catching—was apparently participated in by girls to some extent.[215] In the relatively few allusions to it, there is sometimes deprecation, contempt, and ridicule, much as there was for woman's intellectual efforts. Pliny [216] praises Fundania for being discreet and sparing in indulgence at her play. Ovid would have a woman know how to dance. She may walk profitably "in the Pompeian shade"; she may visit the arena, and should sit in a prominent seat at the theater. Gambling games he recommends also, for these "indolent nature has given to woman," but men play with balls, javelins, hoops, armor, horses.[217]

Most exercises of the gymnasium were thought proper only for men, and were indecent for women. Martial's sixty-seventh epigram [218] is not commonly thought fit to put into English! Juvenal rails at the woman, so bold as to wrap herself in purple, use the wrestlers' oil, and smite the stump with a wooden sword—a woman truly fit "to blow a trumpet at the Floralia!" Perhaps she has even an ambition to appear in public competitions and is practicing for the arena! "See how she pants as she goes through her prescribed exercises; how she

---

[212] Pliny: Letters, v, 6; IX, 15, 36.
[213] Plutarch: Caesar, 17; Suetonius: Julius, 57; Dio, LXXVIII, 11.
[214] Eucharisticus, 141–54; Ausonius, XX, 14.
[215] Mau: "Ballspiel," loc. cit., II, Pt. II, 2832–4.
[216] Letters, v, 16.
[217] Art of Love, III, 349 et seq.
[218] Bk. VII.

bends under the weight of her helmet. . . ." [219] The time did come, indeed, when women appeared in physical contests. They are said to have participated publicly in gymnastics on one occasion (200 A.D.) and vied fiercely with each other; it caused something of an uproar, however, and women, regardless of birth, were forbidden thereafter "to fight in single combat." [220]

Some public baths provided special accommodations for women; others served only for men. Women of high station used the public institutions. The mother of Augustus is said to have gone to the public baths. At Pompeii, a smaller bath, not communicating with the larger, but having about the same arrangements, is believed to have been for women. In smaller towns, where the same institution served both men and women, certain hours were assigned to women, and others to the men.[221] Following the new mores, many went to extremes. The emancipated woman, Juvenal [222] declares, goes to the baths at night and exercises until exhausted. In later days, when laxity ruled at Rome, men and women bathed in common, a practice which Juvenal and Martial mention, and Quintilian condemns as indicative of adultery.[223] How general the custom became is debatable, but Hadrian is said to have ordered the sexes to bathe separately, and provided separate baths for them. Marcus Antoninus also sought to abolish the practice, as did Severus Alexander; Elagabalus, on the contrary, is said to have encouraged the evil by his personal example.[224]

GAMES IN GAUL An interesting and significant testimony to the continuity of Roman life and culture is afforded by the portrait of life in Gaul, drawn by Sidonius in the fifth century. Born at Lyons about 431, he lived nearly sixty years, saw the Romans and Germans fight the Huns, and witnessed the withering of the last pretense of Roman emperors to imperial sway. A member of an old senatorial family, who had turned to the ecclesiastical profession, Sidonius exhibits none of the asceticism of the Christian movement; others might profess much self-denial, but not the Bishop. From his letters one gains glimpses of a life filled with numerous worldly pleasures— those that Romans had either carried to the provinces or had found there indigenous. In general, an air of quiet and peace pervades his pages—the peace of retirement, with slight indication of any stirring Tun und Streben. There is

---

[219] Satire VI, 246 et seq. Trans. by G. G. Ramsay. The Loeb Classical Library. Quoted by permission of Harvard University Press, Cambridge, Mass.; cf. Martial: De Spectaculis, VI–VI B.

[220] Dio, LXXVI, 16.

[221] Suetonius: Augustus, 94; Becker: op. cit., p. 383; Mau: "Bäder," loc. cit., II, Pt. II, 2750.

[222] Satire VI, 419 et seq.

[223] Martial: Epigrams, III, 51; Quintilian, V, 9, 14; Ammianus, XXVIII, 4, 9.

[224] Dio, LXIX, 8; Spartianus: Hadrian, 18; Capitolinus: Marcus Antoninus, 23; Lampridius: Severus Alexander, 24; Elagabalus, 31.

pleasantry and amusing jest; best of all there is no word of officials or taxes; no informers to report; nothing said worth an informer's trouble! [225] The days of youth were spent in sport, as serenely as Roman boys had done for centuries past. Faustinus and Sidonius "played ball and dice together, and vied in leaping, running, hunting, or swimming. . . ." [226] To his brother-in-law, Ecdicius, Sidonius recalls the youthful sports of ball-play, dice, hunting with horses, hawks and hounds, and with the bow.[227]

Ball games are mentioned frequently by Sidonius. To Lupus he writes that Lampridius is delighted with a game of ball.[228] At his estate, Avitacum, near Clermont, is a greensward; and a grove near-by, in whose dense shade they play at ball when Ecdicius comes to visit.[229] Sidonius mentions games involving only two players; another in which two players oppose two others; [230] still a third makes use of many contestants. Sidonius admits himself an ardent player; the ball and book are his "twin companions." Religious services alternate with the ball game and other diversions. The annual church procession has ended; they are compelled to remain near-by to be on hand at the next Mass. The interval of waiting is filled with talk; then some turn to games, both sedentary and active. His description of the game played, while lively, gives but little insight into the manner of play. It is, however, a violent game, and involves two sides; there is much running, collision of the players, intercepting or parrying the ball; and the older players are soon exhausted. The rather vague description suggests the *harpastum*, to which reference has already been made.[231] Properly speaking, Sidonius' descriptions do not seem to justify interpreting any of the games as "tennis." [232]

Dice and the board game are often mentioned, and seem to hold a firm place in the affection of the clerical households. After a ball game, Ecdicius and Sidonius commonly resort to dice, and rest their legs.[233] Again, between the early morning church procession and the next Mass, at near-by Tierce, one group turns to dice, while others play ball. "Brother Domnicius" is most addicted to dice and the board game; and he rattles the bones, "as if he sounded a trumpet-call to play." [234] When visiting Ferreolus and Apollinaris, one hears the dice rattle and the players shout.[235] The board game, probably the *duo-*

[225] *Sidonius*, v, 17, 5.
[226] *Ibid.*, IV, 4, 1. From *The Letters of Sidonius*, translated by O. M. Dalton (The Clarendon Press).
[227] *Ibid.*, III, 3, 2–3.
[228] *Ibid.*, VIII, 11, 8.
[229] *Ibid.*, II, 2, 15.
[230] *Ibid.*, II, 9, 4.
[231] *Ibid.*, v, 17, 3–8.
[232] *Ibid.*, I, cxii.
[233] *Ibid.*, II, 2, 15.
[234] *Ibid.*, v, 17, 6.
[235] *Ibid.*, II, 9, 4.

*decim scripta* of earlier days, suggests backgammon, and is played with dice and two differently colored sets of men.[236] The description of Theodoric II at the board game is unique. Evidently the good Bishop of Clermont knew how to lose one game and win another:

"When inclined for the board-game, he is quick to gather up the dice, examines them with care, shakes the box with expert hand, throws rapidly, humorously apostrophizes them, and patiently waits the issue. Silent at a good throw, he makes merry over a bad, annoyed by neither fortune, and always the philosopher. He is too proud to ask or to refuse a revenge; he disdains to avail himself of one if offered; and if it is opposed will quietly go on playing. You effect recovery of your men without obstruction on his side; he recovers his without collusion upon yours. You see the strategist when he moves the pieces; his one thought is victory. Yet at play he puts off a little of his kingly rigour, inciting all to good fellowship and the freedom of the game: I think he is afraid of being feared. Vexation in the man whom he beats delights him; he will never believe that his opponents have not let him win unless their annoyance proves him really victor. You would be surprised how often the pleasure born of these little happenings may favour the march of great affairs. Petitions that some wrecked influence had left derelict come unexpectedly to port; I myself am gladly beaten by him when I have a favour to ask, since the loss of my game may mean the gaining of my cause." [237]

Hunting is referred to many times. There is apparently plenty of game; the bow, spear, nets, and hounds are the chief means of taking it. Sidonius writes to Agricola, describing the habits of Theodoric II on the chase: the sighting of beast or bird; taking the bow from pages and stringing it; placing the arrow; and his accurate shots.[238] From Namatius he asks news of his work and of his hunting, but warns him not to boast of his prowess in the chase: "It is useless to invite the boar to meet your spears, so long as you take the field alone with those exceedingly merciful hounds of yours; you just rouse the quarry, but not enough to make him run." [239]

Fishing found favor also in fifth-century Gaul. On the estate Avitacum, the fisherman goes to the middle of the lake, lets out the seine, and suspends the lines for trout. One can watch these operations as one sits at the table.[240] To Agricola he writes declining an invitation to visit him and go fishing, because

---

[236] *Ibid.*, II, 216, 249.

[237] *Ibid.*, I, 2, 7–8. From *The Letters of Sidonius*, translated by O. M. Dalton (The Clarendon Press).

[238] *Ibid.*, I, 2, 5.

[239] *Ibid.*, VIII, 6, 10–2. From *The Letters of Sidonius*, translated by O. M. Dalton (The Clarendon Press).

[240] *Ibid.*, II, 2, 12.

of illness in the family. He would like to go; Agricola has a fine, fast boat, excellent steersman and oarsmen.[241]

Boating is also a sport at Avitacum. In mid-lake is an islet with a turning post, round which boat racers were wont to turn, or come to grief.[242] On the Moselle, at an earlier date, Ausonius described the mimic battle of boats in midstream: "They circle in and out, and graze the sprouting blades of the cropped turf along the green banks. The husbandman, standing upon the rise of the green bank, watches the light-hearted owners as they leap about on stern or prow, the boyish crew straggling over the river's wide expanse, and never feels the day is slipping by, but puts their play before his business, while present pleasure shuts out whilom cares." [243]

The bath seems still as necessary to the Bishop of Clermont in the fifth century as it had been to worldly Romans of centuries past. He is filled with admiration for the baths at Octaviana.[244] The estates of Ferreolus and Apollinaris both have permanent baths. On one occasion, however, after a ride to stir the appetite for dinner, an improvised bath was set up because the regular establishments were not in readiness. A deep pit (dug by servants), red-hot stones, a roof of hazel brush and goats' hair coverings, and water—these alone were needed to make a vapor bath in which, he says, whole hours were spent with lively talk and healthy perspiration. Then they revived themselves with fresh water.[245] To Domitius, Sidonius writes, giving a description of his baths at Avitacum. They are on a wooded hill; logs slide down its slope to the furnace which heats them; they are so well lighted as to embarrass modest bathers. The apartments—hot bath, anointing room, cold bath, piscina, and other facilities —follow the usual pattern of Roman baths rather closely. The frigidarium challenges comparison with those of public institutions. Sidonius' description emphasizes the atmosphere of modesty and propriety, quite unlike what might be found elsewhere: on the walls are no nude figures which disgrace the artist; no absurd, painted actors; no fighters or wrestlers in indecent holds; only a few verses, which one may read once, but will not care to read again. Here are neither Parian, Carystian, or other foreign marbles, but the walls provide a satisfactory coolness which an ordinary, plain citizen may desire. It's hot outside; fords are dry; streams scarcely run; the little water in them boils! [246]

Hawking seems to have been unknown to Greek and to Roman, save as they

---

241 Ibid., II, 12, 1–2.
242 Ibid., II, 2, 19.
243 Ausonius, x, 200 et seq. Trans. by H. G. Evelyn White. The Loeb Classical Library. Quoted by permission of Harvard University Press, Cambridge, Mass.
244 Sidonius, VIII, 4, 1.
245 Ibid., II, 9, 7–9.
246 Ibid., II, 2, 1–8; cf. Ausonius, x, 337 et seq.; Statius, I, 5.

learned the art from barbarian neighbors and invaders. The Lombards, however, were skilled in training hawks, and introduced falconry into Italy, as did others in other provinces. Sidonius speaks of hawking as one of the skills in which Avitus is proficient, and names it as one of the youthful sports of Ecdicius.[247] Paulinus Pellaeus, born in Macedonia and educated in Gaul, alludes to his weakness for "a shapely hawk" and other appurtenances of the chase.[248]

[247] Bk. III, 3, 2; Gibbon: op. cit., IV, 37 f.
[248] Eucharisticus, 141 et seq.

# 24

# HEALTH, EXERCISE, DIET, AND DOCTORS

L ivy praised the site of Rome and her "healthful hills," and Strabo noted Italy's generally salubrious climate and hot and cold springs—nature's restoratives of health [1]—but pestilence seems to have been a frequent visitor. Cicero, though he called Rome's location "healthful," with her hills enjoying the breezes and providing shade "to the valleys below," recognized the pestilential character of the region.[2] Horace commented on the Tiber's overflow, laying "low the king's monument and Vesta's shrine"; [3] and flooding was not uncommon. July and August, when the heat was greatest, were marked by highest mortality. Recurrence of epidemics had much to do with promoting certain religious practices. The growth of Apollo's worship was, partly at least, the result of an effort to control disease. A temple was vowed to the god (432 B.C.) because of an epidemic; again a great pestilence of unknown cause and of long duration (399 B.C.) led to consultation of the Sibylline books and supplications to Apollo and other deities for eight days.[4] The Apollinarian Games, instituted 212 B.C., were designed to insure victory over Carthage, Livy says, rather than for reasons of health; but in 208 B.C., when a terrible pestilence swept city and country, supplications were made in every street of the city, and a law fixed the nones of July as the date for their perpetual performance.[5]

Despite numerous pestilences recorded in early times, Varro was of the opinion that Romans then had better health than in his day, for they worked on the land eight days and went to market on the ninth; they had then no need of "citified gymnasia of the Greeks"—of which, in his day, one was not enough—

---

[1] Livy, v, 54; The Geography of Strabo, vi, 4, 1.
[2] The Republic, ii, 6.
[3] Odes, i, 2.
[4] Livy, iv, 25; v, 13.
[5] Ibid., xxv, 12; xxvii, 23; Fowler: The Roman Festivals of the Period of the Republic, pp. 180 f.

and had their farms well tilled besides.[6] Young and old were affected by the transition from an economy of scarcity to one of abundance and luxury. The change in dietetic habits was of fundamental importance. For children of the olden days there was no danger of overeating; in his day, however, Varro observed, it had been discovered to be bad for "immature children" to eat heavily and sleep too much.[7] Seneca, too, assailed the Romans' manner of life, especially gluttonous eating, as the cause of numerous ills. In earlier days they toughened their bodies by hard labors, tiring themselves with running, hunting, and delving in the soil; they had appetite for plain food, and there was no need for medical instruments and pills. The Romans' elaborate diseases were produced by elaborate courses. "How many men are kept busy to humour a single belly!" [8] Medicine then was extremely simple, for it really had very little to do; in Seneca's day it had become remarkably complex, for diseases were as numerous as men! Directly and indirectly, Latin writers frequently criticized their own society, commenting on the superior qualities of the barbarians of whom they were becoming increasingly aware. Ammianus related a common current report that certain primitive people, living in mountainous places, surpassed the Romans in health, strength, and longevity—believed to be "due to abstinence from a conglomeration of diet and from hot baths." [9] Constantius, he said, unlike so many of his day, kept in sound health by moderation in eating and drinking.[10]

Considering the growth in number and complexity of illnesses, Plutarch had potentially a numerous audience in need of his words of *Advice about Keeping Well*. His wisdom, to be sure, was not novel. The science of dietetics, as Celsus said, had been developed by Greek physicians long before his time. He himself had written of foodstuffs extensively, so that those in health might know how to use them properly, and that those who were ill might suit their diet to their particular condition.[11] Plutarch's advice was certainly hard for wealthy Romans of fastidious tastes to follow. Guarding against excess in eating and drinking was the principal rule. One must judge by the stomach, not by the tongue, what to eat; one must be his own judge of food and drink, rather than depend on a physician to tell him.[12] Galen, in later years, gave a much more detailed and thorough account of the properties of foods and juices.[13] Centuries thereafter, when the barbarians put on Roman ways, they learned something of the

---

[6] *On Agriculture*, II, introduction, 2.
[7] *Aulus Gellius, The Attic Nights of*, IV, 19.
[8] *Epistle* xcv, 24.
[9] *Ammianus Marcellinus*, XXVII, 4, 14.
[10] *Ibid.*, XXI, 16, 5.
[11] *Celsus de Medicina*, I, Prooemium, 9; II, 18–33.
[12] Plutarch: *Advice about Keeping Well*, 4, 26.
[13] *Opera*, VI, 453–831.

rules of diet of the older Graeco-Roman culture. Anthimus, physician to Theodoric the Great, advised him, in his *De Observatione Ciborum*, to observe moderation in eating and drinking, as Plutarch and Galen had done before, and added guidance concerning the merits of digestible, well-prepared foods, eating of raw meat, how bread should be baked, the avoidance of doves, the necessary freshness of oysters and fish, the uses of barley gruel, goats' milk, unsalted butter, quince jelly, and cheese.[14]

A prudential philosophy appealed strongly to the Romans. Exercise was for many simply a means to health. In youth, naturally, play is a spontaneous expenditure of superfluous energy; it is only necessary to allow time for it. Martial bids the schoolmaster rest his rod during the heat of midsummer, for health is then a sufficient goal for children.[15] Recreation for health is most stressed in the care of the sick and the old. Cicero says ". . . we must fight, as it were, against disease, and in like manner against old age. Regard must be paid to health; moderate exercises must be adopted; so much of meat and drink must be taken, that the strength may be recruited, not oppressed . . . our bodies, indeed, by weariness and exercise, become oppressed; but our minds are rendered buoyant by exercise." [16]

A great deal of varied, sometimes conflicting, advice on how to keep well by taking proper exercise might be had by anyone in ancient Rome. Much of it was positive; some, purely negative. Certain authors advised the country; others prescribed exercises that took no room and required no journey. Horace considered ball-play bad for sore eyes and dyspepsia,[17] but Galen thought it one of the best forms of exercise.[18] Cicero recommended the country for the old and infirm. Agriculture's mild activities warmed the body as well as, or better than, sun-bathing or sitting by the fire. Fowling and hunting were, he thought, a kind of leisure labor, which stimulated an appetite for country fare. Arms, horses, spears, clubs, balls, swimming, and running were fit for young men, but not for the old. Dice might be allowed to the old, but they could be happy without them.[19]

Juvenal, too, recommended the "country school" of relaxation, which, far from being for the rich only, was really cheaper than living in town! Most of the sick people in Rome, he said, "perish for want of sleep." [20] Only the rich could sleep in town, so mean were the conditions of the poorer sort. If one could forego the circus, he could readily get a little country spot for what a

[14] Riesman: *Medicine in the Middle Ages*, p. 13.
[15] *Epigrams*, x, 62.
[16] *On Old Age*, 11.
[17] *Satires*, I, 5.
[18] "De Parvae Pilae Exercitio," *Opera*, v, 899 ff.
[19] *On Old Age*, 16.
[20] *Satire* III, 223 et seq.

hole in town cost in one year. There, with a garden, a well, and some mild exercise of the hoe, one could produce food for a hundred Pythagoreans, and gain health for the gardener besides. Martial echoed the same thought:

> Why do I seek my poor Nomentan home . . . ?
> Because I cannot find a place in Rome
> Where men as poor as I can sleep or rest.[21]

Sedentary occupations determined to some extent the types of exercise to be employed. Breathing, reading, talking, massage, exercise, the warm bath, and rubbing with oil by the fire were recommended by Plutarch for those devoted to scholarly pursuits.[22] Seneca thought that short, simple exercises—running, jumping, weight-swinging, walking, riding, vociferation—were most conducive to the mental and physical well-being of the studious.[23] Sun baths became common as a means to relaxation and health. Seneca declared that some men spent their whole life in sun-bathing, ball-play, and board games (latrunculi).[24] Cicero recognized the use of sun-bathing, but preferred the warmth of body derived from agricultural labor.[25]

Medical gymnastics of some kind was a necessity when men no longer had active labors to perform, whether in the camp or in the field. Though Romans had no high regard for athletic contests as such, they turned to them readily enough for the sake of health. Celsus advised those busy with public or private affairs to take some part of the day for physical care. For those tired out and troubled with poor digestion, exercise should be moderate; for those less fatigued and having better digestion, it should be more extensive and vigorous. All exercise should come before eating; it should be taken out of doors, rather than indoors; and in the sun, not in the shade. Drill, running, walking, ballplay, and reading out loud are recommended. Horseback riding, useful for certain diseases, is disadvantageous for others. Exercise should generally end with perspiration, but stop short of fatigue. The set regulations and immoderate exercises of the athletes should be avoided. Exercise should be followed by anointing, or a bath, and then rest.[26]

Galen, who was at one time a physician at a gladiatorial school and later attended Marcus Aurelius, gave much thought to exercise for the sake of health. In the "Exhortation to the Study of the Arts" and the treatise on the "Small

[21] Epigrams, XII, 57. Trans. by J. A. Pott and F. A. Wright. Courtesy of E. P. Dutton & Co., Inc., New York.
[22] Keeping Well, 16–7.
[23] Epistle xv, 4–8.
[24] On the Shortness of Life, XIII, 1.
[25] On Old Age, 16.
[26] Celsus, I, 2, 5–8; IV, 26, 30.

FRIGIDARIUM, BATHS OF CARACALLA
(E. M. Viollet-le-Duc, *Entretiens sur l'Architecture*, Pl. VII)

Ball," he set forth his chief convictions regarding the evil effects of certain kinds of exercise and the benefits to be derived from others. Ball-play and hunting, he thought, were best, for they joined exercise of the mind and of the body, and not only one part of the body but all the extremities and the eyes as well. Ball games were preferred to hunting, however, since they required less expenditure of time and money and could be graduated according to the amount and violence of exercise needed. The worst effect of athletic contests was that they not infrequently resulted in maiming the participants; and when carried to extremes, as among the professionals, the mind itself was reduced to the level of the brute.[27]

The use of baths as remedial agents was widely recommended. Celsus thought them useful both during and after certain kinds of fever, but close attention must be given to the time of bathing, extent of it, and avoidance of exposure. In certain forms of wasting disease (*tabes*) bathing might be employed, but in others avoided.[28] For the sick, Galen prescribed the use of the usual bath—the unheated room, the warm room, and the hot room. After

[27] Daremberg: *Oeuvres de Galien*, I, 31–46; Galen: *De Parvae Pilae Exercitio*, 1–2.
[28] *Celsus*, II, 17; III, 12–5, 22.

passing through these, the bather should go back to the *frigidarium*, take a cold bath, and be rubbed dry.[29]

In numerous instances prominent men turned to physical exercises of some sort for the sake of health, or claimed that exercise was the reason of their well-being. Augustus gave up the exercise of the *Campus Martius* after the civil wars, and devoted himself to milder substitutes. He is said to have used moderation in bathing, but was sweated by a fire, or anointed, and then doused with water warmed by the sun. When he had rheumatism, and hot salt and sulphur baths were prescribed, he merely sat on a stool and plunged his hands and feet into the water.[30] Vespasian enjoyed excellent health, but did nothing to secure it except rubbing "his throat and the other parts of his body" while in the ball-court and fasting one day a month.[31] Pliny kept his body well by hunting.[32] Paulinus Pellaeus left off serious study and turned to active sports, such as hawking, hunting, and riding, in order to regain his health.[33]

While some sought health by exercise and proper diet, others turned to doctors. Greek medicine, rooted in the observation of nature,[34] had become emancipated from the thralldom of primitive magic, charms, incantations and the bonds of priestcraft, since the days of Hippocrates (460 B.C.). Medical science, extended by the works of Theophrastus, Celsus, Dioscorides, Galen, Aretaeus, and others, ultimately spread throughout the world.

Early medicine at Rome was a combination of primitive magic of the Italic peoples, the priestly lore of the Etruscans, and infiltrations of superstitions of Greek origin, which scientific medicine never succeeded in fully rooting out. It relied chiefly upon incantation, binding and loosing (magic enthrallment, or freeing, by laying on of hands), name and number magic, lustration, incubation (temple sleep and dream cures), votive gifts and curses, snake-healing, magic waters, wells, images and stones, sympathetic agency, and astrology.[35] Belief in magic cures is reflected in ancient fragments, such as this—a magic charm for "footache"—repeated "thrice nine times" while one spits and touches the ground:

> Earth, take the pest to thee!
> Health, tarry here with me! [36]

That some early cures were more realistic, however, is shown by the Twelve

[29] Galen: *Opera*, x, 706–26; Marquardt: *Das Privatleben der Römer*, pp. 279 f.
[30] Suetonius: *Augustus*, 82–3.
[31] Suetonius: *Vespasian*, 20.
[32] *Letters*, v, 6.
[33] *The Eucharisticus*, 113 *et seq.*
[34] Riesman: *op. cit.*, p. 9.
[35] Allbutt: *Greek Medicine in Rome*, chaps. 1–3.
[36] Lawton: *Classical Latin Literature*, p. 16.

Tables which refer to the use of gold in the teeth, [37] for which Romans were perhaps indebted to Etruscans, whose progress in various kinds of metal work was phenomenal.

The arrival of Greek medical science at Rome was by no means enthusiastically greeted, apparently; or, if so, it soon fell into contempt. Cato the Censor, like many of his countrymen, would have nothing to do with Greek physicians. Instead, he is said to have depended on cabbage, other herbs, duck, pigeon, and hare, spells and prayers, whose uses were set forth in his book of recipes; moreover, he is said to have boasted that he and his family had kept in excellent health. Pliny declared later, when the city was overrun with doctors, that for six hundred years the Romans had gotten along well without any physicians at all.[38] Opposition to Greek medical practitioners was doubtless due largely to their being foreigners. Many other novelties that came from Greece to Rome had aroused similar distrust and opposition, as has been noted. Pliny says Cato warned his son against the Greeks as a "most iniquitous and intractable race"; if they bestowed their literature on Rome, it would mar everything; and their physicians would wreak still speedier havoc. "I forbid you to have anything to do with physicians." [39] Cicero [40] listed medicine as an honorable profession for people of a certain social station, *i.e.* slaves or freedmen—not the native Roman. In general, these classes continued to supply most of the physicians of Rome. Pliny declares that but "very few of our fellow-citizens" have attempted it.[41] Many foreigners became citizens, however, by virtue of their enfranchisement as members of the profession.

With the development of medicine and a vast, lucrative field for practitioners in such a city as Rome, there came specialization of various kinds. Besides surgeons and general practitioners, there were those who devoted themselves to the diseases of the eye, ear, skin, teeth, tumors, fevers, consumption, fractures, female diseases, obstetrics, and many others. Martial knows all the specialists to whom to go for any ailment, but for "a total wreck," well, "Who can mend me?" [42] Professional folk were also divided into several schools—Empirics, Eclectics, Dogmatics, Methodists, Pneumaticists, Hydrotherapists, Vinotherapists, and plain quacks—some of which took the name of their founder.

There being plenty of wealth and no end of diseases, medical men at Rome began to win a rich harvest. Pliny speaks of "the rapacious bargains made with their patients while their fate is trembling in the balance, the tariffs framed

---

[37] Cicero: Laws, II, 24.
[38] Natural History, XXIX, 5, 8; Plutarch: Cato, 23.
[39] Pliny: Natural History, XXIX, 7.
[40] Offices, I, 42; Marquardt: op. cit., pp. 772 ff.
[41] Natural History, XXIX, 8; Friedländer: Roman Life and Manners under the Early Empire, I, 167 f.
[42] Bk. x, 56.

upon their agonies," and declares that only the competition of vast numbers of practitioners kept charges within some degree of moderation. Nevertheless, he informs us that Charmis charged 200,000 sesterces for one cure. Claudius fined the surgeon Alcon 10,000,000 sesterces, who, after returning from exile, soon made it back. Court physicians in the time of Augustus and Tiberius were paid 250,000 sesterces; Stertinius received 500,000, but thought he could have made out much better in private practice. Crinas, a native of Marseilles, is said to have joined medicine with astrology, and left a fortune of 10,000,000 sesterces, having spent almost that sum in rebuilding the walls of his native town.[43]

An extraordinary refinement of knowledge was pretended by some physicians. One remedy was composed of fifty-four elements, not one in the same proportion, some being as small as one-sixtieth of a *denarius*. What gods taught men such trickery? Pliny asks. It's all "vain ostentation," a "monstrous system of puffing off the medical art." [44] To gain celebrity, novelties must be introduced, even at the cost of human lives. No doctor thought it proper to agree with another—hence the doleful discussion over the bed of the ailing patient. Anyone who had the gift of ready speech could easily make himself the arbiter of life and death. Extreme remedies were sometimes employed. Charmis proscribed warm baths, but also urged patients to plunge into cold water in the depth of winter.[45] Augustus is said to have been cured of his illness by the use of cold baths and cold potions, prescribed by Antonius Musa.[46] Aristides, the rhetorician, we are told, was ordered to bathe in an ice-cold river and run in the cold wind when he had a high fever.[47]

How good were the doctors? Quality doubtless had as many degrees as there were physicians. Some were indubitably excellent; others, nothing but opinionated, quarreling quacks. Pliny deplored the disputes over the sickbed; Sidonius shows that wrangling still went on in the fifth century. Only by leaving town and going to the country could his family escape the doctors "who disagree across the bed, and by their ignorance and endless visits conscientiously kill off their patients." [48] The ill effects of doctors' disputes were allegedly augmented by the presence of their pupils. Martial [49] declares he was not seriously ill till Symmachus and his hundred pupils gathered round and "pawed" him with their chilly hands. Some are said to have held aloof from doctors. Tiberius

[43] Pliny: *Natural History*, xxix, 5, 8. Trans. by H. Rackham. The Loeb Classical Library. Quoted by permission of Harvard University Press, Cambridge, Mass.
[44] *Ibid.*, xxix, 8.
[45] *Ibid.*, xxix, 5.
[46] *Dio's Roman History*, liii, 30.
[47] Dill: *Roman Society from Nero to Marcus Aurelius*, p. 465.
[48] Sidonius: *Letters*, ii, 12, 2.
[49] Bk. v, 9.

took good care of his health, according to Suetonius,[50] without aid or advice from physicians. Plutarch thought it ridiculous that a man over sixty should get a physician to take his pulse.[51] Presumably few, however, were hardy enough to take the advice of Marcus Aurelius: "If you are sick do not give doctors a chance to make an ado but let life go on merrily and well." [52]

A new profession—grown rapidly to huge proportions, claiming a high degree of specialization and refinement of knowledge, and harboring doubtless a good many charlatans—provided an excellent theme for serious satire or pleasant raillery. Many there were who enjoyed jibing at the doctors. Pliny cited a tomb inscription: "It was the multitude of physicians that killed me." [53] Martial ribbed the doctors who failed in their profession, and took new jobs—more or less closely related:

> Diaulus, once a surgeon, is now an undertaker;
> At last useful to the sick, the only way he's able.

Another doctor turned gladiator; before, he killed by "force of . . . physic"; now, by "physical force." [54] A man who, cheerful, dined one evening, was next morning dead—not from some terrible disease, but because before him in a dream there stood "the quack Hermocrates." [55] Ausonius tells the story of Doctor Eunomus, whose patient, Gaius, died. The physician met his patient's pallid ghost and, upon inquiry, was informed that it came from *Dis*, to summon doctors. Eunomus froze with fright. "Fear nothing," whispered the sprite, "I said, as all men say, that no man who is wise calls you a doctor." [56]

Greek cities had public doctors by 500 B.C.; and Strabo reported that Masillia had teachers of medicine, as well as other arts and sciences, employed "not only by private persons, but by towns for common instruction." [57] A Peloponnesian, Archagathus, said to have been the first physician to come to Rome (218 B.C.), received the privileges of citizenship and opened a medical clinic, which was "provided for his practice at the public expense." [58] Though welcome for a time, his practices soon led to suspicion and disrepute. Nevertheless, doctors increased; and when they had established themselves extensively, Caesar began a policy of state encouragement of medical science, conferring citizenship on those who practiced it there.[59] Under the Empire, the practice of employing

50 *Tiberius*, 68.
51 *Keeping Well*, 26.
52 Riesman: op. cit, p. 366.
53 *Natural History*, xxix, 5.
54 Bk. viii, 74.
55 *Ibid.*, vi, 53.
56 *Ausonius*, xix, 4.
57 Bk. iv, 1, 5.
58 Pliny: *Natural History*, xxix, 6.
59 Suetonius: *Julius*, 42.

court physicians, the provision of medical men for the armies and fleets, the development of communal medical service, and the demand for medical specialists at gladiatorial schools all combined to place physicians in an enviable position, both from a financial and professional point of view, if not a social one. In later imperial days certain physicians gained the title of *archiater* (ἀρχίατρος), chief doctor—such, for example, were Stertinius Xenophon, physician of Claudius, and Andromochus, Nero's doctor.[60] Severus Alexander had a *medicus palatinus*, with a regular salary, and six other doctors who received double and triple rations.[61] That these court physicians were freed from all civil duties is shown by a decree of 326, which refers to this as a long-established privilege.[62]

As noted, some sort of communal medical service was already known at Masillia in the time of Strabo. Augustus rewarded Antonius Musa handsomely for his services and decreed exemption from taxes not only for him but for the members of his profession in Rome, both for the present and the time to come.[63] This privilege was extended by Vespasian and Hadrian to provincial physicians. Antoninus Pius fixed the number of public doctors in Asia at ten for large cities, seven for smaller ones, and five for the smallest. These physicians were named and paid by local municipal authorities, and were freed from all civil burdens. They could be removed by the same authority. After the second century it seems to have been common for most cities to appoint communal doctors. In larger towns, at least, there were *collegia*, guilds of the profession. Some cities provided halls (*auditoria*) for the use of physicians as dispensaries, offices, and lecture rooms. Severus Alexander is said to have assigned lecture rooms for physicians (as well as for other teachers) and provided rations for such of their pupils as were poor, yet of free birth.[64] The teaching of medicine became widespread not only at Rome but in such provincial towns as Arles, Nîmes, Marseilles, Lyons, and Saragossa. In Valentinian's reign it was decreed (368 A.D.) that the city prefects should name fourteen chief physicians for each of fourteen regions, in addition to one each already provided for the Vestal Virgins and the *Porticus Xysti*, the Athletic Society. These doctors were paid from public funds, and they were to treat the poor free; but they might also take private practice for fees. When vacancies occurred, they were to be filled by a vote of the remaining colleagues, with the confirmation of the Emperor.[65]

[60] Marquardt: *op. cit.*, p. 775.
[61] Lampridius: *Severus Alexander*, 42.
[62] Marquardt: *op. cit.*, p. 776.
[63] *Dio*, LIII, 30.
[64] Lampridius: *Severus Alexander*, 44.
[65] Marquardt: *op. cit.*, pp. 776 ff.; Friedländer: *op. cit.*, 1, 169 f.; Gregory of Tours: *History of the Franks*, 1, 416 f.

Besides encouragement of medical instruction, selection and public approval of head physicians, and the assignment of specified numbers of them to certain areas, there was apparently some effort at quarantine. Ammianus says that, since it "is natural in the capital of the world" for "cruel disorders" to gain such headway that "the healing art is powerless even to mitigate them, it has been provided, as a means of safety, that no one shall visit a friend suffering from such a disease. . . ." [66]

Under Theodoric the Great (c. 454–526) doctors took an oath and were honored with the title *comes archiatrorum*. Though Justinian's Code (533) directed district physicians to minister willingly to the poor and not keep their aid for the rich alone, Procopius informs us that by Justinian's withdrawal of maintenance allowances—previously granted by emperors for the encouragement of scientific endeavor—and by his absorption of the local resources of cities, doctors and teachers were really robbed of their support, and hence could no longer be provided. [67]

Although, due to the encouragement of Roman emperors, practitioners of medicine gained a preferred status throughout a vast territory, it cannot be said that medical science made proportional advancement. Only two major figures, Galen and Celsus, appeared in seven hundred years. After Galen there was a steady decline. At Alexandria at the end of the third century, scarcely "an eminent scientist" is mentioned after the time of "Galen, Soranus, and Julian." [68]

Though the scientific spirit of Greek medicine was regnant in the work of Celsus, Galen, and Aretaeus, the boundary between science and magic was doubtless often shadowy, even in the best days at Rome. With the gradual atrophy of critical intellectual life in the third and succeeding centuries, a general recrudescence of superstition and magic occurred, which ultimately engulfed the world of medical science. The resurgence of unscientific views and practices showed itself in Marcellus Empiricus (c. 410 A.D.) of Bordeaux; and, in some degree, the otherwise sound work of Alexander of Tralles (mid-sixth century) was marked by an admixture of superstitious belief. [69]

Though medicine has been called the chief science of the Merovingian Age, and though Latin translations of Hippocrates, Galen, Soranus, Oribasius, and others were available in the sixth century, the status of medical science was by no means high. Primitive belief and practices were infiltrating the medical

[66] *Ammianus Marcellinus*, xiv, 6, 23. Trans. by J. C. Rolfe. The Loeb Classical Library. Quoted by permission of Harvard University Press, Cambridge, Mass.
[67] Procopius: *The Anecdota or Secret History*, xxvi, 5–7; Grasberger: *Erziehung und Unterricht im Klassischen Altertum*, iii, 461; Gregory: *op. cit.*, i, 417; Riesman: *op. cit.*, p. 12.
[68] Fort: *Medical Economy during the Middle Ages*, pp. 61 f.; Riesman: *op. cit.*, p. 10.
[69] Allbutt: *op. cit.*, p. 39; Dill: *op. cit.*, pp. 459 f.

field, on the one hand, from Teutonic and perhaps also Celtic sources; they were pressing forward, too, under the aegis of religious authority of preachers and saints. According to Teutonic medicine, disease was explained by specific, wind-blown poisons—of which there were nine, and hence nine diseases—and also by various agencies such as worms and the elf-shot. The "possession" theory of disease causation, which emanated from Babylonia and spread through Rome, was accepted by Christians as a rule.[70]

Thus, the medical science of Hippocrates and Galen had to contend against two pseudo sciences. One of them, accepted and practiced by Christian saints, was indeed a formidable rival; for, as Dalton says, "Every deceased saint of repute was a rival . . . [as] were many living holy persons qualifying for saint-hood by austere lives." [71] Bishop Claudius of Turin and others are credited with protesting against saint cures, but "the practice became universal," and there was "one or more saints for nearly every disease." [72] With the growth of Christian and Gnostic sects, says Fort, the healing art declined as a science "in exact proportion as Christianity or Gnosticism progressed"; and when Christianity became dominant, "under the colossal support of secular power, with the new system of religion came remedial adaptations, absurd, irrational, and no longer dependent on the fragile imperfections of human reason, but elevated to celestial or divine manipulation." [73]

[70] Gregory: op. cit., I, 415 ff.; Riesman: op. cit., pp. 12, 15.
[71] Gregory: op. cit., I, 418. From Gregory of Tours: The History of the Franks, translated by O. M. Dalton (The Clarendon Press).
[72] Riesman: op. cit., p. 20.
[73] Fort: op. cit., pp. 61 f.

# 25

# IDLE QUEST FOR HAPPINESS

During the last centuries of the Republic vast changes in respect to private wealth took place in Italy and especially in Rome. At the time of the war in Spain (215 B.C.), when the treasury was exhausted, wealthy men subsidized the state's military operations with loans.[1] The gulf widened rapidly between rich and poor in the next hundred years. The last century of the old era saw the rise of millionaires, the concentration of wealth in few hands. Some fortunes were extremely large. Crassus had land alone valued at 50,000,000 denarii; in 91 B.C., 2,000 citizens probably possessed the wealth of Rome; whether more or fewer, it is certain that a very small, wealthy class was set off sharply from the many (320,000) who were on the grain dole at the middle of the first century. Wealth continued to increase, and was doubtless vaster in the second century A.D. than ever before; but by that time there were fewer great fortunes, the concentration in Rome was less, and many of the greatest holdings were in Asia Minor and Greece.[2]

As fortunes grew, luxury and an idle quest for happiness supplanted the simple life and vigorous activities of an earlier day. A pattern of luxury, as well as the wealth to pay for it, came from Eastern lands. Booty, brought from Asia Minor by Scipio in 189 B.C., seems to have been the initial source of luxury at Rome. Besides luxury goods—fancy tables, couches, tapestries, gems—there came musicians and dancers to entertain one's leisure, and cooks to satisfy the palate with hitherto unknown dishes.[3] At the end of the Republic, with great wealth in hand and an unprecedented era of peace and security, extravagant luxury increased rapidly in the houses of the few.

[1] Livy, XXIII, 48–9.
[2] Abbott: *Society and Politics in Ancient Rome*, pp. 132 f.; Cary: *History of Rome*, pp. 454 f., 672 f.; Johnston: *The Private Life of the Romans*, p. 222.
[3] Pliny: *Natural History*, XXXIII, 53; Livy, XXXVII, 59; XXXIX, 6.

That the great wealth was badly used is the inevitable conclusion to be drawn from Roman writers of the late Republic and the Empire, even when generous allowance is made for exaggeration. It was an age of selfish individualism and spendthrift luxury, and many saw and condemned the growing evil. Polybius commented on the display of public and private wealth after Macedon fell under Roman sway; observed the effect of it on morality; and noted Cato's indignation that pretty boys should bring more than fields, and caviar more than tillers of the land.[4] Many were not aggrieved at wealth, but at the rapid conquest of it by those who had been poor. In Sulla's day, though the old ways were changing, older Romans disapproved both of those who rose swiftly from poverty to riches and those who wasted an inheritance.[5] Many, however, recalling Sulla's victory, hoped to become senators, to feast, and live like kings; and young men of the poorer sort, who had once labored in the fields, were led by public and private doles to prefer the idleness of the city.[6] Those who became freedmen, got wealth, and put on airs aroused contempt. Seneca pours his scorn upon Sabinus who has the "bank-account and the brains of a freedman" and purchases slaves—one to know Homer, one for Hesiod, and others to know each of the lyric poets—to give himself a reputation for learning.[7]

Rome's misfortunes, many thought, arose from war and increase of wealth. Rome at first was poor, says Sallust, but grew in population, territory, and riches; prosperity gave rise to envy, and wars followed with her neighbors.[8] In early days *private* wealth was small, says Horace, and the *common* wealth was large; but now our "piles of royal magnificence" will soon leave no acres for the plow.[9] Ovid joins in: A small hut and river sedge for bedding sufficed our ancestors; senators fed their flocks; the praetor left the plow and came to judgment. Now riches have grown, and frantic lust for wealth drives us on for more and more. Only money counts to-day.[10] In primitive days, Lucretius says, skins were the object of desire; but now gold and purple harass life with care and weary men with conflict. This constant struggle, this failure to learn the limits of true happiness, has ". . . carried life into deep waters" and ". . . stirred up from their depths great tides of war." [11] Tiberius, urged to do something to restrain extravagant tendencies, declared that "victories over the foreigner taught us how to waste the substance of others . . ."; now we have learned how "to squander our own." [12]

4 The Histories, XXXI, 25.
5 Plutarch: Sulla, 1.
6 Sallust: War with Catiline, 37.
7 Epistle XXVII, 5–6.
8 Catiline, 6.
9 Odes, II, 15.
10 Fasti, I, 191–218.
11 Lucretius (Jackson), V, 1434 et seq.
12 Tacitus: Annals, III, 52–5.

In this age of fatted selfishness, materialism was the keynote of Roman life. Money, the ready measure of wealth, became a god; conspicuous parade of it gave social standing. Staberius would have his heirs record the amount of money he left behind, or exhibit one hundred pairs of gladiators, give a great feast, and distribute a whole African corn harvest! Riches are beautiful. Everything bows to them.[13] Again, Horace says, "Money is shameless. It grows and grows . . ." but more is always wanted. Let us be rid of gold and gems, the occasion of all offense, ". . . if we are truly tired of our wickedness." [14] Some men, though wild spendthrifts, appear to have been possessed of the madness of a miser. Caligula, it was said, had such a mania for the mere feeling of money that he poured it out, walked over the coins barefoot, and wallowed in them.[15] No god was revered more than money. "How little you know about the age you live in," says Ovid, "if you fancy that honey is sweeter than cash in hand!" [16] Juvenal concurs. Everything is forgiven, even the stigma of the slave's prison, if one has big moneybags. The first question is about a man's wealth, the last about character. Gaming and adultery are shameful in men of moderate wealth, but the rich who indulge themselves are brave fellows and fine men.[17]

Poverty is "the one great shame," "the worst of moral vices," says Horace.[18] According to Ovid, ". . . the poor man everywhere lies low." [19] Juvenal's portrait of his age emphasizes the evil, seamy side, but it is corroborated by many sources. Knowing the vice and weakness of Roman society of the late first century at first hand, and viewing them realistically, he declares ". . . it is hard not to write satire"; "Honesty is praised and starves." [20] In Rome everything is expensive—a house, a dinner, a toga; we live in "pretentious poverty." The poor should long since have left the city en masse. It is difficult for those hard pressed by poverty to emerge and be something. Grim symbol of the direst poverty of all is Juvenal's newly arrived dead man who shudders at the ferryman, for in his mouth is no copper for the fare.[21]

Juvenal lashes bitterly at the misery and poverty of the city. Seneca, with more detachment, advocates "contentment in poverty," and warns that a "mob of slaves avails not"—but he himself is rich, entertains lavishly, and has a "retinue . . . all but imperial." [22] Unlike either of them, Martial witnesses the

---

[13] Horace: Satires, II, 3.
[14] Odes, III, 24.
[15] Suetonius: Caligula, 42.
[16] Fasti, I, 191–218. Trans. by J. G. Frazer. The Loeb Classical Library. Quoted by permission of Harvard University Press, Cambridge, Mass.
[17] Juvenal: Satire I, 106–16; III, 137–63; XI, 176–8.
[18] Satires, II, 3; Odes, III, 24.
[19] Fasti, I, 191–218.
[20] Juvenal, I, 30, 74; Ramsay: Juvenal and Perseus, xxxiii–xxxiv.
[21] Juvenal, III, 264–7.
[22] Lawton: Classical Latin Literature, p. 244.

same characteristics of Roman life, wisecracks his way about the city, and offers
hints to those who vainly hope to get on there. If one would be a pleader, he
must remember that some, though indeed eloquent, cannot pay their rent.
If literary talents others would exploit, they should take warning from Virgils
and "threadbare Ovids" wandering in the streets. If one thinks to find a generous patron, he must remember that "all have starved excepting three or four."
If one really succeeds in making a go of it in Rome, it's "luck alone" if one's
an honest fellow. One who came to the city gates, already starving, turned
back "again to starve at home," on hearing of the dole in Rome.[23]

The last centuries of the Republic were marked by a great increase of crime,
and many public men sought to protect themselves by using armed slaves and
gladiators. Varro,[24] speaking of an attempted murder, calls it a cause of lament,
but no surprise, that such things are taking place in Rome. Crookedness assumed many forms. Complaisance made friends, but truthfulness was the
source of unpopularity.[25] One entering public life met "shamelessness, bribery
and rapacity" rather than "modesty, incorruptibility and honesty"; public
morals were destroyed by "extravagance and avarice"; lust for power and
money nourished other evils that spread like a plague and changed the very
nature of the state itself.[26] The growth of crime is reflected in the establishment
of a network of special courts for trying magistrates who misused public
moneys, murderers, traitors, forgers, and various other criminals. The destruction of life under Claudius, Caligula, Nero, and others was so great that Vespasian had to recruit "the aristocracy from Italy and the provinces." [27] Gone
were the days when, in Juvenal's phrase, one cell sufficed to hold the nation's
criminals.

Extravagance ran riot; public persons set a grand example to all who could
and would imitate them. Such habits, already developing in the late Republic,
were more extensively indulged in the early Empire. Cicero wrote Atticus of
the games and feasting at Praeneste: "Eight days of games! Picture their
dinners and their extravagant goings on." [28] Caesar fed the public on twenty
thousand dining couches, and gave gladiatorial and naval combats in honor of
his daughter.[29] Augustus gambled lavishly. To Tiberius he wrote of gambling
all day and keeping the game board warm. He lost 20,000 sesterces, but would
have gained 50,000 if he had collected everything won; but he preferred to be

[23] Epigrams, III, 14, 38.
[24] On Agriculture, I, 69.
[25] Terence: Lady of Andros, act 1.
[26] Sallust: Catiline, 3, 5, 10, 12–3.
[27] Dill: Roman Society from Nero to Marcus Aurelius, p. 71; Showerman: Rome and the
Romans, pp. 184 f.
[28] Letters to Atticus, XII, 2.
[29] Plutarch: Caesar, 55.

thought generous, which would exalt him "to immortal glory." To his daughter he sent 250 *denarii*, the sum he gave to all his guests if they wished to play at dice or at odd and even.[30] Caligula tried to outdo everybody in extravagance, threw money to the crowds for several days, bathed in hot and cold perfumed oils, drank pearls dissolved in vinegar, and laid loaves and meats of gold before his guests. Galleys with ten banks of oars, gem-set sterns, and colored sails were provided with spacious baths, banquet halls, colonnades, and even vines and fruit trees, so that he might sail and feast at pleasure.[31] Nero is said to have played dice at 400,000 sesterces a point, fished with a net of gold, never traveled with less than one thousand carriages, had mules shod with silver, and never wore the same clothes twice. On Tiridates he spent 800,000 sesterces a day, and gave him over 100,000,000 when he departed. His friends, too, gave great dinners, on one of which 4,000,000 sesterces were spent.[32] No less spendthrifts were Otho and Vitellius in their day. Domitian depleted the treasury by reckless expenditure, and resorted to property seizures on various pretexts.[33]

Private extravagance kept pace with public. Those unsatisfied by facilities for gayety at home visited resorts at Baiae and Canopus.[34] Private magnificence was exhibited chiefly in elaborate town and country houses, luxurious feasts, and rich personal adornments and equipage. Even Marius had "an expensive house," more luxurious and effeminate than befitted one risen from poverty and schooled in the hard discipline of warfare.[35] Lucullus purchased a house for 2,500,000 drachmas, previously sold for 75,000. A town house of Crassus cost over £60,000. Even Cicero, though not one of the richest by any means and often in debt, had a town house costing 750,000 *denarii* and quite a handful of country places.[36]

Were men happier in many houses than in one? What profit is it to have so many bedchambers, asks Seneca? "You sleep in one." [37] Lucretius pictures the mad race from town to country and back again. A man who is bored at home often leaves his great mansion, and then at once comes back again, finding that he is no happier elsewhere. He rushes off to his countryseat, driving at headlong speed, as if going to a fire; there he yawns the moment he reaches the door, or falls heavily asleep, seeking forgetfulness, or else hastens back to town.[38]

If life in the city was cumbered with an army of slaves, entertainers, dancers,

---

[30] Suetonius: *Augustus*, 71.
[31] Suetonius: *Caligula*, 37.
[32] Suetonius: *Nero*, 27, 30.
[33] Suetonius: *Domitian*, 12; *Dio's Roman History*, LXVII, 5.
[34] Seneca: *Epistle* LI.
[35] Plutarch: *Caius Marius*, 34.
[36] Cary, op. cit., p. 455, credits him with "at least twelve"; Fowler, *Social Life at Rome in the Age of Cicero*, p. 251, says "in all six," besides certain properties owned temporarily.
[37] *Epistle* LXXXIX.
[38] Lucretius, III, 1060 *et seq.*

and musicians, traveling to the country for rest was by no means an easy matter, for carriages and baggage must be taken, also a retinue of slaves, and perhaps even a bodyguard of gladiators. Once in the country, relaxation might be found. Only the dead wear togas in the country, says Juvenal. Cicero complains, however, that his house at Formiae is like a public hall, and wishes he could get away to more secluded Arpinum.[39] Upon the country villa, which was for ostentatious display rather than a productive concern such as Varro described in his work on agriculture, a gentleman usually spent a great deal of care and money. Cicero [40] tells of his efforts to secure proper appointments at one of his country places. Pliny [41] dwells at length on the attractions of his Tuscan villa, lying under the Apennines: the salubrious climate and stirring breezes; the wooded, natural amphitheater, with abundant hunting; the commodious house, its surrounding gardens, terraces, walks, fountains, pavilions, baths, playing courts, riding course, and elaborate servants' establishments. All is peace and quiet, comfort, and rest for mind and body; here a man rejoices, for he can lay aside the heavy toga, no one comes to call him forth to business or to the harrowing pleasures of the city. Juvenal, full of biting condemnation of city luxuries, praises his "Tiburtine farm" and its simple fare: a fat kid, wild asparagus, chickens, fresh eggs, grapes, pears, apples, and wine from the native hills. Besides, there are neither fancy carvers, highly trained servants, nor Spanish girls to entertain with clattering castanets and vulgar dances.[42]

With increased ease of life, professional cooks appeared in private families, and about 170 B.C. public bakeries began to do much of the work formerly done at home.[43] Feasting took the place of normal use of food for proper ends; informal drinking gave way to formal drinking bouts. Fantastic sums, relative to this tendency to extravagance among the rich, are reported by ancient authorities. Lucullus had a number of dining rooms in his house, each of which had a fixed figure for feasts served in it. Fifty thousand drachmas were spent on a dinner served to Cicero in the Apollo dining room. Service was high. Lucullus paid his cooks £1,600 for a single banquet. His fish pond was filled with sea water brought through the mountains.[44] Exotic dishes were most highly prized; the more the expense, the better the dinner. A mullet or sturgeon might cost £100. The rarity of dishes served gave standing to the host. Seven thousand birds and two thousand choicest fishes were served at one dinner; in one enormous platter were mixed pike livers, brains of pheasants and peacocks,

---

[39] To Atticus, II, 14.
[40] Ibid., I, 6, 8–10.
[41] Letters, v, 6.
[42] Satire XI.
[43] Mommsen: History of Rome, III, 123.
[44] Plutarch: Lucullus, 41; Paul-Louis: Ancient Rome at Work, p. 129.

flamingo tongues, and lampreys' milt.[45] This, of course, was a feast to please a brother, and an emperor at that.

Banquets, though not universal, were of frequent occurrence. Varro [46] thought it fair to say that there was a banquet every day in Rome. Their number made prices soar. The tide of luxury, according to Tacitus,[47] reached its flood in the century between Actium and the time of Galba. At the end of this remarkable epoch, Seneca railed at those who combed the earth and the sea for delicate foods and kept an army of hunters, fishermen, and cooks busy trying to please their jaded palates. "Poor wretches, do you not know that your appetites are bigger than your bellies?" From the multitude of such complicated dishes come divers complex diseases which call in turn for various medical treatments.[48]

In the Republic and under the Empire there was no lack of those who knew that something should be done to counteract the corrupting influence of misspent wealth. But, though efforts at restriction of luxury were put forth, Romans failed to become proper masters of their gain. The early laws did not strike at the root of the evil, but only sought to cut off branches. The Oppian Law (215 B.C.) struck at feminine luxury, but ineffectively, because there was little public support behind it. Cato became unpopular because he had all "apparel, equipages, jewellery, furniture and plate" over 1,500 drachmas assessed at ten times its value.[49] During fourscore years numerous other laws (161, 115, 89, 81 B.C.) aimed at restricting or prohibiting delicacies, wines, and the amount of silver plate one might possess. Weights and prices were also fixed, as was the amount that might be expended on ordinary dinners and feasts.[50] Favonius is credited with a rousing attack on luxury: "The leaders in gluttony and luxury declare that an entertainment is not elegant, unless, when you are eating with the greatest relish, your plate is removed and a better, richer dainty comes from the reserves. This to-day is thought the very flower of a feast among those with whom extravagance and fastidiousness take the place of elegance; who say that the whole of no bird ought to be eaten except a fig-pecker; who think that a dinner is mean and stingy unless so many of the other birds and fatted fowl are provided, that the guests may be satisfied with the rumps and hinder parts; who believe that those who eat the upper parts of such birds and fowl have no refinement of taste. If luxury continues to increase in its present proportion, what remains but that men should bid some-

[45] Suetonius: Vitellius, 13.
[46] On Agriculture, III, 2, 16.
[47] Annals, III, 55.
[48] Seneca: Epistle LXXXIX, 22; XCV, 24–9.
[49] Plutarch: Cato, 18.
[50] Mommsen: op. cit., IV, 185 f.

one to eat their dinners for them, in order that they may not fatigue themselves by feeding, when the couch is more profusely adorned with gold, silver and purple for a few mortals than for the immortal gods?" [51]

Few seem to have obeyed the laws; but Rufinus, an ancestor of Sulla, was expelled from the Senate because he had more than ten pounds of silver plate.[52] Luxury, nevertheless, grew more and more extreme. Cicero, living in the midst of it, defended the interests of the wealthy *equites*, but knew full well that the state was depraved wherein "the richest" were rated "the best." [53] The pseudo-Sallustian address to Caesar advised the dictator that, if he wished to right affairs, he must rid Rome of money-hoarders, limit extravagant indulgence, and keep every man's expenditure within his income; for "it has become the custom for mere youths to think it a fine thing to waste their own substance and that of others, to refuse nothing to their own lust and the demands of their fellows. . . . If our youth continue . . . as at present, beyond doubt that eminent renown of yours will come to a speedy end, along with the city of Rome." [54]

The first century of one-man rule saw no improvement; instead, luxury grew worse. "All vice is at its acme," said Juvenal.[55] Some heads of the state, indeed, sought to restrain evil tendencies. Augustus prided himself on fasting one day, he said, as scrupulously as a Jew,[56] but he was extravagant in many respects. Tiberius sought to impose limitations on public games and the price of foods and other luxuries, and encouraged frugality at meals and closeness in money matters by his own example.[57] But Tacitus tells us that he was reluctant to take the lead in trying to restrict freedom of spending by more laws, since those of the past had all been ineffective; if remedies were to be found, they ". . . must be sought in our own hearts." [58] It was not until the reign of Vespasian that extravagance really began to go out of vogue, for his own example was more influential than legal restraints. To this may be added that diminishing wealth at Rome at the end of the century was probably a factor leading to a degree of modesty in expenditures, and a somewhat improved use of wealth.[59] But this improvement was only relative and sporadic, as one may

[51] *Aulus Gellius, The Attic Nights*, xv, 8. Trans. by J. C. Rolfe. The Loeb Classical Library. Quoted by permission of Harvard University Press, Cambridge, Mass.
[52] Plutarch: *Sulla*, 1.
[53] *The Republic*, I, 34, 51.
[54] Sallust: *Speech to Caesar*, 5–6. Trans. by J. C. Rolfe. The Loeb Classical Library. Quoted by permission of Harvard University Press, Cambridge, Mass.
[55] *Satire* I, 147–51.
[56] Suetonius: *Augustus*, 76.
[57] Suetonius: *Tiberius*, 34, 46–8.
[58] Tacitus: *Annals*, III, 54.
[59] *Ibid.*, III, 55; Suetonius: *Vespasian*, 11–2; Frank: *An Economic Survey of Ancient Rome*, v, 59 f.

infer from the tale of extravagant luxury and vice related by later writers.[60]

Petronius' immortal *Satyricon* portrays the great age of money-making and spending. Petronius himself, an elegant, sophisticated idler, is said to have been an intimate of Nero, who sought his advice on matters of taste and elegance in luxurious living.[61] Trimalchio, one of the "new rich," is a "millionaire of millionaires"; he does not even know the meaning of "poor man." He boasts of being "God-fearing, gallant, constant"—a freedman who began with little, left thirty millions, "never listened to a philosopher," and was made a Priest of Augustus.[62] He has sought standing by buying land. Everything that makes his guests' mouths water comes from a new estate which he has not seen, but he thinks it is on the line between Terracina and Tarentum. He hopes to join up all his farms, so that, if he fancies going to Africa, he can do the trip on his own land! He does not despise learning; indeed, he has two libraries, one Greek, one Latin. His little son is already at learning and is to know law, for "law has bread and butter in it." [63] Before dinner he exercises vigorously at a game of ball, bathes, is rubbed down with blankets (not mere towels), and anointed. His wife, Fortunata, dances "the cancan better" than anyone else. He himself thinks acrobats and trumpeters furnish the best of all entertainments.[64]

Ganymede provides vinegar at the feast. He regrets the passing of the good old life when one could play odd and even with a man in the dark, when there was sound religion and no new education. To-day men are dishonest, irreligious, and the gods gouty. No one cares if high food prices pinch the poor man, or whether he gets bread or not. The drought goes on; the famine has lasted a year already. The city fathers are in cahoots with the bakers. The little fellow gets on badly, the upper crust enjoys constant carnival. Ascyltos also hits a sour note, the failure of justice: "Of what avail are laws where money rules alone . . . the knightly juror who sits listening to the case gives his vote as he is paid." [65] But the seamy side gets only fleeting attention from the author of the *Satyricon*. Even Echion, the ragman, sees a rosy future: all depends on how you look at it; if you lived elsewhere, you'd say roasted pigs were walking the streets here. Besides, there is going to be a finish-fight at the amphitheater, for Titus is bound to put on a good show.

60 *Ammianus Marcellinus*, xiv, 6; xxviii, 4.
61 Tacitus: *Annals*, xvi, 18–9; Heseltine: *Petronius*, pp. vii *et seq.*; Dill: *op. cit.*, pp. 120 f.; Frank: *op. cit.*, v, 139.
62 Petronius: *Satyricon*, 71. Trans. by M. Heseltine. The Loeb Classical Library. Quoted by permission of Harvard University Press, Cambridge, Mass.
63 *Ibid.*, 46, 48.
64 *Ibid.*, 27–8, 52–3.
65 *Ibid.*, 14, 44. Trans. by M. Heseltine. The Loeb Classical Library. Quoted by permission of Harvard University Press, Cambridge, Mass.

## LEARNING THE WAYS OF IDLENESS

To be part of a crowd, to watch an exhibition of the skill and power of living beings, and to identify one's self more or less with the contestants is naturally satisfying to man. Primitive men put on shows; civilized nations modify, elaborate, and cultivate them, in one way and another, sometimes to an extraordinary degree. The extent to which exhibitions are developed depends upon numerous factors—a variable human nature, the status of the society which a people has established, notions held by them, and the like.

It has long been said that Romans had a marked, natural love of excitement, and that it was satisfied by the contests of the circus and the amphitheater. It should be remembered, however, that the practices of the late Republic and of the Empire were a result of growth and cultivation, a development which came from natural causes, but ultimately reached unnatural proportions. Romans of the earliest times had few entertainments; their descendants had an extraordinary array of them. Man tends naturally to activity, as Cicero said. The Romans' natural capacity remained fairly constant, doubtless, but the external circumstances of their life changed radically and made them the instruments of futile instead of useful activity. One of the most important factors in this metamorphosis was the concentration of wealth and power, which robbed the mass of men and women of their onetime useful employments by rendering them either impossible or unnecessary, and which enabled the few to rule the many by satisfying their lowest desires, filling their mouths, and diverting their minds. This transformation paralleled other changes in Roman life and education, which followed upon the transition from provincial to cosmopolitan culture. It was, if one considers life whole, a most portentous phase of the "new education."

The teachers of the way of idleness were numerous and of various sorts: political leaders, seeking power by ingratiating themselves with the masses; men in power, wishing to hold it; the inevitable, ubiquitous gossips who went to see, marveled, and spread abroad the delights to be experienced, the thrill of expectancy at not knowing what will happen, but that something will; literary folk who, transposing something of the present into the past, told the Roman people that their primitive ancestors from the very beginning had been participants in spectacular contests and had crowded round to see them. Virgil's vivid portrayal of contests is quite out of keeping with the primitive culture he ostensibly portrays. The shepherds on the hills of Rome and the peasants scattered on the surrounding plains had no time or effort to spend on such displays.

The receptivity of the Roman masses and their betters for this phase of the "new education" is evident on every side. The host of poor citizens, who no longer had any real occupation or income (there may have been more than 300,000 unemployed before Caesar's day), were receptive both to state feeding and entertainment; on the other hand, those who had just become rich were anxious to put on shows to prove their title to men's acclaim. Martial's parvenu "cobbler Kinglet" exhibits gladiators, thus threatening to destroy all that he has won by his awl.[66] The young learn early the ways of their elders. Cicero takes his young son to the country at the time of the games, that he may turn his mind to other studies than the circus; [67] he hastens to reach Antium because Tullia wants to see the games.[68] Tacitus complains of the "passion for play actors, and the mania for gladiatorial shows and horseracing"—vices "taken on," as it were, "in the mother's womb." [69]

The passion for games, with few exceptions, held the learned as well as the unlettered in its grip. There seems to be no barrier between fine, aesthetic development in literature and the enjoyment of the most cruel combats of the arena.[70] Many persons, certainly, had a love both of letters and of the games. Fronto, teacher of Marcus Aurelius, declares that, though ill, he has been "carried to the circus," for he is "again seized with a passion for the games. . . ." [71] Terence, however, is a rueful witness to the preference of the masses for gladiatorial shows.[72] Polybius,[73] too, says that a Roman audience could not appreciate a good troop of actors until they turned their show into a sham battle. Romans would vacate the theater, Horace declared, if a play did not include "a bear or a boxing match." Many students of Roman letters would probably agree that, in the long run, the rise of gladiatorial sports to great importance at Rome combined with other events to hasten the decline of tragedy which had gained a degree of prominence between the days of Andronicus and Attius.[74]

There were, of course, exceptions among the learned and great. Cicero's views are divided. He shows a certain scorn for the games; but he knows their value, and frequently expresses great concern about them. The extensive references in his correspondence with Atticus, Caelius, Quintus, and others, to gladiators, panthers, games, and their bearing on the political situation, show what a place circuses occupied in the minds of serious men. Public, political life and family interests compelled one, otherwise disinclined thereto, to take some notice of the public spectacles. Cicero's philosophy is a prudential one.

[66] Bk. III, 16; Johnston: op. cit., pp. 341 f.
[67] Cicero: Letters to His Brother Quintus, III, 4.
[68] To Atticus, II, 8.
[69] A Dialogue on Oratory, 29.
[70] Abbott: op. cit., pp. 176 f.
[71] Fronto, The Correspondence of Marcus Cornelius, I, 309.
[72] Terence, II, 129 ff.
[73] Bk. XXX, 22.
[74] Lawton: op. cit., p. 23.

BORGHESIAN GLADIATOR  *by Agasias*
(Courtesy, The Metropolitan Museum of Art, New York)

He thinks Milo "beyond endurance, mad" for giving games that cost 1,000,000 sesterces, when they are not really required of him.[75] Of giving gladiatorial combats at funerals, he speaks disparagingly to Curio. The giving of them occasions no real admiration for the giver, for wealth alone, not worth, provides them; anyway, everybody is now sick of them. As for "Greek games," "You

[75] *To Quintus,* III, 8 and 9.

know what I think [of them]," he writes Atticus; he is not surprised that attendance was small at their opening. He advises Tiro, however, to see the gladiators on January 1 and return the following day.[76] When Tullia wants to see the games, Cicero hastens to be at Antium the day before they are to begin. He expresses great interest in Atticus' acquisition of a troop of gladiators, and wants day-by-day news of gladiatorial games. Again he writes Atticus that the games were magnificent and well received, but the *venationes* were postponed. While others were watching the games in the city, Cicero recuperates at Arpinum, enjoying the scenery of the river.[77]

Being a gladiator is contemptible in Cicero's eyes, but he sees them from the standpoint of a politician. If these men cut their friends' throats for sport, what may they not be expected to do to their enemies when they get political power in their hands? [78] Nevertheless, Cicero is much concerned by the punctilios of attending or not attending the games at Rome; even though he is not going, he hopes they will be well attended, and wants full details about their reception.[79] Everything depends, however, not on the merits or demerits of gladiatorial games *per se*, but on particular circumstances with which they are connected. When Caelius Rufus sends mere chitchat about gladiators to him at Athens, Cicero enquires tartly whether he thinks that is the purpose for which he has been commissioned.[80]

Seldom is a voice raised in remonstrance against the inhumanity and brutality of public games. To Marius, Cicero writes, indeed, that he cannot understand what pleasure a cultivated man can find in seeing a human being torn by a beast, or a beast being pierced through by a hunting spear; and he reports that a "certain pity" was aroused in spectators by the elephants, a vague feeling that the big beasts were in some way akin to men. Cicero shows himself herein somewhat more sensitive than most of his compatriots; his view is comparable to that of Pliny later. It is chiefly the monotony that palls; to see them once is enough; ". . . I who was there to see, saw nothing new." He admires anyone who is strong-minded enough to stay away from the spectacles which "others unjustifiably admire." [81] Pliny is happy that he himself is insensible to the pleasures of the circus; he quotes approvingly the sentiment of Junius Mauricus, who wished that gymnastic *ludi* might be abolished at Rome. Nevertheless, though not drawn to bloody sports personally, he congratulates Maximus politely for giving a gladiatorial spectacle in honor of his dead wife, for "greatness of soul" is to be seen in these smaller matters as well as in larger

[76] *Letters to His Friends*, ii, 3; xvi, 20; *To Atticus*, xvi, 5.
[77] *To Atticus*, ii, 8; iv, 4 a, 8, 15; xiii, 37; *To Quintus*, iii, 1, 1.
[78] *Philippic* v, 7; vi, 4; vii, 6.
[79] *To Atticus*, xv, 26.
[80] *To His Friends*, ii, 8.
[81] *Ibid.*, vii, 1.

ones.[82] Marcus Aurelius,[83] conspicuously differing from his imperial colleagues in his sensitivity about shedding the blood of his fellow men, allowed gladiators to fight only with blunt weapons. In the pancratium he saw little merit.

Rome was ruled by a class psychology, and upper-class Romans of refinement and education doubtless generally found it easy to explain their attendance at the games of the circus. Cicero recounts the distinction made by Pythagoras between those who went to games to seek profit or fame and those "free-born men" of the best type who came merely to see the spectacle, to see what was done and how.[84] The hold of games on the minds of people is suggested by the fact that constant allusions and explanations are based on the common knowledge of them. Cicero points to the master of gladiators who meditates constantly on improvement of the knowledge of his art; to explain the difference between *inhibere* and ἐποχή, he turns to charioteers, boxers, and boatmen.[85] Lucretius finds no better example of the lasting effect of deep impressions than the games. Even when absent from the spectacles, one's mind may still retain the impression of its latest lessons. Lucretius notes that men, having spent several successive days intently watching public games, have afterimages of the assembly and the splendor of the adornments hovering before their eyes. Even those who were determined to fight against the seductive influence of the arena might ultimately succumb, as did Alypius, friend of Augustine.[86]

It is hard to think of Rome, with her marked social stratification, as a great happy family; there were forces, however, which tended toward unity in some degree, and among these the public festivals were of some importance. The games, though one of the most brutalizing aspects of Roman life, were in a superficial sense one of its most democratic features. Open to all citizens at the beginning, but excluding foreigners and slaves, the games ultimately drew men and women from every station and from every land in reach of Rome.[87] Here rich and poor shared something in common, even if all did not share alike. The arena and circus were a good sounding board for public opinion. A measure of the popularity of games and the representative character of the audience attending them, once the habit had become well established, is found in the fact that Cicero regarded the approval and disapproval of the assembled crowd as a judgment to which he attached great weight. On one occasion he wrote Atticus (61 B.C.) that both at games and gladiatorial spectacles he had received extraordinary demonstrations and no hisses or catcalls; which he con-

[82] Pliny: *Letters*, IV, 22; VI, 34; IX, 6.
[83] *The Meditations of the Emperor*, XI, 2; Dio, LXXII, 29.
[84] *Tusculan Disputations*, V, 3.
[85] *On Oratory*, III, 23; *To Atticus*, XIII, 21.
[86] *Confessions*, VI, 8; Lucretius, IV, 973 *et seq.*
[87] Fowler: *op. cit.*, p. 298; Friedländer: *Roman Life and Manners under the Early Empire*, II, 16.

sidered evidence that he retained his old influence and had gained some with "the sordid dregs of the populace. . . ." [88] The amount of applause Caesar received when he refused the crown at the Lupercalia was a measure of public approval.[89]

Long experience in the school of observation made the Romans expert connoisseurs of combats. Petronius suggests the contempt felt for mediocre fighters: Norbanus produced only rotten tuppence-ha'penny gladiators, fit to be knocked over by a breath. Over the prospect of a good bloody show, the spirits of the knowing ones rise: "Just think, we are soon to be given a superb spectacle lasting three days; not simply a troupe of professional gladiators, but a large number of them freedmen. And our good Titus has a big imagination and is hot-blooded: it will be one thing or another, something real anyway. I know him very well, and he is all against half-measures. He will give you the finest blades, no running away, butchery done in the middle, where the whole audience can see it." [90]

Ultimately a sturdy folk, which once labored hard all day and went to bed at dark, learned to spend the day at the games and sometimes the night as well, watching the combats by torchlight.[91] Gibbon sums up the way in which Romans had learned a concern for shows when at their height: "The impatient crowd rushed at the dawn of day to secure their places, and there were many who passed a sleepless and anxious night in the adjacent porticos. From the morning to the evening, careless of the sun, or of the rain, the spectators, who sometimes amounted to the number of four hundred thousand, remained in eager attention; their eyes fixed on the horses and charioteers, their minds agitated with hope and fear, for the success of the *colors* which they espoused: and the happiness of Rome appeared to hang on the event of a race. The same immoderate ardor inspired their clamors, and their applause, as often as they were entertained with the hunting of wild beasts, and the various modes of theatrical representation." [92] At the seat of Empire, and in the provinces as well, the mob had learned the somewhat ungrammatical lesson that "'unting . . . bathing and gaming, these is life." [93]

But by no means least among the admiring throng of spectators were the political and military leaders, who came to the headship of affairs in the late Republic and were sole masters during the Empire. With but few exceptions they approved by their presence and their largess the giving of games, and culti-

---

[88] *To Atticus*, i, 16; *Philippic* i, 15; x, 3–4; *Publius Sextius*, 59.
[89] Plutarch: *Caesar*, 61.
[90] Petronius: *Satyricon*, 45. Trans. by M. Heseltine. The Loeb Classical Library. Quoted by permission of Harvard University Press, Cambridge, Mass.
[91] Suetonius: *Domitian*, 4.
[92] *The Decline and Fall of the Roman Empire*, iii, 31.
[93] Cary: *op. cit.*, p. 689.

vated the natural appetite for thrills which, once fully developed, proved embarrassing even to imperial purses. By example, by lavish expenditure, by surrounding the whole business with impressive ceremonies, the emperors made the amphitheater and the circus, filled with thousands upon thousands of spectators, one of the most effective schools of the city. In the late Republic, leaders were already at work satisfying the natural appetite and developing it. Crassus (c. 115–53 B.C.) was unpopular because he was so exceptional as to give "no athletic contests" for the troops! Pompey, on the contrary, satisfied the crowd by dedicating a theater, giving gymnastic and musical contests and wild beast fights in which five hundred lions were slain. Among his novelties were elephants—"a most terrifying spectacle," says Plutarch—all of which won him "admiration and affection." [94] Caesar, at the time of his aedileship (65 B.C.), surpassed previous displays, and exhibited three hundred and twenty pairs of gladiators. After his triumphs he entertained lavishly with banquets and shows, and made gifts to his soldiers. Four celebrations were given on four different days in 46 and 45 B.C. Appian says that a combat of foot soldiers used one thousand on each side; and a cavalry contest, two hundred on each. There was a combat of forty elephants, divided into two groups, a naval fight with four thousand oarsmen, and one thousand fighters on each side.[95]

Augustus carried on the old policy of entertainment so well established under the Republic, providing for many games out of his private resources, and allowing the continuance of those under the praetors and aediles. Gladiatorial contests, especially, became a matter of grave concern on the part of the emperors, and were more and more regulated by them. Augustus was advised to reduce expenditures on games and to limit horse races to Rome, aiming at economy, keeping the populace "from becoming deplorably crazed over such a sport," and also to ensure a plentiful supply of horses for the army.[96] The record of his expenditures and concern for games of all kinds is, however, more impressive than his restraint and economy. It was said that he excelled all predecessors in the number, variety, and splendor of public spectacles, giving them four times on his own account and twenty-three times on behalf of other magistrates. Gladiators in the forum, the circus, and the amphitheater; fights of wild beasts; athletic contests in the *Campus Martius*; naval combats on an artificial lake; chariot races; the game of Troy—all these were among his many exhibitions, provided at great expense for entertainment of the idle multitudes. According to the *Res Gestae*, Augustus gave ordinary *ludi* on twenty-seven occasions; *venationes* (animal hunts), on twenty-six; gladiatorial games, eight

[94] Plutarch: *Crassus*, 17; *Pompey*, 52–3; Dio, XXXIX, 38, 1–5.
[95] Appian: *Civil Wars*, II, 102; Plutarch: *Caesar*, 5, 55; Dio, XLIII, 19, 22–4.
[96] Dio, LII, 30.

times; athletic games, three; a *naumachia* (with three thousand fighting sea-men); the *Ludi Martiales*; and the *Ludi Saeculares*.[97]

Tiberius, an exception to the all but universal imperial mode, is said to have given no public spectacles, and seldom was present at those given by others; moreover, he sought to limit the cost of the games and the number of gladiators that might engage.[98] Caligula, however, taught the Romans that one-man rule and imperial horseplay could cost them dearly, both in money and self-respect. Nevertheless, there were many who offered their lives for his and who vowed to fight as gladiators if he should recover from an illness. These were compelled to fulfill the vow. The wealthiest were killed and their property confiscated, but such lavish sums were spent on horses, gladiators, and the like, that the accumulations of the treasury were soon exhausted. Caligula gave several gladiatorial games, and he himself appeared as a Thracian gladiator, singer, and dancer, and drove in chariot races. Besides, he gave many games in the circus lasting all day long, with panther battles and the game of Troy alternating with the races, and also put on exhibitions in Gaul and in Sicily. The birthday of Drusilla was celebrated with an exhibition of her statue drawn by elephants, horse races, the destruction of five hundred bears and "as many Libyan beasts," competitions in the pancratium, feasting of the populace, and donations to senators and their wives. It was said that, in fact, Caligula was dominated by charioteers and gladiators. He himself was a partisan of the "Greens." To get money he sold those who survived gladiatorial combats; and compelled many men to fight as gladiators, singly and in companies. When a shortage of animals occurred and there were not enough to give to the beasts, he caused some of the mob standing by to be seized and thrown in instead.[99]

Claudius gave each soldier 15,000 sesterces for his allegiance, and was lavish both in largesses to the public and in the provision of games. Besides naval exhibitions, which he gave at Pompey's theater and frequently at the circus built by Gaius, he gave gladiatorial combats in various places, an imitation of a siege in actual warfare, a naval battle between "Sicilian" and "Rhodian" fleets—each with twelve triremes—and a repetition of the secular games which he declared Augustus had exhibited too soon.[100]

Nero's introduction to public life began with a donation to the soldiers in his name and games in the circus to win him favor. His career in profligate entertainment of the public outran all others, and he himself took part exten-

[97] *Res Gestae Divi Augusti*, IV, 22–3; Suetonius: *Augustus*, 43.
[98] Suetonius: *Tiberius*, 34, 47.
[99] Dio, LIX, 2, 5, 10, 13–4, 22; Suetonius: *Caligula*, 14, 18–20, 27, 54. As to the importance of factions into which charioteers were organized, "Greens," "Blues," "Reds," "Whites," "Golds," and "Purples," see p. 731.
[100] Suetonius: *Claudius*, 10, 21.

sively in public exhibitions. From his earliest years he had a passion for horses, talked constantly of the circus games, and soon wanted to drive, himself. He did, in fact, drive in many races, even a ten-horse team at Olympia. It is said that he never failed to take part in equestrian contests. He was dominated by a love of popular acclaim, and was so jealous of others who stirred the mob that he forbade magistrates and procurators in the provinces to exhibit gladiatorial or wild beast fights or give any other entertainment. Not satisfied with acclaim in music and in driving the chariot, Nero is said to have wanted to emulate Hercules, and had a lion in training so that he might kill it publicly in the arena. On one occasion Nero exhibited a wild beast hunt, and then piped water into the theater immediately and displayed a naval battle; after that, the water was drained out and a gladiatorial combat was put on. One of the most unique events in the world of entertainment was his inauguration of the Neronia, a quinquennial festival which included contests in music and gymnastics, in imitation of Greek contests. After his grand tour, filled with all sorts of triumphs, Nero entered Naples through a breached wall, like a conqueror in the Sacred Games. Later he came to Rome, riding in the chariot of Augustus and wearing the Olympic crown, and surrounded by 1,808 others which had been awarded him. Small wonder that the populace hailed him as Olympian Victor, Pythian Victor, Our Hercules, Our Apollo, "The only Victor of the Grand Tour." [101]

Under Vespasian Rome became somewhat more sober, yet he knew the use of games and often provided beast hunts, though it was said he did not "take much pleasure" in the armed combats of men.[102] In Vitellius' brief reign Rome was a place of riot, massacres, spectacles, and feasting. His government is said to have been determined chiefly by the caprices of actors and charioteers. Vitellius himself, "never so absorbed in business as to forget his pleasures," wore the Blue uniform and curried the race horses.[103]

Titus restored the popularity of one-man rule, which, by his time, was sadly in need of rehabilitation. Suetonius says that he took nothing from anyone, respected property, but was, nevertheless, "second to none" in liberality. To render himself more popular, Titus would give gladiatorial games, not according to his own wishes, but those of the onlookers. He himself showed a personal liking for Thracian fighters.[104] At the dedication of baths and amphitheaters, he put on a splendid gladiatorial show, staged a naval battle, and exhibited five thousand beasts in one day. The celebration is said to have lasted a hundred days. There were battles between cranes, elephants, and many other

[101] Dio, LXII, 14–5, 20–1; LXIII, 1; Suetonius: Nero, 12, 22, 24–53; Tacitus: Annals, XII, 41; XIII, 31.
[102] Suetonius: Vespasian, 2; Dio, LXV, 15.
[103] Tacitus: Histories, II, 67; Dio, LXIV, 5; Suetonius: Vitellius, 12.
[104] Suetonius: Titus, 7–8.

animals, of which a total of nine thousand were dispatched, women assisting. Men fought in single and group combats; and on the water there were gigantic contests between "Corcyreans" and "Corinthians," and between "Athenians" and "Syracusans." There were surprises for many, perhaps for everyone, for little wooden balls were thrown down into the crowd, each specifying some prize—a slave, horse, gold or silver vessel, food, or clothing—to be secured by exchanging the balls at proper places.[105]

Domitian entertained the public lavishly with the usual two-horse and four-horse races, put on battles of infantry and horsemen, beast hunts, gladiatorial exhibitions at night by torchlight; and employed not only men but women also. His naval battles engaged almost regular fleets. Martial celebrated the animal hunts—the many tigers that have come "to-day, great Sire, to give delight to Rome." [106] At the secular games, performed according to the calculation of Augustus rather than that of Claudius, a hundred races were run in one day. Two new factions were added by him to the jockeys, the "Golds" and the "Purples." [107]

The century-old custom of satisfying the idle multitudes with brutal, bloody spectacles was honored by the best of emperors, such as Trajan, Hadrian, Antoninus, and Marcus Aurelius. Though Hadrian refused all other circus games in his honor, he accepted those celebrating his birthday; on which occasion, it is said, he slaughtered two hundred lions and gave gifts to men and women. He frequently attended gladiatorial shows. In Athens he visited the public games, and exhibited a hunt with one thousand animals.[108]

Antoninus Pius showed more restraint in games, even a degree of discouragement of the practice, but accepted the circus performances in celebration of his birthday. In 148 he gave elaborate games, exhibiting elephants, corocottae, rhinoceroses, crocodiles, hippopotami, even a hundred lions and tigers at a single show—in fact animals from everywhere. Though there is some evidence of his economy, and he is said to have limited the cost of gladiatorial shows, he was generous to the people, gave largess on nine occasions, and made a donation to his troops at his daughter's marriage.[109]

Marcus Aurelius, though he had no love for them, allowed himself when young to be taken to beast hunts and spectacles. He himself says he learned from his teachers not to be a partisan of either "Greens" or "Blues," nor to take sides in gladiatorial games, nor even to breed fighting quails.[110] His biographer says that he "limited gladiatorial shows in every way," yet elsewhere

---

[105] Dio, LXVI, 25.
[106] Bk. VIII, 26.
[107] Suetonius: Domitian, 4, 7; Dio, LXVII, 8.
[108] Spartianus: Hadrian, 8, 13, 19; Dio, LXIX, 8, 16.
[109] Capitolinus: Antoninus Pius, 5, 8, 10, 12.
[110] Meditations, I, 5–6; Capitolinus: Marcus Antoninus, 4.

informs us that he was "so liberal" as to give a show of one hundred lions, all of which were dispatched with arrows.[111] Likewise, when he armed gladiators and took them away to war, he is said to have arranged that the wealthy folk at Rome should provide plenty of entertainment by games for the people. Aurelius gave customary gladiatorial spectacles at the death of his father and grandfather, and he would not interrupt public games when mourning for his little son.[112] Notwithstanding this participation in a long-established custom, he showed negligence and contempt for it, in some respects, for he was wont to read and sign documents during performances—to the displeasure of the audience. By giving games, Marcus seems to have been buying a certain degree of approval of the public, much as he purchased the good will of the soldiery by paying 20,000 sesterces to every man at his coming to power. Though credited with being sparing in largess, his coins show that he made such gifts to the public on seven occasions.[113]

Profligacy in respect to games became worse in the late second century. Verus, though he shared sway with Marcus Aurelius, was a horse of another color; he took an avid interest in the "Greens," and, when in Asia, gave much time to gladiatorial combats and hunting. Commodus, alleged by a common story to have been the illegitimate son of a gladiator, is said to have fought as Emperor before the people in almost a thousand gladiatorial combats, and to have slain thousands of wild animals with his own hands.[114] A successful gladiator and beast-fighter, Commodus also adopted the Green uniform of the circus and made himself a laughingstock before his people; ultimately he became a terror, for he turned to murdering men—as a respite, as it were, from his sportive career—and was killed at last by those who had reason to fear him. The treasury, depleted by his extravagance, is said to have been replenished in some degree by Pertinax through the sale of articles used in connection with the fighting, charioteering career of Commodus.[115]

This pattern of education in brutality was not altered much during the third and fourth centuries, though a degree of restraint of the regal passion was sometimes necessitated by declining finances. Symmachus (c. 345–410), sometimes called the "last valiant defender of paganism," is said to have given games which cost a fortune when young Symmachus was praetor; [116] and he showed as lively a concern about getting animals for his shows as one could have expected from the most ardent enthusiast of three centuries earlier. Even in the sixth century, despite Christian protest and momentous turns of fortune's

[111] Capitolinus: *Marcus Antoninus*, 11, 17.
[112] *Ibid.*, 6, 8, 21, 23.
[113] *Ibid.*, 7, 15, 23.
[114] Lampridius: *Commodus*, 11-2; Capitolinus: *Marcus Antoninus*, 8, 19; *Verus*, 6-7.
[115] Dio, LXXIII, 14, 16–22; LXXIV, 5.
[116] Dill: *Roman Society in the Last Century of the Western Empire*, p. 150.

wheel, there were still indications that the lessons assiduously taught for centuries had not been completely forgotten.

If the common herd was apt to learn, and if military men who became heads of the state were apt to teach, the noble and polite elements of Roman society were also ready to lend approval to bloody entertainments by their presence, and frequently (though it was held to be disgraceful by some) also by participating in them. A certain Furius Leptinus, of praetorian family, and Quintus Calpenus, a former senator, fought to the end at Caesar's games; but in 38 B.C., senators were excluded from the arena.[117] Augustus set aside the first row at the games for senators; and he used knights in gladiatorial shows till a decree was issued against it. Claudius also provided special seats for senators at the Circus Maximus.[118] Caligula held certain races in which the charioteers were all of senatorial order, and he compelled many knights to fight singly and in groups.[119] In Nero's day men of the greatest families drove in the circus, slew animals, and fought each other in the arena—thus performing publicly those acts which once they had not been willing to watch in others. There were reactions, doubtless, sometimes even in the worst régimes: Vitellius is said to have won approval because he prohibited knights and senators from fighting as gladiators and taking part in other spectacles.[120] Domitian sought to safeguard rank. It appears that thereafter, till the madness of Commodus, senators and knights were not compelled to participate in public spectacles, yet many seem to have done so of their own accord.[121]

Modest domesticity, which women had known almost exclusively in early times, became less marked in the late Republic, and disappeared during the Empire. Cicero's Tullia wanted to see the games at Antium; Ovid advised women to visit the arena.[122] Augustus, keen for reforming morals and manners (of others at least), excluded women entirely from contests of athletes, and decreed that they should view gladiators only from the upper seats, whereas previously men and women had sat together. Vestal Virgins were given a place by themselves.[123] Girls as well as boys had a part in singing the Secular Hymn at the celebration of the Ludi Saeculares in 17 B.C.[124] Caligula gave his sisters the privilege of watching the circus games from imperial seats.[125] Claudius is said to have forced knights and others, "together with women of similar rank," to appear on the stage, not because it pleased him to see them, but to punish

[117] Suetonius: Julius, 39; Dio, XLIII, 23; Friedländer: op. cit., II, 17.
[118] Suetonius: Augustus, 43–4; Claudius, 21.
[119] Suetonius: Caligula, 18; Dio, LIX, 10.
[120] Dio, LXII, 17; LXIV, 6.
[121] Friedländer: op. cit., II, 18.
[122] Art of Love, III, 395 et seq.; Cicero: To Atticus, II, 8.
[123] Suetonius: Augustus, 44.
[124] Wickham: Horace for English Readers, p. 134.
[125] Dio, LIX, 3.

# 716 [EMPIRE OF THE EAST AND WEST]

them for having done so in the time of Caligula.[126] The grandfather of Nero, while Consul (16 B.C.), put knights and matrons on the stage in a farce. At Nero's *Juvenales*, old men and matrons took part, and Vestal Virgins were invited to see the athletic contests, just as did the priestesses of Ceres at Olympia.[127] Dio says that Nero had men and women of the equestrian and senatorial orders appear in the orchestra, the circus, and the arena, just like people of "lowest esteem." "Some of them played the flute and danced in pantomimes or acted in tragedies and comedies or sang to the lyre; they drove horses, killed wild beasts and fought as gladiators, some willingly and some sore against their will." [128] In the time of Titus, women took part in the slaughter of beasts, though they were not of the social elite. Domitian had maidens take part in foot races; dwarfs and women were pitted in combat.[129] In the time of Severus, according to Dio, women took part in spectacles, vied "with one another most fiercely," and gave rise to ridicule, causing a general prohibition against women, regardless of rank, taking part in single combats.[130]

### THE ORIGIN AND GROWTH OF LUDI

MOTIVE FORCES    Originally all games depend on a natural tendency to various kinds of physical activity, which varies in different people, but always exists in some degree. Among equals this drive is the natural basis for competitive sports. An active, virile people, the Romans enjoyed this natural impulse to a marked degree; but as Rome entered upon a career of conquest, the development of sports became, first of all, a means to military efficiency. When that was no longer necessary, games became primarily a source of personal enjoyment, health, and entertainment of spectators. Students of Roman life, ancient and modern, point almost without exception to the deep, pervasive love of frolics, holidays, music, and dancing on the part of the Italian people. Leisure and games were constantly associated with their festivals. One was the complement of the other; the leisure which followed from the cessation of other activities, on the day designated for the honor of the gods, was employed in games and other forms of amusements.[131]

Associated with this basic natural drive to physical activity, there was another causal factor in Roman festival games: the religious motive. All games, it seems, were at the outset associated with religious ceremonies of one kind or

126 *Ibid.*, LX, 7.
127 Suetonius: *Nero*, 4, 11–2.
128 Dio, LXII, 17. Trans. by E. Cary. The Loeb Classical Library. Quoted by permission of Harvard University Press, Cambridge, Mass.; Tacitus: *Annals*, xv, 32.
129 Dio, LXVI, 25; LXVII, 8; Suetonius: *Domitian*, 4.
130 Dio, LXXVI, 16.
131 Ihne: *History of Rome*, i, 568; Fowler: *op. cit.*, pp. 285 f.; Showerman: *op. cit.*, pp. 299 f.

another. Tertullian says that there were many published accounts in his day dealing with the relation between the origin of the games and pagan religious cults.[132] Ultimately, of course, with the decay of the old mores, the religious associations and significance weakened, and were almost, if not wholly, lost.

But games, though at first associated with rites in honor of the gods, were no less intimately and realistically the concern of men. The Roman religion was of a practical, contractual nature, and games were often promised in advance to secure supernatural aid; again, they were an honor paid to the gods for having favored man's success in some past event. A game, vowed in connection with particular events, might become a regularly established festival, ludus sollemnis. Thus, Lucius Tarquinius is said to have celebrated games with unusual cost and glory—after having got more booty by taking Apiolae than was anticipated—and vowed "during a battle" the building of a temple to Jupiter.[133] This, according to traditional accounts, was the beginning of the Ludi Romani. Livy tells of a marvelous warning, on one occasion, that the city would be endangered unless the Great Games were repeated on a magnificent scale; and the Senate decreed the celebration.[134] Camillus vowed a celebration of the Great Games if Veii were captured.[135] The Capitoline Games were ordered in honor of Jupiter, when the city was restored after the Gauls' invasion.[136] At the close of the third century B.C., the consuls were ordered to celebrate certain games, which had been vowed, prior to setting out for war, in order that the gods might be favorably inclined to their efforts.[137] Scipio offered sacrifices and games to the deities for victory in Africa.[138] Augustus founded the Actian Festival in honor of his victory at Actium, 31 B.C.[139] Games might also be given simply to secure some desideratum of a personal nature, or as a gesture of politeness, as when Nero gave games and an animal hunt at the circus so that Claudius, his adoptive father, might have health.[140] Such instances of games given and promised for some return might be multiplied at great length.[141]

The ludi and fasti of the Romans were also associated with religious rites in celebration of the beginning and end of life, as were many games of the Greeks and various primitive peoples. Roman funerals, of the upper class at least, were

---

[132] De Spectaculis, 5; Friedländer: op. cit., II, 1; Sandys: Companion to Latin Studies, pp. 501 f.; Fowler: op. cit., p. 285; Johnston: op. cit., p. 244; McDaniel: Roman Private Life, pp. 147 f.
[133] Livy, I, 35; Cicero: Republic, II, 20; Sandys: op. cit., p. 503; Fowler: op. cit., p. 291.
[134] Bk. II, 36–7.
[135] Ibid., V, 19; Plutarch: Camillus, 5.
[136] Livy, V, 50.
[137] Ibid., XXX, 27.
[138] Appian: Punic Wars, 135.
[139] Dio, LI, 1, 18.
[140] Suetonius: Nero, 7; Dio, LXI, 33.
[141] Livy, IV, 35; VI, 42; VII, 11, 15; Suetonius: Augustus, 23; Ammianus, XXI, 10, 2.

generally marked with much pomp and luxury;[142] so, too, were birthdays. The provision of games and feasts was an item of great expense. For the wealthy the giving of games was a means of proving their financial claim to respect in a money-minded world and cultivating popular good will toward themselves.

Funeral games in honor of Anchises were credited to the very origin of Rome by Virgil: on the ninth morning, weather permitting, contests in the racing of galleys, running, darts, archery, boxing, were to be run off.[143] Down through the centuries funeral games were celebrated, sometimes in honor of private persons, more often for great men of state or their kin. The three sons of Lepidus, augur and twice consul, gave funeral games with twenty-two pairs of gladiators for three days in the forum.[144] When Sextus had been executed (35 B.C.), Caesar gave games in honor of the event, perhaps with mixed motives; again, in honor of his daughter's memory, Caesar shattered precedent by giving a gladiatorial exhibit and a feast.[145] Funeral games were held in Caesar's honor at his death, and a herald recited a Senate decree; at the dedication of his shrine, there were contests of all kinds, animals were slain, and the Troy game was exhibited.[146] Augustus gave gladiatorial games at the death of Agrippa.[147] Sejanus' overthrow and death was to be celebrated with annual horse races and beast hunts.[148] The tribunes gave voluntary games in honor of Augustus' death.[149] Caligula dedicated the shrine of Augustus with many attendant spectacles, and arranged annual funeral games in the circus in his mother's honor.[150] Claudius, though noted for moderation in some respects, honored Livia, his grandmother, with equestrian games and ordered her deification.[151]

Gladiatorial combats came to be common in connection with the Ludi Novemdiales, games given on the ninth day after the burial of the dead. Livy says the practice began about the beginning of the wars with Carthage, when D. Junius Brutus exhibited gladiators (264 B.C.) in honor of his dead father.[152] Cicero, as has been noted, disapproved of them in the instance of Milo, and one would judge, in general.[153] Pliny, however, is full of praise for Maximus because he promised to give gladiatorial games honoring his deceased wife.[154]

---

[142] Friedländer: op. cit., II, 210 ff.
[143] Aeneid, V, 58–71.
[144] Livy, XXIII, 30.
[145] Suetonius: Julius, 26; Dio, XLIX, 18.
[146] Suetonius: Julius, 84; Dio, LI, 22.
[147] Dio, LIV, 29.
[148] Ibid., LVIII, 12.
[149] Tacitus: Annals, I, 15.
[150] Dio, LIX, 7; Suetonius: Caligula, 15.
[151] Dio, LX, 5.
[152] Livy, summary XVI; XXIII, 30; Ausonius, VII, 23.
[153] To Quintus, III, 8 and 9.
[154] Letters, VI, 34.

Horace says that Staberius would have the heirs exhibit one hundred pairs of gladiators at his funeral feast.[155]

The celebration of the beginning of the life process is a ubiquitous practice; in Rome, it was frequently carried to great extremes. Epicurus desired his birth-day to be celebrated after his death; and so it was.[156] In the case of great folk, games had some place in such celebrations. The aediles gave circus games, and slaughtered wild beasts on Augustus' birthday (20 B.C.); Antony's son celebrated it with games (13 B.C.); and it seems to have continued as a regular annual performance, the Augustalia being first observed according to a decree in 11 B.C.[157] Tiberius was unwilling to accept many honors, but he permitted his birth date, which came at the time of the Plebeian Games, to be honored by the addition of a two-horse chariot race.[158] Claudius gave Circensian Games in honor of the birthdays of Drusus and Antonia, his father and mother, but is said to have refused such an honor for his own.[159] Nero welcomed a new daughter, Augusta, decreeing games and other rites in honor of her birth.[160] The birthday of Vitellius was celebrated magnificently with gladiatorial exhibi-tions.[161] Also at the adoption of children, games were sometimes given in cele-bration of the event.[162]

THE CHIEF FESTIVALS AND THEIR INCREASE  The Romans com-monly credited the earliest sacerdotal games to the time of Romulus and Numa. Livy says that games in honor of Neptunus Equestris took place at a festival, the Consualia, arranged by Romulus, at which the Romans acquired wives and doubled the city population.[163] Of the oldest festivals, the Equirria, in honor of Mars, was celebrated on February 27 and March 14; and the Con-sualia, a harvest festival, on August 21 and December 15. The Equirria occu-pied a place in the calendar just prior to the opening of a new year of military operations. To this Ovid alludes, saying: "And now two nights of the second month are left, and Mars urges on the swift steeds yoked to his chariot." [164]

It is commonly accepted that the origin of games at Rome goes back to bor-rowings from Etruria. The Romans themselves had a tradition that linked

[155] Satires, II, 3.
[156] Friedländer: op. cit., III, 310.
[157] Dio, LIV, 8, 26, 34; LV, 6.
[158] Suetonius: Tiberius, 26; Dio, LVIII, 12.
[159] Dio, LX, 5.
[160] Tacitus: Annals, XV, 23.
[161] Tacitus: Histories, II, 95.
[162] Spartianus: Hadrian, 23.
[163] Livy, I, 9, 13; Cicero: Republic, II, 7; Plutarch: Romulus, 14; Tertullian: De Spectaculis, 5; Ausonius, VII, 23.
[164] Fasti, II, 856 et seq.; Fowler: op. cit., p. 300; Sandys: op. cit., p. 503.

both Greece and Etruria with the beginning of the Ludi Romani. According to tradition, Lucius Tarquinius, the son of Demaratus, a refugee from Corinth, and a Tarquinian mother, was chosen King and founded the Great Games. Livy says that the games were constituted of equestrian events and boxing, horses and boxers being brought from Etruria. Tarquin, moreover, by this account, was credited with laying out the Circus Maximus, where the games were thereafter held annually.[165]

During the days of provincial simplicity, a few festivals, each lasting a day at a time, sufficed for the Roman people. But increased fears, uncertainties, and tensions of the Carthaginian wars appear to have been responsible, in some measure, for the introduction of many new celebrations; and the increase of wealth and leisure, arising from victory, occasioned a vast expansion both in the number of festivals and the days allotted to each.[166] The Ludi Plebeii, of ancient but uncertain origin, paralleling in many ways the Ludi Romani, are believed to have been instituted between 293 and 220 B.C.; after the latter date they were celebrated as a public festival in the Circus Flaminius. The Ludi Cereales were also ancient, perhaps as old as the Plebeian Games, or a little less, but apparently were not fully established before 202.[167] The Ludi Apollinares were begun in 212 B.C., and in 208 became a regular, permanent festival.[168] The Ludi Megalenses, in honor of Magna Mater, were instituted in 204; the Ludi Florales were first celebrated in 240 or 238 B.C. at the dedication of the temple of Flora, and became a fixed festival in 173. The Ludi Victoriae, honoring Sulla's success at the Colline Gate, dated from 82 B.C.; and Ludi Victoriae Caesaris were first celebrated at the opening of the temple of Venus Genetrix in 46 B.C.[169]

The days devoted to these festivals varied from time to time, and extraordinary games were often added. On the calendar of festivals, however, at the end of the Republic, the following assignments of time had been made: Ludi Romani, September 4–19 (sixteen, after Caesar's death); Ludi Plebeii, November 4–17 (fourteen); Ludi Cereales, April 12–19 (eight); Ludi Apollinares, July 6–13 (eight); Ludi Megalenses, April 4–10 (seven); Ludi Florales, April 28–May 3 (six); Sulla's Ludi Victoriae, October 26–November 1 (seven); Caesar's Ludi Victoriae, July 20–30 (eleven). Of the sixty-six days (omitting the games for Caesar's victories) there were fourteen days given to races; two

[165] Livy, I, 35; Cicero: Republic, II, 34; Fell: Etruria and Rome, p. 76; supra, pp. 486 f.
[166] Ihne: op. cit., II, 473; Fowler: op. cit., pp. 298 f.
[167] Livy, xxx, 39.
[168] Ibid., xxv, 12; xxvi, 23; xxvii, 23.
[169] Friedlaender: "Die Spiele," Marquardt, Römische Staatsverwaltung, III, 498 ff.; Fowler: The Roman Festivals of the Period of the Republic, pp. 69 f., 72 ff., 91 ff., 179 ff., 252; Sandys: op. cit., pp. 504 f.

to judging race horses; two for sacrifice; and forty-eight for theatrical entertainment.[170]

*Ludi Saeculares*,[171] a three-day-and-night celebration, derived from Etruscan and Greek sources, and associated with penitence and purification for offenses against the gods, were first celebrated in 348 B.C., it is now believed;[172] in 249 B.C., while the Romans were engaged in the Carthaginian struggle, they were repeated and were vowed every hundred years thereafter. A dispute arose, however, as to the correct time for repetition, and this, combined with other factors, made their recurrence irregular. Thus the next repetition came in 146 B.C., not in 149, and the games that would properly have fallen in 46 B.C. were omitted because of civil war. Augustus revived the festival in 17 B.C. Claudius, finding fault with Augustus' calculation, celebrated them in 47 A.D., the eight-hundredth centennial of Rome's founding; but Domitian, repeating them forty-one years later (88), kept to the reckoning of Augustus. Antoninus Pius again celebrated the *saeculum* in 148; Severus, in 204; and Philippus, in 248.[173]

To the *ludi* of Republican days were added many new ones. After victory at Actium, Augustus founded Nicopolis near-by, and established a quadrennial festival, with musical, gymnastic, equestrian, and naval contests in honor of the event.[174] *Ludi Augustales* (19 B.C.) honored the return of Augustus to Rome, became a ten-day festival (October 3–12), and were still celebrated in the fourth century; *Ludi Natalicii*, first performed voluntarily for many years, were established permanently (8 B.C.) to honor his birthday with circus games.[175] Numerous other festivals celebrated the natal days of emperors, and became permanent if they were deified; nineteen of them were still commemorated in the middle of the fourth century. *Ludi Martiales*, instituted at the dedication of the Temple of Mars (2 B.C.), were still being held in the fourth century.[176] Annual circus games were first added (45 B.C.) to the Parilia, an ancient shepherds' festival of springtime, celebrated on April 21 as Rome's birthday. They were soon neglected, however, until Hadrian revived them; thence they continued till the fifth century.[177] The Neronia, a quinquennial

---

170 Friedländer: *Roman Life and Manners*, II, 11.
171 A *saeculum*, a hundred years, or one hundred and ten by another account, was held to be the longest human life span.
172 Taylor: "New Light on the History of the Secular Games," *Am. Jour. Philol.*, LV, 101–20.
173 Suetonius: *Augustus*, 31; *Claudius*, 21; *Vitellius*, 2; *Domitian*, 4; Dio, LIV, 18; Tacitus: *Annals*, XI, 11; Marquardt: *Römische Staatsverwaltung*, III, 385 ff.; Sandys: *op. cit.*, pp. 111 f., 507.
174 Suetonius: *Augustus*, 18; Dio, LI, 1; LIII, 1.
175 Dio, LIV, 10, 34; LV, 6; LVI, 29, 46; Suetonius: *Augustus*, 57.
176 Dio, LV, 10.
177 Plutarch: *Romulus*, 12; Dio, XLIII, 42; XLV, 6; Marquardt: *op. cit.*, III, 207 f.

festival in imitation of Greek contests, established by Nero (60), consisted of athletic, musical, and equestrian events.[178] Though neglected after his death, the Neronian festival was revived by Gordian III in 243. Domitian established the great Capitoline Games, a quinquennial festival in honor of Jupiter Capitolinus (86 A.D.), which included musical, gymnastic, and equestrian features.[179] Victories over the Persians, Goths, Parthians, and other peoples gave rise to ludi of some significance, but fleeting by comparison with the permanence of ancient festivals. Dio notes, for example, that the Ludi Parthici continued for a while after Trajan's death, but were later abolished.[180]

Festival days increased during the Empire; those having games numbered 87 at the time of Tiberius; in the reign of Marcus Aurelius there were 135; and in the middle of the fourth century there were 175. This takes no account of those that were of a special character. At the latter date, ten days were given to gladiatorial combats, sixty-four to the circus, and one hundred and one to theatrical entertainment. Celebrations were often continued by artificial light; sometimes they lasted the entire night.[181]

To these generous assignments for festivals the Romans connived to add many more. According to an ancient, superstitious custom, games had to be repeated in case anything out of harmony with usual procedure occurred; in later times, to extend the holiday, such irregularities were committed purposely and a repetition was then demanded—even as often as ten times. This abuse became so great that Claudius decreed that, in case of a repetition, equestrian contests should last only one day; and he commonly prevented any repetition.[182]

Special occasions frequently called forth unheard of prodigality in spectacles added to the regular calendar. Thus Titus dedicated the Colosseum, the Flavian Amphitheater, with a hundred days' display of sea battles, gladiatorial combats, and an exhibition of five thousand animals in a single day; [183] and Trajan, returning to Rome (107), celebrated his Dacian exploits for one hundred and twenty-three days, slaying over eleven thousand animals, and employing ten thousand gladiators.[184]

Numerous Ludi Privati, given at funerals or in connection with various special events, were open only to particular elements of the population. The Ludi Palatini, given by Livia in honor of Augustus (14 A.D.), were probably

---

[178] Suetonius: Nero, 12; Tacitus: Annals, XIV, 20; Dio, LXII, 21.
[179] Suetonius: Domitian, 4.
[180] Dio, LXIX, 2.
[181] Friedländer: Roman Life and Manners, II, 12 ff.
[182] Dio, LX, 6.
[183] Suetonius: Titus, 7.
[184] Dio, LXVIII, 15.

open only to senators.[185] Also private or semiprivate, perhaps, were the Juvenalia, provided by Nero at the first shaving of his beard, though Dio speaks of the exhibition before the populace and the embarrassment it occasioned; and the various Circensian Games in which Caligula, Caracalla, Commodus, Elagabalus, and Nero took part.[186]

Besides inaugurating numerous new celebrations and increasing the amount of time given to games in connection with the older religious festivals, the Romans brought under their aegis, or actually transferred to Rome, certain Greek festivals. Sulla took the Olympic festival to Rome (80 B.C.). The Augustalia at Naples (1 B.C.) were patterned after the Olympian festival of Greece. Domitian celebrated the Panathenaea with great magnificence.[187] Domitian's Capitoline Games were called Olympian, as were certain other festivals in various parts of the Empire.

THE ENDS AND THE MEANS  Admission to public *ludi* was free, but the wealth to pay for them came indirectly from the people themselves. In early days of simplicity funds were provided from the treasury. Livy mentions games given by the Plebeian aediles (295 B.C.) out of fines levied on farmers of the pastures; again, in 209 B.C., games of a splendid character, considering the circumstances of the day, were given by the Plebeian aediles with money derived from fines.[188] To 217 B.C., 200,000 *asses* were allotted for the *Ludi Romani;* then, as times were troubled, an assignment of 333,333⅓ *asses* was made for them.[189] Only rarely was any subscription received from individual citizens, though this was done in 186 B.C.[190]

The magnificence of games in the late Republic, and their increase already noted, encouraged, if it did not compel, a change in the method of support. If the allotment of public funds was inadequate to provide shows commensurate with an official's ambition to make a good display and please his followers, he supplemented it out of his private funds, or by contributions received from others more or less voluntarily. Gradually, the competition on the part of aediles, eager for higher office, grew to such proportions that it was recognized as pernicious, and some effort was made to restrain it. Livy mentions an act of the Senate (179 B.C.) which directed candidates not to solicit, order, or receive contributions for the games.[191] The gesture was at best only of momentary effect; the practice grew, and aediles and others learned rather well

---

185 *Ibid.*, LVI, 46.
186 Suetonius: *Caligula*, 54; Dio, LXII, 19; LXXIII, 17; LXXVIII, 9–10; Lampridius: *Commodus*, 2; *Elagabalus*, 23; Tacitus: *Annals*, XIV, 14.
187 Dio, LXVII, 1; Gardiner: *Greek Athletic Sports and Festivals*, pp. 165, 169.
188 Livy, X, 23; XXVII, 6.
189 *Ibid.*, XXII, 10.
190 Pliny: *Natural History*, XXXIII, 48.
191 Livy, XL, 44.

how they might spend lavishly on games for their own benefit, squeezing the money out of Italian allies and provincial subjects. Cicero speaks of the "heavy and iniquitous tribute" levied upon Asia for games.[192] He, himself, who had put on several shows while in office, including the *Ludi Romani*, was inclined to agree with Aristotle that such extravagant expenditures were a waste of wealth, pleasing only to the weakest and worst elements of society. Milo he thought mad, to give games costing 1,000,000 sesterces; nevertheless, "the very best men"—Crassus, Hortensius, Lentulus—had to provide them; Pompey's shows, he says, were the most luxurious Rome had ever seen.[193]

What Cicero knew, however, was but a harbinger of more colossal things to come. Caesar was "unsparing" in his expenditures, says Plutarch, but really purchased very cheaply thereby "things of the highest value." Before he had any public office at all, he was 1,300 talents in debt; and, during his aedileship, he put on gladiatorial and other shows so magnificent that the memory of his predecessor's generosity was completely erased from the popular mind. As a result, the people were zealous to offer him new offices and honors; but some criticized him for spending so lavishly on games, and said he had raised the funds unjustly.[194]

Though nothing like a complete picture of expenditure for games can be gained either for Republic or Empire, it is certain that costs mounted to ruinous heights, both as respects many individuals and the public treasury. Even in the middle of the first century, some public men resigned their offices because of the expense of giving *ludi*; many may have left public life for this reason.[195] One's rich friends, of course, might enable him to "stay." Trajan gave Hadrian 2,000,000 sesterces (about $80,000) to aid in giving games during his praetorship; the father of Symmachus laid out about $400,000 for games when the young man was praetor.[196] Justinian is said to have spent close to $1,000,000 on games and other donations when Consul in 521; but there were few who could afford such honorary amusements. Expenses were ultimately so onerous that candidates had to be compelled to stand for office, and they faced the possibility of having to pay all the expenses of games if they sought to evade these public burdens.[197]

As for extravagant public expenditure for games, though there is evidence that the evil was understood, it continued without more than momentary

[192] To Quintus, I, 1, 9; Friedländer: *Roman Life and Manners*, II, 9; Ihne: *op. cit.*, IV, 154 f.
[193] Cicero: *Offices*, II, 16; To Quintus, III, 8 and 9.
[194] Plutarch: *Caesar*, 5; *Dio*, XLIII, 24.
[195] *Dio*, LX, 27; Dill: *Nero to Aurelius*, 71.
[196] Spartianus: *Hadrian*, 3; Dill: *Last Century*, p. 150.
[197] Friedländer: *Roman Life and Manners*, II, 11.

abatement under the Empire. Augustus was advised by Maecenas that cities should not be allowed to waste their resources on a great number and variety of games. They ought to have spectacles, to be sure, but in moderation, and not to the extent of destroying the estates of private citizens and of strangers residing in them.[198] Despite such advice, Augustus left an impressive record of games given on his own account and for others. The victory games alone may have cost as much as 20,000,000 HS. Frank [199] estimates that "practically all the towns of Italy" spent "at least 6,000 sesterces" every year from the treasury; magistrates commonly spent more than that, making perhaps as much as 14,000 sesterces expended each year. In 51 A.D. the state expenditures had risen to 760,000 sesterces for the Ludi Romani; for the Ludi Plebeii, 600,000; and the Ludi Apollinares, which cost only 12,000 asses in 212 B.C., had risen to 380,000 sesterces. The Ludi Augustales, just recently established, cost only 10,000 sesterces. Appropriations from the treasury for games were about 2,000,000 HS in 51 A.D.[200] Caligula, who came to power with two to three billion or more sesterces in the treasury, was in dire straits within a year or two because of lavish expenses for all kinds of shows.[201]

Only occasionally were there serious, or temporarily successful, efforts at retrenchment. Tiberius was conspicuous because, in an age of reckless spending for such purposes, he never gave games himself, and sought to keep expenditures down by cutting the pay of actors and limiting definitely the number of pairs of gladiators that might be exhibited.[202] Claudius was somewhat restricted in his outlays for a time, since the treasury was empty, and his own wealth limited. Nevertheless, by confiscation of certain wealthy estates, he was able to make generous donations to the soldiers and to provide lavish games for the populace.[203] Nerva, who succeeded two lavish spenders, abolished many horse races and other spectacles to cut down expenses; and Antoninus Pius regulated expenditures for games, establishing a maximum limit.[204] The restraint of Antoninus and Marcus was sharply offset by the spendthrift career of Commodus; after him, Pertinax sought to recoup the depleted treasury by selling statues, arms, chariots, horses, and other accouterments that had been collected. The taxation and extortions of Caracalla's brief reign are reflected in Dio's bitter plaint: ". . . we constructed amphitheatres and race-courses wherever he spent the winter or expected to spend it . . . they were all

[198] Dio, LII, 30.
[199] Op. cit., v, 14, 100 f. HS, sestertius, 2½ asses, ¼ denarius.
[200] Ibid., v, 5; Friedlaender: "Die Spiele," loc. cit., III, 488.
[201] Suetonius: Caligula, 37; Dio, LIX, 2.
[202] Suetonius: Tiberius, 34, 47.
[203] Suetonius: Claudius, 9, 21; Tacitus: Annals, XII, 41; Frank: op. cit., v, 42, n. 21.
[204] Dio, LXVIII, 2, 3; Capitolinus: Antoninus Pius, 12.

promptly demolished, the sole reason for their being built . . . being, apparently, that we might become impoverished." [205]

What was the use, the purpose, of this expenditure? Regardless of original ends, which may be only somewhat vaguely perceived, it is evident that in later historic times the exhibition of games became an important agency of social manipulation: a satisfaction of a sense of propriety to some, as conformance with established practice is apt to be; a sure way to win popularity and outright support of the public; a device to keep men occupied; a means of sounding public sentiment; an auditorium where the people could be informed more or less directly of things past and things to come; a place where one might see and be seen. A difference of some importance is to be noted between the earlier games and the later: the former generally were used to inspire, encourage, and solidify the people and lead them to action; the latter served chiefly to lull them to sleep, that they might not be too much concerned with matters of more moment. Romans who once gave commands, says Juvenal, now want just two things: "Bread and Games." [206] To amuse and distract the popular mind became a "prime political necessity." [207] Fronto praised Trajan's interest in actors, stage, amphitheater, and circus; for he knew that "the Roman People" were "held fast by two things" above all others—"the corn-dole and the shows." [208]

How widely and well this general principle was comprehended may be judged from events cited and comments made by ancient authors. The importance of games to ambitious young men is revealed in Rufus Caelius' complaint at the "sublime impudence" of someone bringing an accusation against him at the very moment when his games are at their height.[209] Cicero's letters to Atticus, his brother Quintus, Curio, and others show how well he understood the relation between politics and games. Though he advised Curio to win political distinction by his talents rather than by giving games, he himself gave them as a political necessity, and knew their value; indeed, he felt a certain propriety about giving them, for, as he said on one occasion, "it is a sad disgrace not to preside at the games." [210] Nevertheless, when Rufus Caelius, exceedingly grateful to Curio for beasts from Africa, asked Cicero repeatedly to secure animals from his provincial area, Cicero found it hard to bear, and wrote to Atticus: "[It will be] a blot on my escutcheon that the people of Cibyra

[205] Dio, LXXVIII, 9, 7; LXXIV, 5. Trans. by E. Cary. The Loeb Classical Library. Quoted by permission of Harvard University Press, Cambridge, Mass.
[206] Satire x, 80.
[207] Lot: The End of the Ancient World, p. 178; Friedländer: Roman Life and Manners, II, 1 f.
[208] Fronto, II, 215–7.
[209] Cicero: To His Friends, VIII, 12.
[210] To Atticus, xv, 10, 12, 29; xvi, 4 and 5; To His Friends, II, 3.

should have a public hunt during my governorship."²¹¹ Caesar, wiser than Crassus, who lost standing because he gave no athletic contests for his troops, broke all records with games and feasts to win popular support.²¹²

At the games of the circus was the most appropriate place to render honors to public men. Crowns were offered to Caesar at the Lupercalia; as an honor, he was to "give the signal at all the games in the Circus," and have a special day of his own at all gladiatorial combats in Rome and all Italy; later, he was honored by having his statue and a chariot in a procession at the circus games.²¹³

Games were given to influence public opinion, to honor individual men, to win public attention for them, and to court their favor. Even while very young, many began to cultivate popular opinion. Claudius sought to commend the baby Britannicus to the attention of soldiers and the people at the games; and Silanus was placed before the public eye by "triumphal distinctions" and "a magnificent gladiatorial show." ²¹⁴ Circus games were given to win popular favor for young Nero, and to tell the people by a token who was next to hold sway over them.²¹⁵ Galba began his career by celebrating the Floralia during his praetorship with an exhibition of elephants walking the rope.²¹⁶ Vespasian, though said to have had little enjoyment in combats of armed men, often gave beast hunts in order to win favor: while praetor, he sought the good will of Gaius, and asked that "special games" be arranged because of the Emperor's victory in Germany; to show regard for Barbillus, he allowed Ephesians to hold Sacred Games, an indulgence he granted no other city.²¹⁷ Permission to give Sacred Games was a privilege sometimes bestowed on a city as a mark of favor.²¹⁸

Augustus adopted the political devices of his Republican forerunners, and decided on entertaining the people as a part of public policy—one that was to last to the very end of the Empire. His celebration in honor of completing the Temple of Venus was intended to "win the favour of the populace." ²¹⁹ Though the emperors set out to rule by catering to the crowd, it was sometimes doubtful as to who were rulers and who were ruled, for with all power in their hands, they were nevertheless compelled to conciliate the public. Caligula, it was said, was "ruled" by charioteers, gladiators, and actors; his tactics and threats, and his expressed wish that the Roman people had just one neck,

---

²¹¹ To Atticus, VI, 1. Trans. by E. O. Winstedt. The Loeb Classical Library. Quoted by permission of Harvard University Press, Cambridge, Mass.; To His Friends, VIII, 4 and 8.
²¹² Plutarch: Crassus, 17; Caesar, 5, 55; Appian: Civil Wars, II, 102; Dio, XLIII, 19, 42.
²¹³ Plutarch: Caesar, 61; Dio, XLIII, 14, 45; XLIV, 6.
²¹⁴ Suetonius: Claudius, 27; Tacitus: Annals, XII, 3.
²¹⁵ Tacitus: Annals, XII, 41.
²¹⁶ Suetonius: Galba, 6.
²¹⁷ Suetonius: Vespasian, 2; Dio, LXV, 9, 15.
²¹⁸ Dio, LI, 20.
²¹⁹ Ibid., XLV, 6.

were unusual.[220] Many rulers showed exceedingly great care about the impression they might make on the public mind. Tiberius attended games, though he did not like them, and threw out darts at a boar, hoping to hide his weakened condition from the public.[221] Augustus was fearful of letting Claudius view the games from the imperial box, lest something might occur to render both "him and us" ridiculous in the eyes of the people, who were very ready "to scoff at and deride such things"; and Claudius himself was zealous in showing by applause his respect for the games given by the magistrates.[222] Titus revealed his desire to please the public, telling them to ask what they wished, for he would give the games as they liked, not to suit himself.[223] Hadrian sought to please the populace with Pyrrhic dances and by frequent attendance at gladiatorial shows; and he cultivated Athenian good will by visiting and judging their games.[224] Though Commodus offended some, as did Caligula, he doubtless gained a certain popularity by his exploits in the arena. Justinian won popular favor at once by giving lavish beast hunts and chariot races. Barbarian kings, when they had conquered Rome, gave games and then doubtless truly conquered the hearts of Romans.[225]

[220] Ibid., LIX, 5, 13; Suetonius: Caligula, 26–7.
[221] Suetonius: Tiberius, 72.
[222] Suetonius: Claudius, 4, 12.
[223] Suetonius: Titus, 8.
[224] Spartianus: Hadrian, 13, 19; Dio, LXIX, 16.
[225] Lot: op. cit., pp. 178, 255 f.

# 26

# CIRCUS AND ARENA

Certain limitations on games, unknown in the last mad years of the Republic, were instituted under the Empire. Augustus is said to have placed all festivals in charge of the praetors (22 B.C.), but games continued to be given in the early Empire by the old officials, the Roman and Megalesian under the curule aediles, and the Plebeian Games under the Plebeian aediles.[1] The emperors, of course, gave the public many special shows, particularly gladiatorial contests, which became practically an imperial monopoly.

Of all free public entertainments the greatest favorite was unquestionably the Circensian Games. While chariot races were the most important attraction of the circus, certain other equestrian events, notably the game of *Troia*, the *Pyrrhicha militaris*, and trick riding, were included. These were the most ancient as well as best loved, running back to the dim days of legendary Rome. Romulus, according to tradition, had held a horse race at which the Sabine girls, who came to look on, were seized as wives.[2] Circus games were generally accepted as of Etruscan origin. Livy credited the first design of the circus to Tarquin who sent for horses and boxers from Etruria.[3] The racecourse on the low-lying level ground between the Aventine and the Palatine, commonly known as the Circus Maximus, was the largest in the city. A second Circus, the Flaminian, was built about 220 B.C.,[4] and a third by Caligula and Nero. Outside the city there were three others: that of the *Fratres Arvales*, on the Via Portuensis; the Circus Maxentius, on the Via Appia, built in 309; and the third, more distant from the city, at Bovillae.[5]

---

[1] Dio's Roman History, LII, 30; LIV, 2; Homo: Roman Political Institutions from City to State, p. 312; Cary: History of Rome, p. 570.
[2] Livy, I, 9, 13; Florus: Epitome of Roman History, I, 1.
[3] Bk. I, 35; Tacitus: Annals, XIV, 21; Dennis: Cities and Cemeteries of Etruria, II, 175.
[4] Livy, summary XX.
[5] Johnston: The Private Life of the Romans, pp. 254 f.

The vast number of people who could be accommodated in these circuses, all in easy reach of Rome, is a fair index of the popularity of the races. At Bovillae were places for about 8,000; the Circus of Maxentius would seat about 23,000. The Circus Maximus was enlarged from time to time, and figures varied accordingly: it would seat 260,000 at the time of Caesar, according to Pliny; and had a capacity of 385,000 in the fourth century.[6] If this vast assembly of Rome's population suggests a degree of democratic unity, it is not well to stress the point too far; though citizens and even others entered without charge, care was taken to separate the classes from the masses. In 5 A.D. senators watched the circus separately; knights, too, sat apart from the populace, and this social distinction continued. Augustus is reported to have had a common soldier ousted from a seat which he had taken in the fourteen rows.[7] Women attended as well as men, sat with them, and were among the most enthusiastic supporters.[8] Much care was taken of the spectators' comfort. Caesar sheltered the audiences from the sun, and even covered the Forum and the Via Sacra from his house to the capitol with linen or silk.[9]

Devotion to the racecourse gained vogue rapidly during the first century of the Empire. When the Megalesian Games are beginning, says Juvenal, "all Rome" is at the circus, and if the Green (the favorite faction of the day) should lose, Rome would think it as serious as another battle of Cannae.[10] To see the races once, Pliny thought, should suffice forever. Why should thousands of grown men, some even men of character, be so childish as to watch over and over again the same running horses and men standing in chariots? [11] But Pliny is a rare bird. Ammianus and Symmachus testify to the rapt attention still accorded the circus in the fourth century, and the strenuous efforts made by the rich to keep alive the splendid spectacles.[12] As he leaves Rome in 417, Namatianus cannot forget the cheers for the winning horse and driver in the Circus Maximus. Even Christians, despite their protests against worldly pleasures, were sometimes among the throng of spectators and even among the drivers. In the middle of the sixth century, Totila the Goth regaled the conquered with races.[13]

---

[6] Pliny: Natural History, xxxvi, 24; Friedlaender: "Die Spiele," Marquardt, Römische Staatsverwaltung, iii, 506; Johnston: op. cit., pp. 262 f.; Fowler: Social Life at Rome in the Age of Cicero, p. 301.

[7] Dio, lv, 22; Tacitus: Annals, xv, 32; Suetonius: Augustus, 14.

[8] Ovid: Art of Love, iii, 349 et seq.; The Amores, iii, 2; Juvenal: Satire xi, 202; Friedländer: Roman Life and Manners under the Early Empire, ii, 36.

[9] Pliny: Natural History, xix, 6; Dio, xliii, 24.

[10] Satire xi, 193 et seq.

[11] Pliny: Letters, ix, 6.

[12] Ammianus Marcellinus, xxviii, 4, 29; Symmachus: Epistulae, ii, 78; Dill: Roman Society in the Last Century of the Western Empire, pp. 150 ff.

[13] Friedländer: Roman Life and Manners, ii, 29, 33; Showerman: Rome and the Romans, p. 321.

Many factors doubtless encouraged the increased devotion to the circus, but one of the most important was the lead taken by the omnipotent heads of state. Nero talked constantly of horses and chariots from his earliest years, appeared as a charioteer in public, and was so enamored of horseflesh that he decorated the most famous animals that had passed their prime, and gave them maintenance allowances. At the Olympic Games he is said to have driven a ten-horse team and was crowned victor, though he had fallen from his chariot.[14] Vitellius wore the Blue uniform and curried the horses; Domitian supported the circus enthusiastically, and added two new factions.[15] Though Marcus Aurelius sought to keep aloof, his colleague, Verus, was a partisan of the "Greens," and built a tomb for one of their famous horses, the "Flyer." [16] Commodus had racecourses built everywhere he went, was a follower of the Blue, and drove chariots in public.[17] Sardanapalus was fond of driving the chariot, and was a wearer of the Green.[18]

Another important factor in fostering interest in the races was the organization of the drivers into different factions. Indeed, it appears that the colors of these factions rather than the race itself, or the horse, or the driver, were the objects of devotion on the part of the myriads that frequented the circus. Pliny thought that if in the middle of a race one color were to be exchanged with another, the applause of the partisans would likewise shift instantaneously; so great was the influence of "one cheap tunic." [19] The importance of the factions was not so great at the end of the Republic, but it grew rapidly under the stimulus given by enthusiastic headline supporters, such as Caligula, Nero, Vitellius, Commodus, and others. When first heard of, there were but two colors, the Red and the White; to these were added the Green and the Blue. Domitian created two more, the Gold and the Purple, but these did not last long.[20] In the third century the factions seem to have had less significance than before, but the Greens and the Blues had still enough influence to stir their followers to violence in the first half of the sixth century. Justinian was scarcely able to cope effectively with the rioting of 532, partly, doubtless, because he and Theodora were both partisans. He may well have wished that he had been taught by some wise preceptor, as was Aurelius, to be an adherent of neither Green nor Blue.[21]

Though emperors of more or less dubious character took part in the sports

---

[14] Dio, LXI, 6; LXII, 14–5, 20; LXIII, 1; Suetonius: Nero, 22.
[15] Suetonius: Domitian, 4, 7; Dio, LXIV, 5.
[16] Capitolinus: Verus, 6.
[17] Dio, LXXIII, 9, 10; LXXVII, 7; LXXVIII, 9, 10.
[18] Ibid., LXXX, 14, 15.
[19] Pliny: Letters, IX, 6.
[20] Suetonius: Caligula, 55; Vitellius, 7; Dio, LXVII, 4.
[21] The Meditations of the Emperor, I, 5; Gibbon: The Decline and Fall of the Roman Empire, III, 422 ff.; Friedländer: Roman Life and Manners, II, 28 ff.

of the circus, and thereby won some popularity with the lower sort, Rome generally disapproved of men of high rank participating in such public contests. In earlier days of the Republic, of course, men of standing had exhibited their horses; but racing had now become a professional game. Though Suetonius says that Caligula gave some games in which charioteers were all of senatorial rank,[22] they were almost always of foreign and slave extraction. Like their drivers, the horses, too, mostly came from abroad—Spain, Mauritania, Greece, Africa, and other provinces—and were selected for racing, fed and trained to that end by men who knew the racing game.[23] Games were provided for by men of wealth and high office, but they purchased the services of the factions, and dealt with the *domini factionum*, who attended to all detailed arrangements. These foreigners, slaves, and freedmen often gained wealth and fame, and their names were heralded abroad among the masses, as if they were truly as great as the greatest men Rome had ever known. Gambling flourished. Some of the charioteers had birds, daubed red or green according to their faction, ready to let loose to carry to gamblers the news of their victories as soon as they were won. Magic and superstition have since primitive times often been associated with games, and so it was at Rome. Many appear to have resorted to magic of various kinds, hoping to retard or accelerate appropriately the speed of the horses.[24]

The victories and rewards of certain drivers reached astronomical figures. Great sacks of gold awaited the winner of the chariot race, says Martial.[25] The drivers began young and were soon able to retire. Euprepes won 782 crowns, but was murdered, it was said, because of his conspicuous renown and his support of the wrong faction.[26] Diocles, from Spain, was driving a four-horse chariot at eighteen; he retired at forty-two, having won 1,462 of 4,257 races, and a total purse of 35,863,120 sesterces—worth perhaps from $1,500,000 to $2,000,000.[27] Other famous drivers were Thallus, rival of Diocles; Crescens, a famed driver of the "Blues"; and Scorpus, often named by Martial.[28]

A race began with the throwing of a white cloth by the *dator spectaculorum*, who presided in a box over the entrance opposite the triumphal gate. Below him, but unseen behind the doors of their stations, were the eager drivers and their nervous steeds. At the signal, the charioteers, numbering perhaps as many as a dozen, but often fewer, entered the racecourse, each from his individual

22 Suetonius: *Caligula*, 18.
23 Varro: *On Agriculture*, II, 7, 15–6.
24 Friedländer: *Roman Life and Manners*, II, 27, 34 f.; Fowler: *op. cit.*, p. 302; Davis: *A Day in Old Rome*, p. 387.
25 *Epigrams*, x, 74.
26 Dio, LXXVIII, 2.
27 Friedländer: *Roman Life and Manners*, II, 24; Johnston: *op. cit.*, pp. 267 f.
28 Bk. IV, 67; V, 25; X, 50, 53, 74.

stall to the right and the left of the *porta pompae*, the entrance gate for processions. Their teams, hitched to a light, low-slung chariot, might be of two, three, four, six, or even as many as ten horses; but the most common was the four-horse chariot. The drivers proceeded, at the signal, along one side of a centrally placed low barrier, the *spina*, made a rather sharp turn around the *meta* at the farther end of it, and returned on the other side to complete the lap. The winning color was the one which completed the prescribed number of laps and first crossed a chalk line,[29] fixed some little distance beyond the *meta*, clear of the space required by the turning racers. The winning chariot left by the triumphal gate, located at the end of the circus opposite the *carceres* whence the teams entered. Races were usually seven laps long, but Domitian reduced them to five, owing to a long program at his secular games.[30] To facilitate keeping count of the laps run, there were seven egg-shaped figures at one end of the *spina* and seven dolphins at the other; after a lap, one of each of these was taken down.[31] Widely variant estimates have been made as to the distance covered in the usual seven-lap race. Johnston's estimate is approximately 2.7 miles, if run in the Circus Maxentius; the Circus Maximus was about a hundred yards longer than that of Maxentius.[32] Success was determined partly by speed, but also by cleverness in deception of opponents and by skillful maneuvering, so as to spill them if need be, particularly at the dangerous turns. The number of races varied naturally with the period and the particular occasion. Twelve in a day were usual in the early Empire. Twenty-four were crowded into one day in Caligula's reign, and were common thereafter; and even more were reported.[33]

### GLADIATORIAL GAMES

Originating, as is commonly believed, in Etruria as rites in honor of the dead, gladiatorial contests first appeared at Rome in connection with the funeral of D. Junius Brutus' father in 264 B.C.[34] A few instances followed in the succeeding century, but in contrast with later times, they were all small. The games for Lepidus (216 B.C.) involved twenty-two pairs of fighters and lasted three days; those for Laevinus (200 B.C.) lasted four days, and there were twenty-five pairs of combatants. In honor of Licinius (183 B.C.) one hundred and twenty gladiators fought, and the celebration lasted three days. In 174 B.C. there were many gladiatorial games, but all were small, save those given by

29 Pliny: *Natural History*, xxxv, 58.
30 *Aulus Gellius, The Attic Nights*, iii, 10; Suetonius: *Domitian*, 4.
31 Livy, xli, 27, 6; Dio, xlix, 43.
32 Johnston: *op. cit.*, p. 257.
33 Friedlaender: "Die Spiele," *loc. cit.*, iii, 515.
34 Livy, summary xvi.

Flaminius in honor of his father, which lasted four days and engaged seventy-four swordsmen.[35] By the last century of the Republic such combats had become common; Caesar staged them in honor of his deceased daughter; even the parsimonious Tiberius gave games in honor of his father and grandfather.[36] According to Cicero, gladiatorial games were attended by all kinds of people; it was there that one could get a representative sampling of public opinion.[37]

Gladiatorial games were first given privately; in 105 B.C., however, they were given officially by the consuls; and in 42 B.C., they even took the place of other circus games.[38] Under the Empire such entertainments became extraordinarily common—some being fixed, others given irregularly on special occasions—and were soon practically an imperial monopoly. Augustus (22 B.C.) forbade the praetors to give gladiatorial combats save when the Senate decreed them, and then not more than twice a year nor with more than 120 men.[39] Caligula (39 A.D.) revived the practice of having two praetors named by lot to give gladiatorial games; though Claudius (41) commanded the praetors not to give the customary games for his preservation, he ordered the quaestors to give a gladiatorial exhibition instead of paving certain roads.[40] Dolabella proposed that gladiatorial shows be exhibited each year at the expense of the quaestors, but Nero relieved them of this burdensome requirement.[41] Domitian, in turn, revived the games by the quaestors, which had been given up for a time, and always attended them.[42] Various other acts reveal the government's rather erratic effort to control gladiatorial games. Nero decreed (57) that magistrates and procurators in a provincial government should not exhibit gladiators and beasts and give other entertainments; about the same time the Senate authorized Syracuse to exceed the prescribed number of gladiators in their show.[43] Such was the petty business of that body under Nero. Severus Alexander aimed to divide the gladiatorial games so as to spread them over all the months of the year, but his intent was not realized.[44] Not until 404 do we hear of the last gladiatorial combats at the great Flavian amphitheater.

Growing popularity of gladiatorial combats and an understanding of their use in gaining personal popularity may be read in the acts of leading men of the late Republic and the Empire. In some instances heads of the state actually took part in the combats of the arena. In Cicero's day the purchase of gladia-

[35] Ibid., XXIII, 30; XXXI, 50; XXXIX, 46; XLI, 28.
[36] Plutarch: Caesar, 55; Suetonius: Tiberius, 7.
[37] Publius Sextius, 50, 58.
[38] Dio, XLVII, 40; Friedlaender: "Die Spiele," loc. cit., III, 555.
[39] Dio, LIV, 2.
[40] Ibid., LIX, 14; LX, 5; Suetonius: Claudius, 24.
[41] Tacitus: Annals, XI, 22; XIII, 5.
[42] Suetonius: Domitian, 4.
[43] Tacitus: Annals, XIII, 31, 49.
[44] Lampridius: Severus Alexander, 43.

tors for political purposes had become a commonplace. Cicero relished the trick played by Milo on C. Cato, who had purchased a troop of fighters to act as a bodyguard; and to Atticus he wrote that Domitius' "popular gladiatorial games" would stand to his credit in the election. He felt a keen interest in Atticus' fine troop of gladiators who were "fighting splendidly," wanted to be kept informed about them, and was sure that, if Atticus wanted to hire them out, he could clear all expenses in just two shows. Again, he asked for "news day by day" of the gladiatorial games.[45] Caesar had a band of gladiators which still numbered 640 when the Senate issued a decree requiring a reduction. These he exhibited when aedile.[46] At Caesar's combined triumphs in 46 B.C. there were, among other spectacles, combats with one thousand foot soldiers on each side, and contests of cavalry with two hundred on each side.[47] Augustus gave gladiatorial shows eight times, employing ten thousand fighters, and used for them the Forum, Amphitheater, Circus, and the Saepta.[48] Drusus gloated over bloodshed; Caligula had twenty thousand gladiators in his training school, entertained the public with several gladiatorial games, and himself appeared as gladiator, using genuine weapons.[49] Caligula's intense preoccupation with gladiatorial contests and his unusual cruelties in connection with them must have attracted the closest attention of the audiences, even though they might feel revulsion at such extremes.[50] Claudius is said to have given gladiatorial games constantly, was especially well pleased when many men were destroyed, and enjoyed even the bloodiest spectacles at mealtime.[51] Vitellius' birthday was celebrated with gladiatorial combats of unrivaled brilliance.[52] Titus gained popularity by his gladiatorial shows, showed a personal liking for Thracian gladiators, and himself participated in a combat in heavy armor.[53] Domitian gave gladiatorial games nearly every year at his Alban estate.[54] Even excellent rulers, such as Trajan, took great delight in gladiatorial games; and Hadrian learned how to use the weapons of the gladiators.[55] Probably no ruler outdid Commodus in bloody sports; Dio says that he personally saw him slay animals and fight as a gladiator in the arena. At length, because of his extraordinary fondness for such performances, Commodus is said to have left the palace

[45] Letters to His Brother Quintus, II, 4; Letters to Atticus, IV, 4 a, 8, 16; XIII, 37.
[46] Suetonius: Julius, 10; Plutarch: Caesar, 5.
[47] Appian: Civil Wars, II, 102.
[48] Suetonius: Augustus, 43; Frank: An Economic Survey of Ancient Rome, V, 15; Johnston: op. cit., pp. 271 f.
[49] Tacitus: Annals, I, 76; Suetonius: Caligula, 18, 54; Pliny: Natural History, XI, 54; "20 pairs of gladiators."—Bostock and Riley, The Natural History of Pliny, III, 51.
[50] Suetonius: Caligula, 26–7, 35; Dio, LIX, 10.
[51] Dio, LX, 13, 17; LXI, 30.
[52] Tacitus: Histories, II, 95.
[53] Suetonius: Titus, 7–8; Dio, LXV, 15.
[54] Dio, LXVII, 1.
[55] Ibid., LXVIII, 10; Spartianus: Hadrian, 14.

to live at a gladiatorial school.[56] Kindred in spirit to Commodus were Antoninus and Geta, the sons of Severus, who made gladiators their closest friends.[57]

The growth of a love of gladiatorial fights is reflected in the changing attitude respecting participation in them by men of rank, and even by women. Such participation was sometimes voluntary; again, men and women were forced into combats against their will. In the day of Caesar a Praetorian, Leptinus, and a Senator, Calpenus, engaged in a public gladiatorial contest.[58] In 41 B.C. knights took part in slaying wild beasts in the circus at the *Ludi Apollinares*; shortly thereafter (38 B.C.) the Senate restrained one of its members from fighting, and sought to ban senators in general from fighting as gladiators.[59] A Senator, Quintus Vitellius, took part, however, in a combat at the dedication of Julius' shrine, 29 B.C.; and Augustus (11 A.D.) is said to have permitted knights to fight as gladiators, and even watched their contests, since it was impossible to enforce the law against them.[60] Tiberius again sought to discourage the practice, after one of the knights who had engaged in a combat was killed.[61] Caligula, on the contrary, caused many men of prominence to perish in gladiatorial games; and Nero compelled four hundred senators and six hundred knights to engage in them.[62]

Though Augustus would not allow women to view gladiatorial shows, save from the highest seats,[63] in the course of time they actually became contestants. Though a number of references to this development occur, it is impossible to say just how extensively women entered the arena. Statius speaks of women as a part of the pleasant, swiftly moving scene, the Emperor's Carnival: though by nature strangers to battle, "see how untiringly they essay the weapons of men." [64] Juvenal snarls at the women who are practicing the arts of the arena.[65] At the magnificent gladiatorial shows of Nero both men and women of the senatorial and equestrian orders went into the amphitheater; again, certain women, but not of any prominence, took part in slaughtering beasts at games given by Titus in 80 A.D.; and Domitian staged combats by women as well as by men.[66] The practice fluctuated from time to time, influenced, among other

---

[56] Dio, LXXIII, 17–9; LXXVIII, 6, 19; Friedländer: *Roman Life and Manners*, II, 17.
[57] Dio, LXXVII, 7.
[58] Suetonius: *Julius*, 39.
[59] Dio, XLVIII, 33, 43.
[60] Ibid., LI, 22; LV, 33; LVI, 25.
[61] Ibid., LVII, 14.
[62] Ibid., LIX, 13; Suetonius: *Nero*, 12.
[63] Suetonius: *Augustus*, 44.
[64] *Silvae*, I, 6.
[65] *Satire* VI, 246 et seq.
[66] Tacitus: *Annals*, XV, 32; Dio, LXII, 17; LXVI, 25; LXVII, 8; Suetonius: *Domitian*, 4.

things, by the attitude of those at the head of the state. In 200, a law sought to prohibit women, regardless of their origin, from taking part in single combats of the arena.[67]

Gladiatorial combats were first held in the forum and in the circus; but these were inadequately adapted to the purpose, and the growing popularity of such spectacles, in the late Republic, compelled the construction of new places of exhibition.[68] There was no amphitheater before Caesar's time, when Curio built one of wood. This remarkable structure was two large theaters, so built and poised that they could be turned on a pivot to face each other, thus forming an amphitheater. Due to cheap construction some of the wooden amphitheaters collapsed, as did that at Fidena (27 A.D.), in which fifty thousand were maimed or killed.[69] The first amphitheater of stone, built in 29 B.C. by Statilius Taurus, endured until the burning of Rome, when Nero constructed a new one of wood in the *Campus Martius*.[70] In 80 A.D., Titus finished the Flavian Amphitheater, or Colosseum, begun by Vespasian. This permanent edifice seated nearly ninety thousand spectators, and could accommodate the most stupendous shows imperial minds could imagine. Titus initiated the giant bowl with a spectacular hundred days of bloody battles.[71]

Gladiators came from several sources; they were, Cicero said, "either ruined men or barbarians." [72] First of all they were prisoners taken in war—Germans, Thracians, Gauls, Sarmatians, and others from the frontier struggles—who sometimes were given a chance at life by fighting in combats. In the late fourth century Symmachus secured a troop of Saxon gladiators. Soldiers, direct from the wars, needed no training; ultimately, however, when wars produced only an inadequate supply, schools were established to train men for the arena. These had appeared by the time of Sulla. Those sent to such schools were, at first at least, criminals of the worst sort, judged guilty of murder, treason, arson, robbery, desecration of temples, mutiny in the army. At Athens, Apollonius says, adulterers, fornicators, burglars, kidnappers, and the like were armed and set to fight.[73] When war prisoners and genuine criminals failed to meet the demand, the innocent were easily taken on spurious charges. Little people of no social standing, friendless foreign provincials, Jews, and Christians were also thrown in for the Romans' holiday. Pollio wrote to Cicero about Fadius and others, who had been used as gladiators and thrown to the wild beasts by

[67] Dio, LXXVI, 16.
[68] Dennis: *op. cit.*, I, 71; II, 175.
[69] Tacitus: *Annals*, IV, 62–3.
[70] *Ibid.*, XIII, 31; Dio, LI, 23; Suetonius: *Augustus*, 29; Pliny: *Natural History*, XXXVI, 24.
[71] Suetonius: *Vespasian*, 9; *Titus*, 7.
[72] *Tusculan Disputations*, II, 17.
[73] Philostratus: *The Life of Apollonius of Tyana*, IV, 22; Tertullian: *De Spectaculis*, 12.

Balbus.[74] Hadrian instituted a mild measure of reform, to the effect that no one might sell a slave or maidservant to a trainer of gladiators without giving reasons for so doing.[75] As time went on a number of those of high station took to the arena. Gladiatorial combats became a usual form of training for young men "of good family," and some of them became professionals. Thirty of the equestrian order fought as gladiators at one time in Nero's shows.[76]

Caesar, when planning to build a gladiatorial school, had his scouts keep a sharp lookout for good gladiators whom he might secure. His novices were trained in private houses of men of high rank, skilled at arms, whom he asked to give careful, individual attention to the exercise of their charges.[77] Cicero mentions a letter he wrote to Caesar, answering questions about Caesar's gladiators; the school at Capua, said to have had five thousand heavily armed gladiators in 49 B.C., was so vast that it occasioned public concern.[78]

When emperors became the chief supporters of the games of the arena, they, too, established gladiatorial schools. At Pisaurum imperial gladiators were lent "through the kindness of the emperor." [79] Caligula and Domitian had schools of gladiators; Domitian, indeed, is said to have organized four imperial schools, with elaborate armories, armorers' workshops, mortuaries, and an extensive array of personnel to operate them. At the head was a procurator, a man of high rank, under whose direction were fencing masters, doctors, superintendents of various buildings, and bookkeepers.[80] The number of imperial gladiators naturally varied from time to time, but at Nero's death there were two thousand, and the same figure is mentioned at the celebration of a thousand years of Rome's existence.[81]

Supplying gladiators for the games became a profitable business. Cicero's friend, Atticus, was a man of many affairs, among which was training and hiring out gladiators. There were many schools, apparently, both public and private. One hears of Mamertine, Gallic, and Dacian schools, the *ludus magnus* and the *ludus matutinus*.[82] For these institutions the best possible sites were selected. Ravenna, just such a place, was chosen by Roman governors for the training of gladiators; Praeneste, renowned for its climate, had an endowed gladiatorial school; and Capua, where the uprising of Spartacus occurred, was

[74] Cicero: *Letters to His Friends*, x, 32.
[75] Spartianus: *Hadrian*, 18.
[76] *Dio*, LXI, 9; "Gladiatorial Combats a Usual Form of Exercise," *Am. Jour. Archaeol.*, v, 480.
[77] Suetonius: *Julius*, 26, 31.
[78] *Ibid.*, 10; Cicero: *To Atticus*, VII, 14; VIII, 2.
[79] Frank: *op. cit.*, v, 101.
[80] Suetonius: *Domitian*, 4; Friedlaender: *Darstellungen aus der Sittengeschichte Roms*, II, 376 ff.
[81] Capitolinus: *The Three Gordians*, 33.
[82] Wallon: *Histoire de l'Esclavage dans l'Antiquité*, II, 137; Paul-Louis: *Ancient Rome at Work*, p. 139.

also famous for its training schools.[83] The physical health of gladiators was most carefully guarded by attendants and doctors.[84] Feeding, likewise, was a matter of grave concern, care being taken to provide the best diet for building muscles. *Sagina gladiatoria* was a food especially prepared for the fighters.[85] On the day preceding the combat an unusually elaborate meal was provided for those who were about to pay for what they had eaten.[86]

At Pompeii the ruins of a gladiatorial school show a quadrangular space, 173 feet by 139 feet, surrounded by a colonnade. Rude drawings, representing aspects of gladiatorial life, and announcements of coming contests, with names of the chief contestants, are found upon the walls. Opening on the four sides of the portico are rows of little windowless rooms, about ten to twelve feet square. These prison-like quarters of the gladiators tell a mute story of one aspect of the strict discipline exercised over his dangerous charges by the head of the institution, who might resort to the scourge, burning with hot irons, and confinement in chains and stocks.[87]

Hideous cruelties to gladiators were perpetrated under the Republic and even worse during the Empire. The lot of the gladiator became a synonym for the pitiable.[88] Balbus, we are told, buried Fadius up to the waist at the gladiatorial school, and burned him alive. When Fadius entreated him, saying that he was born a citizen of Rome, Balbus advised him to implore protection, then, of the people.[89] Nero's grandfather was reproved by Augustus because of the inhuman cruelty of his gladiatorial shows; Drusus gloated over bloodshed; Claudius enjoyed the cruelties of the arena, even wishing fighters to be slain so that he could see the expression on their faces.[90] It is said that, for trivial reasons, he compelled carpenters and other assistants around the arena to enter

83 The Geography of Strabo, v, 1, 7; Plutarch: Crassus, 8; Dill: Roman Society from Nero to Marcus Aurelius, p. 239.
84 Friedlaender: Darstellungen, II, 379 ff.
85 Tacitus: Histories, II, 88.
86 Seneca: Epistle XXXVII, 2.
87 Friedlaender: Darstellungen, II, 379; Dill: Nero to Aurelius, p. 242; cf. Overbeck: Pompeji, pp. 193 ff.; Mau: Pompeji in Leben und Kunst, pp. 164–70; Mazois: Les Ruines de Pompeii, III, 12 ff., and Plate II; Schreiber: Atlas, pp. 60 ff. The uses of certain areas, commonly given, despite some uncertainties, are indicated by numbers in the cut, next page: x, colonnade hall; 1, stairs, leading to Forum triangulare; 2, entrance from Stabian Street; 3, portico and passage to theaters; 4, partition wall, later construction, blocking original passage to the Large Theater; 5, space adjacent to the barracks; 6, room, containing remnants of costumes; 7, 8, rooms, ground and second story, for gladiators; 8', guard room; 9, exedra; 10, 11, 12 and 14, kitchen and storerooms; 13, stairway to quarters of the Lanista; 15, room, janitor or guard; 16, dining hall; 17, prison, with stocks; 18, stable. Schreiber gives 100, Overbeck 142, as the number of gladiators the cells may have housed. For photographs of barracks and neighboring structures, see Maiuri, Pompei, pp. 23, 98.
88 Athenaeus, IV, 155.
89 Cicero: To His Friends, x, 32.
90 Suetonius: Nero, 4; Claudius, 34; Tacitus: Annals, I, 76.

contests; and one of his own pages was made to fight in a toga. At one of Domitian's naval combats practically all participants perished, and many of the audience, too, because the monarch would not allow anyone to leave despite a heavy storm.[91]

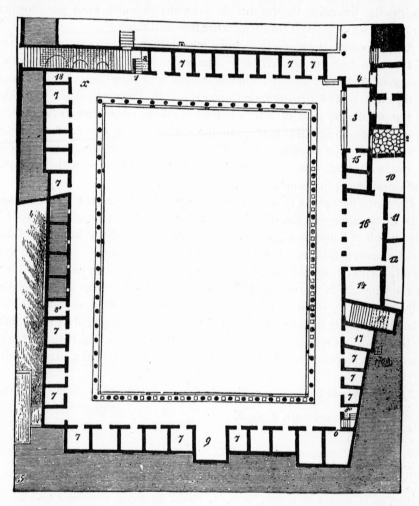

A GLADIATORIAL SCHOOL, POMPEII

(T. Schreiber, *Atlas of Classical Antiquities*, xxx, 11, Macmillan & Co., Ltd., London, 1895)

The life of a gladiator had its horrors; it also had glamour and rewards. Imperial gifts, estates, houses, and honors sometimes fell to their lot; Bato, though killed in combat, was given a glamorous funeral at the Emperor's hands.[92] Vic-

[91] Dio, LXVII, 8.
[92] Ibid., LXXVIII, 6; Suetonius: *Nero*, 30.

torious gladiators, even though physically disfigured, were darlings of women.[93] In a day when everyone was a member of a *collegium*, such a privilege was not denied the fighting entertainers. Some won freedom by the sword, and received in token one of wood; the best of them gained good pay, the choicest care, fame, and even a sort of immortality by virtue of their monuments.[94] All, even the poorest, could not but have felt something of a thrill when, decked out in handsome apparel and gleaming, decorated weapons, they marched into the arena and gave the familiar salute: *morituri te salutamus.* Hope springs eternal: perhaps they may live to carry palms of victory! Moreover, the fact that among the audience not only ordinary people but even emperors were so keenly interested as to designate themselves followers of the Samnites, Thracians, or some other type of fighters; and the solemn circumstance that the gladiator was a member of a group, bound by oath to die bravely without show of emotion, gave an air of professional dignity and prestige to an otherwise fearful and sordid occupation.

Cicero praised gladiators and the excellence of their training. What one "of ordinary merit has ever uttered a groan or changed countenance?" [95] Who has disgraced himself either on his feet or in his fall? Seneca noted that certain gladiators were courageous enough to take their own lives, just like free men.[96] The Saxon gladiators who were to have entertained Symmachus cheated the audience by strangling themselves.[97] Physical training, under the eye of a competent *lanista*, was the best that could be provided. The "gladiator in the school well skill'd" appealed to Cicero as an example of constant, faithful practice.[98] If not steeled by a cool courage, a ready, brutal anger against his opponent inspired his thrusts.[99] Accepting their mode of life as normal, many anticipated their contests with zest. Epictetus says that gladiators of the imperial school complained if they were not matched for combat and brought into the arena. Triumphus, a fighter, is said to have been depressed because there were so few shows in the reign of Tiberius: "What a glorious period of life is wasting." [100]

Types of fighters were numerous, and each used more or less special forms of armor. Some fought in pairs, the oldest and commonest form of combat; but mass fights, though naturally more expensive, were more exciting and hence popular, since they simulated more nearly actual battle. Samnites, probably

93 *Juvenal,* VI, 103 *et seq.*
94 Dill: *Nero to Aurelius,* p. 243.
95 *Tusculan Disputations,* II, 17.
96 *Epistle* LXX, 23–7.
97 Lot: *The End of the Ancient World,* pp. 179 f.
98 *On Oratory,* III, 23.
99 Cicero: *Tusculan Disputations,* IV, 21.
100 Epictetus, *The Discourses,* I, 29; Seneca: *On Providence,* IV, 4.

the oldest gladiatorial type, were armed with short, straight swords and a quad-rangular shield which covered most of the body. The Campanians, it was said, took the armor of their Samnite enemies and used it for their gladiators.[101] *Secutores* (pursuers), mentioned in the time of Caligula,[102] in a match with the *retiarii* (netters) were armed with greaves, swords, and shields, and had helmets equipped with visors. The *retiarii* used large nets, with which they sought to ensnare their adversaries, and were lightly armed with tridents and daggers. *Laqueatores* used lassos in place of the nets. Thracians were heavily armed, used short, curved swords, and had small shields, round or square. Con-tests between light-armed Samnites and heavy-armed Thracians were much in favor. Whether the *Galli* or *myrmillones*, who fought mostly against *retiarii* and Thracians, were heavily or lightly armed is uncertain. The *essedarii*, fighters who used chariots and imitated warriors, described by Caesar, appear to have become popular in consequence of the wars waged in Britain. To whet appe-tites jaded by common forms of combat, variations were introduced, such as fights of blindfolded persons (*andabatae*) and men with two swords (*dima-chaeri*).[103]

Gladiatorial troops were often a danger not only to individuals but to the state as well. Augustus had a narrow escape from a gladiatorial band.[104] Liv-ing together, eating and fighting together,[105] even a small handful of gladiators, being thoroughly trained as soldiers, could offer a hard fight for some of the regular army. Military guards, designed to prevent escape, were not always effective. Spartacus escaped from the school of Lentulus Batiatus at Capua and began a revolt that was finally put down only with great difficulty.[106] Cicero viewed Caesar's gladiators as a danger to the state, as did many others.[107] That the political significance of gladiatorial schools was not limited to the Republic is shown by the fact that sometimes they were even relied upon to strengthen the regular armed forces. Antony's gladiators, it was said, were still his most faithful soldiers when others forsook him.[108] Alfenus' troops de-feated a band of gladiators; Otho increased his army with two thousand gladia-tors; and Vitellius gave gladiators to aid Claudius Julianus.[109]

---

[101] Livy, IX, 40.
[102] Suetonius: Caligula, 30.
[103] Ibid., 35; Claudius, 21; Cicero: To His Friends, VII, 10; Friedländer: Roman Life and Manners, IV, 171 ff.
[104] Suetonius: Augustus, 14.
[105] Seneca: On Anger, II, 8.
[106] Appian: Civil Wars, I, 116; Plutarch: Crassus, 8–11; Tacitus: Annals, XV, 46.
[107] To Atticus, VII, 14; Suetonius: Julius, 10.
[108] Dio, LI, 7.
[109] Tacitus: Histories, II, 11, 23, 43; III, 57.

### VENATIONES

Men, fighting in pairs or in companies, on foot, on horse, or in chariots, competed for the interest of the citizenry of Rome with beast fights, *venationes*. In these spectacles beasts were pitted against other beasts, against trained beast fighters (*bestiarii*), and against untrained, defenseless men who were thrown to them. Like the gladiatorial combats, beast fights were staged at first in the circus, and were sometimes held there even after special structures had been erected. The *ludus matutinus*, one of the schools organized by Domitian to train men for the arena, was a training school for *bestiarii*, the *venationes* being commonly given in the morning. The men so employed were usually captives or condemned criminals, just as were the gladiators, as in the case of Caesar's games. To condemn men "to the lions" was not an infrequent sentence. Throwing provincials to the wild beasts of the arena sometimes caused revolt to rear its head, as was reported of the Isaurians.[110] Women, but not of the prominent sort, it is said, took part in the *venationes* on some occasions.[111]

Though hunting had no longer any serious purpose, beasts of all kinds were already being sought from all the distant reaches of the Empire, at the time of Caesar and Pompey, so as to provide ever fresh supplies to entertain the audiences of the capital. The strenuous effort to get animals for the shows can be glimpsed in the letters of Cicero. Caelius Rufus urged him repeatedly to send animals. Curio had generously sent him some from Africa. Cicero promised to do what he could, but prepared him for failure, for the animals object and have decided to emigrate to another province because they are constantly hunted! [112] In the late fourth century Symmachus bent all energies to secure animals from various places for his shows.[113] Claudian praised Stilicho and called on hunters everywhere to corral wild beasts, whose blood must be spilled only in the arena, to honor his achievements.[114] So extensive and continuous was the drain on animal life in the Mediterranean basin, that animals of some species became extinct.[115]

As early as 186 B.C. beasts made up a part of the games given by Nobilior. Nearly a century later (99 B.C.) lions were shown at Rome, and Sulla (93 B.C.) had a display of one hundred of them. Scaurus (58) is said to have exceeded previous efforts, showing crocodiles and hippopotami swimming in artificial bodies of water. At Pompey's games (55) elephants and lions were slaughtered;

---

[110] Ammianus, XIV, 2, 1.
[111] Dio, XLIII, 23; XLVI, 25.
[112] To His Friends, II, 11; VIII, 4, 8, 9.
[113] Epistulae, II, 76, 77; IV, 58–60, 63; IX, 12, 132.
[114] On Stilicho's Consulship, III, 261 et seq.
[115] Fowler: op. cit., p. 297.

five hundred of the latter were pitted against men, and eighteen elephants against men in heavy armor. Caesar staged beast fights in honor of Julia. At his great joint triumph (46 B.C.), the *venationes* lasted five days, camelopards were first shown at Rome, and forty men fought, mounted on elephants.[116]

The emperors soon put the records of the Republic to shame. Augustus gave beast shows twenty-six times.[117] The shrine of Julius was dedicated (29 B.C.), and the birth of Augustus was celebrated (20 B.C.) with beast slaughters.[118] When the Theater of Marcellus was dedicated (13 B.C.), six hundred African beasts were killed, and the son of Antony gave a beast slaughter on Augustus' birthday.[119] At the celebration of the *Ludi Martiales* (12 A.D.), two hundred lions were killed in the circus when the games had to be repeated.[120] At the death of Sejanus, annual *venationes* and other games of the circus were decreed in his honor.[121] Tiberius' effort to banish beast hunts from the city fared badly, for many people perished (27 A.D.) in the poorly constructed theaters that were put up outside.[122] Caligula quickly made good for Tiberius' restraint, gave shows lasting all day, and again at night. In 37 A.D., when dedicating a shrine to Augustus, four hundred bears and the same number of Libyan beasts were slain; at a two-day celebration of Drusilla's birthday, five hundred bears were slain in one day and five hundred African beasts the next.[123] Caligula varied the performances of the circus by having panther fights between the races; Claudius, who was so fond of beast fights that he went to the arena at dawn, followed the same practice, panthers being pursued by praetorian cavalry, while Thessalian horsemen rode down wild bulls and threw them by their horns when the animals were tired out.[124] In 41 A.D., one contest with camels, twelve with horses, and the slaying of three hundred bears and the same number of Libyan beasts thrilled the audience.[125] Nero's grandfather gave beast fights at the circus and elsewhere in the city. Nero himself made men of high rank fight wild beasts and delighted the crowds by rapid shifts from beast fights to naval battles and gladiatorial combats, all staged on the same ground. At one of his spectacles horsemen rode down bulls, and Nero's bodyguard killed with javelins four hundred bears and three hundred

---

116 Dio, xxxix, 38; xliii, 22–3; Plutarch: *Pompey*, 52; Appian: *Civil Wars*, ii, 102; Suetonius: *Julius*, 39.
117 *Res Gestae Divi Augusti*, iv, 22.
118 Dio, li, 22; liv, 8.
119 *Ibid.*, liv, 26.
120 *Ibid.*, lvi, 27.
121 *Ibid.*, lviii, 12.
122 *Ibid.*, lviii, 1; Tacitus: *Annals*, iv, 62–3.
123 Dio, lix, 7, 13.
124 Suetonius: *Caligula*, 18; *Claudius*, 21, 34; Dio, lx, 23.
125 Dio, lx, 7.

lions.[126] Vespasian was a lover of wild beast fights and gave them often; Titus dedicated the Flavian Amphitheater (80 A.D.) with a slaughter of nine thousand animals, both wild and tame, unique events being a fight between cranes and another of four elephants. Five thousand beasts were shown in one day alone.[127] Martial fancied that Indian hunters never saw so many tigers anywhere as did the citizens who gazed on Domitian's games.[128]

The Christian era saw no decrease of venationes. Eleven thousand beasts were killed (103 A.D.) when Trajan celebrated his Dacian victory. Hadrian gave an animal hunt at Athens with one thousand animals, and entertained at Rome with hunts of great magnificence. At a birthday celebration, it was said, he slew two hundred lions.[129] Commodus, fancying himself a veritable Roman Hercules, killed beasts himself, in public and in private, and in one day shot one hundred bears from the balustrade of the amphitheater.[130] At the tenth anniversary of his rule, Severus put on a great beast fight: a cage resembling a boat suddenly fell apart in the arena, and forth came bears, lions, panthers, wild asses, ostriches, and bisons to the number of seven hundred, all of which were slain. Sixty boars fought together, and an elephant and an Indian corocotta were killed.[131] Antoninus (212 A.D.), who was "for ever killing vast numbers of animals," slew one hundred boars in one day; and the false Antoninus had fifty-one tigers, an elephant, and various other beasts slain at his marriage with Cornelia Paula.[132] At the secular games in honor of Rome's thousandth anniversary (248 A.D.) Philip showed elephants, elks, tigers, wild and tame lions, leopards, hyenas, hippopotami, giraffes, wild asses, wild horses, a rhinoceros, and "various other animals." [133]

In the early sixth century the monotonous routine of beast shows still continued. Justin and Justinian gained their hold on the public by beast fights, races, and gladiatorial games, as had their predecessors for more than five hundred years. The last venationes at Rome, so far as known, were given in 523.[134]

### NAUMACHIAE

Naumachiae, sea battles, were staged from time to time to vary Rome's imperial entertainment, lakes being made by flooding the arena and by excava-

---

[126] Suetonius: Nero, 4, 12; Dio, LXI, 9; LXII, 15.
[127] Dio, LXV, 15; LXVI, 25; Suetonius: Titus, 7.
[128] Bk. VIII, 26.
[129] Spartianus: Hadrian, 19; Dio, LXIX, 8.
[130] Dio, LXXIII, 17–8.
[131] Ibid., LXXVII, 1.
[132] Ibid., LXXVIII, 10; LXXX, 9.
[133] Capitolinus: Gordians, 33.
[134] Lot: op. cit., pp. 255 f.; Showerman: op. cit., p. 349.

tions. Besides elaborate infantry and cavalry displays, Caesar arranged the first great naval display on an artificial lake in the *Campus Martius*. In the contest of the "Tyrian" and "Egyptian" fleets, made up of two-, three- and four-banked ships, there were four thousand oarsmen and two thousand fighting men.[135] Augustus constructed a permanent basin, twelve hundred by eighteen hundred feet, located near the Tiber (2 B.C.), and put on a display of "Athenians" versus "Persians," which engaged three thousand men besides the oarsmen.[136] Other basins were built later. When Lake Fucinus and the River Liris were joined (52 A.D.), Claudius exhibited a famous sea combat between the "Rhodians" and "Sicilians," having three- and four-banked ships, fifty on each side, in which nineteen thousand men were engaged.[137] At Nero's *naumachia*, a battle between "Persians" and "Athenians," sea monsters swam in salt water.[138] In 80 A.D. Titus put on two sea fights, one between "Corcyreans" and "Corinthians," and another between "Syracusans" and "Athenians." Three thousand men fought, the Athenians defeated the Syracusans, landed their forces on an islet, and demonstrated the siege of a city.[139] Domitian staged a naval battle, remarkable for the fact that most of the participants and spectators perished.[140]

Rome's multitudes had a variety of milder entertainments and exhibitions: among them were unusual, exotic animals (which were readily available after the conquest of Africa and Asia), abnormal men, trick horsemanship, the game of Troy, Pyrrhic dances, acrobatic and athletic contests. The arrival of the first hippopotamus and elephant stirred up considerable enthusiasm, judging by the tales of chroniclers. Augustus exhibited a snake fifty cubits long and everything else worth seeing that was brought to town.[141] Caesar's camelopard, the first rhinoceros, and an Indian corocotta taxed Dio's descriptive powers at times.[142] The people doubtless gawked at Augustus' little man (weight seventeen pounds, height scant two feet) with a big voice, gasped at the strong man with his thousand pounds of armor walking across the stage, and held their breath while they gazed at rope dancers and the human fly.[143]

The game of Troy was a popular and frequent equestrian exhibition of the young nobility.[144] The popular Pyrrhic dance, too, was often shown. In

---

[135] Suetonius: *Julius*, 39; Appian: *Civil Wars*, II, 102; Dio, XLIII, 23; Plutarch: *Caesar*, 55.
[136] Suetonius: *Augustus*, 43; Frank: *op. cit.*, V, 15.
[137] Tacitus: *Annals*, XII, 56–7; Suetonius: *Claudius*, 21; Dio, LXI, 33.
[138] Suetonius: *Nero*, 12; Dio, LXI, 9.
[139] Dio, LXVI, 25; Suetonius: *Titus*, 7.
[140] Dio, LXVII, 8.
[141] Suetonius: *Augustus*, 43.
[142] Dio, XLIII, 23; LI, 22; LXXVII, 1.
[143] Suetonius: *Augustus*, 43; Pliny: *Natural History*, VII, 20.
[144] Plutarch: *Cato the Younger*, 3; Dio, XLVIII, 20; XLIX, 43; LIV, 26; LV, 10; Suetonius: *Tiberius*, 6; *Nero*, 7; Tacitus: *Annals*, XI, 11.

Caesar's triumphal games noble youth from Bithynia and Asia gave a Pyrrhic dance; Claudius staged performances of it (41 and 44 A.D.) by boys whom Caligula had sent for, and some of his own retinue later performed in Pyrrhic exhibitions.[145] Nero gave Pyrrhic dances representing various scenes.[146] In Hadrian's reign such military dances were frequently exhibited.[147]

Acrobatic events and trick riding of desultores were often used to vary entertainment of the crowds between races at the circus. From Martial's pen we have a picture of the scene:

> See how they leap, the acrobatic crowd,
> And how the placid bull accepts the load.
> One clasps his horns, one on his broad back stands
> Brandishing shield and sword with careless hands.[148]

### ATHLETIC CONTESTS

Some Romans received the Greek gymnasium and its athletic exercises rather coldly. Pompey admitted he'd wasted oil and toil on them; and Mauricus wished they might be abolished at Rome; [149] nevertheless, both grew in favor rather rapidly, despite criticism heaped upon them by the most conservative. Boxing and wrestling, of course, had long been known in Italy, having been practiced in Etruria.[150] From thence boxers were brought to Rome as a part of the Ludi Romani.[151]

In 186 B.C., a year of many portentous occurrences, athletic contests were introduced from Greece as part of a ten-day spectacle.[152] That boxing was gaining favor is suggested by the fact that in 167 B.C., when Greek flutists sought to give a performance in Rome, they were ordered to box instead, and gave great satisfaction to the audience. Pompey gave gymnastic and musical contests at the opening of his theater, 55 B.C.[153] At Caesar's triumphal games (46 B.C.) the athletic contests lasted for three days, being exhibited in a special stadium on the Campus Martius.[154]

Many of the emperors took a keen interest in athletic performances. Augustus excluded women from a boxing match, but he was fond of watching boxers,

---

[145] Suetonius: Julius, 39; Dio, LX, 7, 23.
[146] Suetonius: Nero, 12.
[147] Spartianus: Hadrian, 19.
[148] Epigrams, V, 31. Trans. by J. A. Pott and F. A. Wright. Courtesy of E. P. Dutton & Co., Inc., New York.
[149] Cicero: To His Friends, VII, 1; Pliny: Letters, IV, 22.
[150] Dennis: op. cit., II, 323 f.; Randall-MacIver: Etruscans, p. 54.
[151] Livy, I, 35.
[152] Ibid., XXXIX, 22.
[153] Dio, XXXIX, 38; Plutarch: Pompey, 52.
[154] Suetonius: Julius, 39.

the inexpert as well as professionals, and matched Roman pugilists with Greek. Augustus provided for athletic exhibitions on three occasions; [155] the Actian Festival included gymnastic events. Caligula had athletes engage in the pancratium at a celebration of Drusilla's birthday; both African and Campanian boxers, the best from both places, took part in an exhibition in the Saepta.[156] Nero was much attracted to wrestling, practiced it constantly, and visited many contests in Greece. Some believed that he himself would soon compete with the athletes at Olympia, after his victories in the theater.[157] Even in the face of the Gallic uprising, Nero is said to have gone calmly to the gymnasium, watched the wrestlers, and "vied in prowess with some athlete." [158]

The deepening influence of Greek contests showed itself in a number of festivals. Nero's quinquennial celebration, Neronia, imitated the Greek pattern, and had three divisions, one being devoted to gymnastic contests, which the Vestal Virgins were permitted to attend, as did Ceres' priestesses at Olympia.[159] These were soon abandoned after Nero's death, but Gordian III revived them in 243, calling them the contests of Minerva. A more important festival, in honor of Jupiter Capitolinus, was established by Domitian in 86 A.D.; one of its three parts was devoted to athletic contests, such as wrestling, boxing, the pancration, long-distance running, and chariot races. Another event, the foot race of girls, did not long survive.[160] That women continued to play some part in public gymnastic exhibitions is evident, however.[161] The importance attached to athletic contests at this time may be judged from the fact that Domitian built a permanent stadium therefor, seating over thirty thousand spectators. Of a few other festivals, partly or wholly athletic, established later, little is known save the name; none of them seem to have compared with the renown of the Capitoline Games. Antoninus Pius established a festival in honor of Hadrian; Games of Hercules, said to have been celebrated by Alexander Severus,[162] were instituted about the time of Caracalla. Aurelius established contests of the sun-god in 274.[163]

The philhellenism of many of the Roman emperors and their enthusiasm for Greek athletic festivals did much to spread the cult of the gymnasium, and placed the conquering athletes on a pedestal of fame. The patronage of the

---

[155] Res Gestae, IV, 22.
[156] Dio, LIX, 13; Suetonius: Caligula, 18.
[157] Suetonius: Nero, 53.
[158] Dio, LXIII, 26.
[159] Suetonius: Nero, 12; Tacitus: Annals, XIV, 20.
[160] Suetonius: Domitian, 4; Dio, LXVII, 8; Friedländer: Roman Life and Manners, IV, 264 ff.
[161] Dio, LXXVI, 16.
[162] Lampridius: Severus Alexander, 35.
[163] Friedländer: Roman Life and Manners, II, 121; Sandys: Companion to Latin Studies, p. 511.

Greekling Hadrian and the magnificent gifts of Herodes Atticus went far to give athletics an unwonted external grandeur. Professionalism flourished as never before.[164] Dio Chrysostom's portrait of the Isthmian festival; Galen's contempt for professional athletes, in his "Exhortation to the Study of the Arts"; Philostratos' account of the decline of athletics and the open sale of contests; and Lucian's appeal to the spirit of an athletic ideal of the Greeks long since dead—all testify to the extremes to which professionalized sports had gone. At Olympia, to be sure, a strict standard seems to have been maintained fairly successfully, and fines were imposed on wrongdoers as late as the second century A.D. Guilds of professional athletes (xystoi) were numerous; some took the name of Augustus, Claudius, and other emperors. One of the most famous was the Herculanei, once located at Sardis, but later established at Rome in the time of Trajan. To their petition for suitable housing Trajan gave a favorable response, assigning them a building equipped with a hall for their deliberations on professional questions (such as examinations, distribution of prizes, erection of statues, the regulation and government·of the gymnasium), a gymnasium, and facilities for the safekeeping of records and relics.[165]

The athletic contests of the professionals wore them out quickly; Fuscus, a runner, having won fifty-three races at Rome, and others elsewhere, died at the age of twenty-four.[166] Men began young and made great records. The stories told of their prowess are often fantastic; they breathe the spirit of professional contests in an age of record-breaking. Pliny notes that it was thought remarkable for Pheidippides to run 1,160 stadia in two days; but later the courier of Alexander the Great ran 1,305 stadia in one day; and now, says Pliny, there are men in the circus who keep running for 160 (128) miles; and a boy eight (eighteen?) years old has covered 75 (68) miles between morning (noonday) and evening.[167]

"Pothunting" became the chief object of athletes. To discourage it and the boasting of the greatest victors, the title, "Successor of Hercules," was abolished, being last awarded in 37 A.D. Almost two centuries later (220? A.D.), Aurelius Helix, a renowned athlete, aspired to contend in wrestling and pancration at Olympia, having already been victorious in both contests at the Capitoline Games. The Eleans, however, refused him the privilege of contending at Olympia, being fearful that he might prove himself the "eighth from Hercules." [168]

[164] Supra, pp. 357 f.
[165] Krause: Die Gymnastik und Agonistik der Hellenen, I, 131.
[166] Daremberg: Oeuvres de Galien, I, 38; Friedländer: Roman Life and Manners, II, 21.
[167] Pliny: Natural History, VII, 20; Rackham's Pliny, II, 561, gives the parenthetical items.
[168] Dio, LXXX, 10.

A BOXER  *Museo Delle Terme, Rome*
(Courtesy, Bettmann Archive, New York)

Athletic contests were increasingly brutalized, and the values of amateur participation in competitive play were lost sight of throughout the Graeco-Roman world. Boxing, wrestling, and the pancration, especially, were fraught with danger of bodily disfigurement and serious injury. Marcus Aurelius refers to injuries by tearing with the nails and dashing the head in athletic exercises; and, though he was himself fond of boxing and wrestling, he attached little value to the pancration.[169] Marcus, however, like a good Stoic, was urging the pursuit of virtue; and his strictures on dancing and the pancration cannot have represented the views of more than a very small minority; most Romans, certainly, would have found boxing and the pancration dull without a little blood. After all, athletic contests at Rome and in her dominions had to compete with gladiatorial combats and venationes.

Privileges of one kind and another and even very substantial rewards fell to the lot of those who made of athletics a life career. To be an athlete, in Egypt for example, meant being in a class with artists and intellectuals who enjoyed exemption from expensive public duties, magistracies, and liturgies.[170] Especially significant, both from the standpoint of the Empire and the athletes, were the maintenance allotments provided for certain victors. Allowances were given to winners of iselastic games—those in which victory gave the right of triumphal entry through a breached wall of their native town. Originally these were only the victors at Olympian, Isthmian, Nemean, and Pythian festivals; but with complete power in the hands of one man, such awards might be made to any victor; new games might be declared iselastic, and others of that class might be abolished. Maecenas urged economy on Augustus in respect to athletes, suggesting that not everyone should have maintenance for life just because he had won an athletic contest; only those victorious at Rome, or in the Olympian and Pythian games, he said, should receive maintenance. Augustus is credited, however, with increasing the privileges of athletes and establishing severe discipline in the wrestling places.[171] An exchange of letters between Trajan and Pliny regarding allowances to iselastic victors is enlightening. Hadrian had abolished some iselastic games, and had decreed new ones. Victors in the new ones petitioned for the allowance between the day of their victory and the time when the contest was declared iselastic, on the ground that now they would be deprived of allowances for their victories in the iselastics that had been abolished. Moreover, the iselastic victors desired that their allowance should begin from the date of their victory, not on the day of their triumphal entry. To Pliny's report and request for directions, Trajan replied that the reward would not be due till the athlete made his entry; nor would

169 Meditations, VI, 20; XI, 2.
170 Chapot: Roman World, pp. 183, 266.
171 Suetonius: Augustus, 44–5; Dio, LII, 30.

payments be made retroactively to victors who might win in games subsequently raised to iselastic status.[172]

In Italy every town had some sort of show, varying in pretentiousness according to its size and prosperity and lasting from two to four or five days. More than ninety amphitheaters and sixty theaters have been discovered, many of them dating from before the Empire. An eminent authority has said that "practically all the towns of Italy" spent "at least 6,000 sesterces per year out of their treasuries," and the magistrates often much more. Legacies, left by men to towns, were commonly assigned for the provision of games.[173]

Wherever Rome's sway extended, there the games of circus and arena were to be found, though less often in northern lands. Many provinces founded quinquennial games in honor of Augustus "in almost every one of their towns." [174] Strabo tells of the beauty of Nicopolis, its constant growth, its stadium and gymnasium, and the Actian Festival, which had been honored and encouraged by Caesar.[175] Caligula gave "Athenian games" at Syracuse and "miscellaneous games" at Lugdunum in Gaul.[176] In remote Galatia, with its hyphenated population of Celtic and Phrygian extraction, the games of the arena were as congenial as they were to the people of Rome itself; and gifts of rich men were commonly devoted to the provision of such entertainments. In the provinces the ancient games and pagan religion went hand in hand, the provincial high priest (sacerdos provincae) presiding at the games.[177] During the first and second centuries of the Empire, it seems, "the passion for cruel excitement was as strong in the provincial towns as it was even at Rome." [178] Even the higher refinement that Athens once knew was not proof against the penetration of ruder pastimes. Gladiatorial games had been known in the Orient for centuries before the Empire's beginning, particularly at Alexandria and Antioch. But now Corinth, first of Greek cities, and then Athens became a center for such entertainments. The vulgarity and inhumanity of the Athenian spectacles stirred Apollonius' boundless contempt.[179] North Africa, Gaul, and Spain, however, saw the most extensive development of the games of the arena and circus. Gladiatorial combats were known at Arles as early as 63 B.C. They were still engaging the attention of her crowds in the sixth century A.D.[180]

---

[172] Pliny: Letters, x, 118, 119.
[173] Frank: op. cit., v, 100; Friedlaender: Darstellungen, II, 422 ff.
[174] Suetonius: Augustus, 59.
[175] Bk. VII, 7, 6; Virgil: Aeneid, III, 280.
[176] Suetonius: Caligula, 20.
[177] Chapot: op. cit., pp. 112 f., 199.
[178] Dill: Nero to Aurelius, p. 235.
[179] Philostratus: Apollonius of Tyana, IV, 21–2.
[180] Friedlaender: Darstellungen, II, 426.

## PAGAN AND CHRISTIAN CRITICISM OF GAMES

Criticism of the spectacles of the circus and the arena found expression to some extent among pagans, Greek and Roman; it increased in volume and vigor under the spur of Christian fanaticism. Apollonius of Tyana, born just before the Christian era, criticized the Athenians for their gladiatorial fights and also for their "lascivious jigs" to which the old dances had given way.[181] Demonax advised Athenians to "destroy the Altar of Pity," before deciding to enter into rivalry with Corinth for brilliance in gladiatorial games.[182] Seneca's understanding of the evil was profound, his criticism severe. To banish sorrow by diverting attention through gladiatorial bouts or other entertainments is in vain. The incessant pursuit of spectacle after spectacle and the enjoyment of human blood cannot enable one to escape from himself.[183] In fact, there is nothing so injurious to good morals as attendance at games. "In the morning they throw men to the lions and the bears; at noon, they throw them to the spectators. The spectators demand that the slayer shall face the man who is to slay him in his turn; and they always reserve the latest conqueror for another butchering. The outcome of every fight is death. . . ." [184] After witnessing combats which are nothing short of murder, one is always more greedy, cruel, voluptuous, and inhuman. To observe such evils is certain to react on the observer.

Christian critics recognized the games of the arena and circus as a great stronghold of paganism and subjected them to vigorous, continuous attack. Minucius Felix (second century) declared: "We, whose values rest on morals and on modesty, have good reason to abstain from the vicious delights of your processions and spectacles; we know the rites from which they originated and condemn their pernicious attractions. At the curule games, who would not shrink from the frenzy of the struggling mob? or the organized bloodshed of the gladiatorial shows?" [185]

Tertullian's theme is the same. As he takes pains to show, the games originated in rites honoring dead men. Gymnastic contests began "with their Castors and Herculeses and Mercuries." Horseback riding, originally in a primitive state, was no sin; but, "brought into the games, it passed from being God's gift into the service of demons." Gladiatorial combats originated as a *munus*

---

181 Philostratus: *Apollonius of Tyana*, iv, 21–2.
182 Lucian: *Demonax*, 57.
183 Seneca: *To Helvia*, xvii, 1; *On Tranquillity of Mind*, ii, 13–5.
184 Seneca: *Epistle* vii, 2 et seq. Seneca, *Epistulae Morales*, trans. by R. M. Gummere. The Loeb Classical Library. Quoted by permission of Harvard University Press, Cambridge, Mass.
185 Minucius Felix: *Octavius*, xxxvii, 11. Trans. by G. H. Rendall. The Loeb Classical Library. Quoted by permission of Harvard University Press, Cambridge, Mass.

(a service) to the dead, founded on belief in the propitiation of "the souls of the dead" by "human blood." This "impiety" has now been turned into pleasure.[186] The stadium is mentioned in Scriptures, Tertullian admits, but what is done in it—giving a "blow, kick, cuff, all the recklessness of the fist, any and every disfigurement of the human face, God's image"—is unfit for men to witness. Running and throwing are idle feats, "idler still is leaping." "Wrestling is the devil's own trade." [187]

Summing up the indictment, Tertullian declares: "Your public games . . . we renounce, as heartily as we do their origins. . . . We have nothing to do . . . with the madness of the circus, the shamelessness of the theatre, the savagery of the arena, the vanity of the gymnasium." [188] The pleasure of the Christian is that of the Greek philosopher—calmness of mind. If the Bible does not specifically condemn the circus, the theater, the spectacle, it does say, "Happy is the man . . . who has not gone to the gathering of the impious, who has not stood in the way of sinners, nor sat in the chair of pestilences." [189]

Over against secular pleasures, Christian ascetics placed their own conception of spiritual joys. Thus Tertullian says: "What greater pleasure is there than disdain for pleasure, than contempt for the whole world, than true liberty, than a clean conscience, than life sufficient, than the absence of all fear of death? than to find yourself trampling underfoot the gods of the Gentiles, expelling demons, effecting cures, seeking revelations, living to God? These are the pleasures, the spectacles of Christians, holy, eternal, and free. Here find your games of the circus—watch the race of time, the seasons slipping by, count the circuits, look for the goal of the great consummation, battle for the companies of the churches, rouse up at the signal of God, stand erect at the angel's trump, triumph in the palms of martyrdom. If the literature of the stage delight you, we have sufficiency of books, of poems, of aphorisms, sufficiency of songs and voices, not fable, those of ours, but truth; not artifice but simplicity. Would you have fightings and wrestlings? Here they are—things of no small account and plenty of them. See impurity overthrown by chastity, perfidy slain by faith, cruelty crushed by pity, impudence thrown into the shade by modesty; and such are the contests among us, and in them we are crowned. Have you a mind for blood? You have the blood of Christ." [190] A host of parallels might be cited, showing the effort that was made to infuse the terms

---

[186] De Spectaculis, 9, 11–2. Trans. by T. R. Glover. The Loeb Classical Library. Quoted by permission of Harvard University Press, Cambridge, Mass.
[187] Ibid., 18; 1 Corinthians, IX, 24.
[188] Apology, XXXVIII, 4. Trans. by T. R. Glover. The Loeb Classical Library. Quoted by permission of Harvard University Press, Cambridge, Mass.
[189] Tertullian: De Spectaculis, 3; Psalms, 1, 1.
[190] Tertullian: De Spectaculis, 29. Trans. by T. R. Glover. The Loeb Classical Library. Quoted by permission of Harvard University Press, Cambridge, Mass.

of the Graeco-Roman sporting world with ascetic, religious meaning. Wrestling the devil is held worthier than contending with a human antagonist. All of life is a combat. The Christian contender needs to keep the body spare, that the soul may be the stronger. To postpone baptism to the deathbed is likened to stripping for a contest when the audience is on the point of leaving. Women, as well as men, can compete in this ascetic discipline of the spirit; and they may even win the race.[191]

Christianity, though its preachers criticized the inhuman practices of the arena unceasingly, was at best only able gradually to alter the minds of men; it was not competent to effect a speedy metamorphosis. The insidious influence of the games drew even Christians and others who resolutely set their will against them, in spite of themselves, as Augustine says of Alypius.[192] Judgments vary respecting the influence of emperors, nominally Christian, at least, upon the bloody sports of Rome. Gibbon speaks of the "piety of Christian princes" which suppressed gladiatorial games; Cary, however, believes that "the Christian emperors of the fourth century gave no heed to the strictures of the Church upon the cruelty of gladiatorial games. . . ." [193] Indeed, little was done. If some emperors considered abolishing the games, most of them held to the contrary opinion and practice. Constantine censured the giving of spectacles in peacetime (326), and ordered that criminals be sentenced to mines instead of the arena; but this was not prohibition. Valentinian's law (365) forbade the condemning of Christians to gladiatorial schools.[194] The imperial gladiatorial schools were abolished in 399. Five years later Honorius abolished gladiatorial combats at Rome, in consequence of the killing by the audience of Telemachus, a monk who sought to interpose himself between men in a gladiatorial contest at the Flavian Amphitheater. Prudentius had pleaded in vain with Honorius to stop the games; but what reason had not effected was now accomplished by more spectacular means.

As long as the old society lasted, some vestige of the splendor of spectacles remained; but with its disintegration came the inevitable atrophy of its dearest pleasures. In the fourth century Ammianus reports with chagrin that though there was a scarcity of food in the city, and foreigners were driven "neck and crop" from the towns, three thousand dancing-girls and as many dancing-masters were allowed to remain. In the middle of the fourth century (359) he tells us that the circus still held Romans in its spell as did nothing else. "Their temple, their dwelling, their assembly, and the height of all their hopes is the

---

[191] Sawhill: *The Use of Athletic Metaphors in the Biblical Homilies of St. John Chrysostom*, pp. 47 ff., 80 ff., 105 f., et passim.
[192] Augustine: *Confessions*, VI, 8.
[193] Cary: *op. cit.*, p. 757; Gibbon: *op. cit.*, III, 31.
[194] Friedländer: *Roman Life and Manners*, II, 80 f.; Lot: *op. cit.*, p. 178.

Circus Maximus." [195] Namatianus still hears the cheers for the winning color ringing in his ears as he sails down the Tiber in 417. While Theodoric ruled (493–526), he held to the principle of bread and circuses for Rome's hordes, and won the praise of Cassiodorus and other Christians. Justin spent more than $1,000,000 (521) on games; and Justinian's reign was seriously disturbed by the rivalries of circus factions in 532. Totila entertained with games the vanquished Romans when he captured the city in 549. Both circus games and beast fights were still of considerable moment in the sixth century. Though the last known *venationes* at the Colosseum occurred in 523, Justinian provided by law (536) that the consuls should give animal fights and other spectacles.[196] When the Germans were threatening the gates of Treves, the populace was still engrossed in the bloody shows of the arena. Procopius says that the German chiefs had coins struck with their own image, and presided like "gentlemen of leisure" at the games in the circus of Arles in 541.[197] Gregory of Tours says that Chilperic (died, 584) ordered amphitheaters to be erected at Paris and Soissons and gave "shows to the people." [198] A reference to a beast being baited by dogs at the palace of Metz is faintly reminiscent of bloodier beast fights of earlier, more glamorous days.[199] By the close of the sixth century, however, the disintegration of the social order itself robbed the spectacles of the encouragement that had so long kept them alive.

[195] Ammianus, xiv, 6, 19; xxviii, 4, 29.
[196] Showerman: op. cit., pp. 321, 349; Lot: op. cit., p. 178; Gibbon: op. cit., iii, 426 ff.; Thorndike: The History of Medieval Europe, p. 126.
[197] Procopius: History of the Wars, vii, 33; Dill: Nero to Aurelius, p. 234.
[198] Gregory of Tours: History of the Franks, v, 11.
[199] Ibid., viii, 36.

# BIBLIOGRAPHY

Abbott, E. A History of Greece. 3 vols. Putnam's: New York, 1900–1906.

Abbott, F. F. The Common People of Ancient Rome. Scribner's: New York, 1911.

———. Society and Politics in Ancient Rome. Scribner's: New York, 1909.

Adamson, J. E. The Theory of Education in Plato's "Republic." Swan Sonnenschein: London, 1903.

Aeschines, The Speeches of. (Trans. by C. D. Adams.) Heinemann: London, 1919. (Now handled by Harvard University Press, Cambridge.)

Allbutt, T. C. Greek Medicine in Rome. Macmillan: London, 1921.

Allier, R. The Mind of the Savage. Harcourt, Brace: New York, 1929.

Ammianus Marcellinus. (Trans. by J. C. Rolfe.) 3 vols. Harvard University Press: Cambridge, 1935–1939.

Anderson, L. F. "Some Facts Regarding Vocational Training among the Ancient Greeks and Romans." Sch. Rev. (Mar., 1912), XX, 191–201.

Andrews, G. F. "Physical Education in India." Jour. Health and Phys. Educ. (Feb., 1933), IV, 10–2, 59.

Ante-Nicene Fathers, The. (Ed. by A. Roberts and J. Donaldson, and rev. by A. C. Coxe.) 9 vols. Christian Lit. Pub. Co.: Buffalo, 1885–1887.

Apollodorus: The Library. (Trans. by J. G. Frazer.) 2 vols. Heinemann: London, 1921. (Now handled by Harvard University Press, Cambridge.)

Apollonius of Rhodes: The Tale of the Argonauts. (Trans. by A. S. Way.) Dent: London, 1901.

Appian's Roman History. (Trans. by H. White.) 4 vols. Heinemann: London, 1912–1913. (Now handled by Harvard University Press, Cambridge.)

Aretaeus, The Cappadocian, The Extant Works of. (Trans. by F. Adams.) Sydenham Society: London, 1856.

757

'Ārifī, M. *Gūī u Chaugān* or *Hālnāma*. (Trans. by R. S. Greenshields.) Luzac: London, 1932.

Aristophanes. (Trans. by B. B. Rogers.) 3 vols. Heinemann: London, 1924. (Now handled by Harvard University Press, Cambridge.)

Aristophanes: *The Frogs*. (Trans. by G. Murray.) Allen and Unwin: London, 1930.

Aristotle, *The Works of*. (Trans. under the editorship of J. A. Smith and W. D. Ross.) 11 vols. Clarendon Press: Oxford, 1908–1931.

Arrian. (Trans. by E. I. Robson.) 2 vols. Heinemann: London, 1929–1933. (Now handled by Harvard University Press, Cambridge.)

Arrian: *The Cynegeticus*. (Trans. by W. Dansey.) Bohn: London, 1831.

Athenaeus: *The Deipnosophists*. (Trans. by C. B. Gulick.) 7 vols. Harvard University Press: Cambridge, 1927–1941.

Augustine, Saint: *The City of God*. (Trans. by J. Healey.) 2 vols. Grant: Edinburgh, 1909.

Augustine's *Confessions*, Saint. (Trans. by W. Watts.) 2 vols. Heinemann: London, 1912. (Now handled by Harvard University Press, Cambridge.)

Aurelius Antoninus, Marcus . . . *His Meditations*. (Trans. by M. Casaubon.) Dutton: New York, 1900.

Aurelius Antoninus, *The Meditations of the Emperor Marcus*. (Trans. by G. Long.) Burt: New York, n.d.

Ausonius [and] *The Eucharisticus* of Paulinus Pellaeus. (Trans. by H. G. Evelyn White.) 2 vols. Heinemann: London, 1919–1921. (Now handled by Harvard University Press, Cambridge.)

Babylonian Talmud. (Trans. by M. L. Rodkinson.) 10 vols. New Talmud Pub. Co.: Boston, 1903.

Babylonische Talmud, Der. (Ed. by L. Goldschmidt.) 9 vols. Calvary: Berlin, 1897–1935.

Badminton Library of Sports and Pastimes, The. (Ed. by the Duke of Beaufort and A. E. T. Watson.) 26 vols. Longmans: London, 1886–1902.

Baikie, J. *The Amarna Age*. Macmillan: New York, 1926.

———. *A History of Egypt from the Earliest Times to the End of the XVIIIth Dynasty*. Black: London, 1929.

———. *The Sea-Kings of Crete*. Black: London, 1913.

Bailey, C. (Ed.) *The Legacy of Rome*. (Essays by C. Foligno, E. Barker, et al.) Clarendon Press: Oxford, 1923.

Bakewell, C. M. *Source Book in Ancient Philosophy*. Scribner's: New York, 1907.

Ball, C. J. *Chinese and Sumerian*. Oxford Univ. Press: London, 1913.

Ballin, H. "Gymnastics in the Bible." *Mind and Body* (Sept., 1895), II, 129–32.

Barnes, H. E. *The History of Western Civilization.* 2 vols. Harcourt, Brace: New York, 1935.

Barrow, R. H. *Slavery in the Roman Empire.* Methuen: London, 1928.

Barton, G. A. *Archaeology and the Bible.* Am. Sunday-Sch. Union: Philadelphia, 1925.

Bauer, L. "Chinese Dances for Children." *Jour. Health and Phys. Educ.* (Sept., 1933), IV, 22–7, 53.

Baumeister, A. *Denkmäler des Klassischen Altertums.* 3 vols. Oldenbourg: München, 1885–1888.

Becker, W. A. *Charicles.* (Trans. by F. Metcalfe.) Appleton: New York, 1866.

———. *Gallus or Roman Scenes of the Time of Augustus.* (Trans. by F. Metcalfe.) Longmans: London, 1866.

Bell, H. I. "Hellenic Culture in Egypt." *Jour. Egy. Archaeol.* (1922), VIII, 139–55.

———. "The Historical Value of Greek Papyri." *Jour. Egy. Archaeol.* (1920), VI, 234–46.

Beloch, J. *Die Bevölkerung der Griechisch-Römischen Welt.* Duncker and Humblot: Leipzig, 1886.

Bernard, T. *Hatha Yoga, The Report of a Personal Experience.* Columbia Univ. Press: New York, 1944.

*Bible, The Holy.* (Am. rev. ed.) Nelson: New York, 1901.

*Bible, The Holy.* (From the Vulgate.) Wildermann: New York, 1911.

Biot, E. C. *Essai sur l'Histoire de l'Instruction Publique en Chine.* Duprat: Paris, 1847.

Blackman, A. M. "On the Position of Women in the Ancient Egyptian Hierarchy." *Jour. Egy. Archaeol.* (1921), VII, 8–30.

Blanco y Sanchez, D. R. *Bibliografía General de la Educación Física.* 2 vols. Hernando: Madrid, 1927.

Blümner, H. *The Home Life of the Ancient Greeks.* (Trans. by A. Zimmern.) Cassell: London, 1895.

Boeckh, A. *The Public Economy of Athens.* (Trans. by G. C. Lewis.) Parker: London, 1842.

Bogeng, G. A. E. *Geschichte des Sports Aller Völker und Zeiten.* 2 vols. Seemann: Leipzig, 1926.

Bondurant, A. L. *Ancient Athletics, Their Use and Abuse.* Banner Press: Emory Univ., n.d.

Bosanquet, B. *The Education of the Young in the Republic of Plato.* Univ. Press: Cambridge, 1908.

Botsford, G. W., and Botsford, L. S. *A Source-Book of Ancient History.* Macmillan: New York, 1927.

———. *The Story of Rome as Greeks and Romans Tell It.* Macmillan: New York, 1927.

Botsford, G. W., and Robinson, C. A. *Hellenic History.* Rev. ed. Macmillan: New York, 1948.

Botsford, G. W., and Sihler, E. G. *Hellenic Civilization.* Columbia Univ. Press: New York, 1915.

Bourguet, E. *Les Ruines de Delphes.* Fontemoing: Paris, 1914.

Bowra, C. M. "Xenophanes and the Olympic Games." *Am. Jour. Philol.* (1938), LIX, 257–79.

Boyd, C. E. *Public Libraries and Literary Culture in Ancient Rome.* Chicago, 1916.

Brav, A. "The Biblical Sanitary Code to Prevent the Spread of Contagious Diseases." *Am. Med.* (Sept., 1917), N.S. XII, 638–44.

Breasted, J. H. *Ancient Times.* Ginn: Boston, 1916.

———. *Development of Religion and Thought in Ancient Egypt.* Scribner's: New York, 1912.

———. *A History of Egypt.* Scribner's: New York, 1912.

Brink, D. B., and Smith, P. *Athletes of the Bible.* Assoc. Press: New York, 1914.

Brown, G. *Melanesians and Polynesians.* Macmillan: London, 1910.

Brown, J. M. *Polo.* Longmans: London, 1891.

Browne, E. G. *A Year amongst the Persians.* Univ. Press: Cambridge, 1927.

Brunn, H., and Arndt, P. J. *Denkmäler Griechischer und Römischer Sculptur.* Ser. 1 and 2. Bruckmann: Munich, 1888.

Brunner-Traut, E. *Der Tanz im alten Ägypten. Ägyptologische Forschungen,* Heft 6. Glückstadt, Hamburg, New York, 1938.

Bryant, A. A. "Boyhood and Youth in the Days of Aristophanes." *Harvard Studies in Class. Philol.* (1907), XVIII, 73–122.

Buckingham, J. S. *Travels in Assyria, Media, and Persia.* 2 vols. Colburn and Bentley: London, 1830.

Büdinger, M. "Die Römischen Spiele und der Patriciat." *Sitzungsberichte der Philosophisch-historischen Classe der Kaiserlichen Akademie der Wissenschaften,* vol. CXXIII, Abh. III.

Bulley, M. H. *Ancient and Medieval Art.* Methuen: London, 1914.

Burn, A. R. *Minoans, Philistines, and Greeks.* Knopf: New York, 1930.

Burnet, J. *Aristotle on Education.* Univ. Press: Cambridge, 1905.

Burns, C. D. *Greek Ideals.* Bell: London, 1917.

Bury, J. B. *A History of Greece.* Macmillan: London, 1922.

————. *The Invasion of Europe by the Barbarians.* Macmillan: London, 1928.

Busolt, G., and Swoboda, H. *Griechische Staatskunde.* 2 vols. C. H. Beck'sche Verlagsbuchhandlung: München, 1920–1926.

Butcher, S. H. *Some Aspects of the Greek Genius.* Macmillan: London, 1893.

Butler, A. J. *Sport in Classic Times.* Benn: London, 1930.

Buttree, J. M. *The Rhythm of the Redman.* Barnes: New York, 1930.

*Cambridge Ancient History, The.* (Ed. by J. B. Bury, S. A. Cook, et al.) 12 vols. Macmillan: New York, 1923–1939.

*Cambridge Medieval History, The.* (By J. B. Bury et al.) 8 vols. Univ. Press: Cambridge, 1911–1936.

Capes, W. W. *University Life in Ancient Athens.* Harper: New York, 1877.

Carcopino, J. *Daily Life in Ancient Rome.* (Trans. by E. O. Lorimer.) Yale Univ. Press: New Haven, 1940.

Carpenter, R. *The Humanistic Value of Archaeology.* Harvard Univ. Press: Cambridge, 1933.

Carus, P. *Chinese Life and Customs.* Open Court: Chicago, 1907.

Cary, H. F. *Pindar in English Verse.* Moxon: London, 1833.

Cary, M. *A History of Rome down to the Reign of Constantine.* Macmillan: London, 1938.

Catlin, G. *Letters and Notes on the Manners, Customs, and Conditions of the North American Indians.* 2 vols. London, 1841.

Cato, Marcus Porcius, *On Agriculture* [and] *Marcus Terentius Varro: On Agriculture.* (Trans. by W. D. Hooper, rev. by H. B. Ash.) Harvard University Press: Cambridge, 1934.

*Catullus and Tibullus, The Poems of.* (Trans. by W. K. Kelly.) Bell: London, 1897.

*Celsus de Medicina.* (Trans. by W. G. Spencer.) 3 vols. Harvard University Press: Cambridge, 1935–1938.

*Censorini de die Natali Liber.* (Ed. by O. Jahn.) Berolini, 1845.

Chait, R. M. "Relics of a Royal Sport in China." *Internat. Studio: Associated with the Connoisseur* (Nov., 1928), xci, 33–6, 90.

Chamberlain, A. F. *The Child: A Study in the Evolution of Man.* Scott: London, 1901.

————. *The Child and Childhood in Folk Thought.* Macmillan: New York, 1896.

Chapot, V. *The Roman World.* (Trans. by E. A. Parker.) Knopf: New York, 1928.

Cheesman, G. L. *The Auxilia of the Roman Imperial Army.* Clarendon Press: Oxford, 1914.

Choris, L. *Voyage Pittoresque autour du Monde.* Paris, 1822.

Chryssafis, J. "Aristotle on Kinesiology." *Jour. Health and Phys. Educ.* (Sept., 1930), I, 14–7, 54–6.

——. "Aristotle on Physical Education." *Jour. Health and Phys. Educ.* (Jan. and Feb., 1930), I, 3–8, 50; 14–7, 46–7.

Cicero: *Brutus* (Trans. by G. L. Hendrickson.) [and] *Orator* (Trans. by H. M. Hubbell.) Harvard University Press: Cambridge, 1939.

Cicero: *De Finibus Bonorum et Malorum.* (Trans. by H. Rackham.) Heinemann: London, 1914. (Now handled by Harvard University Press, Cambridge.)

Cicero: *De Natura Deorum* [and] *Academica.* (Trans. by H. Rackham.) Heinemann: London, 1933. (Now handled by Harvard University Press, Cambridge.)

Cicero: *De Oratore.* (Trans. by E. W. Sutton and H. Rackham.) 2 vols. Harvard University Press: Cambridge, 1942.

Cicero: *De Re Publica* [and] *De Legibus.* (Trans. by C. W. Keyes.) Heinemann: London, 1928. (Now handled by Harvard University Press, Cambridge.)

Cicero: *Letters to Atticus.* (Trans. by E. O. Winstedt.) 3 vols. Heinemann: London, 1912–1918. (Now handled by Harvard University Press, Cambridge.)

Cicero: *The Letters to His Friends* [and] *Letters to Quintus.* (Trans. by W. G. Williams.) 3 vols. Heinemann: London, 1927–1929. (Now handled by Harvard University Press, Cambridge.)

Cicero *on Oratory and Orators; with His Letters to Quintus and Brutus.* (Trans. by J. S. Watson.) Bell: London, 1891.

Cicero, *The Orations of Marcus Tullius.* (Trans. by C. D. Yonge.) 3 vols. Bell: London, 1891–1917.

Cicero: *Philippics.* (Trans. by W. C. A. Ker.) Heinemann: London, 1926. (Now handled by Harvard University Press, Cambridge.)

Cicero: *The Speeches. Pro Lege Manilia, Pro Caecina, Pro Cluentio, Pro Rabirio, Perduellionis.* (Trans. by H. G. Hodge.) Heinemann: London, 1927. (Now handled by Harvard University Press, Cambridge.)

Cicero's *Three Books of Offices . . . On Old Age . . . On Friendship; Paradoxes; Scipio's Dream; [and] . . . Duties of a Magistrate.* (Trans. by C. R. Edmonds.) Bell: London, 1887.

Cicero: Tusculan Disputations. (Trans. by J. E. King.) Heinemann: London, 1927. (Now handled by Harvard University Press, Cambridge.)

Clark, J. W. The Care of Books. Univ. Press: Cambridge, 1901.

Claudian. (Trans. by M. Platnauer.) 2 vols. Heinemann: London, 1922. (Now handled by Harvard University Press, Cambridge.)

Cole, P. R. Later Roman Education in Ausonius, Capella and the Theodosian Code. Teachers College: New York, 1909.

Columella, L. Junius Moderatus. Of Husbandry . . . and Concerning Trees. (Trans. by M. C. Curtius.) London, 1745.

Columella, L. Junius Moderatus, On Agriculture. (Trans. by H. B. Ash.) 3 vols. Harvard University Press: Cambridge, 1941–.

Coomaraswamy, A. The Dance of Siva. Sunwise Turn: New York, 1918.

Corlett, W. T. The Medicine-man of the American Indian and His Cultural Background. Thomas: Springfield, Ill., 1935.

Costello, L. S. The Rose Garden of Persia. Slark: London, 1888.

Couissin, P. Les Armes Romaines. Librairie Ancienne, Honoré Champion, Editeur: Paris, 1926.

Cramer, F. Geschichte der Erziehung und des Unterrichts im Alterthume. 2 vols. Becker: Elberfeld, 1832–1838.

Crosby, H. L. "The Quest of Health in Ancient Greece." Univ. of Pa. Lectures (1916–1917), IV, 309–27.

Cubberley, E. P. Readings in the History of Education. Houghton Mifflin: Boston, 1920.

Culin, S. Games of the North American Indians. 24th Ann. Rep. Bur. Am. Ethnol., 1902–1903. Govt. Printing Off.: Washington, 1907.

Daremberg, C., and Saglio, E. Dictionnaire des Antiquités Grecques et Romaines. 5 vols. Hachette: Paris, 1877.

Davids, T. W. R. Buddhist India. Putnam's: New York, 1903.

Davidson, T. Aristotle and Ancient Educational Ideals. Scribner's: New York, 1901.

———. The Education of the Greek People. Appleton: New York, 1894.

Davies, J. Hesiod and Theognis. Lippincott: Philadelphia, 1873.

Davis, W. S. A Day in Old Athens. Allyn and Bacon: Boston, 1914.

———. A Day in Old Rome. Allyn and Bacon: Boston, 1925.

———. The Influence of Wealth in Imperial Rome. Macmillan: New York, 1910.

DeClercq, L. Catalogue Méthodique et Raisonné Antiquités Assyriennes. 2 vols. Ernest Leroux: Paris, 1888–1903.

Delitzsch, F. J. *Jewish Artisan Life in the Time of Jesus*. (Trans. by B. Pick.) Funk and Wagnalls: New York, 1883.

Della Corte, M. *Ivventvs*. Fraioli: Arpino, 1924.

De Meun, J. *L'Art de Chevalerie*. (From *De Re Militari* of Vegetius.) Librairie de Firmin-Didot: Paris, 1897.

*Demosthenes against Meidias, Androtion, Aristocrates, Timocrates, Aristogeiton*. (Trans. by J. H. Vince.) Harvard University Press: Cambridge, 1935.

*Demosthenes: Olynthiacs, Philippics, Minor Public Speeches, Speech against Leptines*. (Trans. by J. H. Vince.) Heinemann: London, 1930. (Now handled by Harvard University Press, Cambridge.)

*Demosthenes: Private Orations*. (Trans. by A. T. Murray.) 4 vols. Harvard University Press: Cambridge, 1936–.

*Demosthenes, The Public Orations of*. (Trans. by A. W. Pickard-Cambridge.) 2 vols. Clarendon Press: Oxford, 1912.

Dennis, G. *The Cities and Cemeteries of Etruria*. 2 vols. Murray: London, 1883.

Diehl, C. *Excursions Archéologiques en Grèce*. Colin: Paris, 1890.

Diels, H. "Ancient Long Jump." *Am. Jour. Archaeol.* (1900), IV, 539.

Diem, C. *Asiatische Reiterspiele*. Deutscher Archiv-Verlag: Berlin, 1942.

Dill, S. *Roman Society from Nero to Marcus Aurelius*. Macmillan: London, 1937.

———. *Roman Society in Gaul in the Merovingian Age*. Macmillan: London, 1926.

———. *Roman Society in the Last Century of the Western Empire*. Macmillan: London, 1906.

Dio Chrysostom. (Trans. by J. W. Cohoon and H. L. Crosby.) 5 vols. Harvard University Press: Cambridge, 1932–.

Diodorus of Sicily. (Trans. by C. H. Oldfather.) 12 vols. Harvard University Press: Cambridge, 1933–.

*Diogenes Laërtius: The Lives and Opinions of Eminent Philosophers*. (Trans. by C. D. Yonge.) Bell: London, 1915.

*Dionysius of Halicarnassus, The Roman Antiquities of*. (Trans. by E. Cary.) 7 vols. Harvard University Press: Cambridge, 1937–.

*Dio's Roman History*. (Trans. by E. Cary.) 9 vols. Heinemann: London, 1914–1927. (Now handled by Harvard University Press, Cambridge.)

Dobson, J. F. *Ancient Education and Its Meaning to Us*. Longmans: New York, 1932.

Douglas, R. K. *China*. Putnam's: New York, 1904.

Drever, J. *Greek Education*. Univ. Press: Cambridge, 1912.

Duff, J. W. A Literary History of Rome. Unwin: London, 1923.

Dumont, A. Essai sur l'Éphébie Attique. 2 vols. Firmin-Didot: Paris, 1875–1876.

Dutt, M. N. The Mahabharata, A Prose English Translation. Elysium Press: Calcutta, 1895–1897.

Dutt, R. C. A History of Civilization in Ancient India. Thacker: Calcutta, 1891.

Eastman, C. A. Indian Boyhood. McClure, Phillips: New York, 1902.

Edgar, C. C. "A Women's Club in Ancient Alexandria." Jour. Egy. Archaeol. (1917), IV, 253–4.

Egger, J. B. Begriff der Gymnastik bei den Alten Philosophen und Medizinern. Freiburg in der Schweiz, 1903.

Ellis, H. The Dance of Life. Houghton Mifflin: Boston, 1923.

Elmer, R. P. Archery. Penn Pub. Co.: Philadelphia, 1926.

Emmanuel, M. The Antique Greek Dance. (Trans. by H. J. Beauley.) John Lane: New York, 1916.

Epictetus, The Discourses of, With the Encheiridion and Fragments. (Trans. by G. Long.) Burt: New York, n.d.

Erman, A. Aegypten und Aegyptisches Leben im Altertum. (Rev. by H. Ranke.) Mohr: Tübingen, 1923.

——. Life in Ancient Egypt. (Trans. by H. M. Tirard.) Macmillan: London, 1894.

Euler, C. Encyklopädisches Handbuch des Gesamten Turnwesens und der Verwandten Gebiete. 3 vols. Pichler's: Wien, 1894–1896.

Eunapius: The Lives of the Sophists [and] Philostratus. (Trans. by W. C. Wright.) Heinemann: London, 1922. (Now handled by Harvard University Press, Cambridge.)

Euripides. (Trans. by A. S. Way.) 4 vols. Heinemann: London, 1912. (Now handled by Harvard University Press, Cambridge.)

Evans, A. The Palace of Minos at Knossos. 5 vols. Macmillan: London, 1921–1936.

Evans, A. J. Scripta Minoa. Vol. 1. Clarendon Press: Oxford, 1909.

Evans, I. H. N. Among Primitive Peoples in Borneo. Lippincott: Philadelphia, 1922.

Falke, J. von. Greece and Rome; Their Life and Art. (Trans. by W. H. Browne.) Holt: New York, 1882.

Falkener, E. Games Ancient and Oriental and How to Play Them. Longmans: London, 1892.

Fedde, F. *Der Fünfkampf der Hellenen*. Breslau, 1888.

Feldman, W. M. *The Jewish Child*. Baillière Tindall, and Coxe: London, 1917.

Fell, R. A. L. *Etruria and Rome*. Univ. Press: Cambridge, 1924.

Felton, C. C. *Ancient and Modern Greece*. 2 vols. Ticknor and Fields: Boston, 1867.

Ferrero, G., and Barbagallo, C. *A Short History of Rome*. 2 vols. Putnam's: New York, 1918–1919.

Finegan, J. *Light from the Ancient Past; the Archaeological Background of the Hebrew-Christian Religion*. Princeton Univ. Press: Princeton, 1946.

Firdausí, *The Sháhnáma of*. (Trans. by A. G. Warner and E. Warner.) 9 vols. Kegan Paul, Trench, Trübner: London, 1905–1925.

Fletcher, A. C. *Indian Games and Dances with Native Songs*. Birchard: Boston, 1915.

Florus, Lucius Annaeus, *Epitome of Roman History*. (Trans. by E. S. Forster.) (With J. C. Rolfe's *Cornelius Nepos*.) Heinemann: London, 1929. (Now handled by Harvard University Press, Cambridge.)

Forbes, C. A. *Greek Physical Education*. Century: New York, 1929.

Forrer, E. "Die Inschriften und Sprachen des Hatti-Reiches." *Zeitschrift der Deutschen Morgenländischen Gesellschaft* (1922), LXXVI, 174–269.

Fort, G. F. *Medical Economy during the Middle Ages*. Bouton, Quaritch: New York, London, 1883.

Fowler, W. W.: *The Roman Festivals of the Period of the Republic*. Macmillan: New York, 1925.

———. *Social Life at Rome in the Age of Cicero*. Macmillan: New York, 1909.

Frank, T. *A History of Rome*. Holt: New York, 1926.

———. *Roman Imperialism*. Macmillan: New York, 1929.

———. *Rome and Italy of the Empire*. (Vol. v, *An Economic Survey of Ancient Rome*.) Johns Hopkins Press: Baltimore, 1940.

Freeman, K. J. *Schools of Hellas*. Macmillan: London, 1922.

Friedenwald, H. "The Relation of Jews and Judaism to the Medical Art." *Am. Med.* (Sept., 1917), N.S. XII, 615–21.

Friedlaender, L. *Darstellungen aus der Sittengeschichte Roms in der Zeit von August bis zum Ausgang der Antonine*. 3 vols. Hirzel: Leipzig, 1888–1890.

———. "Die Spiele." In J. Marquardt, *Römische Staatsverwaltung*, III, 482–566. Hirzel: Leipzig, 1885.

Friedländer, L. *Roman Life and Manners under the Early Empire*. (Trans. by L. A. Magnus et al.) 4 vols. Routledge: London, 1908–1913.

Fronto, Marcus Cornelius, *The Correspondence of.* (Trans. by C. R. Haines.) 2 vols. Heinemann, Putnam's: London, New York, 1919–1920.

Fuld, L. F. "Physical Education in Greece and Rome." *Am. Phys. Educ. Rev.* (Mar., 1907), XII, 1–13.

Furness, W. H. *Home Life of Borneo Head-Hunters.* Lippincott: Philadelphia, 1902.

Furtwängler, A., et al. *Griechische Vasenmalerei.* 6 vols. Bruckmann: München, 1904–1932.

Galen, C. *Opera Omnia.* (Ed. by D. C. G. Kühn.) 20 vols. Cnobloch: Lipsiae, 1821–1833.

*Galen on the Natural Faculties.* (Trans. by A. J. Brock.) Heinemann: London, 1916. (Now handled by Harvard University Press, Cambridge.)

Galien, *Oeuvres Anatomiques, Physiologiques et Médicales de.* (Trans. by C. Daremberg.) 2 vols. Baillière: Paris, 1854–1856.

Gann, T., and Thompson, J. E. *The History of the Maya.* Scribner's: New York, 1931.

Gardiner, E. N. *Athletics of the Ancient World.* Clarendon Press: Oxford, 1930.

——. "Further Notes on the Greek Jump." *Jour. Hellenic Studies* (1904), XXIV, 179–94.

——. *Greek Athletic Sports and Festivals.* Macmillan: London, 1910.

——. "The Method of Deciding the Pentathlon." *Jour. Hellenic Studies* (1903), XXIII, 54–70.

——. "Notes on the Greek Foot-Race." *Jour. Hellenic Studies* (1903), XXIII, 261–91.

——. "The Pancration and Wrestling." *Jour. Hellenic Studies* (1906), XXVI, 4–22.

——. "Phaÿllus and His Record Jump." *Jour. Hellenic Studies* (1904), XXIV, 70–80.

——. "A School in Ptolemaic Egypt." *Class. Rev.* (1930), XLIV, 211–3.

——. "Wrestling." *Jour. Hellenic Studies* (1905), XXV, 14–31, 263–93.

Gardner, E. A. *A Handbook of Greek Sculpture.* Macmillan: London, 1915.

Gardner, P. "Boat-Races among the Greeks." *Jour. Hellenic Studies* (1881), II, 90–7.

——. "Boat-Races at Athens." *Jour. Hellenic Studies* (1881), II, 315–7.

——. *New Chapters in Greek History.* Putnam's: New York, 1892.

——. "A Stele Commemorating a Victory in a Boat-Race." *Jour. Hellenic Studies* (1890), XI, 146–50.

Gardner, P., and Jevons, F. B. A Manual of Greek Antiquities. Griffin: London, 1895.

Gellius, Aulus, The Attic Nights of. (Trans. by J. C. Rolfe.) 3 vols. Heinemann: London, 1927–1928. (Now handled by Harvard University Press, Cambridge.)

Gerhard, F. W. E. Auserlesene Griechische Vasenbilder. 7 vols. Reimer: Berlin, 1840.

Gibbon, E. The History of the Decline and Fall of the Roman Empire. (With notes by H. H. Milman.) 5 vols. Porter and Coates: Philadelphia, n.d.

Giles, H. A. Adversaria Sinica. Kelly and Walsh: Shanghai, 1914.

———. "Football and Polo in China." Nineteenth Century (Mar., 1906), LIX, 508–13.

Giles, L. "The Awakening of China." Nineteenth Century (Oct., 1906), LX, 521–32.

Girard, P. L'Éducation Athénienne. Hachette: Paris, 1889.

"Gladiatorial Combats a Usual Form of Exercise." Am. Jour. Archaeol. (1901), v, 480.

Glotz, G. The Aegean Civilization. (Trans. by M. R. Dobie and E. M. Riley.) Knopf: New York, 1925.

———. Ancient Greece at Work. (Trans. by M. R. Dobie.) Kegan Paul, Trench, Trübner: London, 1926.

Gomperz, T. Greek Thinkers: A History of Ancient Philosophy. (Trans. by L. Magnus and G. G. Berry.) 4 vols. Scribner's: New York, 1901–1912.

Goodspeed, G. S. A History of the Babylonians and Assyrians. Scribner's: New York, 1902.

Graetz, H. History of the Jews. 7 vols. (Trans. in part by B. Löwy.) Jewish Pub. Society: Philadelphia, 1891–1898.

Grasberger, L. Erziehung und Unterricht im Klassischen Altertum. 3 vols. Stahel'schen Buch- und Kunsthandlung: Würzburg, 1864–1881.

Graves, F. P. A History of Education. 3 vols. Macmillan: New York, 1909–1913.

Gray, J. H. China. 2 vols. Macmillan: London, 1878.

———. "Physical Education in India." Am. Phys. Educ. Rev. (Oct., 1919), XXIV, 373–9.

Green, W. M. "Appropriations for the Games at Rome in 51 A.D." Am. Jour. Philol. (1930), LI, 249–50.

Greenshields, R. S. The Ball and the Polo Stick or Book of Ecstasy. (A trans. of Gūi u Chaugān or Hālnāma by Mahmud 'Ārifī.) Luzac: London, 1932.

Gregory of Tours: The History of the Franks. 2 vols. (Trans. by O. M. Dalton.) Clarendon Press: Oxford, 1927.

Griffith, F. L. "The Teaching of Amenophis the Son of Kanakht." Jour. Egy. Archaeol. (1926), XII, 191–231.

Griswold, H. D. The Religion of the Rig Veda. Oxford Univ. Press: London, 1923.

Groos, K. The Play of Man. (Trans. by E. Baldwin.) Appleton: New York, 1901.

Grote, G. A History of Greece. 4 vols. Am. Bk. Exchange: New York, 1881.

Grove, L. Dancing. Longmans: London, 1907.

Güdemann, M. "Education." Jewish Encyclopedia, v, 42–8.

Gulick, C. B. The Life of the Ancient Greeks. Appleton: New York, 1902.

Gutsch, C. The Greek Games and Their Mythology. Cambridge, 1900.

Gwynn, A. Roman Education from Cicero to Quintilian. Clarendon Press: Oxford, 1926.

Haddon, A. C. "A Few American String Figures and Tricks." Am. Anthropologist (1903), N.S. v, 213–23.

Hall, H. R. Aegean Archaeology. Warner: London, 1915.

———. The Oldest Civilization of Greece. Nutt: London, 1901.

Hambly, W. D. Tribal Dancing and Social Development. Witherby: London, 1926.

Hambly, W. D., and Hose, C. Origins of Education among Primitive Peoples. Macmillan: London, 1926.

Harper, R. F. The Code of Hammurabi. Univ. of Chicago Press: Chicago, 1904.

Hartwig, P. Die Griechischen Meisterschalen. 2 vols. Spemann: Stuttgart, 1893.

Harvey, F. J. The Fighting Gladiators. Phys. Training Pub. Co.: Exeter, Eng., 1903.

Havell, E. B. The History of Aryan Rule in India. Harrap: London, 1918.

Haynes, H. W. "Odysseus' Feat of Archery." Am. Jour. Archaeol. and Hist. of Fine Arts (1890), VI, 487.

Heitland, W. E. The Roman Republic. 3 vols. Univ. Press: Cambridge, 1909.

Heliodorus: An Aethiopian History. (Trans. by T. Underdowne.) Nutt: London, 1895.

Hermann, K. F. Lehrbuch der Griechischen Privatalterthümer. (Ed. by H. Blümner.) Mohr: Freiburg, 1882.

Herodotus, *The History of*. (Trans. by G. Rawlinson.) 4 vols. Appleton: New York, 1893.

Hesiod: *The Homeric Hymns and Homerica*. (Trans. by H. G. Evelyn-White.) Heinemann: London, 1914. (Now handled by Harvard University Press, Cambridge.)

Hippocrates. (Trans. by W. H. S. Jones and E. T. Withington.) 4 vols. Heinemann: London, 1923–1931. (Now handled by Harvard University Press, Cambridge.)

Hirth, F. *The Ancient History of China*. Columbia Univ. Press: New York, 1911.

Hirth, G. *Das Gesamte Turnwesen*. (Ed. by F. R. Gasch.) 4 vols. Lion: Hof, 1893–1895.

Hitti, P. K. *History of the Arabs*. Macmillan: London, 1937.

Hobhouse, W. *The Theory and Practice of Ancient Education*. Stechert: New York, 1910.

Hoffman, W. J. *The Graphic Art of the Eskimos*. Ann. Rep. Smithsonian Institution, Pt. II. Washington, 1897.

Hogarth, D. G. "The Zakro Sealings." *Jour. Hellenic Studies* (1902), XXII, 76–93.

Hoh, G. *Physical Education in China*. Commercial Press: Shanghai, 1926.

Holmes, J. H. *In Primitive New Guinea*. Putnam's: New York, 1924.

Holmes, T. R. *The Roman Republic and the Founder of the Empire*. 3 vols. Clarendon Press: Oxford, 1923.

Homer, *The Iliad of*. (Trans. by A. Lang, W. Leaf, and E. Myers.) Macmillan: London, 1923.

Homer, *The Iliads of*. (Trans. by G. Chapman.) 2 vols. J. R. Smith: London, 1865.

Homer, *The Odyssey of*. (Trans. by S. H. Butcher and A. Lang.) Macmillan: London, 1900.

Homer, *The Odysseys of*. (Trans. by G. Chapman.) Reeves and Turner: London, 1897.

Homo, L. *Primitive Italy and the Beginnings of Roman Imperialism*. (Trans. by V. G. Childe.) Kegan Paul, Trench, Trübner, London; Knopf, New York, 1926.

——. *Roman Political Institutions from City to State*. (Trans. by M. R. Dobie.) Knopf, New York; Kegan Paul, Trench, Trübner, London, 1929.

Horace. (Trans. by A. F. Murison.) Longmans: London, 1931.

Horace for English Readers. (Trans. by E. C. Wickham.) Clarendon Press: Oxford, 1903.

Hose, C. *Natural Man: A Record from Borneo*. Macmillan: London, 1926.

How, W. W., and Leigh, H. D. *A History of Rome to the Death of Caesar*. Longmans: London, 1917.

Hrozny, B. *Die älteste Geschichte Vorderasiens und Indiens*. Melantrich: Prague, 1943.

———. *Kretas und Vorgriechenlands Inschriften, Geschichte und Kultur*. Kohlhammer: Stuttgart, Prague, 1943.

Huart, C. *Ancient Persia and Iranian Civilization*. (Trans. by M. R. Dobie.) Knopf: New York, 1927.

Hyde, W. W. "Athlete Reliefs from the Themistoclean Wall at Athens." *Art and Archaeol*. (Mar., 1923), xv, 117–24.

———. *Greek Religion and Its Survivals*. Marshall Jones: Boston, 1923.

———. *Olympic Victor Monuments and Greek Athletic Art*. Carnegie Institution: Washington, 1921.

———. "Our Debt to Greek Athletics." In *School Athletics in Modern Education*. Wingate Mem. Foundation: New York, 1931.

———. "The Pentathlum Jump." *Am. Jour. Philol*. (Oct., 1938), LIX, 405–17.

*Iamblichus' Life of Pythagoras*. (Trans. by T. Taylor.) London, 1818.

Ihne, W. *The History of Rome*. 5 vols. Longmans: London, 1871–1882.

Im Thurn, E. F. *Among the Indians of Guiana*. Kegan Paul, Trench: London, 1883.

*Isocrates*. (Trans. by G. Norlin and L. Van Hook.) 3 vols. Heinemann: London, 1928–1945. (Now handled by Harvard University Press, Cambridge.)

Jackson, A. V. W. (Ed.) *History of India*. 9 vols. Grolier Society: London, 1906–1907.

———. *Persia Past and Present*. Macmillan: New York, 1906.

Jaeger, O. H. *Die Gymnastik der Hellenen*. Weychardt: Eszlingen, 1850.

Jaeger, W. *Paideia: The Ideals of Greek Culture*. (Trans. by G. Highet.) 3 vols. Oxford Univ. Press: New York, 1943–1945.

James, W. *The Principles of Psychology*. 2 vols. Holt: New York, 1890.

Jardé, A. *The Formation of the Greek People*. Knopf: New York, 1926.

Jastrow, M. *The Civilization of Babylonia and Assyria*. Lippincott: Philadelphia, 1915.

Jerome, St., *Select Letters of*. (Trans. by F. A. Wright.) Heinemann: London, 1933. (Now handled by Harvard University Press, Cambridge.)

Johns, C. H. W. *Babylonian and Assyrian Laws, Contracts and Letters*. Scribner's: New York, 1904.

Johnston, H. W. *The Private Life of the Romans.* (Rev. by M. Johnston.) Scott, Foresman: Chicago, 1932.

Johnstone, M. A. *Etruria Past and Present.* Methuen: London, 1930.

Jordanes: *The Origin and Deeds of the Goths.* (Trans. by C. C. Mierow.) Princeton, 1908.

Joseph, M. *Judaism as Creed and Life.* Macmillan: New York, 1910.

Josephus. (Trans. by H. St. J. Thackeray and R. Marcus.) 9 vols. Harvard University Press: Cambridge, 1926–.

Judson, H. P. *Caesar's Army: A Study of the Military Art of the Romans in the Last Days of the Republic.* Ginn: Boston, 1894.

Julian the Emperor . . . *Gregory Nazianzen's Two Invectives . . . Libanius' Monody with Julian's Extant Theosophical Works.* (Trans. by C. W. King.) Bell: London, 1888.

Jullien, E. *Les Professeurs de Littérature dans l'Ancienne Rome.* Ernest Leroux, Éditeur: Paris, 1885.

Jüthner, J. "Gymnastik." *Real-Encyclopädie,* vii, Pt. ii, 2030–85.

———. *Körperkultur im Altertum.* Fischer: Jena, 1928.

———. *Über Antike Turngeräthe.* Hölder: Wien, 1896.

Juvenal and Persius. (Trans. by G. G. Ramsay.) Heinemann: London, 1928. (Now handled by Harvard University Press, Cambridge.)

Karsten, R. *The Civilization of the South American Indians.* Knopf: New York, 1926.

Keay, F. E. *Ancient Indian Education.* Oxford Univ. Press: London, 1918.

Kees, H. *Der Opfertanz des Ägyptischen Königs.* J. C. Hinrichs'sche Buchhandlung: Leipzig, 1912.

Keil, J., and Premerstein, A. *Bericht über eine Reise in Lydien und der südlichen Aiolis, 1906. Denkschriften der Kaiserlichen Akademie der Wissenschaften in Wien,* Band liii. Wien, 1908.

Keller, A. G. *Homeric Society.* Longmans: New York, 1902.

Keller, R. M. "An Oriental Dance on an Attic Vase." *Bul. Fogg Mus. Art* (Nov., 1940), ix, 56–8.

Kenyon, F. G. "A Rescript of Marcus Antonius." *Class. Rev.* (Dec., 1893), vii, 476–8.

Kidd, D. *Savage Childhood: A Study of Kafir Children.* Black: London, 1906.

King, L. W. *A History of Babylon.* Chatto and Windus: London, 1919.

———. *A History of Sumer and Akkad.* Chatto and Windus: London, 1923.

Klebs, L. *Die Reliefs und Malereien des Neuen Reiches . . . Material zur Ägyptischen Kulturgeschichte. Teil I: Szenen aus dem Leben des Volkes.* Abhandlungen der Heidelberger Akademie der Wissenschaften, Nr. IX. Carl Winters Universitätsbuchhandlung: Heidelberg, 1934.

Klostermann, A. *Schulwesen im Alten Israel.* Deichert'sche Verlags Buchhandlung: Leipzig, 1908.

Kluckhohn, C., and Wyman, L. C. *An Introduction to Navaho Chant Practice.* Memoirs, Am. Anthrop. Assoc., no. 53, 1940.

*Knyghthode and Bataile.* A XVth Century Verse Paraphrase of Flavius Vegetius Renatus' "De Re Militari." (Ed. by R. Dyboski and Z. M. Arend.) Oxford Univ. Press: London, 1935.

Kober, A. E. Bedrich Hrozny's *Die älteste Geschichte Vorderasiens und Indiens,* and *Kretas und Vorgriechenlands Inschriften, Geschichte und Kultur.* Am. Jour. Archaeol. (Oct.–Dec., 1946), L, 493–5.

Korrigan, P. *Causerie sur la Pêche Fluviale en Chine.* La Mission Catholique: Chang-Hai, 1909.

Kraemer, C. J. "A Greek Element in Egyptian Dancing." *Am. Jour. Archaeol.* (1931), XXXV, 125–38.

Krause, J. H. *Die Gymnastik und Agonistik der Hellenen.* 2 vols. Barth: Leipzig, 1841.

———. *Die Pythien, Nemeen und Isthmien.* Barth: Leipzig, 1841.

———. *Geschichte der Erziehung, des Unterrichts und der Bildung bei den Griechen, Etruskern und Römern.* Pfeffer: Halle, 1851.

———. *Olympia oder Darstellung der Grossen Olympischen Spiele.* Beck: Wien, 1838.

———. *Theagenes oder Wissenschaftliche Darstellung der Gymnastik, Agonistik und Festspiele der Hellenen.* Anton: Halle, 1835.

Krishnayya, P. G. "The Yoga Asanas—An Important Phase of Physical Education Practiced in the Indigenous Schools and Seats of Learning in India from Time Immemorial." *Jour. Health and Phys. Educ.* (Feb., 1933), IV, 13–5, 55–6.

Kuo, P. W. *The Chinese System of Public Education.* Teachers College: New York, 1915.

Kyle, J. W. "The Maidens' Race on Attic Vases." *Am. Jour. Archaeol.* (1902), VI, 53.

Laistner, M. L. W. *A Survey of Ancient History to the Death of Constantine.* Heath: Boston, 1929.

Lamb, H. *Genghis Khan.* Garden City Pub. Co.: Garden City, 1927.

Lane, E. W. *An Account of the Manners and Customs of the Modern Egyptians.* 2 vols. Murray: London, 1871.

Lane, F. H. *Elementary Greek Education.* Bardeen: Syracuse, 1895.

Laufer, B. "The Early History of Polo." *Polo* (Apr., 1932), VII, 13–4, 43–4.

Laurie, S. S. *Historical Survey of Pre-Christian Education.* Longmans: London. 1895.

Law, B. C. *Ksatriya Clans in Buddhist India.* Thacker: Calcutta, 1922.

Lawton, W. C. *Introduction to Classical Greek Literature.* Scribner's: New York, 1903.

――――. *Introduction to Classical Latin Literature.* Scribner's: New York, 1904.

――――. *The Soul of the Anthology.* Yale Univ. Press: New Haven, 1923.

――――. *The Successors of Homer.* Macmillan: New York, 1898.

――――. *Three Dramas of Euripides.* Houghton Mifflin: Boston, 1889.

――――. "Womanhood in the Iliad." *Atl. Mo.* (June, 1893), LXXI, 784–801.

Layard, A. H. *The Monuments of Nineveh.* 2 vols. Murray: London, 1853.

――――. *Nineveh and Its Remains.* 2 vols. Murray: London, 1854.

Lee, J. *Play in Education.* Macmillan: New York, 1922.

Legge, J. *The Chinese Classics.* 8 vols. Trübner: London, 1861–1872.

Legrain, L. "L'Art Sumérien au Temps de la Reine Shoubad." *Gazette des Beaux-Arts* (July, 1931), ser. 6, VI, 1–26.

Leonard, F. E. *A Guide to the History of Physical Education.* (Ed. by R. T. McKenzie.) Lea, Febiger: Philadelphia, 1923.

Letourneau, C. *L'Évolution de l'Éducation dans les Diverses Races Humaines.* Vigot: Paris, 1898.

Levy-Brühl, L. *Das Denken der Naturvölker.* (Trans. by W. Jerusalem.) Braumüller: Wien, 1921.

Lewis, I. B. *The Education of Girls in China.* Teachers College: New York, 1919.

Lexová, I. *Ancient Egyptian Dances.* (Trans. by K. Haltmar.) Oriental Institute: Praha, 1935.

Liu, S. "The Physical Education Movement in China." *Jour. Health and Phys. Educ.* (Apr., 1932), III, 17–21, 61–2.

Livius, Titus, *The History of Rome.* (Trans. by D. Spillan and C. Edmonds.) 2 vols. Harper: New York, 1871.

Livy. (Trans. by B. O. Foster et al.) 13 vols. Harvard University Press: Cambridge, 1919–.

Loebker, G. *Die Gymnastik der Hellenen.* Deiters: Münster, 1835.

Loftus, W. K. *Travels and Researches in Chaldæa and Susiana.* Robert Carter: New York, 1857.

Longman, C. J., and Walrond, H. *Archery*. Longmans: London, 1894.

Lot, F. *The End of the Ancient World and the Beginnings of the Middle Ages*. (Trans. by P. Leon and M. Leon.) Kegan Paul, Trench, Trübner: London, 1931.

Lowell, A. "Songs of the Pueblo Indians." *Dial* (Sept., 1920), LXIX, 247–51.

Lucan: *The Civil War*. (Trans. by J. D. Duff.) Heinemann: London, 1928. (Now handled by Harvard University Press, Cambridge.)

Lucian of Samosata, *The Works of*. (Trans. by H. W. Fowler and F. G. Fowler.) 4 vols. Clarendon Press: Oxford, 1905.

*Lucreti Cari, T., de Rerum Natura*. (Trans. by H. A. J. Munro.) 3 vols. Deighton Bell: Cambridge, 1886.

*Lucretius Carus, Titus, on the Nature of Things*. (Trans. by T. Jackson.) Blakewell: Oxford, 1929.

*Lucretius: De Rerum Natura*. (Trans. by W. H. D. Rouse.) Heinemann: London, 1924. (Now handled by Harvard University Press, Cambridge.)

*Lucretius on the Nature of Things*. (Trans. by C. Bailey.) Clarendon Press: Oxford, 1910.

Luehring, F. W. *Swimming Pool Standards*. Barnes: New York, 1939.

*Lyra Graeca*. (Trans. by J. M. Edmonds.) 3 vols. Heinemann: London, 1922–1927. (Now handled by Harvard University Press, Cambridge.)

*Maccabees*. In *The Holy Bible* . . . and . . . *Apocrypha*, by H. Wace. 2 vols. Murray: London, 1888.

McCrindle, J. W. *Ancient India as Described by Megasthenês and Arrian*. Trübner: London, 1877.

McDaniel, W. B. *Roman Private Life and Its Survivals*. Longmans: New York, 1927.

Macdonell, A. A. *A History of Sanskrit Literature*. Heinemann: London, 1917.

McDougall, W. *Outline of Psychology*. Scribner's: New York, 1929.

Mace, A. C. "Hathor Dances." *Jour. Egy. Archaeol.* (1920), VI, 297.

Mackay, D. "Mohenjo-Daro and the Ancient Civilization of the Indus Valley." *Ann. Rep. Bd. Regs. Smithsonian Institution*, 1932. Pt. I, 429–44. Govt. Printing Off.: Washington, 1933.

Mackay, E. *The Indus Civilization*. Lovat Dickson and Thompson: London, 1935.

Mackay, E. J. H. *Further Excavations at Mohenjo-Daro*. 2 vols. Manager of Publications: Delhi, 1937–1938.

*Macrobivs*. (Ed. by F. Eyssenhardt.) Lipsiae, 1893.

Maddox, J. L. *The Medicine Man*. Macmillan: New York, 1923.

Mahaffy, J. P. *Greek Life and Thought.* Macmillan: New York, 1896.

———. *Old Greek Education.* Harper: New York, 1881.

———. *Social Life in Greece.* Macmillan: London, 1913.

Maiuri, A. *Pompei.* La Libreria Dello Stato: Roma, 1931.

Malinowski, B. *A Scientific Theory of Culture and Other Essays.* Univ. of N. C. Press: Chapel Hill, 1944.

Manning, C. A. "Professionalism in Greek Athletics." *Class. Wkly.* (Dec. 17, 1917), XI, 74–8.

Margolis, M. L., and Marx, A. *A History of the Jewish People.* Jewish Pub. Society of Am.: Philadelphia, 1927.

Marquardt, J. *Das Privatleben der Römer.* Hirzel: Leipzig, 1886.

———. *Römische Staatsverwaltung.* 3 vols. Hirzel: Leipzig, 1881–1885.

Marshall, J. *Mohenjo-Daro and the Indus Civilization.* 3 vols. Probsthain: London, 1931.

*Martial: Epigrams.* (Trans. by W. C. A. Ker.) 2 vols. Heinemann: London, 1919–1920. (Now handled by Harvard University Press, Cambridge.)

*Martial: The Twelve Books of Epigrams.* (Trans. by J. A. Pott and F. A. Wright.) Routledge, London; Dutton, New York, 1925.

Martin, W. A. P. *The Awakening of China.* Doubleday: New York, 1910.

———. *The Chinese.* Harper: New York, 1881.

———. *The Lore of Cathay.* Revell: New York, 1912.

Maspero, G. *The Dawn of Civilization: Egypt and Chaldaea.* (Trans. by M. L. McClure.) S.P.C.K.: London, 1901.

Matthews, W. "The Mountain Chant." *5th Ann. Rep. Bur. Am. Ethnol.* (1883–1884), pp. 379–467. Govt. Printing Off.: Washington, 1887.

———. *The Night Chant.* Memoirs, Am. Mus. Nat. Hist., vol. VI. New York, 1902.

Mau, A. "Bäder." *Real-Encyclopädie*, II, Pt. II, 2743–58.

———. "Ballspiel." *Real-Encyclopädie*, II, Pt. II, 2832–4.

———. *Pompeji in Leben und Kunst.* Engelmann: Leipzig, 1908.

*Maximus Tyrius, The Dissertations of.* (Trans. by T. Taylor.) 2 vols. Evans: London, 1804.

Mazois, F. *Les Ruines de Pompeii.* 4 vols. Didot: Paris, 1824–1831.

Means, P. A. *Ancient Civilizations of the Andes.* Scribner's: New York, 1931.

Mehl, E. *Antike Schwimmkunst.* Heimeran: München, 1927.

———. "Über Antike Schwimmkunst und Wasserspringstile." *Die Leibesübungen* (Aug. 20, 1925), I, 377–82.

Meissner, B. *Babylonien und Assyrien*. 2 vols. Carl Winters Universitätsbuch-handlung: Heidelberg, 1920–1925.

Menander. (Trans. by F. G. Allinson.) Heinemann: London, 1921. (Now handled by Harvard University Press, Cambridge.)

Milne, J. G. "Egyptian Nationalism under Greek and Roman Rule." *Jour. Egy. Archaeol.* (1928), XIV, 226–34.

Minucius Felix. (Trans. by G. H. Rendall.) (With T. R. Glover's *Tertullian*.) Heinemann: London, 1931. (Now handled by Harvard University Press, Cambridge.)

Modi, J. J. *Education among the Ancient Iranians*. Times Press: Bombay, 1905.

Mohler, S. L. *The Cestus*. Univ. of Pa. Ph.D. Thesis. Philadelphia, 1926.

Mommsen, A. *Feste der Stadt Athen im Altertum*. Teubner: Leipzig, 1898.

Mommsen, T. *The History of Rome*. (Trans. by W. P. Dickson.) 5 vols. Scribner's: New York, 1903.

Monroe, P. *Stereopticon Views in the History of Education*. New York, 1915.

Montell, G. "T'ou Hu—The Ancient Chinese Pitch-pot Game." *Ethnos* (1940), V, 70–83.

Montgomery, J. A. (Ed.) *Religions of the Past and Present*. Lippincott: Philadelphia, 1918.

Mordell, P. *The Origin of Letters and Numerals According to the Sefer Yet-zirah*. Mordell: Philadelphia, 1914.

Morgan, L. H. *Ancient Society*. Holt: New York, 1907.

Morley, S. G. "Chichen Itzá, an Ancient American Mecca." *Nat. Geog. Mag.* (1925), XLVII, 63–95.

Mosso, A. *The Dawn of Mediterranean Civilization*. (Trans. by M. C. Harrison.) Unwin: London, 1910.

———. *The Palaces of Crete and Their Builders*. Unwin: London, 1907.

Mourlot, F. *Essai sur l'Histoire de l'Augustalité dans l'Empire Romain*. Librairie, Émile Bouillon, Éditeur: Paris, 1895.

Müller, C. O. *The History and Antiquities of the Doric Race*. 2 vols. (Trans. by H. Tufnell and G. C. Lewis.) Murray: London, 1839.

Müller, F. M. (Ed.) *The Sacred Books of the East*. 50 vols. Clarendon Press: Oxford, 1879–1910.

Müller, K. O. *Die Etrusker*. (Rev. by W. Deecke.) Heitz: Stuttgart, 1877.

Myers, A. C. *The Boy George Washington . . . His Own Account of an Iroquois Indian Dance, 1748*. Author: Philadelphia, 1932.

Myers, A. C. *William Penn: His Own Account of the Lenni Lenape or Delaware Indians, 1683*. Author: Moylan, Pa., 1937.

Nepos, Cornelius. (Trans. by J. C. Rolfe.) (With E. S. Forster's *Florus: Epitome of Roman History*.) Heinemann: London, 1929. (Now handled by Harvard University Press, Cambridge.)

Newberry, P. E. *Beni-Hasan*, Pts. I and II. Archaeol. Survey of Egypt, ed. by F. L. Griffith. Egypt Exploration Fund: London, 1893.

Niebuhr, B. G. *Römische Geschichte*. Reimer: Berlin, 1853.

Nilsson, M. P. *Griechische Feste von Religiöser Bedeutung mit Ausschluss der Attischen*. Teubner: Leipzig, 1906.

Nizami of Ganja. *The Haft Paiker*. (Trans. by C. E. Wilson.) 2 vols. Probsthain: London, 1924.

Nowack, W. *Lehrbuch der Hebräischen Archäologie*. 2 vols. Mohr: Freiburg, 1894.

Oldfather, C. H. *The Greek Literary Texts from Greco-Roman Egypt*. Univ. of Wis. Studies, Soc. Sc. and Hist., no. 9. Madison, 1923.

Olmstead, A. T. *History of Assyria*. Scribner's: New York, 1923.

Oman, C. W. C. *The Art of War in the Middle Ages*. Blackwell: Oxford, 1885.

———. *A History of Greece*. Longmans: New York, 1910.

Opler, M. E. *An Apache Way of Life*. Univ. of Chicago Press: Chicago, 1941.

Oppian. (Trans. by A. W. Mair.) Heinemann: London, 1928. (Now handled by Harvard University Press, Cambridge.)

Ouseley, W. *Travels in Various Countries of the East; More Particularly Persia*. 3 vols. Rodwell and Martin: London, 1819–1823.

Overbeck, J. *Pompeji in Seinen Gebäuden, Alterthümern, und Kunstwerken*. Rev. by A. Mau. Engelmann: Leipzig, 1884.

Ovid: *The Art of Love, and Other Poems*. (Trans. by J. H. Mozley.) Heinemann: London, 1929. (Now handled by Harvard University Press, Cambridge.)

Ovid: *Heroides and Amores*. (Trans. by G. Showerman.) Heinemann: London, 1921. (Now handled by Harvard University Press, Cambridge.)

Ovid: *Metamorphoses*. (Trans. by F. J. Miller.) 2 vols. Heinemann: London, 1916. (Now handled by Harvard University Press, Cambridge.)

Ovid: *Tristia* [and] *Ex Ponto*. (Trans. by A. L. Wheeler.) Heinemann: London, 1924. (Now handled by Harvard University Press, Cambridge.)

Ovid's *Fasti*. (Trans. by J. G. Frazer.) Heinemann: London, 1931. (Now handled by Harvard University Press, Cambridge.)

*Ovid's Metamorphoses.* (Trans. by Dryden et al.) 2 vols. Tonson and Draper: London, 1751.

Parker, H. M. D. *The Roman Legions.* Clarendon Press: Oxford, 1928.

Pater, W. *Greek Studies.* Macmillan: New York, 1901.

*Paterculus, Velleius, Compendium of Roman History* [and] *Res Gestae Divi Augusti.* (Trans. by F. W. Shipley.) Heinemann: London, 1924. (Now handled by Harvard University Press, Cambridge.)

Paul-Louis. *Ancient Rome at Work.* (Trans. by E. B. F. Wareing.) Knopf: New York, 1927.

Paulinus Pellaeus: *The Eucharisticus* [and] *Ausonius.* (Trans. by H. G. Evelyn White.) Heinemann: London, 1921. (Now handled by Harvard University Press, Cambridge.)

*Paulys Real-Encyclopädie der Classischen Altertumswissenschaft.* (Ed. by G. Wissowa, W. Kroll, et al.) Ser. 1 and 2, 51 half vols.; supp., 7 vols. Metzlerscher Verlag: Stuttgart, 1894–1940.

*Pausanias's Description of Greece.* (Trans. by J. G. Frazer.) 6 vols. Macmillan: London, 1898.

Pavlov, I. P. *Conditioned Reflexes.* (Trans. and ed. by G. V. Anrep.) Oxford Univ. Press: London, 1927.

————. *Lectures on Conditioned Reflexes.* (Trans. by W. H. Gantt.) International Publishers: New York, 1928.

Peet, T. E. *The Stone and Bronze Ages in Italy and Sicily.* Clarendon Press: Oxford, 1909.

————. "The Year's Work at Abydos." *Jour. Egy. Archaeol.* (1914), 1, 37–9.

Peet, T. E., and Woolley, C. L. *The City of Akhenaten.* Egypt Exploration Society: London, 1923.

Pelham, H. F. *Outlines of Roman History.* Putnam's: New York, 1900.

Peritz, I. J. *Old Testament History.* Abingdon Press: New York, 1915.

Perrot, G., and Chipiez, C. *Histoire de l'Art dans l'Antiquité.* 10 vols. Hachette: Paris, 1882–1914.

Perry, W. C. *Greek and Roman Sculpture.* Longmans: London, 1882.

Petersen, C. *Das Gymnasium der Griechen nach Seiner Baulichen Einrichtung.* Perthes-Besser, Mauke: Hamburg, 1858.

Petrie, W. M., and Quibell, J. E. *Naqada and Ballas.* Quaritch: London, 1896.

Petrie, W. M. F. *Egypt and Israel.* S.P.C.K.: London, 1912.

Petrie, W. M. F., et al. *A History of Egypt.* 6 vols. Scribner's: New York, 1899–1901.

*Petronius.* (Trans. by M. Heseltine.) (With Seneca's *Apocolocyntosis.*) Heinemann: London, 1925. (Now handled by Harvard University Press, Cambridge.)

Philadelpheus, A. "Three Statue-Bases Recently Discovered at Athens." *Jour. Hellenic Studies* (1922), XLII, 104–6.

*Philostratos: Concerning Gymnastics.* (Trans. by T. Woody.) Reprinted from *The Research Quarterly* (May, 1936), VII, no. 2.

*Philostratos: Über Gymnastik.* (Trans. by J. Jüthner.) Teubner: Leipzig, 1909.

*Philostratus: Imagines* [and] *Callistratus: Descriptions.* (Trans. by A. Fairbanks.) Heinemann: London, 1931. (Now handled by Harvard University Press, Cambridge.)

*Philostratus: The Life of Apollonius of Tyana.* (Trans. by F. C. Conybeare.) 2 vols. Heinemann: London, 1912. (Now handled by Harvard University Press, Cambridge.)

*Philostratus: The Lives of the Sophists* [and] *Eunapius.* (Trans. by W. C. Wright.) Heinemann: London, 1922. (Now handled by Harvard University Press, Cambridge.)

Pisan, Christine de. *The Book of Fayttes of Armes and of Chyualrye.* (Trans. by W. Caxton.) Oxford Univ. Press: London, 1932.

Platner, S. B. *A Typographical Dictionary of Ancient Rome.* (Rev. by T. Ashby.) Oxford Univ. Press: London, 1929.

*Plato, The Dialogues of.* (Trans. by B. Jowett.) 5 vols. Oxford Univ. Press: New York, 1892.

*Plato, The Works of.* (Trans. by H. Cary, H. Davis, and G. Burges.) 6 vols. Bohn: London, 1849–1854.

*Plautus.* (Trans. by P. Nixon.) 5 vols. Harvard University Press: Cambridge, 1916.

*Pliny: Letters.* (Trans. by W. Melmoth; rev. by W. M. L. Hutchinson.) 2 vols. Heinemann: London, 1915. (Now handled by Harvard University Press, Cambridge.)

*Pliny: Natural History.* (Trans. by H. Rackham.) 10 vols. Harvard University Press: Cambridge, 1938–.

*Pliny, The Natural History of.* (Trans. by J. Bostock and H. T. Riley.) 6 vols. Bohn: London, 1855–1857.

Plummer, E. M. "Athletic Games among the Homeric Heroes." *Am. Phys. Educ. Rev.* (Dec., 1897), II, 197–208.

———. "The Olympic Games in Ancient Times." *Am. Phys. Educ. Rev.* (Mar., June, 1898), III, 1–18, 93–106.

———. "Toys and Games for Children among the Ancient Hellenes." *Am. Phys. Educ. Rev.* (Sept., 1898), III, 157–69.

Plutarch, The Roman Questions of. (Trans. by H. J. Rose.) Clarendon Press: Oxford, 1924.

Plutarch's Lives. (Trans. by B. Perrin.) 11 vols. Heinemann: London, 1914–1926. (Now handled by Harvard University Press, Cambridge.)

Plutarch's Lives and Writings. (Ed. by A. H. Clough and W. W. Goodwin.) 10 vols. Little, Brown: Boston, 1909.

Plutarch's Moralia. (Trans. by F. C. Babbitt et al.) 14 vols. Harvard University Press: Cambridge, 1927–.

Pollucis, Iulii, Onomasticon cum Annotationibus Interpretum. 5 vols. Curavit Guilielmus Dindorfius: Lipsiae, 1824.

Polybius: The Histories. (Trans. by W. R. Paton.) 6 vols. Heinemann: London, 1922–1927. (Now handled by Harvard University Press, Cambridge.)

Poulsen, F. Etruscan Tomb Paintings. (Trans. by I. Andersen.) Clarendon Press: Oxford, 1922.

Pratt, J. B. India and Its Faiths. Houghton Mifflin: Boston, 1915.

Preston, H. W., and Dodge, L. The Private Life of the Romans. Sanborn: Chicago, 1923.

Procopius. (Trans. by H. B. Dewing.) 7 vols. Harvard University Press: Cambridge, 1914–1940.

Pumpelly, R. Explorations in Turkestan, Expedition of 1904. 2 vols. Carnegie Institution: Washington, 1908.

Quintilian, The Institutio Oratoria of. (Trans. by H. E. Butler.) 4 vols. Harvard University Press: Cambridge, 1921–1936.

Radcliffe, W. Fishing from the Earliest Times. Dutton: New York, 1921.

Ragozin, Z. A. The Story of Media, Babylon, and Persia. Putnam's: New York, 1898.

Ramsay, W., and Lanciani, R. A. A Manual of Roman Antiquities. Griffin: London, n.d.

Randall-MacIver, D. The Etruscans. Clarendon Press: Oxford, 1927.

———. The Iron Age in Italy. Clarendon Press: Oxford, 1927.

———. Villanovans and Early Etruscans. Clarendon Press: Oxford, 1924.

Raum, O. F. Chaga Childhood. Oxford Univ. Press: London, 1940.

Rawlinson, G. The Five Great Monarchies of the Ancient Eastern World. 3 vols. Dodd, Mead: New York, 1881.

———. The Story of Ancient Egypt. Putnam's: New York, 1888.

Rawlinson, H. G. Intercourse between India and the Western World. Univ. Press: Cambridge, 1926.

Reed, V. Z. "The Ute Bear Dance." *Am. Anthropologist* (1896), O.S. IX, 237–44.

Reid, A. *The Principles of Heredity.* Chapman and Hall: London, 1906.

Reinach, S. *Orpheus.* (Trans. by F. Simmonds.) Liveright: New York, 1930.

Renan, E. *History of the People of Israel.* 5 vols. Roberts: Boston, 1894–1895.

*Res' Gestae Divi Augusti* [and the] *Roman History* of Velleius Paterculus. (Trans. by F. W. Shipley.) Heinemann: London, 1924. (Now handled by Harvard University Press, Cambridge.)

Richardson, B. E. *Old Age among the Ancient Greeks.* Johns Hopkins Press: Baltimore, 1933.

Richardson, R. B. "The Gymnasium at Eretria." *Am. Jour. Archaeol. and Hist. of Fine Arts* (1896), XI, 152–65.

Richardson, R. B., and Heermance, T. W. "Inscriptions from the Gymnasium at Eretria." *Am. Jour. Archaeol. and Hist. of Fine Arts* (1896), XI, 173–95.

Richter, W. *Die Spiele der Griechen und Römer.* Seemann: Leipzig, 1887.

Ridington, W. R. *The Minoan-Mycenaean Background of Greek Athletics.* Author: Philadelphia, 1935.

Riesman, D. *The Story of Medicine in the Middle Ages.* Hoeber: New York, 1935.

*Rig-Veda.* (Trans. by H. Grassmann.) 2 vols. Brockhaus: Leipzig, 1876–1877.

Riley, E. B. *Among Papuan Head-Hunters.* Lippincott: Philadelphia, 1925.

Ringwood, I. C. *Agonistic Features of Local Greek Festivals Chiefly from Inscriptional Evidence.* Columbia Univ. Ph.D. Thesis. Poughkeepsie, 1927.

Rivers, W. H. R. *The History of Melanesian Society.* 2 vols. Univ. Press: Cambridge, 1914.

Robinson, C. E. *A History of Greece.* Crowell: New York, 1929.

Rogers, R. W. *A History of Babylonia and Assyria.* 2 vols. Abingdon Press: New York, 1915.

Rostovtzeff, M. "Frumentum." *Real-Encyclopädie,* VII, Pt. 1, 126–87.

———. *A History of the Ancient World.* 2 vols. (Trans. by J. D. Duff.) Clarendon Press: Oxford, 1926–1927.

———. *The Social and Economic History of the Hellenistic World.* 3 vols. Clarendon Press: Oxford, 1941.

———. *The Social and Economic History of the Roman Empire.* Clarendon Press: Oxford, 1926.

Sachs, C. *World History of the Dance.* (Trans. by B. Schönberg.) Norton: New York, 1937.

St. John, J. A. *The History of the Manners and Customs of Ancient Greece.* 3 vols. Bentley: London, 1842.

*Sallust.* (Trans. by J. C. Rolfe.) Heinemann: London, 1920. (Now handled by Harvard University Press, Cambridge.)

Sandys, J. E. *A Companion to Latin Studies.* Univ. Press: Cambridge, 1925.

Sawhill, J. A. *The Use of Athletic Metaphors in the Biblical Homilies of St. John Chrysostom.* Princeton Univ. Press: Princeton, 1928.

Sayce, A. H. *The Ancient Empires of the East.* Scribner's: New York, 1884.

———. *Babylonians and Assyrians.* Scribner's: New York, 1900.

———. "The Early Geography of South-Eastern Asia Minor." *Jour. Hellenic Studies* (1923), XLIII, 44–9.

———. *The Early History of the Hebrews.* Macmillan: New York, 1897.

Schäfer, H., and Andrae, W. *Die Kunst des Alten Orients.* Propyläen-Verlag: Berlin, 1925.

Schanz, M. *Geschichte der Römischen Literatur.* (4th ed. by C. Hosius.) C. H. Beck'sche Verlagsbuchhandlung: München, 1927–1935.

Schleyer, W. *Bäder und Badeanstalten.* Carl Scholtze: Leipzig, 1909.

Schliemann, H. *Mycenae; a Narrative of Researches and Discoveries at Mycenae and Tiryns.* Scribner's: New York, 1880.

Schmidt, R. *Fakire und Fakirtum im Alten und Modernen Indien.* Hermann Barsdorf: Berlin, 1908.

Schoolcraft, H. R. *Archives of Aboriginal Knowledge.* 6 vols. Lippincott: Philadelphia, 1868.

Schreiber, T. *Atlas of Classical Antiquities.* (Ed. by W. C. F. Anderson.) Macmillan: London, 1895.

Schröder, B. *Der Sport im Altertum.* Hans Schoetz: Berlin, 1927.

Schuchhardt, C. *Schliemann's Excavations.* (Trans. by E. Sellers.) Macmillan: London, 1891.

Scott, E. *Dancing in All Ages.* Swan Sonnenschein: London, 1899.

*Scriptores Historiae Augustae, The.* (Trans. by D. Magie.) 3 vols. Heinemann: London, 1922–1932. (Now handled by Harvard University Press, Cambridge.)

Sears, J. M. J. "A Greek Bath." *Am. Jour. Archaeol.* (1904), VIII, 216–26.

Senart, É. *Caste in India.* (Trans. by E. D. Ross.) Methuen: London, 1930.

*Seneca ad Lucilium Epistulae Morales.* (Trans. by R. M. Gummere.) 3 vols. Heinemann: London, 1917–1925. (Now handled by Harvard University Press, Cambridge.)

Seneca: Apocolocyntosis. (Trans. by W. H. D. Rouse.) (With M. Heseltine's Petronius.) Heinemann: London, 1925. (Now handled by Harvard University Press, Cambridge.)

Seneca: Moral Essays. (Trans. by J. W. Basore.) 3 vols. Harvard University Press: Cambridge, 1928–1935.

Senecae, M. Annaei, Rhetoris Suasoriae, Controversiae, Declamationumque Excerpta. (Ed. by A. Schott.) Amsterdam, 1628.

Seymour, T. D. Life in the Homeric Age. Macmillan: New York, 1907.

Showerman, G. Rome and the Romans. Macmillan: New York, 1931.

Shryock, J. K. The Origin and Development of the State Cult of Confucius. Century: New York, 1932.

Sidonius, The Letters of. (Trans. by O. M. Dalton.) 2 vols. Clarendon Press: Oxford, 1915.

Simon, J. L'Éducation et l'Instruction d'après la Bible et le Talmud. Leipzig, 1879.

Simpson, D. C. "The Hebrew Book of Proverbs and the Teaching of Amenophis." Jour. Egy. Archaeol. (1926), XII, 232–9.

Sinclair, T. A. A History of Classical Greek Literature. Macmillan: New York, 1935.

Sloley, R. W. "Primitive Methods of Measuring Time." Jour. Egy. Archaeol. (1931), XVII, 166–78.

Smith, A. H. Chinese Characteristics. Revell: New York, 1894.

———. Village Life in China. Revell: New York, 1899.

Smith, H. P. Old Testament History. Scribner's: New York, 1903.

Smith, S. Early History of Assyria. 2 vols. Chatto and Windus: London, 1928–.

Smith, V. A. The Early History of India. Clarendon Press: Oxford, 1914.

Speiser, E. A. Mesopotamian Origins. Univ. of Pa. Press: Philadelphia, 1930.

Spencer, F. C. Education of the Pueblo Child. Macmillan: New York, 1899.

Spencer, W. B., and Gillen, F. J. The Arunta: A Study of a Stone Age People. 2 vols. Macmillan: London, 1927.

———. The Native Tribes of Central Australia. Macmillan: London, 1899.

———. Northern Tribes of Central Australia. Macmillan: London, 1904.

Spiegelberg, W. "Note on the Feminine Character of the New Empire." Jour. Egy. Archaeol. (1929), XV, 199.

Spiers, B. The School System of the Talmud. Stock: London, 1898.

Springer, A. Die Kunst des Altertums. (12th ed.) 6 vols. Alfred Kröner Verlag: Leipzig, 1923–1929.

Statius, *The Silvae of*. (Trans. by D. A. Slater.) Clarendon Press: Oxford, 1908.

Staunton, G. *An Authentic Account of an Embassy from the King of Great Britain to the Emperor of China*. 2 vols. Nicol: London, 1798.

Stevenson, M. C. "Zuñi Games." *Am. Anthropologist* (1903), N.S. v, 468–97.

———. *The Zuñi Indians. 23d Ann. Rep. Bur. Am. Ethnol., 1901–1902*. Govt. Printing Off.: Washington, 1904.

Stobart, J. C. *The Glory That Was Greece*. Lippincott: Philadelphia, 1911.

Strabo, *The Geography of*. (Trans. by H. C. Hamilton and W. Falconer.) 3 vols. Bell: London, 1903–1906.

Strabo, *The Geography of*. (Trans. by H. L. Jones.) 8 vols. Heinemann: London, 1917–1932. (Now handled by Harvard University Press, Cambridge.)

Suetonius. (Trans. by J. C. Rolfe.) 2 vols. Heinemann: London, 1914. (Now handled by Harvard University Press, Cambridge.)

Swift, F. H. *Education in Ancient Israel*. Open Court: Chicago, 1919.

Swindler, M. H. *Ancient Painting from the Earliest Times to the Period of Christian Art*. Yale Univ. Press: New Haven, 1929.

Sykes, P. M. *Ten Thousand Miles in Persia or Eight Years in Iran*. Murray: London, 1902.

Symmachi, Q. *Avrelii, Qvae Svpersvnt*. (Ed. by O. Seeck.) Berolini, 1883.

Symonds, J. A. *Studies of the Greek Poets*. 2 vols. Harper: New York, n.d.

Tacitus, *Annals of*. (Trans. by A. J. Church and W. J. Brodribb.) Macmillan: London, 1921.

Tacitus: *Dialogus*. (Trans. by W. Peterson.) *Agricola* [and] *Germania*. (Trans. by M. Hutton.) Heinemann: London, 1925. (Now handled by Harvard University Press, Cambridge.)

Tacitus, *The Histories of*. (Trans. by G. G. Ramsay.) Murray: London, 1915.

Tarbell, F. B. "The Palm of Victory." *Class. Philol.* (1908), III, 264–72.

Tarn, W. W. *Hellenistic Military and Naval Developments*. Univ. Press: Cambridge, 1930.

Taylor, J. W. "The Athenian Ephebic Oath." *Class. Jour.* (Apr., 1918), XIII, 495–501.

Taylor, L. R. "New Light on the History of the Secular Games." *Am. Jour. Philol.* (1934), LV, 101–20.

Terence. (Trans. by J. Sargeaunt.) 2 vols. Heinemann: London, 1912. (Now handled by Harvard University Press, Cambridge.)

Tertullian: *Apology* [and] *De Spectaculis.* (Trans. by T. R. Glover.) (With G. H. Rendall's *Minucius Felix.*) Heinemann: London, 1931. (Now handled by Harvard University Press, Cambridge.)

Theocritus, *The Idylls of.* (Trans. by J. H. Hallard.) Rivingtons: London, 1913.

Theodosianus, *Codex.* (New ed. by J. D. Ritter.) 6 vols. Weidmann: Lipsiae, 1736–1743.

Thomas, R. *Swimming.* Sampson Low: London, 1904.

Thomas, W. I. *Sex and Society.* Univ. of Chicago Press: Chicago, 1907.

Thomason, A. D. F. "Physical Education in India." *Mind and Body* (Mar., 1929), xxxv, 407–16.

Thorndike, E. L. *Educational Psychology.* 3 vols. Teachers College: New York, 1913.

Thorndike. L. *The History of Medieval Europe.* Houghton Mifflin: Boston, 1928.

Thucydides. (Trans. by B. Jowett.) 2 vols. Clarendon Press: Oxford, 1900.

Tixier's *Travels on the Osage Prairies.* (Ed. by J. F. McDermott; trans. by A. J. Salvan.) Univ. of Okla. Press: Norman, 1940.

Tod, M. N. "Teams of Ball-Players at Sparta." *Ann. Brit. Sch. Athens* (1903–1904), x, 63–77.

Todd, A. J. *The Primitive Family as an Educational Agency.* Putnam's: New York, 1913.

Trachtenberg, J. *Jewish Magic and Superstition: A Study in Folk Religion.* Behrman's Jewish Bk. House: New York, 1939.

Tsountas, C., and Manatt, J. I. *The Mycenaean Age.* Houghton Mifflin: Boston, 1897.

Tucker, T. G. *Life in Ancient Athens.* Macmillan: New York, 1929.

———. *Life in the Roman World of Nero and St. Paul.* Macmillan: New York, 1936.

Twitmyer, E. B. *A Study of the Kneejerk.* Univ. of Pa.: Philadelphia, 1902.

Tylor, E. B. *Anthropology.* Appleton: New York, 1899.

———. *On American Lot-Games, as Evidence of Asiatic Intercourse before the Time of Columbus.* Repr., *Internationales Archiv für Ethnographie,* supp. to vol. ix, 1896. Leiden, 1896.

———. *Primitive Culture.* 2 vols. Murray: London, 1913.

Ueberweg, F. *History of Philosophy.* 2 vols. (Trans. by G. S. Morris.) Scribner's: New York, 1893.

Ussing, J. L. *Darstellung des Erziehungs-und Unterrichtswesens bei den Griechen und Römern.* (Trans. by P. Friedrichsen.) Mentzel: Altona, 1870.

*Valerius Maximus*. (Ed. by C. B. Hase.) 2 vols. Lemaire: Paris, 1822–1823.

Van Aalst, J. A. *Chinese Music*. Statistical Dept., Inspectorate General of Customs: Shanghai, 1884.

Van Hook, L. *Greek Life and Thought*. Columbia Univ. Press: New York, 1923.

Varro, Marcus Terentius: *On Agriculture* [and] Cato: *On Agriculture*. (Trans. by W. D. Hooper; rev. by H. B. Ash.) Harvard University Press: Cambridge, 1934.

Varro: *On the Latin Language*. (Trans. by R. G. Kent.) 2 vols. Harvard University Press: Cambridge, 1938.

*Vegeti, Flavi Renati, Epitoma Rei Militaris*. (Ed. by C. Lang.) Lipsiae, 1885.

Venkateswara, S. V. *Indian Culture through the Ages. Vol. I: Education and the Propagation of Culture*. Longmans: London, 1928.

Venturi, L. *History of Art Criticism*. (Trans. by C. Marriott.) Dutton: New York, 1936.

Viollet-le-Duc, E. M. *Entretiens sur l'Architecture*. A. Morel et Cie: Paris, 1863–1872.

*Virgil, The Aeneid of*. (Trans. by H. H. Ballard.) Scribner's: New York, 1930.

*Virgil, The Works of*. (Trans. by A. H. Bryce.) Bell: London, 1902.

*Vitruvius on Architecture*. (Trans. by F. Granger.) 2 vols. Heinemann: London, 1931–1934. (Now handled by Harvard University Press, Cambridge.)

Vlachos, N. P. *Hellas and Hellenism*. Ginn: New York, 1936.

Vuillier, G. *A History of Dancing from the Earliest Ages to Our Own Times*. Appleton: New York, 1898.

Walden, J. W. H. *The Universities of Ancient Greece*. Scribner's: New York, 1909.

Wallon, H. A. *Histoire de l'Esclavage dans l'Antiquité*. 3 vols. Dezobry, E. Magdeleine, Libraires—Éditeurs: Paris, 1847.

Ward, W. *Account of the Writings, Religion, and Manners of the Hindoos*. 4 vols. Mission Press: Serampore, 1811.

Watson, J. B. *The Ways of Behaviorism*. Harper: New York, 1928.

Way, A. S. *The Odes of Bacchylides*. Macmillan: London, 1929.

———. *The Odes of Pindar*. Macmillan: London, 1922.

Webster, H. *Primitive Secret Societies*. Macmillan: New York, 1908.

Weege, F. *Etruskische Malerei*. Niemeyer: Halle, 1921.

West, G. *A Dissertation on the Olympick Games* [and a trans. of the] *Odes of Pindar*. Dodsley: London, 1749.

Westaway, K. M. *The Educational Theory of Plutarch.* Univ. of London: London, 1922.

Westermann, W. L. "Apprentice Contracts and the Apprentice System in Roman Egypt." *Class. Philol.* (1914), IX, 295–315.

———. "The Castanet Dancers of Arsinoe." *Jour. Egy. Archaeol.* (1924), X, 134–44.

———. "Entertainment in the Villages of Graeco-Roman Egypt." *Jour. Egy. Archaeol.* (1932), XVIII, 16–27.

———. "The Ptolemies and the Welfare of Their Subjects." *Am. Hist. Rev.* (Jan., 1938), XLIII, 270–87.

———. "Vocational Training in Antiquity." *Sch. Rev.* (1914), XXII, 601–10.

Wheeler, B. I. *Alexander the Great.* Putnam's: New York, 1900.

Whibley, L. *A Companion to Greek Studies.* Univ. Press: Cambridge, 1905.

Wiesen, J. *Geschichte und Methodik des Schulwesens im Talmudischen Alterthum.* Strasburg, 1892.

Wietersheim, E. von. *Geschichte der Völkerwanderung.* 2 vols. Weigel: Leipzig, 1880–1881.

Wilamowitz-Moellendorff, U. *Aristoteles und Athen.* 2 vols. Weidmannsche Buchhandlung: Berlin, 1893.

Wilkins, A. S. *National Education in Greece.* Strahan: London, 1873.

———. *Roman Education.* Univ. Press: Cambridge, 1905.

Wilkinson, J. G. *The Manners and Customs of the Ancient Egyptians.* 3 vols. Cassino: Boston, 1883.

Williams, E. T. *China Yesterday and Today.* Crowell: New York, 1923.

Williamson, A. *Journeys in North China.* 2 vols. Smith, Elder: London, 1870.

Wilson, E. (Ed.) *Egyptian Literature.* Colonial Press: New York, 1902.

Wilson, J. A. "Ceremonial Games of the New Kingdom." *Jour. Egy. Archaeol.* (1931), XVII, 211–20.

Windelband, W. *A History of Philosophy.* (Trans. by J. H. Tufts.) Macmillan: New York, 1938.

Wissowa, G. *Religion und Kultus der Römer.* C. H. Beck'sche Verlagsbuchhandlung: München, 1902.

Wolff, C. *Öffentliche Bade- und Schwimmanstalten.* G. J. Göschen'sche Verlagshandlung, 1908.

Woodworth, R. S. *Contemporary Schools of Psychology.* Ronald Press: New York, 1931.

———. *Experimental Psychology.* Holt: New York, 1938.

Woodworth, R. S. *Psychology*. Holt: New York, 1929.

Woody, T. "The Fair Sex in Greek Society." *Research Quarterly* (May, 1939), x, 57–71.

———. *A History of Women's Education in the United States*. 2 vols. Science Press: Lancaster, 1929.

———. "Professionalism and the Decay of Greek Athletics." Repr. from *Sch. and Soc.* (Apr. 23, 1938), XLVII, 521–8.

Wright, F. A. *Greek Athletics*. Cape: London, 1925.

———. *Greek Social Life*. Dent, London; Dutton, New York, 1925.

Wright, F. A., and Sinclair, T. A. *A History of the Later Latin Literature*. Routledge: London, 1931.

Wright, W. C. *A Short History of Greek Literature*. American Book Co.: New York, 1907.

Wyman, L. C., and Kluckhohn, C. *Navaho Classification of Their Song Ceremonials*. Memoirs, Am. Anthrop. Assoc., no. 50, 1938.

Xenophon: *Anabasis*. (Trans. by J. S. Watson.) Bell: London, 1915.

Xenophon: *Memorabilia and Oeconomicus*. (Trans. by E. C. Marchant.) Heinemann: London, 1923. (Now handled by Harvard University Press, Cambridge.)

Xenophon: *Scripta Minora*. (Trans. by E. C. Marchant.) Heinemann: London, 1925. (Now handled by Harvard University Press, Cambridge.)

Xenophon: *Symposium and Apology*. (Trans. by O. J. Todd.) (With C. L. Brownson's *Anabasis*.) Heinemann: London, 1922. (Now handled by Harvard University Press, Cambridge.)

Xenophon, *The Works of*. (Trans. by H. G. Dakyns.) 4 vols. Macmillan: London, 1890–1897.

Xenophon's *Cyropaedia, or Institution of Cyrus, and the Hellenics*. (Trans. by J. S. Watson and H. Dale.) Bell: London, 1891.

Young, C. V. P. *How Men Have Lived*. Stratford: Boston, 1931.

Zend-Avesta, The. (Trans. by J. Darmesteter and L. H. Mills.) 3 vols. Clarendon Press: Oxford, 1880–1887.

Ziebarth, E. "Juvenes." *Real-Encyclopädie*, x, Pt. II, 1357–8.

———. "Schulen." *Real-Encyclopädie*, ser. 2, II, Pt. I, 758–68.

# INDEX

Mental and physical education (*continued*)
289, 298–315; in China, 118, 121, 132,
146; Plato on, 441ff.; Socrates on, 431f.
Mental discipline, Aristotle on, 455f.; He-
brew, 109; Plato on, 437f.; Quintilian on,
603
Mental education (see education)
Merchants, Athenian, 281f.; Babylonian, 78;
Chinese, 112; Cicero on, 502; Cretan,
200; emergence of, 5; Hindu, 159, 160;
Plato's view of, 432, 440; Roman, 562,
564f.; Spartan, 236
Mercury, 533
Merneptah, 215
Merodach, 77, 78, 81f.
Mesopotamian, agriculture, 75, 77, 79; cul-
ture, rediscovered, 75; education of work
and play, 84–94; government, 77; neolithic
culture, 3; occupations, 80
Metals, used by, Assyrians, 80; Athenians,
273, 276; Chinese, 113; Cretans, 198, 200,
202ff.; Dorians, 233; Egyptians, 48;
Etruscans, 477, 479; Hindus, 161; Mo-
henjo-Daro, 153, 156; Romans, 519, 562
Metellus Numidicus, 619
Metempsychosis, Hindu concept of, 158; in
Plato, 427, 569; in Pythagoras, 426; in
Virgil, 569
Method of teaching, alphabetic, 304; apprenticeship, 20ff., 441 (see, also, apprenticeship); imitation, 21f., 29ff., 35,
57, 579; individualized, 305; memoriza-
tion, 58, 109, 118f., 163, 304; play as a,
437, 442, 455, 579; writing, 579f.
Methodists, medical, 689
Metz, beast baiting at, 756
Micah, 97
Militarism, and Persian sports, 188; Chinese
opposition to, 120, 139; Persian, 177ff.
Military displays, at Athens, 347f.; at Rome,
718, 729, 746
Military training, Aristotle on, 451, 458; as
physical culture, 9; Athenian, 315–27,
330ff.; Chinese, 120, 121, 122; Egyptian,
59ff.; Hindu, 165–72; Mandan, 29ff.;
Persian, 182–8; Plato on, 436f., 442f.;
Roman, 520–6, 632–45; Spartan, 244f.,
248–72
*Millenary Classic*, 118
Milo of Crotona, 331
Mind and body, balance of, in Greek education, 6, 289, 298–315, 431f., 441ff.,
453ff.; opposed by Christian ascetics, 6
(see mental and physical education, balance of)
Mind, Aristotle on, 456; enriched by letters,
6; injured by excessive physical exercise,
359f.; inseparable from body, 9, 16, 569
Minerva, 481, 533, 592, 675, 748

Minoan, collapse, and fusion with Hellenic
culture, 215; life and culture, 197–215;
trade, 199
Minos, 199, 200, 210, 230
Minucius Felix, on spectacles, 753
Miriam, 96, 102
*Mishna*, 109
Mithraism, at Rome, 567
Mithridates, 498, 564
Mixolydian music, 456
Mohammedanism, 179
Mohammedans, in India, 157
Mohenjo-Daro, and the Indus civilization,
152ff.; agriculture, 152; antiquity of, 152;
architecture, 152, 154f.; art, 153, 175;
bath, 154f.; cereals, 153; dancing figure,
175; domesticated animals, 153; folk, 152;
hunting and fishing, 155f.; industries, 153;
religion, 153f.; script, 154; wildlife, 153,
155
Monasticism, Buddhist, 141, 148, 163, 164;
Chinese, 114
Monogamy, 114
Monotheism, Babylonian, 82; Christian,
754; Greek, 421; Hebrew, 96f.; Hindu,
158
*Mora*, 663, 664
Moral codes and education, Athenian, 287,
289, 294, 296; Chinese, 116ff.; Egyptian,
53f., 57f.; Hebrew, 97f.; Hindu, 162;
Homeric, 222; Persian, 181f.; Roman,
503–9, 575, 576, 577; Spartan, 239f.
Morality, Egyptian standards of, 54
Moses, 95, 97, 102, 106
*Mothaces*, 250
Mother Goddess, Cretan, 199, 206, 208,
210f., 214; in India, 154; in Rome, 531,
720
Mother Matuta, 531
"Mountain Chant," 32f.
Mummius, 391, 398
Musea, 309
Music, Aristotle on, 455f.; Chinese, 122,
123, 124, 127ff.; Cretan, 211f.; Dorian,
456; Egyptian, 69f., 72; Hebrew, 102ff.,
107; Hindu, 175; Homeric, 223; Meso-
potamian, 90, 92ff.; Mixolydian, 456;
Persian, and the chase, 188; Phrygian,
456; Plato on, 435f.; Pythagoras on, 426;
Spartan, 243, 267
Music and dancing, Athenian, 301, 302, 303,
309; Chinese, 118, 121, 122, 126ff.;
Cretan, 211f.; Egyptian, 69ff.; Etruscan,
483f.; Homeric, 231f.; in India, 173ff.;
Roman, 628f., 654f.; Spartan, 245f., 265ff.
Music school, Athenian, 298ff., 424
Musonius, 501, 575, 593, 616, 630
Mycenae, 198, 199, 201, 204, 205, 212, 216,
233

644f.; tug-of-war, 145, 306, 308, 315;
tumbling, 164, 414, 486; walking, 164,
255, 404, 405, 406, 407, 414, 659, 660,
661, 662, 669, 686; war games, 21, 29f.,
35, 36, 61, 65; weights, lifting, throwing,
swinging, 64, 105, 229, 659, 669, 686;
"white man," 36; willows, fights with, 36;
windmills, imitating, 164; wrestling, 22,
36, 38, 61, 64, 65f., 67, 74, 90, 93, 101,
105, 140, 165, 170, 190ff., 209, 226,
228f., 231, 244, 254, 255, 256, 257, 259,
305, 307, 308, 314, 315, 320, 321, 337,
338, 341, 343, 346, 348, 351, 353, 354,
356, 360, 361, 363, 367, 371, 377, 378,
380, 381, 385f., 388, 389, 391, 393, 394,
405, 406, 408, 411, 427, 432, 442,
443, 457, 466, 469, 486, 511, 525, 607,
624, 638, 648, 654, 657, 658, 659, 660,
661, 662, 668, 669, 670, 747, 748, 749,
751; Yoga, 165
Spring and Autumn Annals, 115, 119
Spurinna, 569, 669; exercises of, 661, 665
Staberius Eros, 581
Stabian Baths, 653
"Stable for education," Egyptian military
school, 60
State and education, 244ff., 287f., 419, 425,
432, 435ff., 448ff., 458ff., 506
State service and physical training, Athenian,
287f., 315–27, 351f., 361; Chinese,
121–6; Hindu, 159f., 165–72; Persian,
182ff.; Roman, 520–6, 632–45; Spartan,
241–72
Statius, 582, 613, 629, 652; on dancing,
655; on swimming, 671; on women at
gladiatorial games, 736
Status of women, Athenian, 291ff.; Baby-
lonian, 80f.; Chinese, 113f.; Egyptian,
52f.; Etruscan, 489; Hebrew, 96; Hindu,
161f.; Persian, 180f.; Roman, 503ff.;
Spartan, 244ff.
Stertinius, 690
Stesichorus, 581
Stilicho, 546, 743
Stilo the Penman, 581
Stoicism, 471, 615, 616, 617
Strabo, 59, 65, 84, 157, 159, 161, 170, 180,
181, 182, 183, 184, 185, 190, 193, 194,
197, 198, 264, 265, 365, 368, 369, 375,
390, 469, 476, 477, 485, 587, 683, 691,
692, 752; on Assyrian warriors, 86; on
Egyptian dancing, 73
String-games, Indian, 42
Student life, at Athens, 587ff.
Studies named, agriculture, 598; architecture,
587, 598; arithmetic, 57, 109, 118, 162,
182, 290, 303, 437, 442, 509, 577, 580,
598, 603, 607; art, 242, 573; astrology, 82,
83, 84; astronomy, 108, 438, 442, 583,

598, 603, 607, 629; behavior, 118, 296,
302, 303; botany, 108; carpentry, 328;
carriage and posture, 308; chronology, 83,
108; dancing, 118, 122, 126–32, 150; dialectic, 598; divination, 84; drawing, 303,
455; embroidery, 298; engineering, 84;
geography, 83, 84, 108, 298; geometry,
57, 320, 437f., 580, 598, 603f., 607, 629;
grammar, 83, 84, 162, 320, 572f., 584,
585, 592, 597, 598, 607; Greek, 107, 108,
572, 573, 574, 596, 597, 603; history,
83, 109, 507, 583, 584, 607; languages,
109, 320, 527, 607; Latin, 597, 603; law,
82, 83, 107, 108, 109, 162, 289, 303, 311,
318, 441, 507, 527, 528, 587, 595, 598,
604; liberal studies, 597, 606f.; literature
and letters, 57, 83, 108, 109, 119, 162, 163,
242, 300, 302, 303, 320, 326, 441, 460,
466, 527, 580f., 582, 583f., 587, 592,
595, 596, 607, 628, 629; logic, 607; manners, 509; mathematics, 57, 73, 83, 84,
108, 118, 121, 122; mechanical science,
587; medicine, 82, 83, 328, 587, 598;
mensuration, 442, 580; military arts, 122,
137, 165f., 438, 441, 442, 598; military
gymnastics, 435, 442, 457, 458; moral instruction, 98, 109, 604; music, 69, 70,
72, 74, 107, 108, 109, 118, 121, 122,
128f., 132, 175, 242f., 244, 267, 289, 296,
300, 302, 303, 304, 320, 372, 435f., 437,
438, 440, 441f., 455f., 460, 466, 583, 598,
603, 604, 607, 628, 629; mythology, 181,
296; natural history, 83; oratory, 585, 587;
orthography, 583; painting, 303, 607;
philology, 83, 84, 572; philosophy, 84,
108, 161, 162, 320, 325, 438, 573, 575,
583, 585, 587, 595, 597, 603, 604, 606,
607, 614f., 629f.; physical education, 121,
163, 166, 182, 242, 243, 244, 246, 248f.,
253, 254, 289, 300, 302f., 308, 309f.,
320, 325, 332, 351f., 359, 435, 436, 437,
438, 440, 441, 442, 455, 456f., 466, 573,
575, 604, 655; playing on musical glasses,
166; "polite" conversation, 118; psalms
and prayers, 162; reading, 55, 56, 82, 108,
109, 118, 162, 175, 182, 241, 296, 302,
303, 304, 441, 455, 507, 509, 527, 577,
579, 581, 583, 603; religion, 82, 83,
98, 107, 109, 162, 604; rhetoric, 320,
573, 575f., 584f., 586f., 592, 594,
595, 597, 598, 604, 607; "rites," 121;
rituals, 118; sciences, 109, 162, 298; sewing, 298; singing, 175, 303, 304, 309;
speech, 118, 119, 509, 583, 596, 597, 598;
spinning, 298, 509; surveying, 84; theology, 162; weaving, 298, 509; weights,
measures, money, 107; word study, 162;
writing, 55, 82, 108, 109, 118, 119, 121,
162, 175, 182, 241f., 296, 298f., 300,